Praise for *The Blackwell Companion to the Bible in English Literature*

"This is indeed a true companion, one that succeeds in its aim of being both scholarly and accessible to all lovers of English literature. In short, all students of English literature ought to put aside a month to read and study this book before going up to university."

Church Times

"Probably what comes across most clearly is how, and that, many of the writers chose deliberately to draw on the Bible, and for students increasingly unfamiliar with the Bible, this approach challenges as well as informs."

Reference Reviews

"An extremely useful volume."

The Year's Work in English Studies

Wiley-Blackwell Companions to Religion

The *Wiley-Blackwell Companions to Religion* series presents a collection of the most recent scholarship and knowledge about world religions. Each volume draws together newly-commissioned essays by distinguished authors in the field, and is presented in a style which is accessible to undergraduate students, as well as scholars and the interested general reader. These volumes approach the subject in a creative and forward-thinking style, providing a forum in which leading scholars in the field can make their views and research available to a wider audience.

Recently Published

The Blackwell Companion to the Bible in English Literature

Edited by

Rebecca Lemon, Emma Mason,
Jonathan Roberts, and Christopher Rowland

WILEY-BLACKWELL

A John Wiley & Sons, Ltd., Publication

This paperback edition first published 2012
© 2012 Blackwell Publishing Ltd

Edition History: Blackwell Publishing Ltd (hardback, 2009)

Blackwell Publishing was acquired by John Wiley & Sons in February 2007. Blackwell's publishing program has been merged with Wiley's global Scientific, Technical, and Medical business to form Wiley-Blackwell.

Registered Office
John Wiley & Sons Ltd, The Atrium, Southern Gate, Chichester, West Sussex, PO19 8SQ, UK

Editorial Offices
350 Main Street, Malden, MA 02148-5020, USA
9600 Garsington Road, Oxford, OX4 2DQ, UK
The Atrium, Southern Gate, Chichester, West Sussex, PO19 8SQ, UK

For details of our global editorial offices, for customer services, and for information about how to apply for permission to reuse the copyright material in this book please see our website at www.wiley.com/wiley-blackwell.

The right of Rebecca Lemon, Emma Mason, Jonathan Roberts, and Christopher Rowland to be identified as the authors of the editorial material in this work has been asserted in accordance with the UK Copyright, Designs and Patents Act 1988.

Library of Congress Cataloging-in-Publication Data

The Blackwell companion to the Bible and English literature / edited by
Rebecca Lemon . . . [et al.].
    p. cm. – (Blackwell companions to religion)
Includes bibliographical references and index.
ISBN 978-1-4051-3160-5 (hbk.) – ISBN 978-0-470-67499-4 (pbk.)
1. English literature–History and criticism. 2. Bible and literature. 3. Bible–
Influence. 4. Bible–In literature. I. Lemon, Rebecca, 1968– II. Title. III. Series.
                                                                              2008047964

PR149.B5B5 2009
820.9′3822–dc22

A catalogue record for this book is available from the British Library.

Set in 10/13 pt Photina by Toppan Best-set Premedia Limited
Printed in Malaysia by Ho Printing (M) Sdn Bhd

1   2012

Contents

Contributors

Daniel Anlezark, University of Durham
Helen Barr, University of Oxford
Bernard Beatty, University of Liverpool
Dinah Birch, University of Liverpool
Kirstie Blair, University of Oxford
Ward Blanton, University of Glasgow
Penny Bradshaw, University of Cumbria
Andrew Bradstock, University of Otago
Catherine a. M. Clarke, Swansea University
Elizabeth Clarke, University of Warwick
Valentine Cunningham, University of Oxford
Graham Davidson, Coleridge Society
Sister Mary Clemente Davlin, OP, Dominican University, River Forest
John Drury, University of Oxford
Paul S. Fiddes, Regent's Park College
William Franke, Vanderbilt University
David Fuller, University of Durham
Michael Giffin, independent scholar
Douglas Gray, University of Oxford
Hannibal Hamlin, The Ohio State University
Wolf Z. Hirst, University of Haifa
Douglas L. Howard, Suffolk County Community College in Selden
David Jasper, University of Glasgow
Elisabeth Jay, Oxford Brookes University
Carol V. Kaske, Cornell University
Mark Knight, Roehampton University
Charles LaPorte, University of Washington
Edward Larrissy, Queen's University Belfast
Rebecca Lemon, University of Southern California
Michael LIeb, University of Illinois at Chicago
Elizabeth Ludlow, University of Warwick

Emma Mason, University of Warwick

Julie Maxwell, independent scholar and novelist, Oxford

Kevin Mills, University of Glamorgan

Roger Pooley, Keele University

Jane Potter, Oxford Brookes University

Stephen Prickett, University of Glasgow

Gerard Reedy, S.J., Fordham University

Jonathan Roberts, University of Liverpool

Christopher Rowland, University of Oxford

Jeanne Shami, University of Regina, Canada

Michael F. Suarez, S.J., Fordham University in New York, and Campion Hall, Oxford

Annie Sutherland, Somerville College, Oxford

Andrew Tate, Lancaster University

Marianne Thormählen, Lund University

J. R. Watson, University of Durham

Deeanne Westbrook, Portland State

Christiania Whitehead, University of Warwick

T. R. Wright, University of Newcastle upon Tyne

Rivkah Zim, King's College London

PART I

Introduction

CHAPTER 1
General Introduction

Rebecca Lemon, Emma Mason, and Jonathan Roberts

"The Bible and literature" is a more specific field than it might first appear, and differs significantly from the ostensibly similar fields of: (a) "literature and theology"; (b) "Christianity and literature"; (c) "religion and literature"; and (d) "the Bible *as* literature." We begin by taking a moment to differentiate these projects as a means to showing where this volume sits in relation to them.

Literature and Theology

A writer can be theologically complex but have comparatively little of the Bible in his or her work (for example, T. S. Eliot), or, by contrast, may freely deploy biblical allusion but have little obvious theology (such as Virginia Woolf). For this reason there is only a partial intersection between "theology and literature" and "the Bible and literature." Studies within the former field are often strongly theorized, not least because of the symbiotic relationship between literary studies and theology. The theo-philosophical work of thinkers such as Paul Tillich, Paul Ricoeur, Hans Georg Gadamer, Walter Benjamin, Jacques Derrida, Hélène Cixous, and Martin Buber, for example, has fore-shadowed a modern theoretical re-evaluation of literature that in turn has given way to a renewed interest in religious questions. The religiously inflected critical inquiry of writers such as Geoffrey Hartman, Luce Irigaray, J. Hillis Miller, Terry Eagleton, and John Schad has developed this tradition further, and provoked Stanley Fish, writing in *The Chronicle of Higher Education* (2005), to declare that religion might "succeed high theory and race, gender and class as the centre of intellectual energy in academe." The field is well served by the journal *Literature and Theology*, as well as the recent *Oxford Handbook of English Literature and Theology*.

Christianity and Literature

"Christianity and literature" is distinct from "the Bible and literature" both because the former (like "literature and theology") need not address the Bible itself, and because

"Christianity and literature" implies a focus on a faith perspective, whereas "the Bible and literature" does not (one need not identify as Jewish or Christian to draw on the Bible). "Christianity and literature" has a different range from "literature and theology" because the former might consider, for example, ecclesiastical or liturgical matters that do not necessarily coincide with theology. The presence of vicars and parsonage life in eighteenth- and nineteenth-century fiction may have much to say about the lived experience of Christianity as life under a social institution, but does not necessarily entail discussion of conventional theological concerns such as the Incarnation, Trinity, or Resurrection. In practice, however, the faith orientation of "Christianity and literature" does tend to press it in a more reflective, didactic, or occasionally evangelizing direction. In one sense, the field is as old as the New Testament, as Christian writers (such as Paul) can be seen rereading Jewish Scripture in the light of their new faith within the Bible itself. These early typological readings are extended through a long history of attempts to read Christian echoes in texts from *The Odyssey* through to *The Lord of the Rings*. In the twentieth century, J. R. R. Tolkien and C. S. Lewis became both proponents and subjects of this approach, as Lewis's 1944 essay "Myth Became Fact" and Joseph Pearce's 1998 *Tolkien: Man and Myth* exemplify.

As with "literature and theology," in addition to these author-based studies, there are numerous journals dedicated to the topic: "The Conference on Christianity and Literature" and its associated journal *Christianity and Literature* is one of the longest-standing. There have also been numerous anthologies of essays in this field including David Barratt et al, *The Discerning Reader: Christian Perspectives on Literature and Theory* (1995), and, more recently, Paul Cavill and Heather Ward's *The Christian Tradition in English Literature: Poetry, Plays, and Shorter Prose* (2007).

Religion and Literature

"Religion and literature" is of a different order of magnitude, as it no longer deals with one religious text, but potentially with many texts, many gods, and many varieties of religious experience. It overlaps with "literature and theology" but goes beyond the Judeo-Christian traditions into the major world religions (see Tomoko Masuzawa's *The Invention of World Religions* for a helpful introduction to this area). The most inclusive of the categories discussed here, this area also includes work on psychology (Carl Jung), belief (Slavoj Žižek and John D. Caputo), and ethics (Richard Rorty and Donna Haraway). Journals such as *Religion and Literature* have long been connected with this field, while new series like Continuum's eclectic "New Directions in Religion and Literature" are suggestive of the evolving range of approaches and relevant texts opened up by the interplay between the two disciplines.

The Bible *as* Literature

The ongoing debate over the relationship between literature and the Bible is not a historical curiosity, but is grounded in the fact that the Bible itself is literature. As writers such as Murray Roston (*Prophet and Poet: the Bible and the Growth of Romanticism*, 1965) argue, this idea materialized in the sixteenth century with the translation of the Bible into the vernacular, and again in the eighteenth century due to a newfound interest in the principles of Hebrew poetics. The story of that rediscovery can be found in this volume (see Stephen Prickett's introduction to the eighteenth century), but the reception of the Bible as a book of (among other things) poetry seems to have been a discovery for – and a surprise to – every generation since. The Romantic recognition of the biblical prophets as poets (and therefore Romantic poets' self-recognition as prophets) segued into newly articulated forms of agnosticism in the nineteenth and twentieth centuries that found "the Bible as literature" an agreeable solution to a text at the center of their culture, the nature of which had gradually come to seem less clear. One result of this is that the Bible itself comes to be repackaged in editions such as Charles Allen Dinsmore's *The English Bible as Literature* (1931) and Ernest Sutherland Bates's *The Bible Designed to be Read as Literature* (1937).

The current sustained wave of interest in the Bible as literature owes much to Frank Kermode and Robert Alter's *Literary Guide to the Bible* (1987), which was preceded by Kermode's *The Genesis of Secrecy* (1979) and Alter's *The Art of Biblical Narrative* (1981). At a time when literary theory was at the height of its influence in the 1980s, Kermode and Alter's work showed that it was of equal significance to the work of biblical scholars, and that the Bible is composed of many diverse and disruptive examples of linguistic play and meaning.

"The Bible and Literature"

The range of studies pertaining to the fields outlined above is extensive. Nonetheless, many of the works (particularly academic monographs) written on "religion" and particular authors would not fall into any of these categories. This is because while religion has been the subject of an increasing focus in literary studies in recent years, this has taken place primarily via the recovery of historical contexts and period discourses. To take one example, the past decade or so has witnessed the publication of many books on Romantic religion. These books, however, have focused almost exclusively on the recovery of, for instance, the dissenting cultures of William Blake's London, rather than his engagement with the Bible itself. This is a generalization, but indicates a trend. So, while the recovery of a history and hermeneutics of religion has been wide-ranging and essential to the very field of religion and literature to which this volume speaks, consideration of the uses that specific writers have found for the Bible has been comparatively underplayed. The foundations for this collection, David Lyle Jeffrey's *A Dictionary of Biblical Tradition in English Literature* (1992), Stephen Prickett and David Jasper's *The Bible and Literature: A Reader* (1999) and David Norton's *A History of the Bible as Literature* (2000), have begun to redress this anomaly. Jeffrey presents the reader with an encyclopedic resource book detailing the appearance of biblical images and characters in later literature; Prickett and Jasper construct a helpful teaching book, offering groupings of extracts of literary texts by theme; and Norton provides a thorough historical trajectory of the subject. The present volume supplements these works by offering sustained and detailed analyses of the use of the Bible by specific authors, the majority of whom receive an entire chapter written by an expert on that particular writer. This volume also supplements these earlier studies by providing discussions, within many of the chapters, of the versions of the Bible available to, and influential on, these authors. As a result of this historical attention to Bible translation, both terms – "Bible" and "literature" – as engaged in this volume are capacious and mobile: there are varieties of Bibles influencing these authors, just as there are varieties of literature (drama, poetry, prose, memoir). The descriptor "the Bible and literature," then, is a means to taking a kind of textual engagement as a common denominator, rather than any more qualitative judgment grounded in adherence to a particular tradition, or maintenance of a particular belief.

Accessibility has been a key aim of this volume, and we have attempted to commission essays that will be usable by the widest audience. As the principal audience is expected to be students of literature, we have sought to include authors who typically appear on undergraduate syllabi; this has meant a selection that could certainly be described as canonical, and located within a specific geography, since we have concentrated on writers who are British or who worked substantially in the British Isles. We hope that this volume might help to inspire scholars and/or students to undertake other, complementary studies of literature and the Bible, in languages other than English, in countries outside of Britain, and through a selection of authors more wide-ranging than we could undertake here. We thus offer this volume as an aid in understanding the vast influence of the Bible on English literature, rather than as a definitive and exhaustive study of the topic. There are, inevitably, omissions: while in the case of some authors, we would have liked to invite several scholars to have written on them, in the case of others, we had great difficulty commissioning anyone at all. This was an unexpected but instructive aspect of compiling the volume. We learned that the authors whom one might most quickly identify as "religious" and in whose critical reception "religion" has featured may not, in fact, have stimulated much (if any) discussion of their biblical usages; and often it is the least religious (or at least the most anti-clerical) writers – Byron, Blake, Lawrence, for example – who are the most biblical.

Perhaps the most difficult editorial decision concerned the date range of the volume. After much discussion and consultation we decided to stop at what is sometimes called "high modernism": the writer born latest in the collection is T. S. Eliot. However, this was not, perhaps surprisingly, due to a diminished interest in the Bible among later twentieth and twenty-first century writers. Quite the reverse: had we gone later, there would be a wealth of choices: Douglas Coupland, William Golding, Graham Greene, Elizabeth Jennings, David Jones, C. S. Lewis, Philip Roth, J. R. R. Tolkien, and Jeanette Winterson, to name just a few. Amidst this range it would be difficult to make the sort of canonical selection that characterizes the rest of the volume; and length restrictions would mean that looking at some of the more interesting modern authors here would mean losing authors from earlier periods. As mentioned above, here too we hope that the volume offers a foundation for further study and research both into those authors we were unable to include and into new perspectives on those writers that are discussed here.

One of the most illuminating aspects of editing the collection has been seeing the different approaches that our contributors have taken to the subject matter. Without wishing to attempt to provide a typology of approaches, a selection of the chapters that follow is noted here to indicate the variety of critical approaches to be found in this collection.

Catherine Clarke's essay on Old English poetry begins the medieval section, offering a history of the Bible as an object of aristocratic exchange. Clarke's approach helps to illuminate how, to a large degree, the study of the Bible and literature concerns the history of the book itself. In contrast to her attention to book and manuscript circulation in England, other authors such as Douglas Gray (the medieval religious lyric), Christiania Whitehead (Chaucer), and Carol Kaske (Spenser) illuminate the range of specific ways in which authors engage with the Bible in their literary production. We see how historical authors draw on the Bible in numerous ways: typologically, allegorically, figuratively, affectively, and liturgically, to name only a few. These chapters are suggestive of the flexibility of biblical engagement, which extends beyond intertextual reference. Yet close attention to the nature of intertextual reference is itself revealing and several essays in these opening sections concentrate on how authors favour specific sections of the Bible. Here, Jeanne Shami's essay on Donne is exemplary. In tracking Donne's engagement with both the Psalms and Paul, her chapter engages Donne's vast meditations on the Bible, ranging from his essays to his sermons to his devotions to his poems, demonstrating continuity within his diverse writings. Yet another approach in our medieval and early modern sections illuminates the relation between biography and faith. Michael Lieb's essay is particularly instructive on how and why Milton engages with the Bible; Lieb gives a keen sense of the drama of this engagement, tracing the variations and continuities in the form of Milton's biblical influences. Similarly, Rivkah Zim's essay illuminates how Mary Sidney, Countess of Pembroke, produces her translation of the Psalms from her position as an activist Protestant aristocrat.

The chapters in the remaining three parts of the volume are no less various. Valentine Cunningham, for example, grants the reader access to Defoe's biblical world through an anatomy of Defoe's use of particular scriptural words. Michael Giffin, by contrast, steps back and discerns a set of grand biblical themes in Austen's work, locating a particular worldview and faith position that he shares as an Anglican priest. For Deanne Westbrook, Wordsworth's hidden biblical allusions materialize as figure and parable, modes of linguistic articulation able to accommodate divine mystery even as they acknowledge the "fallen" nature of language so prevalent in *The Prelude*. Penny Bradshaw's approach to Romantic women's poetry, on the other hand, implements a historio-feminist methodology to highlight how these writers engaged with the ostensibly patriarchal traditions of divine and biblical poetics. Focusing on Hannah More and Felicia Hemans, Bradshaw suggests that they interrogate their relationship with the Bible as a way of finding an otherwise unavailable perspective on contemporary questions of gender and female voice. Ruskin too felt compelled to reassess the scriptural authority he had so meticulously studied in his youth, Dinah Birch shows us, but did so by sustaining a textual scrutiny of the Bible. Andrew Tate uses the framework of *fin de siècle* decadence to read Wilde's aesthetic exegesis of the Gospels, one that continually collapses into a Gospel-driven moralism removed from the sensuous spirituality with which Wilde is conventionally associated. By the time we arrive at Joyce,

William Franke shows, the "Word" of the Bible can be realized only in a fractured human language comprising biblical, colloquial and liturgical allusions alike.

As this brief overview indicates, the contributions to this volume are rich and diverse, and the insight they offer into the Bible and literature lies not only in their individual content, but in their range as a collection: they show the Bible and literature to be an infinitely complex topic, as the Bible changes in the hands of each author that reads it, modulating according to the style and theme of each literary work, and in the forms of belief and disbelief that underlie them.

Each of the five period sections in this volume – medieval literature, early-modern literature; eighteenth-century and Romantic literature; Victorian literature; and Modernism – is preceded by a general introduction. The volume begins, however, with two broad essays that set the scene: Christopher Rowland offers a perspective from biblical studies on the nature and genre of the Bible; and then David Jasper surveys interpretive approaches to that text in his chapter on biblical hermeneutics and literary theory.

Note on Terms

A number of terms used in this volume have alternative, regional, or contested forms. These include the use of "Old Testament" or "Hebrew Bible"; of BC/AD or BCE/CE; of "the King James version" or "the Authorized Version"; and of variants such as "Paul," "St Paul," and "Paul the Apostle." Rather than theologically or politically sanctioning one or other sets of these terms, we have left them as contributors have used them, thereby indicating their current diversity of usage.

References

Alter, Robert (1981) *The Art of Biblical Narrative*. Basic Books, New York.

Alter, Robert, and Kermode, Frank (1987) *The Literary Guide to the Bible*. Belknap Press of Harvard University Press, Cambridge, MA.

Barratt, David, Pooley, Roger, and Ryken, Leland, eds (1995) *The Discerning Reader: Christian Perspectives on Literature and Theory*. Apollos, Leicester.

Bates, Ernest Sutherland, ed. (1933) *The Bible Designed to Be Read as Literature*. Heinemann, London.

Cavill, Paul, and Ward, Heather (2007) *The Christian Tradition in English Literature: Poetry, Plays, and Shorter Prose*. Zondervan Publishing House, Grand Rapids, MI.

Dinsmore, Charles Allen, ed. (1931) *The English Bible as Literature*. George Allen & Unwin, London.

Fish, Stanley (2005) "One University, Under God?" *Chronicle of Higher Education* January 7 (http://chronicle.com/weekly/v51/i18/18c00101.htm). Accessed November 17, 2008.

Jasper, David, and Prickett, Stephen (1998) *The Bible and Literature: A Reader*. Blackwell, Oxford.

Jeffrey, David Lyle, ed. (1992) *A Dictionary of Biblical Tradition in English Literature*. W. B. Eerdmans, Grand Rapids, MI.

Kermode, Frank (1979) *The Genesis of Secrecy: On the Interpretation of Narrative*. Charles Eliot Norton lectures. Harvard University Press, Cambridge, MA.

Lewis, C. S. (1996) "Myth Became Fact," in *God in the Dock: Essays on Theology and Ethics*. W. B. Eerdmans, Grand Rapids, MI.

Masuzawa, Tomoko (2005) *The Invention of World Religions: Or, How European Universalism Was Preserved in the Language of Pluralism*. University of Chicago Press, Chicago.

Norton, David (2000) *A History of the English Bible as Literature*. Cambridge University Press, Cambridge.

Pearce, Joseph (1998) *Tolkien: Man and Myth*. Harper Collins, London.

Roston, Murray (1965) *Prophet and Poet. The Bible and the Growth of Romanticism*. Faber & Faber, London.

CHAPTER 2

The Literature of the Bible

Christopher Rowland

What Is the Bible?

In November 2003 Chief Justice Roy Moore was removed from office for refusing to remove a two-ton granite monument of the Ten Commandments from the Alabama Supreme Court building, after the monument had been ruled an unconstitutional endorsement of religion.[1] The event is a reminder that these verses from Exodus 20 are embedded in the popular psyche as epitomizing what the Bible teaches. The Bible is often seen as a book of moral instruction or a relic of a previous age, and also as a forbidding reminder of a more puritanical environment from which a modern age is glad to be free. Many would sympathize with William Blake's protest against dominant models of eighteenth-century Christianity that appropriated the Bible as a moral, doctrinal rulebook, authoritatively sanctioning the kind of religion summarized in the Ten Commandments, which Blake characterizes by the words "Thou shalt not." Yet the Ten Commandments are only one fragment of an enormously diverse book: open the Bible at random, and you may find a legal code, but you are equally likely to turn up a genealogy, or a long account of the doing of the kings of Judah in the Old Testament, or a set of complex arguments about the Jewish law and justification by faith in some New Testament epistle. Even a Gospel like that of John portrays a rather elusive and eccentric Jesus whose words are often opaque. While the Bible can be (as Moore would like it to be) a stern arbiter of morality, it is simultaneously full of sexual scandal and violence on the grand scale.

The complexity of the Bible is belied by its very name: the Bible. The definite article gives the impression – confirmed by two thousand years of two major-faith traditions endorsing the view – that the Bible is a single book rather than a motley collection made up (depending on your tradition) of fifty-six works in the (Christian) Old Testament and twenty-seven in the New Testament. To describe it in this way is to point to its highly heterogeneous composition, composed of, among other things, narrative, poetry, prophecy, law, and personal communication. The heterogeneous has only come to appear homogeneous due to the religious communities that have asserted that its contents represent the Word of God. The logic of the argument is that there is a unique divine mind behind the various parts of the Bible, and it is therefore the responsibility of frail human minds to discern the unified mind of God behind these diverse texts. There is no doubt about the ingenuity that has existed (and still exists) to discern the unity of the Bible, and many sharp interpreters have set themselves to find that coherence. The result is that this collection has become special not as books but as THE Book to be set part from others and regarded with reverence as a collection of words which not only cohere, but despite their ordinariness, are also somehow imbued with a holy quality. Hence the Holy Bible – it is a book set apart.

The time span that covers the earliest and the latest biblical books is enormous. Even the most conservative estimate would be around five hundred years, and a more generous estimate might well double that to take account of the fact that the biblical books include traditions that emerged half a millennium before they were committed to writing in their present form. In itself, that time span should flag up the heterogeneity of the biblical texts, confirming their emergence from various and different cultures and environments. Not only is the time span great, but we cannot with any certainty track a chronology of the biblical texts. Genesis, for example, was not written first nor Revelation last. The reality is infinitely more complex: it has been suggested, for example, that the earliest books include the Song of Deborah or the Succession narrative at the beginning of 1 Kings, as well as those mythological elements that indicate a debt to the Canaanite religion, such as Daniel 7:9–13. Despite the commitment of some orthodox scholars to the idea of a coherent message in the Bible, their vision owes more to the creative imagination of systematic Christian theologians than to the biblical texts that are part of our canon.

The Bible as Literature

Stephen Prickett argues in *Origins of Narrative: The Romantic Appropriation of the Bible*[2] that our idea of what constitutes literature is strongly influenced by the development of the novel, so much so that it is almost impossible not to read those expectations back into the biblical text and find it wanting. As modern readers, when we look at the Bible we notice that there is little attention to the description and exploration of character and historical context. There are deficiencies in plot, for example, while characterizations of figures such as Joshua appear two-dimensional to modern readers. Even the portrayals of Moses and Jesus give few glimpses into the internal psychological struggle that presumably accompanied the development of these two men into revolutionary leaders. Despite some of the best efforts of biblical scholars, the biblical stories make poor narrative and even worse biography. Ancient characters are judged less by motivation and more by action: "by their fruits ye shall know them" is an appropriate maxim for anyone striving to understand what is going on in character portrayal in ancient biblical narrative. Modern biblical scholarship has attempted to rectify the shortcomings of the Bible by trying to fill in the gaps, whether psychological or historical, thereby seeking to make the Bible more "user friendly" for an age where the inner workings of heroes and their historical backgrounds are a "sine qua non" for any meaningful understanding. Such attempts have been at best inadequate and at worst futile.

The Biblical Genres

The Bible in all its variety of genre has prompted many later texts. The survey offered in this chapter attempts to chart that variety in both the Old and New Testaments.

Narrative

The Bible begins with a story, with the account of creation and the cause of human sinfulness and its ongoing effects. The opening chapters of Genesis are universal in their scope, and it is only with the story of Abraham and his descendants that we find the peculiar Jewish story emerging. This narrative then winds its way through much of the Pentateuch. The story of a covenant, whether with Abraham, the whole people at Sinai, or later, King David, forms a Leitmotiv though the whole of the story. The settlement and the establishment of the monarchy prompt a peculiar kind of didactic history, where the writing is told less for information and more as a morality tale and explanation of the great crisis in Jewish history: the exile of the elite from Judah to Babylon. This event, about which we know so little, has become for modern historical scholarship the decisive moment in Jewish life, when much of what is now contained in the Hebrew Bible began to take shape.

The narrative form so central to the Hebrew Bible was taken up in the Christian New Testament, which looked back on the Hebrew Bible as an antecedent "older testament." The early Christian narratives are themselves distinctive. Written (comparatively) soon after the events that they recount, they are a curious mix of anecdote and saying focusing on the central story of the Christian gospel, that of Jesus of Nazareth. The first three gospels (only one of which – Mark – is actually called a "gospel") are closely related, almost certainly with Mark being the earliest, supplemented by other pre-existing sources. Matthew and Luke had access to a source, including one known as Q (from the German *Quelle*), which was almost entirely a collection of Jesus' sayings, and which supplemented Mark's story in different ways, in Matthew's and Luke's gospels. The Gospel of John in all likelihood had a separate origin, hatched in a community with a very different kind of story, laying claim to its origin in the life of Jesus through an anonymous figure, called the Beloved Disciple (Jn 21:24). Its sayings and narrative content overlap with the Synoptic Gospels but the differences have persuaded many commentators that it had its origin in early Christian circles, perhaps of a sectarian character, which had little contact with emerging mainstream Christianity.

One of the gospels was then taken further and did not stop with the death and resurrection of Jesus. The Acts of the Apostles, traditionally attributed to the author of the Gospel of Luke, continues the narrative of Jesus with the account of what his key followers, especially Paul, did. In this way, the story of the Jewish origins of Christianity in Palestine is taken via a meandering route, providentially guided, to Rome, the capital of the ancient world.

Law

The heart of the Hebrew Bible is the story of God giving a code of law to the emerging Jewish nation. That law formed the basis of a covenant relationship and a kind of thank offering to God for the deliverance of a people from Egypt. The law takes various forms in Exodus, Leviticus, Numbers, and Deuteronomy and probably reflects different contexts in which such traditions were handed down. Deuteronomy is particularly distinctive, and has linguistic echoes in other parts of the Bible (notably the Books of Kings and the prophecy of Jeremiah), suggesting the existence of a particular school of priests or prophets that kept the laws alive. Such a school may have been responsible for the production of the law book that was found in the temple in the reign of King Josiah (2 Kings 22:8, 11), and which was to revolutionize the life of the ailing Judean nation. The biblical laws relate to civic, personal as well as ritual matters and exemplify the quality of life that enables an elect people to be considered "holy" or special. As well as the civic or political laws there are regulations, which concern the administration of the cult. These laws are set in the context of the emerging nation wandering in the wilderness, where its life is one that is "on the move" with a temporary religious shrine – the tabernacle – awaiting some kind of future settlement in the promised land, the entry into which is recorded in the Book of Joshua.

There are affinities between the legal material in the Bible and various ancient law codes and the traditional wisdom which regulated life. Thus, elsewhere in the Bible the aphoristic morality of books such as Proverbs and Ecclesiastes, and later the Wisdom of Jesus ben Sirach (the book Ecclesiasticus in the Christian Apocrypha, a Hebrew version of which has been found at Masada), reflect a traditional morality that was passed down from generation to generation and that may well explain the origin of the biblical laws. Nevertheless, what is characteristic of the biblical laws is that despite their specificity, their application required ongoing contextualization; thus casuistry was the basis for the emerging Judaism, and is exemplified in legal collections such as the Mishnah and the Talmud. These books, which are the collections of legal debates by later interpreters, codify the rulings, and the discussions, of the later teachers, and are only loosely related to the themes of the biblical law as the requirements of being a holy nation were interpreted in different cultures and places down history. Thus, while it is clear that the inspiration for the subject matter of debate comes from the Bible (Sabbath observance, the regulations for worship and festivals, and the application of laws), these are collections of case-law that are only rarely a detailed exegetical discussion of the meaning of the laws as they are found in the text of the Bible.

This is a crucial point to make about the Bible, especially for those who are part of a primarily Christian culture. Judaism's relationship with the Bible is much more nuanced than that of Protestant Christianity. Just because laws (such as the Ten Commandments) are given divine approbation, it does not mean that they are (to quote a phrase) set in tablets of stone and to remain binding in their literal sense at all times and in all places. The biblical laws are themselves frequently general rather than providing sets of detailed prescriptions. One searches in vain, for example, to find out what it means to "remember the Sabbath day, to keep it holy" (Exodus 20:8). As in other instances of Jewish legal interpretation, Jewish teachers, or rabbis, explored the application of a general principle to specific circumstances (in the practice of casuistry). They were not literal minded in the way we might consider some Protestants to be. Instead, they showed a flexibility in interpretation and application that did not deny the value of the original, but saw it less as a prescription and more as a catalyst or ingredient for future interpretation. This point is crucial for modern readers brought up on a denigration of law and an exaltation of gospel. Ironically, it is the Christians who have been more literal minded than Jews in their lack of readiness to apply words to new circumstances in ways that have convinced millions that one has to believe, and practice, a million impossible things before breakfast, all of them derived from a literal reading of the Bible. Rabbinic Judaism could not be further from this kind of religion.

Prophecy

Prophecy is usually linked with prediction, but that is too simple a view of biblical prophecy that is rightly designated as including both "foretelling" and "forth telling." That is, prediction about the future as compared with explanation of the present. The emergence of the biblical prophets is a peculiar phenomenon within antiquity, marginal figures arising to challenge a nation and a society with judgment rather than approbation. This is typical both of figures such as Samuel and Elijah, who appear in the narrative books, and of the so-called "writing prophets" such as Amos and Isaiah who appear from the eighth century BCE and onwards. The preservation of what are now the canonical, prophetic, words probably has much to do with the Exile and the vindication of the words of people who were widely disbelieved or regarded in their day as "false prophets" over against those who proclaimed peace and plenty and thereby curried the favor rather than the opprobrium of their contemporaries. Three different kinds of prophetic writing are set out below: oracles, myth and historical prediction, and different kinds of visions.

Oracles   Prophecy is part of human culture and in antiquity the Sibyl and the Delphic Oracles, which were widely consulted sources of information about the future are but two examples of the ways in which the mysteries of the world were interpreted and illuminated. This was done by a variety of means, embracing the whole gamut of theurgic practice and magic. In literary terms this only occasionally makes its appearance. Nevertheless, the prophetic oracles sometimes take the form of riddles such as that of Samson (Judges 14:14) and the famous Immanuel oracle (Isaiah 7:10–14). For the prophet, almost any object in the natural world – be it a plumb line or an almond tree – could serve as a means of discernment of the divine will (cf. Jeremiah 1:11). More often, however, writing prophets find themselves being channels of divine words. These words are usually prefaced by "Thus says the Lord," and consist most often of judgment, and occasionally of encouragement and hope. In some cases the prophetic message is enacted in the prophet's life. Jeremiah was remembered due to the vindication of the truth of his words of warning. He was thought to be a troublemaker because he predicted the destruction of Jerusalem and its temple and the carrying of its king and elite into exile in Babylon. Ezekiel communicates extraordinary visions that encompass mind-bending journeys through time and space in order to view that which was taking place hundreds of miles away. Ezekiel's imaginative reconstruction of Jerusalem provides the clearest blueprint of hope for a restored city and temple. This would become an important model not only for utopian prophets but also for the restoration of Jerusalem and for later visionaries such as John of Patmos (e.g. Rev 21).

Prophetic books in the Bible are linked with particular figures, but most were a kind of oracular magnet that, over time, accumulated words from anonymous prophets. This is nowhere better seen than in the case of the Book of Isaiah. By common consent the book falls into three major sections. The first thirty-nine chapters more or less (bar chapters 24–7) derive from the years before the sixth century and are concerned with the career of Isaiah of Jerusalem and the crisis surrounding the invasions of Judea by the King of Assyria in 622. The second part begins with the memorable words "Comfort, ye, comfort ye my people," spoken by the anonymous prophet of the Jewish elite in exile in Babylon who promises a peculiar restoration of their fortunes. The last chapters (55–66) come historically later, and may reflect the situation of more disillusioned circles whose political hopes had not come to fruition, when a different kind of political arrangement had been established, in which prophetic voices had become marginal.

Myth and historical prediction   Myth and history are blended throughout the prophetic texts. The stories of creation and the slaying of mighty monsters are used as ways of describing the impact of the divine in history (Isiah 51:9). Such imagery is a hallmark of prophetic literature and prophecy depends on the lens of myth as a means to interpret history. In addition, ancient biblical themes such as the Exodus are (for example, in the writings of Second Isaiah) a potent way of recapitulating the divine promise. This is the root of typology, as one story becomes the means of telling another. The Exodus from Egypt becomes the means of narrating the return from Babylon, and both describe the political deliverance of a people. In the same way, the language of redemption is used in a text such as 1 Peter (1:18) in the New Testament to describe the effects of salvation on a nascent Christian community.

Varieties of visionary experience   By and large the prophets are depicted as channels of the divine word but in addition visions become decisive to the prophetic message. This is true of Ezekiel as we have seen. His vision of the divine throne chariot (Ezekiel 1) with its eyes and wheels and the fiery enthroned figure became a central resource for Jewish visionaries down the centuries, of whom John of Patmos is only the most famous (Rev. 4). Along with Isaiah's temple vision (Isaiah 6), with which it has so many affinities, Ezekiel's *merkabah* (chariot) vision (not described as such by Ezekiel but by later writers who noticed the affinities between what the prophet described and a chariot with its wheels and movement) was the basis of a mystical tradition that infuses later literature from Dante to Blake.

It is in Ezekiel particularly, and also in the later prophecy of Zechariah, that we find the visionary descriptions that were to be a key part of what is termed "apocalyptic literature" later exemplified in the biblical canon in Daniel and Revelation. Both books contain visions, with Daniel containing also angelic verbal interpretations. This type of literature continues the concern of the prophetic literature to reveal the divine will but now less by divine fiat or words but through pictures of visions. It probably represents a later development of prophecy in the later part of the Second Temple period (which came to an end with the destruction of the Temple constructed after the Exile in 70 CE, only forty years after the death of Jesus of Nazareth).

Wisdom literature

"Wisdom literature," exemplified by the Books of Proverbs and Ecclesiastes, is a very different kind of writing. In varied ways it describes the way of the world as it is, not as it might be. On the basis of experience, wisdom literature describes the type of conduct that might bring the person success. Its origin in pedagogy, probably linked with the royal court, is a kind of traditional wisdom that is not given any divine sanction via revelation such as the Law at Sinai. It is the wisdom that is hallowed by time and experience. Of course, such wisdom didn't always work, and the challenge to traditional wisdom is nowhere better seen than in the Book of Job. Here the view that the practice of inherited wisdom necessarily leads to the good life is ruthlessly exposed. The Book of Job offers no easy answer to this problem, and instead depicts the inability of comprehending the inscrutability of God. It is that kind of pessimism about predicting the outcome of human life and the mystery of the divine purposes that also underlies books such as Qoheleth (Ecclesiastes), where the point of life is to make the best of what one has, and not to assume that everything will go to plan.

The aphoristic literature is also typical of large parts of the gospel tradition. The narrative structure of all four canonical gospels cannot disguise the fact that the teaching attributed to Jesus in all of the gospels consists of pithy sayings or stories from everyday life that are used as analogies (parables) of how one might comprehend theological truths: "the Kingdom of God may be compared with ...," and so on. Collections of Jesus' sayings may well have circulated independently from any narrative structure and were perhaps only later put within such a narrative framework. This is even true of the Gospel of John where Jesus speaks in a series of enigmatic sayings that individually have an oracular, or parabolic, quality. The discovery of The Gospel of Thomas in the Nag Hammadi library indicates what such a text may have looked like. Such aphoristic collections were widespread in Judaism. There are several collections of rabbinic sayings: for example, Pike Aboth (now preserved in the Mishnah), the Sayings of the Fathers, and Pirke de Rabbi Eliezer, a much later rabbinic collection. The paradigm offered by such aphoristic collections was taken up and used, for example, in William Blake's "Proverbs of Hell," part of The Marriage of Heaven and Hell.

The Marriage reflects the mix of narrative (in which Blake describes dialogues or journeys with devils and angels) and aphorisms in a complex form such as we find in the canonical gospels.

The Song of Songs is less easily categorized. It is an extraordinary love poem that has been interpreted in both Judaism and Christianity as an allegory of the relationship between the human and the divine. Such an interpretation may have a long history and the erotic imagery became a key part of the mystical exploration of the divinity in both Judaism and Christianity.

Psalms

Throughout the Hebrew Bible we find hymns of praise to God. These became a central part of Jewish life in the various temples in Jerusalem. How much of what now constitutes the Book of Psalms actually goes back to the temple of Solomon has been a matter of much debate. Clearly there are ancient themes that reflect the Canaanite background, probably of the old Jebusite religion that preceded the settlement of the city by Jews under David and Solomon (Psalm 82:1 may be an example). Nevertheless, many Psalms were collected during or after the exile as exemplified by Psalm 137 ("By the waters of Babylon we sat down and wept"), Psalm 19 (in its growing concern to exalt the law of God), and Psalm 119. The collection of Psalms we now have nonetheless combines praise, lament, and the recitation of the divine acts in concise form in a number of different situations that transcend Temple, or any other place of worship. It is no surprise that this collection above all else has been a resource and inspiration for worshippers within both Judaism and Christianity.

Letters

Already in the Hebrew Bible letters as modes of communication have their place (Jeremiah: 45:1), but in the New Testament this mode of personal discourse became a crucial part of social organization and doctrinal development in the hands of Paul. Paul was of course a key founder of the Christian movement, who had converted from Pharisaism. Some of the extant letters were personal: most notably those offering advice about his former slave to Philemon, and those written to his apostolic companions Timothy and Titus (though the tone of these suggests that they might come from a hand later than Paul). But such personal correspondence is overshadowed by the extraordinary extension of the letter form by Paul into a mode of discourse, the reading of which was clearly intended to have a catalytic effect on a nascent community seeking in the absence of the author to bring about a semblance of order and conformity to apostolic rule. This is most clearly seen in the Corinthian correspondence, where the mix of personal apology, exhortation, detailed advice, and doctrinal exploration represents a concerted attempt to offer a peculiar manual of practice for those who were separated from the author by hundreds of miles.

Biblical Hermeneutics

Hermeneutics is about interpretation. It is a word that is used in a variety of different ways in modern writing. The more obvious usage is to describe reflection on how it is one goes about reading a text and the methods used, whether consciously or unconsciously. It is, therefore, a second order activity in which one stands back and attempts a considered contemplation of what has been happening in one's own reading practice or in that of others. It is also used to describe the ways in which ancient texts are related to the contemporary world. In this mode it functions as a kind of mediating activity, bridging the gap between an authoritative text like the Bible and the time of the reader. This approach to reading is something that is as old as the Bible itself, for New Testament writers were constantly trying to see how the ancient Jewish Scriptures related to their belief and practice. Thus, typology and allegory are two ways in which the gap could be bridged and related to the experience of the writers and their readers.

Types of Exegesis

Exegesis means interpretation. From the beginning of the engagement with received tradition, different ways of reading were established. There is a basic distinction between literal and figurative, or allegorical, exegesis: the first is about attempting accurately to describe what the text actually says, while the second means probing the text for its deeper meaning.

Literal exegesis of Scripture is an enterprise in which the basic tasks, such as consultation of the best manuscripts and accurate construal and translation of passages in the original, enable a reader to know what the text actually says and means. The early Christian writer Augustine (354–430 CE) sets this out in his influential manual of biblical and doctrinal exposition:

> The student who fears God earnestly seeks his will in the holy scriptures. Holiness makes him gentle, so that he does not revel in controversy; a knowledge of languages protects him from uncertainty over unfamiliar words and phrases, and a knowledge of certain essential things protects him from ignorance of the significance and detail of what is used by way of imagery. Thus equipped, and with the assistance of reliable texts derived from manuscripts with careful attention to the need for emendation, he should now approach the task of analysing and resolving the ambiguities of the scriptures. When in the literal usages that make scripture ambiguous, we must first of all make sure that we have not punctuated or articulated the passage incorrectly. Once close consideration has revealed that it is uncertain how a passage should be punctuated and articulated, we must consult the rule of faith, as it is perceived through the plainer passages of the scriptures and the authority of the church. (Augustine, *De Doctrina Christiana* iii.1)

What Augustine sets out here is basically what is often described as "lower criticism." This is contrasted with the "higher criticism" that characterizes modern historical exegesis, one that is less concerned with what the text tells us about doctrine and morals, and more with the history and the circumstances of its writings and its sources.

Biblical studies witnessed a significant shift at the end of the eighteenth century with the rise of the historical method. This meant that a method of interpretation based on the received wisdom of the Christian tradition was over time replaced with a form of interpretation that either had only loose ties to the earlier tradition or rejected it completely. The character of traditional Christian exegesis is set out in Augustine's *De Doctrina Christiana* ii.16–21:

> It is therefore necessary above all else to be moved by the fear of God towards learning his will: what it is that he instructs us to see or avoid. ... After that it is necessary, through holiness, to become docile, and not contradict holy scripture – whether we understand it (as when it hits at some of our vices) or fail to understand it (as when we feel that we could by ourselves gain a better knowledge or give better instruction) – but ponder and believe that what is written there, even if obscure, is better and truer than any insights that we may gain by our own efforts. After these two stages of fear and holiness comes the third stage, that of knowledge. ... This is the area in which every student of divine scripture exerts himself, and what he finds in them is simply that he must love God for himself, and his neighbour for God's sake. ... It is vital that the reader first learns from the scriptures that he is entangled in the love of this present age. ... It is at this point that the fear which makes him ponder the judgement of God, and holiness which makes it impossible for him not to admit and submit to the authority of the holy books, compel him to deplore his condition. ... When he beholds this light ... he strenuously occupies himself with the love of his neighbour and becomes perfect in it. (Translation R. P. H. Green, 1995)

The task of understanding meaning almost always moves beyond the literal through recourse to analogies, such as parallels drawn from other texts, whether inside or outside the Bible, or through historical reconstruction. Allegorical interpretation presupposes that the letter of the text points to another level of reality as well as other dimensions of meaning. The literal sense of Scripture thereby yields a "deeper," "transcendent" meaning as may be seen in the contrast between two cities and two covenants (for example, Galatians 4:24). Allegorical exegesis, therefore, involves the ability of the interpreter to discern in a piece of biblical text subject matter different from the apparent subject, even though the latter may suggest it.

Typology is the juxtaposition of types (including people, institutions, or events), and is employed in exegesis when a biblical scene or figure is taken up and viewed as an interpretative analogy for a contemporary belief or practice.[3] The relationship between type and antitype is suggested by the accumulation of points of correspondence between two (or more) narratives or characters. The type and the antitype are not identical and cannot be one and the same person, institution, or event, since, by definition, typology involves a process of describing one thing in terms of another. The correspondences are consequently based on difference as well as similarity. Thus Paul in 1 Corinthians 10 can see an analogy between what had happened to the disobedient people of Israel in the wilderness and the Corinthian Christians with whom he has to deal. What Paul seems to suggest is that the earlier story is not primarily about what happened to the people of Israel in the past but is written specifically as a warning for the recipients of the letter. Indeed, it seems as if Paul wants to suggest to erstwhile pagans that the story of Israel and its origins was now their story and they too could find both warning and solace in it. The type functions, therefore, as a warning to readers not to pursue a path similar to that followed in the original story.

Allegory differs from typology in one key respect. Whereas typology depends for its success on the interplay between figures or incidents – Isaac and Christ, for example, or the serpent lifted up by Moses versus the Son of man being lifted up in John 3:14 – allegory opens up another, "deeper" level of meaning latent within a text's literal sense. In the complex reference to allegorical exegesis made by Paul in Galatians 4:24, the Sarah/Hagar story of Genesis 16 and 21 becomes a gateway to another level of understanding: what the text REALLY means is that the two women represent two covenants or two cities, Sinai and the new covenant, or the Jerusalem below and the Jerusalem above. The literal sense of the text in allegorical exegesis becomes a signifier of another dimension of meaning.

The tradition of figurative and allegorical exegesis was pioneered in particular by Origen (c.185–254), one of the founders of the Alexandrian school of exegesis. Despite his reputation as an allegorical exegete, Origen was also a careful philologist, who made use of the best critical methods of his day. For all his critical brilliance, however, Origen was interested not in philological or historical analysis for its own sake, but in how it could serve a more important goal: the training of the soul so as to lead it back to God. The excesses of allegorical interpretation led to a significant reaction, as the literal sense became little more than an excuse for the most fanciful of moralistic and doctrinal exposition. Followers of the so-called Antiochene school of exegesis (for example, Theodore of Mopsuestia, c.350–428) sought to drag Christian biblical interpretation back to the letter of the text. Antiochenes had a concern with the literal sense that included reference to historical context as well as purely spiritual exposition. In many ways they pointed forward to the reaction against allegorical and other forms of figurative interpretation in the early modern period when Luther, Calvin, and other protestant exegetes, stressed the indispensable foundation of the pursuit of the literal sense of Scripture.

The issue of criteria has always been important in the developing tradition of Christian exegesis, particularly as emerging orthodoxy sought to distinguish its own approach to Scripture from rival interpretations. In the face of conflicting interpretations of the Scriptures, there emerged the rule of faith, a concise summary of the basic articles of the Christian faith, the origins of which can be found in New Testament passages (e.g. Philippians 2:6–11; 1 Timothy 3:16). Christian interpreters formulated exegetical rules to assist with interpretation and to set the bounds of interpretative possibility. The Reformation saw a reaction against dominant trends in exegesis that in some ways resembled the earlier reaction against the allegorical exegesis of Origen. John Calvin's (1509–64) commentaries take up grammatical and historical matters. Martin Luther's (1483–1546) concerns are more overtly theological and interpretative, as he sought to find a basic principle for interpreting Scripture. Luther stressed the importance of the plain statement of the gospel as the heart of the Christian message, and stressed it was this by which all else in the Bible and Christian interpretation should be judged.

In the last decades of the twentieth century there emerged a variety of contextual theologies, including feminist theology and liberation theology. These models involve a conscious avowal of the importance of the ways in which readers' social contexts determine exegesis. Within these methodologies, connections are made between contemporary commitments and the experience of oppression on the one hand and biblical passages on the other. This way of reading the Bible has many affinities with earlier appropriations of Scripture in that there is an imaginative interface between the biblical text and the existential situation of the interpreter. Modern exegesis of the Bible is increasingly polarized between those who appeal to the letter of the Bible as the basis for doctrine and ethics, and those who seek to allow the insights of the modern world to have their part to play in determining meaning.

Notes

1   http://www.cnn.com/2003/LAW/11/13/moore.tencommandments/
2   Stephen Prickett, *Origins of Narrative: the Romantic Appropriation of the Bible* (Cambridge University Press, Cambridge, 1996).
3   On the importance of typology for Christian biblical exegesis, see Hans Frei *The Eclipse of Biblical Narrative* (Yale University Press, New Haven, 1974).

CHAPTER 3

Biblical Hermeneutics and Literary Theory

David Jasper

Although most contemporary studies of literary theory rarely if ever mention the Bible and usually look back to classical texts such as Aristotle or Horace's *On the Art of Poetry*, much in our theory of literature and understanding of literary processes derives from hermeneutical practices both within the canon of biblical literature and within the tradition of its interpretation. As a word, *hermeneutics* has its origins in the activity of the Greek god Hermes, the messenger whose task it was to interpret to people of the earth the messages and secrets of the Olympic gods. Hermeneutics, therefore, comes to mean the theory of interpretation, and specifically interpretation that seeks to bridge the gap between the divine and the human realms. Inasmuch, therefore, as the Christian Bible is understood as "the word of God," its role as sacred Scripture is traditionally perceived as being to reveal the divine message and activity to human readers. But the truth in texts is never simply self-evident, and texts must be interpreted, interpretation always presupposing some kind of theory: how we read is always in the context of necessary presuppositions, and this can be seen even within and between the biblical texts themselves. For example, the opening chapters of St Matthew's Gospel presuppose a particular way of reading and interpreting the literature of the Hebrew Bible as itself interpretative of the events of Jesus birth, which begins to turn this literature into what the Christian tradition knows as the Old Testament.

Before we turn to a brief review of biblical hermeneutics *within* the Bible, we should recognize the largely accepted claim that what Terry Eagleton has called "the rise of English"[1] as an academic study in the nineteenth century and the development of modern literary theory are to some degree the consequence of the decline of the Bible received as a sacred text. It is sometimes said that with the decline of formal religion, the status of the Bible as a *literary* and *aesthetic* paradigm grew.[2] Literature, then, begins to appropriate the Bible so that a Professor of English Literature early in the twentieth century, George Gordon, remarked that, with the failure of the Churches, the function of English literature is "to delight and instruct us, but also, and above all, to save our souls and heal the state."[3] Some years later, in 1935, T. S. Eliot expressed the view that the end of the Bible as a *sacred* text spelled the end also of its literary influence: "The Bible has had a *literary* influence upon English literature *not* because it has been considered as literature, but because it has been considered as the report of the Word of God."[4] I am inclined to think that he was probably right.

Yet the Bible, or at least a great deal of it, is certainly worthy of the title literature, though not, as the author of one book entitled *The Bible as Literature* has suggested, "in any normal sense."[5] But within the biblical canon there are poems and lyrics, narratives and stories that function and relate to one another in complex ways "as literature." It is probable, for example, that the book of Job is based on a much more ancient epic poem, adapted for later use. Modern literary theory has compared and contrasted the literature of the Bible with the classical traditions of poetry,[6] and acknowledged the importance of ancient Rabbinic forms of scriptural interpretation for contemporary literary understanding.[7] The texts and the drive to understand them *theologically* gave rise to forms of interpretation that have continued to be important in literary hermeneutics. For example, in typological readings, figures and events in the Hebrew Bible are seen as prefigurements of persons and events in the Christian story and thus their authenticity is guaranteed by ancient foreshadowings. Thus Isaiah 7:14 with its reference to the birth of a child called Immanuel is linked to the identity of Jesus. Not far removed from typology is Dryden's allegorical satire *Absalom and Achitophel* (1681), which links 2 Samuel 13–19 with contemporary politics and intrigues.

But it is in the interpretations of Scripture by the early Christian Church that many of the ground rules of subsequent literary readings are firmly established, and we can here be no more than highly selective. St Augustine of Hippo's *De Doctrina Christiana* (*c.*427 CE) begins with a clear statement of purpose.

> There are certain rules for interpreting the scriptures which, as I am well aware, can be usefully passed on to those with an appetite for such study to enable them to progress not just by reading the works of others who have illuminated the obscurities of divine literature, but also by finding illumination themselves.[8]

In book two of this work, Augustine outlines a remarkably clear exposition of what we would now call *semiotics* – the study of signs – in anticipation of what literary theory knows as *structuralism*, and it is extraordinary that a standard modern text such as Terence Hawkes's *Structuralism and Semiotics* (1977) does not even acknowledge Augustine. In his reading of the Bible, Augustine also elaborates on the issue of *intentionality*, establishing his principle of charitable intention in reading, another theme in literary theory since the American New Critics of the 1940s and W. K. Wimsatt's seminal 1946 essay "The Intentional Fallacy." Referring to the pattern suggested in Galatians 4:22–7, Augustine develops an allegorical approach to the reading of the Bible that has permeated English literature, the greatest example being found, perhaps, in John Bunyan's *The Pilgrim's Progress* (1678–84). In fact, the allegorical interpretation of Scripture was much more ancient than Augustine, and in the work of Origen of Alexandria (*c.*185 to *c.*254), especially *De Principiis*, he proposes allegorical readings on the principle that the invisible world pervades the whole universe through discernible signs and symbols. Everything is to be perceived in its corporeal and spiritual aspect, so that, for example, a respect for the historical details of the Fourth Gospel is combined with a complex symbolism such that Christ's seamless robe (John 19:23) is understood both as an actual garment and as symbolizing the wholeness of Christ's teaching.[9]

Origen's capacity to read the biblical text on a number of different levels at once, a characteristic he has in common with biblical interpreters until well into the Middle Ages but which was largely discouraged after the Reformation, was also, though for less theological reasons, a characteristic of Romantic poetics as they developed through the nineteenth century,[10] and is recovered in the varieties of open-ended readings within postmodern literary theory.[11] In fact, it is remarkable how contemporary biblical exegetes like Augustine and Origen seem to the eye of the modern literary theorist, a salutary reminder to those who subscribe to the notion, still widespread, that the roots of literary theory lie in the essentially secular and post-religious fields of various forms of Marxism, psychoanalysis, and liberation movements.[12] In some respects this sense of literary modernity is sustained even through the long centuries of medieval biblical readings and up to the new flowering of European thought in the High Renaissance. For example, St Bernard of Clairvaux's magnificent sermons on the Song of Songs (*Super Cantica Canticorum*, c.1135–53) pursue Origen's allegorical and even mystical readings, but with a freedom and flexibility approaching the postmodern. In his first sermon he reflects upon the kiss – "Let him kiss me with the kiss of his mouth," understood in a thoroughly intimate manner. The text leads the reader on:

> Surely this way of "beginning without a beginning," this freshness of expression in so old a book, must capture the reader's attention? It is clear that this work was not written by human wit, but was composed by the art of the Spirit. As a result, even if it is difficult to understand, it is nevertheless a source of delight to him who looks into it.[13]

The sense of open textuality, freedoms from beginnings and endings, the acknowledgment of the intentional fallacy, the accommodation to difficulty as a legitimate element in response, all have a contemporary ring. Bernard's imaginative energy also anticipates the poetics of Renaissance literature, as in, for instance, Sir Philip Sidney's *Apology for Poetry* (1595), in which, like Erasmus, Sidney stresses the necessity of the imagination, and it is there in the Bible, as an antidote to the philosopher's jargon of "genus and difference" and mere doctrines "which, notwithstanding lie dark before the imaginative and judging power, if they be not illuminated or figured forth by the speaking power of poesy."[14] Sidney then refers the reader back to Christ's teaching through parables that, by their claims upon the imagination "More constantly ... inhabit both the memory and the judgement."

One of the greatest glories of the Reformation is the translation of the Bible into vernaculars, in George Steiner's words, into a "more concrete translation of Christ's teaching both into daily speech and daily life."[15] William Tyndale prefaces his magnificent translation into English of the New Testament (1534) – one of the most influential works in English literature and forming the basis of all English Bibles until the middle years of the last century – with remarks on the nature of textuality that biblical criticism as it developed from the end of the eighteenth century too often neglected. Tyndale seeks to unlock the text from the "dark learning" of academic sophistry in way that anticipate the principles of formalism and New Criticism, and warns the reader that the text must be taken as a whole so that we do not founder over the particular difficulties of decontextualized verses. "And in many places, where the text seemeth at the first chop hard to be understood, yet the circumstances before and after, and often reading together, maketh it plain enough etc."[16] Tyndale not only attends to the process of reading, he anticipates what we would now call "reader response criticism" in his emphasis on the circumstances of the reader in the process of interpretation.[17] Nor is Tyndale the first in this: the same focus is found in his translation of Erasmus's *Exhortations to the Diligent Study of Scripture* (1529), and it was Erasmus who was also eager to contextualize the reading of the Bible in the wide sea of Western literature, in the "sensible reading of the pagan poets and philosophers."[18] This anticipation of the placing of the Bible in the context of *Weltliteratur* by Goethe and Romanticism centuries later was diametrically opposite to Martin Luther's principle of *sola scriptura* – the Bible alone, which insists that if "Homer, Virgil, and other noble, fine, and profitable writers, have left us books of great antiquity ... they are nought to the Bible."[19] The consequence of Luther's isolation of Scripture, as well as his emphasis on the literal sense alone, actually strikes a division between the sacred and the secular realms of literature that set the seal on the Enlightenment's prioritizing of reason in the process of interpretation, the setting apart of the Bible as a "sacred" text, and finally the crisis of biblical authority in the separation between readings driven by piety and readings driven by critical analysis. But before we review the rise of the historical critical paradigm in biblical studies, we need to acknowledge the achievement of Robert Lowth (1710–87), Oxford Professor of Poetry and later Bishop of London, and his remarkable work *Lectures on the Sacred Poetry of the Hebrews* (1753).[20] Lowth, we might say, rediscovered the form and structure of Hebrew poetry, based on the principle of *parallelism*, in a work of close reading of the Bible that constitutes a major achievement in structural analysis, and sets apart the *literary* study of the Bible (the Bible *as* literature) from the more formal, historical and theological studies of the enterprise of "biblical criticism" (more interested, at best, in the Bible *and* literature). With Lowth we are, undoubtedly, within the history of literary criticism with his emphasis on the nature of poetic language. He begins his fourth lecture in the following way.

> The origin and first use of poetical language are undoubtedly to be traced into the vehement affections of the mind. For what is meant by that singular frenzy of poets, which the Greeks, ascribing to divine inspiration, distinguished by the appellation of *enthusiasm*, but a style and expression directly prompted by nature itself, and exhibiting the true and express image of a mind violently agitated?[21]

What this sets up is a tension between literature on the one hand, and the theological and historical underpinnings of the future of biblical criticism on the other, that has only now begun to dissolve as the roots of much literary theory in more ancient biblical hermeneutics have slowly begun to be acknowledged.[22]

In the eighteenth century, the technical study of the Bible, shaped by such works as Edward Gibbon's *The History of the Decline and Fall of the Roman Empire* (1776–88), became both learned and skeptical, focusing on both the historicity of the biblical narratives and the historical roots of the texts themselves. Thus the German scholar H. S.

Reimarus (1694–1768) embarked on what was to become an ultimately fruitless but continually renewed quest for the historical Jesus by his reading of the gospels as no more than early Christian elaborations on the simple "facts" by speculation and mythologizing. Another German scholar, Johann Gottfried Eichhorn (1752–1827), the author of massive "Introductions" to both Old and New Testaments, dismissed much of the literature of the Old Testament as merely primitive outpourings of an unsophisticated people, their greatest poetry simply the ramblings of an almost prehistoric race.[23] As we look ahead into the nineteenth century we can see the implications of such thinking expressly stated in the controversial work of David Friedrich Strauss, *Das Leben Jesu* (1835), quietly translated into English by Marian Evans, the future novelist George Eliot, as *The Life of Jesus Critically Examined* (1846), a task that drove her, significantly, from her youthful Evangelicalism and theology into the vocation of a writer of serious fiction. Writing of the gospels, Strauss concludes, in George Eliot's translation:

> we stand here upon purely mythical-poetical ground; the only historical reality which we can hold fast as a positive matter of fact being this: – the impression made by John the Baptist, by virtue of his ministry and his relation to Jesus, was so powerful as to lead to the subsequent glorification of his birth in connection with the birth of the Messiah in the Christian legend.[24]

The division here is absolute: between truth grounded in history alone, and the "purely" literary, which is the stuff of legend and mere fanciful unrealities. Thirty years after Strauss's work, another *Life of Jesus*, by the Frenchman Ernest Renan, a Professor of Semitic Languages,[25] was to be hailed by Albert Schweitzer as "an event in world literature,"[26] but judged as wanting because it was *bad* literature, abounding in distressing lapses of taste, and "the art of the wax image." In every sense, the Bible and its critics were losing ground in wider cultural discussions as, on the one hand, an increasingly academic historical critical byway, and, on the other, productive of bad literature that is not really to be taken seriously anyway in matters of truth.

But this is not the whole story. Of necessity our reference to two figures, one German and one English, will be brief, but that hardly represents their importance both in the history of biblical interpretation and in the establishment of the principles of literary criticism, that is, of literary theory. Friedrich Schleiermacher (1768–1834) was born of German pietist stock, but at the same time a formidably learned theologian and philosopher. Although barely acknowledged in the history of literary theory, he was in fact a major figure in the establishment of modern principles of hermeneutics such as to overcome the increasing isolation of the biblical text from other literature. For Schleiermacher insisted that the processes of interpretation must be universal and that the Bible should be offered no privileges. He regarded reading as an art and the reader must therefore be as much of a creative artist as the author. The negotiations that go on between text and reader are born out of two anxieties: the first is the anxiety to be understood (which is why we write), and the second is the anxiety to understand (which is why we read). One hundred and fifty years later, the literary critic Harold

Bloom was to write an influential "theory of poetry" entitled *The Anxiety of Influence* (1973), in which there is not one mention of Schleiermacher. Furthermore, Bloom's book was dedicated to William K. Wimsatt, the author of the essay "The Intentional Fallacy," and again, it was Schleiermacher who formulated the task of the interpreter as "To understand the text at first as well as and then even better than its author."[27] In other words, in principle we must go beyond the conscious intention of the author, to which we have no direct access, and "try to become aware of many things of which he himself may have been unconscious."

The second figure within Romanticism is the English poet and critic Samuel Taylor Coleridge (1772–1834). In the posthumously published series of "letters" entitled *Confessions of An Inquiring Spirit* (1840), in the words of the Advertisement to the first edition, "the Reader will find ... a key to most of the Biblical criticism scattered throughout the Author's own writings."[28] Coleridge is careful to define his critical terms, such as inspiration, the literal, and the figurative, but above all he compares the Bible with his greatest literary hero, William Shakespeare, insisting, like Schleiermacher, that the principles of interpretation are the same in each case, and that we should interpret St Paul like "any other honest and intelligent writer or speaker."[29] Furthermore, just as Shakespeare's canon of writings must be taken as a whole from the greatest of the tragedies to *Titus Andronicus*, in order to gain a necessary sense of "unity or total impression," so also must the Bible be taken as a whole, not selected for reasons of theology or aesthetics. It is a good literary principle. But perhaps the key to Coleridge's reading of the Bible is his sense that meaning and significance do not lie hidden within the text, to be excavated, so to speak, by interpretative procedures, but are found in the interactive process between the reader and the book, reading being seen as a kind of voyage of discovery in this exchange. He hates what he calls "bibliolatry," that is, the unthinking assumption that the truth is simply and absolutely there within the text, to be dug out. But it is in the interactive process between text and reader, and only in this, that the particular nature of the Bible is to be discovered. As Coleridge says in Letter II of the *Confessions*:

> in the Bible there is more that *finds* me than I have experienced in all other books together; ... the words of the Bible find me at greater depths of my being, and that whatever finds me brings with it an irresistible evidence of its having proceeded from the Holy Spirit.[30]

The conclusion, of course, may be different, but the principle is familiar to modern literary theory in Wolfgang Iser's phenomenological approach to the "reading process," as he states that

> the literary work has two poles, which we might call the artistic and the esthetic: the artistic refers to the text created by the author, and the esthetic to the realization accomplished by the reader. From this polarity it follows that the literary work cannot be completely identical with the text, or with the realization of the text, but in fact must lie half-way between the two. The work is more than the text, for the text only takes on life when it is realized, and furthermore the realization is by no means independent of the individual disposition of the reader.[31]

But Coleridge's most underestimated and neglected work on biblical interpretation is his "Lay Sermon" of 1816 entitled *The Statesman's Manual, or The Bible the Best Guide to Political Skill and Foresight*, "addressed to the higher classes of society."[32] Here he explores the living power of words in Scripture, and addresses the growing critical division between historical and "literary" critical approaches to the text, that is, between what we might now call the diachronic and the synchronic, or in his words between the *Temporal* and the *Eternal*. "In the Scriptures therefore both Facts and Persons must of necessity have a two-fold significance, a past and a future, a temporary and a perpetual, a particular and a universal application. They must be at once Portraits and Ideals."[33] Not only does this recognize the growing problem of historical criticism of the Bible, and suggest a way of reading Scripture that was only picked up again well over a hundred years later in work of the Oxford New Testament critic and philosopher of religion Austin Farrer and the literary critic Frank Kermode,[34] but it relates reading, through an understanding of the symbolic, to a sacramental understanding of religious experience that the study of literature and theology has barely yet acknowledged let alone pursued. Coleridge's achievement in the face of the rise of historical criticism of the Bible, with its almost scientific and clearly poentially disintegrative claims, is well described by Eleanor Shaffer in her book *"Kubla Khan" and The Fall of Jerusalem* (1975):

> In order to salvage Christianity, historical criticism had to be made constructive as well as destructive; the result was a new form of history. If what was of prime importance was not the eternal message of the gospels, but the particular historical circumstances of their origin, then these circumstances represented an enabling milieu in which sacred events of this kind could take place. If the sacred writings of other nations were examined n their historical setting, then one might arrive again at a general view of the conditions of religious experience. It was the work of several generations to grasp this possibility and to carry it out. But it was in such a mythologized history that the solution to both the literary and the religious problem was to be found.[35]

Coleridge, it must be admitted, never attracted a wide reading public, and until the work on the *Collected Edition* of his writings and his *Notebooks* in the second half of the twentieth century has been known largely as a poet and colleague of Wordsworth. But one of his disciples, the Broad Church clergyman F. D. Maurice, attributed his lack of a readership to the difficulty of his work and the unwillingness of people to take "the trouble of examination," asserting that "thought can only address itself to thought, and truth be won only by those who will toil to gain her." He further remarked that "Wordsworth and Coleridge belong to the coming ages, and we need not fear that any honour which those ages can pay them will be withheld."[36] Yet even in the nineteenth century, the effect of Coleridge's reading of the Bible was filtered through the influential writings of Matthew Arnold, and through him their influence has been felt on such modern literary critics as Frank Kermode and Northrop Frye.

In such works as *Literature and Dogma* (1873) and *God and the Bible* (1975), Arnold does manage to make St Paul seem like a rather genteel Victorian rationalist, but seeks to rescue the Bible in literary terms and reintroduce it to critical reading as an indispensable foundation to culture.[37] In such important essays as "The Function of Criticism at the Present Time" (1864), Arnold, learning from his father Thomas Arnold, Coleridge, and before them Spinoza, sought to recover the Bible from those who would pick it apart as a historical document, or on "scientific" principles, and this, he suggests, is the function of criticism. The role of the literary critic is to stand between the imagination (literature) and understanding (science), offering a sound theoretical basis to the appreciation of poetry – and not least the poetry of the Bible, for the word "God" itself, he suggests in *Literature and Dogma*, is "a term of poetry and eloquence." Literary criticism, then, can heal the modern rift between heart and head, between thought and feeling. "The main element of the modern spirit's life," he said, "is neither the senses and understanding, nor the heart and imagination; it is the imaginative reason."[38] But this suggestion, is not, for Arnold, merely an escape from religion into literature. In "The Function of Criticism" he looks back to Coleridge and refers to Renan as examples of those who are not making war on the Bible but seeking "a fresh synthesis of the New Testament *data*,"[39] using the tools of culture and literature, and they are not insignificant. Later in our story we will review the return of the Bible to literary studies in the later years of the twentieth century in such monuments to scholarship as Frank Kermode and Robert Alter's *Literary Guide to the Bible* (1987), as a serious, if limited, contender with the still largely historical tools of the "biblical critics," and this project owes much to the work of Arnold.

Yet Arnold's tone is melancholic. The ebbing tide of Dover Beach and Victorian "honest doubt" deeply underlie his reading of the Bible. Something is missing in his biblical hermeneutics. Stephen Prickett has argued that the rising prestige of the Bible as a literary and aesthetic model resulted in its "appropriation" into literature; not, that is, its replacement *by* literature as Professor George Gordon seems to suggest, but its absorption into, above all, the narratives of the Victorian novel, which as it lends itself to them, so it becomes interpreted through the forms of nineteenth century fiction. What, in Thomas Carlyle's phrase in *Sartor Resartus*, we might call the "natural supernaturalism" of the secular pilgrims of the Victorian novel,[40] mirrors the pilgrims of biblical literature, the Bible translated yet again into the language and culture of the time. Yet the Bible is never quite absorbed into literature, its hermeneutics still demanding a distinct attention, which is why literary theory, although deeply rooted in the traditions of biblical interpretation, nevertheless remains uneasy with them, unwilling finally to acknowledge them. The point may be illustrated by reference to one of the most celebrated of all nineteenth century fictions, Charlotte Brontë's *Jane Eyre* (1847). As St John Rivers tries to persuade Jane to focus her sense of duty on her heavenly home he reads from Revelation 21, the source of "natural supernaturalism": "he sat there, bending over the great old Bible, and described from its page the vision of the new heaven and the new earth – told how God would come to dwell with men."[41] But for Rivers this is never literally true. Jane will eventually find its fulfillment in her love for Rochester (while Rivers "put love out of the question"), and not in the heavenly mansions to which Rivers calls her. In *Jane Eyre*, the biblical vision is appropriated by and absorbed into the Romantic vision – yet the end, disconcertingly, is not with Jane and Rochester in their married bliss "buried deep in a wood," but with the unmarried Rivers in the mission field and approaching death and "his sure reward, his incorruptible crown."[42] The novel ends with the final words of the book of Revelation, awkwardly outside the romantic story, somehow beyond interpretation yet, in the figure of St John Rivers, somehow belittled and somewhat less than fully human.

Jane Eyre forces us to acknowledge what T. S. Eliot was to insist upon in his essay "Religion and Literature" (1935): that the Bible can never be considered simply *as* literature, can never be simply absorbed into the literary canon, and has an enduring and somehow unique influence upon literature and literary interpretation. As a character in Antonia Byatt's novel *Babel Tower* (1997) puts it, "the narrative of the Novel in its high days was built on, out of, and in opposition to the narrative of the One Book, the source of all Books, the Bible."[43] That opposition is supremely important, and why D. H. Lawrence's description of the Bible as "a great confused novel" that is not about God but "is really about man alive" does not go far enough.[44] For the Bible is, irreduceably, about God, and God's dealing with his people, and that is precisely why it remains at the very heart of the hermeneutical enterprise of literary criticism, since hermeneutics derives its name from the Greek god Hermes, the messenger of the Olympian gods, whose task it was to convey messages from the divine heights to the people of earth, a bridge between two realms of discourse that endlessly prompts and resists theory, and this paradox is identified by Paul de Man (though he would not have attributed his thoughts to a biblical origin) in his essay "The Resistance to Theory": "The resistance to theory which ... is a resistance to reading, appears in its most rigorous and theoretically elaborated form among the theoreticians of reading who dominate the contemporary theoretical scene."[45] Thus the Bible cannot be finally appropriated by literature, and in this sense, de Man is curiously at one with, though at the same time very different from, T. S. Eliot in Eliot's claim that "literary criticism should be completed by criticism from a definite ethical and theological standpoint," though at the same time "we must remember that whether it is literature or not can be determined only by literary standards."[46]

Eliot's essay in some way opened the door to the flowering of a form of literary criticism that emerged in the later years of the twentieth century that we might call "Bible and literature," which set itself up against the venerable project of "biblical criticism" as professionally pursued and underwritten by historical assumptions. It was self-consciously "new," as is clear from the General Introduction of the somewhat immodestly entitled *The Literary Guide to the Bible* (1987), edited by Frank Kermode and Robert Alter. They write:

> The effectiveness of this new approach – or approaches, for the work has proceeded along many different paths – has now been amply demonstrated. Professional biblical criticism has been profoundly affected by it but even more important, the general reader can now be offered a new view of the Bible as a work of great literary force and authority, a work of which it is entirely credible that it should have shaped the minds and lives of intelligent men and women for two millennia and more.[47]

This somewhat mandarin claim – it is by no means clear that *intelligence* has necessarily much to do with the ancient and continuing authority of the Bible – is not only almost diametrically opposed to the position of Eliot. In opposition to Eliot also is the suggestion that the Bible can be wholly "accommodated" to the literary canon.[48] But in the project to explore new ways of reading the Bible,[49] what is most strange is the deliberate avoidance of literary theory or "those who use the text as a springboard for cultural or metaphysical ruminations."[50] By and large this avoidance of theory has characterized a great deal of the "literary readings of the Bible" from the work of Amos N. Wilder to Kermode and Alter themselves in such works as, respectively, *The Genesis of Secrecy* (1979) and *The Art of Biblical Narrative* (1981), and in more recent works like Shimon Levy's *The Bible as Theatre* (2000) or David Jasper and Stephen Prickett's *The Bible and Literature* (1999). The reason for this avoidance of the literary theoretical in literary readings of the Bible has been sharply suggested by Mieke Bal, a professor of comparative literature, in a lengthy review of the work of Robert Alter, Meir Sternberg, and Phyllis Trible, first published in the journal *Diacritics* in 1986.[51] Bal's fundamental criticism of these authors is their refusal to "challenge the traditional acceptance of social and theological ideologies that are assumed to underlie biblical literature."[52] In other words, their literary readings leave substantially undisturbed the ancient assumptions about biblical authority, while for Bal, literary theory offers the possibility of new *political* readings that seek to destabilize or deconstruct, for example, the patriarchal undercurrents of biblical theology. Thus, in her own feminist readings of the book of Judges in *Death and Dissymmetry* (1988), Bal employs such readings "to substantiate the countercoherence" in a radical feminist perspective and "its inherent power to underscore power; its adequacy, in its relation to the narrative structures and their semiotic status; its workability, in the direct relation between terms and heuristic questions."[53] Bal admits to the limitations of her feminist perspective, but claims that the very limitations allow her criticism to overturn neglected stones in the text, to tell a story in the biblical narrative that centuries of religious interpretation have ignored and left undisturbed at the cost of terrible suffering.

Bal's approach to the Bible is a self-consciously hermeneutical one in its deliberate exploration of the traditional assumptions that underlie the reading and appropriation of the Bible. Furthermore, like Hans-Georg Gadamer, in his monument to modern hermeneutical thinking, *Truth and Method* (1960), and other essays, she reminds us that the processes of understanding the biblical text should always acknowledge our experience of the whole of life.[54] Reading the Bible can never be an abstract experience, and thus Gadamer appeals primarily to "truth" rather than to "method" in the process of biblical interpretation. In his essay "Aesthetic and Religious Experience,"[55] he draws a close connection between poetic and religious speech. Each is a creative event, related to the concept of "play," which, for Gadamer, is deeply serious, "absorbing the player into itself" and its world. At the heart of biblical interpretation must be our response to the proclamation of the Gospel message in sermon and in liturgy or order of service. In other words, the Bible within the Christian tradition is a world to be entered into with radical consequences because, says Gadamer, "the Christian message represents a challenge that shatters all our natural expectations."[56] If our understanding is defined by our openness to the radical "other" it is also dependent on a serious acknowledgment of our own historical situation. In other words, our relationship with the biblical literature is unavoidably political.

The political and theological threat within more recent postmodern literary theory to the interpretation of the Bible, dating from the 1980s, is graphically portrayed by

Stephen D. Moore, a self-styled *enfant terrible* of New Testament critics, and an Irishman brought up on the imagery of W. B. Yeats. He writes:

> What are the prospects, actually, for a demythologized, postmodernist, or philosophical biblical criticism? Unwanted by so many, will it dare to crawl forth from the womb – or will it scuttle back into the darkness? More specifically, what are the chances of gospel literary criticism taking a broad philosophical turn? Literary criticism of the Gospels at present, while it does manifest a variety of forms, clusters around a few preferred foci. ... Narrative criticism ... with reader-in-the-gospel criticism leaning on its arm, seems to be the most successful literary approach. ... But if narrative criticism sometimes presents the aspect of a genial reform movement within historical criticism, philosophical or poststructuralist biblical criticism – for now they amount to the same thing – presents the forbidding aspect of a millenarian sect and has had as little general appeal.[57]

Moore was a member of a group of scholars who described themselves as the Bible and Culture Collective and produced a volume entitled *The Postmodern Bible* (1995) offering seven approaches to the Bible, including criticism from a psychoanalytic and ideological perspective. Their confessed purpose was to expose "the still highly contested epistemological, political, and ethical positions in the field of biblical studies,"[58] that is, a radical overturning of the assumptions inherent in tradition biblical interpretation and an exposure of the power of the Bible in culture and society both for good and ill. An even more recent development of such political criticism has been in the field of postcolonial studies and their examination of forms of interpretation of the biblical texts in their capacity to legitimate oppressive imperialist regimes.[59]

One of the characteristics of postmodern literary readings of the Bible has been a new attention to forms of textuality, and an important volume edited by Regina M. Schwartz, a member of the Bible and Culture Collective, is entitled *The Book and the Text: The Bible and Literary Theory* (1990). An essay by Gerald L. Bruns in this book signals a postmodern return to the hermeneutics of midrash, a ancient rabbinic practice of interpretation of the Bible that celebrates an abundance of conversation in the profuse play of the text, always contemporary and always open-ended.[60] Significantly, two great contemporary Jewish scholars, Emmanuel Levinas and Jacques Derrida, feature in a companion volume to *The Postmodern Bible*, *The Postmodern Bible Reader* (2001). In an essay entitled "Whom to Give to (Knowing Not to Know)," the central figure in postmodern literary theory, Derrida, returns to Jewish understanding of the nature of textuality in his reference to St Paul in the context of Kierkegaard's meditation on Genesis 22, the sacrifice of Isaac in *Fear and Trembling*.

> One can understand why Kierkegaard chose, for his title, the words of a great Jewish convert, Paul, in order to meditate on the still Jewish experience of a secret, hidden, separate, absent, or mysterious God, the one who decides, without revealing his reasons, to demand of Abraham that most cruel, impossible, and untenable gesture: to offer his son Isaac as a sacrifice.[61]

The Pauline text in question is Philippians 2:13: "For it is God which worketh in you both to will and to do of his good pleasure." It gives rise to Derrida's intertextual reflection on both Genesis and Kierkegaard, a reflection on the nature of theological discourse, from which he proposes that "we don't speak with God or to God, we don't speak with God or to God as with others or to our fellows."[62] In a way, therefore, postmodern criticism is a return, by an odd route, to the traditional sense of the Bible (though perhaps its intertexts in literature and philosophy as well) as a different kind of discourse from all other conversations that we hold with our fellow human beings. To return to where we began in this essay, literary criticism *has* become "a kind of substitute theology."[63] Yet, at the same time, modern hermeneutics and literary theory is rooted in biblical hermeneutics, and most particularly in postmodern theory there has been a recovery of the ancient Rabbinic tradition of textuality that celebrates multiplicity, open interpretability, intertextuality, and the sense of interpretation itself as a divine act.

Literary criticism of the Bible has taken its place alongside the more established historical critical methods of biblical criticism as it has emerged as a distinct discipline in the past two hundred years or so. But only more recently in forms of postmodern or poststructuralist theory and practice has there been a more radical shift, at once new and, as we have seen, with ancient roots. It can perhaps be described most succinctly in what A. K. M. Adam has called the practice of "thinking the opposite,"[64] that is, a shift away from the common wisdom of biblical interpretation and an exposure, as Jacques Derrida has demonstrated, of the way in which theology and metaphysics has affected, directed, and even infected all our thinking about the texts of the Bible, both for good and, often, for ill.[65] Such thinking had led us to see that St Paul and other writers in the Bible are far more "postmodern" than we might have imagined, and that therefore the theology that we think through them needs to be revisited and reassessed. It is thus no accident that in recent years Paul has attracted the attention of a number of contemporary and often radical social and cultural thinkers such as Slavoj Žižek, Alain Badiou, and Giorgio Agamben.[66]

Biblical hermeneutics will always be odd, for there is no book like the Bible in its origins and in its reception. Yet at the same time it is locked within the very heart of literary and artistic culture, and therefore its broader interpretative and theoretical reaches. What is clear is that these exchanges will not cease with our own time, as the nature of biblical authority in an increasingly post-ecclesial age continues to change. Furthermore, as our reading of texts changes in an age of electronic media, the recovery of a new and vibrant sense of the visual in culture (as opposed to the merely verbal text), and the shifts in the graphic and visual arts, so the interpretation of the Bible must also respond to the growing range and availability of interpretative media, challenging scholarship and the traditional appropriation of the scriptural texts.

Notes

1   Terry Eagleton, *Literary Theory: An Introduction,* 2nd edn (Blackwell, Oxford, 1996), chapter 1, "The Rise of English," pp. 15–46.
2   A study that makes this a central claim is Stephen Prickett's *Origins of Narrative: The Romantic Appropriation of the Bible* (Cambridge University Press: Cambridge, 1996).

3   Quoted in Eagleton, op. cit., p. 20.

4   T. S. Eliot, *Selected Essays*, 3rd edn (Faber & Faber, London, 1951), p. 390.

5   T. R. Henn, *The Bible as Literature* (Lutterworth Press, London, 1970), p. 9. The phrase persists in the title of a more recent and widely read book: John B. Gabel, Charles B. Wheeler, and Anthony D. York, *The Bible as Literature: An Introduction*, 3rd edn (Oxford University Press, New York and Oxford, 1996).

6   See the famous essay "Odysseus' Scar," comparing a passage in Homer's *Odyssey* with Genesis 22, by Erich Auerbach, *Mimesis: The Representation of Reality in Western Literature*, trans. Willard R. Trask. (1946. Princeton University Press, Princeton, 1968), pp. 3–23.

7   See Susan A. Handelman, *The Slayers of Moses: The Emergence of Rabbinic Interpretation in Modern Literary Theory* (New York University Press, Albany, 1982).

8   St Augustine, *On Christian Teaching*, trans. R. P. H. Green (Oxford World Classics, Oxford, 1997), p. 3.

9   See further M. F. Wiles, *The Spiritual Gospel: The Interpretation of the Fourth Gospel in the Early Church* (Cambridge University Press, Cambridge, 1960), chapter 3, "Historicity and Symbolism."

10 See George P. Landow, *Victorian Types, Victorian Shadows: Biblical Typology in Victorian Literature, Art and Thought*. (Routledge & Kegan Paul, Boston and London, 1980).

11 See The Bible and Culture Collective, *The Postmodern Bible* (*Yale* University Press, New Haven, 1995).

12 Another good example of this modern spirit in patristic biblical exegesis is Gregory of Nyssa's Life of Moses (*c.*350 CE). There is an excellent recent translation by Abraham J. Malherbe and Everett Ferguson (Paulist Press, New York, 1978).

13 Bernard of Clairvaux, *Selected Works*, trans, G. R. Evans (Paulist Press, New York, 1987), p. 212.

14 Sir Philip Sidney, An Apology for Poetry, in Edmund D. Jones, ed., *English Critical Essays* (*Sixteenth, Seventeenth and Eighteenth Centuries*) (Oxford World Classics, Oxford, 1947), p. 15.

15 George Steiner, *After Babel: Aspects of Language and Translation*, 2nd edn (Oxford University Press, Oxford, 1992), p. 258.

16 *Tyndale's New Testament*, modern spelling edition by David Daniell (Yale University Press, New Haven, 1995), p. 3.

17 See Mark G. Brett, "The Future of Reader Criticisms?" in Francis Watson, ed., *The Open Text: New Directions for Biblical Studies?* (SCM, London, 1993). "The rise of literary theory has been associated with a new and unsettling attention to factors which influence the process of interpretation, factors like gender, race, culture and class" (p. 13). Such attention, I am suggesting, is not so new.

18 Erasmus, *The Handbook of the Militant Christian* (1503) in *The Essential Erasmus*, trans. John P. Doolan (New American Library, New York, 1964), p. 36.

19 Martin Luther, *Table Talk*, trans. William Hazlitt (Fount Classics, London, 1995), p. 3. Hazlitt's translation is itself a classic of English literature.

20 Lowth's lectures were delivered in Oxford in Latin, and not translated into English until 1787, by Richard Gregory. It is astonishing that Lowth is not even given a mention in the *Oxford Companion to English Literature*.

21 Robert Lowth, *Lectures on the Sacred Poetry of the Hebrews*, Lecture IV, in John Drury, *Critics of the Bible*, 1724–1873 (Cambridge University Press, Cambridge, 1989), p. 71.

22 An example of this division is expressed in T. R. Wright's influential work *Theology and Literature* (Blackwell, Oxford, 1988), p. 1. "Much theology ... tends towards unity and coherence, a systematic exploration of the content of faith which attempts to impose limits

on the meaning of words, while literature, as Ezra Pound insisted, is often dangerous, subversive and chaotic, an anarchic celebration of the creative possibilities of language." This, it seems to me, is a dangerous distinction, but one embedded in the history we are following.

23   For further comments see David Jasper, *A Short Introduction to Hermeneutics* (Westminster John Knox Press, London, 2004), chapter 4, "Friedrich Schleiermacher and the Age of Romanticism."

24   David Friedrich Strauss, *The Life of Jesus Critically Examined*, ed. Peter Hodgson (SCM, London, 1973), p. 107.

25   Renan's *La Vie de Jesus* was published in Paris in 1863, and only a year later published in English.

26   Albert Schweitzer, *The Quest of the Historical Jesus* (1906), trans. W. Montgomery, J. R. Coates, Susan Cupitt and John Bowden (SCM, London, 2000), p. 159.

27   The most accessible excerpts from Schleiermacher's hermeneutical work, taken from lecture notes that he never himself published, are to be found in Kurt Mueller-Vollmer, ed., The *Hermeneutics Reader* (Blackwell, Oxford, 1986), pp. 72–97. His discussion on authorial intention is on p. 83. For a more extended selection see Friedrich Schleiermacher, *Hermeneutics and Criticism, and Other Writings*, ed. Andrew Bowie (Cambridge University Press, Cambridge, 1998).

28   S. T. Coleridge, *Confessions of an Inquiring Spirit*, facsimile of the 1840 edition (Scolar Press, Menston, 1971), p. i.

29   Ibid., p. 26.

30   Ibid., p. 13.

31   Wolfgang Iser, *The Implied Reader: Patterns of Communication in Prose Fiction from Bunyan to Beckett* (Johns Hopkins University Press, Baltimore, 1974), p. 274.

32   In a letter to a friend Coleridge commented that "the Title ... ought to have been, and I had so directed it – addressed to the Learned and Reflecting of all Ranks and Professions, especially among the Higher Class." See, S. T. Coleridge, *Lay Sermons*, ed. R. J. White, *The Collected Works*, vol. 6 (Princeton University Press, Princeton, 1972), p. 3.

33   Ibid., p. 30.

34   For a further discussion of Farrer and Kermode in the tradition of Coleridgean thought, see David Jasper, *Coleridge as Poet and Religious Thinker* (Macmillan, London, 1985), chapter 8, "Conclusion: Inspiration and Revelation," pp. 144–55.

35   E. S. Shaffer, *"Kubla Khan" and The Fall of Jerusalem: The Mythological School in Biblical Criticism and Secular Literature, 1770–1880* (Cambridge University Press, Cambridge, 1975), p. 32.

36   F. D. Maurice, quoted in Charles Richard Sanders, *Coleridge and the Broad Church Movement* (Russell & Russell, New York, 1972), p. 189. Maurice's prediction has been realized in the field of Coleridge's anticipation of modern critical literary theory. See, for example, the work of Kathleen Wheeler, *Sources, Processes and Methods in Coleridge's Biographia Literaria* (Cambridge University Press, Camrbidge, 1980), p. 159: "There has still not been an adequate appreciation of the similarity of these critical developments [e.g. in the work of Wolfgang Iser, Stanley Fish, R. H. Jauss, et al.] with the theories of the German Romantic Ironists. Aside from the similarities of modern critical theory to Coleridgean practice, this historical dimension would strengthen and elucidate the parallels, since it is related both to Coleridge and to modern critical theory."

37   The influential work *The Postmodern Bible* (Yale University Press, New Haven, 1995), by The Bible and Culture Collective, begins with an Arnoldian claim: "The Bible has exerted more cultural influence on the West than any other single document," p. 1.

38 Matthew Arnold, quoted in James C. Livingston, *Matthew Arnold and Christianity: His Religious Prose Writings* (University of South Carolina Press, Columbia, 1986), p. 108.

39 Matthew Arnold, *Essays in Criticism. First Series* (J. M. Dent & Sons, London, 1964), p. 28.

40 See Barry Qualls, *The Secular Pilgrims of Victorian Fiction* (Cambridge University Press, Cambridge, 1982).

41 Charlotte Brontë, *Jane Eyre*, ed. Jane Jack and Margaret Smith (Clarendon Press, Oxford, 1969), p. 532.

42 Ibid., p. 578.

43 A. S. Byatt, *Babel Tower* (Vintage, London, 1997), p. 311.

44 D. H. Lawrence, "Why the Novel Matters," in *Selected Literary Criticism*, ed. Anthony Beal (Heinemann, London, 1967), p. 105.

45 Paul de Man, *The Resistance to Theory* (Manchester University Press, Manchester, 1986), pp. 17–18.

46 T. S. Eliot, "Religion and Literature," in *Selected Essays*, p. 388.

47 Robert Alter and Frank Kermode, eds, *The Literary Guide to the Bible* (Collins, London, 1987), p. 2.

48 Ibid., p. 4.

49 See also the book edited by Michael Wadsworth, *Ways of Reading the Bible* (Harvester Press, Brighton, 1981), with essays by a combination of biblical scholars and literary critics from John Drury and Duncan Forrester to Gabriel Josipovici and Stephen Prickett.

50 *The Literary Guide to the Bible*, p. 6.

51 The works reviewed are Robert Alter, *The Art of Biblical Narrative*, Meir Sternberg, *The Poetics of Biblical Narrative*, and Phyllis Trible, *Texts of Terror*.

52 Mieke Bal, "The Bible as Literature," in *On Story-Telling* (Polebridge Press, Sonoma, 1991), p. 59.

53 Mieke Bal, *Death and Dissymmetry: The Politics of Coherence in the Book of Judges* (University of Chicago Press, Chicago, 1988), p. 38.

54 See also David E. Klemm, *Hermeneutical Inquiry. Volume 1: The Interpretation of Texts* (Scholars Press, Atlanta, 1986), p. 174. "Gadamer's basic point, hinted at in the title of *Truth and Method*, is that modern methods of explanation and understanding lose sight of our experience of the whole of life."

55 Hans-Georg Gadamer, *The Relevance of the Beautiful and Other Essays*, ed. Robert Bernasconi, trans. Nicholas Walker (Cambridge University Press, Cambridge, 1986), pp. 140–53.

56 Ibid., p. 149.

57 Sephen D. Moore, *Literary Criticism and the Gospels: The Theoretical Challenge* (Yale University Press, New Haven, 1989), p. 177.

58 Taken from the cover of *The Postmodern Bible* (Yale University Press, New Haven, 1995)

59 See R. S. Sugirtharajah, *Postcolonial Criticism and Biblical Interpretation* (Oxford University Press, Oxford, 2002).

60 See further Geoffrey H. Hartman and Sanford Budick, eds, *Midrash and Literature* (Yale University Press, New Haven, 1986).

61 Jacques Derrida, in David Jobling, Tina Pippin and Ronald Schleifer, eds, *The Postmodern Bible Reader* (Blackwell, Oxford, 2001), p. 337.

62 Ibid.

63 Susan A. Handelman, op. cit., p. xiii.

64 A. K. M. Adam, *What Is Postmodern Biblical Criticism?* (Fortress Press, Minneapolis, 1995), p. 74.

65 See further Stephen D. Moore, *Poststructuralism and the New Testament: Derrida and Foucault at the Foot of the Cross* (Fortress Press, Minneapolis, 1994).

66 Slavoj Žižek, *The Puppet and the Dwarf: The Perverse Core of Christianity* (MIT Press, Cambridge, MA, 2003); Alain Badiou, *Saint Paul: The Foundation of Universalism* (Stanford University Press, Stanford, CA, 2003); Giorgio Agamben, *The Time that Remains: A Commentary on the Letter to the Romans* (Stanford University Press, Stanford, CA, 2005).

PART II
Medieval

CHAPTER 4

Introduction

Daniel Anlezark

One of the most contentious disputes during the English Reformation concerned the translation of the Bible into English. Conservative hostility to the English Bible at the time has left a legacy in popular perception that the medieval Church was also hostile to translations of the Bible. The historical reality is more complex. There can be no doubt that a number of churchmen were concerned that translated books of the Bible could confuse uneducated laymen, and maybe even lead them astray. Writing around the turn of the first millennium, the monk Ælfric expressed his reluctance to undertake translation from Latin (the sacred language of medieval Scripture) for his lay patron Æthelweard:[1]

> Now it seems to me, dear one, that the work is very dangerous for me or any other man to commence, because I dread, lest some foolish man read the book or hears it read, that he will suppose that he might live now under the New Law, just as the patriarchs did in the time before the Old Law was established, or just as men lived under Moses' law.

Ælfric's concern does not represent a refusal to translate the biblical text, however, and this passage introduces the reader to his version of the first half of Genesis. A full translation of Genesis is found with his preface in the mid-eleventh-century Old English Heptateuch, an illustrated compendium of the first seven books of the Bible in English. The complex medieval attitude to English Scripture is indicated in Ælfric's comment to another lay patron, Sigeweard, for whom he made an English summary of biblical history, divided up into the ages of the world:[2]

> How can the man do well who turns his heart away from these books? And is so self-conceited that he would rather live according to his own vain imaginings, so different from these, so that he knows nothing of Christ's commands?

The contradictions implied by Ælfric's position, and that of later churchmen who not only questioned but condemned and prohibited the translation of Scripture into English, indicate the diversity of ideas and practice in medieval approaches to biblical translation. Medieval churchmen might be wary of making the Bible available to vernacular readers, but authors were also aware that sacred Scripture could edify and entertain. Indeed, within a century of the first Roman missionaries' arrival in 597 to preach the gospel to the pagan Anglo-Saxons (who had invaded Britain in the fifth century, and would become the English), a range of biblical poetry was circulating in Old English. Some of this poetry, like *Genesis A*, retold scriptural stories in a straightforward way, while *The Dream of the Rood* could lead audiences into more profound reflections on the meaning of biblical events. Like much biblical literature in Old English, both these poems reveal a debt of influence to the Church's liturgy. This liturgical debt is evident in a different way in the enormously popular Middle English lyrics, discussed in the second part of this chapter. It is unlikely that English lyrics were sung at Mass; instead they were an expression of the devotional life of the laity, sung in celebrations associated with the great feasts of the Christian calendar. Their inspiration was a new emotional form of piety that emerged from *c.*1100, and imaginatively meditated on the biblical text, with the aim of engaging the heart of the reader, listener, or singer. In the following centuries authors would also provide English readers with longer narrative versions of biblical books, and sermon writers would translate portions of the Bible used in their preaching.

Whatever its form and intended audience, biblical literature in both Old and Middle English is best comprehended in the light of the medieval understanding of where the Bible fitted into the life of the Church. For the medieval Christian the sacred texts of the Old and New Testament were a part of a great inheritance bequeathed to the Church by the apostles of Jesus. They had passed on to their followers a scriptural tradition that included the Jewish Scriptures and their own writings, and for the medieval mind the role of the Scriptures was more to support Christian life than to demonstrate Christian faith. The liturgy of the medieval English Church was conducted in Latin, a language not understood by the laity, and probably only poorly comprehended by many clergy. As pastoral care of the laity became a more important part of the life of the Church across the Middle Ages, and the spirituality of the laity was fostered by new movements, biblical literature in English also became popular. It is evident that from Ælfric's time until the sixteenth century, large parts of the Bible were available in the vernacular, whether in Old English (readable well into the twelfth century), Anglo-Norman French (the language of most of the ruling class from 1066 until the late thirteenth century), or Middle English. None of these literary texts ever enjoyed the status of "official" translations, and few aimed to translate the whole Bible with close accuracy. Instead this body of literature emerged to meet needs that ran parallel to the regulated liturgical life of the Church: lyrics could stir the heart, while biblical narratives, often augmented by apocryphal legend, could entertain and moralize.

1

The history of the Bible in English literature begins in the late seventh century in the northeast of England, at the newly founded monastery of Whitby, under the Abbess Hild. In his *Ecclesiastical History of the English Nation* (completed 731), Bede relates the story of the cowherd Cædmon, who "received the gift of song freely be the grace of God."[3] His first short poem in praise of the Creator (*Cædmon's Hymn*) was the first Christian poem in Old English verse, a form based on alliterating half lines with roots in oral tradition. This was followed by the composition of a whole corpus of Old English poetry based on biblical stories and Christian doctrine. Whether or not any surviving biblical verse might be attributable to the illiterate Cædmon himself is impossible to say; Bodleian Library Junius XI, a partially illustrated manuscript containing the bulk of surviving Old English biblical poetry, came to be called the "Cædmon Manuscript" only in modern times. Nevertheless, Bede's story, written for a Northumbrian audience in the generations after the event, must preserve an authentic tradition that Cædmon was the first vernacular Christian poet, and testifies to a corpus of Old English scriptural verse circulating in the early eighth century.

The anonymous authorship of most Old English poetry is complemented by the fact that it is notoriously difficult to date. However, it is generally agreed that one of the earliest narrative poems is *Genesis A* (found in Junius XI), which presents the story of Genesis as far as the sacrifice of Isaac. It would appear that most of the audience was not especially learned, and probably did not know the text in Latin. The poem begins by stating that it is right for us to praise the "glorious King of hosts," a doxology echoing the Preface to the Canon of the Mass, the climax of Christian life and worship in the Middle Ages (*Genesis A* 1–8).[4] This is no accident, and recalls the fact that the medieval reading of Scripture was more a part of devotional life than of doctrinal controversy. This opening invitation to praise the creator is followed by an account of the rebellion of Lucifer and the fall of his angels – a story elaborated nowhere in canonical Scripture (but based ultimately on an interpretation of Isaiah 14:13–14). For the medieval reader, however, the distinction between canonically received books (those with full ecclesiastical sanction and divine authority) and apocrypha (those whose authority was dubious) was not always important – all had the power to edify.

The poem continues to narrate the events of Genesis, omitting repetitive verses and details that would mean little to the Christian audience (such as Abraham's circumcision). The choice to end the poem with Abraham's sacrifice of Isaac might seem abrupt to the modern reader. However, given the opening echoes of the Mass and the eucharistic sacrifice, it is entirely apt (2932–6):

> Brandishing the sword he coloured the burnt offering,
> The smoking altar with the ram's blood,
> Offered that gift to God, said his thanks for the rewards
> And all of the gifts that he had been given
> Both early and late, by the Lord.

The story was universally understood in the Middle Ages as representing in allegory a prophecy of both the sacrifice of Christ on the cross, and the commemoration of this singular event in the Mass. Genesis 22 offers no parallel to this exchange of gifts or to this expression of thanks, the theological core (and Greek meaning) of Eucharist. The parallels between the sacrifice of Isaac and of Christ made this obvious to the spiritual reader: a father is sacrificing his son, who has carried the wood for the sacrifice up the hill on his back, and so on. The incomplete sacrifice of Isaac (the type), whose father is to be father of many nations, is completed in Christ (the antitype), whose death reconciles to the Father the Gentile nations, among whom, of course, the English are numbered.

Most Old English biblical poetry focuses on the more public or moral aspects of religion, perhaps suggesting a public rather than a private audience. The poem *Judith*, for example, is unusual in its celebration of female violence, but does not enter into normal human experience or motivations. In a variety of ways the poems of Junius XI generally share *Genesis A*'s objective and instructive stance: *Exodus* celebrates God's protection of his chosen with a careful development of biblical typology; *Daniel*, based on the first five chapters of the biblical book, is concerned with personal and national repentance; *Christ and Satan* with its fascination with devils and hell is removed from the daily concerns of normal human beings. *Genesis B* does show interest in the psychology of sinfulness in its treatment of the temptation of Adam and Eve, but unfortunately this remains underdeveloped in a poem that has been interpolated incompletely into *Genesis A*.[5] Biblical stories also found their way into texts whose connection to the Bible might appear tangential at best. Both the murder of Abel by Cain and the biblical Deluge are referred to directly in the Old English poem *Beowulf*. This epic, apparently composed between the second half of the eighth century and the first half of the tenth, tells of the monster-slaying feats of the pre-Christian Scandinavian hero, Beowulf. The first monster he kills is the cannibalistic giant Grendel, whom the poet includes among the descendants of Cain, echoing a range of apocryphal traditions that saw Adam's cursed son as the progenitor of monstrous races.[6] The destruction of these monsters by the Flood is evoked as a key metaphor in Beowulf's own contest with the forces of chaos.[7] The use of mythic events from the earliest part of Genesis reveals a Christian poet whose imaginative world has thoroughly integrated the biblical account of the early world as a past shared by the Anglo-Saxons.

A far more conventional focus for the Christian poet is the crucifixion of Christ, a key event in Christian faith and liturgy. This conventional focus, however, is the object of unconventional treatment in *The Dream of the Rood* (or *Cross*), one of the most celebrated achievements of Old English poetry, which draws on a range of literary conventions and genres, most notably the dream vision. The narrator begins by recalling a midnight dream of long ago, in which a bright cross appeared in the heavens (4–9):[8]

> It seemed to me that I saw a most marvellous tree
> Led up into the sky, wrapped in light,
> The brightest of beams. The beacon was completely
> Covered with gold; gems stood
> Fairly on the plains of the earth – there were also five
> Of these up on the crossbeam.

The imagery of the poem draws on a range of medieval apocalyptic traditions, most notably the belief that a cross will appear in the heavens announcing the Last Judgment. Before turning to the theme of judgment, however, the poem recounts the story of the crucifixion, drawing on the gospel accounts but also diverging from them. Most remarkably, the story is told by the cross itself (28–30):

> "That was long ago, I remember it still,
> When I was cut down at the edge of the wood,
> Torn from my trunk."

The imagery of *The Dream of the Rood* reflects the liturgical uses of the cross and a sophisticated understanding of doctrinal controversies concerning the relationship between the human and divine natures of Christ.[9] However, the poet's recasting of the crucifixion story is guided more by two related thematic concerns: the desire to emphasize Christ's courage according to the traditions of Old English heroic verse; and a desire to create an empathetic, rather than intellectual, response in the reader.

The poet not only embraces the central paradox of the crucifixion – that God should die – but intensifies this by presenting Christ as a victorious hero. The silence of the young warrior who strips himself and submits to death in battle contrasts with the tortured narration of the cross, which reproaches itself for having slain its Lord (39–43):

> "Then the young hero stripped himself – that was God almighty –
> Strong and resolute, he climbed onto the high gallows,
> Brave in the sight of many, when he wished to redeem mankind.
> I trembled when he embraced me, but I did not dare bow to the earth,
> Fall to the plains of the earth. Rather, I was compelled to stand still."

The rhetorical device of prosopopoeia, whereby an inanimate object is personified and speaks, is exploited fully. The emphasis on remembered physical closeness and self-reproach recalls the Old English elegiac poem *The Wanderer*, and the intimacy of the cross's disclosure to the dreamer gives way to the familiarity of the dreamer's own address to the reader, as he recalls the death of loved ones and growing solitude since the time of the vision. The reader's own life experience becomes an important part of the poem's dynamic, and the invitation to salvation that the poem extends rests on shared emotion rather than intellectual insight, despite the poem's theological density. The reflective and emotional quality of *The Dream of the Rood* anticipates elements of later medieval lyrics, and has no parallel in other early European vernaculars. The Old English *Advent Lyrics*, the first poem in the *Exeter Book*, anticipate the lyric tradition in another way. These poems present meditations on the "O antiphons" of the Office in the days before Christmas, reflecting on the Old Testament prophecies of Christ's birth. The Marian piety they express would become the focus of many later medieval writers' creative efforts.

2

The Norman Conquest of 1066 brought in its wake a general displacement of English by Anglo-Norman French speakers in the upper ranks of the Church and government. The alliterative poetic tradition, insofar as written transmission was concerned, largely went underground, having lost its sources of patronage among the social elite. The following century also gave rise to new popular literary forms, in both French and English; one of the most popular of these was the short lyric. Many secular and religious lyrics survive, though the majority are religious, and many of these draw their inspiration from the text of the Bible. The best – like their counterparts across Europe – express common emotions (mostly love) with a deceptive simplicity and clarity, adopting a humble pose and shunning excessive ornament. Sacred lyrics reflect the interests of contemporary religious movements, which emerged in new social contexts. In the course of the twelfth century European society underwent profound changes, and England was no exception. Urban life expanded with the rise of trades and the merchant classes, a shift paralleled by the growth of bureaucracy in secular government and the Church. The new middle classes in the growing towns and at court were literate, and experienced and expressed their Christian faith in new ways. New forms of professional religious life also emerged at this time: the Cistercians fled this modern society to recreate the monastic ideal, while new preaching orders engaged with urban life.

The new piety of the age, fostered by figures like Anselm of Canterbury, Bernard of Clairvaux, and Francis of Assisi (a son of the merchant class, and a composer of lyrics), used the imagination to meditate on scriptural narratives, and focused on the emotional response of the individual to the life and death of Christ. The lyrics also drew on the liturgical tradition, and it is no surprise that the principle feasts of the Church's year, such as Easter and Christmas, form the subject of the many sacred lyrics, some of which would have been sung in connection with liturgical celebrations. The mystery of the incarnation and the suffering of Christ in his passion also contain profound theological paradoxes – such as the idea that God could be born of a woman, and could suffer and die. Another feature of many lyrics is their intense Marian piety, as they reflect on Mary's experience of the annunciation, in the birth of Christ, or at the foot of the cross, using the viewpoint of her humanity to enter the unfolding story. The English lyrics are a part of a wider continental tradition, but should not be seen simply as imitative. As we have seen, the impulses behind the lyrics are found in earlier English poetry. So while the new poetic forms were transmitted through French and Latin sources, the best English authors make these forms their own, and do so very early, often with an awareness of national tradition.

The advent of the religious lyric in England can be associated with the eccentric character of Godric of Finchale, born in Norfolk three years after the Conquest (1069).[10] Godric's early career was on the sea, until a visit to Holy Island (Lindisfarne) and the inspiration of the great Anglo-Saxon hermit, St Cuthbert (d. 687), brought radical change; like Cuthbert he became a hermit, and was also a friend of animals. After distant pilgrimages and time in the Holy Land, Godric spent the last sixty years of his life at Finchale, close to the new Norman monastic cathedral at Durham, until his death in 1170. Godric was of Anglo-Saxon stock, but his poetry reveals the influence not of the native alliterative tradition, but of his wide travels in southern Europe and his time among crusaders in the Holy Land. His poetry also refects new devotional emphases:[11]

> Sainte Marye Virgine,
> Moder Jesu Christes Nazarene,
> Onfo, schild, help thin Godric,
> Onfang, bring heyilich with thee in Godes riche.

onfo: receive; onfang: having received (him); heyilich: on high

This prayer to the Virgin is a simple plea for maternal protection, with a none-too-subtle play on his own name (*Godes riche*, "God's kingdom"). According to tradition Godric received his lyrics, with music, in visions, and it was the Virgin herself who led him to sing in the new style (*canticum quoddam novum*). The parallels with the story of the first English Christian poet, Cædmon, are clear: poetry is a visionary gift, and this represents a starting point for English Christian verse. The stories of Cuthbert and Cædmon were certainly well known in the northeast of England in the twelfth century, and the adoptive Northumbrian Godric emerges, with the help of his biographers, as a fusion of both.

Not all medieval English composers of lyrics were centenarian hermits who enjoyed visions. Most were anonymous, but almost all draw on the New Testament for inspiration; this is evident in *Ecce, ancilla domini* ("Behold the handmaid of the Lord").[12] The poem presents an extended meditation on the Annunciation (also called Lady Day), which was New Year's Day in medieval England. The opening refrain is taken from the Vulgate text (Luke 1:38):

> "Ecce, ancilla Domini!"
> Thus seyde the virgine wythuten vyse,
> Whan Gabryll grett hure gracyously:
> "Hayle be thou, virgine, ipreved on prys,
> Thou shalt conceyve a swete spyce."
> Then seyde the virgine so myldely:
> "Therto I am ful lytel of prys,
> Ecce, ancilla Domini."

spyce: spice; alther: of all

The text paraphrases the scriptural narrative, but the exchange in the poem evokes courtly refinement. Gabriel "greets graciously," and Christ is a "sweet spice," recalling the popular idea that courtesy came down from heaven with Gabriel's message. The poet also makes extensive use of alliteration, loosely combining the lyric form with a native English tradition reaching back to the Anglo-Saxons. Medieval developments of doctrine are also evident; praise of the Virgin's lack of vice is developed in the second stanza into a fuller evocation of the hotly debated doctrine of her Immaculate Conception:

> "Hayle be thou, gracious, wythuten gilt,
> Mayden iboren alther best,
> Al en thy body schal be fulfyllyt
> That profytes haveth ypreched ful prest –
> He wyl be boren of thy brest."
> Then sayde the virgine so myldely:
> "He ys to me a welcome gest,
> Ecce, ancilla domini."

prest: eagerly

The belief that Mary's own conception had left her free from the stain of Adam's sin, a preparation for the body which would hold Christ within it, was generally accepted in the Middle Ages, but appears first to have been celebrated in the West by the English Church in the mid-eleventh century.

The poem reflects medieval doctrinal developments in the context of a recollection of conventional Old Testament prophecies of the birth of Christ, much as the Old English *Advent Lyrics*, which also declared the Virgin Mary had been foretold by the prophets (Isaiah 7:14).[13] Other more complex scriptural traditions are also evoked:

> The sayde that angel: "Conseyve thou schalt
> Within thyn holy body bryght
> A chyld that Jesus schal be icallyt,
> That ys gryte Godes sone of myght;
> Thou ert hys tabernacle idyght."
> Then seyde the virgine mildely:
> "Syth he wroght never ayeyn the ryght,
> Ecce, ancilla domini."
>
> "Kalle hym Jesus of Nazareth,
> God and man in on degre,
> That on the rode schalle suffre death,
> And regne in Davidys dignite:
> Wel goude tydynges he hath sente to the."
> Then seyde the virgine so myldely:
> "He schal be dyre welcome to me,
> Ecce, ancilla domini!"

idyght: called; ayeyn: against

The figure of the Virgin as a "tabernacle," a dwelling place for God, was a commonplace of the tradition, often associated with (Vulgate) Psalm 18:1. In this light the reference to David is doubly significant, as through his mother Jesus is a descendant of the royal house of David, who as the supposed author of the Psalm also prophesied the coming of Christ. The poem achieves great theological intricacy, recalling Old Testament types and prophecies. Adding to the complexity of the poem's ideas is the articulation of Mary's sinlessness, and also the central mystery of the incarnation it anticipates. In her "bright body" Mary herself – born before Christ and therefore within the Old Testament – contains Christ, the New Testament, just as the Old Testament contains the promise of his advent. The courtly grace with which the angel announces his message is also the theological grace that Mary's obedience makes possible. However, the subtle complexity of the angel's announcement and description of Mary's historical role are contrasted in the lyric with the simplicity of Mary's own part in the dramatic dialogue. In each stanza the Virgin is given only one line, declaring her unworthiness, her trust in God's goodness, and that the child will be to her a dear welcome guest; together these obedient sentiments combine in the meaning of the biblical refrain, "Behold the handmaiden of the Lord." The homely familiarity of Mary's language is prevented from slipping into banal acquiescence by the promise of suffering – even before her child is born, she is promised her dear son will suffer a miserable death.

One of the driving forces behind devotion to Mary was the desire to use the humanity shared with her as a way of entering the direct human experience of the Divine. This familiarity allowed sacred lyrics to shift between an objective stance towards biblical stories and a shared subjectivity with a character like Mary. But this was true of Christ, also fully human, and lyrics of the Passion at times endeavoured to enter Christ's human perspective on his suffering. A short lyric associated with John Grimestone, a fourteenth-century Franciscan preacher, adopts the point of view of Christ praying in the Garden of Gethsemane before his arrest:[14]

> A sory beverich it is and sore it is abouht
> Nou in this sarpe time this brewing hat me brought.
> Fader, if it mowe ben don als I have besouht,
> Do awey this beverich, that I ne drink et nouht.
>
> And if it mowe no betre ben, for alle mannis gilt,
> That it ne muste nede that my blod be spilt,
> Suete fader, I am thi sone, thi wil be fulfilt,
> I am her thin owen child, I wil don as thou wilt.

beverich: beverage, brew; abouht: bought; sarpe: sharp, bitter

The opening of the poem recalls the great number of medieval songs dedicated to drinking, and only with the reference to the "Father" do we find ourselves in a sacred lyric.[15] The first two lines evoke not the enjoyment of drink, but a hangover, and recall the lively depiction of drunkenness in another fourteenth-century poem, William Langland's *Vision of Piers Plowman*.[16] What follows, however, draws on the gospel account of Gethsemane (see Matthew 26:39–42), as Christ prays that "this cup pass" from him. The emotion is intense, and the reader is reminded that Christ's suffering is not for his own guilt, but sinful humanity's. In a sustained metaphor it is the corruption of human sin that, like yeast, has brewed Christ's drink, a sorry beverage that will be bought with sorrow. The loving relationship between the "sweet father" and his "own child" also suffers because of mankind's need for redemption; no beer will be spilled, but Christ's blood will be. The poem is more emotional, and the homely image of brewing, with the tender words of the Son to the Father, invite remorse from the sinner who has contributed to the brewing, perhaps even by excessive drinking. While Christ's obedience in paying the price is exemplary, this is not developed as overtly as Mary's in *Ecce ancilla domini*, and for medieval audiences Christ's humanity generally remained less approachable than Mary's.

Running alongside the development of the Middle English sacred lyric was a tradition providing fuller accounts of biblical history for readers of English. These biblical paraphrases began to appear against the background of shifting linguistic politics in the thirteenth century as the use of French as a literary language declined in England. The Middle English *Genesis and Exodus* and *Jacob and Joseph*, made about 1250, seem to have been the first long poetic paraphrases made in English since before the Norman Conquest.[17] *Genesis and Exodus* is a relatively straightforward rendition in rhyming couplets, echoing French models; *Jacob and Joseph* is mostly concerned with Joseph's adventures in Egypt. French translations – undoubtedly circulating in England – were a popular source for English translators, presenting as they did texts already adapted to lay readers' needs.[18] The Psalms, always a popular devotional text, had been translated into Old English poetry and prose,[19] and a number of Middle English versions survive, one by the fourteenth-century mystic Richard Rolle, who also composed lyrics.[20] Adaptations the New Testament include the stanzaic *Life of Christ*, made in Chester in the middle of the fourteenth century.[21]

The greater part of Middle English biblical literature originated either from the Church's devotional life, or in authors' desire to edify and entertain a vernacular audience. The only full English translation of the Bible, the well known Wyclifite Bible, was made for a different reason, in the last decades of the fourteenth century, by the followers (popularly called Lollards) of John Wyclif. Controversy surrounded the figure of Wyclif, and his preaching against Church abuses brought him censure, and led to condemnation as a heretic.[22] While no doubt its authors wished to edify, their systematic Englishing of the Bible was based on the ideological conviction that the word of God should be directly accessible to all. The Wyclifite Bible is in fact two versions of the Bible, an Early and a Late. The Early is a painfully literal translation of the Vulgate, while the Late is more obviously designed to be read. Despite official prohibition, this English Bible was enormously popular and survives in over 200 manuscripts. A contemporary work also concerned with Church corruption, and similarly ambitious, is Langland's *Piers Plowman*, a vast allegorical dream vision peppered with biblical imagery and quotations from the Latin Bible's text. Langland presents a dream landscape in which those pulled simultaneously toward heaven and hell must learn how the live well and be saved. Their teachers, not all of whom are to be trusted, instruct using scriptural glosses, which often distort the text. Ultimately the only hope is found in the figure of Piers, whose character fuses with Christ in an allegorical retelling of scriptural history.

Two other works also present the full panorama of the biblical narrative. Ranulph Higden's Latin *Polychronicon*, a universal history, written in the middle of the fourteenth century, covered history from Genesis to his own day, and was translated into English in 1387 by John Trevisa, an Oxford scholar associated with, though not a follower of, Wyclif.[23] The other is the *Cursor Mundi* ("Cursor of the World"), a vast poem originally composed in the north of England in the early thirteenth century, surviving in nine medieval manuscripts.[24] The "Cursor" is a "cursor" because it runs over the history of the world. The terminology draws from the practice in medieval universities of introducing beginners to masses of material by "running" through texts cursorily, with a minimum of comment, and little disruption to narrative flow. While the panoramic scope of Langland's poem and the Wyclifite Bible have attracted a great deal of critical attention, the *Cursor Mundi* is not matched with a comparable amount of scholarship. Nineteenth-century editions have not made the poem easily accessible, but the poem's combination of linguistic nationalism, comprehensive scope, and evident popularity make it a forerunner of translations proper. At nearly 30,000 lines of rhyming couplets this anonymous poem is enormous, and presents an ambitious retelling of the whole of biblical history, drawing on a range of sources. The most obvious of these is the Bible, though the author made use of two French biblical translations as well, which furnished him with the legendary elaborations and interpolated interpretations also incorporated into the story. The *Bible* of Hermann of Valenciennes and the *Traduction anonyme de la Bible* are presumably the books the author has in mind when he discusses in his prologue the problem encountered by English audiences listening to "vernacular" French Bibles, who have a poor understanding of the language (lines 231–50). His intention, "for the commun at vnderstand", evokes the growing English linguistic nationalism of the thirteenth century, as do other comments about the need for English in England.

The preface sets out the poet's intention of competing for attention with a range of less edifying material his readers can find. The Bible can compete with romance, offering exciting characters and stories (21–6):

> Storis als o serekin thinges
> O princes, prelates and o kynges;
> Sanges sere of selcuth rime,
> Inglis, frankys, and latine,
> to reder and here Ilkon is prest,
> the thynges that tham likes best.

Serekin: various; selcuth: wondrous

The author, pointing out the superiority of Bible narrative, goes on to suggest that those who are drawn to worldly stories reveal that their hearts are inclined to worldly things. The *Cursor Mundi* is divided into seven sections corresponding to the ages of the world: the first ranges from the Creation to Noah; the second up to the tower of Babel; the third from Abraham to Saul; the fourth from David to the Exile in Babylon; the fifth brings the reader to the end of the Old Testament, but is preoccupied with Jesus' ancestry and apocryphal accounts of his childhood; the sixth age (also called the age of grace, following the age of the Law, which Moses had initiated) extends from the baptism of Jesus until the Judgment; the seventh age will see the establishment of the kingdom of God, and the poem includes a collection of prayers, exhortations, and instructions that prepare the soul for the Kingdom. The same process of elaboration found in other medieval biblical literature is found here – legendary and apocryphal material is woven into the narrative at the appropriate juncture, and as usual the most dramatic of these is the fall of the angels. Small details are also added, such as the medieval commonplace that the sun and moon shone brighter before the fall.

The dramatic, though reticent, biblical account of Cain's killing of Abel – the world's first act of violence – is carefully elaborated upon. Where in the Bible Cain's sacrifice is simply refused, the *Cursor Mundi* adds a traditional reason: it is refused because it is offered reluctantly. Abel is killed here with the jawbone of an ass, another medieval commonplace, echoing Sampson's weapon of choice (Judges 15:15). A striking inclusion in this early part of the biblical story is a riddle (1187–90):

> This es that man men sais was born
> Bath his fader and moder beforn.
> He had his eldmoder maiden-hede,
> And at his erthing all lede.

bath: both; eldmoder: grandmother's; erthing: burial; lede: people

Neither Adam nor Eve was born, Abel was the first buried in the earth (his grandmother because Adam had been formed from the earth), and the whole population of the world was at his funeral. The audience evoked by this kind of detail is not learned, but one with a taste for the marvellous and anecdotal, and which enjoys challenges to its wits. The *Cursor Mundi* also provides the modern reader with a range of insights into what the "Bible" was in medieval imagination. To the scholar it might have been the authoritative text in matters of theological dispute, but to more popular audiences it existed as a great story, presenting the history of the world and the marvellous lives of those favoured or cursed by God in his dealings with humanity. It is unlikely that the audience of the *Cursor Mundi* would have had a rigid sense of the division of the Bible into books, and the author uses the more popular, and memorable, structural division in the ages of the world. It was important that the text should be remembered, as it is more than likely that large sections of the poem's audience were unlettered, but also had the capacious memory characteristic of oral societies.

The transformation of the many books of the Bible into one book in the *Cursor Mundi* creates an original work with its own points of unity. One of these is the recurrent motif of the three holy trees, which anticipate and lead to Christ's cross. The motif is introduced with a legend concerning Seth, Adam and Eve's good son born after the death of Abel. As Adam approaches death he instructs Seth to visit paradise in search of the oil of mercy (1327–1432). Continuing the poem's riddling quality, Seth asks two questions of the angel at the gate: when will Adam die, and will he receive the oil promised at his expulsion? Seth is told by the angel to look in three times. On the first he sees a great dead tree in the midst of the beautiful green garden; on the second a serpent coiled around the tree; on the third a newborn child weeping in the upper branches and in the roots of the tree, extending to hell, his dead brother Abel. The angel explains the vision: the child is God's son, weeping for Adam's sin, which he will one day cleanse – this is the oil of mercy. Before Seth is sent back to Adam he is given three seeds from the tree of knowledge. These are to be buried under Adam's tongue when he dies three days later, eventually growing into the three healing trees, the cedar, cypress, and palm, each of which flourishes in the valley of Hebron until the time of Moses. The three trees later fuse into one, and go on to serve as a link between great figures of the Old Testament with whose stories they intersect.

After many adventures, the fused tree is preserved in the Temple until it is used, in fulfillment of both narrative expectation and prophecy, as the wood of the cross on which Christ is crucified (16573–6):

> The rode thai scop than as thai wald,
> als we the taken se,

> O cedre, cipres, and o pine,
> Als writen es on that tre.

rode: cross; scop: shaped; taken: sign

The beam, which two hundred of Caiaphas's men can not budge, is tenderly greeted and lifted by Christ (16585–92):

> Quen he come to that suete tre
> til him thaa feluns said,
> "Tak it up," coth thai, "thou seis
> hu it es to the graid."
> He luted dun and kist it sun,
> and at the first braid,
> Wit-uten ani help on man
> apon his bak it laid.

graid: prepared; luted: bent; sun: soon; braid: lift

The intimate tone – as Christ kisses his own cross – recalls *The Dream of the Rood* and lyrics of the passion. The theological metaphor at this point is easily comprehended: Christ alone can lift the burden that men cannot lift, and with the tree he will heal humanity of sin. The legend of the "Holy Rood Tree" is not unique to *Cursor Mundi*, but was widely developed in the literature and art of the Middle Ages. The typology associating Christ's cross and Adam's tree is Pauline in origin (Romans 5:14), but here given full imaginative expression. The incorporation of the legend reveals something of the poet's art and purpose: the vernacular verse Bible, with all its additions, presents a unified narrative designed to entertain, educate, and save.

The medieval dramatic impulse emerges from the same sources and with similar emphases to the *Cursor Mundi*. The medieval cycles of plays had their historical origins in the liturgy of the medieval church, specifically with the institution from 1311 of the midsummer Feast of Corpus Christi, and were also popular, and designed to entertain, educate, and save. The English plays of this European phenomenon survive in four cycles – York, Chester, Wakefield (or Towneley) and "Coventry" – in addition to numerous non-cycle plays.[25] These were performed by the laity, and offer a dramatic presentation in English of the full course of history from the biblical perspective, from Creation to Judgment. Very like the *Cursor Mundi* they use popular devotion and legendary material to animate biblical stories and create vibrant characters recognizable to medieval audiences. Female characters – usually glossed over in the Bible – are imaginatively developed, often revealing the biases of medieval antifeminism. In the Wakefield play of Noah, his wife emerges as an argumentative shrew, with whom he exchanges blows, and who initially refuses to enter the ark. The comedy is intense, and the moral (developed beside more complex typological themes) is simple – Noah's obedience to God cannot save her, she too must submit. Another woman whose role is amplified is Pilate's wife. In the York cycle he is the proud and boastful ruler, while she is warned in a dream that the innocent Christ must not be condemned. In a dramatic twist it is a flattering devil ("O woman, be wise and ware") who appears in the dream, and uses the woman in an attempt to prevent the crucifixion; the irony, evoking Adam's "obedience" to Eve, intensifies as Pilate's refusal to listen to his wife leads to the redemptive death of the Second Adam.

This medieval dramatic tradition is evoked in *The Miller's Tale* by Geoffrey Chaucer, whose own use of the Bible is tied to other literary interests.[26] The drunken Miller rants "in Pilates voys," insisting he will tell his tale, which concerns an elderly Oxford carpenter who marries a young and sexually adventurous wife. The story loosely evokes the plays of Noah at various points – Noah himself is very old, and has problems with his wife – and climaxes in a scene where John the carpenter comes crashing from his attic sitting in a tub, convinced a second universal deluge has come: "Allas, now comth Nowellis flood!"[27] Chaucer's interest lies more in the humor to be generated by the carpenter's muddled reception of the Bible through plays and Christmas carols, as "Noah" fuses with "Nowell." Chaucer assumes and uses his audience's familiarity not only with the story of the Flood, but also with its medieval dramatic embodiment, to intensify the humor of his own exploration of the relationship between the sexes. Chaucer's irony is also in evidence in *The Monk's Tale*, where a range of biblical characters, including Lucifer and Adam, are included in a list of illustrious victims to Fortune. The Monk's use of the biblical text gives the narratives a fatalistic rather than a moral interpretation. Another pilgrim who does not hesitate to draw morals from the Bible is the Pardoner, who preaches on 1 Timothy 6:10 ("The love of money is the root of all evils"), in the ironic hope of making money. Much less ironic is the preaching of the Parson at the end of the *Canterbury Tales*. The Parson, whom the Host suggests has the odor of a Lollard, denounces fiction and tales, and does not tell a story himself, invoking the authority of St Paul against fiction (1 Timothy 1:4, 4:7; 2 Timothy 4:4). Instead, he preaches at great length on Jeremiah 6:16: "Stondeth upon the weyes, and seeth and axeth of olde pathes (that is to seyn, of olde sentences) which is the goode wey, and ye shal fynde refresshynge for youre soules, etc." The chosen verse is appropriate for the pilgrims on the way to Canterbury, and in this context the Parson's very literal sermon presents an allegorizing gloss on the whole of the pilgrimage, an earthly enactment of the journey to "Jerusalem celestial." The Parson does not emerge as a Lollard, but instead offers a comprehensive treatise on penance, and with a closing touch of Chaucer's humour, offers a remedy for the sinfulness characterizing the *Tales*.

There is no doubt that when Chaucer was writing in the late fourteenth century, the York and Chester play cycles were fully established. This was also the time that witnessed the composition of *Piers Plowman*, the translation of the Wyclifite Bible, and Higden's *Polychronicon*. This time of growing nationalism, and confidence in the literary potential of the English language, also saw the composition of a group of four poems in a regional English dialect by one of the great poets of the age. These poems survive uniquely in the British Library MS Cotton Nero A.x: *Cleanness; Patience; Pearl;* and *Sir Gawain and the Green Knight.* Writing, like Langland, in the English alliterative verse tradition, this writer remains anonymous. *Gawain* is the only one of the four poems in the manuscript that does not draw in detail on the Bible in its composition. This is not to say that *Gawain* is devoid of religious or biblical interest – it is set around the Feast of Christmas, while

Gawain's shield shows the Star of Solomon (a pentangle) on the outside, and an image of the Virgin Mary inside. Nevertheless, *Gawain* is not a biblical poem, but a medieval romance. This presents a striking contrast to the other three poems, *Cleanness*, *Patience*, and *Pearl*, each of which draws closely on the Bible for its narrative. *Cleanness* recounts episodes from Genesis and Daniel to illustrate the virtue of sexual purity. *Patience* tells the story of Jonah, a man full of rage who must learn patience through obedience. *Pearl*, less dependent on biblical narrative but rich in the imagery of Revelations, is a consolation poem treating the painful experience of the death of a child.

The least discussed of the poems is *Cleanness*, though it perhaps deserves more attention than it is normally accorded. An interest is shown at the outset in the purity of priests celebrating the Mass, in which, according to Catholic theology, they make present the sacrifice on Calvary, and Christ is physically present in the bread and wine (1–8):[28]

> Clannesse who so kyndly cowthe comende,
> And rekken vp alle the resounz that ho by right askez,
> Fayre formez myght he fynde in forthering his speche,
> And in the contraré, kark and combraunce huge.
> For wonder wroth is the Wygh that wroght alle thinges
> Wyth the freke that in fylthe folghes hym after –
> As renkez of religioun that reden and syngen,
> And aprochen to hys presens, and prestez arn called.

cowthe: can; ho: she; kark: trouble; combraunce: difficulty; wygh: man; freke: man; folghes: pursues; renkez: men

This poem lacks the light touch and humor found in the other three, a problem which may have its origin in the lack of focus on a principal character, such as Jonah in *Patience*, *Pearl*'s dreamer, or Gawain. In *Cleanness* the abstract virtue of purity dominates, and is pursued across a range of biblical stories. These are introduced with a reflection on a parable from Matthew's Gospel, in which a rich man invites many people to a banquet (22:1–14). Those first invited make excuses and do not come, so servants are sent out to the highways and byways to find guests to replace them. The parable as told develops the banquet theme, so the reader is aware that the heir's wedding equates with the Lamb's as described in Revelation (19:9).

Both the developing emphasis on sexual purity and this apocalyptic theme echo ideas developed in detail in *Pearl*, where the dreamer encounters the Pearl, arrayed in Pearls, who is gradually revealed as the lost child, glorified as a bride of the apocalyptic Lamb. One of the guests at the banquet in *Cleanness*, however, is dressed in working clothes (145–8):

> "Thow art a gome vngoderly in that goun febele;
> Thou praysed me and my place ful pover and ful gnede,
> That watz so prest to aproche my presens hereinne.
> Hopez thou I be a harlot thi erigaut to prayse?"

gome: man; praysed: valued; gnede: beggarly; harlot: villain; erigaut: robe

With a heavy-handedness not found in the other (perhaps later) poems, the poet explains that Christ is talking here about the kingdom of heaven, and warns the reader not to approach the Prince who hates impurity as much as hell. The poet's use of the parable is significant. He presents something of his own art, using fiction to present spiritual truth, a practice based on Christ's use of parables and metaphor. In the late fourteenth century both the spiritual value of fiction and attention to the literal truth of Scripture were contentious issues. The Lollards – the poet's contemporaries – rejected the allegorizing tendency of medieval exegesis, preferring the plain text. Not only the Lollards' translations, but also the literal ways in which they read them, were condemned by ecclesiastical authority.

The *Cleanness*-poet, like Chaucer, would have been aware of contemporary theological debates. The poet's sophistication in biblical exegesis is well demonstrated in *Pearl*, where the dreamer debates with the Pearl the significance of the parable of the workers in the vineyard, with those arriving late paid the same as those who have laboured all day (Matthew 20:1–16). The Dreamer disputes the assertion that this means the dead child can claim the highest rewards of heaven. *Cleanness* develops a more straightforward use of Scripture, following medieval preaching practice, whereby an abstract theme is illustrated through a range of *exempla*. The poet presents a number of stories revealing the results of impurity of the flesh (line 202). The first, surprisingly, is Lucifer, who has no body, and who was cast out of heaven and into hell with his angel followers. However, Lucifer's pride is presented as rooted in Narcissistic self regard (line 209): "He segh noght bot hymself how semly he were." The root of all the sins of the flesh, it would seem, lies in contemplating the creature rather than the Creator. Adam's fall is briefly retold (lines 235–48), with no clear explanation of the impurity it represents, though a sexual element was usually understood by medieval commentators: Adam here violates "trawthe" (line 236; truth, loyalty), but the reference to Eve's "eggyng" him on (line 241) is suggestive.

More directly linked to sexual impurity is the punishment meted out in the Flood. Living before Moses, the people of Noah's time had no other law to obey than that of nature, which they rejected in their sin (263–8):

> Ther watz no law to hem layd bot loke to kynde,
> And kepe to hit, and alle hit cors clanly fulfylle.
> And thenne founden thay fylthe in fleschlych dedez,
> And controeued agayn kynde contraré werkez,
> And vsed hem vnthryftyly vch on on other,
> And als with other, wylsfully, upon a wrange wyse.

watz: was; kynde: nature; vnthryftyly: wickedly; uch: each; wylsfully: perversely; wrange: twisted; wyse: manner

The poet shows no interest in the controversy surrounding the nature of the sins of the generation before the Flood (Genesis 6:1–4), but clearly understands they were sexual. The reader's mind is given scope to imagine what kind of perversity was practiced – the poet himself is not interested in titillating. The reference to the law of nature recalls the poem's opening line, which asserts that purity itself is recommended by nature, and the themes of sexual purity, nature, and grace are developed in more detail in both *Pearl* and *Gawain*. The emerging pattern in *Cleanness* is clear: sexual impurity is punished by God, ultimately in hell. Noah and his family (all married) are delivered from the punishment of the Flood by Noah's obedience, but they also embody a heterosexual natural ideal, with the pairs of male and female animals that will repopulate the world. The next exemplum, the destruction of Sodom and Gomorrah, told in much greater detail than any so far, presents the reader with the perversion of this ideal, in another standard medieval interpretation (693–700):

> Thay han lerned a lyst that lykez me ille,
> That thay han founden in her flesch of fautez the werst:
> Vch male matz his mach a man as hymseluen,
> And fylter folyly in fere on femmalez wyse.

fautez: faults; uch: each; matz: mate; fylter: embrace; in fere: together

The description of the punishment of the cities is conventional, though the stress on infertility, where ripe fruit is full of ashes, emphasizes the perversion of nature that the people of Sodom practiced, contrasting with the fecund regenerative life in the ark.

Before turning to his longest *exemplum* the poet exhorts his readers to purity in a homiletic aside lasting more than one hundred lines, and discusses the Virgin Mary's purity which brought Christ into the world. Purity, he says, is a pearl that can be kept clean by polishing, but even if by neglect it should be tarnished, it can be made white again by washing in wine. The earlier *exempla* provide simple moral readings grounded in the letter of the text; sinners sinned, and were punished. The same pattern is found in the account of Belshazzar's feast, though the sin here is not of sexual impurity, but the defiling of the sacred vessels of Solomon's Temple. The *Cleanness*-poet provides the reader with the historical background to the sacrilegious feast, with the destruction of the Temple after the fall of Jerusalem. The poet's characteristic interest in courtly opulence is found in the description of Babylon, which the splendour of Belshazzar's feast takes further, involving the Temple vessels from which his drunken courtiers drink (1497–1500):

> Soberly in His sacrafyce summe wer anoynted,
> Thurgh the somones of Himselfe that syttes so hyghe;
> Now a boster on benche bibbes therof,
> Tyl he be dronkken as the deuel, and dotes ther he syttes.

somones: summons; boster: boaster; bibbes: drinks; dotes: raves

The destruction of Babylon wrought by the Medes is described in much greater detail than in the Book of Daniel, and the poet takes delight in describing the defilement of the king's body, much as he had defiled the Temple vessels. But how does this last *exemplum* relate to the earlier part of the poem? The image of the banquet recalls the wedding feast of the parable, itself an image of the celestial banquet, linked to the recollection of the sacrificial function of the vessels in the Temple liturgy, which also recalls the opening lines of the poem demanding cleanness from priests at the altar. These emphases suggest that a clerical audience has been in mind throughout: their sexual purity is required lest they defile the sacred vessels in the Mass. The image of the human body as a vessel is also a commonplace, and it is unlikely that an exclusively clerical audience is to be imagined. The poet's three biblical poems represent a highpoint in the medieval English tradition. While *Cleanness* might not be the most acclaimed of the three, it perfectly combines the use of scriptural narrative within the medieval tradition of biblical interpretation. The choice of texts centers on human dramas in a way that draws out the tension between human feeling and desire on one hand, and God's will on the other, and so balancing emotion and intellect in a way that draws on the tradition represented by sacred lyrics and medieval biblical drama. The poet's identity remains unknown, but *Gawain*, a poem interested in the foundation of Britain and the virtue of its ruling elite, suggests someone not far removed from courtly circles. The choice of poetic medium – alliterative verse combined with complex metrical schemes – evokes a poet more at home with this traditional national form than Chaucer was.

Discussion of the full range of biblical literature of the English Middle Ages lies beyond the scope of this survey, but certain distinctive features of this literary tradition have emerged. The rich liturgical and devotional life of the medieval Western Church gave rise to a vernacular lyrical tradition, which in England, as elsewhere, emotionally expressed the connection between the lives of ordinary believers and the great narrative of their salvation. The earliest traditions surrounding English biblical literature evoke a nascent linguistic nationalism, evident in the visionary inspiration and poetic innovation of both Cædmon and Godric of Finchale. The story of Cædmon suggests that a body of Old English verse presenting the stories of the Bible circulated in early Northumbria, and the emergence of this biblical poetry from the great monastic teaching center of Whitby in the generation after the Christian conversion probably indicates a demand for the "Bible" in English in the seventh century. The poems of Junius XI are not by Cædmon, but the compilation of the manuscript in the late tenth century again points to a desire for something like an Old English Bible, and English prose translations suggest this demand continued, and was met despite Ælfric's reservations. In the following centuries Old English books would fall out of use, but the growing demand for biblical literature in an understandable language was met in a variety of ways: by French versions; the *Cursor Mundi*; the populist cycle plays; a range of short works; and ultimately the Lollard Bible. Renderings of the Latin Bible into the medieval vernacular are characterized by the desire of authors to edify, save, and entertain – not always equally balanced. The introduction of legendary materials and authorial commentary served to engage the reader's imagination, but also to ensure that readers and listeners understood the text correctly. By the late fourteenth century a tradition of biblical literature in English had developed to the point where Chaucer could ironically evoke its conventions. In time the linguistic nationalism that was always a feature of medieval

English biblical literature would find an extreme expression in the polemics of the Reformation, which ironically would relegate the contribution of most medieval authors to relative obscurity.

Notes

1   *The Old English Version of the Heptateuch: Ælfric's Treatise on the Old and New Testament and his Preface to Genesis*, ed. S. J. Crawford, EETS os 160 (London, 1922), p. 76; Old English texts are translated; Middle English is glossed.

2   Crawford, ed., *Heptateuch*, p. 71.

3   Bertram Colgrace and R. A. B. Mynors, eds, *Bede's Ecclesiastical History of the English People* (Oxford, 1969), IV.24.

4   George P. Krapp, ed., *The Junius Manuscript, Anglo-Saxon Poetic Records* (New York, 1931).

5   A. N. Doane, ed., *The Saxon Genesis* (University of Wisconsin Press, Madison, WI, 1991).

6   See Andy Orchard, *Pride and Prodigies: Studies in the Monsters of the Beowulf Manuscript*, rev. edn (University of Toronto Press, Toronto, 2003), pp. 58–85.

7   See Daniel Anlezark, *Water and Fire: The Myth of the Flood in Anglo-Saxon England* (Manchester University Press, Manchester, 2006), pp. 291–346.

8   *The Dream of the Rood*, ed. Michael Swanton (Exeter, 1987).

9   See Éamonn Ó Carragáin, *Ritual and the Rood: Liturgical Images and the Old English Poems of the Dream of the Rood Tradition* (British Library, London, 2005).

10 See Reginald of Durham, "Life of St. Godric," in *Social Life in Britain from the Conquest to the Reformation*, ed. G. G. Coulton (Cambridge University Press, Cambridge, 1918), pp. 415–20.

11 R. T. Davies, ed., *Medieval English Lyrics: A Critical Anthology* (London, 1963), p. 51.

12 The poem survives in two manuscripts: Cambridge University Library MS Add 5943, f. 182 v; a longer version exists in National Library of Scotland MS Advocates, 19.3.1; see Douglas Gray, ed., *English Medieval Lyrics* (Oxford, 1975); J. A. W. Bennet, *Poetry of the Passion: Studies in Twelve Centuries of English Verse* (Clarendon Press, Oxford, 1982).

13 See R. B. Burlin, *The Old English Advent: A Typological Commentary* (Yale University Press, New Haven, CT, 1968).

14 National Library of Scotland MS Advocates 18.7.21, fol 119v, written in Norfolk in 1372, the MS contains material for sermons, and a larger number of English verses.

15 See *Selections from the Carmina Burana: A Verse Translation*, trans. David Parlett (Penguin, Harmondsworth, 1986).

16 See William Langland, *The Vision of Piers Plowman: A Critical Edition of the B-Text*, ed. A. V. C. Schmidt (London, 1978).

17 *The Story of Genesis and Exodus*, ed. Richard Morris, EETS os 7 (Truebner, London, 1873); *Iacob and Iosep*, ed. A. S. Napier (Clarendon Press, Oxford, 1916).

18 An example is found in the Gospel harmony in Magdalen College Cambridge MS Pepys 2498.

19 Preserved in the Paris Psalter; see *The Paris Psalter: MS. Bibliothèque nationale Fonds Latin 8824*, ed. Bertram Colgrave (Rosenkilde and Bagger, Copenhagen, 1958).

20 See *English Writings of Richard Rolle, Hermit of Hampole*, ed. Hope Emily Allen (Oxford University Press, London, 1931).

21 *A Stanzaic Life of Christ: Compiled from Higden's Polychronicon and the Legenda aurea*, ed. Frances A. Foster, EETS os 166 (Oxford University Press, London, 1926). For a full

discussion see David Fowler, *The Bible in Early English Literature* (London, 1977); and his *The Bible in Middle English Literature* (Seattle, 1984).

22   See Margaret Deanesly, *The Lollard Bible and other Medieval Versions* (Cambridge, 1920).

23   *Polychronicon Ranulphi Higden monachi Cestrensis*, ed. Churchill Babington and Joseph Rawson Lumby, Rolls Series 41 (Longman, London, 1865–86).

24   *Cursor Mundi: A Northumbrian Poem of the XIVth Century*, ed. Richard Morris, EETS os 57, 59, 62, 66, 68 99, 101 reprint (Oxford University Press, London, 1961–6).

25   See Peter Happé, ed., *English Mystery Plays* (Penguin, Harmondsworth, 1975).

26   This is not to say that his knowledge and use of the Bible is not extensive; see Lawrence Besserman, *Chaucer and the Bible: A Critical Review of Research, Indexes, and Bibliography* (Garland, New York, 1988).

27   *The Riverside Chaucer*, 3rd edn, ed. Larry D. Benson (Oxford University Press, Oxford, 1988).

28   Malcom Andrew and Ronald Waldron, eds, *The Poems of the Pearl Manuscript* (London, 1978); the letter þ has been transliterated as th, ȝ as gh.

CHAPTER 5

Old English Poetry

Catherine A. M. Clarke

The Exeter Book, an anthology of Old English poetry produced in the late tenth century, includes a collection of almost one hundred riddles, at least two of which may be solved as "book" or, more specifically, "Bible." Among these, Riddle 26 perhaps offers the best encapsulation of the ways in which the Bible was conceptualized in Anglo-Saxon England and represented in its literature. The riddle reveals a fascination with the physical artifact of the book itself and emergent technologies of writing and literacy, as well as an awareness of the Bible's material value as a precious treasure or commodity. The text then moves on to catalogue the more abstract benefits contained within the book – ranging from allusions to the Bible as a source of spiritual grace and redemption to a very pragmatic list of the worldly advantages to be gained by its readers.

> Mec feonda sum   feore besnyþede,
> woruldstrenga binom,   wætte siþþan,
> dyfde on wætre,   dyde eft þonan,
> sette on sunnan,   þær ic swiþe beleas
> herum þam þe ic hæfde.   Heard mec siþþan
> snað seaxses ecg,   sindrum begrunden;
> fingras feoldan,   ond mec fugles wyn
> geondsprengde speddropum   spyrede geneahhe,
> ofer brunne brerd,   beamtelge swealg,
> streames dæle,   stop eft on mec,
> siþade sweartlast.   Mec siþþan wrah
> hæleð hleobordum,   hyde beþenede,
> gierede mec mid golde;   forþon me gliwedon
> wrætlic weorc smiþa,   wire bifongen.
> Nu þa gereno   ond se reada telg
> ond þa wuldorgesteald   wide mære
> dryhtfolca helm,   nales dol wite.
> Gif min bearn wera   brucan willað,
> Hy beoð þ wuldorgesteald   wide mære
> dryhtfolca helm,   nales dol wite.
> Gif min bearn wera   brucan willað,

> hy beoð þy gesundran   ond þy sigefæstran,
> heortum þy hwætran   ond þy hygebliþran,
> ferþe þy frodran,   habbaþ freonda þy ma,
> swæstra ond gesibbra,   soþra ond godra,
> tilra ond getreowra,   þa hyra tyr ond ead
> estum ycað   ond y arstafum
> lissum belicgað   ond hi lufan fæþmum
> fæste clyppað.   Frige hwæt ic hatte,
> niþum to nytte.   Nama min is mære,
> hæleþum gifre   ond halig sylf.[1]

A certain enemy robbed me of life, deprived me of physical strength, then dipped and wetted me in water, took me out again and placed me in the sun, where I quickly lost all the hair that I had. Then the hard edge of a sharpened knife cut me, fingers folded me, and the bird's joy [feather] repeatedly made tracks over my brown body with useful drops; it swallowed wood-dye mixed with water, stepped over me again, moved on in its black tracks. Then a man enclosed me between boards covered with hide and adorned me with gold, so that the wondrous work of the smiths, woven wires, embellished me. Now those ornaments and the red dye and the glorious decorations glorify widely the Protector of peoples, not the punishment of folly. If the children of men are willing to make good use of me, they will be the healthier and the surer of victory, more courageous in heart and happier in mind, wiser in spirit. They will have the more friends, kinsmen and dear ones, loyal and good, more excellent and true, who will gladly increase their honor and prosperity and surround them with favors and kindnesses, and hold them fast in the embraces of love. Ask what I am called, a benefit to people. My name is great, useful to men, and itself holy.

Written within the traditional Old English alliterative verse form, and packed with the dense metaphors typical of vernacular riddles, this text claims the voice of the Bible itself, speaking of its own identity, material origins, and spiritual powers. The process of the production of a book is evoked in vivid detail, focusing in particular on the physical effort and even violence inherent in the steps from the slaughtered calf to prepared vellum to written page. Indeed, the depiction of the wetting, stripping, and cutting of the calf-skin suggests the influence of the Gospel passion narratives and later hagiographic traditions, with the Bible itself here claiming a kind of physical suffering and martyrdom as part of its material identity. Riddle 94, another Exeter Book verse with the possible solution of "Bible," reflects a similar fascination with the material artifact of the book itself and the technologies of its production. Where Riddle 26 confronts the brutality of many aspects of the process, Riddle 94 focuses on the mystery of literacy and the power of the Bible to transmit knowledge in silence via the written word. The Bible's voice proclaims: "ic monigum sceal / wisdom cyþan;   no þær word sprecan" ("I shall reveal wisdom to many without speaking words").[2] Both riddles also represent the finished Bible as an object of treasure and literal value and prestige. Riddle 26 lingers over the gold, jewels, and precious red dye (another resonance with the martyrdom imagery) that adorn the book. This picture is concordant with the evidence of real Bibles surviving from Anglo-Saxon England, which functioned as symbols of the owners' riches and power, and could be used as commodities in gift exchanges or transactions between wealthy parties. Certainly, this Riddle demonstrates awareness of the practical uses of the Bible in Anglo-Saxon society, presenting a surprisingly pragmatic list of the benefits available to its readers. The advantages to be enjoyed by those who read the book include greater health, surer victory, more friends, and greater happiness and prosperity. Here the value of the Bible is advertised in terms that might appeal to an audience with predominantly secular or worldly concerns. Yet many of these assertions have spiritual resonances too. The idea that the Bible might help one to acquire "freonda þy ma / swæstra ond gesibbra,   soþra ond godra" ("more friends, kinsmen and dear ones, loyal and good") recalls the idea of a new Christian family of readers and believers, and the promise of being "þy sigefæstran" ("the surer of victory") might suggest the spiritual triumph over sin and death offered by the Bible and its teachings rather than success in earthly battles. The Riddle concludes with a confident assimilation of spiritual and secular heroic values into the identity of the Bible. Like a mythical hero the Bible claims greatness or fame ("min nama is mære"), addresses its audience as heroic warriors ("hæleþum"), and finally asserts that its very name is holy ("halig"). Exeter Book Riddle 26 enables us to recognize several key issues regarding the Bible in Old English poetry: its role in the developing literacy and textual culture of Anglo-Saxon England, its relation to concepts of treasure and worth (both material and spiritual), and its assimilation into traditional literary heroic culture. The Bible is an enormous influence on Old English poetry, yet biblical texts and images emerge transformed by the idioms of vernacular poetry and the traditions of the Germanic warrior ethos.

The centrality of the Bible to Anglo-Saxon intellectual and literary culture is attested by a range of sources.[3] Yet Frederick Biggs has cautioned that our understanding of "the Bible" itself must be nuanced and adapted in order to relate to its form and function in Anglo-Saxon England. Biggs observes that "the modern English word 'bible' ... is not attested from the period," noting that the terms used most commonly before the conquest are either Latin *bibliotheca* or the Old English *gewrit*. He goes on to explain that "one reason for this more general terminology is that single volumes containing the entire Bible were rare" and that "the text itself is not as firmly fixed during the period."[4] Thus the biblical texts encountered by Anglo-Saxon readers may have been either independent Books or more limited collections (for example, the many Psalters and Gospel-books in circulation), or indeed ones that no longer form part of the canonical Bible (such as the apocryphal Book of Judith; see discussion below). Readers and translators might also have had access to either the Vulgate Bible or a number of different Old Latin versions.[5] In whatever form, study of the Bible was certainly a fundamental aspect of Anglo-Saxon religious culture, and played a particularly central role in Benedictine monasticism. Efforts were also made during the period to make the Bible more widely available in the Old English vernacular to lay audiences beyond clerical or monastic circles. When asked by his patron, the nobleman Æthelweard, to produce a prose translation of the Old Testament for the laity, the abbot Ælfric prefaced his work with a discussion of the tribulations and pitfalls of rendering the Latin Bible in the vernacular. He laments the task as "hefigtime" ("burdensome, heavy") and further warns that it may also be "swiðe pleolic" ("very dangerous") to make the literal biblical text available to those who may not be trained to recognize the "gastlice andgit" ("spiritual meaning").[6] In marked contrast to the anxieties and troubled efforts of

Ælfric's Preface, Bede's story of the poet Cædmon in the *Ecclesiastical History* offers a mythical paradigm for the translation of biblical material into vernacular poetry as spontaneous, instantaneous inspiration. In a dream, Cædmon sees a figure who commands him to sing. He sings a song in English about God the Creator and, on waking, finds himself able to transform biblical texts easily into beautiful vernacular verse. Bede emphasizes both the brilliance and effortlessness of Cædmon's divinely inspired composition.

> Et quidem et alii post illum in gente Anglorum religiosa poemata facere temtabant, sed nullus eum aequiperare potuit. Namque ipse non ab hominibus neque per hominem institutus canendi artem didicit, sed diuinitus adiutus gratis canendi donum accepit.

> It is true that after him other Englishmen attempted to compose religious poems, but none could compare with him. For he did not learn the art of poetry from men nor through a man but he received the gift of song freely through the grace of God.[7]

Cædmon's method of composition, though apparently mystical and miraculous, in fact mirrors processes of reading and textual meditation familiar to Anglo-Saxon monastic audiences. We are told that:

> At ipse cuncta, quae audiendo discere poterat, rememorando secum et quasi mundum animal ruminando, in carmen dulcissimum conuertebat, suauiusque resonando doctores suos uicissim auditores sui faciebat.

> He learned all he could by listening to them and then, memorizing it and ruminating over it, like some clean animal chewing the cud, he turned it into the most melodious verse: and it sounded so sweet as he recited it that his teachers became in turn his audience.[8]

Cædmon's "rumination" over biblical texts fits neatly with his previous occupation as a humble cow-herd. Yet there are echoes here of the Latin term *ruminatio*, used to describe a specific kind of contemplative, creative reading practiced by early medieval monks.[9] Thus Bede's story offers a kind of mythical pattern for the Bible study, commentary, and translation familiar to religious audiences in the period.

"Cædmon's Hymn," the song first sung by Cædmon in his dream, functions similarly as a paradigm for the transformation of biblical material into the idioms of vernacular poetry. The poem responds to the Genesis story of creation with a radical transformation into the conventions of heroic verse and the traditional formulae of secular praise poetry.

> Nu sculon herigean   heofonrices weard,
> meotodes meahte   ond his modgeþanc,
> weorc wuldorfæder,   swa he wundra gehwæs,
> ece Drihten,   or onstealde.
> He ærest sceop   eorðan bearnum
> heofon to hrofe,   halig scyppend;
> þa middangeard   moncynnes weard,
> ece Drihten,   æfter teode
> firum foldan,   frea ælmihtig.[10]

> Now we must praise the Guardian of the heaven-kingdom, the power of the Maker and his design, the work of the glorious Father, as he, eternal Lord, founded the beginning of each of the wonders. He first created heaven as a roof for the children of earth, holy Creator; then the middle-earth, the Guardian of mankind, eternal Lord, afterwards ordained the world for people, Lord almighty.

The secular terminology of power and authority (*weard*, *Drihten*, *frea*, and so on) is here transposed to articulate spiritual concepts. The central metaphor of the creation story here is not the six-day sequence of commands as in the Genesis narrative, but instead the image of building a hall – the structure most central and emotive within Anglo-Saxon community and culture – with heaven "to hrofe" ("as a roof") and "middange-ard" ("middle-earth") protected below. The word "Nu" ("now") which opens the poem is emphatic and crucial: the pivotal moment of transition and change as words, praise and allegiance are repositioned toward the Lord in heaven. The recurrence throughout the poem of forms related to *scieppan* ("to create") is also significant. Cædmon – the first English *scop* ("poet") to create biblical verse in the vernacular – honors God as the ulti-mate "Scyppend" ("Creator") who "sceop" ("created") the earth from nothing. This self-referentiality underscores the poem and simultaneously celebrates Cædmon's own unique status even as it praises God. Ironically, the Old English text of the Hymn cited here derives from the West Saxon translation of Bede's *Ecclesiastical History* in the ninth century. Bede's original (early eighth-century) narrative is in Latin and, despite the centrality of the vernacular to this story, Cædmon's Hymn does not appear in English. Instead, the suppressed vernacular text of the Hymn creeps slowly back into the main narrative via marginal inscriptions in the early manuscripts. So, while Bede's story ostensibly offers a celebration and endorsement of English and the powers and possibili-ties of its poetry, anxieties evidently linger regarding the status of the vernacular, the appropriate range of its subject-matter, and the potential for its inclusion in a "canoni-cal," authoritative text such as Bede's *History*. And, as Allen Frantzen notes, "The account is never – not even in the oldest manuscript – the whole and satisfying com-plete moment of origin that Anglo-Saxonists desire."[11]

The Cædmon story, however, has proved a compelling myth for both medieval and modern scholars of Old English poetry. The major extant codex of Old English biblical verse, the Junius Manuscript (Oxford, Bodleian Library, MS Junius 11 or "Junius 11"), produced around the turn of the millennium, was conventionally referred to until the early twentieth century by the alternative title of the "Cædmon" or "Cædmonian" Manuscript. The name reflected a genuine belief (or, certainly, a tenacious desire) that its constituent poems were indeed the products of Bede's divinely inspired cowherd. While this view is no longer accepted, Bede's catalogue of the biblical subjects under-taken by Cædmon provides a fitting index to the contents of Junius 11.

> Canebat autem de creatione mundi et origine humani generis et tota Genesis historia, de egressu Israel ex Aegypto et ingressu in terram repromissionis, de aliis plurimis sacrae scripturae historiis.

> He sang about the creation of the whole world, the origin of the human race, and the whole history of Genesis, of the departure of Israel from Egypt and the entry into the promised land and of many other stories taken from the sacred scriptures.[12]

The Junius Manuscript includes a series of poems known by the editorial titles *Genesis A*, *Genesis B*, *Exodus*, *Daniel*, and *Christ and Satan*. All these poems deal with biblical material and include biblical narratives. Yet there are also marked differences across their treatments of biblical texts. While some poems and passages are relatively close to biblical content and chronology, others draw together episodes from across biblical Books and radically transform scriptural material. Throughout all the works in the codex, the text of the Vulgate Bible meets vernacular sources, traditions, and idioms, resulting in rich and challenging poems that have provoked hugely divergent critical evaluations.

The two Genesis poems are divided editorially into *Genesis A* and *Genesis B*, an originally distinct text worked into the main narrative. E. Sievers argued in 1875 that *Genesis B* derived from hypothesized Old Saxon sources, and this was dramatically proved in 1894, when analogous fragments of an Old Saxon Genesis were discovered in the Vatican Library.[13] There is evidence, then, that at least part of the Genesis narrative in Junius 11 engages with a wider vernacular poetic tradition of biblical translation. *Genesis A* includes a reworking of the Fall of the angels and God's creation of the world, expanded from the biblical text and reimagined through the conventions of vernacular poetry. This section of the poem provides some of the most striking uses of traditional Old English elements, yet presents a point of difficulty for some critics. God's casting out of the rebel angels is imagined in terms of an Anglo-Saxon lord's response to treacherous retainers, using emotive vocabulary of oath-breaking, malicious boasting, and rebellion.

> Sceof þa and scyrede   scyppend ure
> oferhidig cyn   engla of heofonum,
> wærleas werod.   Waldend sende
> laðwendne here   on langne sið,
> geomre gastas;   wæs him gylp forod,
> beot forbosten,   and forbiged þrym,
> wlite gewemmed.[14]

Then our Creator thrust out and cut off the arrogant kin of angels from the heavens, that treacherous company. The Ruler sent out the hateful army, the wretched spirits, on a long journey; their bragging was undermined, their boast [or vow] was broken, and their glory cast down, their beauty destroyed.

The text positions its audience united in allegiance with God "scyppend ure" ("*our* Creator") and in opposition to these outcast traitors. The representation of the angels conforms to a series of Old English poetic conventions for depicting treachery or dishonour, with their broken boasts ("gylp") recalling the empty bragging of the malicious Unferth in *Beowulf*, and their betrayal of loyalty resonating with the oath-breaking deserters in *The Battle of Maldon*.[15] Indeed, the semantic potential of the word *beot* ("beot forbosten," line 70) to include both "vow, oath" and "boast, brag" calls attention to the angels' parody and perversion of the rituals of heroic allegiance. The passage here exploits all the resources of Old English as a literary language: alliteration is intense, poetic variation juxtaposes different titles for God ("scyppend," "waldend"), and the

series of verbs with the intensifying prefix *for-* ("forod," "forbosten," "forbiged") underlines the violence of the angels' rebellion and their punishment. Crucially, the angels
are envisioned in recognizable terms as an army ("werod," "here"), and their fate is
typical for a traitor in Anglo-Saxon society: that of exile ("on langne sið").

The account of creation that follows again draws on Old English poetic idioms, most
effectively in the tautly understated description of the emptiness of the earth before God
brings forth life.

> Folde wæs þa gyta
> græs ungrene;   garsecg þeahte
> sweart synnihte,   side and wide,
> wonne wægas.[16]

The ground was then still ungreen, without grass. Far and wide black sinister night hid
the ocean, the dark waves.

Loosely translating Genesis 2:4–6, these lines rework the biblical account with arrest-
ing intensity and vividness. The earth is literally "*un*-green" ("ungrene") – almost a wry
litotes here, which imagines the earth before life only in terms of that which is not *yet*,
that which is absent. This single Old English adjective effectively condenses several
phrases of Genesis into a single astonishing concept.[17] Such powerful rhetoric is juxtaposed with the more commonplace "side and wide" ("far and wide"), grounding this
disconcerting, disturbing imagery at least within a familiar poetic formula.

In his edition of *Genesis A*, A. N. Doane focuses on this reworking of biblical material
through Old English, "Germanic" cultural values and literary idioms. Doane observes
that, in both the Genesis poems,

> a system of traditional [English] formulaic expressions is being utilized as the technical
> means for giving form and expression to the words, concepts and actions thought to be
> intrinsic to the [biblical] original. The better of these poets are attempting to create verbal
> structures which will elicit by familiar means (formulaic poetry) spiritual or doctrinal
> responses deemed similar to those which the sacred texts are supposed to elicit from trained
> audiences.[18]

Doane further extends his argument, asserting that, in *Genesis A*, we see Old English
poetic traditions responding to the challenges of new material.

> Germanic alliterative poetry had been developing for hundreds of years before *Genesis A*
> was composed and had evolved its own highly elaborate techniques and vocabulary. It had
> developed in a certain pre-Christian cultural environment to meet certain limited cultural
> demands. While working within this fully-fledged poetic-linguistic system, the poet of
> *Genesis A* was deriving his statements, content and meaning from sources external to his
> verse tradition and developing them according to demands entirely alien to it. ... Thereby
> arose a confrontation of styles, a gap between source and product.[19]

Finally, Doane claims that:

> The poet must have been aware of the deficiencies of his style for rendering a text expressed in a style so alien to his own. ... Certainly nothing in the native rhetoric could match the syntactical resources which the Vulgate offered.[20]

Doane's argument is worth close examination as it typifies many critical approaches to Old English "biblical" poetry. For Doane, *Genesis A* represents a retelling of biblical material through the traditional conventions – and limitations – of Old English alliterative formulaic poetry. The relation of the vernacular poetic style to the biblical source is one not only of difference, but also of deficit: the Old English poetic idiom lacks the vocabulary and rhetorical resources to match the sophistication of the Vulgate original. Implicit in Doane's argument is also the suggestion that a poem in the vernacular must be designed for unlearned audiences – not the "trained" readers skilled in biblical exegesis whom he imagines for the Latin Bible. Yet the alternative articulation of biblical narrative in the vernacular need not be regarded as inferior. The passages from *Genesis A*, discussed above, exploit traditional poetic idioms and the resources of the Old English language to imagine the biblical narrative in new and powerful ways. Similarly, the use of Old English need not indicate an unlearned audience, incapable of dealing with the biblical text in the original. The choice of the vernacular opens up new textual and cultural associations for contemplation, and, as in the case of the treacherous angels, may allow more affective responses to be elicited. Indeed, recent work on the Junius manuscript argues that these vernacular poems demand skills of exegesis, *ruminatio*, and textual interpretation just as sophisticated as those required by biblical or patristic Latin texts.[21]

A poem in the Junius Manuscript that has inspired perhaps even greater critical debate and controversy is the editorially titled *Exodus*. *Exodus* uses biblical material in a less straightforward way than the two Genesis poems, presenting a more ambitious synthesis of sources and interpretative traditions and confounding scholarly attempts to trace a linear historical narrative within the text. Earlier evaluations of the poem saw the absence of a clear chronological narrative as evidence of the text's lack of coherence and integrity, and dismissed anything beyond recognizable biblical material as idiosyncratic authorial addition. In his edition and translation of the poem, Tolkien asserts that *Exodus* exists only in a "dislocated and mutilated form," and that in all probability the "original poem" has been "curtailed, adapted, accidentally dislocated, interpolated and expanded deliberately, or patched with alien material where chance damage left a gap."[22] In his earlier 1907 edition of the poem, Francis Blackburn also argues that it is fragmentary and marred by interpolation, and comments that "the *Exodus* uses its source with great freedom and is indebted to the author's own fancy for the great mass of its details."[23] One of the major critical problems presented by the poem is that, despite the editorial title *Exodus*, the text includes narrative episodes from elsewhere in the Bible, such as the story of Noah and the Flood and Abraham and Isaac, and these episodes are drawn together apparently without attention to chronology or original biblical order. Successive editions of the poem have attempted to solve this supposed problem by disentangling it into distinct sections and even offering new editorial titles for a hypothesized series of shorter poems.[24]

The most recent edition of the poem, by Peter J. Lucas, aims to justify the poem's coherence and integrity in its extant manuscript form, arguing against suppositions of interpolation or corruption of an imagined "original." Lucas asserts the unity of the poem under the central theme, which he articulates as "Salvation by Faith and Obedience."[25] Indeed, Lucas's statement of theme might provide a more satisfactory title for the poem than the evidently misleading nineteenth-century heading *Exodus*, which has led to so many charges of deviation, interpolation, and confusion. The importance of sources far beyond the biblical Book of Exodus itself is shown strikingly by the *Fontes Anglo-Saxonici* database entry for the poem. In addition to Exodus, the poem draws on a wide range of other biblical Books (Old and New Testaments), and patristic and exegetical texts from Augustine to Jerome to Bede.[26] It is also now widely accepted that the poem is influenced by the liturgy of Holy Saturday, and in particular the sequence of readings (the pre-baptismal lections) assigned to the Easter Vigil. This connection was first suggested by J. W. Bright in 1912, who recognized that the poem was the product of "a well-endowed and skilful craftsman ... resourceful in diction, accurate in versification, masterful in condensation and uniformly elevated in mood," and sought to dismiss arguments that the poem was the victim of interpolation.[27] The liturgy of Holy Saturday brings together the disparate biblical narratives that are also combined in *Exodus*, drawing parallels and allegorical associations that relate to the themes of salvation, resurrection, and baptism (which was traditionally performed on Easter Eve). In the Old English *Exodus*, it seems that we see biblical material mediated and modified by liturgical context and allegorical interpretation.

A good example of this sophisticated allegorical treatment and interweaving of different biblical texts occurs at lines 105 to 119 of the poem, which describes the Israelites being guided through the desert by the pillar of fire.[28] The imagery here at first seems startling and incongruous: the Israelites are imagined as "sæmen" ("seamen," line 105b) traveling over the "flodwege" ("ocean-way," line 106a). Yet this imagery might appeal directly to an Anglo-Saxon audience familiar with sea-faring, and its metaphor of passing through water to reach salvation resonates with both the crossing of the Red Sea and the symbolism of baptism. This apparently inappropriate sea imagery also links the narrative of the Israelites in the desert with the poem's account – once dismissed as interpolation – of Noah's Flood. The protective fire-pillar is imagined as "heofoncandel" ("heaven-candle," line 115b), a characteristic Old English *kenning* or metaphorical compound used more conventionally for the sun, but here raising associations with the Paschal Candle at the center of the Easter Vigil liturgy. Allegorical connections and typological readings resonate between the poem's different narrative episodes, and imagery of darkness, light, and water recurs throughout the work. Without any explicit commentary or gloss alongside the poem, these connections demand sophisticated interpretative skills and exegetical experience. As Lucas comments:

> On the basis of the available evidence it looks as if MS Junius 11 was intended for devotional reading in the vernacular. (In the unlikely event that such reading was regarded as elementary, because in the vernacular, then the inclusion of *Exodus* in the manuscript was ill-considered.)[29]

Exodus presents again a brilliant synthesis of traditional vernacular and Christian Latin literary traditions and aesthetics. With its interwoven episodes, rather than single linear narrative, the poem's structure recalls the "interlace" designs of Anglo-Saxon art and vernacular poetry.[30] Such meditative connections and associations also resonate with the monastic practice of *ruminatio*, or contemplative reading. The poem's challenging, allegorical, and figurative style might also be aligned with either the vernacular riddle tradition or the difficult "hermeneutic" Latin characteristic of some contemporary Anglo-Saxon monastic texts.[31] The complexity of the poem and its treatment of biblical material is now becoming more widely recognized and studied.

Beyond the biblical poetry of the Junius Manuscript, other Old English poems also engage with biblical narratives and ideas. *Judith*, found in the Beowulf Manuscript (MS Cotton Vitellius A. XV), reworks the apocryphal Book of Judith (from the Vulgate Old Testament) into a powerful – and problematic – heroic poem. Judith's beheading of the drunken Holofornes, who had planned to rape her, is described in vivid and violent detail.

> Sloh ða wundenlocc
> þone feondsceaðan   fagum mece,
> heteþoncolne,   þæt heo healfne forcearf
> þone sweoran him,   þæt he on swiman læg,
> druncen ond dolhwund.   Næs ða dead þa gyt,
> ealles orsawle.   Sloh þa eornoste
> ides ellenrof   oðre siðe
> þone hæðenan hund,   þæt him þæt heafod wand
> forð on ða flore.[32]

Then the woman with braided hair struck the enemy, the hostile one, with the bright sword, so that she cut through half of his neck and he lay in a stupor, drunken and wounded. He was not yet dead then, not completely lifeless. The courageous woman struck the heathen dog bravely a second time, so that his head rolled away on the floor.

The contrasting epithets here place Judith the "courageous woman" ("ides ellenrof") in stark opposition to Holofornes the "heathen dog" ("hæðenan hund") and "hostile one" ("feondsceaðan"). Judith's double attempt to cut through Holofernes's neck is both an affecting reminder of her frailty and physical vulnerability as a woman, and a further grotesque detail that underscores the violence of the scene. Indeed, the Old English Judith has proved a problematic figure for many critics, as she performs here the traditionally masculine heroic role of violence and vengeance, rather than any of the conventional female roles of mourner, advisor, or "peace-weaver."[33] The manuscript context of the poem adds further disturbing resonances to Judith's transgression of literary heroic gender norms, with clear echoes in this scene of Grendel's mother's fight with Beowulf. Like Grendel's monstrous mother, Judith also seems to usurp the masculine role of violent, warrior vengeance. Yet Judith's violence is not an indulgence of her own resentment and anger, but instead an act inspired and enabled by God who "Hi ... mid elne onbryrde" ("inspired her with great courage," line 95) and works through her. Before she kills Holofernes, Judith prays to God for "victory and sure faith" ("sigor ond soðne geleafan," line 89) and "salvation" ("gesynta," line 90b), and asks *Him* to avenge Holofernes's wickedness ("Gewrec nu, mihtig Dryhten," line 92b). Yet the Old English poem still presents a complex and challenging portrayal of Judith. Whereas Ælfric's Old English homily on Judith emphasizes her chaste widowhood and focuses on her potential as an allegorical type for God's Church, the Old English poem returns repeatedly to images of Judith's beauty, femininity, and allure.[34] Most strikingly, she is described as "ides ælfscinu," a "woman shining with elfin beauty" (line 14a), which both captures her rare beauty but also recalls the sinister, otherworldly "eotenas ond ylfe   ond orcneas" ("giants and elves and evil spirits") who stalk the margins of human culture in *Beowulf*.[35] The poem's refusal to simplify or allegorize Judith's character ensures ongoing critical challenges and puzzles.

The "giants and elves and evil spirits" of *Beowulf* are traced back in the poem to the kin of Cain, the Bible's first murderer ("Caines cynne," line 107a; see also lines 1260–3). As with all Anglo-Saxon poetry, biblical echoes and allusions recur throughout *Beowulf*, confounding any attempts to distinguish between Old English "secular" and "sacred" verse. The magical sword that Beowulf finds at the bottom of the Grendelkin's haunted mere has inscribed upon it

> fyrngewinnes,   syðþan flod ofsloh,
> gifen geotende   giganta cyn –
> frecne geferdon.

the ancient strife, when the flood, the surging water, killed the race of giants: they had behaved badly.

The sword's mysterious runes ("runstafas," line 1695) meld the biblical Flood with vague, allusive memories of Germanic myth and legend. At the end of the poem, as twelve mourners ride around Beowulf's barrow, the poem recalls the biblical apostles and invests Beowulf with a (perhaps ironic) Christ-like stature.[36] As with most uses of the Bible in Old English poetry, it is likely that these elements are introduced via wider Christian traditions, rather than direct access to a biblical text.

Perhaps the best-known Old English poem that deals with biblical material, and again offers an interweaving of Germanic heroic and Christian Latin traditions, is *The Dream of the Rood*, in the late tenth-century Vercelli Book. With close analogues in the inscriptions of the eighth-century Ruthwell Cross and the late tenth- or early eleventh-century Brussels Cross, *The Dream of the Rood* is a powerful reworking of the crucifixion story from the perspective of the cross itself. The text draws loosely on the Gospel accounts, modifying details and compressing narrative for poetic effect, and resonates with both vernacular riddle and Latin hymn traditions.[37] Its literary techniques, then, are not without precedent: there are late antique and early medieval analogues for use of prosopopoeia in the presentation of the cross, and Venantius Fortunatus's well known hymns *Pange lingua* and *Vexilla regis* exploit similar martial or warrior metaphors.[38] Yet the radical impact of *The Dream of the Rood* stems from its use of these devices to confront paradoxes and tensions that are particularly acute and problematic in the context of transitional secular-heroic/Christian Anglo-Saxon England. At the center of the poem is the revisioning of Christ as a warrior-hero embracing his chosen destiny and welcoming battle. The cross recalls the moment of Christ's crucifixion,

> Ongyrede hine þa geong hæleð –   þæt wæs God ælmihtig –
> strang ond stiðmod;   gestah he on gealgan heanne,
> modig on manigra gesyhðe,   þa he wolde mancyn lysan.
> Bifode Ic þa me se beorn ymbclypte;   ne dorste Ic hwæðre bugan to eorðan,
> feallan to foldan sceatum,   ac Ic sceolde fæste standa.
> Rod wæs ic aræred.   Ahof Ic ricne Cyning,
> heofona Hlaford;   hyldan me ne dorste.
> Þurhdrifan hi me mid deorcan næglum;   on me syndon þa dolg gesiene,
> opene inwidhlemmas; ne dorste Ic hira nænigum sceððan.
> Bysmeredon hie unc butu ætgædere.[39]

He stripped himself then, the young hero – that was God almighty – strong and resolute, he climbed onto the high gallows, brave in the sight of many, when he intended to redeem mankind. I trembled when the warrior embraced me; yet I did not dare bow down to the earth, fall to the corners of the earth, but I had to stand fast. I was raised as a cross. I lifted up the powerful King, Lord of the heavens; I did not dare to bend. They drove me through with dark nails; the marks can still be seen on me, the open wounds of wickedness: I did not dare to harm any of them. They mocked us both together.

This passage adapts the Gospel narratives to depict Christ not as passive victim but as active, heroic warrior. He strips *himself* ("Ongyrede hine," line 39a), and, as throughout the poem, his own active intention and volition are emphasized ("he wolde," line 41b). The lines here also play with the paradox of Christ's dual identity as both man ("geong hæleð," line 39a) and God ("God ælmihtig," line 39b). Similarly, throughout the poem, the paradoxical identity of the cross is explored as it shifts from a symbol of suffering and shame (for example, the "gallows" of line 40b) to an icon of triumph and glory, adorned with treasure (see lines 4 to 17).

The passage cited here centers on the shared experience and intimacy of Christ and the cross, imagined in terms of the close relationship between a warrior lord and his loyal retainer. It is in fact the cross that speaks of being driven through with nails, drawing attention to his complete engagement and empathy with Christ's suffering. Indeed, the Old English "þurhdrifan" (line 46) might be a vernacular approximation of the Latin devotional concept of *compunctio*, becoming popular at this time, which urges the individual's emotional involvement with Christ's suffering on the cross through the contemplation of emotive artistic and literary representations.[40] Here the cross even claims that the nail-wounds remain visible upon it – a daring transfer of the idea of the *stigmata* onto the cross itself. The intimacy and unity between Christ and the cross is further underlined in affective vocabulary, exploiting both the heroic tradition of the close bond between lord and retainer and the particular resources of the early English vernacular. The cross trembles as Christ embraces him ("Bifode Ic þa me se beorn ymbclypte," line 42), recalling the intense homosocial bonds familiar from heroic poetry such as *Beowulf*,[41] and the Old English dual pronoun (no longer available in Modern English) is invoked to articulate the absolute unity between the two protagonists ("unc butu ætgædere," line 48). Like Christ, the cross is imagined in terms of active obedience to his lord rather than passive submission: the passage is full of verbs of compunction and obligation (for example, "ne dorste Ic," lines 42b and 47b, "Ic sceolde," line 43b). Yet despite this absolute allegiance and obedience to his lord, the cross is ultimately the instrument of Christ's destruction. Germanic tradition insists that the worst offence imaginable is betrayal or destruction of one's Lord: here the cross appears to commit that crime. At line 66 of the poem the cross is even described, astonishingly, as Christ's slayer (*bana*). In his recent major study of *The Dream of the Rood*, Éamonn Ó Carragáin stresses the impact of these tensions within the poem.

> Beguiled by romantic notions of what Germanic heroism involved, scholars have not sufficiently considered how disturbing it must have been for an early English audience to imagine the Crucifixion in this new way. ... To present the Cross as aware that it must slay its Lord was deliberately to emphasize that its role was problematic: a risky thing to do in the very centuries when the liturgy had begun to celebrate the Exaltation of the Cross.[42]

Once again, use of the vernacular in *The Dream of the Rood* does not imply an elementary or introductory function. The poem uncovers tensions between Germanic heroic and Christian values and ideologies, and reveals difficult paradoxes at the heart of the crucifixion narrative. Again, this poem presents major spiritual and intellectual challenges for its audience.

Near the beginning of *The Dream of the Rood*, the cross describes the violent process by which it was hacked down from its roots in the forest and made into an instrument of execution (lines 28 to 33). As with the account of the Bible's production in Riddle 26, the cross claims for itself its own passion and martyrdom, so that we see Christ's redemptive suffering mirrored in the material fabric of these two central artifacts of the Christian faith. Like the cross, the Bible is an accessible symbol of salvation and God's relationship with mankind. Yet Old English poetic versions of the Bible are challenging, allusive meditations on scriptural texts, rather than simplifications or straightforward mediations for the laity. In the earliest English poetry, translation of the Bible represents daring ambition and aspiration for the vernacular, sophisticated reflection on scriptural texts and traditions, and a desire to explore the meeting-points between Christian and Germanic heroic cultures.

Notes

1 Bernard J. Muir, ed., *The Exeter Anthology of Old English Poetry*, 2 vols (Exeter, 1994), vol. 1, pp. 306–7. The riddle numbering used here is Muir's.
2 Muir, *The Exeter Book*, vol. 1, p. 382.
3 For a good general discussion of the ways in which the Anglo-Saxons encountered biblical texts, see Paul Remley, *Old English Biblical Verse* (Cambridge, 1996), pp. 30–90.
4 Frederick M. Biggs, "Bible in Old English Literature," in Paul E. Szarmach et al., eds, *Medieval England: An Encyclopaedia* (New York and London), pp. 128–9, p. 128.
5 See Peter J. Lucas, ed., *Exodus* (Exeter, 1994), pp. 52–3.

6   S. J. Crawford, ed., *The Old English Version of the Heptateuch*, Early English Text Society Ordinary Series 160 (London, 1922), p. 76.

7   Bede, *Bede's Ecclesiastical History of the English People*, ed. and trans. Bertram Colgrave and R. A. B. Mynors (Oxford, 1969), pp. 414, 415.

8   Bede, *Ecclesiastical History*, pp. 418, 419.

9   See Jean Leclercq, *The Love of Learning and the Desire for God*, trans. Catharine Misrahi (New York, 1982), p. 73.

10   Thomas Miller, ed. and trans., *The Old English Version of Bede's Ecclesiastical History of the English People*, Early English Text Society Ordinary Series 95 (London, 1890), p. 344.

11   Allen J. Frantzen, *Desire for Origins. New Language, Old English, and Teaching the Tradition* (New Brunswick, NJ, 1990), p. 143.

12   Bede, *Ecclesiastical History*, pp. 418, 419.

13   See B. J. Timmer, *The Later Genesis* (Oxford, 1948), p. 11.

14   *Genesis* in George Philip Krapp, ed., *The Junius Manuscript* (London and New York, 1931), lines 65–71.

15   See D. Scragg, ed., *The Battle of Maldon* (Manchester, 1981), ll. 185–201, and George Jack, ed., *Beowulf: A Student Edition* (Oxford, 1994), lines 499–532a.

16   *Genesis*, lines 116b–119a.

17   Genesis 2:5: "when no plant of the field was yet in the earth and no herb of the field had yet sprung up."

18   A. N. Doane, ed., *Genesis A. A New Edition* (Madison, WI, 1978), p. 49.

19   Doane, *Genesis A*, p. 70.

20   Doane, *Genesis A*, p. 70.

21   The illustrations (and planned illustrations) for the Junius Manuscript are also often cited as evidence that the book was intended for an unlettered audience. Yet Catherine Karkov's recent study of the existing images argues persuasively that these are not simple narrative illustrations, but are loaded with complex symbolism and allusion. See Catherine E. Karkov, *Text and Picture in Anglo-Saxon England* (Cambridge, 2001).

22   Joan Turville-Petre, ed., *The Old English* Exodus: *Text, Translation and Commentary by J. R. R. Tolkien* (Oxford, 1981), pp. 33 and 35.

23   Francis A. Blackburn, ed., *Exodus and Daniel* (Boston and London, 1907), p. xix.

24   See Lucas, *Exodus*, pp. 30–1.

25   Lucas, *Exodus*, p. 61.

26   D. C. Anlezark, "The Sources of *Exodus* (Cameron A.1.2)," 2001, Fontes Anglo-Saxonici World Wide Web Register (http://fontes.english.ox.ac.uk/), accessed December 2006.

27   J. W. Bright, "The Relation of the Cædmonian *Exodus* to the Liturgy," *Modern Language Notes* 27 (1912), 97–103, p. 97.

28   See Lucas, *Exodus*, pp. 92–5.

29   Lucas, *Exodus*, p. 29.

30   See Andrew J. G. Patenall, "The Image of the Worm: Some Literary Implications of Serpentine Decoration," in J. Douglas Woods and David A. E. Pelteret, eds, *The Anglo-Saxons. Synthesis and Achievement* (Waterloo, Ontario, 1985), pp. 105–16.

31   See Michael Lapidge, "The Hermeneutic Style in Tenth-Century Anglo-Latin Literature," *Anglo-Saxon England* 4 (1975), 67–111.

32   Mark Griffith, ed., *Judith* (Exeter, 1997), lines103b–111a.

33   See Jane Chance, "Grendel's Mother as Epic Anti-Type of the Virgin and Queen," in R. D. Fulk, ed., *Interpretations of* Beowulf (Bloomington and Indianapolis, 1991), pp. 251–63, especially p. 260.

34   Andy Orchard, *Pride and Prodigies. Studies in the Monsters of the Beowulf-Manuscript* (Toronto, 1995), p. 9.

35   Jack, ed., *Beowulf*, line 133.

36   See *Beowulf*, lines 3169–82.

37   See Bruce Dickins and Alan S. C. Ross, eds, *The Dream of the Rood* (London, 1945), pp. 18–19.

38   See Earl R. Anderson, "Liturgical Influence in *The Dream of the Rood*," *Neophilologus* 73 (1989), 293–304, p. 293. For the Venantius Fortunatus hymns, see *Venanti Honori Clementiani Fortunati presbyteri italici opera poetica*, ed. F. Leo, *Monumenta Germaniae Historica Auctores Antiquissimi* 4, 1 (Berlin, 1881), 27–8 and 34–5.

39   Dickins and Ross, eds, *The Dream of the Rood*, lines 39–48.

40   See Leclercq, *The Love of Learning*, p. 30.

41   For example, the relationship between Hrothgar and Beowulf, see lines 1866–79.

42   Éamonn Ó Carragáin, *Ritual and the Rood. Liturgical Images and the Old English Poems of the Dream of the Rood Tradition* (London, 2005), p. 2.

CHAPTER 6
The Medieval Religious Lyric

Douglas Gray

Chaucer famously said of his Physician that his study was but little on the Bible. Rather curiously, in the popular mind this remark seems to have been extended to the whole of medieval culture. Curiously, because to anyone who looks more closely, it is evident that the Bible underlies and informs a mass of commentary, exegesis, and exposition, and is deeply significant in the devotional life and literature of the period, and in ordinary life as well. It is true of course that the "study" of the Bible was different from what it came to be in Reformation and post-Reformation times: a learned theologian might well pore over the pages of a biblical book and produce a learned commentary in Latin, but a humble layman who had no Latin and often could not read at all derived his knowledge of scriptures from different sources – through the ear, from the sermons of preachers and from hearing vernacular books that paraphrased biblical stories, and through the eye, from visual representations of scenes and figures – which were long called "laymen's books." In the later Middle Ages when both the literacy and the cultural importance of the laity increased there was evidently a desire to be able to read the scriptures in the vernacular, to which the large number of surviving copies of the Wycliffite version (in spite of much ecclesiastical hostility) eloquently testifies. But even in the fifteenth century when many layfolk as well as priests were able to read these, or various paraphrases and retellings, this seems to have been largely a private activity, and anything resembling later group "Bible study" was largely confined to groups of "dissenters." It is therefore not surprising that at first sight at least religious lyrics in the vernacular (written mostly by clerics for other clerics and layfolk) biblical materials are not as immediately apparent as they are in later, and especially in Protestant, examples. But it is there, sometimes mediated through commentary or paraphrase, and always seen through medieval eyes. Here three traditions were especially influential, each of which this chapter discusses in turn: the use of biblical material in the liturgy; the "typological" reading of the Bible; and the widespread tradition of "affective" devotion. In tracking these three modes of engagement with biblical sources, this chapter spends its most significant energies on the "affective mode," since this is the predominant tradition: as we will see in the depiction of Mary and the passion in particular, the affective mode was particularly well suited to the lyric form, moving the viewer to pity and piety. Yet the liturgical and typological modes also produced some of the period's most remarkable lyrics, as this chapter discusses in its opening pages. Finally this chapter turns, in conclusion, to consider the legacy of these three modes on poetic form. Before we start, it is worth noting that the study of the Middle English religious lyric is based on foundations laid by two great American scholars, Carleton Brown and R. L. Greene, who collected, edited, and annotated a vast amount of the materials available in manuscript. It is their work in the field that has provided the groundwork for its subsequent flourishing.[1]

To begin with the first of the three interpretative modes: the use of biblical material in the liturgy is one significant tradition influencing the poets' knowledge and use of Scripture. Some of the shorter introits, offertories, and graduals based on biblical verses are already virtually lyrics in miniature. The "Reproaches" or *Improperia* of the Good Friday liturgy, a series of contrasting statements of God's grace known to man in the Old Testament, and of man's cruel responses in the passion (which were brilliantly used later by George Herbert in "The Sacrifice"), underlie some of the "complaints" of Christ to man. Sometimes they were translated (not brilliantly) in this period – once, curiously, by an earlier Herbert, William Herebert, a learned fourteenth-century Franciscan ("Ich delede [divided] to see for the, / And Pharaon dreynte[drowned] for me; / And thu to princes sellest me. / My folk, what habbe [have] I do thee / Or in what thing toened [harmed] thee?" etc.). More usually, however, they will suggest an idea or a word or phrase that can form the basis of a lyric. Thus the idea of *felix culpa*, the widely used paradox of the fortunate fall, which appears in the *Exultet* sung in the Easter Saturday liturgy ("O cerrte neccessarium Adae peccatum. O felix culpa, quae talem ac tantum meruit habere redemptorem!"), is cheerfully and ecstatically transformed into a brief lyric:

> Adam lay iboyndyn [bound],
>   bowndyn in a bond,
> Fowre thowsand wynter
>   thowt [thought] he not to [too] long.
>
> And al was for an appil,
>   an appil that he tok,
> As clerkes fyndyn wretyn [written],
>   wretyn in here [their] book.
>
> Ne hadde the appil take,
>   the appil take ben,
> Ne hadde never our lady
>   a [have] ben hevene qwen [queen].
>
> Blyssid be the tyme,
>   that appil take was,
> Therfore we mown [may] syngyn [sing]
>   *Deo gracias* [thanks be to God]

Similarly, a verse from an Advent Epistle (Romans 13:11–12), "now it is high time to awake out of sleep; for now is our salvation nearer than when we believed," inspires a triumphant carol:

> Nowel, Nowel, Nowel,
> Nowel, Nowel, Nowel, Nowel
>
> Owt of your slepe aryse and wake
> For God mankynd now ytake
> Al of a maide without any make [mate, peer];
> Of al women she bereth the belle [apparently a rustic prize for excellence].
>   Nowel!
>   Nowel, Nowel, etc.

It celebrates the redemption of mankind ("now man is brighter than the sunne," "now man may to heven wende"), who can now address God as brother: "Now blessyd brother, graunte us grace / A [on] domesday to see they face."

Another influential tradition was much older, going back to the early church, the practice of finding "figures" of the Redemption in the events or characters of the Old Testament, often in fact reading Christ's name in those pages. This typological method continued through the Middle Ages in both literature and art (we see four prophets carrying the Evangelists on their shoulders; the devotional image of the seated figure of "Christ in distress" is the fulfillment of the Old Testament figure of Job setting *in sterquilinio*), and continued beyond, appearing still for instance in the seventeenth-century East window of the chapel of Lincoln College, Oxford. Some were especially associated with the Virgin Mary and the virgin birth – the burning bush seen by Moses, which was not consumed, the fleece of Gideon mentioned above, the closed gate of Ezekiel. Some are so common that they may simply be alluded to as in the poem "I syng of a mayden that is makeles," or when Chaucer's Prioress addresses Mary directly as "bussh unbrent, brennynge in Moyses syghte." Typology often underlies and gives strength and texture to a lyric. As a common mode of thought it explains the practice in some Marian lullabies of alluding, even in this happy moment, to the sufferings and torments that were to befall the Christ child. All this produced a "stock" of meaningful images that could be used in a variety of ways by the English lyric poets. When a lyric addresses Mary – "Moder, loke on me / With thine suete eyen [eyes]" – we are apt to think first of the influence of cross-fertilisation from the secular love lyric. This may well be the case, but even here biblical images of turning eyes or face toward a person as a sign of favor may also be lurking.

The most important, however, was an intense and "affective" devotional tradition encouraged by the writings of St Anselm and St Bernard and spread by spiritual teachers and preachers to the laity, which emphasized a personal meditation on the humanity of Christ, dwelling on the details of his life and passion in such a way that the individual became as close to the events of the sacred story as if, in the vivid eye of their imagination, they were really there and could, as it were, participate ("follow the mother as she goes to Bethlehem; go with her into the inn; stand by and assist her when she bears the child," a religious sister is counselled). In the intensely devout this could be taken to extremes: Margery Kempe in the fifteenth century weeps and cries when she sees a *pietà*, and is reproved by a priest, who says "damsel, Jesus is dead long since," but she has the last word: "sir, his death is as fresh to me as he had died this same day, and so me thinketh it ought to be to you and to all Christian people." Emile Mâle said without too much exaggeration that the Christians of the Middle Ages had their souls filled with Jesus Christ – "they sought him everywhere and they saw him everywhere" and "read his name on all the pages of the Old Testament."

This intense concentration on the figure of Christ explains much of the power of the medieval religious lyric and also explains its apparent selectivity – Old Testament material tends to be used in a markedly Christocentric way. The many devotional cults that clustered around the figure of Christ – his Five Wounds, his sacred Heart and sacred Blood, his Holy Name (using the Old Testament verse from *The Song of Songs*, "oleum effusum est nomen tuum") – are all echoed in the lyrics "Crist makith to man a fair present, / His blody body with love brent [burnt, consumed by]," and others, some of which remind us of the later Cowper hymn "There is a fountain filled with blood" (there are even verses purporting to give the exact number of drops of blood that Christ shed). The Nativity scene is sometimes evoked in lyrics, usually suggested by a detail – in one the Virgin Mary addressing her son says "on porful [poor] bed list thou here ... / For thi cradel is ase a bere, / Oxe and asse beth [are] thi fere [companions]: / Wepe ich [I] mai tharfore," and tenderly tells him to place his feet on her breast to guard against the cold. The human emotion of the scene is emphasized in a number of lullabies sung to the child ("his mouth ofte she dyd kysse / And sayd, 'sweete hert myne, / I pray you make good chere'").

Specifically these affective approaches to the Bible celebrate the Virgin Mary, the object of a very significant medieval cult, both as a loving mother and as the powerful "empress of heaven." The Angelic Salutation (Luke 1:28) is at the center of a number of lyrics. One of the very best lyrics celebrates her voluntary "choice" as the key to the mystery of the Incarnation in imagery filled with biblical echoes (the dew, for instance, recalls that which fell on Gideon's fleece in Judges 6:37–8):

> I syng of a mayden
>   that is makeles [peerless, without a mate]
> Kyng of alle kynges
>   to here sone she ches [chose]
>
> He cam also [as] stylle [silently]
>   ther his moder [mother] was
> As dew in Aprylle
>   that fallyt [falleth] on the gras.
>
> He cam also stylle
>   ther his moder lay
> As dew in Aprille
>   that fallyt on the spray [branch]
>
> Moder and maydyn
>   was never non but she –
> Wel may swych [such] a lady
>   Godes moder be!

The best of the Nativity lyrics contrive to combine celebration of the great significance of the Incarnation with an expression of joy. In one this is charmingly done through a humble "bystander," a shepherd "Joly Wat." He is introduced sitting on a hill with his cloak, hat, and pipe, his dog tied to his girdle, and surrounded by his sheep. He hears the angelic "gloria in excelsis" and sees a star as red as blood. He hastens to Bethlehem, where he find Jesus in "a sympyll place / Betwen an ox and an asse," offers presents – his kilt, tar-box (shepherds used tar as a salve for their sheep), and saying farewell to Mary and Joseph hurries back to his sheep: "Now may I well both hop and syng, / For I have bene a [at] Crystes beryng [birth]." However, the Passion, and especially the scene of the Crucifixion, which is the most common subject, is often intensely realized: "The mynde [memory] of thy sweet passion, Jesu – / Teres [tears] it tolles [draws], / Eyene [eyes] it bolles [swells], / My vesage it wetes, / And my hert it swetes [makes sweet]" says one. Sometimes Christ is imagined to utter a lament from the cross, an appeal to sinful man, or a reproach ("thi garland is of grene, / Of floures many on [one]; / Myn of sharpe thornes." [Your hands have fine gloves, mine are pierced by nails, etc.]).

One of the most striking versions of the crucifixion is an adaptation of a verse in Lamentations (1:12), "O vos omnes qui transitis per viam, attendite et videte si est dolor sicut meus" ["all yet that pass by, behold and see if there be any sorrow like my sorrow"].

> Ye that passen be the wey,
> abideth [pause] a litil stounde [while]:
> Beholdeth, al me felawes,
> Yef [if] ani me like is founda.
> To the tre with nailes thre
> Wel fast I hange bounde;
> With a spere al thuru [through] mi side
> To min herte is made a wounde.

The sorrow of the scene is deepened by the presence of Mary ("stabat autem juxta crucem Jesu mater eius ..." ["now there stood by the cross of Jesus his mother ..."], John 19:25), the source of some of the finest art and literature of the Middle Ages. The lyrics often use it, sometimes simply:

> Jesu cristes milde moder
> Stud, beheld hire sone o [on] rode [cross]
> That he was ipined [tortured] on;
> The sone heng, the moder stod
> And beheld hire childes blod
> Huy [how] it of hise woundes ran

Here Mary seems to stand without weeping, showing the fortitude noted by St Ambrose ("stantem illam lego, flentem non lego," "I read that she stood, but I do not read that she wept"), not needing the support of bystanders, as the artists show, and certainly not the emotional prostration of Mary Magdalene, who has been likened to a "maenad beneath the cross."

However, the urge to represent the human emotions of the crucified Christ found an outlet in other lyric forms (the earlier prophecy of Simeon in Luke 2:35, that a sword would pierce her soul, also was taken to refer to her sorrow at the scene, and contrasted with the painless childbirth of Christ). In the words of the famous Franciscan poem *Stabat mater dolorosa* she stood sorrowing at the foot of the cross, as vividly imagined in some meditations. The scene inspired a fine dialogue between mother and son, which was set to music:

> "Stond wel, moder, under rode,
> Bihold thi child with glade mode [heart],
> Blithe [happy] moder might thou be."
> "Sone, how may I blithe stonden?
> I se thin feet, I se thin honden [hands],
> Nayled to the harde tre."

As it continues, Mary laments her son's torments, and allude to her own – "Sone, I fele the dethe-stunde [hour of death], / The swerd [sword] is at min herte-grunde [depths of my heart], / That me byhyghte [promised] Symeon." Christ says that his death is to release Adam and save all mankind; she says she will suffer with him: "Sone, I wylle with thee funden [go], / I deye [die] ywis [truly] of thine wunden [wounds], / So rueful [piteous] ded [death] was nevere non." Even more emotional scope was offered by the form known as the lament of Mary or *planctus Mariae*. These are formal laments, imagined to have been uttered by her at the foot of the cross or to the dead body of her son lying in her lap (the *pietà* of medieval art). These may be very simple, as a direct appeal to the tormentors ("Why have ye no reuthe [pity] on my child? / Have reuthe on me ful of mourning! / Taketh doun on rode my dar-worthi [precious] child, / Or prek [hail] me on rode with my derling!"), much more elaborate, in a visionary setting ("Sodenly afraide, half waking, half slepyng, / And gretly dismayed – a woman sat weeping. And of hir sore weeping this was the enchesone [reason], Hir son in hir lap lay ... slayne by treason": her refrain is "who cannot wepe, come lerne at me"), or in a reproachful lament addressed to other women ("O alle women that ever were born / That berys childur, abyde and see / How my sone liggus [lies] me beforn / Upon my skyrte, taken fro tree."). The Passion of Christ is always seen as a sacrifice of love, which demands in the worshipper a recipro-cal act of love, leading in mystics like Richard Rolle of Hampole to an intense "love-longing," often crystalized in verse from the Song of Songs (2:5, 5:8), *quia amore langueo* (because I languish with love). Intense love-longing is also found in some lyrical meditations on the Passion: in one, "Jesu that hast me dere ibought [redeemed], / Write thou gostly [spiritually] in my thought," the poet asks Christ to write in his heart with nail and spear all the stages of suffering, and prays "Jesu, make me glad to be / Sympil and poor for love of thee"; as Julian of Norwich said, "love was our lord's meaning."

The poets' reading of the Bible is evident throughout the lyrics. The many poems on death make use of biblical, especially Old Testament, sources: phrases and images on the transience of life are echoed again and again in devotional poetry. The psalms (with their wide emotional range) are understandably important, and were the object of close devotional reading, but they do not seem to inspire individual lyrics. We have to wait until a later period and for the influence of Savonarola's meditations to see this flourish. There are Middle English paraphrases, but they are not distinguished. There are also some dull, workaday paraphrases of various biblical material, the Ten Commandments or lists of patriarchs, for instance.

If lyrical engagements with the psalms are limited, and if other biblical paraphrases are rather uninspired, nevertheless rather surprisingly the book of Ecclesiastes produced an original, powerful, and rather gloomy reflection on mortality with the refrain "this worlde fareth as a fantasy [illusion]." It opens in a questioning way: "I wolde witen [know] of sum wise wiht [person] / What this world were." Echoing the Preacher he remarks

> The sunnes cours, we may wel kenne [perceive],
> Ariseth est [east] and goth doun west;
> The ryvers into the see thei runne [run],
> And it is never the more [greater] almest [hardly].
> Wyndes rosscheth [rush] here and henne [hence],
> In snouw and reyn is non arest [ceasing];
> Whon [when] this wol stint [stop] who wot [knows], and whenne [for what cause],
> But only God on grounde grest [greatest]?

The earth remains, but each man glides forth like a guest. Generations come and go, "summe are foryete [forgotten] clene as bone," and so shall we be. Man melts away as a moth does. Who knows except the creator of all where man goes when he must die? As in the biblical book, the nature and fate of man is like that of beasts:

> Dieth mon, and beestes dye,
> And al is on [one] occasion [occurrence]
> And al o [one] deth bos [must] bothe drie [suffer],
> And ham on incarnacion ...
> Who wot yif monnes soule styye [rises],
> And beestes soules synketh doun?
> Who knoweth beestes entencioun,
> On heore [their] creatour how thei crie.
> Save only God, that knoweth heore soun [utterance]?
> For this world fareth as a fantasye

This combination of scepticism, pessimism, and a fideistic trust in God is characteristic of the poem as a whole. It even questions the usefulness of discussion, argument, and disputation. Man's intellect is no more of avail than his strength:

> Thus men stumble and sere [blight] heore witte,
> And meveth [raise] maters mony and fele [numerous]
> Summe leeveth [believe] on hym, summe leveth on hit,
> As children leorneth [learn] forto spele [speak]
> But non [no one] seoth [sees] non [anyone] that abit [survives]
> Whon stilly [silently] deth wol on hym stele.

Why do we wish to know "the poyntes [details] of Godes priveté [secret purpose]"? "An idel bost is forto blowe [brag] / A maister of divinité." After all our reasonings and disputations are dismissed ("the more we trace the Trinité / the more we falle in fantasye"), there is a brief moment of resigned cheerfulness ("make we murie and sle [slay] care, / And worschupe we God whil we ben here") before a final prayer that "the prince that hath to pere / Tak us hol [entirely] to his merci / And kepe our conscience lere").

This remarkable poem is exceptional. Rather than being direct paraphrases of biblical passages, the lyrics are often inspired by single biblical verses used in the liturgy – like that from Lamentations mentioned above, which was used in Good Friday services (where it was already applied to Christ).

By now something of the nature of the medieval religious lyrics will have become evident. In general they do not seem to be markedly "personal," in the sense of recording an individual religious experience of "struggling" with God or with doubt: they seem instead to be "practical," destined for the use of other Christians – to be read aloud, to be used for prayer or for meditation (the lyric mentioned above in which the poet asks Christ to write in his heart is in one MS accompanied by a rubric that seems to imply its use by an individual in a church – "saying of this orison pause and wait at every cross and think on what you have said; for a more devout prayer I never found of the Passion for whoever would say it devoutly"). They are sometimes (but not usually) accompanied by music, for singing; in the later part of the period they are sometimes accompanied by devotional images for the eye of the reader. It would obviously be rash to attempt to exclude a personal experience on the part of the poet, but if it is there it is concealed beneath a more "anonymous" appearance – even the few known authors who compose them seem to adopt this mode of writing. The style is usually simple, but sometimes vivid and colloquial (in this it is akin to that of the preachers, and may well have been influenced by that); it is rare (and usually in the later period) that we find writers striving to "literary" eloquence and adornment.

Finally, two lyrics may serve to illustrate how the lyric writers make use of the different ways of reading the Bible. "What is he, this lordling, that cometh from the fight?" by the Franciscan William Herebert is a paraphrase of a passage in Isaiah 63 (*Quis est iste qui venit de Edom, tinctis vestibus de Bosra?*), which was used for one of the readings for Wednesday in Holy Week. The Old Testament Messiah coming from battle in Edom is already a "figure" of Christ the conqueror of death (and Herebert has removed the unfamiliar place-names of Edom and Bosra). The imagery becomes ambiguous, and sometimes ironic. The "dyed garments" are both the triumphal robes of the conqueror stained with the blood of his enemies and the blood-stained garment of the suffering Christ. "I have trodden the wine-press alone" says the Old Testament Messiah, using an image for a crushing slaughter: this has become a common medieval image suggesting that Christ trod the winepress in which he was trodden and conquered the Passion that he suffered (it was sometimes given a literal representation in art, with the body of Christ being pressed in the winepress, and his blood flowing out): the idea is still found in the seventeenth century, where it is used by the later and greater Herbert ("much more him I must adore, / Who of the Law's sour juice sweet wine did make, / E'en God himself, being pressed for my sake"). Christ is both champion and sufferer (in his "answer" to the opening question he says "Ich [I] hyt [it = he] am that ne speke bute right / Chaunpyon to Helen [heal] mon kunde [mankind] in fight" (a rather bold paradoxical interpretation of *propugnator … ad salvandum*, "a defender to save"). Isaiah's words, "I looked about, and there was none to help; I sought and there was none to give aid," suggest to him a more "affective" moment – "Ich loked al aboute some helping mon [man]; Ich souhte al the route [crowd], bote [but] help nas [was not] ther non." It is an unusual lyric, not only because it is a paraphrase, but because Christ here has (momentarily at least) a more terrible and forbidding aspect than a suffering and pathetic one. A later lyric that uses the phrase *Quia amore langueo* as a refrain (and is throughout suffused by the imagery of The Song of Songs) has a imaginative visionary opening:

> In the vaile of restles mynd
>   I sowght in mowntayn and in mede [meadow],
> Trustyng a treulofe [true love] forr to fynd.
>   Upon an hyll than toke I hede,
> A voise I herd (and nere [nearer] I yede [went])
>   In gret dolour [grief] complaynyng tho [then],
> "See, dere soule, my sides blede,
>   Quia amore langueo."

On the mount is a tree, and beneath it a man sitting, wounded from head to foot, "a semely man to be a kyng." As the poem continues, it becomes clear that this sitting figure is the wounded "Christ in distress" of medieval art sitting beneath the cross). He is "treulofe" and his wounds are because he languished for love. He loves his sister, man's soul, and left his kingdom to seek her (this is an imaginative allusion to the medieval story of "Christ the lover-knight"). In the manner of the "Reproaches" he laments her treatment of him ("I saved hyr from betyng and she hath me bett; / I clothed hyr in grace and hevenly light, / This blody surcote she hath on me sett"). His red gloves will never come off: "thes handes full friendly for hyr fowght." His feet are "buckled" with hard nails. In his side he has made her nest: "Loke in me, how wyde wounde is here! / This is hyr chamber, here shall she rest, / That she and I may slepe in fere." Boldly the poet combines the language of medieval secular love poems with that of the Song of Songs: "My swete spouse, will we goo play? / Apples ben rype in my gardine." The poet piles up ecstatic images: Christ is man's lover, husband, brother, and even mother. He seems to have assimilated not only the images of the Song of Songs but also something of its poetic technique.

Note

1   See Rosemary Woolf, *The English Religious Lyric in the Middle Ages* (Clarendon Press, Oxford, 1968) and subsequent studies, including the excellent essay by Christiania Whitehead in Thomas G. Duncan's *A Companion to the Middle English Lyric* (D. S. Brewer, Cambridge, 2005), a volume that contains a full bibliography.

CHAPTER 7
The Middle English Mystics

Annie Sutherland

In the late fourteenth-century English mystical treatise *The Cloud of Unknowing*, we read:

> Godes worde, ouþer wretyn or spokyn, is licnid to a mirour. Goostly, þe iȝe of þi soule is þi reson; þi conscience is þi visage goostly. & riȝt as þou seest þat ȝif a foule spot be in þi bodily visage, þe iȝe of þe same visage may not see þat spotte, ne wite wher it is, wiþoutyn a myrour or a teching of anoþer þan itself; riȝt so it is goostly. Wiþouten redyng or heryng of Godes worde, it is inpossible to mans vnderstondyng þat a soule þat is bleendid in custom of synne schuld see þe foule spot in his concyence.[1]

This statement is noteworthy for two reasons. First, it emphasizes the centrality of the Word of God to the living of an authentic Christian life. Second, rather than deferring specifically to the Bible as authoritative, it refers twice to the rather more amorphous "Godes worde." Both of these points raise questions integral to an understanding of the role of the Bible in the Middle Ages. First, given its centrality to the Christian faith, how might one expect to gain access to the Bible? And second, what exactly was meant by the term "Bible" and by the phrase "Godes worde"? Although this chapter cannot hope to offer full answers to either of these questions, it does aim to provide some insight into them and into the nature and role of the Bible in the Middle Ages by means of analyzing its deployment in the English mystical literature of the period.

The category of "Middle English Mystics" has long been taken to include Richard Rolle (d. 1349), Walter Hilton (d. 1396), Julian of Norwich (b. 1342) and the anonymous author of the late fourteenth-century *Cloud of Unknowing*.[2] To this group, the East Anglian laywoman Margery Kempe (b. *c.*1373) has often been added.[3] Although united by their interest in matters of the spirit, the writings associated with these five figures are in fact somewhat disparate; while direct links between them cannot be proved, it is arguably more revealing to view them as reactions to each other than it is to view them as uncomplicated relations of each other.[4] The Yorkshire mystic Richard Rolle is the earliest and one of the more idiosyncratic of the group. Never recognized officially by any religious order, he lived as a self-styled, self-regulating hermit.[5] Both biblical commentator and devotional advisor, in his early literary career he produced several Latin treatises before turning to the vernacular as a language of spiritual guidance.[6] Frequently addressed directly to religious women, manuscript evidence tells us that Rolle's English writings in fact reached a wide and diverse audience.[7] His resolutely cataphatic, affirmative mysticism is echoed by Walter Hilton, whose devotional works, not infrequently circulating alongside those of Rolle, reached a similarly diverse audience.[8] An Augustinian canon with a legal background, Hilton is nonetheless a more austere figure, his devotional guidance marked by its mistrust of the sensory mysticism apparently popularized by Rolle.[9] The excesses associated with Rollean devotion are also confronted and dismissed by Hilton's contemporary, the anonymous author of *The Cloud of Unknowing* and associated works.[10] The *Cloud* author stands apart from his English contemporaries in avowing a decidedly apophatic mysticism and in explicitly attempting to limit the circulation of *The Cloud* at least to the devotionally competent; unlike Rolle and Hilton, the *Cloud* author never intended his material for the spiritual novice and his work does not survive in quite the same numbers.[11]

However, despite their obvious differences, the treatises of Rolle, Hilton, and the *Cloud* author are linked generically by their assured instructional emphasis; each of them is clearly writing for an attentive audience. The audience intended for – and, indeed, reached by – the *Revelations* of Julian of Norwich is less easily defined. Extant in two distinct versions and in only four relatively late manuscripts, Julian's *Revelations* detail her own Passion-based visionary experience, but provide us with little information regarding their author or audience (she talks only generally of her "evenchristen").[12] The generic uncertainty that characterizes Julian's prose is due in part to her gender (how could a woman presume to instruct?) and is also evidenced in the *Book* of Margery Kempe, which survives in only one manuscript and appears similarly unsure of its intended audience.[13] Indeed, Margery's *Book* is the most anomalous of the treatises investigated in this chapter; neither a manual of devotional guidance nor, specifically, a reflection on visionary experience, it is an often anxiously self-justifying autobiographical account of a life lived in the world.[14] However, what links Margery's *Book* with the writings of the other "Middle English Mystics" is its emphasis on hearing and responding to the word of God.

Yet – to return to a question raised at the outset of this chapter – what did the mystics understand "Godes worde" to be and how did they respond to it? Of all the treatises examined in this chapter, only Margery's *Book* explicitly mentions the "Bible" as material entity.[15] The *Cloud*, as highlighted above, refers to "Godes worde, ouþer wretyn or spokyn," Julian's *Revelations* also speak of the grounding of our faith in "Goddes worde" and Rolle's *Form of Living* refers to "holy writynge, þat is Goddis word."[16] Specific reference to the Bible is by no means rare in Middle English literature (it is found, for example, in the writings of Chaucer, Langland, and Gower) so that it finds no place in the mystical material mentioned above is noteworthy. Its absence suggests an understanding of divine revelation as something more fluid and less fixed than that which we find on the written page. "Godes worde," while obviously encompassing the Bible, also includes inspired patristic commentary in addition to individual mystical insight into God's nature as revealed through the Scriptures. It is interesting that even Walter Hilton (unusual among the authors examined in this chapter in his sustained and explicit reference to "holy scripture") refers to the Bible as spoken word more often than as written authority, the former arguably more immediate and malleable than the latter.[17]

Indeed, the identity of the Bible was the subject of much debate between Wycliffite reformers and ecclesiastical authorities in the late Middle Ages. Was its potency found on the written page or did it inhere in the rather more elusive intention of God? Wycliffite theory, at least, located divine authority in the "sententia sacra" (sacred meaning) rather than in "nudum scriptum materiale" (bare written material), but it was the "bare written material" of the Bible that was most contested at this time.[18] At the heart of this contention was the language in which the Scriptures ought to be preserved and read. Should the Vulgate Bible remain the property of the Latinate or was it appropriate for it to be translated into the vernacular and rendered accessible to a wider and more diverse audience? The Wycliffite translation project is the most obvious of late medieval attempts to broaden the Bible's circulation and audience, yet the vernacular Scriptures – or at least excerpts of the vernacular Scriptures – reached a diverse audience by many other means in the Middle Ages. Not least among these is the English mystical literature explored in this chapter. It is no exaggeration to claim that the Bible lies at the very center of such literature; scriptural quotation and allusion provide the bare bones around which the devotional narrative constructs itself. It is to these devotional narratives that attention now turns.

Each treatise examined in this chapter relies on the Bible as a source of wisdom, yet each does so very differently. Richard Rolle's English epistles, for example, veer between quotation from the Latin text of the Vulgate and Rolle's own vernacular translations of biblical verses in bolstering the authority of his devotional prose. Walter Hilton's *Scale of Perfection*, in contrast, is punctuated with Vulgate quotation followed by vernacular (pre-eminently Augustinian) exegesis, while the roughly contemporary *Cloud of Unknowing* contains many vernacular allusions to the Bible but absolutely no Latin scriptural quotation.[19] Julian of Norwich's *Revelations* differ even further; characterized by their "scripturally inflected" prose, they nonetheless contain almost no direct quotation from the Bible.[20] Lastly, while the *Book* of Margery Kempe alludes to the Scriptures as authoritative, and contains some Vulgate and vernacular quotation, it cannot be said to establish a biblical "voice" or "character" in quite the same manner as the other texts explored in this chapter.

These stylistically diverse biblical voices may be attributable in part to varying individual responses to the theological climate of the late fourteenth century. Rolle, writing in the first half of the century, prior to the development of the Wycliffite heresy and attendant anxieties over the translation of the Bible, could afford to be relatively relaxed in his deployment of scriptural quotation.[21] However, it may well be that somewhat later Hilton's predominantly Latinate biblical voice is part and parcel of his orthodox response to a Wycliffite threat associated with demands for the increased availability of the vernacular Scriptures. It could also be argued that Julian's "imbedding" of biblical material in her own devotional prose is a product of her concern that she, as a woman in the contemporary climate, ought not exhibit too close a familiarity with the intricacies of the Scriptures.[22]

However, such stylistic variety should not be interpreted as motivated simply by different responses to a highly charged contemporary debate. Instead, we need to recognize that these diverse biblical voices are the result of very different personal experiences of "Goddes worde." For Walter Hilton, apparently educated at Cambridge, trained in canon law and, latterly, Augustinian canon at Thurgarton Priory, we can assume that the Vulgate Bible (accompanied by extensive glosses) would have been accessible.[23] His confident scriptural familiarity is thus likely to result from personal engagement with the Bible, mediated by the authority of patristic exegesis.[24] The same can be said of Hilton's contemporary, the anonymous *Cloud* author, and of his predecessor, Rolle. Direct access to the Vulgate Scriptures and to the traditions of patristic exegesis is, however, very unlikely to account for the biblical familiarity exhibited in either the *Revelations* of Julian of Norwich or the *Book of Margery Kempe*. While Julian probably possessed a degree of liturgically inspired Latin, it is doubtful that either education or opportunity would have provided her with access to a complete Vulgate.[25] Instead, we must assume that her undeniable scriptural knowledge and understanding was a result of reading or hearing devotional material, of liturgical familiarity and, of personal communication with ecclesiastical figures. Indeed, hinting at the aurality of her learning environment, in the shorter (earlier) version of her *Revelations*, she tells us that she:

> *harde a man telle of halye kyrke of the storye of Sainte Cecille*, in the whilke shewinge I understode that she hadde thre woundes with a swerde in the nekke, with the whilke she pinede to the dede. (Short Text, section 1, 65/36–8, italics added)

She writes that this prompted in her a "mighty desire" for her own "thre woundes" from God (section 1, 65/39–40). Providing us with a more explicit variation on Julian's remark, Margery Kempe also informs us that it was through "comownyng in scriptur whech sche lernyd in sermonys" (chapter 14, 97/941–8/942) and through "heryng of holy bokys" that she "evyr encresyd in contemplacyon and holy meditacyon" (Chapter 59, 280/4832–281/4834).[26] Furthermore, she tells us that a priest acted as her "reader" for "the most part of vii yer er viii yer" and that among their shared texts were:

> many a good boke of hy contemplacyon and other bokys, as the Bybyl wyth doctowrys thereupon, Seynt Brydys boke, Hyltons boke, Bonaventur, *Stimulus Amoris*, *Incendium Amoris*, and swech other.[27] (Chapter 58, 280/4818–21)

That Margery should refer to "Hyltons boke" (most probably his *Scale of Perfection*) and to Richard Rolle's *Incendium Amoris* in addition to "the Bybyl wyth doctowrys thereupon" (presumably a Latin glossed version that the priest would have translated orally for her) is noteworthy in the context of this chapter, emphasizing the major role that such treatises of devotional guidance must have played in communicating biblical material to their audiences.

We ought not, however, assume a simple divide between men as active communicators of "Goddes worde" and women as passive recipients, nor should we suppose that it is only in male-authored devotional writing that we encounter penetrating, scripturally inspired thought.[28] Instead, we need to recognize that, despite the stylistic variety of their scriptural voices and despite their different experiences of the Bible, all the authors explored in this chapter rely on "Goddes worde" as *auctoritas*. With this in mind, it is now time to focus on specific manifestations of "Goddes worde" in the mystical literature under discussion. This analysis will begin with a brief survey of the scriptural books most often referenced before proceeding to an exploration of the different roles that the Bible plays in this category of literature.

For all the stylistic variety of biblical quotation and citation in the writings explored in this chapter, it is noteworthy that much Middle English mystical literature is bolstered by its reliance on a shared stock of well worn Biblical authorities.[29] It is the voice of the Psalmist that resounds most insistently in devotional narratives of the period, a dominance that is unsurprising given the Psalter's liturgical prominence in Church and Cloister.[30] In particular, devotional audiences are encouraged repeatedly to imitate the example of David in their own intercessory lives; to borrow the *Cloud* author's metaphor, they are to see in the "myrour" of the repentant David a reflection of themselves as they could be. Hilton, for example, illustrates the efficacy of spoken prayer by appeal to the words of the Psalmist (Psalms 58:2 and 40:5) as model; when "a man or a woman" cries out to God for "succor and help," he is:

> like a man in peril among his enemies, or like someone in sickness showing his sores to God as a doctor, and saying thus: *Eripe me de inimicis meis Deius meus* (Ah, Lord, deliver me from my enemies); or else thus: *Sana, Domine, animam meam, quia peccavi tibi* (Ah, Lord, heal my soul, for I have sinned against you). (*Scale I*, chapter 29, p. 100)

And warning his audience against over-enthusiastic ascetic practice, Rolle also presents us with the example of David: "For þe prophet seith, Lord, I shal kepe my streynth to þe" (*Form of Living* 4/66; Psalm 58:10).

But David's is not the only scriptural voice to resound in medieval mystical writing; St Paul also makes his presence felt. Perhaps surprisingly, given his misogynistic reputation (he is invoked in opposition to Margery speaking in Church (chapter 52, 253/4210–11)), he appears to have been particularly influential in the thought of both Margery and Julian. He is presented as communicating directly with Margery (chapter 17, 115/1263 and chapter 87, 378/7246) and his is one of the few biblical voices cited explicitly in her *Book*:

> So ther was neithyr worschep ne preysyng, lofe ne lakkyng, schame ne despite that myth drawyn hir lofe fro God, but, aftyr the sentens of Seynt Powle, "To hem that lovyn God al thyng turnyth into goodnes," so it ferd wyth hir. (Chapter 72, 322/5828–31)[31]

The *Book* also portrays Julian of Norwich as influenced by Paul; in recalling her encounter with the anchoress, Margery presents Julian's voice as indebted explicitly to Romans 8:26:

> Seynt Powyl seyth that the Holy Gost askyth for us wyth mornynggys and wepyngys unspekable; that is to seyn, he makyth us to askyn and and preyn wyth mornynggys and wepyngys so plentyvowsly that the terys may not be nowmeryd. (Chapter 18, 121/1363–122/1367)

In characterizing Julian's voice thus, the *Book* may be far from inaccurate. For although this specific Pauline quotation does not appear in the *Revelations*, Julian does refer explicitly to St Paul on two occasions. The first of these recalls Romans 8:38–9 ("For I am sure that ... [nothing] ... shall be able to separate us from the love of God which is in Christ Jesus our Lord"):

> And in the time of joye I myght hafe sayde with Paule: "Nathinge shalle departe me fro the charite of Criste." (Short Text, section 9, 81/30–1; Long Text, chapter 15, 177/13–15)

The second alludes to Philippians 2:5 ("For let this mind be in you, which was also in Christ Jesus"):

> Swilke paines I sawe that alle es to litelle that I can telle or saye, for it maye nought be tolde. Botte ilke saule, aftere the sayinge of Sainte Paule, shulde "feele in him that in Criste Jhesu." (Short Text, section 10, 83/21–3)[32]

And these invocations of St Paul are all the more striking when one considers that he is the only biblical *auctor* of whom Julian's *Revelations* ever make explicit mention.[33]

Although such repeated Pauline borrowings are notable, the biblical voices explored in this chapter also exhibit marked resemblances in other areas. For example, resonant in each of these authors (with the exception of Julian, whose mysticism is particularly uneroticized) is a turn of phrase influenced by the Song of Songs. The specific text recalled most frequently in this context is Song of Songs 5:2 ("I sleep and my heart watcheth ..."). For centuries, the Western mystical tradition had understood these words as referring to the dormancy of the discursive consciousness in contemplation of the divine splendour of God. And it is within this interpretative framework that Rolle, Hilton, and the *Cloud* author deploy the text. It is, in fact, one of only two texts that Rolle quotes in its Vulgate form in his English epistles (*Ego Dormio*, 26/1–3). And although Hilton is in general suspicious of the sensory excesses that he associates with the interpretation of Song of Songs, he too quotes the Vulgate version of this text. Further, he can, like Rolle, be heard to echo it in the vernacular:

> The more I sleep from outward things, the more wakeful I am in the knowledge of Jesus and of inward things. ... The more that the eyes are shut in this kind of sleep from the appetite of earthly things, the keener is the inner sight in the lovely beholding of heavenly beauty. (*Scale II*, chapter 40, pp. 284–5)

The Cloud of Unknowing, by contrast, does not quote from Song of Songs directly in either Latin or English. Yet the anonymous author does exhibit familiarity with its conventional exegetical framework, and seems to expect his readers to grasp the same.[34]

Also apparent in several of the works relevant to this chapter are echoes of Song of Songs 4:9 ("Thou hast wounded my heart, my sister, my spouse: thou hast wounded my heart with one of thy eyes, and with one hair of thy neck"). Indeed, the metaphorical association of love and pain reverberates throughout the *Cloud of Unknowing*, where the addressee is encouraged repeatedly to "smyte apon þat þicke cloude of vnknowyng wiþ a scharp darte of longing loue."[35] The notion of anguished "love-longing" that permeates so much of the writing under discussion also owes itself at least in part to the terminology of Song of Songs 2:5 ("I languish with love.") Along with Song of Songs 5:2, this is one of only two biblical verses from the Vulgate text of which Rolle quotes directly in his English epistles (*The Form of Living*, 15/489–94). And at opposite ends of the mystical spectrum, while the *Cloud* author is not averse to recalling the sentiment of this biblical love-longing, we also hear Christ instructing Margery Kempe to "languren in lofe" (chapter 7, p. 79).[36]

That Christ is presented as directing Margery by means of recourse to biblically inspired language highlights the instructional role that the Scriptures play in much mystical literature, and it is to an examination of this particular role that attention now turns. Indeed, it is as devotional guide that the Scriptures function most essentially in much Middle English mystical writing, for not only do the mystics present themselves as guided by biblical authority, but they also offer their audiences guidance by means of the same. The nature of this guidance varies dramatically from author to author and text to text. For example, *The Cloud of Unknowing*, as already stated, contains no quotation from the Vulgate Scriptures, choosing instead to emphasize the exemplary behavior of biblical *figurae* in encouraging its addressee towards spiritual excellence.[37] Such reliance on the exemplary role of biblical *figurae* is, of course, found in other mystical literature, including Hilton's *Scale of Perfection*, but it is in this latter text that we find most apparent a conventional emphasis on the Vulgate Scriptures as authoritative guide *par excellence*. Throughout both books of this treatise it is emphasized that the learned do not have a monopoly on the "grace" of biblical understanding. Instead, "This grace may be – and is – in the unlettered as well as in the learned as regards the substance and the veritable feeling of truth, and the spiritual savor in general" (*Scale II*, chapter 43, p. 295). Yet despite his emphasis on the fact that "by a little pouring of [Christ's] wisdom into a pure soul [Christ] makes the soul wise enough to understand all holy scripture" (p. 293), the resolutely orthodox Hilton is not comfortable in allowing his audience direct access to the Scriptures. Instead, he is almost entirely consistent in offering a vernacular interpretation of any Vulgate text that he quotes, ensuring that his non-Latinate audience have access to biblical guidance only when it is supplemented by his orthodox, allegorical glossing. So, for example, in *Scale I*, he quotes from Matthew 13:44: "Simile est regnum caelorum thesaurum abscondito in agro; quem qui invenit homo prae gaudio illius vadit et vendit universa quae habet et emit agrum illum." He goes on to provide a straightforward translation: "The kingdom of heaven is like treasure hidden in a field. When a man finds it, for joy he goes and sells all that he has and buys that same field." But he then proceeds immediately to explain how this parable should be understood, and what a spiritually sensitive response to it might entail: "Jesus is treasure hidden in your soul; then if you could find him in your soul and your soul in him, I am sure you would for joy of it want to give up all your pleasure in all earthly things in order to have it" (Chapter 49, p. 122).

Of course, such interpretative glossing serves not only as a clarification of moral instruction for one's audience. It is also a device that an author can use to foreground his or her own spiritual intelligence and, importantly, his or her own orthodoxy. This latter concern certainly plays a part in Hilton's exegetical practice in the *Scale*, but it is seen at its most obvious in Margery Kempe's *Book* where, in addition to being instructed by means of Biblical wisdom, Margery also proves herself an astute scriptural exegete. Faced repeatedly with a suspicious audience, Margery is depicted on more than one occasion as having to "prove" her orthodoxy, and in narrating one notable incident, the *Book* tells us that "Another tyme ther cam a gret clerke onto hir, askyng thes wordys how thei schuld ben undirstondyn, *Crescite et multiplicami*." Presenting her with the words of Genesis 1:22, the "gret clerke" is apparently attempting to trap Margery into interpreting the phrase in a heretically literal manner.[38] She surprises the cleric, however, with her grasp of its allegorical meaning:

> Sche, answeryng, seyd: "Ser, thes wordys ben not undirstondyn only of begetyng of chyl-
> dren bodily, but also be purchasing of vertu, whech is frute gostly, as be heryng of the
> wordys of God, be good exampyl yevyng, be mekenes and paciens, charite and chastite,
> and swech other, for pacyens is more worthy than myraclys werkyng."

And this is an interpretation with which we are told that the cleric is "wel plesyd" (chapter 51, 243/4010–19).[39] Whether we read this foregrounding of "correct" scriptural interpretation as a deliberate tactic on the part of the clerical scribe, anxious to protect Margery against further accusations of heterodoxy, or as Margery's own shrewd assertion of her spiritual credentials, the important point is that biblical understanding is here seen to function as a gauge of orthodoxy.

In deploying the Bible as a gauge of orthodoxy, one might also say that the Middle English mystics use it as a means of identifying and positioning themselves in relation to their audience. Indeed, in addition to functioning as authoritative devotional guidance, this is one of the principle ways in which the Bible operates in Middle English devotional writing. Of all the authors explored in this chapter, it is Richard Rolle (blessed with a keen sense of the dramatic) who boasts the most fully developed biblical persona.[40] Yet in a rather more allusive manner, Julian of Norwich can also be said to model herself on scriptural *exempla*, most notably that of Christ himself. Indeed, her initial prayer, that she "might have the more true mind in the passion of Christ," is articulated in terms that recall clearly Christ's words prior to his Crucifixion:

> Therfor I said: "Lord, thou wotest what I would. If it be thy wille that I have it, grant it me.
> And if it be not thy will, good lord, be not displesed, for I will not but as thou wilt." (Long
> Text, chapter 2, 129/30–1. See Matthew 26:39 etc.)

Her insistence that her suffering lasted for "three days and three nightes" (Long Text, chapter 3, 129/2) could be read as reinforcing a link between her pain and that of Christ.

Perhaps surprisingly, the sober and measured Walter Hilton also relies on biblical authority as a means of characterizing himself as author. This is witnessed at its most effective toward the end of *Scale II* when, attempting to describe the opening of the "spiritual eye to gaze upon Jesus by the inspiration of special grace," Hilton admits:

The greatest scholar on earth cannot with all his wit imagine what this opening of the spiritual eye is, or fully declare it with his tongue, for it cannot be acquired by study or through human toil alone, but principally by the grace of the Holy Spirit, together with the work of man.

He continues: "I am afraid to speak of it at all, for I feel myself to be ignorant; it goes beyond my experience, and my lips are unclean" (chapter 40, p. 280). An ostensible protestation of linguistic ineptitude, this is in fact an accomplished example of Hilton's adaptation of scripturally allusive language to his own prose. For a biblical scholar of learning such as he would surely not be unaware that with the disclaimer "my lips are unclean," he is implicitly allying himself with the prophet Isaiah:

> And I said: Woe is me, because I have held my peace; because I am a man of unclean lips, and I dwell in the midst of a people that hath unclean lips, and I have seen with my eyes the King the Lord of hosts. (Isaiah 6:5)

In thus appropriating biblically inspired language to their own voices, Hilton and other mystics suggest a mutually informing relationship between themselves and the Scriptures. Not only is the Bible useful to them (and their audience) in providing authoritative wisdom, but they in turn are also "useful" to the Bible in acting as incarnate examples of its precepts in action.

Earlier in this chapter I stated that the Bible lies at the very center of Middle English mystical writing – and indeed it does. But there is also a sense in which mystical authors can be said to position themselves at the very center of the Bible. In many cases, as explored above, this is achieved through their adoption of scripturally inspired personae. But in others it is achieved through the rather more dramatic positioning of themselves at the heart of biblically inspired narrative. Drawing on the traditions of pseudo-Bonaventuran meditation, much Middle English devotional writing encourages one to further one's spiritual development by imagining oneself present at various episodes during the life of Christ.[41] The most notable of these episodes is, of course, the crucifixion, central to the mystical experience of Julian of Norwich and key in the devotional enterprises of Rolle and Hilton.[42] The crucifixion also plays a vivid role in Margery Kempe's spiritual life, but it is her meditative involvement in the circumstances surrounding Christ's nativity that provides us with the most vivid example of mystical "inhabitation" of biblical narrative. In chapter six of her *Book*, unsure of an appropriate subject for spiritual reflection, Margery is advised by Christ to "thynke on my modyr" (75/545–6). She does so, and her vivid meditation witnesses her engaged enthusiastically in the practicalities of childbirth and care:

> And than went the creatur [i.e. Margery] forth wyth owyr Lady to Bedlem and purchasyd hir herborwe every nyght with gret reverens, and owyr Lady was receyved with glad cher. Also sche beggyd owyr Lady fayr white clothys and kerchys for to swathyn in hir sone whan he wer born; and whan Jhesu was born, sche ordeyned beddyng for owyr Lady to lyg in wyth hir blyssed sone. And sythen sche beggyd mete for owyr Lady and hir blyssyd chyld. (77/578–84)

In thus inserting herself into scripturally based narrative, Margery Kempe bears striking witness to the fact (witnessed more quietly by the other authors explored in this
chapter) that late medieval mystical engagement with the Bible was profoundly varied
and remarkably imaginative. As penetrating readers – and enactors – of "Goddes
worde," Margery and others remind us that they, the recipients of scriptural wisdom,
are as central to the effectiveness of the Bible as the Bible is central to the effectiveness
of their mystical enterprise.

To conclude this chapter by returning to the quotation with which it began, in
Middle English mystical literature, the Bible reveals itself to be a "myrour" and for all
the mystics, and it is a mirror in which they see themselves reflected. In the case of
Margery Kempe, this mirror reflects back to her biblical scenes into which she has
inserted herself as a key player, and for Julian, it is a mirror that allows her to perceive
and articulate herself and her experiences in a distinctively scriptural mold. The Bible
functions in a very similar way for Richard Rolle, although for him it is also a mirror
that he holds up to us as his audience, asking us to judge ourselves against the standard
of perfection that we perceive therein. This notion of a corrective mirror is also key to
the scriptural hermeneutic of *The Cloud of Unknowing*, in its focus on the exemplary role
of biblical *figurae*. For Walter Hilton, however, the mirror of the Bible is often presented
as opaque to anyone who attempts to perceive a reflection therein without the clarify-
ing guidance of a spiritually intelligent individual.

Of course, a mirror is of no use unless one looks into it; in order for it to perform its
function, it is necessary for us to interact with it. And this is essentially how "Godes
worde" operates in the writings of the mystics; it stands at the center of each narrative,
absolutely stable and authoritative, yet at the same time it reflects and embodies motion,
requiring our active engagement. Indeed, throughout the corpus of Middle English
mystical literature, the Bible reveals itself as a text that asks to be *lived* as much as *read*;
it demands that we interact with it, that we understand ourselves by means of reference
to it, and that we articulate ourselves by means of recourse to its authoritative voice.

Notes

1   See Hodgson, *The Cloud of Unknowing* (1944 for 1943), chapter 35, 39/37–40/3. The notion
    of the Bible as "myrour" is commonplace; for a summary of its background, see Clark
    (1995/6), volume 2, p. 152.

2   For a useful and accessible introduction to the English mystical tradition, see Glasscoe
    (1993).

3   For the purposes of this chapter, attention is focused on the three English epistles of Richard
    Rolle: *The Commandment*, *The Form of Living*, and *Ego Dormio* (all reference is taken from
    Ogilvie-Thomson, 1988). Some reference is also made to Rolle's *English Psalter* (Bramley,
    1884). While it is recognized that Hilton may have been responsible for several vernacular
    writings, this chapter focuses on *The Scale of Perfection* (in the absence of a full critical edition
    of the Middle English *Scale*, throughout this chapter I quote from the translation by Clark
    and Dorward, 1991). Similarly, while it is recognized that the *Cloud* author may have com-
    posed and translated several English texts, this chapter concentrates on *The Cloud of Unknow-
    ing* (all quotation is taken from Hodgson (1944 for 1943) with some reference to *Privy*

Counselling (Hodgson, 1955 for 1949). All reference to Margery Kempe's *Book* is derived from Windeatt (2000) and all reference to Julian of Norwich's *Revelations* is taken from Watson and Jenkins (2006).

4 The one figure who does supply us with evidence of a direct link to another "Middle English Mystic" is Margery Kempe, who claims to have met Julian of Norwich (Windeatt, 2000, chapter 18, 119/1335–123/1381). The *Book* also refers explicitly to the writings of "Richard Hampol, hermyte" (chapter 62, 295/5171) and to "Hyltons boke" (chapter 58, 280/4820). In addition, the *Cloud* author does refer, on three occasions, to "anoþer mans werk," thought by many critics to be the first book of Hilton's *Scale of Perfection*.

5 For a quasi-hagiographical account of Rolle's life, see Perry (1867). For an autobiographical account of various key moments in Rolle's life, see his *Incendium Amoris* (Deanesly, 1915).

6 For Rolle's Latin material, see Arnould (1957), Deanesly (1915), and Watson (1995). For his biblical commentaries, see Bramley (1884), Boenig (1984), and Moyes (1988).

7 English writings attributed to Rolle appear in over fifty manuscripts. His *English Psalter* (uninterpolated by Lollard material) appears in a further nineteen manuscripts.

8 Like Rolle, Hilton wrote in Latin as well as English. For his Latin works, see Clark and Taylor (1987). For the English works definitely attributable to him, see Ogilvie-Thomson (1985) and Clark and Dorward (1991). Hilton's enormous popularity is testified by the fact that forty-three surviving manuscripts contain the complete English text of *The Scale of Perfection*.

9 *Of Angels' Song*, a short treatise very probably by Hilton, is most explicit in its denouncement of sensory mysticism. For an edition, see Windeatt (1994).

10 For dismissal of sensory excess, see, for example, chapter 57 of *The Cloud of Unknowing*.

11 For the author's deliberate attempt to restrict the readership of his text, see the Prologue to the *Cloud*. The *Cloud* itself survives in seventeen manuscripts.

12 Julian's *Revelations* survive in Short ("A Vision Showed to a Devout Woman") and Long ("A Revelation of Love") Versions – the latter is generally agreed to be later. For background material on Julian, see the introduction to Watson and Jenkins (2006).

13 The single manuscript of Margery's *Book* (British Library Additional MS 61823) was only discovered in 1934. Until then, Margery was known only in the context of a 1501 Wynkyn de Worde pamphlet (followed by a 1521 Pepwell print). Entitled " ... a shorte treatyse of contemplacyon taught by our Lorde Jhesu Cryste, or taken out of the boke of Margerie Kempe of Lynn," this short compendium of twenty-eight extracts from the *Book* "normalizes" Margery, removing much of the original's distinctive character.

14 Margery states that her *Book* was dictated to a series of scribes. For interrogation of this claim, see Johnson (1991).

15 See Chapter 58, 280/4819. This reference is discussed in more detail later in the chapter.

16 Although the *Cloud* does not mention the Bible specifically, it does refer to the New Testament gospels, and to "Scripture" (chapter 16) and "Holy Writte" (chapter 55). For Julian, see *Long Text* chapter 32, 223/31–2. For Rolle, see Ogilvie-Thomson (1988, 24/862).

17 To offer just one example of many, introducing a quotation from Ephesians 3:17–18, Hilton writes "This is what St. Paul *says*" (*Scale I*, chapter 12, p. 86, italics added). Although the *Scale* does not mention the Bible as an entirety, it does mention individual biblical books; for example, "the gospel" (*Scale I*, chapter 15, p. 88), "the Psalter" (*Scale I*, chapter 28, p. 100), "the Apocalypse" (*Scale II*, chapter 10, p. 206), and "The Book of the Songs of the Spouse" (*Scale II*, chapter 45, p. 298). In referencing these particular books by name, Hilton is by no means unusual among the Middle English Mystics.

18 G. V. Lechler, *Joannis Wiclif Trialogus Cum Supplemento Trialogi* (Oxford, Clarendon Press, 1869), 239/3–5. For background to the Wycliffite controversy, see Hudson (1988).

19   It is unfortunately beyond the scope of this chapter to examine the peculiarity that while the *Cloud* contains no Latin quotation from the Bible, *Privy Counselling* (a later treatise apparently by the same author and for the same audience) does. For an edition of *Privy Counselling*, see Hodgson (1955 for 1949).

20   I borrow the phrase from Windeatt (2004, p. 79). For close examination of Julian's biblical voice, see Sutherland (2004).

21   Of course, English anxieties regarding biblical translation were not unique to the late Middle Ages. On the contrary, such anxieties surfaced much earlier in Anglo-Saxon writing. See, for example, Aelfric's hesitations in the preface to his translation of Genesis (B. Mitchell and F. Robinson, *A Guide to Old English* (1964), 191/7–12).

22   For discussion of Lollard attitudes toward women see, for example, Cross, C., " 'Great Reasoners in Scripture': The Activities of Women Lollards 1380–1530," in D. Baker, ed., *Medieval Women*, Studies in Church History Subsidia 1 (Blackwell, Oxford, 1978).

23   For discussion of the likelihood that Hilton studied in Cambridge, see Clark (1992). For reference to his early career in Canon Law, see Clark and Taylor (1987).

24   For exploration of Hilton's background and sources, see Clark (1992). As Clark demonstrates, Hilton is profoundly influenced by Augustinian and Gregorian traditions. Among more recent authors, he is indebted to Bernard of Clairvaux, Anselm, Gilbert of Hoyland, and William Flete.

25   For an alternative viewpoint, see Colledge and Walsh (1978). For exploration (and dismissal) of the possibility that Julian might have had access to a vernacular Wycliffite Bible, see Colledge and Walsh (1976).

26   For further references to the aurality of Margery's learning environment, see chapter 58, 278/4778–82, and chapter 69, 314/5641–5.

27   For identification of the texts to which Margery refers, see Windeatt (2000, p. 280).

28   For example, although Hilton's *Scale* is informed by the most conventional awareness of biblical authority, in a rather different way the *Book* of Margery Kempe also foregrounds repeatedly the authoritative weight of the Scriptures. This is most apparent in Margery's retellings of "stor[ies] of scriptur" in her interactions with suspicious clerics (chapter 13, 93/869), some of whom attribute her knowledge of the "Gospel" to the fact that "she hath a devyl wythinne hir" (Chapter 52, 252/4208–9). Additionally, for appeals to the authority of the Bible in Margery's *Book*, see also the "story of Holy Writte" in chapter 40 (207/3210) and the appeal to "Holy Writte" in chapter 48 (235/3832). Margery's awareness of the authority of the Bible can also be seen in her own intercessory communications with God: "In Holy Writte, Lord, thu byddyst me lovyn myn enmys, and I wot wel that in al this werld was nevyr so gret an enmye to me as I have ben to the" (chapter 77, 335/6162–4) (See Matthew 5:44; Luke 6:27 and 35).

29   For detailed exploration of the role of the Bible in the writings of the Middle English mystics, see Sutherland (1999).

30   The Psalter is one of the relatively few biblical books actually referred to by name in Middle English mystical literature. For the Psalmist's comparative silence in the works of the *Cloud* author (and for speculation on the possible reasons for this) see Sutherland (2002).

31   See Romans 8:28.

32   For speculation on possible reasons for the deletion of this Biblical reference from Julian's *Long Text* see Sutherland (2004). All modern versions of biblical texts quoted in this chapter are taken from *The Holy Bible Translated from the Latin Vulgate* (Rheims, 1582; Douay, 1609).

33   Further Pauline resonances can be heard throughout Middle English mystical writing. Indeed, they are woven into the fabric of authorial prose to such an extent as to suggest

that by the late fourteenth century they had simply become an unconscious adjunct of the religious vernacular. Perhaps most insistent are recollections of 1 Corinthians 6:17 ("But he who is joined to the Lord is one spirit"), a cornerstone text of the Western mystical tradition, and of the well worn triad of 1 Corinthians 13:13 ("And now there remain faith, hope and charity, these three; but the greatest of these is charity"). And less common, yet conspicuous nonetheless, are echoes of the sentiment of Romans 8:17 ("And if sons, heirs also; heirs indeed of God and joint heirs with Christ").

34   See Hodgson (1944 for 1943, 110/19–22, 151/23–6, and 152/3–4).

35   For Rolle, see Ogilvie-Thomson (1988, 18/615–18 and 31/203). For the *Cloud* author see Hodgson (1955 for 1949, 72/14–19 and 72/23–5).

36   For the *Cloud*, see Hodgson (1944 for 1943, 45/18–19).

37   To take just one instance of this, impressing upon us the importance of coupling our awareness of sin with the confidence to approach God in love, the *Cloud* author offers us the scriptural example of Mary Magdalene. Telling us to do "as Mary did," he writes, "Scho, þof al scho myȝt not vnfele þe depe hertly sorrow of hir synnes ... neuerþeles ȝit it may be seide & affermyd by Scripture þat sche had a more hertly sorrow, a more doleful desire, & a more deep siȝing, & more sche languischid, ȝe! niȝhonde to þe dee p, for lacking of loue, þof al sche had ful mochel loue ... þan sche had for any mynde of hir synnes" (chapter 16, 45/12–21).

38   Windeatt (2000, p. 243) records that "among some contemporary Continental heretics, this text was used to justify free love."

39   For an alternative, very literal interpretation of Genesis 1:22, one might turn to Chaucer's Wife of Bath. Of course, literal biblical interpretation was often associated with the Wycliffite heresy.

40   For examination of Rolle's biblical character, see, for example, Alford (1973) and Sutherland (2005).

41   For background to the pseudo-Bonaventuran meditative tradition and its influence in late medieval England, see Sargent (2005).

42   Julian's revelations are founded on a vision of a bleeding crucifix. For Hilton, see, for example, Clark and Dorward (1991, *Scale I*, chapter 35, p. 106). For meditative writing attributed to Rolle, see the "Meditations on the Passion" in Ogilvie-Thomson (1988). Christ's Passion plays little part in the anonymous *Cloud of Unknowing*, though it does receive more attention in the later *Privy Counselling*.

Bibliography

Primary

Arnould, E. J. F. (1957) *The Melos Amoris of Richard Rolle, Hermit of Hampole*. Blackwell Publishing, Oxford.

Boenig, R. (1984) *Richard Rolle: Biblical Commentaries*. Salzburg Studies in English Literature. Elizabethan and Renaissance Studies 92: 13. Institut für Anglistik und Amerikanistik, Universität Salzburg, Salzburg.

Bramley, H. R. (1884) *The Psalter Translated by Richard Rolle of Hampole*. Clarendon Press, Oxford.

Clark, J. P. H. and Dorward, R. (1991) *Walter Hilton – The Scale of Perfection*. The Classics of Western Spirituality. Paulist Press, Mahwah, NJ.

Clark, J. P. H. and Taylor, C. (1987) *Walter Hilton's Latin Writings*. Analecta Cartusiana 124, 2 volumes. Institut für Anglistik und Amerikanistik, Universität Salzburg, Salzburg.

Colledge, E. and Walsh, J. (1978) *A Book of Showings to the Anchoress Julian of Norwich*. Studies and Texts 35. Pontfical Institute of Medieval Studies, Toronto.

Deanesly, M. (1915) *The Incendium Amoris of Richard Rolle of Hampole*. Manchester University Press, Manchester.

Hodgson, P. (1944 for 1943) *The Cloud of Unknowing and the Book of Privy Counselling*. EETS 218. Oxford University Press, London.

Hodgson, P. (1955 for 1949) *Deonise Hid Divinite and Other Treatises on Contemplative Prayer Related to The Cloud of Unknowing EETS 231*. Oxford University Press, London.

Moyes, M. (1988) *Richard Rolle's Expositio super Novem Lectiones Mortuorum: An Introduction and Contribution towards a Critical Edition*. Salzburg Studies in English Literature: Elizabethan and Renaissance Studies 92: 12, 2 volumes. Institut für Anglistik und Amerikanistik, Universität Salzburg, Salzburg.

Ogilvie-Thomson, S. J. (1985) *Walter Hilton's Mixed Life Edited from Lambeth Palace MS 472*. Mellen Studies in Literature/Elizabethan and Renaissance Studies. The Edwin Mellen Press, Lewiston, Queenston, Lampeter.

Ogilvie-Thomson, S. J. (1988) *Richard Rolle: Prose and Verse*. EETS 293, Oxford.

Perry, G. G. (1867) *Officium de Sancto Ricardo de Hampole et Legenda de Vita Eius*.

Sargent, M. G. (2005) *The Mirror of the Blessed Life of Jesus Christ. A Full Critical Edition*. University of Exeter Press, Exeter.

Watson, N. (1995) *Emendatio Vitae: Orationes ad Honorem Nominis Ihesu*. Pontifical Institute of Mediaeval Studies, Toronto.

Watson, N. and Jenkins, J. (2006) *The Writings of Julian of Norwich: A Vision Showed to a Devout Woman and A Revelation of Love*. Medieval Women: Texts and Contexts, volume 5. Brepols, Turnhout.

Windeatt, B. (1994) *English Mystics of the Middle Ages*. Cambridge University Press, Cambridge.

Windeatt, B. (2000) *The Book of Margery Kempe*. Longman Annotated Texts. Pearson Education Limited, Harlow.

Secondary

Alford, J. A. (1973) "Biblical *Imitatio* in the Writings of Richard Rolle." *English Literary History* 40, 1–23.

Alford, J. A. (1995) "Richard Rolle's *English Psalter* and *Lectio Divina*." *Bulletin of the John Rylands Library* 77, 47–59.

Blamires, A. (1995) "The Limits of Bible Study for Medieval Women," in L. Smith and J. Taylor, *Women, the Book and the Godly*. D. S. Brewer, Cambridge, pp. 1–12.

Clark, J. P. H. (1992) "Late Fourteenth-Century Cambridge Theology and the English Contemplative Tradition," in M. Glasscoe, ed., *The Medieval Mystical Tradition in England*. Exeter Symposium V. D. S. Brewer, Woodbridge, pp. 1–16.

Clark, J. P. H. (1995–6) *The Cloud of Unknowing: An Introduction*. Analecta Cartusiana 119: 4, 5, 6. 3 volumes.

Colledge, E. and Walsh, J. (1976) "Editing Julian of Norwich's *Revelations*. A Progress Report," *Medieval Studies* 38, 404–27.

Glasscoe, M. (1993) *English Medieval Mystics: Games of Faith*. Longman, London.

Hudson, A. (1988) *The Premature Reformation: Wycliffite Texts and Lollard History*. Clarendon Press, Oxford.

Johnson, L. S. (1991) "The Trope of the Scribe and the Question of Literary Authority in the Works of Julian of Norwich and Margery Kempe," *Speculum* 66, 820–38.

Renevey, D. (2001) *Language, Self and Love: Hermeneutics in the Writings of Richard Rolle and the Commentaries on the Song of Songs*. University of Wales Press, Cardiff.

Sutherland, A. (1999) "Biblical Citation and Its Affective Contextualisation in Some English Mystical Texts of the Fourteenth Century," unpublished DPhil Thesis, Oxford.

Sutherland, A. (2002) "The Dating and Authorship of the Cloud Corpus: A Reassessment of the Evidence," *Medium Aevum* 71, 82–100.

Sutherland, A. (2004) " 'Oure feyth is groundyd in goddes worde' – Julian of Norwich and the Bible," in E. A. Jones, ed., *The Medieval Mystical Tradition in England*. Exeter Symposium VII. D. S. Brewer, Cambridge, pp. 1–20.

Sutherland, A. (2005) "Biblical Text and Spiritual Experience in the English Epistles of Richard Rolle," *Review of English Studies*, n.s. 56, 695–711.

Watson, N. (1995) "Censorship and Cultural Change in Late-Medieval England: the Oxford Translation Debate, and Arundel's Constitutions of 1409," *Speculum* 70, 822–64.

Windeatt, B. (2004) "Julian of Norwich," in A. S. G. Edwards, ed., *A Companion to Middle English Prose*. D. S. Brewer, Cambridge.

CHAPTER 8
The *Pearl*-Poet

Helen Barr

Introduction

The *Pearl*-poet's engagement with the Bible produced some of the most challengingly profound works of poetry in Middle English literature. For three of the four poems contained in British Library MS Cotton Nero Ax, biblical stories and teachings provide their narrative structure and their plot. Further, individual lines and local episodes are saturated with biblical allusions, quotations, and cross-references. The Bible was the primary and most fertile source for the poet's theological imagination, providing the springboard for searing meditation on how, in the later fourteenth century, one might come to terms with God. The language of the Vulgate finds its equal in a writer able to rework its words into a poetics that moves with ease between the sublime, the grotesque, the intellectual, and the comic. But this is not mere virtuosity; it is a measure of the poet's integrity that his word-craft is inseparable from his examination of often harrowing social and theological problems.

Who was this poet? The dialect of the manuscript suggests north Derbyshire, or the Staffordshire/Cheshire borders (Bennett, 1983, 1997; Cooke and Boulton, 1999). The poet was clearly well versed in theology and is most likely to have been a priest attached to a provincial aristocratic household, but he also seems to have had intimate knowledge of London (Bowers, 2001). The audience for the poet's work is likely to have been one that was aristocratic (or one that at least had pretensions to such a station) for it to have been able to appreciate the insistent courtly texture of the poetry. The *Pearl* poems do not appear to have been designed for a clerical audience well versed in matters of arcane theology. More probably, the poems were addressed to an educated secular elite who were part of the newly educated laity to whom instruction in matters of vernacular theology was becoming increasingly important (Watson, 1997). This putative target audience, whatever its precise regional borders, is very important for the ways in which the *Pearl*-poet translates (both in sense and place) his biblical texts. Like the writers of Mystery Plays, he brings the Bible home – in all the apparently comfortable, yet ultimately terrifying, implications of that phrase.

In each of *Pearl*, *Patience*, and *Cleanness*, the poet draws on both the Old and New Testaments. *Patience* can be seen as a retelling of the Book of Jonah but is framed by a retelling of the Beatitudes from Matthew 5:1–10. Also inserted into the narrative are references to the Psalms and to New Testament interpretations of the Old Testament story. *Cleanness* ranges very freely through both Testaments. Like *Patience*, though less overtly, the poem begins with the Beatitudes, but moves swiftly on to a retelling of the parable of the Wedding Guest. The poet draws on both New Testament sources for this parable: Matthew 22:1–14 and Luke 14:16–24. The rest of the poem is indebted to major biblical stories from Genesis 6:1–9, Genesis 18, Exodus, the Chronicles, Jeremiah, and Daniel. The biblical sources for major narrative stretches of *Pearl* are the parable of the vineyard (Matthew 20:1–16) and the description of the heavenly Jerusalem from the Book of Revelation (Newhauser, 1977).

The *Pearl*-poet shows knowledge of the standard institutional usages of the biblical texts on which he draws. But he translates the Bible from these contexts and invests biblical text with a significance that is idiosyncratic and unique. Whatever the precise institutional context toward which the poet gestures, his handling of biblical texts always exceeds the discipline of the discursive frameworks he invokes. Patristic commentary, typological interpretation, liturgical settings, and homily are all summoned, but all are supplemented by the complexities of poetic (and hence theological) practice. The *Pearl*-poet's Bible is extra-institutional (Somerset, 1998).

Translating the Bible

Paramount in this extra-institutional translation is, of course, the *Pearl*-poet's persistent rendering of the Vulgate Latin into English. However late into the fourteenth century we care to date the *Pearl* poems, the official text of the Bible was in Latin, situating it firmly within the institutional hands of the male clerical elite. Preachers, of course, would cite their pericope text in English, and continue to expound its significance in the vernacular, but until followers of Wyclif translated the Bible into English in the 1380s and 1390s, a lay readership had no access to this privileged text, unless it were read for them. *Piers Plowman* envisages a cleric doing precisely this for Mede (a secular aristocratic woman) in an early part of that poem (B.III.347). Biblical translation was not formally condemned as heretical when the *Pearl*-poet was writing, but nor was it a resolutely orthodox activity, and the association of biblical translation with heresy was certainly part of common cultural currency (Hudson, 1988, p. 190).

There is a striking absence of Latinity in these *Pearl* poems. In *Piers*, the majority of scriptural citations are in Latin, even if they are subsequently Englished. The single use of Latin in all three *Pearl* poems is not even a complete scriptural citation; "sancta sanctorum" in *Cleanness* 1491 refers to the holy vessels in the temple of Solomon in Jerusalem. When, in the same poem, the poet paraphrases the mysterious writing on the wall at Belshazzar's feast, described in Daniel 5:26, he preserves the mysterious words "Mane, Techal and Pharec" but paraphrases their meaning in English. For example, "PHARES: divisum est regnum tuum et datum est Medis et Persis" (Daniel 5:28) is expanded to fit the contours of the alliterative line. Belshazzar's kingdom will be divided, he deposed, and the Medes will become masters (1738–40). In the final comment, "and þou of menske [renown] schowued" (1740), the dynamic energy of the

Old English verb "schowued" (shoved) muscles out completely the factual Latin of the bible.

For learned clerics, the Latin Vulgate would have been familiar to them, encased and enclosed (quite literally) in more Latin; the extensive paraphernalia of glosses acquired through ages of patristic tradition, and in glossed gospels, written around the margins of the text. Of this Latin carapace to the Vulgate, there is, in the *Pearl* poems, almost no sign; and where it is discernible, the hard shell of the Latin learning is split open. Consider the raven, the bird that in Genesis Noah sends to spy out the land when it has finally stopped raining, and it is possible to throw open the previously water-locked windows of the ark. The biblical text says simply "and after that forty days were passed, Noe, opening the window of the ark which he had made, sent forth a raven: Which went forth and did not return, till the waters were dried up upon the earth" (Genesis 8:6–7). In *Cleanness*, the raven is greatly amplified:

> Þat watz þe rauen so ronk, þat rebel watz euer;
> He watz colored as þe cole, corbyal vntrwe.
> And he fongez to þe flyȝt and fannez on þe wyndez,
> Halez hyȝe vpon hyȝt to herken tyþyngez.
> He croukes for comfort when carayne he fyndes
> Kast vp on a clyffe þer costese lay drye;
> He hade þe smelle of þe smach and smoltes þeder sone,
> Fallez on þe foul flesch and fyllez his wombe,
> And sone ȝederly forȝete ȝisterday steuen,
> How þe cheuetayn hym charged þat þe chyst ȝemed.
> Þe rauen raykez hym forth, þat reches ful lyttel
> How alle fodez þer fare, ellez he fynde mete. (453–66)

That was the raven, so proud, which was always a rebel; the disloyal raven was as black as coal. And he takes to the flight and flaps on the winds, sweeps up on high to listen for news. He croaks for pleasure when he finds carrion, thrown up on the cliffs where the regions lay dry. Having smelt the flavour, he sets off there right away. He seizes on the foul flesh and fills his stomach, and promptly forgot yesterday's instructions; how the master who ruled the ark had given him commands. The raven roams forth, giving no heed to how all the people there are faring, just so long as he finds food.

In patristic glosses, the raven is given various figurations: the devil, the Jews, heretics, the unbaptized. Augustine interprets the raven's previous cohabitation in the ark with the dove, as the coexistence of different peoples within the Church. The Prologue to the Wycliffite Bible equates the raven with foul prelates encumbering the institutional Church (chapter 10). None of this ecclesiology finds its way into *Cleanness*. Instead, the poet focuses on beast lore interpretations that emphasize the raven's blackness, its wanderings, its refusal to obey command, its croaking, and above all, its delight in feeding on carrion. In deleting the ecclesiological in favor of lore of the characteristics of the natural world, the poet has relocated the raven from the world of church scholarship to a palpable world of stinky dead flesh. In place of scholarly diction that spells out the meaning of the raven to the learned ("intelligens," "significatur," or simply "est") the poet has given us a dramatized sensory perception of the "smelle" (461) of the carrion, and the greedy eagerness with which the raven guzzles its prey until its guts are full. The eating of dead flesh can be found in a patristic biblical interpretation,[1] but not with the graphic realization of the *Pearl*-poet. The vignette relocates the biblical episode and its interpretation from one of the inhabitants of the Church, to a vivid contrast between the lord of the ship and a disreputable, foul, rebellious servant.

The poet is no less daring in his revision of another important mode of biblical scholarship, namely typological interpretation. In an attempt to reconcile the two testaments of the Bible, typological interpretation argues that what is narrated in the Old Testament is a prefiguration of what comes to pass in the New. Even the laity might have been familiar with how this works in the story of Jonah, which forms the narrative basis of *Patience*. Jonah's three days and three nights in the belly of the whale were understood to prefigure the time between Christ's crucifixion and his resurrection, and hence the stomach of the whale signified Hell. The great fish of the Vulgate was pressed visually into service to remind parishioners of the dangers of Hell. Dooms in parish churches, painted over the chancel arch, painted Hell mouth as the gaping jaws of a great sea monster gulping into its maw the flailing limbs of the desperate damned. Typically, the *Pearl*-poet renders such typological connections much more complicated than a visual deterrent to sin.

The typological connection between Jonah and Christ is explicitly forged in the Bible when Jesus tells the scribes and Pharisees that, just as Jonah was three days and three nights in the belly of the whale, so the Son of Man will be three days and three nights in the heart of the earth (Matthew 12:40). This refers back to the three days and three nights of Jonah 1:17, a timespan explicitly mentioned in *Patience* 295. But, as commentators have often observed, the characterization of Jonah in the poem renders the typological connection between Jonah and Christ theologically fraught. The poet takes a typological connection forged from the comparison of identical time periods and the likening of a big fish to hell, and presses so hard on these neat parallels as to render them troublesome. Unwilling to go to Ninevah, Jonah is given lines that have no parallel in the biblical text:

> "Oure Syre syttes," he says, "on sege so hyʒe
> In His glowande glorye and gloumbes ful lyttel
> Þaʒ I be nummen in Nunniue and naked dispoyled,
> On rode rwly torent with rybaudes mony." (93–6)

"Our Lord sits," he says, "on such a high seat, in his glowing glory, and frowns not at all if I be captured in Ninevah and stripped naked, pitifully torn apart on a cross by many vagabonds."

The diction here, imagining Jonah stripped naked and torn apart on "rode" by vagabonds, unmistakably suggests Christ's crucifixion. Shockingly, the poet has Jonah imagine God, sitting in glory, far out of reach, complacently indifferent to the slaughter of his own Son, which He himself commanded. The typological connection between Jonah and Christ, which in the biblical text offers the comfort of deliverance after three days of torment, is transformed into a speech that is heretical. Did one member of the

Trinity kill another? That the speech is in Jonah's mouth, and that Jonah is clearly an unreliable commentator (witness his faulty logic in thinking that if he escapes to Tarshish, then God will be unable to see him (86)), cannot dilute the theological indecency of these lines. While *Patience* is ostensibly a poem about fortitude and selflessness, the poet's treatment of typology raises deeply disturbing questions about God's relationship to human beings, even His own Incarnate son. Does He care? Or is God simply capricious and vindictive, a distant puppeteer who feels nothing should He, on a whim, simply snap the strings of His creatures dangling from his hands? Neat parallels between Old and New Testaments, institutionally tried and tested, become a source of extra-institutional problem-raising about the scope of God's power.

The poet positions *Patience* extra-institutionally right from the start. He tells how he "herde on a **halyday**, at a hyʒe masse / How Matthew melede þat his Mayster His meyny con teche" (9–10) and then rehearses the Beatitudes from Christ's Sermon on the Mount (Matthew 5:1–11). The Beatitudes passage did not form the basis for the Gospel reading on an ordinary Sunday, but for the Feast of All Saints (November 1), and was also one of the Gospels appointed for a Feast of several martyrs. Having placed this text within appointed Church liturgy, however, the poet's subsequent rendition takes the words right out of the church and into a sexualized, courtly context. His personification of Matthew's virtues creates a retelling that was surely never any part of church liturgy on a formal saints' day:

> These arn þe happes alle aʒt þat vus bihyʒt weren,
> If we þyse ladyes wolde lof in lyknyng of þewes:
> Dame Pouert, Dame Piteé, Dame Penaunce þe þrydde,
> Dame Mekenesse, Dame Mercy, and miry Clannesse,
> And þenne Dame Pes, and Pacyence put in þerafter.
> He were happen þat hade one; alle were þe better. (31–4)

These are all the eight beatitudes that were promised us, if we would love these ladies in imitation of virtues; Dame Poverty, Dame Pity, Dame Penance the third, Dame Humility, Dame Mercy and merry Purity. And then Dame Peace and Patience placed after. He were a lucky man that had one of them; much better to have them all.

In Matthew, the Beatitudes are told to promise those that follow their teaching that their reward shall be great in heaven. Hence the liturgical use of this text on All Saints' Day. In the words of the *Pearl*-poet, these virtues become "ladyes," and heavenly reward their possession. Fortunate is he who has one of them, smirks the narrator, but much better to have them all (34). Virtue is translated into the possibility of serial sexual conquests. The interpolated figurative diction dilutes the seriousness both of church teaching and of church liturgy. The Bible is translated out of its church setting into a household joke.

This translation in *Patience* sets the scene for the unruly treatment of biblical text for the whole poem. Why, if the poem is to teach the virtue of patience, choose to narrate the story of Jonah in the first place when the story of Job would have been so clearly more suitable? Such translation of biblical text from a straightforward teaching context is a characteristic of all three poems, perhaps nowhere more challenging than in *Pearl*, where the Maiden tells the notoriously difficult parable of the Vineyard (Matthew 20:1–16), to explain to the narrator that reward in heaven is justly equitable. Traditionally, allegorical interpretations read the laborers' varying times of entry into the Vineyard to represent the different times of life at which virtuous Christians were converted; the eleventh hour, for instance, was taken to represent the life of a baptized Christian in childhood (Putter, 1996, pp. 173–4; Bishop, 1968, pp. 122–5). The retelling of this parable in *Pearl* upsets such tidy reading of a story, which at its literal level offends so sourly a human sense of justice. As in *Patience*, this teaching is located with liturgical precision: "As Mathew melez in your messe / In sothful gospel of God almyȝt" (497–8). As the line suggests, the Vineyard parable was used as a gospel preaching text for the Sunday mass – for Septuagesima Sunday. While earlier the poet relocated the Beatitudes from the church to the court, here the Sunday gospel is placed within the fully realized fourteenth-century social setting of a manorial lord who employs discontented seasonal laborers. The "patrifamilias" or householder of Matthew 20:1 becomes a "lord" who has an unbiblical "reue" who negotiate with their "werkemen" at a particularly crucial time that is unmentioned in the biblical text:

> Of tyme of ȝere þe terme watz tyȝt,
> To labor vyne watz dere þe date.
>
> Þat date of ȝere wel knawe his hyne. (503–5)

The beginning of the season had come; the time was right to labor the vineyard. His laborers knew that time of year well.

It is vital that the vineyard is harvested "now" – the implication is that otherwise, the grapes will rot and the harvest be lost. An economic sense of urgency is injected into the biblical narrative. Crucially, the laborers ("his hyne") are also well aware of the "date of ȝere." Without their labor, the yield will spoil and there will be no profit for the lord. This economic framing significantly alters the pitch of the telling of the parable. In Matthew 20:4, the householder tells his workers that if they go to work in his vineyard, "I will give you what is just." The householder in *Pearl* is given the non-biblical lines: "What resonabele hyre be naȝt be runne / I yow pay in dede and þoȝte" (523–4). "Reasonable hire" is not semantically equivalent to "quod justum fuerit." The phrase brings the biblical reward up to date with fourteenth-century arguments over inequitable wage structures. Successive bouts of plague had caused labor shortages, and as a consequence, endowed agricultural journeymen with an acute sense of their economic power and importance. Fourteenth-century legislation sought to regulate wages that laborers might legitimately earn; "resonabele hyre" might well be a reference to a particular Statute of Labourers passed in 1388; further, the lord's promise to pay "in dede and þoȝte" suggests a legal obligation (Watkins, 1995; Barr, 2001; Bowers, 2001). No wonder, then, there is outrage when all the laborers are paid an equal wage, irrespective of the time they have spent labouring. In Matthew 20:11, the recipients grumble at the householder, saying, "these last worked one hour, and you have made them equal to us, who have borne the burden of the day and the heat." In *Pearl*, the voice of the workmen is made recognizable in contemporary economic terms:

> "More haf we serued, vus þynk so,
> Þat suffred han þe dayes hete,
> Þenn þyse þat wroȝt not **hourez two**,
> And þou dotz hem vus to **countrefete**."
> Þenne sayde þe lorde to on of þo:
> "Frende, no waning I wyl þe ȝete;
> Take þat is **þyn owne**, and go.
> And I hyred þe for a peny agrete
> Quy bygynnez þou now to **þrete?**
> Watz not a pené þy **couenaunt** þore?
> Fyrre þen **couenaunde** is noȝt to plete;
> Wy schalte þou þenne ask more?" (553–64)

"It seems to us that we, who have endured the heat of the day, have deserved more than these who have not worked two hours, and you make them equal to us." Then said the lord to one of them, "Friend, I will make no reduction. Take what is your own and go. I hired you for an agreed penny. Why do you begin now to make threats? Was not the agreement for a penny? No one can claim more than is agreed. Why must you ask for more?"

The diction highlighted introduces an economic and legal register into the biblical source. It points up a disparity in the rewarding of labor. The initial agreement to work for a penny a day, proposed by the lord, is challenged by the laborers' computation of the merit of their works by the hour. The discussion of spiritual reward in the gospel is translated to acerbic wage negotiations in which the laborers' sense of injustice makes economic human sense. It is not surprising that this retold parable fails to convince the dreamer of *Pearl*:

> Me þynk þy tale vnresounable;
> Goddez ryȝt is redy and euermore rert,
> Oþer holy wryt is bot a fable.
> In sauter is sayd a verce ouerte
> Þat spekez a point determynable:
> "Þou quytez vchon as hys desserte,
> Þou hyȝe Kyng ay pertermynable." (589–96)

It seems to me that your account is unreasonable. God's justice is always ready and supreme; otherwise the Bible is simply a fable. There is a clear verse in the Psalter that makes an incontrovertible point: "You, High King, supreme in judgment, reward each person according to his merit."

Far from explaining the equality of reward in heaven, the Maiden's sermoning of the gospel leaves the narrator ready to condemn holy writ as nothing more than a fiction. To prove his point, he is given a translation of a verse from Psalm 61:12–13 that does contradict what the Maiden has told him: "you reward each person according to his deserving" (595–6). This has implications over and above the poet's economic translation of his scriptural source. The subsequent altercation between dreamer and maiden effects another type of translation – and arguably, one that is even more significant.

What are we to make of a woman (even if dead) arguing the toss about the interpretation of biblical text with a narrator who is clearly a member of the laity – each of them
adducing Englished scriptural texts to support their cause? This extra-institutional
relocation of Matthew's gospel raises profound questions about salvation. How does
God reward human beings – according to the works they have performed, according
to strict justice, or according to merciful dispensation incomprehensible to human
judgment? An acute theological problem is being discussed, not by the clergy in Latin,
in a formally recognized institutional setting, but by two fictionalized members of the
laity in a Middle English poem. There is no easy pastoral didacticism in this use of the
gospel preaching text. Instead, the lay are seen to be taking the Bible into their own
hands and actively questioning the interpretation of what it has to say; interpretation
nourished not by Latin patristic glosses, but by the economic wage structures of fourteenth-century England.

Social Theology

The *Pearl*-poet's relocation of the Bible into socially recognizable settings raises acute
theological issues. Even when the poet is most adamant that what he is writing are the
words of the Bible, he cunningly tells us something significantly altered: the repeated
claim in *Pearl*, for instance, that the vision of the heavenly Jerusalem that concludes
the poem is drawn from the Book of Revelation "as deuyses þe apostel John" (983). The
poet does give us the words of John the Divine Englished, but imped in with diction
that brings the Heavenly Jerusalem down to earth as the city of London (Barr, 2001;
Bowers, 2001):

> So sodanly on a wonder wyse
> I watz war of a **prosessyoun.**
> Þis noble cité of ryche enpresse
> Watz sodanly ful, **wythouten sommoun**
> Of such vergynez in þe same gyse
> Þat watz my blysful anvnder croun:
> And **coronde** wern alle of þe same fasoun,
> **Depaynt in perlez** and wedez qwyte. (1095–102)

> Hundreth þowsandez I wot þer were,
> And alle **in sute her liuréz** wasse. (1107–8)

> Þise **aldermen**, quen He aproched,
> Grouelyng to his fete þay felle. (119–20)

> To loue Þe Lombe his **meyny inmelle**
> Iwysse I laʒt a gret delyt. (1127–8)

Suddenly, miraculously, I was aware of a procession. This noble city, of royal renown, was
suddenly full, without summons, of virgins in the same dress as was my blessed crowned
one; and crowned all in same fashion, adorned with pearls and white clothes. ... I think
that there were a hundred thousand there, and all their liveries were identical. ... When

he approached, these aldermen fell grovelling to his feet. ... I conceived a great delight to love the Lamb among his retinue.

There is no biblical justification for the diction that is highlighted in the passages quoted. In Revelation 5 and 14:1–4, the 144,000 virgins have the Father's name written on their foreheads. They stand before the Lamb while a song is played. In *Pearl*, aristocratic women crowned in pearls form a rich procession without any formal summons, and city aldermen (the elders of Revelation) grovel before the paraded Lamb. The Father's name is translated into a livery of pearls turning the Lamb into an aristo-cratic lord with the 144,000 queens as his retainers.

This is not as John the Divine devised it. What the poet has done is to embellish the Bible to create a socially recognizable vignette of aristocratic power: a royal entry into a city. And the head of that power is God. This is part of a pattern in all three poems in which the poet figures relations between God and human beings in terms of recogniz-able earthly formations of power and social relationships. There is an intense focus on the display of aristocratic culture. The poet gives to his courtly audience a presentation copy of the Bible, but, as I shall argue, this display book has theological terror glossed into its gold leaf. While the audience can see in these poems a reflection of their own sophisticated practices, the use to which the poet puts his aristocratic Bible simultane-ously asks searching questions about human cultural achievement, and about the relationship of human beings to God.

The uselessness of human achievement, when measured against the wrath of God, is emphasized in *Patience* by the changes the poet introduces to the biblical account of Jonah inside the whale. Verse 17 simply states that the Lord appointed a great fish to swallow up Jonah and Jonah was in the belly of the fish three days and three nights. What the poet tells us is that Jonah glides into the whale like a mote of dust entering a *cathedral* door ("munster dor," line 151). He hurls head over heels until he lands in part of the gut as broad as a *hall* (line 155). This is the *bower* ("bour," line 159) for the man who did not want to suffer pain. Jonah looks to see where he might find the best *castle/ shelter* ("le," line 160), but finds nothing but stinky slime through which he must slither and slip. There is no civilized shelter for Jonah. In these lines the poet reinvents typology to create a profoundly disturbing exposure of the fragility of human existence. The grandest achievements of human civilization, far from protecting humans from the elements, are reduced to human waste.

The poet frequently introduces such crushing commentary on human existence into his rendering of the Bible. In *Cleanness*, the destruction of Sodom and Gomorrah is described with the following simile: "And clouen alle in lyttel cloutes þe clyffez any-where / As lauce leuez of þe boke þat lepe in twynne" (965–6). The reduction of a city to smoking ash is compared to leaves that burst from a book once the sewing is broken. That books were considered among the most valuable of human possessions is attested by the fact that in wills, they were the most popular bequeathed objects – apart from beds. Which takes us to the brutally shocking death of Belshazzar, the Chaldean king, at the end of *Cleanness*. The Bible has a single verse, which states that Belshazzar the Chaldean king was slain and Darius the Mede received the kingdom (Daniel 5:30). In *Cleanness*, Darius and his followers scale the walls of a palace previously described in another biblical embellishment as surpassing all "of werk and of wunder," with its elaborate crenellations, skillfully carved crockets, and mathematically precise dimensions (1377–85). Belshazzar, who in the poem presides over one of the most gorgeously sumptuous feasts ever wrought out of alliterative poetry (1393–528), ends his days thus:

> Baltazar in his bed watz beten to deþe,
> Þat boþe his blod and his brayn blende on þe cloþes;
> The kyng in his cortyn was kaȝt bi þe heles,
> Feryed out bi þe fete and fowle dispysed.
> Þat watz so doȝty þat day and drank of þe vessayl
> Now is a dogge also dere þat in a dyche lygges. (1787–92)

Belshazzar was beaten to death in his bed so that both his blood and his brain mingled on the bedclothes. The king inside his bedcurtains was seized by the heels, dragged out by his feet, and cruelly abused. He who was so proud that day and drank from the sacred vessel is now as precious as a dog that lies in a ditch.

All the elaborate carving on the battlements is finally shown to be useless as Darius and his followers enter unimpeded. To be beaten to death in one's own bed is an inversion of all that might be considered courtly and refined. The elaborate bedclothes are mingled not just with Belshazzar's blood but also with his mashed brain that has been cudgelled out of his head. The finery of the bedcurtains can do nothing to prevent Belshazzar's being dragged out of his bed by his heels. The king who presided over such exquisite displays of courtly culture is now as "dere" (precious or worth, 1727) as a dog that lies in a ditch. The aspiring pinnacles of Belshazzar's castle become a channel dug to drain human effluence; the curtained bed becomes a ditch that houses a skulking dog.

The *Pearl*-poet's introduction of aristocratic culture into his biblical paraphrase – only to dash it to pieces – is not ultimately reducible to something as simple as punishing the guilty. The poet's symptomatic recourse to courtly materials when translating the Bible has a deeper theological purpose. His exposure of what lies behind the veneer of courtliness, that is, brutality, feebleness, and wilful destruction, is a commentary, not just on the horror at the heart of the civilized aristocratic world, but also on the horror of the felt puniness of human beings in the face of the mighty power of the Lord in heaven.

The ugliness of Belshazzar's death is not simply a punishment for excessively proud courtliness. This is evident from the poet's treatment of the sacred vessels used in the feast. What is so shocking about Belshazzar's feast, both in the Bible and in *Cleanness*, is that Belshazzar drinks out of the sacred vessels that were made by Solomon, dedicated to God, yet ransacked from the Temple of Jerusalem. Belshazzar's actions in drinking from them are acts of defilement and for this he is punished. In the biblical account the vessels are described simply as being made of gold and silver (Daniel 5:3). The poet amplifies that stark biblical reference into a passage of twenty-one lines (1456–76), completely without trace in the Bible, which forms a catalogue of the most exquisitely described courtly objects in the whole oeuvre of the *Pearl*-poet.

There can be nothing sinful in these vessels themselves; they are sacred. The passage describes lavishly basins of burnished gold (1456), enamelled with azure (1457), ewers in the same fashion (1457), cups with covers arrayed like castles with elaborate buttresses beneath the battlements with skillfully made stepped corbles, and fashioned into figures of marvellous shapes (1458–61). The ornamental tops of the lids on the cups have turrets with pinnacles elegantly projected onto them (1462–3). Upon the pinnacles are magpies and parrots pecking at pomegranates, flowers, and fruits picked out in a vast array of precious stones (1462–74). The goblets are engraved and the bowls inlaid with flowers and golden butterflies (1475–6). The splendor and craft of these vessels exceeds even that of Belshazzar's elaborate platter-covers. All this copious decoration paints a courtly vignette of civilized human practices conquering nature. The battlements are wonderfully wrought, the elegant castles are protected, and creatures of the natural world – butterflies and magpies – are turned into precious human worked materials. In this dizzyingly wrought description, aristocratic finery at its finest is crafted onto the vessels sacred to God. From this description, the exquisite signs of nobility that characterized Belshazzar's court are seen to grace the holiness of God.

This is not the first time in *Cleanness* that God is invested with the trappings of aristocratic culture. The description of God at the start of the poem compares the kingdom of heaven with an aristocratic household:

> He is so clene in His court, þe Kyng þat al weldez
> And honeste in His housholde and hagherlyche serued
> With angelez enourled in alle þat is clene,
> Boþe withinne and withouten in wedez ful bryȝt. (17–21)

The King that rules over everything is so pure in his court, and honest in his houeshold and fittingly served, surrounded by angels in all that is pure, both inside and out, in shimmering clothes.

These lines embellish a single verse from Matthew 5:8, "blessed are the pure in heart, for they shall see God." They seem to present an idealized version of a court, but as the poem develops, this vignette of God as a pure, virtuous Lord is put under strain. The first instance of this is in the retelling of the Parable of the Wedding Guest. The poet conflates two biblical versions of this story: Matthew 22:1–14 and Luke 14:16–24. Contemporary sermons preached on this parable interpret the lord's ejection of the guest who arrives at the feast "not clothed in a wedding garment" (Matthew 22:11) as God's rejection from heaven of those who have not performed good works in their earthly lives. The absence of a wedding garment is interpreted as the absence of virtuous living (Mirk, *Festial*, p. 131; *Middle English Sermons*, pp. 16–19). But in none of these contemporary sermons is there the fully realized social picture that the *Cleanness* poet creates in his expansion from his biblical sources. Having set the Lord up in his fine aristocratic household, the poet describes his aristocratic displeasure should there arrive:

> a ladde ... lyþerly attired,
> When he were sette solempnely in a sete ryche.
> Abof dukez on dece, with dayntys serued?

> And þe harlot with haste helded to þe table,
> With rent cokrez at þe kne and his clutte traschez.
> And his tabarde totorne, and his totez oute. (36–41)

A fellow, ... badly dressed, when he were placed in solemnity on a noble seat, above nobles on the dais, being served with delicacies, and then the rascal approached the table, with his leggings torn at the knee, his rags all patched, his tunic torn, and his toes sticking out of his shoes.

There is no prompt in either biblical source to suggest the presentation of the badly dressed wedding guest as a *poor laborer*. But that is exactly how the guest is presented here, especially given that he wears a tabard (41). His torn and tattered working clothes contrast to the lord seated on his dais served with dainties. Both here and in a later paraphrase of the same biblical passage (133–68), the poet's addition of contemporary social details presents a lord at a luxuriously ordered feast expelling a laborer soiled with his toil from the lord's aristocratically clean court. The poet expands on the discomfiture of the wedding guest. Matthew tells us that, when confronted with his lack of wedding garment, he "fell silent" (22:12). In *Cleanness*, the poet takes four lines to amplify his terror (Wallace, 1991). In Matthew, the "man" (never *laborer*) is cast into outer darkness (22:13); in *Cleanness*, the lord commands his hands to be bound, his feet fettered, he is then to be stuck in the stocks and thereafter placed "depe in my dungeoun þer doel euer dwellez" (155–8). Texts closely contemporary with *Cleanness*, such as *Piers Plowman, Pierce the Ploughman's Crede*, and Julian of Norwich's *Revelations of Divine Love*, depict poor, ragged, laboring clothing as a sign of virtue, and in Julian's Lord and Servant analogy, God desires to redeem his poorly dressed servant and transform him into "cleness wyde and syde."[2] The theological force of the socially recognizable clothing in *Cleanness* presents an opposite scenario. God, as aristocratic lord, unilaterally and arbitrarily, punishes a laborer for wearing clothes appropriate to his station and to his humble, but necessary labor. The fetters, the stocks, and the dungeon recreate the biblical outer darkness to conform to contemporary criminal punishment. There is no theologically, or socially, comfortable reading that can be extracted from the poet's alterations to his biblical source.

By translating his biblical texts into narratives saturated with recognizable contemporary social details, the poet creates a God who is aristocratic and fully aware of the feudal power that he wields. While the biblical parable of the Wedding Guest is used in contemporary sermons to remind human beings that they cannot expect to be received in the court of heaven soiled with sin, the *Pearl*-poet adds a new dimension to the biblical fear. Replicating the cruelty and brutality that the poet reveals underneath all the civilized practices that his poetry so lovingly recreates, the God of biblical narrative becomes a contemporary tyrant; indifferent to the welfare of his subjects and arbitrary in his decisions to save or to destroy. But this is not the whole story, and while it is hard to find much theological comfort about the relationship of God to his creation in *Cleanness*, and problematic to do so in *Pearl*, the repointing of biblical details in *Patience* tells a slightly different tale, as well as shedding light on why the poet might have retold his Bible in such a frightening fashion.

God's first entry into *Patience* describes him whispering right in Jonah's ear with "a roghlych rurd" that startles the unwilling prophet (64–5). There is nothing of this in the Bible; simply a reference to the word of the Lord (Jonah 1), nor is there any equivalent to the lines that the poet adds about God's power over all created things "at wylle" (131) before he summons the storm. In a further addition, the poet stresses God's power to intervene in the natural order of things. Jonah is able to survive in the whale's guts despite "lawe of any kynde" (259). Here, however, God's miraculous power is seen to protect what he has made: "he watz sokored by þat Syre þat syttes so hiȝe" (261). *Patience* shows us how God has the power to do with creation just as he wills: either to destroy it or to save it. It is this apparent contrariness that so vexes Jonah. In a further interpolation of the biblical story, the narrator tells us that when God, although he had promised otherwise, withheld his vengeance from the Ninevites, Jonah "wex as wroth as þe wynde towarde oure Lorde" (408–10). Jonah's anger with God is that he has not kept his word. Further, the poet greatly expands Jonah's prayer to God from the whale's belly. He calls upon God to grant him mercy and promises that if he does so, he shall keep God's word. The changes to the biblical source emphasize that Jonah is predicting how God ought to behave: "þou **schal** releue, me Renk, whil þy ryȝt slepez, / þurȝ myȝt of þy mercy þat mukel is to tryste" (323–4). And in praying to God to spare him, as a further additional line makes clear, Jonah thinks he can hold God to a bargain He has made: "**halde goud** þat þou me hetes: **haf here my trauthe**" (336). The poet gives Jonah diction that belongs to that of contemporary feudal pledges. Jonah demands of God that He honors His word. These changes to the biblical source create a Jonah who stands as a figure for the perplexed difficulties confronted by every Christian in thinking about the ultimate fate of their own soul.

Through God's atonement for human sin through the crucifixion, God could be seen to have entered into a kind of covenant with human beings that held out the promise of salvation. But how could human beings, however virtuous their deeds, be sure of that salvation, without that knowledge supremely compromising God's absolute power and will? These were issues, as a number of critics have shown, that wrestled the minds of prominent theologians (Coleman, 1981; Wallace, 1991). The changes the *Pearl*-poet makes to his biblical source material can be seen to dramatize the human dilemma of reconciling a human notion of just reward that is rational and proportional to deeds performed with God's idea of just reward, which is suprarational, possibly merciful and possibly brutal, and neither just nor merciful as humans understand these terms. How can human beings hope for God to be just, and to expect his justice, without simultaneously compromising his Omnipotence (Coleman, 1981)? How can humans live comfortably in *this* world when all such measurements of human justice and mercy cannot be counted on at the Day of Doom?

It is this necessary inscrutability of God's will and power that is dramatized in *Patience*. Despite his rough treatment of Jonah, God is ultimately merciful, both to his petulant prophet and to the Ninevites. But he is not merciful in the way that Jonah expects him to be. Jonah wants a God he can count on. The changes the poet has made to his source show that it is rather more complicated than this. Jonah can count on God, but not, in ways (necessarily) that Jonah can either predict or like. *Patience* shows us a more merciful God than the aristocratic tyrant whom the poet forges from his biblical sources in *Pearl* and *Cleanness*; but He is still an inscrutable God, whom neither the wishes nor even the virtuous deeds of human beings can constrain.

The Book of Jonah, as retold by the *Pearl*-poet, dramatizes a vital and anxious dilemma for human beings, and as in *Pearl*, we see things very much from the perspective of the confused, and often comically limited, human viewpoint of either Jonah or the dreamer. The poet adds comic touches to the Bible that bring the audience closer to the protagonist than to God. But the poet also adds something else equally significant, especially in *Patience*. God's biblical rebuke to Jonah for taking God to task for destroying his woodbine runs: "You pity the plant for which you did not labor, nor did you make it grow, which came into being in a night and perished in a night. And should I not pity Nineveh, that great city, in which there are more than twenty thousand persons who do not know their right hand from their left, and also much cattle" (Jonah 2:10–11). With the strangely after-thoughted cattle, the text falls silent. The *Pearl*-poet greatly distends this speech. God tells Jonah that having labored for such a long time to create human beings, should he destroy Ninevah, the pain of losing such a place would sink into his heart (507). The poet expands on those people who should be lost; not only those with reduced mental capabilities (510), but also the innocent (513), unlearned women, and sinless dumb beasts (514–17). The poet's repointing of his source emphasizes God's sorrowful reluctance to destroy the innocent. In a striking addition, God upbraids Jonah: "could I not **þole** bot as þou, þer þryued ful fewe" (521, emphasis added). "Few should thrive," says God, "if I *suffered*, or *endured* only as you do." For all his dramatization of God's omnipotence, inscrutable to human rationality, here the poet has God tell us of His own suffering. If the poem teaches the virtue of patience as the endurance of suffering, then it also begs a profound question: who suffers more than God?

The *Pearl*-poet's Bible

Religious texts produced for aristocratic households might be accompanied with flattering portraits of their patron in full aristocratic regalia – as in the Psalter for Geoffrey Luttrell. In some ways, the *Pearl*-poet presents his courtly household with a Bible in which they might see a gorgeous reflection of their own courtliness in its richly crafted poetry. But to see only a mirror image of aristocratic sumptuousness mistakes the surface for depth. The Bible is relocated from a Latin scholarly context, and requisitioned from the established church to teach a lesson to the lay nobility. But this extrainstitutional Bible is not a source for the sweet end of pastoral care. Stark theology engraves its cultured leaves. In offering up a vision of the ultimate uselessness of courtliness in the face of God's power, and in revealing how the codified brutalities of aristocratic human power can be seen as a figure for God's majesty, the poet creates an embellished biblical text of great profundity, as well as of great beauty. God does remain inscrutable in this Bible retold; his capacity for mercy or for forgiveness remains beyond the ken of even the most virtuous human beings. Yet, as *Patience* reveals, there is more to this aristocratic God than the tyrant who stocks a ragged peasant who hasn't washed his hands. God suffers for His Creation, and suffers more than man can know. That's why, in *Pearl*, the prophecy of Revelation 22:14 ("Blessed are they that wash their robes in the blood of the Lamb: that they may have a right to the tree of life, and may enter in by the gates into the city") is translated into a contemporary aristocratic pageant in the glittering city, which has, at its center, a lamb dripping red blood. The narrator is too ignorant to recognize his complicity in Christ's wound: the freshly wet gash so palpable a sign of Jesus's suffering on the cross. "Alas," says the dreamer, "who did þat spyt?" (evil deed) (1138)? So intent is this grief-addled man on assuaging his own pain by straining to gaze on his "lytel quene" that he misses what stares him in the face: a sign of sacrifice that cannot bring him certainty, but can offer him hope.

Notes

I am grateful to Vincent Gillespie for reading this chapter and for his sage advice on its content.

1   "arca continent corvum et columbam" S.Augustine, vol. 33 "cadaveris detento," Hieronymus Stridonensis, *Patrologia Latina*, vol. 26; "qui avidate fententis cadaveris," Goffridus Vindocinensis, *Patrologia Latina*, vol. 157; "cadaveribus inventis forsitan supersedit," Hugo de Folieto?, *Patrologia Latina*, vol. 177.
2   2 *Piers Plowman*, XI.184–5; *Pierce the Ploughman's Crede*, 420–32; Julian of Norwich, *Revelations*, ch. 51.

References and Further Reading

Primary Texts

English Wycliffite Sermons, volume 2, ed. Pamela Gradon. Oxford, 1988.
Julian of Norwich, *Revelation of Love*, ed. Marion Glasscoe. Exeter, 1976.
Langland, William, *Piers Plowman: A Complete Edition of the B-Text*, rev. edn, ed. A. V. C. Schmidt. London, 1987.
Middle English Sermons Edited from British Museum MS Royal B xiii, ed. W. O. Ross. EETS OS 209, 1940.
Mirk, John, *Mirk's Festial*, ed. T. Erbe. EETS OS, 1905.
Patrologia Latina accessed through Chadwyck Healey database.
Pierce the Ploughman's Crede in The Piers Plowman Tradition, ed. Helen Barr. London, 1993.
The Poems of the Pearl Manuscript, rev. edn, ed. Malcolm Andrew and Ronald Waldron. Exeter, 1987.

Secondary Texts

Aers, David (1997) "Christianity for Courtly Subjects: Reflections on the *Gawain*-poet," in D. Brewer and J. Gibson, eds, *A Companion to the Gawain-poet*. Cambridge, pp. 91–104.
Barr, Helen (2001) *Socioliterary Practice in Late Medieval England*. Oxford.
Bennett, Michael J. (1983) *Community, Class and Careerism: Cheshire and Lancashire Society in the Age of Sir Gawain and the Green Knight*. Cambridge.

Bennett, Michael J. (1997) "The Historical Background," in D. Brewer, and J. Gibson, eds, *A Companion to the Gawain-poet*. Cambridge, pp. 71–90.

Bishop, Ian (1968) *Pearl in Its Setting*. Oxford.

Bowers, John (2001) *The Politics of Pearl: Court Poetry in the Ages of Richard II*. Woodbridge.

Brewer, D. and Gibson, J., eds (1997) *A Companion to the Gawain-poet*. Cambridge.

Coleman, Janet (1981) *"Piers Plowman" and the Moderni*. Edizioni di Storia e Letteratura, Rome.

Cooke, W. G. and Boulton, D'A. J. D. (1999) "Sir Gawain and the Green Knight: a Poem for Henry of Grosmont?" *Medium Aevum* 68, 42–51.

Hudson, Anne (1988) *The Premature Reformation*. Oxford.

Johnson, Lynn Staley (1991) "The Pearl dreamer and the eleventh hour," in J. Wasserman and M. Youngerman, eds, *Text and Matter: New Critical Perspectives on the Pearl-poet*. New York, pp. 3–15.

Levy, B. S., ed. (1992) *The Bible in the Middle Ages: Its Influence on Literature and Art*. New York.

Newhauser, Richard (1997) "Sources II: Scriptural and Devotional Sources" in D. Brewer, and J. Gibson, eds, *A Companion to the Gawain-poet*. Cambridge, pp. 257–76.

Nicholls, Jonathan (1985) *The Matter of Courtesy: Medieval Courtesy Books and the Gawain Poet*. Cambridge.

Putter, Ad (1996) *An Introduction to the Gawain Poet*. London.

Riddy, Felicity (1997) "Jewels in Pearl," in D. Brewer, and J. Gibson, eds, *A Companion to the Gawain-poet*. Cambridge, pp. 143–56.

Somerset, Fiona (1998) *Clerical Discourse and Lay Audience in Late Medieval England*. Cambridge.

Spearing, A. C. (1970) *The Gawain-Poet: A Critical Study*. Cambridge.

Spearing, A. C. (1980) "Purity and Danger," *Essays in Criticism* 30, 293–310.

Wallace, David (1991) "Cleanness and the Terms of Terror," in J. Wasserman and M. Youngerman, eds, *Text and Matter: New Critical Perspectives on the Pearl-poet*. New York, pp. 93–104.

Watkins, John (1995) "'Sengeley in syngulere': *Pearl* and late medieval individualism," *Chaucer Yearbook* 2, 117–36.

Watson, Nicholas (1997) "The *Gawain*-poet as vernacular theologian," in D. Brewer and J. Gibson, eds, *A Companion to the Gawain-poet*. Cambridge, 293–314.

CHAPTER 9

William Langland

Sister Mary Clemente Davlin, OP

"We cannot restate too often the fact that the most pervasive single influence upon *Piers Plowman* was that of the Bible" (Salter, 1968, p. 84). To understand this influence, one must look at a number of elements in the poem. Six elements warrant particular attention:

1   The vast number of quotations in *Piers Plowman* from the Bible, their sources, their order, and the degree to which they shape the structure of the poem.
2   The ways various characters in the poem read, understand, or misunderstand the Bible.
3   The poem's retelling of Bible stories and re-creation of biblical characters.
4   Personifications of the Bible in the poem.
5   The ways in which biblical genres and styles form the poem.
6   The way the poem is centered on biblical ideas and ideals.

These various modes of engagement with the Bible constitute what Morton Bloomfield has called Piers Plowman's "echoes and paraphrases" of the Bible:

> *Piers Plowman* is impregnated with the Bible. ... It has been said of Bernard of Clairvaux that he speaks Bible as one might speak French or English. Langland speaks Bible, too; phrases, echoes, and paraphrases crop out everywhere. His whole mind is steeped in the Bible; it is a real language to him. (Bloomfield, 1961, p. 37)

In concentrating on Langland's "speaking Bible," this chapter surveys the vast range of biblical influences on *Piers Plowman*, offering an introduction both to the poem and, more generally, to the understanding of the Bible in fourteenth-century England.

Biblical Quotations

Looking at almost any page of *Piers Plowman* makes a reader aware that "Langland's poem differs from all other vernacular books that have come down to us" (Hort, 1936,

p. 43) because each page is threaded with Latin quotations, roughly one for about every eighteen lines,[1] although they are not distributed evenly. John Alford estimates that such quotations "could be said to account for nearly half the poem's substance, and, if some critics are right, for much of its form as well" (Alford, 1992, p. 2). At least three-fourths of these quotations are from the Bible, which in the Middle Ages was usually read in Latin in a version called the Vulgate. The public prayer of the people, the liturgy, was also celebrated in Latin, and sometimes in those prayers a different Latin version of the Bible was used, the *Vetus Latina*. These Latin versions of the biblical text with "its commentaries and the liturgy certainly account for the vast majority of Langland's quotations" (Alford, 1992, p. 22).

How did Langland come to know the Bible so well and to feel so much at home with Latin? We know almost nothing about his life with any certainty. Most scholars think that he must have studied as a boy in a monastic school and continued afterwards to educate himself, as there is no certain evidence that he attended university.[2] Although Judson Boyce Allen concluded that "Langland almost certainly owned" a Bible "or at least ... much of one," this would have been most unusual, because manuscripts were so expensive. Yet he quotes from forty-six of the biblical books.[3] Perhaps he was allowed to use the library of a monastery. He knew the liturgy well and would have memorized many biblical prayers, perhaps by serving Mass; he may also have practiced meditation upon biblical passages, learning them "by heart" so that one passage reminded him of others in a process of memory called "verbal concordance." He uses such concordance in his poem. In addition to people's trained memories, books of concordances existed, too, listing various themes in alphabetical order as helps for preachers, and books of biblical commentary also used concordance. Langland is thought to have used such common study aids. Alford comments, "That Langland read the Bible with the help of a commentary is beyond doubt" (Alford, 1992, p. 19). Yet, as Michael Kuczynski concluded after thorough study of the use of the biblical psalms in the poem, the words of the Bible themselves are far more important to Langland than any commentary. Quotation itself is essential in the poem (Kuczynski, 1995, p. 22).

Sometimes Latin quotations are only a single word or phrase fitted into an English sentence. It has become quite clear that such a word or phrase needs to be understood in the context of the whole biblical passage from which it comes, as the poet seems to take it for granted that readers know the context of each particular quotation. Sometimes an entire Latin line is quoted, or several lines, either from the same biblical passage or from more than one. The reader then needs to ask what these biblical passages have in common. Whether the quotation is short or long, one needs to ask how it relates to the English text. Sometimes English and Latin express and reinforce the same theme; sometimes the Latin quotation is the authority (the "proof text") for the English; sometimes one text, English or Latin, raises questions about the texts near it and they reinterpret one another (Rogers, 2002, p. 22). So, for example, Lady Holy Church explains to Will:

> "Whan alle tresors arn tried," quod she, "treuthe is the beste.
> I do it on *Deus caritas* to deme the soothe;
> It is as dereworthe a drury as deere God hymselven." (1.85–7)

> "When all treasures are tried," she said, "truth is the best.
> I base [my words] on *God is love* to judge the truth;
> It is as precious a treasure as dear God himself."

Holy Church quotes a single phrase here, "God is love" from 1 John 4:8 and 4:16, in an inviting but puzzling way. She does not translate the Latin; presumably the passage she is quoting is well enough known that translation is unnecessary. She says that this Latin phrase is the basis of her belief that truth is the best treasure, but she does not explain how love and truth are related, except that both are names for God. If *treuthe* is God, as she has said at 1.12–14, and if God is love, then *treuthe/caritas* certainly is the best treasure. But the passage, simple as it appears with its short quotation, demands a great deal of interpretative thought to put together the biblical links that help make sense of the apparent synonymy of truth and love in the passage.

In Passus 9, the theme of likeness to God brings together three Latin biblical quotations from three sources:

> That lyven synful lif here, hir soule is lich the devel.
> And alle that lyven good lif are lik God almyghty:
> *Qui manet in caritate, in Deo manet ...*

> Allas! That drynke shal fordo that God deere boughte,
> And dooth God forsaken hem that he shoop to his liknesse:
> *Amen, dico vobis, nescio vos. Et alibi, Et dimisi eos secundum desideria eorum.* (9.63–6b)

> Those who live sinful lives here, their souls are like the devil.
> And all who live a good life are like almighty God:
> *One who lives in love, lives in God ...*

> Alas! that drink shall undo what God bought so dearly,
> And that it should cause God to forsake them that he made to his likeness:
> *Amen, I say to you, I do not know you. And elsewhere, And I dismissed them according to their desires.*

The three Latin quotations, from 1 John 4:6, Matthew 25:12, and Psalm 80:13, are related in sharing the theme of being like or unlike God. The first quotation, *Qui manet in caritate, in Deo manet*, is the second half of Holy Church's quotation, *deus caritas*. This part of the quotation demands knowledge of the other half. With that knowledge, it "proves" that "all who live a good life are like almighty God," since "God is love," and living a good life means dwelling in love like God, even dwelling in God. But the second quotation, *Amen, dico vobis*, warns that although God made all people in "his liknesse," abuse of drink (as a concrete example of living "synful lif") could lead to becoming less and less like God so that eventually God would have to say, "I don't know you." Then, if all likeness were gone from them, all they would have left would be the desires that formed them to be unlike God and God's creatures: they would have what they chose (*Et alibi, Et dimisi*). These quotations are not translated, but they would have been heard regularly, in Latin, in church. For someone like the poet, who knows the Bible well, each quotation recalls or suggests another, and the reader who works to understand how these three quotations are thematically connected comes to a deep realization of something profound: that love makes people like God, and that sin is a destruction of that likeness. Again, Langland's use of the Bible here invites the reader to explore various portions of the text, since only with knowledge of the biblical context for each quotation can the reader reach appropriate conclusions concerning right living and sin.

Reading *Piers Plowman*: Two Scholarly Disputes

While Langland invites the reader to explore the text's variety of biblical quotations, he also exercises their interpretative skills through the depictions of characters. Specifically, within the narrative, different characters provide examples of different ways of reading and using biblical quotations. Thus *Piers Plowman* is an important text for understanding how people read (and misread) the Bible, and how the Bible was understood in fourteenth-century England, at least by this brilliant reader. As James Simpson shows,

> Holy Church, for example, uses biblical texts in Passus I as illustrations of didactic moral points. Will uses them in the third vision as counters in an intellectual, theological argument. Patience, in the fourth vision, uses especially Gospel texts in an inspiring, paradoxical way; and here in the fifth vision, biblical time itself informs the narrative, as Old Testament figures are seen from a New Testament perspective, standing for and calling forth the Christian epoch of charity. The Bible is now being "read" by Will, as it were, in an inward, sophisticated and dynamic way. (Simpson, 1990, p. 199)

The many ways of reading biblical quotations within the narrative raise important questions. One of these is: how should the Biblical quotations fit into the English text, or how does the English text support them? This is a key question "more pertinent than any other to the art of *Piers Plowman*" upon which scholars do not yet agree (Alford, 1977, p. 80). A natural way to read *Piers Plowman* is to pay attention only to its English lines, following the narrative and treating the many biblical quotations as extraneous, redundant, or non-essential though enriching. Certainly the poem may be read that way, but it is not easy reading, and its structure is not obvious. The English narrative is filled with surprises: characters suddenly appear or speak out unexpectedly, whole narrative sequences break off before they come to any satisfying conclusion, moods change, and there are apparent digressions and repetitions in pattern. Many scholars have offered explanations for this narrative oddity, including the possibility that the poem reflects the uncertainties of the time,[4] that it dramatizes the human struggles of a life of faith,[5] or that it reflects fourteenth-century acceptance of mixed styles or Langland's deep awareness of change and the need for change.[6]

John Alford suggested reversing the ordinary way of reading the poem when he wrote "In general, scholarship has looked for the structure of *Piers Plowman* in the English portions of the poem; I shall be looking for it in the Latin" (Alford, 1977, p. 82), suggesting that the poem is structured not by its English narrative, but by its biblical quotations organized as batches of texts about single themes connected by verbal concordance. Judson Boyce Allen (1984) showed that in the Pardon Passus where the priest attacks Will, the Latin texts are probably all taken from Hugh of St Cher's commentary on the psalms, forming a connected group of texts called a "*distinctio*," about God's protection of good people against others' hostility. David Allen (1989) discussed another *distinctio* which he thinks Langland composed by drawing together quotations to structure Passūs 10–13. In the view of these and some other scholars, the English narrative simply explicates and connects the Latin text. "The text of the poem obeys no logic of its own, but occurs as a commentary on or development of an array of themes already defined elsewhere as an ordered set – usually by the Bible" (Judson Allen, 1982, p. 275).

However, no one has yet offered an explanation of the whole structure of *Piers Plowman* based entirely upon its biblical quotations, and although most scholars are probably still open to evidence of such a structure, some insist that the Latin quotations are not the skeleton of the poem but "are characteristically proof texts supporting or confirming some point made in the vernacular" (Hill, 2001, p. 217).

At this point, we can be certain that Langland knew the Bible intimately and quoted it constantly, and that biblical quotations may have been put into the poem not individually, but in groups, either groups of his own devising or groups that he found in commentaries. We know that it is possible that these biblical quotations may form the "skeleton" of the poem. Scholars, however, are not agreed on this point. Anne Middleton, for example, notes that biblical quotations are borrowings from the past and sees them as important not because of structure, but because "the subject of the poem is the combined outrage and salvific necessity of this ceaseless borrowing from those who have gone before us" (Middleton, 1992, p. 138). Regardless of critical conclusions on whether it is the English or Latin text that forms the foundation of the poem's structure, such a debate reveals the poem's depth of engagement with the Latin Bible as well as with vernacular traditions, making *Piers Plowman* unusual in its range.

A second major dispute about how to read this biblical poem began with an argument by D. W. Robertson and Bernard F. Huppé that *Piers Plowman* is based entirely upon the Bible, and that since each part of the Bible could be read on four levels, "historically ... allegorically ... anagogically ... tropologically" (Robertson and Huppé, 1951, p. 14), *Piers Plowman*, too, could be read on four levels. Other scholars had little difficulty accepting that *Piers* is about the same things that the Bible is about, but many thought, with Elizabeth Salter, that *Piers* was "badly served by subjection to precise and thoroughgoing analysis in terms of allegory, and especially in terms of fourfold allegory, the 'allegory of the theologians'" (Salter, 1968, p. 75). Today, although everyone recognizes the importance of the Bible in *Piers Plowman*, few give *Piers Plowman* the fourfold allegorical reading that Robertson and Huppé advocated.

Bible Stories and Characters

Besides being present in Latin quotations, the Bible permeates the poem through the retelling of stories in English from both the Hebrew Scriptures and the New Testament.[7] Some gospel stories are retold several times in the poem, in different ways, with different purposes and effects. The annunciation story, for example, comes from Luke 1:26–38:

the angel Gabriel was sent from God into a city of Galilee called Nazareth to a virgin espoused to a man whose name was Joseph, of the house of David, and the virgin's name was Mary. And the angel being come in said to her, Hail, full of grace, the Lord is with thee: blessed art thou amongst women. ... Behold, thou shalt conceive in thy womb, and shalt bring forth a son, and thou shalt call his name Jesus. ... And Mary said to the angel, How shall this be done, because I know not man? And the angel answering said to her, The Holy Ghost shall come upon thee, and the power of the most High shall overshadow thee. And therefore also the Holy which shall be born of thee shall be called the Son of God. ... And Mary said, Behold the handmaid of the Lord. Be it done to me according to thy word.

Passus 11 retells the story this way:

> Jesu Crist on a Jewes doghter lighte: gentil womman though she were,
> Was a pure povere maide and to a povere man ywedded. (11.246–7)

> Jesus Christ descended on a Jew's daughter, [who] though she was a gentlewoman
> Was a pure, poor maiden married to a poor man.

No biblical quotation is used or needed, as the story is so well known. This passage is brief and spare, without descriptive or sensory words. The adjectives "gentil," "pure," "povere" are rather abstract. Mary is not given her proper name: she is simply "a pure, povere maide," "a Jewes doghter," a remarkable reminder in fourteenth-century English society, which was often anti-Semitic. The verb "lighte" uses the metaphor of spatial relationship (moving downward from on high) as visual artists do in paintings of this scene, with God "descending."

The character Ymaginatif retells the same story in the next Passus, combining the annunciation story with the Christmas story of Jesus' birth:

> For the heighe Holy Goost hevene shal tocleve,
> And love shal lepe out after into this lowe erthe,
> And clennesse shal cacchen it and clerkes shullen it fynde:
> *Pastores loquebantur ad invicem.*

> For the high Holy Spirit shall cleave heaven open,
> And love shall leap out after into this low earth,
> And cleanness shall catch it and scholars shall find it.
> "*The shepherds said to one another.*" (12.140–2a)

Here, each character except the Holy Spirit and the shepherds is turned into an abstraction or generalization: Jesus is "love," Mary is "clennesse," and the wise men from the east are "clerkes." Yet verbs fill the lines with drama and life: the Holy Spirit cleaves heaven open, love leaps down, and cleanness makes an unforgettable catch. This is farther from the original Bible story, more of an interpretation than a simple retelling. It explains the reason for the incarnation – love – and the involvement of both heaven and earth in Jesus' coming.

A third retelling immediately follows Piers's rush to defeat the devil:

> And thanne spak *Spiritus Sanctus* in Gabrielis mouthe
> To a maide that highte Marie, a meke thyng withalle,
> That oon Jesus, a justice sone, moste jouke in hir chambre
> Til *plenitudo temporis* time comen were ...

> And then the Holy Spirit spoke in the mouth of Gabriel
> To a maiden called Mary, a meek person,
> That one Jesus, the son of a justice, must stay in her chamber
> Until the fullness of time came. (16.90–3)

This begins with a style closer to that of the gospel story though it includes interpretation: Gabriel really speaks not his own words but the words of the Spirit to Mary, who is "meke." Thus far, the text is literal. But in line 92, Mary becomes a householder with a room to rent or lend out, and Jesus "a justice sone," a punning phrase that could mean the son of a judge, the son of justice, or (by sound, though not by spelling) the sun of justice. The latter possibility identifies him beyond doubt as the *sol iustitiae* mentioned in liturgical morning prayer. Mary's "chamber," of course, is her own body, where, accepting the divine invitation, she welcomes him to dwell for nine months until "the fullness of time." Latin is retained for the name of the Holy Spirit and the phrase "*plenitudo temporis*" from the Divine Office, both of which would be heard in church services.

These three uses of the same Bible story show the economy and lack of direct emotional emphasis that characterize Langland's use of the Bible. Its statement of faith ("spak *Spiritus Sanctus*") is direct and unquestioned; the word play on "justice sone" demands thought and offers the pleasure of recognizing a meaningful pun; "jouke in hir chambre" is a homely, concrete metaphor, startling at first, emphasizing the personhood of both Mary and the newly conceived Jesus. This is thought poetry, which Walter Ong called "wit poetry,"[8] leading the reader to a deeper understanding of the Bible story and only then, through thought, to an emotional reaction.

Certain other gospel stories, too, such as the birth of Christ, the crucifixion, and the resurrection, are retold several times in *Piers*. They are told not in order, except in Passus 18 (B), but wherever they are needed to illustrate some point in the English narrative.

The use of the Bible becomes dramatic when Will actually encounters some biblical figures and either sees their stories re-enacted or hears them retell what happened to them. So, for example, he meets Abraham, who tells him the story of the visit God made to Sarah and himself promising them a son. Later, he sees the Good Samaritan care for the man wounded on the way to Jericho and runs to follow him, and then watches the whole passion, death, and harrowing of hell by Jesus.

It is during the liturgy of Holy Week that Will "sees" the passion of Jesus. For example, Matthew's gospel reads:

> And plaiting a crown of thorns, they put it upon his head, and a reed in his right hand. And bowing the knee before him, they mocked him, saying: Hail, king of the Jews. And spitting upon him, they took the reed, and struck his head. (27:29–30)

Will sees the event this way:

"*Crucifige!*" quod a cachepol, "I warante hym a wicche!"
"*Tolle, tolle!*" quod another, and took of kene thornes,
And bigan of kene thorn a garland to make,
And sette it sore on his heed and seide in envye,
"*Ave, raby!*" quod that ribaud – and threw reedes at hym. (18.46–50)

"Crucify him!" said an officer, "I swear he's a witch!"
"Away with him! Away with him!" said another, and took sharp thorns
And began to make a garland of sharp thorn
And set it painfully on his head and said in envy,
"Hail, Rabbi!" said that evil fellow – and threw reeds at him.

The Latin words are some of those that people would hear several times every year when the Passion was read in Latin during Mass. They weave the gospel directly into the poem. Yet the smooth rhythms of the gospel narrative are broken by short dialogue. The scene seems busy; the malevolence of the characters is explicit. The words "kene" and "sore," added to the gospel account, intensify the reader's awareness of the torture involved in this scene, and the soldiers are given motives for their hostility, envy, and fear of witchcraft. The reader is reminded of the influence the morality plays seem to have had on the poem (Skeat, 1886, II, pp. 4–5).

In considering Langland's engagement with particular biblical episodes, then, we might say that he dramatizes these episodes repeatedly, doing so with immediacy, fluidity, and emotion; his use of language at once condenses the biblical tales, and makes them pointed for his contemporary audience.

Personifications of the Bible in *Piers Plowman*

Beyond directly quoting Scripture and dramatizing biblical episodes, Langland introduces two characters in the poem who probably represent the Bible itself. One is called "Scripture" and the other "Book." In Passus 10, Will is told by Wit and his wife Study to go to another couple: Clergy, who represents book learning, probably in Latin, or perhaps theological learning (Simpson, 1990, p. 106) or "revealed understanding" (Zeeman, 1999, p. 207), and his wife Scripture, in order "to know what Do Well is" (Zeeman, 1999, p. 219). Will greets Clergy and Scripture and tells them that he has been sent "to learn Do Well and Do Better and Do Best" (Zeeman, 1999, p. 231). Believing that Do Well means power and position, Will misunderstands what Clergy tries to teach him about following the Bible and being loving, so Scripture explains that riches do not help a person get to heaven unless she or he is good to the poor. Will resists this, argues with the couple about how to be saved, using his understanding of scripture against Scripture (!), and finally insults Clergy, saying that learning is useless and even dangerous. As Passus 11 begins, Scripture "scorns" Will and makes him weep and fall into a dream within a dream. After Will lives a dissipated life for a period of time within this inner dream, he sees Scripture again, who is preaching on the theme that "Many are called but few are chosen," and he is terrified that he will not be saved, but Scripture comforts him by reminding him that mercy is above all God's other works (Psalm 144:9; *Piers* 11.107–39a).

Scripture in this section seems to be the Bible, but not just its surface words: she tries through biblical words to make Will understand that learning is valuable, that good works are essential, and that God is merciful; in other words, she teaches love, the deep meaning of the words of the Bible: "And thus bilongeth to lovye, that leveth to be saved" (10.357): "And thus one who hopes to be saved needs to love." The episode makes it clear that if one is to learn from Scripture, one needs to be humble; Will's arrogant approach keeps him from learning what Wit and Study hoped he could learn from her.

The second personification that is usually interpreted as the Bible is called "Book,"[9] who enters the poem in the middle of the climactic section of the poem, Passus 18 (229–59). Will has been observing a dispute among four other personifications, Mercy and Peace, Truth and Righteousness. They are "characters" from Psalm 84:11, and they continue the argument about salvation that Will had begun with Scripture. All four women argue from texts of the Bible, but while Truth and Righteousness read without compassion for human beings, seeing only the literal surface meanings of the Bible, sometimes missing possible ambiguities of meaning,[10] Mercy and Peace understand figurative language, connotation, and word play, and read lovingly, with compassion for sinners (Peace, for instance, saying that the psalms are letters from Love). The four can never agree since they understand and use language so differently, and so a figure called Book appears, presumably to resolve their problems. Yet Book, too, fails to resolve the problem of human salvation. Most of his talk is a poetic profession of faith in Christ and his victory (231–56), but his last lines are a puzzling condemnation of the Jews who do not believe in Christ (257–9). Some scholars attribute this simply to anti-Semitism. However, Book here displays the same kind of error of understanding that Truth and her sister, Righteousness, have made when he says that Jesus will comfort all his kin but the Jews will be lost. Since the Jews *are* Jesus' kin, this makes little sense, and scholars have written many articles about these lines. But the fact that Book fails to solve the sisters' intellectual muddle may suggest that the words of the Bible by themselves cannot resolve the problems of its interpreters since people read so differently.

Something more is needed to make the Bible's message clear and to enable people to read it correctly, and that seems to be loving understanding shared through the community of the church.[11] Much of Will's (and Langland's) engagement with the Bible is filtered through the liturgy, the public prayer of the whole community. Bible readings during liturgy are set in a rich context of sacrament and symbol. For example, in the harrowing of hell episode that follows the conversation with Book, Christ explains salvation more clearly and more lovingly than Book does, as he defeats the devils on the night before Easter. His appearance as a light is based on the liturgy of the Easter vigil, when a large lighted paschal candle is brought into the dark church where the community is assembled. Christ's spirit of triumph and joy in the poem was familiar to the community through this liturgy, as well: the chanting of the "Exultet," the range of readings, the use of incense, music, and beautiful vestments, and the celebration of the sacraments of baptism, penance, and Eucharist on this night. In such a context, the Bible narrative of Christ's resurrection comes to life and can be deeply understood as part of the lives of the individual and community. In the liturgy, Book does not stand alone, but is embedded within action and symbol, so that together they reveal the truth of God. This may be the reason why Christ's words in the liturgical harrowing passage are so much clearer and kinder than Book's words a little earlier.

Fuelled in part by Langland's inclusion of figures like Scripture and Book in his text, recent scholarly study of the works of John Wyclif (1320–84) and his followers (the "Lollards" or "poor preachers")[12] has raised the question whether Langland was a Wycliffite. Scholars do not agree about this. Langland clearly shared with the Lollards (and with others, like faithful friars) admiration for simplicity of life and a conviction that the Bible was an essential rule of life for believers. Of course, the Bible was important to more than Lollards. It was the basic study of all students of theology and men hoping to become priests in the medieval university, the central text of monastic prayer and study, and the basis of good friars' preaching. Lay persons learned parts of it even if they could not read Latin, from prayers, services, sermons, paintings, stained glass, and other art works, and (if they were well-to-do) Books of Hours. Also, some of Langland's beliefs were significantly different from those that Wyclif developed: for example, his view of the Eucharist. Thus, although the early sixteenth-century reformers claimed Langland as a precursor of Protestantism, there is almost universal agreement today among scholars that he was a devout Catholic who, like Dante, satirized sinful and foolish church officials out of love for the church. In this passage, it would seem that neither Will nor the poet is particularly concerned, as the followers of Wyclif came to be, with individual reading of the Bible in the vernacular, since Will seems to understand and use Latin freely as the author clearly does. Here the emphasis seems to be not so much on the need for translation (although Langland translates many of his biblical quotations) but on how to read or hear Scripture in a profitable way.

The Influence of Biblical Forms and Styles

Besides personifying the Bible and quoting and retelling portions of it, Langland's work shows that he was deeply influenced by the forms and styles of the biblical books he knew. No one has been able to classify *Piers* satisfactorily as an example of a particular "genre" or type of literature, since it seems to contain many genres. Morton Bloomfield identified eight different genres or forms that help to shape it: "the allegorical dream narrative; the dialogue, *consolatio*, or debate; and the encyclopedic (or Menippean) satire ... the complaint, the commentary, and the sermon" (Bloomfield, 1961, p. 10), the autobiography, and the apocalypse. Examples of most of these forms are to be found in the Bible: dream visions are common in the prophetic and other books; dialogues or debates occur in some of the Wisdom Books; and pieces, at least, of complaint, commentary, sermon, satire, and autobiography are also used by biblical authors. Other scholars note other genres and forms, some of them biblical, in different parts of the poem.

Two biblical forms wider than genres, each of them including more than one genre within itself, seem to have had an especially telling effect on *Piers*: the apocalypse and the wisdom book. Apocalypses like the Bible's *Book of Revelations* are sometimes defined as "symbolic revelations of eschatological secrets." As Bloomfield (1961, p. 9) explains, "The classic Judeo-Christian apocalypse is cast in dream form, or consists of several dreams, is a revelation from some superior authority, is eschatologically oriented, and constitutes a criticism of, and warning for, contemporary society." He and others see *Piers* as an apocalypse, especially because apocalypses usually deal with "the end time," and the disastrous attack on the Church by Antecrist in *Piers Plowman* 19–20 is clearly based upon the terrifying destruction, battles, and plagues of the "end-time" in the Bible's *Book of Revelations* or *Apocalypse*. However, *Piers* is a unique apocalypse since it is also a quest, a search for a guide, and a personification allegory (Bloomfield, 1961, p. 9), and its "end-time" is not final. E. T. Donaldson (1985, pp. 75–7) notes, however, that both books have a sense of urgency, a mixing of the time sequence and of the literal and metaphorical levels of allegory.

The other form that seems to have influenced Langland particularly is that of the Books of Wisdom, five books from the Hebrew Scriptures, and parts of other biblical texts. They include Proverbs, Job, Ecclesiastes (Qoheleth), Sirach (Ecclesiasticus), the Wisdom of Solomon, some of the psalms, the Song of Songs, Tobias, Baruch, Daniel (which is also classified as an apocalypse), the parables of Jesus, the letter of James, parts of the letters of Paul, the prologue of the gospel of John, and 1 John 2:3–11; 4. *Piers* resembles both apocalypses and wisdom books in form and style by having more than one genre, abruptly switching points of view, using puns, riddles, and other kinds of word play, and in other ways being "supralogical,"[13] that is, not illogical, but going beyond logic, for example, with puns like "a justice sone" mentioned above, which says more than a purely logical statement could: Jesus is both child of justice and child of a judge, Only Son and radiant sun whose light is justice. It also shares a theme with wisdom books, the theme of wisdom, *hokmah* in Hebrew, *kynde knowyng* in certain passages of *Piers*. Within this wisdom tradition, *Piers* was particularly influenced by the gospel and first letter of John.

This is not to suggest that the Bible tells us the genre of the poem. But these two forms from the Bible help us see that the roughness of *Piers*, its difficulty, its inconsistencies, its refusal to follow a clear, simple narrative line, its constant surprises, its shifts from one genre to another without warning, may be not failures but deliberate choices made by a poet who knew this sort of literary composition from the Bible and perhaps believed that it would achieve his religious purposes better than clear, logical exposition or narration. One has only to face the difficulties of the *Book of Revelations/Apocalypse* or *Job* or the *Song of Songs* to see that he had such a literary tradition at hand.

Biblical Ideals

Langland's whole poem is biblical in its ideas as well as its language and narratives. He understood the Bible in an unusually profound way. It seems to have expressed his thoughts and feelings, to have answered his questions or sharpened them, and to have helped his characters make sense of life. Some of the key concepts of the poem are those of the Bible; the Middle English *treuthe* and *kynde knowyng* (in its fullest meaning of "wisdom"), for example, are translations of the Hebrew *emet* (truth) and *hokmah* (wisdom), words that express central biblical ideas.

Langland's urgent sense of the necessity of social justice in care for the poor and even in acceptance of groups marginal in his society, like Jews, heretics, prostitutes, and the poor themselves, is a new expression of the prophetic and New Testament emphases on justice and charity. In the Hebrew Scriptures, God's compassion demands human compassion toward the weakest in the community; for example, "You shall not molest a stranger or afflict him, for yourselves also were strangers in the land of Egypt. You shall not hurt a widow or orphan. ... If thou take of thy neighbor a garment in pledge thou shalt give it him again before sunset, For that same is the only thing wherewith he is covered ... and if he cry to me I will hear him, because I am compassionate" (Exodus 22:21–2, 26–7). In the New Testament, salvation depends upon compassion, for God identifies himself with the poorest: "As long as you did it to one of these my least brethren, you did it to me" (Matthew 25:40). *Piers* is directly countercultural in adopting this biblical ideal in a period (like ours) dominated by "work ethos" and "aggressive individualism" (Aers, 1988, pp. 34, 55, 59), when the poor were usually blamed and contemned for their poverty. Langland's poem is, as Christopher Dawson (1953, p. 250) wrote, "the first and almost the only utterance in literature of the cry of the poor":

> Wo in winter tyme for wantynge of clothes
> And in somer tyme selde soupe to the fulle. (14.178–9)

> Misery in winter time for lack of clothing
> And in summer time rarely enough to eat.

The poet warns the rich that wealth is a dangerous burden, only made safe when shared with the poor out of love. Most strikingly, the title character, symbolic of human goodness, of prophets, Christ, and Peter the apostle, is a plowman. Elizabeth Kirk has noted that making a plowman a moral leader was a "bold move" because it honored a poor laborer, and did so in a new way, since the Bible usually shows shepherds and fishermen, not plowmen, as models. This choice "seems to have fallen, so to speak, into a powder keg" (Kirk, 1988, p. 11) at the time of the Peasants' Revolt, when the poem was quoted by peasant leaders. Langland was not a revolutionary, but his vivid depiction of the misery of poverty and his unrelenting insistence on the dignity and rights of the poor (e.g. 9.80–1) was the startling, radical result of his deep understanding of the biblical ideal and of his conviction that God is love.

Just as the Bible introduces the Jewish and Christian communities to the nature of God through its laws (e.g. "Be holy because I am holy," Leviticus 11.44, 46), and through the experiences of Adam and Eve, Abraham and Sarah, Moses, the prophets, Jesus, and Mary, so *Piers Plowman*, through its naming of God (*Treuthe, Loue, Grace, Kynde*) and through its debates and events, seeks to illuminate the divine nature. Indeed, it could be argued that the whole of *Piers Plowman* is centered on one biblical quotation, the line from the first letter of John in the New Testament, 4:8, repeated at 4:16, "God is love." Holy Church's words, "I do it on *deus caritas*" ("I base it [what I say] on [the text] "God is love") could almost be Langland's words, as he seems to base the poem on that phrase and belief. Finally, as the Bible dramatizes and illuminates the relationships of humans with God through story and history, psalmic prayers, wise sayings, and the life of Jesus, so *Piers Plowman*, too, centers on relationships of God with humans as beloved creatures made in God's likeness, capable of living in love; children of God; "kin" of Jesus and therefore of God.

Conclusion

Questions and discoveries about the use of the Bible in *Piers Plowman* have been a persistent theme in the scholarship that has come to surround the poem in the past century and a half. Gradually the sources of most of the biblical quotations have been identified and their number agreed upon, so that the weight of biblical quotation in the poem has been revealed. New awareness of the uses of biblical commentaries and concordances in the later Middle Ages has made it clear that Langland had various possible means of accessing the biblical text. Understanding of verbal concordance, both mental and written, has thrown light on the way he remembered and used many of his quotations and the connections between them. Study of his use of some of his favorite texts, such as the Psalms, and comparisons of his genres and styles with those of certain biblical books have at least been begun, and work on the processes of reading in the Middle Ages has shed some light on ways of reading the Bible in *Piers*. Even the disputes about whether Latin or English structures the poem, and about whether or not the poem is to be read on several levels at once, have made Langland scholars much more aware of the depth and breadth of Langland's use of the Bible and of the importance of paying close attention to the Latin as well as the English parts of the poem. As one scholar writes of the awareness of the Bible in *Piers Plowman*, "it is as if the black and white print has broken into colour."[14] These areas will continue to be sites of further study and deeper understanding of the poem as a whole, the many ways in which the Hebrew Scriptures and the New Testament helped to form *Piers Plowman*, and how much the poem tells us about understandings of the Bible in fourteenth-century England.

Notes

1 There are three or four different manuscript versions of the poem, called A, B, C, and Z, though there is no general agreement on whether Z is indeed a separate version. B and C are each over 7,700 lines long; A and Z are much shorter. I am concerned here with the long versions, principally B. By a rough count (as no two editions of any version are identical), the poem contains about 422 Latin quotations, as well as some French quotations, and Hort estimated that "of these 422 quotations no less than 301 are of biblical origin" (Hort, 1936, pp. 43–4). Kuczynski shows that psalms are quoted most frequently in the middle of the poem and in passūs 5 and 18; there are few psalm quotations at the beginning and end of the poem. This suggests a designed structure of quotation, but no particular studies have been made of the placement of other biblical quotations, though one could do such a study using Alford's *Guide*. New Testament quotations below are from the Douai version.
2 But see Baldwin (2007, p. 5).
3 Alford (1977, pp. 80–99).
4 Muscatine, *Poetry* 107.
5 Davlin (1989, pp. 116–20).
6 Salter, *Fourteenth* 107.
7 Actually, however, Bible stories do not make up the bulk of Langland's use of the Bible. Helen Barr points out that "The most frequently quoted sections of the Bible ... [are] the Sermon on the Mount and the Psalms" (440).

8   Ong (1947, p. 323).

9   He may simply represent books, including the Bible, or the New Testament, or the "letter" or words of the New Testament; scholars do not agree.

10 For further discussion, see Davlin (1989, pp. 98ff) and Simpson (1990, p. 216).

11 As Simpson (1990, p. 219) points out, it is necessary both to "read" and to "see" and this happens to Will through the liturgy.

12 See, for example, Anne Hudson's (1978) edition of *Selections from English Wycliffite Writings* (Cambridge University Press, Cambridge) and Anna Baldwin's (2007) comments in *A Guidebook to Piers Plowman* (Palgrave, New York), especially pp. 15, 115, 138–9.

13 See Davlin (1988).

14 Blick, personal email, 18 August, 2006.

Bibliography

Some Helps, Editions, and Translations of Piers Plowman

There are four versions of *Piers Plowman*, presumably written at different times of Langland's life. The shortest is called the Z-Text. The A-Text has eleven chapters. The B- and C-Texts both have a Prologue and twenty chapters though they are numbered differently.

Attwater, Donald and Attwater, Rachel (1907) *The Book Concerning Piers the Plowman, Rendered into Modern English*. Everyman edn, J. M. Dent, London, 1957.

Baldwin, Anna (2007) *A Guidebook to Piers Plowman*. Palgrave, Basingstoke and New York.

Bennett, J. A. W., ed. (1972) *Piers Plowman: the Prologue and Passus I–VII of the B-Text*. Clarendon Medieval and Tudor Series. Clarendon Press, Oxford [Middle English, with notes].

Covella, Francis Dolores, SC, trans. (1992) *Piers Plowman: the A-Text. An Alliterative Verse Translation*. MRTS, Binghamton.

Donaldson, E. T. (1990) *Piers Plowman: an Alliterative Verse Translation*, ed. E. D. Kirk and J. H. Anderson. Norton, New York.

Economou, George (1996) *William Langland's Piers Plowman: the C-Version. A Verse Translation*. University of Pennsylvania, Philadelphia.

Fowler, David et al. (1992) *Piers Plowman: A-Text. Alliterative Verse Translation*. Pegasus.

Goodridge, J. F. (1959) *Piers the Ploughman, Translated into Modern English*. Penguin, Baltimore, 1966.

Kane, George et al. (1988–97) *The Three Versions* [text]. University of California Press.

Pearsall, Derek, ed. (1978) *Piers Plowman by William Langland: an edition of the C-Text*. Edward Arnold, London [Middle English, with notes].

The Penn Commentary on Piers Plowman (2006) 5 volumes. Pennsylvania University Press, Philadelphia.

Piers Plowman Electronic Archive (2000) T. Turville-Petre et al., eds. University of Michigan, Ann Arbor.

Rigg, A. G. and Brewer, C. eds (1983) *Piers Plowman: the Z Version*. Pontifical Institute, Toronto.

Robertson, Elizabeth and Shepherd, Stephen H. A., eds (2006) *Piers Plowman: A Norton Critical Edition*. Norton, New York [with Middle English text, translation, and critical essays].

Rose, Margaret (1996) "*The Ragged and the Rich: A Modern Interpretation of William Langland's Piers the Plowman*." Pickpockets, Hastings.

Salter, Elizabeth and Pearsall, Derek, eds (1969) *Piers Plowman*. York Medieval Texts. Northwestern University Press, Evanston [B: selections in Middle English, with notes].

Schmidt, A. V. C., ed. (1992) *Piers Plowman, a New Translation of the B-Text*. World's Classics. Oxford University Press, Oxford.

Schmidt, A. V. C., ed. (1995a) *The Vision of Piers Plowman*, 2nd edn. Everyman, Tuttle, VT [B-Text, Middle English, with notes].

Schmidt, A. V. C., ed. (1995b) *Parallel Text Edition of A, B, C, Z Versions*. Longmans, White Plains, NY.

Skeat, W. W., ed. (1886) *The Vision of William Concerning Piers the Plowman, in Three Parallel Texts*. 2 volumes. Oxford University Press, London [Middle English, with notes in volume 2].

Wells, Henry W. (1945) *The Vision of Piers Plowman newly rendered into Modern English*. Sheed and Ward, New York.

Williams, Margaret, R. S. C. J. (1971) *Piers the Plowman. William Langland*. Random House, New York [B: translation].

Wittig, Joseph, ed. (2005) *Concordance [to] Piers Plowman*. Continuum, London.

References and Further Readings on the Bible in Piers Plowman

Adams, Robert (1976) "Langland and the Liturgy Revisited," *Studies in Philology* 73, 266–84.

Adams, Robert (1988) "Langland's Theology." In *John Alford*, ed., *A Companion to Piers Plowman*. University of California Press, Berkeley, pp. 87–114.

Aers, David (1988) *Community, Gender, and Individual Identity*. Routledge and Kegan Paul, London.

Alford, John (1977) "The Role of the Quotations in Piers Plowman." *Speculum* 52, 80–99.

Alford, John (1992) *Piers Plowman: A Guide to the Quotations*. MARTS, Binghampton.

Allen, David G. (1989) "The Dismas *Distinctio* and the Forms of *Piers Plowman* B 10-13," *Yearbook of Langland Studies* 3, 31–48.

Allen, Judson Boyce (1982) *The Ethical Poetic of the Later Middle Ages*. University of Toronto Press, Toronto.

Allen, Judson Boyce (1984) "Langland's Reading and Writing: *Detractor* and the Pardon Passus," *Speculum* 59, 342–62.

Ames, Ruth M. (1970) *The Fulfillment of the Scriptures: Abraham, Moses, and Piers*. Northwestern University Press, Evanston, IL.

Anderson, J. J. (1995) "Some Aspects of Scriptural Quotation in Piers Plowman: Lady Holy Church," *Bulletin of the John Rylands University Library of Manchester* 77, 19–30.

Barney, Stephen (1973) "The Plowshare of the Tongue: the Progress of a Symbol from the Bible to Piers Plowman," *Medieval Studies* 35, 261–93.

Barr, Helen (1986) "The Use of Latin Quotations in *Piers Plowman* with Special Reference to Passus XVIII of the 'B' Text," *Notes and Queries* December, 440–8.

Bennett, J. A. W. (1982) *Poetry of the Passion*. Clarendon Press Oxford.

Besserman, Lawrence (1998) *Chaucer's Biblical Poetics*. University of Oklahoma Norman.

Bethurum, Dorothy, ed. (1960) *Critical Approaches to Medieval Literature*. Selected Papers from the English Institute 1958–9. Columbia University Press, New York.

Blick, Gail (2006) "*Langland's Use of Latin in certain Biblical Quotations and their Context in in Passus VI*," dissertation in progress, Cardiff University.

Bloomfield, Morton W. (1961) *Piers Plowman as a 14th-Century Apocalypse*. Rutgers University Press, New Brunswick, NJ.

Chadwick, Dorothy (1922) *Social Life in the Days of Piers Plowman*. Cambridge University Press, Cambridge.

Chamberlin, John (2000) *Medieval Arts Doctrines on Ambiguity and Their Place in Langland's Poetics*. McGill-Queens University Press, Montreal.

Coghill, Nevill (1944) "The Pardon of Piers Plowman," *Proceedings of the British Academy* 30, 303–57.

Coleman, Janet (1981) *Medieval Readers and Writers 1350–1400*. Columbia University Press, New York.

Davlin, Mary Clemente (1988) "*Piers Plowman* and the Books of Wisdom," *Yearbook of Langland Studies* 2, 23–33.

Davlin, Mary Clemente (1989) *A Game of Heuene*. Cambridge: Boydell and Brewer.

Davlin, Mary Clemente (1996) "*Piers Plowman* and the Gospel and First Epistle of John," *Yearbook of Langland Studies* 10, 89–127.

Davlin, Mary Clemente (2001) *The Place of God in Piers Plowman and Medieval Art*. Ashgate, Burlington, VT.

Davlin, Mary Clemente (2003) "*Piers Plowman* as Biblical Commentary," *Essays in Medieval Studies* 20, 85–94.

Dawson, Christopher (1953) *Medieval Essays*. Sheed and Ward, London.

Donaldson, E. T. (1985) "Apocalyptic Style in *Piers Plowman* B XIX–XX," *Leeds Studies in English* 16, 74–81.

Donaldson, E. T. (1966) "The Grammar of Book's Speech in *Piers Plowman*," in M. Brahmer, S. Helsztynski and J. Krzyzanowski, eds, *Studies in Language and Literature in Honour of Margaret Schlauch*. Panstwowe Wydawnictwo Naukowe, Warsaw, pp. 103–9.

Dunning, T. P. (1980) *Piers Plowman: An Interpretation of the A-Text*, 2nd edn. Clarendon Press, Oxford.

Dyas, Dee and Hughes, Esther (2003) *The Bible in Western Culture: The Student's Guide*. Routledge, New York.

Fowler, David C. (1961) *Piers the Plowman: Literary Relations of the A and B Texts*. University of Washington Press, Seattle.

Fowler, David C. (1984) *The Bible in Middle English Literature*. University of Washington Press, Seattle.

Frank, R. W. Jr (1957) *Piers Plowman and the Scheme of Salvation*. Yale Studies in English 136. Yale University Press, New Haven, CT.

Griffiths, Lavinia (1985) *Personification in Piers Plowman*. D. S. Brewer, Cambridge.

Halmari, Helena and Adams, R. (2002) "On the Grammar and Rhetoric of Language Mixing in Piers Plowman," *Neuphilologische Mitteilungen* 103, 33–49.

Harwood, Britton J. (1973) "'Clergye' and the Action of the Third Vision in Piers Plowman," *Modern Philology* 70, 279–90.

Hill, Thomas (2001) "The Problem of Synecdochic Flesh: *Piers Plowman* B 9.49–50," *Yearbook of Langland Studies* 15, 213–18.

Hoffman, Richard L. (1964) "The Burning of 'Boke' in Piers Plowman," *Modern Language Quarterly* 25, 57–65.

Hort, Greta (1936) *Piers Plowman and Contemporary Religious Thought*. Folcroft Press, Folcroft, PA (1969).

Jusserand, J. J. (1894) *Piers Plowman*. Russell and Russell, New York (1965).

Kaske, R. E. (1959) "The Speech of 'Book' in Piers Plowman," *Anglia* 77, 117–44.

Kaske, R. E. (1960) "Patristic Exegesis in the Criticism of Medieval Literature: the Defense." In Dorothy Bethurum, ed., *Critical Approaches to Medieval Literature*, pp. 27–60. N. Y.: Columbia University Press.

Kaske, R. E., Groos, A. M. and Twomey, W., eds (1988) *Medieval Christian Literary Imagery*. Toronto: University of Toronto Press.

Kean, P. M. (1969) "Justice, Kingship and the Good Life in the Second Part of *Piers Plowman*," in S. S. Hussey, ed., *Piers Plowman*. Methuen, London, pp. 143–79.

Kee, James M. (2004) "Northrop Frye and the Poetics in Biblical Hermeneutics," In Jeffrey Donaldson and Alan Mendelson, eds, *Frye and the Word*. University of Toronto, Toronto, pp. 251–64.

Kerby-Fulton, Kathryn (1999) "Piers Plowman," in David Wallace, ed., *Cambridge History of Medieval English Literature*. Cambridge University Press, Cambridge, pp. 513–38.

Kirk, Elizabeth (1988) "Langland's Plowman and the Recreation of Fourteenth-Century Religious Metaphor," *Yearbook of Langland Studies* 2, 1–22.

Kuczynski, Michael (1995) *Prophetic Song*. University of Pennsylvania Press, Philadelphia.

Libby, Bonnie L. (2004) "A Language of Incarnation: the Gospel Parables in Piers Plowman," *Dissertation Abstracts International A* 649.

Middleton, Anne (1986) "Piers Plowman," in A. E. Hartung, ed., *Manual of Writings in Middle English 1050–1500*. Connecticut Academy of Arts and Sciences, New Haven, pp. 2211–34, 2419–48.

Middleton, Anne (1988) "Introduction: the Critical Heritage," in John Alford, ed., *A Companion to Piers Plowman*. University of California Press, Berkeley, pp. 1–25.

Middleton, Anne (1992) "Langland's Lives: Reflections on the Medieval Religious and Literary Vocabulary," in J. M. Dean and C. K. Zacher, eds, *The Idea of Medieval Literature*. Newark, NJ, pp. 227–42.

Muscatine, Charles (1972) *Poetry and Crisis in the Age of Chaucer. Ward-Phillips Lectures in English Language and Literature*. University of Notre Dame Press, Notre Dame, IN.

Ong, Walter, S. J. (1947) "Wit and Mystery: A Revaluation in Mediaeval Latin Hymnody," *Speculum* 22, 310–41.

Pearsall, Derek (1979) "*Introduction*." Piers Plowman by William Langland: an Edition of the C-Text. University of California Press, Berkeley, pp. 9–24.

Pearsall, Derek (1990) *An Annotated Bibliography of Langland*. University of Michigan Press, Ann Arbor.

Rhodes, Jim (2001) *Poetry does Theology*. University of Notre Dame Press, Notre Dame.

Robertson, D. W. (1951) "The Doctrine of Charity in Medieval Literary Gardens," *Speculum* 26, 24–49.

Robertson, D. W. and Huppé, B. F. (1951) *Piers Plowman and Scriptural Tradition*. Octagon, New York (1969).

Rogers, William Elford (2002) *Interpretation in Piers Plowman*. Washington, DC.

Ryan, William M. (1968) *William Langland*. Twayne, New York.

Salter, Elizabeth (1962) *Piers Plowman: An Introduction*. Harvard University Press, Cambridge, MA.

Salter, Elizabeth (1968) "Medieval Poetry and the Figural View of Reality," *Proceedings of the British Academy* 54, 73–92.

Salter, Elizabeth (1983) *Fourteenth-Century English Poetry*. Clarendon Press, Oxford.

Salter, Elizabeth and Pearsall, Derek, eds (1969) *Piers Plowman*. Northwestern University Press, Evanston, IL.

Schleusener, Jay (1978) "*Langland's Inward Argument: the Poetic Intent of 'Piers Plowman' B. XV–XVIII*," unpublished dissertation, Columbia University.

Schmidt, A. V. C., ed. (1978) "Introduction," in *The Vision of Piers Plowman: a Complete Edition of the B-Text*. Dent, London, xi–xlvii.

Scott, Anne M. (2004) *Piers Plowman and the Poor*. Dublin: Four Courts.

Simpson, James (1990) *Piers Plowman: An Introduction to the B-Text*. Longman, London.

Simpson, James (2002) *Reform and Cultural Revolution: The Oxford Literary History*. Volume 2 1350–1547. Oxford University Press, Oxford.

Smith, Ben H. Jr (1966) *Traditional Imagery of Charity in Piers Plowman*. The Hague: Mouton.

Szittya, Penn (1986) *The Anti-fraternal Tradition in Medieval Literature*. Princeton University Press, Princeton, NJ.

Wurtele, Douglas (2003) "The Importance of the Psalms of David in William Langland's *The Vision of Piers Plowman*," *Cithara* 42(2), 15–24.

Zeeman, Nicolette (1999) " 'Studying' in the Middle Ages – and in Piers Plowman," *New Medieval Literature* 3, 185–212.

Zeeman, Nicolette (2006) *Piers Plowman and the Medieval Discourse of Desire*. Cambridge University Press, Cambridge.

CHAPTER 10
Geoffrey Chaucer

Christiania Whitehead

Lawrence Besserman concludes his recent survey of Chaucer's biblical poetics with the comment that Chaucer rendered greater quantities of biblical passages into English prose and verse than ever before.[1] How did Chaucer select and utilize these passages, and in what ways did he set them to work in relation to contemporary debates upon biblical authority, interpretation, and vernacular translation? To equip ourselves to address these questions more fully, and as a prelude to an informed engagement with Chaucer's texts, it will be helpful to turn initially to the late fourteenth-century biblical milieu in which Chaucer operated. As this examination of Chaucer in his contemporary context will show, he possessed an extensive, dexterous knowledge of the Bible, and was able to make it work for him in the most varied and flexible of ways. In the course of his poetic career, Chaucer toys with a whole spectrum of modes of biblical response: he generates figuration, typology, allegory, literal exposition, homily, and *exemplum*. On balance, however, it can be said that his interest in the effects of scriptural distortion and ironic usage outweighs his commitment to scriptural didacticism, and to reformist practices of plain quoting (such straight practices are too often shown to be tedious, simplistic, or uncompelling), and that it is the former, the comic, that sees him functioning at his most artistically successful. This chapter explores Chaucer's comedic/ironic biblical hermeneutics by tracing his relation to the reform movement. While it might seem that Chaucer's moments of plainer, non-ironic engagement with the Bible most closely resemble the calls of Wycliffite reform, in matter of fact, Chaucer's use of irony, at the level of plot, character, and word, arguably offers a more complex and committed response to central aspects of reformist concern, as we shall see by inspecting his poetry and tales.

Chaucer's Biblical Milieu

Insofar as Chaucer worked directly from the Bible, his principal source of reference would have been the Latin Vulgate Bible of St Jerome. This Vulgate Bible could well have been a vast, many-volumed compilation, separating out the different books of Scripture, and supplying each with an extensive textual apparatus of prefaces, glosses, and marginal commentaries (Chaucer's poetry makes clear that he was well aware of this overlay of commentary and interpretation).[2] Alternatively, it could have been a smaller, single-volume, "pocket" Vulgate, one of the many to originate from Paris and circulate widely from the early thirteenth century onward.[3] Whatever the style of manuscript that Chaucer made primary use of, it is likely that his reception of the Scriptures would also have been assisted by additional volumes of Latin *distinctiones* (alphabetized lists of biblical citations of specific objects or topics), gospel harmonies (weaving the narration of the four gospels into a single master-narrative), sermon handbooks and collections, and by "moralized" Bibles and lectionaries, in which passages from the Old and New Testaments were juxtaposed in such a way as to suggest a typological relationship between the two.

It appears unlikely that Chaucer made any direct use of the English translation of the Bible prepared by Wycliffite scholars during the last twenty years of the fourteenth century.[4] However, he would certainly have been familiar with much of the extensive vernacular "biblical literature" available to late fourteenth-century England:[5] metrical biblical paraphrases and versifications of biblical and salvation history, such as *Cursor Mundi* (c.1300); vernacular homily cycles, combining extracts from the Scriptures with extensive exposition; "lives" of Christ and religious lyrics, fleshing out the narrative of the gospels or isolating individual episodes for affective treatment; ambitious poetic renderings of biblical stories, such as *Cleanness* and *Patience*;[6] and the regional mystery play cycles. The extent and richness of this "biblical literature" attests to the variety of means by which the non-Latinate laity were able to gain access to some form or portion of scriptural narrative. Nonetheless, before the advent of the above-mentioned Wycliffite Bible there existed no full translation of the Scriptures, while the preparation and appearance of this translation were soon to lead to problems of their own.

Chaucer's biblical poetics were composed at a moment of unusual intensity and crisis within English church history. For, in addition to the usual debates being waged within the universities upon various theological *quaestiones* and niceties of biblical interpretation, new reformist voices were beginning to emerge. The writings of John Wyclif, the Oxford philosopher and theologian, dating between the mid-1360s and early 1380s, mounted a challenge to many central doctrines and practices of the medieval church. However, in this context, it is most relevant to take note of their observations upon the Bible. Wyclif and his followers believed that the text of sacred Scripture had become distorted and obscured over the centuries by the weight of the scholastic glosses and commentaries that surrounded it. They recommended a return to a "plain" text, stripped of gloss and interpretation, in which the hermeneutic function was relinquished wholesale into the hands of the devout reader. The Wycliffites (or Lollards) were also committed to vernacularization – to the principle of direct lay access to a vernacular Scripture. This should not be taken to suggest their endorsement of the many types of "biblical literature" listed above. On the contrary, they tended to disapprove of poetic treatments and paraphrases, preferring translation into a literal prose that remained free of imaginative embellishment. Third, the Wycliffites were committed to the principle of the *unity* of Holy Scripture. Scripture should be read whole, not piecemeal or in disconnected fragments. And finally, making their own radical contribution to the debate upon the locus of divine textual authority, they insisted that authority subsided solely in the unembellished Word of God – the Bible – rather than in the composite teachings of the established Church.

The positions assumed by the Wycliffites inevitably met with an adverse ecclesiastical reaction. Following condemnations of elements within Wyclif's teachings in 1382, 1388 and 1397, legislation of 1401 branded Lollardy a heresy punishable with death.[7] Subsequent to this, in specific reaction to Wycliffite advocacy of a vernacular Bible, Archbishop Arundel's *Constitutions* of 1408 issued a wholesale prohibition on the making or possession of vernacular Scriptures, unless by special license from a bishop.[8] It is well known that the *Constitutions* exercised a stifling effect upon many different kinds of early fifteenth-century religious literature; nonetheless, it is important to realize that in the period in which Chaucer was writing – even in the late period of the 1380s and 1390s, when most of his biblically imbued composition took place – the related questions of biblical translation and valid biblical interpretation could still be debated with comparative openness, *without* any necessary imputation of heresy.[9] As David Lawton puts it: "orthodoxy [remained] an unstable judgement before 1407."[10] Partially as a consequence of this brief climate of unstable orthodoxy, in which many reformist ideas circulated far beyond the immediate circle of Wyclif's followers attracting widespread sympathy and support, it is difficult to gauge Chaucer's exact relation to Lollardy. We know that for a time Chaucer and Wyclif shared a common patron in John of Gaunt; also, that Chaucer numbered many Lollard supporters among his most intimate friends. As we shall see, it would also seem to be the case that several of the pilgrims on Chaucer's Canterbury pilgrimage air views or exemplify vices consistent with Wycliffite positions.[11] Nonetheless, definite evidence of Chaucer's stance *vis-à-vis* Wycliffitism has so far proved impossible to come by, very possibly intentionally so. So, while the following discussion highlights Chaucer's affinity with reformist standpoints in certain of the ways in which he locates the Bible, it also comes preceded by the important qualification that, in the last twenty years of the fourteenth century, sympathy for reformist positions upon a variety of textual and institutional matters should not be taken as a necessary indication of fully fledged Wycliffite allegiance.

Serious and Non-ironic References to Scripture in Chaucer's Poetry

Reference to a lack of irony must seem an odd way to begin a close examination of Chaucer's usages of Scripture. But since so much of Chaucer's biblical *oeuvre* is governed by varying degrees of satire or irony, it makes sense to start with the not unimportant instances where Chaucer indubitably employs Scripture to orthodox effect: to instruct, to induce repentence, or to heighten reverence or pathos.

It would appear that Chaucer willingly aligns himself with *both* traditional and more reformist exegeses of Scripture to achieve the effects that he desires in these instances. To explain more fully, traditional exegesis of Scripture tended to prioritize the *figural* interpretation of Scripture: its *allegorical* or *typological* message, over and above the *literal* meaning on the page. Through the thirteenth and fourteenth centuries, this priority gradually lost momentum, and exegetical emphasis was shifted toward a preference for the literal sense, culminating in due course in Wyclif's ringing demands for a solely *literalistic* understanding of Scripture.[12] Nonetheless, figuration did not vacate the scene entirely. It remains implicit in the juxtaposition of Old and New Testament passages in the lectionary, implying the first as a prefiguration of the second, and continues to determine the arc of salvation history inscribed by the great mystery cycles. In addition, biblical quotations used in accordance with their figural meaning adorn many of the extravagently mannered religious lyrics composed in praise of Mary, Queen of Heaven, from the eleventh to the fifteenth centuries. It is this tradition of figural embellishment that seems primarily to underpin Chaucer's *ABC*, an early abecedarian poem in praise of the Virgin,[13] in which Mary is successively compared to a haven of refuge, the burning bush of Exodus, a devout temple for God's indwelling, and a well of mercy, cleansing sinners from their sin.[14] A number of these figural epithets reappear in the Marian *Prologues* to the *Prioress's* and *Second Nun's Tales*,[15] where, as though impressed by the institutional hermeneutic mode they represent, Chaucer carries a loose imaginative thread of typological reference over into several of the religious tales themselves, implying the young boy murdered by the Jews in the *Prioress's Tale* as a second Christ-child, labeling his bereft mother a "newe Rachel,"[16] and validating the religious worth of Custance's travails at sea, in the *Man of Law's Tale*, by locating them as post-figurations of the travails of Daniel in the lions' den, Jonah in the whale's belly, and David confronting Goliath.[17]

In terms of the tales themselves, these figurations seem relatively straight-faced, designed either to ramp up emotionalism (in the case of the *Prioress's Tale*), or to help cultivate an atmosphere of miraculous grandeur and awe. The only hint of dubiety – if we choose to allow this method of interpretation – arises from the hypocrisy and worldliness of both tale-tellers,[18] giving us the option of locating scriptural figural embellishment as a potentially *insincere* mode of narrative hyperbole.

The serious use of figuration to support reverential religious narrative is, as we shall see later, heavily outnumbered by ironic instances elsewhere in Chaucer's poetry, in which the main effect of the figural relation is not support but incongruity. Given this inexorable pull toward the ironic (and the difficulty of sustaining seriousness even within the religious tales without certain counterthrusts – the questionable caliber of the narratorial voices), it is tempting to conclude that Chaucer judged the whole enterprise of traditional figural exegesis as strained and unconvincing. As a consequence of this, one might argue that he resolved to make trial of the hermeneutic practices of the reformers, turning to an approach to Scripture that eschewed poetry for prose, fanciful tale-telling for non-fictive didacticism, and figural hyperbole for an unmitigatedly *literal* exposition of the Word.

The *Parson's Tale* is Chaucer's most extended exercise in biblically rich writing along these lines, opening, in its *Prologue*, with the Parson's famous avowal, validated in part by St Paul himself, to reject fiction, rhyme, and all forms of "glossed" exposition:

> Thou getest fable noon ytoold for me,
> For Paul, that writeth unto Thymothee,
> Repreveth hem that weyven soothfastnesse,
> And tellen fables and swich wrecchednesse ...

> I kan nat geeste "rum, ram, ruf," by lettre,
> Ne, God woot, rym holde I but litel bettre;
> And therfore, if yow list – I wol nat glose –
> I wol yow telle a myrie tale in prose. (ParsT X.31–4, 45–6)

Insofar as the *Tale* then continues with the Parson's translations of "hundreds of biblical verses … from Latin into English for [his listening] lay audience,"[19] accompanied by their literal exposition, it would seem that it self-consciously embodies many of the pastoral and hermeneutic principles of Wyclif and his followers. Indeed, the Host himself jocularly encourages that association: "'I smelle a Lollere in the wynd,' quod he" (MLEpi II.1173). Nonetheless, these associations need to be weighed carefully against the orthodoxy and conventionality of the Tale's subject matter: a long-winded exposition of the "parts" of penance, drawn from thirteenth-century Dominican sources,[20] its cautious avoidance of areas of contemporary controversy,[21] and the Parson's initial, twice-repeated determination to subject his teaching to the "correccioun / Of clerkes" (ParsT X.56–7), that is, to the authority of the Church.

Extensive vernacular translations from Scripture in a pedagogic prose milieu materialize again in Chaucer's *Tale of Melibee*, in which Dame Prudence draws upon many scores of "proof-texts" from the Bible (interspersed with classical and patristic *auctoritee*) to validate her advice to Melibee *vis-à-vis* his reaction to his political enemies: "as seith Seint Peter in his Epistles … For Salomon seith … therfore seith Seint Jame in his Epistle" (Mel VII.1500, 1511, 1516). *Melibee's* affinity with reformist thought is further extended by its pedagogical gendering. Dame Prudence is the unexceptional product of a textual tradition of feminized personifications of authority that stretches back to Boethius's Philosophy. Nonetheless, she is returned to centerstage,[22] and positioned as an incontestable expositor of vernacular Scripture, at precisely the moment in the late 1380s and early 1390s when Wycliffite reformers were exploring the possibility that a woman might defensibly proclaim and expound the Bible.[23]

The *Parson's Tale* and *Melibee* represent Chaucer's closest overt engagements with the new attitudes to Scripture taking hold in the 1380s and 1390s. But while they may succeed in the extent of their scriptural vernacularity and literal exposition, they fare far less well when judged against the fictive shapeliness and comic verve of the majority of the other Tales. We need to be careful here to distinguish between modern literary judgments and those of Chaucer's contemporaries and immediate predecessors. In the fifteenth century, *Melibee* was the second most independently copied tale of the entire *Canterbury* corpus. Helen Cooper writes that "Modern taste ranks the literary dazzle and the wit of the Nun's Priest above the scholastic moralizing of the Parson. To Chaucer, both were valid."[24] Nonetheless, there is a certain joylessness about both treatises. Even in their own period, when set against the irreverent pyrotechnics of the *Miller's Tale* or the *Merchant's Tale*, they seem to show the dogged amassing of biblical authority to didactic ends to be a dull business. Purely by implication and juxtaposition, their rejection of poetry and fable in favour of (particularly in the case of the Parson's sermon) an unremitting biblicalism, albeit an openly understandable one, does *not* ultimately serve to support the reform movement. Reformist textual practices are made to appear intelligible certainly, but simultaneously nigh-on unreadable. It remains to be seen to what extent Chaucer can succeed in revitalizing scriptural reference in a succession of markedly less illustrious textual settings that "sownen [mainly] into synne" (Ret X.1085).

Comic and Ironic References to Scripture in Chaucer's Poetry

By far the greater number of scriptural references in Chaucer's poetry are made to connect with their fictive referents in a way that creates a primary relationship of *dissimilarity* or *irony*. Chaucer delights in bringing Scripture to bear in settings that cause us to reflect upon the *distance* between the events described and their nominal co-relative within the Bible. So, for example, in the *Miller's Tale*, when the lecherous clerk, Nicholas, sings *Angelus ad virginem*,[25] we are *entertained* by the distance between Gabriel's interaction with Mary and Nicholas's bawdy tryst with Alison. Mary's carpenter husband's anxieties about her infidelity are benignly reassured in the gospel narrative; Alison's carpenter husband has far more reason to fear the prospect of cuckolding. In addition to allusions to the Holy Family, the specter of the popular Old Testament narrative of Noah's Flood also underpins much of the story. John the carpenter constructs a series of homely vessels to save his household from drowning, comically ignorant of God's promise never to send a second flood. To cement the association, his wayward young wife intentionally brings to mind the recalcitrant Mrs Noah of the mystery plays.[26]

The effect of these biblical references has never been altogether easy to determine. On the one hand, scriptural event and the bourgeois contemporary are connected and then fractured from one another in a way that signals their absolute *dissimilarity* – arguably making a judgment upon the contemporary bourgeois mores. Yet, inversely, it could equally be said that the countercultural exuberance of the tale more than holds its own against these divine shadows. In this reading, these references then force a reassessment of the relevance of the ideal in the light of the powerful energies of the real. It would certainly not be out of keeping with what we know of Chaucer for him to wish to lead us in this primarily experiential direction.

References to Scripture premised upon this "incongruous congruence"[27] proliferate throughout the *Tales*, and, while the optional interpretations sketched above arguably resonate beyond the immediate environment of the *Miller's Tale*, it needs also to be said that the effect of each incongruous connection remains, to some extent, individual to the tale that produces it. While lack of space precludes a thorough investigation of each and every comically dissimilar or fissured link to Scripture, it is worth noting the playful and satirical allusions to the Eden story and Fall of Man in the *Nun's Priest's Tale* (Adam and Eve reborn as chickens) and the *Merchant's Tale* (where May plays a mercenary Eve to January's elderly and lascivious Adam); to Pentecost at the conclusion of the *Summoner's Tale* (in which twelve friars congregate to receive a blast of bad air); and to the *mulier fortis* of Proverbs 31:10–31 in the Wife of Bath's *Prologue* and *Shipman's Tale* (in which, in both cases, the wives' thrift and facility for business are utilized to trick rather than to advance their husbands).[28] Looking further afield, a little unusually among the early dream-vision poems, Chaucer's *House of Fame* employs a number of oblique biblical references to comedic ends, relating Chaucer's enforced journey sky-wards in search of "tydynges ... of love" (HF 1888–9) to the Old Testament assumptions of Enoch and Elijah ("I neyther am Ennok, ne Elye": HF 588), and parodically linking the enthroned figure of Fame to the many-feathered, many-eyed beasts surrounding the throne of final judgment in Revelation:

> ... as feele eyen hadde she
> As fetheres upon foules be,
> Or weren on the bestes foure
> That Goddis trone gunne honoure,
> As John writ in th'Apocalips. (HF 1381–5)

In both instances, the effect of these links is *contrastive*. The heaven Chaucer is being brought toward is only a land of caprice, stuffed full with very earth-bound jockeyings for favor. Similarily, Fame soon transpires to be an intrinsically partial, unreliable judge of conduct. Her wild variations and whimsy in allocating good or bad fame make us long for a veracious judgment that "sees to the heart" – some firm ground within the poem upon which to set our step. The reference to the throne of Revelation dangles that veracity of judgment then withdraws it cruelly. And while it may bring satisfaction to know that the possibility of true judgment exists somewhere, beyond the boundaries of the poem, it is equivalently unsettling to find that it plays no part in the allegorical cosmos of fame and favoritism that Chaucer, and by implication, we, inhabit.

Misuses of Scripture by Chaucerian Characters: (i) Unwitting Misuses

So far we have considered instances in Chaucer's *oeuvre* in which ironic links with scriptural event can be accredited directly to the design of the author. However, there is also a sizable body of biblicalism that occurs *indirectly*, in which inept or inappropriate scriptural reference is voiced through one or other of the tale-tellers or characters *within* a tale. In such cases, the irony is generally targeted primarily toward the speaking voice. The incongruity of the relation between narrative and scriptural event is shown to emerge from the poor or flawed understanding of the *character* who posits the link, rather than necessarily critiquing the event itself.

Chaucer's characters cite Scripture wrongly for a number of reasons. First, they may fail in their ability to apprehend the meaning of Scripture truly and apply it to their lives out of a kind of ignorance about themselves and their true motivations that Chaucer most commonly represents as blindness. January, in the *Merchant's Tale*, whose ultimate literal blindness only encapsulates his ongoing symbolic blindness about his masculine capacity and motivations for marriage, and Chanticleer, in the *Nun's Priest's Tale*, who fatally shuts his eyes when he should see, blinded by vanity and pride, offer relevant examples. January cites a succession of laudable women from the Old Testament – Rebecca, Judith, Abigail, and Esther[29] – in the course of his rumi-nations about the blessings of a wife, entirely failing to realize that the laudable conduct of these women generally serves to benefit their sons or their Israelite people with very unpleasant consequences for their husbands. Later, shortly before the denouement of the tale, January invites May into his enclosed garden with words drawn from the Song of Songs:

> Rys up, my wyf, my love, my lady free!
> The turtles voys is herd, my dowve sweete;
> The wynter is goon with alle his reynes weete.
> Com forth now, with thyne eyen columbyn! (MerT IV.2138–41)

Once again he fails to see the inapplicability of this divine love-song of reciprocal eroticism, commonally glossed in the Middle Ages as an expression of the love between Christ and his Church, to the lusts and manipulations of his own marriage. Chanticleer cites the Old Testament narratives of Daniel and Joseph as proof of the prophetic capacity of dreams with avian pomposity, following his own bad dream of a yellow-red animal with black-tipped ears and tail, and glowing eyes.[30] The reference is quite in order. The *exempla* of Daniel and Joseph *do* support the prophetic capacity of dreams. However, the comedy in this instance lies in Chanticleer's complete inability to move from the rhetorical flourish to any practical application to his own life. Chanticleer becomes so entranced with his talent for embellished speech and for the mesmerizing citation of textual authority that he entirely loses sight of the *meaning* of what he says, in particular of what these proofs from Scripture may mean *for him*. As a result, the fox takes him wholly unawares, inviting him to literalize his blind vanity by shutting his eyes to sing. Insofar as the tale comments on biblical usage, it would seem to suggest that this usage has become dangerously *inert*. Scriptural examples function as rhetorical tools to dress up masterful speech; their speakers learn nothing serviceable from them. It remains to be seen whether it will be more appropriate to explain January's and Chanticleer's hermeneutic shortcomings by reference to the institutional position on biblical exposition – that lay readers lack the clerical learning and authorization necessary to deploy Scripture correctly[31] – or whether both simply fall short of the Wycliffite perception that, lay or religious, "a proper understanding of the Bible depends upon the virtue of the interpreter."[32]

Misuses of Scripture by Chaucerian Characters: (ii) Knowing Clerical Misuses

We have already surveyed the biblical discourse of the Parson, in which transparently "correct" biblical expositions, clerical authorization, and personal virtue all intersect. However, by far the greater number of Chaucer's ecclesiastical pilgrims – in particular, his Latinate male clergy, the only ones unquestionably authorized to expound Scripture – are represented as abusers of the *verbum Dei*, commandeering it to support manifestly corrupt ends. The Pardoner and Friar John in the *Summoner's Tale* are the most developed examples of this abusive approach, although the Friar himself, the Monk, and the Summoner in the *Friar's Tale* all deliver further variations upon this underlying idea.

The *Pardoner's Tale* contains many of the key elements of a medieval sermon – an initial text from Scripture: *Radix malorum est Cupiditas* (1 Timothy 6:10); a series of admonitions against the "tavern" vices of drunkeness, gluttony, gambling, and swearing; and an *exemplum* – the well known fable of the three rioters who set out to murder Death – showing the evils of the love of money in action.[33] Scripture abounds throughout the narrative. The initial admonitions amass citation after citation to prove their point. Lot slept with his daughters and committed incest because he was drunk. Herod ordered the execution of John the Baptist when drunk. Adam and Eve were expelled from the Garden of Eden as a result of their gluttony. Jeremiah the prophet ordained that we should swear only in truth, judgment, and righteousness.[34]

Critics have found it hard to gauge the intended caliber of these citations. At first glance, many seem patently reductive, willfully isolated from their broader textual context simply to prove a point. In the original context, for example, Lot's daughters made their father drunk and then slept with him to preserve the family line; the act was not regarded as a vice.[35] Yet, on closer inspection, it emerges that many of these examples, used to an identical purpose, derive from Jerome's *Adversus Jovinianum* and Pope Innocent III's *De miseria condicionis humane*, seminal texts for Chaucer and within the canon of medieval biblical exegesis. So, perhaps the *Tale* is designed to point up the questionable quality of the interpretation in many of these intermediary commentaries and patristic treatises. That may well be true, but it is disconcerting to learn in addition that several of the examples given above are reused, to the same end, in the relevant sections of the *Parson's Tale*.[36] If we continue to maintain that Chaucer means us to take the Parson seriously as an exemplary figure (which I think we must do), then we must conclude that it is not the scriptural examples themselves that are at fault but the integrity of the voice that cites them. The Pardoner patently fails to practice what he preaches; he gorges, drinks, and swears idly (" 'It shal be doon,' quod he, 'by Seint Ronyon! / But first,' quod he, 'heere at this alestake / I wol bothe drynke and eten of a cake' ": PardIntr VI.319–22), and tells a powerful *exemplum* on the destructiveness of avarice to the explicit end of wheedling money from a credulous congregation. We are helped by the extravagance and unnatural candor of his self-revelation, in his *Prologue* to the tale. This particular wolf in sheep's clothing is not at all hard to see through. Nonetheless, despite the clarity with which the *Tale* exposes the practices of hypocrisy, it is less easy to be sure of its stance with regard to contemporary debates upon valid and invalid biblical interpretation. Does the *Pardoner's Tale* defend the institutional position, aligning interpretative validity with clerical office, by showing that a bad cleric can still tell a spiritually useful tale? Or, in line with reformist attitudes, is the didacticism of the tale irrevocably compromised by the hypocrisy of the teller? The answer would seem to lie in the respective responses of the recipients. The *Pardoner's Tale* and the *Parson's Tale* both make significant use of identical biblical materials. However, while Chaucer, the author, reacts to the *Parson's Tale* with a confession of textual sin (the effect of the Parson's teachings on penance even extends, apparently, to his author), at the close of the *Pardoner's Tale*, the pilgrims react not to the message of the *Tale* (they are wholly silent on *that* front), but to the charlatanism of its teller, confronting his vicious motivations with equiva-

lently shocking language: "thy coillons ... shul be shryned in an hogges toord!" (PardT
VI.952, 955). Reformist emphasis upon the necessary virtue of the expositor seems
pre-eminent.

Many similar themes and concerns reappear in the *Summoner's Tale*, in which a
hypocritical friar uses his homiletic and expository offices to attempt to extort money
from a bedridden peasant. Once again, the dichotomy between practice and preaching
is rendered in black and white. Friar John preaches fasting and abstinence, and counsels against the sin of ire, offering an exemplary tale and numerous tags from Scripture.[37] He simultaneously calls for capon, soft bread, and roast pork, and gives way to
fury after receiving a fart from his disaffected victim. Many of his quotations from
Scripture are no more questionable, removed from the context of his extortionary
intent, than the quotations upon gluttony and ire within the *Parson's Tale*, and again,
parallels can be found. Nevertheless, similar to the *Pardoner's Tale*, several of the friar's
quotations seem to have been culled not first-hand from Scripture (the Parson's predominant method[38]), but second-hand, from Jerome's *Adversus Jovinianum*, where they
are already being pressed into service to support a specific moral agenda.[39] Jovinianus
even receives an explicit mention within the friar's discourse; Friar John is obviously
well acquainted with this particular supplementary text.[40]

The prominence of Jovinianus, and by implication St Jerome, within the Friar's
private reading, points toward a further theme, explored more fully here than in the
Pardoner's Tale. Friar John prefers the *gloss* to the letter of Scripture – knows it better
indeed, because, so he tells us, it supplies him with validations missing from the plain
biblical text:

> "But herkne now, Thomas, what I shal seyn.
> I ne have no text of it, as I suppose,
> But I shal fynde it in a maner glose,
> That specially oure sweete Lord Jhesus
> Spak this by freres, whan he seyde thus:
> 'Blessed be they that povere in spirit been.'" (SumT III.1918–23)

When the Friar preaches in church, he refers to the gloss rather than to the Scriptures
themselves. The gloss is easier, he says. The letter kills, but the spirit (or gloss) gives
life.[41] Judging by what he uses the gloss primarily to achieve – money and goods for his
friary, what abides is the impression that the gloss is *morally* easier; certainly, more
easily malleable.

The Friar's willful preference for biblical glosses and his easy fashioning of them to
support his campaign of avarice conforms to the pejorative treatment of glossing elsewhere in the *Canterbury Tales* (we will return to this subject in our discussion of the
Wife of Bath).[42] More broadly, his characterization would seem to engage with contemporary debates on valid and invalid styles of biblical interpretation, and to originate in
positions very similar to those outlined within Wycliffitism – that biblical glosses should
be treated with suspicion, the Scriptures should stand alone; that the *verbum Dei* should
be made directly available to the congregation, not withheld in favor of the gloss; that
the friars were particularly reprehensible for, among other things, their penchant for

manipulative readings of Scripture. Again, it is awkward to try and pin Chaucer down to a Wycliffite allegiance; at the time at which he was writing, these ideas had not yet become isolated and rigidly categorized; they were part of a wider currency of reformist thinking. It is also harder than in the *Pardoner's Tale* to obtain an entirely stable vantage-point from which to evaluate this performance of antifraternalism. We need to bear in mind that the narrative voice is the Summoner's, and that he tells the tale that he does to "quit" the Friar's preceding Tale of a corrupt summoner. Antifraternalism is performed by a speaker who has his own axe to grind. It is *one* way of responding to the prevalence of mendicancy and to the expository and homiletic strategies of the friars, but not necessarily the *only* way, nor is it certainly Chaucer's way.

Misuses of Scripture by Chaucerian Characters: (iii) Knowing Female Misuses

As if in response to the gathering sense that, if most clerical readings of Scripture seem irrevocably corrupt then perhaps we are indeed intended to support the right of the laity and of laywomen to read and interpret Scripture, Chaucer next presents us with the Wife of Bath. But what a pugnacious and ambivalent representative of lay female biblical reading practice she turns out to be! For the Wife of Bath confronts Scripture head-on. In order to vindicate her own five marriages, she spends the first two hundred or so lines of her Prologue disputing St Paul's evaluations of marriage, virginity, and remarriage[43] by measuring them against other, less hardline, passages from the Bible ("God bad us for to wexe and multiplye": WBPro III.28;[44] "I woot wel Abraham was an hooly man, / And Jacob eek ... And ech of hem hadde wyves mo than two": WBPro III.55–8). In the same vein, she raises the key gospel episodes used exegetically to prove the immorality of remarriage – the wedding at Cana, Christ's meeting with the Samaritan woman at the well – and simply asserts that their meaning is unclear: "What that he mente therby, I kan nat seyn" (WBPro III.20).

An older generation of critics has taken considerable delight in decrying the partiality of the Wife of Bath's scriptural reading in her Prologue. She cites one half of a verse and not the other; she extracts verses from their scriptural context; she willfully ignores the fact that Old Testament marital practice was superseded by the teachings of Christ and of Paul. D. W. Robertson Jr attacks her as a "carnal" exegete, who reads according to the letter but not the spirit of the text.[45] These criticisms cannot be discounted. Indeed, in many ways, they may well tally closely with contemporary reactions to the Prologue. In the face of Wycliffite assertions that women should have the right to read and even expound Scripture, the Wife of Bath's outrageous facility to use this to validate multiple marriage and sexual voracity would seem to support the viewpoint of the antireformist churchmen who declared that female access to Scripture invariably resulted in profound hermeneutic distortion.[46]

Nonetheless, as is so often the case with Chaucer, it proves untenable to consider this the whole story. Certain recent criticism has sought to recuperate the Wife of Bath's exegetical integrity by emphasizing the extent to which the Wife takes issue, not with Paul, but with St Jerome, in these opening paragraphs of her Prologue.[47] Who was it who interpreted Christ's single appearance at the wedding in Cana as an indication that he only wished Christians to be given in marriage once? St Jerome, in his *Adversus Jovinianum*.[48] The Wife dismisses the illustration without comment. Who wrote that the genitalia were purely created for the expulsion of urine and for purposes of gender differentiation? St Jerome.[49] The Wife begs to differ, based on her own experience: "ese of engendrure" (WBPro III.127–8) also plays its part. The *Adversus Jovinianum* rematerializes again in the closing pages of the Wife's Prologue – one of the texts transcribed to make up Jankyn's book of "wikked wyves," written, the Wife sarcastically remarks, by aged churchmen who have lost their sexual capacity (WBPro III.707–10). The treatise's repeated reappearance as a butt for contestation, both here and in the *Summoner's Tale* (see above), suggests that, for Chaucer, the *Adversus Jovinianum* sums up all that is most prejudiced about patristic scriptural exposition and its use in later biblical glossation (on both occasions when the Wife talks about men "glosen up and doun," she is referring to interpretations from the *Adversus Jovinianum*[50]). If we allow that the Wife takes St Jerome as her prime target, rather than the Bible per se, we can then explain the partiality of her citations of Scripture by locating them as perhaps the only possible response to the equivalent partiality of the *Adversus Jovinianum*. Jerome distorts Scripture to serve his antifeminist, antimatrimonial agenda; the Wife of Bath is left with no alternative but to quote back in an equivalently skewed manner to support her oppositional campaign for sex and remarriage. As Robert Longsworth usefully puts it: "she has merely used Jerome as Jerome has used St Paul."[51] What this effectively lays bare (and what a radical exposure it is) is the difficulty of reaching any conclusion whatsoever about the *true* meaning of Scripture, amidst the exchange of contestive interpretations. In addition, it also raises the question: what possible criteria can we bring to bear to judge that St Jerome's interpretation is *worth more* in any sense than the Scripture reading of the Wife of Bath? That question is left disarmingly wide open for the reader, for Chaucer gives us no props upon which to construct any definite answer within the text as it stands.

So, we have moved from a position in which the Wife of Bath demonstrates the validity of ecclesial fear about female access to Scripture, to a position in which she seems to show considerable sympathy for the reformist viewpoint – in particular, in her concern about the distorting effect of glosses in mediating Scripture, and in her exposé of the dubious prominence accorded patristic exegetes, such as Jerome. The authority of this concern needs to be weighed with reference to other more undesirable side-effects of the Wife of Bath's penchant for self-revelation – her promiscuity, mercenariness, and monstrous will to domination. It also needs to be viewed alongside other female expositions of Scripture within the *Tales*: Prudence's scriptural citations, scrupulously orthodox but dulled by her allegorical stature, and the Second Nun's – like the Prioress, the Second Nun confirms her gendered religious orthodoxy by giving nigh-on *no* direct exposition of Scripture. Instead, she offers up a saint's legend, uncontroversial devotional reading for nuns, confining her not-inconsiderable hermeneutic powers to a linguistic analysis of the symbolic etymology of St Cecilia's name. Within her legend, Cecilia preaches and teaches – within the home (SNT VIII.342–3, 538–9) – but shows no first-hand engagement with Scripture. Instead, the presence of Scripture within the tale is confined to a visionary visitation from St Paul bearing a "book with

lettre of gold in honde" (SNT VIII.202). This book, the Bible, proves seminal in converting Cecilia's husband, Valerian – St Paul reads from Ephesians, Valerian responds with
a statement of Christian allegiance – but interestingly, in an otherwise predominantly
female text, this is a solely *male* transaction, overseen only by Pope Urban. The implication seems clear. In the world of Chaucer's religious women, the Bible is sky-borne and
gold and univocal, and largely out of reach. Men fine-tune their Christianity by engaging with it, women must make do (although in fact, the effects are more powerful) with
the enabling presence of guardian angels, or, in the case of the *Prioress's Tale*, with the
divine protection of Mary.

A similar rationale regarding scriptural absence underpins the *Prioress's Tale*. Neither
the Prioress in her *Prologue* nor the infant Christian protagonist in her story shows any
real first-hand knowledge of Scripture, nor, in the orthodox world that they inhabit, is
it suitable that they should. Instead, their untutored devotions, expressed via rote-
learned liturgical song, facilitate the miracle that elevates them to become objects of
reverence for the monastic *literatti*: "whan this abbot hadde this wonder seyn ... gruf
he fil al plat upon the grounde, / And stille he lay as he had ben ybounde. / The covent
eek lay on the pavement / Wepynge" (PrT VII.673, 675–8).[52] This apparent corrective
to normative hierarchies of erudition cuts both ways. On the one hand, the tale shows
the untutored devotion of the female and innocent ascending far above the miriad
scriptural engagements of the local monastery – the monks presumably read the
Vulgate Bible, draw from its glosses to write homilies, perhaps even generate their own
commentaries. Yet, on the other, the tale constructs a world of supernatural ratification
in which there is simply *no need* for women to gain access to the *verbum Dei*. Purity of
heart and intention are all that it takes. For all its surface play with the empowerment
of the meek, deep down, the tale actually promulgates something very traditional:
women and children are sanctified through their devout unlearnedness and *innocence*
of Scripture.

These contrasting tales by religious women, implying the irrelevance of Scripture to
female spirituality, are a far cry from the spectacular awkwardness and obfuscation of
the Wife of Bath's contentions with Scripture. Yet, despite their clarity of rendition, the
juxtaposition does not necessarily work in their favor. Chaucer uses these tales to show
the simplified, heightened, unrealistic, narrative landscape that results from the reiteration of traditional ideas about gendered spirituality. He uses the Wife of Bath's *Prologue*
to show how inchoate is the alternative. The Wife of Bath stumbles over herself; she
digresses; she trips herself up as often as she trips up her clerical detractors. But all
because she is doing something new and unimaginable. A woman is expounding Scripture. Unlike the closed texts of the religious women's tales, this is a discourse that stands
wide open to the contemporary world of hermeneutic debate. And the greatest testament to that openness is the buzz that it engenders among the pilgrims. Her activities
leave a trail. Everyone reacts to her. Nearly every tale is formed, in some way, in reaction to what she stands for.

The most implicitly menacing of those reactions, and the most relevant for our
purpose, is that of the Merchant. He takes the Wife of Bath's contestations of scriptural
auctoritee, her skill in exposition, and her frustration with clerical antifeminism, and
puts them wholesale in the mouth of Proserpina:

> What rekketh me of youre auctoritees?
> I woot wel that this Jew, this Salomon,
> Foond of us wommen fooles many oon ...
> Though that he seyde he foond no good womman,[53]
> I prey yow take the sentence of the man;
> He mente thus, that in sovereyn bontee
> Nis noon but God, but neither he ne she ...
> What though he were riche and glorious?
> So made he eek a temple of false goddis.
> How myghte he do a thyng that moore forbode is?
> Pardee, as faire as ye his name emplastre,
> He was a lecchour and an ydolastre,
> And in his elde he verray God forsook. (MerT IV.2276–8, 2287–90, 2294–9)

The tone and subject matter are the Wife of Bath's to the letter. The educated skill in biblical exposition (Proserpina's interpretation of Ecclesiastes 7:29 to mean that no one is good before God replicates the reading given in the *Glossa ordinaria*) suggests that the Merchant views the Wife as a *serious* exegete rather than simply a specious misreader of Scripture. But the relocation is disturbing. For the Wife of Bath's views are now uttered by a denizen of hell; by a pagan goddess, part of the stage set of an enlarged fabliau – that most amoral and unscriptural of genres. Effectively, they become grist to the mill of Proserpina's intention to help May get away with her adultery scot free. Or, as Besserman shrewdly puts it, the tale shows the scholarly explication of biblical material being brought to bear "to allow ... [a] biblically unacceptable ... outcome [to] the plot."[54]

The Merchant aims to divert and manage the challenge of the Wife's biblical reading by redirecting it to comically scurrilous ends. Yet whether or not he achieves these aims is ultimately of less consequence than the fact that he *feels the need* to do this. Distinct from almost any other rendition of the Bible within Chaucer's *oeuvre*, the Merchant feels compelled to ventriloquize the Wife's scriptural method within his own tale to enclose her disturbing openness. Testament again to the fact that her voice and feisty, intimate relationship with Scripture touch an extraordinarily raw nerve within many fields of late fourteenth-century bourgeois and ecclesial culture.

Conclusion

In his engagement with the Bible, Chaucer uses techniques of irony and biblical distortion for comic effect. He packs narratives such as the *Miller's Tale* with a biblical underlay to give additional texture and richness to this irrepressible tour de force. He makes various of his characters misquote or misapply Scripture to expose the blindspots in their vision of themselves – biblical awareness becomes a kind of touchstone for the evaluation of self-knowledge. But Chaucer also uses irony and misapplication in fiercer, more socially concerned ways. He channels his attacks upon corrupt and extortive clerics via their abuse of Scripture. That is, their misrepresentations of Scripture come to *stand for* their betrayals of vocation. If smooth-tongued clerics, those professionals of explication, can abuse Scripture so readily as a tool of predation, to whom can we turn for a *true* exposition of the Bible? Concern about this question leads Chaucer to review glosses – malleable in the extreme, they aid the process of abuse, and patristic exegeses – but if St Jerome is anything to go by, they divert Scripture to the service of preset agendas. Are the reformers right then? Should dissatisfaction with the clerical estate, and with the accumulated clutter of glosses and commentaries, lead to lay access to a vernacular text? The Wife of Bath's *Prologue* becomes a first halting step in that direction, beset by defensiveness and incoherence admittedly – in a sense, she does little more than fight Jerome's glosses – but commanding *attention* and *reaction*. Whom, in the last count, do we attend to more fully – the Wife's indefatigably personal scriptural trysts or the Parson's impersonal didacticism (both have elements of reformist culture about them)? If the former, then we should identify that vitality, amateur though it is, as a sign of things to come.

Chaucer tries out many of the tenets of reformist biblical thought in the course of his tales. He also shows himself to be sensitive to many of the uncertainties and anxieties it provokes. Having cut away the majority of the traditional vendors of scriptural interpretation – clergy, church, and tradition – Wyclif and his followers lay the stress of godly interpretation firmly upon the lay vernacular reader. Will this not produce many kinds of truth and many readings? Will meaning not become a private good (perhaps many private goods), rather than a single, communal commodity? These questions have far-reaching implications for Chaucer's sense of his own text and its meaning and reception. How ought he to ensure the transmission of a *right* meaning? How ought he to direct reception? The *form* of the *Canterbury Tales* as it stands – where the pilgrims respond variously and reactively to the tales that they hear, and in which the dissociate truths of different tales are simply amassed alongside each other – should be viewed as Chaucer's answer. He *cannot* control or confine meaning. He *cannot* prescribe reception. David Jeffrey writes aptly that: "on the primacy of the reader's will in achieving interpretation of a text, there is no writer so forceful as Wyclif in the fourteenth century, *except* Chaucer, whose whole approach to reader-centred hermeneutical difficulties in *The Canterbury Tales* offers a brilliantly imaginative outworking of Wyclif's synthetic literary theory."[55] What more forceful indication could there be of the centrality of the Bible to Chaucer's *oeuvre*? The debates upon biblical hermeneutics of the 1380s and 1390s serve crucially to determine the form and intention of the major literary achievement in English of the late Middle Ages.

Notes

1   L. Besserman, *Chaucer's Biblical Poetics* (University of Oklahoma Press, 1998), p. 203.

2   The *Glossa ordinaria*, compiled by Anselm of Laon, became the standard Bible commentary from the second half of the twelfth century. It was frequently supplemented from the early fourteenth century, with the *Postillae* of Nicholas of Lyra, which placed greater emphasis on the *literal* meaning of the Scriptures.

3   See Laura Light, "The New Thirteenth-Century Bible and the Challenge of Heresy," *Viator* 18 (1987), 275–88.

4   It should be noted that parts of Wyclif's teaching had already been condemned at the "Earth-quake Synod" of the Archbishop of Canterbury in 1382.

5   I take the phrase from J. H. Morey's informative *Book and Verse: A Guide to Middle English Biblical Literature* (University of Illinois Press, 2001).

6   Composed by the *Gawain Poet*, these two poems retell the biblical stories of Noah's flood, the destruction of Sodom and Gomorrah, and Belshazzar's Feast, and of Jonah and the Whale, respectively.

7   The statute in question: the 1401 statute, *De haeretico comburendo*.

8   A short extract from the Continuator of Henry Knighton's *Chronicle* provides us with a polemical reason for this antipathy to vernacular Scripture: "This Master John Wyclif translated from Latin into English ... the Gospel that Christ gave to the clergy and doctors of the Church ... so that by his means it has become vulgar and more open to laymen and women who can read it than it usually is to quite learned clergy of good intelligence, And so the pearl of the Gospel is scattered abroad and trodden underfoot by swine" (quoted in H. Hargreaves, "The Wycliffite Versions," in G. W. H. Lampe, ed., *The Cambridge History of the Bible, volume 2: The West from the Fathers to the Reformation* (Cambridge University Press, 1969), pp. 387–415, p. 388.

9   A good example of such a debate, carried out textually, which comes down wholeheartedly in the side of vernacular translation, is John Trevisa's *Dialogue between the Lord and the Clerk on Translation* (*c.*1387).

10 D. Lawton, "Englishing the Bible 1066–1549," in D. Wallace, ed., *The Cambridge History of Medieval English Literature* (Cambridge University Press, 1999), pp. 454–82, p. 459.

11 For an essay that makes much of Chaucer's sympathies with and affinities to Wycliffitism, see D. L. Jeffrey, "Chaucer and Wyclif: Biblical Hermeneutic and Literary Theory in the Fourteenth Century," in D. L. Jeffrey, ed., *Chaucer and Scriptural Tradition* (University of Ottawa Press, 1984), pp. 109–40.

12 For a classic discussion of the spiritual and literal senses of Scripture and the decline in the spiritual sense, see B. Smalley, *The Study of the Bible in the Middle Ages* (University of Notre Dame Press, 1964; repr. 1978), pp. 214–63, 281–307.

13 It should be noted that the *ABC* is a close translation of a prayer in Guillaume de Deguileville's long allegorical poem, *Le Pèlerinage de la vie humaine*. All citations of Chaucer's poetry and their abbreviated references are taken from *The Riverside Chaucer*, ed. L. D. Benson et al. (Oxford University Press, 1988).

14 *ABC*, lines 14, 89–94, 145, 177–8; referring to Ps. 46:3, 107:30, Exod. 3:2, 1 Cor. 3:16, and Zech. 13:1 respectively.

15 PrPro VII.468; SNPro VIII.37, 75.

16 PrT VII.627.

17 MLT II.470–6, 484–7, 932–8. Further examples of this type include Griselda as a post-figuration of Job, in ClT IV.932–8.

18 Critics differ significantly on the extent to which tale can be read as a reflection of teller. For a respected reading largely hostile to the the relationships between the two, see D. Pearsall, *The Canterbury Tales* (Routledge, repr. 1994).

19 Besserman, *Biblical Poetics*, p. 100.

20 Specifically, the *Summa de poenitentia* (1222–9) of Raymund of Pennaforte, and the *Summa vitiorum* (1236) of William Peraldus.

21 Besserman details the Parson's reluctance to expound the Ten Commandments and the Pater Noster, and his canny omission of references to Matt. 26:52 (a pacifistic verse closely associated with Lollard thinking in the 1380s and 1390s), *Biblical Poetics*, pp. 96–8.

22   It should be noted that Chaucer's *Tale of Melibee* is a close translation of Renaud de Louens's *Livre de Melibée et de Dame Prudence* (late 1330s), itself a translation of the *Liber consolationis et consilii* (1246) of Albertanus of Brescia.

23   See M. Aston, "Lollard Women Priests?" in her *Lollard and Reformers: Images and Literacy in Late Medieval Religion* (Hambleton, 1984), pp. 49–70. Walter Brut, the principal Lollard voice associated with these sentiments, was put on trial for heresy in 1391–3. It should be noted that Chaucer avoids any similar unpleasantness by carefully maintaining Prudence's personified veneer and staging her scriptural teaching within a nominally private and domestic environment.

24   H. Cooper, *The Canterbury Tales*, 2nd edn (Oxford University Press, 1996), p. 407.

25   MilT I.3216.

26   See also many less developed scriptural references within the tale – Absolon's name evokes 2 Sam. 14:26; Alison dismisses Absolon from her window (MilT I.3712) with a reference to John 8:7; Absolon uses a ploughshare as a weapon, comically inverting Isa. 2:4.

27   The phrase is Teresa Coletti's, "Biblical Wisdom: Chaucer's *Shipman's Tale* and the *Mulier fortis*," in Jeffrey, ed., *Scriptural Tradition*, pp. 171–82, p. 181.

28   Ibid., pp. 171–82.

29   MerT IV.1362–74. For the relevant scriptural references see Gen. 27:1–29; Judith 11–13; 1 Sam. 25:1–35; Esther 7:1–10.

30   NPT VII.2898–907, 3126–35.

31   For comments in support of this position, see FrPro III.1271–7.

32   V. Edden, "The Bible," in S. Ellis, ed., *Chaucer: An Oxford Guide* (Oxford University Press, 2005), pp. 332–51, p. 339.

33   Recent studies tend to modify the older view of the *Pardoner's Tale* as a sermon, arguing that while it retains many key elements, it omits others and does not exemplify the structure of a typical sermon.

34   PardT VI.485–91, 505–11, 635–7.

35   Gen. 19:30–6.

36   Adam and Eve as examples of gluttony reappear in ParsT X.819; the quote from Jeremiah reappears in ParsT X.592. In fact, large portions of the admonitory material on gluttony, drunkeness, and swearing reappear, complete with biblical citations, in ParsT X.819–22, 587–93.

37   See, for example, SumT III.1876–7, quoting Luke 16:19–31; SumT III.1884–90, quoting Exod. 34:28; SumT III.1988–91, quoting Ecclus. 4:35; SumT III.2085–8, quoting Prov. 22:24–5.

38   The vast majority of the Parson's quotations from Scripture seem to be first-hand. Where he quotes from a patristic source or gloss, that source is usually identified explicitly (that is, it is differentiated from Scripture). It may be noted that the Parson makes very little use of Jerome's *Adversus Jovinianum* (in *Sancti Eusebii Hieronymi Epistulae*, ed. I. Hilberg, CSEL 54–6, [Tempsky, 1910-18], hereafter abbreviated as Adv.Jov.), which the Pardoner and Friar John both rely heavily upon in their citations of Scripture (generally without acknowledgment).

39   See, for example, SumT III.1877–901, drawn from Adv.Jov. 2; SumT III.1937, found in Adv.Jov. 2.3.

40   SumT III.1929. Chaucer seems to have found this popular patristic epistle particularly questionable, for the Wife of Bath also contends with it at length in her *Prologue* to her *Tale*.

41   SumT III.1788–96, quoting 2 Cor. 3:6.

42   For detailed discussions of Chaucer's references to "glossing," see Besserman, *Biblical Poetics*, ch. 5; Edden, "Bible," pp. 343–6.

43 The bulk of these evaluations appear in 1 Cor. 7.

44 See Gen. 1:28.

45 D. W. Robertson Jr, *A Preface to Chaucer* (Princeton University Press, 1962), pp. 317–30, p. 321.

46 For a useful discussion of ecclesial perception of the female mind as inherently heterodox, see A. Blamires, "The Limits of Bible Study for Medieval Women," in L. Smith and J. Taylor, eds, *Women, the Book, and the Godly* (D. S. Brewer, 1995), pp. 1–12.

47 See W. S. Smith, "The Wife of Bath Debates Jerome," *Chaucer Review* 32 (1997), 129–45; R. Longsworth, "The Wife of Bath and the Samaritan Woman," *Chaucer Review* 34 (2000), 372–87.

48 Adv.Jov. 1.14. See also, in the same passage, Jerome's reading of Christ's meeting with the Samaritan woman at the well as a condemnation of remarriage.

49 Ibid., 1.36.

50 WBPro III.26; III.119. Besserman discusses the way in which the Wife of Bath diminishingly re-evaluates glossing in sexual terms, as sexual cajoling or foreplay, in *Biblical Poetics*, pp. 154–5.

51 Longsworth, "Wife of Bath and the Samaritan Woman," p. 383.

52 I take as understood the identification between the Prioress and the child-victim of the Tale, implicitly mooted by the Prioress in the *Prologue* to her *Tale* VII.481–7.

53 Eccles. 7:29.

54 Besserman, *Biblical Poetics*, p. 131.

55 Jeffrey, "Chaucer and Wyclif," p. 140.

PART III
Early Modern

CHAPTER 11
Introduction

Roger Pooley

The English Bible was the single most printed and authoritative source book of ideas and narratives in the early modern period, and its impact on everyday life was immense. It was argued over, revised, rewritten, and reinterpreted within a public domain not always controlled by the church and had become easily searchable with the new availability of Bible concordances. The marginal notes to the Geneva Bible established a doctrinally Protestant reading of the text, while Tyndale's introductions were key to the early Reformation. Arguing about and from the Bible is a central feature of what David Katz (2005, p. 70) calls "the all-pervasive nature of biblical culture in seventeenth-century England," the Bible generally acknowledged as a source of literal truth. The early Reformers stressed the plain sense of Scripture, Tyndale claiming in his "Preface" to his 1526 New Testament: "Mark the plain and manifest places of the Scriptures, and in doubtful places see thou add no interpretation contrary to them." Tyndale also intimated here that in arguing from Scripture, believers must distinguish between Law and Gospel, and follow St Paul's mode of arguing from the Old Testament while insisting that Christ has also done something new. In other words, Tyndale observes, the Bible, rather than the church, had come to occupy the central pedagogic role in early modern religious culture. At the later end of the early modern period, Archbishop Laud's godson, William Chillingworth, continued to remark on the importance of biblical interpretation in reinforcing Protestantism's dominance as the best route to salvation. "The Bible, and the Bible only, is the religion of Protestants," he wrote, in a phrase that has become almost proverbial.

While the Bible was one authority among many, there was still a hierarchy of authority, as Francis Bacon's *Essays* attest. Here, Bacon deftly sets the Bible against the classics in some matters, while in others suggests that the two discourses agree. At the beginning of his essay "Of Vicissitude of Things," for example, he interweaves Plato and the book of Ecclesiastes: "Solomon saith, *There is no new thing upon the earth*. So that as Plato had an imagination, *that all knowledge was but remembrance*, so Solomon giveth his sentence, *that all novelty is but oblivion*" (Bacon, 1985, p. 228). In his essay "Of Anger," however, Bacon sharply decides for the Bible against Stoicism: "To seek to extinguish anger utterly is but a bravery of the Stoics. We have better oracles: *Be angry, but sin not. Let not the sun go down upon your anger*" (ibid., p. 226).

For humanist writers like Bacon, educated as he was in the classics, great thinkers from the past are to be revered and tested, while the Bible is to be only revered and understood. An intellectually critical attitude to the Bible really only emerges at the end of the seventeenth century, and even then it remains a movement within rather than against Christianity.

This chapter shows that the biblical culture of early modern Britain was vernacular, largely Protestant (but sometimes Catholic too) and sprang from the availability of the text for everyone who could read – and beyond. After exploring the ingrained nature of the Bible in early modern everyday life, this chapter goes on to discuss the role of biblical drama in the period, a genre seriously threatened by contemporary Protestant censorship laws. This is followed by an assessment of the significant place of poetry as an instrument of imaginative biblical instruction, and the chapter concludes by thinking about not just those who rewrote the Bible but the reception of such revisions by readers in the period.

The Availability and Pervasiveness of the Bible

I begin this section with two examples that affirm the various ways in which the English Bible became part of everyday early modern life, in oral and printed culture alike. First is the service of Morning Prayer, as conducted by Rev. Thomas Traherne, among others after the reimposition of the Book of Common Prayer in 1662. Its considerable length, despite there being no hymns or sermon, is due to its dependence on the Bible: two long readings from the Old and New Testaments, and three Psalms set for the day. The average churchgoer in this period (and there were penalties for not going, so that was virtually everyone) would have encountered a large amount of the Bible, even if he or she were not functionally literate, or did not share the contemporary appetite for hearing sermons based on the analysis and application of biblical texts.

Second is a second edition of a 1566 verse translation of a selection of Horace's poetry, which characteristically of the period appeared with a lengthy title page: *A medicinable morall, that is, the two bookes of Horace his satyres, Englyshed accordyng to the prescription of saint Hierome. The wailyngs of the prophet Hieremiah, done into Englyshe verse. Also epigrammes.* The mixture of sources here is symptomatic of the sixteenth-century marriage of the classical and the biblical, the humanist and the reformed. Both Renaissance and Reformation involved a return to textual origins, to the Bible and the Greek and Roman classics. This expressed itself in editions in the original languages, and also a series of translations, paraphrases, imitations, and appropriations. Consequently, this one volume includes English translations of both poems of a great moral Latin writer (Horace) alongside passages from the Bible (Jeremiah's Lamentations). Thomas Drant, the author of this volume of verse, was better known as a preacher, and was domestic chaplain to Archbishop Grindal. (Mukherjee, 2000) This was not the first English translation of Lamentations, but it is one of the earliest versions of Horace, thirty years before the great vogue for Roman-style satire. In the Preface Drant defends his decision to mix the two: "I have brought to pass that the plaintive Prophete Jeremie should wepe at synne: and the pleasant poet Horace should laugh at sinne." The Bible is rarely thought of as a source of humor in this period; but in any case, no one would read Jeremiah for laughs. At the same time, the notion that one should appeal to classical and biblical models together for justification is an important indicator of the early-modern literary culture in which the English Bible was read.

In such an intellectual and cultural context, the presence of the Bible in early modern literature is substantial and varied. Some of the greatest writers of the period engage with the text directly, in recreating some of its central narratives (Milton, most obviously); in exploring its key doctrines, as they became newly visible and redefined in the period; in reworking some of its principal genres; and in working out a sometimes vexed relationship with its authority. As Brian Cummings (2002, p. 6) has argued, "Without reference to religion, the study of early modern writing is incomprehensible"; and, summarizing Erasmus, he shows how the early modern version of Christianity is indebted to metaphors of reading and writing. "Christ is our author; his authorship is present in his words; his presence guarantees truth; the truth is delivered in these words, written in scripture" (ibid., p. 105).

Which versions of the Bible did English writers use? We must acknowledge the supreme importance of Tyndale's biblical translations into English, and those that followed closely in his footsteps, particularly the Geneva Bible and the King James, or Authorized Version. Coverdale's versions of the Psalms, which remained in the Book of Common Prayer until the twentieth century, were also important. The story of the English Bible, with Tyndale as its hero, is an important narrative, but it needs to be supplemented. Education in the period is organized around Latinity; and so, while the Englishness of the English Bible is important for many writers – Bunyan is unimaginable without it – the availability of printed Latin Bibles is also a factor in the increased awareness of the Bible. For European Protestants, the new Latin translation of the Bible by Junius and Tremellius was an important step toward the availability of the Bible based on more reliable texts, if not as much as the great vernacular translations of Tyndale and Luther, or the Greek New Testament of Erasmus, or the Polyglot Bibles, which set Hebrew and Greek alongside Latin and Syriac. Many of the sermons of Lancelot Andrewes begin with the text in Latin rather than English. Although Donne's sermons begin with the text in English, the actual sermon, especially when he is preaching to scholarly congregations, sets up a dialogue between the English of the Bible and the Latin of the church fathers. Preaching to Lincoln's Inn in 1618 on Psalm 38:4, he says of David, "he was overflowed, surrounded, *his iniquities were gone over his head*, and in that S. Augustine notes *Ignorantiam*, his in-observance, his inconsideration of his own case."[1] Moving between Latin and English, for the postgraduate law students of the Inns of Court, was easy enough; however, the implication that the Bible should be seen as an English text would have been unusual a century earlier.

This also points to a problem in identifying biblical allusion in this period. For Bunyan in the mid-seventeenth century, and indeed from then on until quite recently, a biblical allusion is often identifiable as a verbal echo of the King James translation. For earlier writers, the Tyndale tradition is still recognizable, especially once the Geneva Bible became cheap and portable enough to be on a writer's desk. If, however, the writer's reading version of the Bible was Latin (or even Greek or Hebrew), this will not work in the same way. As a rule of thumb, the writers who were not university educated, like

Shakespeare and Bunyan, use the English versions available to them. As the Bible becomes embedded in the (linguistically) English imagination, so the nature of the literary debt to it changes.

David Daniell goes further than this: he argues that "Tyndale found, uniquely, a language register which made a 'plain style' for long after" (Daniell, 2003) This is not to say that the Bible is always plain, but the clarity of Tyndale's work would often reveal the difficulty or strangeness of the original Greek or Hebrew. More than that, says Daniell: "it established a form of prose for what can only be called un-courtly writers, the mass of ordinary women with something important to say" (p. 252). He traces its widespread influence beyond Bunyan to Defoe and the early novel, to the Royal Society's interest in plain style, to Hobbes, and to Addison's journalism. It is a large claim, and downplays the other pressures from classical and Middle English literature that create the plain style; but it is one account of the influence of the English Bible that does not have to wait for a more "literary" admiration for the Authorized Version that David Norton rightly sees as a later eighteenth-century phenomenon.

Tyndale's plain Englishness was, in part, an expression of his Protestantism. The vernacular Bibles of Europe began as part of the Reformation movement. However, this was paralleled by a revival of Catholic biblical scholarship. The Complutensian Polyglot Bible of 1516 was sponsored by Cardinal Ximenez of Spain, and was started before the Reformation with the aim of setting the best and oldest versions of the Bible in various source languages alongside each other. It represents the best of the scholarly Renaissance, with its aim of encouraging morality and religion by investigating the oldest, and therefore least corrupt texts of the Bible. However, Catholics tended to argue against laypeople having direct access to the Bible. The great Catholic humanist Sir Thomas More seems to have changed his mind, being all for a regulated, official English Bible before the Reformation, and then changing his mind when he saw some of the consequences. So, in his later, embattled phase, he praises the King "for the while to prohibit the scripture of God to be suffered in English tongue among the people's hands, lest evil folk by false drawing of every good thing they read in to the colour and maintenance of their own fond fantasies, and turning all honey into poison might both deadly do hurt unto themselves and spread also that infection farther abroad." (*The Confutation of Tyndale's Answer*, 1532, in More, 1963). This notion of general readers turning honey into poison lay at the heart of Catholic concerns about biblical translation and dissemination.

As my opening example from Drant shows, the early modern English Bible also exists in a number of paraphrases, some distinguished, many little more than workmanlike. Paraphrase can be a means of adapting a text for a different audience or purpose; for example, the versified Psalm books of Sternhold and Hopkins, or the Bay Psalm Book, make them available for congregational singing in public worship. For young writers like the seventeen-year-old Thomas Middleton, still an undergraduate at Cambridge, writing them was a way of starting out, while stating Protestant loyalties for the benefit of patronage as well as personal piety. His *The Wisdom of Solomon Paraphrased* (1597) was dedicated to the Earl of Essex, and versifies much of Proverbs. Middleton retains and develops a doctrinal acuteness in his better-known plays. For Thomas Wyatt, writing in the earliest years of the English Reformation, it was a way of exploring Protestant doctrine as part of the Bible's revelation. Wyatt's versions of the Penitential Psalms (a group of Psalms, 6, 32, 38, 51, 102, 130, and 143, used from the Middle Ages on as a means of preparing for the sacrament of Penance) are not simply versions of the Psalms, but they include a narrative prologue, and narrative and doctrinal links between them. Wyatt's editors identify a number of translations and paraphrases that Wyatt draws on, in Italian, Latin, and English, some by reformers like Tyndale and Zwingli, others not (Wyatt, 1978). We know that a number of Wyatt's other poems engage with Italian and other European, mostly Petrarchan, poetry, so that they might be viewed as, if not strict translations, imitations and adaptations of existing poems. His adaptations of the Psalms show an even more complex pattern of research and indebtedness, creativity and commentary, delving into the emotions of David with comments like "He, then inflamed with far more hot affect / Of God than he was erst of Barsabe [Bathsheba]."

For Hannibal Hamlin (2004), this interweaving of paraphrase and commentary may have been picked up by the Elizabethan poet George Gascoigne in his version of Psalm 130. In the earlier version (in *An Hundreth Sundrie Flowres*, 1573), it is prefaced by a prose comment by a (possibly fictional) editor, who gives the occasion for composition (riding between Chelmsford and London) and a spiritual and psychological context as well: "*he gan accuse his owne conscience of muche time misspent.*" In the second version (in *Posies*, 1575), the prose has gone, and there is just a sonnet describing the same occasion before the paraphrase of the Psalm. Gascoigne tries to identify himself with the arch-example of the penitent sinner, David. Is this any more than a pose? Perhaps – it is often hard to tell with Gascoigne – but it shows how the Psalms in particular lend themselves to an imaginative exercise that can also be a spiritual exercise. The greatest of the Psalm paraphrases in the period is a collaboration between Philip Sidney and his sister Mary, for its liveliness and rhythmic inventiveness. The Psalms are always recognized as poetry, even as contemporaries admitted their ignorance of the precise metrical rules of the Hebrew: poets at many levels of competence and sophistication rewrote them. The remainder of this chapter examines more closely the impact of genre on biblical revision, and begins with an exploration of the sharp decline in the popularity of biblical drama.

The Paradoxical Death of Biblical Drama

In the early part of the sixteenth century biblical drama was commonplace. As well as surviving cycles of mystery plays in various provincial centers, new plays based on Bible stories continued to be written and performed until some time after the English Reformation. However, by the end of the sixteenth century, with Protestantism, the religion of the Bible, dominant, drama based on the Bible has virtually died out, despite the fact that the new public theaters (the first was founded in 1579) and the court-based performances by the same companies meant that there was an enormous demand for play scripts. Why is it that while, arguably, the greatest period of English drama coincides with the golden age of biblical translation and the consequent availability of the Bible, the incidence of biblical drama actually declines? There is an oversimplified narrative to account for this, which might run as follows. Popular drama based on the Bible continued to be performed in the provinces, and even in the court after the Reformation. However, the combination of state and ecclesiastical censorship, the philistinism of an increasingly Puritan Protestantism, and the sophistication of the new, secular public theater companies meant that drama based on the Bible dies out in the middle of Elizabeth's reign. As Peter Womack (2006) puts it, "Ironically, then, the effect of Protestantism upon the theatre was to *make* it irreligious. The actors were forbidden to engage seriously with sacred matters; they were released from every obligation to the church." Such a narrative is not untrue, but it could give the wrong impression. First of all, to what extent were the mystery cycles biblical, and how widely were they performed? Would they have seemed inaccurate, or second best, once people could read accurate translations for themselves? Isn't there an element of selective nostalgia in the picture of popular enactment of biblical stories in the Middle Ages? Second, to what extent were the plays of the period constrained by the apparatus of censorship and control exercised by the state and the church? Did it become impossible to deal with biblical stories directly, or were they just not interested?[2] Third, how effective and pervasive was Puritan antitheatricalism? Certainly, it is matched by theatrical anti-Puritanism. The figure of Malvolio in *Twelfth Night*, to say nothing of Zeal-of-the-Land Busy and numerous other comically corrupt Puritans in Ben Jonson's plays, is evidence enough that it is hard to find a sympathetic Puritan in the drama of the period.[3]

Of course, it is also quite difficult, though not impossible, to find sympathetic Catholic clerics as well. In a period where patriotic Englishness is increasingly becoming defined as anti-Catholicism, a Cardinal is likely to be portrayed as hypocritical as well as Machiavellian. Even those writers like Jonson, who converted temporarily to Catholicism in prison, and Shakespeare, whose father was a recusant and is often thought of as retaining Catholic sympathies, do not people their plays with admirable clerics. The Cardinal in Webster's *Duchess of Malfi* (1613–14) is a fair example of the general picture; though he is also an example of the murderous corruption that is standard in English portrayals of Italian courts. He employs the malcontent assassin Bosola, who has an understandably bitter view of him, having spent seven years in the galleys as a result: "Some fellows, they say, are possessed with the devil, but this great fellow were able to possess the greatest devil and make him worse" (1.1.44–6). He is angry about his sister, the Duchess, remarrying, but he keeps a mistress, in flagrant contradiction of his vows of chastity, although he is not as sexually obsessed as his brother Ferdinand. Webster counters this with the Christian stoicism of Antonio and the Duchess. In their courtship scene, Antonio advises the widowed Duchess to remarry: "Begin with that first good deed begun I'th'world / After man's creation: the sacrament of marriage" (1.1.386–7), a clear allusion to Genesis 2. However, in calling marriage a sacrament, Webster partly distances Antonio from the figure of the ambitious, Protestant, reliable middle-class steward who – heroically in Deloney's fiction, villainously in Shakespeare's Malvolio – would marry his social superior. The Church of England only recognized two sacraments, baptism and Holy Communion; according to Article 25 of the 39 Articles, marriage is not strictly a sacrament because it was not "ordained of Christ our Lord in the Gospel." Webster also makes the third madman, sent by the brothers to torment their sister, a Puritan, who claims "we are only to be saved by the Helvetian translation," in other words the Geneva Bible with its Calvinist marginal comments. There is also a passing reference to Laban's sheep in Genesis. So Webster shows himself knowledgeable about the Bible, as well as taking part in the anti-Catholic discourse of the time; but without going into the extreme Protestant version of this.

Finally, was biblical drama, at least as it was practiced in the sixteenth century, just too crude to survive in the face of the new dramatic experiments of the London public theaters? Biblical drama before the opening of the public theaters is, by and large, educational and sometimes aimed specifically at the young. So, for example, John Bale's biblical plays, such as *A Comedy, or Interlude of John Baptist's Preaching in the Wilderness* and *The Temptation of our Lord*, are prefaced by the figure of Bale himself, "Baleus Prolocutor," who acts as a chorus, or commentator; so much so, that they might be described as illustrated sermons. The control exerted by such a figure means that the evil or disruptive characters are not allowed to subvert the central message of the Bible. John Bale (1495–1563) was a prominent Carmelite monk who converted to Protestantism and was made Bishop of Ossory in Ireland by Edward VI. He was under the protection, if not the patronage, of Thomas Cromwell in the 1530s, and his players performed before Cromwell in 1538. He was the author of *King Johan*, the first English history play. Only four of his biblical plays survive: *The Chief Promises of God, John the Baptist's Preaching, The Temptation of Christ*, and *The Three Laws*, probably first printed in 1547–8; there may have been as many as twenty others.

When it comes to the plays performed in the public theaters of the 1580s onwards, such schoolmasterly control is absent, and the audience is cut free to find its own way. For example, the Vice figure, already a potential subversive in the humanist interlude (of which Bale's drama is an unusual, specialized example), can be seen as an ancestor figure of a number of seductive villains in the public theater. The figure of Falstaff in Shakespeare's second history tetralogy is one obvious example; not least because he figures as a dangerous alternative for the young Prince Hal in his education. Falstaff has a complex, parodic relationship to religious language in general, the sermon and the catechism particularly. The language of the Bible is less prominent in that mix.

At the beginning of *Dr Faustus* (1594), the hero is alone in his study, and he reads from his Bible, which appears to be the Vulgate, Jerome's Latin Bible used by the Roman Catholic church:

> *Stipendium peccati mors est. Ha! Stipendium, etc.*
> The reward of sin is death? That's hard.
> *Si pecasse negamus, fallimur,*
> *Et nulla est in nobis veritas*:
> If we say we have no sin
> We deceive ourselves, and there's no truth in us.
> Why then belike we must sin,
> And so consequently die, an everlasting death.
> What doctrine call you this? *Che sera, sera,*
> What will be, shall be? Divinity, adieu! (1.1.39–49)

Thus Faustus turns to magic and necromancy. Marlowe's original audience may have known some Latin, but if they didn't, he is translating as he goes along anyway. The question is, would they have known the text from 1 John 1:8 that Faustus finds so discouraging? And would they have been able to recognize the irony that, had he read another line on, to verse 9, he would have found the promise of forgiveness: "If we acknowledge our sins, he is faithful and just, to forgive us our sins, and to cleanse us from all unrighteousness" (Geneva Bible, 1560)? They would not have to have been students of the Bible to spot it; it is quoted before the confession in Morning Prayer in the Prayer Book, though in the 1559 version current at the time verse 8 and not verse 9 is all that is set, just as in this soliloquy.

The Bible does not disappear from English drama just because of the hostility between the new public theaters and the increasingly antitheatrical viewpoint of Protestantism in the 1580s and 1590s. Many of the biblical plays produced in this period survive only as titles, but there is something different about George Peele's *The Love of King David and Fair Bethsabe: with the Tragedy of Absolon*, published in 1599, and probably performed between 1594 and then; and possibly after then as well, if the entry in Henslowe's diary of 1602 for the poles needed "for to hange absolome" refers to the same play. The play is based on a series of narratives in 2 Samuel, which results in an interesting mixture of genres, characteristic of the late 1590s. Peele also demonstrates his familiarity with other biblical stories, which allies his play with the typological habits of reading common in the period. Bethsabe is compared to "Eva" when David first sees her. Hardly a sophisticated form of typology, true, but then David in his lust seems blind to the comparisons between him and Adam. The object of his desire is not. In the song that is so often anthologized, she prays "Let not my beauty's fire / Enflame unstayed desire"; but then the following lines are rather more sensual:

> Come gentle Zephire trickt with those perfumes
> That erst in Eden sweetned Adams love
> And stroke my bosome with thy silken fan.

The play has many interesting scenes, and takes advantage of the twists and turns of the plot in the biblical story. It is one counter to the image of biblical drama being too unsophisticated to survive in the rapidly developing public theater of the 1590s, but it remains a relatively isolated example.

One curious literary consequence of the Reformation is the increased role of the devil. Satan is often present in pre-Reformation drama, but he is often balanced by good angels and saints. The effective abolition of the cult of the saints, and the ban on representations of God on the stage, give devil figures the stage by default. Keith Thomas (1978, p. 589) relates the story of the annual procession by St George's Guild in Norwich, which was altered under Protestant influence after 1558; the saints, George and Margaret, would no longer appear, but the dragon would. There are the devils in *Dr Faustus*, of course, but the play is enough in the miracle play tradition to have a Good Angel – not a very persuasive one, but that's Marlowe, and the source material. Subsequent devil plays have even fewer alternatives. It could be argued that, because devils are part of a dualistic world picture, their very presence implies some sort of God. In the early modern drama, God cannot be named except in the plural or as a Latin deity because of the censorship; or he is there by implication. Is biblical reference in the drama effectively marginalized by the very forces that sought to curb the new drama's perceived godlessness?

Attacking and Defending Literature from the Bible

The idea of reading the Bible "as" literature in this period presents problems because it implies a fictional element. Yet many of the writers of this period recognized that some of the Bible was poetry, and saw no conflict between this recognition and an acknowledgment of its unique inspiration. Sir Philip Sidney's *Apology for Poetry*, for example (published posthumously in 1595, and also known as *The Defence of Poetry*), actually takes the teaching style of Jesus as a justification for regarding poets as more effective than philosophers, who only teach in abstractions:

> Certainly, even our Saviour Christ could as well have given the moral commonplaces of uncharitableness and humbleness as the divine narration of Dives and Lazarus; or of disobedience and mercy, as that heavenly discourse of the lost child and the gracious father; but that His through-searching wisdom knew the estate of Dives burning in hell, and of Lazarus being in Abraham's bosom, would more constantly (as it were) inhabit both the memory and judgement. Truly, for myself, me seems I see before my eyes the lost child's disdainful prodigality, turned to envy a swine's dinner: which by the learned divines are thought not historical acts, but instructing parables. (pp. 108–9)

Sidney's own adventures in moral narrative, the two versions of *Arcadia*, are more like epic romance than parable, though perhaps some of the individual incidents might work like that. What is interesting here is that Sidney sees the parables of Dives and Lazarus (Luke 16:19–31) and the Prodigal Son (Luke 15:11–32) as teaching stories that work because they are memorable, and they affect people. In most of the *Apology* Sidney is more concerned to show that biblical fictions work than he is to assert their difference in kind from other writings we might call secular. He has already confronted the question of whether calling the Psalms poetry is a profanity. His argument to his fellow Protestants who would have poetry "scourged out of the Church of God" is that poetry is there in the Bible already, and that it is there to teach.

This notion of poetry as an instrument of imaginative instruction for life has a long history in classical and English critical thinking and was an important component in the rise of "English" as a school subject and an academic discipline. But here, Sidney is not arguing against modern defenders of literature as a site of play, of power, or of multiplying meanings. He may be taking to task those like Stephen Gosson, minor playwright turned scourge of the theater in *The School of Abuse* (1579), or he may simply be working out a justification for his own practice as a Protestant poet in the 1580s.

As we have established, the Puritan attack on the theater was responded to in the plays they sought to have abolished – and, eventually, succeeded in 1642. Of these attacks, the most comprehensive, virulent, and indeed biblical was that of William Prynne in *Histrio-mastix, The Players Scourge* (1633), over a thousand pages long.

While Sidney, with classical as well as biblical precedent, sees pleasure as a means of making teaching work, Prynne is not keen on pleasure. Like Tertullian, one of the early Church Fathers, he regards not going to plays as a badge of a true Christian. It is tempting (if that is the right word) simply to quote with relish phrases from Prynne's polemic: "That all popular, and common Stage-Playes, whether, Comicall, Tragicall, Satyricall, Mimicall, or mixt of either ... are such sinfull, hurtfull, and pernitious Recreations, as are altogether unseemely, and unlawfull unto Christians" (p. 6). He does have a number of specific reasons: the encouragement of effeminacy among actors and spectators, of which dressing up in women's clothes is only the beginning, the viciousness of actors, the effect of plays that satirize religion, and the fact that they break all the Ten Commandments (pp. 551ff). As his citing of Tertullian shows, Prynne is not inventing a Christian suspicion of dramatic art. Instead, he shows that a return to the biblical text can cause its reader to be highly suspicious of literature, just as often as it can cause a Christian humanist to identify the imaginative powers of the Bible, as well as the best of classic literature, and to value both.

One consequence of this dichotomy is that the great Puritan texts of the Restoration are very anxious to display the thoughtfulness and the biblical basis of their poetics. So we have the sequence of invocations of the "heavenly muse" several times in *Paradise Lost*, and the "Author's Apology" at the start of *The Pilgrims Progress*, both texts not just soaked in the Bible, but keen to show that the Bible permits their art.

Ways of Reading, Ways of Writing

In order to understand how early modern writers appropriated the Bible we also need to think about how they read it, especially given the availability of the Bible in versions that literate people, lay and ordained, could buy; and its use in public worship, in sermons, and alluded to and argued over in all sorts of discourse. The perceived authority of the Bible meant that proof texts are cited in every conceivable kind of context. The assumptions about the authority of the Bible that stem from the Reformation are important to recognize. But so are habits of reading. In the discussion of paraphrases, we have seen how translation and imitation generate new poetic and dramatic texts. There are other modes of reading popular in the period that provided ways of understanding the text and also imaginative discipline and a route to creativity. Think of the example of allegory, which begins as a way of reading, of disciplining pagan texts such as Ovid's *Metamorphoses* by seeing allegorical versions of Christian truth hidden within them, but very soon turns into a mode of composition as well. So, Arthur Golding's Elizabethan version of Ovid moralizes the tales:

> As for example, in the tale of Daphnee turnd to Bay,
> A myrror of virginitie appeere unto us may,
> Which yeelding neyther unto feare, nor force, nor flatterye,
> Doth purchase everlasting fame and immortalitye. (Book 1)

Golding also paraphrased the Psalms, and was one of Calvin's translators.

Closely allied to allegory is typology, where, for example, various Old Testament figures are seen as "types" of Christ, thus bringing Old and New Testaments into harmony. It is a habit of reading and interpreting that is encouraged in the New Testament itself. In the Letter to the Hebrews, the writer compares Christ to Melchizedek, an obscure figure from the Old Testament, who was a priest as well as a king. There are examples in St Paul as well, particularly Colossians 2:16–17: "Let no man therefore judge you in meat, or in drink, or in respect of an holyday, or of the new moon, or of the Sabbath days; which are a shadow of things to come; but the body is of Christ." The Old Testament laws about diet, for example, are not just to keep the Israelites holy. They can be ignored by Christians, after the dispensation given to Peter in a vision in Acts 10:15 ("What God hath cleansed, that call not thou common"). In his *Solomon's Temple Spiritualised*, Bunyan takes every detail of the temple building and translates them into gospel. Spiritualizing and moralizing the biblical text are similar interpretative strategies, turning stories and images into lessons for behavior or devotion. In the poetry of the period they are also modes of self-examination – as George Herbert finds in "The Bunch of Grapes," an explicit reference to the great bunches brought back from the Promised Land by the spies in Exodus. In the story of wanderings in the wilderness he finds an image of his own lack of spiritual progress, and in the bunch of grapes an image of potential refreshment. Here is his account of the process of reading that enables him to find this:

> For as the Jews of old by Gods command
> Travell'd, and saw no town;
> So now each Christian hath his journeys spann'd;
> Their storie pennes and sets us down. (Lines 8–12)

The story of the people of God in the Old Testament thus becomes, analogically, the story of contemporary Christians reading that story.

The idea of Christ as the second Adam, already found in Paul, is very common in religious poetry of this period. The Christ of Milton's *Paradise Regained* is explicitly seen as repairing Adam's disobedience with his own obedience:

> I who erstwhile the happy garden sung,
> By one man's disobedience lost, now sing
> Recovered Paradise to all mankind,
> By one man's firm obedience fully tried
> Through all temptation, and the tempter foiled
> In all his wiles, defeated and repulsed,
> And Eden raised in the waste wilderness. (Lines 1–7)

A similar combination is made use of in Donne's "Hymn to God My God, in My Sicknesse," where he sees the two Adams inscribed on his sick and dying body. He begins with a conceit that has no geographic basis in the Bible, though it has some typological justification:

> We thinke that *Paradise* and *Calvarie*,
> *Christs* Crosse, and *Adams* tree, stood in one place;

> Looke Lord, and find both *Adams* met in me;
> As the first Adams sweat surrounds my face,
> May the last *Adams* blood my soul embrace. (Lines 21–5)

The reference is a little complex. The primary allusion is to two verses in 1 Corinthians 15, "For as in Adam all die, even son in Christ shall all be made alive" (verse 22) and "The first man is of the earth, earthy: the second man *is* the Lord from heaven" (verse 47). The allusion to Adam's sweat recalls part of God's punishment for his disobedience: "In the sweat of thy face shalt thou eat bread, till thou return unto the ground" (Genesis 3:19). Christ's blood as a guarantee of eternal life for Christians runs through the New Testament epistles; but there might also be a half-reference to Christ sweating what looked like blood in Luke 22:44.

The close involvement of the reader in the biblical text is clear enough; but this was sometimes aided by a conscious discipline of reading. The most influential treatment of this is Louis Martz's (1954) *The Poetry of Meditation*. Martz suggests that "meditative" is a more helpful term for religious poetry than "metaphysical" because it points to a method of self-examination and reading Scripture that is found in Europe, in the Counter-Reformation, and particularly in the writings of Ignatius Loyola, the founder of the Jesuits. This enormously influential book focused on Donne, Herbert, and Crashaw, but also pointed to the Puritan writer Richard Baxter and the neglected Catholic poet William Alabaster as making use of the same method. Eventually it was countered by Barbara Lewalski's *Protestant Poetics and the Seventeenth-Century Religious Lyric* (1979), which recovered more of the distinctive Calvinist emphasis in poems about biblical subjects. As Martz has now recognized, and more recently R. V. Young, in a chapter in *Doctrine and Devotion in Seventeenth-Century Poetry* (2000), which has the merit of looking at continental poems as well as English, it is complex. It is not just that Protestant poets like Herbert followed Calvin and Luther, and Catholics like Southwell followed Loyola. Doctrinally, there are key distinctions; but the text of the Bible is common to both, and a desire for self-examination is common, too, even if it springs from different theological premises. So, for that matter, is the legacy of St Augustine. Catholic writers might have a more liturgical emphasis, but that liturgy is often based on biblical events like the Last Supper. One point that certainly emerges from this conflicted history of devotional poetry is that the identification of the Christian's self with aspects of Old Testament figures, or New Testament disciples, is a highly imaginative mode of reading, which issues in biblical poetry that takes biblical poetry beyond paraphrase.

The Beginning and End

The biblical books most focused on beginnings and endings (Genesis and Revelation) are of particular fascination to early modern writers. At first glance it may seem that poems about creation tend to be epic in scope – Milton's *Paradise Lost* obviously, but Lucy Hutchinson's recently rediscovered *Order and Disorder* as well. Before them there is the European hexaemeral tradition (so named because it was about the six days of creation), represented by the translation by Sylvester of the French writer Du Bartas, published as *The Divine Weeks and Works* in 1598. These are long poems that expand on the sometimes rather terse biblical accounts, not just by way of decoration, but as explorations and arguments. Genesis is particularly important for this kind of work because of the peculiar authority vested in origins in the period. The first eleven chapters of Genesis are about the origin of the universe, and also of marriage, of murder, and of language. There are the compelling images of the Tower of Babel and Noah's Ark. For more radical political thinkers, like Gerard Winstanley, the early chapters of Genesis have to be rewritten. Adam and Eve in the garden is such a compelling image, as well as the beginning of the biblical story of sin and redemption, that it is constantly in the background even when not overtly present. Every garden poem is, at some level, a garden of Eden poem. Marvell's "The Garden" is archly knowing about this: "Such was that happy garden state / When Man there walked without a mate." For God in Genesis, man needed company (2:18), but Marvell reminds us that the consequences were mixed.

Revelation, the book of the end of the world, the last judgment, and the vision of the New Jerusalem, attracted more esoteric attention but became particularly powerful in revolutionary times, as it so often does. The interpretation of it that identified the Pope with the antichrist was common enough in Protestant England; the main literary consequence of this is in Book I of *The Faerie Queene* by Edmund Spenser. Marvell gives a typically teasing version of this in "To His Coy Mistress," where the (no doubt fictional) woman is allowed to refuse "Till the conversion of the Jews," which was supposed to be just before the last judgment. The language of Revelation gets its most confident citation at the end of Part One of *The Pilgrim's Progress*; perhaps its most uncertain in Kent's horrified "Is this the promised end?" in the last scene of *King Lear*. I am not sure what early modern readers expected at the end of the world and the last judgment any more than their Christian predecessors. What they did have was a more precise and detailed language for it that derived from the Bible, as the following chapters make clear.

Notes

1   http://contentdm.lib.byu.edu/cdm4/document.php?CISOROOT=/JohnDonne&CISOPTR=3135&REC=8 (accessed November 15, 2007).

2   See Cyndia Susan Clegg, *Press Censorship in Elizabethan England* (Cambridge University Press, Cambridge, 1997); Debora Shuger, *Censorship and Cultural Sensibility: The Regulation of Language in Tudor-Stuart England* (University of Pennsylvania Press, Philadelphia, 2006); and Annabel Patterson, "Censorship and Interpretation," in David Scott Kastan and Peter Stallybrass, eds, *Staging the Renaissance: Reinterpretations of Elizabethan and Jacobean Drama* (Routledge, London, 1991), pp. 40–8.

3   See Kristin Poole, *Radical Religion from Shakespeare to Milton: Figures of Nonconformity in Early Modern England* (Cambridge University Press, Cambridge, 2000); and Peter Lake, *The Antichrist's Lewd Hat: Protestants, Papists and Players in Post-Reformation England* (Yale University Press, New Haven, CT, 2002).

References

Bacon, Francis (1985) *Essays,* ed. John Pitcher. Penguin, Harmondsworth.

Cummings, Brian (2002) *The Literary Culture of the Reformation: Grammar and Grace.* Oxford University Press, Oxford.

Daniell, David (2003) *The Bible in English, its History and Influence.* Yale University Press, New Haven & London.

Hamlin, Hannibal (2004) *Psalm Culture and Early Modern English Literature.* Cambridge University Press, Cambridge.

Katz, David (2005) *God's Last Words. Reading the English Bible from the Reformation to Fundamentalism.* Yale University Press, New Haven & London.

Lewalski, Barbara (1979) *Protestant Poetics and the Seventeenth-Century Religious Lyric.* Princeton University Press, Princeton, NJ.

Martz, Louis Lohr (1954) *The Poetry of Meditation: A Study in Religious Literature of the Seventeenth Century.* Yale University Press, New Haven, CT.

More, Thomas (1973) *The Confutation of Tyndale's Answer (1532)* in *Collected Works* vol.8, ed. Louis A. Schuster, Richard C. Marius and James P. Lusardi. Yale University Press, New Haven & London.

Mukherjee, Neel (2000) "Thomas Drant's Rewriting of Horace" *Studies in English Literature 1500–1900* 40:1.

Sidney, Philip (1965) *Apology for Poetry,* ed. Geoffrey Shepherd. Nelson, London.

Thomas, Keith (1978) *Religion and the Decline of Magic.* Peregrine, Harmondsworth.

Womack, Peter (2008) *English Renaissance Drama.* Blackwell, Oxford.

Wyatt, Sir Thomas (2008) *The Complete Poems,* ed. R. A. Rebholz. Penguin, Harmondsworth.

Young, R. V. (2000) *Doctrine and Devotion in Seventeenth-Century Poetry.* D. S. Brewer, Cambridge.

CHAPTER 12
Early Modern Women

Elizabeth Clarke

In that most popular of early modern exemplary lives of women, *A Christal Glasse for Christian Women* of 1591, Katherine Stubbes's obsessive Bible reading was held up as a particular virtue for godly women to emulate: "you could seldom or never have come into her house, and have found her without a bible, or some other good booke in her hands. And when she was not reading, she would spend the time in conferring, talking and reasoning with her husband of the worde of God."[1] Ian Green suggests there were about thirty-four editions of this work in the next 100 years, establishing Katherine Stubbes as the ideal early modern woman, and Bible reading as a key aspect of her ideal womanhood.[2] It is less easy to discern exactly what Katherine Stubbes did with her Bible reading. When asked why she read the Bible so much, she replied, "if I should be a friend unto this world, I should be an enemie to GOD."[3] Within the short pages of this biography, Katherine Stubbes is indeed constructed as someone who was a friend to God and an enemy to the world, so much so that at the age of twenty, and with a newborn baby boy to care for, she was happy to die of a fever and go to God. Quite a few pages of this pamphlet are given over to her own deathbed speech, "set downe word for word, as she spake it, as neere as could be gathered" (sig. A1r). However, it consists less of anything profound she may have learned from her Bible reading, than a confession of faith that is orthodoxly Church of England. The constant presence of the Bible, it seems, is no more than a token of Katherine Stubbes's conformity and exemplarity.

It is very difficult to find an early modern space in which women could express their individual thoughts on, or reactions to, the Bible. This is not because of any restrictions on women reading the Bible: on the contrary. In 1645, the *Annotations Upon All the Books of the Old and New Testament* was published, an important commission of the Parliamentary Committee on Religion that specifically extended the right of reading and interpreting Scripture to women, in contrast with the unenlightened practices of the past. The statute of Henry VII's reign prohibiting the reading of the Bible to certain classes, including all women, is indignantly quoted: "no woman, Artificers, Apprentices, Journey-men, Servingmen, none of the degrees of Yeomen, or husbandmen, nor labourers."[4] The result of such enfranchisement for women should have been more writing about Scripture, but such work is scarce and difficult to find. This is because there is a general reluctance by women to express themselves in writing, or at least in published writing, in the sixteenth and early seventeenth centuries.[5] Thus there is a problem with identifying a distinctive female voice in responses to the Bible in the early modern period. Since those who produced printed works are on the whole exceptional for one reason or another, what set them apart from other women was at least as important in their writing as what they had in common. Early modern women do not seem to have had a particular interest in reading texts by other women: there is little sense of sisterly solidarity.[6] Any attempt to make generalizations about early modern women's use of Scripture is fraught with difficulty. This chapter traces the efforts of a few early modern women who were by definition unusual because they wrote down some of their responses.

Mary Sidney Herbert, Countess of Pembroke, produced one of the most famous versions of a biblical book in the early modern period, and what made her exceptional was that she was the sister of Sir Philip Sidney, the man who was to attain cult status as one of the most prized poets of the late sixteenth century. She consciously assumed his mantle to edit his *Arcadia*, and to complete his paraphrase of the Psalms. It was undoubtedly useful to be able to represent herself as the sister of the author of *Astrophil and Stella*.[7] However, there was another, and perhaps more important, role that Philip had played, and that Mary perhaps felt impelled to take on. He had been leader of the strong Protestant faction involving Robert Dudley, Earl of Leicester, and the Earl of Essex.[8] By 1601 all three men were dead. Mary's authorship activities, including translating the work of her brother's Huguenot friend Philippe Duplessis-Mornay, show her assuming his mantle, at least in her written work.

There was perhaps little part for her femininity to play in this politico-religious leadership, yet Mary Sidney showed herself very conscious of the perceived limits on female authorship. She limited herself to translation, rather than conventional authorship, in her printed works; and for perhaps her most important poetic work, the paraphrase of the Psalms which her brother had begun, but for which she completed the vast majority of chapters, she chose manuscript as her means of publication. This choice was as much driven by her elite status as by her feminine gender. For aristocrats, the medium of print still had connotations of vulgarity, and Mary Sidney wanted to reach the highest readership available, the monarch herself, as one of the manuscript versions with a dedication to Queen Elizabeth reveals. There are in existence at least eighteen manuscript versions of the Sidney Psalter, indicating a serious attempt to reach a wide section of an elite audience.[9] As Margaret Hannay has pointed out, there was a political message inherent in Mary Sidney's sources, the Geneva Bible with its often radical glosses, the French psalter by Marot and Beza, Beza and Calvin's commentaries on the Psalms.[10] The dedicatory poem to Queen Elizabeth, "Even Now that Care," equates Elizabeth with David and therefore makes the Psalter relevant specifically to the politics of England: "ev'n thy Rule is painted in his Raigne" says Mary Sidney to her monarch.[11] In this context the translator of the Psalms takes on the admonitory role which, it has been argued, was that of Anne Lok in 1560, publishing Calvin's sermons and what is probably her own version of Psalm 51 from exile in Geneva.[12] In some ways Mary Sidney could be seen as the inheritor of the Genevan exiles' radicalism. However, by this time, rather than the fight for a purer liturgy and church hierarchy in England, Mary Sidney was espousing military support for French and Dutch Calvinists. The first stanza of the dedicatory poem makes it clear that Mary Sidney, and the spirit of her dead brother, hold Elizabeth responsible for what happens in Europe: "On whom in chiefe dependeth to dispose / What Europe acts in theise most active times" (p. 47).

Mary Sidney's tactics are revealed in one of the first psalms that she was responsible for, Psalm 45. This psalm is addressed to Solomon and his Bride, the daughter of Pharaoh, a queen in her own right, and Sidney delights in the opportunity to imply an address to Queen Elizabeth while remaining perfectly faithful to her sources. The gloss to the Geneva Bible version of verse 2 makes clear that Solomon is being praised in the context of military politics: "Salomons beautie and eloquence to winne favour with his people, and his power to overcome his enemies, is here described."[13] The Bride of Solomon is seen by the Geneva glossers, as was conventional, as a type of the Church. This gives Mary Sidney licence to admonish the sixteenth-century Queen in the guise of the biblical queen, and to give the foreign policy advice that is perhaps relevant to an early modern Europe torn by religious strife. Elizabeth is to receive the tributes of rich foreign nations, which the Genevan gloss specifies as those who "do not give perfect obedience to the Gospel": Spain, perhaps. The royal trappings are certainly those of Tudor England: even her underclothes are embroidered gold, and she is attended by "Maids of Honour," which was the correct term for Elizabeth's ladies in waiting.[14]

Courtly rhetoric is an important characteristic of Mary Sidney's psalm versions: English paraphrases, above all the ubiquitous but notorious Sternhold and Hopkins, tended not to do justice to the rhetorical richness of the original.[15] One of the rhetorical features that Mary Sidney was at pains to reproduce was the recapitulation of the first half of a verse in different terms that formed the second half. The layout of Psalm 127 in Sidney's working manuscript makes this parallelism clear.[16]

> The house Jehova builds not   We vainly strive to build it
> The Town Jehova guards not   We vainly watch to guard it.

This psalm also demonstrates other features of Sidney's paraphrase. The Geneva gloss identifies the city of stanza 1 as "The public estate of the commonwealth," making this psalm a statement of God's providential upholding of the Christian state: Sidney does not make this identification. Also interesting is her rendering of the gendered rhetoric of the latter part of the Psalm, about God's gift of children: "No not thy children hast thou   By choice by chance by nature."[17]

While Sidney keeps the rhetoric of "chance" and "nature" from Beza's commentary, she ignores his tactless comment that children are obtained "not by labour or industrie."[18] Hannay comments that her version is "an example of male commentaries read with a female eye," but Sidney's sensitivity to feminine issues does not extend to correcting the part of the psalm where children are seen as the property of men, and women's part in childbearing is not mentioned at all.[19] This is typical of Sidney's authorial persona, however, which tends to be gender-neutral and is never explicitly female. It would be strange if Mary Sidney perceived her authorial identity as specifically feminine when there were so many other constructs available to her: spokesman for her politico-religious faction, representative of her dead brother.

No other woman in the early modern period was to do what Mary Sidney had achieved – circulate at the highest level translations of the Bible that influenced George Herbert and were praised by John Donne.[20] Another woman at the court of James I did try the same strategy: she clearly also intended to circulate her poems to the monarch, in an effort at scribal publication. Anne, Lady Southwell, was a witty, well educated woman who seems to have moved in court literary circles that involved John Donne and Sir Thomas Overbury.[21] Her *magnum opus*, however, was a poetic version of the Ten Commandments, which exists in two partial manuscript drafts.[22] Her second husband, Henry Sibthorpe, describes "The Decalogue" in this way:

> when yf she chaunce to worke by imitation
> shee goes beyond her patternes commendation.[23]

It seems that Anne Southwell starts with an "imitation" of each commandment – the Lansdowne manuscript, which seems to be a more polished draft of the third and fourth commandments, begins with a quotation from Deuteronomy and then a verse paraphrase. After that, however, she does indeed go beyond "her patternes commendation." For example, after an exposition of the fourth commandment, "Remember the Sabbath day to keepe it holy," she runs through "Gods first weekes worke" day by day, in a kind of imitation of Du Bartas's *Devine Weekes and Workes*, which was very popular at the Jacobean court. She ends on the sixth day with a rather horrified description of the heresiacs who were created then: "Turks & Popes & other brutish factions." At this point she imagines a misogynist interlocutor asking "how dares this foolish woman be so bold," and defends herself robustly with the invocation of Jael and Judith, whose violence on men was divinely inspired (p. 147). She continues in no less bold a vein. Southwell's satire could not be more direct: every species has a king, and it is strange that kings should be the highest rank mankind aspires to:

> monkeis have cheeftaines, ther's a king mongst bees
> should angells Iuniors looke for naught but this
> the Chaldeeen tyrant fared not much amisse. (p. 150)

Suddenly her target becomes that favorite of literary aristocrats, those who write for money. By contrast her own authorship activity is decorously "private," and piously "inspired":

> For mee, I write but to my self & mee
> What gods good grace doth in my soule imprint. (p. 151)

Elsewhere she has bracketed poets with "Popelings" as objects of scorn: "whoe deales too much wth eyther, is an Asse" (p. 26). Here, she defends rhyme with a rather fine metaphor, which conveys the extra rhetorical impact it can give:

> nor marres it truth, but gives wittes fire more fuell
> & from an Ingott formes a curious Iewell. (p. 152)

Although she is not speaking specifically as a woman here, a lyrical passage follows, highly derivative of the Song of Songs, in which she declares her love for God:

> love doth love this fashion,
> To speak in verse, yf sweet & smoothly carried
> to true proportions love is ever maryed. (p. 152)

Identification with the Bride of Christ seems to bring to Anne Southwell's mind the topic of femininity, and she begins with conventional denunciations of women's pride, adding a comment that she could boast of her looks as much as any woman (p. 154). Such vanity gives rise to the heresy that women have no souls, a doctrine on which her friend John Donne had written one of his Paradoxes and Problemes.[24] The men who could possibly imagine such a thing of women become the target of Anne Southwell's wrath, and she embarks on criticism of the double standard for men and for women in early modern society. If women lift their eyes "but to see theyr fellow spheare, the sunne" they are accused of trying to seduce men (p. 156). The woman who has the temerity to put pen to paper is in real trouble:

> Dare you but write, you are Minervaes bird
> that owle at wch these battes & crowes must wonder.

Anne Southwell points out that the sanguine temperament is thought of as the best: it is the disposition of the witty, learned poet, who is also amorous and likes a drink.[25] Of course, such a woman, who cannot help making jokes, is "of all accurst": patriarchal culture does not believe that in a woman "goodnes & mirth should hold a simpathye" (p. 157). With resignation, Southwell looks forward to the time when difference in gender will not matter, and both sexes will stand before their divine Judge (pp. 157–8).

Anne Southwell's religious politics are shown in the final stanzas, which were initially crossed out. She starts with a denunciation of the Family of Love, but soon moves on to a group readily recognizable as extreme Puritans, whom she calls "deformed reformers of the word." She attacks these "angry prophetts," these "sects & schismes," and finally returns to the topic she started with: "Such cannot keepe the peacefull sabbath day" (p. 160). In the circuitous route she has taken from one meditation on the fourth commandment to another, she has covered a fair amount of ground and given vent to some of her strongest opinions. It is hard to know whether her poem ever reached the king to whom it was dedicated, or whether it would have been welcome if it had. Like Mary Sidney, Anne, Lady Southwell was a moderate Calvinist and Protestant internationalist: she was a friend of Daniel Featley and her second husband fought the English Protestant cause with Horace Vere in the Netherlands.[26] As such, she would have opposed the growing power of Arminianism in the 1620s, which would have made her meditations particularly unwelcome to Charles I, if, as Jean Klene believes, he was the monarch to whom the poetry was eventually addressed.[27]

A mere handful of works by women had come into print before the Civil War of the mid-seventeenth century, and several of these were marketed as "mother's legacies" – documents whose primary readership was apparently the authors' children, and which were usually introduced by prominent men.[28] Female authorship is allowed here because it is posthumous, a criterion that of course applies to the apparent verbatim reporting of Katherine Stubbes's words, which constitute a kind of authorship. As Wendy Wall has shown, the combination of the limited audience, apparently the author's own family, and the recent decease of the author herself, offered one space for women's authoritative writing in which the bounds of her submission to men were not deemed to have been transgressed.[29] It was impossible to accuse a dead woman of the self-display, deemed inherent in the activity of authorship, that for women was often seen as akin to bodily display: publication of her writing was seen as equivalent to prostitution.[30] This suspicion of female authorship undermined the freedom to interpret that the Reformed doctrine of the perspicacity of Scripture to all believers should have given to women.

Thus it is important that these "mother's legacies" were prose works, with no rhetorical or literary virtuosity on show: psalm-like meditations in prosaic metre were often added as appendages to the prose texts, as if to indicate what an acceptable kind of woman's literary activity might be. Ordinary women had started writing their own psalms of praise for events in their own lives – Frances Cooke for her deliverance from shipwreck off Ireland, Mary Cary for what she saw as divine protection in the fearful circumstances of miscarriage and stillbirth – but it was important that there was no hint of rhetorical sophistication on display.[31] Dorothy Leigh's *The Mothers Blessing*, which went into perhaps twenty-three editions between 1616 and 1674, was a posthumous work, and was prefixed by a poem called "Counsell to My Children."[32] The relevant children seem to have been male, which leads Dorothy to worry about inverting the normal hierarchy whereby men teach women: but she does so in order to entreat her sons to write about what they have learned from reading the Word of God (p. 24). She tells them that if they pray to the Holy Spirit they will read the Bible with great profit (p. 42). However, there is little in Dorothy Leigh's treatise to illustrate her own reading of Scripture: her legacy is in passing on the social and cultural prescriptions of Puritanism, although her suggestions are everywhere supported with references from Scripture. Thomas Goad, who edited Elizabeth Joscelin's *The mothers legacie, to her unborne childe* in 1624, ignored her poetry, and her notes on divinity, in order to publish an unfinished treatise that fitted perfectly into his construction of her in his prefatory "Approbation." Sylvia Brown has edited the manuscript of *The mothers legacie* without Goad's corrections in order to try to recover Elizabeth Joscelin's own thoughts, but Goad did not have to edit the manuscript thoroughly to produce her as an ideal Stuart woman.[33] Not knowing the sex of her unborn child, Joscelin debates with herself as to whether a daughter ought to be learned, deciding in favor of a rather more conservative "learning the Bible as my sisters doe" (p. 107). Reading the Bible is suggested as a cure for possible female pride (p. 117). Nowhere is Elizabeth Joscelin expounding the Bible in an original or systematic way, although her rhetoric shows an immersion in the Geneva Bible (p. 98).

Even the manuscript writing of early modern women shows that their response to the Bible is highly mediated by the authoritative men of their culture.[34] It might have been expected that the gendered restriction on publication by women would have led to them writing their own Bible study in private: however, surviving manuscripts abound in personal statements of faith, spiritual diaries, and meditations, rather than Bible study as such. These documents are, of course, full of biblical verses, but these are usually referenced as proof texts to support the orthodoxy of the writing. The most popular and deferential of female scriptural writing was the taking of sermon notes (pride in which was seen as making "multitudes of women unfortunate").[35] It is difficult to escape the conclusion that women's commitment to religion was judged in terms of obedience to orthodoxy rather than intellectual engagement with the Bible. No women had the university education that would qualify them to translate the Bible, or comment on it. One exception is Elizabeth Brackley's manuscript notes on every chapter of the Bible, but her short summaries are not in any way original.[36]

There was one group of women who escaped the limitations imposed on them by their gender: their lack of education was eclipsed by the fact that God interpreted the Scriptures for them. In fact, Sue Wiseman has argued that the special circumstances of their writing meant that they did not think of themselves as women at all, but were speaking "for" God, and therefore not engaging with patriarchal authority in a way that makes sense to modern feminists.[37] These were the women prophets, who, even in mainstream culture of the late 1640s and 1650s were perceived as being particularly open to the Holy Spirit.[38] Their works, which were often printed, show that they were immersed in the biblical texts: Elaine Hobby points out that many radical women show signs of having studied the Bible systematically.[39] Mary Pope, who has often been thought of as a royalist prophet, does not feel the need for testimonies of support by men. Her 1647 treatise, formed as an address to Parliament, claims an authority for herself: she sets out her own credentials for authorship. She has been "an observer of the ebbings and flowings up and downe of Gods providence" over twenty years, and she has "gotten understanding."[40] The main appeal throughout the treatise is to the authority of her own interpretation of Scripture, "having good warrant out of Gods word" both for her message and for her right to give it as a woman (sig. C2v). Her volume is full of scriptural examples of women who have contributed to the work of God, or who have authoritatively spoken the words of God to their community. In her epistle to Parliament, however, her role model is the woman of Tekoah, who, in 2 Samuel 14, spoke to David on behalf of Absalom, to bring him home from exile. She specifically asks Parliament to bring the King home from imprisonment at Holmby (sig. C1r). In the epistle to the reader she elaborates on this: the treatise is the product of co-operation between God and herself, "God ... forcing of me on, and as it were improving of the tallents which he has given for his glory, and serving of my generation." She answers the objection that her writings are nonsense with a statement of faith in her own interpretation and knowledge of Scripture, and her use of "right reason" (sig. C3r). The climax of her treatise is her interpretation of the image of an extremely complicated candlestick in Zechariah 4:

> And now that God hath by his poore weak worthless, and unworthy handmaid (I say) God hath by me a contemptible woman, made out the full directory which is in his Word, and Government of his Church ... all of it infolded, and comprehended, under the type of this golden Candlestick. (p. 59)

At this point, her rational, discursive treatise becomes more characteristic of prophetic discourse, as she assigns meanings to each part of the candlestick's mechanism, employing typology to set out her particular model of how ministry and magistracy cooperate to the advantage of the Church. Zechariah 4:10 also provides the source text for her warning at the end of the epistle to the reader, "Despise not the day of small things," which clearly refers to the supposed weakness of her sex. Mary Pope's willingness to contribute her own "widow's mite" to Parliament in the form of her biblical insights shows the logic of Reformed theology, with its stress on the perspicacity of Scripture and the importance of every individual, whatever the handicaps of poverty, lack of education, or gender. Despite Pope's argument for the power of Christian ministry and magistracy, and ultimately the restoration of the King as Head of the Church, her tracts are evidence of a profoundly unhierarchical approach to the Scriptures, which could allow women such as herself to consider their opinions worth printing, as long as they were divinely inspired.

Diane Purkiss has suggested that prophetesses find authority for their voice in the seventeenth-century marriage law of the *femme couverte*, in which the husband is responsible for the crimes or debts of his wife.[41] This law was explicitly cited by Nonconformists later in the seventeenth century to describe the freedom they experienced on being "married" to Christ. Women, from the mid-seventeenth century onwards, seem to have gained authority and confidence from identifying with the female-gendered Bride of Christ. The best known prophetess of the period, Anna Trapnel, dated her genuine spiritual experience from the age of fourteen when she heard Hugh Peters speak on the mystical marriage: "he opened the marriage Covenant that is between God and his spouse."[42] Despite her precocious spirituality she did not know God as she ought: a period of intense anxiety and grief was brought to an end on January 1, 1642. Thereafter she experienced the bliss characteristic of a prophetess – "raptures of joy," and "ravishings of spirit" (p. 12) – and she began expounding Scripture to those who were close by. The 1654 volume *The Cry of a Stone* contains some of that exposition.

Many of Anna Trapnel's visions are extrabiblical, or combine biblical elements with other visual features. However, the text of Scripture is never far from her mind, even if God suggests contemporary and political interpretations for the actual words:

> bringing that of *Iudges 7*, to me, to prove *Oliver Cromwell*, then Lord General, was as that *Gideon* ... that as sure as the Enemy fell when *Gideon* and that army blew their trumpets, so surely should the Scots throughout Scotland be ruinated.[43]

At other times, Trapnel uses the method beloved of Bible-worshippers throughout the ages, opening the text at random to find guidance:

> at which time, opening my Bible, this was given to me in Job, Thou has been tried in Fetters, and holden in chains of Affliction ... now he openeth thine ear to discipline, and he commandeth that thou return from Iniquity; Lord said I, what is my work? Reply was, that I should go forth to the tempted, and whatever their temptations were, I should have to speak forth to them. (p. 9)

Nigel Smith believes that an untitled folio volume in the Bodleian was published by some of Anna Trapnel's wealthy Fifth Monarchist friends.[44] The first page of the first section – dated October 11, 1657 at 9 o'clock precisely – sets out the role of the Spouse, which is, alongside the Holy Spirit, to sing of Christ: to "bring / Tydings unto the world of / Christ the most glorious King." Soon after the start of her poem, Trapnel is situated in exactly the situation of the Spouse in chapter 5 of Canticles, being attacked by the watchmen: "they at her do strike. For they did tear and rent the vail / Of Christs beloved Wife." Some of the biblical metaphors are used in her description of Christ – his eyes are "Dove-like," he is like the cedar, his countenance is "like Lebanon" (Canticles 5:15). Some of this early discourse, on the second page, is taken straight from Canticles: "Ten thousand can't compare" with Christ (5:10), she is "ravish'd" with his eye (4:9), "O how lovely is he!" (5:16). Trapnel herself, or her scribe, has obviously received the text of the Canticles as a female-authored document, and it is the role of the Bride as singer that is appropriated for her. Clearly this identification with the Spouse of Canticles helps to validate her prophecy at this key point in the volume. The Song of the Bride is referred to later in the volume as a way of constructing the text itself: a paraphrase of parts of Canticles is included, so that Trapnel's poem is grounded in the authority of the Bride's song, from which it branches out (p. 14). At one point this poem seems to be identified as the same kind of discourse as the song of Deborah, and another biblical woman, Jael, is mentioned as the heroine of Deborah's song (p. 69). The choice of these figures is clearly meant to authorize and reinforce the author's femininity here as in other female-authored texts.

However, no point about the validity of women's discourse in general is being made. Midway through the volume a conventional condemnation of women's utterance as "idle talk" occurs (p. 211), and a criticism of women as being too ready to speak. Moreover, Eve is censured as a representative of sinning woman:

> he made Creation rue,
> Through the yeilding of *Eve* to that
> Which did so tempt and ensnare;
> And therefore, Hand-maids, you ought now
> To have the greater care.
> O let some learn what evil hath been,
> And how it actively doth grow;
> And do not you go tattling, and
> With such a tongue to and fro.

The affirmation and validation of Trapnel's prophecies is found in the extraordinary women of the Bible: that affirmation is not extended to women in general. In fact, women's own words will always be unacceptable: the lesson to be learnt from Eve's example is that female human utterance should be replaced by divine discourse.

> This should learn Females to be slow of speech
> To have very few words from self,
> Because this Sex had such a first voice,
> But to look to the Lord for help. (p. 211)

Trapnel's power as a prophetess is in emulating a divine feminine voice in the Scripture: she is an extraordinarily receptive woman, whose voice is that of the Spouse. As an exception to the majority of women, she can ventriloquize the speaking voice of the Holy Spirit. Ironically, this is far from the spirit in which Reformed commentary interpreted the Bride, as a privileged relationship with Christ for all believers, accessible in theory to all women.

One woman who was very aware of her Reformed heritage, as well as of her own substantial abilities, was the Republican writer Lucy Hutchinson. By social status and education she was already superior in standing to most women, but she was also conscious that she needed to respect the gendered conventions of the day with regard to publication of her writings. Thus, her translation of Lucretius's *De Rerum Natura* remained in manuscript, as did her sophisticated theological treatise, which was packaged as a "mother's legacy" addressed to her daughter.[45] Despite its modest claims, this work showed intellectual ambition which went far beyond the well known moralizing of Elizabeth Joscelin and Dorothy Leigh, which was still available in the 1670s when Hutchinson was writing. Her spiritual journal, while remaining in manuscript, seems to have been sent by her to the Earl of Anglesey, who was reading it in 1682.[46]

This unwomanly concern with an audience for her scriptural writing seems to have led, in 1679, to the anonymous publication of her poetic version of Genesis, *Order and Disorder*, a rare example of women's writing appearing anonymously in print. This work makes an interesting contrast with another poetic version of Genesis that is fully aware of its limitations as the writing of a woman. "The Sacred Historie" is, strictly speaking, anonymous, although its dedicatory prayer makes clear that it is the work of a woman named Mary, probably Mary Roper.[47] In the tradition of Renaissance women such as Mary Sidney and Anne Southwell, the author dedicates her work to a monarch, not King Charles II but his wife, Catherine of Braganza. She is very conscious of her inferior status as a woman. Like many early modern women before her, she likens her work to the widow's mite, and compares her praise of God to that commanded "out of the Mouths of Babes and Sucklings." She situates herself in the role of biblical women like Miriam, Deborah, and Hannah, who all composed songs of praise to God (p. 156). By contrast, Lucy Hutchinson's preface reads like the prefatory sentiments of many Puritan male authors. She regrets "the vain curiosity of youth," which had drawn her to work on pagan authors (probably Lucretius).[48] She excuses her use of poetry by referring, as male Christian poets such as Philip Sidney had done, to the poetic nature of much of the Holy Scriptures: she echoes the fear of Andrew Marvell when considering that other epic version of Genesis, *Paradise Lost*, that human imagination would corrupt divine truth: "Had I a fancy, I durst not have exercised it here; for I tremble to think of turning Scripture into a romance."[49]

Nevertheless, it is interesting that both authors are obviously drawn to the many vivid stories in Genesis in which a woman is the central protagonist. The plight of Lot's wife turning into a pillar of salt, of Hagar left to watch her baby die of thirst in the desert, of Rebekah feeling her twins fight in the womb and giving birth to them painfully feature in both poems, although Hutchinson is obviously much the better poet.[50] She tends to allow the women to complain in their own voice, as in this lament from Hagar, who, abandoned in the desert, has removed herself from her child because she cannot bear to see him die:

> "O that I could" said she "thaw to a spring
> Which might my Ishmael some refreshment bring!
> With what content should I my life resign
> Could I prolong his day by losing mine. ...
> Neither with death a quick deliverance bring
> We must endure a tedious languishing
> And while he doth in wretched torture pine
> His death augments the bitterness of mine." (*Order and Disorder*, pp. 190–1)

Roper's description of Hagar is also pitiful.

> Nothing she sees but Stones, and Rocks, and Woods
> Roarings of Wilde Beasts in their Dismall Shades
> Torments Her Eares. She Feares to be a prey
> Or Lett some Tiger take her Son Away. (p. 71)

As so often in the writing of seventeenth-century women, however, the different politics of Mary Roper and Lucy Hutchinson mean that the contrasts between the two poems are as striking as the similarities. Mary Roper is very aware that in versifying Genesis she is portraying the excellence of the Patriarchs. It is tempting to think that she had read Robert Filmer's *Patriarcha*, which was finally published in 1680 and dedicated to Charles II but which had been written as early as 1630.[51] Filmer, of course, uses the patriarchs of Genesis to clinch his argument about the "Absolute Dominion" of monarchs. For Filmer, Adam is proof that men are not all born equal, since Adam was created first (p. 11). Moreover, the primacy of Adam can be used to justify monarchy: "not only Adam, but the succeeding Patriarchs had, by Right of Father-hood, Royal Authority" (p. 12). Roper's Adam, too, is explicitly a king (p. 14). As an example of this *"Patriarchal Power"* Filmer cites Abraham in his dealings with Abimelech (p. 13). Lucy Hutchinson, however, is clearly not impressed by Abraham's cowardice in giving his beautiful wife to Abimelech in order to pre-empt any jealous anger, and treats the episode with epic seriousness. Her account stresses Abimelech's essential decency and the embarrassment and shame with which Abraham has to listen to bewildered questioning of his motives for bringing the wrath of God down on his court (p. 186). By contrast, Mary Roper calls him "a Wicked Man" and God's wrath is punishment for Abimelech's lust, despite the fact that Sarah is returned to Abraham undefiled ("The Sacred Historie," p. 45). Most striking is the difference in the way Hutchinson and Roper deal with the story of Noah's drunkenness. Roper is at pains to excuse Noah's intoxication – "He Sinned through Ignorance," unaware of the effects of the fermented grape – and it is his son Ham who drew attention to the exposure of his genitals who is wicked, cursed for his irreverence ("The Sacred Historie," p. 37). By contrast, Hutchinson is scornful of Noah, and moralizes for 170 lines on the evils of drink (*Order and Disorder*, pp. 136–41).

Reverence for the patriarchs is important for Mary Roper, as she is clearly using one of them – Joseph – as a type of Charles II. Lucy Hutchinson does not get as far as the story of Joseph in her versification of Genesis, but for Roper it is the climax of her book. She traces the betrayal of Joseph by his brothers, his slavery in Egypt, and his imprisonment, during which he gains a reputation of an interpreter of dreams, and then with delight describes his subsequent fame in a section she calls "Josephs Glory." At this point Roper breaks off her narration to deal with contemporary events in a section called "May 29 1669," the ninth anniversary of Charles's entry into London, and she makes the comparison of Charles II with Joseph explicit.

> God who Joseph Did in Prison Save
> > Deliverance unto our Soveraigne Gave
> Our King, Like Joseph, was in Great Distresses
> > But God Brought Him from troubles Wildernesses ("The Sacred Historie," p. 157).

The rest of the poem is panegyric for Charles and praise for God who has "Chosen him a Lott": the providential care of God in providing for Charles is illustrated by a picture of Boscabel Oak, where Charles hid after his defeat at Worcester in 1651. The tree theme is continued: Charles is "Our Royall Cedar" and "The Bramble God Cut Downe" is presumably Cromwell (p. 158). After this Roper returns to Genesis and Joseph's story until he reveals himself to his brothers, which is the cue for four poems relevant to seventeenth-century political history: "Our Kings Sorrows and Suffrings" (in which Charles is called "Our Joseph"), "Englands Misery," "Englands Sad Lamentation," and "Englands Thanksgiving." In all of these Roper's Royalism is made explicit. Not that Lucy Hutchinson's version of Genesis is irrelevant to contemporary politics, although she does not break into her narrative with contemporary poems, as Roper does. The first five cantos, which were printed, are relatively uncontroversial. In the rest of the poem, which remained in manuscript, she does use the technique of digression and a change of tense to signal that she is addressing contemporary evils. The long digression about drunkenness, mentioned above, is clearly based on the observation of Restoration debauchery. The licentiousness of women is presented as a conspiracy of Hell: the excuse for this digression is the moral laxity of Cain's daughters but the clothes they are dressed in are Restoration fashions (*Order and Disorder*, pp. 102–3). Cain himself is identified even more specifically as a seventeenth-century high churchman, a "formal hypocrite" (p. 98). The reason his sacrifice is not accepted is that there is no sincerity in his heart. Like the Laudians whom the Restoration Anglican church explicitly celebrated, he merely enjoys the holy ceremonies: they are "performances" (p. 90).

It is not surprising that the Bible can speak to women on opposite sides of the political divide in ways that seem to support completely opposed causes. The close emotional engagement that characterizes Reformed reading of the Bible together with the doctrine of perspicuity, which stresses its accessibility to every believer, is bound to result in such subjectivity. This partiality was of course a feature of men's dealings with the Bible in the seventeenth century, as well as women's, but it is exaggerated in women's writing because they tend to eschew biblical scholarship in favor of a personal appropriation of the text. Each of the women here, whether a Calvinist aristocrat like Mary Sidney, or shipwright's daughter and Fifth Monarchist Anna Trapnel, found the Bible relevant to their own deepest political and personal concerns. It is almost true to say, then, that their writing about the Bible is a manifestation of the original authorship that was officially denied them: through writing about the Bible they were able to speak, however indirectly, about their own passions and politics.

Notes

1   Phillip Stubbes, *A christal glasse for Christian women containing, a most excellent discourse, of the godly life and Christian death of Mistresse Katherine Stubs, who departed this life in Burton upon Trent, in Staffordshire the 14. day of December. 1590. With a most heavenly confession of the Christian faith, which shee made a little before her departure* (London, 1592), sig. A2r.
2   Ian Green, *Print and Protestantism in Early Modern England* (Oxford University Press, Oxford, 2000), p. 661.
3   Stubbes, *A Christal Glasse*, sig. A3v.
4   *Annotations upon all the books of the Old and New Testament* (London, 1645), sig. B3r.
5   Jill Millman and Gillian Wright, eds, *Early Modern Women's Manuscript Poetry* (Manchester University Press, Manchester, 2005), p. 1.
6   One rare exception to this apparent ignorance of other women's writing is Elizabeth Ashburnham's manuscript treatment of Mary Sidney's *A Discourse of Life and Death* (1592). See Margaret Hannay, "Elizabeth Ashburnham Richardson's Meditation on the Countess of Pembroke's *Discourse*," in *English Manuscript Studies*, 8 (2000), 114–28. Sylvia Brown argues that Elizabeth Joscelin had read Dorothy Leigh's *The Mother's Blessing* (1616). See Sylvia Brown, ed., *Women's Writing in Stuart England: The Mothers' Legacies of Dorothy Leigh, Elizabeth Jocelin and Elizabeth Richardson* (Sutton, Stroud, 1999), p. 98. Jill Millman points out that Margaret Cunningham's "Life" echoes almost verbatim Ann Lok's dedication of her 1590 volume to the Countess of Warwick: Faith Eales, "Context and Purpose," National Library of Scotland: MS 874, fos 363–84 in Perdita catalogue, http://human.ntu.ac.uk/research/perdita/frames/html/index.htm.
7   For Mary Sidney's role as Philip's "literary executor" see Danielle Clarke, "Mary Sidney Herbert and Women's Religious Verse," in Patrick Cheney, Andrew Hadfield and Garrett Sullivan, eds, *Early Modern English Poetry: A Critical Companion* (Oxford University Press, Oxford, 2006), p. 184.
8   Margaret P. Hannay, "'Doo What Men May Sing': Manuscript and the Admonitory Dedication," in Hannay, ed., *Silent But for the Word: Tudor Women as Patrons, Translators, and Writers of Religious Works*. Kent State University Press, Kent, OH 1985), pp. 149–50.
9   *Early Modern Women's Manuscript Poetry*, p. 21.
10 For the connections of each of these texts with the Sidney-Dudley alliance, see Danielle Clarke, ed., *Isabella Whitney, Mary Sidney and Aemilia Lanyer: Renaissance Women Poets* (Penguin, Harmondsworth, 2000), pp. xx–xxi.
11 *Renaissance Women Poets*, p. 49.
12 See Ros Smith, "'In a mirrour clere': Protestantism and Politics in Anne Lok's *Miserere Mei Deus*," in Danielle Clarke and Elizabeth Clarke, eds, *"This Double Voice": Gendered Writing in Early Modern England* (Basingstoke: Macmillan, 2000), pp. 41–60. Louise Schleiner, having charted the Cooke sisters' efforts in an admonitory direction in the 1570s (in which Ann Lok had a part), sees Mary's admonitory function in a more European context: Louise

Schleiner, *Tudor and Stuart Women Writers* (Indiana University Press, Bloomington, 1994), p. 52.

13   *The Bible and Holy Scriptures conteyned in the Olde and Newe Testament. Translated according to the Ebrue and Greke, and conferred with the best translations in divers langages. With moste profitable annotations upon all the hard places, and other things of great importance as may appeare in the epistle to the reader* (Geneva, 1560), p. 244.

14   *Renaissance Women Poets*, pp. 308–9.

15   *Early Modern English Poetry*, p. 189.

16   Bodleian MS Rawlinson 25 is derived from one of Sidney's working copies, and Danielle Clarke's edition is based on it.

17   *Renaissance Women Poets*, p. 166.

18   Theodore de Bèze, *The Psalmes of Dauid truly opened and explaned by paraphrasis, according to the right sense of everie Psalme* (London, 1581), p. 315.

19   Margaret P. Hannay, "'House-confinéd maids': The Presentation of Woman's Role in the *Psalmes* of the Countess of Pembroke," *English Literary Review* 24 (1994), 64–5.

20   Barabara K. Lewalski, *Protestant Poetics and the Seventeenth-Century Religious Lyric* (Princeton University Press, Princeton NJ, 1979).

21   Jean Klene, "Southwell, Anne, Lady Southwell (bap. 1574, d. 1636)," *Oxford Dictionary of National Biography* (Oxford University Press, Oxford, 2004).

22   Folger MS V. b. 198. See *The Southwell-Sibthorpe Commonplace Book* pp. 44–8, 54–87: B. L. Lansdowne MS 740.

23   *The Southwell-Sibthorpe Commonplace Book*, p. 163.

24   John Donne, *Iuvenilia or Certaine paradoxes and problemes* (London, 1633), p. 36.

25   Henry Peacham, *Minerva Britanna or A garden of heroical deuises furnished, and adorned with emblemes and impresa's of sundry natures* (London, 1612), p. 127.

26   *The Southwell-Sibthorpe Commonplace Book.*

27   Klene, "Southwell, Anne, Lady Southwell (bap. 1574, d. 1636)."

28   See Sylvia Brown, *Women's Writing in Stuart England* (Sutton, Thrupp, Gloucestershire, 1999) for an annotated edition of three such "Mother's Legacies."

29   Wendy Wall, *The Imprint of Gender: Authorship and Publication in the English Renaissance* (Cornell University Press, Ithaca, NY, 1993), pp. 283–96.

30   Diane Purkiss, "Producing the Voice, Consuming the Body: Women Prophets of the Seventeenth Century," in Isobel Grundy and Susan Wiseman, eds, *Women, Writing, History 1640–1740* (B. T. Batsford, London, 1992), p. 140. See Richard Lovelace's opinion on the woman poet: "Now as her self a Poem she doth dresse, / And curls a Line as she would so a tresse; / Powders a Sonnet as she does her hair / Then prostitutes them both to publick Aire," *Poems* (1657), p. 200. For male reaction to even a sober religious treatise written by a woman, see F. W. van Heertum, *A Critical Edition of Joseph Swetnam's The Arraignment of Lewd, Idle, Froward and Inconstant Women* (The Cicero Press, Nijmegen, 1981), pp. 87–8.

31   Frances Cooke, *Mrs Cooke's Meditations, being an humble thanksgiving to her Heavenly Father, for granting her a new life, having conclnded [sic] her selfe dead, and her grave made in the bottome of the sea, in that great storme. Jan. the 5th. 1649* (London, 1650); *Lady Carey's Meditations, & Poetry* (Bodleian Library MS Rawlinson D. 1308).

32   Ian Green, *Print and Protestantism in Early Modern England* (Oxford University Press, Oxford, 2000), p. 637; Sylvia Brown, ed., *Women's Writing in Stuart England* (Sutton, Stroud, 1999), p. 18.

33   *Women's Writing in Stuart England*, p. 100.

34 See my treatment of this topic in the context of elegy in " 'A heart terrifying Sorrow': the Deaths of Children in Seventeenth-Century Women's Manuscript Journals," in Kimberley Reynolds, ed., *Representations of Childhood Death* (Macmillan, Basingstoke, 2000), pp. 65–86.

35 Elizabeth Anne Taylor, "Writing Women, Honour and Ireland 1640-1715," unpublished PhD thesis, University College Dublin, 1999, II, p. 285. See Gillian Wright, "Mary Evelyn and Devotional Practice," in Frances Harris and Michael Hunter, ed., *John Evelyn and His Milieu* (British Library, London, 2003), pp. 221–3, for a study of Mary Evelyn's sermon notes.

36 Huntingdon Library MS EL 8374. See Betty S. Travitsky, *Subordination and Authorship in Early Modern England* (Mediaeval and Renaissance Texts and Studies, Tempe, AZ, 1999), p. 137.

37 Wiseman, "Unsilent Instruments," pp. 187–9. See also Hilary Hinds's chapter on "The disappearing author" in her book *God's Englishwomen; Seventeenth-Century Radical Sectarian Writing and Feminist Criticism* (Manchester University Press, Manchester, 1996).

38 See Longfellow, *Women and Religious Writing*, pp. 149–79.

39 Elaine Hobby, " 'Discourse So Unsavoury': Women's Published Writings of the 1650s," in Isobel Grundy and Susan Wiseman, eds, *Women, Writing, History 1640–1740* (B. T. Batsford, London, 1992), p. 25.

40 Pope, A Treatise of Magistracy, sig. C2r.

41 Diane Purkiss, "Producing the Voice, Consuming the Body: Women Prophets of the Seventeenth Century," in Isobel Grundy and Susan Wiseman, eds, *Women, Writing, History 1640–1740* (B. T. Batsford, London, 1992), p. 157.

42 Anna Trapnel, *A Legacy for Saints* (London, 1654), p. 3.

43 Anna Trapnel, *The Cry of a Stone* (London, 1654), p. 6.

44 This volume is catalogued as "Poetical addresses or discourses delivered to a gathering of 'Companions' in 1657 and 1658."

45 See British Library Add MS 19333 and Northamptonshire Record Office: Fitzwilliam Collection, misc., volume 793.

46 David Norbrook, "Lucy Hutchinson's 'Elegies' and the Situation of the Republican Woman Writer," *English Literary Renaissance* 27 (1997), 485.

47 See *Early Modern Women's Manuscript Verse*, pp. 10–11, for the evidence of Mary Roper's authorship.

48 Lucy Hutchinson, *Order and Disorder*, ed. David Norbrook (Oxford: Blackwell, 2000), p. 3.

49 *Order and Disorder*, p. 3. Compare Marvell, "On Mr Milton's Paradise Lost" (*Miscellaneous Poems*, 1681): "That he would ruine (for I saw him strong) / The sacred Truths to Fable and old Song."

50 Hutchinson, *Order and Disorder* pp. 174, 190–1, 216–17; Roper?, "The Sacred Historie," p. 64, 71–, 84–5.

51 Glenn Burgess, "Filmer, Sir Robert (1588?–1653)," *Oxford Dictionary of National Biography* (Oxford University Press, Oxford, 2004).

CHAPTER 13
Early Modern Religious Prose

Julie Maxwell

Imagine the following dystopia. A student of literature, you are allowed access to literary criticism, but not to primary texts. Only university professors have copies of *The Divine Comedy*, *Don Quixote* and *War and Peace* – all in original language editions that few English students can read. A handful of underground manuscript translations circulate, but you can't afford to buy one. Your knowledge of literary masterpieces is restricted to the parts the professors happen to quote or describe in lectures and critical studies. Unfortunately, they seem far more interested in each other's arguments than, say, Goethe or Proust. Sometimes, you suspect, they are being fanciful. But without reading the texts for yourself, you cannot possibly challenge what they say.

Before the early modern period, reading or hearing religious prose could be just like this. It summarized, interpreted, elaborated, and generally put itself in the place of a text that was known directly only to a few: the Bible. Legends of the saints, not the letters of St Paul, were familiar material. But in the sixteenth century this changed, and what happened to religious prose across the next 150 years is the subject of this chapter. An unwieldy category – which ranged from pastoral writing to polemical, devotional to doctrinal, exegetical to ecclesiastical – religious prose dominated publishing.

Tyndale and Citation

"When I allege any scripture," the pioneering English Bible translator William Tyndale advised readers of his prose writings, "look thou on the text, that I interpret it right" (Tyndale, 2000, p. 30). An unprecedented number of English readers were now *able* to look: criticism was democratized by Tyndale's determination to make even the ploughboy biblically conversant. The Bible couldn't be missed – Hugh Latimer, not quite Tyndale's ploughboy but a yeoman farmer's son, "began to smell the word of God" and to preach a socially egalitarian gospel (Latimer, 2000, p. 334). The appearance of the Bible and its preachers made a stink. The unhygienic early modern world was plagued with stenches – but in this case, the stink was also a fragrance. The Bible, as John Bunyan would later write, "smelt after the manner of the best Perfume, also it was

Written in Letters of Gold" (Bunyan 2003, p. 171). Not only an olfactory triumph, then, but a typographic one too. In other words, It Stood Out.

Like any great work, however, the Bible was not transparent. Tyndale exhorted readers not just to look at the text, but to look at it very hard indeed, particularly at the *circumstances*, or original context, of any scriptural quotation:

> When Paul preached (Acts 17), the others searched the scriptures daily, whether they were as he alleged them. Why shall not I likewise, whether it be the scripture that thou allegest? Yea why shall I not see the scripture and the circumstances and what goeth before and after, that I may know whether thine interpretation can be the right sense or whether thou jugglest and drawest the scripture violently unto thy carnal and fleshly purpose? (Tyndale, 2000, p. 64)

The careful attention that Tyndale recommends, and the double-dealing he fears, are expressed in his legalistic vocabulary. *Alleged*, used for quoting an authority for or against an argument, was also used for giving testimony for or against a defendant (OED *allege* v.2). And *circumstances* would become legalized too: Shakespeare's Richard III asks leave to acquit himself "By circumstance," or circumstantial evidence (1.2.77). For Tyndale, the pulpit is in the dock. Scriptural evidence may be alleged, but it must be carefully scrutinized. This legality is shared with Scripture – in the Johannine metaphor of Jesus as the one who bears true witness, in the cross-examination of texts that both he and Paul employ as a rhetorical strategy. Tyndale's legal consciousness also arises from historical circumstance, specifically from the threat of interrogation for heresy, which affected how the Bible was used. In John Foxe's *Acts and Monuments of the Christian Martyrs* (first English edition 1563), where Tyndale's story and many others are told, the Bible is most often introduced in an ecclesiastical trial situation.

Or rather, cited. It is no accident that the legal term *cite* has a new sense in English – of quoting in order to adduce an authority – once Tyndale starts writing. George Joye, who famously fell out with Tyndale, after ignorantly and silently correcting his New Testament, is the first to use *cite* in this way. Eventually – the OED takes the first clear example from Thackeray – English speakers refer to "chapter and verse – a phrase, derived from the layout of material in the Bible, which has come to mean the minutiae of evidence, the citation of detailed, clinching proof, exactitude, certainty, a sense of truth" (OED *chapter* 10b; Raine, 2000, p. 281). Tyndale's prose originated all the ideas associated with this phrase, although his translations did not actually use numbered verse divisions. If anything, though, the lack of verse divisions actually made Tyndale and his followers look even more forensically at the minutiae of biblical evidence.

Take John Bale's *The Image of Both Churches* (1548). This was a clause-by-clause (and the first full-length Protestant) exposition of Revelation as a key to world epochs, a new idea in English writing. The commentary was keyed to a numbered biblical text. It begins like this: "1 The revelation of Jesus Christ, 2 which God gave unto him, 3 for to shew unto his servants the things which must shortly come to pass: 4 and he sent and showed by his angel unto the servant John" (Bale, 1849, p. 264). Intratextual verse divisions had still not been introduced to Bibles and Bale's division is extreme:

what would become the standard verse one of chapter one has been divided fourfold here.[1] It is theology by numbers: a difficult subject divided into tiny pieces.

So far, so simple. There is a procedure in place. But compare the beginning of Tyndale's *The Obedience of a Christian Man* (1528) and it is already clear that there is an unforeseen difficulty. "Grace, peace and increase of knowledge in our Lord Jesus Christ be with the reader" (Tyndale, 2000, p. 3). The reader may recognize that this is like the opening of a New Testament epistle, that Tyndale owes an appropriate stylistic debt to parts of the Bible that advocate religious revolution. In other words, this is not just prose writing *about* the Bible, which *cites* the Bible. It is prose writing that takes on some literary characteristics *of* the Bible. And here we reach our problem, or, in true Renaissance style, paradox.

Tyndale's warning about scrutinizing how people use Scriptures sounds simple enough – but the introduction of the English Bible had complicated effects on religious prose. Tyndale himself is not always explicitly alleging Scriptures, or offering up for our inspection his use of the Bible. The Bible does not arrive in discrete plastic bags – here is Exhibit A, here is Exhibit B – in his prose. Instead his writing is full of absorbed scriptural phraseology, fragments embedded in new circumstances, as well as of neobiblical cadences. It is as though the lawyer for the defence has started talking like his most important witness. Pastiche just isn't part of the procedure.

What are we to make of writing that sounds like the Bible, but isn't? Neobiblicism has not been considered odd in the translator who created the Bible in his own language (82 percent of the King James Bible is Tyndale, and 90 percent of its New Testament is his). But it is odd. In fact it is a paradox. Tyndale, anxious to shared gospel truth, also supplied a language for faking the Bible, which would allow later writers to claim their words had a status equal to the Bible. They sounded biblical – which they put down to the inspiring influence of the Holy Spirit, and which we may discover in shared habits of syntax and lexis. Tyndale's legacy was not simply the Bible in English, then, but biblical English. He modeled an idiom that could roam well beyond the text to which it had first belonged. Fearing ignorance and hypocrisy, Tyndale sought to banish them by providing a Bible. But what he never feared – what he never, in his innocence of literary ambitions, even conceived – was the power of his own words. Increased familiarity with the contents of biblical narratives and texts also conduced to their creative reimagination by writers. And again, paradoxically, Tyndale had supplied the material – gospel for fiction.

Southwell and Paraphrase

Tyndale was not alone at this time in writing "biblically," rather than strictly what was in the Bible. In 1548, the year that Bale's *Image* appeared, the *Paraphrases on the New Testament* (1517–24) of the Dutch humanist Erasmus began to be placed in every church in England, along with a copy of the Great Bible. Some readers were upset that Erasmus put words into the mouths of the apostles, and even Christ. Paraphrasing the biblical text had an ancestry in Jewish scriptural interpretation, specifically the Targums that rendered the Hebrew Bible into Aramaic. Ultimately, paraphrasing was ascribed a biblical origin: on a famous occasion Ezra and Nehemiah had read the law of Moses to the people "and gave the sense, and caused *them* to understand the reading" (Bible, 1997, Nehemiah 8:8). This story also indicates one purpose of paraphrasing: the pioneering works of religious prose after Tyndale were expository. The Bible required introduction to beginners. Explanation was often achieved through expansion – putting the Bible into alternative, diffuser, easier words.

But if biblical paraphrase was sometimes an elementary, homiletic genre, it could also be a self-consciously literary one, designed for sophisticated readers, as was Robert Southwell's *Marie Magdalens funeral teares* (1591). It might be written not neobiblically, but neoclassically. Tyndale's imitation of biblical style and genre was not inevitable for religious prose writers: it would take time for his biblical English to become a native tongue, as it is in *The Pilgrim's Progress* (1678) or *The Journal* (1694) of George Fox; also, there was stiff literary competition. Biblical teaching often appeared in non-biblical genres. The dialogue form of George Gifford's *A Brief Discourse of ... Countrie Divinitie* (1581), or Arthur Dent's *The Plaine Mans Pathway To Heaven* (1601), is Socratic, not scriptural. The spiritual autobiography is Augustinian. The sermon has an obviously biblical origin, although in its early modern incarnations it is massively distended – longer, like the limbs of an El Greco saint, or the nether parts of the fallen Satan in *Paradise Lost*. Generic transformations and substitutions occurred because early modern religious prose writers did not respond to the Bible in a literary vacuum. How could, say, any writer with aspirations in the London of the 1590s be unaware of experiments in contemporary prose fiction, love poetry, or the theater?

The cases of Robert Southwell and John Donne, who write several decades after Tyndale but also several decades before Bunyan, illustrate this amply. The effects are worth considering in some detail.

Southwell, later martyred for his Catholic faith, hoped to divert readers from "the popular vaine" of "patheticall discourses" in English prose writing to his biblical paraphrase, *Marie Magdalens funeral teares* (Southwell, 1591, unpaginated preface). By the time Southwell was writing, it was not only the Reformation but the Renaissance that had happened to English religious prose – and it shows.

Southwell's work was an amplification of a few biblical verses – "the ground thereof being in Scripture, and the forme of enlarging it, an imitation of the ancient doctours" (Southwell, 1591, unpaginated preface). The verses, from John's gospel, describe Mary seeking in vain Jesus's body in the tomb where he has been laid, her encounter with the angels, and Jesus's appearance to her. How can it be, Southwell asks, that *she mistakes him for the gardener*? Southwell's enlargement drew on the contemporary literature of which he was officially contemptuous. His imitation of patristic sources – especially the *Homilia de Beata Maria Magdalena*, traditionally attributed to Origen – employed Renaissance conventions. Mary Magdalene steps out of pastoral romance, weeping and despairing in a cave like the lovelorn figures of Philip Sidney or Lady Mary Wroth. Pathetical, indeed. While Southwell can be skeptical of romantic excess – "if thy eyes were melted ... how wouldst thou see him ... ?" – he also finds it useful in explaining puzzles in the biblical text (ibid., p. 20). Why did the angels ask Mary why she was weeping (surely fairly self-evident) instead of telling her out straight that Jesus was resurrected? Because of the emotional instability that is typical of lovers in literature: "And this O *Mary* I ghesse to be the cause why the Angels would not tell thee thy Lords estate. For if it had béen to thy liking, thou wouldest have died for joy, if otherwise thou wouldst have suncke downe for sorrow" (ibid., p. 34a). Because, in romance, a bipolar disorder is perfectly in order.

Mary's tears, which supply Southwell with his title, might flow just as readily in a Shakespearean sonnet. Like Mary, Love's eye can't see clearly in sonnet 148: "How can it, O, how can love's eye be true, / That is so vexed with watching and with tears?" (9– 10). Marvell, too, ponders these cross-purposes in "Eyes and Tears" and thinks of Mary: "So *Magdalen*, in Tears more wise / Dissolv'd those captivating eyes" (29–30). Early modern love poets strive ingeniously to discovery the advantage of misery. Happy are those who mourn because they will be comforted – because, especially when the Bible meets the classics, they have company. Thus Southwell's Mary imagines that the whole natural world is wailing with her, as it would in Greek pastoral elegy: "thy ears per-suade thee, that all sounds and voices are tuned to mourning notes, and that the Eccho of thy own wailings, is the cry of the very stons & trées, as though (the cause of thy teares being so unusuall) God to the rocks and woods, had inspired a feeling of thine and their common losse" (Southwell, 1591, pp. 27a–28). A similar *idea* occurs else-where in the gospels – "if these [Jesus's disciples] should hold their peace, the stones would immediately cry out" – but Southwell's *expression* of it is a Renaissance echo of the classical Echo (Luke 19:40).

Mary's literary-inspired mistakes, delusions, and doubts dominate the text. They are how Southwell smuggles in the imagination. Fanciful legends and apocryphal anec-dotes (which Protestants denounced in Catholics, and which vernacular translation of the Bible was designed to stamp out) may be avoided, but invented thoughts and speeches abound. Suppose, Mary speculates, she were to thieve Jesus's body from the thieves she supposes to have stolen it? Speculation is soon heaped on speculation, briefly creating a counterfactual gospel according to which Mary attempts to recover Jesus's body and is beaten and killed by a tyrant, who repents and conceals her body (she is posthumously pleased to observe) beside her Lord's. This isn't written in neobibli-cal English, but it might be dubbed "neobiblical plotting."

If speculation is Mary's weakness, plausibility is Southwell's strength. Take his ratio-nalistic, realistic enquiries about details in the biblical narrative:

> Would any théefe thinkest thou have béen so religious, as to have stollen the body and left the clothes? yea would he have béene so venturous, as to have staied the unshrowding of the corse, the well ordering of the sheets, and folding up of the napkins? Thou knowest that mirrhe maketh linen cleaue as fast, as pitch or glue: and was a théefe at so much leisure, as to dissolve the mirrhe and uncloath the dead? (Southwell, 1591, p. 24)

Valuable abandoned clothes, folded sheets and napkins, the properties of myrrh – Hercule Poirot meets the Bible. In Southwell's detective imagination, biblical hyperbole is replaced with hypothesis. Jesus had said, "the very hairs of your head are all num-bered" (Matthew 10:30). Southwell suggests, "Looke then into the shéete, whether there remaine any parcel of skinne, or any one haire of his head" (Southwell, 1591, p. 24a). It is not a superhuman activity to spot a hair on a white sheet.

Tyndale had put the Bible citer in the dock: Southwell returns us to the scene of the crime. There is a vivid flashback of events – the verbal equivalent, we might say, of the explanation scene at the end of an Agatha Christie film adaptation. Southwell imagines the participants moving around, existing in physical space. Why was Jesus not insulted when Mary addressed him as a gardener – and a thieving gardener at that? "Thy whole person presented such a paterne of thy extreame anguish, that no man from thy presence could take in anie other impression" (ibid., p. 50a). In short, "what thy wordes wanted, thy action supplied" (ibid.) Southwell suggests the stage direction that the Bible doesn't: perhaps there was something in Jesus' voice and demeanor that inclined Mary to think her question would be well received.

Entering imaginatively into such moments, Southwell often writes as if they are happening right now. Frequently he addresses the characters directly, in the second person, in order to question, counsel, and encourage them. As though the Bible were a playbook, and this a rehearsal. It is appropriate that Southwell introduces this theatrical feeling to his detective paraphrase, because detection, as represented in literature, is inherently dramatic: it holds us in long suspense for the denouement. And this was an idea in the London air. The domestic tragedy *Arden of Faversham*, published in 1592, the year after *Marie Magdalens funeral teares*, is the first English drama to involve a piece of detective work.

But if the Bible could be reimagined as romance, pastoral elegy, and even detective drama, it could also be *analysed* as a poem. In the early modern period, no one did this better than John Donne, the poet who became the prelate, the Dean of St Paul's.

Donne and the Poetry of Prose

Donne said that the writers of the Bible were "ever inserting into their writings some phrases, some metaphors, some allusions taken from that profession which they had exercised before" (Donne, 1987, p. 144). Donne was once a student of law and, as we will see, his version of Tyndale's legalistic interrogation is a thrilling courtroom performance. But more importantly Donne was a poet and he wrote about the Bible as though it were a poem.

Of course, the Bible *is* poetry in parts – including the Psalms, which Donne especially loved – but Donne reads biblical prose poetically too. In his sermons, biblical scholarship turns frequently into a marvellous exercise of practical criticism. Take Donne's recourse to the Bible's original languages. What does he notice about Hebrew? Tellingly, its sound effects. For instance, the swish of "*Ishe*, which is the first name of man, in the Scriptures, and signifies nothing but a *sound*, a *voyce*, a word; a Musical ayre dyes, and evaporates, what wonder if man, that is but *Ishe*, a *sound*, dye too?" (Donne, 2003, p. 32). Mortality is onomatopoeic. We fade away like the tail end of a song. In Pope's *The Dunciad* (1743), a young man dissipates into thin sound: "And last turn'd *Air*, the Echo of a Sound!" (4:322). But Pope is slighting, while Donne offers our slightness for serious contemplation. This is onomatopoeia as theology, the argument of a poet alive to the sounds that others are dead to. Poetry is written for the ear. So is Donne's biblical exegesis. He argues, with reference to Psalm 90:14, that "Prayer and

Praise is almost the same word" (Donne, 2003, p. 47). In what sense? Again, in our aural experience: "the names agree in our eares" in English translation, and "the Originall differs no more then so, *Tehillim* and *Tephilloth*" (ibid.). This is assonance as ecclesiology.

By comparison to a contemporary expert like Lancelot Andrewes, Donne had small Hebrew and less Greek. Donne defended vernacular translations of Scripture, but his practice was to quote the Latin Vulgate translation, the Bible of his childhood. That is one reason why he doesn't write biblical English: Tyndale's idiom was an acquired language, not his mother tongue. And he doesn't invent neobiblical plot either: narrative is not, after all, necessary to poetry. In fact Donne is most likely to allegorize biblical narratives – and very summarily at that: "finde thy Saviour in a *Manger*, and in his *swathing clouts*, in his humiliation, and blesse God for that beginning," i.e. of spiritual humility (Donne, 2003, p. 141). Nothing could be more different from Southwell, who discusses imaginary plot possibilities exhaustively and then rushes a lot of moralistic allegories into the last page.

But Donne does paraphrase images into being. At the creation of the world, the Holy Ghost "sate upon the waters, and he *hatched* all that was produced" (ibid., p. 113, italics added). In most translations, the Holy Spirit hovers. Alternatively, it is the wind that sweeps (prosaically) past. But in the Junius-Tremellius translation that Donne is using here, the spirit incubates the water. He isn't hovering – as Donne's paraphrase makes clear, he gets stuck in, he exhibits the paternal diligence of a penguin. So does Milton's: "Dovelike satst brooding on the vast abyss / And mad'st it pregnant" (*Paradise Lost*, 1:21–2). The development of this image, like the sound effects Donne records, works to transcend the linguistic barriers presented by the Bible's ancient languages. Everyone can hear the swish of *Ishe*. Quite a few will be able to visualize a huge broody bird. Donne makes the Bible's effects accessible to his audience.

Often Donne hears the Bible not in isolated sounds, but as a voice. This is particularly true of his *Devotions Upon Emergent Occasions*, written after a serious illness in 1623. In the first prayer he reflects on the value of hearing God's Word the Bible, or, as he calls it, God's *voice*:

> *A faithful ambassador is health*, says thy wise servant Solomon. Thy voice [the Bible] received in the beginning of a sickness, of a sin, is true health. If I can see that light betimes, and hear that voice early, *Then shall my light break forth as the morning, and my health shall spring forth speedily* [Isaiah 58:8] ... if I take knowledge of that voice then, and fly to thee, thou wilt preserve me from falling, or raise me again, when by natural infirmity I am fallen. (Donne, 1959, p. 11–12)

Prayer is a conversation that the believer generally gets to dominate. But the Word gets a word in very frequently here. God's Word, or voice, is in fact an entire cast of voices – all the characters that are in the Bible. "In all these voices," Donne says to God, "thou sendest us to those helps which thou hast afforded us" (ibid., p. 26). The *Devotions* is, like a dramatic poem, full of unembodied voices. Sometimes they are heated: God "grudges not to be chidden and disputed with. ... Not to be directed and counselled by *Jonas*. ... Nor almost to be threatened and neglected by *Moses*" (ibid., p. 117). Donne is not a passive hearer of the polyphony: he prompts the lines he would like to hear. "But wilt not thou avow that voice too, *He that hath sinned against his Maker, let him fall into the hands of the physician* [Ecclesiasticus 38:15] ... ?" (ibid., p. 26). Donne also speaks in the Bible's tongues: "My God, my God," he appeals continually, borrowing Christ's words on the cross; likewise, "we do not say with Jacob, *Surely the Lord is in this place*" (ibid., p. 9, 10, passim).

In the *Devotions* Donne's attention to the voices of the Bible derives not only from his typically alert poetic ear, but from the fact of his illness. A person on a sickbed, unable to move about very much, listens out for approaching sounds instead. His mind may also distort perfectly ordinary sounds into extraordinary ones – just as Southwell's distraught Mary distorts woodland chatter to mourning notes. Donne himself can very nearly make out the General Resurrection: "Then I shall hear the angels proclaim the *Surgite mortui*, Rise, ye dead. Though I be dead, I shall hear the voice" (ibid., p. 15). God's own hearing, by Donne's account, is utterly exceptional. "*Gods* eares are so open, so tender, so sensible of any motion, as that *David* formes one Prayer thus, *Auribus percipe lachrimas meas*, O Lord, heare my teares; hee puts the office of the *Eye* too, upon the *Eare*" (Donne, 2003, p. 76). Donne is sensitive to the literary device (synaesthesia), while God is sensible even of silent weeping.

Donne hears the Bible as a poem, then, and, in the *Devotions*, turns it into a dramatic one. He also thinks it is written with the concentration of a poem: every word there for a reason. There is no surplus stylistic fat, no superfluous synonym, no Erasmian *copia* or Lylyan euphuism:

> The Holy Ghost is an eloquent Author, a vehement, and an abundant Author, but yet not luxuriant; he is far from a penurious, but as far from a superfluous style too. And therefore we doe not take these two words in the Text [Psalm 90:14], *To rejoice*, and *to be glad*, to signifie merely one and the same thing.

Donne is concerned to characterize the style of the Bible, not least because he believes this is evidence of its divine authorship. Were a Christian to plead for the Bible and a Muslim for the Koran before a disinterested party, "the Majesty of the *Style*" of the former would win out (Donne, 2003, p. 139). John's books, in particular, "rather seem fallen from Heaven, and writ with the hand which ingraved the stone Tablets, then a mans work" (ibid., p. 125). What, then, are the characteristics of this style? Style has been well defined, not simply as "prose style – its lexis, its taxis, its habitual quirks, its peculiarities, its allegedly distinguishing features," but as the "attitudes, ways of thinking" that prompt these stylistic choices (Raine, 2006, p. 23–4). In short, as personality. Or what we call *voice*. And Donne's Bible bears the imprints of a particular authorial personality – of one who is generous but not redundant, neither "penurious" nor "superfluous." Someone, that is, worth having a conversation with. This personality expresses itself, in the excerpt quoted above, in a doublet (to rejoice *and* to be glad) that Donne explains is not a tautology but a denotation of two kinds of joy: one external, one internal. Synonymous phrases would later be identified as the poetic principle of psalmody: parallelism. In Donne it is interpreted as a personality trait.

This idea of the Holy Spirit's personality is why he thinks of the Bible's style as singular, although its authors were multiple. "All say what any of them say. ... Yet not so precisely, but that they differ in words" (Donne, 2003, p. 124). Because early modern authors believed that Bible writers were all saying the same thing, they could legitimately put the words of one writer or character into another's mouth. John Lyly, for instance, "quotes" the high priest Eli saying words from all parts of the Bible in *Euphues* (1578).

Donne, too, differs in words. He does not write neobiblically – his own style is too distinct, his personality too strong – but his understanding of the Bible's sparing style does govern the way he writes about it. Exegesis is best done economically too. "Abundant, but yet not luxuriant" doesn't merely say the same thing as neither "penurious" nor "superfluous." And a doublet is one thing – a stylistic bow to the synonymous phrases of the biblical text in this example – but sextuplets are another. "There is no necessity of that *spirituall wantonnesse* of finding more then necessary senses" (Donne, 2003, p. 134). Critical over-ingeniousness is wanton – that is, promiscuous. It loves, not the text, but the self-gratification.

Donne argues that "when you have the *necessary sense*, that is the meaning of the holy Ghost in that place, you have sense enow, and not till then, though you have never so many, and never so delightfull" (ibid., p. 134). The correct interpretation is satisfying, whereas fanciful ones easily become satiating. Not that the Bible is mathematics, of course, as Donne also points out: "we have not a *Demonstration*; not such an Evidence as that one and two, are three" (ibid., p. 139). Instead, interpreting the Bible is more like law: a plausible case can be made. "It is not a cleare case," he will admit (ibid., p. 37). Donne can construct a plausible case breathtakingly. He puts on a brilliant courtroom performance in the pulpit when he proposes the preposterous – "But did Christ not die then?" "Is that fabulous?" – to create anticipation for his solution (ibid., p. 40). Christ *did* die, but not like anyone else, because he was able to control his dying.

Small pieces of evidence are particular favorites with Donne: the Bible is still undergoing the forensic examination begun by Tyndale. Even "a For" or "a But" in the Bible has significance (ibid., p. 120). Like a Renaissance Christopher Ricks, Donne finds self-reflexivity or mimetic meaning in phrases that appear entirely unexceptional to other readers. The very modesty of a word like "For," for instance, expresses the modesty Jesus had when praying and which we ought to imitate: "he gave us a convenient scantling for our *fors*, who prayed, Give me enough, for I may else despair, give me not too much, for so I may presume" (ibid., p. 121). Keep your requests, like the word *for*, scant in scope.

Dante (whom we know Donne read) imagined God as a point of light, infinitesimally omnipotent. Donne found power in verbal pinpricks – connectives, short texts, even punctuation marks. He wrote a whole sermon on "*Jesus wept*" [John 11:35] (ibid., p. 157). "Whoever," he says, was responsible for introducing verses divisions to the Bible "seemes to have stopped in an amazement in this Text ... making an intire verse of these two words, *Jesus wept*. ... There is not a shorter verse in the Bible, nor a larger Text" (ibid., pp. 157–8). Similarly, it took only a semi-colon, Donne explains, for the Arians to deny the Trinity. Still, he adds tiny things to the Bible himself. A single tear to Ezekiel, for instance. "And remember still, that when *Ezechias* wept, *Vidit lachrymam,*

God saw his Teare, His Teare in the *Singular*" (ibid., p. 92). In fact, Donne is misremembering: Ezekiel's tears flow plurally in the Bible. But because Donne is a writer, his memory makes the Bible even better than it is. And he is a brilliant writer – which is why he recognises the right word when he sees it. Remarking on Christ's extraordinary words on the cross ("Father, forgive them, for they know not what they do," Luke 23:34), he explains: "There was no one word, by which he could so nobly have maintained his Dignity, kept his station, justified his cause, and withal expressed his humility and charity, as this, Father" (ibid., pp. 115, 119). Donne exudes the qualifications to comment.

All these small things add up. Donne tells us that the book of Psalms has been called "The book of Heapes, where all assistances to our salvation are heaped" (ibid., p. 121). He advises us to collect metaphorical droplets of Christ's sweat and blood. He also likes to gather together in one place a concordance of images: all the wings in the Bible, or all the hands, or all the beds. In the *Devotions* he is nervous to find himself in bed when there are so few favorable mentions of them in the Bible. "The bed is not ordinarily thy [God's] scene, thy climate" (Donne, 1959, p. 19).

Donne's own metaphors are often small-scale. "All this that is temporall, is but a caterpillar got into one corner of my garden" (Donne, 2003, p. 99). This imitates the homeliness of Jesus' similes, but it is also a deliberate shrinking: our problems are not so vast, there are limits to the voracity of a caterpillar. Similarly, in Donne's reading of Psalm 11:3 ("If the foundations be destroyed, what can the righteous doe?"), domestic perspective rebukes puritan exaggerations: "Call not the *furniture* of the *House, Foundations*," nor "the cracking of a pane of glasse, a *Destroying of foundations*" (ibid., p. 90). This isn't Günter Grass's *The Tin Drum* (1959), where the hero's miraculous ability to shatter the church glass calls into question the powers of a plastic Jesus.

Donne squints, beyond smallness, into nothingness. While puritan contemporaries were busy denouncing what couldn't be found in the Bible (bishops and surplices), Donne was concerned with absences relating to literary form and genres. He notices, for instance, the apotheosis of the vocative apostrophe "O thine altars," where "there is in the Originall in that place, a patheticall, a vehement, a broken expressing expressed" (Donne, 2003, p. 101). Or, to take another example, he enlists God's *lack* of arms: "When the Poets present their great Heroes, and their Worthies, they always insist upon their Armes, they spend much of their invention upon the description of their Armes. ... But God is invulnerable in himselfe, and is never represented armed; you finde no shirts of mayle, no Helmets, no Cuirasses in Gods Armory" (ibid., p. 108). God easily exceeds any epic hero. As Milton would later say, this is an "argument / Not less but more heroic" for its canning of cannonry (*Paradise Lost*, 9:13– 14).

Clearly Donne is, like Southwell and Milton, full of literary sophistication. But what if you were a reader or writer for whom the Bible *is* the whole of culture? "Our shepheards, sayes *S. Hierome*, here, have no other Eclogues, no other Pastoralls; Our labourers, our children, our servants no other songs, nor Ballads, to recreate themselves withall, then the Psalmes" (Donne, 2003, p. 65). What, in short, if you were John Bunyan, the untutored son of a tinker?

Bunyan and Neobiblicism

Donne says it is considered "a meere Hebraisme [Hebrew idiom] to say, that every man shall *see death*" (Donne, 2003, p. 33). That is because Donne is interested not in replicating Hebraisms, but in reading large meanings into their small bounds. He does not imitate biblical idiom for extended passages, which is a major characteristic of the masterpieces of later seventeenth-century religious prose. Because Donne's primary Bible is the Vulgate, he is not steeped in biblical English. But the writer we turn to now – John Bunyan – certainly was.

At first, it terrified him: the ease with which one might think up a sentence that sounded like the Bible, but in fact wasn't. This is because, in Bunyan's marvellous spiritual autobiography *Grace Abounding to the chief of Sinners* (1666), his state of mind depends heavily on what part of the Bible pops into his head at any given moment. It is a mental sortilege. "But one day, as I was passing in the field, and that too with some dashes on my Conscience, fearing lest yet all was not right, suddenly this sentence fell upon my Soul, *Thy righteousness is in Heaven*" (Bunyan, 1998, p. 65). Cheered up, he is soon dashed to discover it isn't a biblical text, after all. In such situations he comforts himself by thinking of other Scriptures, preferably ones that appear to relate to the invented one.

Shakespeare knew, or imagined, people like Bunyan: unsure if they are saved, they quote apparently contradictory texts on the subject in *Richard II* (Maxwell, 2007). But these people are not, like Shakespeare and Bunyan, great writers. Bunyan translated his continual mental agony into a literary mode. Instead of tormenting himself with neobiblical sentences, he could unburden them onto the page. "And as I slept I dreamed a Dream. I dreamed, and behold *I saw a Man cloathed with Raggs, standing in a certain place, with his face from his own House, a Book in his hand, a great Burden upon his back*" (Bunyan, 2003, p. 10). The polyptoton (dreaming a dream, redundantly) is biblical. So is the repeated connective *And*, which Bunyan, however, soon gives up, presumably sensing that it can quickly become wearying or knee-jerk. "Behold I saw" – or, see what I saw – is a command from a biblical visionary. As for the man's appearance, Bunyan's own margin directs us to a range of Scriptures.

Coleridge said that Bunyan's "piety was baffled by his genius, and the Bunyan of Parnassus had the better of the Bunyan of the Conventicle – and with the same illusion as we read any tale known to be fictitious, as a novel – we go on with his characters as real persons" (Coleridge, 1968, p. 475). In fact, it is fiction that offers to solve Bunyan's religious perplexity – and not only because it provides an outlet for the sentences preoccupying his consciousness. It is because fiction justifies making things up. That is what fiction is *for*. It gives invention a purpose. Bunyan is very clear about saying that what he is writing is feigned, a fable, an allegory. And, in his view, this makes neobiblicism permissible.

Contrast *The Journal* of George Fox, the founder of the Quakers. Fox, unfazed by, if not completely unaware of, his neobiblical imprecisions, has no need for fiction, because what matters to him isn't the exact words of the Bible, but the spirit that inspired them.

He can be a new Paul, his words a new Bible. A great crack goes through the earth and a great smoke arises – not symbolically, as it would in *The Pilgrim's Progress*, as an explicit part of the fiction, but actually, in the year 1648, as Fox sits in a Friend's house in Nottinghamshire.

In modern times, the counterpart of the terrorized Bunyan is the amanuensis in Salman Rushdie's *The Satanic Verses* (1988). One day he records the words of the prophet Mahound – the words that will become the Koran – incorrectly. "Little things at first. If Mahound recited a verse in which God was described as *all-hearing, all-knowing*, I would write, *all-knowing, all-wise*" (Rushdie, 1988, p. 367). Reminiscent of Bunyan's emotions, he is shocked, frightened, and finally saddened when Mahound doesn't even notice this profane erring. Divine truth turns out to be a human invention. It is an allegory of the writer's life in any religious community: eventually, he must supply the Words himself.

But ironically, in post-Reformation England, it was Tyndale's biblical English that showed some writers how.

Note

1   Marginal verse numbers had been used for decades in printed editions of the Psalms and latterly throughout the whole Bible by the Hebraist Santes Pagnini in 1528 (see Saenger, 1999). Robert Stephanus introduced the verse divisions we use today in the mid-sixteenth century.

References and Further Reading

Bale, J. (1849) *Selected Works of Bishop Bale*, ed. H. Christmas. Cambridge University Press, Cambridge.

Bible (1997) *The Bible Authorised King James Version*, ed. R. Carroll and S. Prickett. Oxford University Press, Oxford.

Bunyan, J. (1998) *Grace Abounding with Other Spiritual Autobiographies*, ed. J. Stachniewski with A. Pacheco. Oxford University Press, Oxford.

Bunyan, J. (2003) *The Pilgrim's Progress*, ed. W. R. Owens. Oxford University Press, Oxford.

Coleridge, S. T. C. (1968) *Coleridge on the Seventeenth Century*, ed. R. F. Brinkley. Greenwood Press, New York.

Donne, J. (1959) *Devotions Upon Emergent Occasions*. University of Michigan Press.

Donne, J. (1987) *Selected Prose*, ed. N. Rhodes. Penguin, Harmondsworth.

Donne, J. (2003) *John Donne's Sermons on the Psalms and Gospels*, ed. E. M. Simpson. University of California Press, Berkeley.

Fox, George (1998) *The Journal*, ed. N. Smith. Penguin, Harmondsworth.

Latimer, H. (2000) *The Sermons*, ed. A. Pollard. Carcanet Press, Manchester.

Marvell, A. (1993) *The Complete Poems*, ed. George deF. Lord. David Campbell Publishers, London.

Maxwell, J. (2007) "How the Renaissance (Mis)Used Sources: The Art of Misquotation," in L. Maguire, ed., *How To Do Things With Shakespeare*. Blackwell, Oxford.

Milton, J. (1998) *Paradise Lost*, ed. A. Fowler. Longman, New York.

Pope, A. (1989) *Poetical Works*, ed. H. Davis. Oxford University Press, Oxford.

Raine. C. (2000) *In Defence of T. S. Eliot*. Picador, London.

Raine, C. (2006) "Italics: Kundera's Style." *Areté* 21, 23–45.

Rushdie, S. (1998) *The Satanic Verses*. Vintage, London.

Saenger, P. (1999) "The Impact of the Early Printed Page on the Reading of the Bible," in K. Van Kampen and P. Saenger, eds, *The Bible as Book*. The British Library, London, pp. 31–51.

Shakespeare, W. (1981) *Richard III*, ed. Anthony Hammond. Methuen, London.

Shakespeare, W. (1999) *The Sonnets and A Lover's Complaint*, ed. John Kerrigan. Penguin, London.

Southwell, R. (1591) *Marie Magdalens funeral teares*. London.

Tyndale, W. (2000) *The Obedience of a Christian Man*, ed. D. Daniell. Penguin, Harmondsworth.

CHAPTER 14
Edmund Spenser

Carol V. Kaske

The present chapter proceeds from simple, statistical points to those that are complex and controversial. It argues that Spenser was remarkably free in his use of the Bible.[1]

Spenser uses the Bible pervasively in the first book of *The Faerie Queene* and the "Hymne of Heavenly Love" in the *Fowre Hymnes*, as well as occasionally throughout his poems, his letters, and the prose *Vewe of the Present State of Ireland*. When Spenser demonstrably uses the Bible, what parts does he turn to? "Spenser alludes to Revelation more than any other book of the Bible" Landrum (1926, p. 517) replies.[2] Book I contains forty-two out of the sixty citations of it in the *Faerie Queene*, according to Shaheen (1976, pp. 181–2). Many of these references (e.g. FQ I.vii.16–18, viii.6, 14) are associated with Duessa in her role, closely derived from Revelation, as biblical Whore of Babylon (Revelation 17–19:3), interpreted by Protestants of Spenser's day as the corrupt church, and thus identified with the Roman Catholic Church. The contrast between her and the Woman Clothed with the Sun (Revelation 12, interpreted as the true, the Protestant Church and reincarnated in Una) provided Protestants with a scriptural defense against the charge of having split the church. Revelation also provided *Faerie Queene* Book One with a common and appealing plot – a good and a bad woman who compete for the hero's soul. This Protestant politico-religious reading of Revelation was a popular subject, one stressed by many commentaries on Revelation, of which an exceptional number existed in English, including the long commentary by Van der Noot in *Theatre for Worldlings* (1569), where Spenser's first work was published. Revelation brings with it apocalypticism – the sense that current events are predestined and have been prophesied as signs that the world is about to end and that humanity is polarized "in two flocks, two folds – black, white; right, wrong"(Gerard Manley Hopkins, "Spelt from Sibyl's Leaves").

Next to Revelation in number of clear borrowings come the Psalms (Landrum, 1926, p. 517; Shaheen, 1976, p. 181) – the best-known book of the Bible, perhaps even more so then than now, because at least one Psalm was included in every church service and they were also recommended for private and family devotions. The Book of Psalms also existed in more versions than any other book because in addition to that included in the various versions of the Bible as a whole, it sometimes stood alone

– the version in the Prayer Book and the innumerable private metrical paraphrases, of which the Sternhold and Hopkins version had subsequently been authorized for use in churches. So great was the latitude of the variations that in one of them – the Sternhold and Hopkins metrical version as revised early on by Whittingham – there is no "shepherd" in the Twenty-third Psalm. The Sternhold and Hopkins version was often sung in church to various tunes, which are indicated in Elizabethan psalters, e.g. their version of Psalm 100 was sung to a tune which has ever since born its name: "Old Hundredth."

The poet could choose to echo different translations in different places, as Shaheen (1976, pp. 21–35) has proved that Spenser did. Consequently the Psalms were remembered not only in clear verbal borrowings like "The Lord is my Shepherd" – they may be just the tip of the iceberg – but in typical sentiments, in imagery, in sub-genres, or perhaps, like a secular book, in mere form and style. Little was known of Hebrew poetics, but realizing this left Elizabethan poets free to use any verse form they chose, and this was a greater freedom than they had with other books of the Bible.

Much has recently been written on these metrical paraphrases, especially since most of one of them was written by a woman, Mary Sidney, Countess of Pembroke. Spenser is said to have translated "The seven Psalmes" – i.e. the Penitential Psalms, 6, 32, 38, 51, 102, 130, and 143, as reported in *Complaints*, "The Printer to the Reader" – though his versions are no longer extant. Translating the Psalms must have directed attention to biblical poetics. Spenser borrows some of the poetic form of the Psalms. Most pervasive is their syntactic parallelism: this device is also characteristic of the *Faerie Queene* as a whole, especially of the first three books, and elegantly exemplified in Una's lament (I.vii.22–5). Two Messianic Psalms claim the king is God's son: Psalms 2:7 and 89:26–7. Spenser echoes this in the notion that Gloriana is "heavenly born" (FQ I.x.59); and that Eliza in the "April" eclogue of the *Shepheardes Calender* is "O dea certe" and begotten by the god Pan (see lines 50–4, 91–4, Thenot's emblem and the last line of the gloss thereto). Spenser's description of the birth of Belphoebe, another of Elizabeth's surrogates, as "of the wombe of Morning dew" echoes the beautiful but mysterious verse 3 in 110, a Messianic Psalm that in some versions (not the Geneva), reads "the deawe of thy birth, is of the wombe of the morning" (chiefly, the Psalter in the Book of Common Prayer; for a conspectus of versions of this verse, see Shaheen, 1976, appendix C, example 29).

A further section of the Bible, labeled Apocrypha by Protestants, held a fascination for Spenser that seems Romanist because nowadays it is considered canonical only by the Catholic and the Greek Orthodox denominations. Landrum (1926, p. 518) finds thirty-three uses of the Apocrypha in Spenser's works. In his time, these books were not considered so Romanist in that all Bibles contained them: English Protestant Bibles inserted most of them between the Old Testament and the New. Though the Geneva Bible cautions that they be "not received by a common consent to be read and expounded publikely in the Church" (Apocrypha, The Argument), the Church of England – following Melanchthon and the Catholics rather than the Geneva editors on this issue – recommended that they be read not for doctrine, it is true, but for morality (Article 6 of the 39 Articles, which can be found in most Books of Common Prayer before the 1970 revisions). She actually ordered some of them to be read in church: Judith, Tobit,

Wisdom of Solomon, Ecclesiasticus, and Baruch once made up most of the Old Testament lessons for Morning and Evening Prayer in October and November of the liturgical year (see the successive Lectionaries in the oldest Books of Common Prayer). 2 Esdras 14:9 inspired the theme of the degeneration of the world in FQ IV.viii.31 and V Proem; 2 Esdras 4 and 2 Maccabees 9:8 inform the image of the Leveling Giant with the scales.[3]

A long-recognized, striking, and extended use of the Apocrypha is the portrayal of Sapience in *An Hymne of Heavenly Beautie* (183–288). Spenser's Sapience represents one of the three developed biblical characters in his works, the other two being Christ in the *Hymne of Heavenly Love* and Duessa as the Whore of Babylon in *Faerie Queene* I. Spenser's Sapience derives not only from the canonical Proverbs 1–9, especially 9, but also from the Apocryphal Wisdom 6–9, Ecclesiasticus (now known as Sirach) 1, 4, 6, 14–15, 24, and 51, and Baruch 3:28–32. The character Gloriana owes much to Sapience or Wisdom – both the book and the character (see, for example, A. C. Hamilton's note to I Proem 4.7). Spenser's calling Elizabeth "mirrour of grace and majesty divine" in I Proem 4.2, as A. C. Hamilton notes, is tantamount to equating her with the similarly described Sapience in Wisdom 7:26. Sapience "reacheth from one ende to another mightily, and comely doth she order al things" (Wisdom 8:1). Sapience's imperial attribute could justify the rule of a female monarch like Gloriana and her real-life counterpart Queen Elizabeth (Fruen, 1990, p. 66).

Una has sometimes been regarded as another surrogate for Queen Elizabeth; and Una like Gloriana is said to be "borne of hevenly birth" (I.x.9), even though she has earthly parents. Having earthly parents does not disqualify Una from being Wisdom; it only makes her a lower emanation in the same chain of being. A material cause for Spenser's linking of Elizabeth to Sapience by the attribute of heavenly birth is the presence of sacral monarchy in the Royal Psalms, as explained above. A final cause is feminism: the link with Sapience functions as a scriptural counterweight to the Pauline strictures invoked by those misogynists like John Knox who objected to having a female as the head or supreme governor of the church – which office since Henry VIII had been a prerogative of the English crown. True, the typical exegete allegorized Sapience as Christ, thus downplaying her gender; but the very existence of a feminine sign for Christ would have strengthened the claim of a woman to a Christlike office. Besides, as Fruen has shown, Melanchthon and in a sense even Calvin equated the biblical Sapience not with Christ but with natural law and natural revelation – things that could be personified in a woman (Fruen, 1990, p. 65–70). When her surrogates are apotheosized, so is Queen Elizabeth herself. Thus Scripture and exegesis can sometimes serve the poet as a political tool. The biblically-inspired poet not only absorbs but on occasion attempts to manipulate his culture.

Another section of the Bible of predictable importance to Spenser is the Gospels, which are particularly pervasive in the *Hymne of Heavenly Love*. Three surprising allusions to them, surprising in view of their secular context, are "the bird, that warned Peter of his fall" (FQ V.vi.27); the association of the parthenogenesis of Amoret and Belphoebe with that of Christ (III.vi.3, 27); and the associations of the goddess Nature with the transfigured Christ (VII.vii.7). The first two Gospel references could be seen as portraying Britomart and Belphoebe as types, respectively, of Peter and of Christ, or as antitypes, focusing on their differences, or as remote analogues to them on a natural level. I compare and contrast Britomart and Peter below.

When Spenser demonstrably uses the Bible, how does he use it? This question dominates the rest of the present chapter. Verbatim quotation is the most direct, unless it is ironical (on which see below). The Renaissance recognized three looser degrees of fidelity to a source-text – translation, paraphrase, and the still looser types of imitation. The second most direct uses are translation or paraphrase, and these types of imitation, while not always mechanical, exhibit the least degree of creativity. Of this sort may have been Spenser's supposed translations of The Seven (Penitential) Psalms, Ecclesiastes, and Canticum canticorum (Song of Solomon). He is generally believed to have translated the four "sonnets" paraphrased by his French source from Revelation in the *Theatre for Worldlings*.

Reverential imitation comes in other and looser varieties, and these will occupy us for the middle portion of this chapter. Spenser's uses of the Bible range from a literal to an allegorical sense, whether moral or typological; from the direct to the oblique – parodic, allegorical, analogic, or otherwise far-fetched; and from the political to the purely aesthetic.

Some borrowings are relatively direct and literal: for instance, "And eke with fatnesse swollen were his eyne" (FQ I.iv.21) from "Their eyes swell with fatnesse" (Psalter of Book of Common Prayer, Psalm 73:7). Spenser's only change here is to adapt what in the Bible is a metonymy for the general prosperity of the wicked to a literal symptom of gluttony. Another literal imitation is longer but still simple and straightforward: Artegall's re-enactment of the Judgment of Solomon upon rival claimants to a desired person – in the Bible, between two women about a baby (1 Kings 3:26–7); in Spenser, between Sanglier and a squire about a lady (FQ V.i.26–8). In both Spenser and the Bible, the test of ownership is the same: willingness to give up the person to the rival rather than to see him or her killed (see A. C. Hamilton's note ad loc.).

A surprisingly literal use, almost as if the Bible were just another book of stories, is the one referred to above where Britomart on her quest for her beloved forces herself to stay awake when lodged by the sinister Dolon – a struggle that climaxes at the first crowing of "the native bellman of the night / The bird that warned Peter of his fall." According to Spenser, Peter "fell" when he repeatedly denied knowing Christ and then heard the cock crow. That fall had nothing to do with sleep – the temptation with which Britomart is currently wrestling. But just before that in the Bible – and immediately after Christ had warned Peter of his future denial (Matthew 26:34) – Peter and his two compatriots had thrice deserted Christ by falling asleep; though the verb "fall asleep" is not used, it is implied, especially in verse 43, "He ... found them asleepe againe, for their eyes were heavy"(Matthew 26:36–46, 69–75). That Spenser is thinking also of the sleepy disciples and thus conflating Peter's two falls is shown by Britomart's repeated injunction to her eyes to "watch," that is, stay awake (V.vi.25–26), paralleling Christ's injunction to the sleepy disciples, "What? Could ye not watch with me one hour? Watch, and pray, that you enter not into tentation; the spirit indeed is ready, but the flesh is weake" (Matthew 26:40–1, 43, 45–6). Britomart is the antitype of Peter: she has not experienced and will not experience a moral fall (though in accepting Dolon's invitation, she has deviated "a little wide by West," the direction she is supposed to be taking; V.vi.22.4, see Hamilton's note), but she is in danger of literally falling through the floor when the perilous bed does, escaping because unlike Peter she has resisted *falling* asleep. The allusion is creative and oblique; it is not religious or allegorical but only stoical, prudential, and characteristic of chivalric romance. The sacredness of the subtext contributes nothing beyond the hint that love is a bit like religion and Britomart the antithesis of Peter. When the artist is imitating at such a great distance, he is quite free. (For a straightforward and condemnatory reading of this biblical imitation as being what Greene and I would call sacramental, see Dunseath, 1968, pp. 168–71.)

At the opposite extreme is a biblical allusion whose relevance could not be fully understood without the tradition of biblical allegory – in other words one where Spenser has retained the clothing of allegory that the character or action wore or allegedly wore in the Bible. One example of this is the aforementioned Duessa as the Whore of Babylon in Revelation 17–19:3. Without her assumed symbolism of the false, the Roman Catholic Church, Redcrosse's fornication with her, meaning his starting to entertain Catholic ideas, would not be a sin so serious as to merit hell as it does: "ever burning wrath before him laid, / By righteous sentence of th'Almighties law" (I.ix.50).

Another instance of filtering the Bible through allegorical exegesis is Redcrosse's unexpected announcement after the dragon-fight that he cannot marry Una right now but must first go back to Gloriana whom he has promised to serve for six years (xii.17–19, 41). Redcrosse then promises Una's father that he will come back in the mystic seventh year to consummate their marriage (I.xii.19). This deferral sounds like his promised return to the Hermit Contemplation in old age and final departure to the New Jerusalem (I.x.60–1, 63–4). We can begin to see the point just from the text alone. We have already been told in a cryptic passage that Gloriana and Una both have a claim on Redcrosse's "love" (I.ix.17.1–3). When the knight says his love of Una will be "next to that lady's love" he parallels Lovelace's later statement in "To Lucasta, going to the wars": "I could not love thee half so much loved I not honor more," and I submit that Redcrosse's departure from Una illustrates the same complex priorities. Gloriana as we know symbolizes glory and honor, and at this point, her symbolism is more prominent than that of Una, who seems to be just an earthly beloved (but see the allegory below); also Gloriana is for the moment literally Redcrosse's sovereign, so he should not let his personal affection for Una interfere with his patriotic duty.

Now Redcrosse's two good women parallel Jacob's two women in the Bible. Jacob serves Laban for seven years, allegedly to win as his wife Rachel, the woman he passionately loves (Genesis 29:15–30). The morning after the wedding night, however, Jacob finds that Laban has substituted in the bed his other daughter, the unwanted Leah, and that to get Rachel he has to serve yet another seven years. This alternation is like Redcrosse winning Una by his deeds, then serving Gloriana for a specified number of years, then marrying Una. Serving the woman in Spenser corresponds to serving the woman's father to win her hand in marriage in the Bible. Redcrosse disappoints Una and her father just as Laban disappointed Jacob; but Redcrosse has not deceived them insofar as he has forewarned the father and on that occasion claims to have already forewarned Una (I.xii.18).

Medieval exegesis provides the point of Spenser's imitation. Every sincere Christian wants to experience ecstatic contemplation, symbolized in the Bible by Rachel and in the poem by Una as religious truth. A literal instance of it which Redcrosse also desires is the lifestyle of the Hermit Contemplation and the city he contemplates, the New Jerusalem or heaven (I.x.55–64). But for various reasons every Christian must perform some work for society. In theology and biblical exegesis this social obligation is called the active life and is symbolized by Jacob's other woman, Leah, who is not passionately loved but who needs him (for instance, in Aquinas's *Summa Theologica* II IIae, 2, 179, 2, and in Dante's *Purgatorio* 27.94–108 and Sinclair's note ad loc.). That Redcrosse's alternative woman is not only a personification of honor and glory but a literal queen who assigns quests to knights and records their successes (I.x.59) makes her a perfect symbol of the active life, with its devotion to achievement and its motive of winning glory. Serving the two women in Spenser corresponds to serving the exacting father of the two women in the Bible.

The numerology provides further evidence of the allusion. Spenser has revised the biblical sequence and years of service: Redcrosse wins contemplation first in what may be seen as year number one and what in mystical theory is called the spiritual betrothal, corresponding to the betrothal ceremony in I.xii.36–40; but he cannot enjoy her fully until he serves the active life for six years. Spenser has borrowed from the numbers of years Jacob served to win each lady only the idea of seven as the number of consummation, by giving the less passionately desired lady, or life, not another seven as in the Bible but the obviously incomplete number six. The spiritual marriage, the Union with Truth, will occur only with the Beatific Vision in the afterlife, which is described as the Sabbath or seventh day (FQ VII.viii.2). Redcrosse's desire to remain with Una is analogous to and symbolic of his desire to either remain on the mountain or go straight to heaven expressed to the Hermit (I.x.63–4, see also 60–1), and tells us that he wants to become a full-time contemplative while in this life. His contrary reluctant return to his worldly duty on both occasions (I.xii.18, 41) obeys the Hermit's imperative of good works (I.x.55–64) and adds an ethical dimension to Redcrosse's desertion of Una. This second good woman in Redcrosse's life represents his further and somewhat conflicting obligations. Spenser, like the allegorists of Leah and Rachel, is making the point that the believer must practice both the active and the contemplative lives, even though contemplation is obviously better and indeed the climax of one's earthly life and the chief pleasure in the life to come. This meaning is both moral and anagogical. It reaffirms Una's lofty symbolism without downgrading that of Gloriana. Redcrosse's initial view of contemplation as a possible full-time job (x.63–4) could be seen as Catholic, and the Hermit's refusal to take him on just yet and his resulting departure from both symbols of Contemplation – the personification of it and Una – to the workaday world of Gloriana could be seen as Protestant, though this same image and theme had been voiced frequently in the Catholic Middle Ages as well (see King, 1990, pp. 217–18). Thus Spenser does not distinguish between a Catholic and somewhat far-fetched allegorical exegesis like this one and a Protestant one (the Whore) but uses the Catholic one when it fits his story and the stage of his hero's spiritual development.

Another oblique and thus creative use of Scripture is the parodic. Although the Bible retains its normative character and the irony is not at the expense of the sacred text but at the expense of the extrabiblical being who does not measure up and who may actually be using the Scripture sophistically, the tone is not reverential but witty, comical, or cynical. Sophistry is displayed when Phaedria deviously misapplies "consider the lilies of the field" (FQ II.vi.15–16; cf. Matthew 6:28–9) to authorize her frivolous idleness. In Spenser's social satire, *Mother Hubberd's Tale*, when the formal priest, recommending to the Fox and the Ape the easy life of Protestant clergy, says "Ne is the paines so great, but beare ye may" (445), he is misapplying "There hath no tentation taken you, but ... ye may be able to beare it" (1 Corinthians 10:13). Some entire plots are parodic. The Giant with the scales (FQ V.ii.37–8, 42–6) not only reflects Apocryphal villains but parodies almost blasphemously God's leveling of mountains and weighing of unquantifiable things (Isaiah 40:4, 12; Wisdom 11:17; Job 28:25). Enjoyment of these ironies depends on the reader's recognition of the scriptural echo.

Spenser uses the Bible in the various allegorical senses ascribed to it by exegetes. The medieval mnemonic jingle defines them as follows: "Littera gesta docet, quid credas allegoria, / Moralis quid agas, quo tendas anagogia" ("The *letter* teaches the events, the *allegory* what you should believe, the *moral* what you should do, the *anagogy* where you should be going"). The last three are pigeonholes for the different kinds of subject matter the literal sense can sustain: salvation-history, morality, and the afterlife, the three topics the Middle Ages considered important, just as today the three "relevant" subjects to be found in literature are gender, class, and ethnicity. Rarely are all three of the allegorical senses found in a single passage either in the Bible or in secular literature, but they are there potentially for the poet to turn on or off.

The anagogical subject-matter – allegories or direct portrayals of the future life, also known as eschatology – is rare both in the Bible and in literature. In *The Faerie Queene* it is exemplified on a large scale only in the New Jerusalem, which Redcrosse glimpses from the Mount of Contemplation (FQ I.x.55–7) and in "that same time when no more change shall be / But steadfast rest of all things firmly stayed / Upon the pillars of eternity" in the last stanza of the poem as we have it (FQ VII.viii.2).

Conventionally, then as now, "allegory" is of course the general name for every sense outside the literal. In the peculiar narrow sense used only in biblical exegesis, and not universally there, "allegory" is only one of them: "what you should believe." In the Judeo-Christian tradition generally, what you should believe is not a set of doctrines but a story about God's dealings with mankind, which is called salvation-history. Typical allegories of this sort occur when an Old Testament person like Abel or Melchisidek "allegorizes," or better "typifies," Christ (see, for example, Psalm 110:4; Hebrews 7:1–15; 12:24), or when St Paul the persona of Romans 7, according to commentators, re-enacts the Fall of Man. When a person resembles a biblical person she or he is called a type, a figure, or a figura.[4] The *Faerie Queene* contains seven clear and widely recognized figural or typological episodes, on which see Kaske, "Bible," in Hamilton et al. (1990). Being an analogy of one person or event to another, typology or figura lends itself to what Fowler calls "extended symbolism."

The remaining sense is the moral one, which hardly needs explanation. It is practically ubiquitous in sacred and even secular texts, or at least it was once claimed to be in order to justify secular literature. While somewhat restrictive, this hermeneutical principle at least allowed a reader to investigate whether a given passage – in the Bible or in literature – is not praising but subtly critiquing a supposedly exemplary character, as exegetes rightly do with David and as Spenserians rightly do with Redcrosse, Arteg-all, and Calidore, thus painting these heroes in shades of gray. Spenser in the *Letter to Raleigh* professes to deliver "doctrine by ensample [example] not by rule," and thus implies that everything that happens in the *Faerie Queene* is somehow moral in either a positive or a negative sense.

Alastair Fowler, in a book arguing that the *Faerie Queene* is organized astrologically, presents another and a helpful classification of Spenser's methods of biblical imitation: "Sometimes Spenser handled the Biblical material as Bunyan was later to do: combin-ing a large number of short texts, directly applied to contemporary life [I think he means to the reader's daily life] into a single but multi-partite allegorical fable" (Fowler, 1964, p. 66). This method is exemplified, I presume, in Spenser's House of Holiness in Book One, Canto Ten, especially a stanza like the following on Fidelia's miracles of faith in which A. C. Hamilton discovers short biblical texts:

> She would commaund the hasty Sunne to stay,
> Or backward turne his course from hevens hight [Joshua 10:12–13 and 2 Kings 20:10],
> Sometimes great hostes of men she could dismay [Judges 7:19–22],
> Dry-shod to passe, she parts the flouds in tway [Exodus 14:21–31];
> And eke huge mountaines from their native seat
> She would commaund, themselves to bear away,
> And throw in raging sea with roaring threat [Matthew 21:21].

"At his best, however," Fowler continues,

> he worked in a different manner. He would develop a few of the Biblical images in a more extended symbolism [including, I presume, typology], and make these the dominating poetic features of the Book. Thus, the character of Una, and the outline of her story, are based on the passage in the twelfth chapter of Revelation about "a woman clothed with the sun" who fled into the wilderness to escape a persecuting dragon.

In addition, as Fowler (1964, p. 66, n1) notes in this connection, John E. Hankins "shows that Spenser has conflated this biblical passage with another, traditionally associated with it: the account of the Bride's search for her lover (allegorically, Christ) in the Song of Songs," and this parallel too, I would add, is extended at length, up to Canto Eight, where the pair is reunited. I would add that Spenser has conflated with the above rather helpless females the character of Sapience in his portrayal of Una's magisterial relationship to Redcrosse (I.i.; I.ix–xii) and the Satyrs (I.vi). Thus Una brings with her at least three biblical subtexts, as well as representing on the literal level the conflation of two romance characters: the romance damsel in distress and the romance damsel as guide. Such polysemy exhibits another kind of freedom that imitation even of a sacred subtext allows.

Extended development occurs with less explicitness than do the bouquets of proof texts. Although Landrum rightly finds no explicit biblical echoes in *Muiopotmos*, the doomed butterfly's loose analogy to the Fall of Adam in a garden – a parallel of one entire story with another – subtends the entire last part of this poem. Una and the but-terfly Clarion constitute biblical types – items that seldom show up in tabulations and commentary notes to Spenser. Extended symbolism often goes unnoticed, like the largest names on a map. Spenser's allegory of Gloriana and Una as Leah and Rachel is an example not only of allegorical exegesis but of extended symbolism. Spenser's use of the apocalyptic and exegetical Whore of Babylon as a model for Duessa is extended and amplified – for example, by the addition of Lucifera as an ally and of Timias as Arthur's inferior double, and of both him and Fradubio as other victims and thus conditional parallels (that is, parallels with significant contrasts) to Redcrosse.

A clear yet richly complex instance of "extended symbolism" emerges from the way in which Redcrosse and Arthur in their respective duels with the giant Orgoglio (vii.7–15, viii.2–25) enter into conditional parallels with David in his confrontation with Goliath (1 Samuel 17:38–49) – another event of Old-Testament history. David puts aside the armor (sword, helmet, coat of mail) given him by Saul and approaches Goliath with only a staff, his sling, and a pouch of smooth stones (1 Samuel 17:38–40). But David declares that the Lord will "deliver" Goliath into his hand (1 Samuel 17:45–7). Redcrosse has also laid aside his armor, including his shield, for a quite different reason, but he makes no such profession of faith. Attacked by Orgoglio "ere he could get his shield," he cannot defeat Orgoglio as he would have had he possessed that faith which Ephesians (6:16, cited at the end of the *Letter to Raleigh*) depicts as a shield ("above all, take the shield of Faith, wherewith yee may quench all the fierie dartes of the wicked"). David doesn't need literal armor (passing over his quite effective slingshot) because of his faith in God. Redcrosse may look like the unarmed David, but he is merely a parody of him because that which David substituted for armor, i.e. faith, is here symbolized by armor, and he lacks it.

In contrast, Arthur, fully armed and, above all, shielded, prevails against both Duessa's seven-headed beast (FQ I.vii.7–8) and, later, Orgoglio (viii.18, 19, 20, and 21), where the crucial shield is mentioned in each stanza). Faith is the metaphorical meaning of his shield (as in Ephesians). His shield enables those same miracles of defeating "unequal armies of his foes," dismaying monsters, and harming the very heavens – effects which are later said to be wrought by Fidelia, personification of faith, in x.20 (see above). Spenser thus develops a biblical character (David) by reflecting him in both a foil and a skewed analogue. We have seen three examples of extended symbolism in Duessa as the Whore of Babylon with her extra allies and victim (a distinctively Protestant exegesis), Redcrosse and Arthur as two different Davids fighting Orgoglio as Goliath, and Gloriana and Una as Leah and Rachel. To cover imitations as complex as these, and sometimes as literal, we need a broader term than just "symbolism" – a term like "development" or "amplification." By extending biblical symbolism with extra allies, victims, and antitypes, Spenser employs great ingenuity.

One would think that biblical imitation would stifle creativity because the normativity of the text would seem to allow only a reverential, uncritical, unmediated imitation – scarcely more than a translation, one that aims to transfer to the new work some of the primary text's authority. This type of imitation Thomas M. Greene in his study of Renaissance imitation of the classics would label sacramental, and he gives it short and scornful shrift (Greene, 1982, pp. 38–9, 47, 57). True, he never mentions imitating the Bible, though it would seem to be a perfect example of sacramental imitation because the authority with which a classical text oppresses its author applies *a fortiori* to a sacred text, which may even be a means of grace. This oppression may be the reason for the phenomenon noted by Greenslade, that few works that are heavily influenced by Bible stories or scenes attain the highest rank, the exception being *Paradise Lost*. Greenslade (1963, pp. 496–7) praises Spenser among others for finding his plots elsewhere. Greene praises as sophisticated a "dialectical" imitation by those writers who know that their subtext was written a long time ago, perhaps on other shores, and is not applicable to their generation without considerable reinterpretation. Such *cognoscenti* either supply this or put the original nugget between quotation marks as a naive period-piece. Some of Spenser's imitations of the Bible are reverential, especially *Hymne of Heavenly Love* and parts of *Faerie Queene* Book I – works whose aim clearly is to enlist the Bible's salvific power to make the reader a better Christian (see *Letter to Raleigh* on Book I). Such truly sacramental imitations are supported when the Bible or a portion thereof is mentioned explicitly, as Spenser does in the *Vewe*, the *Letter to Raleigh*, the *Shepheardes Calender*, especially the glosses (whether he authored or just authorized them), and above all in Book I, but nowhere else. In the *Letter to Raleigh*, he cites Ephesians (6:11–17) to explain that Redcrosse's armor is "the armour of a Christian man." Redcrosse gives Arthur as a parting gift "a booke, wherein his Saveours testament / Was writ ... / A worke of wondrous grace, and able soules to save" (I.ix.19). Such a view supports reverential imitation.

Descriptions of the Bible in the House of Holiness are jaundiced; and such an attitude supports dialectical imitation of it. We can see from Spenser that a Christian can utilize the Bible against itself by criticizing, relativizing, and historicizing the Old Testament along the lines of St Paul and of Christ's "Antitheses" (Matthew 5:17–47). The Ten Commandments given to Moses on Mount Sinai are characterized as what St Paul calls the "letter" that "killeth" (2 Corinthians 3:6–7), namely as the "bitter doome of death and balefull mone," which is "writ in stone / With bloudy letters by the hand of God" (x.53). Greene would call this echo a dialectical imitation of the account of the giving of Mosaic Law – even a combative or an adversarial one (43–48, passim). Such an imitation is authorized provided that the criticisms are those voiced or implied by Paul and the Epistle to the Hebrews. In the House of Holiness, Fidelia holds a "sacred Booke, with bloud ywrit." All things considered, it seems to be the entire Bible: it is "signd and seald with blood" (x.13), and out of it she teaches "Of God, of grace, of justice, of free will" (x.19). Spenser sometimes says the Bible may harm its readers – a warning stressed by Catholics. Fidelia's book contains "darke things ... hard to be understood" (x.13, 19; cf. 2 Peter 3:15), and when Redcrosse hears them, he is filled with despair at his own unworthiness and wishes to die (x.21–9; cf. ix.50–1). This warning is the nearest Spenser ever comes to criticizing the Bible as a whole, and he seems to question as Catholics did the sufficiency of Bible-reading for salvation if an optimistic instructor (Speranza or Hope) is not present.

Furthermore, such relativizing and historicizing of a subtext as Greene admires in poets is only one kind of poetic freedom. Another way of using Scripture independently is by combining it with another text or discourse, as when Spenser boldly inserts between the expected heaven of "happy soules" and the heaven of angels a mezzanine "where those Idees on hie / Enraunged be, which Plato so admyred" (HHB 82–3). This project is called syncretism – a viewpoint neither wholly religious nor wholly secular –

and it is common in the Middle Ages (most notably with Aristotle) and the Renaissance (most notably with neoplatonism).

Another way of declaring one's independence from the Bible is to avoid mentioning it at all. This makes for a secular discourse – classical or courtly-chivalric or merely ethical or prudential, giving a view of humanity in itself – independent of God or the devil. Such a poem is *Prothalamium*, a poem celebrating a double betrothal. It is absent from Landrum's (1926, pp. 538–44) tabulations. The almost complete absence of Scripture from *Faerie Queene* III and IV means that, like Shakespeare, Spenser does not regard the Bible as containing the answer to every question – for example, the question dominating Britomart's quest, whom to marry.

An imitation both more and less direct than verbal and thematic imitation is biblical poetics. It must be admitted that Spenser often uses personification – two of his most powerful being Despaire in *Faerie Queene* I.ix and Mutabilitie, the protagonist of Book Seven. Personifications are not typical of biblical poetics, except for Sapience and Love in 1 Corinthians 13. In mode, Despaire and Mutabilitie resemble the *Roman de la Rose* more than they do the Bible.

Two kinds of biblical poetics are adversarial enough to meet Greene's criteria – images *in bono* and *in malo* and contradictory propositions. In addition to psalmic parallelism, moral examples, and typology, all mentioned above, an element of biblical poetics that Spenser demonstrably employs throughout the *Faerie Queene* and in the *Amoretti* is the repetition of images in good and bad senses (*in bono* and *in malo*) – a biblical structure explored by patristic and medieval exegesis and recognized in the Renaissance even by some Protestants. In *Faerie Queene* Book One appear alternating good and bad cups, wells, women, castles, allegorical houses, garlands, and reptilian beasts. Spenser also repeats with this variation what one might broadly call "motifs" – themes and actions, such as pride/self-confidence, fasting, magic, glory-praise-honor, bidding of beads, communities (good, bad, and imperfect), and abandoning one's shield. Redcrosse and Arthur are giant-fighting Davids – Redcrosse *in malo*, Arthur *in bono*. The good instance and the bad one are not always diametrically opposite as they are in the previous example because they are sometimes in different areas of life. Whereas the bad dragon represents Satan, an originary and cosmic principle of evil, the good dragon, forming the crest on Arthur's helmet (I.vii.31), is just a dynastic and political symbol (see *Spenser Encyclopedia*, "Heraldry," p. 354). Nevertheless Spenser's effort to include a good dragon is unmistakable and biblical. Shifting evaluations of altars, pride, and a laurel leaf complicate *Amoretti and Epithalamium* (*Amoretti* 27–8, 58–9; *Epithalamium* 162–4). These tergiversations, especially when they are in the same area of life, give the feeling of a progressive self-correction, yielding the Aristotelian conclusion that vice is to virtue as abuse is to the proper use of the same thing. Despite its biblical precedent, the strategy is versatile and adaptable to secular literature such as the later books of the *Faerie Queene* because it is tied not to religion nor to allegory but to categories of good and evil, better and worse. It is more text-based than is allegory. At the same time, the progressive self-correction is hermeneutically unsettling because no one passage can be trusted to give Spenser's last word about an image or practice; at the end of the poem one has to construct a complex distinction to cover everything he says, and some of those things may be contradictory. The Tenth Canto of Book One contradicts previous condemnations of certain religious practices such as fasting. The resulting indeterminacy is meant to lead the reader toward a position of adiaphorism – a position favored by Anglicans that allowed a certain latitude provided that the practice was not explicitly condemned by Scripture and could serve a good cause (Kaske, 1999, pp. 86–97).

Sometimes not only evaluations of images but whole propositions are contradicted, especially on two questions. Do we obtain heaven by God's indefectible, irresistible grace springing ultimately from his predestination or by our own good works? And if we do so by works – winning merit, avoiding serious sin, and repenting after we fail to do so – are they performed through divine grace or through our own free will? Spenser presents all these positions (see I.ix.53 versus I.x.41 and II.i.32; and I.x.1 versus I.vii.41 and II.i.33). By exposing contradictions – what some would consider a flaw in the Bible – Spenser imitates the Bible dialectically or even "eristically," that is, combatively.

It can now be seen how I fit into existing scholarship on Spenser and the Bible. I alone take this as my prime subject. I read both works with a more empirical closeness. Five other recent critics resemble me, have influenced me, and should be read along with me for their unique data and their differing perspectives on the subject. Darryl Gless, *Literature and Theology in Renaissance England* (1994) and the many works of John N. King, especially *Spenser's Poetry and the Reformation Tradition* (1990), focus on English sources: "practical divinity" (Gless) and popular literature (King). Some textual and theological precision is unattainable by King and Gless because neither attends to the many Latin Bibles (not only Romanist but Protestant) or to their commentaries that in the sixteenth century were written and reprinted overwhelmingly in Latin. Only Gervase Babington's commentaries and a substantial share of the many Protestant commentaries on Revelation were written in English. This was because Latin was the lingua franca of all educated European men from grammar school onwards, especially on intellectual subjects. (For a survey of the Bibles and commentaries available to Spenser at Cambridge, see the bibliographical appendix to Kaske, 1999.) I disagree with King about the extent of the Romanism in Spenser owing to my use of these Latin sources (especially of the conciliatory Melanchthon) and to King's assumption that the *Faerie Queene* and the *Shepheardes Calender* give one consistent doctrinal position throughout (i.e. moderate Protestantism). I contend that Spenser is a disciplined pluralist, that he offers a theology in Book I (mostly scripturalist, though also stressing sacraments and sacramentals) that differs not only from that in Book II (infrequent Scripture mostly syncretized with the predominant Aristotelian ethics), but also from that in the remaining books of this poem (broadly humanistic). The same degrees of Christianity are found in the *Fowre Hymnes*, namely the "Hymne of Heavenly Love" (based mostly on the Bible and the Creeds), the "Hymne of Heavenly Beauty" (vaguely Christian but syncretized with Jewish and Platonic ideas), and the "Hymne of Love" and the "Hymne of Beauty" (secular).

Darryl Gless departs from King and resembles me in his acceptance of Spenser's religious contradictions. He locates each pole of a contradiction, couched in sophisticated theological vocabulary (e.g. "intrinsic versus extrinsic causes of salvation"), in the mind of an individual reader – a reader-response approach leading to indeterminacy. This interpretation, being minimalist, is plausible, especially regarding Spenser's equivocations on "mercy" in I.x. But I also attempt to see patterns in the contradictions (e.g. fasting *in bono* and *in malo*) and reasons for them within the text, such as the virtue treated in the individual book or the hero's current stage of religious development. Unlike King and me, Gless limits his focus to *Faerie Queene* Book I. In addition there are two currently undervalued, theologically precise, and heavily scriptural interpretations of Spenser's doctrinal contradictions arguing for Augustinian influence and allusion as the key: James Schiavoni's (1989) "Predestination and Free Will: The Crux of Canto Ten" and Åke Bergvall's (2001) book, *Augustinian Perspectives in the Renaissance*.

As a biblical poet, Spenser excels with respect to his patterns of images *in bono* and *in malo* and to his vast exfoliating structural variations on biblical events and characters. Modern readers must exert themselves to "trace" Spenser's "fine footing" among the Scriptures. They will discover a good deal of artistic freedom.

Notes

1   Many points in this chapter owe much to my entry "Bible" in the *Spenser Encyclopedia*, ed. A. C. Hamilton et al. (Toronto, 1990), my book, *Spenser and Biblical Poetics* (Ithaca, NY, 1999), and my essay "Spenser's *Amoretti*: A Psalter of Love," in Daniel Doerksen and Christopher Hodgkins, eds, *Centered on the Word* (Newark, NJ, 2004). Unless otherwise noted, biblical citations are taken from the Geneva Bible. Spenser citations are from *The Faerie Queene*, ed. A. C. Hamilton et al. (New York, 2001) and from *Shorter Poems*, ed. Richard A. McCabe (Harmondsworth, 1999). I have normalized u-v-w and i-j-y. *Faerie Queene* is abbreviated FQ and *Hymne of Heavenly Beautie* HHB in documentation.

2   Landrum's list provides the only statistics we have on the shorter poems and the *Vewe*. Unfortunately, she overlooks many allusions, and her comparison of versions is illogical. Since his publication in 1976, the more discriminating Shaheen has replaced Landrum on *The Faerie Queene*: he has collected hundreds of verbal borrowings and proved that Spenser usually, though by no means always, employs the Geneva version.

3   V.ii. On the imitation of Esdras here, see Dunseath (1968, pp. 97–8) and Hazard (2000, pp. 163–70, passim).

4   For example, by Erich Auerbach, "Figura," in *Scenes from the Drama of European Literature* (New York, 1959), and, with more theological rigor, by A. C. Charity, *Events and Their Afterlife: The Dialectics of Christian Typology in the Bible and Dante* (Cambridge, 1966), 1–2, 171–8, passim.

Bibliography

Auerbach, Erich (1959) *Scenes from the Drama of European Literature*. New York.

Bergvall, Åke (2001) *Augustinian Perspectives in the Renaissance*. Acta Universitatis Upsaliensis, Studia Anglistica Upsaliensia, 117. Uppsala.

Bible, [Geneva] (1594) *The Bible, that is, the Holy Scriptures conteined in the Olde and Newe Testament*. London.

Charity, A. C. (1966) *Events and Their Afterlife: The Dialectics of Christian Typology in the Bible and Dante*. Cambridge.

Dante (1961) *Purgatorio*, trans. and commentary by John D. Sinclair. New York.

Dunseath, T. K. (1968) *Spenser's Allegory of Justice in Book Five of "The Faerie Queene."* Princeton, NJ.

Fowler, Alastair (1964) *Spenser and the Numbers of Time.* London.

Fruen, Jeffrey P. (1990) "The Faery Queen [sic] Unveiled? Five Glimpses of Gloriana," *Spenser Studies* 11, 53–88.

Gless, Darryl (1994) *Interpretation and Theology in Spenser.* Cambridge.

Greene, Thomas M. (1982) *The Light in Troy: Imitation and Discovery in Renaissance Poetry.* Elizabethan Club Series, 7. New Haven, CT.

Greenslade, S. L. (1963) "Epilogue," in S. L. Greenslade, ed., *The Cambridge History of the Bible, Volume Three: The West from the Reformation to the Present Day.* Cambridge.

Hamilton, A. C. et al., eds (1990) *The Spenser Encyclopedia.* Toronto.

Hazard, Mark (2000) "The Other Apocalypse: Spenser's Use of 2 Esdras in the Book of Justice," *Spenser Studies* 14, 163–87.

Hopkins, Gerard Manley (1948) "Spelt from Sibyl's Leaves," in *Poems*, 3rd edn, ed. Robert Bridges and W. H. Gardner. New York.

Kaske, Carol V. (1999) *Spenser and Biblical Poetics.* Ithaca, NY.

Kaske, Carol V. (2004) "Spenser's *Amoretti*: A Psalter of Love," in Daniel Doerksen and Christopher Hodgkins, eds, *Centered on the Word: Literature, Scripture and the Tudor-Stuart Middle Way.* Newark, NJ.

King, John N. (1990) *Spenser's Poetry and the Reformation Tradition.* Princeton, NJ.

Landrum, Grace Warren (1926) "Spenser's Use of the Bible and His Alleged Puritanism," *PMLA* 41, 517–44.

Lovelace, Richard (1944) "To Lucasta, Going to the Wars," in Richard Aldington, ed., *The Viking Book of Poetry of the English-Speaking World.* New York, 446–7.

Schiavoni, James (1989) "Predestination and Free Will: The Crux of Canto Ten," *Spenser Studies* 10, 175–95.

Shaheen, Naseeb (1976) *Biblical References in "The Faerie Queene."* Memphis, TN.

Spenser, Edmund (1989) *The Yale Edition of the Shorter Poems*, Ed. William A. Oram et al. New Haven, CT.

Spenser, Edmund (2001) *The Faerie Queene*, ed. A. C. Hamilton, text ed. Hiroshi Yamashita and Toshiyuki Suzuki. New York.

CHAPTER 15
Mary Sidney

Rivkah Zim

When feminist critics of the 1980s first encountered the literary works of Mary Herbert, countess of Pembroke (1561–1621) they read them in the context of a "societal norm" that had oppressed women and denied them access to higher learning. Although there were exceptions, even "protestant emphasis on the Word of God," it was argued, "encouraged education for women so that they could read the Bible and the appropriate commentaries, not so that they could speak or write their own ideas ... [thus] the enforced rhetorical ignorance of women was maintained."[1] Upon this premise early modern women were "silent but for the word," and those few aristocratic women who were allowed space on the "margins of discourse" could only become distinct literary personalities by "subverting" this construct of a "societal norm." Yet, as a sympathetic reviewer pointed out, "To the extent that women participated in religious translation, we must see them not on the margins but on the broad highway"; these topics predominate in literary and scholarly works by all writers in the period – male and female.[2] A further misconception about the status of translation as a subservient, non-creative activity – and thus one suitable for females – compounded the effect of gender-based theories on approaches to the countess of Pembroke's writing. Yet another distortion involved the so-called "stigma of print": gentlemen poets avoided print publication because they thought it vulgar, while women feared a charge of immodesty if their writing circulated widely. Many of these generalizations have since been modified as a result of developments in the history of the early modern book. It is now recognized from studies of the functions, status, and extent of the circulation of texts in manuscript copies that print did not simply supersede handwriting.[3]

If modern critics still tend to study Pembroke as a woman writer, Mary herself never forgot that she was born a Sidney. Her father, Sir Henry Sidney, served as Queen Elizabeth's deputy in Ireland, and as President of the Council in the Marches of Wales, in which positions he was expected to control and organize civil and military power in the queen's name. Through her mother, the daughter of the duke of Northumberland, Mary Sidney was related to some of the most powerful Elizabethan grandees: Robert Dudley, earl of Leicester, the queen's favorite, and Henry Hastings, earl of Huntingdon, were Mary's uncles. This background conditioned the upbringing and education that prepared her for life as the consort of a similarly distinguished and powerful man. After two years at court, as one of Queen Elizabeth's ladies, Mary Sidney married Henry Herbert, second earl of Pembroke, in 1577.[4] The new countess was sixteen and would have been made aware of the privileges and responsibilities of her rank and of her role in the enlargement of her family's sphere of influence and power. She would never have subscribed to ideas of her own inferiority, whether social, cultural, or spiritual, based on gender. By 1593 she was described as a model poet who "enjoyes ... wise Minervaes wit, / And sets to school, our poets everywhere": [5] "Pembroke a pearle, that orient is of kind, / A Sidney right, shall not in silence sit." Women of Mary Sidney's social class and generation were encouraged to develop their expressive powers. According to Thomas Hoby's appendix to his translation of Castiglione's *Book of the Courtier*, published in the year of Mary's birth, a lady at court was expected to have the education and "livelie quicknesse of wit" that would enable her not only to converse with any of the company there but also to judge and influence people of power. She was expected:

> To have an understandinge in all thinges belonginge to the Courtier, that she maye gyve her judgemente to commend and to make of gentilmen according to their worthinesse and desertes.
> To be learned.
> To be seene in the most necessarie languages.[6]

The duties of the court lady, like those of the court gentleman, required intelligence and rhetorical dexterity. Girls and boys were trained to develop their minds and the necessary communication skills by learning languages (especially Italian, French, and Latin), and by reading good literature. Translation and imitation of model texts, including the biblical poetry of the Book of Psalms, were essential components of the humanist methods of education that were adopted by the Sidneys, among others in the mid-sixteenth century, for their sons and daughters.[7] Such literary culture constituted essential life skills.

If her family's advantages gave Mary Sidney the education, personal confidence, and, hence, the option of becoming a writer, their misfortunes may also have generated incentives for her writing. All her surviving literary works belong to a period of about twelve years following the disastrous year 1586, in which her father, then her mother, and, finally, her elder brother Philip died within a few months of each other. Her writing is dominated by themes of death or commemoration and a search for religious consolation.[8] Her *Antonius*, an English version in iambic pentameters of the French neo-Senecan tragedy by Robert Garnier, dramatizing the story of Mark Antony and Cleopatra, cannot be earlier than the 1585 edition of Garnier's text that she used. In her prose *Discourse of Life and Death*, translated by 1590 from Philippe de Mornay's French, the countess selected an opportunity to study a Christian (but equally neo-Stoical) approach to death.[9] De Mornay, a distinguished Protestant theologian and political theorist, was a longstanding friend of her brothers, Philip and Robert. Both of these translations from French were widely disseminated in print for a mass readership. By contrast, her translation from Italian into English terza rima of Petrarch's *Triumph of Death* survives in only one manuscript copy.[10] Towards the end of the *Triumph* the voice of the poet's dead beloved, Laura, tries to console him by revealing her happiness in heaven and confirming her soul's eternal love for him. The editors of Pembroke's *Collected Works* point out that in adding an allusion to her brother Philip's metrical version of Psalm 42, she emphasized Laura's representation of her death as "An unrepentant syghe."[11] The addition of this allusion is suggestive of Pembroke's incentive in pursuing her greatest literary endeavor: her completion of Philip Sidney's English sequence of metrical psalms, which was left unfinished, at Psalm 43, when he died unexpectedly in October 1586.

She was not only a Sidney by birth and affection; she was also an Elizabethan Protestant by education and conviction. However, none of the countess's other poems makes any specific use of biblical texts. These include "The Dolefull Lay of Clorinda," a pastoral elegy written for Philip in her voice and name as Sidney's sister, that was published with other elegies for Sidney by Edmund Spenser, and friends, in *Astrophel* (1595); and two poems found in one manuscript of the Sidney–Pembroke metrical psalms. "Even now that Care which on thy Crowne attends" dedicates these psalms to the "thrice sacred Queene" Elizabeth. "To the Angell spirit of the most excellent Sir Phillip Sidney" addresses her dead brother, offering him their "coupled worke," which she has been inspired to complete by his example. She grieves for his loss and invokes "Truth, sacred Truth" to commemorate his "Angells soule with highest Angells plac't" now, and forever, in heaven. Finally, striving with sorrow (much as Petrarch's persona had done in confronting the death of Laura), the poet-speaker is comforted by the "just cause" that might reunite their souls in heaven, at the death – "Oh happie chaunge" – of the poet who identifies herself as "the Sister of that Incomporable Sidney."[12]

How and why did Mary Sidney approach the biblical poetry of the Book of Psalms? She described her versions of Psalms 44 to 150 as "theise dearest offrings of my hart / dissolv'd to Inke, ... sadd Characters indeed of simple love," intended for no "other purpose but to honor" him, "the wonder of men." She speculated about how his psalm paraphrases would have been "Immortall Monuments of [his] faire fame" and therefore completed them as her tribute to his life and writing career.[13] Although he was only thirty-one when he died, according to some contemporary ideas about the different stages of man's life, Philip had already reached an age of maturity that would make it appropriate for him to write about religious subjects.[14] It is possible therefore that in imitating him, the countess intended these psalms, their "coupled worke," to celebrate and conclude her own writing career as much as her brother's. (The psalmist's voice is not gendered.) It also seems unlikely that she could have produced such an extensive body of thoughtful and vigorous poetry without gaining some gratification or intellectual satisfaction.

She worked to the same criteria, using the same sources that he had consulted, and by the same literary methods. This involved working through the whole Book of Psalms since Philip had not selected particular psalms for personal reasons as, for example, his uncles had done when they were imprisoned in 1554.[15] The main aesthetic attribute of his paraphrases was their metrical variety accomplished with a level of versatility that was unprecedented in English. Many of the different verse and stanza forms in Philip's forty-three psalms correspond to precedents in the French metrical psalms by Clement Marot and Theodore Beza, which had been known in England since Edward VI's reign. Mary Sidney continued, matched, and, inevitably, exceeded Philip's formal variety in her greater number of metrical paraphrases. It is also possible to demonstrate how, like her brother, she had immersed herself in studying the biblical texts and worked with English, French and Latin sources open before her: often borrowing words, or ideas to develop metaphors. In particular, she relied extensively on Beza's original Latin commentaries and his neo-Latin metrical paraphrases, or *carmina*, and not simply on Anthony Gilby's English version of Beza's prose texts. Beza, a Greek and Hebrew scholar as well as Calvin's deputy and successor, brought the insights of a poet to his biblical interpretations.[16] (Evidence from the countess's version of Psalm 104 will be discussed below.)

In following these patterns of reading and writing, established by Philip, Mary respected his achievement, and fulfilled her own ambition to create an image that represented her family's lost aspirations. This was part of a larger picture; during the 1590s, this self-appointed agent for his "Angell Spirit," did more than anyone else to shape and promote Sidney's literary reputation. She may have caused pirated first editions of his sonnet sequence *Astrophel and Stella* (1591) to be called in by the authorities; in 1598 it was reprinted as part of a larger folio edition of Sidney's works, most likely from her manuscript copy. She lent her name to protect his pastoral romance – *The Countess of Pembroke's Arcadia* – which he claimed to have written for her, much of it in her presence and at her command. In 1593 the Pembrokes' secretary described the newly printed work as "now by more than one interest *The Countess of Pembroke's Arcadia*; done, as it was, for her; as it is, by her." And he promised: "Neither shall these pains be the last (if no unexpected accident cut off her determination) which the everlasting love of her excellent brother will make her consecrate to his memory."[17]

Yet, when she completed her brother's project for new English metrical psalms, by 1594, the countess also claimed a share of his reputation as a poet of distinction for herself. This claim was based on her rhetorical display and command of versification, on contemporary ideas about the nature and value of the personal expression inherent in processes of paraphrase, and, above all, on the significance of the Psalms as "a heavenly poesie" containing divine instruction and inspiration.

The wording on the title page of an early seventeenth-century scribal copy of the Sidney–Pembroke Psalms assures its readers that the texts are presented under her name and authority.[18] Although she did not write for a mass readership, and thus had no incentive to publish them in print, it is clear from the number and variety of eighteen surviving manuscript copies that she frequently allowed their circulation among favored readers, and at different stages in the evolution of her texts which were much revised. This scribal copy advertises itself as: "The Psalmes of David translated into divers & sundry kindes of verse, more rare, & excellent, for the method & varietie then ever yet hath bene don in English." This emphasis on formal variety was designed to appeal to readers of superior literary taste, experience, and judgment. But the associated names of its authors would also have attracted attention and assured the quality of the product: "begun by the noble & learned gent. Sr P. Sidney Kt., & finished by the R. honnorable the Countesse of Pembroke, his Sister, & by her dirrection & appointment." "Verbum Dei manet in aeternum" is inscribed beneath an ink ruling at the bottom of the page. The enduring eternal life of the Word of God in these biblical texts would also carry the names and reputations of both Mary and Philip Sidney into an eternity of fame as English poets of learning, piety, spiritual insightfulness, and virtuosity.

The effectiveness of this tribute in "immortall monuments" of fame depended on contemporary attitudes to the Psalms. Some time after her death in 1621, John Donne celebrated the "Sydnean Psalmes," describing their biblical models as "The highest matter in the noblest forme."[19] Donne's statement evokes traditional views of the Psalms that were shared by many sixteenth-century English Protestants, among others. The Book of Psalms was regarded as the "Treasure house of the holye Scripture" because this one part of the whole, it was thought, "contaynethe what so ever is necessary for a christen man to know."[20] Typological interpretations, transmitted by the works of patristic and medieval exegetes to sixteenth-century Christians, caused the English translators of the Geneva Bible to proclaim: "here is Christ our onely redeemer, and mediator moste evidently described." But this convenient, representative quality was not their principal attribute. By the end of the sixteenth century Richard Hooker was assured of his readers' agreement when he asked rhetorically: "What is there necessarie for man to know which the Psalmes are not able to *teach?*"[21]

Early Christian commentators had also recognized that, owing to their variety of tone, mood, and attitudes to spiritual matters, as well as to their many personal and vivid forms of expression, the Psalms contained "the alterations of every mans hart and conscience described and lively paynted to his owne sight."[22] In the sixteenth century all kinds of Christians echoed this view and recommended them as model prayers that provided immediate relief, in "moste present remedies," for all temptations and "troubles of minde and conscience."[23] Their usefulness was considered universal: they were an "Anatomy of all the partes of the Soule, inasmuch as a man shalnot find any affection in himselfe, wherof the Image appeereth not in this glasse" or mirror.[24] The first-person singular forms, I and me, which predominate in so many psalms, have always encouraged individuals to identify with the psalmists' suggestively open expressions, and to apply them personally. Thus, despite their doctrinal differences, sixteenth-century Christians continued to participate in a long and relatively stable tradition of personal devotion, based on biblical psalms regarded as models for self-examination and a ready-made source of spiritual comfort. Anthony Gilby, the translator of Beza's commentary on the Psalms, which Gilby dedicated to the countess of Huntingdon, Philip and Mary Sidney's aunt, summarized their special appeal and significance by stating: "whereas al other scriptures do teach us what God saith unto us, these praiers ... do teach us, what we shall saie unto God."[25]

When humanist scholars such as John Calvin, and Immanuel Tremellius who had been brought up in Jewish traditions of biblical scholarship, went back to study the Hebrew language of the original texts, supplemented by medieval rabbinic commentaries, they revitalized early Christian scholars' insights into the poetic qualities of David's "songs."[26] The lyricism and other poetic qualities of the Psalms were especially evident because their metaphors, similes, apostrophes, and structural patterns of parallelism, and other varieties of rhetorical arrangement of ideas, were appreciable when translated into other languages. Philip Sidney was moved by such imaginative qualities in the Psalms to declare "holy Davids Psalms ... a divine Poeme." The psalmist's "handling his prophecie," "the often and free chaunging of persons, ... his telling of the beasts joyfulnesse, and hils leaping," and other rhetorical devices, were evidence of "a heavenly poesie" or art of poetry; and Sidney referred to learned "Hebricians," such as Tremellius, to validate these ideas.[27] His *Defence of Poesie* is probably the best guide to the Sidneys' intentions in becoming English metrical psalmists, since it implies that in striving to honor God's name and teach others how to speak to God, "in some worthy phrase," they were also offering personal thanks, as poets, for "the immortall goodnes of that God, who giveth us hands to write, and wits to conceive" or think. Of all the different kinds of poet, Sidney considered the "chiefe both in antiquitie and excellencie" to be those who "imitate[d] the unconceiveable excellencies of God."[28] Sidney would have regarded his imitations of psalms as a fulfillment of his "vocation" as a poet. But it was the vision and the determination of his sister that allowed this ambition to be realized, and transmitted to others.

Generations of readers had recognized that the poetic qualities of David's "songs" made them especially memorable as instructions, and affective, and therefore efficacious, personal prayers. Yet these were "heavenly fruites, both private and publike."[29] The significance of the countess of Pembroke's metrical paraphrases needs to be understood in all these contexts.

In a private context, she would have turned to the Psalms, like any other Christian, for thanksgiving and celebration, or to explore her grief and spiritual needs. At the end of her version of Psalm 88, for example, she softens the resentful tone of the distraught psalmist by emphasizing the distance, rather than the cause of the speaker's separation from those

> Who erst [i.e. formerly] were neare and deare
>   far now, o farr
>   disjoined ar:
>
> ...
>
> as darknesse they to me appeare. (Lines 73–5, 78)

Contemporary English Bibles translate this final clause as a statement either that God hid the psalmist's friends, or that they hid themselves. Gilby's Beza supplied her with the two distinctive elements of her imitation: references to distance and darkness. But whereas Beza had focused on the situation of the psalmist, Pembroke's subject is the situation of the speaker's near and dear ones. This emphasis, aided by the layout of the short lines and repetition of "far," imparts a wistful quality and an impression of this speaker's helplessness in confronting personal loss and fading memories. Yet, however suggestive and intimate this seems in the context of the Sidney family, the subtlety of her interpretation means that it is not exclusive.

In a public context, it is clear from the number of surviving copies that by following Philip's ideals and example, she succeeded in creating versions of these universal, necessary, and familiar texts that could be used by anyone who shared her literary and religious sensibilities.[30] This was an important and altruistic achievement. In her judgment, the substance of these divine poems remained unchanged in their new metrical paraphrases; she assured Philip's "Angell spirit"

> That heaven's King may deigne his owne transform'd
> in substance no, but superficiall tire
> by thee put on. (Lines 8–10)

Nevertheless, because of the nature of human individuality, each of their new versions reveals the style or character of the mind that has transformed or regenerated it. The "heavenly fruit" was private and public, but the process of production, in changing the dress of thought, was personal.

Translation, paraphrase, and similar forms of close imitation of model texts were not considered subservient activities and the new works they produced were not therefore considered inferior to any created by other literary processes. The countess of Pembroke's imitations of the Psalms reflect the creativity of her approach, in terms of her meditative readings of the biblical models, as well as her characteristic English style in regenerating them as Elizabethan poetry.

In the mid-sixteenth century Roger Ascham, the queen's Greek tutor, had defined literary "imitation" as "a facultie to expresse livelie and perfitelie that example which ye go about to folow."[31] Paraphrase required a high level of skill and was best reserved for those with learning and discretion. An interpretation of a text such as a paraphrase was a new work in which a writer offered readers a well judged elucidation of the model by speaking alongside it in language appropriate for those readers. It was an ancient truism, repeated in the sixteenth century by humanists such as Erasmus, that every individual writer's style was peculiar to him (or her) and thus every imitation of a model text was a new work since it inevitably bore the character, or stamp, of the mind that had created it. Erasmus, echoing Quintilian and Seneca, explained:

> what you have consumed in varied and prolonged reading has to be digested, and transferred by a process of reflection [*meditatione*] into the grain of the mind ... so that your natural talent ... will of itself bring forth a discourse ... redolent of your character.[32]

According to Philip Sidney, by "attentive translation" one could make other authors' works wholly one's own. It was, as Horace had advised the young Roman poet, a matter of taking out private rights over public property.[33] This depended on a combination of personal qualities in terms of one's capacities as a reader or critic and scholar, and one's expressive eloquence as a writer: the "learned discretion" of a "right poet."

Therefore, although Mary Sidney followed her brother's example in composing her metrical paraphrases in various English verse forms and by consulting the same literary and scholarly resources, it was inevitable that her new poems would reflect her critical faculties and literary sensibilities. G. F. Waller identified her "muscular syntax" and "terse" metaphors; John Rathmell noted the "sense of involvement that gives the finest of [her] psalms their force."[34] Analysis of her working methods shows her understanding and imagination in entering into the psalmist's situation, speaking alongside his words and representing his feelings in graphic terms and her favorite rhetorical devices: "I as I can think, speake, and doe the best" (Psalm 56, line 11). In some of her best writing the countess is as logical, dramatic, decisive, and rhetorically artful as any metaphysical poet. Donne praised the authors of the "Sydnean Psalmes" as "this Moses and this Miriam": sibling prophets (and singers) who had led and protected God's chosen people of Protestant England (as the biblical siblings had led the ancient Hebrews). He did not disparage their literary methods; instead he understood and celebrated the ways in which their "formes of joy and art" had "re-reveal[ed]" those songs previously "whisper'd to David" by "heavens high holy Muse."[35]

Mary Sidney's metrical paraphrase of Psalm 104 is one of her finest. It was one of three "trulie devine" psalms by her – "in Poesie the mirrois of our Age" – that John Harington sent to the countess of Bedford in 1600.[36] The biblical model epitomizes the joyful song of the psalmist; it celebrates the divine work of creation described in all its varied glory as an integrated system. Anthony Gilby, translating Beza, defined it as "this heavenlie poetical invention"; it was amplified "with such an excellencie of words, and gravitie of sentences [i.e. thoughts], that nothing can be thought to be spoken either more elegantlie, or more learnedlie"[37] – a concept to which Mary Sidney responded with idiosyncratic vitality and thoughtfulness.

Each of her fourteen eight-line stanzas carefully transposes the sense of two or three biblical verses, and some of the wording from Coverdale's version used with the Book of Common Prayer. Her apostrophe, "O my soule," is a direct quotation from Coverdale, and her metaphor for God's glory, imagined as "all roiall pompes ... clothed ... in state" (lines 3–4), derives from her response to Coverdale's word choice, "majesty," and by analogy with the literal signs of a contemporary English monarchy. Elsewhere it is evident that she responded to the stimulus of different translations, paraphrases, and commentaries. The popularity of Psalm 104 also enables comparisons to be made with metrical versions by King James VI of Scotland, "translated out of Tremellius" in twelve eight-line stanzas, and Abraham Fraunce who dedicated his poetry to the countess.[38] As soon as there is more than one version, all may be perceived in relation to each other. For each of these poets the absolute original text was the biblical psalmist's *Hebraica veritas*; but none of these poets demonstrates direct experience of the Hebrew-language text.[39] Pembroke depended on the commentaries of learned "Hebricians."

The countess's artistry and sensitivity in speaking alongside the biblical psalmist creates the impression of a tightly organized world of sound and sense based on various patterns of repetition. The lyricism of her poem is in part the product of her virtuosity in sustaining 112 lines of iambic pentameter verse with only two rhymes in each stanza (ababbaba) or a maximum total of twenty-eight rhymes. Repeating patterns of sound-play within lines include figures of alliteration: "birdes ... brickle neastes ... on ... branches borne" (lines 58–9); reduplication (where the last word or sound is repeated at the beginning of the next line "to rest: / they rest ...": lines 74–5); and *traductio*, one of her favorite figures, in which a word stem is repeated in different forms within the same unit, "hastning their haste with spurr of hasty feare" (line 24).

Throughout her imitation of this psalm she was as careful to ensure the clarity of the logical connections between her ideas as to extend their emotional force. At the beginning of her fourth stanza she emphasized the consequences of the actions described in the previous stanza, tying all the main subjects into a logical train of thought, signaled by repetitions of the connecting word "So ... so ... so. ..." Similarly, she began stanza 7 by repeating the word "Thence ..." in order to connect her new subjects with their origins. She also demonstrates a new expressive link between form and ideas in lines 89–90, where the rhythm of her short phrases sustains the sense of the reciprocal relationship between God and his creatures, and where the repetition of "thy hand" imitates the circularity of the concept it represents:

> Thou giv'st, they take; thy hand it self displaies,
>   they filled feele the plenties of thy hand.

The artfulness of her paraphrase is most expressive in her rendering of verse 12, at the end of stanza 5:

> by these in their self-chosen mansions stay
>   the free-borne fowles, which through the empty way
> of yelding aire wafted with winged speed,
>   to art-like notes of Nature-tuned lay
> make earelesse bushes give attentive heed. (Lines 36–40)

Compare: "Beside them shall the foules of the ayre have theyr habitacion, & singe amonge the branches" (Coverdale as BCP); "Hard by we heir / The chirping birds among the leaves" (James VI); "There shall sweete-beckt byrds theyr bowres in bows be a building, / And to the waters fall theyr warbling voyce be a tuning" (Fraunce).

Here, a reader's attention is drawn to her rhetorical prowess in the prominence of expressive flourishes, so often to be found in the last lines of her stanza: in this stanza, the mental challenge of the paradox in bushes (without organs of hearing, but where the birds roost) heeding their song. While the birds' natural music mimics art, the long fluid rhythm of her phrase running over from line 37 pushes through the empty white space on the page to mimic their flight through yielding air. The complex detail behind her regeneration of this one simple idea reflects Mary Sidney's imaginative empathy with her subject. King James hardly lifts his mind above the sound of chirping birds, but his psalmist is present to hear them. Fraunce's version is so dominated by alliteration that his idea of the sensory parallel between warbling birds and running water is obstructed. Neither of these poets has lavished so much care or been so prolific with ideas as the countess was in recreating this biblical verse.

From the Geneva Bible's translation of verse 13 she took the image of God watering the mountains from his "chambers" in the heavens and extended its practical implications by specifying: "Thou, thou of heav'n the windowes dost unclose" (line 41). When the psalmist went on to sing of the consequences of this water as the earth's being "filled with the frute of thy workes," the countess personified this image of fecundity, imagining that the female "Earth greate with yong hir longing doth not lose" (line 43). In the next verse she avoided the specific words "food" (as BCP) or "bread" (as Geneva), but perhaps guided by the wording of Thomas Wilcox's exposition of this verse, which refers to "al thinges" necessary for life's "maintaynaunce,"[40] concluded: "all things in breef, that life in life maintaine, / from Earths old bowels fresh and yongly growes" (lines 47–8). A glance at Gilby's Beza would have provided her with the metaphor of the "bowels of the earth" but the paradox of the pregnant Earth's old bowels generating young growth was the countess's invention, tactically placed at the end of her stanza for maximum effect.

Her independence in handling the familiar phrases of this psalm also emerges in her personal interjection, "I say," when she disagrees with Golding's Calvin, who had included bread among other "dainties" produced by the earth. Mary Sidney confirms bread as our best food, agreeing with the biblical sense of its function to strengthen man's heart, but she cannot commend it as our "daintiest fare": "thence bread, our best, I say not daintiest fare, / prop yet of hartes, which els would weakly bow" (lines 51–2). Elsewhere, however, she followed Calvin's learned exposition in developing her image of the moon, "the Empresse of the night" (line 65). The editors of her *Collected Works* note that in this epithet Pembroke follows the traditional phrasing of secular poetry. However, Calvin's commentary at this point suggests that the priority given by the psalmist to the moon (also gendered feminine) reflects the importance of the moon in the Jewish calendar, which uses "hir as the director of their festival dayes ... holy assemblies, as [well as] for their meetings about politike affaires."[41] This last detail may have strengthened a potential political significance in the Empress of the night's holding "constant course with most unconstant face" (line 66); if the countess was also tempted to evoke consideration of Queen Elizabeth who had become associated with the myth of Cynthia (and favored wearing the colours of the moon, black and white), this paradox could indicate more than a poetic convention. Contemporary reference may arise from verbal associations. In verse 30 when God sends forth his "spirit" (as in the Geneva Bible) all kinds of life "are created" and the "face of the earth" is renewed. Gilby's Beza explains further that "the kinds of things do not decaie." From these cues the countess went her own way in extending her image of "troopes" of sea creatures (line 83) to a fully developed military metaphor using language associated with the Elizabethan militia:

> thy life-giving sp'rit doe mustering raise
>   new companies, to reinforce each band,
> which still supplied, never whole decaies. (Lines 94–6)

Finally, the countess, like the biblical psalmist, places herself in this cycle of life as she dedicates her voice to praise the creator "in song":

> I framed have a resolute decree,
> and thankfull be, till being I forgoe. (Lines 103–4)

Compare: "I wyll prayse my God whyle I have my beinge" (as BCP verse 33); "this is the same with that which went before, the doubling of it noteth the resolute purpose which the Prophet had to performe this his vow."[42]

The Sidneian Psalms remain her last known literary work, as well as her brother's latest poetry, and her only direct use of the Bible. From Chaucer onwards, poets had conventionally written retractions of their secular and amorous verses, and offered instead to turn to biblical and religious subjects in their maturity; some even did so.[43] If either of the Sidneys had thought that retractions were required, these psalms would have set the seal of godliness upon the lasting reputations of "this Moses and this Miriam." The achievement of their "coupled worke" that mingled her "mortall stuffe" with Philip Sidney's remnants of divinity may also have given the countess hope that her aspiration to be reunited with him (and the other "saints," or godly Christians) in heaven was more, rather than less, likely. No "work" could confirm or earn her soul its theological salvation among the Protestant "elect." However, the countess could still have seen these psalm versions as an antidote to the ordinary but brief triumph of death.

These divine poems bear testimony to Mary Sidney's eloquence and the image of her mind; they would therefore commemorate her literary personality according to the ancient poets' concept of the eternity of fame, so long as they were known. And they were known. Texts were copied throughout the seventeenth century; plans were even made to publish them in print, and new poets responded to her ideas.[44] The style and substance of George Herbert's "Providence" shows how well one poet assimilated her example in Psalm 104. The Psalms became so much part of her image that, in 1618, she was portrayed in a printed engraving by Simon de Passe, holding an open volume of "Davids Psalmes."[45] In 1594, in one of the earliest references to "Those Hymnes that thou doost consecrate to heaven," her protégé, Samuel Daniel, assured her that they

> Unto thy voyce eternitie hath given,
> And makes thee deere to him from whence they came.
> In them must rest thy ever reverent name,
> So long as Syons God remaineth honoured;
>
> ...
>
> And this is that which thou maist call thine owne,
> Which sacriligious time cannot confound.[46]

After four hundred years they remain "Immortall monuments" in her voice, ready "to teach us what we shall saie unto God." As her first modern editor recognized, by "recreating the Psalms as Elizabethan poems, the Countess compels us to read them afresh."[47]

Notes

1   M. P. Hannay, ed., "Introduction," in *Silent But for the Word: Tudor Women as Patrons, Translators, and Writers of Religious Works* (Kent, OH, 1985), pp. 7–8.

2   E. Rosenberg, "Review of *Silent But for the Word*," *Renaissance Quarterly* 39 (1986), 769–73.

3   See further A. F. Marotti, *Manuscript, Print, and the English Renaissance Lyric* (Ithaca, NY and London, 1995); H. R. Woudhuysen, *Sir Philip Sidney and the Circulation of Manuscripts 1558–1640* (Oxford, 1996); and G. L. Justice and N. Tinker, eds, *Women's Writing and the Circulation of Ideas. Manuscript Publication in England, 1550–1800* (Cambridge, 2002), especially the introduction, and Margaret Hannay's superb chapter, "The Countess of Pembroke's Agency in Print and Scribal Culture," pp. 17–49.

4   The standard biography is M. P. Hannay, *Philip's Phoenix. Mary Sidney, Countess of Pembroke* (Oxford, 1990).

5   Thomas Churchyard, *A Pleasant Conceite*, quoted in J. Buxton, *Sir Philip Sidney and the English Renaissance* (London, 1954), p. 193.

6   T. Hoby, "Of the chief conditions and qualityes in a wayting gentylwoman," in B. Castiglione, *The Book of the Courtier*, ed. V. Cox (London, 1994), pp. 372–3.

7   See further R. Zim, *English Metrical Psalms: Poetry as Praise and Prayer, 1535–1601* (Cambridge, 1987, reprinted 2011), pp. 31–4.

8   Even her 1599 "Dialogue ... in praise of Astrea," written in anticipation of a visit by the queen, is a form of commemoration. See further, on death and dialogue with the dead, G. Alexander, *Writing After Sidney: The Literary Response to Sir Philip Sidney* (Oxford, 2006), p. 103.

9   Pembroke's translations from French, printed together in 1592, had the widest circulation of all her works. *Antonius* was reprinted in 1595; *The Discourse* was reprinted in 1600, 1606, 1607, and 1608.

10   The text was copied for Lucy Russell, countess of Bedford, together with works by Sir John Harington of Kelston and three of Mary Sidney's psalm versions (in different modes: Psalms 51, 104, 137), in 1600.

11   "But when the panting soule in God take's breath; / And wearie heart affecteth heavenlie rest, / An unrepented syghe. Not els, is death." *The Collected Works of Mary Sidney Herbert Countess of Pembroke*, ed. M. P. Hannay, N. J. Kinnamon and M. G. Brennan, 2 volumes (Oxford, 1998), 1, p. 271. All quotations from Pembroke's works are taken from this edition; see volume 2 for her versions of Psalms 44–150. *The Sidney Psalter: the Psalms of Sir Philip and Mary Sidney* (Oxford 2009) is a revised edition, in one volume, by H. Hamlin and the original editors.

12   "To the Angell spirit," ibid., 1, pp. 105–12; see especially lines 2, 52, 59, and 90–1.

13   "To the Angell spirit," lines 78–9, 82, 30, 37, and 71.

14   Cf. R. Zim and M. B. Parkes, "Sacvyles olde age: a Newly Discovered Poem by Thomas Sackville," *Review of English Studies* 40 (1989), 1–25, at 4–6 and literature cited.

15   On Sidney's psalms see Zim, *English Metrical Psalms*, pp. 152–84; cf. on his uncles' psalms, pp. 80–2, 104–11.

16   See further ibid., pp. 185–202. On Beza's influence see also *Collected Works*, 2, pp. 22–5.

17   "To the Reader," in Sidney's, *The Countess of Pembroke's Arcadia (The Old Arcadia)*, ed. J. Robertson (Oxford, 1973), pp. xlix–l, at l.

18   Oxford, Bodleian Library, MS Rawlinson poet. 24. The title page is illustrated in *The Psalms of Sir Philip Sidney and the Countess of Pembroke*, ed. J. C. A. Rathmell (New York, 1963), facing p. xxxii. Alexander (*Writing After Sidney*, p. 107) points out that not all the known manuscript copies mention the countess of Pembroke.

19   "Upon the translation of the Psalmes by Sir Philip Sydney, and the Countesse of Pembroke his Sister," line 11, in Donne's *Divine Poems*, ed. H. Gardner (Oxford, 1978), pp. 33–5.

20   Thomas Becon, *Davids Harpe* (London, 1542), STC 1717, sig. A7v.

21   "Argument" prefixed to the Psalms in *The Bible and Holy Scriptures* (Geneva, 1560), STC 2093, fo. 235r. Hooker, *Of the Lawes of Ecclesiasticall Politie. The fift Booke* (London, 1597), chapter 37, p. 74 (emphasis added).

22   Athanasius on the Psalms, cited by Archbishop Matthew Parker in his *The Whole Psalter translated into English Metre* (London, 1567), STC 2729, sig. B4v.

23   Geneva Bible "Argument," fo. 235r.

24   See Calvin's letter to the reader (dated 1557), in Arthur Golding's translation: *The Psalmes of David and others. With M. John Calvins Commentaries* (London, 1571), STC 4395, sig. *6v.

25 *The Psalmes of David* (London, 1581), *STC* 2034, sig. a3v. Gilby, a former Marian exile to Geneva, took a major part in the new English translation of the Bible produced there in 1560. On his return to England he became a prominent Calvinist clergyman in Leicestershire where he enjoyed the patronage of Henry Hastings, earl of Huntingdon. See further Claire Cross's article on Gilby in *Oxford DNB* (2004).

26 See B. Smalley, *The Study of the Bible in the Middle Ages*, 3rd edn (Oxford, 1984), pp. 149–72, 329–55; J. L. Kugel, *The Idea of Biblical Poetry: Parallelism and Its History* (New Haven and London, 1981); and I. Baroway, "Tremellius, Sidney and Biblical Verse," *Modern Language Notes* 49 (1934), 145–9. On Tremellius in England see *Oxford DNB*.

27 P. Sidney, *The Defence of Poesie* (London, 1595), *STC* 22535, sig. B4r.

28 Ibid., sigs I 2v and B4r.

29 Ibid., sig. I 2v.

30 Two manuscripts, in John Harington's ownership by late 1609, have been marked up for use at morning and evening prayer. See *Collected Works*, 2, pp. 317, 321, and 342; and M. G. Brennan, "Sir Robert Sidney and Sir John Harington of Kelston," *Notes and Queries* 34 (1987), 232–7 at 235.

31 *The Scolemaster*, in Roger Ascham, *English Works*, ed. W.A. Wright (Cambridge, 1904, reprinted 1970), p. 264.

32 D. Erasmus, *Dialogus Ciceronianus* (1528), cf. discussions of this passage by T. C. Cave, *The Cornucopian Text: Problems of Writing in the French Renaissance* (Oxford, 1979), p. 45, and T. M.Greene, *The Light in Troy: Imitation and Discovery in Renaissance Poetry* (New Haven and London, 1982), pp. 182–3.

33 *Defence of Poesie* (1595), sigs I 3v and C2. Cf. Horace, *On Poetry: the "Ars poetica,"* ed. C. O. Brink (Cambridge, 1971), p. 60, lines 131–5. (English translations appeared in 1567 and 1586.)

34 G. F. Waller, "The Text and Manuscript Variants of the Countess of Pembroke's Psalms," *RES* 26 (1975), 1–18, at 9; *Psalms*, ed. Rathmell, p. xxiii.

35 Donne, "Upon the translation," lines 50, 46, 34, 31–2.

36 For the text of Harington's covering letter to Bedford, see J. Scott-Warren, *Sir John Harington and the Book as Gift* (Oxford, 2001), p. 147.

37 *The Psalmes of David* (1581), *STC* 2034, p. 243.

38 Cf. James VI, "The CIIII Psalme," in *Essayes of a Prentis, in the Divine Art of Poesie* (Edinburgh, 1584), *STC* 14373, sigs N3–N4v; and A. Fraunce, *The Countesse of Pembrokes Emanuel ... with certaine Psalmes ... in English hexameters* (London, 1591), *STC* 11339, sig. E3.

39 For different views on the possibility of Pembroke's knowledge of Hebrew, see C. Goodblatt, "High Holy Muse: Christian Hebraism and Jewish Exegesis in the Sidneian *Psalmes*," in C. Goodblatt and H. Kreisel, eds, *Tradition, Heterodoxy and Religious Culture: Judaism and Christianity in the Early Modern Period* (Beersheva, 2006), pp. 287–309 and literature cited.

40 Wilcox, *A very Godly and learned Exposition, upon the whole Booke of Psalmes* (London, 1591), *STC* 25626, pp. 339–48, at p. 343. This newly recognized addition to Pembroke's sources suggests her independence from Sidney, who was unlikely to have had access to Wilcox's *Exposition* first published in 1586 (i.e. after Sidney had left England), and also the priority of her incentive to seek out guides to the *Hebraica veritas*. See further P. Collinson on Wilcox in *Oxford DNB*.

41 *The Psalmes ... with ... Calvins Commentaries*, trans. Golding (1571), fos 98-104, at fo. 101r (dainties) and 101v (calendar).

42 Wilcox, *Exposition*, p. 346.

43   On retractions, see above n.14. Cf. "Leave me o Love, which reachest but to dust, / And
     thou my mind aspire to higher things ... Eternal Love maintaine thy life in me." "Certain
     Sonnets," 32, in *The Poems of Sir Philip Sidney*, ed. W. A. Ringler (Oxford, 1962), pp.
     161–2.

44   See further *Collected Works*, 1, pp. 47–9; Hannay in Justice and Tinker, eds, *Women's
     Writing*, pp. 35–8; and Alexander, *Writing After Sidney*, p. 85. For discussion of the Sidneian
     psalms and their influence on Herbert, and other poets, see *Collected Works*, 1, pp. 49–52
     and literature cited.

45   For this engraving, published by John Sudbury and George Humble, see London, National
     Portrait Gallery/NPG D 19186, illustrated in Hannay, *Philip's Phoenix*, facing p. 59. De
     Passe was associated with 147 similar portraits.

46   See Daniel's dedication to Pembroke of his verse drama *Cleopatra*, printed after a separate
     title page in *Delia and Rosamond augmented* (London, 1594), STC 6243.4, sig. H5–7, at H6.

47   *Psalms*, ed. Rathmell, p. xx.

CHAPTER 16

William Shakespeare

Hannibal Hamlin

Although *Measure for Measure* has an overtly biblical title (from Matthew 7:2, "with what measure ye meate, it shalbe measured to you agayne"), Shakespeare did not write any biblical dramas along the lines of George Peele's *David and Bethsabe* or Robert Greene's (lost) *The History or Tragedy of Job*. Nor did he contribute to the popular genre of biblical paraphrase that interested so many Renaissance poets, including Wyatt and Surrey, Gascoigne, Philip and Mary Sidney, Spenser (though his paraphrases are lost), the Fletchers, Crashaw, Herbert, and Milton. Yet despite his wide reading in classical and early modern literature, Shakespeare alludes to no book so often as the Bible, and it is in terms of allusion – direct or indirect reference by means of recognizably biblical language, situation, or scenic arrangement – that Shakespeare should be considered a biblical writer. All of his plays and many of his poems contain significant biblical allusions. Some plays, like *The Comedy of Errors, The Merchant of Venice*, and *Hamlet*, are not fully comprehensible without some biblical knowledge. This is hardly surprising, since the Bible was the most important book in Shakespeare's culture. The Protestant Reformation had brought about a wave of Bible translation; Shakespeare and his audience were in only the second generation of those able to read and listen to the Bible in English. The experience of the English Bible was still new and exciting, and the many translations and editions of the Bible produced during Shakespeare's lifetime testify to people's eagerness to read the Scripture in their own tongue.

I

There were many English translations of the Bible in the sixteenth century, but the two most important for Shakespeare were the Geneva Bible, translated by Protestant exiles during the reign of the Catholic Queen Mary and first published in Geneva in 1560, and the Bishops' Bible, translated under the leadership of Archbishop Matthew Parker, and published in 1568. According to the Elizabethan Injunctions of 1559, every church in England was to have a copy of the whole Bible, in English, in the largest format available. From 1568 on, it was the Bishops' Bible that served this official function, being read in church services across the country. Shakespeare, like everyone else, was required by law to attend church on Sundays and holy days, and he would therefore have heard much of the Bible read aloud in the Bishops' version. Despite the official status of the Bishops' Bible, however, the Geneva Bible remained the most popular in print. This was partly because it was produced in small, relatively inexpensive formats, but also because it came with a helpful editorial apparatus for the common reader. In addition to maps, guides to reading, biblical chronologies, and useful indices, hundreds of marginal notes guided the reader on matters of language and interpretation, and also pointed the reader to relevant passages in other parts of the Bible.

Many of Shakespeare's biblical allusions use the language of the Geneva Bible. *As You Like It*, for instance, is one of many Elizabethan plays that allude to the Parable of the Prodigal Son (Luke 15). When Orlando says to his brother, "Shall I keep your hogs and eat husks with them?" (1.1.37–8),[1] Shakespeare's audience would have recognized the allusion to Luke 15:16, "And he wolde faine have filled his bellie with the huskes, that the swine ate: but no man gave them him." But only the Geneva Bible, not the Bishops', has the word "husks." There are also cases where Shakespeare alludes to biblical passages in wording that derives from the Bishops' Bible. In *Richard II*, for instance, Mowbray declares, "if ever I were traitor, / My name be blotted from the book of life" (1.3.201–2). The allusion is to Revelation 3:5, "I will not blot out his name out of the booke of life," but only the Bishops' translation uses "blot." The other Bible translations use "put out" (Shaheen, 1999, pp. 38–48). It is clear therefore that Shakespeare was reading the Bible on his own in the Geneva translation, but also hearing the Bishops' in church.

Shakespeare was also familiar with the version of the Psalms translated by Miles Coverdale for the Great Bible of 1539. Long after this Bible had ceased to be widely used, Coverdale's Psalms continued to be regularly bound with the Book of Common Prayer and were therefore the English Psalms used most often in worship. In *The Merry Wives of Windsor*, Pistol says of Falstaff that "He woos both high and low, both rich and poor, / Both young and old, one with another" (2.1.113–14). This fine sentence, with its rhetorical antitheses, is taken from Psalm 49: "High and lowe, rich and poore: one with another" (verse 2). The Geneva Bible does not use the phrase "one with another," while the Bishops' Bible, which does have it, doesn't have the parallelism of the several antitheses ("As well lowe as high: riche and poore"). Pistol's language clearly adheres most closely to the Prayer Book version.

There are few biblical books to which Shakespeare does not allude. This applies as well to the Apocrypha, which were included in Elizabethan Bibles and in the proper lessons of the Book of Common Prayer. Some books, like Genesis, Exodus, Samuel, Job, and the Gospels, are the richest in character and narrative. Others, like Proverbs, Ecclesiastes, the Apocryphal books Wisdom and Ecclesiasticus, and the New Testament Epistles, indicate Shakespeare's interest in philosophical ideas. His extensive use of the Psalms (more than any other biblical book) shows an attraction to their powerful poetic language. Furthermore, some biblical passages were natural loci for topics of concern in early modern England or that Shakespeare was exploring in particular plays. For instance, early modern Christians considering the nature of love, marriage, or relationships between the sexes, the core subjects of comedy, would naturally turn to the seminal story of Adam and Eve in Genesis 1–3, as well as to some of the pertinent writings of Paul. For the biblically minded, the subject of kingship or government, on the other hand, the focus of Shakespeare's English Histories, would naturally suggest the stories of Saul, David, and other Old Testament rulers. Similarly, for Shakespeare and his contemporaries the ultimate model of human suffering and persecution, in various configurations the subject matter of tragedy, was that of Jesus in the Gospels.

It is important to recognize that his reading of the Bible doesn't necessarily mean Shakespeare was more pious than his contemporaries, nor does it indicate the specifics of his particular religious beliefs. But, for a writer interested in good material, the Bible was a particularly rich source for complex and fascinating characters and stories not just of faith, but of love, heroism, battle, and betrayal – even incest, fratricide, idolatry, and genocide. The story of Susannah and the Elders, for instance, one of the apocryphal additions to the Book of Daniel, was very popular. Shakespeare alludes to the decisive judgment of Daniel against the Elders in *The Merchant of Venice* (4.1.223–4), but for many readers some of the appeal of the story probably lay in Susannah's naked bathing. (A similarly titillating scene, Bathsheba's bathing that King David spies on in 2 Samuel 11:2, was often visually reproduced, gratuitously, in Renaissance Bibles, prayer books, and psalters).

The Bible was not only the foundation of Christian religious worship and belief, it was also the basis of English popular culture. Biblical characters and episodes were depicted on painted cloths hung in the local tavern, on dinner plates, purses, jewelry, swords, and furniture. Biblical ballads like "When Jesus Christ Was Twelve" were among those sold by real-life pedlars like Shakespeare's Autolycus in *The Winter's Tale*. Regular church attendance meant that everyone heard hundreds of sermons explaining biblical texts, and the packed crowds (in the thousands) at public open-air sermons at places like Paul's Cross in London suggest that this was a popular entertainment, not just something to be endured on Sunday mornings. The great preachers of the day, such as Lancelot Andrewes or Henry "Silvertongued" Smith, were celebrities. The Bible pervaded virtually every aspect of culture, shaping ideas not just about religion, but about politics, marriage and social relations, trade and exploration, warfare, agriculture, even astronomy and medicine.

Allusions to the Bible in Shakespeare's writing sometimes come indirectly by way of the church liturgy, sermons, commentaries, or religious art and literature. When Hamlet condemns the player who "out-Herods Herod," for instance (3.2.14), he is on the one hand referring to the Jewish King from Matthew's Gospel account of the Nativity, but he is more specifically alluding to the traditionally bombastic acting associated with the character of Herod in the English Mystery plays. A liturgical allusion can be observed in *King John*, when Constance says to Queen Elinor, "This is thy eldest son's son ... / Thy sins are visited in this poor child" (2.1.177–9). The ultimate source of these lines is Exodus, in which God is said to visit "the iniquitie ["sinne" in Bishops'] of the fathers upon the children, upon the third generation" (Exodus 20:5). But Shakespeare likely also had in mind the repetition of the second commandment in the Communion Service. In the latter, for instance, the wording is closer to Shakespeare's: "For I the Lord thy God am a jealous God, and visit the sin of the fathers upon the children, unto the third and fourth generation." The wording used in the Catechism, which all children learned in school, is even closer, since it has the plural "sins" (Shaheen, 1999, p. 393). So, while the commandments were obviously biblical, they may have been more familiar to Shakespeare and his audience from schoolroom rote exercises or the liturgy.

Furthermore, the Bible is only one of many sources flowing into Shakespeare's creative imagination, so that references to biblical stories and characters sometimes exist alongside, or even intertwine with, those from Classical or Renaissance literature or English folklore. It was an age when people could believe both that England was the new Israel, God's chosen Protestant kingdom on earth, and that it was founded by Brute, the grandson of Aeneas, hero of Virgil's *Aeneid* and survivor from the fall of Troy. One of Shakespeare's most culturally scrambled, or syncretic, plays is *A Midsummer Night's Dream*, which takes place in ancient Athens, yet combines characters out of Greek myth, young Greek lovers (who really seem to be Renaissance Italian), fairies from English folklore, and tradesmen seemingly from the streets of Elizabethan London. One of the latter, Bottom the Weaver, is magically given the head of an ass as part of Oberon's revenge plot. Eventually, Bottom's enchanted body is restored to normal, and he wakes up to reflect on the "dream" he believes he has had:

> I have had a most rare vision. I have had a dream, past the wit of man to say what dream it was. Man is but an ass, if he go about t'expound this dream. Methought I was – there is no man can tell what. Methought I was, and methought I had – but man is but a patch'd fool, if he will offer to say what methought I had. The eye of man hath not heard, the ear of man hath not seen, man's hand is not able to taste, his tongue to conceive, nor his heart to report, what my dream was. (4.1.205–14)

Bottom's speech seems like nonsense, but the humor and its meaning is intensified if one recognizes its allusion to Paul's First Epistle to the Corinthians:

> The eye hathnot seen, & the eare hath not heard, neither haue entred into the heart of man, the thynges which God hath prepared for them that loue hym. (1 Corinthians 2:9, Bishops' Bible)

Bottom is not simply scrambling senses, or mixing up nouns and verbs, he is parodying Paul's description of the wondrous mysteries of God's love. Bottom himself cannot be conscious of either the allusion or the parody, since, despite his English appearance and language, he is supposedly living in pre-Christian Athens. Yet when the audience catches the allusion, the scene is enriched in complex ways. For example, in one sense "Bottom's Dream," which "hath no bottom," is nonsense, since eyes can never hear, and ears can never see. In another sense, however, Bottom's experience could be said to be even more transcendent than the one described by Paul. In Paul's description, the mysteries of God's love are beyond anything the eye has seen or the ear heard; Bottom's dream goes beyond even what we can conceive, let alone experience, since we simply cannot imagine eyes hearing, ears seeing, or hands tasting. Bottom's dream is truly extrasensory. Ultimately, despite its biblical allusions, *A Midsummer Night's Dream* is not a "Christian" play in any narrow sense. After all, the Pauline allusion is used to describe Bottom's experience among the fairies, as he and his fellow mechanicals prepare for the wedding in Athens of an Amazon queen and the half-son of the god Poseidon.

II

Shakespeare alludes to the Bible in a variety of modes and with a variety of effects. Some allusions, for example, are comical, whereas others are acutely serious. One disturbingly serious example is Iago's statement in *Othello*, "I am not what I am" (1.1.65). The allusion is to the name of God in Exodus 3. Having been called to bring Israel out of Egypt, Moses asks God by what name he should be identified. God replies, "I AM THAT I AM," the English rendering (in the Geneva Bible) of the Hebrew Tetragrammaton, the four letters that are also rendered as "YHWH," "Yahweh," or "Jehovah." Though the latter renderings may seem like names, God is in fact refusing to be named. God has no need of a name, because he is the one and only God, and does not need to be differentiated from other "gods." God's answer to Moses also indicates God's eternal immutability; in the Hebrew, verbs have no tense, so it could also mean, "I am what I was," "I will be what I am," and every other possible permutation. God is, has been, and always will be just what he is. Iago's allusion inverts this. Not only is he not what he seems to be, in keeping with his prior admission that his "outward action" does not "demonstrate / The native act and figure of my heart" (1.1.61–2). But he actually *is* not what he is, which is on the one hand a logical impossibility, but on the other an expression of utter negation and vacuity. In other words, if God is ultimate plenitude, then Iago is absolute emptiness. Shakespeare's audience would likely have remembered this allusion, when, at the end of the play, Othello says of Iago, "I look down towards his feet; but that's a fable" (5.2.286). Othello half-expects to see the cloven hooves normally included in depictions of the Devil. For the audience, Iago's devilishness has already been established through the earlier allusion: as the one who is not what he is, Iago is the opposite of God. Iago isn't really the Devil, but the allusions that represent him as such enhance the sense of his undiluted wickedness.

By contrast, the passage from *The Merry Wives of Windsor* cited above is an example of a light, comical allusion. Another example can be observed in *The Winter's Tale*, when the Clown (i.e. country bumpkin) says to the conman Autolycus, "We are but plain fellows, sir." Autolycus replies, "A lie; you are rough and hairy" (4.4.721–22). The audience laughs not only at the obvious insult, which puns on the two senses of "plain" (simple and smooth-skinned), but at the clever allusion to the story of Jacob and Esau. Jacob says to Rebecca, "Beholde, Esau my brother is a heary man, and I am smoothe" (Genesis 27:11; here Shakespeare blends together the Bishops' Bible and the Geneva, since the former has "heary" and the latter "rough"). The allusion is meaningful, since Jacob's statement comes just before he tricks his brother out of his birthright. (Rebecca puts animal skins on Jacob's arms to make him seem "heary" to his blind father, Isaac.) Since Autolycus is a trickster too, the allusion draws an appropriate parallel.

Shakespeare's biblical allusions may also be roughly classified in terms of their relative conspicuousness and the greater or lesser extent of their implications for a given play. The most conspicuous allusions are outright quotations from or references to the Bible, in which the character making the allusion is fully conscious of making it. If Othello does indeed compare himself to "the base Judean" just before he kills himself (5.2.347 in the Folio; this is a notorious textual crux), and if "Judean" refers to Judas Iscariot, who betrayed Christ, this would be a good example. Othello, realizing he has betrayed the person who most loved him, compares himself to the biblical exemplar of treachery and betrayal. Another conscious reference occurs in *Henry IV, Part One*, when Falstaff cites Paul's injunction, "Let everie man abide in the same vocation wherein he was called" (1 Corinthians 7:20), in support of following his own "vocation" of thievery (1.2.104–5). Falstaff is a stage parody of the stereotypical Puritan, often quoting Scripture, but, in his case, usually to blasphemous or self-serving purposes (Poole, 2000, pp. 16–44).

Some instances of biblical language in Shakespeare's plays are simply cases of biblical idioms having become commonplace or proverbial in English speech. In *Timon of Athens*, for instance, Timon curses the young, calling on "Lust, and liberty" to infect them, so that "'gainst the stream of virtue they may strive, / And drown themselves in riot!" (4.1.25–8). While Ecclesiasticus does indeed urge its readers to "strive ... not against the streame," there was also a popular English proverb, "It is hard to strive against the stream." So Shakespeare's reference may be to one or the other source – or both (Shaheen, 1999, p. 677). Similarly, in *Twelfth Night*, Feste says to the Duke, trying to joke another coin from him, "Put your grace in your pocket, sir, for this once, and let your flesh and blood obey it" (5.1.32–3). The phrase "flesh and blood" is scriptural (Matthew 16:17, 1 Corinthians 15:50, etc.; the earliest citations in the OED are from Bible translations), but it had become a popular idiom long before Shakespeare used it, and no biblical allusion seems especially relevant or meaningful here. On the other hand, it can be difficult to distinguish the commonplace from the allusive with any precision. In *Titus Andronicus* Tamora likens a king (specifically Saturninus) to an eagle that "suffers little birds to sing" while knowing it could silence them with "the shadow of his wings" (4.4.85). The phrase "shadow of his wings" occurs in a number of Psalms (17:8, 36:7, 57:1, 63:7, the Geneva note to 143:9) as an image of divine protection, but it may, like "flesh and blood," have become a commonplace (Shaheen, 1999, pp. 506–7). However, knowing the biblical context of Tamora's phrase, that it is a metaphor for God's protection and grace, ironizes her advice about "imperious" monarchy, which is not about mercy but about the arrogant expression of absolute power.

Some of Shakespeare's biblical allusions illuminate a single speech or short scene. One of these localized allusions, for example, occurs in Macbeth's soliloquy deliberating the murder of Duncan. He begins, "If it were done, when 'tis done, then 'twere well / It were done quickly" (1.7.1–2). An attentive listener or reader might hear behind these lines Jesus' words to Judas after Satan had "entred into him": "That thou doest, do quickly" (John 13:27). As in the example from *Othello* cited above, Macbeth is here allusively linked to Judas, the exemplar of betrayal. This further undermines any justification Macbeth can offer for the murder of his king. Another localized allusion occurs in *Romeo and Juliet*, when Juliet, on hearing that Romeo has killed her cousin Tybalt, calls her lover a "wolvish ravening lamb" (3.2.76). The audience would have recognized the well known metaphor of hypocrisy from the Gospel of Matthew: "Beware of false Prophets, which come to you in sheepes clothing, but inwardely they are ravening wolves" (Matthew 7:15). But, while adding weight to Juliet's bitter outburst, the allusion doesn't resonate far beyond this scene; even within a few lines, Juliet's love for Romeo has reasserted itself.

By contrast, many of Shakespeare's biblical allusions have a substantial impact, connecting to predominant themes of a given play, especially when they are links in an allusive chain involving the same or related biblical passages. Such extended patterns of allusions are woven into a number of the plays, including *Coriolanus*, *Richard II*, and *Pericles*. (On the first two, see Hamlin 2002, 2004, pp. 242–5.) In *Pericles*, for example, a series of allusions invokes the Book of Jonah. Initially, the shipwrecked Pericles is cast up on the shores of Pentapolis. Three fisherman discuss the wreck of his ship, which they have just witnessed. They compare human society to the sea that they know so well, and one describes a miser as being like a whale:

> I can compare our rich misers to nothing so fitly as to a whale: a plays and tumbles, driving the poor fry before him, and at last devours them all at a mouthful. Such whales have I heard on a'th'land, who never leave gaping till they swallowed the whole parish, church, steeple, bells, and all. (2.1.28-32)

To this the second fisherman replies that "if I had been sexton I would have been that day in the belfry," explaining further,

> Because he should have swallowed me too, and when I had been in his belly, I would have kept such a jangling of bells that he should never have left till he cast bells, steeple, church, and parish up again. (2.1.34–40)

The social satire here is clear enough, but the fisherman's little allegory also suggests the biblical story of Jonah, who was swallowed by a fish and then cast up again on land. (The fishermen – who, living in ancient Pentapolis, are presumably pagans – are not conscious of their allusions to Jonah, but the audience is.) Pericles, who is listening unseen, has just been through an experience at least somewhat similar to the Old Testament prophet's: both characters have had misfortune at sea, yet are ultimately tossed up on land.

Later in *Pericles*, Shakespeare alludes more overtly to Jonah. Once again, Pericles is on the sea, this time with his new wife Thaisa, who is pregnant with his child. Another storm blows up that threatens to sink their ship, and Pericles, following the traditional equating of a storm with the voice or hand of the divine, calls on the powers behind the storm to break it off. The excitement sends Thaisa into premature labor, and she gives birth to a girl, seemingly at the cost of her own life. Alerting the audience to the symbolic implications of his own journey – the life-as-a-sea-voyage metaphor – Pericles refers to his "poor infant," soon to be named Marina after the sea that gave her birth, as "this fresh new seafarer" (3.1.42). Without giving him time to grieve, however, the superstitious sailors insist that the body of Thaisa must be cast overboard, since

> the sea works high,
> The wind is loud and will not lie till the ship
> Be cleared of the dead. (3.1.48–50)

In other words, the sailors see the body of Thaisa as a source of bad luck at sea, what early modern mariners actually termed a "Jonah" in reference to the bad luck brought on by the errant prophet (*OED*). Thaisa's body is thus jettisoned, and Pericles's eulogy makes the parallel with Jonah explicit:

> A terrible child-bed hast thou had, my dear:
>
> ...
>
> The air-remaining lamps, the belching whale,
> And humming water must o'erwhelm thy corpse
> Lying with simple shells. (3.1.56–64)

Although she doesn't actually end up in the belly of whale, Thaisa is indeed belched up out of the "belly" of the sea. As Cerimon, the physician who saves her, puts it: "If the sea's stomach be o'ercharged with gold, / 'Tis a good constraint of fortune it belches upon us" (3.2.53–4).

Such references to Jonah add more than superficial resonance to *Pericles*. The key lies in the tradition of typological reading of the Bible, the way in which characters, episodes, or language from the Old Testament were interpreted by Christians as prefiguring their "fulfillment" in the New Testament. Shakespeare's allusions therefore often suggest chains of association between biblical verses, books, and testaments, reflecting a widespread habit of reading Scripture that George Herbert described: "This verse marks that, and both do make a motion / Unto a third, that ten leaves off doth lie."[2] Traditionally, Christians interpreted Jonah's three days in the whale and his escape typologically, as a foreshadowing of Christ's death and resurrection. This interpretation was reinforced in the marginal glosses to the Book of Jonah in the Geneva Bible. However, the ultimate source for reading Jonah as a type of Christ comes from Christ's own words:

> Then answered certeine of the Scribes and of the Pharises, saying, Master, we wolde se a signe of thee. But he answered, and said to them, An evil and adulterous generacion seketh a signe, but no signe shal be give unto it, save the signe of the Prophet Jonas. For as Jonas was thre dayes, and thre nights in the whales bellie: so shal the Sonne of man be thre dayes and thre nights in the heart of the earth. (Matthew 12:38–40)

Given the typological association of Jonah's "resurrection" with Christ's, then, the allusions to Jonah in *Pericles* seem significant not only in relation to Pericles himself but also for Thaisa. First, Thaisa's body is a "Jonah," the offensive passenger who must be cast overboard into the "belly" of the sea in order to satisfy the "god of this great vast."

Like Jonah, she is cast up on shore, and like both Jonah and Jesus, she "dies" and is miraculously brought back to life. The allusion does not seem to suggest that Thaisa is a "Christ-figure." Instead, it reinforces the sense that there is something miraculous and mysterious about Thaisa's "resurrection," while nevertheless remaining in the fantastical, and secular, realm of Romance.

Shakespeare's biblical allusions sometimes operate ironically, in the sense that the dramatic characters themselves cannot be aware of the biblical sources of their own words. In plays such as *Pericles*, the Roman plays, or those featuring pagan characters, such as *King Lear*, the time period and geographical setting make biblical awareness on the part of the characters historically impossible. The allusions are thus deliberately anachronistic. This would have seemed less puzzling to Shakespeare's audience than it may to us, however. For an early modern Christian audience, for instance, any experience of extreme suffering or sacrifice would inevitably have been compared, on some level, to the ultimate model of sacrifice in the Crucifixion of Christ. This applied even to characters who lived before the time of Christ, like Thaisa, Cordelia, or Julius Caesar, since for those Christians the Bible was held to contain truths that were universal and eternal. When pre-Christian characters such as Adam, David, and Jonah were understood as types foreshadowing Christ, then comparing other pre-Christian (but nonbiblical) pagans to Christ would have been seen as typologically or morally valid rather than historically anachronistic.

Another function of Shakespeare's biblical allusions is that they often concern matters of character, suggesting parallels between a dramatic character and a biblical one. The allusions comparing Thaisa with Jonah, or Orlando with the Prodigal Son, are examples of this technique. A number of characters, like Coriolanus and Julius Caesar, are compared through allusions with Christ himself, usually to the disadvantage of the character on stage (Fisch, 1999, pp. 3–33; Hamlin, 2002). In fact, Shakespeare frequently uses allusions in this way: to emphasize contrast rather than similarity. Often the dramatic irony involved in characters making allusions of which they are not conscious is intensified by the contrastive effect of the allusion, the biblical background undercutting the conscious intention of the speech in which it occurs. Such an example is found in *Hamlet*. Claudius, believing he is alone, meditates on his crime of murdering his brother and wonders about the possibility of God's forgiveness:

> What if this cursed hand
> Were thicker than itself with brother's blood,
> Is there not rain enough in the sweet heavens
> To wash it white as snow? (3.3.45–6)

Though Claudius shows no signs of being aware of it, these lines allude to Psalm 51, "wash me, and I shalbe whiter then snowe" (verse 7). The authorship of Psalm 51 was traditionally attributed to King David as the expression of his guilt and contrition after having committed adultery with Bathsheba and ordering her husband Uriah's death (2 Samuel 11). Shakespeare's allusion is appropriate, since Claudius is another king, guilty of murder and (perhaps) adultery with the wife of his victim (at least he has married his victim's wife). Yet, while David was genuinely contrite (according to the Psalm, this requires a "broken and contrite heart"), Claudius only feels regret and cannot bring himself to repent. Furthermore, he is not willing to give up the spoils of his crime. (The attentive Bible reader might note that David gets unfair special treatment: he actually keeps Bathsheba after all. This point was generally ignored in traditional interpretations of the story.) Thus, the biblical allusion is primarily contrastive, ultimately underscoring the profound dissimilarity between the kings Claudius and David.

Another allusion in the same speech affirms Claudius's persistent sinfulness; this allusion works in a non-contrastive way. In describing his offense, Claudius says that "It hath the primal eldest curse upon't, / A brother's murder" (3.3.37–8), a straightforward reference to the murder of Abel by Cain in Genesis 4. His previous reference to "brother's blood" similarly recalls the blood of Abel that God says "cryeth unto me from the grounde" (Genesis 4:10). These are not the first allusions to Cain, however, since in 1.2, Claudius tries to console Hamlet, saying reason has cried that death "must be so" from "the first corse till he that died to-day" (1.2.104–6). The first corpse was Abel's. Both allusions draw the parallel between Claudius's and Cain's sin, a parallel that in this case is persuasive. A final reference to Cain comes from Hamlet, as he watches the gravedigger dig up a skull that he compares to "Cain's jaw-bone, that did the first murder" (5.1.77), reminding the audience that *Hamlet* is, among other things, a play about the consequences of fratricide.

Additional examples of non-contrastive biblical allusions occur in *King Lear*. On the level of allusion, Cordelia is several times linked to Christ. For instance, after she returns to England, late in the play, Cordelia says of her still-absent father Lear, "O dear father, / It is thy business I go about" (4.4.23–4). This is an allusion to Christ's remark to his parents in the Temple, where they finally find him after becoming separated from him: "Knewe ye not that I must go about my father's [i.e. God's] business?" he asks (Luke 2:49). Two scenes later, an anonymous gentleman states of the mad Lear:

> Thou hast one daughter
> Who redeems nature from the general curse
> Which twain have brought her to. (4.6.201–3)

The most obvious "twain" referred to here are Goneril and Regan, Cordelia's wicked sisters who have "cursed" nature by their "unnatural" behavior (conspiring against father, sister, and husbands). But in biblical terms, a "general curse" was brought upon nature and all subsequent humanity by another twain, Adam and Eve. In Christian theology, this general curse was redeemed by *the* Redeemer, Christ; in the play Cordelia "redeems nature" in her own way. A final suggestion of Cordelia as a Christ-figure is visual rather than verbal. This mode of allusion is peculiar to drama, where aspects of staging may visually mirror the conventional iconography of biblical images. Lear's final entrance, for example, with the dead Cordelia in his arms has been described as a gender-inverted Pietà (Goodland, 2007). Nothing specific in the text demands this, but the earlier allusions establish the parallel between Cordelia and Christ, so the scene could plausibly be staged to resemble the iconography of Mary cradling her dead son, familiar from religious art. Cordelia is not to be equated with Christ, nor is she divine herself, but the ultimate model for her innocent suffering and her self-sacrifice to save her father is Christ. The biblical allusions add depth and resonance for those who recognize them.

Some biblical stories were especially familiar, because they were fundamental to Christian theology and the history of God's plan for human salvation. The Crucifixion, for instance, provides allusions for many Shakespeare plays, including *King Lear*, as well as *Richard II* and *Julius Caesar*. Another widely recognizable biblical story was that of the Fall, the first sin of Adam and Eve that resulted in their banishment from Eden and the corruption of the world. Eve is the first to succumb to the serpent's temptation to disobey God, and she then passes the forbidden fruit to Adam. As noted earlier, Claudius is compared to Cain, but he is also described as a "serpent" by his dead brother's ghost, and it is when old Hamlet was sleeping in his edenic orchard that this "serpent" killed him (1.5.39, 35–6). Young Hamlet's focus, however, is more on the betrayal of his dead father by his mother. Even before he knows that Claudius has murdered old Hamlet, young Hamlet condemns what he feels is Gertrude's sexual appetite, which has led her into Claudius's bed before her first husband has been properly mourned. "Frailty thy name is woman!" Hamlet cries, evoking Eve, the first to be named "woman," whose moral frailty (traditionally interpreted in sexual terms) corrupted her husband and the world. The world for Hamlet is a fallen Eden, "an unweeded garden" in which "things rank and gross in nature / Possess it merely" (1.2.135–7). Thus, after the Fall, even the garden of Paradise may have become corrupt, not to mention Denmark, a state in which, according to Marcellus, "something is rotten" (1.4.90).

While Genesis represents the beginning of the Christian narrative, and the Crucifixion its most theologically essential moment, the Book of Revelation describes its ending. Millenarianism – the expectation of the end of days – has a long history. Religious turmoil caused by the Protestant Reformation and subsequent Protestant–Catholic conflicts, such as the threat of the Spanish Armada and the Gunpowder Plot in England, rekindled millennial expectations in the sixteenth and seventeenth centuries. This may partly explain the frequent allusions to the Apocalypse in Shakespeare's plays. These allusions and references appear in early plays, as in *1 Henry VI*, when Henry V's war against the French is compared to "the dreadful Judgment Day" (1.1.29). But apocalyptic images from Revelation seem to have taken on a greater interest for Shakespeare later in his career, especially in the Romances. This is also true of *Antony and Cleopatra*, which, with its exotic Egyptian scenes, its flitting across the entire Mediterranean world, its unearthly music, and Cleopatra's final apotheosis, is the most Romance-like of the tragedies.

In the first scene, Antony expresses a desire for a "new heaven" and a "new earth" that could contain the infinite overflow of his and Cleopatra's mutual love (1.1.17). As the audience, though not Antony, will recognize, this alludes to John's statement in Revelation that he "sawe a new heaven, & a new earth: for the first heaven, and the first earth were passed away" (Revelation 21:1). Later, when Antony describes his own downfall, he admits that this is a time

> When my good stars that were my former guides
> Have empty left their orbs and shot their fires
> Into the abysm of hell. (3.13.145–7)

A similar image of stars falling into hell occurs in Revelation. John writes, "I sawe a starre fall from heaven unto the earth, and to him was given the keye of the bottomless pit. And he opened the bottomless pit, and there arose the smoke of the pit, as the smoke of the great furnace" (Revelation 9:1–2). The image of the fallen star returns later in the response of the guards to Antony's botched suicide. "The star is fall'n," says one, and the other responds, "And the time is at his period." Both cry "Alas, and woe" (4.14.106–7). Shakespeare combines several passages from Revelation here:

> & there fell a great starre from heaven burning like a torch. (8:10)
> And he sware ... that time shulde be no more. (10:6)
> Wo, wo, wo to the inhabitants of the earth. (8:13)

Such allusions to the Apocalypse seem dark and cast a shadow on Antony's character, since the falling star in Revelation is usually interpreted (in fulfillment of Isaiah 14:12) as a reference to Lucifer or Satan, the rebel angel and "bearer of light" cast out of heaven. Such a biblical parallel reflects (anachronistically) the Roman perspective on Antony, who, seduced by Egypt's "serpent of old Nile," rebelled against Rome, and whose final defeat marked the triumph of Caesar Augustus, who ushered in Rome's golden age. Shakespeare's play, however, offers more than one perspective on Antony. For instance, the allusions to Revelation continue after Antony's death, and for Cleopatra, Antony is not a demon but a god:

> His face was as the heav'ns, and therein stuck
> A sun and moon, which kept their course and lighted
> The little O, the earth.
>
> ...
>
> His legs bestrid the ocean; his reared arm
> As all the tuned spheres, and that to friends;
> But when he meant to quail and shake the orb,
> He was as rattling thunder. For his bounty,
> There was no winter in't; an autumn 'twas
> That grew the more by reaping. (5.2.78–87)

This passage alludes not to Satan but to one of the Angels of the Apocalypse (Seaton, 1946):

And I sawe another mightie Angel come downe from heaven, clothed with a cloude, and the raine bowe upon his head, & his face was as the sunne, and his feete as pillers of fyre

... and he put his right fote upon the sea, and his left on the earth, and cryed with a lowed voice, as when a lyon roareth: and when he had cryed, seven thondres uttered their voices. ... And the Angel which I sawe stand upon the sea and upon the earth, lift up his hand to heaven, And sware ... that time should be no more. (Revelation 10:1–6)

The image of reaping comes from a later verse, "Thrust in thy sickle and reap, for the time is come to reap, for the corn of the earth is ripe" (14:15). In terms of biblical allusions, then, for Caesar, Antony is a fallen angel, a devil to be cast out; for Cleopatra, he was an angel on earth, whose death has brought time (their time anyway) to its close, and who awaits her in heaven.

Finally, the emphatic repetition of promises and entreaties to "come" in the final scenes of *Antony and Cleopatra* echoes the final lines of Revelation that bring the whole Christian Bible to its end: "He which testifieth these things, saith, Surely, I come quickly. Amen, even so come, Lord Jesus" (Revelation 22:20). For example, Antony calls "Come Eros, Eros!" "Come, then!" and "Draw, and come" (4.14.54, 78, 84). Similarly, Diomedes is sent by Cleopatra who is worried that Antony may act rashly, but he is "come ... too late" (4.14.126–7). Antony is taken to the monument, where Cleopatra calls "come, come Antony." He replies, "O quick, or I am gone." "O come, come, come," she responds (4.15.29, 31, 37). The repetition of the word culminates in Cleopatra's cry, "Husband, I come!" (5.2.287). Shakespeare's use of the verb "come" includes all the ordinary senses that Revelation employs, as well as John's apocalyptic urgency to "come quickly." But Shakespeare may be adding a sexual dimension that would ordinarily be bawdy, but here seems strangely transcendent. Cleopatra's only use of the word "husband" in the play expresses and enacts a consummation with her lover through death. Cleopatra's cry implicitly combines two favorite English sexual puns on orgasm: Cleopatra "dies" and "comes" at once. The senses of both words entwine in a peculiarly Shakespearean version of the *Liebestod*. Its impact is heightened by the allusions to Revelation, which describes the end of time in terms of a marriage between Christ and his Church: John sees Jerusalem come down "from God out of heaven, prepared as a bride adorned for her husband" (Revelation 21:2).

Since debates about religious ideas were fundamental to English Renaissance culture, Shakespeare not surprisingly demonstrates an interest in them. He explores the nature of grace (*Measure for Measure, Pericles*), providence (the English histories, *King Lear*), redemption (*1 Henry IV, Measure for Measure*), and resurrection (*All's Well that Ends Well, Cymbeline, The Winter's Tale*). Biblical allusion is his principal technique for engaging his audience with such explorations. But ultimately Shakespeare was a playwright rather than a theologian, and he often co-opted religious ideas for ironic or theatrical purposes. In other words, Shakespeare's biblical allusions do not seem to have been intended for doctrinal purposes. Instead, Shakespeare alluded to the Bible primarily because it was a vast storehouse of readily recognizable, powerful stories, characters, and language, the same reasons for which he alluded to Ovid and Virgil. Yet many more members of his audience knew the Bible than the *Metamorphoses*, as is likely still the case today. This made, and continues to make, biblical allusion a powerful tool for manipulating his audiences and for enhancing the emotional and intellectual resonances of his plays.

Notes

1   All Shakespeare citations are from *The Riverside Shakespeare*, second edition, ed. G. Blakemore Evans et al. (Houghton Mifflin Company, Boston, 1997).
2   "The H. Scriptures II," in *The Works of George Herbert*, ed. F. E. Hutchinson (Clarendon Press, Oxford, 1941), p. 58.

Further Reading

Bloom, Harold (1989) *Ruin the Sacred Truths: Poetry and Belief from the Bible to the Present.* Harvard University Press, Cambridge, MA.

Fisch, Harold (1999) *Biblical Presence in Shakespeare, Milton, and Blake: A Comparative Study.* Clarendon Press, Oxford; Oxford University Press, New York.

Goodland, Katherine (2007) "Inverting the Pietà in Shakespeare's *King Lear*," in Regina Buccola and Lisa Hopkins, eds., *Marian Moments in Early Modern British Drama.* Ashgate, Aldershot, pp. 47–74.

Groves, Beatrice (2007) *Texts and Traditions: Religion and Shakespeare 1592–1604.* Clarendon Press, Oxford.

Hamlin, Hannibal (2002) "The Bible, *Coriolanus*, and Shakespeare's Modes of Allusion," in Jennifer Lewin, ed., *Never Again Would Birds' Song Be the Same: New Essays on Poetry and Poetics, Renaissance to Modern.* Beinecke Library, New Haven, CT, pp. 73–91.

Hamlin, Hannibal (2004) *Psalm Culture and Early Modern English Literature.* Cambridge University Press, Cambridge.

Hunt, Maurice (2004) *Shakespeare's Religious Allusiveness: Its Play and Tolerance.* Ashgate, Aldershot.

Jackson, Ken and Arthur F. Marotti (2011) *Shakespeare and Religion: Early Modern and Postmodern Perspectives.* University of Notre Dame Press, Notre Dame, IN.

Marx, Steven (2000) *Shakespeare and the Bible.* Oxford University Press, Oxford and New York.

Milward, Peter (1987) *Biblical Influences in Shakespeare's Great Tragedies.* Indiana University Press, Bloomington and Indianapolis.

Noble, Richmond (1935) *Shakespeare's Biblical Knowledge.* Society for Promoting Christian Knowledge, London.

Poole, Kristen (2000) *Radical Religion from Shakespeare to Milton: Figures of Nonconformity in Early Modern England.* Cambridge University Press, Cambridge.

Seaton, Ethel (1946) "Antony and Cleopatra *and the* Book of Revelation." *The Review of English Studies* 22, 219–24.

Shaheen, Naseeb (1999) *Biblical References in Shakespeare's Plays.* University of Delaware Press, Newark and London.

Shell, Alison (2011) *Shakespeare and Religion.* Arden Shakespeare, London.

Sims, James H. (1966) *Dramatic Uses of Biblical Allusions in Marlowe and Shakespeare.* University of Florida Press, Gainesville, FL.

CHAPTER 17
John Donne

Jeanne Shami

The Bible permeates Donne's universe, providing the fabric and texture of his epistemology, psychology, spirituality, and sense of self, and the raw materials for his witty, imaginative explorations of experience. Engagement with God's word is the foundation of audacious reading practices extending to all aspects of Donne's life, and ultimately to his calling as a Church of England preacher. Biblical allusions pervade the *Songs and Sonets, Elegies*, and early poems: Mary Magdalen in "The Relique," "spider love" in "Twicknam Garden" that transubstantiates "Manna" to "gall," the speaker as naked Adam in "Elegy: Going to Bed" at the end of his fantasy about Edenic sex with his new-found-land, Nebuchadnezzar in the epigram "The Lier." In the *Satyres*, too, Donne "turns to biblical aesthetics ... to formulate a [prophetic] spokesman appropriate to the times in which he lived and wrote" (Hester, 1982, p. 6). Here, we see how "Ask thy father" (Deuteronomy 32:7) is central to the inquiry after truth in *Satyre III*; how *Satyre V*, Donne's poetic oration on the corruption of the Elizabethan legal system, is framed by passages from Esther, Genesis, Isaiah, Micah, Numbers, and the Psalms that offer warnings to foolish suitors and corrupt officers. In the *Holy Sonnets, Divine Poems, Pseudo-Martyr, Biathanatos*, the *Anniversaries*, and the *Verse Letters*, we see elements that will characterize the later Donne's full engagement with Scripture – in particular, hermeneutical and exegetical principles that navigate competing and apparently contradictory controversial interpretations of the Bible's revealed truths. The *Essays in Divinity* – likely written between 1611 and 1615 when Donne was contemplating his vocation – inaugurate Donne's most thorough engagement with Scripture, demonstrating his paradoxical sense that the Bible is both a stable text that can rectify errors, and a text that requires hermeneutic "salvation" from the corruptions of misinterpreters. Because of their pivotal position in Donne's canon, written during Donne's transition from secular professions to the pulpit, these *Essays* can introduce Donne's later, more nuanced, treatment of Scripture in the *Devotions Upon Emergent Occasions* and sermons. Beginning with the *Essays*, this chapter analyzes Donne's use of multiple biblical translations, and his attraction to certain sections of the Bible, particularly the Psalms and the Pauline epistles. These biblical texts anchor Donne's wide-ranging biblical engagement, enabling a biblical poetics derived from the Psalms and a complex hermeneutics of the "middle way" favoring diverse biblical commentators and interpretations over dogmatic scriptural pronouncements. In tracking Donne's engagement with both the Psalms and Epistles, this chapter considers Donne's vast meditations on the Bible, ranging throughout his entire oeuvre but embodied most fully in his sermons.

In the *Essays*, Donne identifies the Bible as one of *three* books that reveal God, framed by the "eternall Register of his Elect" and the Book of God's creatures. The contents of the "eternall Register" are "impossible" to comprehend; the book of creatures expresses the will of God, but does not teach all the particularities of the Christian religion; but the Bible, though "difficult," is the historical record of God's revelation and the final authority in matters of faith. While it cannot be approached "without inward humility, and outward interpretations," this book, Donne says, has "*Certainty*, ... *Dignity*, ... And ... *Sufficiency*; ... for it is written by *revelation*; yea the first piece of it which ever was written, which is the Decalogue, by *Gods own finger*" (8).

For Donne, Scripture is salvific not only because it is the revealed word of God, but also because of its eloquent literary qualities: "There are not so eloquent books in the world as the Scriptures: ... we may be bold to say, that in all their Authors, Greek and Latin, we cannot finde so high, and so lively examples of those Tropes, and those Figures, as we may in Scriptures: whatsoever hath justly delighted any man in mans writings, is exceeded in the Scriptures. The style of the Scriptures is a diligent, and an artificial style; and a great part thereof in a musical, in a metrical, in a measured composition, in verse" (2.170–1). Elsewhere, Donne observes that "the Holy Ghost in penning the Scriptures delights himself, not only with a propriety, but with a delicacy, and harmony, and melody of language; with height of Metaphors, and other figures, which may work greater impressions upon the Readers, and not with barbarous, or triviall, or market, or homely language" (6.55). The eloquence of the Holy Ghost extends beyond musical cadence, tropes, and figures, including even "wit" (Doerksen, 2004, p. 155), a quality that Donne exhibits in all his writings, and a source of "holy delight" (*Letters*, 259) for his hearers. For Donne, the Bible is the ideal medium – the source and the expression of eloquent truth, a model of rhetorical decorum, perfectly fitted to its audience.

However, just as Donne acknowledged the Bible as the eloquent repository of saving truth, he also understood that the Holy Ghost's intentions were mediated through fallible human translators. Consequently, Donne consulted all known versions of the Bible, including Aramaic, Syriac, and Arabic Bibles, the Septuagint, and the Greek New Testament (*Sermons*, 10.295–328). As a Christian Hebraist (Goodblatt, 2003, p. 223–7), he also used Hebrew (Allen), as well as rabbinic commentaries, to correct or corroborate readings of the Authorized Version. However, Donne preferred the Latin Vulgate (the Bible of his Catholic upbringing), other Latin translations, and available English translations. Of these latter, Donne refers most often to the Geneva and Authorized versions (with the exception of the Psalms, which he cites as they are translated in the *Book of Common Prayer* [Bishop's Bible]). Donne often quoted from memory, transposing words, altering tenses, and omitting or adding particles, a practice he defended by saying that "neither Christ in his preaching, nor the holy Ghost in penning the Scriptures of the New Testament, were so curious as our times, in citing Chapters and Verses, or such distinctions, no nor in citing the very, very, very words of the places" (5.44).

Donne's choice of Bible retains not only theological, but political and polemical resonance, although it is unwise to measure Donne's religious allegiances by his patterns of biblical quotation, which weigh and compare texts, rather than championing singular readings. Typically, Donne compares texts, selecting the reading he judges to be most accurate linguistically, historically, or etymologically, but reserving the discretion to choose readings that are edifying, even if not doctrinally foundational. In choosing his text for a sermon on Psalm 2:12, for example, Donne finds that the King James and the Vulgate texts differ dramatically. Rather than dismissing the Vulgate (which reads "Embrace knowledge" rather than "Kisse the son"), Donne notes that "the Chalde paraphrase (which is, for the most part, good evidence) and the translation of the Septuagint, (which adds much weight) and the currant of the Fathers (which is of importance too)" all support the Vulgate. However, although he calls the Vulgate "a reverend Translation," (8.207) he chooses the Authorized Version, which rightly follows the Hebrew. In another sermon, although cautious of "singular" translations, Donne commends the translators of the Authorized Version for departing from all translations in rendering their text from Malachi: "Whereas all other *Translations*, ... read that place thus, *If a man hate her, let him put her away*, (which induced a facility of *divorces*) our *Translators* thought it more conformable to the *Originall*, and the wayes of *God*, to read it thus, *The Lord the God of Israel saith, that hee hates putting away*" (7.88).

Although Donne valued every word of the Bible, his spiritual appetite was best satisfied by the Psalms of David, for a first course, and the Epistles of Paul, for a second course, esteeming these especially "because they are Scriptures, written in such forms, as I have been most accustomed to; Saint *Pauls* being Letters, and *Davids* being Poems" (2.49–50). Citing Basil on the Psalms, Donne observed frequently that "If all the other Books of Scripture could perish, there were enough in that one, for the catechising of all that did believe, and for the convincing of all that did not" (4.91). Donne's deep engagement with the Psalms is readily documented. He preached thirty-four of his extant sermons on Psalm texts (more than from any other biblical book, and second only to the Gospels), including five sermons on Psalms 62 through 66 for which, as prebendary for Chiswick, he had special responsibility.

The Psalms are efficacious not only for their doctrine but for their poetry, particularly their "metrical" qualities: "The highest matter in the noblest forme," as he says in "Upon The Translation of the Psalms" (line 11). In this poem, Donne praises Philip and Mary Sidney, whose psalm translation circulated in manuscript, for being the final link in the historical chain of revelation from God to humanity. They "But told us what, and taught us how to doe ... They tell us *why*, and teach us *how* to sing" (lines 20–2). As part of a coherent divine plan "The songs are these, which heaven's high holy Muse / Whisper'd to *David*, *David* to the Jewes: / And *Davids* Successors, in holy zeale, / In formes of joy and art doe re-reveal / To us so sweetly and sincerely too" (lines 31–5). In this poem, God's ability to create coherence by subsuming seemingly fragmented experiences into himself is manifested through a series of double actions in which binaries (figured by the "cloven tongue" of the inspiring Spirit which fell on David) are made to function as integers (Frontain, 1996, p. 105) through the creation of harmony: "Harmonized singing is the action by which humans restore unity where there had previously been division and duplicity, and by which the splintered world is gradually re-formed. Similarly, by aligning their wills with God's, Moses and Miriam, although physically two, acted as one; likewise Philip and his sister Mary" (ibid., 106). The poem is about the making of two literary saints: the Sidneys have been canonized for poetry that when sung or recited can bridge the gap between heaven and earth (joining the choirs of "heaven, earth and sphears": line 23), and move the fallen world closer to its prelapsarian coherence (the translators themselves having been "translated" into heaven). Donne's engagement with the Psalms is further demonstrated in his paraphrase of "The Lamentations of Jeremy, for the Most Part According to Tremellius" and in his alleged translation of Psalm 137, "the quintessential psalm" for Renaissance translators and paraphrasers who found in it "a source of consolation for a variety of conditions of exile, alienation, loss, and estrangement" (Hamlin, 2004, p. 251). Donne's fondness for the Psalms has led one scholar to argue for Donne's authorship (Crowley, 2008), based on extant manuscript evidence, bolstered by biographical and stylistic elements. Currently, however, most editors continue to ascribe "Psalme 137" to Francis Davison.

But the impact of the Psalms on Donne's religious imagination – expressed in his uniquely biblical poetics – is not limited to his sermons, or to his poems explicitly dealing with Psalms. Donne found the biblical *figura* of David the Psalmist an apt model for the Christian lyric poet: "[David's] example is so comprehensive, so generall, that as a well made, and well placed Picture in a Gallery looks upon all that stand in severall places of the Gallery, in severall lines, in severall angles, so doth Davids history concerne and embrace all" (5.299). As tools of self-examination (anatomy) and instruments in the exegesis of experience (Mueller, 1968), the psalms connect with many of Donne's works, particularly the *Anniversaries, Holy Sonnets*, and *Devotions*.

The penitential psalms (especially the *anima mea* psalms that employ dialogue between a man and his soul) inform several of the *Holy Sonnets* (Radzinowicz). Donne is not original in using the psalms devotionally as a penitential exercise, but his dramatizations of experience modulating into prayer are characteristic. For example, Donne addresses the sonnet "O my blacke Soule!" to his own soul, using this psalmic pattern of spiritual address to contrast his idolatrous past with the contrite present, and place "a solitary and single worshiper within the traditions of a commonly experienced faith" (Radzinowicz, 1987, pp. 49–50). Again, Donne finds the refrains of Psalms 42 and 43 ("Why art thou cast down, O my soul") both "restorative and dangerous," but considers the self-address effective "to reintegrate that broken and scattered heart, by enabling him to expostulate" (Radzinowicz, 1987, p. 45).

As the word "expostulation" suggests, Donne's *Devotions* also follow Old Testament models for stance and language, producing the genre of "holy soliloquy." "This model," Narveson (2004, p. 113) explains, "requires the use of 'scripture phrase,' an exuberant pastiche from throughout Scripture to express the range of one's devotional affections, with chapter and verse glossed in the margins." And, in fact, although Donne wrote the *Devotions* without benefit of library, they contain over 500 Bible references taken from thirty-one Old Testament and twenty-three New Testament books, testifying to Donne's familiarity with the Bible and his lifelong habit of using it to interpret matters of faith and of experience. The *Devotions* comprise twenty-three repeated cycles of meditation, expostulation, and prayer, and Narveson notes that, like David, Donne develops expostulation as a component "distinct from and equal to meditation and prayer," thereby adapting "toward even greater expressivity a genre that already encouraged public, exemplary confession of sin and doubt as well as faith" (Narveson, 2004, p. 129).

Like his attraction to the Psalms, Donne's preference for Paul's epistles extends to his secular writings. For Donne, famously, letters "mingle Soules" ("To Sir Henry Wotton," line 1) and are part of "his second religion, friendship" (*Letters*, 85). They are "conveyance[s]" (*Letters*, 105), conduits of the self, and instruments of community. And, just as Donne's analogic thinking led him to adapt David's psalmic persona, so, too, does it allow Donne to follow a *via Pauli* (Kneidel, 2001). However, Donne applies Paul not only internally or psychologically but historically as well, concluding that Paul's paradoxes and struggles are not merely psychological but rhetorical and communal, problems of an audience in a church made up of Gentiles and Jews, and part of the communal context in which God's word is understood (Kneidel, 2001, p. 229). Crucial for Donne's exegetical strategies, his *via Pauli* sanctions rhetorical adaptability of character, thus stressing pastoral as well as confessional emphases, the Biblical Word as expressing communal values and doctrine rather than the absolute opinion of a single exegete.

Reference to Donne's rhetorical use of the Bible emphasizes that an important context for understanding Donne's interpretive strategies is the proliferation of controversy that followed the Reformation and Counter-Reformation and Donne's concomitant sense of the Bible as requiring hermeneutic salvation. Because Donne's belief that "*Gods own finger*" produced a text – the canonical Scriptures – imbued with certainty, Donne rejects the fragmenting, controversial thrust of sermons as spiritually and politically dangerous. A sermon preached before the king in 1621 distinguishes between Christ's plain doctrine, which exercises faith, and the "curiously disputed" doctrines of men, which exercise the understanding. Donne structures the sermon to contrast "Christs plaine doctrine" (the "Text" of the Bible) and "the interlineary glosses, and the marginal notes" (3.208) added by commentators. The evidence for salvation, Donne insists, is "matter without controversie" (3.210). Yet, Donne acknowledges, this truth, paradoxically, is a mystery that can only be seen by the eyes of faith, and then only "organically, instrumentally, by the Church," which "proposes all that is necessary to my salvation, in the Word, and seales all to me in the Sacraments" (3.210). Donne's caution against misinterpretation often dominates his prose, and occasionally emerges in his earlier poetry. In the preface to *Biathanatos*, for example, Donne rejects the "politics of quotation" (Shami, 1995) practised by controversialists: "If any small place of Scripture, misappeare to them to be of vse, for iustifying any opinion of theyrs then (as the Word of God hath that precious Nature of Gold, that a litle quantity thereof, by reason of a faithfull tenacity and ductilenes, will be brought to couer 10000 tymes as much as any other Mettall) they extend it so farre, and labor, and beat it to such a thinnesse, as it is scarse any longer the Word of God, onely to giue theyr other Reasons, a little tincture and colour of Gold, though they haue lost all the weight and estimation" (110). In the *Essays*, he compares verses torn out of context to stones torn from the foundation of a solid city wall, and refers to Cabalists as interpreters who "torture" the biblical text until it says exactly what they wish it to say (40–1; 13–15).

Because Donne recognizes the proliferation of erroneous interpretive practices, his writings search for hermeneutic methods of overcoming these. In "A Litanie," for example, probably written when Donne was surveying controversial literature in preparation for *Pseudo-Martyr* (his tract defending James I's Oath of Allegiance), he already recognizes obstacles to religion posed by biblical interpretation, specifically singularity, or its opposite, slavish adherence to authority: he urges the apostles to "decline / Mee, when my comment would make thy [God's] word mine" (lines 80–1), and prays that whatever the Doctors of the Church "have misdone / Or mis-said, wee to that may not adhere; / Their zeal may be our sin. Lord let us runne / Meane waies, and call them stars, but not the Sunne" (lines 114–16). Donne's writings, more than those of his contemporaries, show a deeply self-conscious analysis of interpretation modelled for his audience.

The most important thing about Donne's hermeneutics is that he understands the Bible as profoundly typological, a unified, coherent, poetic text requiring close reading to recover its full meaning and to reveal the individual's place in sacred history. This complex reading code (as distinguished from allusion, allegory, and analogy) was based on three fundamental principles: that types and antitypes were historically real; that the imperfect order of the law prepared for the more perfect order of grace; and that the New Testament was superior to the Old Testament, because Christ fulfilled all of the biblical prophecies (Dickson, 1987, p. 260). Typology was, in fact, established by Paul in defense of the early Christians, transforming Jewish history into a universal history of Christianity in which Christ's coming was foreshadowed by the Old Testament. Donne inherits and advances this Christian universalist way of reading the Old Testament / Hebrew Bible, contributing to the textual and religious polemic (Catholic/Protestant and Jewish/Christian) involved in biblical exegesis (Goodblatt, 2003, p. 223). Despite an expansive sense of God's inclusiveness that sometimes extends even to "some ancient Jews who lived before Christ" (6.162), Donne sees Jews as grammar-school boys, "always spelling and putting together Types and Figures," compared to the Christian graduates, "come from the school to the University, from Grammar to Logick, to him that is Logos it self, the Word" (8.351). They are always subsumed by Christian history, and denied any current theological significance.

However, Christological typology is only one of three kinds (the other two being the "sacramental" types [through which the individual's salvation history imitates Christ's] and the "eschatological" types ["through which the ultimate glorification of Christ, man, and the universe is foreshadowed and fulfilled"]) (Dickson, 1987, p. 254). This typological symbolism forms the figurative center of Donne's "Hymne to God my God, in my sickesse," in which Donne perceives his personal drama in terms of the typological drama staged in Scripture: "We thinke that *Paradise* and *Calvarie*, / *Christs* Crosse, and *Adams* tree, stood in one place; / Looke Lord, and find both *Adams* met in me; / As the first *Adams* sweat surrounds my face, / May the last *Adams* blood my soule embrace" (lines 21–5). Dickson has shown how the Christological typology (with allusions to Romans: 5:14 and 1 Corinthians 15:45) is complicated by the speaker's role in the same drama, as he finds "both *Adams* met in me." "The Christological fulfillment, that is, has made possible a sacramental recapitulation whereby the speaker can hope to be transformed into a Christ-like, second Adam himself" (Dickson, 1987, p. 267). Further, the allusion to "*Adams* tree" suggests eschatological fulfillment of this type, where Adam's tree (of the knowledge of good and evil), redeemed by Christ's tree (the cross), is fulfilled in the tree of life in the New Jerusalem that gives eternal life to the faithful (Revelation 22:2).

Thinking typologically, Donne invites listeners to see themselves as New dispensation types of Old Testament figures and finds the entire nexus of typological relationships embodied in his Christian auditory. Donne also treats events in the order of nature – emergent occasions – as types, using typological symbolism, for example, as a means of self-analysis in the *Devotions* and a vehicle of praise in *Anniversaries*. Moreover, biblical *figurae* chosen by the poet are also typological (Moses and his song from Deuteronomy 32, Jeremiah of the *Lamentations* in the first *Anniversary*, John of Patmos in the second *Anniversary*). For Lewalski, this application of the Scripture to the self is a particularly Protestant emphasis, reinforced by linking meditation to sermons, as Donne does when he urges his hearers to preach the sermon to themselves at home. "As every man is a world in himself, so every man hath a Church in himself; and as Christ referred the Church for hearing to the Scriptures, so every man hath Scriptures in his own heart, to hearken to" (7.403). Most important, Donne does not relinquish the historical ground of typological symbolism, relating all events to the three orders of nature, grace, and glory, as in the sermon for Margaret Washington on Hosea 2:19. "The marriage in this Text hath relation to both those marriages [the first marriage, in Paradise, and the last marriage, in Heaven]: It is it self the spirituall and mysticall marriage of Christ Jesus to the Church, and to every marriageable soule in the Church: And it hath a retrospect, it looks back to the first marriage; ... And then it hath a prospect to the last mariage" (3.255). R. V. Young (2000a, pp. 85–9), however, provides compelling evidence that Donne's poetics, while biblical, were not exceptionally Protestant, and that focus on private interpretation and application to the self, which Lewalski (1979, pp. 31–146) says is distinctly Protestant, is also evident in Catholic engagements with the Bible from the earliest Christian periods through Erasmus and the Catholic humanists, in the biblical commentaries of figures such as Cardinal Robert Bellarmine, and in Renaissance Catholic continental writers (Lewalski, 1979, pp. 167–217; Young, 2000b). Not to recognize that Renaissance biblical poetics were the product of a long tradition of Christian, and specifically Catholic, engagement with the Bible is to oversimplify these poetics, and to lose the power of their resonance for Donne, whose engagement with them is filtered through the Catholicism into which he was born as well as the English Church in which he matured.

Donne uses typology as an instrument of self-definition and analysis, and in a series of articles on Donne's biblical self-fashioning Frontain has argued that every biblical identity assumed allows Donne the authority to negotiate a critical moment in his life or in the life of God's people to whom he ministers. Masselink has shown how Donne uses biblical types as both typological pattern and illustration, a use of precedents suggesting Donne's political conservatism ("do nothing for which thou hast not a rule"), but which might better be understood as Donne's rejection of singular examples. He urges his hearers, for example, not to presume on God's mercy by examples of either Paul (who converted suddenly) or the thief (who was converted finally): "One instance to the contrary destroys any peremptory Rule, no man must say, God never doth it; He did it to *Saul* here, He did it to the Thiefe upon the Crosse. But to that presumptuous sinner, who sins on, because God shewed mercy to One at last, we must say, a miserable Comforter is that Rule, that affords but one example" (6.208). Even in considering the singularly good example of Christ, Donne recognizes that its very singularity renders it ineffective: "every Christian is not Christ; and therefore as he that would fast forty dayes, as Christ did, might starve; and he that would whip Merchants out of the Temple, as Christ did, might be knockt downe," so we should acknowledge that "it is not always good to go too far, as some good men have gone before" (4.329).

While typology – as a symbolic mode – might flatten complexity, erase difference (as it most surely does when Donne uses it to compare Jewish with Christian understandings of Scripture), or dull historical and experiential particulars (the source, perhaps, of criticism of the *Anniversaries*'s lament as incommensurate with the loss of Elizabeth Drury), it can also participate in more complex biblical reading practices. Characteristically, Donne demonstrates his appreciation of interpretive paradox and plurality as a means of ensuring rigorous interpretation. In part, paradox exists to expose the pride of biblical commentators: "So he is pleased that his word should endure and undergo the opinion of contradiction, or other infirmities, in the eyes of Pride (the Author of Heresie and Schism) that after all such dissections, & cribrations, and examinings of Hereticall adventures upon it, it might return from the furnace more rein'd, and gain luster and clearness by this vexation" (*Essays*, 57). Conversely, a proper reading of the Bible teaches readers to look upward to God's beautiful complexities, and to stop wielding scriptural passages as weapons; thus, consideration of the paradoxical multiplicity of names attached to single biblical characters leads directly to the understanding that, if God allows paradox in his Word, it is narrow of Christians to jettison such paradox when they speak of differing denominations (*Essays*, 49–52). For Donne, the Scriptures are "a litle wicket, and he that will enter, must stoop and humble himselfe" (*Essays*, 5), a metaphor suggesting that humans must sacrifice their desire for clear, simple answers (their reason must "stoop") if they are to become immured in the holy tangle of the scriptural text. Thus, the paradox inherent in the Bible becomes a defense against those who would appropriate it for controversial or polemical ends, which usually involves oversimplifying rather than amplifying the text.

Closely connected with Donne's trust in biblical paradox is his trust in plurality among biblical interpreters. Rather than confining himself to commentators from a single theological tradition, Donne juggles the opinions of multiple commentators, and often does not resolve the paradoxes that occur as the result of this theological pastiche; rather, the paradoxes become the means of humbling interpretive pride, and thereby work to reveal the text's meaning. As Donne's practice of reconciling "some such places of Scripture, as may at first seem to differ from one another" (2.325) further indicates, Donne, like many of his contemporaries, believed that the Bible brought its own hermeneutic key – to collate one text with another to recover meaning. The advice of such divines not to use the Bible as a collection of scattered prooftexts for controversial purposes was congenial to Donne, who often reverts to the biblical image of Scripture as a seamless garment torn into rags by controversialists. Pico, for example, "being a man of an incontinent wit, and subject to the concupiscence of inaccessible knowledges and transcendencies," is excoriated in the *Essays* for "vexing, and transposing, and anagrammatizing" the text (13–14). Donne is wary of incurring "the fault of them, who for ostentation and magnifying their wits, excerpt and tear shapeless and unsignificant rags of a word or two, from whole sentences, and make them obey their purpose in discoursing" (39). One of Donne's first exercises in reconciling contradictions occurs in the *Essays* in the discussion of the number of those who issued from Jacob's loins, the Bible in three places offering the numbers 66, 70, and 75. Donne says that these "varieties" are God's way of making men sharp and industrious in the inquisition of truth. Having considered how both 66 and 75 might be accurate, Donne argues for the aptness of the number 70, outlining the works of God or his servants which this number "reduces to our memory" (60). Again, in the *Essays*, he concludes that the variety of names used for a single person (e.g. Esau, Edom, Seir) implies that, as various names can apply to a single person, so various denominational labels can apply to a single, catholic church: "so Synagogue and Church is the same thing, and of the Church, Roman and Reformed, and all other distinctions of place, Discipline, or Person, but one Church, journeying to one Hierusalem, and directed by one guide, Christ Jesus" (51). The unity of the Scriptures is also how Donne counters "inordinate dejection" (3.303) or despair, a crippling religious state that Donne says is seven times more prevalent than presumption, its opposite (8.249). Donne says "the written Word of God is light of light too, one place of Scripture takes light of another" (5.39). Such an interpretive practice mitigates partial readings that "agree to thy particular tast and humour," "for the Scriptures are made to agree with one another" (5.39).

A corollary of the rule of using the whole Bible is that in the Scriptures nothing is superfluous. When the Holy Spirit uses "image" and "likeness" in Genesis 1:26, for example, Donne – working from the principle that "there can be no word thought idle, in the Scriptures" and that the holy Ghost is "ever abundant, and yet never superfluous in expressing his purpose, in change of words" – distinguishes between the two by noting that "God proposes to thee in his Scriptures, and otherwise, Images, patterns, of good and holy men to goe by" but also ensures that the image is not copy, "no other man, but the originall it selfe, God himself" (9.71–3, 76). Similarly, in a sermon on Psalm 6:1, Donne considers the weighty differences between "*To rebuke in anger*" and "*to chasten in hot displeasure*," concluding that God's anger is an assurance of his love while his hot displeasure is "that poison of the soule, obduration here, ... finall impenitence in this life, and an infinite impenitiblenesse in the next" (5.336).

As Donne developed as an exegete, he ensured that his interpretations were founded on the literal sense. Most Reformed theologians, unlike medieval exegetes, insisted that the figurative meaning was a dimension of the literal text. For Donne, however, "many times by altercation and vehemence of Disputation, the truth of the literal sense is indangered" (4.114). For this reason, the primacy of the literal sense must be supported by a definition that rescues this sense from an absurd literalism while at the same time eschewing mystical readings of historical events: "The literall sense is always to be preserved," Donne says, "but the literall sense is not always to be discerned, for the literall sense is not always that, which the very Letter and Grammer of the place presents, as where it is literally said, *That Christ is a Vine*, and literally, *That his flesh is bread*," concluding that the literal sense is "the principall intention of the Holy Ghost," but an intention that might be to express things "by allegories, by figures; so that in many places of Scripture, a figurative sense is the literall sense" (6.62). Capturing the right sense of the literal, however, is challenging, but enabled by the "Rule ... which is Not to admit a figurative sense in interpretation of Scriptures, where the literall sense may well stand" (7.193).

The exegete who wants to edify or exercise devotion using senses other than the literal should take care: "though it be ever lawfull, and often times very usefull, for the raising and exaltation of our devotion, and to present the plenty, and abundance of the holy Ghost in the Scriptures, ... to induce the diverse senses that the Scriptures do admit, yet this may not be admitted, if there may be danger thereby, to neglect or weaken the literall sense it self" (3.353). Donne blames the Roman Church for this forced reliance on the literal sense because the Council of Trent, Donne says, advanced "mischievous" doctrines upon moderate positions of "former reverent men," and corrupted these less authoritative senses. The anti-Catholic thrust of Donne's exegesis is based in part, then, on their excesses in scriptural interpretation, either too literal (as in debate over transubstantiation) or too figurative (as in debate over purgatory).

Donne's profound experience of Christ's "real" bodily presence in his sermons does not tolerate what he sees as the superstitious literalism of "that new article of *Transubstantiation*" (3.95), particularly as articulated at the Council of Trent. If understood literally, in fact, the doctrine requires God to contradict himself (something he cannot do), and multiplies miracles absurdly, thus trivializing the transformation (and the grace it conveys). A sermon preached on June 18, 1626 speaks to Donne's uncharacteristically polemical purpose in it, provoked by the ways in which his text has been "detorted, and misapplied by our Adversaries of the Roman Church, for the establishing of those heresies [namely Purgatory], which we have formerly opposed" (7.190). Donne's complaint is with Robert Bellarmine's figurative interpretation, contradicting Donne's methodology whereby "the sense that should ground an assurance in Doctrinall things, should be the literall sense" (7.192). Not only does Bellarmine insist on reading "baptism" figuratively (as a baptism of tears meaning penance, discipline, and suffering), but he also contends that this reading is "the true and naturall sense of the place" (7.192). Donne's thorough examination of expositions of this text shows that only by allowing figurative senses – and many of these far-fetched – can this text be made to provide evidence for purgatory and the indulgences sold to gain entrance to it. Moreover, Donne raises the main interpretive issue, which is how Bellarmine's figurative reading can prove the resurrection of the body, which is Paul's purpose in this text. Johnson (2003a, pp. 104–6) concludes that because Bellarmine insists on a reading that is blind to "the commonsense and literal reading of the passage," his argument is specious. By contrast, Donne selects comments by Luther and Melanchthon, praising their adherence to the "plaine, the naturall, and the true signification of the place" (7.207). Lest these literal interpretations be calumniated because their followers "follow as Sheepe," Donne cites a different literal interpretation – by Piscator – "a learned and narrow searcher into the literal sense" and also a Roman Catholic, to prove that his argument is not with Bellarmine as he is Catholic, but as he is a poor expositor in this case. In the end, however, Donne erects a massive foundation of the doctrinally literal to support practical application of this text to the figurative "resurrection from sin" that is the thrust of his sermon. The "literal" sense *is* sometimes "metaphorical"

(Johnson, 2003a). On other occasions, Donne consulted Bellarmine's Psalm commentary, aligning himself with Bellarmine on matters of grace and justification to distance himself, discreetly, from Calvin's rigorous double predestinarian theology. As Young (2000b) has demonstrated, Donne accepted much of the Catholic tradition, albeit equivocally, especially in its pre-Tridentine form, proving that his relationship to the Bible was forged through a Reformation that was neither monolithic nor consistent.

Donne's exegesis strives for perceptual wholeness, a way of comprehending that enlarges the literal sense rather than pitting it against the metaphorical. Characteristically, Donne walks a middle path between what he terms "left-handed" and "right-handed" interpretations of Scripture (3.74). Though both are not equal, because not equally according to the letter, both can be useful. Frequently, in fact, Donne figures interpretive infirmities as perceptual handicaps, literally as "imperfect sense[s]": hearing with only one ear (7.74), or seeing things with a "squint-eye" (3.229). These perceptual flaws commonly produce interpretations that are "singular," both in their limited focus and in their one-sided distortion of truths. Papist exegetes are condemned for making these "left-handed" interpretations the "right-handed" ground for resolving controversy (Shami, 2004).

Clearly, Donne accepted the Bible as the final authority in matters of faith, and insisted that the scriptural doctrines essential to salvation were "without controversie." That said, however, he believed that individuals need the testimony of men called as interpreters: "It is not a bare reading, but a diligent searching, that is enjoyned us. Now they that will search, must have a warrant to search; they upon whom thou must rely for the sense of the Scriptures, must be sent of God by his Church" (4.219). Paradoxically, Donne acknowledges, scriptural truth is a mystery that can only be seen by the eyes of faith, and then only "organically, instrumentally, by the Church" (3.21). The Church as the communal eyesight of the faithful is crucial to Donne's relationship with the Bible, for "howsoever it be Gospel in it self, it is not Gospel to us if it be not preached in the Congregation" (1.291). Donne does not discourage auditors from reading the Scripture at home (something he terms a "pious" exercise). But in the Church, the Holy Ghost is there "as a Doctor to teach thee; First learne at Church and then meditate at home, Receive the seed by hearing the Scriptures interpreted here, and water it by returning to those places at home" (8.227). "Not that the Church is a Judge above the Scriptures, (for the power, and the Commission which the Church hath, it hath from the Scriptures) but the Church is a Judge above thee" (8.228). This mutual relationship has God's authorization between a Bible "inanimated" by God in the preacher and "actuated" in the hearers (6.282). As Donne says, "He is a perverse servant, that will receive no commandment, except he have it immediately from his Masters mouth; so is he too, that pretendeth to rest wholly in the Word of God, the Scriptures, as that he seeks not interpretation, no exposition, no preaching" (6.102). Authority to interpret God's word is crucial to Donne in *Satyre IV* where he compares the satirist to the apocryphal and the preacher to the canonical books, and in the *Essays*, where he denigrates his exegesis because his essays are not sermons, and he is not a preacher. Donne's relationship with the Scripture also involves the public, communal, liturgical experience of the word "preached" efficaciously in the Church. By contrast, the Roman Church, he says, does not afford this ordinance of salvation, but "Scripture it self is locked up from us; and the soule of the conveyance, the sense, and interpretation of the Scriptures, is locked into one mans [the Pope's] breast" (7.401–2).

To correct these "squint-eyed" interpretations, Donne develops a "discourse of perspective," founded on the biblical trope of the "dark glass," which stimulated exegetes to coin new metaphors for spiritual sight (Shami, 2003). So, too, is Donne's "hermeneutic of the centre." As Johnson argues, "The center Donne seeks is not some flabby compromise, some unsatisfying, because ill-matched, mingling of Roman Catholic tradition and Protestant ingenuity. Instead, he works toward a hermeneutic that avoids losing itself in the peripheries of divisive wrangling by locating the center where those who are 'divers' and 'contrary' can meet, as well as by struggling to gain the difficult ground of the 'cousening,' spiral path to Truth [so famously described in *Satyre III*]" (Johnson, 2003b, pp. 130–1). This same hermeneutic "is not only based upon, but ... also promotes union and community" by establishing an interpretive model by which "the individual and community are stabilized by the very tension that seeks to pull the other down" (Johnson, 2003b, p. 131).

Donne's exegesis tends toward saving truth and application to the self: Augustine's "analogy of faith" and "charity" as hermeneutic standards. A 1629 sermon expresses the *charitable* aspect of this hermeneutic clearly: "Where divers sense arise, and all true, (that is, that none of them oppose the truth) let truth agree them. But what is Truth? God; And what is God? Charity; Therefore let Charity reconcile such differences ... Let us use our liberty of reading Scriptures according to the Law of liberty; that is, charitably to leave others to their liberty, if they but differ from us, and not differ from Fundamentall Truths" (9.94–5). The analogy of faith is as clearly expressed in a sermon on Psalm 38:3 where Donne says that "the book of Psalms is a *mysterious* book; and, if we had not a lock, every man would thrust in, and if we had not a key, we could not get in our selves" (2.72). The "lock" he calls the analogy of the Christian faith, "That wee admit no other sense, of any place in any Psalm, then may consist with the *articles* of the *Christian faith* ... such a sense as agrees with other Truths, that are evident in other places of Scripture, and such a sense as may conduce most to edification" (2.72). In a Lincoln's Inn sermon on Genesis 18:25, Donne shows how this hermeneutic can allow interpretations that are not strictly according to the letter. In the most crucial passage of the sermon, which treats the question "whether he [Abraham] apprehended not an intimation of the three Persons of the Trinity" (3.142), Donne attempts to replicate Abraham's charity in an exegetical context: "But yet, between them, who make this place, a distinct, and a literall, and a concluding argument, to prove the Trinity, and them who cry out against it, that it hath no relation to the Trinity, our Church hath gone a middle, and a moderate way, when by appointing this Scripture for this day, when we celebrate the Trinity, ... it is an awakening of that former knowledge which we had of the Trinity, to heare that our onely God thus manifested himselfe to *Abraham* in three Persons" (3.143). Donne concedes his doubt about the possibility of discovering definitive proof of the Trinity at the "literall" level of the text. However, faithfulness to this primary textual intention is only one element of Donne's homiletic obligations; another is the question of how he can "doe this congregation the best service." Later in the sermon, Donne re-emphasizes the moral implications of his approach when he remarks that "We must not proceed alike with friends and enemies" (3.144). Donne draws his former colleagues at the Inn into an interpretive community – unless they open themselves, charitably, to Donne's textual negotiations, they cannot reap the spiritual benefit offered by Abraham's example. What the preacher argues here, effectively, is that the structures of accommodation between text and occasion are written into the law itself; God's word anticipates charitable deviations from its literal meaning – it contains "divers senses," which may "all" be "true." On the terms of this model, an interpreter can realize figurative readings that benefit his audience while still respecting the integrity of the Scriptures. The Bible thus means many things and yet remains perfectly at one with itself. As Donne is quick to emphasize, though, such liberty is not to be confused with hermeneutic licence. Non-literal readings are only admissible if they conduce to devotion and edification (Ettenhuber, 2007).

In the end, Donne's various strategies of engagement with the Bible, especially in the *Essays, Sermons*, and *Devotions*, but also in his poems (where the biblical engagement is more polemical, parodic, and less sustained), apply the Bible to individual Christians as an instrument of salvation. A true searching of the Scriptures is "to finde all the *histories* to be example to *me*, all the *prophecies* to induce a Saviour for *me*, all the *Gospell* to apply Christ Jesus to *me*" (3.367). "This is *Scrutari Scripturas, to search the Scriptures*, not as though thou wouldest make a *concordance*, but an *application*; as thou wouldest search a *wardrobe*, not to make an *Inventory* of it , but to finde in it something fit for thy wearing" (3.367). Such application is possible because God speaks to all Christians in all parts of the Bible and on every emergent occasion, whether it be a deadly sickness, the death of a young girl, a trip on horseback on Goodfriday 1613, or the Annunciation and Passion falling on the same day in 1608. The radically figurative language of the Bible as well as the examples of its historical characters can all be applied by focusing on the eloquent and metaphorized literal sense of the Bible. By this strategy, the Bible accommodates itself to the devotion and salvation of willing hearers who are not "Sermon-proofe" (6.219). In it, God speaks to every particular soule "in that voice, and in that way, which I am most delighted with, and hearken most to. If I be *covetous*, God wil tel me that heaven is a pearle, a treasure. If cheerfull and affected with mirth, that heaven is all *Joy*. If ambitious, and hungry of preferment, that it is all *Glory*. If sociable, and conversable, that it is a *communion of Saints*" (10.110). Just as God speaks metaphorically of heaven in language that builds on foundations of earthly loves, so Donne came to see tropes as the Holy Spirit's chosen formulations of revealed truth. The Bible is the central authority and inspiration to which Donne always returns to gain his bearings.

Note

1   I would like to acknowledge the assistance of my research assistant, Karl Persson.

References

Allen, Don Cameron (1943) "Dean Donne Sets His Text," *English Literary History* 10, 208–29.
Crowley, Lara (2008) "Donne, not Davison: Reconsidering the Authorship of 'Psalme 137'," *Modern Philology* 105:4, 603–36.

Dickson, Donald R. (1987) "The Complexities of Biblical Typology in the Seventeenth Century." *Renaissance and Reformation* 11:3, 253–76.

Doerksen, Daniel (2004) "Discerning God's Voice, God's Hand: Scripturalist Moderation in Donne's Devotions." In Daniel Doerksen and Christopher Hodgkins, eds, *Centered on the Word: Literature, Scripture, and the Tudor-Stuart Middle Way*. University of Delaware Press, Newark, pp. 148–72.

Donne, John (1984) *Biathanatos*, ed. Ernest W. Sullivan II. University of Delaware Press, Newark.

Donne, John (1952) *Essays in Divinity*, ed. Evelyn Simpson. Clarendon Press, Oxford.

Donne, John (1651) *Letters to Severall Persons of Honour*. London.

Donne, John (1985) *The Complete English Poems*, ed. C. A. Patrides. Knopf, New York.

Donne, John (1953–62) *The Sermons of John Donne*, ed. George Potter and Evelyn Simpson, 10 volumes. University of California Press, Berkeley. All references are taken from this edition and indicated parenthetically by volume and page number.

Ettenhuber, Katrin (2007) " 'Take heed what you hear': Re-reading Donne's Lincoln's Inn Sermons," *John Donne Journal* 26, 127–57.

Frontain, Raymond-Jean (2003) "Donne's Protestant Paradiso: The Johannine Vision of the Second Anniversary." in Mary Arshagouni Papazian, ed., *John Donne and the Protestant Reformation: New Perspectives*. Wayne State University Press, Detroit, pp. 113–42.

Frontain, Raymond-Jean (1999) "Law, Song and Memory: The Mosaic Voice of Donne's First Anniversarie," *Literature and Belief* 19:1/2, 155–74.

Frontain, Raymond-Jean (2004) " 'The Man Which Have Affliction Seene': Donne, Jeremiah, and the Fashioning of Lamentation." In Daniel Doerksen and Christopher Hodgkins, eds, *Centered on the Word: Literature, Scripture, and the Tudor-Stuart Middle Way*. University of Delaware Press, Newark, pp. 127–47.

Frontain, Raymond-Jean (1996) "Translating Heavenwards: 'Upon the Translation of the Psalmes' and John Donne's Poetics of Praise," *Explorations in Renaissance Culture* 22, 103–25.

Goodblatt, Chanita (2003) "From 'Tav' to the Cross: John Donne's Protestant Exegesis and Polemics." In Mary Arshagouni Papazian, ed., *John Donne and the Protestant Reformation: New Perspectives*. Wayne State University Press, Detroit, pp. 221–46.

Hamlin, Hannibal (2004) *Psalm Culture and Early Modern Literature*. Cambridge University Press, Cambridge.

Hester, M. Thomas (1982) *"Kinde Pitty and Brave Scorn": John Donne's Satyres*. Duke University Press, Durham, NC.

Johnson, Jeffrey (2003a) "John Donne and Paolo Sarpi: Rendering the Council of Trent." In Mary Arshagouni Papazian, ed., *John Donne and the Protestant Reformation: New Perspectives*. Wayne State University Press, Detroit, pp. 90–112.

Johnson, Jeffrey (2003b) " 'One, four, and infinite': John Donne, Thomas Hariot, and Essayes in Divinity," *John Donne Journal* 22, 109–43.

Kneidel, Gregory (2001) "John Donne's *Via Pauli*," *Journal of English and Germanic Philology* 100, 225–46.

Lewalski, Barbara (1979) *Protestant Poetics and the Seventeenth-Century Religious Lyric*. Princeton University Press, Princeton, NJ.

Masselink, Noralyn (1992) "A Matter of Interpretation: Example and Donne's Role as Preacher and as Poet," *John Donne Journal* 11:1/2, 85–98.

Mueller, Janel (1968) "The Exegesis of Experience: Dean Donne's *Devotions Upon Emergent Occasions*." *Journal of English and Germanic Philology* 67, 1–19.

Narveson, Kate (2004) "Publishing the Sole-Talk of the Soul: Genre in Early Stuart Piety." In Daniel Doerksen and Christopher Hodgkins, eds, *Centered on the Word: Literature, Scripture, and the Tudor-Stuart Middle Way*. University of Delaware Press, Newark, pp. 110–26.

Radzinowicz, Mary Ann (1987) " 'Anima Mea' Psalms and John Donne's Religious Poetry." In Claude Summers and Ted-Larry Pebworth, eds, *"Bright shootes of everlastingnesse": The Seventeenth-century Religious Lyric*. University of Missouri Press, Columbia, pp. 40–58.

Shami, Jeanne (2003) *John Donne and Conformity in Crisis in the Late Jacobean Pulpit*. D. S. Brewer, Cambridge.

Shami, Jeanne (1995) "John Donne and the Absolutist Politics of Quotation." In Raymond-Jean Frontain and Frances Malpezzi, eds, *John Donne's Religious Imagination: Essays in Honor of John T. Shawcross*. University of Central Arkansas Press, Conway, pp. 380–412.

Shami, Jeanne (2004) "Squint-Eyed, Left-Handed, Half-Deaf: *Imperfect Senses* and John Donne's Interpretive Middle Way." In Daniel Doerksen and Christopher Hodgkins, eds, *Centered on the Word: Literature, Scripture, and the Tudor-Stuart Middle Way*. University of Delaware Press, Newark, pp. 173–92.

Shami, Jeanne (2008) "Troping Religious Identity: Circumcision and Transubstantiation as Tropes in Donne's Sermons." In Jeanne Shami, ed., *Renaissance Tropologies: The Cultural Imagination of Early Modern England*. Duquesne University Press, Pittsburgh, pp. 89–117.

Young, R. V. (2000a) *Doctrine and Devotion in 17th-Century Poetry*. D. S. Brewer, Cambridge.

Young, Robert V. (2000b) "Donne and Bellarmine." *John Donne Journal* 19, 223–34.

CHAPTER 18

George Herbert

John Drury

In his life of George Herbert, Izaak Walton relates that when the poet was dying at Bemerton in 1633, he entrusted a "little book" that contained his English poems to his friend Nicholas Ferrar, with the instruction that if he thought it would help people in their struggles and afflictions, he might publish it. If not, he should burn it. It was published at Cambridge within the year under the title *The Temple: Sacred Poems and Private Ejaculations* with a foreword, "The Printers to the Reader," in which Ferrar related that Herbert used to refer to Jesus Christ in New Testament Gospel terms as "My Master" and that:

> Next God, he loved that which God himself hath magnified above all things, that is, his Word: so that he hath been heard to make solemne protestation, that he would not part with one leaf thereof for the whole world, if it were offered him in exchange.

So Herbert's verse came to the public as the work of a biblical poet, one familiar with a century of biblical translation and excitement and so reflective of a culture deeply and widely scriptural. This chapter shows that Herbert has a claim, rivaled only by his younger contemporary Milton, to be *the* biblical poet of the period. He achieved this status through a deft ability to portray devotional love in his reworkings of the Psalms, notably in *The Temple*, but also through overt and covert allusions to Scripture that have a powerful capacity to transform the content of his poems. The chapter also discusses Herbert's role as both an exegete and maker of the Bible, linking his imaginative approach to the Bible with other Scripture-creating poets like Milton and Blake.

The Praise and Use of Scripture

The supreme importance of the Bible to Herbert was confirmed when his prose work *A Priest to the Temple, or, The Country Parson* was published in 1652. In its fourth chapter, "The Parsons Knowledg," he wrote that:

The chief and top of his knowledge consists in the book of books, the storehouse and maga-
zene of life and comfort, the holy Scriptures. There he sucks and lives. In the Scriptures
he findes four things; Precepts for life, Doctrines for knowledge. Examples for illustration,
and Promises for comfort: these he hath digested severally.

"Digested" is key. It may well have derived from the collect for the second Sunday in
Advent in his Anglican *Book of Common Prayer*. It concerns the Scriptures and prays
that we may "inwardly digest them." Herbert then propounds the ways in which Scripture is digested. First and foremost is "a holy Life"; second is prayer; followed by "diligent collation of Scripture with Scripture" and "the consideration of any text with the
coherence thereof, touching what goes before, and what follows after." The last of these
is historical: "the Law [The Old Testament] required one thing and the Gospel [The
New] another: yet as diverse, not as repugnant." Finally, "Commenters and Fathers"
are useful. All of these are found, in similar order of importance, in Herbert's poetry:
life is the locus for digesting Scripture; prayer is the usual and dominant mode of the
poems; pondering the differences and connections between the Old Testament and the
New is a frequent preoccupation. Commentaries, the final resort, are less obviously
used, though there is a strong case for the influence of Lancelot Andrewes's great commentary on Christ's sufferings in his *Sermon of the Passion* of 1604 on Herbert's *The
Sacrifice*. Herbert owned the works of St Augustine and probably used Calvin's commentaries, which were widely circulated.

Which Bible, precisely, did Herbert digest? He was highly proficient in Greek and
Latin, writing verses in both, Cambridge public orations and letters in the latter. As a
boy at Westminster he did the daily exercise of turning Scripture readings into Latin
verse. So the Greek New Testament, the Septuagint, and the Vulgate were open to him.
Printed English translations had been available since Tyndale's New Testament in
1526 and Coverdale's English Bible of 1535. From 1560 onwards, the Geneva Bible
held the field, even surviving in popularity the publication of that official masterpiece,
the King James Version of 1611. Herbert's friend and mentor Lancelot Andrewes,
although in charge of the translation of one-third of the Old Testament for King James,
kept on using Geneva (as well as a dazzling array of other versions) in his sermons well
after 1611. Chana Bloch[1] has noticed signs of Herbert's use of the Geneva Bible's "right
profitable and fruitful Concordances" – one of its justly popular features – in Herbert's
various uses in his poetry of "rocke" and of the likely influence on his poem "Aaron"
of its woodcut illustration of the garments of the High Priest and commentary on the
Urim and Thummim on his breastplate as signifying light and perfection (Herbert:
"Light and perfections on the breast") There are also signs of Herbert's knowledge of
the King James Version, which came out when he was a young fellow of Cambridge's
royal college, Trinity. Calling the Bible a "book of starres" while celebrating how one
verse of it leads to another in "The H. Scriptures. II" looks like a clear reference to the
little stars or asterisks that enabled such connections in the otherwise sparsely annotated King James Version. Also, the altar with its sacrificed lamb, which stood at the
center of the elaborate engraved frontispiece of the King James Version, is just the same
shape as the altar-shaped poem "The Altar," which opens the section of *The Temple*
headed *The Church*.

As with his theological theme of themes, love, he gave the Scriptures a set of two consecutive sonnets, "The H. Scriptures I" and "The H. Scriptures II," the Bible took over the form and the content of desire and praise of the favorite form of secular love poetry. Here are the sonnets in full:

I

Oh Book! infinite sweetnesse! Let my heart
　Suck ev'ry letter, and a hony gain,
　Precious for any grief in any part;
To cleare the breast, to mollifie all pain,
Thou art all health, health thrvining till it make
　A full eternitie; thou art a masse
　Of strange delights, where we may wish & take.
Ladies, look here; this is the thankfull glasse,
That mends the lookers eyes: this is the well
　That washes what it shows. Who can indear
　Thy praise too much? Thou art heavn's Lidger here,
Working against the states of death and hell.
　Thou art joyes handsell: heav'n lies flat in thee,
　Subject to ev'ry mounters bended knee.

II

Oh that I knew how all thy lights combine,
　And the configurations of their glorie!
　Seeing not onely how each verse doth shine,
But all the constellations of the storie.
This verse marks that, and both do make a motion
　Unto a third, that ten leaves off doth lie;
　Then as dispersed herbs do make a potion,
These three make up some Christian's destinie:
Such are thy secrets, which my life makes good,
　And comments on thee: for in ev'ry thing
　Thy words do finde me out, & parallels bring,
And in another make me understood.
　Starres are poore books, & oftentimes do misse:
　This book of stares lights to eternall blisse.

The first half of the first sonnet exploits the trope of Scripture as sweet, medicinal nourishment, derived from Psalm 19:10 and Ezekiel 3:1–3, with vigorous sensuality. "He sucks and lives" as in *The Country Parson* chapter 4. In the second half the poet is a huckster, gallantly soliciting the ladies with the Bible as magic mirror and cleansing water. Then it is heaven's ambassador ("Lidger" – his brother Edward was ambassador in Paris) on earth, where sin and death have to be worked against. Finally, a surreal metaphor from horsemanship has the Bible, as horse cum material book, being laid out flat and its reader bending his knee to mount, i.e. in reverent prayer. The high spirits are evident and infectious.

In the second sonnet the "diligent collation of Scripture with Scripture" of *The Country Parson* chapter 4 is more exhilarating than diligent: a delighted hopping from star, or asterisked verse, to star. Joined together, like various herbs in a single potion (practical pharmacology was one of Herbert's accomplishments: see *The Country Parson*, chapter 23), they make the framework of a Christian's life – "which my life makes good." Such a life is, again as in *The Country Parson* chapter 4, the prime divinely intended commentary on Scripture, which finds out and understands the individual Christian. This was a welcome thought to Herbert's admirer Coleridge and the fundamental reason for the intimately autobiographical or confessional character of Herbert's greatest verse, which describes his struggles and reconciliations with the God revealed in the Word: in Christ and Scripture.

For poetry as prayer and prayer as poetry, the Psalms, the Bible's anthology of passionate poetry that spans so many moods, are Herbert's model. His cousins, Philip and Mary Sidney, had translated them all, varying meter and form from psalm to psalm with a variety comparable to The Temple. They circulated in manuscript. There is every reason to suppose that Herbert knew them – which may be why he did not repeat the exercise, with the solitary exception of "The 23d Psalme." Instead, the psalms were to him an example and encouragement. There the feeling self expressed that self in hope and fear, repentance and praise, affliction and contrition, anger and love. And so did he, the priest who recited them all at Morning and Evening Prayer every month of the year, in his verses. The Temple is a kind of Christian psalter in its variety and scope of address to God. On its title page Psalm 29:9, in the Prayer Book version of Herbert's monthly recitation of it, is prominent: "In his Temple doth every man speak of his honour."

Scripture the Way into *The Temple*

The Temple is firmly and deliberately marked and structured by the Bible from the first quotation on its title page. The "Dedication" is an offering of first fruits, as by the devout Old Testament pilgrim to the Jerusalem Temple in Deuteronomy 26, and an echo of the sentiments of the dying King David making provisions for the building of that temple in 1 Chronicles 29:14: "all things come of thee, and of thine own have we given thee." Under the heading of "The Church Porch," indicating that we are still in approach rather than arrival mode, there follows a long poem of moral advice in seventy-seven stanzas. Its erudite subtitle, "Perirrhanterium," means nothing grander than a bunch of twigs with which to sprinkle water on people to cleanse them, as enjoined in the books of Leviticus and Numbers, in preparation for cult. The aphoristic poem itself, though sensible and vivacious, is not as popular with modern critics as it would have been with Herbert's contemporaries, who enjoyed collecting proverbs, native and foreign. Chana Bloch is the exception, her biblical sensitivity alerting her to its importance for readers of Herbert.[2] Very like *The Book of Proverbs* in its tireless efforts to knock a bit of prudence into the heads of young men, it shows Herbert as a biblical poet in an unusually complete sense. The Old Testament matters to him along with the New. Law and rules are as important to his practical, pastoral purposes as grace, daylight common sense as essential to the good life as revelation.

The Church Porch is followed by *Superliminare*, a brief crossing from secular ethics onto holy ground, where the reader is confronted by "The Altar," a poem fitted into the shape of an ancient altar, classical or Hebrew. Within the shape there is the content: Old Testament references to the sacrifice of the broken and contrite heart of Psalm 51:17; the altar of unworked stone commanded in Exodus 20:25; and the law inscribed in the heart of Jeremiah 31:33, echoed by St Paul at 2 Corinthians 3:3; finally the stones that would cry out if Christ's disciples were silent from Luke 19:40. It is not a eucharistic holy table, which Herbert reserves for later in *The Temple* ("The H. Communion" and "Love (III)"). It is a biblical altar, just like the one in the center of the frontispiece of the King James Version, which bears the sacrificed lamb.

Sacrifice is the subject of the following long poem and also its title. "The Church Porch" was an imitation of a biblical genre, the proverb collection, and a modern assertion of biblical attention to ethical wisdom. "The Sacrifice" is a retelling of the New Testament Gospel narratives, St Matthew's in the lead, which are quoted in every one of its sixty-six stanzas. It is an uncanonical fifth passion narrative, which is boldly put into the mouth of Christ himself, making it *his* passion story in a double sense. Christ's refrain to each verse, "Was ever grief like mine?" quotes Lamentations 1:12 as insistently as Lancelot Andrewes did (but in Latin) in his 1604 Good Friday sermon. This first person singular of Lamentations perhaps suggested to Herbert the powerful coup of making Christ the narrator of his own fate. The theology of the poem is biblical. St John's irony of the world's divine maker subjecting himself to it and the sacrificial atonement doctrine of St Paul, including the Epistle to the Hebrews, bear on the gospel-derived narrative throughout. Old Testament references are woven into the fabric. Lines 161–9, dealing with Christ's crown of thorns from Matthew 27:29, are typical:

> Then on my head a crown of thorns I wear:
> For these are all the grapes *Sion* doth bear,
> Though I my vine planted and watred there:
>   Was ever grief, &c.
>
> So sits the earth's great curse in *Adams* fall
> Upon my head: so I remove it all
> From th'earth unto my brows, and bear the thrall:
>   Was ever grief like mine?

The movement or transaction here is the redemptive transfer of God's curse on transgressing Adam to obedient Christ on which all St Paul's thinking and writing turns (Galatians 3:13, Romans 8:32, 1 Corinthians 15, etc.). It is a movement effected by Christ himself ("I remove it all") with the divine power that underlays his suffering in St John's gospel and is hinted at in St Matthew's (e.g. 26:53). Herbert goes back behind St Paul to Genesis 3:17 and 18 for God's curse on Adam: "cursed is the ground for thy sake. ... Thorns also and thistles shall it bring forth to thee." Christ's crown of thorns comes precisely from there. The association of thorns with grapes comes from the song of the vineyard, a figure for Jerusalem ("*Sion*"), in Isaiah 5. God tended it carefully but "He looked that it should bring forth grapes, and it brought forth wild grapes." In revenge, God lays it waste: "It shall not be pruned, nor digged; but there shall come up briers and thorns." This is the "diligent collation of Scripture with Scripture" of *The Country Parson* 4, the configuration of scattered verses into a destiny of "The H. Scriptures II" carried off with tragic power.

Scripture at the Far End of *The Temple*

The Temple is not only robustly and energetically scriptural from the start, where the two long poems are an essay in a biblical wisdom genre and a presentation of the mystery of redemption by refashioning Scripture by Scripture. The Bible is there at the end of it all too, once again in two different ways: overt and covert. The penultimate poem in the collection is "Heaven." It is an Echo poem, a form used by Herbert's cousin Sir Philip Sidney, but with greater grace and mastery by Herbert, who turns it to the praise of Holy Scripture as the Echo of heavenly bliss.

> O who will show me those delights on high?
> *Echo.*   I.
> Thou, Ech, thou art mortal, all men know.
> *Echo.*   No.
> Wert thou not born among the trees and leaves?
> *Echo.*   Leaves.
> And are there any leaves that still abide?
> *Echo.*   Bide.
> What leaves are thy? Impart the matter wholly.
> *Echo.*   Holy.
> Are holy leaves the Echo then of blisse?
> *Echo.*   Yes.
> Then tell me, what is that supreme delight?
> *Echo.*   Light.
> Light to the minde: what shall the will enjoy?
> *Echo.*   Joy.
> But are there cares and businesse with the pleasure?
> *Echo.*   Leisure.
> Light, joy, and leisure; but shall they persever?
> *Echo.*   Ever.

Wit and the utmost art turn tiresomely exacting formal requirements into sheer happiness. Equally, they turn a pagan/pastoral genre to a devout Christian end: the enjoyment of God by Bible reading. The poem is not laden with biblical references, though God's word as light and delight derive from Psalm 119, lines 105 and 35 – a psalm in praise of Scripture, the Law. Apart from that, to praise Scripture, Herbert stands objectively apart from Scripture and questions it, so giving his piety the dignity of freedom expressed in free dialogue.

The Temple concludes by using Scripture in a quite different way. It is so thoroughly digested, so much part and parcel of the piece like leaven in a loaf, that it can be read and admired by the biblically ignorant:

> Love (III)
> Love bade me welcome: yet my soul drew back
>   Guiltie of dust and sinne.
> But quick-ey'd Love, observing me grow slack
>   From my first entrance in,
> Drew nearer to me, sweetly questioning,
>   If I lack'd any thing.
>
> A guest, I answer'd, worthy to be here:
>   Love said, You shall be he.
> I the unkinde, ungratefull? Ah my deare,
>   I cannot look on thee.
> Love took my hand, and smiling did reply,
>   Who made the eyes but I?
>
> Truth Lord, but I have marred them: let my shame
>   Go where it doth deserve.
> And know you not, sayes Love, who bore the blame?
>   My deare, then I will serve.
> You must sit down, sayes Love, and taste my meat:
>   So I did sit and eat.

This poem (the most beautiful in the world, according to Simone Weil) is supported on the twin pillars that Herbert placed at the outset of *The Temple*. It is a commonplace scene of domestic hospitality in which table manners matter – the world of "The Church Porch"; and it turns on the redemptive mystery of "The Sacrifice" – "And knowe you not, sayes Love, who bore the blame?" But it also takes assiduous scrutiny by a scriptur-ally informed eye to detect the wealth of covert biblical references. They include the shame of Adam, man of dust and sin, when he heard God calling him in the garden (Genesis 3:9 and 10) and the confessed unworthiness of Moses, Isaiah, and Jeremiah when divinely summoned; the Old Testament conviction that humanity cannot look at God's face (Exodus 10:28, etc.); the Song of Solomon 2:4 where "He brought me into the banqueting house, and his banner over me was love"; Psalm 23 with "thou hast prepared a table before me against them that trouble me"; Psalm 94 with "he that made the eye, shall he not see?"; the Christ of the Gospels eating with sinners and telling parables about banquets for the unworthy, such as the prodigal son (Luke 15:23); and the Lord who girds himself and makes his servants sit down and eat while he serves them (Luke 12:37). The list is indicative, not exhaustive. Scripture and life belong together (we might look to *The Country Parson* 4 again in relation to this connection).

The covert and the overt in Herbert's use of Scripture are further combined in "Coloss. 3.3. Our life is hid with Christ in God," a favorite text of his. The gossipy antiquary John Aubrey relates that he adorned his church at Bemerton with scriptural texts:

> In the Chancell are many apt sentences of the Scripture. At his Wive's Seat, My life is hid
> with Christ in God (he hath verses on this text in his Poems). Above, in a little windowe
> – blinded, with a Vaile (ill painted) *Thou art my hideing place*.[3]

The second text is from Psalm 32:7: in the poem the Colossians text is expanded with a precis of Matthew 13:44, "the kingdom of God is like treasure hid in a field; the which when a man hath found, he hideth, and for joy thereof goeth and selleth all that he hath, and buyeth that field." The combined text is ostentatiously hidden in italics.

> *My* words & thoughts do both express this notion.
> That *Life* hath with the sun a double motion.
> The first *Is* straight, and our diurnal friend,
> The other *Hid* and doth obliquely bend.
> One life is wrapt *In* flesh and tends to earth:
> The other winds towards *Him*, whose happie birth
> Taught me to live here so, *That* still one eye
> Should aim and shoot at that which *Is* on high;
> Quitting with daily labour all *My* pleasure,
> To gain at harvest an eternall *Treasure*.

The artificiality serves living truth as we see the Christian lead a double life. His straight line through day-by-day earthly existence, like the lines of the poem, is always "obliquely" cut through by the heavenly life of which Scripture is the echo, and aimed at the last "harvest."

Beginnings and Endings

There are also poems in which the Bible exerts its main force from the title at its head. "The Pearl. Matth. 13. 45," refers to Jesus' parable: "Again, the kingdom of heaven is like unto a merchant man, seeking goodly pearls: who, when he had found one pearl of great price, went and sold all that he had, and bought it." The reader needs to have that text in mind, for what follows is not scriptural but instead a positive and lively description of Herbert's advantages in life and his easy familiarity with them. Each of the first three verses begins in the same way: "I know the wayes of Learning"; then "of Honour"; then "of Pleasure." All these verses also end with the same refrain: "Yet I love thee." Not until the fourth and final verse does Scripture surface again. It recapitulates the first three verses and binds them into "Matth. 13. 45" with its theme of sale, commodities, rate, and price:

> I know all these, and have them in my hand:
> Therefore not sealed, but with open eyes
> I flie to thee, and fully understand

> Both the main sale, and the commodities;
> And at what rate and price I have thy love;
> With all the circumstances that may move:
> Yet through these labyrinths, not my grovelling wit,
> But thy silk twist let down from heav'n to me,
> Did both conduct and teach me, how by it
>   To climbe to thee.

But St Matthew's text has here undergone a sea change. St Paul's doctrine, beloved of the protestant reformers, of salvation by God's grace alone, overlays the human initiative of St Matthew's "merchant man." And it does so by resort to the ancient Greek myth of Ariadne's "silk twist" guiding her lover Theseus safely out of the labyrinth. Scripture modifies Scripture and secular literature assists the process. Herbert is a free man within his Bible: free to modify St Matthew by St Paul and to elucidate St Paul with a pagan legend.

"Ephes. 4. 30. Grieve not the Holy Spirit, &c." is a similar instance of a directive scriptural title. The six stanzas of the poem itself ponder the text's extraordinary assertion that divinity can suffer and that "the God of love doth grieve." In the face of it, the poet can only "adjudge myself to tears and grief" – but never enough, for "flesh would fail" to keep it up. The poem ends, again, with resort to scriptural emphasis on Christ's saving sacrifice: "Lord, pardon, for thy Sonne makes good / My want of tears with store of blood." The two poems entitled "Jordan" belong in this category. Commentators are not curious enough about this title, contenting themselves with references to Israel's crossing and Christ's baptism. Neither of these has very much to do with the poems, which are preoccupied with Herbert's search for an honest and clean poetics that is obediently responsive to God's word. Direct relevance to Herbert's two "Jordans" stands instead in the entertaining story in 2 Kings 5 of Naaman, the haughty but leprous Syrian general who eventually obeys Elisha's direction to bathe in the Jordan and is cleansed. It shares the poem's concerns of manners, style, status, and cleansing. A seventeenth century biblically literate reader would pick up this clue and read accordingly.

Just as Herbert sometimes makes Scripture call the tune at the outset of a poem, so, conversely, it can conclude one with transforming force on all that has gone before. Here are two examples of it. "A true Hymne" shares the concern of the two "Jordan" poems with the nature of true, as against false, poetry:

> He who craves all the minde,
> And all the soul, and strength, and time,
>   If the words onely ryme
> Justly complains, that somewhat is behinde
> To make his verse, or write a hymne in kinde.
>
> Whereas if th'heart be moved,
> Although the verse be somewhat scant,
>   God doth supplie the want.
> As when th'heart sayes (sighing to be approved)
> *O could I love!* and stops: God writeth, Loved.

It all turns on Christ's command to love God with all one's mind, soul and strength (Mark 12:30). But then it turns again. The human attempt and ardent longing to obey Christ's order "stops": it is unfulfilled. But that is not the end of the matter at all. "God writeth (scripture!) Loved." That wonderful ending condenses John 3:16, "So God loved the world, that he gave his only-begotten Son, to the end that all that believe on him should not perish, but have everlasting life" into a monosyllable that caps and covers all the preceding struggle for sincerity. (John 3:16, it is worth noticing, was particularly familiar to Herbert as one of the "comfortable words" in the Communion service of his Book of Common Prayer.)

"The Crosse" is a further example. Its concern is with the problem of suffering, particularly of having one's positive aims and aspirations "crossed" by bitter disappointments. It ends, crying to God:

> ... these crosse actions
> Doe winde a rope about, and cut my heart;
>   And yet since these thy contradictions
> Are properly a crosse felt by thy Sonne,
> With but foure words, my words, Thy will be done.

The last four words there are *both* Christ's prayer in the garden of Gethsemane (Matthew 26:42) when his will is "crossed" by his Father's, and from the prayer that he gave to his disciples (Matthew 6:10) and that they have used ever since. The reader may first feel that the last three lines are inconclusive or incomplete (where is the main verb?) but looks again and finds that it could not be more complete and conclusive. Precisely in affliction and "crosses" are we with Christ and he, "with but foure word, my words," with us in a union of wills. This is scriptural exegesis of the utmost economy and strength.

Herbert as Scriptural Maker

Herbert is not just a great exegete. He is a maker, a poet, too, and well up to the Bible's own genres and inventions – though he might be displeased to hear such an opinion, which puts him alongside the Scripture-creating poets, Milton and Blake. He writes his own stories of God creating man and redeeming him. "The Pulley" shows God benevolently at work in his kitchen or dispensary:

> When God at first made man,
>   Having a glasse of blessings standing by;
> Let us (said he) poure on him all we can:
> Let the worlds riches, which dispersed lie,
>   Contract into a span.

The blessings of strength, beauty, wisdom, honor, and pleasure are combined into the human mixture. Only rest remains in the bottom of the glass. God hesitates. If he included that, man would be content within nature, "so both should losers be." Better to leave it out. Herbert knew Augustine's famous prayer in his *Confessions* 1.1: "Thou hat made us for Thyself, and our hearts are restless till they rest in Thee." So God concludes (his pun testifying to his good mood):

> Yet let him keep the rest,
> But keep them with repining restlessnesse:
> Let him be rich and wearie, that at least,
> If goodnesse leade him not, yet wearinesse
> May tosse him to my breast.

The winner, of course, is love. And so it is in "Redemption." The poem is constructed in terms of the law of property, of which the redemption of alienated goods is part. So the New Testament doctrine of redemption can run along behind the scenes of the secular story. The "I" of the poem is a longstanding tenant "to a rich Lord" and is "not thriving." So he decides to ask for: "A new small-rented lease, and cancel th'old." To this purpose, he goes to the Lord's manor in heaven, only to hear:

> ... that he was lately gone
> About some land, which he had dearly bought
> Long since on earth, to take possession

So the "I" goes off to look for him in the "great resorts" where such a personage was likely to be:

> In cities, theatres, gardens, parks and courts.
> At length I heard a ragged noise and mirth
> Of theeves and murderers: there him I espied,
> Who straight, Your suit is granted, said, & died.

At which point, confronted with a squalid and fatal mugging in a side street and the kind words of its omniscient victim, the "I" and the reader find themselves at the cross, landed on biblical *terra firma* and fully, heart-breakingly, redeemed.

Old Testament / New Testament

The frontispieces of both the Geneva and the King James bibles showed their contents in schematic images. The tents of the twelve tribes of the Old Testament are stacked up and down the left side of the page, the twelve apostles of the New Testament on the right. Down the center go the three persons of the Trinity: the Father's sacred name in Hebrew characters, the Holy Spirit in the form of a dove, Christ as the lamb of God (in the King James Version, slain on an altar and surrounded by the four evangelists). It is a diagram of Christian biblical world-history, turned on its axis of divine initiative from old to new and from promise to fulfillment. It was embedded in Herbert's mind and heart. Though superseded by the New Testament, the Old held its value as

Holy Scripture for the Christian Church: as prophecy, law (despite St Paul), wisdom, history, and a wealth of warnings and examples. In Herbert's biblically reformed Church of England it was read every day at Morning and Evening Prayer. He knew it as well as his New Testament and was deeply interested in the relations between the two.

In "Decay" he compares the world of the Old Testament very favorably indeed with his own present. Then, God was familiar and much around the place. Now, in contrast, God is imprisoned and opposed:

> Sweet were the dayes, when thou didst lodge with Lot,
> Struggle with Jacob, sit with Gideon,
> Advise with Abraham, when thy power could not
> Encounter Moses strong complaint and mone:
>   Thy words were then, *Let me alone.*
>
> One might have sought and found thee presently
> At some fair oak, or bush, or cave, or well:
> Is my God this way? No, they would reply
> He is to Sinai gone, as we heard tell:
>   List, ye may heare great Aaron's bell.
>
> But now thou dost thyself immure and close
> In some one corner of a feeble heart;
> Where yet both Sinne and Satan, thy old foes,
> Do pinch and straiten thee, and use much art
>   To gain thy thirds and little part,
>
> I see the world grows old, when as the heat
> Of thy great love, once spread, as in an urn
> Doth closet up it self, till it return,
>   And calling Justice, all things burn.

In the first two verses, multiple Old Testament references are combined to make a picture – a landscape with figures of great everyday charm (the everydayness of God being the point) and nostalgia. Aaron rings his bell like a country parson calling every-one to prayer. Remarkably and powerfully, Herbert makes no reference here to redemp-tion in Christ. All went well in the old days, it is implied, but at Doomsday God will return with a vengeance.

"Sion" starts off on the same course, celebrating the architectural glories of Solo-mon's temple, drawn from 1 Kings 6. But then it changes. Old Testament prophets and New Testament apostles alike distrusted ritual splendor. And in Herbert's own day there was hot debate over the rich church furnishings beloved of Lancelot Andrewes and John Cosin:

> Yet all this glorie, all this pomp and state
> Did not affect thee much, was not thy aim;
> Something there was that sow'd debate

That something was the priority of inward piety over ritual performance, well witnessed within the Old Testament. God in the heart is what matters. But, as in "Decay" this is a hard place for God, "struggling with a peevish heart." The fight produces groans but this is good. "All Solomon's sea of brasse and world of stone / Is not so deare to thee as one good grone." St Paul too had propounded a very positive doctrine of groaning in Romans 8. The whole creation groans: "and not only they, but ourselves also, which have the firstfruits of the Spirit, even we ourselves groan within ourselves, waiting for the adoption, to wit, the redemption of our bodies." More and better still: "The Spirit itself maketh intercession for us with groanings which cannot be uttered."

The poem progresses from Old Testament splendors, through the Old Testament/ New Testament consensus about the priority of inner piety over outward display, to the importance of groaning as basic prayer in the New Testament. There is also a progress from architecture to music, Herbert's chief earthly delight:

> And truly brasse and stones are heavie things,
> Tombes for the dead, not temples fit for thee:
>   But grones are quick, and full of wings,
>   And all their motions upward be;
> And ever as they mount, like larks they sing;
> The note is sad, yet musick for a King.

"The Bunch of Grapes" is a tour de force of the time-honored (St Paul started it) allegorical Christian interpretation of the Old Testament. The title refers to the colossal bunch of grapes that the Israelite spies brought back from Canaan, the Promised Land, in Numbers 13:23–7. It has a resoundingly New Testament conclusion, Pauline and eucharistic. But it starts with the everyday fury of someone who has carefully locked up a domestic animal only to find it gone – and thoughtlessly blames someone for it: "Joy, I did lock thee up: but some bad man / Hath let thee out again." Some sharp disappointment has set Herbert back – by seven years, he reckons. He steadies himself and the reader by recollecting that this is like the fate of the Jews in the Book of Numbers. When the spies brought back the grapes they also reported that Canaan was populated by giants. Struck with terror, the Jews rebelled against Moses and wanted to go back to Egypt. God therefore condemned them to forty years wandering, taking them right back to the Red Sea where they had begun, before they could regain their destination. It was a detour daily remembered by Herbert at Morning Prayer with the recitation of Psalm 95 (Venite):

> Forty years long was I grieved with this generation and said: it is a people that do err in their hearts, for they have not known my ways. Unto whom I sware in my wrath: that they should not enter into my rest.

"Their storie pennes and sets us down," Herbert writes, and rapidly rehearses features of those forty years that match "our" experience: not least murmuring against God and his representatives. Last on the list – and at long last – comes the bunch of grapes advertised in the title:

> But where's the cluster? where's the taste
> Of mine inheritance? Lord, if I must borrow,
> Let me take up their joy, as well as sorrow.
> But can he want the grape, who hath the wine?

The questions themselves cluster toward a positive answer. "Wine," sang the psalmist, "maketh glad the heart of man" (Psalm 104:15 – and Herbert approved of a couple of glasses of it, but not three, in "The Church Porch" 25, 41 and 47). Righteous Noah invented wine. Christians drink it eucharistically as the blood of Christ, whom they believed to be the mysterious figure in the dialogue in Isaiah 63:1–3:

> Wherefore art thou red in thine apparel, and thy garments like him who treadeth out the winepress? I have trodden out the winepress alone; and of the people there was none to help me.

With brilliant economy, Herbert works all this, along with St Paul's doctrine of Christ's sacrifice superseding the old Law, into a Christian resolution of his Old Testament antetypes in the last verse:

> But can he want the grape, who hath the wine?
>   I have their fruit and more.
> Blessed be God, who prospered Noahs vine
>   And made it bring forth grapes good store.
>   But much more him I must adore,
> Who of the Laws sowre juice sweet wine did make,
> Ev'n God himself, being pressed for my sake

Rich variety in emotional range and poetic forms, truth in everyday and theological matters, common sense and mystical urgency – many things combine to make Herbert one of the few great religious poets. The Bible nourished him in all these things, to the point of giving him independence from it as well as dependence on it. But perhaps a particularly endearing trait of his handling of his wide and deep biblical knowledge is its sheer wit – a noun with connotations of spirit, penetrating lightness, skill, and intelligence. This is a quality generally and sadly absent from later modern biblical use of Scripture, more common among those of his contemporaries who are called "metaphysical" poets, but most brilliantly and subtly present in his verse.

Notes

1   *Spelling the Word: George Herbert and the Bible* (University of California Press, 1985), pp. 55–6, 123–4, 135n.
2   Op. cit., pp. 176–97.
3   *Aubrey's Brief Lives*, ed. Oliver Lawson Dick (1950), p. 137.

Further Reading

The best text is *The Works of George Herbert*, edited by F. E. Hutchinson (Oxford University Press, Oxford, 1945). Ann Pasternak Slater's *George Herbert, The Complete English Works* (Everyman's Library, London, 1995) has valuable notes that supplement Hutchinson's. *A Concordance to the Complete Writings of George Herbert* by Mario A. Di Cesare and Rigo Mignani (Cornell University Press, Ithaca, NY, 1977) is extremely useful. *George Herbert, His Religion and Art* by Joseph H. Summers (Chatto and Windus, London, 1954) remains the best general introduction. *The Poetry of George Herbert* by Helen Vendler (Harvard University Press, Cambridge, MA, 1975) is full of brilliant close readings but short on biblical matters. For those, Chana Bloch's *Spelling the Word: George Herbert and the Bible* (University of California Press, Berkeley, 1985) is unrivalled and the resort for readers needing more than there is in this chapter.

CHAPTER 19
John Milton

Michael Lieb

The Psalmist

The influence of the Bible on the writings of John Milton (1608–74) can hardly be overestimated. In many respects, Milton was among our most "biblical" of authors. This means that as a source of both inspiration and belief, the Bible was crucial to him throughout his career as writer and as thinker.[1] As a young poet in his teens, he sought to do the Psalmist one better by paraphrasing Psalms 114 and 136, in anticipation, no doubt, of his later, more mature translations of Psalms 80–8, and, shortly thereafter, Psalms 1–8, during the tumultuous mid-century period culminating in the Protectorate. First published in the second edition of Milton's *Poems* (1673), the two sets of Psalm translations are important both in their own right and for what they say about Milton's self-conception as an aspiring biblical poet.[2] For both reveal Milton's poetic practices as he conceives himself in the act not just of translating but of rewriting Scripture. The first set contains the explanatory headnote "April 1648. J. M.," followed by the statement: "*Nine of the Psalms done into Metre, wherein all but what is in a different Character* [that is, italics], *are the very words of the Text, translated from the Original*" (*Poems*, I, 86). From the outset, the statement alerts the reader that the poet conceives his role as essentially that of a "translator." As such, he seeks to be as accurate as possible in rendering the Hebrew Bible into English verse. Adhering to this principle, Milton is careful not just to italicize words or phrases that he inserts into the translation but also to provide marginal glosses as appropriate. Here, he is acting as a scholar, as well as a translator. Consistent with prevailing hymnals and psalters, among them the Sternhold and Hopkins edition *The Whole Book of Psalms Collected into English Metre* (London, 1562), Milton's translations appear in the form conventionally known as "common meter," a quatrain with alternating lines of iambic tetrameter and iambic trimester.

With the second set of translations, the text provides no explanatory headnotes as such, other than the dates when the individual psalms were "done into verse," that is, during the week of August 7 (?) to August 14, 1653, a period of intense political uncertainty, one that witnessed the coming into power of Oliver Cromwell as Lord Protector on December 16, 1653.[3] Reflecting the upheavals of the times, these psalm translations are remarkable as representations of Milton's capabilities not simply as a translator but as a poet of importance. Eliminated are such qualifiers as "*the very words of the Text, translated from the Original.*" Gone are the marginal glosses as well. Rather than strictly subscribing to the conventional form discernible in the hymnals and psalters, these poems represent occasions for prosodic experimentation and the creation of new forms. No two of the eight psalms possess the same form. Whereas the first psalm assumes the form of a sixteen-line poem written in decasyllabic couplets, the second psalm, as the headnote indicates, assumes the form of "*Terzetti,*" a scheme reminiscent of the Italian influence made evident most famously in Dante's *Commedia*, among other works; and the third psalm appears as a twenty-four line poem with a complex rhyme scheme and lines of various length that alternate catalectic as well as acatalectic feet. The other psalm translations in the set are correspondingly complex in form and texture. This mode of poetic discourse is, in turn, complemented by the presence of enjambment, as well as in the adoption of *caesurae* that occur variously throughout the lines. In short, Milton's translations of Psalms 1–8 are compositions that qualify as "poems" in their own right. They are as much Milton's as they are the Psalmist's. As such, they provide the occasion for Milton as a poet veritably to assume the role of the Psalmist himself. As a poet, Milton, in effect, writes his own Scripture. He himself becomes "the Psalmist" par excellence.

Biblical Vocation

The biblical basis of Milton's self-conception as a poet is discernible throughout his works, both early and late. While still a young man fresh from his undergraduate years at Cambridge, Milton made known his poetic vocation in a Latin epistle (*Elegy*, 6) to his dear friend Charles Diodati, "Sojourning in the Country." Whereas the tone of this verse epistle is ostensibly jocular at times, the poem makes a serious point of providing the opportunity for the poet to delineate himself in both prophetic and priestly terms as one sacred to the gods and empowered thereby to appear before them (77–8). In keeping with this exalted view, the poem culminates in an account of Milton's poetic activities. "I am," the poet declares, "singing the King, bringer of peace by his divine origin / and the blessed times promised in the sacred books." Milton dedicates his poem to "the birthday of Christ" (81–7). What Milton has in mind is his early poem *On the Morning of Christs Nativity*, a work that represents a testament to his view of himself as a poet of things sacred and things biblical early in his evolving sense of his poetic vocation. It is this kind of view that underscores his determination to establish himself as a true votary of the life of Christ. Corresponding poems in this venue include *Upon the Circumcision* and *The Passion*, a poem that is particularly notable because of its unfinished state. It appears that the subject of Christ's Passion, so germane to medieval and Renaissance poems on the life of Christ, proved unsuitable for Milton, either because he did not respond to the Passion as an event that his poetic temperament could embrace or because he felt that the subject was finally beyond his powers. In either event, he did not hesitate to publish *The Passion*, along with his *Nativity* and *Circumcision* poems, in the 1645 and 1673 editions of his "minor" poems, as well as to append an explanatory note underscoring the fact that he left *The Passion* a fragment: "This Subject the Author finding to be above the yeers he had, when he wrote it, and nothing satisfi'd with what was begun, left it unfinisht." Even so fragmentary a poem as *The Passion* Milton determined to publish as a testament to the extent of his devotion to delineate the crucial biblical events that constitute the life of Christ. Such a self-reflexive move underscores Milton's desire to make known to the world as many aspects of his sensibility as possible. This sense of self-reflexivity permeates his poems.

Milton's poem *On the Morning of Christs Nativity* is a case in point. In the introductory stanzas (or proem) to the "Hymn" proper, Milton conceives himself in almost disarmingly childlike terms by calling upon his Muse to get to the manger even before "the Star-led Wisards" arrive with their "odours sweet," because the young poet wishes to be the first one to lay his own gift (that is, his "humble ode") before the feet of "the Infant God." The gesture is at once charming and playful, both of which elements are implicit in the title of the poem. For *On the Morning of Christs Nativity* implies not only that this is a poem *about* Christ's Nativity and all that it signifies but also that this is a poem the action of which occurs "*on*" the very morning of Christ's Nativity. The poet, in effect, rewrites biblical history to "place" himself at the scene of the holy event itself. So, in his race to get to the manger before the Wise Men do, the poet calls out to his Muse: "O run, prevent them with thy humble ode, / And lay it lowly at his blessed feet; / Have thou the honour first, thy Lord to greet, / And joyn thy voice unto the Angel Quire, / From out his secret Altar toucht with hallow'd fire" (15–28). At issue is Isaiah's account of his receipt of the prophetic vocation in the sixth chapter of his prophecy. There, Isaiah envisions himself as having penetrated to the most sacred place of the temple, the Holy of Holies, where he beholds the Enthroned Deity with all his accoutrements. According to Isaiah's account of the event, the Lord appears to him "sitting upon a throne, high and lifted up," where the glory of his train envelops the temple. Above the throne, the seraphim appear: "each one had six wings; with twain he covered his face, and with twain he covered his feet, and with twain he did fly." They cry unto each other "Holy, holy, holy, *is* the Lord of hosts: the whole earth *is* full of his glory." Isaiah reacts disarmingly: "*Woe is* me! For I am undone; because I *am* a man of unclean lips; for mine eyes have seen the King, the Lord of Hosts." One of the seraphim responds, in turn, by taking a "live coal" from off the holocaustal altar and laying the coal on Isaiah's lips, after which the seraph proclaims, "Lo, this hath touched thy lips; and thine iniquity is taken away, and thy sin purged." At this point, Isaiah hears "the voice of the Lord, saying, Whom shall I send, and who will go for us?" Now purified, Isaiah is able to declare: "Here *am* I; send me" (Isaiah 6:1–8). Like Isaiah, Milton conceived himself as one who has penetrated to the Holy of Holies in order to behold the theophany of God, who bestows upon him the poet a calling all his own.

The Celebrant

Although Milton reconceives both the setting and the terms of the Isaiah narrative to suit his poetic needs, the biblical event represents the allusive world in which Milton views himself an active participant. Such is particularly true of his festive poem *At a solemn Musick*. As a magnificent celebration of the Enthroned Deity surrounded by the angelic choirs this poem becomes the occasion for Milton to portray himself as one called upon to "present / That undisturbed Song of pure concent / Ay sung before the saphire-colour'd throne / To him that sits theron" (5–8). His purpose is to "renew that Song" sung before the throne of God and there "live with him [God]" and "sing in endless morn of light" (25–8).[4] Implicit in the setting is not only Isaiah 6 but Revelation 4. In the Revelation account (drawn from Isaiah, among other prophecies), St John the Divine experiences his own celestial vision of God on his throne. Here, the vision is at once tumultuous and festive. If the tumultuous elements are discernible in "lightnings and thunderings and voices" that proceed from the throne, the festive elements are embodied in the "four beasts full of eyes before and behind" that John witnesses round about the throne. Like the seraphim of Isaiah, the four beasts or living beings "rest not day and night, saying Holy, holy, holy, Lord God Almighty, which was, and is, and is to come" (Revelation 4:1–8). Their "undisturbed Song of pure concent" is commonly known as the *trisagion* ("thrice holy"). Milton's *At a solemn Musick* is his own *trisagion*. That is, he not only produces such a poem to celebrate the Enthroned Deity but, rather like the four creatures of Revelation, he portrays himself as an actual participatant in the *trisagion*. In that way, his poem becomes the occasion through which he incorporates himself as celebrant into the divine setting. This remarkable gesture is later articulated in the angelic hymn to God that culminates the celestial dialogue in book 3 of *Paradise Lost* (372–415). If the hymn begins in the third person ("Thee Father first they sung Omnipotent"), it concludes in the first person ("Hail Son of God, Saviour of Men, thy Name / Shall be the copious matter of my Song / Henceforth, and never shall my Harp thy praise / Forget, nor from thy Fathers praise disjoin"). It is only too easy to miss the crucial transition here. Almost imperceptibly, the pronominal references in this hymn move from the angelic choir ("they sung") to the poet himself ("my Song ... my Harp"). If the hymn is that of the angels surrounding the throne, Milton as poet/celebrant is as much a member of that celestial company as any one of the other members of the angelic throng.

Prophetic Milton

What is true of the poetry is no less true of the prose works. In the introduction to the second book of *The Reason of Church-Government* (1642), he re-enacts the visionary drama delineated in Isaiah by situating it in the polemical context of his tracts against the prelates. Distinguishing between himself and other poets (such as "the vulgar Amorist" or the "rhyming parasite") who do nothing more than invoke "Dame Memory and her Siren daughters" to inspire them, Milton promises to produce a major poem inspired by "devout prayer to that eternall Spirit who can enrich with all utterance and knowledge, and sends out his Seraphim with the hallow'd fire of his Altar to touch and purify the lips of whom he pleases" (I, 820–1). With the Spirit of God as his Muse, he bears witness to the fact that he, as much as any of the biblical prophets, is the one who has been chosen to be purified for the sake of undertaking the vocation of the prophet both in his poetry and in his prose. The vocational dimension of biblical prophecy is transformed into the polemical setting of Milton's self-conception as poet-prophet. If for Milton, the office of the biblical prophet was not easy, it was also one that he could not refuse. As he states earlier in the introduction to *The Reason of Church-Government*, "when God commands to take the trumpet and blow a dolorous or a jarring blast, it lies not in mans will what he shall say, or what he shall conceal" (compare Jeremiah 20:8–10). Such an allusion, Milton observes, puts his own times on notice "not suddenly to condemn all things that are sharply spoken" (I, 803). Particularly in the polemical context of Milton's prose, the burden of the prophet was palpably present throughout his writings both before and after total blindness overcame him later in life (1652).

The experience of that burden underscores Milton's determination to make use of his God-given talents and his deep-seated anxieties about his putative "belatedness" in failing to fulfill his obligations as a true servant of God. These issues haunted him his entire life. At the center of his anxieties lay the all-important experience of the unprofitable servant depicted in the Parable of the Talents. According to the parable, a man traveling into a far country called upon his servants to look after his goods, that is, his "talents," which the text conceives both as a form of currency and as the sign of ability. "And unto one he gave five talents, to another two, and to another one; to every man according to his several ability." Whereas the first two servants double the number of talents their lord has bestowed upon them, the third "went and digged in the earth, and his lord's money." Upon returning from the far country, the lord rewards the first two servants for their respective labors, but when he calls upon the third servant to account for his actions, the man responds, "Lord, I knew that thou art an hard man, reaping where thou hast not sown, and gathering where thou hast not strawed: And I was afraid, and went and hid thy talent in the earth: lo, *there* thou hast *that* is thine." In response to the third servant's statement, the lord accuses him of being "wicked and slothful" and commands that the talent be taken from him and bestowed upon the first servant, the one who already has more than the rest. "For," the lord says, "unto every one that hath shall be given, and he shall have abundance; but from him that hath not shall be taken away even that which he hath." Having issued this pronouncement, the lord has the unprofitable servant cast into "outer darkness," where we are told "there shall be weeping and gnashing of teeth" (Matthew 25:14–30). The terror associated with the harsh lord of this parable culminates in the coming of the Son of man to sit upon his throne of glory to judge all the nations of the world.

From the time he was a young man, Milton revealed an ever-present awareness of the biblical implications of his vocational anxieties. Thus, as early as his "Letter to an Unknown Friend" (1631–3? or 1637?), he responded to the admonitions of one who reminded him "that the howres of the night passe on" and that the day "is at hand wherin Christ commands all to Labour while there is light" (John 9:4). Although the precise identity of the friend has never been disclosed, the dark mystery surrounding his identity serves to underscore, rather than to alleviate, the anxieties Milton experienced in his need to justify himself before God. In the letter, Milton conceives the friend as "a good watch man" (compare Ezekiel 33:7; Isaiah 21:12; Matthew 20:6) whose responsibility is to make certain that Milton make appropriate use of his gifts. But Milton does not need the watchman to remind him of what is at hand. His own conscience is sufficient to that end. Accordingly, Milton thinks himself "bound though unask't" to provide "an account, as oft as occasion is" of his "tardie moving," in accord with the urging of his conscience, which he avers "is not without god." With the coming judgment in mind, he places himself in the context of one ever mindful of the need to obey "that command in the gospell set out by the terrible seasing of him that hid the talent." Paradoxically, it is the "very consideration of that great commandment," he says, that prevents him from pressing forward with his great work but that obliges him instead to hold off with "a sacred reverence & religious advisement how best to undergoe," that is, to undertake and fulfill the terms of his vocation. He justifies his belatedness through an allusion to the Parable of the Vineyards, in which the householder rewards all those who labored for him according to his will, whether they were the first to serve or the last: "So the last shall be first, and the first last: for many be called, but few chosen" (Matthew 20:1–15). It is through the consolation afforded by the Parable of the Vineyard that Milton responds to the terrors of the Parable of the Talents. So he views himself as "not taking thought of beeing late so it give advantage to be more fit, for those that were latest lost nothing when the maister of the vineyeard came to give each one his hire" (I, 319–21).

As much as the Parable of the Vineyard might be invoked to relieve the anxieties wrought by the Parable of the Talents, it is this parable that represents the cornerstone of Milton's view of his vocation. Once again, the introduction to the second book of the *Reason of Church-Government* is germane. Milton begins that introduction by declaring that "God even to a strictnesse requires the improvement of these his entrusted gifts." Prompted by that awareness, Milton "cannot but sustain a sorer burden of mind, and more pressing then any supportable toil, or waight, which the body can labour under; how and in what manner he shall dispose and employ those summes of knowledge and illumination, which God hath sent him into this world to trade with" (I, 801). One notes immediately the extent to which the language of the discourse is infused with the harsh mercantilism of the Parable of the Talents itself. (Compare the version of this parable in Luke 19:12–27, which in the Authorized Version substitutes "pounds" for "talents.") Although the mercantilism of this parable would appear to be directly at odds with biblical mandates against the evils of usury (for example, Exodus 22:25–7; Leviticus 25:35–7; Deuteronomy 23:19–20, etc.), such an outlook bespeaks the anxieties Milton experienced as one who felt that "burden of mind," as well as that "toil" and "waight," under which he labored in order to prove his worth before a God who would ultimately come to judge him. These anxieties underscore Milton's poetry as well.

The Sonnets

Anxieties are already present, for example, in Sonnet 7 ("How soon hath Time the suttle theef of Youth"), which Milton appended to his "Letter to an Unknown Friend" as a way providing poetic insight into the dilemma he was facing in the establishment of his accountability at that early juncture in his career. Commemorating the passing of his "three and twentieth year," the sonnet becomes the means by which the poet takes stock of his accomplishments to date and professes his faith in God's providence. The octave of this Petrarchan sonnet articulates the dilemma. Although the poet's "haysting dayes fly on with full career," his "late spring" at this point in his maturation reveals as yet "no bud or blossom." The first quatrain of the octave recalls Milton's own statement in the "Letter to an Unknown Friend" that he remains "suspicious" of himself and continues to "take notice of a certaine belatedness" in himself that he is frankly incapable of dispelling. The sonnet represents a poetic confirmation of this stance. The sestet, on the other hand, represents a kind of resolve that attempts to reconcile the underlying anxieties that arise from belatedness with a corresponding sense of resignation to the inscrutable ways of God: "Yet be it less or more, or soon or slow, / It shall be still in strictest measure eev'n / To that same lot, however mean or high, / Toward which Time leads me, and the will of Heav'n," a statement that culminates in the declaration of faith in God's ways and a realization that the dilemma of belatedness can be overcome only with an awareness that the providential eye of God sees and foresees everything: "All is, if I have grace to use it so, / As ever in my great task-maisters eye" (compare Exodus 33:13; Romans 12:3, 6). If such a statement provides at best a momentary sense of resolution and reconciliation, the ever-present anxieties that characterize the "Letter to an Unknown Friend" find expression at various points throughout Milton's career, perhaps, because of the lingering sense that to be ever in the eye of the "great task-maister" is as much a source of disquietude as it is a source of comfort.

It is this "great task-maister" with his all-seeing eye that haunts Milton's Sonnet 19 ("When I consider how my light is spent"). In its own way, this sonnet, more than any other in the Miltonic canon, bespeaks the dread that the poet experiences in his account of what he had earlier called "the terrible seasing of him that hid the talent." Reinforced no doubt by the devastating fact of Milton's own blindness (1652), the prospect of that seizure assumes an especially grim and unsettling irony, one that further intensifies the anxieties that Milton experienced earlier in life. With the blindness in both of Milton's eyes fully realized, the bearing of the unprofitable servant invoked earlier in his career is now conceived not just as trope but as fact. The death that comes from unwillingly burying one's talent within oneself becomes the occasion for the dread of being cast into "outer darkness" as a result of one's inability to fulfill his God-given talents, despite his intense desire to please the "great task-maister." What a cruel joke appears to have played on the blind poet! Thus, he cries out: "Doth God exact day labour, light deny'd"? As it recalls John 9:4 ("I must work the works of him that sent me, while it is day: the night cometh, when no man can work"), among other texts, the outcry that anticipates the *volta* in Sonnet 19 has already been sounded in Milton's statement in his "Letter to an Unknown Friend" that "the day is at hand wherin Christ commands all to Labour while there is light" (I, 319). Whereas in the letter the idea is framed as an observation, in the sonnet it becomes a "murmur" putatively countermanded by the serene voice of "patience," through which the consolation afforded by the sestet is articulated. How effective that consolation is in ameliorating the anxieties brought about by Milton's blindness remains to be seen. Clearly, that "great task-maister's eye" remains focused, indeed riveted, on the blind poet until his death.

The Trinity College Manuscript

Whether in the form of poems on biblical themes early in his career or in the form of the great epics on the loss and regaining of paradise and the drama on the fallen hero of Judges published at the end of his career, Milton conceived himself throughout his life as a poet who aspired to refashion the Bible in his own terms. To that end, he maintained a list of biblical subjects that appear in what is known as the Trinity College Manuscript, now in the archives of Trinity College, Cambridge. Available in facsimile, this holograph and scribal notebook contains not only drafts of poems such as *A Mask* (later known as *Comus*) and *Lycidas*, as well as certain sonnets; it also contains detailed lists of subjects that might serve as the basis of possible works that Milton had in mind to execute on some later occasion. Although a goodly number of the items are drawn from the earliest periods of English history, a more extensive series of subjects (some accompanied by rather elaborate plans and outlines) are drawn from the Bible, both the Old Testament and the New. (The subjects drawn from the Bible are interspersed with those drawn from English history; and, among the subjects drawn from the Bible, the preponderance of these find their source in the Old Testament, as opposed to the New.) Milton, it would seem, looked upon himself as one through whom sacred biblical narrative, on the one hand, and secular historical narrative, on the other hand, found something of a common ground. In either case, it appears that, at some point in his career, Milton sought inspiration in the appropriate sources (sacred and secular) to discover essential sites that might serve as the basis of his creativity. More than any other text, the Bible represented his most important source of his desire to refashion sacred history, to transform it, to make it his own.

The subjects noted in the lists drawn from the Bible are especially illuminating, for they suggest an entire range of possibilities Milton found appropriate to his calling and deemed important enough to inspire him to embark upon major poetic undertakings. In citing the various topics of interest to him, Milton both provides a title and at times specifies the precise biblical text that his proposed work seeks to illuminate. Thus, one finds entries such as "Athalia 2 Reg. 10," "Asa or Æthiopes. 2 chron. 14," "Moabitides Num. 25," "Abimelech the usurper. Jud. 9," and "David Adulterous," among many others. Inventive with his titles, Milton often conceives them in a form that imbues his biblical subjects with a Greek sensibility, such as "Elias Polemistes." Those topics that truly catch his attention receive detailed description, as, for example, his plans for a drama to be called "Cupids funeral pile. Sodom Burning," with its source in Genesis 19. In this proposed drama, the angels rescue Lot from the barbarous behavior of the citizens of Sodom, and love is seen to triumph over lust. Both in theme and in tone, the proposed drama recalls *Comus*. Other topics of this sort receive detailed attention as well.

In the Trinity College Manuscript Milton first provides detailed outlines and plot summaries for the action of a proposed tragedy on the theme of what would later emerge as *Paradise Lost*. Beginning with two lists of personages, Milton fleshed out his plans first with a five-act prospectus for a drama to be called "Paradise Lost" and several pages later with a detailed summary of another drama titled "Adam unparadiz'd" (as

well an apparently rejected title, "Adams *Banishment*"). Accordingly, the act of reworking or rearticulating biblical narrative is at the very heart of Milton's plans for his great
epic. The same is true for *Paradise Regained* and *Samson Agonistes*. In both cases, Milton
draws inspiration from specific biblical narratives that he would reconceive in his own
terms. In anticipation of the brief epic on the figure of Christ, Milton thus entertains
subjects drawn from the gospels such as "Christ born," "Christ bound," "Christ crucifi'd,"
"Christ risen," and "Christus patiens," subjects that ultimately assumed the form of
Paradise Regained, which focuses on the temptations in the wilderness recounted in
Luke 4. Finally, Milton's dramatic poem *Samson Agonistes* may be said to find its ground-
ing in the list of subjects on the strong man of Judges 13–16, including "Samson pur-
sophorus," that is, Samson the fire-bearer; Samson "Hybristes," that is, the insolent
Samson; Samson marrying, that is, the episode concerning the woman of Timnath;
Samson in Ramath-Lechi, that is, the overcoming of the Philistines with the jawbone
of an ass; and the "Dagonalia," that is, the overthrow of the temple of Dagon in Gaza.
Clearly, for this poet-in-the making, biblical subjects on an entire range of subjects
represented the basis of his outlook and his imagination from the very outset of his
career and culminated in the masterpieces published at the very end of his career.[5]

Hebraism versus Hellenism

As made apparent thus far, the Bible played a crucial role in what might be called Milton's biblical poetics. If such is the case, it played no less crucial a role in his vocation
as an interpreter of the biblical text. A child of the Reformation, Milton was a figure for
whom the Bible assumed a primacy that superseded that of all other sources, including
the very Greco-Roman classics upon which the notion of Renaissance humanism was
grounded. In *Paradise Regained*, Milton's Jesus becomes the spokesman for this kind of
radical view as he is subjected to the barrage of temptations that Satan places before
him in the wilderness. Having been unsuccessful in his attempt to seduce Jesus by his
earlier temptations, Satan plays what he hopes is a trump card, that is, the temptation
to wisdom. In this case, it is wisdom of a particular sort that Satan has in mind. Rather
than relying solely upon "the *Pentateuch* or what the Prophets wrote," Satan advises
Jesus, seek to know the world of the gentiles: "The *Gentiles* also know, and write, and
teach / To admiration, led by Natures light" (4.225–8). What does Satan mean by the
word *Gentiles*? These are the individuals whose home is "*Athens* the eye of *Greece*,
Mother of Arts / And Eloquence." They include philosophers such as Plato and Aristotle, orators such as Demosthenes and Pericles, and poets such as Homer, Sappho, and
Pindar (4.240–84). To counter the tenor of such a temptation, Jesus "sagely" replies
that the doctrines these figures espouse and the world they represent are "false, or little
else but dreams, / Conjectures, fancies, built on nothing firm" (4.291–2). Jesus' allega-
tions are harsh, to say the least. Calling into question all aspects of the culture embraced
by the gentiles, Jesus finds particularly repugnant "the vices of their Deities" as portrayed in their "Fable, Hymn, or song." For the Jesus of Milton's epic, the gentile gods
are "ridiculous" and those who worship them "past shame." As iconoclast, Jesus seeks
to lay bare or denude these false deities as one would strip a harlot of her finery. In place

of the world of the gentiles, Jesus extols his own culture, his own heritage, and his own language, all of which are summed up in Hebrew Scriptures. Whether in the area of government, statesmanship, or law, the divine teachings of the Bible are unsurpassed. Such is true of oratory as well: the Bible is so eloquent that it surpasses "all the Oratory of *Greece* and *Rome*." In the Bible, Jesus finds "All our Law and Story strew'd / With hymns, our Psalms with artful terms inscrib'd." These, he calls "*Sion*'s songs," a poetic form with which the literature of the gentile world is "unworthy to compare." Unlike this "pagan" literature, the songs of the Hebrew Bible are divinely inspired by God (4.293–364). Jesus' critique of the Greco-Roman world is as much literary as it is theological, political, or legal. That is, Jesus adopts the role of aesthetician and literary critic as much as he assumes the function of philosophical or theological commentator. In all respects, his response to Satan's temptation is an indictment of everything the world of the gentiles represents in contradistinction to the Hebraism implicit in Jesus' endorsement of the Bible as the true source of knowledge and wisdom.

Needless to say, the radical nature of Jesus' response to the temptation to wisdom has generated a great deal of debate in the scholarly community about the extent to which Milton himself actually embraced such an outlook. Assuming that Milton projected his own views onto those of Jesus, critics have been understandably chagrined that the great spokesman for Renaissance humanism would have placed the temptation to study Homer, Plato, and Aristotle in the mouth of Satan, especially since the study of the Bible in all its aspects is as much a part of Renaissance humanism as is the mastery of the classics. It is not the purpose here to address the dilemma. Instead, the issue is raised simply to frame the subject so that one is made aware from the outset that any attempt to explore the place of the Bible in Milton's works is immediately fraught with difficulties. Those difficulties are not made any easier in an analysis of what Milton says about the Bible in his theological treatise *De Doctrina Christiana*, a work the very canonicity of which has been questioned at various times since the manuscript was first discovered and subsequently published in the early nineteenth century. Assuming that in some form the work was authored by John Milton, one might well conclude that his treatment of the Bible in the theological treatise would obviously be of major significance to any understanding of the place of the Bible in his thought. What is true of *Paradise Regained* is no less true of *De Doctrina Christiana*: nothing can be taken for granted, and just about everything is problematical.

The Hermeneut

At first blush, Milton's attitude to the Bible in the theological treatise is crystal clear. As he maintains in his prefatory epistle to the reader, the Bible for him represents the most authoritative source of knowledge concerning all matters of Christian doctrine. Rather than "depend[ing] upon the belief or judgment of others in religious questions," he maintains that the "only authority" he accepted in such matters is "God's self-revelation" as manifested in the biblical text. Accordingly, he explains his exegetical method by asserting that "he read and pondered the Holy Scriptures themselves with all possible diligence" (VI, 118). Whereas other exegetes adopt the practice of relegating biblical references to the margins with only "brief reference to chapter and verse," he has "striven to cram [his] pages even to overflowing, with quotations drawn from all parts of the Bible and to leave as little space as possible for his own words" (VI, 122). Here is a theological treatise that allows the Bible to take centerstage, to speak for itself. This is a fascinating revelation of compositional practice or method, for it willingly privileges not the doctrinal assertions that the exegete seeks to advance but the scriptural evidence that the exegete draws upon to underscore his assertions. What results is a renewed emphasis upon the primacy of Scriptures as the source of interpretative insight and doctrinal belief. At the very point that Milton claims the liberty to sift and winnow each doctrine before advancing it, he makes certain that his conclusions are grounded in scriptural authority. "For my own part," Milton maintains, "I devote my attention to the Holy Scriptures alone. I follow no other heresy or sect" (VI, 123).

When Milton addresses the subject of the Holy Scriptures in the treatise (book 1, chapter 30), the whole question of "authority" re-emerges in a new form, that having to do with the concept of the "double scripture," the external and the internal. Accordingly, Milton distinguishes between "the external scripture of the written word and the internal scripture of the Holy Spirit." The internal scripture is that which God has engraved "upon the hearts of believers." Although it might be argued that such a dichotomy, in one form or another, is consistent with Reformation theology, Milton's emphasis upon it is crucial to his interpretative posture as one who does not hesitate throughout his writings to justify the bold act of moving the seat of authority from the external to the internal, the visible to the invisible. Thus, he observes that "Nowadays the external authority for our faith, in other words, the scriptures, is of very considerable importance and, generally speaking, it is the authority of which we first have experience. The pre-eminent and supreme authority, however, is the authority of the Spirit, which is internal, and the individual possession of each man" (VI, 587). This is a remarkable statement, for followed to its logical conclusion, it calls into question the viability, if not the primacy, of the very text upon which Milton professes to base his entire theological system. What occurs, in effect, is an act of displacement: external authority grounded in the text as object is replaced by an internal authority grounded in the world of spirit. The text as object disappears. To reinforce his argument for such an act of displacement, Milton makes a point of calling attention to the "corruptions" inherent in the biblical text as it has been transmitted over the centuries. Focusing especially on the New Testament (the very basis of Christian belief), he maintains that the act of transmission (and, along with it, preservation) has given rise to codices that are of questionable authority. That is because those responsible for copying and disseminating the codices are themselves not to be trusted. (Although better preserved and more carefully transcribed, the Old Testament, Milton implies, is not without its problems as well.) One is confronted by such "an assortment of divergent manuscripts" and such a "medley of transcripts and editions" that knowing which version to adopt as truly authoritative for the purpose of exegesis represents in itself a major undertaking (VI, 587–8).

Whether in reference to the Bible, the church, or the implementation of God's decrees, the movement from external to internal (and correspondingly, visible to invisible) is an essential constituent of Milton's stock-in-trade. One thinks immediately of the proem to book 1 of *Paradise Lost*. Moving from sources of inspiration as embodied in the teachings inscribed by God on the tablets that Moses receives on Sinai or in the events portrayed at such sites as "*Sion* Hill" or "*Siloa's* Brook that flow'd / Fast by the Oracle of God," the site of the temple in Jerusalem, the poet invokes as his consummate source of authority the Spirit of God itself: "And chiefly Thou O Spirit, that dost prefer / Before all Temples th' upright heart and pure, / Instruct me, for Thou knowst" (1.6–19). Clothed in the trope of poetic discourse, this testament to the power of the spirit within reflects the radical terms in which Milton conceives the Bible as the ultimate source of authority in the theological treatise.

Milton's Bibles

In the production of his theological treatise, Milton had available to him a multiplicity of scriptural versions.[6] These include versions that he owned or that were said to be in his possession. Among them are a 1612 edition of the Authorized Version (now extant), the Geneva Bible (1650), and a Hebrew Bible (given to him by his tutor) including the *Biblia sacra polyglotta* (1657), compiled by Brian Walton. Providing Hebrew, Greek, Latin (of the Vulgate), Arabic, Aramaic, Ethiopic, Persian, and Syriac transcriptions in separate columns (along with an interlinear Latin translation of the Hebrew), this multivolume work has been offered as one of the possible sources for the proof-texts cited in *De Doctrina Christiana*. Vying for equal, if not greater, claim to that distinction is the Junius-Tremellius-Beza translation of the Old and New Testaments (Junius-Tremelius for the Old Testament and Beza for the New). The version of choice for seventeenth-century Reformed dogmatics and exegesis, this edition assumed the reputation of a veritable *textus receptus* during the period when Milton's theological treatise was being produced. These are only two of the likely sources behind the proof-texts Milton cites. As worthy as these editions are, Milton was painfully aware of their shortcomings in his attempt to ferret out the "truths" embedded in the "original" or "foundational" text. The point is not to discover the precise version (or versions) that Milton drew upon to produce his theological treatise but to acknowledge Milton's awareness that the *ur*-text (of both the Old Testament and the New) is finally not to be had. This means that, despite (or, perhaps, because of) the range of versions available to him, Milton was sensitive to the limitations they represented in his quest to generate his theological treatise.

The Major Poems

Each of Milton's major poems is grounded in the Bible, a fact to which the Trinity College Manuscript fully attests. Each poem self-consciously elaborates certain core texts of the Bible that influenced Milton profoundly. Well before the appearance of any of the major poems, he looked forward to his vocation as biblical poet by reflecting upon his ambitions. Those ambitions characteristically placed the Bible at the very center of his reflections. Once again, the introduction to the second book of his prose treatise *The*

Reason of Church-Government (1642) is germane. Here, he considers the appropriate models upon which to found his future endeavors, be they epics or dramas. In his consideration of epic, his reflections move him to distinguish between what calls the "diffuse" model and the "brief" model. One thinks of *Paradise Lost*, on the one hand, and *Paradise Regained*, on the other. Moving between ancient and contemporary epics, as well as dramas of various kinds, he invokes classical and biblical forms through which his pursuit of a Christian hero might be realized. An entire range of possibilities presents itself. Notable are the references to the Bible as a source-book both for subjects and for forms. Searching for the ideal model of the brief epic, he invokes the book of Job, which leads in its own way as much to *Paradise Regained* as it does to *Samson Agonistes*, both later published in one volume (1671). Corresponding references to the Song of Songs and to the book of Revelation further suggest the esoteric and apocalyptic course of his thinking (I, 812–13). As he moved on with his plans, it became clear that the major poems, which lay ahead, would essentially be biblical in nature.

As indicated by the citations in the Trinity College Manuscript, such an approach is entirely consistent with Milton's artistic practices. At the core of his thinking is the complex of narratives that constitutes the biblical text. This is as true for *Paradise Regained* and *Samson Agonistes* as it is for *Paradise Lost*. Each work represents in epic or dramatic form an encounter with the Bible very much as subtext. As indicated, the essential core text for *Paradise Regained* is the fourth chapter of Luke, the base narrative having to do with the temptations in the wilderness. Although the account of Jesus' sojourn in the wilderness is also the subject of the fourth chapter of Matthew, the order of the temptations differs markedly between Matthew and Luke. The reader is immediately presented with a conundrum: why did Milton choose Luke over Matthew? The very first questions we ask about the major poems are in response to their respective adoptions of the biblical texts as core. In the case of the dramatic poem *Samson Agonistes*, Milton has so altered the base narrative of Judges 13–16 that an entirely new fable, along with entirely new characters, makes its way to the fore. Harapha is a figure that never makes an appearance in Judges. Although Delilah most certainly makes her appearance in Judges, her reappearance in Milton's poem in the form of Dalila is striking in the significance Milton bestows upon her not simply as one of the strong man's sexual conquests but also as the symbol of another marriage gone bad. (Whereas Judges nowhere indicates that Delilah and Samson are married, Milton's Dalila and Samson certainly are. This "revision" of the Judges narrative points to Milton's willingness to alter the sacred text and to transform it into a text all his own.)

The core text upon which *Paradise Lost* is grounded is Genesis 1–3. As is well known, the first chapter provides the fundamental account of the creation of the universe (including the heavens and the earth, living things such as plants, animals, fish, and the like) and the creation of humankind. This event represents the culminating creative act that anticipates the celebration of divine rest toward which the chapter ultimately moves. Here, there is no prohibition of any sort. Instead, humankind (in the form of male and female) is to be fruitful and multiply and to have dominion over every living thing that moves upon the earth. The purpose of all such beings is finally to sustain humankind, which, as the crowning achievement of God's creative acts, assumes a truly regal stature. It would take the next two chapters to introduce disharmony into this sublime moment. In the next two chapters, Milton found such discordant enactments as the first prohibition (against the eating of the fruit from the Tree of the Knowledge of Good and Evil), as well as the first disobedience as a result of the willingness of the first man ("Adam") and of the first woman ("Eve") to fall victim to the wiles of the serpent. It to this dark narrative that Milton looked for evidence of the primal act that brought death into the world and that prompted the expulsion of Adam and Eve from the garden of God, known as Eden.

As Milton was well aware, the linkage of Genesis 1 with Genesis 2 and 3 offered its own unique problems and challenges. But this text remained at the core of *Paradise Lost*, as it anchored the narrative throughout the epic but especially in those books having to do with the creation of the universe and the relationship between Adam and Eve both before and after the Fall. But, of course, such concerns represent only one aspect (albeit a crucial one) of Milton's epic. To tell the story of all things, Milton was obliged to draw upon other seminal biblical texts that he appropriated for his own particular use. One might consider, for example, the issue of Satan's rebellion depicted in Milton's narrative of the war in heaven. Genesis 1–3 says nothing about that crucial event, but it is an event fully attested in Revelation 12:7–9: "And there was a war in heaven: Michael and his angels fought against the dragon; and the dragon fought against his angels, And prevailed not; neither was their place found any more in heaven. And the great dragon was cast out, that old serpent, called the Devil, and Satan, which deceiveth the whole world; he was cast out into the earth, and his angels were cast out with him." At issue is not only the "fact" of celestial warfare, but also the "characters" in that warfare, including Michael and the angels, on one side, and the dragon, also known as the old serpent, called the Devil and Satan, along with his angels, on the other. Here, Milton would have most immediately found the link between the serpent of the Genesis story and the serpent of Revelation, who is at once dragon and devil and Satan to boot. But this tie in is already anticipated in such seminal texts as Isaiah 14:12–24, which alludes to the fall of "Lucifer, son of the morning," and Ezekiel 28:12–19, which provides an account of the "covering cherub" who once inhabited "Eden the garden of God" but is now doomed to destruction. Customarily associated with Satan, both "Lucifer, son of the morning" and the "covering cherub" have their own distinct associations and translational histories, but for Milton they represented different dimensions of a very complex character. These are only a few of the many crucial texts upon which Milton as biblical poet grounded the narrative of his great epic.

Conclusion

As indicated at the beginning of this chapter, one can hardly overestimate the influence of the Bible on the writings of John Milton. This is a poet who does not hesitate to conceive of himself and his art in biblical terms. Whether as psalmist, as prophet, or as celebrant, he transforms the Bible and makes it his own. He conceives of his vocation or calling as an experience that empowers him to fill out the interstices of the biblical text, to tell of "secret" things unspoken in the narratives he recreates, whether that having to do with the creation of the universe or that having to do with the temptations of Jesus in the wilderness. At the same time, he is aware that the gift of this vocation is potentially as much a curse as it is a blessing. He is ever aware that, if he fails to make proper use of this God-given talents, he might well find himself in the untenable position of the unprofitable servant cast into "outer darkness," where we are told "there shall be weeping and gnashing of teeth" (Matthew 25: 30). For Milton, the Bible was not simply a source of poetic experience but the means by which he forged an identity and a career centered on the conviction that the biblical text was in a very real sense his own.

Notes

1   Unless noted otherwise, references to Milton's poetry in my text are to *The Complete Poetry of John Milton*, ed. John T. Shawcross (New York, 1971). References by volume and page number in my text to Milton's prose are to *The Complete Prose Works of John Milton*, 8 volumes in 10, gen. ed. Don M. Wolfe et al. (New Haven, CT, 1953–82).

2   References by volume and page number in my text to Milton's psalm translations are to the facsimile edition *John Milton's Complete Poetical Works*, ed. Harris Francis Fletcher, 4 volumes (Urbana, IL, 1943).

3   Although the text does not provide a specific headnote date for the translation of Psalm 1, logic suggests that it dates to August 7, because the headnotes for the remaining psalm translations follow sequentially from August 8 to August 15, 1673.

4   In a manuscript still extant in the library of Trinity College, Cambridge (and therefore referred to as the Trinity College Manuscript) one can find, among many of Milton's early poems and other jottings (some in Milton's own hand), the first drafts of *At a Solemn Musick*. These drafts are especially interesting because they suggest that it is not only the angelic choirs that sing but also God himself: So the poet would "live & sing wth him [God] in endlesse morn of light" (28). Music encompasses the entire setting, one in which God is a participant in his own *tri-sagion*. See John Milton, *Poems Reproduced in Facsimile from the Manuscript in Trinity College, Cambridge* (Menston, England, 1972), pp. 4–5.

5   See *Poems Reproduced in Facsimile from the Manuscript in Trinity College, Cambridge*, pp. 36–41.

6   See the entry on "Bibles," in *A Milton Encyclopedia*, gen. ed. William B. Hunter, 9 volumes (Lewisburg, 1978–83), I, p. 163. In the same volume, see the entry on Milton and the Bible, I, pp. 142–63.

List of Milton's Works Cited

The Complete Poetry of John Milton, ed. John T. Shawcross (New York, 1971).

John Milton's Complete Poetical Works, ed. Harris Francis Fletcher, 4 volumes (Urbana, IL, 1943).

The Complete Prose Works of John Milton, gen. ed. Don M. Wolfe 8 volumes in 10 (New Haven, CT, 1953–82).

Poems Reproduced in Facsimile for the Manuscript in Trinity College, Cambridge (Menston, England, 1972).

A Milton Encyclopedia, gen. ed. William B. Hunter, 9 volumes (Lewisburg, 1978–83).

Suggested Reading

Baldwin, Edward C. (1929) "Some Extra-Biblical Semitic Influences upon Milton's Story of the Fall of Man," *Journal of English and Germanic Philology* 28, 366–401.

Conklin, George N. (1949) *Biblical Criticism and Heresy in Milton*. King's Crown Press, New York.

Dobbins, Austin C. (1975) *Milton and the Book of Revelation: The Heavenly Cycle*. University of Alabama Press.

Evans, J. M. (1968) *"Paradise Lost" and the Genesis Tradition*. Clarendon Press, Oxford.

Fisch, Harold (1984) "Creation in Reverse: The Book of Job and *Paradise Lost*," in James H. Sims and Leland Ryken, eds, *Milton and Scriptural Tradition: The Bible into Poetry*. University of Missouri Press, Columbia, pp. 104–16.

Fixler, Michael (1984) "All-Interpreting Love: God's Name in Scripture and in *Paradise Lost*," in James H. Sims and Leland Ryken, eds, *Milton and Scriptural Tradition: The Bible into Poetry*. University of Missouri Press, Columbia, pp. 117–41.

Gallagher, Philip J. (1990) *Milton, the Bible, and Misogyny*. University of Missouri Press, Columbia.

Hamlin, Hannibal (2004). *Psalm Culture and Early Modern English Literature*. Cambridge University Press, Cambridge.

Hannay, Margaret (1976) "Milton's Doctrine of the Holy Scriptures," *Christian Scholar's Review* 5, 339–49.

Kerrigan, William (1974) *The Prophetic Milton*. University Press of Virginia, Charlottesville.

Kirby, R. Kenneth (1984) "Milton's Biblical Hermeneutics in The Doctrine and Discipline of Divorce," *Milton Quarterly* 18, 116–25.

Labriola, Albert C. (1981) "'Thy Humiliation Shall Exalt': The Christology of Paradise Lost," *Milton Studies* 15, 29–42.

Lewalski, Barbara K. (1966) *Milton's Brief Epic: The Genre, Meaning, and Art of "Paradise Regained."* Brown University Press, Providence, RI.

Lewalski, Barbara K. (1970) "*Samson Agonistes* and the 'Tragedy' of the Apocalypse," *PMLA* 85, 1050–62.

Lieb, Michael (1981) *Poetics of the Holy: A Reading of "Paradise Lost."* University of North Carolina Press, Chapel Hill.

Lieb, Michael (2006) *Theological Milton*. Duquesne University Press, Pittsburgh, PA.

MacCallum, Hugh (1962) "Milton and the Figurative Interpretation of the Bible," *University of Toronto Quarterly* 31, 397–415.

Park, Youngwon (2000) *Milton and Isaiah: A Journey through the Drama of Salvation in "Paradise Lost."* Peter Lang, New York.

Patrides, C. A. (1966) *Milton and the Christian Tradition*. Clarendon Press, Oxford.

Pecheux, Mother Mary Christopher (1971) "Sin in *Paradise Regained*: The Biblical Background," in Joseph Anthony Wittreich Jr, ed., *Calm of Mind: Tercentenary Essays on "Paradise Regained" and "Samson Agonistes" in Honor of John S. Diekhoff*. Press of Case Western Reserve University, Cleveland, OH, pp. 49–65.

Radzinowicz, Mary Ann (1983–4) "*Paradise Regained* as Hermeneutic Combat," *University of Hartford Studies in Literature* 15–16, 99–107.

Radzinowicz, Mary Ann (1989a) "How Milton Read the Bible: The Case of *Paradise Regained*," in Dennis Danielson, ed., *The Cambridge Companion to Milton*. Cambridge University Press, Cambridge, pp. 207–223.

Radzinowicz, Mary Ann (1989b) *Milton's Epics and the Book of Psalms*. Princeton University Press, Princeton, NJ.

Reichert, John (1992) *Milton's Wisdom: Nature and Scripture in "Paradise Lost."* University of Michigan Press, Ann Arbor.

Ryken, Leland (1984) "*Paradise Lost* and Its Biblical Epic Models," in James H. Sims and Leland Ryken, eds, *Milton and Scriptural Tradition: The Bible into Poetry*. University of Missouri Press, Columbia, pp. 43–81.

Sadler, Lynn Veach (1973) "Coping with Hebraic Legalism: The Chorus in Samson Agonistes," *Harvard Theological Review* 66, 353–68.

Sansone, David (2006) "How Milton Reads: Scripture, the Classics, and that Two-Handed Engine," *Modern Philology* 103, 332–58.

Schwartz, Regina M. (1988) *Remembering and Repeating: Biblical Creation in "Paradise Lost."* Cambridge University Press, Cambridge.

Schwartz, Regina M. (2003) "Milton on the Bible," in Thomas Corns, ed., *A Companion to Milton*. Blackwell, Oxford, pp. 37–54.

Shawcross, John T. (1975) "The Etymological Significance of Biblical Names in Paradise Regain'd," *Literary Onomastics Studies* 2, 34–57.

Shawcross, John T. (1984) "Milton and Covenant: The Christian View of Old Testament Theology," in James H. Sims and Leland Ryken, eds, *Milton and Scriptural Tradition: The Bible into Poetry*. University of Missouri Press, Columbia, pp. 160–91.

Shawcross, John T. (1993) *John Milton: The Self and the World*. University Press of Kentucky, Lexington.

Shawcross, John T. (2003) "Confusion: The Apocalypse, the Millennium," in Juliet Cummins, ed., *Milton and the Ends of Time*. Cambridge University Press, Cambridge, pp. 106–19.

Sims, James H. (1962) *The Bible in Milton's Epics*. University of Florida Press, Gainesville.

Sims, James H. (1979) "Milton, Literature as a Bible, and the Bible as Literature," in J. Max Patrick and Roger H. Sundell, eds, *Milton and the Art of Sacred Song*.: University of Wisconsin Press, Madison, pp. 3–21.

Sims, James H. and Ryken, Leland, eds (1984) *Milton and Scriptural Tradition: The Bible into Poetry*. University of Missouri Press, Columbia.

Steadman, John M. (1984) *Milton's Biblical and Classical Imagery*. Duquesne University Press, Pittsburgh, PA.

Urban, David V. (2004) "'Rousing Motions' and the Silence of God: Scripture and Immediate Revelation in *Samson Agonistes* and *Clarel*," in Robin Grey, eds., *Melville and Milton: An EditiOn and Analysis of Melville's AnnotatiOns On Milton*. Duquesne University Press, Pittsburgh, PA, pp. 87–107.

Wall, John N. Jr (1978) "The Contrarious Hand of God: *Samson Agonistes* and the Biblical Lament," *Milton Studies* 12, 117–39.

Wittreich, Joseph (1986) *Interpreting "Samson Agonistes."* Princeton University Press, Princeton, NJ.

Wittreich, Joseph, ed. (1975) *Milton and the Line of Vision*. University of Wisconsin Press, Madison.

Wittreich, Joseph (1975) "'A Poet amongst Poets': Milton and the Tradition of Prophecy," in Anthony Joseph Wittreich Jr, ed., *Milton and the Line of Vision*. University of Wisconsin Press, Madison, pp. 97–142.

Wittreich, Joseph and Patrides, C. A., eds (1984) *The Apocalypse in English Renaissance Thought and Literature: Patterns, Antecedents, and Repercussions*. Cornell University Press, Ithaca, NY.

CHAPTER 20
John Bunyan

Andrew Bradstock

"*Pilgrim's Progress* seems to be a complete reflection of Scripture," wrote Matthew Arnold of John Bunyan's most famous literary work.[1] It was an opinion endorsed by the historian J. R. Green: "So completely had the Bible become Bunyan's life that one feels its phrases as a natural expression of his thoughts. He had lived in the Bible til its words became his own."[2] By comparison, Bunyan's own assessment of his attitude to Scripture at the time of his coming to faith seems a touch modest: "I was then never out of the Bible, either by reading or meditation."[3] This chapter explores Bunyan's relationship with Scripture – as he defends it against those who take a lower view of its authority, as it leads him to conversion and (after much wrestling) to an assurance of his eternal salvation, as he relates it to the practice of the church, and as he explores its truth metaphorically. That biblical truth can operate at the level of metaphor gives him the courage to adopt the same approach, to powerful effect.

Bunyan's literary output is truly phenomenal for one who enjoyed little formal education. Between 1656 and his death in 1688 he published no fewer than forty books, with another twenty appearing posthumously. Some of his better-known and most enduring works – including *Grace Abounding* and Part One of *The Pilgrim's Progress* – were written during his two spells of imprisonment (November 1661 to March 1672 and December 1676 to June 1677), while a third of the writings published during his lifetime were penned in his last five years. What is also remarkable is the influence his better-known writings have enjoyed: most commentators suggest that, since its first publication, *The Pilgrim's Progress* has outsold all other books excepting the Bible, having been translated into more than two hundred languages and received approbation from literary giants as diverse as Johnson, Pushkin, Kipling, and Shaw.

Yet, despite this phenomenal legacy, the literary influences on Bunyan himself may well have been few. He tells us that his (unnamed) first wife, whom he married in 1649 at the age of twenty, brought to the marital home Arthur Dent's *Plaine Man's Path-way to Heaven* and Bishop Lewis Bayly's *Practice of Piety*, both of which they read together and in which Bunyan found things that were "somewhat pleasing."[4] Both helped to shape his thinking at an impressionable age, the latter being particularly important in encouraging him to devote his life to religion. Bunyan also immersed himself in Martin

Luther's *Commentary on the Epistle to the Galatians* – which he knew in a translation of 1575 – and his dependence on the German reformer surfaces particularly strongly in his spiritual autobiography, *Grace Abounding to the Chief of Sinners*. He wrote that he preferred Luther's book before all others he had seen, excepting the Holy Bible, "as most fit for a wounded conscience" (though he seems unaware of who Luther was, supposing that he lived hundreds of years before him).[5] During his first period of imprisonment he bought a copy of Foxe,[6] which would both have deepened his appreciation of Luther and provided inspiration for the torments Christian endures on his journey. But it was the Bible, in the Geneva, King James, and (occasionally) Tyndale versions, that inspired, informed, and infused his thinking throughout his life: it permeates not one but each of his more than sixty writings.[7] In the last writing published during his lifetime, *Solomon's Temple Spiritualized*, he specifically acknowledges not having "fished in other men's waters; my Bible and Concordance are my only library in my writings."[8] In prison in 1665 he counted himself, having the Bible still with him, "far better furnished than if I had without it all the libraries of the two universities."[9]

Bunyan's emphasis on the Bible over university-learning may well have been a function of his education. Bunyan enjoyed only the most basic formal training: "my parents ... put me to school, to learn both to read and write ... though, to my shame I confess, I did soon lose that little I learned" is how he himself describes it in *Grace Abounding*.[10] He acknowledges his ignorance of Aristotle and Plato and admits to having borrowed the Latin he uses in his writings.[11] It is therefore unsurprising that in his approach to the Bible he eschews scholarship and is concerned instead, as John Knott has suggested, "with recovering the original simplicity of the Word of God and conveying what [he] perceived to be its extraordinary power to transform the individual and society."[12] With others in the Reformed tradition Bunyan upheld the right of all to read and interpret Scripture for themselves, and saw positive danger in that work being left to the educated divines and "carnal priests" who "tickle the ears of their hearers with vain philosophy and deceit."[13] If it was necessary to know Greek in order to understand the Scriptures, he asserted, "then but a very few of the poorest sort should be saved."[14] An admirer of Bunyan, Charles Doe, who produced an early catalogue of his writings, recorded an argument between Bunyan and "a scholar" over who had the original of Scripture. Bunyan sent the scholar packing by "proving" that the English version he had was as true a copy of the original as the other's.[15] Bunyan made a virtue of his humble station: the saints of God "are for the most part a poor, despised, contemptible people" he wrote.[16]

This triumph of the humble believer over the educated scholar reveals not only Bunyan's conviction that his own Spirit-taught understanding of Scripture is of infinitely more value than any formal education in "divinity," but also, as both Christopher Hill and E. P. Thompson have argued, his class politics. Hill, whose seminal studies of the seventeenth-century radicals from a Marxist perspective have influenced generations of scholars and activists, notes how Bunyan consistently attacked the rich and gave his unsavory characters the titles of gentlemen and lords: "more servants than masters, more tenants than landlords, will inherit the kingdom of heaven," he notes Bunyan writing in 1658, concluding that his writings "were seen to have subversive social content, whether or not he subjectively so intended."[17] Hill and Thompson both stress the extraordinary influence Bunyan's works have had in the radical dissenting tradition. Hill observes, with tongue only slightly in cheek, that Bunyan's great allegory might even have become China's "earlier little red book" had the Taiping rebels succeeded, as they so nearly did, in conquering China in the mid-nineteenth century. Next to the Bible it was the favorite book of the leader of this radical Christian sect, Hong Xiuquan, who may well have made it compulsory reading in what he called the New Jerusalem, his capital city, Nanjing.[18] Edward Thompson famously described *The Pilgrim's Progress* as, with Paine's *Rights of Man*, "one of the two foundation texts of the English working-class movement." In Bunyan, Thompson suggests, "we find the slumbering Radicalism which was preserved through the eighteenth century and which breaks out again and again in the nineteenth" – though, as Wakefield dryly notes, "the effect of *The Pilgrim's Progress* in Nonconformist homes was not to encourage revolution"![19] Thomas Cooper, the Chartist leader, esteemed Bunyan's classic allegory the "book of books."

Yet, however much Thompson and Hill find Bunyan the champion of working-class rights, he betrays little interest in formal politics. Indeed, considering that he lived through one of the most turbulent, unstable, and revolutionary periods in English history, Bunyan conveys little of this political context in his writings. In the year following his birth in Bedford, 1629, Charles I began his eleven-year "personal rule," and Bunyan was just fourteen when the tension between king and Parliament spilled over into civil war. At sixteen he was conscripted into the parliamentary army and posted to the garrison at Newport Pagnell, in the neighboring county of Buckinghamshire, where he remained until demobilization in 1647. Newport Pagnell was a center of radical debate at that time, where Bunyan would undoubtedly have encountered the ideas of the Levellers, who argued that no one owed obedience to any ruler for whom they had not had the opportunity to vote; the Fifth Monarchists, with whom he may have associated at one time and who anticipated the imminent return of King Jesus in fulfillment of a prophecy in Daniel once the last great empire had ended with the execution of Charles Stuart; and perhaps also the Diggers, who believed that no land should be privately owned, the Earth having been created a "common treasury" for all. He certainly witnessed the anarchic and shockingly irreligious behavior of the Ranters because he tells us about it in *Grace Abounding*. Shortly before his demob the King surrendered, and very soon after it the rank and file of the New Model Army and its leaders debated the future shape of government in Putney church. Bunyan was twenty when the King was executed, the House of Lords abolished, and – for the only time in English history – a republic proclaimed. With the Restoration in 1660, Bunyan was convicted and imprisoned for ten years for preaching – technically for holding "unlawful meetings and conventicles" – released following a relaxation of the law, and then briefly imprisoned again some five years later. Bunyan lived to see the death of Charles II and succession of James II, and died three months before William of Orange landed at Torbay.

One can only imagine the impact that the experience of serving in Cromwell's army and openly debating hitherto proscribed subjects might have had on a young country boy like Bunyan. In the case of many of his contemporaries it led to engagement in political struggle and identification with the various movements and sects that took advantage of the breakdown of censorship in the 1640s to come together to pursue their aims. Bunyan, however, appears not to have joined any political movement or espoused any particular cause, notwithstanding that his writings display an evident sympathy with the "common people" over against the nobility, as suggested above, and that, in later life, he fell foul of the civil and ecclesiastical authorities who found both the fact and content of his preaching profoundly subversive. His main preoccupations throughout were his preaching, writing, pastoral responsibilities, and the well-being of his own soul. He shared the millenarian expectations of most of his radical contemporaries – he wrote in 1658 that he thought the judgment day was "at hand," the graves "ready to fly open," and the trumpet "near the sounding"[20] – but unlike some did not try to read out of the Book of Revelation a schedule for the last days. He shared the widespread belief that Antichrist was the Pope.[21]

In his preaching and writing Bunyan certainly took on some of the key religious, if not political, conflicts of his day. He disliked, for example, the approach to Scripture adopted by many of the Quakers with whom he came into contact. Some denied outright that the Bible was the Word of God, and all put more emphasis on the "spirit within" than the plain word of Scripture. Like many mystics, Quakers lived by the dictum "the letter killeth, the spirit giveth life," and saw little merit simply in a belief in a set of doctrines or the historicity of events as described in the Bible: it was the inner working of the Spirit, the "light within," that changed people. Bunyan, however, though he saw a vital role for the Spirit in applying Scripture to the human heart, understood salvation to be dependent upon the literal, historical birth, death, resurrection, and second coming of Jesus of Nazareth as related in the Bible, and employed some of his most vivid prose to challenge Quakers to say whether "the very Man" who was "crucified on Mount Calvary between two thieves" is "with that very body," within them. "What Scripture have you to prove, that Christ is, or was crucified *within* you, dead within you, risen within you, and ascended within you?" he asks in *Some Gospel Truths Opened*, proving his own case by reference to the Lucan account of the resurrected Jesus inviting the disciples to touch his body to prove he is not mere spirit.[22] Interestingly, while many Quakers would not have shared Bunyan's assumption that the matter could be resolved by reference to Scripture, his chief opponent, Edward Burrough, in taking up Bunyan's challenge, did attempt to refute him using biblical texts.

For a time Bunyan saw Quakers in the same light as Ranters, who regarded doctrines such as the Resurrection and Second Coming as metaphors for inward transformation. Ranters thought the Bible should be as open to criticism as any other historical document. Radical antinomians who held sin, heaven, and hell to be wholly imaginary, Ranters were noted for their sexual immorality, drunkenness, and blasphemy, and Bunyan's hostility to them may have arisen in part from his awareness of how close he came to joining them. The temptations they laid before him, he admitted, were "suitable to my flesh, I being but a young man, and my nature in its prime."[23] The Ranters' skepticism about concepts such as bodily resurrection or final judgment also appealed to Bunyan in his times of spiritual doubt, providing a convenient solution to the fears he experienced when he encountered references in Scripture to sin and damnation but no means to counter them in the book itself.

In contrast to the Quakers and Ranters, Bunyan upheld the Bible itself as the word of God, and his propensity to see scriptural texts as both feeding and relieving spiritual anxiety lies at the heart of his approach to the Bible. For Bunyan, the Bible is crucial for an understanding of the essentials of salvation – namely knowledge of one's self and of God – and therefore the Scriptures must be searched until satisfaction is found. This approach is seen most clearly in *Grace Abounding*, in which texts flash into his mind from all parts of the Bible, one minute to comfort, the next to disturb. In this Bunyan's debt to Luther, with whom he feels a deep empathy, is palpable: just as the latter, desperate to find peace with a God who could never accept him on account of his sins, wrestled with Paul's teaching on justification by faith in Romans 1 until it became for him "the very gate of heaven," so Bunyan, no less weighed down (like Christian) by the demands of the law of God, finds himself "trembling under the mighty hand of God, continually torn and rent by the thunderings of his justice" and thus led, "with great seriousness, to turn over every leaf, and with much diligence, mixed with trembling, to consider every sentence, together with its natural force and latitude."[24]

"His torment is that of an unlearned man who must search the Scripture with the conviction that any one verse can save or damn him," writes Knott of the author of *Grace Abounding*.[25] One minute he can "look into the Bible with new eyes" and find the epistles of Paul "sweet and pleasant," the next he can alight upon another text from Paul and find himself questioning whether he had any faith at all, fearing the word had "shut me out of all the blessings that other good people had given them of God."[26] On one occasion Bunyan notes how the words "my grace is sufficient" darted in upon him, but they did not give him the assurance he needed because the remainder of that Scripture, the words "for thee," was left off. Eventually the full verse did break in upon him, three times in succession, but despair returned again as he recalled the plight of Esau who, having sold his birthright, "found no place of repentance, though he sought it carefully with tears." In a particularly poignant passage Bunyan recalls wondering, if both these Scriptures should meet in his heart at once, which of them would get the better of him.[27] Sometimes a text would come to him that he could not find in Scripture at all, leading him to search until he did locate it. On one occasion he searched for "above a year" until he eventually discovered an elusive phrase in the Book of Ecclesiasticus in the Apocrypha.[28]

Bunyan records in *Grace Abounding* his gratitude to his pastor, John Gifford, whose preaching and friendship clearly had a stabilizing effect on him. Bunyan seems to have joined Gifford's church in Bedford around the age of twenty-five and to have been impressed by his counsel not to put his trust in the teaching of any human being but to implore the Almighty to give him conviction "by his own Spirit, in the holy Word."[29] Such conviction was, of course, exactly what Bunyan needed, buffeted as he was by texts warring against themselves in his consciousness – a process that seems to have continued despite Gifford's intervention. Bunyan's salvation, like Luther's, eventually came through a discovery of the righteousness of God, by an understanding that nothing he could do himself could make him right with God: his righteousness is "Jesus Christ himself, the same yesterday, and to-day, and for ever."[30] But it was a tortuous process, not least since Bunyan saw Satan himself at work in the struggle, pulling him this way and that and disputing his interpretation of Scriptures that should have given him comfort. Satan could even persuade him that a verse such as "him that cometh to me I will in no wise cast out" could not include him.[31]

Bunyan's struggle only makes sense if one understands the authority that he invested in Scripture as the Word of God. The role that the Bible played in Bunyan's conversion cannot be underestimated, which is why he defended it so passionately against Quakers and other skeptics. The verses Bunyan reads and remembers may seem to contain contradictory messages, but Scripture is the only source of the knowledge he craves – assurance of his place among the elect of God – and therefore a resolution must be found within its pages. As Roger Sharrock has put it, Bunyan, like the majority of Puritan English people of his day, "believed that each verse of the Bible, taken out of its context, still held a message of truth" – a message that applied directly to him.[32] Thus, when he is beset by fear that he has committed the unforgivable sin, he considers the gory fate of Judas Iscariot recorded in Acts 1 will be his. He admits to turning his head on hearing Jesus' words to Peter in Luke 22, "Simon, Simon, behold, Satan hath desired to have you": "I thought verily … that somebody had called after me," he records, "and although that was not my name, yet it made me suddenly look behind me, believing that he that called so loud meant me." He identifies with Esau as he sells his birthright and with it any hope of salvation, yet he also has no doubt that when Christ spoke the words "and yet there is room" he did so specifically with Bunyan in mind, knowing that he would be afflicted with fear that there was no place left for him in his bosom.[33] In a very real sense did Bunyan "live in the Bible."

A powerful example of the authority Bunyan invests in the Bible, and in every part of the Bible in equal measure, is found in *A Few Sighs From Hell, or The Groans of a Damned Soul*, a very early work published in 1658. This is an extended reflection on the parable of Dives and Lazarus (Luke 16:19–31), in which the writer presents an urgent, pastoral warning to his readers to heed the fate of the one damned into Hell before it is too late. Bunyan takes the opportunity in this book, upon reaching the point where Abraham advises Dives that those he has left behind do not need a special visitor but should heed Moses and the prophets, to expound on the text "all Scripture is given by inspiration of God, and is profitable for doctrine, for reproof, for correction, for instruction in righteousness" (2 Timothy 3:16, 17). For Bunyan the "all" is pivotal – "Do but mark these words, 'All scripture is profitable.' ALL; take it where you will, and in what place you will, 'All is profitable'" – and as proof thereof he presents a lengthy quasi-catechism drawing upon the broad sweep of Scripture to answer a wide range of existential questions he imagines his reader might pose.

"Wouldst thou know what thou art, and what is in thine heart? Then search the Scriptures and see what is written in them" is Bunyan's premise, which he follows with a series of questions concerning the whole gamut of Christian doctrine from Creation, Fall, and original sin through the vicarious death of Christ to the final preservation of the saints – each question being answered by references drawn from every part of Scripture with, in many cases, invitations to compare other Scriptures.[34] A page or two later Bunyan again demonstrates the coherence of Scripture, marshaling texts from Job, Isaiah, Matthew, Acts, 1 Corinthians, Hebrews, Jude, and Revelation in one short paragraph devoted to forewarning sinners of the danger of unbelief.[35] But despite his sustained appeal to Scripture and palpable mastery of the text, what is essential for

Bunyan is that his readers do not simply search the Scriptures and become conversant with them but experience a "real application of him whom they testify of" to their souls. Bunyan is clear that those who read the Bible often, encountering regularly the "sad state of those that die in sin, and the glorious estate of them that close in with Christ" yet "lose Jesus Christ," will "fare a great deal the worse," notwithstanding their "reading so plentifully of him" than others.[36]

Bunyan felt that one of the worst temptations he experienced was to question the being of God and the truth of his Gospel, and argued that even if, at times, the Scriptures will be "a dead letter, a little ink and paper," there is no alternative to them if one is to discover the light of God.[37] Not that Bunyan escaped doubting the authority of the Bible on occasions. In 1649 a translation of the Qur'an began circulating in England, and Bunyan records in *Grace Abounding* how, "for about the space of a month," he was led to ask how one can tell "but that the Turks had as good Scriptures to prove their Mahomet the Saviour, as we have to prove our Jesus is?" Succumbing once again to the condition we would now recognize as "obsessive compulsive disorder," Bunyan speaks of being subject to floods of blasphemous thoughts that led him to doubt whether God or Christ existed and "whether the holy Scriptures were not rather a fable, and cunning story, than the holy and pure Word of God." "Every one doth think his own religion rightest," Bunyan reflects with disarming honesty, "both Jews and Moors, and Pagans! and how if all our faith, and Christ, and Scriptures, should be but a think-so too?"[38] Hill considers Bunyan unique in owning up to such subversive beliefs.[39]

Bunyan saw Scripture as normative not only for the individual Christian life but also for the practice of the church. In *A Case of Conscience Resolved*, published in 1683, he considers whether there is scriptural warrant for meetings that only part of the church may attend – a question occasioned by the practice of some women in his Bedford congregation to meet for prayer without men present. Bunyan was concerned about such meetings, believing they "wanted for their support, a bottom in the word," but also recognized that the church could ill afford to lose its women members, many of whom "for holiness of life have outgone many of the brethren."[40] (Women also constituted two-thirds of the membership.) In making his case that sections of the church ought not to separate themselves for worship, Bunyan lists the types of assembly for worship recorded in the Bible and admits his inability to find any occasion where women meet for worship by themselves (he discounts the example in Philippi recorded in Acts because there was no church in the city at that time). He also argues that the (male) elders of the church cannot perform their duties if they are precluded from attending certain meetings of the church. Whatever the private views of the pastor, elders, members, or even women of the church, for Bunyan only what Scripture says matters: "Take heed of letting the name, or good show of a thing, beget in thy heart a religious reverence of that thing: but look to the word for thy bottom, for it is the word that authorizeth, whatever may be done with warrant in worship to God; without the word things are of human invention, of what splendour or beauty soever they may appear to be."[41] Fortunately for Bunyan (and the other males in the church), bringing the women's meetings to an end did not cause dissension in the church, Bunyan noting that the women were "so subject to the word ... and so willing to let go what by that could not be proved a duty for them."[42]

While Bunyan justifiably claims to lean on Scripture to settle the matter, other factors clearly influenced him, including his knowledge that it was a tenet of the Ranters and Quakers that women should enjoy a degree of autonomy within the church. Bunyan also understands appointing meetings for divine worship to be "an act of power," and elsewhere takes a literal interpretation of references in St Paul to women being subject to their husbands and without authority to teach[43] (notwithstanding that when Christian and his companions reach the House Beautiful in *The Pilgrim's Progress* it is women who decide whether they should be admitted). A number of dissenting congregations took a different line, some allowing women to preach, teach, prophesy, and have other leadership roles, and it was a paper possibly from a minister of a similar theological hue (a "Mr K," perhaps William Kiffin) that sparked the controversy in Bunyan and Gifford's church when circulated among the women members.

Bunyan is very clear that biblical truth operates at the level of metaphor. In his apology for writing *The Pilgrim's Progress* he notes how the prophets "used much by metaphors to set forth truth" and how the Bible is full of "dark figures, allegories." St Paul may have warned his prodigy Timothy against indulging in "old wives' fables" but he never forbade the use of parables. The paradox for Bunyan is that, while Scripture employs shadows and types and dark forces at every turn, it does so the more to illuminate its truth. As darkness is followed by light, as a pearl needs bringing to the surface, so allegory enables truth to casts forth its golden rays. And Bunyan's logic is that, if such a literary form is to be found working so effectively in Holy Writ, none can gainsay his humble employment of it also: "My dark and cloudy words they do but hold / The truth, as cabinets enclose the gold."[44] Bunyan most powerfully employs metaphor in relation to the Christian's journey, of which the exodus experience of the Israelites, and Abram's obedience to the call of God to leave his country for an undisclosed destination, are the pre-eminent models. A passage in *The Heavenly Footman* – of uncertain date though presumed to have been written several years before *The Pilgrim's Progress* – clearly demonstrates Bunyan's dependence on this narrative, in this and his later work: "Because the way is long (I speak metaphorically), and there is many a dirty step, many a high hill, much work to do, a wicked heart, world, and devil, to overcome; I say, there are many steps to be taken by those that intend to be saved, by running or walking, in the steps of that faith of our father Abraham. Out of Egypt thou must go through the Red Sea; thou must run a long and tedious journey, through the vast howling wilderness, before thou come to the land of promise."[45] As Knott perceptively points out, Bunyan's use of metaphor operates on two levels: "The way is the path of all Christians through the wilderness of the world, the way 'From This World To That Which Is To Come,' and simultaneously the inner way of faith of the individual believer." Bunyan draws upon images in the Psalms of walking in the way of the righteous, and those Paul uses of walking "in the Spirit" and "in newness of life." Here his dependency on both testaments of Scripture to make his case is again evident, though, as Knott rightly says, the New Testament meaning trumps the Old: "Faith must be attested by a genuine 'newness of life'."[46]

Bunyan's use of metaphor can also be quite subversive: in *The Water of Life*, published shortly before his death in 1688, he compares the grace of God to water, which "naturally descends to and abides in low places, in valleys and places which are undermost," but which does not flow over steeples. This grace is held in "low esteem ... with the rich and the full" because it is primarily "for the poor and needy." "They that can drink wine in bowls ... come not to this river to drink."[47] Hill finds political comment in the narrative in *The Pilgrim's Progress* where Christian and his companion Great-heart are persecuted by giants who enclose public lands and the king's highway; "hedges" in the radical literature of Bunyan's day, Hill notes, represent private property over against land held in common, and it is not until Christian and his companion reach Immanuel's Land that land becomes common property.[48] "The great ones of the world," Bunyan notes in *A Few Sighs from Hell*, "will build houses for their dogs, when the saints must be glad to wander, and lodge in dens and caves of the earth."[49] The whole of *The Pilgrim's Progress* is arguably a metaphor of the lifestyle forced upon many of the poor and lowly in Bunyan's day, the itinerants and "masterless" folk.[50]

Scripture may have been an indispensable feature of Bunyan's conversion experience but, as *The Pilgrim's Progress* demonstrates, it must be the believer's constant companion through the whole of life, the key to understanding the right path, to avoiding pitfalls and temptations. When trapped in the Slough of Despond, Christian is reminded by his rescuer, Help, that the Lawgiver has provided "certain good and substantial steps" to enable the traveler to pass through it in safety. When tempted away from his path by Mr Worldly-wiseman to seek freedom from his burden by an easier means, he needs to be reminded by Evangelist of texts from Hebrews warning of the peril of refusing to hear "him that speaketh from heaven" (12:25) and of "drawing back" from the way of faith (10:38). Christian is only able to overcome Apollyon when he is in possession of his two-edged sword, a metaphor for the word of God Bunyan would have found in Hebrews 4:12. The nearest Christian comes to being devoured by his adversary is when his sword flies from his hand, and on recapturing it he quotes Scriptures from Micah ("Rejoice not against me, O mine enemy: when I fall, I shall arise," 7:8) and Romans ("Nay, in all these things we are more than conquerors, through Him that loved us," 8:37).[51] Christian benefits much from the instruction in the gospel that he receives from the good companions he meets on his journey, and finds in the Word both the wherewithal to overcome the many trials and temptations he encounters and what he needs in terms of comfort and consolation. Yet, as throughout, he needs also the Spirit of God to bring him, as his pastor John Gifford pointed out, conviction of the truth of the Word. As Knott has argued, Christian's difficulty in winning his duel with Apollyon suggests a certain shortfall in faith requiring the intervention of the Spirit to enable him to handle his sword aright. Bunyan would be clear that all Christians need the aid of the Spirit in order to understand Scripture.[52]

Bunyan's genius was to make the Bible accessible to the ordinary woman and man, the humble pilgrim weighed down with their burden of sin in a dangerous and hostile world. Bunyan's qualification for this task was his own humble origins and lack of learning and sophistication, his identification with the carpenter of Nazareth who was also rebuked for presuming to speak from such a lowly station. His heroes are all simple folk, characters with whom his readers could identify: his villains all gentry and titled folk, people with authority and learning who, like Pilate, might know Hebrew, Greek, and Latin yet miss the life-changing truth of the gospel. Christ's "little ones," Bunyan explicitly tells us, "are not gentlemen," whereas "sins are all lords and great ones."[53]

Employing what Frei and Lindbeck have called an "intratextual" approach to Scripture,[54] where the whole of Scripture is understood as a unified narrative against which one interprets one's experience, Bunyan enables his reader to "live in the Bible" as he himself does. Bunyan shows that the ordinary believer might attain heaven, might lose his or her burden at the cross, and might understand, with the aid of the Spirit, how the Scriptures can make them "wise unto salvation."

Notes

All references to Bunyan's own writings are taken from George Offor, ed., *The Works of John Bunyan*, 3 volumes (Blackie, Glasgow, 1854; Banner of Truth Trust edition, 1991).

1   Norman Mable, *Popular Hymns and Their Writers* (Independent Press, London, rev. edn 1951 (1944)), p. 52.
2   Edmund Venables, *Life of John Bunyan* (Great Writers Series, London, 1888), ch. IX.
3   Offor, I, p. 11.
4   Offor, I, p. 7.
5   Offor, I, p. 22.
6   He refers to Foxe in *Grace Abounding*: Offor, I, p. 41.
7   Offor notes that occasionally Bunyan quotes Scripture from memory, confusing various versions: III, p. 382.
8   Offor, III, p. 464.
9   Offor, III, p. 398.
10 Offor, I, p. 6.
11 Offor I, p. 495; III, p. 202.
12 John R. Knott Jr, *The Sword of the Spirit: Puritan Responses to the Bible* (University of Chicago Press, 1980), p. 4.
13 Offor, III, p. 715–16.
14 Christopher Hill, *A Turbulent, Seditious and Factious People: John Bunyan and his Church* (Oxford University Press, Oxford, 1989), p. 140; cf. Offor, III, p. 695.
15 Offor, III, p. 767.
16 Offor, III, p. 676.
17 Christopher Hill, *The World Turned Upside Down: Radical Ideas During the English Revolution* (Penguin, Harmondsworth 1975 (1972)), p. 405; Hill, *A Turbulent, Seditious and Factious People*, p. 372.
18 Hill, *A Turbulent, Seditious and Factious People*, p. 375.
19 E. P. Thompson, *The Making of the English Working Class* (Penguin, Harmondsworth 1968), p. 34; Gordon Wakefield, *John Bunyan the Christian* (HarperCollins, London, 1992), p. 3.
20 Offor, III, p. 722.
21 See *Of Antichrist, and his Ruin* (published posthumously), Offor, II, pp. 41–82, esp. p. 76.
22 Offor, II, p. 175.
23 Offor, I, p. 11.
24 Offor, I, p. 38.
25 Knott, *The Sword of the Spirit*, p. 132.
26 Offor, I, pp. 11–12.
27 Offor, I, pp. 31–33.
28 Offor, I, p. 13.

29   Offor, I, p. 20.
30   Offor, I, pp. 35–6.
31   Offor, I, p. 33.
32   Roger Sharrock, *John Bunyan* (Macmillan, London, 1968), p. 64.
33   Offor, I, pp. 26, 17, 30–1, 14.
34   Offor, III, pp. 708–9.
35   Offor, III, p. 714.
36   Offor, III, pp. 709–10.
37   Offor, III, 711.
38   Offor, I, 17; on Bunyan's state of mind see Gaius Davies, *Genius and Grace*, London: Hodder & Stoughton, 1992, ch. 2.
39   Christopher Hill, *The English Bible and the Seventeenth-Century Revolution* (Penguin, London, 1993), p. 235.
40   Offor, II, pp. 659–60.
41   Offor, II, p. 671.
42   Offor, II, p. 660.
43   For example, in *Christian Behaviour* (1663), Offor, II, pp. 548–74, esp. 560ff.
44   Offor, III, p. 86.
45   Offor, III, p. 382.
46   Knott, *The Sword of the Spirit*, p. 140.
47   Offor, III, pp. 541, 543, 545.
48   Hill, *The English Bible*, p. 131.
49   Offor, III, pp. 676–7.
50   Hill, *The World Turned Upside Down*, p. 406 and ch. 3 passim.
51   Offor, III, pp. 92, 95, 113.
52   Knott, *The Sword of the Spirit*, pp. 147–8.
53   Offor, III, pp. 695, 130.
54   David Dawson, "Allegorical Intratextuality in Bunyan and Winstanley," *Journal of Religion* 70 (1990), pp. 189–201.

CHAPTER 21
John Dryden

Gerard Reedy, S.J.

Enlightenment philosophers sometimes reduced complex matters to a provocative simplicity. With regard to the canon of the Bible and the authority to interpret it, for example, Thomas Hobbes opined: leave it to the King. Likewise, Spinoza answered competing biblical interpreters: read it as you would nature. These remarks were repeated again and again in radical circles between 1660 and 1700 (Hobbes, 1651, pp. 294, 303; Spinoza, 1670, pp. 98–106). John Dryden (1631–1700) eschewed these rationalist sound bites. In almost all matters, but especially when reason tentatively met faith, as in Scripture, he liked to set out opposites, even extremes, study them, and present tentative conclusions. As the expertise needed to read Scripture grew, he preferred a "more modest" way than rationalist truisms about how and by whom Scripture could be read. This chapter explores Dryden's approach to Scripture, and in doing so positions him in relationship to the political and biblical controversies of his day.

We might begin by acknowledging the vast range of Dryden's references. When John Dryden celebrated or condemned a person or subject in verse, in prose, and in dramatic dialogue, he tended to write within four areas of reference, none uncommon for a learned man of his day. First, he saw himself as part of an evolving history of English writing, which he himself depended upon and continued. He was conscious of an evolution that began in Chaucer, and continued through Shakespeare, that he and others, whom his poems and prose honored, carried on in the current age. He also understood that his age had a new attitude to the physical world. Very conscious of the work of the Royal Society in creating experimental, rather than deductive, natural science, he also advanced the idea that a new prose was being written of which he was an exemplary practitioner. This plain style communicated, as the Royal Society desired, rather than disguised reality. Third, he wrote within the context of Latin and Greek models and languages that he knew very well. His education at Westminster School and at Trinity College, Cambridge, gave him an excellent knowledge of Latin and Greek and the best literature written in them from Homer through Aristotle, Horace, and especially Virgil. Of these frames of reference, Dryden perhaps most naturally moved in a classical frame of thought and composition.

Lastly, Dryden lived in a world interpreted by Scripture. For Dryden, "Scripture" meant the Authorized Version of 1611, the King James Bible, of whose style and (as they were told) accuracy English men and women were proud. Those more interested in the subject could take up, as Dryden no doubt did, the magnificent six volume *Biblia Sacra Polyglotta*, edited and published by Brian Walton and a group of ejected Anglicans and Presbyterians in the late 1650s. Assembling rare manuscripts and typefaces, inventing more economical publication, Walton published in nine languages all the reputable translations of Scripture he could find. In his Latin preface, Walton praised the unity of Scripture: although often translated, it everywhere witnessed common doctrine (Wrangham, 1827, p. 321). While conscious of succeeding criticism, Dryden accepted the state of affairs given by Walton as he began serious discussion of Scripture in the 1680s, namely that the often translated text remained accurate in essentials.

Dryden relied on Scripture for political and poetic verse. Besides offering metaphors of creation and deluge, and sin and redemption, Scripture founded discussion on a number of topics relatively new in the late seventeenth century. It was debated whether and which heroes and histories of the Old Testament, for example, provided useful parallels for the characters and events of contemporary history. Dryden exhibits particular interest in the Old Testament, drawing most of his biblical engagements from a few books: a survey of his poetry shows that he found only the Old Testament useful in providing ancient, religious analogies to what went on about him in the 1660s and later. Even in the Old Testament, only parts of Genesis, Exodus, and 2 Samuel provided the most useful parallels to him of the current events he wanted to interpret.

In addition to this analogical use of the bible, Dryden also weighed into a new, original development in approaches to Scripture: Dryden and his contemporaries subjected the very text of Scripture to critical analysis, for the mistakes of copyists in the Scripture manuscripts themselves questioned whether even the essential doctrines of Christianity were faithfully transmitted and taught. The conflict between authority and impartiality found in Scripture study also being played out in Dryden's own field, literature and literary criticism. Dryden immersed himself in these controversies and became a spokesperson for the proper analysis of Scripture. Thus what makes Dryden unique in the study of the relations between Scripture and literature is that he not only used scriptural imagery, but also wrote about current controversies concerning the text of Scripture, and what guides best helped a true reading.

Scriptural Politics

Charles II arrived from his exile on the continent in late May 1660, was crowned King of England on April 23, 1661, and reigned until his death in 1685. During these years Dryden occasionally disagreed with individual political positions Charles advocated, although he was in the main a strong supporter. Recent scholarship supports the idea that by the early 1680s Dryden was in fact a government propagandist.

Because Charles crossed the English Channel in 1660, writers who sought scriptural parallels to his brief journey naturally settled on the figures of Noah, who survived the great flood, and Moses, who crossed safely through the Red Sea. There are hundreds of examples of these tropes. In his own poem on Charles's coronation in 1661, Dryden

joined this host of parallel-seekers to situate the year 1660–1 in the context of Noah.
This is what Dryden wrote at the start of his coronation poem:

> In that wild Deluge where the World was drownd,
> When life and sin one common tombe had found,
> The first small prospect of a rising hill
> With various notes of Joy the Ark did fill:
> And when that flood in its own depths was drownd
> It left behind it false and slipp ry ground;
> And the more solemn pomp was still deferr'd
> Till new born Nature in fresh looks appeard:
> Thus (Royall Sir) to see you landed here
> Was cause enough of triumph for a year:
> Nor would your care those glorious Joyes repeat
> Till they at once may be secure and great:
> Till your kind beams by their continued stay
> Had warmd the ground, and calld the Damps away. (Dryden, I, p. 33)

How and why does Dryden create this complicated analogy? First of all, I think, it is
for political reasons that Dryden isolates for metaphorical use not Noah, the full journey
of one man; nor the sins of the many and their punishment by flood; nor the covenant
of the rainbow, which seems one of the principal points of the story of Noah in Scripture.
Dryden picks an exact time in the Genesis story (8:6–12), when Noah keeps sending
out a dove to see if the earth is dry, until the dove returns with an olive branch. While
the passage reinforces no obvious theme of Genesis, Dryden finds that it usefully answers
a political question asked between May 1660, when the King arrived home, and his
coronation almost a year later: why did the King experience such trouble during this
period? For in this year, even during general rejoicing, there is a rebellion in London,
armed though easily put down; Charles suffers deaths in his family; and old and new
friends scrap for places in church and state. That many properties had old (Stuart) and
new (Cromwellian) owners added to the wealth of public dispute that had to be settled
by the King.

The comparison of 1660–1 to an obscure period in the saga of Noah enables Dryden
to answer the political question (why so much trouble?) in a non-political way. The
analogy with Noah indicates simply that divinely ordered events may take place in a
way and time that are unpredictable, with the divine ordering presumed, not argued.
Only once, when Dryden calls the ground "false and slipp'ry," does he let his guard
drop, for, although there are no immoral characters in this part of Noah's story, Dryden
slips them in to cover his present-day judgment. Though the biblical analogy does not
fully cover what Dryden thinks of opposition to Charles, God can write in crooked lines;
thus troubles in 1660 and 1661, which have a happy ending, do not deny divine
design.

Dryden's scriptural analogies can be read within two continuums, one between
scriptural and secular history, and a second between the rhetorics of amplification and
irony. When we note that Dryden adds a detail to strengthen contemporary reference
at the cost of fidelity to Scripture, we are reading inside the first continuum. Secular

history overcomes scriptural. But the question of Dryden's intention, amplification or irony, remains. Hyperbolic scriptural analogies to political leaders were commonplace for parliamentary leaders during the 1650s. Stuart poets of the 1660s had to do better, but did not want to abandon the genre of amplification, evidenced by the introduction of a Noah, Moses, or David. Indeed probably both Dryden and Charles II would bore easily at amplification without irony. Although the coronation poem elevates Charles in comparing him to Noah, the countervailing irony arises from a self-regard and self-satisfaction in the verse. The verse showily contains, in its last three couplets, complex actions: the country needs recuperation from the joy of Charles's landing at Dover in May 1660 before it can rejoice again; the King's "care" would not stage another cele-bration before public safety and a proper degree of magnificence was assured; and the King, sun-like, should warm the hearts of all his subjects. Both amplification and the poet's self-satisfaction vie pleasantly for our attention. Indeed, whenever Dryden creates complicated scriptural analogies, a sense of his own accomplishment intrudes.

This relationship of Dryden's biblical poetry to political affairs continued throughout the reign of Charles II, reaching full expression with the Exclusion Crisis and Dyrden's poem *Absalom and Achitophel*. This poem emerges at a fraught political moment. Broadly speaking, tension surrounded the reign of Charles II. First, Charles II's father and pre-decessor was beheaded in London in January 1649; his brother and successor, James II, fled into exile at the end of 1688. In contrast to both father and brother, Charles II brought about many diplomatic and domestic triumphs, especially a long reign. Many political and religious tensions that he both inherited and caused also harried him. Roman Catholics and nonconformists sought legal protection within the framework of the Anglican establishment. The King's spending patterns needed deeper and steadier revenues than he could provide. England continually had to situate herself against varying postures of European states, especially France and Spain. Most of all, as his reign progressed, Charles was unable to solve the problem of the constitutional rights of his brother, James II, a not so secret Roman Catholic. More specifically, especially in the early 1680s, figures hostile to Charles II and his brother tried to bring into the Houses of Lords and Commons legislation that would exclude James from the throne, substituting James, Duke of Monmouth, an illegitimate son of King Charles, as the logical, Protestant heir. Partisan pamphlets, plays, sermons, and poems announced an "Exclusion Crisis," and affirmed or denied the reality of a "Popish plot."

Phillip Harth has accomplished a definitive ordering of phases of the Exclusion Crisis and its aftermath. He situates Dryden's great poem, *Absalom and Achitophel* (1682), in the third stage of the Crisis, when public opinion had begun to turn toward the King and when the reality of an alternative "Protestant plot" against Charles began to be widely believed (Harth, 1993, pp. 94–102). Based on 2 Samuel 13–19, Dryden's poem compares and contrasts Charles as King David; his illegitimate son, Monmouth, as Absalom, son of David; and the Duke of Buckingham as Achitophel, Absalom's mentor. Never before or after did Dryden attempt biblical parallelism on such a large scale. His extended narrative has an elaborate cast of characters, a temptation scene, and a final triumph for David-Charles, and apparently is equaled by no other poet of the time, even though many used the section from 2 Samuel as the basis for their commentary on current events. Harth shows how King Charles, by dismissing Parliament at the poem's end, saves not only himself but the nation, and thereby becomes a figure of special divine providence. Charles-David is fallible in his hesitation in acting against Absalom, but at the same time, at the beginning and end of the poem, "Godlike." Chosen as leader of a nation, like David, he saves the English monarchy and polity from the disastrous chaos planned by his enemies.

In molding materials from 2 Samuel, Dryden shows his originality by creating a long and consistent narrative, by making David the central character in the drama, and by his masterful blend of history and irony. As he accommodates the narrative of 2 Samuel to his current needs as an activist historian of contemporary politics, he elicits the presence of the two continuums mentioned above: he plays secular against sacred history, and brilliantly modifies typology with irony.

Dryden's satiric use of biblical parallel begins in the first verse paragraph of the 1682 poem:

> In pious times, e'r Priest-craft did begin,
> Before *Polygamy* was made a sin;
> When man, on many, multiply'd his kind,
> E'r one to one was, cursedly, confin'd:
> When Nature prompted, and no law deny'd
> Promiscuous use of Concubine and Bride;
> Then, *Israel*'s Monarch, after Heaven's own heart,
> His vigorous warmth did, variously, impart
> To Wives and Slaves: And, wide as his Command,
> Scatter'd his Maker's Image through the Land. (Dryden, II, p. 5)

As in the coronation panegyric, Dryden begins his scriptural parallels in one corner of the political map: Charles II's bastards. Without Monmouth/Absalom, there would be no Exclusion Crisis, and no poem. So Dryden approaches the King's promiscuous fatherhood first.

Restoration divines believed that scriptural exegesis should build on the historical background of the text; in the poem Dryden parodies the historical introduction of many sermons by unexpectedly supplying an irreligious background. He begins his biblical apology for the King's promiscuity by describing a pseudohistorical time when Kings could legally have many spouses and when nature, not censorious priests, set the rules. The introduction praises the warmth of Charles's sexual activity, outrageously suggestive of the divine command to Adam to multiply. In this never-never land that parodies contemporary scriptural interpretation, virtue is stingy and the King's promiscuity good and divinely ordered. The books of Samuel of course do not offer a justification of polygamy. Dryden does not let such digressions from sacred history bother the poem's speaker. Indeed, how one characterizes the speaker thus notes his placement on a continuum from typology to irony. The speaker's tone varies as the poem moves along – sometimes justifying David's actions by biblical paralleling, sometimes judging them by more complex strategies.

Politics and poetics continue to unite in Dryden's verse after the ascension of James II. After Charles II died in 1685, his Roman Catholic brother, James II, lasted only three years on the throne, in great part owing to the ferocity with which he pressed his religion on the government, church, and universities. Sometime during this period, Dryden became a Roman Catholic, a point to which I shall return later in this chapter. Moreover, it appears Dryden felt that a Roman Catholic Renaissance was imminent in England. This feeling animates a beautiful ode that Dryden wrote, probably between 1685 and 1688, celebrating the union of two Roman Catholic families in marriage, "On the Marriage of the Fair and Vertuous Lady Mrs. Anastasia Stafford with a Truly Worthy and Pious Gent. George Holman, Esq. A Pindarique Ode." After Holman had voluntarily exiled himself to France around 1680, he became a leader and benefactor of Catholics also in exile. Anastasia Stafford was a child of the Viscount Stafford executed – or, for Dryden, martyred – in the Popish Plot in 1680.

At the end of the present version of the poem, Dryden imagines Holman in France as Joseph feeding the Israelites (Genesis 47:12):

> For Providence designed him to reside,
>   Where he, from his abundant stock,
>   Might nourish God's afflicted flock,
> And, as his steward, for their wants provide.
>   A troop of exiles as his bounty fed,
>   They sought, and found him with their daily bread;
> As the large troop increast, the larger table spread.
>   The cruse ne'er emptied, nor the store
>   Decreas'd the more;
> For God supplied him still to give, who gave in God's own stead.
>   Thus, when the raging dearth
>   Afflicted all the Egyptian earth;
>   When scanty Nile no more his bounty dealt,
>   And Jacob, even in Canaan, famine felt:
>   God sent a Joseph out before:
>   His father and his brethren to restore. (Dryden, III, p. 206)

As is his wont, Dryden uses only a small part of the Joseph story for his poetic needs: Joseph's supplying grain to his brothers and father. In *The Hind and the Panther* (1687) and *Eleanora* (1692), he uses different parts for different needs. The abundance of Joseph's gifts in the wedding ode, like many other images therein, suggests the abundance of resources and graces about to befall English Catholics.

Secular and sacred history evenly animate this imagery: each element from Scripture illuminates Holman's accomplishment. Moreover, Dryden's self-congratulatory ingenuity, though present, provides no strong ironic counterpart to Holman's noble generosity. In fact, in recalling Stafford earlier in the poem, Dryden cautions against rationalized reading of human experience:

> Now, let the reasonable beast, called man;
>   Let those, who never truly scan
>   The effects of Sacred Providence,
>   But measure all by the grosse rules of Sence:
>   Let those look up and steer their sight,
>   By the great Stafford's light. (Dryden, III, p. 205)

In their immediate context, these lines challenge an interpretation of Stafford or Holman that does not allow them to be God's providential agent, as Joseph was. In the full context of Dryden's life, the lines form part of the package of changes that his conversion brought and that are rarely outlined. The weighty words to "the reasonable beast, call'd man" address not only whether God works in the late seventeenth century as he had in biblical times, but also what place reason and science have in reading history, and what place the "grosse rules of sence" have in the proper reading of Scripture that so interested Dryden. One might be grateful that Dryden had never before publicly exhibited what might be an annulling seriousness, for he would therefore significantly have diminished his wit. Although the formal needs of this "ode" differ from those of the coronation "panegyric" and the "poem" *Absalom and Achitophel*, Dryden's Catholic hopes and dreams also modify the continuum between typology and irony so that the irony, in this historical moment, fades.

Interpretation

In the 1680s Dryden, along with many other English virtuosi, turned their attention to problems in Scripture. For centuries the principal denominational arguments about Scripture concerned the meaning of individual passages, especially the meaning of passages dealing with miracles, Holy Communion, the primacy of Peter, the Trinity, and the divinity of the Son. In the late seventeenth century, however, writers such as Thomas Hobbes, Spinoza, and Richard Simon began to question Scripture in a way that undermined not only its content, but also its textual integrity. These authors showed that Scripture, owing to the carelessness of the scribes, was full of errors that had occurred, it was alleged, not through malice, but simply through the carelessness necessarily involved in centuries of copying and transmission. For example, the French Roman Catholic priest Richard Simon amassed evidence of scribal changes and mistakes in chronology in commonly used Old Testament editions. Specifically Simon shattered the proof for truth by authorship by giving empirical evidence that the Old Testament books were written by multiple authors at different times from different cultures. Moses, he argued, was a committee. Cutting the cord from God that let an individual author give life to his individual work, Simon allowed the possibility that each work was an assembly of discrete passages untraceable to one hand (Simon, 1682, pp. 18–23, 24, 26–7, among others). Truth came not from the authorial person, but from the content of the fragments as reason judged them. When Simon presented his evidence in *A Critical History of the Old Testament*, translated in 1682, Dryden appended a long answer to it in the poem he was writing that became *Religio Laici* (1682) (Harth, 1968, pp. 174–200). *Religio Laici* seems interested in both types of truth, emerging from author and reader, although its argument, which ends but doesn't close, cannily switches sets of opposites, from author and content to scholarly speculation and the religion of the common man.

This issue of the inaccuracy of Scripture excited significant controversy among Dryden and his contemporaries. Liberal church of England apologists, usually called Latitudinarians, answered the growing evidence of inaccuracies in the text by means of a distinction. Some matters and places in Scripture were more important than others. Some essential matters have been faithfully, exactly preserved in transmission. Other matters and places perhaps have admitted errors of transmissions, but these places contain teaching that is not essential to human salvation (Reedy, 1985, pp. 101–4). Although apologists were reluctant to enumerate doctrines that were essential, a few important doctrines concerning the Jesus event would be on the assumed list. Whenever Anglicans use the word Socinian, they mean theologians who questioned the accuracy of essential texts on matters such as the Trinity and the divinity of Jesus.

Such questioning of the accuracy of texts essential to salvation had to be answered, as Dryden tries to do in *Religio Laici*. In doing so, Dryden approaches a problem that concerned both Protestants and Catholics. Most obviously inaccuracies alarmed Protestants who based their faith directly upon the Bible: as William Chillingworth wrote in 1638, the Bible is the religion of Protestants. Indeed, seventeenth-century English Protestants minimized the need for anything but a knowledge of Scripture and common sense to reach the essential truths of Christianity. Even as "High" Anglicans also acknowledged a need for scholarly help, nevertheless the basis of Anglican religious faith was undermined if it were shown that the biblical text itself was so confusing as not to support consistent truths. Furthermore, the research of critics such as Richard Simon revealed that biblical issues caused not only a Protestant but also a Catholic problem. The Catholic problem involved notions of authority. If religious truth could not be based on Scripture, then an institution like the papacy, with a united front that made official Scripture readings, assured religious stability. But at what price to notions of individual freedom? Some Catholics balked at so strengthening the power of Rome. For them the word "tradition" came to mean not only the Pope but also the General Councils of the Church. Dryden discusses the Protestant problem in the second half of *Religio Laici*. He discusses the Catholic problem in *The Hind and the Panther* (1687). In both discussions, he follows for the most part a moderate position.

These two poems on interpreting the Bible illustrate Dryden's brilliant use of a customary shape of his verse: the heroic couplet. Dryden's couplet reaches perfection in these poems in both discipline and variety. The perspicacious student of Dryden, reading the couplets of these two poems, notices (a) caesuras changing places in the central feet of succeeding lines; (b) how the parts of speech of the rhymes vary; and (c) the complex, ever changing relationship between the couplets and the syntax of the sentences that compose them. The first line of a couplet, for example, can be the subject of the sentence, a whole sentence, or several options in between. All these effects change mere skill to brilliance as Dryden builds a creative tension between repetition and novelty.

Dryden introduces a further constraint into the composition of *Religio Laici* and *The Hind and the Panther*. The theological sources of the two poems, readily available in research libraries and, now, on the Internet, state the Anglican and Roman Catholic orthodoxy on guides for reading Scripture that Dryden, mostly without exception, wanted to follow. It is challenging to write hundreds of lines of lucid heroic couplets, and doubly so to convey others' complex ideas in them. Dryden's great success at this conveyance not only renders theological texts accurately, but also allows us to see how and when he departs from them.

In the period after 1660, the line between politics, theology, and literature was not so finely drawn. In his education at Westminster School and Trinity College, Dryden would have known and made friends with a number of men who later became leaders of the Church of England, and wrote significant apologetical works. Dryden made great use of Latitudinarian theology in *Religio Laici*. He thanks a clergyman in his preface, perhaps John Tillotson, a prominent Latitudinarian; he borrows his arguments in both halves of his poem from works by Tillotson and others. Although Dryden presses the radical questions posed by Richard Simon somewhat harder than his contemporaries do, his arguments are, in the main, Latitudinarian commonplaces.

In *Religio Laici* Dryden marvelously condenses an Anglican view of why Scripture is true.

> If on the Book it self we cast our view
> Concurrent Heathens prove the Story *True*:
> The *Doctrine, Miracles*; which must convince,
> For *Heav'n* in *Them* appeals to *Humane Sense*. (Dryden, II, pp. 113–14)

He first argues from comparative history: non-religious history confirms sacred history. "The *Doctrine, Miracles*," especially complex, refers to a common Anglican argument: Moses, Matthew, Paul, and so on, wrote the books that bear their names; the Bible also attests to the miracles these writers caused; God allows them to do so as a way of certifying the truth of the doctrines they taught (Reedy, 1985, pp. 47–50). Although contemporary critics recognized the circularity of the argument, it had a lasting currency. Since the argument ties Scripture's truth to the character of its authors, any evidence that establishes authorship was valuable. Parts of Edward Stillingfleet's *Origines Sacrae*, a studied compendium of orientalia, amount to an intellectual biography of Moses (Stillingfleet, 1666, pp. 107–49). Employers of the authorship argument noted that we have as much evidence that Moses wrote Exodus, and Luke the gospel assigned to him, as we have that Herodotus wrote the *Histories*.

Articulating Laditudinarian beliefs in *Religio Laici*, at the start of the second half of his poem, Dryden versifies the troubling arguments of Simon (1682, pp. 258–69). He adds the possibility that only "tradition" can unerringly guide the believer searching for the meaning of scriptural texts. Dryden repeats the answer to these voices by many Anglicans:

> More safe, and much more modest 'tis, to say
> *God wou'd not leave mankind without a way*:
> And that the *Scriptures*, though not *everywhere*
> Free from Corruption, or intire, or clear,
> Are incorrupt , sufficient, clear, intire,
> *In all* things which are needfull Faith require. (Dryden, II, p. 118)

This in the last analysis is how Anglicans during the seventeenth century responded to the new research on the biblical text that suggested it was unreliably corrupt. In answer to a wealth of empirical data, Anglicans (including Dryden) give a theological, a priori answer: God would not leave mankind without a way. But in *Religio Laici*,

Dryden both accepts the a priori response, and adds a disruptive paragraph that poses the true threat in the arguments of Simon and others. What if, asks Dryden, even points necessary to saving faith remain obscure in Scripture because the texts are corrupt (pp. 306–7)? What if even the divinity of Christ, truly a necessary point of belief, has been left uncertain? What if the Socinians are correct in this?

Dryden never answers these questions. He moves the discussion to topics like freedom of speech in England and unlettered Christians who do not have an intellectual view of Scripture. He also advocates consulting the work of learned divines. His honesty consists in bringing up the importance of Socinian arguments, while claiming the innocence of a layman in being unable to answer them properly. Dryden insists that God has exercised his providence over the text and truths of Scripture, but acknowledges problems he cannot answer about the stability of important Christological texts. The argument ends, but it does not close.

Between *Religio Laici* and the anonymous publication of *The Hind and the Panther* in 1687, Dryden in unknown circumstances became, as mentioned above, a Roman Catholic. Although he never documents the process of his conversion, we know that he had to grapple with many issues as he changed denominations. Though the king, James II, was now a Roman Catholic, dissimilarities of religious culture and worship remained, as well as the problem of confronting his own previous attacks on Catholic doctrine. His problems with Anglican scriptural interpretation had often posed questions: who can say, for example, whether needful matters in Scripture are doubtfully expressed? By 1687 he had begun to constitute a new self, sometimes a harsh self that could satirize what the author himself quite recently was. Dryden now regarded Anglican directions for resolving textural ambiguities as a hodge-podge. They were like, he said, a mule:

> But you who fathers and traditions take,
> Garble some, and some you quite forsake,
> Pretending church auctority to fix,
> And yet some grains of private spirits mix,
> Are like a mule made of different seed,
> And that's the reason why you never breed. (Dryden, III, p. 147)

Roman Catholics, Dryden alleged, had an unambiguous means of deciding religious truth:

> I then affirm that this unfailing guide
> In Pope and gen'ral councils must reside;
> Both lawful, both combin'd, what one decrees
> By numerous votes, the other ratifies:
> On this undoubted sense the church relies. (Dryden, III, p. 142)

Because some Roman Catholics in Dryden's time held that the Pope, without a council to help him, could decide what was true in Scripture, Dryden's lines place him among the moderates at this point. Dryden suggested that the two authorities should be "combined."

In one major line of thought, however, Dryden was not a moderate. In *Religio Laici*, with authority from his Anglican sources, he confirmed the primacy of the written text of Scripture: "*Tradition written* therefore more commends / *Authority*, then what from *Voice* descends" (Dryden, II, p. 119). In *The Hind and the Panther*, perhaps five years later, Dryden had changed his mind in a radical way. Joining the Catholic far right, he argued that the primary Christian revelation occurred orally, from Jesus, then the apostles, then others; that this was summarized from time to time in written forms; and that the church's interpretation is needed to recognize and prioritize the oral and written material.

> No written laws can be so plain, so pure,
> But wit may gloss, and malice may obscure,
> Not those indited by his first command,
> A Prophet grav'd the text, an Angel held his hand.
> Thus faith was e're the written word appear'd,
> And man believ'd, not what they read, but heard.
>
> So great Physicians cannot all attend,
> But some they visit, and to some they send.
> Clearness by frequent preaching must be wrought,
> They writ but seldome, but they daily taught. (Dryden, III, p. 149)

Helpful as these remarks are to affirming the need for church interpretive authority, mindful as they are of criticism of the text of Simon and others, they also completely reject the privileging of the Bible that had been Protestant orthodoxy for over one hundred years. Even future development in Catholicism did not support Dryden. In succeeding centuries, mainstream Catholicism taught a theory of two traditions, both text and church, thus rejecting the strange argument of the primacy of oral tradition.

Laditudinarian divines fairly owned English scriptural interpretation from 1660 on, as Dryden acknowledged by his reliance on them in 1682. Given his conversion, it is not surprising that in 1687 Dryden rejected latitudinarian principles. In *Religio Laici* Dryden had preferred to adopt an open, mildly skeptical self as he examined opinions he found doubtful. In *The Hind and the Panther* he blasted both latitudinarian doctrine and its defenders, who openly campaigned for "fat Bishopricks" (III, pp. 172, 181–90). Similar attacks color his 1690 tragedy, *Don Sebastian* (Dryden, XV, pp. 107–9). Dryden's changing stands on Scripture, its text, and its interpretation, accompanied other religious and political decisions he had to make in the late 1680s.

Conclusion

Dryden, during a period of significant political and religious change, charted an interpretative approach to the Bible at once moderate and modest. That he deviated from this rule of modesty in *The Hind and the Panther* only highlights, I think, his usual practice. Certainly, in mediating between scriptural and secular history Dryden's wit occasionally overruled his reverence for the text: he changed a detail or two to make

Scripture fit, or he exaggerated a scriptural virtue or vice. The speakers of his poems leave it to readers to decide whether Charles II is a national savior and the equivalent of David in the 1680s, or whether George Holman is like Joseph, a gift to his people. But in whatever key it is played, the theme of divine providence is presented as a plausible choice for the reader. Even though it is disguised behind human qualities and events that are comically not divine, providence can be seen in experience. That God had worked and was working in history were themes Dryden played in various keys throughout his writing years.

The years 1660 to 1700 in England were an era when vast amounts of new data entered human consciousness, and also new categories of interpretation in which to catalogue that data. Scientific study moved from the accumulation of experiment by the Royal Society to the mathematicization of the physical world by Isaac Newton. Political theorists debated how much authority descended from God, and to whom, a debate that ended in the theories of toleration and consent of John Locke, who also announced a new way of knowing and of reading Scripture. In this last area, Dryden enjoyed a special role, at least in discussing and analyzing the findings of specialists about the text of Scripture, as he reconciled traditional faith with a new empiricism. Lastly, as different norms were bought forward for correct literature, Dryden took preeminence as an arbiter of the rules for this, and, inevitably, as the father of English prose criticism.

Although the historian of Dryden has the right to ask whether his scriptural interpretation resembles his literary, few have ventured into this field. Before one creates the appropriate models to unify the explosion in interpretation that characterize the era, Dryden, a major figure, must be addressed and understood in his approaches to secular and religious texts. I have always found that terms like "rationalist in principle" or "enlightenment" are too heavy handed, self-fulfilling, and distant from the text to be helpful as unifying devices. Dryden's practice turns out to be both sensitive to conflicting issues and evident in the different genres in which he wrote.

Dryden's sage encounter with new and old ideas of the scriptural text offers a good model for assessing his critical readings of secular literature. His literary criticism offers similar sets of oppositions between which he mediates without letting the oppositions cave in. Most importantly, Dryden's literary criticism, like his scriptural criticism, cannot be judged in small doses. Between "An Essay of Dramatic Poesy" (1668) and "A Preface to the *Fables*" (1700), some essays, or parts of essays, may argue what appear to be extremes, but the whole accomplishment of almost fifty long and short essays must qualify our judgment of individual parts. Nor can we easily ascertain a linear progression in his literary criticism. Dryden stopped writing because he died, not because he had solved the problems he returned to again and again.

The extremes in Dryden's literary criticism remain consistent in his forty-year career. He is drawn to the newer, rationalist, often Gallic position that classical, universal norms for genres, action, language, and character exist, with which native English exuberance often conflicts. Works that follow these valuable norms will perdure, as have Greek and Roman plays, from which the norms arise. Yet Dryden also loved the English tradition, which he enumerated and praised. Chaucer, Shakespeare, Jonson, and others intuitively communicated their individual greatness to him. He kept a portrait of Shakespeare before him as he wrote; he knew that Shakespeare's great accomplishment compensated for his violation of the classical norms.

Dryden's way of reading Scripture and literature have nothing and everything to do with one another. Of course, no miracles and inerrancy mark his literary theory. Yet both critical activities reveal an anxiety about the dissociation of textual evaluation from personal values intuitively communicated to an elite towards an objective standard that is democratic, impersonal, and dangerously mechanical. This anxiety – which Dryden admittedly reveals with wit – deeply penetrates his entire pattern of interpretation, whatever text he faces.

References

Dryden, John (1961–) *Works*, 20 volumes. University of California Press, Berkeley and Los Angeles.

Harth, Phillip (1968) *Contexts of Dryden's Thought*. University of Chicago Press, Chicago.

Harth, Phillip (1993) *Pen for a Party: Dryden's Tory Propaganda in Its Contexts*. Princeton University Press, Princeton, NJ.

Hobbes, Thomas (1651) *Leviathan*. Barnes and Noble, New York (2004).

Reedy, Gerard, SJ (1985) *The Bible and Reason. Anglicans and Scripture in Late Seventeenth-Century England*. University of Pennsylvania Press, Philadelphia.

Simon, Richard (1682) *A Critical History of the Old Testament (1678)*, trans. Henry Dickinson. London.

Spinoza, Benedict de (1670) *A Theologico – Political Treatise*, trans. R. H. M. Elwes. New York, Dover (1951).

Stillingfleet, Edward (1666) *Origines Sacrae*, 3rd edn. London.

Wrangham, Francis (1827) *Biblia Polyglotta Prolegomena Specialia*, ed. Briani Waltoni STP. Cambridge.

PART IV
Eighteenth Century and Romantic

CHAPTER 22
Introduction

Stephen Prickett

The changing understanding and status of the Bible in the eighteenth century cannot be appreciated except in relation to the prevailing print-culture – without which such matters could have had little meaning. Printing, moreover, was a political act. At the beginning of the century the Bible had only existed as a printed commercial artifact for about two hundred years, and in that time it had already led to civil wars in Germany, England, and Scotland, and – to say the least – major civil disturbances in many other European countries, including Bohemia, France, the Netherlands, Poland, and Sweden. Religion and politics were, similarly, inextricably entwined. Luther's great translation had reshaped both European history and the German language itself. In England, there had been a series of translations, culminating, of course, in the King James Version of 1611, which, though its initial impact was muted, was also to reshape the English language in scarcely less dramatic ways throughout the following centuries.[1]

Though we should not forget Samuel Butler's assertion that in his own (nineteenth) century, volumes of sermons were given – unread – and were displayed – similarly unread – by the recipients, neither should we allow even the most pardonable cynicism to obscure how the secular and commercial impact of the Bible intermeshed with its perceived spiritual content. It is sometimes difficult for the modern observer to grasp fully the centrality of the Bible, with its associated commentaries, sermons, and theological controversies, to the eighteenth-century British printing industry. The best figures we have available at the moment suggest that whereas there were some five hundred books published during the period, there were over fifty thousand sermons.[2] Present estimates suggest that for every page of secular fiction published in the eighteenth century there were about fifteen pages of sermons or other explicitly religious material. If we recognize that many of the other works in that very heterogeneous category of "books," from Swift's *Proposal for the Abolition of Christianity*, to Hartley's *Observations on Man*, to Sterne's *Tristram Shandy*, or Wordsworth and Coleridge's *Lyrical Ballads*, have a strong undercover "biblical" content, we can begin to get a feeling for the omnipresence of the Bible – affecting the commerce, aesthetics, philosophy, and – not least, if least quantifiable – the spirituality of the age. The world of William Blake was, as much as that of Isaac Watts, the Wesley brothers, or George Whitfield, a world where the printed word was still dominated by the Word of God.

What changed radically in the course of the century, however, was the way in which that Word was understood. Like many great shifts in aesthetic and imaginative consciousness, this was something that would have been better understood in retrospect than it would have been by contemporary observers. Indeed, the very strength of the Evangelical Revival mid-century, with its stress on the unchanging nature of God, and of his Word and Providence, probably obscured rather than highlighted this change. But over time the trend is clear. If one had asked a poet in the early years of the century – say Joseph Addison, author of that well known hymn "The Spacious Firmament on High" (1712) – what should be the models for artistic endeavor, he would have answered with reference to the Greek and Latin classics – especially the latter. "The Psalmist," Addison wrote of Psalm 19 in his prefatory essay, "has very beautiful strokes of poetry to this purpose in that exalted strain. As such a bold and sublime manner of Thinking furnished out very noble Matter for an Ode."[3] In other words, the Bible offered the raw material, but the classical form – the ode – was the appropriate modern form of expression. In contrast, by the end of the century Blake's claim that "The Bible is the Great Code of Art" is probably one of his least eccentric slogans. Similar views are to be found from Coleridge in England, from Chateaubriand in France, or from Schleiermacher or Friedrich Schlegel in Germany.[4]

Yet even in Addison's time other more radical voices were emerging from the most conservative sources. For the modern reader, the description of the Bible by John Sharp, Archbishop of York, in a sermon of 1714, as containing "the great drama and contrivances of God's providence," sounds conventional enough, yet according to the OED this was the first time that the metaphor of the theater had been applied to the Bible.[5] If it has now become a cliché, the image was nevertheless then momentous: the action of the Bible, that is, the outworking of God's sacred purposes, was being viewed – even explained – in terms that were primarily aesthetic. It is no accident that the word "aesthetic" (and to some extent, even the concept itself) dates from the late eighteenth century.[6] In Germany, what was virtually a new subject, "aesthetics," had come into being following Kant's hint in the third *Critique* that the gap between pure and practical reason might be bridgeable by art, and was to become a central plank of Romanticism.

Such profound shifts in sensibility have no one simple explanation. In the light of these aesthetic arguments it would be easy, for example, to point from the drama to the popular literary influence of the great seventeenth-century biblical epics. It has been said that from mid-century almost every household with pretensions to literacy would possess at least three books: *The Bible*, Milton's *Paradise Lost*, and Bunyan's *Pilgrim's Progress*. In the crudest commercial publishing terms these were staples of the book trade – outselling even the most popular novels of the day. At another level they were part of a widespread climate of feeling, expressed at one level by a legion of "Miltonizers" – both English and Continental. Four separate translations of *Paradise Lost* appeared in French during the "long eighteenth century" (1729, 1754, 1787, and 1805) and it was so much admired that it had spawned a host of Francophone imitations. During the same period Milton was also translated into German and Italian (four times each) and into Dutch (twice), not to mention translations into Swedish and Spanish.

But behind this new emphasis on aesthetic form is something else, essentially foreign to the Bible, but that had, from Chaucer to Shakespeare, become increasingly central to English literature: the idea of "character." Though Milton may not have been aware of it when he began his epic, it was an idea that was to transform both the narrative and even the *theology* of the Fall. For Chateaubriand, one of the greatest Romantic admirers of Milton and his finest French translator,[7] writing at the very beginning of the nineteenth century, Milton's creation of character was evidence for the *literary* superiority of Christian civilization over its antecedents. Taking *Paradise Lost* as one of his prime examples, he argued in *The Genius of Christianity* (1802) that Christianity and the Bible had transformed the nature of European literature: "by mingling with the affections of the soul, [it] has increased the resources of drama, whether in the epic or on the stage."[8] Only when Christianity replaced paganism was the modern European idea of character free to develop. It was "a double religion":

> Its teaching has reference to the nature of intellectual being, and also to our own nature: it makes the mysteries of the Divinity and the mysteries of the human heart go hand-in-hand; and, by removing the veil that conceals the true God, it also exhibits man just as he is. Such a religion must necessarily be more favourable to the delineation of *characters* than another which dives not into the secret of the passions. The fairer half of poetry, the dramatic, received no assistance from polytheism, for morals were separated from mythology.[9]

Yet however much Milton may have assisted in the eighteenth-century shift in sensibility concerning the Bible, it is clear that the way in which Milton was interpreted *also* changed radically during the course of the century. Chateaubriand's reading of Milton in terms of dramatic character would have had little traction in the seventeenth century. If, for the neoclassical critics like Addison, Milton's claim to "justify the ways of God to Man" was to be taken at face value, for Blake, eighty years later, he was "of the Devil's party without knowing it." More generally, the swing of the pendulum that had made Milton, the Cromwellian rebel of the mid-seventeenth century, into the upholder of orthodoxy by the early eighteenth, had swung back to Milton the intellectual rebel and upholder of liberty – at least among the pro-French Revolutionary romantics of the 1790s. Perhaps the final stage in the re-evaluation of Milton was to come in 1818 with the publication of Mary Shelley's *Frankenstein*. In this strange defamiliarized retelling of the biblical Creation story, the monster acquires a copy of *Paradise Lost* from the De Lacy household (presumably in one of the four French versions listed above) as part of his crash-course in European history and culture.[10] For him, the Monster tells us, it was a story of tyranny and injustice in which Satan was a fit "emblem" of his condition.[11]

Such a revolution in interpretation of a single "biblical" poet suggests not so much that Milton's influence *caused* any revolution as that it was itself carried along by something much larger and more complex. For some, there is an inherent paradox that the century that saw the advent of the Higher Criticism of the Bible, and the consequent questioning of both its historicity and its veracity, was also the century that saw it rise to new heights as an aesthetic model. This is a paradox present in the very origins of the Higher Criticism itself. Robert Lowth's Oxford lectures on *The Sacred Poetry of the Hebrews* (1753) were not intended in any way to be revolutionary. Much of his framework seems to be derived from the work of Richard Simon in France in the 1680s.[12] Moreover, Lowth published, as he had lectured, in Latin, and he was not even translated into English until 1778. An able Hebrew scholar, he had been elected to the Professorship of Poetry at Oxford in May 1741, and since he was obliged to start lecturing almost at once without time to prepare by consulting the normal academic sources, he seems to have turned to his theme of the Psalms almost by default. Nevertheless, for an age still accustomed to typological and figural interpretations, his first lecture struck a quite new note:

> He who would perceive the peculiar and interior elegancies of the Hebrew poetry, must imagine himself exactly situated as the persons for who it was written, or even as the writers themselves; he is to feel them as a Hebrew ... nor is it enough to be acquainted with the language of this people, their manners, discipline, rites and ceremonies; we must even investigate their inmost sentiments, the manner and connexion of their thoughts; in one word, we must see all things with their eyes, estimate all things by their opinions: we must endeavour as much as possible to read Hebrew as the Hebrews would have done it.[13]

Instead of trying to deduce the medieval fourfold (or sevenfold or twelvefold) meanings divinely encoded within the sacred texts, or following what might be called the "Miltonic" exploration of narrative and character, Lowth was, almost for the first time, trying to understand the biblical writers historically as people of their time within what was known of their social framework. The result was to transform both biblical criticism, and, what was entirely unforeseen, the status of poetry and literature as well.

For Lowth, the prophets and poets of the Old Testament were one and the same:

> it is sufficiently evident, that the prophetic office had a most strict connexion with the poetic art. They had one common name, one common origin, one common author, the Holy Spirit. Those in particular were called to the exercise of the prophetic office, who were previously conversant with the sacred poetry. It was equally part of their duty to compose verses for the service of the church, and to declare the oracles of God.[14]

The Hebrew word "Nabi," explains Lowth, was used to mean "a prophet, a poet, or a musician, under the influence of divine inspiration." The word "Mashal," commonly used to mean a "poem" in the Old Testament, is also the equivalent of the (Greek) word translated in the New Testament as "parable." In other words, the parables of Jesus, so far from being an innovation, were an extension, by the greatest of the biblical "poets," of the existing Hebrew prophetic tradition.

Discussing biblical language, Lowth anticipates and sets the agenda for Wordsworth's theory of poetic diction by implicitly rejecting the stilted conventions of Augustan poetic diction, and praising instead the "simple and unadorned" language of Hebrew verse, which gained its "almost ineffable sublimity" not from artificially elevated diction, but from the depth and universality of its subject matter. In his humble origins, and in the simplicity and directness of his language, Jesus also continues the poetic tradition of the Old Testament. Unlike contemporary European poets, the Hebrew ones had never been part of a courtly circle, but had remained in close touch with the rural and pastoral life of the people, using in their verse (or "parables") the homely metaphors of agriculture and domestic existence.

For Lowth this is evidence for the "sublimity" of biblical language – by which he means naturalness, as against artificiality; the irregular, as against the regular; the mysterious as against the comprehensible. Here he anticipates Burke's *Enquiry into the Sublime and the Beautiful* by a decade or so. For him, as for Burke, sublimity is the ultimate criterion of greatness in art. Foreshadowing Blair and Wordsworth, Lowth goes on to describe the language of poetry as the product of "enthusiasm" "springing from mental emotion." This is another striking innovation: "enthusiasm" was commonly a word of abuse rather than praise – applied more usually to ranters, Methodists, or Quakers. Through Lowth's influence the Bible was to become for the romantics not merely a model of aesthetic sublimity, but also a source of literary style, and a touchstone of true feeling.

Nevertheless, Lowth is not uncritical of his material. In his comments on Isaiah (1778) he discusses the problems of a corrupt text, noting that some sections are "improperly connected, [and] without any marks of discrimination." This was too much for at least one of his admirers, Thomas Howes, Rector of Thorndon, who, in 1783, published his *Doubts Concerning the Translation and Notes of the Bishop of London to Isaiah, Vindicating Ezechiel, Isaiah, and other Jewish Prophets from Disorder of Arrangement*. Howes has no doubts that Lowth's critical method is sound, but in suggesting that there might be breaks in the text, or mistakes in ordering, Lowth is being untrue to his own principles. Taking another giant step toward romantic aesthetics, Howes, by implication, enlists the authority of the Holy Spirit for the new ideas of organic form. Challenging Lowth's preference for chronological order, he suggests either "historic order," that in which the prophecies were actually accomplished, or, "still better," "poetic arrangement," that which "is best suited to the purpose of *persuasion and argumentation*."[15]

> For it has been long conceived, that these prophecies are replete with bold poetic ideas and expressions; the translator [Lowth] with his usual learning and accuracy, has convinced the public, that they are even composed in a similar metre to the other antient poetic works of the Jews: I have only ventured, in pursuance of his example, to advance one step farther in novelty, by shewing, that there are equally good reasons to conceive these prophecies to be put together in a connected method and order, agreeably to such modes of poetic and oratorical arrangement, as were customary in the most antient ages, and this apparently by the respective authors of each prophetic work.[16]

Howes's arguments provide the final tread for the new Jacob's ladder by which the poet has ascended from the neoclassical role of craftsman and decorator to divine authority and prophet.

But if Howes also reinforced the historical argument that poetry is older than prose[17] by claiming that the Holy Spirit used it, this debate was to some extent bypassed by Lowth's second great contribution to critical history, which was nothing less than what he believed to be the construction of Hebrew verse itself. Whereas all European poetry had depended upon such aural effects as rhyme, rhythm, and alliteration, no such forms could be discovered in Hebrew verse – even in the psalms, which were obviously intended to be songs. Nor could contemporary Jews explain the lost art of Hebrew poetry. Lowth was now able to explain in his lectures that the poetry of the ancient Hebrews had depended primarily upon a feature that he called "parallelism."

> The Correspondence of one verse, or line, with another, I call parallelism. When a proposition is delivered, and a second subjoined to it, or drawn under it, equivalent, or contrasted with it in sense; or similar to it in the form of grammatical construction; these I call parallel lines; and the words or phrases, answering one to another in the corresponding lines, parallel terms.[18]

The origins of parallelism, Lowth argued, like the origins of European poetry, lay in the previous oral tradition – in this case in the antiphonal chants and choruses we find mentioned in the Old Testament. He cites, for instance, 1 Samuel 18:7, where David, returning victorious from battle with the Philistines, is greeted by women chanting "Saul hath slain his thousands"; to be answered with a second chorus with the parallel, "And David his ten thousands."[19] Lowth distinguishes no fewer than eight different kinds of parallelism, ranging from simple repetition, to echo, variation, contrast, and comparison – as in the particular case cited, where the implications were not lost on Saul, who promptly tried to have David assassinated.

Here, in eighteenth-century terms, was a source of both character and drama. If, before, dramatic irony had been limited to such obvious moments as Nathan's denunciation of David, it was now possible to see biblical poetry, and much of biblical prose as well, in terms of dramatic narrative. Moreover, in linking Jesus's parables with the prophetic metaphors of the Old Testament, Lowth is further encouraging a sense of ironic and literary meanings – as distinct from figural ones – in the New Testament texts. In the Preliminary Dissertation to his *New Translation of Isaiah*, written in 1778, some thirty years after his ground-breaking *Lectures*, Lowth insists that his quest for scholarly accuracy is grounded in what he calls "the deep and recondite" readings of Scripture.

> The first and principal business of a Translator is to give us the plain literal and grammatical sense of his author; the obvious meaning of his words, phrases, and sentences, and to express them in the language into which he translates, as far as may be, in equivalent words, phrases, and sentences. ... This is peculiarly so in subjects of high importance, such as the Holy Scriptures, in which so much depends on the phrase and expression; and particularly in the Prophetical books of scripture; where from the letter are often deduced deep and recondite senses, which must owe all their weight and solidity to the just and accurate interpretation of the words of the Prophecy. For whatever senses are supposed to be included in the Prophet's words, Spiritual, Mystical, Allegorical, Analogical, or the like, they must all entirely depend on the Literal Sense.[20]

This is not so much a stress on the literal sense for its own sake[21] as a belief that all figurative interpretation must rest on an accurate text. In discussing Isaiah 35:5–6 ("Then shall the eyes of the blind be opened, and the ears of the deaf shall be unstopped. Then shall the lame man leap as an hart, and the tongue of the dumb sing") Lowth is at pains to link it with its standard New Testament antetype: Matthew 9:4–5 ("that the lame walked and the deaf heard"). Indeed, his commentary suggests more a typical medieval fourfold reading than simply the kind of two-level typology more common in eighteenth century commentaries.

> To these [Matthew's words] the strictly literal interpretation of the Prophet's words direct us. ... According to the allegorical interpretation they may have a further view: this part of the prophecy may run parallel with the former, and relate to the future advent of Christ; to the conversion of the Jews, and their restitution to their land; to the extension and purification of the Christian Faith; events predicted in the holy Scriptures as preparatory to it.[22]

Such apparent conservatism would hardly ring alarm bells, yet it is difficult to think of any secular term except "dramatic irony" for what Lowth here sees as conventional biblical typology. Once again, changes in the meanings of words reflect changes in sensibility and outlook. It is significant also that this new meaning of the word "drama," to describe non-theatrical narratives, coincides with the introduction of the theatrical metaphors "scene" and "scenery" to describe landscape.

Lowth's work inaugurated a critical revolution.[23] The Latin text of his *Lectures* was quickly republished in Göttingen (1758) with a new preface and extensive notes by the pioneer biblical scholar Johann David Michaelis, and was partially translated into German by C. B. Schmidt in 1793. Lowth's translation of Isaiah was translated into German the year after its English publication in 1778. They were to prove vital catalysts in German historical criticism of the Bible. For such figures as Eichhorn, Lessing, Reimarus, and Herder, the Bible had to be read not merely as one might read any other book, but specifically as a record of the myths and aspirations of an ancient and primitive Near Eastern tribe. Accounts of God's appearances and other miracles were to be understood primarily as constituents of a particularly powerful and eclectic mythology. Contemporary research had begun to reveal how much of Genesis, in particular, had been appropriated from older Egyptian, Babylonian, and Near Eastern religions. What meaning there was in such stories was moral and developmental rather than historical – illustrating what Lessing, in the title of one of his best-known books, had called *The Education of the Human Race* (1780). If such narratives were to be given a different status from those, say, of ancient Greece or Rome, it was for their "moral beauty" or the profoundly ethical nature of their teachings.

Yet for all the long-term importance of the German Higher Criticism, the fact remains that in Britain its influence on the eighteenth century was slight. In part, the reasons for this were political. During the earlier part of the 1790s, the critical ideas of Michaelis, Reimarus, Lessing, Eichhorn, and even Herder had begun to filter into progressive circles in Britain, often through Unitarian circles. There were even British scholars of international repute, such as the Scottish Catholic priest Alexander Geddes. It is significant that Geddes's work, like that of Richard Simon a century before, was initially seen by his superiors as a new weapon in the conservative armory against Protestantism rather than something that might destabilize the whole subject.[24]

For the English-speaking world in the eighteenth century the most thoroughgoing historical analysis of biblical sources came not from Germany (a source of few translations during this period) but from France. C. F. Volney's *Ruins of Empires* (1791) was a work of massive syncretistic scholarship, drawing in many cases on the work of the German scholars mentioned above. But Volney was also an expert in his own right. In 1781 he had gained an international scholarly reputation by his study of Herodotus's chronology. His next book, *Voyage en Syrie et en Egypt* (1787), had confirmed his status as an Orientalist and earned him a decoration from Catherine the Great. To prepare for that expedition he had spent some time in a Coptic monastery and learned Arabic. Like Herodotus, his first subject, he had been overwhelmed by his first-hand experience of the historical *difference* of past cultures from his own culture and society. For Volney, all the world's major religions could be traced by way of Persia to a common origin in the sun cults of ancient Egypt: "Jews, Christians, Mahometans, howsoever lofty be your pretensions, you are, in your spiritual and immaterial system, only the blundering followers of Zoroaster."[25] Understandably, it was an immediate success in radical circles. No fewer than three editions of two different English translations (both of which Volney thought were unduly moderate in tone) were brought out in 1795–6, and it was a major influence on figures as different as Tom Paine, Godwin, and his-son-in-law Shelley.

By the mid-1790s, however, war against revolutionary France had led to an anti-Jacobin backlash. Unitarianism, with its dangerous radical associations, became politically suspect. Joseph Priestley, the internationally famous scientist, philosopher, and political theorist, perhaps the best-known Unitarian in the country, was forced to flee to America after his house and laboratory was burned by a loyalist mob in 1794. Paine's own attack on religion, *The Age of Reason* (1793), lost him popularity and his natural position as leader of the radical reformers, and he was forced to follow suit. Other influential academics suspected of Unitarian sympathies, such as William Frend (Coleridge's tutor at Cambridge) and Thomas Beddoes at Oxford, were expelled from their fellowships.

Because of these political associations, Higher Criticism – whether French or German – was generally deemed to be Jacobin, unpatriotic and unchristian, and for the next thirty years was virtually ignored in Britain. Not until the 1820s was the intellectual climate again sufficiently favorable for the introduction of continental ideas. Indeed the priorities and standards of the time were revealed by the fact that when, in 1823, the future Tractarian leader and Oxford Professor of Divinity, Edward Bouverie Pusey, wanted to learn about Lutheran theology, he could find only two men in Oxford who knew any German.[26] Cambridge was marginally better off. Herbert Marsh, who had translated Michaelis's *Introduction to the New Testament* (1793–1801), and who had prudently returned to Leipzig for a while after the persecution of Frend, became Lady Margaret Professor of Divinity in 1807. Julius Hare, who became a Fellow of Trinity in the 1820s, and, before becoming rector of Hurstmonceaux, was tutor to both John Sterling and F. D. Maurice, had more than 2,000 books in German.

There were, however, other, more complex, reasons for the different receptions of historical criticism in Britain and Germany. Hans Frei, in *The Eclipse of Biblical Narrative*, argues that though conditions leading to a critical and historical approach to the Bible in the first half of the eighteenth century were roughly comparable in both England

and Germany, the reason why the ways in which they subsequently developed were so markedly different was primarily due to the relative status of prose fiction in the two countries:

> In England, where a serious body of realistic narrative literature and a certain amount of criticism of that literature was building up, there arose no cumulative tradition of criticism of the biblical writings, and that included no narrative interpretation of them. In Germany, on the other hand, where a body of critical analysis as well as general hermeneutics of the biblical writings built up rapidly in the latter half of the eighteenth century, there was no simultaneous development of realistic prose narrative and its critical appraisal.[27]

Frei, of course, is primarily interested in the way in which what we now, following the German, call the "Higher Criticism" failed to be influenced by the development of the English novel, and why English literary criticism correspondingly failed to influence biblical criticism. But in fact there is good evidence to suggest that the rise of the novel in the eighteenth century *did* have a profound effect on the way in which the Bible was read in England – though it did not, as Frei assumes it should, lead to the Higher Criticism. What happened in Britain was that the Bible – and in particular the Old Testament – ceased to be read as though it spoke with a single omniscient dogmatic voice, and began instead to be read as dialogue, with a plurality of competing voices. At the same time, what had been universally accepted as an essentially polysemous narrative, with many threads of meaning, was progressively narrowed into a single thread of story, but instead of interpreting this as being "historical," there is an increasing tendency to read it in terms of narrative fiction.[28]

Laurence Sterne's Sermon 18, for instance, is on the Levite and his concubine (Judges 19). Here the tendency to break into dialogue is so powerful that it completely runs away with the traditional form of the sermon. It opens in a way that, however startling it might have been to the congregation, is instantly familiar to anyone coming to it with the hindsight of *Tristram Shandy*:

> A CONCUBINE! – but the text accounts for it; "for in those days there was no king in Israel;" and the Levite, you will say, like every other man in it, did what was right in his own eyes; – and so you may add, did his concubine too, – "for she played the whore against him, and went away."
>
> – Then shame and grief go with her; and wherever she seeks a shelter, may the hand of Justice shut the door against her!
>
> Not so; for she went unto her father's house in Bethlehem-judah, and was with him four whole months. – Blessed interval for meditation upon the fickleness and vanity of this world and its pleasures! I see the holy man upon his knees, – with hands compressed to his bosom, and with uplifted eyes, thanking Heaven that the object which had so long shared his affections was fled!
>
> The text gives a different picture of his situation; "for he arose and went after her, to speak friendly to her, and to bring her back again, having his servant with him, and a couple of asses; and she brought him unto her father's house; and when the father of the damsel saw him he rejoiced to meet him."

    – A most sentimental group ! you'll say; and so it is, my good commentator, the world talks of everything. Give but the outlines of a story, – let Spleen or Prudery snatch the pencil, and they will finish it with so many hard strokes, and with so dirty a colouring, that Candour and Courtesy will sit in torture as they look at it …

    … Here let us stop a moment, and give the story of the Levite and his concubine a second hearing. Like all others, much of it depends upon the telling; and, as the Scripture has left us no kind of comment upon it, 'tis a story on which the heart cannot be at a loss for what to say, or the imagination for what to suppose; the danger is, Humanity may say too much.[29]

Here a single biblical narrative has become a debate. The congregation's "comments" to the preacher are, in turn, subverted by the conventional wisdom of the "good commentator" ("Then shame and grief go with her"). Nor is this voice the last of these phantom speakers, for no sooner has the speaker fantasized the Levite on his knees thanking God that the woman in his life has at last left him, than we get the dry corrective: "The text gives a different picture." In the final cast all the gossipy qualities of the mind are crowding in: Spleen and Prudery, Candour and Courtesy, the heart and imagination are all offering us their own unasked-for opinions, not to mention squabbling among themselves. In previous sermons Sterne had taken a third-person biblical narrative and "novelized" it with elaborate characterization and direct dramatic speech. But this is something different. Here the dialogue involves partici-pants, critics, and even our own responses and prejudiced opinions: Sterne has in effect turned the biblical commentators *themselves* into dramatic participants in his biblical epic.

    Not all Sterne's sermons work in this dialogic manner. But Sterne was not merely a good preacher, he was, at least in the York area, a famous one.[30] The way in which he can turn biblical narrative into metacritical dialogue is extraordinary – suggesting how far *Tristram Shandy* itself is rooted in the Bible. We should also remember that the sermon, not the novel, was the dominant literary form of the age. Nevertheless, this particular sermon suggests an answer to Hans Frei's problem: historical criticism of the Bible did not take hold in England as in Germany precisely *because* England had a more highly developed novel tradition and theory of prose fiction. For the next generation of English critics, such as Coleridge, it was not the scholarly distancing of historicism so much as the psychological intimacies of hermeneutics that was to fascinate. When Coleridge says that he takes up the Bible to read it for the first time as he would "any other work,"[31] that "other work" is most often the English novel. His assumptions about the nature of the Bible were shaped less by Eichhorn and more by Sterne than he was probably aware of.

    Though one can hardly argue the case for a fundamental shift in the sensibility of a nation on the originality of one novelist, however influential, it is possible to see in Sterne both the beginning and a symptom of a much larger trend. It is there again in the early nineteenth century in Lamb's parallel desire to appropriate Shakespeare into prose narrative: internalized, psychologized, and novelized. If Sterne had begun by choosing to turn certain passages of the Bible into dialogue, Byron could follow by turning others into a play. His *Cain* is one of the first of a whole series of nineteenth-century dramatizations of biblical stories.[32] More significantly, by the early nineteenth century that hermeneutic sea-change had affected even the most conservative biblical commentaries. Though Mrs Trimmer, for instance, makes gestures in the direction of traditional polysemous interpretations, she has no real stomach for any but the literal meaning – and the most obvious of morals to be deduced from it. She has a barely concealed embarrassment in the case of the Levite's concubine. Seventeenth-century commentaries can still quote Ambrose with equanimity, and find in the story a typological condemnation of the laxity of the time;[33] one eighteenth-century commentary examines and rejects a crudely psychologized version from antiquity. Mrs Trimmer, however, finds the whole episode so disturbing that she can only comment on Judges 19, 20, and 21 that:

> These chapters give an account of some shocking and dreadful things that happened in Israel in the days of Phineas the high priest ... when the Israelites had in a great measure forsaken the LORD, particularly the tribe of Benjamin, and committed all kinds of aboninable deeds, which at last occasioned a civil war, and almost all the tribe of Benjamin was cut off.[34]

All opportunity for typology has been abandoned and her response is now entirely dominated by the historical narrative. This is in keeping with her own introduction to the Bible, which, without denying the possibility of figural interpretations, insists on their strictly secondary status:

> it has pleased GOD to cause the HOLY SCRIPTURES to be written with such clearness and plainness, that all who will study them with humility and diligence may understand, as much at least of them as is necessary for their comfort in this world, and their salvation in the next. Those who have but little leisure, therefore, have no occasion to puzzle themselves to find out *hidden meanings* in difficult passages.[35]

A casual reading might suggest that this rejection of hidden meanings and polysemous interpretations represents the triumph of the historical method, but that perpetuates the confusion of Hans Frei's analysis. Mrs Trimmer's criterion is not historical versimilitude; nor does she apparently suspect for a moment that there might be textual problems. On the contrary, she is totally engrossed in the narrative before her and reads it with the same attention to character and plot as she might any secular novel. But, of course, as she reminds us, this is self-evidently much *more* than any secular novel – and hence, in part, her horror at this story once it is read in purely human terms. Here is her introduction to the historical narratives themselves:

> The Books that follow, as far as the BOOK OF ESTHER, are called the HISTORICAL BOOKS. The Histories they contain differ from all the other histories that ever were written, for they give an account of the ways of GOD; and explain *why* GOD *protected and rewarded* some persons and nations, and *why* he *punished* others; also, *what led* particular persons mentioned in Scripture to *do* certain things for which they were approved or condmened; whereas writers who compose histories in a common way, without being *inspired of God,* can only form guesses and conjectures concerning God's dealings with mankind, neither

can they know what passed in the hearts of those they write about; such knowledge as
this, belongs to *God* alone, whose ways are *unsearchable and past finding out*, and *to whom
all hearts are open, all desires known!*[36]

Henry Fielding in *Tom Jones* had compared the novelist to a Calvinistic God, but this is
a Calvinistic God as novelist. Gone are any "hidden meanings," fourfold readings of
Scripture, and the figural interpretations of an Ambrose or an Augustine. This is,
instead, Sterne's novelized and internalized version of the Scriptures read back into the
Bible as a commentary. Its narratives are treated as those of a novel, peopled by characters with recognizable psychological motivations and feelings. The only difference is
that these are *not*, of course, fictional characters, but *real* ones, described for us by the
only truly omniscient Author.

The significance of Mrs Trimmer is that so far from being an original like Sterne,
she is consciously addressing the "unlearned" and writing for "common apprehen-
sions." Indeed, she stresses that her biblical commentary is no more than a compilation
of the most learned and "approved" authorities. She may, nevertheless, be rather more
original than her modesty implies. Though David Norton recognizes a revolution in
taste concerning the literary qualities of the Bible between about 1760 and 1790, his
evidence suggests that claims for the Bible in terms of its characterization (as distinct
from its literary style) were still comparatively rare. Indeed, among his examples only
Samuel Pratt's *The Sublime and the Beautiful of Scripture* (1777) comes anywhere near
such a discussion.[37] But Mrs Trimmer's claim is not about the creation of *literary* character, but the much more literalistic one that God understood the protagonists of the
Old Testament as no human historian or novelist possibly could. And here her modest
disclaimer of originality is itself of interest. If her commentary is indeed no more than
a popular distillation of the conventional wisdom of the time, then it is possible to argue
that what we are looking at is, in effect, the result of a fundamental and permanent
change in the way in which the Bible was read around the end of the eighteenth
century.

To see Lowth, together perhaps with Richard Simon, as fathers of the Higher Criticism is certainly accurate as far as it goes, but that does not exclude an opposite effect:
that the ways of reading the Bible begun with him, so far from leading *only* towards the
Higher Criticism, had also created a new dialogic fiction – eventually so powerful and
all-pervasive that those coming afterwards are scarcely conscious that there might
have been other ways of reading the sacred history. Without anyone apparently being
aware of what has been happening, the new "sentimental" and novelistic way of
reading the Bible had become the accepted norm by the early nineteenth century. The
problem is whether the new way of reading was, as is usually assumed, fundamentally
"historical," or whether it involved something that at first glance looked very like this,
but was in fact much more concerned with seeing the biblical protagonists as individual
characters of the kind made familiar through the new literary genre of the novel and
possessed of a quite new kind of inner consciousness.

At the same time in poetry, Lowth's biblical criticism had triggered off a quite different aesthetic revolution. As we have seen, his *Lectures* not merely opened up a new
historical approach to the context of the biblical writings, but allowed the poet to claim

biblical precedents for a new status: not as a decorator or supplier of "supernumerary ornaments," but as a prophet, seer, and mediator of divine truth. Thus Smart and Cowper, Blake and Wordsworth were given scriptural warrant to cast themselves in a biblical role unimaginable, for instance, to Pope or Gray.

Hugh Blair, first Professor of Rhetoric at Edinburgh University and, in effect, the first professor of English literature in the world, devoted a whole chapter of his *Lectures* (1783) to summarizing Lowth. Not surprisingly, these lectures were one of Wordsworth's main sources for his preface to the *Lyrical Ballads*. But Blair had also seized upon some significant corollaries to Lowth's arguments. Because Hebrew poetry relied on parallelism rather than the rhymes and rhythms of European verse, it was, Lowth claimed, best translated not into verse, but into prose.[38] This, as Blair saw, meant that whereas European and even classical poetry was extremely difficult to translate into another language with any real equivalence of tone or feeling, the Bible was peculiarly, and, by implication, providentially, open to translation. For Blair, such "poetic" prose could still be distinguished from ordinary prose, and the results could be felt in the rhythms and cadences of the King James Bible.

> It is owing, in great measure, to this form of composition, that our version, though in prose, retains so much of a poetical cast. For the version being strictly word for word after the original, the form and order of the original sentence are preserved; which by this artificial structure, this regular alternation and correspondence of parts, makes the ear sensible of a departure from the common style and tone of prose.[39]

Moreover, this was an argument that would work both ways. If the Holy Spirit could be shown to have bypassed conventional forms of verse to write prose – however elevated in tone – traditional distinctions between prose and verse could no longer be held inviolate. To speak of a prose piece as "poetic" could now be much more than a metaphor.

Nor was this shift in critical theory dependent on the writer's own religious beliefs. If such poets as Blake, Coleridge, Cowper, Southey, and Wordsworth were all Christians of a kind, Shelley had been expelled from Oxford specifically for his atheism. He nevertheless centers his *Defence of Poetry* (1821) on Lowthian principles: "Poets, according to the circumstances of the age and nation in which they appeared, were called in the earlier epochs of the world, legislators or prophets; a poet essentially comprises and unites both these characters." "The distinction between poets and prose writers," he continues, "is a vulgar error." "Plato was essentially a poet" – so were Moses, Job, Jesus, Isaiah, Bacon, Raphael, and Michaelangelo. To "defend" poetry he extends his definition to embrace the whole of literature – and, indeed, art in general. Following Lowth, the prophetic function of the artist has become more important than any particular linguistic form. Common to Romanticism right across Europe at this period is a new concept of "Literature" as of inherent value in itself over and above its ostensible subject. The OED lists this value-added variant as the third, and most modern, meaning of the word, defining it as "writing which has a claim to consideration on the ground of beauty of form or emotional effect" – adding the rider that it is "of very recent emergence in both France and England."

If Lowth's biblical criticism had had the unintended effect of transforming both narrative fiction and secular poetry, it was, paradoxically, no less influential in blurring traditional distinctions between the two. His stress on the literary power and "sublimity" of the Bible was to help (though not inaugurate) new ways of appreciating it as an aesthetic work. Though the progressive secularization of the written word has been attributed to many origins, there is no doubt of the part played by the Romantic reading of the Bible. But there is a great deal of evidence to suggest that this new value attached to good writing, whether prose or verse, was already gaining ground in both Britain and Germany as an extension of the Protestant approach to reading the Bible before either Lowth or Kant was published. It is possible to follow a process whereby the intense self-searching and self-constructing relationship to the text fostered by the personal Bible study of Protestantism was subsequently transferred first to the study of the "book" of Nature in seventeenth-century science, then to history, and finally, with the rise of the new art form, the "novel," in the eighteenth century, to the reading of secular fiction as "literature."[40] Not least among the many ironies of critical history is the way in which, just as a literal historical interpretation of the Bible was becoming increasingly impossible for an educated readership, it was to regain much of its old status in a secularized form, as "literature."

Notes

1   See David Norton, *History of the Bible as Literature*, 2 volumes (Cambridge University Press, Cambridge, 1993).

2   That ratio seems likely to increase rather than diminish with further research. Some 12,000 sermons were published individually and, in addition, there were about 2,500 published collections. Estimates are made more uncertain by three complicating factors: (a) because sermons are also recorded in the *English Short Title Catalogue* under such alternative titles as "discourses," or "lectures," it is impossible to be sure how to classify entries without inspection of every text; (b) the great majority of sermons were published in collections, and many title pages do not list their contents; (c) non-Anglican sermons are often not held in research libraries – especially Roman Catholic material but also a lot of the "fringe" dissenting material. I am indebted to Bob Tennant of the English Pulpit project for this information.

3   *The Spectator*, August 23, 1712.

4   See Stephen Prickett, *Origins of Narrative: the Romantic Appropriation of the Bible* (Cambridge University Press, Cambridge, 1996).

5   Sharp, we are told, was a great lover of poetry and the theatre, and was wont to say that the Bible and Shakespeare had made him archbishop. G. Burnet, *History of his own Time, volume III* (London, 1827), p. 100.

6   Though it is, of course, associated with Kant's Third Critique, it seems to have been first used by Baumgarten. See David Bowie, *Aesthetics and Subjectivity: from Kant to Nietzsche* (Manchester University Press, 1990), and *From Romanticism to Critical Theory: the philosophy of German literary theory* (Routledge, London, 1997).

7   His version did not appear until 1836.

8   René François Auguste de Chateaubriand, *The Genius of Christianity* (1802), trans. C. White (Baltimore, 1856), p. 299.

9   Ibid., p. 232.

10 The other volumes being Plutarch's *Lives*, Goethe's *Sorrows of Werther*, and Volney's *Ruins* – also, in its strange way, a biblical epic.

11 Mary Shelley, *Frankenstein or The Modern Prometheus* (Everyman, London, 1912), pp. 133–6.

12 See Françoise Deconinck-Brossard, "England and France in the Eighteenth Century," in Stephen Prickett, ed., *Reading the Text: Biblical Criticism and Literary Theory* (Blackwell, Oxford, 1991), pp. 137–47.

13 Robert Lowth, *Lectures on the Sacred Poetry of the Hebrews*, trans. G. Gregory (1787), vol. i, pp. 113, 114.

14 *Lectures*, vol. ii, p. 18.

15 Thomas Howes, *Critical Observations on Books, Antient and Modern*, 4 volumes (1776–1813, reprinted Garland, New York, 1972), vol. ii, p. 139.

16 Ibid., vol. ii, pp. 442–3.

17 An argument that had been fiercely resisted by such critics as Joseph Trapp, who believed that as the more sophisticated form, it must be later than prose. *Lectures on Poetry* (1742), trans. William Bowyes, asst. William Clarke (reprinted Scolar Press, Menston, 1973).

18 *Lectures*, vol. ii, p. 32.

19 Ibid., vol. ii, p. 53.

20 Robert Lowth, *Isaiah: A New Translation* (1778), 5th edn, 2 volumes (Edinburgh, 1807), p. lxviii.

21 A long tradition of Reformation divines had stressed the importance of the literal meaning, e.g. William Perkins: "there is only one sense and that is the literal," *The Art of Prophecying* (1592).

22 *Isaiah*, vol. ii, p. 232.

23 For a fuller discussion of the implications of Lowth's work see Stephen Prickett, *Words and the Word: Language, Poetics and Biblical Interpretation* (Cambridge University Press, Cambridge, 1986).

24 See R. C. Fuller, *Alexander Geddes* (Almond Press, Sheffield, 1983).

25 C. F. Volney, *The Ruins: or A Survey of the Revolutions of Empires*, first published 1795 (London, 1881), p. 83.

26 David Newsome, *The Parting of Friends* (London, 1966), p. 78.

27 Hans Frei, *The Eclipse of Biblical Narrative: A Study in Eighteenth and Nineteenth Century Hermeneutics* (Yale University Press, New Haven, CT, 1974), p. 142.

28 See Stephen Prickett, *Origins of Narrative*, ch. 3.

29 *Works of Laurence Sterne*, ed. James P. Browne, 2 volumes (1885), vol. II, p. 218.

30 Arthur H. Cash, *Laurence Sterne: the Early and Middle Years* (Methuen, London, 1975), p. 216.

31 S. T. Coleridge, *Confessions of an Inquiring Spirit*, 2nd edn (1849), p. 9.

32 Coleridge had, of course, earlier attempted a "dramatic poem" on the same theme – much of the material of which was later to appear in *The Rhyme of the Ancient Mariner* (1798).

33 See, for instance, Richard Blome, ed., *The History of the Old and New Testaments Extracted from the Sacred Scriptures, the Holy Fathers, and Other Ecclesiastical Writers*, 4th impression (1712), p. 72.

34 Mrs Sarah Trimmer, *Help to the Unlearned in the Study of the Holy Scriptures*, 2nd edn (1806), p. 144.

35   Ibid., p. v.
36   Ibid., p. iii.
37   David Norton, *History of the Bible as Literature*, vol. II, pp. 116–17.
38   Hugh Blair, *Lectures on Poetry and Belles Lettres* (1783), 2 volumes (Edinburgh, 1820), vol. i, pp. 71ff.
39   Ibid., vol. ii, pp. 270–1.
40   See Stephen Prickett, *Origins of Narrative*; and Wesley A. Kort, *Take Read: Scripture, Textuality and Cultural Practice* (Pennsylvania State University Press, Philadelphia, 1966).

CHAPTER 23

Eighteenth-Century Hymn Writers

J. R. Watson

Eighteenth-century hymn writing in English must be seen in the context of the particular course of the Reformation in Britain and its subsequent development. The Bible was the authority upon which the whole practice of Puritan religion was based. As William Chillingworth put it, "I cannot find any rest for the sole of my foot, but upon this rock only."[1] One consequence of this was that throughout the seventeenth century, metrical psalms (psalms translated into metrically regular verse) were produced in version after version: Dod's psalms, Ainsworth's psalms, Wither's psalms, Rous and Barton, the Scottish Psalter, the Bay Psalm Book in America, Patrick's psalms, and finally, *A New Version of the Psalms of David* by Tate and Brady (1696). From this it was a short step to the paraphrasing of texts from the Bible outside the Book of Psalms. One of the best known examples, conveniently dated (for this chapter) at 1700 and the *Supplement* to Tate and Brady's *New Version*, is the paraphrase of the account of the Nativity in Luke 2, "While shepherds watched their flocks by night," in which the narrative is gracefully organised into common meter:

> The heavenly Babe you there shall find
>   To human view displayed,
> All meanly wrapped in swaddling bands
>   And in a manger laid.
>
> Thus spake the seraph; and forthwith
>   Appeared a shining throng
> Of angels praising God, who thus
>   Addressed their joyful song:
>
> All glory be to God on high,
>   And to the earth be peace;
> Goodwill henceforth from heaven to men
>   Begin and never cease.

The singer's task is to repeat the biblical chapter, without trying to apply it or interpret it; although the final verse, taken straight from Luke 14, becomes, in its doxological character and function, a fitting conclusion to the hymn as well as a paraphrase. The song of the angels becomes the verse that gives expression to the feelings of the worshipper, praising God at the news of the Nativity.

Isaac Watts's *Hymns and Spiritual Songs* of 1707 and his *Psalms of David* of 1719 must be seen in this context of paraphrasing and renewing. Book I of the 1707 book is entitled "Collected from the Holy Scriptures" and almost every one of the 150 hymns has a biblical text prefaced to it. In a preface (written much later, 1719–20), Watts described two principles. The first was that of selection, for some parts of the Old Testament were, in his view, either too violent or too exclusively Jewish:

> When we are just entering into an evangelic frame, by some of the glories of the gospel presented in the brightest figures of Judaism, yet the very next line perhaps which the clerk parcels out to us, hath something so extremely Jewish and cloudy, that it darkens our sight of God the Saviour. Thus by keeping too close to David in the house of God, the veil of Moses is thrown over our hearts. (p. i)

The second was to remain faithful to the text, even if it meant a diminution of poetic inspiration (something that Watts set great value by, as can be seen from his poem "The Adventurous Muse" in *Horae Lyricae*). In Book I, he noted:

> I have borrowed the sense and much of the form of the song from some particular portions of scripture, and have paraphrased most of the doxologies in the New Testament, that contain any thing in them peculiarly evangelical; and many parts of the Old Testament also, that have a reference to the times of the Messiah. In these I expect to be often censured for a too religious observance of the words of scripture, whereby the verse is weakened and debased, according to the judgment of the critics.

He went on to defy the critics, deliberately concentrating on readers with "serious" minds, some of whom wanted the Bible because it was dear to them, and some of whom believed, in the Calvinist tradition, that it would be wrong to introduce anything else into worship:

> But as my whole design was to aid the devotion of Christians, so more especially in this part: And I am satisfied I shall hereby attain two ends, namely, assist the worship of all serious minds, to whom the expressions of scripture are ever dear and delightful, and gratify the taste and inclination of those who think nothing must be sung unto God but the translations of his own word.

The hymns of Book I are therefore paraphrases of the text, sometimes with a brief exposition. They allow the text to be revisited metrically, and (as with the last verse of "While shepherds watched") renewed in a sung context. This is one reason why Watts's psalms and hymns were often taken over and adapted by the Scottish church later in the eighteenth century. The transmission of the text is clear and effective, as Watts wanted it to be: his ideas on rhetoric were that it should be the servant of truth, and he distrusted its ability to persuade. He preferred to see rhetoric as producing clarity. His transmission of Holy Scripture, therefore, concentrated on the clear presentation of the text in a new metrical form, making it simultaneously old and new, manifestly from the Bible yet also contemporary. Hymn 3, for example, follows Tate and Brady in recounting the Nativity story from Luke 2, though using short meter:

> "Go humble swains," said he;
> "To David's city fly;
> The promis'd infant born to-day,
>   Doth in a manger lie":
>
> "With looks and hearts serene,
>   Go visit Christ your King;"
> And straight a flaming troop was seen,
>   The shepherds heard them sing:
>
> "Glory to God on high,
>   And heavenly peace on earth,
> Good-will to men, to angels joy,
>   At the Redeemer's birth!"

Here Watts differs from Tate and Brady by keeping the song of the angels as part of the narrative: it is not possible to transfer this text to make it a *Gloria Patri*. But the opportunity of revisiting the narrative of Luke 2 is also valuable: it is a rehearsing of old truths in a form that can be easily sung and remembered.

Human lessons are learned from the Bible, but for the most part Watts does not enlarge upon them. He will open a hymn (hymn 7) with "Let every mortal ear attend," which is a preacher's opening. This hymn, which paraphrases Isaiah 55, does so from a New Testament standpoint:

> Let every mortal ear attend,
>   And every heart rejoice;
> The trumpet of the gospel sounds
>   With an inviting voice.

Watts then launches into his versification of Isaiah's "Ho, every one that thirsteth, come ye to the waters," with a final verse that takes the singer back to the gospel of verse 1:

> The happy gates of gospel grace
>   Stand open night and day,
> Lord we are come to seek supplies,
>   And drive our wants away.

The Old Testament is framed by the New. At other times, Watts can reverse the process and insert an Old Testament reference into a New Testament hymn, as he does in Hymn 125, "With joy we meditate the grace," which is a paraphrase of Hebrews 4:15, 16, and 5:7 linked to Matthew 12:20, but which inserts an image from Isaiah 42:3 as the penultimate verse:

> He'll never quench the smoking flax,
> But raise it to a flame;
> The bruised reed he never breaks,
> Nor scorns the meanest name.

Watts's typological practice is as near as he ever comes to modifying the paraphrase and providing a kind of interpretation. Many of his hymns simply present the text versified for singing, with attendant verses beginning "Praise," or "Come," or "Awake." These also frame the paraphrase, as they do in the celebrated version of Psalm 90. It begins with "Our God" (John Wesley altered this to "O God"), as a reminder that God is "*our* God," the God of those who believe in him, perhaps even the Protestant British God (there are plenty of references to the British Isles in Watts's psalms and hymns), possibly even the dissenters' God. The first lines also offer us a God of the past and the future: "Our God, our help in ages past, / Our hope for years to come." The verses that follow are a straightforward paraphrase of the psalm, bringing out the contrast between "man frail, and God eternal" (as the metrical version is headed). The final verse closes the psalm within Watts's frame, by picking up the first two lines and adding a prayer:

> Our God, our help in ages past,
> Our hope for years to come;
> Be thou our guard while troubles last,
> And our eternal home.

Watts is very clear about where his knowledge of the properties of God comes from:

> 'Tis from the treasures of his word
> I borrow titles for my Lord:
> Nor art, nor nature can supply
> Sufficient forms of majesty. (Book I, hymn 147)

Because art and nature are inadequate, the Bible has a special place in the ordering of Watts's spiritual understanding. We need to remember that he lived in a great age of scientific discovery, and took a great interest in it, so that there is unusual force in

> We learn Christ crucified,
> And here behold his blood;
> All arts and sciences beside
> Will do us little good.

This is from hymn 120 in Book II of *Hymns and Spiritual Songs*, entitled "The Law and Gospel joined in Scripture," one of two hymns on the Bible. The first, hymn 119, is entitled "The Holy Scriptures," and begins by insisting that

> Laden with guilt, and full of fears,
> I fly to thee, my Lord,
> And not a glimpse of hope appears
> But in thy written word.

The Bible is "thy written word," the word of God, and we are fortunate to be able to understand it. We do so because God has permitted his majesty to be communicated to us in images and names. Book I hymn 150 begins by admitting that anything we can say is inadequate, but continues by proposing "all the glorious names" that we can use: prophet, counsellor, shepherd, surety, high priest, advocate, lord, conqueror, king. These are metaphors that allow our limited understanding to perceive something of God, because he "condescends." Although "all names" are "too mean to speak his worth, / Too mean to set my Saviour forth," Watts reflects on the grace that allows us to have an idea of him through linguistic constructs:

> But O what gentle terms,
> What condescending ways,
> Doth our Redeemer use
> To teach his heav'nly grace!
> Mine eyes with joy and wonder see
> What forms of love he bears for me.

God is made accessible through words, and is revealed as love. It is the perpetual need to emphasize the redemption of the world that drives Watts's practice in both psalms and hymns. His paraphrases are consistent in one thing: the need to present redeeming grace as the supreme benefit for humankind. They presuppose a pattern of meaningful life that involves a subscribing to the doctrine of redeeming love as prefigured in the Old Testament and set out in the New Testament, followed by a life in heaven: so "glory ends what grace begun." As one of the greatest hymns from Book III, entitled "Prepared for the Holy Ordinance of the Lord's Supper," puts it, "Nature with open volume stands," displaying the wonders of creation,

> But in the grace that rescu'd man
> His brightest form of glory shines;
> Here, on the cross, 'tis fairest drawn
> In precious blood, and crimson lines.

It is in the service of this message that Watts re-presents the Bible, not adapting it, but setting and framing it. His hermeneutics is simple, because his motives for writing these hymns were to provide not just a paraphrase, or to enlarge on human spiritual experience, but to strengthen faith. As Horton Davies has observed, "the great significance of this eighteenth-century Dissenting hymnody was that if 'enthusiasm' was banned from the sermon it was reintroduced in the praise, and thus the emotions were not starved, as was so often the case in Established worship during this period."[2] These hymns exhort the heart and mind to "awake" and the tongue to speak:

> Awake my heart, arise my tongue,
>   Prepare a tuneful voice,
> In God, the life of all my joys,
>   Aloud will I rejoice.

Watts's hymns and psalms show a firm adherence to the Bible, and they celebrate, either openly or implicitly, the fundamental importance of Holy Scripture. His example was followed by other dissenting writers, who regarded the Bible as justifying their conscience. The Bible was their authority for not being a part of "Established worship": naturally it was the subject of their expository sermons, but it was also the explanation for who they were, the people of God on pilgrimage, strangers and pilgrims here below, the saints proceeding in fellowship together toward the Promised Land. So two of Watts's followers, Philip Doddridge and Benjamin Beddome, wrote hymns on biblical texts to follow the sermon, no doubt in an attempt to imprint the message of the preaching more deeply on the minds of the hearers, but also to generate the emotional response that Horton Davies has noted. As they did so, the biblical texts became more vivid, set as they were in the context of exposition and instruction. The pattern of their chapel worship was one of text/exposition/return to text, the last movement being that of the new hymn. To this end Doddridge wrote the hymns that were collected and published after his death by his friend Job Orton under the title *Hymns founded on Various Texts in the Holy Scriptures* (1755). "It was his Design," said Orton in the Preface, "that they should bring over again the leading Thoughts in the Sermon, and naturally express and warmly enforce those devout Sentiments, which he hoped were then rising in the Minds of his Hearers, and help to fix them on the Memory and heart" (p. iv).

Orton summarized the different types of paraphrase in Doddridge's work:

> There is a great Variety in the Form of them: Some are devout Paraphrases on the Texts: others expressive of lively Acts of Devotion, Faith, and Trust in GOD, Love to Christ, Desire of divine Influences, and good Resolutions of cultivating the Temper and practising the Duties recommended: Others proclaim an humble Joy and Triumph in the gracious Promises and Encouragements of Scripture, particularly in the Discovery and Prospect of eternal Life. (p. v)

This indicates that the very act of paraphrasing the text was seen as one of devotion. Beyond that, however, was the recognition that the modern metrical versions were capable of encouraging the spiritual life. They fostered faith and love, taught the duty of a practicing Christian, and led the believer toward the hope of eternal life in Christ. To this end the Old Testament was capable of being used for New Testament purposes, as it had been by Watts:

> In this Collection there are many Hymns formed upon Passages in the Old Testament, particularly in the Prophets, directly relating to the Case of the Israelites, or some particular good Man among them, which the Author hath accommodated to the Circumstances of Christians, where he thought there was a just and natural Resemblance; and he apprehended, that the Practice of the inspired Writers of the New Testament warranted such Accommodations. (p. vi)

Doddridge's use of the Bible was that of a shepherd, gently leading and admonishing his flock; and the guiding principle of his hermeneutics was that of the Covenant between God and his people, found in the Old Testament and fulfilled in the New. One of his best known hymns, "O God of Bethel, by whose hand" ("O God of Jacob" in 1755), ended with a bargain:

> If thou through each perplexing path
>   Wilt be our constant guide;
> If thou wilt daily bread supply,
>   And raiment wilt provide;
>
> If thou wilt spread thy shield around
>   Till these our wanderings cease,
> And at our Father's loved abode
>   Our souls arrive in peace;
>
> To thee as to our Covenant-God
>   We'll our whole selves resign,
> And count that not our tenth alone
>   But all we have is thine.

Doddridge always draws lessons from Scripture: "Ye servants of the Lord" (entitled "The active Christian") is based on the parable of the wise and foolish virgins (Matthew 25:1–13), and "My gracious Lord, I own thy right" was entitled "Christ's service the fruit of our labours on earth; Philippians 1:22." His hymn for Advent, "Hark the glad sound! The Saviour comes," however, does something more: it carries a very powerful message of the righting of wrongs and the freeing of the imprisoned spirit:

> He comes the broken heart to bind,
>   The bleeding soul to cure,
> And with the treasures of his grace
>   To enrich the humble poor.

That hymn, entitled "Christ's message, from Luke iv. 18, 19," contains a verse that is now never found in hymn books but that indicates the way in which Doddridge is playing with the ideas in the text:

> He comes, from the thick films of vice
>   To clear the mental ray,
> And on the eyeballs of the blind
>   To pour celestial day.

The humble poor are no doubt the actual poor, the hungry of the *Magnificat* who were "filled with good things" while the rich were sent empty away (Luke 1:53). But they are also those who are poor in the gospel, those who do not have the hope of salvation and the grace of mercy: Christ comes to enrich their lives with the treasures of his grace. It is a simple metaphor, but it transforms the New Testament narrative.

Equally, the pouring of celestial day is the dawn of a new era, "whereby the dayspring from on high hath visited us" (Luke 1:78), clearing away the films of vice that have coated the mind and giving light "to them that sit in darkness" (Luke 1:79). Doddridge is taking phrases from the *Benedictus* and privileging them to emphasize the new life promised at the Nativity. In so doing he begins a process of change, in which the employment of biblical texts becomes less a matter of reproduction and more a matter of developing them into indicators of human need and divine grace.

Doddridge was an Independent minister, Beddome a Baptist pastor. Both spoke and wrote with the authority of the pulpit. Anne Steele, on the other hand, was a member of the congregation, and even more disadvantaged by being a woman.[3] Her first hymn in *Poems on Subjects Chiefly Devotional*, published under the pseudonym of "Theodosia" in 1760, makes her position plain:

> Great God, accept the humble praise,
>   And guide my heart, and guide my tongue,
> While to thy name I trembling raise
>   The grateful, though unworthy song.

Nancy Cho has shown that the idea of Anne Steele as a solitary and unhappy woman was a fictional construct of the nineteenth century,[4] and certainly she has the confidence to express herself: she has no need of ministerial authority. Because the poems are hers, rather than those of her teachers from the pulpit, the Bible is of central importance in directing her thoughts. It becomes a comfort and guide:

> Father of mercies, in thy word
>   What endless glory shines!
> For ever be thy name ador'd
>   For these celestial lines.

In this, Steele's most famous hymn, the images are those of richness, food, and wealth. The Bible is a precious jewel, beside which "the glittering gem no longer glows / And India boasts no more." It is a place where "the wretched sons of want / Exhaustless riches find," and where "the fair tree of knowledge grows," where the blind and hungry can come and receive light and food, and where the thirsty can find "sweet refreshment." The Bible has become no longer a source of doctrine that is to be respected but a force that is nourishing and sustaining in itself. The narratives that it contains are now the subject of an intense recapitulation. Her verse shows an intense devotion based on the narratives of the Bible, especially of the Passion:

> Stretch'd on the cross the Saviour dies;
> Hark! his expiring groans arise!
> See, from his hands, his feet, his side,
> Runs down the sacred crimson tide!

This shows an obvious debt to Watts, but Steele has an individual voice that comes from her own insight. Volume II of her *Poems on Subjects Chiefly Devotional* (1760) has a frontispiece depicting a young woman with a telescope, or "glass." That telescope is the Bible, and in her poem "To Florio" she urges the reader to

> Upward point that glass of truth, and see
> A fairer guest, descending from the sky,
> Celestial hope!

The Bible brings hope, and comfort, and the light of understanding. As Beddome wrote, echoing Watts in the use of "crimson" as the color of Christ's blood:

> Here in the records of his grace,
>   God's brightest glory shines;
> Here mercy's varied form we trace,
>   As drawn in crimson lines.

The "crimson lines" are not the lines of type, but the lines of blood running down the body of the crucified Savior. In this evangelical age, the concentration on the Passion of Christ draws writers such as Watts, Steele, and Beddome to the narrative of the Gospels and to the blood of the dying Lamb. We shall find this again in Newton and Cowper; but before them – indeed, before the publication of Doddridge, or Steele – comes Charles Wesley.

It is a commonplace that Charles Wesley used the Bible extensively in his hymns. J. Ernest Rattenbury once said, extravagantly, that "a skilful man, if the Bible were lost, might extract much of it from Charles Wesley's Hymns."[5] This is a teasing proposition: it suggests a dependency so great that the process of intertextuality could somehow be reversed, that the lines of Wesley could be used to reconstruct their source. In fact, Rattenbury's claim would be far truer of Watts than of Wesley, and the bracketing of those two hymn writers together (as in the title of Bernard Manning's book[6]) does a disservice to each. Watts is a consummate artist in the adaptation of the Bible into metrical form; Wesley is closer to Doddridge in his translation of narrative into metaphor.

This is particularly true of his hymns from the Old Testament. In "Earth, rejoice, our Lord is King!," a hymn that emerges from early Methodist experience of confrontation and violence, and entitled "To be sung in a Tumult," Wesley celebrates the victory of Christ. In two verses he suddenly turns back to 2 Kings 6:15–17, with the story of Elisha:

> Though the sons of night blaspheme,
> More there are with us than them:
> God with us, we cannot fear;
> Fear, ye fiends, for Christ is here!
>
> Lo! to faith's enlightened sight,
> All the mountain flames with light;
> Hell is nigh, but God is nigher,
> Circling us with hosts of fire.

This is from the story of the young man who saw the Syrian army encamped around Elisha, and said "Alas, my master! how shall we do?," whereupon the prophet prayed that his eyes should be opened, "and, behold, the mountain was full of horses and chariots of fire round about Elisha." Narrative here is pressed into the service of a contemporary problem (violent opposition to the Wesley brothers in places such as Wednesbury or Evesham), which is also a permanent problem (the need to hold on to difficult or improbable faith in the face of the objections of easy and obvious unbelief). The command in the same hymn to "Sing ye in triumphant strains, / Jesus our Messiah reigns!" has to combat the very real objection that in many parts of the world he very often seems not to reign. Charles Wesley's response is that of Elisha to the servant – "Fear not; for they that be with us are more than they that be with them." The hymn becomes both a record of Wesley's heroic resolve and a test of the faith of subsequent generations who are bold enough to sing it. The original narrative is subsumed into a personal statement; the myth becomes a metaphor of the spiritual condition.

Rattenbury was right, up to a point: Wesley's hymns are intricately woven tapestries of quotation and allusion. But to the biblical text Wesley brings his own experience: he handles the Bible – not least in his juxtapositions of one text to another – with a freedom that is quite unlike anything before him. An example is the hymn written on Leviticus 6:13, "The fire shall ever be burning upon the altar; it shall never go out":

> O thou who camest from above
> The pure celestial fire t'impart,
> Kindle a flame of sacred love
> On the mean altar of my heart!

The passage from Leviticus is concerned with some complicated instructions to Aaron and his sons about the rituals to be observed. In Wesley's hands it becomes a prayer to the Holy Spirit, using Acts 2 for lines 1 and 2, and then praying that the inspiration that came to the apostles might also come to him to kindle sacred love. Aaron's altar becomes his heart. The most remarkable of all these transformations is the hymn or poem entitled "Wrestling Jacob," in which the narrative of Jacob's encounter with the angel at the ford of Jabbok becomes an emblem of the soul's wrestling with the Christ figure. The speaker encounters the Other, not as a comfortable or companionable presence, but as a terrifying opponent in the dark. It allows Wesley to explore the paradoxes of the spiritual life:

> What tho' my shrinking flesh complain,
>   And murmur to contend so long,
> I rise superior to my Pain,
>   When I am weak then I am strong,
> And when my All of Strength shall fail,
> I shall with the God-man prevail.

My strength is gone, my Nature dies,
   I sink beneath Thy weighty Hand,
Faint to revive, and fall to rise;
   I fall, and yet by faith I stand,
I stand, and will not let Thee go,
   Till I Thy Name, Thy Nature know.

The name, which is heard in the whisper of one wrestler to another, is Love, and the poem ends with the modern Jacob going on his way rejoicing. As a treatment of the original text it is the opposite of Watts (who admired it greatly[7]) because it explores a spiritual condition, using the Old Testament narrative as a myth to illuminate the psychodrama of the human self in relation to Christ. In its method of working, the process is closer to Freud than to Watts: as Freud used the Oedipus story to explore the hidden relationships between children and parents, so Wesley uses the Jacob story to present a contemporary account of the soul in a situation of intense and ultimately joyful conflict:

Lame as I am, I take the Prey,
   Hell, Earth, and Sin with Ease o'ercome;
I leap for Joy, pursue my Way,
   And as a bounding Hart fly home
Thro' all Eternity to prove
Thy Nature, and Thy Name is LOVE.

The verse incorporates references from Isaiah 33:23 ("The lame take the prey") and Isaiah 35:6 ("Then shall the lame man leap as an hart") in addition to the Genesis story. But Genesis has at this point been left behind, as Jacob's limping away from the fight has become an image for someone who has been marked for life by the struggle with God, and whose final act is a "flying home" to the Christ who is the God of love.

The image of heaven as home, later to become a common image of nineteenth-century gospel hymns, is found again in Wesley's "Hymn for Ascension-Day":

Grant, tho' parted from our Sight,
High above yon azure Height,
Grant our Hearts may thither rise,
Following Thee beyond the Skies.

Ever upward let us move,
Wafted on the Wings of Love,
Looking when our Lord shall come,
Longing, gasping after Home.

This was one of five hymns in *Hymns and Sacred Poems* (1739) on the great festivals of the church's year, for Christmas Day ("Hark how all the Welkin rings"), the Epiphany "Sons of men, behold from far"), Easter Day (" 'Christ the Lord is ris'n today' "), Ascension Day ("Hail the day that sees him rise") and Whitsunday ("Granted is the Saviour's prayer"), all in the same meter of 7777. They celebrate the God of love and mercy, the Christ of the New Testament, whose story is told in the Gospels and taught in the Epistles. They demonstrate again the "Wrestling Jacob" technique, in which the narrative survives but is transformed. The "Hymn for Easter-Day," for example, begins by echoing the earlier "Jesus Christ is ris'n today" (from *Lyra Davidica*, 1708):

> "Christ the Lord is ris'n to Day,"
> Sons of Men and Angels say,
> Raise your Joys and Triumphs high,
> Sing ye Heav'ns, and Earth reply.

But by verse 5 Wesley has begun to explore the full implications of his own Incarnational theology. If Christ is made like us, we are like him:

> Soar we now, where Christ has led:
> Following our Exalted Head,
> Made like Him, like Him we rise,
> Ours the Cross – the Grave – the Skies!

The sudden leap at the end is characteristic of an element of Charles Wesley's verse that is common in his New Testament hymns, the spectacular. It is found at its most remarkable, perhaps, in "Glory be to God on high" from *Hymns for the Nativity of our Lord* (1744). It is based on Luke 2:14, the source of the traditional *Gloria Patri* that was often found at the end of eighteenth-century hymn books, often in several versions. Wesley takes it, paraphrases it, and then transforms it. He begins simply enough:

> Glory be to God on high,
>   And Peace on Earth descend;
> God comes down: He bows the Sky:
>   He shews Himself our Friend!

"He bows the sky" is from the awe-inspiring Psalm 18:9, "He bowed the heavens also, and came down." But then comes the God of Exodus 3:14:

> God th'Invisible *appears*,
>   God the Blest, the Great I AM
> Sojourns in this Vale of Tears,
>   And Jesus is his Name.

Moses knew that the people would ask, when told of the God of their fathers, "What is his name?" Now we know. And at his Nativity the angels sang:

> Him the Angels all ador'd
>   Their Maker and their King:
> Tidings of their Humbled LORD
>   They now to Mortals bring:
> Emptied of his Majesty,
>   Of His dazzling Glories shorn,
> Being's Source *begins to* Be,
>   And GOD himself is BORN!

The verse leaps from Luke 2 to the commentary of Philippians 2, "he humbled himself," and then begins its own display of verbal wit. At such a point, says Donald Davie (quoting this verse), "we encounter audacities, imaginative abstracting, that ... ought to leave us gasping."[8] It is indeed an astonishing sound-play, with "Be-ing" leading to "to-Be," linked in the middle by "begins." It is also almost beyond our intellectual ability to conceive of a meaning: how does "Being's Source" commence being? It is a riddle that is only solved by understanding that God began at the Nativity to "be" in a particular sense, to be visible, incarnate, human, the Word made Flesh.

Here and elsewhere Wesley applies such verbal and intellectual energy to the New Testament that it is as if he is trying to invest the original text, which is already powerful enough, with an attention-grabbing immediacy. I have concentrated on the Nativity story because that is the point at which the Old Testament turns into the New, as God himself is born. It is fully told by St Luke only, and it is part of what I believe to be a particular affinity with the third gospel in Wesley's hymns: Luke's compassionate understanding of human hearts and minds is fundamental to Wesley's doctrine of repentance and salvation, and I have argued elsewhere that the Lucan writings have a special place in his affections and his understanding.[9] But to that emphasis on mercy and compassion there is, in Wesley's hymns, an almost violent poetic energy: it presents the reader with a remarkable and very unusual combination of the comfort of salvation with a supercharged expression of it.

During the Evangelical Revival, the doctrine of salvation was enthusiastically expressed in hymns, which asserted their orthodoxy by referring continually to the Bible. Martin Madan's *Collection of Psalms and Hymns* (1760) printed its verses with letters at the end of every line, referring the reader to a text, or sometimes two. The result is a collage of varied elements:

> Who hath our report believed? (a)
> Shiloh come is not received, (b)
>   Not received by his own, (c)
> Promis'd branch from Root of Jesse (d)
> David's offspring sent to bless ye, (e)
>   Comes too meekly to be known. (f)

(a) Is. liii. 1. (b) Gen. xlix. 10. (c) John i. 11. (d) Is. xi. 1. Jer. xxiii. 5. (e) Rev. xxii. 16. Acts iii. 26. (f) Zech. ix. 9. Mat. xxi. 5.

This had the effect not only of sending the reader back to the Bible but of proving the authenticity of the poetry. On a larger scale, John Newton (following Watts) headed Book I of *Olney Hymns* (1779) "On select Texts of Scripture." The 141 hymns follow the order of the books of the Bible, with a "Table" printed at the end for easy reference. In Book II there are two hymns on the Holy Scripture, one by Newton and one by his collaborator, William Cowper. Newton's defies the world, in the spirit of a true Evangelical enthusiast of the eighteenth century:

> Precious Bible! What a treasure
> Does the word of God afford?
> All I want for life or pleasure,
> FOOD and MED'CINE, SHIELD and SWORD:
> Let the world account me poor,
> Having this I need no more.

Cowper's hymn is less strident in tone, and more conventional, using the traditional image of the light of the gospel. That gospel was inspired by the Holy Spirit:

> The Spirit breathes upon the word,
> And brings the truth to sight;
> Precepts and promises afford
> A sanctifying light.
>
> A glory gilds the sacred page,
> Majestic like the sun;
> It gives a light to ev'ry age,
> It gives, but borrows none.

Also traditional was Cowper's perception of typology in "Old-Testament gospel":

> Israel in ancient days,
> Not only had a view
> Of Sinai in a blaze,
> But learn'd the gospel too:
> The types and figures were a glass
> In which they saw the Saviour's face.

Cowper was a member of Newton's church at Olney: indeed, he and Mary Unwin went to live at Olney *because* an evangelical minister of the gospel was the incumbent. And Cowper and Newton at Olney were part of a network of Evangelicals within the Church of England who produced hymn books: Madan and Toplady in London, Richard Conyers at Helmsley. The biblical texts that they privileged were favorite ones of the Evangelical movement, such as John 21:15–17 with its description of Jesus' meeting with Peter at the sea of Tiberias. Cowper's "Lovest thou me?" is a dramatic rewriting of the event in terms of the individual experience of redeeming love:

> Hark, my soul! It is the Lord;
> 'Tis thy Saviour, hear his word;
> Jesus speaks, and speaks to thee;
> "Say, poor sinner, lov'st thou me?"

Cowper is capable of using the Bible with great freedom. Zechariah 13:1 ("In that day there shall be a fountain opened to the house of David and to the inhabitants of Jerusalem for sin and for uncleanness") becomes

> There is a fountain fill'd with blood
>   Drawn from EMMANUEL's veins;
> And sinners, plung'd beneath that flood,
>   Loose all their guilty stains.

The text resonates with a new meaning at the introduction of the word "Emmanuel," the word that bridges the Old and the New Testaments (Isaiah 7:14, Matthew 1:23); and with a new force at "plung'd beneath." The blood fountain is shocking enough, but to be plunged not just in but beneath is overwhelming. And this is as it should be: the image depends on a series of impeccable references (Leviticus 7:14, Hebrews 12:24, 1 Peter 1:2) given a new immediacy because applied to the self and charged with the same kind of verbal energy that is found in Charles Wesley's work.

Cowper and Newton follow Charles Wesley in the application of biblical texts to the individual condition. John Wesley made a virtue of this when he compiled *A Collection of Hymns for the Use of the People called Methodists* (1780) by making the book a record of Christian experience, from "Exhorting and beseeching to return to God" to being "brought to the Birth" and "Groaning for full redemption." It is this momentous change that distinguishes the later eighteenth-century use of the Bible from the time of Watts and the other metrical psalmists.[10] When Newton writes "Amazing grace! (how sweet the sound)" he is appropriating the New Testament to his own condition; and Cowper is often disturbingly (and engagingly) open about his own condition, as in "The Waiting Soul" (Book II, hymn 10):

> I wish, thou know'st, to be resign'd,
>   And wait with patient hope;
> But hope delay'd fatigues the mind,
>   And drinks the spirit up.

Here the subjectivity is pushing toward the age of feeling (Henry Mackenzie's *The Man of Feeling* dates from 1771, when Newton and Cowper were writing hymns together in the summer house at Olney) and toward the Romantic period. These hymns had a powerful effect, and left a remarkable legacy, from Eliza Westbury to F. W. Faber.[11] They mark a significant departure from the use of the Bible in the early part of the eighteenth century; and if the genius of Charles Wesley was the pivot upon which this movement turned, the other Evangelicals were also important in transforming the hymn-writing process from the reproduction of the Bible for singing to the use of its texts for the exploration of the human condition and the individual soul.

Notes

1   William Chillingworth, *The Religion of Protestants* (*Works*, vi.56)
2   Horton Davies, *Worship and Theology in England, from Watts and Wesley to Maurice, 1690–1850* (Princeton University Press, Princeton, NJ, 1961), p. 100.

3   The discussion of the work of Anne Steele that follows is indebted throughout to the work of Nancy Cho. See Cho's unpublished PhD dissertation, "'The Ministry of Song': Unmarried British Women's Hymn Writing, 1760–1936," University of Durham, 2007.

4   See J. R.Watson and Nancy Cho, "Anne Steele's Drowned Fiancé," *British Journal of Eighteenth-Century Studies* 28 (2005), 117–21.

5   J. Ernest Rattenbury, *The Evangelical Doctrines of Charles Wesley's Hymns* (London: Epworth Press, 1941), p. 48.

6   Bernard Manning, *The Hymns of Wesley and Watts* (London, 1942).

7   John Wesley's obituary tribute to Charles at the Methodist Conference of 1788 noted that Watts had said that "that single poem, *Wrestling Jacob*, was worth all the verses he had himself written" (Frank Baker, *Representative Verse of Charles Wesley*, 1962, p. 37).

8   Donald Davie, *Dissentient Voice* (University of Notre Dame Press, 1982), p. 21.

9   J. R. Watson "The Hymns of Charles Wesley and the Writings of St Luke," the A. S. Peake Memorial Lecture, the Methodist Conference, 2005, reprinted in Farmington Papers, Modern Theology 17 (Farmington Institute for Christian Studies, Harris Manchester College, Oxford, 2005).

10 It must be remembered that metrical psalms continued to be produced during the eighteenth century by writers such as Sir Richard Blackmore (1721), James Merrick (1765), Christopher Smart (1765), and Basil Woodd (1794). Smart's delightful and often eccentric use of biblical texts could be the subject of an essay in itself.

11 For Eliza Westbury, a Northamptonshire lace-maker and her hymns, see Sibyl Phillips, *Glorious Hope: Women and Evangelical Religion in Kent and Northamptonshire, 1800–1850* (Compton Towers Publishing, Northampton, 2004). Faber strove to write verse "that should contain the mysteries of faith in easy verse ... with the same unadorned simplicity, for example, as the O for a closer walk with God of the *Olney Hymns*" (Preface to *Jesus and Mary; or, Catholic Hymns for Singing and Reading*, 1849), preface, p. xvii.

CHAPTER 24
Daniel Defoe

Valentine Cunningham

Daniel Defoe, father of the English Novel, was a lifelong Dissenter. He was brought up from the age of two in the "gathered" congregation of the Revd Samuel Annesley to which his parents resorted after the Restoration of the monarchy in 1662, refusing, like their pastor, and hundreds of other Presbyterian-minded clergy, to submit to the hegemony of a monarchist-episcopalian national church. He was schooled by Dissenters, most notably at the so-called Dissenting Academy at Newington Green run by the Revd Charles Morton, another ejected Puritan.[1] He became and remained the kind of staunch biblicist which that upbringing and training encouraged and endorsed. Until he decided in the early 1680s to opt instead for a career in business he was actually intended for the Presbyterian ministry. The daily Bible reading and meditation on and discussion of the Bible that was normal in the Puritan family, years of "sitting under" preachers and public "lecturers" (Bible "readers," or expositors) busily and vividly interpreting the "Word of God," had their intended effect of ingraining in Defoe biblical text, biblical narrative, and interpretations of that text. (It appears from Defoe's huge repertoire of direct quotation that the principle version he used was the 1611 King James Version, though he is also obviously familiar with the Geneva Bible (1st edn 1560), the Puritan version.) "Interpretation" meant taking all the biblical words and passages as directly applicable to life, the spiritual and ethical life of the individual, but also wider national and international affairs. Especially rich as an interpretative practice was strong figurative, or tropological, rereading, taking biblical stories, episodes, and characters as allegories of contemporary being.

There was nothing to which the Bible was not deemed applicable. It contained all of meaning and truth. It was necessary. It comprised all of the "imaginaire," or image-repertoire – as that great French Protestant interpreter Roland Barthes put it[2] – that was necessary to negotiate the nature of belief and action and the meanings of history. An image-repertoire implanted early (there is even that astonishing story of little Defoe being set to make a shorthand copy of all of the Bible, when it was rumored that the Restoration authorites planned to take away the Dissenters' Bibles: he dropped out at the end of the Pentateuch). Paula Backscheider has shown how the biblical allusions in Defoe's Letters reveal a habit of self-knowing in his political life, especially his relationship with his spymaster Robert Harley – self-fashioning as one would now say –

through the mirror of Bible characters and stories: the cripple at the pool of Bethesda, Blind Bartimaeus, David, Shimei, Adonijah, and so on.[3] It was an imaginaire Defoe never stopped carrying in his head, and which became a persistent mark of his writing – writing that reveals him as a constant Bible reader and rereader, Bible commentator, explicator, rewriter, in short a Christian midrashist.

The Bible appears with great regularity in Defoe's writing as genetic, foundational, and thus absolute, final. He was obsessed with geneses, how and where things began, and the Bible keeps providing him with origin truths. Law is founded in the the Torah: "the great Original of statuted Justice" is "the Israelites Law."[4] The Depravity which that Law has to deal with goes back to the "original" Fall in Genesis 2 when "the Tree of Knowledge and Good and Evil ... were taken in together" – "they are still inseparable" (This is in Defoe's protracted meditation on states of "natural" being excited by the Europe-animating discovery of a feral German boy in 1725.[5]) Defoe, the arch-projector, traces all human projecting back to the Book of Genesis. "The Building of the Ark by Noah, so far as you will allow it a human Work, was the first Project I read of." Insofar as "the true definition of a Project, according to Modern Acceptation, is ... a vast Under-taking, too big to be manag'd, and therefore likely enough to come to nothing," then the "Building of Babel" was a foundational model.[6] The origin of alphabeticism and of writing is found in the Book of Exodus, when God writes on the "the two Tables" at Sinai:

> As to *Writing*, and the knowledge of Letters, the first we meet with in Scripture, and *Scripture is the oldest as well as the truest Account of the Things in the World*, was the two *Tables of Stone*, written by the Finger of GOD himself; containg the written Law of God.

Here began all literature, all reading, all communication by writing:

> MANKIND had no idea of such a thing among them, it was not in them to make a peice [sic] of Paper speak, and to stamp them on a Paper, and empower other People to speak over again, by the help of those dumb Figures, the same Words that the first Person had uttered at a hundred or a thousand Miles distance; no Man could imagin [sic] such a Thing feasible, nor did it ever, as I have Reason to believe, enter into any Man's Thoughts to contrive any thing of such a kind.
>
> BUT God from Heaven giving Laws to Men, gave not an oral, but a written Law, and it was from him, that Letters were cloathed with Sounds, to be convey'd to any distance, and by the sight, and upon any occasion that requir'd it, repeated Articulately as often as was requir'd, by which the Sense of things was convey'd from Man to Man, and from Age to Age. It was his own doing, and from him alone it deriv'd.
>
> HERE I place the true Original of Writing, and indeed all Literature.[7]

The Bible's word are prime; they come first, and about firstness. The Bible also has the last word, is the ultimate authority. On doctrine, of course – on, for instance, the question of the equality of God and Jesus, hotly contended in the Dissenters' "Salter's Hall" debates of 1717–19. To think otherwise brings "the Truths of God declar'd in his Word to be doubtful, inextricable, and past our Understanding."[8] But the Bible's finality is universal. Part III of Defoe's *Mere Nature Delineated* ends with a gibing account of a society of "Gentlemen of Distinction" who agreed they needed no improvements in the matter of knowledge to be got from books; they were wise enough, especially after "Two Bottles":

> This so verified *Solomon*'s wise Words of *a Fool in a Mortar*, that I could not but call him to Mind, and with that Text of Scripture, we may venture to close the Consideration of it; for they who choose Ignorance, should always have it; and the *Fools which hate Knowledge*, should always go without it. As Wisdom and Virtue are their own Reward, so Vice and Ignorance are their own Punishment; and they who choose them, as *Solomon* says of other Criminals, *Let them flee to the Pit; let no Man stay them*.[9]

Scripture closes the consideration. Defoe is calling to mind a clutch of words from the Book of Proverbs: Proverbs 27:22 ("Though thou shouldest bray a fool in a mortar among wheat with a pestle, yet will not his foolishness depart from him"), Proverbs 1:7 ("fools desire wisdom and instruction"), and Proverbs 28:17 ("A man that doeth violence to the blood of any person shall flee to the pit; let no man stay him"). Proverbs has the last word, in this case about fools. Arrestingly he doesn't give chapter and verse, and nor does he complete his quotations. He assumes that the verses in his mind will be in his readers' as well, that they will share his sense of the Book of Proverbs shutting down an argument. Proverbs is certainly conclusive for him – especially on the key question for his novels of how criminals are created by poverty. Moll Flanders, Roxana, Colonel Jack are all, we are repeatedly told, driven to steal for want of bread.[10] Necessity is the devil tempting to lives of crime. Repeatedly Defoe appeals to a cut-down version of Proverbs 30:8–9: "Give me not poverty, lest I steal." Proverbs is not to be appealed against. It has the last word, a last word that is, paradoxically, part of a sequence of last words. Defoe can go on in that passage about fools, piling up a sequence of quotations from Proverbs: finalities piled on finalities, a field or flow of last words that enables their contemporary repetition, sanctions their continuing repeatable life.

The Bible is reliable because its words are *sure*. Defoe has no time for ghosts and apparitions, or the likes of the soothsayers, omen readers, and prophetic naked Quakers jeered at in *A Journal of the Plague Year* (1722) for claiming knowledge of the future of London. There have, of course, been plenty of supernatural apparitions in the past – God himself, angels, Satan, the resurrected Jesus – this is apparent from the Bible. Defoe's Essay *Upon the History and Reality of Apparitions* (1727) relishes the word *apparently* in Numbers 11:8. "*With him* [Moses] *will I* [God] *speak Mouth to Mouth, even* APPARENTLY, *and not in Dark Speeches, and the Similitude of the* LORD *shall he* BEHOLD": "HERE is a positive Declaration from Heaven, that GOD would appear visibly to *Moses* ... The Word *Apparently* is plain, it can be no otherwise understood, without gross Equivocating with the Text." But now what is apparent from the Bible is a new apparentness: "*We have* now *a more sure Word of Prophecy*"; 2 Peter 1.19 says so; "[that is] that since the Preaching of the Gospel, and the Revelation of God by a Written Word, there is no more need of what the Text calls *a ministration of Angels*. The Scripture is a daily Revelation, and the Spirit of God, who is promised to lead us, is a daily Inspiration, there is no more need of Vision and Apparition."[11] Daily revelation, revelation for the daily, is now available, with the inspiring help of the Holy Spirit, only from this source. The "more sure word": reliable because truly apparent – open, obvious.

The talk of non-biblical oracles, prophets, modern wits, is an "unscrew'd Engine."[12] The Bible's engine is never unscrewed. Reading it is the only way to salvation. And a merciful Providence keeps providing this apparent Book for the opening. Robinson Crusoe has three Bibles, and Providence leads him to open one of his three at relevant places: Hebrews 13:5, "I will never, never leave thee, nor forsake thee"; Psalm 5:15, "Call on me in the Day of Trouble, and I will deliver, and thou shalt glorify me"; Acts 5:31, "He is exalted a Prince and a Saviour, to give Repentance, and to give Remission." Defoe's Providence is perennially bibliomantically inclined like this. The religiously quite ignorant Colonel Jack happens to take up the Bible ("This blessed Book") of his "Tutor" in Virginia, the penitent deportee,

> and the Book open'd at the *Acts* 26.v.28. where *Foelix* says to *St.* Paul, *almost thou per-swadest me to be a Christian.* I think, says I, here's a Line hits me to a Tittle, upon the long Account, you have given of yourself, and I must say them to you, as the Governor here said; and so I read the Words to him. He blush'd at the Text, and returns, I wish I could answer you in the very Words the Apostle return'd to him in the next Ver. *I would thou wert both almost, and altogether such as I am, except these Bonds.* (p. 169)

Wanting "direction" whether to stay in London during the Plague of 1665, seeking reassurance that he would be "kept" if he did so, Defoe's HF, narrator of *A Journal of the Plague Year*, "turns over" the Bible that "lay before me," cries "Lord, direct me,"

> and at that juncture I happened to stop turning over the book at the 91st Psalm, and casting my eye on the second verse, I read on to the seventh verse exclusive, and after that included the tenth, as follows: "I will say of the Lord, He is my refuge and my fortress: my God, in him will I trust. Surely He shall deliver me from the snare of the fowler, and from the noisome pestilence. He shall cover thee with His feathers and under His wings shalt thou trust: His truth shall be thy shield and buckler. Thou shalt not be afraid for the terror by night; nor for the arrow that flieth by day; nor for the pestilence that walketh in dark-ness; nor for the destruction that wasteth at noonday. A thousand shall fall at thy side, and ten thousand at thy right hand; but it shall not come nigh thee. Only with thine eyes shalt thou behold and see the reward of the wicked. Because thou hast made the Lord, which is my refuge, even the most High, thy habitation; there shall no evil befall thee, neither shall any plague come night thy dwelling." (p. 14)

Everywhere in Defoe, in the non-fiction as in the fiction, there is on hand, like this, what is called in *Moll Flanders* some "proper quotation from the Bible." The phrase comes where Moll, in prison and sentenced to death, is counselled by a "serious," i.e. Puritan, even Dissenting, minister, "unfeignedly to look up to God with my whole soul and to cry for pardon in the name of Jesus Christ." "He backed his discourses with proper quotations of Scripture encouraging the greatest sinner to repent and turn from their evil way" (p. 253). Proper quotations. The Bible is the always appropriate Word; it has the appropriate words, for all seasons. And Defoe's texts are stocked with "proper" quotations because, plainly, Defoe's mind and memory are.

Much of the time Defoe seems to be reeling off his quotations by heart. His ideolect is intensely biblical. The biblical words keep coming to him and to his post-conversion characters as it were naturally. HF, for instance, goes on after his reading of Psalm 91:

> I scarce need tell the reader that from that moment I resolved that I would stay in the town, and casting myself entirely upon the goodness and protection of the Almighty, would not seek any other shelter whatever; and that, as my times were in His hands, He was as able to keep me in a time of the infection as in a time of health; and if He did not think fit to deliver me, still I was in His hands, and it was meet He should do with me as should seem good to Him.

This is a way of talking (and thinking) that is almost embarassingly laden with biblical idiom: "Casting all your care upon him; for he careth for you" (1 Peter 5:7); "my times are in thy hands" (Psalm 31:15); "he is able to keep" (2 Timothy 1:12); "it was meet" (Luke 15:32); "it seemed good to the Holy Ghost and to us" (Acts 15:28). And so on. HF talks Bible, and so does Defoe. It is a discourse so at home with its as it were naturalized biblicisms that they keep seeping into the mouths even of characters apparently quite ignorant of the Bible – as they leaked, as time went on, into common English under the impress of the Authorized Version being dinned into the English-speaking people's ears in church and chapel and at school.

Roxana, to take one of many examples from her novel, tells how "we had eaten up almost everything, and little remain'd, unless, like one of the pitiful Women of Jerusalem, I should eat up my very Children themselves" (p. 18). Her kindly neighbors "sat around like Job's three Comforters, and said not one Word to me for a great while" (p. 17). Sympathetic people question the little London street arab Colonel Jack about his unknown name and missing parents: "I lay'd up all these things in my heart," he says (p. 8). And from where, you wonder, realistically, did irreligious Roxana, daughter admittedly of Huguenot refugees, but always worldly and by her own admission rarely in church, get this fluent familiarity with the story of Job and with Lamentations 2:2 ("Shall the women eat their fruit, and children of a span long?"), or the illiterate Jack catch the thought and rhythm of the Virgin Mary in Luke 2, who "kept all these things, and pondered them in her heart"?

It is possible that some of the patent biblical echoes and allusions circulating in Defoe's English had already achieved the kind of Bible-free life they would later enjoy and were already in the common language by Defoe's time. But these are early days for any confidence about that. Even when some biblicism is apparently getting wider circulation it seems to find it hard to shed its original biblical flavor. Take Roxana's Job's Comforters. The OED gives 1680 as the date for their entry into ordinary English as a proverbial presence – which would be well in time for Roxana, who is supposedly writing in the early eighteenth century. But, interestingly indeed, the Dictionary's 1680 occurrence comes from the ranting anti-episcopal and anti-Dissent sermon *Curse Ye Meroz, or the Fatal Doom*, by the immensely controversial presbyterian and monarchist, and one-time Baptist, Anglican minister Edmund Hickeringill – the kind of Bible-based polemic Defoe was very familiar with, and indeed engaged in. The sermon's title is taken from the Song of Deborah, Judges 5:23, "Curse ye Meroz, said the angel of the

Lord, curse ye bitterly the inhabitants thereof": a curse for their inaction against the enemies of Deborah that Hickeringill redirects at disloyal religious rebels. His Job's Comforters are London's disobedient clerics, whether purveyors of Popery, or of "Foppery" (the radical Dissenters). The sermon was preached in the Guildhall chapel before the then Mayor of London, the great anti-Papist banker and money-man Sir Robert Clayton. He and his partner John Morris essentially invented the mortgage. Defoe, in his own capacity as would-be money-maker and economic theorist, admired Clayton greatly. With "the Assistance of the famous Sir Robert Clayton" Roxana obtains a substantial mortgage on an estate that brings in sizeable rent (p. 164). But it is Clayton the banker ("my faithful Counsellor" in money matters) rather than Clayton the intent follower of political applications of Judges and Job whom Roxana is interested in. And it is, surely, Defoe, rather than Roxana, who has at his fingertips the knowledge of the Comforters, let alone that fine detail from The Book of Lamentations.[13]

It is better, I take it, to think that Defoe is just forgetting for the moment that he is not Roxana or Colonel Jack; forgetting that they are in no position to share his own immense Bible recall. And occasional forgetting happens to be one of this memory man's great charms. Notorious cases of memory lapse are scattered all across his narratives – Crusoe swimming out to his wrecked ship apparently naked and filling his "pockets" with biscuits in the ship's bread-room, and so on. And Defoe's memory does occasionally betray him in its recallings of Scripture. When Colonel Jack is inclined to use starvation as an excuse for theft, his counsellor in Viginia, the deported penitent thief, "replied very sharply, that shows us the need we have of the Petition in the Lord's Prayer: *Lead us not into Temptation*; and of *Solomon's* or *Agar's* Prayer: *Give me not Poverty, least I steal*" (p. 163). But Proverbs 30 ascribes the words to Agur. Agar is the name of an "Arabian" mountain in Galatians 4. It is an understandable metaleptic slip. It nicely shows how biblical texts are echoing and jingling around in Defoe's mind, indicating how all of the Bible, Old and New Testament, are as it were Defoe's parish, making all of it a kind of repetitive space, where Agur and Agar rhyme busily together. But still the rhyme is not a whole one, only a half- or para-rhyme. Confusing the two is a mistake. It is an indicator of how intense verbal taking – remembering, appropriating – of Defoe's sort can involve mistaking – misremembering, in effect misappropriation. That they often do so is not only a fact of the best kind of memory life (it is the case that almost every time a poet recalls a predecessor with aplomb and approval – here is something truly wonderful, important, and above all memorable – they misquote the admired passage) but also a trope of modernist and postmodernist hermeneutic. And, it would seem, of Defoe's hermeneutic.

"Give me not poverty lest I steal" is not, actually, what is ascribed to Solomon/Agur in Proverbs 30. That is an edited version of Proverbs 30:8–9: "Remove far from me vanity and lies: give me neither poverty nor riches; feed me with food convenient for me: Lest I be full, and deny thee, and say, Who is the Lord? or lest I be poor, and steal, and take name of my God in vain." Defoe cuts it down to simplify and specialize its point. A prayer against the effects of both riches and poverty is reduced to a matter of poverty only. So quoting the Scripture affirms its apparentness and apparent finality, but editing it in effect denies that apparentness and finality. Pointing the text has its appropriateness, but effecting that appropriateness involves a deliberate misappropriating. This is precisely recall as deliberate misrecalling. It is what Bible interpreters and preachers did and do – it is even arguably necessary to their interpretative performances – and it is what Defoe does. The biblical epigraph to Defoe's *Due Preparations for The Plague* (1722) pointedly makes the point. Defoe's texts often come, as this one does, with Bible epigraphs. *Preparations* invokes Psalm 91:10: "There shall no evil befall thee, neither shall any plague come nigh thy dwelling." Except that the epigraph has "*the* plague."[14] Of course Defoe wants to claim the promise in particular, for the plague of his own time. That is the point, he wants us to believe, of the Scripture. But this deictic act, pointing the text interpretatively, involves a patent tampering with the authoritative given text. So in claiming the contemporary performativity of the "sure word of prophecy" Defoe is actually undoing it. But of course this literal rejigging is a most effective way of affirming the point of Scripture, and – in an intense paradox – of laying claim to the original authoritative sureness of that word. And such is Defoe's customary hermeneutic praxis.

> Solomon was certainly a friend to business, as it appears by his frequent good advice to them. In Prov. XVIII.9, he says, *He that is slothful in business, is brother to him that is a great waster*: and in another place, *The sluggard shall be clothed with rags*, Prov. XXIII.1, or to that purpose.[15]

That is how Letter V of *The Complete English Tradesman*, "Of Diligence and Application in Business," begins. As usual Defoe's favorite Book of Proverbs has the apt words of wisdom for the commercial ephebe. The Letters being "Calculated for the Instruction of our Inland Tradesmen; and especially of young Beginners," here is one more of Defoe's biblically based geneses – the genetic and final word about business. Except that it is not quite that. Once again Defoe has rewritten the sure word. Proverbs has "He also that is slothful in his work." Work, not business. In applying the text to businessmen, Defoe has rewritten it. Once more, appropriating as misappropriating. He hasn't greatly perverted the meaning in converting the text slightly – after all businessmen are a sort of worker – but he has turned it for the purposes of the application. And, arrestingly, he seems to be asserting that this way with the text is fine so long as the gist of the text is made present. As a matter of textual fact, "The sluggard shall be clothed with rags" is not to be found at Proverbs 23:1, as alleged (and alleged in all versions of *The Complete Tradesman*); nor anywhere else in Proverbs. The sluggard is regularly threatened with a bad end in Proverbs, and Defoe's "quotation" is close-ish to Proverbs 23:21, "the drunkard and the glutton shall come to poverty: and drowsiness shall clothe a man with rags." But still, in order to point Proverbs, and Proverbs 23:1, at the sluggardly businessman Defoe is making up the words. And admitting it. "[O]r to that purpose" suggests the words might be in another place than Proverbs 23:1, or they might even be other words, words "to that effect." Either way, his memory is failing him; but this doesn't matter because the chapter and verse and the words are close enough. So the essence of the meaning of Proverbs is good, and being got across, without the detail. Which seems rather like a claim that proper applications of Scripture might actually be contingent upon this dual act of remembering and misremembering.

This hermeneutic double act, the convergence between apparent or actual forgetting of a text and its strong application, is so common in Defoe that it usually fails to stick out as odd. But there is one place where the Bible reader with a memory is pulled up rather short. This is where the massively biblicist Robinson Crusoe, forever applying Bible words to himself and his condition, describes his need for more room for his burgeoning stores as a wish "to build my Barns bigger" (p. 123). How, you think, can Crusoe, how can Defoe, have forgotten that the rich man in Jesus's parable in Luke 12, whose ground "brought forth plentifully" so that he needed to "pull down my barns and build greater" is called a fool by God for putting material prosperity before spiritual? Everett Zimmerman's way around the shock of this seeming hermeneutic waywardness is to dwell on the complex figurality of Jesus' parables – here is a sower with a plentiful harvest turning into a foolish rich husbandman – and to ascribe Defoe's apparent casualness to his awareness of such overdetermination in biblical stories.[16] Explanation certainly seems called for. And Zimmerman's is a good try; but it won't do. The figurality of the parable of the foolish barns-builder is pretty plain; no appeal to overdeterminism can strip out the fact that Jesus' barnsman is a materialist fool – and thus that Crusoe, and Defoe, appear foolish to let such an undesirable suggestion seep into their narrative. But neither Crusoe nor Defoe seem put out by their interpretative push on the parable. It would seem as if this is a rather stark case of Defoe's customary practice of application as more or less strong misreading – a stark example of this interpreter's persistent working against the given apparentness of the text. Which is say his constant sense that the Bible's alleged apparentness, its openness, is always in need of being opened out. Or translated. As on the occasion in *Mere Nature Delineated* referred to above where he has "Solomon" saying "of other Criminals," in a slightly adapted version of Proverbs 28:17, "Let them flee to the Pit; Let no Man stay them," and adds: "that is, as I should translate it, Let them be as miserable as they desire to be." The Bible needs translating, or annotating.

"I am no Annotator," Defoe declares, disarmingly, in *An Essay on the History and Reality of Apparitions* in a discussion of the "remarkable place" in Matthew 27:52 where multiple resurrections of "Saints" occur at Jesus' resurrection. It "would admit of a long Exposition; but I must not preach."[17] But he, so familiar with preachers and expositors and annotators, repeats all of their ways with the Bible. He knows the apparent text apparently cries out for the elucidations of annotators. He himself relies heavily on commentators. Again and again, on Presbyterian minister Matthew Poole (1624–79), the fourth edition of whose two-volume *Annotations Upon the Holy Bible* appeared in 1700 (this was the English version (1683–5) of Poole's vast five-volume Latin *Synopsis Criticarum* (1667–76)). The claim made by some interpreters of Jude 14:15, that Enoch's "prophecy" suggests there was ancient writing rather than mere oral production before Defoe's preferred origin point of Moses's Tablets, is scotched with reference to "the learn'd Commentators upon this Text: the Continuators of the Learned Mr Pool" – and he quotes from the 1696 continuation of Poole, done "by certain judicious and learned divines."[18] Defoe readily adduces the authority of the (often strongly polemical) marginal comments of the Geneva Bible. The nature of the books said to be written "in that memorable Text of apocryphal Scripture," 2 Esdras 14, "is evident from the 24th Verse, where he is bid to bring many Box-Trees with him, as well as Writers; this in the

Margin of some of our Bibles, is explain'd in direct Words to be Box-Tables to write on, or Tables made of Box-Wood, which confirms also what has been said of those Tables in the former part of this Work."[19] Just so, Defoe will cite the Geneva Bible's running headings, whose format and most of whose content were retained in the Authorized Version, which, however, eliminated all the Geneva marginal comments. Joshua, for example, perceives "the Man" who appears to him in Joshua 5 as an Angel – as the "Heads or Contents ... expresly" say.[20]

Defoe is, after all, a rational Bible reader. For example, his sense of history won't allow the "iron pen" of Job 19 to be a stylus.

> Oh that my words were now written! Oh that they were printed in a Book! That they were graven with an iron pen and lead, in the rock for ever! ... I think that these were only translated according to the Author that wrote the Book; for as to the best Account we have of Job himself, he lived and died before the Knowledge of Letters was in the World, and the Pen-Man of his History might be allow'd to Express the Sense of the Good Man in the Manner of the Age in which he then wrote.[21]

Of course Defoe grants that other commentators do see a stylus in Job 19. He is very alert to possible and actual conflicts of interpretation. He continually brings disputes about biblical meaning out into the open. Friday's questions about the Devil – why doesn't God put an end to the Devil now, and if wicked humans can and be pardoned, why can't the Devil? (p. 219) – flummox Crusoe because they bear in on scriptural difficulties not resolved by simply quoting the biblical words about Christians quenching the Devil's fiery darts, and Satan's being reserved for the "last" judgment of the Bottomless Pit. *A Journal of the Plague Year* is, not least, a battleground of opposed readings of the Plague in matters of divine providence and intervention, and the will of God for sinners and saints, which all come down to differences of Bible interpretation and application.

Defoe's narrator HF is resistant to the enthusiastic prophets who read London figuratively as Nineveh, and see themselves as Jonahs sent to preach destruction to the city (pp. 23ff). Is London really to be "an Aceldama," a deserted "Field of Blood," "a space of ground designed by Heaven ... to be destroyed from the face of the earth" (p. 21) – with reference to ST Peter's discussion (Acts 1), the field he bought with the thirty pieces of silver: a "fulfilment" of Psalm 69:25, "Let his habitation be desolate, and let no man dwell therein"? For is not this a day of visitation, a day of God's anger, and those words came into my thought, Jer. V.9: 'Shall I visit for these things? saith the Lord: and shall not My soul be avenged of such a nation as this!' So this is all God's visitation on sinners – which it would be wrong, however, to think you should not take precautions against. HF is hostile to what he calls "a kind of a Turkish predestinarianism" (p. 218). "Means" – taking rational precautions, leaving town, isolating yourself, and so on – are not to be avoided in the name of extreme Calvinism, a "presumptuous" fatalism: which is to say, literalism about the Bible's promises about plague not coming "nigh you," an absolutism of belief in God's irresistible plan for every individual's life. The "best physic against the plague is to run away from it. I know people encourage themselves by saying God is able to keep us in the midst of danger; and this kept thousands in the town, whose carcases went into the great pit by cartloads, and who, if they had fled from the danger, had, I believe, been safe from the disaster" (p. 223).

The plague has a dual explanation: it is all at once the will and the action of God; but it also arises from the "natural causes" which "Divine Power" has set in place; so that "I must be allowed to believe that no one in this whole nation ever received the sickness or infection but who received it in the ordinary way of infection from some-body, or the clothes, or touch, or stench of somebody that was infected before" (pp. 219–20). And Defoe does not feel what Zimmerman calls the "clash" between figural interpretation and an "analytico-referential discourse" as a self-cancelling contradic-tion – but rather as a complementary set of differential readings. So what began in 1719 in *Robinson Crusoe* as a rather tentative complementary, binary explanation for Defoe's experience has set in place three years later in the *Plague Year* as mature reflection.

In *Robinson Crusoe*, famously, some barley unexpectedly springs up, to be rational-ized as all at once completely providential and completely natural. When Crusoe first sees the shoots of English barley he supposes it God's miraculous provision. Then he remembers that he had earlier shaken out a "little Bag" of corn that had been reduced to "Husks and Dust" by rats, and this natural explanation abated "my religious thank-fulness to God's Providence." But then he has the further thought that "it really was the work of Providence as to me," in that the rats must have left "10 or 12 Grains of Corn" unspoiled in the bag, and he happened to shake them out in a place where they would flourish. So the whole sequence was, in fact, "as if it had been dropped from Heaven" (pp. 77–9). And thus it is across all of Crusoe's island experience: the sanctified and the natural readings run in parallel. There are human "means" and there is Provi-dence. The containers of useful goods that keep arriving at the island come by both natural accident and divine arrangement. "But God wonderfully sent the Ship in near enough to the Shore, that I have gotten out so many necessary Things as will either supply my Wants, or enable me to supply my self as long as I live" (p. 66). God supplies him; he supplies himself. Crusoe is in a biblical story: the living enactment of the biblical "figures" (the biblical texts and narratives that are read as pre-enactment, proleptic versions of post-biblical being to come, texts and stories that contain the future "in a figure" as Hebrews 11:19 has it of Isaac's "resurrection" from the dead of the "Akedah," the murderous Binding of Genesis 22: *en parabole*, as the New Testament's Greek has it, *in a parable*). And Crusoe is also in a story of empirical, rational, non-biblical explana-tion. The binary is midrashic indeed: simultaneously the biblical and the post-biblical, with the latter never canceling out the former but, as midrash always does, keeping it intact at the same time as rewriting it.

It is a genuine dualism – the dualism in fact of those often Dissenting scientists of the recently formed Royal Society, whose new rationalism went commonly hand in hand with their older providentially minded assumptions. This is a complementarity misperceived by recent Defoe criticism that thinks a contemporary scientific rational-ism is as it were kicking into touch a worn-out providentialism. This slanted reading goes back to the nineteenth century when Karl Marx in *Das Kapital* notoriously wafted aside "the prayers" of Crusoe as of no moment beside the novel's story of work, of *Homo economicus*, and continues in the foundational critique of Ian Watt in his extremely influential *The Rise of the Novel* (1956) and the associated article in *The Pelican Guide to English Literature* (1957). The theological, the biblical material is present in *Crusoe*, Watt thought, only as "Sunday religion," as the worn-out remnants of a once vibrant puritan orthodoxy, a mere religious sop thrown to an already outmoded religious market; much as if, in Watt's vivid analogy, the star utilitarian reporter on a newspaper, the business correspondent, had to give way from time to time to a "distant colleague" on the paper's religious pages for a few conventional spiritual commentaries.[22] But Defoe's discourse is completely double; we keep getting, persistently, back to back and side by side, in the words of Leopold Damrosch's title of 1985, both God's Plot and Man's Stories.[23]

One very apparent thing Defoe got from the English Bible is style. He promises in *The Political History of the Devil* that, after paying due attention to Milton's misleadings about Satan in Paradise Lost, he will "return to honest prose again, and persue the duty of an Historian."[24] He will get things right; say them straight; in prose. Prose is honest, the historian's, the storyteller's prose. Honesty of prose is central to the ethical claim of the Puritan's plainness of language – what Thomas Sprat desired of the Royal Society's efforts to reform English orthography: "a mathematical plainness of language." It is what Defoe's writing strives for: the simplicity, clarity, perspicuity of the Bible in English; the language of Tyndale, of course, affirmed and transmitted through the Authorized Version.

> And Noah began to be an husbandman, and he planted a vineyard: And he drank of the wine, and was drunken; and he was uncovered within his tent. And Ham the father of Canaan, saw the nakedness of his father, and told his two brethren without. And Shem and Japheth took a garment, and laid it upon both their shoulders, and went backward, and covered the nakedness of their father, and they saw not their father's nakedness. And Noah awoke from his wine, and knew what his younger son had done unto him. And he said, Cursed be Canaan.

That is Genesis 9:20–5 in the Authorized Version. And ... and ... and ... , one clause, one sentence after another, a narrative sequence, narrative as a connected sequence of event and life and meaning, registered in plain, simple words. The paratactic mode of the Hebrew text (waw ... waw ... waw ...) transposed into English by Tyndale and after him by the Authorized Version translators; the plain English of Tyndale and of the AV. It was the English Bible's stylistic and narrative gift to English narrativity, and, as mediated through biblicist, biblicizing Daniel Defoe, the Bible's endowment of English fiction.

> In this juncture who should come by but young *Canaan*, say some; or, as others think, this young Fellow first attack'd him by way of Kindness and pretended Affection; prompted his Grandfather to drink, on Pretence of the Wine being good for him, and proper for the Support of his old Age, and subtilly set upon him, drinking also with him, and so (his head too strong for the old Man's) drank him down, and he, *Devil* like, triumph'd over him; boasted of his Conquest, insulted the Body as it were dead, uncovered him on purpose to expose him, and leaving him in that indecent Posture, went and made Sport with it to

his father Ham, who in that Part, wicked like himself, did the same to his Brethren *Japhet* and *Shem*; but they like modest and good Men, far from carrying on the wicked Insult on their Parent, went and cover'd him, as the Scripture expresses it, and as may be supposed inform'd him, how he had been abus'd, and by who.

That is Defoe in his Noahic nouvelle in *The Political History of the Devil* (VI, p. 121), doing his fictionalizing midrash on Genesis 9, in obvious English Bible style.[25] And here is that same plain style, and fundamentally paratactic mode, as the engine driving *Robinson Crusoe*'s narration:

> I ... walk'd back to my Retreat, and went up over my Wall, as if I had been going to Bed, but my thoughts were sadly disturb'd, and I had no Inclination to Sleep; so I sat down in my Chair, and lighted my Lamp, for it began to be dark: Now as the Apprehension of the Return of my Distemper terrify'd me very much, it occurr'd to my Thought, that the *Brasilians* take no Physick but their Tobacco, for almost all Distempers; and I had a Piece of a Roll of Tobacco in one of the Chests, which was quite cur'd, and some also that was green and not quite cur'd.
>
> I went, directed by Heaven no doubt; for in this Chest I found a Cure, both for Soul and Body, I open'd the Chest, and found what I look'd for, *viz.* the Tobacco; and as the few Books, I had sav'd, lay there too, I took out one of the Bibles which I mention'd before, and which to this Time I had not found Leisure, or so much as Inclination to look into; I say, I took it out, and brought both that and the Tobacco with me to the Table.
>
> What Use to make of the Tobacco, I knew not, as to my Distemper, or whether it was good for it or no; but I try'd several Experiments with it, as I was resolv'd it should hit one Way or other: I first took a Piece of a Leaf, and chew'd it my Mouth, which indeed at first almost stupefy'd my Brain, the Tobacco being green and strong, and that I had not been much us'd to it; then I took some and steeped it an Hour or two in Rum, and resolv'd to take a Dose of it when I lay down; and lastly, I burnt some upon a Pan of Coals, and held my Nose close over the Smoke of it as long as I could bear it, as well for the Heat as almost for Suffocation. (p. 93)

John Bunyan's *The Pilgrim's Progress* (1678), that ur-novel which is as it were Crusoe's Puritan-Protestant stablemate, is the first English prose work to extensively employ the biblicist – the plain and paratactic – mode. In employing it, *Robinson Crusoe*, the first English novel proper, lays it down as foundational for the English novel.

In the "Conclusion" to *Robinson Crusoe: Myths and Metamorphoses*, the collection of essays edited by Lieve Spaas and Brian Stimpson that rather finely examines fictional afterlives of Defoe's novel, the so-called "Robinsonaden," novels midrashic on *Crusoe*, which are produced in number right down to the present, Lieve Spaas suggests that Crusoe is a revised Genesis myth – "a post-paradise situation of hard labour on a desert island threatened by the incursion of canibals" that rewrites the Bible story's attempted grip on its gender-differentiated "self–other-dichotomy" in terms of "new dichotomies of race and ethnic superiority."[26] Be the detail of that rewriting as it may, the large point about a rewriting of Genesis cannot be gainsaid. It needs expanding, though, to take in, in effect, the whole Bible. For what happens in *Robinson Crusoe*, the genetic English novel, is a new fictional beginning, a Genesis of this new genre, as a multidimensional biblicized practice: this new thing, the novel, originating as utterly biblicized in all its ways and means, as to form and content, to its sense of what self is, and how a life-story is to be known and narrated: all a revision of the Bible's "plot," all midrashic, in one way or another, on the Big Book.

Notes

1   Biographical details are from Paula R. Backscheider, *Daniel Defoe: His Life* (Johns Hopkins University Press, Baltimore, 1989), still the best life. There is good detail about his sectarian history in John Robert Moore, "Defoe's Religious Sect," *RES* 17:68 (1941), 461–7.

2   Roland Barthes, *La Chambre claire: note sur la photographie* (Cahiers du cinéma, Gallimard, Paris, 1980), trans Richard Howard, *Camera Lucida: Reflections on Photography* (Flamingo, London, 1984).

3   Paul Backscheider, "Personality and Allusion in Defoe's Letters," *South Atlantic Review* 47:1 (1982), 1–20. For the full-on tropological treatment of Scripture, see *Tropologia: a Key to Open Scriptural Metaphors* (1682) by the Particular Baptist and Calvinist, Benjamin Keach (imprisoned and pilloried for his preaching as a Dissenter) and the Baptist Thomas Delaune (imprisoned in Newgate for the "sedition" of *A Plea for Non-Conformists* (1683), where he and his wife and children died in 1685). Defoe wrote a Preface to the 1706 reprint of the *Plea*.

4   *A Review of the State of the British Nation*, Saturday 11 February 1710: *Selected Poetry and Prose of Daniel Defoe*, ed. Michael F. Shugrue (Holt, Rinehart & Winston, New York, 1968), p. 144.

5   *Mere Nature Delineated: Or, A Body Without a Soul. Being Observations Upon the Young Forester Lately Brought to Town from Germany. With Suitable Applications* (1726), in Daniel Defoe, *Writings on Travel, Discovery and History*, ed. W. R. Owens and P. N, Furbank, volume V, *Due Preparations for the Plague (1722) and Mere Nature Delineated (1726)*, ed. Andrew Wear (Pickering and Chatto, London, 2002), p. 181.

6   "The History of Projects," in *An Essay upon Projects* (1697), The Stoke Newington Daniel Defoe Edition, ed. Joyce D. Kennedy, Michael Seidel and Maximillian E. Novak (AMS Press, New York, 1999), p. 13.

7   *An Essay Upon Literature: Or, An Equiry into the Antiquity and Original of Letters* (1726), in *Writings on Travel, Discovery and History*, volume IV, ed. P. N. Furbank (Pickering & Chatto, London, 2001), pp. 227, 230, 237–8.

8   *A Letter to the Dissenters* (May 1719), quoted in Backscheider's *Life*, p. 402. For those debates, see Russell E. Richey, "Did the English Presbyterains Become Unitarian?" *Church History* 42:1 (1973), 58–72.

9   *Mere Nature Delineated*, edn cited, p. 208.

10   Referencing Defoe's novels is difficult because they don't employ chapter divisions. Where necessary I shall give page references to the following editions of Defoe's novels: *The Life and Strange Surprizing Adventures of Robinson Crusoe, of York, Mariner* (1719), ed. J. Donald Crowley, 1972 (Oxford World's Classics, Oxford, 1998); *The Fortunes and Misfortunes of the Famous Moll Flanders* (1722), Signet Classics edn, with afterword by Kenneth Rexroth (New American Library, New York, 1964); *A Journal of the Plague Year* (1722), Everyman Paperback, intro G. A. Aitken (J. M. Dent, London, 1908); *The History and Remarkable Life of the Truly Honourable Col. Jacque, Commonly Call'd Jack* (1722), ed. S. H. Monk (Oxford University Press, Oxford, 1970); *Roxana, The Fortunate Mistress* (1724), ed. Jane Jack (Oxford University Press, Oxford, 1969).

11 Daniel Defoe, *Satire, Fantasy and Writings on the Supernatural*, ed. W. R. Owens and P. N. Furbank, volume VIII, *An Essay Upon the History and Reality of Apparitions* (1727), ed. G. A. Starr (Pickering & Chatto, London, 2005), pp. 51, 56–7.

12 Ibid., p. 72.

13 Katherine Clark is surely wrong to suppose that Roxana's avarice as an investor is obviously condemned by her choice of Clayton as adviser: *Daniel Defoe: The Whole Frame of Nature, Time and Providence* (Palgrave, Basingstoke, 2007), p. 144. Defoe may well have disapproved of Clayton's alleged freemasonry and his friendship with the Arian John Toland, but there is no gainsaying his admiration in *A Tour Round the Whole Island of Great Britain* (1724–6) for Clayton's self-made success as a financier: see Pat Rogers, *The Text of Great Britain: Theme and Design in Defoe's Tour* (University of Delaware Press, Newark, NJ), p. 193. There is no evidence that Clayton sat on the Bench at Defoe's trial that put him prison for *The Shortest-Way With The Dissenters* (1702), *pace* Richard West, *The Life and Strange Surprising Adventures of Daniel Defoe* (1997; Flamingo Press, London, 1998), p. 300. F. Bastian's suggestion that Defoe might have used Clayton for his large mortgages to buy land on the Essex Marshes is more plausible as well as more attractive: *Defoe's Early Life* (Macmillan, London, 1981).

14 *DUE PREPARATIONS FOR THE PLAGUE, as well for Soul as Body. Being some seasonable THOUGHTS upon the Visible Approach of the present dreadful CONTAGION in France; the properest Measures to prevent it, and the great Work of submitting to it* (1722), in *Writings on Travel, Discovery and History*, volume V, p. 27.

15 *The Complete English Tradesman in Familiar Letters; Directing him in all the several Parts and Progressions of Trade* (George Ewing, Dublin, 1726), 37.

16 Everett Zimmerman, "From Figure to Trace: Bunyan and Defoe," in *The Boundaries of Fiction: History and the Eighteenth-Century British Novel* (Cornell University Press, Ithaca, NY, 1996), p. 69.

17 Edn cited, volume VIII, p. 77.

18 *An Essay Upon Literature*, edn cited, volume IV, p. 255.

19 Ibid., p. 282.

20 *Of Apparitions*, edn cited, volume VIII, pp. 55–6.

21 *Essay Upon Literature*, edn cited, volume IV, p. 286.

22 Ian Watt, *The Rise of the Novel* (Chatto & Windus, London, 1956), p. 84. See also "Defoe as Novelist," in Boris Ford, ed., *From Dryden to Johnson, The Pelican Guide to English Literature*, IV (Penguin, Harmondsworth, 1957), pp. 203–16.

23 Leopold Damrosch Jr, *God's Plot and Man's Stories* (University of Chicago Press, Chicago, 1985).

24 *Satire, Fantasy*, edn cited, VI, p. 57.

25 I do wonder whether precocious little Maggie Tulliver's reading *Defoe's History of the Devil* at the beginning of *The Mill on the Floss* – that novel which is a kind of midrash on the Noah's Flood story – should be taken as George Eliot's covert acknowledgment of Defoe's biblicized narrative endowment of the great tradition Eliot is consciously writing in. It is difficult to find any other explanation that holds water.

26 Lieve Spaas, "Conclusion," in Lieve Spaas and Brian Stimpson, eds, *Robinson Crusoe: Myths and Metamorphoses* (Macmillan, Basingstoke, 1996), p. 320.

CHAPTER 25
Jonathan Swift

Michael F. Suarez, S.J.

Writing to the Duke of Dorset to ask a favor for a fellow clergyman in financial distress, Jonathan Swift, Dean of St Paul's, Dublin, employed an unusual form of the humility topos: "My Lord; I will as a Divine, quote Scripture. Although the Childrens meat must not be given to Dogs; yet the Dogs eat the Scraps that fall from the Childrens tables" (December 30, 1735, Swift, 1965, 4:450; Matthew 15:26–7; Mark 7:27–8). Lest he seem preachy or pompous, Swift justifies his adducing the gospel passage by virtue of his profession. Yet, the text Swift employs in his suit for the Duke's charity places Dorset in the position of Christ who grants a petitioner's request – and situates Swift in the place of the importunate foreign woman rewarded for her great faith in Jesus' generous goodness and his ability to effect the remedy she seeks (Matthew 15:22–8; Mark 7:25–30). The correspondence between Swift and the woman is further strengthened by the fact that neither asks a boon for himself or herself, but on behalf of another in dire need. By means of these identifications, then, the Dean creates a quasi-typological parallel that would make it hard for the Duke to say no. Thus, Swift evinces a high degree of scriptural wit, a knowing gift for adducing the biblical text that will produce the desired effect.

As a divine, satirist, poet, and correspondent, Swift routinely quotes Scripture. A recent catalogue of Swift's own library lists twenty-one different texts under "Bibles," indicating how central the Bible was to Swift's own understanding and sensibilities (Passmann and Vienken, 2003). Although the Bible repeatedly appears in Swift's writings, it has rarely been studied as an essential element of his rhetorical strategies or his habits of mind. The sole monograph devoted to the subject, *Swift's Use of the Bible* (1965) by Charles Allen Beaumont, has been deservedly neglected by scholars of Swift and of the Bible's reception alike. This chapter, part of a larger work on Swift and Scripture, attempts to offer some small redress for the surprising paucity of scholarly attention devoted to Swift's uses of the sacred page.

There are four basic uses of the Bible in Swift's writing: the homiletic, chiefly but not exclusively found in his sermons; the proverbial, when he adduces biblical texts as ordinary proverbs more than theological teaching; the jocular, using the biblical text or allusion to make a joke, but not of any satirical consequence; and, finally, the mock biblical, employing the Bible (and, often, invoking its normative status) for satirical purposes. Swift's mock biblical satire can typically be divided into two kinds. The first is the quick thrust, in which the obvious meaning and incongruity of the verse itself makes its satirical point. The second type of mock biblical is a more intricate and intriguing use in which the text Swift adduces must be understood in its larger context if we are to attend to its full resonance in a new context. In the pages that follow, I briefly delineate Swift's four principal uses of the Bible, devoting most attention to the mock biblical as an instrument of Swiftian satire.

The Homiletic/Sermonic

Swift himself denigrated his sermons as "preaching pamphlets," but the small number of his extant homiletic texts (see Swift, 1939–68, volume 9, pp. 139–250) show him to have been highly accomplished in the pulpit. (Swift's attitude to preaching and homiletic practice are most ably treated in Steele, 1978, pp. 74–81.) His "A Letter to a Young Gentleman" (1720) leaves us in no doubt as to his convictions about either the seriousness with which the duty of delivering sermons should be regarded, or how carefully the preaching cleric ought to prepare. Yet, the Dean's sense of genre and decorum means that – although his command of rhetoric is far superior to that of virtually all of his contemporaries – his treatment of biblical texts is almost altogether unexceptional. Nigel Dennis acutely observes that Swift so "closely and vigorously ... hewed to his rule of the unmodified Word" in his sermons "that they emit hardly a breath of his fabulous spirit and are severely unadorned in respect of wit and fancy" (Dennis, 1964, p. 24). Given that his handling of the Scriptures deliberately resembles contemporary homiletic practice as closely as possible, it seems most fitting that we move on to other uses of the sacred page that more conspicuously bear the stamp of Swift's mind and the signature of his personality.

The Proverbial

Swift often quotes biblical texts as maxims, adages, or aphorisms. In his "Letter concerning the sacramental test," he comments on the bondage of the citizenry – a favorite Swiftian theme – by recalling a stock phrase from the Old Testament,

> and, in the mean Time, the common People without Leaders, without Discipline, or natural Courage, being little better than *Hewers of Wood, and Drawers of Water*, are out of all Capacity. ("A Letter Concerning the Sacramental Test," Swift, 1939–68, volume 2, p. 120; Joshua 9:21, 23, 27)

Likening their condition to slavery, Swift has no profound scriptural or theological truth to reveal; the phrase "hewers of wood, and drawers of water" is merely a shorthand for their subjugation.

Swift typically adduces the sacred page merely to call to mind a parallel situation that his audience will recognize. Complaining to Stella in 1711, he moaned:

Pox on that bill; the woman would have me manage that money for her. I do not know what to do with it now I have it. I am like the unprofitable steward in the gospel: *I laid it up in a napkin; there thou has what is thine own* etc. ("Letter 33, November 1711," Swift, 1948, p. 400; Luke 19:20; Matthew 25:25)

Often for Swift, the Bible serves as a store of proverbial truths or loose parallels. He employs a well known scriptural image in *The Examiner* to identify the Dissenters as enemies of the Kingdom: "I believe there are few Examples in any *Christian* Country of so great a Neglect for Religion; and the Dissenting Teachers have made their Advantages largely by it; *Sowing Tares among the Wheat while Men slept*" ("The Examiner No. 42, May 24, 1711," Swift, 1939–68, volume 3, p. 160; Matthew 13:25). The allusion reinforces a polarization already well established in the writings of this Tory Anglican, but it does little other textual work. In these instances, the Bible is not so different from the *Aeneid* or some other classical text that might furnish recognizable situations, tags, or tropes: in Swift's proverbial use of the Bible, the sacred status of the text rarely comes into play.

The Jocular

When Swift marshals the Bible for playful or jocular ends, he is often writing tongue-in-cheek, as in this passage from "A Serious Poem" (1724):

When Foes are o'ercome, we preserve them from Slaughter,
To be *Hewers of Wood and Drawers of Water*,
Now, although to *Draw Water* is not very good,
Yet we all should Rejoyce to be *Hewers* of wood. (Swift, 1958, volume 1, p. 334, lines 1–4; Joshua 9:21, 23, 27)

The comic effect depends upon a pun, as Swift devilishly suggests that he and his audience would delight in slaying William Wood, the English entrepreneur who had been authorized to mint coins for Ireland (Wood's halfpence), a privilege the Dean believed would seriously damage the nation's already fragile economy. "Hewing Wood" is thus a revenge fantasy made safe by the author's biblical paranomasia. Swift enjoyed such harmlessly transgressive jokes, as when a friend told him that he "was a Beast forever after the order of Melchisedec" ("Letter 12, 23 Dec. 1710," Swift, 1948, p. 54; Psalm 110:4; Hebrews 5:6), or when he quipped,

It is said of the Horses in the Vision [i.e. Revelation], that their Power was in their Mouths and in their Tails. What is said of Horses in Vision [Revelation 9:19], may be said of Women in reality. ("Thoughts on Various Subjects," Swift, 1939–68, volume 4, p. 253)

These waggish jests do not appeal to the revealed nature of Scripture in any way, though they are all the more facetious for their incongruity with the source text.

In his correspondence, Swift flippantly refers to his "vineyard field" as "Naboth's Vineyard" and to the garden within as "Sheba's garden" (see, for example, "Swift to

John Worrall, 27 August 1725," Swift, 1965, volume 3, p. 91; "Swift to Thomas Sheridan, 18 September 1728," ibid., p. 298; "Swift to A. Pope, 20 April 1731," ibid., p. 458). These mischievous references to 1 Kings 21 – the story of Jezebel's nefarious arrogation of Naboth's property for Ahab – and to 1 Kings 10 – the plentitude Sheba brings from her kingdom – usefully remind us that the word *allusion* comes from *ludere*, to play. In much the same vein, Swift calls the second son of Lord Chief Justice Rochfort "Nim" (for Nimrod, the "mighty hunter" of Genesis 10:9) because of his love of hunting ("Swift to Daniel Jackson, 26 Mar. 1722," Swift, 1965, volume 2, p. 423). Several of Swift's correspondents – most memorably Pope and Bolingbroke, whose views about Scripture were markedly different than Swift's own – also casually engage in such droll biblical banter.

Inverting the sense of a biblical text is one of Swift's most common gambits, both in his playful writings – as in "The Answer," below – and elsewhere in his more serious satirical enterprises. In these verses, the Dean questions the soundness of the supposedly inerrant text purely for the pleasure of a trivial demonstration:

> And, though the gospel seems to say,
> What heavy burthens lawyers lay
> Upon the shoulders of their neighbor,
> Nor lend a finger to the labour,
> Always for saving their own bacon:
> No doubt the text is here mistaken:
> The copy's false, and sense is rack'd:
> To prove it I appeal to fact;
> And thus by demonstration show,
> What burthens lawyers undergo. ("The Answer," Swift, 1958, volume 2, p. 434, lines
> 61–70; Luke 11:46)

Typically, this jocular use of the sacred page is more about the mirthful display of wit for its own sake than about the subject's genuine relevance to biblical truths. In such cases, Swift merely exploits the Bible as a vehicle for secular comic ends.

The Mock Biblical

The quick thrust

The most engaging way in which Swift deploys the sacred page is his use of the Bible to create satirical effects. The mock biblical – marshaling scriptural quotations, types, and tropes as a means of producing satire – is almost never about mocking the Bible itself. Instead, the mock biblical almost invariably seeks a target outside the ambit of its immediate reference. In this regard, as in many others, it resembles its rhetorical cousin, the mock epic, also a favorite rhetorical strategy in the Restoration and early decades of the eighteenth century. Fiercely combative, the Dean of St Paul's often uses the Bible to deride his adversaries, skewering them on the terrible Swiftian sword of his mock biblical rhetoric with a sharp, quick thrust. In "Remarks upon Tindall's *Rights of the Christian Church*," he assails the Freethinkers – who reject revelation and miracles – and their spurious reasoning:

> It must be allowed in their Behalf, that the Faith of Christians is not as a Grain of Mustard Seed in Comparison of theirs, which can remove such Mountains of Absurdities, and submit with so entire a Resignation to such Apostles. (Swift, 1939–68, volume 2, p. 73; Matthew 17:20; cf. 1 Corinthians 13:2)

In Swift's lacerating inversion, it is the atheists who have tremendous faith in the miraculous and the Christians who have comparatively none, so foolish are the Freethinkers' reasoning and creed. Thus does Swift turn the tables on the unbelievers with consummate wit, by charging them not with skepticism, but with credulity.

Unlike the examples we have already been surveying, Swift's satirical swipe at Matthew Tindall and his Deist disciples draws a great deal of its satirical force from the biblical texts to which he adverts: the relevant pericope in Matthew 17 concerns Jesus' distress both generally at the "faithless and perverse generation" (verse 17) he must teach, and specifically at the ways in which the "unbelief" (verse 20) of the disciples hinders them from doing the work of the kingdom. The biblical resonances Swift excites into motion are all the more satirically suggestive because the occasion of the Teacher's pronouncement is the need to exorcize a demon who has turned the possessed into a "lunatick" (verse 15). Therefore, although the effect of Swift's quick-witted jab is immediate, the damage it inflicts is not merely superficial. The more thoroughly one understands the Scripture that Swift employs, the more one recognizes how apposite it is to his critique. Both the biblical text and its context are adroitly brought into play.

The quick thrust typically depends upon a clever similitude and, then, an inversion, often achieving a comic effect even as its satire stings. In *The Drapier's Letters*, Swift created a typological satire, casting himself as the young David, principally equipped with his courage and wit, and William Wood, the would-be minter of the brass halfpenny for Ireland, as the ungodly, foreign Goliath:

> I was in the Case of *David* who *could not move in the Armour of* Saul; and therefore I rather chose to attack this *uncircumcised Philistine* (*Wood* I mean) *with a Sling and a Stone*. And I may say for *Wood's* Honour, as well as my own, that he resembles *Goliah* in many Circumstances, very applicable to the present Purpose: For *Goliah* had *a Helmet of* Brass *upon his Head, and he was armed with a Coat of Mail, and the Weight of the Coat was five Thousand Shekles of* Brass, *and he had Greaves of* Brass *upon his Legs, and a Target of* Brass *between his Shoulders*. In short, he was like Mr. *Wood*, all over Brass; and *he defied the Armies of the living God*.

So far, so good. Swift presents us with a typology that establishes a loaded moral calculus. The humor of the mock correspondence allows its author to get away with proclaiming himself the righteous hero and Wood the perfidious Philistine. But Swift takes matters a step further:

> *Goliah's* Conditions of Combat were likewise the same with those of *Wood: If he prevail against us, then shall we be his Servants*. But if it happen that I *prevail* over him, I renounce

the other Part of the Conditions; he shall never be a *Servant* of mine; for I do not think him fit to be trusted in any *honest* Man's shop." ("Some Observations upon the Report ... ," Swift, 1939–68, volume 10, p. 48, or Swift 1935, p. 63; 1 Samuel 17)

In this clever reversal, Swift moves from the biblical landscape of the Elah valley to the streets of Dublin. Goliath/Wood is not merely the foe of Israel/Ireland, he is also not to be trusted near the shop till. This deflationary move brings the conflict with Wood and his London masters back to the hard realities of daily trade, even as it enables Swift to advert to his favorite theme of Irish servitude. In addition, using the David-and-Goliath story allows the pamphleteer to introduce a hopeful prolepsis. Swift's readers all knew how the narrative ends: like the idol Dagon (1 Samuel 5:3–4), the evil giant falls with his face to the ground, never to rise again (1 Samuel 17:49).

The slow burn: Swift's more extended use of mock biblical satire

Beyond the quick-witted and instantly impressive attacks of the kind we have been examining, Swift also routinely made use of a more deliberative form of mock biblical to advance his satirical program. Here his method is more subtle, more nuanced, and hence requires a more thoroughgoing exegesis if we are to glean the full import of his meaning. Accordingly, what follows is a fairly extensive investigation of two representative mock biblical moments in the Swift's satires.

Written in defense of the Test Act to address those who were calling for its repeal, Swift's "An Argument against Abolishing Christianity" (comp. 1708, pub. 1711) maintains that abrogating the Sacramental Test would attenuate the power of the Established Church, jeopardizing the practice of orthodox Christianity and, hence, the very foundations of virtue and morality upon which English civil society depends. To repeal the Test, Swift claims, would be to give license to licentiousness, to encourage profligacy, and to promote irrationality and vice. Tolerating heterodoxy leads to atheism and debauchery. A stance at once so conservative and well rehearsed might seem an unpromising starting place for a satirical triumph. The genius of the essay, however, is that Swift makes this slippery-slope argument through the persona of an urbane and rakish character unconcerned about theology and unconstrained by secular convention.

Early on in Swift's essay, the persona, who is conducting a kind of mock disputation rooted in the Scholastic tradition of theological argument since at least the appearance of Peter Abelard's *Sic et Non* (c.1123), considers the case of "two young Gentlemen ... of profound Judgment, who ... without the least Tincture of Learning," came to the decision "that there was no God, and generously communicating their Thoughts for the Good of the Publick; were ... upon I know not what *obsolete* Law, broke *only* [i.e. merely] for *Blasphemy*" (Swift, 1939–68, volume 2, p. 28). Although the Lord Rochester-like persona finds blasphemy unobjectionable and belief in God untenable, he nevertheless discovers in this prosecution a warrant for the maintenance of the Established Church. His reasoning is somewhat eccentric, however. "I think this [case] rather shews the Necessity of a *nominal* Religion among us," he writes, explaining:

> Great Wits love to be free with the highest Objects; and if they cannot be allowed a *God* to
> revile or renounce; they will *speak Evil of Dignities*, abuse the Government, and reflect upon
> the Ministry; which I am sure, few will deny to be of much more pernicious Consequence.
> (Ibid., p. 29)

Giving the libertines "a God to revile or renounce" as a palliative for their itching wit
will keep them from the much more serious activity of training their skepticism on the
established social order and the current political scene. Unlike the trifling business of
religion, the text ironically implies, politics genuinely affects the public's personal and
corporate fortunes. If religion is preserved by the state, albeit nominally, then God is a
sop thrown to the free-thinkers in order to keep them from tearing the political status
quo to pieces and engendering civil unbelief.

Swift's devil quotes Scripture, though only once. The phrase "speak Evil of Dignities"
comes from a passage in the Second Letter of Peter in which the pseudonymous author
issues a polemic against heretics, emphasizing the relationship between error and vice,
and proclaiming the certainty of God's judgment against those whose hearts are
corrupt:

> But there were false prophets also among the people, even as there shall be false teach-
> ers among you, who privily shall bring in damnable heresies, even denying the Lord
> that bought them, and bring upon themselves swift destruction. And many shall follow
> their pernicious ways; by reason of whom the way of truth shall be evil spoken of. And
> through covetousness shall they with feigned words make merchandise of you: ... The
> Lord knoweth how to deliver the godly out of temptations, and to reserve the unjust
> unto the day of judgment to be punished: ... chiefly them that walk after the flesh in the
> lust of uncleanness, and despise government. Presumptuous are they, selfwilled, they are
> not afraid *to speak evil of dignities*. ... these, as natural brute beasts, made to be taken and
> destroyed, speak evil of the things that they understand not; and shall utterly perish in
> their own corruption; And shall receive the reward of unrighteousness, as they that count
> it pleasure to riot in the day time. Spots they are and blemishes, sporting themselves with
> their own deceivings while they feast with you; Having eyes full of adultery, and that
> cannot cease from sin; beguiling unstable souls: an heart they have exercised with covet-
> ous practices; cursed children: Which have forsaken the right way, and are gone astray.
> (2 Peter 2:1–3a, 9–10, 12–15, emphasis added)

I have quoted at some length because this passage represents the essence of Swift's
"Argument": false teaching fosters heresy, which leads to the breakdown of the moral
and social order and the debasement of its members.

Swift's urbane rake takes an extremely liberal stand: his citation of Scripture *en
passant* is meant to promote a nominal Christianity that is tolerant of all positions, even
free-thinking and atheism, though he ironically condemns the view for which he argues
by the very biblical passage he adduces. He maintains that it should be acceptable to
blaspheme, but not to speak evil of dignities and, hence, to threaten the social order. In
contrast, the biblical text shows that these systems of authority are inextricably linked.
This scripturally rooted understanding of the relationship between the ecclesiastical
and civil spheres is, after all, the whole point of Swift's essay – England cannot have a

secure society without a stable doctrinal and ecclesiastical order. The secularists who would erode Erastianism, or the *jus divinum* of episcopacy, or the state's ability to regulate heterodoxy, do not understand that – in their attempt to make neat divisions between the sacred and the secular, and between public and private morality – they undermine the very foundations of English society. The second chapter of 2 Peter makes this abundantly clear, but the persona's failure to comprehend the truth of the authority he cites betrays his lack of understanding and demonstrates that the very concept of a nominal Christianity for England must be riddled with ignorance and the perversion of truth. Thus, the Scripture that the "enlightened" libertine employs satirizes not only his thesis but the very cast of mind – or rather habit of soul – that could produce such a bankrupt and dangerous view. The collision of the rake's secularizing position with the hortatory New Testament epistle exposes the persona – and all who would similarly abridge the powers of the Established Church – as those "false teachers" who will turn a noble people into "brute beasts," leading them to their slaughter on the way of perdition.

Therefore, the rhetorical strength of Swift's thoroughly undermining mock biblical whisper is not so much that it subverts the arguments and attitudes of the urbane rake, for these are hardly in need of such demolishing. Just as the rhetorical purpose of the persona is not to lampoon the views of freethinking libertines, but to strike out against those moderate Anglicans who would accommodate Dissent, so too is Swift's mock biblical satire meant to do more than achieve the simple comic effect of illustrating that an atheistic rake does not have the faintest understanding of the Scripture he cites. Instead, simultaneously normative and satirical, the biblical text from 2 Peter – strategically positioned in the very first case that the persona considers – provides the sum and substance of Swift's own position even as it satirically casts all those holding a contrary view as belonging to the rake's camp. Thus, the manner in which Swift's biblical allusion functions is altogether commensurate with the slippery-slope argument he develops throughout the essay, associating toleration with atheism, moderation with secularism, liberty of conscience with libertinism, and heterodoxy with heresy. Reduced to a simple proposition – "abrogating the Sacramental Test is the first step on a way that leads inexorably to Deism and freethinking, the deterioration of the Established Church, and moral decay; therefore, the Test must be upheld" – Swift's argument is hardly compelling. Accordingly, Swift addresses those in favor of moderation under the expedient of satire: the persona foretelling what they will become, and the Bible prophesying what will become of them.

In his *A Vindication of His Excellency John, Lord Carteret, from the charge of favouring none but Tories, High-Churchmen and Jacobites* (1730), Swift writes in the persona of an "old Whig" to defend the Lord Lieutenant of Ireland and to attack the "new Whigs," especially Sir Richard Tighe and Joshua Viscount Allen. With effective irony, Swift's Whig "of the *old fashioned Stamp*" apologizes for Carteret's virtues, while praising Tighe and Allen for qualities they obviously do not possess (Swift, 1939–68, volume 12, p. 156.) Carteret's learning, judiciousness, and fair-mindedness are contrasted with the ignorance, imprudence, and zealous partisanship of Swift's adversaries until it becomes clear that the Lord Lieutenant is a public-spirited Whig statesman, while Tighe, Allen, and their confederates are merely self-interested Whig politicians. The simplicity of

Swift's inverted praise-and-blame topos is complicated by the old Whig persona's defense of Carteret: even though the Lord Lieutenant has been handicapped by the "great Disadvantage" of "great natural Talents" (ibid., pp. 155, 154), he is nevertheless innocent of the new Whigs' accusation that he has favored the Tories in the "Preferments and Employments" he has conferred (ibid., p. 168).

Swift was particularly enraged by Allen, who had denounced him in both the Privy Council and the House of Lords, charging the Dean with disloyalty to both God and King, and accusing him of having libeled the government (Ehrenpreis, 1962–83, volume 3, pp. 652–3). Swift's venomous poems "Traulus, Part One" and its less successful sequel "Traulus. The Second Part" indicate the strength of his hatred of this "*honest* Gentleman for the bitterest Invectives against one, to whom he professeth the greatest Friendship" (Swift, 1939–68, volume 12, p. 157). In the "Vindication," Swift gives the lie to Allen by defending the Lord Lieutenant's decisions against the criticisms of Tighe, Allen, and their allies; in this way he creates a fine situational irony through a reversal of roles: it is Swift the Tory who is the loyal government apologist, writing to set the record straight in reply to the defamatory accusations of the faithless Whigs. Thus, there is a double apology in this essay as Swift associates himself with Lord Carteret, whom he deeply admired in a manner akin to his regard for Sir William Temple. (On Swift's admiration of Carteret, see Ehrenpreis, 1962–83, volume 3, p. 224.) Both the Dean and the Lord Lieutenant are learned servants of the Irish people; both are falsely accused by the fanatical new Whigs on account of their high principles. Though the "Vindication's" mock biblical satire is typically spare, appearing in just two succeeding paragraphs, it is also characteristically well aimed, striking at the extremist Whigs – whose attitudes and actions are so contrary to the principles and practices of Lord Carteret – and at the epitome of this debased form of Whiggery, Lord Allen himself. Not surprisingly, both instances of the mock biblical allude to the Whigs' wrongful charge that Carteret has favored "none but Tories, High-Churchmen and Jacobites," and to Allen's slanderous remarks about Swift.

In the first of these satirical assaults, we learn that, unlike the scholarly Carteret, who "could never wipe off the Stain, nor wash out the Tincture of his University Acquirements and Disposition [in favor of erudition as a path toward wisdom]" (Swift, 1939–68, volume 12, p. 154),

> It is certain, the high-flown Loyalists in the *present* Sense of the Word, have their thoughts, and Studies, and Tongues, so entirely diverted by political Schemes, that the *Zeal* of their *Principles* hath *eaten up* their *Understandings*; neither have they Time from their Employments ... to amuse themselves with ... [learned] Speculations which are utterly ruinous to all Schemes of rising in the World. (Ibid., p. 160)

Swift alludes to Psalm 69:9a, "For the zeal of thine house hath eaten me up," a text that would have been well known to his readers, not only on account of its appearance in the Psalter, but also because it is quoted in John's Gospel: "And his disciples remembered that it was written, The zeal of thine house hath eaten me up" (John 2:17). In the context of the "Vindication," the scriptural citation obviously indicates that the fanatic Whigs are so consumed with their ideology (sarcastically rendered as

"Principles") and selfish ambition ("Schemes of rising in the World") that they have no chance to think, no room for balanced judgment or disinterested understanding. This idea is intimated earlier in Swift's essay when the persona suggests that the old Whigs – in contrast, we are led to infer, with the new breed now ascendant – "having nothing to ask for themselves, and therefore more Leisure to think for [i.e. on behalf of] the Publick," could direct their thoughts toward redressing the "melancholly Prospects, concerning the State of their Country," including "the Decay of Trade, the Want of Money, [and] the miserable Condition of the People ... all which do equally concern both *Whig* and *Tory*" (Swift, 1939–68, volume 12, p. 156). On one level, then, the slightly modified psalm verse draws attention to the idea that the high-flying Whigs' zeal for party makes them unfit for government. Behind this notion is Swift's defense of Carteret: that if he has given a few preferments to deserving Tory clergymen, it is because he has had the insight to discern their genuine worth without being blinded to timeless values by the passing squabbles of party politics (see ibid., pp. 162ff).

On a deeper level, however, Swift uses the two contexts of the biblical text to satirize particular instances of the new Whigs' lost understanding and to attack the disordered nature of their fanaticism. The primary source of his quotation, Psalm 69, is the lament of one who, falsely accused by his enemies, appeals to God for justice. The verse Swift partially cites brings this theme at once to mind, for it reads in its entirety: "For the zeal of thine house hath eaten me up; and the reproaches of them that reproached thee are fallen upon me" (Psalms 69:9). Those who have dared to rebuke God now reprimand an innocent and righteous man. Given the circumstances of the "Vindication of His Excellency John, Lord Carteret" and Swift's transparent satirical treatment of the new Whigs and Lord Allen in that pamphlet, could contemporary readers have failed to apprehend that, transported into this secular context, the psalm adverts to the Whigs' false charge against the Lord Lieutenant and to Allen's slanderous remarks on Swift? The typically Swiftian satirical reversal of persecuted and persecuting, of innocence and guilt, is effected by having the old Whig persona, who inverts praise and blame, cast the new Whigs as those who are wrongly accused. Because the Psalm is the lament of one man surrounded by powerful and lying antagonists – "They that hate me without a cause are more than the hairs of mine head: they that would destroy me, being mine enemies wrongfully, are mighty" (Psalm 69:4) – the imaginative transposition required to locate Carteret or Swift as the Psalm's upright individual, and the high-flying Whigs as the mendacious assailants, comes quite readily.

Just as Psalm 69 is highly apposite for Swift's satirical purpose, so too is the second chapter of John's Gospel. It is Jesus' cleansing of the temple that leads his disciples to recall the Psalm, applying it to him, though ironically unknowing of their master's persecution that was to come (on irony as a characteristic device of John's Gospel, see MacRae, 1973). In the case of Swift's Dublin, it is the Whigs' zeal, not for the house of the Lord, but for the House of Lords and the House of Commons, that consumes them. In a characteristic satirical reversal, purification in the first instance is paired and, hence, compared with profanation in the second, as the sacred trust of governance is sacrificed to the petty selfishness of party and personal advantage. If Jesus restores his Father's house to its proper purpose, then the new Whigs, typified by Allen in the Lords and Tighe in the Commons, debase the legislative houses of their fathers by perverting the mission for which they were founded. It is this notion of a corrupt "House" that links the essay's first mock biblical foray with what follows a few sentences further on in the "Vindication."

Swift's old Whig, having freely admitted to "his Excellency's Failings," such as "Memory, Judgment, Comprehension, Eloquence and Wit ... the Gifts of Nature and Education" (Swift, 1939–68, volume 12, pp. 155, 154), then concedes it is certainly possible that a modern Whig "Favourer of the Times, might [also] have been born to those useless Talents, which, in former Ages qualifyed a Man to be a Poet, or a Philosopher" (ibid., p. 160). Nevertheless, he is adamant that the extreme partisanship and immoderate conduct of political life as practiced by the new Whigs would quickly annul the effect of these disabilities for holding office and exercising power in an advantageous manner. "All I contend for," he writes, "is that where the true Genius of Party once enters, it *sweeps the House clean*, and leaves room for many *other Spirits* to take joint Possession, until the *last State of that Man is exceedingly* better *than the first*" (ibid., p. 160).

The persona's words are, of course, adapted from Jesus' condemnatory remarks to "certain of the scribes and of the Pharisees." The relevant text in the Gospel of Matthew runs thus:

> When the unclean spirit is gone out of a man, he walketh through dry places, seeking rest, and findeth none. Then he saith, I will return into my house from whence I came out; and when he is come, he findeth it empty, swept, and garnished. Then goeth he, and taketh with himself seven other spirits more wicked than himself, and they enter in and dwell there: and the last state of that man is worse than the first. Even so shall it be also unto this wicked generation. (Matthew 12: 43–5)

By simple substitution, "the true Genius of Party" is equated with "the unclean spirit," a deeply ironic correspondence that casts a dark moral shadow. In the gospel, the spirit finds the house swept upon its return, whereas in the old Whig's rendition it is the "genius" itself that "*sweeps the House clean*." As in the "Vindication's" earlier instance of the mock biblical, cleansing and corruption of "the House" are reversed; the diabolical spirit of faction and party interest spreads its contagion throughout the legislature until virtually all are infected. In telling us that this contamination "leaves room for many *other Spirits*," Swift intimates that, where the preoccupation with partisan advantage replaces governance for the common good, a legion of abuses will quickly follow. Similarly, Swift's employment of the legal term "joint Possession" may be more than a playful paronomasia, for it suggests that the extreme form of party politics practiced by the new Whigs results in the ownership not only of votes and seats, but of the MPs themselves. The depravity of the old Whig's inverted moral calculus is then fully exposed in the climax of this mock biblical passage: the state of the one possessed is said to be "*exceedingly* better" than it was before. The persona's perversion of the sacred text, though less comic, is reminiscent of Jack's foolishness in "Sect. XI" of *A Tale of a Tub*. Scripture is turned upside down and the "useless Talents" that might have equipped one for the richest civil and cultural attainments have been driven out by motives of a far baser nature.

Following an old mock biblical contrivance, the last sentence of the final verse remains unwritten and is left to be supplied by the reader. This condemnation, "Even so shall it be also unto this wicked generation," being the antithesis of the old Whig's commendation, brings into relief the inverted quality of his moral sensibility and further compromises his praise of Tighe and Allen. The drive to complete the unfinished verse then sets in motion considerations about the context of the adapted passage. Although the verses that immediately follow begin an unrelated narrative, Jesus' denunciation of the scribes and Pharisees reverberates throughout the Matthean pericope and is especially germane to the "Vindication's" most satirically lively purpose: rebuking the Whigs for their unjust incrimination of Carteret and humiliating Allen for his wrongful reprehension of the Dean. The gospel pericope reads in part:

> For out of the abundance of the heart the mouth speaketh. A good man out of the good treasure of the heart bringeth forth good things: and an evil man out of the evil treasure bringeth forth evil things. But I say unto you, That every idle word that men shall speak, they shall give account thereof in the day of judgment. For by thy words thou shalt be justified, and by thy words thou shalt be condemned. ... The men of Nineveh shall rise in judgment with this generation, and shall condemn it. ... The queen of the south shall rise up in the judgment with this generation, and shall condemn it. ... When the unclean spirit is gone out of a man. ... (Matthew 12:34–7, 41a, 42a, 43a)

It is difficult to imagine a Scripture passage more apposite for the political incidents and rhetorical designs that occasioned Swift's pamphlet.

Intriguingly, Luke's Gospel also includes the illustration of the unclean spirit return- ing to the swept house with "seven other spirits more wicked than himself" (Luke 11:24–6). A biblically literate reader of the "Vindication" might just as likely recall this Lucan passage, which would give a different, though still highly appropriate, context for Swift's satire. In the Lucan account, Jesus replies to the charge that he casts out devils by the power of Beelzebub: "Every kingdom divided against itself is brought to desolation; and a house divided against a house falleth. ... He that is not with me is against me: and he that gathereth not with me scattereth" (Luke 11:17, 23). Although this text has no relevance for Swift's secondary purpose of attacking the slanderous Allen, it does powerfully address the primary subject of his essay: the strident Whigs' unfounded and narrow-minded accusation of party disloyalty against their own leader, Lord Carteret, the diplomatic and capacious Whig statesman. High- lighting the folly of their actions, the Lucan context of the "unclean spirit" establishes that the falsehood and factionalism that characterize the ironically named "true Genius of Party" are self-destructive and ultimately highly damaging to the national interest.

Though it lacks the ringing denunciation against false speech found in the Matthean passage, Luke's text is nevertheless pertinent in a way that must leave us either won- dering at the felicitous coincidence or admiring of the Bible's plasticity. It is impossible to know which gospel Swift himself had in mind, or if he hoped to capitalize on the satirical possibilities that a double resonance would offer. It is certain, however, that – whether the mind of the reader well schooled in Scripture alights on Matthew's text, or Luke's, or both – the mock biblical satire surrounding the persona's encomium of "the true Genius of Party" helps Swift to establish how fallacious and debased Whig ideology truly is. In a work that castigates primarily by irony and other methods of indirection, Swift conscripts the biblical text to speak authoritatively on his behalf. The "Vindication's" mock biblical moments do more than invoke holy writ as a corrective to the wrong-headedness of the old Whig persona. Significantly, Swift uses the Scriptures as a moral yardstick to take the measure of the Whigs' behavior, and to beat them for the evil they have done.

Conclusion

Writing a birthday poem to the fatally ill Stella in 1726, the Dean of St Patrick's, Dublin, only half jokingly implored her, "From not the gravest of Divines / Accept for once some serious Lines" ("Stella's Birthday, March 13, 1726," Swift, 1958, volume 2, p. 764, lines 13–14). Deeply committed to the office of his priesthood and to the Anglican church, Swift nevertheless deployed the sacred page in witty, sometimes transgressive ways. We must distinguish, however, between the innocent liberties he takes in his private writings and the masterfully calculated scriptural salvoes that characterize Swift's use of the Bible as an instrument of reform in his public oeuvre. For all his comic exuberance and imaginative plentitude, Swift, though never moralistic, is a relentlessly moral writer. Even when being self-deprecatory about his achievement, the Dean was adamant about his authorial purpose: "I have been only a Man of Rhimes, and that upon Trifles," he explains, "yet never any without a moral View" ("To Charles Wogan, July–2 Aug. 1732," Swift, 1965, volume 4, p. 52). A maestro of the mock biblical, Swift, perhaps more adroitly than any author of his age, was able to transpose the measures of the Authorized Version into a secular key, to season reasoned argument with revelation. Simple distinctions between the profane and the sacred take on a rich complexity in his scriptural satires, where the agora and the temple are wonderfully met.

References

Beaumont, C. A. (1965) *Swift's Use of the Bible*. University of Georgia Press, Athens.

Dennis, N. (1964) *Jonathan Swift*. Macmillan, London.

Ehrenpreis, I. (1962–83) *Swift: The Man, His Works, and the Age*, 3 volumes. Methuen, London.

MacRae, G. W. (1973) "Theology and Irony in the Fourth Gospel," in R. J. Clifford et al., eds, *Essays in Honor of Frederick L. Moriarty: The Word in the World*. Harvard University Press, Cambridge, MA.

Passmann, D. F. and Vienken, H. J., eds (2003) *The Library and Reading of Jonathan Swift: A Bio-bibliographical Handbook*. Peter Lang, Frankfurt am Main.

Steele, P. (1978) *Jonathan Swift: Preacher and Jester*. Clarendon Press, Oxford.

Swift, Jonathan (1935) *The Drapier's Letters to the People of Ireland against receiving Wood's Half-pence*, ed. H. Davis. Clarendon Press, Oxford.

Swift, Jonathan (1939–68) *The Prose Works of Jonathan Swift*, ed. H. Davis, 14 volumes. Blackwell, Oxford.

Swift, Jonathan (1948) *Journal to Stella*, ed. H. Williams, 2 volumes [paginated continuously]. Clarendon Press, Oxford.

Swift, Jonathan (1958) *The Poems of Jonathan Swift*, 2nd edn, ed. H. Williams, 3 volumes [paginated continuously]. Clarendon Press, Oxford.

Swift, Jonathan (1965) *The Correspondence of Jonathan Swift*, ed. H. Williams, 5 volumes. Clarendon Press, Oxford.

CHAPTER 26

William Blake

Jonathan Roberts and Christopher Rowland

The thesis of this chapter is that Blake contests the Bible insofar as it promotes division, disintegration, and a view of the divinity as separate from creation and the imaginative and practical lives of humans. Such a Bible leads to a world fractured by the elevation of some and the rejection of others. Blake offers a reading of the Bible that says that forgiveness of sins (a mutual activity) is central, and that all that militates against this is false religion. He does this by protesting against the way in which Old Testament (Hebrew Bible) law is made the heart of Christianity and uses the Jesus stories to point to the priority of forgiveness of sins. Confronted by an eighteenth-century model of Christianity that is hierarchical and oppressive and that promotes moral virtue, Blake declares that God's people are prophets who must engage in mental fight to build a different kind of polity.

There is no linear path through Blake's art, but for the purpose of this chapter we begin with a pair of beginnings:

> In the beginning God created the heaven and the earth. And the earth was without form, and void; and darkness was upon the face of the deep. And the Spirit of God moved upon the face of the waters. And God said, Let there be light: and there was light And God saw the light, that it was good: and God divided the light from the darkness.

> 1. Lo, a shadow of horror is risen
> In Eternity! Unknown, unprolific!
> Self-closd, all-repelling: what Demon
> Hath form'd this abominable void
> This soul-shudd'ring vacuum? – Some said
> "It is Urizen," But unknown, abstracted
> Brooding secret, the dark power hid.

> 2. Times on times he divided, & measur'd
> Space by space in his ninefold darkness
> Unseen, unknown! changes appeard
> In his desolate mountains rifted furious
> By the black winds of perturbation

> 3. For he strove in battles dire
> In unseen conflicts with shapes
> Bred from his forsaken wilderness,
> Of beast, bird, fish, serpent & element
> Combustion, blast, vapour and cloud. (Erdman, 1990, p. 69)

The two passages above are, respectively, the opening verses of Genesis, and the opening verses of *The Book of Urizen*, Blake's reimagining of Genesis. As these and subsequent stanzas show, Blake's creator-God ("Urizen") is not the commanding, benevolent patriarch of Genesis, but an inadequate and pathologically motivated demiurge frantically struggling to order the world the way he wants it. Blake's radical inversion of Genesis extends from the creator to the created: Urizen's world is not a garden of Eden, but a forsaken wilderness. In fact, the Creation itself – as Blake depicts it – is not a benevolent synthesis, but a series of violent ruptures and divisions: light from darkness, humans from God, good from evil, and so on. Blake is not being perverse here, he is working with the recognition that the God of Genesis is a systematizer who dislikes categorical confusion and who brooks no suggestion that humans might be like gods (Genesis 3). *The Book of Urizen* brings that aspect of Genesis to the fore, depicting "creation" as a tearing apart of an original dynamic unity: Blake presents Creation as destruction.

Blake engages with Genesis for several reasons. Although the Genesis creation narrative is short, because of its subject matter it has a high profile and abiding cultural presence (still manifest today in the ongoing arguments between creationists and evolutionists). Moreover, as Blake recognizes, Genesis lays the ground for considering the whole Bible to be a code book to distinguish good from evil, the sacred from the profane, and to consequently think of Christianity as a religion of morality.

This preoccupation with the systematic division of good from evil is unquestionably a central component of the Old Testament, but it is not its only component, and it is a preoccupation that is questioned, as Blake recognizes, by Jesus himself, who throughout his ministry collapses sacred / profane distinctions by, for example, living with "sinners." Through this sort of activity, Jesus foregrounds a different facet of the Old Testament, whereby the emphasis is on impulse and compassion rather than moral judgment. This is why *The Marriage of Heaven and Hell* culminates with a discussion of how Jesus broke the ten commandments, Blake's devil arguing that "no virtue can exist without breaking these ten commandments: Jesus was all virtue, and acted from impulse: not from rules" (plates 23–4).

In adopting this different focus, Blake is at odds with the prevailing Christian interpretations of the New Testament that are predicated on the sacred/secular binary of the Old Testament. As Blake shows, Christians who read the Bible as a book of moral law concomitantly come to focus their religious lives on moral uprightness. This interpretation of the Bible as a moral lawbook is, in Blake's view, not only hermeneutically mistaken, it is also at the basis of individual and social inequality and suffering. More specifically, in his analysis of his contemporary context, Blake argues that a focus on moral judgment and on the separation of sacred and profane leads to a priestly elite enabling a privileged ruling class to disregard the miseries of those whom they deem to be morally or spiritually insignificant or beyond the pale. Blake's critique of that perspective is evident throughout *Songs of Experience*. For example, in "The Chimney Sweeper" the child is left weeping and neglected in the snow by parents who have gone to church. The child says:

> And because I am happy, & dance & sing,
> They think they have done me no injury:
> And are gone to praise God & his Priest & King
> Who make up a heaven of our misery.

In their zeal to worship the sacred, the parents have neglected what they think of as (comparatively) insignificant: their own child. Blake shows, however, that this is not simply an isolated issue of child neglect, for the parents' behavior is directly connected to wider hierarchical issues within society, as these lines make clear. What is sanctified under this system is not just "God," but also his "Priest & King," which is to say the national Church in collusion with the state. Yet there are no easy solutions here: as poems such as "The Sick Rose" and the *Innocence* version of "The Chimney Sweeper" make clear, these destructive concepts are not merely implemented from above by those in power, but are internalized by the exploited themselves as what Blake calls "mind-forg'd manacles" ("London"). In the words of the *Innocence* chimney sweep, "if all do their duty, they need not fear harm."

A key characteristic of Blake, which distinguishes him from, for instance, Ludwig Feuerbach or Karl Marx, is that while he wishes to attack both contemporary religion and the Bible, he does so from a Christian perspective. One example of this is his comment about the famous victories of God's chosen people over the Canaanites (Joshua 7–9), Blake writes: "To me who believe the Bible & profess myself a Christian a defence of the Wickedness of the Israelites in murdering so many thousands under pretence of a command from God is altogether Abominable & Blasphemous." Here Blake states that he is a Christian, and believes the Bible, but critiques a central biblical narrative as "abominable & blasphemous." His own more compassionate understanding of God and Christianity thus offers him a critical vantage point from which to engage with the Bible. It is this approach to the Bible that connects him with an ancient pattern of biblical interpretation that does not, paradoxically, identify God or God's word with the Bible itself.

Blake was influenced by a view of the Bible which has a long history in Christianity and may have been part of the radical religious underground of which he was an inheritor. In this view the Word of God is not a book, but a person: Christ (see John 1:14, "And the Word was made flesh, and dwelt among us" and Hebrews 1:1–2, "God ... Hath in these last days spoken unto us by his Son"). In short, the Bible bears witness to the Word of God (that is, Christ), but is not in itself the Word of God. Blake manifests this view when he writes:

> The Bible or <Peculiar> Word of God, [when read] exclusive of conscience or the Word of God Universal, is that Abomination which like the Jewish ceremonies is for ever removed & henceforth every man may converse with God & be a King & Priest in his own house. (Erdman, 1990, p. 614)

Here Blake exalts "the Word of God Universal" (Christ, or conscience) over the "Peculiar Word of God" (the Bible as the exclusive mode of divine communication).[1] This distinction between the two "Words" (Christ and the Bible) means that an individual inspired by the former (through conscience, the Divine Spirit within) might contest and criticize the latter. This is exactly what Blake does in the passage above in which he suggests that when the Bible (the "peculiar Word of God") is disconnected from Christ ("the Word of God Universal") the former becomes an "abomination." Consequently the radical tradition within which Blake stands enables the individual, by means of his or her conscience, to speak out against the tradition of interpretation of clergy and church.[2] Jesus is positioned as the incarnate God bringing the divine and the human together in a relationship that no longer needs to be mediated by state religion: hence Blake's comment that "henceforth every man may converse with God & be a King & Priest in his own house."

This emphasis on the importance of individuals (and their social contexts) in interpreting the Bible means that Blake is particularly concerned with replacing a literalist hermeneutic with one that considers the Bible to be a stimulus to the imagination. This means above all engaging readers in the interpretation of the text, rather than demanding they accept it as an object above and beyond them. To this end Blake provides a consistent polemic against the preoccupation with the literal sense of the text, and against a reverence for that text which comes at the expense of what an imaginative and life-affirming encounter with the Bible might offer. These two tasks required a thoroughgoing assault on the ways in which the Bible had been construed and reduced to a focus on the sacrificial death of Jesus and a religion of moral virtue. Blake would have no truck, for example, with the view that humans are inherently sinful; that God must be appeased by a sacrifice (of Christ); and that God – having made this sacrifice – then expects humanity to behave morally in order to stay in relationship with him (i.e. by keeping his commandments). Such an outlook, Blake thought, led to a denial of aspects of the human person and the subjection of some human beings by others.

So, as an author, Blake seeks to develop strategies to overturn this kind of hermeneutic and to press his reader into imaginative (and inevitably radical) new relationships with the text. Such strategies abound in *The Book of Urizen*, where the relationship between text and images offers an immediate and striking contrast. To take one example, the image that accompanies those initial stanzas quoted in the opening of this chapter depicts a naked human figure, face turned away from the reader, leaping through flames. The text itself appears to be participating in the imagery, as the etched words become entwined with tendrils, leaves, and birds, yet importantly this figure doesn't appear to be that described in the text: there is no obvious connection. Immediately the book's reader is put to the test. Most books use illustrations to clarify or interpret the text, but in Blake there is often no obvious relationship between text and image, and the images serve to complicate (not resolve) our understanding the text. Blake demands the involvement of his audience in creating meaning from works in which there is no definitive meaning waiting to be discovered. Any meaning that is found there is provisional and partial, the product of an imaginative effort on the reader's part to make sense of the relationship, often the hiatus, between (for example) the text and image.

The text–image relationship in Blake is a helpful way to understand the dialectical relationship of his texts to the Bible. In the same way that his images complicate his text, so his books complicate the Bible, revealing it as a dynamic and shifting text. Blake's work is not, then, an explanation of the Bible (as a theological commentary seeks to be), but a problematization and a liberation that casts the text in a new light, and lets it become, afresh, a stimulus to the imagination.

The kind of interpretative process set up by Blake is illustrated by a letter to one of his patrons in which he provides a rare insight into his hermeneutics. Blake writes:

> You say that I want somebody to Elucidate my Ideas. But you ought to know that What is Grand is necessarily obscure to Weak men. That which can be made Explicit to the Idiot is not worth my care. The wisest of the Ancients considerd what is not too Explicit as the fittest for Instruction because it rouzes the faculties to act. I name Moses Solomon Esop Homer Plato ...
>
> Why is the Bible more Entertaining & Instructive than any other book. Is it not because they are addressed to the Imagination which is Spiritual Sensation & but mediately to the Understanding or Reason. (Letter to Trusler, Erdman, 1990, p. 703)

Here Blake articulates the art of a critically reflective practice. He also explains the delicate balance between reason and imagination, and the priority of the latter in the interpretative engagement with the Bible. The redressing of the balance between reason and imagination is the cornerstone of Blake's critical work.

Blake uses the term "Imagination" to point to a kind of thinking that is qualitatively different from what might be termed "legalistic" thinking. There are many models of Christianity that are about following inflexible rules, but being open to the Spirit means having to improvise, to engage attentively in new situations. "Imagination," therefore, is one way of describing a non-legalistic way of interpreting, an alternative to the moralistic forms of religion discussed above. Blake is clear about the centrality of the imagination to his understanding of Christianity, as he explicitly identifies the imagination as "the Divine Body," Blake's term for what Paul (in 1 Corinthians 12 and elsewhere) calls "the Body of Christ." In other words, the Imagination – open-ended, Spirit-oriented interrelating – is what brings all people together in the body of Christ.

Blake challenges the legalistic, moral Christianity of his contemporaries by unveiling its incompatibility with the gospels, and showing that in the New Testament itself, a preoccupation with moral law is identified with Jesus' opponents, the Scribes. For Blake, the consequence of this identification is that when we judge one another we take on the role of the accuser, which is, in biblical terms, the role of Satan (see Job 1:6). Blake thinks the conflict between Jesus and the Scribes arises precisely because Jesus comes to replace a religion of moral virtue (which blocks relationships between people) with one of compassion (which opens us to the experience of God in one another).

In Blake's view, then, Jesus offers the paradigm of how moral idolatry can be overcome through the forgiveness of sins. The forgiveness of sins means a relinquishment of the barriers of judgment that block relationships between people, and it reopens the possibility of collaborative hermeneutics and of the denial of selfhood and false forgiveness (cf. *Milton* 15). The forgiveness of sins therefore constitutes an act of the imagination. In his later work, Blake came more and more to concentrate on the "forgiveness of sins" and the overcoming of selfhood as the key to human flourishing. Blake sees forgiveness – rather than morality – as the central concept of Christianity and stresses that Jesus brings the former, not the latter, to the world through his teachings. This is apparent in his late engraving *Laocoön* (1826–7), in which he writes: "If morality was Christianity, Socrates was the Saviour. The Gospel is Forgiveness of Sins & has no moral precepts – these belong to Plato & Seneca & Nero" (Erdman, 1990, p. 618). And also in "The Everlasting Gospel" (*c.*1818):

> There is not one moral virtue that Jesus inculcated but Plato & Cicero did Inculcate before him. What then did Christ Inculcate? Forgiveness of Sins. This alone is the Gospel & this is the Life & Immortality brought to light by Jesus. Even the Covenant of Jehovah, which is this: "If you forgive one another your trespasses so shall Jehovah forgive you [so] that he himself may dwell among you. But if you avenge, you murder the Divine Image & he cannot dwell among you [and] because you murder him he arises again & you deny that he is arisen & are blind to Spirit." (Erdman, 1990, p. 874)

Here – and elsewhere in passages such as *Jerusalem* plate 61 – Blake argues that when we live in that spirit of mutual love and forgiveness, God lives in us, and we in him.

Forgiveness is qualitatively different from Law, Blake suggests, because it cannot be codified in a book: it requires imagination, not legislation. The point is exemplified in the gospels by Jesus' response when his disciple, Peter, seeks to establish the limits of forgiveness: "Then Peter came to Jesus and asked, 'Lord, how many times shall I forgive my brother when he sins against me? Up to seven times?' Jesus answered, 'I tell you, not seven times, but seventy-seven times'" (Matthew 18:21–2). There is a clear contrast here with the law of retaliation formulated in Exodus: "if there is serious injury, you are to take life for life, eye for eye, tooth for tooth, hand for hand, foot for foot, burn for burn, wound for wound, bruise for bruise" (Exodus 21:23–5). Unlike retaliation, forgiveness cannot be quantified, and is always particular to each life situation.

Blake exemplifies the meaning of forgiveness of sins in his reimagining of the brief, but allusive, account at the end of Matthew 1 (18–25) in which Joseph discovers that his betrothed, Mary, is pregnant:

> 1:18 Now the birth of Jesus Christ was on this wise: When as his mother Mary was espoused to Joseph, before they came together, she was found with child of the Holy Ghost. 1:19 Then Joseph her husband, being a just man, and not willing to make her a publick example, was minded to put her away privily. 1:20 But while he thought on these things, behold, the angel of the Lord appeared unto him in a dream, saying, Joseph, thou son of David, fear not to take unto thee Mary thy wife: for that which is conceived in her is of the Holy Ghost. 1:21 And she shall bring forth a son, and thou shalt call his name JESUS: for he shall save his people from their sins. 1:22 Now all this was done, that it might be fulfilled which was spoken of the Lord by the prophet, saying, 1:23 Behold, a virgin shall be with child, and shall bring forth a son, and they shall call his name Emmanuel, which being interpreted is, God with us. 1:24 Then Joseph being raised from sleep did as the angel

of the Lord had bidden him, and took unto him his wife: 1:25 And knew her not till she
had brought forth her firstborn son: and he called his name JESUS.

Blake's reimagining of this scene occurs in *Jerusalem: The Emanation of the Great Albion*
(1804–20):

> [Jerusalem] looked & saw Joseph the Carpenter in Nazareth & Mary
> His espoused Wife. And Mary said, If thou put me away from thee
> Dost thou not murder me? Joseph spoke in anger & fury. Should I
> Marry a Harlot & an Adulteress? Mary answerd, Art thou more pure
> Than thy Maker who forgiveth Sins & calls again Her that is Lost
> Tho She hates. he calls her again in love. I love my dear Joseph
> But he driveth me away from his presence. yet I hear the voice of God
> In the voice of my Husband. tho he is angry for a moment, he will not
> Utterly cast me away. if I were pure, never could I taste the sweets
> Of the Forgive[ne]ss of Sins! if I were holy! I never could behold the tears
> Of love! of him who loves me in the midst of his anger in furnace of fire.
>
> Ah my Mary: said Joseph: weeping over & embracing her closely in
> His arms: Doth he forgive Jerusalem & not exact Purity from her who is
> Polluted. I heard his voice in my sleep O his Angel in my dream:
> Saying, Doth Jehovah Forgive a Debt only on condition that it shall
> Be Payed? Doth he Forgive Pollution only on conditions of Purity
> That Debt is not Forgiven! That Pollution is not Forgiven
> Such is the Forgiveness of the Gods, the Moral Virtues of the
> Heathen, whose tender Mercies are Cruelty. But Jehovahs Salvation
> Is without Money & without Price, in the Continual Forgiveness of Sins
> In the Perpetual Mutual Sacrifice in Great Eternity! (Erdman, 1990, p. 614,
>   *Jerusalem*, 61.1–46, Erdman, 1990, pp. 210–11)

This passage may seem uncharacteristic to readers who are familiar with Blake principally through the *Songs* and *The Marriage*. It is from a later prophetic work, and represents one of Blake's slightly awkward attempts to dramatize a biblical scene. It is very
much an eighteenth-century literary mode: the passion, sighing, weeping, and embracing could have been lifted from a sentimental novel of that period. Blake uses this mode
to evoke a fraught emotional scene lying behind the gospel narrative, and he imagines,
from there, the significance of Mary and Joseph's reconciliation.

Mary is confronted by Joseph's challenge about her supposed infidelity as he discovers that she is pregnant. In response to this, Blake imagines Mary bluntly declaring the
consequence of her rejection: in effect Joseph would be murdering her as she could have
been stoned to death under Jewish law as a suspected adulteress (cf. Deuteronomy
22:21). Joseph the righteous man speaks "in anger and fury" and questions why (in
the light of the law) he should marry "a Harlot & an Adulteress." Mary's question in
return is to point to the character of God who goes on forgiving his bride Israel. Mary
says she hears the voice of God in the voice of Joseph, and it is a God who forgives sins.
The exquisite possibility of the forgiveness of sins cannot happen, if she were always
holy and pure. The experience of the tears of love comes as the result of "anger in the
furnace of fire."

Joseph's initial response is to embrace Mary and query the idea that God might exact a price for forgiveness. But this is immediately followed by the voice of an angel questioning this reparatory theology by intimating that forgiveness does not come simply by making oneself pure, as such a debt is not really forgiven. Indeed, this is the religion of dictatorial "gods," "the Moral Virtues of the Heathen, whose tender Mercies are Cruelty," whereas God's "salvation is without Money & without Price, in the Continual Forgiveness of Sins." Joseph's tone thus changes from condemnation of the sin to the recognition of the person before him: "Ah, my Mary."

This is immediately followed by sentiments that echo the Lord's Prayer – "Forgive us our trespasses as we forgive those who trespass against us" – reflecting "the Perpetual Mutual Sacrifice in Great Eternity." The portrayal of God's covenant with humanity as a state in which forgiveness is mutual and shared echoes Matthew 18:15–20: "If you Forgive one-another, so shall Jehovah Forgive You: That He Himself may Dwell among You." God dwelling with humans is conditional on the establishment of the covenant with humanity, the "Perpetual Mutual Sacrifice in Great Eternity." Such sentiments also recall some of Blake's much earlier ideas recorded in his marginal notes to Lavater's *Aphorisms on Man*, in which he consistently focuses on the human person rather than the offense.

At the beginning of this chapter, we stated that Blake wished all God's people to be prophets. This desire for prophecy is centrally connected to Blake's focus on alternatives to the legalistic tradition embedded in the Bible. As we mentioned earlier, Blake considered his contemporaries to be preoccupied with the Old Testament emphasis on morality, Law, and separation of the sacred from the profane, and by interpreting the New Testament in the light of these elements, they were engaging a judgmental, moralistic form of Christianity. Blake, by contrast, sought to prioritize the imaginative, compassionate, radical elements of the New Testament, and takes those as his guide to the Old Testament. In doing so he identifies the prophetic tradition of the Old Testament as primary, and not the hegemonic legislative tradition (Matthew 12:7, "I desire mercy and not sacrifice" – a quotation of Hosea 6:6). As a result, Blake understands prophecy to be at the heart of Christianity: prophecy locks together with the imagination and the forgiveness of sins.

Blake's call for all individuals to embrace their role as prophets is especially apparent at the conclusion to the preface to his long poem *Milton* (popularly known as "Jerusalem"), Here Blake added the words "Would to God that all the Lord's people were prophets," giving the biblical reference Numbers 11:29, and reminding his reader of prophecy's key place in his work, and his own role as a prophet. Blake recognized the prophets of the Bible as kindred spirits, dining with Isaiah and Ezekiel and questioning them about their prophetic ministries in *The Marriage of Heaven and Hell* (plates 12 and 13). He wrote in their style and used their images but as a prophet for his own time, seeking to unmask the extent of human delusion and the forgetfulness of the practice of love and the forgiveness of sins. Like John, the visionary of Patmos (Revelation 22:19), Blake called his own books "prophecies." However, Blake regarded prophecy not as some kind of arcane activity reserved solely for an eccentric elite, but something everyday and democratic: "Every honest man is a prophet," ("On Watson," E616). Moreover, his prophecies were not intended to predict what would happen in the future, for they were written after the events that are described. In his annotations to Watson's *An Apology for the Bible* (1797), Blake declared that:

> Prophets in the modern sense of the word have never existed. Jonah was no prophet, in the modern sense, for his prophecy of Nineveh failed. Every honest man is a prophet; he utters his opinion both of private and public matters. Thus: If you go on So, the result is So. he never says, such a thing shall happen let you do what you will. A Prophet is a Seer, not an Arbitrary Dictator. ("On Watson," Erdman, 1990, p. 616)

One purpose of prophecy, then, is to lay bare the inner dynamic of all revolutions, and to show their potential for both positive change and corruption. The book Blake thought most achieved this laying bare was the Book of Revelation, and his relationship to it is particularly informative. He did not read Revelation as if it were a riddle that had to be solved, but understood it instead as a gateway through which the Imagination can "open the Eternal Worlds, to open the immortal eyes of Man inwards into the Worlds of Thought, into Eternity" (*Jerusalem*, 5.18). Blake reads Revelation (and other prophetic works) not as an end in itself but as a means to an end: the permeating of consciousness with the apocalyptic outlook.

In summary, Blake was not an expositor of the Bible, but an artist who regarded it as a stimulus to his imagination and inventiveness. Biblical imagery appears in the context of Blake's own mythological creations, which he believed were in continuity with prophetic texts such as the books of Isaiah and Ezekiel, and the Book of Revelation, however different their form and content. Thus Blake's relationship with his literary antecedents, the Bible included, is less that of a reverent expositor and much more that of a querulous partner, who is always ready to point out the flaws in what he has received. What he has received, however, is complex, it is not so much a book as a history of interpretations of a text, and in offering something different, he thereby shows his active engagement with this book. This is no simple biblical critique. The thoroughgoing radicalism of its hermeneutic is matched only by that of its forms: the astonishingly diverse array of poems, engravings, and paintings that make Blake simultaneously both England's greatest "Christian" artist and its most radical biblical interpreter.

Notes

1 This distinction is an important part of a long tradition of radical Christian hermeneutic of the Bible, which was especially prevalent in England from the sixteenth century onwards. It is crucial to understanding the wider context of biblical interpretation of which Blake was a part.

2 See Lerner (1972) for the late medieval antecedents.

Further Reading

The subject of Blake and the Bible is an enormous one. This chapter has provided one way into thinking about topic. A range of other – and often very different – approaches are listed below.

Burdon, Christopher (1997) *The Apocalypse in England: Revelation Unraveling, 1700–1834*. St Martins Press, New York.

Davies, John (1948) *The Theology of William Blake*. Clarendon Press, Oxford.

Erdman, David V., ed. (1990) *Blake and His Bibles*, intr. Mark Trevor Smith. Locust Hill, West Cornwall, CT.

Lerner, Robert E. (1972) *The Heresy of the Free Spirit in the Later Middle Ages*. University of Notre Dame Press, Notre Dame, IN.

Paley, Morton D. (1998) "To Defend the Bible in This Year 1798 Would Cost a Man His Life," *Blake, An Illustrated Quarterly* 32:2, 32–43.

Prickett, Stephen and Stratham, Christopher (2006) "Blake and the Bible," in Nicholas M. Williams, ed., *Palgrave Advances in William Blake Studies*. Palgrave Macmillan, Basingstoke.

Rowland, Christopher (2003) "Blake and the Bible: Biblical Exegesis in the Work of William Blake," in John Court, eds., *Biblical Interpretation: The Meanings of Scripture – Past and Present*. T & T Clark, London.

Rowland, Christopher and Jonathan Roberts (2008) *The Bible for Sinners: Interpretation in the Present Time*, SPCK, London.

Ryan, Robert (2003) "Blake and Religion," in *The Cambridge Companion to William Blake*. Cambridge University Press, Cambridge.

Tannenbaum, Leslie (1982) *Biblical Tradition in Blake's Early Prophecies*. Princeton University Press, Princeton, NJ.

CHAPTER 27
Women Romantic Poets

Penny Bradshaw

The linking of poetry and prophecy in the latter part of the eighteenth century plays a crucial role in the development of concepts of poetry and the poet within the Romantic period (Jasper and Prickett, 1999, p. 27). Yet that which forms such a profound justification and high purpose for male poetry of the period presents special problems for the female poet who shares the wider aesthetic and ideological framework of Romanticism but who is excluded from what appears to be an exclusively patriarchal tradition of divinely inspired and visionary poetics. Some of the prominent female writers of the period, such as Mary Robinson and Charlotte Smith, sidestep this difficulty by negotiating their poetic voices in relation to a range of alternative secular sources of authority, including classical mythology and scientific writings. Other writers, such as Anna Barbauld and Helen Maria Williams, frequently deploy the language of prophecy and religious discourse in politicized contexts, in their political hymns and tracts, but tend to avoid the more direct engagement with biblical writings that we find in the work of their male contemporaries and that often relates to the assertion of a divinely inspired poetics.[1] Two major women poets of the period who do attempt to interrogate more fully their relationship with sacred and divinely inspired poetry and with the Bible itself, Hannah More and Felicia Hemans, both explore the role of women within scriptural narratives as a means of negotiating the dilemma of gender in relation to high prophetic discourse. Somewhat paradoxically, these poets use the authority of the master patriarchal text to explore the possibility of less restrictive and more meaningful roles and voices for women than those sanctioned by Romantic contexts.

Hannah More

Hannah More has recently been described as "the most influential woman living in England in the Romantic era" (Mellor, 2000, pp. 15–16) and while her work has received increasing critical attention of late, most critics focus on her post-revolutionary tracts and conduct works, and have tended to sideline her biblical literature. Her 1782 *Sacred Dramas* is, however, a compelling early Romantic engagement with the Bible that provides a precursory and in some ways more radical working through of the ideas that would come to dominate her later prose works, in particular those relating to the nature of women's influence within society.

More manages to elide the criticism that might be attached to a woman writer in directly engaging with biblical material in this way, by utilizing the educational mode as a legitimate justification for venturing into sacred territory; the subtitle indicates that the dramas are "Chiefly Intended for Young Persons," and it is likely that the impetus behind the collection was More's involvement with the teaching of privileged young ladies at the school that she and her sisters ran in Bristol. The texts are thus written, overtly at least, for educational purposes, but under the relatively safe cover of producing pedagogical, morally instructive literature, More ventures into the realm of biblical hermeneutics and presents a confident imaginary revisioning of the original canonical narratives.

Although they are described as dramas, More makes clear in the prose advertisement that these texts are not intended for stage production and are therefore more properly described as closet dramas or dramatic poems, intended to be read aloud rather than enacted. While More began her literary career as a playwright, she later abandoned the writing of plays for public performance in reaction to what she viewed as the immoral tastes of the theatergoing public. She retained, however, a commitment to the possibilities presented by dramatic forms and continued to assert the value of drama over and above other forms of literature as the only genre with the "combined advantage of addressing itself to the imagination, the judgement and the heart" (More quoted in Mellor, 2000, p. 46). In the 1780s she shifted her attention therefore to the production of dramatic poems, which allowed her to evade the problematic associations of stage production, while continuing to utilize what she saw as the benefits of dramatic writing. These verse-dramas enabled her to explore the human and emotional dimensions of the Bible and to bring about a response from readers that simultaneously drew on their imagination, their emotions, and their intellect. The effect of this is to render biblical narrative and theological ideas more directly affecting and meaningful as we enter into the imagined emotional, psychological, and spiritual dilemmas of specific characters.

The biblical incidents and characters focused on are mainly drawn from the staple Sunday school repertoire, including "Moses in the Bulrushes," "David and Goliath," "Belshazzar," and "Daniel," but her handling of this material positions her firmly within the aesthetic climate of Romanticism. More's own account of the attributes of dramatic writing owes much to changing aesthetic preferences in the late eighteenth century, in particular the emphasis on the role of the imagination and the attempt to engage the reader in a more direct and emotional way with the subject matter. The stories she chose also tackle a number of Romantic tropes and themes, such as the plight of the marginalized outsider – which is explored in the stories of Moses and David – and the corrupting influence of absolute power, that "dangerous pinnacle of power supreme!" from which one grows "giddy," beholding the "gazing prostrate world below" (More, 1825, p. 127). Daniel's speech to Belshazzar, in which he rejects the king's offer of wealth and worldly status, also in some ways prefigures the aspirational language of Byron's transgressive heroes, but here the speaker's ambitions are divinely legitimized and validated by biblical authority:

> O mighty king, thy gifts with thee remain,
> And let thy high rewards on others fall.
> ... Honour, fame,
> All that the world calls great, thy crown itself,
> Could never satisfy the vast ambition
> Of an immortal spirit: I aspire,
> Beyond the pow'r of giving; my high hopes
> Reach also to a crown – but 'tis a crown
> Unfading and eternal. (pp. 126–7)

There is also a subtle attempt within the collection to link the role of the poet with that of the divine songmaker and prophet, which again relates to Romantic contexts, but the gender of the author presents problems in this respect and the introduction of this tension at the opening of the collection draws attention to the ways in which More's gender impacts on her literary negotiation with sacred material.

The blank verse introduction begins and ends in fairly conventional terms, with the Christian woman poet wistfully asking for the "sacred energy" of the male biblical prophets and psalmists or for "one faint ray, / ... Of that pure spirit which inflam'd the breast / Of Milton, GOD'S own poet!" before acknowledging that she lacks the "proph-et's burning zeal" and the Miltonic "muse of fire" (p. 11). More appears here to accept the conventional exclusion of women from high, divinely inspired poetic discourse, yet her very Romantic critical argument for the validity of treating the Bible as appropriate poetic subject matter over and above classical source material contains a subtle sug-gestion that women poets might be particularly successful within this genre of Scrip-ture-inspired literature. She notes that poets have so far failed to really feel and empathize with the divine message:

> Truth has our reverence only, not our love;
> Our praise, but not our heart: a deity,
> Confess'd, but shunn'd; acknowledg'd, not ador'd;
> Alarm'd, we dread her penetrating beams;
> She comes too near us, and too brightly shines. (p. 13)

In this invocation to "love" spiritual truths, to experience them with our "heart" and allow them to come "near us," More seems to be arguing for a more emotional engage-ment with biblical material and this is precisely what her dramas offer. *Sacred Dramas* was published together with a poem entitled "Sensibility," and this pairing offers a clue to More's intended project here. "Sensibility" has been described as "an advocacy of the religion of the heart" (Stott, 2003, p. 83), and in the *Dramas* her strategy is essentially to bring the "heart" to religion, to present the characters in such a way that we *feel* their dilemmas and experience their stories in an emotional way. On one level, this relates to the changing aesthetic tastes of the late eighteenth century but this appeal for a new way of responding to sacred material is also gendered, since More argues repeatedly in her writing that women have a more intense engagement with the emotions and thus a special and unique access to the Christian message: "In their Christian course women have every superior advantage. ... Their hearts are naturally soft and flexible, open to impressions of love and gratitude; their feelings tender and lively" (More, 1830, p. 238).

In "Moses in the Bulrushes," the most provocative of the dramas and that which opens the collection, More not only displays this theory in practice but also develops the story in other, more surprising ways, which emphasize the crucial role played by women within biblical narrative. Despite her assertion in the advertisement to the volume that "I have seldom ventured to introduce any persons of my own creation: still less did I imagine myself at liberty to invent circumstances," More offers a far from conventional retelling of this standard Sunday school narrative (More, 1825, p. 5). She specifies at the outset that her drama is based on Exodus 2 and she proceeds to dramatize the events of this chapter through the female figures in the story. The four speaking characters in the drama are all women: Jochebed, mother of Moses; Miriam, sister of Moses; the Pharaoh's daughter; and Melita, an attendant of Pharaoh's daughter. By focusing on these figures, the first three parts of the drama work to emphasize a range of virtues such as pity, love, and sympathy, which are identifiably Christian but which are here as elsewhere in More's writings also explicitly connected to women, and which are juxtaposed in the drama with Pharaoh's masculine cruelty, his "oppression" and his "unrelenting hate" (p. 29). In this More does not actually deviate from the biblical version but in retelling the story as a female-orientated drama and empathetically engaging with the female characters, she emphasizes the pivotal role played by the women and moves their collaboration and virtues to the center of the story's meaning, thus developing an aspect of the narrative that is merely latent in Exodus. The women are united across racial and religious divides through their shared feminine qualities, illustrated most graphically by the sympathy of the Egyptian Pharaoh's daughter, who describes how her "heart has bled / In secret anguish" for the "Unhappy" Hebrew mothers and their "slaughter'd sons" (pp. 28–9). Jochebed's vital maternal role in filling Moses's "tender soul with virtue" and warming "his bosom with devotion's flame" (p. 37) is also emphasized, showing how this helps to prepare him for his subsequent role in rescuing the Hebrew people from their bondage. Through this maternal spiritual guidance he is:

> furnish'd, 'gainst the evil day,
> With God's whole armour, girt with sacred truth,
> And as a breastplate wearing righteousness;
> Arm'd with the Spirit of God, the shield of faith. (p. 37)

More is clearly rehearsing ideas here that would dominate her influential female conduct book, *Strictures on the Modern System of Female Education* (1799), in which she argues powerfully for the role of woman as mother in shaping the nation itself:

> the great object to which YOU, who are or may be mothers, are more especially called, is the education of your children. ... On YOU depend, in no small degree, the principles of the whole rising generation. To your direction the daughters are almost exclusively committed; and until a certain age, to YOU also is consigned the mighty privilege of

forming the hearts and minds of your infant sons. To YOU is made over the awfully important trust of infusing the first principles of piety into the tender minds of those who may
one day be called to instruct, not families merely, but districts; to influence, not individuals,
but senates. (More, 1830, p. 40)

In this drama, published some seventeen years earlier, More enacts this process for her
audience and demonstrates the far-reaching effects of the maternal role throughout
history. In all of this More is of course reaffirming conventional eighteenth-century
gender roles, albeit in a way that emphasizes the central role played by women in
scriptural history and the role of the mother in the construction of man and thus
society itself. In the fourth part of this drama, however, More begins to deviate more
fully from the time frame of the original biblical version of this story as well as from
the realist mode of dramatic presentation, and in so doing suggests a more powerful
and transgressive female role, which does not find such full exploration anywhere else
in her writing.

Moses reaches manhood at verse 11 of Exodus 2 and from this point onwards in the
biblical account the focus shifts from the women who saved him to the man himself,
telling of how he begins to respond to the suffering of the Hebrews. The chapter ends
with Moses's marriage and with God hearing the suffering of the Israelites in bondage.
In More's radical retelling, however, the focus stays with the women and the time frame
remains within the infancy of Moses, immediately after his rescue by Pharaoh's daughter. We do learn of his adulthood in the final section of the verse-drama but this is
achieved quite startlingly through the dramatic device of prophetic speech. Part 4 of
the drama is a dialogue between Jochebed and her daughter Miriam in which Miriam,
suddenly "wrapt in extasy," is visited by a "prescient spirit ... from on high" who
"Reveals the hidden things of unborn time, / And leads my view through dim futurity"
(More, 1825, p. 39). Through this device More actually moves beyond the confines of
Exodus 2 and travels forward through subsequent chapters; "successive scenes in order
pass" (p. 40) before Miriam's vision, including Moses leading the Israelites on their
journey through the desert and through the parting waves of the Red Sea. Miriam
foresees not only the events of Moses's life and his role in the deliverance of the Israelites, however, but also, in the final vision, Christ's future redemption of mankind:

> Hear further wonders:
> Moses, though great, is but the type of ONE
> Far greater; ONE predestin'd to redeem
> Not Israel only, but the human race;
> ONE who in after time shall rescue men,
> Not from the body's slav'ry, the brief bondage
> Of life and time; but who shall burst the chains
> Which keep the soul enthrall'd, the chains of sin;
> Shall free the captive from the galling yoke
> Of Satan; rescue from eternal death,
> And finally restore, Man's ruin'd race. (p. 46)

In this final prophecy More extrapolates from the very slight biblical hints about
Miriam's prophetic character in a surprisingly audacious way. She was clearly aware

that her construction of Miriam took liberties with biblical authority and adds an apologetic but defensive footnote:

> The Author is fearful that she may be thought, in this last part, to have exceeded the bounds of poetical licence. For though Miriam, in the chapter which contains the Song of Moses, is called a prophetess; and though the prophet Micah, in his sixth chapter, speaks of Miriam assisting jointly with her brothers, Moses and Aaron, in the redemption of Israel from captivity, yet we hear little or nothing of her elsewhere in her prophetic character. (p. 46)

More's engagement with biblical material here is complex and combines the imaginative with the hermeneutic. While in her *Strictures on the Modern System of Female Education* she asserts that the "profession[s]" sought by women should be those of "daughters, wives, mothers, and mistresses of families" (More, 1830, p. 71) and while much of the emphasis of this drama reasserts the power and value of these traditional roles for women, she is nonetheless keen here to pick up on the very slight biblical hints of a woman in the role of seer and prophet. She brings these buried elements of Miriam's story back to the surface and reconstructs the idea for dramatic purposes. Given that the text was written ostensibly as an educational tool, it might be supposed that such a portrayal of female inspiration would work against her advocation of meekness and humility in the female sex. The representation of Miriam here aligns More with a specific branch of feminist biblical scholarship, which focuses on bringing to light those submerged elements of the Bible that are suggestive of a hidden narrative of female power and authority. Such critics set out to "retrieve from the palimpsest of patriarchal narrative what the narrative attempts to bury and deny," the "traces or tracks of the female story" (Ostriker, 1997, pp. 164–5) and then attempt to "rewrite women back into the text and ... break the conspiratorial silence regarding their role in biblical narrative" (Davis, 2003, p. 86). These later feminist scholars have, like More, been particularly drawn to the possibilities presented by Miriam:

> there are some indications in the Hebrew Bible to suggest that Miriam occupied a position of prominence and prestige in Israel. ... But while the biblical text gives tantalizing hints of Miriam's importance and influence, she is not accorded the attention the few passages concerning her suggest she deserves. ... Thus, for example, ... although she is called a "prophet," there are no examples of her prophecies or any clues as to the nature of her prophetic activity. ... Miriam's role was minimized and suppressed by the biblical authors and her contribution was practically submerged within the male-orientated framework of the biblical text. (Ibid.)

In her attempt to present us with an imaginary reconstruction of Miriam's submerged prophetic voice, More seems to step beyond the bounds of her better known identification of the domestic and the maternal as the locus of women's power. She stakes a claim here for a much more radical role for women as having special access to spiritual truths, thus transgressing into the masculine sphere of divine revelation. More's latest biographer describes her as "a paradoxical figure, who worked for change while supporting existing hierarchies ... though deeply hostile to overt feminism, she longed for women to realize their spiritual and intellectual potential" (Stott, 2003, p. xi). More's feminist act of literary reconstruction within this drama is perhaps her most powerful intimation of this desire being realized.

Felicia Hemans

As in the case of Hannah More, the recent resurgence of critical interest in the work of Felicia Hemans has tended to sideline her biblical poetry, which is no doubt seen as "resistant to the highly secularised ... progressivism of much academic discourse" (Kelly, 2002, p. 85). Yet an understanding of Hemans's sacred poetry and especially her engagement with biblical source material, is central to reaching a fuller conclusion about her work, since here she not only reaffirms the ideas about female roles and gender that dominate her more widely studied poetry, but also presents a more powerful case for the value and worth of those roles in society.

Hemans's earliest reworking of biblical narrative is a poem published just four years after Byron's successful *Hebrew Melodies*: "Heliodorus in the Temple" appeared in an otherwise secular poetic collection, *Tales and Historic Scenes*, in 1819 and critics have tended to read this collection as a whole as a nationalistic response to the Napoleonic conflicts and their immediate aftermath (Kelly, 2002, pp. 26–7). Wolfson describes the Heliodorus story as a "tale of divine protection," which in Hemans's reworking "speaks to Britain's boast, in the wake of its defeat of Napoleon, of being a modern Jerusalem, providentially protected" (editorial notes in Hemans, 2000, p. 148). Such a reading of this poem is complicated, however, by the emphasis on gendered language in Hemans's reworking of the Heliodorus narrative, an emphasis that might suggest a rather different interpretation of her presentation of this tale of sacrilege and divine nemesis. The poem in fact seems to prefigure what would become the central motif of her later more influential collection, *The Records of Woman*, in describing and critiquing male destruction of a sacred feminized domestic space. That the sacred temple in the poem functions on one level as a metaphor for this idealized place is suggested by the fact that Heliodorus's crime is depicted initially through women's misery:

> A sound of woe in Salem! – mournful cries
> Rose from her dwellings ...
>
> Thy daughters, Judah! weeping, laid aside
> The regal splendor of their fair array,
> With the rude sackcloth girt their beauty's pride,
> And throng'd the streets in hurrying, wild dismay. (Hemans, 2000, pp. 148–9)

The "sacred chambers" of the "bright" and "beautiful" temple are subtly feminized and Heliodorus himself is figured merely in symbolic terms, as "man, with eye unhallow'd" (p. 149); the absence of the definite article before "man" makes this act of sacrilege read less like the crime of a specific man, as we might expect in an allegory of Napoleonic conquest, and more like a generic male crime against that which is both sacred and closely associated with women.

In the apocryphal account of this story in 2 Maccabees 3, the fear of the high priest Onias is the focus of attention and it is the people and the priest who call out for God's intervention; in Hemans's poem the male voice is silenced and instead the voice of the female poet calls out to God to avenge the crime:

> Wilt thou not wake, O Chastener!
>
> ...
>
> Oh! yet once more defend thy loved domain,
> Eternal one! Deliverer! rise again! (p. 149)

As the "sanctuary" is being ransacked this prayer for divine vengeance is answered and a horse and rider appear within the temple, crushing Heliodorus beneath trampling hooves. The horse and rider are figured as the wrath of God incarnate and Hemans lingers over this awful vision of vengeance:

> Away, intruders! – hark! a mighty sound!
> Behold, a burst of light! away, away!
> A fearful glory fills the temple round,
> A vision bright in terrible array!
> And lo! a steed of no terrestrial frame,
> His path a whirlwind, and his breath a flame!
>
> His neck is clothed with thunder – and his mane
> Seems waving fire – the kindling of his eye
> Is as a meteor – ardent with disdain
> His glance – his gesture, fierce in majesty!
> Instinct with light he seems, and form'd to bear
> Some dread archangel through the fields of air.
>
> But who is he, in panoply of gold,
> Throned on that burning charger? bright his form,
> Yet in its brightness awful to behold,
> And girt with all the terrors of the storm!
> Lightning is on his helmet's crest – and fear
> Shrinks from the splendor of his brow severe. (pp. 149–50)

As the tone of the poem at the beginning is one of righteous anger at male acts of plunder and betrayal, so at the end there is clearly a lingering pleasure in the vision of God's intervention to protect the sacred temple; this "scourge of God" leaves Heliodorus as one dead and he is carried out of this "inviolable" space; light returns to the temple and Salem "exult[s]" in her triumph (p. 150).

Hemans's tendency throughout her career to focus on the suffering of women and man's mistreatment of the sacred domestic space has been linked to her own abandonment by her husband, and this poem was published just one year after Captain Hemans finally left the family home, a pregnant wife, and four sons for Rome, never to return. At some level the engagement with biblical material here seems an attempt to work through her own suffering and her sense of anger at this act of male sacrilege. As Anne

Mellor (1993) has argued, while "Hemans' poetry locates ultimate human value within the domestic sphere," it simultaneously

> emphasizes just how precarious, how threatened, is that sphere – by the passage of time, by the betrayals of family members, by its opposition to the dominant ideology of the masculine public sphere, the domain of ambition, military glory and financial power. We need to read her lyrics … as parts of a corpus that constantly reminds us of the fragility of the very domestic ideology it endorses. (p. 124)

This poem could be read as an attempt to position God on her side within this gender conflict and to explore ways of countering the fragility of the domestic space, since casting the allegory through biblical narrative allows her to rewrite the ending. While in most of the poems that deal with this motif the conclusion is inevitably woman's fortitude in the face of ongoing suffering, by contrast, the women in this poem – the daughters of Judah – are not left sobbing and weeping at the end, since God intervenes to protect them and wreak revenge on the male oppressor. Because the temple here is literally sacred, this analogy works and is valorized by biblical, albeit apocryphal, authority. When Hemans turned to biblical material more extensively at the very end of her career, she seemed to remember this lesson and moved toward a closer identification of women with God.

From around 1830 Hemans made a public and private decision to turn her attention more fully to the production of sacred poetry, culminating in the publication of *Scenes and Hymns of Life* in 1834, the year before her death. In a letter describing this shift, she flags up its significance in terms of her self-construction as a poet:

> I have now … passed through the feverish and somewhat visionary state of mind, often connected with the passionate study of art in early life: deep affections and deep sorrows seem to have solemnized my whole being, and I now feel as if bound to higher and holier tasks. … I hope it is no self-delusion, but cannot help sometimes feeling as if it were my true task to enlarge the sphere of sacred poetry, and extend its influence. (More quoted in Melnyk, 2001, p. 76)

Like More, Hemans feels it necessary to defend her foray into sacred territory, but the notion that this is in some sense her "true task" and that she has received a calling to produce sacred works legitimizes her transgression into a "higher and holier" realm. In making this assertion, as Julie Melnyk (2001, p. 76) notes, Hemans is claiming "the vatic power that male Romantic poets represented as their birthright, but that female poets were popularly denied" and there are certainly moments within these late poems when she seems to assert an inspired and visionary poetic power: "The gift, the vision of the unsealed eye, / To pierce the mist o'er life's deep meanings spread" (Hemans, 1887, p. 625), which elsewhere in her poetry she had rejected in favor of a more acceptable discourse of the domestic affections.

Melnyk (2001, p. 74) argues that this turn to religious poetry was a means of "freeing" Hemans "from the confines of an affectional tradition," but in her preface to *Scenes and Hymns of Life*, Hemans makes claims for her ability as a woman to transform the genre of sacred poetry in a way that suggests she is instead bringing that feminized affectional poetic tradition to bear on a religious poetry:

> I trust I shall not be accused of presumption for the endeavour which I have here made to enlarge, in some degree, the sphere of religious poetry, by associating with its themes more of the emotions, the affections, and even the purer imaginative enjoyments of daily life, than may have been hitherto admitted within the hallowed circle. (Hemans, 1887, p. 607)

As well as "enlarging" religious poetry in this way, Hemans also presents us with a strategically selected body of material from the Bible, which emphasizes and focuses on women's role within sacred history. This connects to what Kelly (2002) has identified as her ongoing attempt to "refeminize history":

> Hemans and other liberal Romantic writers ... saw historiography, written almost exclusively by men, as a record of conflict, war, and destruction caused by and for men. Such history ... victimizes women and what they represent. ... Hemans, like other women writers of the time, suggests that the way to break the cycle of masculine history is to refeminize history for the future. (p. 29)

Within her 1834 collection, *Scenes and Hymns of Life*, along with poems dealing quite broadly with spiritual and Christian themes, Hemans also presents a more direct poetic engagement with the Bible in a series of sonnets on "Female Characters of Scripture." This can be viewed as the culmination of her attempt to "break the cycle of masculine history" by focusing on women's important contributions to Christian history, and through this pointing to an alternative set of values that are both feminized and divinely authorized.

The sequence opens with two Invocation sonnets, which mourn the absence of important female figures in our understanding of biblical history:

> Your tents are desolate; your stately steps,
> Of all their choral dances, have not left
> One trace beside the fountains. (Hemans, 1887, p. 641)

The first Invocation then calls on these silenced women to rise up and provide her with the poetic inspiration and role models she needs:

> Come with the voice, the lyre,
> Daughters of Judah! with the timbrel rise!
> Ye of the dark, prophetic, Eastern eyes,
> Imperial in their visionary fire;
> Oh! steep my soul in that old, glorious time,
> When God's own whisper shook the cedars of your clime! (p. 641)

In this powerful depiction of the "Daughter of Judah" it is clear that Hemans is interested in alternative and more powerful traditions of female poetry represented by these women prophets. She locates a hidden tradition of female voices that have been sup-pressed and silenced but that were inspired by the authority and the "whisper" of God.

This idea is developed in a poem about Miriam that follows the two Invocations and, like More, Hemans picks up on the subversive possibilities inherent in the biblical hints regarding Miriam's prophetic power. While Hemans does not attempt the imaginary reconstruction of Miriam's voice found in *Sacred Dramas*, nor would such a detailed reconstruction be possible within the confines of the sonnet form, she does contemplate the possibility of more powerful female role models in what the Bible leaves unsaid, and gestures toward the perplexity of the later silencing of this woman's voice:

> When Miriam's voice o'er that sepulchral realm
> Sent on the blast a hymn of jubilee.
> With her lit eye, and long hair floating free,
> Queen-like she stood, and glorious was the strain,
> E'en as instinct with the tempestuous glee
> Of the dark waters, tossing o'er the slain,
> A song for God's own victory! Oh, thy lays,
> Bright poesy! were holy in their birth:
> How hath it died, thy seraph-note of praise,
> In the bewildering melodies of earth!
> Return from troubling, bitter founts – return,
> Back from the life-springs of thy native urn! (Ibid., p. 642)

Hemans's poetic approach to Scripture here involves another recognized model of femi-nist hermeneutics, one that, according to critics, first began to emerge in the nineteenth century: "the study and lifting up of historical women or female literary characters in the Bible ... as role models for women" (Yarbro-Collins, 1985, p. 4). This portrayal of the female prophet is, however, situated within a much wider exploration of possible female role models and in the context of the sequence as a whole is shown to be just one of many examples of women's important interventions within spiritual history. Following the portrayal of Miriam, Hemans celebrates, or "lifts up," a range of other female figures who mostly conform to more traditional feminine roles. While for modern readers the powerful prophetic figure of Miriam may be more appealing, the celebration of the gendered qualities of meekness, submission, humility, gentleness, and a capacity for selflessness in the other female biblical characters should not be dismissed since ironically, for Hemans, it is precisely these qualities that cause those women to be "Chosen of heaven" (Hemans, 1887, p. 643). These gendered traits are shared by virtu-ally all the Old and New Testament female characters depicted in the sonnet sequence, and indeed are traits shared by female figures elsewhere in Hemans's poetry, where they are often identified as an alternative to more aggressive masculine gender roles. Here these qualities are raised to a position of ultimate worth, rendering women par-ticularly suited to fulfill and communicate the will of God. More than this, though, these gendered attributes also find their echo in Christ himself, who is subtly identified with women both through his patient suffering and through the strength of his love, the latter being linked by Hemans on more than one occasion to that of a mother for her child. In another sonnet from *Scenes and Hymns of Life*, "On a Remembered Picture of Christ," Hemans describes the lasting impression made on her by a youthful encounter with Da Vinci's depiction of Christ in *Ecce Homo*. The sonnet describes how the older female poet and mother experiences a moment of empathy with Christ's suffering and love:

> Now that, around the deep life of my mind,
> Affections, deathless as itself, have twined,
> Oft does the pale, bright vision still float by;
> But more divinely sweet, and speaking *now*
> Of One whose pity, throned on that sad brow,
> Sounded all depths of love, grief, death, humanity! (Hemans, 1887, p. 646)

Women are subtly raised up in these late poems not only by the fact that they are shown to be chosen by God, but also because in some sense they represent and embody most fully the qualities associated with Christ.

The sequence ends strategically with Mary Magdalene, who endorses Hemans's argument that women's special qualities of empathy and love befit them to play important roles in Scripture and perhaps by extension in society. Mary begins as a "meek listener at the Saviour's feet" with her "woman's heart of silent worship" (p. 643) and then in the final sonnet in the sequence is given the task of revealing the truth of Christ's divinity and thus mankind's redemption through the resurrection:

> Then was a task of glory all thine own,
> Nobler than e'er the still small voice assigned
> To lips in awful music making known
> The stormy splendours of some prophet's mind.
> *"Christ is arisen!"* – by thee, to wake mankind,
> First from the sepulchre those words were brought! (p. 645)

Mary's role in carrying forth the message of this direct revelation is "Nobler" even than Miriam's voice of prophecy and there is a sense in these late poems that Hemans sees herself as continuing the noble work commenced by Mary, in reaffirming the Christian message and also in continuing to valorize those qualities that she depicts as both feminized and Christ-like.

While Hemans's attempt to "refeminize history" in secular contexts was doomed to end in the portrayal of further female suffering, as she was repeatedly forced to show women to be the victims of a patriarchal, militarist world, the shift to sacred contexts at the end of her career provided her with the opportunity to explore much more positive images of women. The narrative told by these sonnets – that women are chosen by God to prophesize, to nurture and attend Christ, to carry forth the central message of Christianity, and to provide an earthly model for Christ – has both spiritual and social implications, and works to challenge the subsequent suppression of women's role within scriptural history as well as the silencing and victimization of women within the dominant nineteenth-century model of patriarchal ideology.

Conclusion

It is perhaps not surprising, given her own interest in biblical exegesis, to find that More had developed a similar argument to the one suggested by Hemans's sonnet in her 1799 *Strictures on the Modern System of Female Education*, a text in which she analyzes and attempts to define the chief female characteristics in order to bring about a "transformation of the role played by women ... in the formation of national culture" (Mellor, 2000, p. 25). Within this text More rehearses the argument put forward poetically by Hemans in the sonnets and offers a subtle challenge to women's exclusion from influence in modern society by pointing to their central role within Scripture.

> The religion of Christ has even bestowed a degree of renown on the [female] sex beyond what any other religion ever did. ... Some of the most affecting scenes, the most interesting transactions, and the most touching conversations which are recorded of the Saviour of the world passed with women. *Their* examples have supplied some of the most eminent instances of faith and love: *they* are the first remarked as having "ministered to him of their substance:" *theirs* was the praise of not abandoning their despised Redeemer when he was led to execution, and under all the hopeless circumstances of his ignominious death; *they* appear to have been the *last* attending at his tomb, and the *first* on the morning when he arose from it: *theirs* was the privilege of receiving the earliest consolation from their risen Lord: *theirs* was the honour of being first commissioned to announce his glorious resurrection. (More, 1830, pp. 243–4)

More's and Hemans's biblical verse-dramas and sonnets deploy strategies by which these female Romantic-era poets sought to transcend the restrictions of the gender categories assigned to them and claim the authority of God to produce the high prophetic and divinely inspired discourse from which they were culturally excluded. More that this, though, both writers engaged in what later biblical scholars would classify as an early feminist hermeneutics of the Bible. In their attempts to imaginatively reconstruct submerged female voices and to lift up and identify with positive female characters within an overwhelmingly patriarchal text, they were seeking to find a place for women within that master narrative and, having done so, to use the authority of that text to challenge the restrictions placed on women both culturally and ideologically within the Romantic period.

Note

1   Within this chapter I have focused on examples of very direct literary engagements with the Bible by women Romantic poets and have not therefore dealt with Barbauld and Williams's deployment of religious discourse in political contexts or indeed with Barbauld's major sacred work, her influential *Hymns in Prose for Children* (1781). The latter, although more broadly a pedagogical presentation of Christian theology rather than a direct reworking of the Bible per se, is nonetheless interesting in relation to the treatment of the Bible by women Romantic writers, especially in terms of Barbauld's attempts to rework certain biblically authorized theological ideas from what is both a rationalist and a Romantic perspective.

References and Further Reading

Brenner, Athalya and Fontaine, Carole, eds (1997) *A Feminist Companion to Reading the Bible: Approaches, Methods and Strategies*. Fitzroy Dearborn, London and Chicago.

Davis, Eryl Wynn (2003) *The Dissenting Reader: Feminist Approaches to the Hebrew Bible*. Ashgate, Aldershot.

Demers, Patricia (1993) *Heaven upon Earth: The Form of Moral and Religious Children's Literature, to 1850*. University of Tennessee Press, Knoxville.

Hemans, Felicia (1887) *The Poetical Works of Mrs. Hemans*. Frederick Warne, London.

Hemans, Felicia (2000) *Felicia Hemans: Selected Poems, Letters, Reception Materials*, ed. Susan J. Wolfson. Princeton University Press, Princeton, NJ.

Jasper, David and Prickett, Stephen, eds (1999) *The Bible and Literature: A Reader*. Blackwell, Oxford.

Kelly, Gary (2002) "Introduction," in Gary Kelly, ed., *Felicia Hemans: Selected Poems, Prose, and Letters*. Broadview Press, Lancashire and Ontario, pp. 15–85.

Mason, Emma (2006) *Women Poets of the Nineteenth Century*. Northcote House, Tavistock.

Mellor, Anne K. (1993) *Romanticism and Gender*. Routledge, London and New York.

Mellor, Anne K. (2000) *Mothers of the Nation: Women's Political Writing in England, 1780–1830*. Indiana University Press, Bloomington and Indianapolis.

Melnyk, Julie (2001) "Hemans' Later Poetry: Religion and the Vatic Poet," in Nanora Sweet and Julie Melnyk, eds, *Felicia Hemans: Reimagining Poetry in the Nineteenth Century*. Palgrave, Basingstoke and New York, pp. 74–92.

More, Hannah (1825) *Sacred Dramas: Chiefly intended for young persons, the subjects taken from the Bible. To which is added, Sensibility: An Epistle*. Cadell, London.

More, Hannah (1830) *Strictures on the Modern System of Female Education, vol. 5 of The Works of Hannah More*, 11 volumes. Cadell, London.

Myers, Mitzi (1986) "Hannah More's Tracts for the Times: Social Fiction and Female Ideology," in Mary Anne Schofield and Cecilia Macheski, eds, *Fetter'd or Free? British Women Novelists, 1670–1815*. Ohio University Press, Athens, pp. 264–84.

Ostriker, Alice (1993) *Feminist Revision and the Bible*. Blackwell, Oxford.

Ostriker, Alice (1997) A Triple Hermeneutic: Scripture and Revisionist Women's Poetry, in Athalya Brenner and Carole Fontaine, eds, *A Feminist Companion to Reading the Bible: Approaches, Methods and Strategies*. Fitzroy Dearborn, London and Chicago, pp. 164–89.

Stott, Anne (2003) *Hannah More: The First Victorian*. Oxford University Press, Oxford.

Sunderland, Kathryn (1991) "Hannah More's Counter-Revolutionary Feminism," in Kelvin Everest, ed., *Revolution in Writing: British Literary Responses to the French Revolution*. Open University Press, Milton Keynes and Philadelphia, pp. 27–63.

Sweet, Nanora and Melnyk, Julie, eds (2001) *Felicia Hemans: Reimagining Poetry in the Nineteenth Century*. Pandora, Basingstoke and New York.

Wolfson, Susan J. (1994) " 'Domestic Affections' and 'the spear of Minerva': Felicia Hemans and the Dilemma of Gender," in Carol Shiner Wilson and Joel Haefner, eds, *Re-Visioning Romanticism: British Women Writers, 1776–1837*. University of Pennsylvania Press, Philadelphia, pp. 128–66.

Wolfson, Susan J., ed. (2000). *Felicia Hemans: Selected Poems, Letters, Reception Materials*. Princeton University Press, Princeton.

Yarbro-Collins, Adela, ed. (1985) *Feminist Perspectives on Biblical Scholarship*. Scholars Press, California.

CHAPTER 28

William Wordsworth

Deeanne Westbrook

Go forth from Babylon, flee from Chaldea,
Declare this with a shout of joy, proclaim it,
Send it forth to the end of the earth. (Isaiah 48:20)

O welcome messenger! O welcome friend!
A captive greets thee, coming from a house
Of bondage, from yon city's walls set free. (*The Prelude* 1:5–7)[1]

O, blank *confusion*, and a type not false
Of what the mighty city is itself. (*The Prelude* 7:696–7)

The first fifty-four lines of *The Prelude*, a passage Wordsworth called his "glad pream-ble" (*The Prelude* 7:4), insinuate major themes developed in that work. There are the "glad" themes of inspiration, blessing, "miraculous gift," freedom, election, and dedi-cation to the poetic/prophetic calling. But as a muted ground bass, scarcely noticeable themes of confusion, wandering, lost direction, bondage, captivity, and exile may also be heard. Both sorts of theme are carried in intertextual allusions that demonstrate the complexity of the poet's integration of the Bible and its poetics into his master-work, a complexity marked by a separation between the poet's mind and body and between "the spirit" and "the letter." Pertinent to this discussion is the fact that the biblical plot of humanity's fall and redemption finds an echo in the equally devastating myth of fallen language. In that myth, an originally perfect language lapses into con-fusion, a garbled speech that will endure through history, finally to be redeemed at the apocalypse when it takes the form of a hymn of praise sung in unison by those few singled out for salvation.[2] This myth is grounded in two key biblical figures: the ruined Tower of Babel (Genesis 11:1–9) and the City/Whore of Babylon (Revelation 17–19). The biblical idea that human language has fallen from an original perfection creates an understandable bias against polyphony, ambiguity, and hidden meaning, yet in order to record sacred history or speak the divine message, biblical authors resorted to parable, allegory, figure, and image. For it was to these very "Babylonians" in their own "confused" language that God's instructions and prophecies were spoken and reported.[3] This chapter demonstrates that the myth of fallen language plays a crucial and structuring role in *The Prelude*, and that it is a muted theme in the opening lines.

Wordsworth's poetic career reflects conflicting attitudes toward language – its triumphs and its inadequacies – its potential, as an "awful ... instrument for good and evil." Words, he declared, "hold above all other external powers a dominion over thoughts" (*Prose Works* 2:84). From the biblical perspective, after the confusion, humans speak the language of confusion; all the world's languages are descendants of Babel. These include the languages of Scripture: Hebrew, spoken by Old Testament patriarchs, prophets, and lyricists; Aramaic and Greek, used by the four evangelists, by Paul and John of Patmos, and, of course, by Jesus. Human language is unable to produce the congruity of thought, imagination, word, and act said to exist at both the beginning and the end of history, manifest in the first divine fiat (Genesis 1:3) and "The Word of God" (Revelation 19:13).

An examination of *The Prelude*'s opening lines reveals some of the intricacies of Wordsworth's artistry in response to biblical authors and texts and introduces a theme pervasive in the work – that of wandering and lost direction. As Wordsworth begins his epic work, he finds himself, like the Old Testament patriarchs and prophets, confronted by a seemingly transcendent entity, an animate, personified breeze who delights the poet by blessing him, and whom he welcomes as a "messenger" and "friend":

> A captive greets thee, coming from a house
> Of bondage, from yon city's walls set free,
> A prison where he hath been long immured. (*The Prelude* 1:5–8)

Using biblical metaphors, the narrator characterizes himself, rather insistently, as socially beleaguered. He is a freed Babylonian captive, an escaped Egyptian slave, and a convict. The poet's joyous declaration might have been made in response to Isaiah's instruction in the epigraph to "go forth from Babylon" with joy. Two biblical events are invoked within these three lines – the release of the Israelite captives from the city of Babylon (home of confusion)[4] and the fearful, even reluctant, escape from Egypt, the "house of bondage" (e.g. Exodus 13:3). The destination of the former Egyptian slaves is Canaan, the Promised Land; the destination of the freed Babylonian captives is Jerusalem, the holy city. Bringing together two biblical events separated by hundreds of years during which the Promised Land has been gained and lost raises intriguing questions: how are these situations alike? how different? how do they comment on each other? Adding further complexity, Wordsworth figuratively associates the departures from Egypt and Babylon with the exile of Adam and Eve from the Garden of Eden: in an echo of Milton's description of the expulsion of the first couple from paradise, the poet exclaims, "The earth is all before me" (*The Prelude* 1:15; cf. *Paradise Lost* 12:646–7). Is the speaker to be thought of as an escaped slave, a released captive, a lapsed soul, a universal Everyman whose wandering and exile are figured in the expulsion? As the biblical intertexts meet and resonate, their already figurative meanings are multiplied and deepened. If it is desirable to be released from Babylon, is it also desirable to be expelled from paradise? Or, conversely, if it is disastrous to be expelled from Eden, is it likewise disastrous to be freed from Babylon? Milton provides "Providence" to guide the first couple as they leave Eden "with wandering steps and slow" (*Paradise Lost* 12:646–7); Yahweh as pillar of cloud and fire guides the forty-year wanderings of the Israelite slaves. In either case, how much freedom is implied? Tension resides in the fact that although Wordsworth's persona makes a motif of freedom and self-determination ("and should the guide I chuse / Be nothing better than a wandering cloud / I cannot miss my way"), his astonishing choice, as he says, might be "nothing better" than a "wandering cloud"! The wandering cloud is an image of an image representing the God who led the Israelites in their protracted and torturous wandering in the wilderness. Is there anything better? Anything worse? The passage ends with further irony:

> Whither shall I turn,
> By road or pathway, or through open field,
> Or shall a twig or any floating thing
> Upon the river point me out my course?

Wordsworth's unlimited possibilities for wandering and "turning" suggest what Northrop Frye calls "an image of lost direction," to be distinguished from the "apocalyptic way":

Corresponding to the apocalyptic way or straight road, the highway in the desert for God prophesied by Isaiah, *we have in this world the labyrinth or maze, the image of lost direction.* ... The labyrinthine wanderings of Israel in the desert, repeated by Jesus when in the company of the devil ... fit the same pattern. (*Anatomy of Criticism* 150; emphasis added)

Although the poet insists that he cannot miss his way, to introduce the song of the self as Wordsworth does – as a tale of escape, flight, exile, wandering, and turning – is to make the "image of lost direction" the central trope of the poet's life and the growth of his mind. Yet at the same time, as the biblical echoes suggest, if the wandering is guided by God or Providence, the way of the poet is not free but determined. The released captive, the freed slave, the paroled prisoner is given a one-way ticket that bears no indication of its destination. To complicate the situation further, the narrator's future seems to consist in relating the story of his own (past) wandering and captivity. The future and its task are thus as constrained as was the recent captivity and enslavement. Like the Old Testament prophets, the poet understands that he has been "clothed in priestly robe" and "singled out ... / For holy service."[5] The conscription of a divine spokesperson is never "free,"[6] so when the poet says that "poetic numbers came / Spontaneously" (*The Prelude* 1:60–3), he suggests not only a usurpation of his language, but also the imposition of another sort of captivity. The joyous announcement of freedom – from captivity, from poetic silence – is shadowed by an ironic denial of freedom, that escape and freedom are played against exile and lost direction, and that the compulsion to speak "spontaneously" is at once an image of divine inspiration and utter loss of poetic freedom. It is in the collision of such irreconcilable concepts that the poem reveals the direction of its unfolding.

My point here is not to exhaust the interpretative possibilities of these opening lines, but simply to suggest that the references to biblical texts and images and even individual words lend Wordsworth's preamble multiple meanings and ironic reversals characteristic of the language of Babylon and quite distinct from the prelapsarian language depicted in Genesis when Adam at God's direction names (co-creates) the animals (2:19) or when "the whole earth was of one language, and of one speech" (11:1). My concern is with the appeal of biblical language as it manifests itself in two key, but related, respects: first, in what Stephen Prickett (2002, p. 38) identifies as the irony of the "unspoken or 'hidden' meaning" in biblical texts, the sense that divine revelation cannot be spoken directly in human speech; second, in the motifs associated with the Tower of Babel, the confusion of tongues, the subsequent wandering, and the city of Babylon, site of the ruined Tower. In the biblical account, interruption of the building of the Tower had put an end to an era of perfect communication and cooperation, when human beings had only to imagine and to speak in order to accomplish. As God observes the building of the Tower to heaven, he remarks, "Behold the people is one, and they have all one language; and this they begin to do: and now nothing will be restrained from them, which they have imagined to do" (Genesis 11:6). His response is to "confuse the tongues" of earth's inhabitants and thereby to initiate a history of human wandering (scattering) across the face of the earth, of confusion and inability to say exactly what one means. The Tower, confusion, and wandering form an imbricated pattern in the biblical narrative, making the Tower a vertical "image of lost direction" corresponding to the horizontal labyrinthine way of the world. Though Wordsworth's persona may claim that he cannot miss his way and that cloud or floating twig will guide him, both "guides" are suspect, and *The Prelude* itself takes the very form of wandering, confusion, and lost direction in a landscape that is both physical and mental. M. H. Abrams has observed that "*The Prelude* is an involuted poem which is about its own genesis, a prelude to itself. Its structural end is its own beginning; and its temporal beginning ... is Wordsworth's entrance upon the stage of his life at which it ends." The temporal beginning is recorded in the "glad preamble." The stage of his life at which *The Prelude* ends is the flight from London/Babylon. A bit later Abrams adds, "the narrator, moving bewilderingly back and forth through time, is persistently concerned with the nature of voluntary and involuntary memory" (Abrams, 1971, pp. 79, 81), another variation on the conflicting themes of freedom and restraint.

As mentioned, God's confusion of tongues at Babel imposed the necessity of his using now-fallen language for his own messages, even as it rendered some matters inaccessible through human speech. Too high or mysterious, they could not be spoken of directly, but only imperfectly through figure or parable. It became necessary, as Jesus suggests in his parables purporting to speak of "things hidden since the foundation of the world," to "accommodate" sublime mystery to fallen human speech (Matthew 13:35). As Steven Goldsmith has shown, biblical authors, working with confused language in a fallen world, return obsessively to the story of the Tower, failed language, and the cultural trauma of captivity in Babylon.[7] In Psalm 137, a lament "by the waters of Babylon," a poet who has hung up his lyre asks, "How shall we sing the Lord's song in a foreign land?" (137:4). The question identifies what Wordsworth saw as a universal difficulty for a poet singing in the world of wandering, the foreign land of captivity. Attempting to articulate the "genius, power, / Creation, and divinity" that "passed within" him in childhood, Wordsworth declares the inadequacy of language, for what passed within is unspeakable: "It lies far hidden from the reach of words." All the poet can do is "make breathings for incommunicable powers" (*The Prelude* 3:174, 185–8).

Addressing the "daughter of Babylon," the psalmist anticipates Babylon's destruction and the joy of one "who takes your little ones / and dashes them against the rock!" (137:9). Such shocking attitudes toward the city of captivity and confusion are carried into the New Testament, where the city provides figural form not only for Rome, but for the entire degenerate world, all its evils and injustices, its incessant clamor of voices.[8] The thematic crescendo of Revelation with its intense apocalyptic longing discloses at the apocalypse the defeat and destruction of Babylon (the city now personified as the Whore of Babylon) along with the linguistic confusion she has come to embody, all enunciated figuratively in the word *mystery* emblazoned upon *her* forehead: "Upon her forehead was a name written, MYSTERY, BABYLON THE GREAT, THE MOTHER OF HARLOTS AND ABOMINATIONS OF THE EARTH" (Revelation 17:5). The refrain of fall and destruction of Babylon continues in chapter 18, when the captives (now representative of the world's population of the righteous) are admonished once more to flee from the city, where light and life, poetry and music are soon to be extinguished: "And the voice of the harpers, and musicians, and of pipers, and trumpeters, shall be heard no more at all" (Revelation 18:22). Thus Babylon and the Tower of Babel draw to themselves a cluster of meanings: evils of every ilk (the abominations of the earth), foreign nations and religions associated with the ubiquitous biblical theme of harlotry in the worshiping of "other gods," the confusion of tongues, and the failure of meaning in the resulting cacophony. The poet approaching the Bible as poetic model is confronted by a tension between, on the one hand, admiration for the rich complexity of common language pressed into service for uncommon ends and, on the other, what may be called the biblical bias against *all* human language – poetic or prosaic – the babble of "nations and tongues."

Wordsworth's Parabolic Style

> Visionary Power
> Attends upon the motions of the winds
> Embodied in the mystery of words. (*The Prelude* 5:619–21)

The genius of Wordsworth lies in part in his singular ability to fuse the literal with the figurative so that readers, if they are so inclined, may ignore the figurative altogether; an intriguing alternative is that they may discount the literal, as readers tend to do in approaching, for example, biblical or literary parables and fables. Robert Lowth's term "parabolic style" is an apt name for this aspect of Wordsworth's poetic practice. It is a style constituted of different forms of irony. It consists in part of the irony that Harold Bloom (1989, p. 4) discovers in the Yahwist's strand of biblical narratives: "It is the irony ... in which absolutely incommensurate realities collide and cannot be resolved." A collision of incommensurates will inevitably result when intertextual allusion and the language of nature and society are made to speak of things and conditions, spiritual or psychological, that lie "hidden from the reach of words." Biblical ideas of escape and exile in the opening lines of *The Prelude* are incommensurate – both by themselves and as figurative for the narrator's outrageously indeterminate/overdetermined circumstances.

In Wordsworth's parabolic style the irony of incommensurates is joined with another sort – the irony of the "hidden."[9] This is the irony Robert Lowth explores at length in his *The Sacred Poetry of the Hebrews* and his introduction to his *New Translation of Isaiah*. It is one in which "from the letter" one must deduce "deep and recondite senses" (Lowth, *Isaiah* 1:ixviii).[10] Lowth's metaphors of depth and obscurity imply that in sacred discourse, beneath a text's literal surface, there extends, perhaps infinitely, an abyss of meanings of which even an author may be ignorant, and the task of whose discovery may well prove endless. Nevertheless, the way to the "deep and recondite" lies through the intricacies of the surface.[11] On this point Paul de Man (1983, p. 211) comments, "Curiously enough, it seems to be only in describing a mode of language which does not mean what it says that one can actually say what one means."[12]

The question arises, what is it about a text that invites readers to "see" that it contains hidden depths of meaning? Is it something that strikes one as too obvious, too obscure, too elliptical, or absurdly contradictory? Is it a perceived echo of an earlier text? Prickett offers possible answers in his analysis of a passage from Kierkegaard's *The Concept of Irony*, where Kierkegaard argues that in Socratic irony there is "what amounts to a prototype of the *via negativa*," the way to God or truth through negation. Kierkegaard explains what he means by the Socratic "ironic totality, a spiritual condition that was infinitely bottomless, invisible, and indivisible," by the example of a print called *Napoleon's Tomb*. As Kierkegaard describes it,

> Two tall trees shade the grave. There is nothing else to see in the work, and the unsophisticated observer sees nothing else. Between the two trees there is an empty space; as the eye follows the outline, suddenly Napoleon himself emerges from this nothing, and now it is impossible to have him disappear again. Once the eye has seen him, it goes on seeing him with almost alarming necessity.

Socrates' words are like the two trees. Meaning lies in the blank spaces surrounding his words as it does in the relationship between the trees, and in the emptiness between them – "this nothing ... [that] hides that which is most important" (quoted in Prickett, 2002, p. 43). Prickett comments, "that image of the Napoleonic profile in the outline of the trees ... hidden, yet once seen, quite unmistakable, re-shaping our reading of everything else in the frame, is one of the great metaphors of irony" (ibid.).[13] The trees are the manifest or literal; the absent Napoleon, made present in his name, a haunting void between the trees, is a painterly trope, a virtual abyss of potential meaning.[14] However, one might further observe that one's eye lingers on the print because of an incongruity, an odd relationship between the title and the picture. There is no grave, no tomb visible; the trees dominate one's view and invite the viewer's attention. Implicit in this metaphor of irony is the notion that there are those who do not see (Kierkegaard's "unsophisticated observer") and those who do. For those who see, who question the oddness, perhaps, everything changes in that glimpse into the emptiness that hides *and* reveals what is "most important." Irony, especially biblical irony, engages readers in the discovery of hidden meaning; it exploits the virtues of the indirect, the obscure, the aphoristic, and the sententious. Thus, once seen, the incongruities and absurdities of *The Prelude*'s opening lines – the clashes of sense among escape, flight, and expulsion, between finding one's way and potentially endless wandering – shape one's reading of everything that follows.

Jesus relates his ironic parables purporting to speak of what has been "hidden since the foundation of the earth" to "those outside" – "so that they may indeed see but not perceive, and may indeed hear but not understand" (Mark 4:12). The disciples are supposedly sophisticated observers, who can "read" the true meanings because they have been given a key – "the secret of the kingdom of God" – but nevertheless they seem as mystified as the outsiders. As Frank Kermode (1979, p. 3) comments, "Outsiders must content themselves with the manifest, and pay a supreme penalty for doing so." Parabolic style is the appropriate form for expressing this supreme irony – the use of language to conceal as it reveals its important meanings, the meanings that often lie "far hidden from the reach of words" (*The Prelude* 3:185).

Speaking of sacred literature, Lowth emphasizes the relationship between the surface of a text (the manifest or literal) and its depths, between what he thinks of as the fictional and the true. Speaking specifically of biblical parables, he says, "Parable is thus the paradoxical way through fiction to truth." The parabolic allegory allows "no room for literal ... expressions; every word is figurative" (*Lectures* 1:233). Yet it must be the case that at times "every word" *becomes figurative* only after the hidden is uncovered. This possibility is suggested by Harold Bloom – that texts considered spiritual may be "literally true, as well as metaphorically" (Bloom, 2005, p. 211). Wordsworth understood that the genuine could, and perhaps should, exist in both the manifest and hidden meanings of a text, and that literal language may be, like the trees in the print, the *Tomb of Napoleon, manifestly* "true" even though they shelter important but hidden meanings. One might argue that the irony would dissolve into naive allegory, and the hidden would not be hidden, if the trees did not strike viewers as "real."

In this vein Wordsworth stressed that the first requisite power for the production of poetry was "the ability to observe with accuracy things as they are in themselves, and with fidelity to describe them, unmodified by any passion or feeling existing in the mind of the describer." This first power, that of faithful representation in which the "higher faculties" are passive, must, however, be augmented by other powers – "sensibility," "reflection," and, most crucially, "imagination" and "fancy" (Preface of 1815, *Prose Works* 3:26). Imagination is the poet's ability "to glance from earth to heaven, whose spiritual attributes body forth what his pen is prompt in turning to shape; fancy "insinuat[es] herself into the heart of objects with creative activity." Imagination is a word "denoting operations of the mind upon [external] objects and processes of creation or of composition, governed by certain fixed laws" (Preface of 1815, *Prose Works* 3:30–1). What is of interest in Wordsworth's remarks is their explicit identification of the essentially double nature of imaginative works – the literal (accurate description) and the figurative expressed through language that "bodies forth" glimpses of "heaven" and "spiritual" or psychological attributes. According to Wordsworth, this imaginative doubleness is epitomized in biblical texts: "The grand storehouses of enthusiastic and meditative Imagination, of poetical ... Imagination, are the prophetic and lyrical parts of the Holy Scriptures, and the works of Milton" (Preface of 1815, *Prose Works* 3:34).

"Lines Written with a Slate-Pencil upon a Stone"

I have discussed Wordsworth's parabolic style elsewhere;[15] here I would like to examine briefly Wordsworth's "Lines Written with a Slate-Pencil upon a Stone, the Largest of a Heap Lying Near a Deserted Quarry, upon One of the Islands at Rydale." I call this poem a parable, and in my discussion I want both to demonstrate the poet's irony of the hidden and the incommensurate and to prepare the way for the discussion of Babylon to follow.

The poem begins, "Stranger!" – an address to the reader, as well, perhaps, as an announcement of theme or attitude. A linguistic strangeness certainly follows:

> this hillock of misshapen stones
> Is not a ruin of an ancient time,
> Nor, as perchance thou rashly deem'st, the Cairn
> Of some old British Chief ...

In calling attention to the stones and saying what they are not, the poet takes the *via negativa*. Naming the thing that is not there – the ancient ruin or monumental pyramid of rough stones – calls up their images and has the effect of making the absent present, and so the ruin and the cairn "appear" despite the effort to dismiss them.[16] Before the poet identifies the hillock of misshapen stones in positive terms it has taken on an elusive significance in the minds of readers. Even then the poet dismisses the pile as "nothing":

> 'tis nothing more
> Than the rude embryo of a little dome
> Or pleasure-house, which was to have been built
> Among the birch-trees of this rocky isle.

Wordsworth's "'tis nothing more" echoes the denials of the opening lines and parallels the ironic characterization at the opening of *The Prelude* of the poet's potential guide as "nothing better than a wandering cloud." This is no great matter, the poet asserts, merely the "rude embryo" of an aborted building project. But by now the specter of the ancient ruin that is not and is, which, like the profile of Napoleon in the anonymous print, haunts the scene, assumes a new facet. The ancient ruin that represents an interrupted building project is the Tower of Babel – that structure "conceived" and reared toward the heavens by perfect language before the work was "rudely" interrupted by God's confusion of tongues (Genesis 11). The "quarry and the mound," the poet says, "Are *monuments* of [the Knight's] unfinished task" (emphasis added).

Cynthia Chase (1987, pp. 66–7) has emphasized the ambiguity of the word *monument*, whose multiple meanings permit the word to refer to objects commemorating the past (historical persons and events and the dead) as well as to written documents, legal and literary (especially a classic work of literature). Monuments to past events and the dead typically carry their own inscriptions and thus may be monuments in both senses. The narrative of the Tower of Babel in Genesis, one might say, is a monument of literature; its subject is a monument to devastating, world-changing events in the past. The Genesis account does not appear inscribed on the ruined Tower, but the name *Babel*, "confusion," taken from that narrative and its interpretation of the name,[17] has been so intimately attached that the narrative might well have been inscribed thereon. In "Lines," the "monument" of the unfinished task, once inscribed by the poet, embodies both monumental functions and fuses the unfinished building project with Wordsworth's poem, which as a result takes on a stony density and permanence.

Wordsworth's "Lines" are written on what he thinks of as "the corner-stone / Of the intended pile." In this scene this stone corresponds to the biblical "stone which the builders refused" (Psalm 118:22) or the "stone which the builders rejected" (Matthew 21:42).[18] In both cases, the stone becomes primary – the cornerstone. New Testament echoes of Psalm 118 make the refused or rejected stone a metaphor for Jesus, the Word. In Wordsworth's "Lines," an ironic juxtaposition of a stone of confusion (from Babel's ruin) with the figure of perfect language – the Logos – renders the tale of Sir William's failed building project intriguingly parabolic. As parable, the poem requires yet resists interpretation.[19] The explanation the poet offers, like Jesus' explanations of his own parables, raises more questions than it answers. Wordsworth addresses a reader who might be "on fire," "disturbed / By beautiful *conceptions*" (an ironic echo of Sir William's aborted and "rude *embryo*" and the "ill-conceived" attempt of the Tower builders to build beyond the realm of nature) to construct a "mansion" of "snow-white splendour." The juxtaposition of *mansion* and *snow-white* suggests the too ambitious or grand aspiration or other-worldly perfection[20] – another sort of reaching beyond nature. His advice: "leave / Thy fragments to the bramble and the rose" (the thorns of fallen nature and the rose of perfection). "Fragments" is, of course, a common enough word for unfinished texts. Human pride figured in the Tower of Babel and human mortality figured in the cairn (both under erasure) are merged in the image of the interrupted building project and its rejected cornerstone, now become a bearer of the word, if not the Word. The tower of language, the poet advises, should – indeed must – be left unfinished, in fragments, a broken text, and the "outrage"[21] entirely forgiven.

This analysis of Wordsworth's "parable" of the interrupted building project is intended merely to demonstrate the ironic ways of the text, which as in the *Tomb of Napoleon* hides what is most important: The "rude embryo" as degraded image of absent tower and tomb is a sort of historical abstract of the relationships among human beings, their aspirations, their pride, their failures, and their ruined "monuments" – of both stone and word (Word). Confusion, fragmentation, hidden meanings, parabolic speech – these, for good or ill, are the legacy of Babylon and its rubble of language. And these, too, characterize Wordsworth's record of wandering through the "mighty city."

Wordsworth in Babylon

> The quick dance
> Of colours, lights and forms, the Babel din. (*The Prelude* 7:156–7)

I behold Babylon in the opening Street of London. (William Blake, *Jerusalem* 74:16)

After his richly crafted and problematic opening of *The Prelude*, with its ironic invocations of Eden, Babylon, and wilderness wandering, Wordsworth indeed wanders figuratively into his own mind and leads readers through a maze of memories and years (years recalled and years spent in writing about those years) from childhood to manhood. It is noteworthy that, after a long silence, the first mention of that highly charged opening occurs some six books and, Wordsworth says, five years[22] later as he opens Book 7, "Residence in London," by reminding readers of his "glad preamble":

> Five years are vanished since I first poured out,
> Saluted by that animating breeze
> Which met me issuing from the city's walls,
> A glad preamble to this verse. (7:1–4)

Reference to the opening lines of Book 1 at the outset of the London books recalls and stresses the warring themes of flight, release, exile, freedom, restraint, and wandering. In Wordsworth's parabolic style, London is merely and literally – at the level of the dead letter – London. The poet names landmarks, events, and activities of the "real" city. At the figurative level, however, it is Babylon, the city of captivity and fallen language, the city of earthly corruption; more broadly, it is all cities (including Paris and Goslar), and the very image of lost direction – in the labyrinthine way of the world as in the spiritual and textual wandering way of the mind.

As he begins to describe the "look and aspect" of London, Wordsworth singles out for attention the "broad highway appearance," the "quick dance / Of colours, lights and forms," and the "Babel din, / The endless stream of men and moving things" (*The Prelude* 7:154–8).[23] Babel/Babylon in Revelation is seated "upon many waters" (17:1), and the waters are "peoples and multitudes and nations and tongues" (17:15). These waters appear as Wordsworth's "endless stream of men" and "the tide" of humanity that flows through London (*The Prelude* 7:206). The wanderer hears the sound of the "Babel din" as a "roar" punctuated by "some female vendor's scream" (*The Prelude* 7:197), the scream perhaps a metaphor for the death cry of the biblically doomed Babylon, the fallen world. Certainly London, as Wordsworth encounters it, is a form of Babylon, a city of "peoples and multitudes and nations and tongues" – "all specimens of man / Through all the colours which the sun bestows" (*The Prelude* 7:236–43). "Foolishness, and madness on parade" are "most at home" there (*The Prelude* 7:589–90). Nevertheless, one reaction belongs "to this great city by exclusive right":

> How often in the overflowing streets
> Have I gone forwards with the crowd, and said
> Unto myself, "The face of every one
> That passes by me is a mystery." (*The Prelude* 7:593–8)

Mystery, as noticed above, is another name for Babylon; it is the name written her forehead. Goldsmith (1993, p. 62) has suggested that *mystery* "designates Babylon as a figure of indeterminacy ... with the danger of proliferating unregulated meanings," such unregulated meanings an attribute of fallen human language. A case in point is the word *mystery* itself: *mystery* has its etymological roots in secret ritual and religious truth, especially a truth "known or understood by divine revelation"; but *mystery* in another sense, as "the obscure" or "enigmatic," is difficult to reconcile with truth. When Wordsworth declares that "The face of every one / That passes by me is a mystery," the very statement carries the dual senses of enigma and truth. "Mystery" written on the forehead of Babylon, this figure of fallen humanity and confusion of language, implies as well a startling glimpse of truth. To be confronted by *mystery* (in the sense of enigma) is also the common condition of humankind and its struggles with fallen language. Wordsworth's blind beggar, "Wearing a written paper, to explain / The story of the man," is a metaphor for the human condition. Wordsworth suggests that we are all blind beggars, citizens of Babylon, with "mystery" on our foreheads, and our written papers – the indeterminacy of our labels, texts, Scriptures – to explain our story:

> ... it seemed
> To me that in this label was a type
> Or emblem of the utmost that we know
> Both of ourselves and of the universe,
> And on the shape of this unmoving man,
> His fixed face and sightless eyes, I looked,
> As if admonished from another world. (*The Prelude* 7:610–23)

Just as Wordsworth singles out the blind beggar (with the haunting image of "fixed face and sightless eyes") as a figure for humanity, so he represents Bartholomew Fair as a type of London, and her ancestress, Babel ("confusion"), or Babylon ("mystery"); London, like Babel, comes indeed to mean "confusion" – "blank confusion"; like Babel it represents all manner of evils and all failure of meaning and purpose:

> O, blank confusion, and a type not false
> Of what the mighty city is itself
> To all, except a straggler here and there –
> To the whole swarm of its inhabitants –
> An undistinguishable world to men,
> The slaves unrespited of low pursuits,
> Living amid the same perpetual flow
> Of trivial objects, melted and reduced
> To one identity by differences
> That have no law, no meaning, and no end. (*The Prelude* 7:696–705)

Blank suggests a sheer emptiness – of law, meaning, and end – and *confusion*, the "mighty city" itself, a metonymy of "an undistinguishable world." The "hubbub" (7:213) of the unreal city is a roar like that which might have issued from Babylon on the very day of the confusion, as from Milton's Chaos: "A universal hubbub wilde / Of stunning sounds and voices all confus'd / Borne through the hollow dark" (*Paradise Lost* 2:951–3); for Wordsworth, it is produced by "all specimens of man / Through all the colours which the sun bestows" (7:236–7). As the poet wanders through the city, surveying its various languages – not only of its residents, but also of theater, court, parliament, and church – the deceit and confusion multiply:

> I glance but at a few conspicuous marks,
> Leaving ten thousand others that do each –
> In hall or court, conventicle, or shop,
> In public room or private, park or street –
> With fondness reared on its own pedestal,
> Look out for admiration ... –
> Lies to the ear, and lies to every sense –
> Of these and of the living shapes they wear
> There is no end. (7:567–77)

It is from this "city" – this blank confusion, this "universal hubbub," this place of failed language, of "Lies to the ear, and lies to every sense" – that the poet flees and to which the poet's "glad preamble" to his tale of wandering and lost direction will lead again. As mentioned, it is not a tale that proceeds chronologically as along a straight road through the desert to the Promised Land or the holy city. In fact the "autobiography" is a retrospective that tends to conceal the chronology of the life lived. The departure from London – figured in the preamble as a flight from Babylon, Egypt, and Eden – is the chronological end of the tale, and it is where the narrative will begin to recount a life of wandering in time and space, in the "real" world and the figurative reaches of the mind. Central to the poet's journey is his paradoxical celebration of confusion – the real, but fallen, language of the poet and of men. The confusion of Babel encompasses all of human time and place, a confusion that characterizes the difficult and miraculous language of biblical poetry – the model Wordsworth selects for himself.[24]

A recurrent image in Wordsworth's poetry is that of ascending voices, songs, murmurs, and roars, often associated with water. The "Babel-din" and "roar" of London/Babylon is human language, seeming to arise from a figurative "endless stream of men" (*The Prelude* 7:157–8, 184) that reaches like the Tower of Babel toward heaven. This roar is echoed – with a difference – in the climactic Snowdon vision in the last book of *The Prelude*. There, from a "deep and gloomy breathing-place" the poet hears "the roar of waters, torrents, streams / Innumerable, roaring with one voice" (13:57–9). This roar, unlike that of London/Babylon, seems to be undergoing a transformation toward the "one song" of nature heard when the physical ear sleeps (*The Prelude* 2:431–4) and the song sung in unison by the living beings and the elders surrounding God's throne in Revelation. Ideally, Wordsworth suggests, the human din of confusion would be adapted to nature's song, and nature's song to a universal harmony. Wordsworth's late poems reveal increasingly that his admiration for the richness and complexity of fallen human language wanes as he abandons, one might say, Babylonian lyric for kiddusha, a "hallelujah sent / From all that breathes and is" (*The Prelude* 13:262–3).[25] Wordsworth's dilemma is that of the psalmist: "How shall we sing the Lord's song" in Babylon? (137:4). Wordsworth's flight from Babylon will take him step by step from acceptance of – even reverence for – the tropological, deceptive, ambiguous, confused, and beautiful language of the biblical authors and the "real language of men" to a longing for perfect communication and communion, a desire celebrated most overtly in the magnificent late poem, "On the Power of Sound":[26]

> O for some soul-affecting scheme
> Of moral music, to unite
> Wanderers whose portion is the faintest dream
> *Of memory!* – O that they [angels] might stoop to bear
> Chains, such precious chains of sight
> As laboured minstrelsies through ages wear!
> O for a balance fit the truth to tell
> Of the Unsubstantial, pondered well. (169–76; emphasis added)

If angels could wear chains of physical sight, if the unsubstantial could be weighed in a *true* balance, the scattered wanderers of the world might once more become one people with one language (Genesis 11:6). "O for a balance fit the truth to tell / Of the Unsubstantial, pondered well" – this is Wordsworth's version of the psalmist's lament, "How shall we sing the Lord's song in a foreign land?" Where is the balance in which to weigh, to tell (speak) the truth, of "the Unsubstantial"? Poets of the ages elapsed since the confusion (the "laboured minstrelsies") are Babylonian captives, slaves in a mundane house of bondage – in chains to the material realms that prevent their hearing and participating in the song of praise to the "Unsubstantial," the "Ever-living" (195), the universal hymn (the kiddusha) from all of creation transmitted to heaven "by flaming Seraphim" and poured "Into the ear of God." The longed-for harmony is the Alpha and Omega – the Word of the beginning and the end – timeless, divine, and perfect. Harmony's "stay / Is in the Word, that shall not pass away" (223–4).

If the rift between thought and expression, between imagination and speech, inflicted at the fall of Babel were healed in the perfect language of the Word, there would be no confusion. A monoglot society would speak as one and would sing one song – carried in a single word – Hallelujah. In the Apocalypse of Paul, an angel explains to Paul the meaning of the word: "Let us bless him all together." He instructs that "whoever is able, and does not join in the singing, you know that he is a despiser of the word" (Hennecke, 1964, vol. 2, pp. 778–9). In Revelation, John of Patmos hears "what sounded like the roar of a great multitude in heaven shouting: 'Hallelujah! Salvation and glory and power belong to our God' " and then "what sounded like a great multitude, like the roar of rushing waters ... shouting: 'Hallelujah! For our Lord God Almighty reigns' " (Revelation 19:1, 6). When the confused voices of Babylon have been silenced, yielding to the Word, all the redeemed will shout one hymn of praise, whereupon poets and the need for poets will have been eliminated: "And the voice of the harpers, and musicians, and of pipers, and trumpeters, shall be heard no more at all" (Revelation 18:22).

Although he may flee from Babylon and the voice of its harpers, Wordsworth's attitude toward the elimination of earthly music is not settled in *The Prelude*. In Book 5, for example, contemplating the perishable nature of human texts, he comments, "Tremblings of the heart / It gives, to think that the immortal being / No more shall need such garments" (21–3). And though his final vision in Book 13 is of "one song," it is a song like and eerily unlike that heard by John from heaven: "a roar of waters, torrents, streams / Innumerable, roaring with one voice" but emerging darkly as a "homeless voice" through Nature's "dark, deep thoroughfare," seat of the "imagination of the whole" (13:57–65). The roar from the fractured mist seems not to be "Hallelujah"; it is not yet the "*moral* music" of "On the Power of Sound" that will unite earth's wanderers; and its univocal harmony is not yet that of the perfect Word "that shall not pass away" (170–1; 224).

Notes

1   Unless otherwise indicated, citations to *The Prelude* are to the 1805 version.
2   M. H. Abrams argues that *The Prelude* is a secular, personal, and figurative recapitulation of biblical history and the "sharply defined plot with a beginning, a middle, and an end" (Abrams, 1971, p. 35, and see pp. 278–92. William A. Ulmer intriguingly claims that "in *The Prelude* Wordsworth creates a *modern religious* myth, a *secularized* reaffirmation of Christian insights into the way of the soul" (Ulmer, 2006, p. 278; emphasis added). Ulmer's argument is that Wordsworth's "Fall" is framed by the Simplon and Snowdon visions, representing a movement from a "disruptive confrontation with the sublime" to a "saving return to the beautiful" (ibid., p. 272). My position is that such architectural structure disguises the thematic coherence carried in the emphasis on language and what I am calling the "flight from Babylon."
3   Stephen Prickett (1986, pp. 37–94) provides an excellent history of evolving understanding of the relationship between the religious and the poetic and the adaptation of biblical to secular poetics.
4   Goldsmith (1993, p. 63) draws attention to the "embedding of Babel within the figure of Babylon," in later millenarian traditions, citing as an example a seventeenth-century hymn that associates Babylon with the tower and both with fallen humanity: "The Whore that rides in us abides, / A strong beast is within ... / Alas, we may most of us say / We're stones of Babel's tower."
5   In this same passage, Wordsworth declares, "To the open fields I told / A prophecy," which invokes God's instruction to Ezekiel, "Prophesy to the wind [or breath]" and recalls the breeze that blesses the poet in the opening lines.
6   Moses's poignant plea, "Oh, my Lord, send, I pray, some other person" (Exod. 4:13), is typical of the chosen prophet's unsuccessful attempt to avoid the divine commission. The Lord rejects Jeremiah's similar request and declares, "Behold, I have put my words in your mouth" (Jer. 1:9).
7   Biblical references to Babylon are numerous and insistent. In all, there are some 300 mentions of Babel, Babylon, or forms thereof in the King James Version of the Bible.
8   As Goldsmith (1993, p. 58) asserts, "the polyglot of history" is in Revelation rendered in the formula "peoples and multitudes and nations and tongues."
9   In my discussion of the irony of the hidden, I am indebted to both Frank Kermode (1979) and Stephen Prickett's (2002) fine analysis of irony.
10   Taking his metaphors from the Bible, Wordsworth refers to the literal as "the dead letter" as opposed to the figurative "spirit of things" (*The Prelude*, 1850, 8:296–7).
11   Stephen Prickett (2002, p. 37) shows that, although he does not mention the word, Lowth recognized a pervasive irony in biblical texts: "for Lowth, irony – the contrast between explicit and implied meaning – lay right at the structural centre of Hebrew poetry ... it was now possible to see biblical poetry, and ... much of biblical prose as well, in terms of dramatic and ironic narrative."

12 De Man's sharp distinction between allegory and irony is not as useful as Kevin Hart's observation that the sort of reading both require leads to the conclusion that "allegory supplies the necessary structure for its ironic subversion, and of course the subversion brought about by irony is itself open to be overturned to the extent to which the ironic becomes canonized as 'literature' ... or 'philosophy' " (Hart, 1989, p. 158). De Man denies that Wordsworth is an ironic writer (although he does raise the interesting possibility of an allegory that is "meta-ironic"; de Man, 1983, p. 223) and wishes to make a clear distinction between allegory and irony, even though, as he says, in both "the relationship between sign and meaning is discontinuous" (ibid., p. 209).

13 The *Tomb of Napoleon* is reproduced as the frontispiece of Prickett's *Narrative, Religion and Science*.

14 Of interest here is the fact that Napoleon was buried beneath weeping willows, the trees associated with Babylon.

15 See Westbrook (2001), especially chapters 4, 5, and 6.

16 J. Hillis Miller speaks of what he calls the poetic "act of displacement, substitution or stepping aside" which "mark a thing so that it ceases to be itself and becomes a sign pointing toward something absent." He says, "That absent something exists, already and elsewhere, or not yet. It exists ... in the signs for it." (Miller, 1985, p. 96).

17 *Babel* meant "gate of God" in Babylonian; the interpretation of the word as "confusion" comes from a similarity between *Babel* and the Hebrew verb *balal*, "to confuse." The creative misinterpretation ironically demonstrates the very confusion which is the subject of the narrative.

18 This same language is found in Mark 12:10 and Luke 20:17. Similar language occurs in Acts 4:11.

19 See my chapter "Wordsworth's Prodigal Son" for a fuller discussion of the problems presented by parables (Westbrook, 2001, pp. 99–121).

20 *Mansion* seems to echo Jesus' description of heaven as consisting of "many mansions" (John 14:2), and *snow-white* suggests a condition of righteousness or perfection – associated with God and Jesus (Ps. 51:7, Dan. 7:9, Matt. 28:3, Rev. 1:14).

21 "Outrage" seems too big a word to describe the knight's "conception" and aborted building project, but not for the human attempt, using perfect, prelapsarian language, to build a tower to heaven.

22 In the 1850 *Prelude*, Wordsworth calculates the interval as six years, rather than five.

23 It is intriguing to notice that in the more orthodox and conservative 1850 *Prelude* "Babel din" is revised to "deafening din" (7:155).

24 For an argument to this effect, see chapter 1 of Westbrook (2001).

25 Goldsmith (1993, chapter 1) offers a fine analysis of the kiddusha and the language of End Times. I discuss Wordsworth's "one song" as kiddusha (Westbrook, 2001, chapter 7).

26 Wordsworth thought that "some passages in 'The Power of Sound' [are] equal to anything I have produced" and gave it the emphatic last position in both *Yarrow Revisited* and "the Poems of Imagination" in the "last edition" of his poems (*The Major Works*, p. 725n).

References

Abrams, M. H. (1971) *Natural Supernaturalism: Tradition and Revolution in Romantic Literature*. W. W. Norton & Company, New York.

Blake, William (1966) *Complete Writings with Variant Readings*, ed. Geoffrey Keynes. Oxford University Press, London.

Bloom, Harold (1989) *Ruin the Sacred Truths, Poetry and Belief from the Bible to the Present*. Harvard University Press, Cambridge, MA.

Bloom, Harold (2005) *Jesus and Yahweh, The Names Divine*. Riverhead Books, New York.

Chase, Cynthia (1987) "Monument and Inscription: Wordsworth's 'Lines'," *Diacritics* 17:4, 66–77.

de Man, Paul (1983) *Blindness and Insight: Essays in the Rhetoric of Contemporary Criticism*, 2nd edn, rev. intro. Wlad Godzich. University of Minnesota Press, Minneapolis.

Frye, Northrop (1967) *Anatomy of Criticism: Four Essays*. Princeton University Press, Atheneum, NY.

Goldsmith, Steven (1993) *Unbuilding Jerusalem: Apocalypse and Romantic Representation*. Cornell University Press, Ithaca, NY.

Hart, Kevin (1989) *The Trespass of the Sign: Deconstruction, Theology and Philosophy*. Cambridge University Press, Cambridge.

Hennecke, Edgar (1964) *New Testament Apocrypha*, ed. R. McL. Wilson, 2 volumes. The Westminster Press, Philadelphia.

Kermode, Frank (1979) *The Genesis of Secrecy: On the Interpretation of Narrative*. Harvard University Press, Cambridge, MA.

Larue, Gerald A. (1969) *Babylon and the Bible*. Baker Book House, Grand Rapids, MI.

Lowth, Robert (1787) *Lectures on the Sacred Poetry of the Hebrews*, trans. G. Gregory, 2 volumes. London, reprinted Georg Olms Verlag, Hildesheim, 1969.

Lowth, Robert (1807) *Isaiah: A New Translation; With a Preliminary Dissertation and Notes*, 5th edn, 2 volumes. George Caw, Edinburgh.

Miller, J. Hillis (1985) *The Linguistic Moment from Wordsworth to Stevens*. Princeton University Press, Princeton, NJ.

Milton, John (1968) *Paradise Lost and Paradise Regained*, ed. Christopher Ricks. New American Library, New York.

Owen, W. J. B. and Worthington Smyser, Jane, eds (1974) *The Prose Works of William Wordsworth*, 3 volumes. Clarendon Press, Oxford.

Prickett, Stephen (1986) *Words and The Word: Language, Poetics and Biblical Interpretation*. Cambridge University Press, Cambridge.

Prickett, Stephen (2002) *Narrative, Religion, and Science: Fundamentalism versus Irony, 1700–1999*. Cambridge University Press, Cambridge.

Said, Edward W. (1975) *Beginnings: Intention and Method*. Basic Books, New York.

Ulmer, William A. (2006) "Simplon Pass to Moount Snowdon," in Stephen Gill, ed., *William Wordsworth's The Prelude: A Casebook*. Oxford University Press, Oxford, pp. 259–92.

Westbrook, Deeanne (2001) *Wordsworth's Biblical Ghosts*. Palgrave, New York.

Wordsworth, William (1974) *The Prose Works of William Wordsworth*, ed. W. J. B. Owen and Jane Worthington Smyser, 3 volumes. Clarendon Press, Oxford.

Wordsworth, William (1979) *The Prelude, 1799, 1805, 1850*, ed. Jonathan Wordsworth, M. H. Abrams, and Stephen Gill. W. W. Norton & Company, New York.

Wordsworth, William (1984) *The Major Works*, intro. and ed. Stephen Gill. Oxford University Press, Oxford.

CHAPTER 29

S. T. Coleridge

Graham Davidson

Coleridge was born in 1772, and before he was three, he could read a chapter of the Bible. He continued to read both testaments all his life, and he read them in the hope that they would reveal, and help create in him, the being of Christ. He valued the Bible above all other books, but as we shall see he was no bibliolater. His early work was suffused with the belief that the good life was that which imitated Christ, an ambition discernible in short poems such as *Pity* and *The Eolian Harp*, and long and once major works such as *Religious Musings* and *The Destiny of Nations*. The dogmatic assertions we find in these poems soon give way to a working out of the processess by which this mode of consciousness, and its corollaries, can be achieved. Some of these poems are clearly based on biblical sources – *The Wanderings of Cain*, for example, which proved to be a rehearsal for the ideas and energies that drive *The Ancient Mariner*; others are less obviously indebted, and we might think *Christabel* has no distinct biblical background, though some critics have seen significance in the name – ChristAbel. But even when the subject matter of a poem has no obvious biblical source, it will often be redolent with biblical imagery: *Kubla Khan* and *Religious Musings* are suffused with images drawn from *Genesis* and *Revelation*. His political thinking was equally dependent on the Bible – one lecture he called a lay sermon and entitled it *The Statesman's Manual or The Bible the best guide to Political Skill and Foresight*.

This chapter will look primarily at the method by which Coleridge read and commented on the Bible, but early and long-lived ambitions of writing a biblical epic influenced his reading. In 1802 he declared that "I have since my twentieth year meditated an heroic poem on the Siege of Jerusalem by Titus ...," (CL II 877) and 18 years later, described it as "the one only fit subject remaining for an Epic Poem ... ." (CL V 28) Why did Coleridge choose the beginning of the diaspora as his potential subject? Because he believed that it was the apotheosis of Jewish history, and that St Paul's assurances "respecting the Ascension of Christ to the Throne of Divine Providence" were co-incident with "the Jewish War and the Destruction of the City and Temple." (CN IV 5612) He believed that the Old Testament should be read in the light of the New, that "the Law and the Prophets speak throughout of Christ" and that "the termination of the first revealed national religion" would instigate "the spread of a revealed mundane religion … ." (TT 28 April 1832) He conceived this moment as the key to all history, because Jewish history "is the very Tap-root and Trunk of the Moral and therein of the physical History of the whole Planet …," (CN V 6282) or as he said of Christianity itself, "The history of all historical nations must in some sense be its history."[1] Those may seem hyperbolical, Casaubon-like claims to us, but it was the frame of mind in which Coleridge read his Bible; and during his last fifteen years, from about 1819 to 1834, the Bible became increasingly the focus of his studies, until in the final decade it was almost his sole occupation.

Nature, the Bible, and the Imagination

In *The Statesman's Manual*, published in 1816, when he was 44, Coleridge re-iterates a claim he first made when a very young man – that Nature is "another book, likewise a revelation of God" (CC 6 70). This is no metaphor, for he goes on to challenge the reader with the assertion, "That in its obvious sense and literal interpretation it [Nature] declares the being and attributes of the Almighty Father, none but *the fool in heart* has ever dared gainsay." In his *Lectures on the History of Philosophy* in 1819, he called "the book of nature" "the other great Bible of God." (CC 8, 541) In *Frost at Midnight*, Nature is the "Great universal Teacher", whom Coleridge imagines will mould his son's spirit, and by giving make it ask. He believed at that time that we should receive the "sweet influences" of Nature with "a wise passiveness," and so allow them to create a living soul within us. To some extent, we have inherited this attitude to the images of nature: we expect or hope that they may stimulate some positive response within us, as we suppose that just through the act of reading, the Bible, or any other book, will convey its truths to us.

And yet a few years later, in the early 1820s, Coleridge had changed his mind so completely in respect of Nature that he is reported as saying, "No! Nature is not God; she is the devil in a strait waist-coat." (CC 6, 71) This change is reflected throughout his later works, and in 1827, for instance, he described Nature as "the Ens non vere ens, [the being not truly a being] the Opposite of God, as the Spirit of Chaos, but made Nature by the Word." (CN V, 5632) This change requires explanation, and the explanation will illustrate how Coleridge read his Bible.

At the heart of this transformation is the relationship between Nature, or the objective world, and the mind. In his early work, Coleridge was willing to believe, with Wordsworth, that "One impulse from a vernal wood/ May teach you more of man,/ Of moral evil and of good,/ Than all the sages can"; that the sensory impulses from the external world act on and form the mind, and that Nature, as the language of God, is active and benign. The mind is thus the sum of its experience, and Coleridge briefly adopted the logical extension of this view when he became a necessitarian. God made and is immanent in the natural world, and we continually remake it in our perception of it – "a repetition in the finite mind of the eternal act of creation in the infinite I AM." This is Coleridge's definition, in 1815, of the primary imagination, which he holds "to be the living Power and prime Agent of all human Perception." (CW 7, 1, 304) But, as I hope to show, the key word is "human". He had come to believe that the mind had its own powers, was not merely passive or receptive, and here, in what he later called a "muddled and immature" formulation, the imagination appears to be the power that can recall or produce the concepts by which we read the sensory world. Bit by bit he had rejected the view that nature is mind-making, until he asserted something that is harder for us to understand, that Nature is mind-made. Wordsworth believed that Nature could teach us about good and evil; Coleridge, finally, rejected such a view outright. He came to believe that Nature remained meaningless in respect of our humanity unless we organize our conceptions using powers from within ourselves; these powers are distinct from our conceptual abilities, which we probably share with other animals, and it is the confusion of those two that has made the 1815 definition of the imagination problematic.

The question he wrestled with is, What are those powers, and how can they be described or defined? His one constant answer, which he wove into many different shapes, was a distinction between Reason and Understanding. In this definition, Reason is not logical thinking. It is that which belongs to us specifically as human beings, unlike the Understanding, which animals share with us to a greater or lesser extent. And in the light of this distinction, which he developed from Plato and Kant, we can separate ideas from concepts. The ideas co-ordinate with Reason are, for Coleridge, the ideas of our humanity, all those abstract nouns Blake made such good use of – mercy, pity, peace, love, truth, beauty, justice, power, freedom – and so on. These ideas, however defined, constitute our humanity; the concepts by which we perceive the world do not belong specifically to us, but are shared by other forms of being, who otherwise would presumably not manage their habitation with much success. And vice-versa, we do not need these ideas for our perception of, or our success in, the natural world. We could survive perfectly well as concept-capable animals. However the natural world makes no sense in respect of our humanity unless we bring these ideas to it, ideas which Nature does not reveal. They belong to our mind as our distinctly human mind. As he expressed it in *Aids to Reflection*:

> whatever things in visible nature *have* the character of Permanence, and endure amid continual flux unchanged like a Rainbow in a fast-flying shower, (ex. gr. Beauty, Order, Harmony, Finality, Law,) are all akin to the *peculia* of Humanity, are all *con-genera* of Mind and Will, without which indeed they would not only exist in vain, as pictures for Moles, but actually not *exist* at all ... (AR p. 347 (1825))

We could argue with this, and culturally we have: why impose our ideas on nature? Let it be, observe it, and that will be our poetry. But such was not Coleridge's way – nor probably any great poet's.

These ideas, "the *peculia* of Humanity, are *con-genera* of the Mind and Will": that is they depend upon the will; and although potential in all of us, they need to be realized. This is where the imagination steps in: activated by the will, the human and religious life begins with the ideas generated by the imagination:

> But only as a Man is capable of Ideas ... and as far only as he is capable of an Ideal (practical product having its cause & impulse in *Ideas* ...) is Man a *Religious* Being. But neither the

one nor the other is possible except thro' the Imagination ... by force of which the Man ... creates for himself, and for the use & furtherance of his *Thinking*, Representations or rather *Presences*, where *Experience* can supply no more, but had already stopt payment. (CN IV 4692)

These "*presences*" are the prime agents of *human* perception. Their realization is not dependent on any experience, any external stimulus; not on the images of nature, nor words from the page. And neither nature, nor text, can act on us, as human and religious beings, unless we permit our imagination to create these ideas, these presences. This places us, as readers, in a position of responsibility. If we do not bring these ideas, as living powers, to our reading of the text, it will remain unresponsive, as it will for sceptical readers. And in Coleridge's mind, the source of these ideas could not have a greater authority, for he was willing to say, "God is Reason." He defined faith as "Feälty to Reason" and declared "that any articles of faith that were not Ideas of Reason were jargon for Traitors to conjure with ..." (CN V 5619). He expressed this radical belief colourfully in a letter of 1815: "For even the Bible is but the Pool of Bethesda, of no avail till the Angel, whom angels and archangels worship by the working of his Holy Spirit in the human spirit, troubles the waters, before stagnant to the inward eye." (CL IV 580) The authority of the Bible does not lie in the ability of the text to act on the mind, but in the relationship established between what the reader brings and what the text says.

One of the consequences of Coleridge's method is that he believed that Reason might compensate for any inadequacies in phenomenal reality, any failure of the historical or providential scheme of revelation. In the *Opus Maximum* he writes:

The fruits and attainments of the reason are at hand to compensate ... for whatever diminution, either of the proofs or their influence on the mind, may be inherent in the nature of all historical testimony by the ravages or even the mere lapse of time. (CW 16, 16)

Not only do the ideas of Reason fill in the gaps created, for example, by lost documents, but should the biblical texts themselves represent the process imperfectly or inadequately, then Reason can repair their intention. The Bible is not so much a teacher as a collaborative – but potentially fallible – partner in this enterprise. All of this puts Coleridge very close to Blake in his method of reading the Bible, but reduces the risk of the subjectivity incurred by claiming a prophetic mantle.

Confessions of an Inquiring Spirit

Coleridge knew he would be running into serious trouble with those who took the Bible as gospel or literal truth, the fundamentalists of his day. In the 1820s he began a series of letters, published posthumously as *Confessions of an Inquiring Spirit*, in which he attempts to reconcile this radical approach with his belief in the inspired authority of the Bible. Since the 1790s, the Bible had been steadily undermined, as a reliable source of historical truth, by German Higher Criticism;[2] literal readings became a way of reasserting its validity. The interpretations derived from the doctrine of literal truth could do a lot of damage, even at the domestic level. For instance, of the text "He that spareth the Rod, spoileth the Child", Coleridge noted that "translating the *Rod* literally" constitutes an "unmerciful Despoliation of the sweetest Gardens of Human Nature – the sweet sunshiny meadows of Childhood." (CN III, 3852) Coleridge was flogged regularly at home as well as at school, but only regarded one of his beatings as just – when James Bowyer, his headmaster at Christ's Hospital, flogged infidelity out of him. Thus the view he attacks is that the Bible was "dictated by an infallible intelligence." (CW 11, 2, 1122) The view he defends is that it was "composed by men under the actuating influence of, the Holy Spirit." (Ibid) Coleridge wants to read the Bible as he does other human documents: the doctrine of infallibility "petrifies at once the whole Body of Holy Writ" and turns the Scriptures

> into a colossal Memnon's Head, a hollow Passage for a Voice, a Voice that mocks the voices of many men and speaks in their names and yet is but one voice and the same! – and no man uttered it, and never in a human heart was it conceived! (ibid.)

Much better, in his experience, to take up the Bible as one would any other body of ancient writings, in a tranquil and reflective state of mind; such a reader, he believes, will soon be impressed by its superiority to all other books, "till at length all other Books and all other Knowlege will be valuable in his eyes in proportion as they help him to a better understanding of his Bible." (CC 11, 2, 1164) And Coleridge is prescient in realizing that the Bible cannot be used as an authority in arguments outside the conditions of its creation: thus, commenting on a book attempting to make Genesis speak the truths of geology, Coleridge writes

> the Pressing of Moses & the Bible into the Service of Geological Theory … must end in the triumph of Infidels. If there be one sure Conclusion respecting the Bible, it is this – that it not only uniformly speaks the language of the Senses, but adopts the inferences which the Childhood of the Race drew from the appearances presented by the Senses. The Bible must be interpreted by its known objects and Ends; & these were the moral and spiritual Education of the Human Race. – These ends secured, the truths of Science follow of their own accord. (CL V 372)

The Role of Sense Experience

Given Coleridge's belief in the primacy of the ideas of Reason, sense experience might be expected to vanish utterly in this idealist scheme, but it does not. Coleridge argues that the images of sense may prime the pump of Reason, and he devotes a whole chapter to this in the *Opus Maximum* (CW 16, I, iv). As he puts it in a note, though he would reject the notion that our mind at birth is a blank sheet, he admits that "whatever characters may have been impressed on the sheet, are written in *Sympathetic* Ink, and need an exciting cause to render them apparent" (CN V, 5530). Thus Reason and history as forms of revelation work hand in hand for Coleridge. Although he is willing to provide incisive definitions – such as "Religion is: Ideas contemplated as Facts" – Coleridge follows up that particular entry with a lengthy caveat that recognizes that ideas cannot constitute religion until they are incorporated into specific historical events. The same note continues as follows:

> "There is a God" is a philosophic Dogma: but not of itself a Religion. But that God mani-fested himself to Abraham or Moses, and sent them to make known that he *made* the World and formed Man out of the Ground, and breathed into him a living Soul – this is Religion. (CN IV, 5299)

In another note, he treats facts rather like nature's sense impressions, to be reunited with ideas in order to substantiate the revelation they offer:

> Now this is my Aim – to bring back our faith & affections to the simplicity of the Gospel Facts, by restoring the facts of the Gospel to their union with the Ideas or Spiritual Truths therein embodied or thereby revealed. (CN IV, 5421)

This is why Coleridge's reading of the Bible is so hugely engaged: simultaneously he is testing what he finds there against the ideas of Reason, and allowing the Bible to bring those ideas to life in him; and though he realizes that not every event in the Bible will be established as fact, a religion without a factual history is no religion. It is a difficult position to adopt, and easily unsettled.

Coleridge Reads Genesis

On November 1, 1829 Coleridge began reading *Genesis* for a second or third time, though on this occasion apparently intending a consecutive study of, and commentary on, the books of the Old Testament.[3] The record of the event is fascinating because it embodies: first, Coleridge's philosophically charged desire to make coherent sense of the text; second, his utter failure to do so; and, third, his contemplation of a poetic approach as a possible hermeneutical improvement. His first note comments on chapter 1 and the first three verses of chapter 2, and opens with these words: "In whatever point of view I contemplate this venerable Relic of ancient Cosmogony ... I find difficul-ties." If considered as a religious document, he thinks that verses 1 ("In the beginning God created the heaven and the earth") and 26 ("And God said, Let us make man in our image") "seem to say all that Religion requires." Trying to account for the story as it stands, Coleridge suggests that it may have been intended for the people, and "addressed to the Senses and grounded in the *Appearances* of Things"; but if so, why is "the Vegetable creation [verse 11] anterior to the *Sun* [verse 14]?" This looks to him like a "Physiogony" or scheme for the generation of nature; but if so, what is the func-tion of verses 6 to 8, "so obviously built on the popular fancy of the Earth floating, like a square Garment (hence the 4 *Corners* of the Earth) on an Ocean, and the sky being an Arch of blue Stone or Sapphire?" The questions multiply without solution, and

Coleridge appears to retire from the fray with the Parthian shot, "This seems addressed to Men in the Childhood of Thought." But he hasn't quite given up:

> To make this Cosmogony ... a Morning Hymn ... in which every Dawn *re-creates* the World to us, [as] it was created by God – only with pre-determined Epochs – First, all indistinction, darkness – then a Breeze – then Break of Light – then the distinction of Sky – then of Land and Water – then of Trees & Grass – then the Sun rises – the animals next are seen and first the Birds – afterwards the Cattle – and lastly, Man the High Priest comes forth from his Cottage – this is beautiful! But, I fear, far too refined and sentimental, to be received as sound interpretation. (CN V, 6124).

So the note closes, the poet in Coleridge more satisfied than what he elsewhere calls the "historico-critical *intellective*" reader (CN V, 6241).

What the above extract illustrates is that the mood in which Coleridge reads the Bible is very much the mood in which modern readers might take it up. There is an attention to the status of the text: whom does it address; what purpose does it serve; in what context was it written; is it a genuine document? A variety of possible answers are provided, and the value of each is rationally assessed. Coleridge's method is more or less our method, even if certain events, possible for him, such as a universal flood, are no longer possibilities for us. There are other features of his reading that should also help to make us feel at ease with his commentary: he is, for instance, quite prepared to admit that he doesn't understand. He is puzzled, for example, by the episode in which Jacob wrestles with God, remarking that "I have as yet had no Light given to me. ... The symbolic Import, & the immediate purpose, are alike hidden from me ... The whole passage is a perfect episode – a sort of parenthesis in the narrative" (CN V, 6198).

In fact what to make of Genesis continues to puzzle Coleridge, and a few notes later he has another stab at it, identifying his idea of the Fall in the process. He considers the first chapter

> a scheme of Geogony, containing the facts and truths of Science adapted to the language of Appearances. ... It is throughout literal – and gives the *physical* Creation/ then from v. 4 of C. II comes the *Moral* Creation – the formation of the *Humanity* ... with the moral cause, the spiritual process of the Fall, the *Centaurization* of Man, – and that the whole is symbolic or allegorical. (CN V, 6129)

Coleridge discriminates between what may be taken literally and what symbolically – although he seems here to conflate the distinction between symbol and allegory that he had made in *The Statesman's Manual*; but it is certainly characteristic that he reads many events in both Testaments, particularly the miracles, symbolically. *Genesis*, at this point, is open to such a reading because God warns Adam, before the birth of Eve, that if he should eat of the tree of Good and Evil, "thou shalt surely die" (Genesis 2: 17). Of course, in the event, Adam and Eve do not die, or at least not as the immediate consequence of their act. Coleridge treads cautiously at this point. Whereas he is willing to say "I seem myself to understand" of the rest of chapter 3, of "the precise import of the Tree of Knowledge ... and of the several Particulars appertaining thereto ... I have at present only a *gleam.*" His gleams are revealed in the next paragraph:

> The Death of the Man is not [considered as] the extinction of all Being in him; but a Descent into a lower Being – a demersion and suffocation of his proper Humanity – the loss of the Divine Idea, the Image of God, which constituted it. (CN V, 6134)

This symbolic treatment of the Fall is not an isolated case. As one might expect, the sense that Hell, and consequently the Resurrection, are moral and spiritual conditions, not material facts, also runs through Coleridge's writings. Indeed, he finds the impoverished spiritual state of the contemporary Church represented in its very literal understanding of the resurrection. "The way, the Life, and the *Resurrection,*" he writes, underlining "Resurrection," and then comments,

> Oh what a poor fraction of the import of this last term do those Divines content themselves, who think of the Resurgence out of Hades as a mere Rising again from the Sexton's Grave – from the Church-yard. / And alas! alas! that "*those* Divines" should be all but all- 999 in every 1,000! (CN V, 5814 f.38v)

The true sense of the resurrection, the scriptural sense he believed, was "To act creatively, to beget a new creature, a new Spirit, in the Soul ... capable of communion and of final union (n.b. not indistinction) with the Son of God, the divine Humanity, so as to reveal his spiritual omnipresence ... entire in each believer" (CN V, 5814 f.40 & v).

This symbolic reading of central biblical ideas is not without difficulties. For example, such is Coleridge's determination to see all mention of Death or Hades in the Bible as of this spiritual or metaphysical order that he finds it very difficult to deal with statements that suppose death ends all modes of consciousness. Thus he has a real struggle with verse 5 of Psalm 6: "For in death there is no remembrance of thee: in the grave who shall give thee thanks?" It is a short Psalm, and clear in its import – a petitionary prayer for God "to confuse and confound" the Psalmist's enemies. It does not look to another life. But Coleridge cannot read it in this historically specific light:

> I see but one rational conclusion, viz. that the Psalmist was praying for a deliverance from that state of merely *potential* Being, into which on the dissolution of it's [sic] bodily organ ... the Soul must necessarily fall – and in which but by a divine Awaking, but by a resurrection into another Body, the Soul must remain. (CN V 6328)

The Place of Narrative

I have given most of my attention so far to Coleridge's discovery of the outworkings of certain key ideas in the Bible, and how his ideas and hopes can lead to readings that are sometimes difficult to reconcile with the evidence he has before him. But where ideas central to his belief are not in question, where the narrative or story is uppermost in his mind, Coleridge is a patient, generous, and sensitive reader. Here are two examples, the first from *Genesis* 45:24: Joseph is sending his brothers home, to their father and his. The verse is this: "So he sent his brethren away, and they departed, and he said unto them, See that ye fall not out by the way." Coleridge comments:

> There is something so truly natural in this gentle reproach, implied rather than expressed. … Not till they were leaving – when he saw them all together, with the presents they had received, & and then could not [but] recall the fact of their having sold him into Slavery, from Jealousy and lust of Lucre, that borrowed from some actual tho' slight apprehension of their quarreling under the influence of the same passions a pretext for, and at the same instant a *diversion* of, the involuntary feeling or resentment – this is the Drama of the Heart. (CN V, 6233)

Behind a verse we might pass over without reflection, Coleridge astutely sees the inherent tension in the apparently resolved relationship between Joseph and his brothers. He understands how a person of fundamental good will might deal with feelings of resentment, having himself been sold into the educational slavery of Christ's Hospital. There are suggestive enough parallels between Coleridge and Joseph for us to understand why he might have been sensitive to the motions of Joseph's heart and mind.

The second example is from chapter 12 of Numbers, and we witness Coleridge's tenderness for the sinful and the suffering, his merciful view of necessary punishment. Miriam has offended the Lord by speaking against Moses, and is punished by God with leprosy. Aaron pleads to Moses who pleads to God, who mitigates her punishment by reference to the Hebraic custom of a daughter being in disgrace for seven days if her father spits in her face:

> Even a Sister, who hath so offended, that the Heavenly Father hath spit into her face, is to find a Sabbath, a Seventh Day on which she is to be received again! O of such as are permitted to live … let us not hear of irrecoverable Backslidings, excommunication *sine die* – of a poor Miriam. She may yet be called to make sweet music before the Lord![4]

Coleridge completed his reading of Genesis sometime in the winter of 1829–30, and writing a note on the occasion, gave it the title, "Sundry General Remarks and Reflections on a studious Re-perusal of the Book of Genesis." What is noticeable about this two page entry is Coleridge's reversion to the establishment of ideas in Genesis; no attention at all is given to Genesis as a story or as a form of history – both of which Coleridge has commented on in his previous notes. Thus he first draws our attention to the fact that Genesis "begins with an *Act*, a revelation of a *Will* –" but further still "yea, and of a Will in it's own form! of *the* Will – of an Absolute Identity antecedent in order of Thought, to the Unity of Personal Being. – of the Absolute Will, as the Ground and eternal Antecedent of all Being" (CN V, 6239).

Study and Prayer

Finding the right balance between the text and its interpretation is clearly a question raised by his treatment of the Bible's opening verse, yet there is no hint in Coleridge's notes that he himself thinks that he might be reading too much into the text. Indeed, later in the same note, he feels that "this first Verse might with great propriety have been detached and presented as the First Chapter" – having said which he then begins his philosophical disquisitions afresh. However, although we might think the main question is whether the Bible supports the philosophical insights that he ascribes to it, Coleridge himself thinks that more important is the state of mind we bring to our reading. Those who bring nothing to their readings of the Bible can take nothing from it and Coleridge is conscious that those who only bring scholarly skills to their reading bring only a little more than nothing: "O the difference, the unspeakable difference, between an historico-critical *intellective* Study of the Old Testament, and the *praying* of the same! I mean the perusal of it with a personal moral and religious Interest" (CN V, 6241).

Scattered through his notes and letters during the last fifteen years of his life are references to parts of the Bible he has read in the spirit of prayer; thus in a letter of August 31, 1826, which describes much physical suffering, he adds at the end, "I have derived great comfort from praying the 71st. Psalm" (CL VI, 607). Earlier in the same year he felt it a "duty of Love and Charity" to study the Apocalypse because rumors had reached him of his friend Edward Irving's "Aberrations" in his treatment of the same book. Coleridge found that the rumors proved true. "But," he says, "these studies were against my inclinations and cravings. I needed Prayer for my Comfort: I needed unction and tenderness of heart for my Prayers: and this I could not hope to find from the thorns and brambles of critical disquisition."

As we have seen, Coleridge's philosophy rested on the premise of an originating act of will, absolute or infinite in God, relative or finite in man and that, acting on the Hades or Chaos of his natural self, elevates him into his true humanity. He defined prayer, which he believed to be the focus of religion, as "the relation of a Will to a Will, the Will in each instance being of a Person to a Person" (CN V, 5566); or as he put it in an earlier note, "The Personal in me is the ground and condition of Religion: and the Personal alone is the Object" (CN V, 5530 f.65v).

So we have a concatenation of terms essential to Coleridge's belief that prayer is the focus of religion: the absolute will meets the finite in the relation of a person to a person, each of which is known through and constituted by their ideas. These ideas are not there to be passively observed as we observe phenomena, but evolved through an act of will; this is prayer, and is of a broad definition in which, for instance, Coleridge is happy to include meditation (CN V, 5566). The ideas evolved are a power, and when, and however, that power is known, Coleridge is sure of his faith and secure in his understanding of the Bible. The following note is dated "27 Octob^r 1827 Ramsgate," and he is perhaps reacting against his own "historico-critical *intellective*" reading:

> Why do I ever suffer myself even for a moment to forget, that respecting all of Christianity … my Conscience & my reason are more than satisfied, and even my Understanding is convinced. When the Ideas rise up within me, as independent Growths of my Spirit, and I then turn to the Epistles of Paul and John and to the Gospel of the latter, these seem a Looking-glass to me in which I recognize the same truths as the reflected Images of my Ideas. … Why should I trouble myself with questions about the precise character, purpose

and source of the supposed Matthew's, of Mark's, or even of the less difficult Gospel of Luke? (CN V, 5624)

That simple phrase – "When the Ideas rise up within me" – bespeaks the essential nature of Coleridge's enterprise, the will empowering the imagination to educe the ideas of Reason. It ends on Highgate Hill, perhaps with a faint echo of its beginnings on the hills of Somerset, invoking the ground and unity of all being, in prayer or meditation, and seeking the "Faith that inly feels." But Coleridge's last note, written in the month he died, has a particularity we miss in his poetic meditations of the 1790s:

> O Grace of God! if only a believing Mind could indeed be possessed by, and possess, the full Idea of the Reality of the Absolute Will, the Good! … if in short, the Idea, the Mystery of absolute Light save in the beams of which all else would struggle in the Mystery of hopeless Darkness & Contradiction, were present to him – o with what deep devotion of Delight, Awe and Thanksgiving would he read every sentence of [chapters 13–17] of St. John's Gospel!! (CN V, 6918)

Those chapters record Jesus' reflections, in his consciousness of the approaching passion, on who and what he is. Jesus is preparing to leave life, and Coleridge is willing in himself what he believed Jesus' death symbolized: "[the] final entire detachment and deradication of the human Principium Individualitatis from the *Ground* (Hades, Nature) and its transplantation into the Substance (or divine ground) of the Logos." This last note is an almost ruthless invocation of the absolute, the prayer of a man who was also willing to write this simple, rough couplet: "O! might Life *cease,* and selfless *Mind /* Whose Being is *Act,* alone remain behind!" By the end, Coleridge had outgrown life, and as Charles Lamb said, "hungered for eternity."

Notes

This article was first published, in a very different form, in *The Coleridge Bulletin, New Series 23 (NS)* pp. 63–81 (Spring 2004)

1   CW 11, 2, 1119. Coleridge's idea of history was one of progressive revelation, gradually embodying the being of Christ; it is also the impetus behind his *Lectures on the History of Philosophy, CW* 8. In the next sentence, Causabon is a figure from George Eliot's *Middlemarch.*
2   A rather too general collective term, and better considered author by author: see Harding 3–16 for an account of the authors and their various approaches.
3   His first critical reading of Genesis may have been as early as 1810, and he took it up again in 1818. See, for instance, CN III, 4325, 4418, 4625; Harding (2008, p. 110).
4   CN V 6362, Harding 255–6; Coleridge is probably referring to Exodus 15.20, where Miriam sings to the Lord in celebration of the crossing of the Dead Sea, though this happened prior to the events of Numbers 12.

Bibliography

Barbeau, Jeffrey W. (2008) *Coleridge, the Bible, and Religion.* Palgrave, Basingstoke.
Beer, J. B., ed. (2002) *Coleridge's Writings, Vol. 4: On Religion and Psychology,* Palgrave.

Harding, Anthony, ed. (2008) Coleridge on the Bible, vol. II of John Beer, ed., *Coleridge's Responses*, 3 volumes. Continuum, London.

Coleridge, Samuel Taylor (1969–2002) *The Collected Works of Samuel Taylor Coleridge (CW)*, 16 volumes. Princeton University Press, Princeton, NJ. All references to Coleridges works in this chapter can be found in this collection.

Coleridge, Samuel Taylor (1957–2002) *The Notebooks of Samuel Taylor Coleridge (CN)*, ed. Kathleen Coburn and Anthony Harding, 5 volumes. Princeton University Press, Princeton, NJ.

Coleridge, Samuel Taylor (1957–71) *The Collected Letters of Samuel Taylor Coleridge (CL)*, ed. E. L. Griggs, 6 volumes. Oxford University Press, Oxford.

CHAPTER 30
Jane Austen

Michael Giffin

When thinking about Austen and the Bible, it is useful to recall how common it was for our forebears to relate chapter and verse of scripture to their personal and communal lives, and to national and international events. We do not know whether Austen did the same, but she could have, as a clergy daughter with a strong personal faith and an astute awareness of the world within and beyond her domestic frame. As alien as it may seem to us, her family would have said morning and/or evening prayer daily. If they used the prayer book lectionary, which was highly likely, Austen would have read or heard most of the Psalms once a month, most of the Jewish Scriptures once a year, and most of the Christian Scriptures twice a year. She cherished her copy of *A Companion to the Altar*, a primer of meditations for those preparing to receive Holy Communion. She wrote eloquent intercessory prayers.

Understanding Austen's period is challenging, as it has become foreign to us in many ways. At least since Alistair Duckworth's *The Improvement of the Estate* (1971) and Marilyn Butler's *Jane Austen and the War of Ideas* (1975), most critics support the view that her novels are commentaries that participate in the intellectual ferment of her period and situate themselves in relation to genres and sub-genres of contemporary heroine-centered novels. She belongs to what is increasingly referred to as a long eighteenth century between the Restoration in 1660 and the end of the Georgian period in 1830. During this period the State and Church were united in a way that will not be as apparent to us as it was to her contemporaries. She accepted that unity, which is why it is difficult to separate her literary vision into distinct secular and religious spheres.

Austen's novels are simultaneously biblical and contemporary. On a biblical level they present the story of the fall and the drama of salvation in contemporary terms. On a contemporary level they interrogate neoclassicism and romanticism in biblical terms. In each novel, these presentations and interrogations are firmly focused on marriage and family, where the condition of the domestic economy mirrors the national economy, both of which are measured against what theologians call the divine economy. Husbands and wives exercise joint headship, effectively or ineffectively. Marriage and parenthood determine whether the domestic economy is ordered or disordered.

Austen intends to establish her heroines and heroes in effective marriages, as a means of promoting domestic economy. This is not an easy process as all the heroines and heroes, with the possible exception of Catherine Morland in *Northanger Abbey* (1818), have been raised in families that are disordered in some way; consequently they lack necessary qualities in an effective partner. None of these marriages is easily achieved and neither are they established by fate or accident or providence. They are the hard won product of conflict and misunderstanding and growth. They are forged in difficult social and economic and moral circumstances. They occur at the end of a journey into maturity that, in most cases, is analogous with those undertaken by many characters in the Jewish and Christian Scriptures, including Abraham, Moses, the followers of Jesus, and Jesus himself.

Everything depends on the heroine and hero maturing. Jesus' maturity comes after the journey of his earthly ministry in Galilee and its gradual progress toward and beyond Jerusalem. The heroine and hero undertake a similar journey. Their maturity depends on how they exercise their free will, and learn from their circumstances and the consequences of their choices. Expressed in theological terms, a fallen and continually falling humanity is called to follow the human example of the earthly Jesus, in order to participate in the divine example of the risen Christ, and thereby share the physical preservation (*soteria*) and metaphysical salvation (*soteria*) the following and participation confer. Notice how these two terms, preservation and salvation, are the same in biblical Greek.

The need for preservation and salvation was wide ranging in the Georgian period. Social life was still determined by property and patronage. Economic life was still dominated by a market economy subject to cycles of surplus and shortage, boom and bust, and extended periods of high inflation. Public health was still poor, filled with inequalities, and even the wealthy suffered from what we now regard as unacceptable levels of preventable sickness and premature death. There were high degrees of social mobility, upward and downward. Every class was restless and insecure and under threat. In this period of individual and communal vulnerability, the Austen heroine and hero need to discover answers to the questions: How have I fallen? How can I be preserved and saved? This is a difficult physical and metaphysical discovery among the extremes of a Georgian reality very different from, and much less secure than, our reality, where marriage was much more crucial to survival than it is now.

Let us see how Austen's narrative scheme appears in three of her novels.

Sense and Sensibility

Both biblical and contemporary themes are woven together in the first chapter of *Sense and Sensibility* (1811). Mrs Henry Dashwood and her daughters are in precarious circumstances, caused by her late husband's inability to secure their future and the greed of his son and daughter-in-law. With each sentence Austen heightens an awareness of how the commandment to honor thy father and mother, and the injunction to care for the widowed and orphaned, have been violated. Once that violation is described, and its consequences are revealed, Austen presents the different temperaments of two sisters, Elinor's reason (sense) and Marianne's feeling (sensibility), which determine their neoclassical and romantic responses to their circumstances.

Mr John Dashwood, already wealthy through maternal inheritance and advantageous marriage, inherits his father's estate. At the deathbed he promises to do everything in his power to care for his stepmother and stepsisters but once the paternal inheritance is conveyed his wife persuades him to change his mind and not provide for them at all. As a result, they are ejected from their home and descend to a lower class. This violation was common and contemporary readers would recognize it as something that could happen to them.

The plight of Mrs Henry Dashwood and her daughters is mitigated when Sir John Middleton, her cousin, offers her a small cottage on easy terms on his estate. Their removal to Barton Cottage solves the immediate problem of how they can live within their means. It also allows the central action of the novel to unfold: the drama of two young women whose preservation and salvation depend on negotiating an effective marriage. Central to this drama is the way Elinor's neoclassical sense is portrayed as appropriate, because it protects her and allows her to survive, and Marianne's romantic sensibility is portrayed as inappropriate, because it makes her vulnerable and self-destructive.

This does not mean Elinor is without feeling and Marianne cannot reason. Austen maintains an exquisite symmetrical sense of the balance each sister needs to achieve depending on whether she is destined for Church or Estate. After her trials, Elinor is rewarded with an effective marriage to a priest, Edward Ferrars, in which feeling provides a corrective balance to reason. After her trials, Marianne is rewarded with an effective marriage to a squire, Colonel Brandon, in which reason provides a corrective balance to feeling.

Early in the novel, before her removal from Norland Park, Elinor's reason tells her Edward Ferrars, a candidate for ordination, is interested in and temperamentally suited to her. Her great drama is maintaining her faith in reason, even when it seems to have failed her, and the outcome of that faith is a hard won vindication of her rationality. Soon after her arrival in Barton Cottage, Marianne's feeling tells her John Willoughby, a flawed Byronic character, is interested in and temperamentally suited to her. Her great drama is suffering the consequences of her misguided faith in feeling as it betrays her and leads her close to self-destruction. Both sisters suffer greatly, Elinor privately and Marianne publicly, as Austen leads them to and through their respective passions before rewarding them as Mrs Ferrars and Mrs Brandon.

Reason is what will make Elinor an ideal priest's wife, in Austen's narrative scheme. Her discretion and caution, proportion and propriety, refusal to prejudge or misjudge, and repression of will and desire are important because her preservation and salvation depend on them. That does not mean she is passionless. Elinor has deep feelings, even of anger, but she regulates her behavior in a way Marianne refuses to. When Edward does not behave as she wishes, or senses he wishes, she reasons that his life, like hers, might be full of difficult circumstances she may not be aware of. More importantly, she accepts that his happiness may not involve her and must take precedence over hers.

Elinor's reason turns out to be right. Edward is wrestling with his conscience. He is faced with the prospect of following a difficult vocation, as a poor man, disinherited by his wealthy and manipulative mother and burdened with an unsuitable wife. Yet

Edward refuses to cultivate his inheritance and, youthful and misguided though it was, he knows he freely entered into an engagement with Lucy Steele. He is morally obliged to marry her regardless of the consequences. In choosing to be true to his principles over his earthly happiness, Edward is at odds with the values of the world. His actions reflect the cost of discipleship described in the three Synoptic Gospels: denying one's self and taking up one's cross and following Jesus, for whoever would save his life will lose it and whoever would lose his life for Jesus' sake will find it (Matthew 16:24–5; Mark 8:34–5; Luke 9:23–4). Since Edward is prepared to lose his life for Jesus' sake, Austen finally rewards him with both Elinor and Jesus.

Elinor's selfless behavior requires great emotional forbearance and sacrifice. She places Marianne's needs above her own, which brings her reader sympathy because Marianne is a sympathetic heroine in spite of her behavior. Placing the needs of Edward's fiancé above her own brings Elinor less reader sympathy because Lucy is not a sympathetic character. In spite of this, Elinor is obliged to uphold the law of perfect love described in Matthew: we must love our enemies and pray for those who persecute us, for God makes his sun rise on the evil and the good and sends his rain on the just and the unjust (Matthew 5:43–5). Everywhere in Austen's novels evil coexists with good, as it does in the parable of the wheat and the tares, where Jesus reminds us to leave ultimate moral judgments for God to make on the last day (Matthew 13:24–30). According to human justice, Elinor should take a stronger moral position against Willoughby; according to divine justice, she forgives him in spite of his treatment of Marianne, marriage of convenience to Miss Grey, and ruin of Eliza Brandon's character. If the reader wants to see Willoughby held to account for his actions, and is in sympathy with Colonel Brandon's failed attempt to duel with him, ultimately the coals of forgiveness Elinor heaps upon him are more effective.

Feeling is what will make Marianne an ideal squire's wife in Austen's narrative scheme. Her abilities are in many respects equal to Elinor's and she embodies several necessary qualities in a young woman destined to preside over the Estate rather than the Church. There are dangers, however, which Austen highlights by making her a damsel in romantic distress. Before Marianne can be elevated to her pedestal she needs to mature within Austen's critique of romanticism.

In the Platonic model of mind still dominant in Austen's period, Elinor is guided by reason (head) and Marianne is guided by feeling (heart) but, according to this model, feeling is more easily corrupted by base appetite (lower abdomen) than reason is. Feeling is a dangerous guardian of conscience and Marianne is a romantic accident waiting to happen. When she meets the handsome Willoughby, through a fall, he literally sweeps her off her feet, but she is unaware he is a rake who has recently seduced and impregnated and abandoned a young woman much like herself in temperament. She is overcome by her desire for Willoughby, and her feeling is soon overtaken by base appetite and degenerates into an unhealthy passion. At no stage is Marianne a victim. Her passion is fed by her will, and she can be understood as an early example of a prototype that develops throughout the nineteenth-century novel, culminating in characters such as Rosamond Vincy and Mr Kurtz. Once her friendship with Willoughby is established, Marianne's personality alters. She becomes selfish and arrogant and her thinking becomes disordered, especially about Colonel Brandon.

The chivalrous colonel, a knight in a flannel waistcoat, wants to protect Marianne from as much harm as he can, while remaining in the background, vigilant while nursing his unrequited love for his beautiful lady. He is the only character who knows what kind of suffering and self-destruction Marianne's romantic sensibilities are capable of, because he shares those sensibilities and in his youth he saw their capabilities unleashed in and against a similar young woman.

Once her feeling is corrupted by base appetite, Marianne starts to believe that social propriety, ethical value, and moral behavior can all be judged through a pleasure principle. This is hedonism, which Austen associates with romanticism and uses to strengthen Marianne's delusion so the moral weight of her disillusionment, and the physical and mental breakdown it causes, will be more keenly felt. The outcome of Marianne's disillusionment is her recognition of her errors of judgment and the promise that her painful memories of Willoughby will be regulated "by religion, by reason, and by constant employment." This is Marianne's admission that for much of the novel she abandoned these three things, which upheld Elinor in her darkest hour: religion, reason, and constant employment.

Marianne's greatest mortifications, and greatest lessons, are realizing how much emotional suffering she brought to those who love her, including her failure to see Elinor was suffering as intensely over Edward as she was over Willoughby, and her inability to see Colonel Brandon as temperamentally suited to her. Much more than Willoughby, the Colonel is in every sense an ideal husband for Marianne: socially, economically, morally, romantically, and even sexually.

At the end of the novel, the Reverend and Mrs Ferrars and the Colonel and Mrs Brandon begin their interdependent lives at Delaford, peacefully and happily. The fallenness that began the novel, and the disorder that characterized most of its story, are resolved. The heroines, who represent neoclassical reason and romantic feeling, have been balanced and achieve preservation and salvation. Delaford is now an idealized model in which the effective marriages of male and female, and of Church and Estate, perform complementary roles in a domestic economy that mirrors the national economy, both of which are measured against the divine economy.

Pride and Prejudice

When read through the prism of hermeneutics, or theory of interpretation, *Pride and Prejudice* (1813) becomes less a love story of a middle-class heroine and an upper-class hero and more a moral story about how Elizabeth Bennet and Fitzwilliam Darcy learn to interpret "correctly," in biblical and contemporary terms, by overcoming their first impressions, recognizing their sins of pride and prejudice, and learning to give and receive human love as a proxy for divine love. The novel is about how they mature, and after they mature Austen places them as equals at the pinnacle of her symbolic order, which is hierarchical but also a meritocracy, where their shared headship is of both public and private importance.

According to the logic the novel proposes, their marriage overcomes the bad economy of Longbourn in Hertfordshire, where their horizons clash, improves the good economy of Rosings and Hunsford in Kent, where their horizons dialogue, and perfects the ideal economy of Pemberley in Derbyshire, where their horizons fuse. Elizabeth's pilgrimage into preservation and salvation is a gradual discovery of self, which moves from south to north, beginning in an earthly purgatory and ending in an earthly paradise. However, Austen interrupts that ascent on two occasions, after Elizabeth's first trip to Kent, and again after her first trip to Derbyshire, and returns her to purgatory to reflect. During that slow and painful ascent, and its necessary interruptions, Elizabeth's attitude to Darcy gradually changes from contempt, to ambivalence, and finally to gratitude, John Gregory's contentious precondition for love and successful marriage, described in his popular female conduct book *A Father's Legacy to his Daughters* (1774).

Having established Longbourn (long + borne) as an earthly purgatory in volume I, Austen uses Elizabeth's confident assertion to her sister Jane, "one knows exactly what to think," to measure the pride and prejudice of both heroine and hero. Before the gulf between them can be bridged, they must change how they interpret. Austen uses the language of danger, fear, and mortification to describe that change because, as Paul tells the Philippians, we must work out our preservation and salvation in fear and trembling (Philippians 2:12).

Elizabeth's pride and prejudice cannot be defended but can be understood. She is contemptuous because Darcy believes her connections are inferior but everything her family does proves him right. Beneath her defences, she is aware of belonging to a dysfunctional family. Mr and Mrs Bennet are ineffective managers, primogeniture has operated against their daughters, and what remains of Mr Bennet's estate is entailed in favor of his cousin Mr Collins. The future depends on the Bennet sisters finding good husbands, but they are leaving too much to chance, are temperamentally unsuited to the task, and their parents are not providing them with guidance or the right example.

The contrast between Elizabeth and Charlotte Lucas is instructive. Charlotte is plain, her parents cannot provide for her future, even though they are more secure than the Bennets, and she does not intend to leave finding a husband to chance because chance is a poor finder of husbands. While Austen does not believe Charlotte's engagement to Mr Collins is ideal, and intends something better for Elizabeth, it is wrong to assume Elizabeth's view of the Collins marriage is Austen's view.

Darcy's pride and prejudice cannot be defended but can be understood. If he is highly aware of class, his own and everyone else's, so are most other characters that have ulterior motives for cultivating his acquaintance. In fact, Darcy is less of a snob than those vying for his attention. He can accept social change but needs to learn he cannot dictate the terms of change or remain invulnerable in the face of change. Also, the qualities that attract him to Elizabeth are, ironically, the qualities that will make her refuse him when he proposes to her in Kent. He is willing to overlook her inferior connections, because of his feelings for her, but she cannot be grateful to a man who has tried to ruin her sister's chances of happiness, or who is insensitive enough to offer her a marriage that will apparently exclude her family. In spite of her inferior connections, Elizabeth must remain loyal to her family. Disloyalty would disqualify her from becoming the kind of Mrs Darcy Austen wants her to become in Derbyshire.

Unlike that of volume I, the leitmotiv of volume II is one does not know what to think. At the center of the volume, also the center of the novel, the great confrontation between Elizabeth and Darcy challenges the way they interpret. Following this confrontation, Elizabeth begins a process of seeking understanding, and she uses John Locke's formula of reason, revelation, and reflection on experience to do so.

Austen accomplishes many things during Elizabeth's visit to Kent. She is seen as equal to the society of Rosings and her manners are better than Lady Catherine's. She learns the truth about George Wickham, a flawed Byronic character similar to John Willoughby. She observes the unity of the relationship between Estate and Church. Rosings and Hunsford represent good economy, certainly much better than Longbourn, but it is less than ideal. In spite of her caricatures of Lady Catherine and Mr Collins, Austen portrays life in Kent as a model of decency and good order compared with life in Hertfordshire, although a better model awaits the heroine in Derbyshire.

Elizabeth notices Mr Collins's manners have not changed with marriage but apart from that she is unable to fault him. He is hospitable and kind, is pleased to be married, loves his home and garden, and is assiduous in performing his clerical duties. He is proud of his connection with Lady Catherine and although he may hope for advancement in the Church he is neither ruthless nor political. Elizabeth would find marriage to Mr Collins oppressive but the pragmatic Charlotte appears quite happy because her expectations are lower than Elizabeth's and may be more realistic.

Elizabeth is returned to the purgatory of Longbourn to reflect on what she has learned at Rosings and Hunsford. She now knows that if her younger sister Lydia follows Wickham's regiment to Brighton there will be dire consequences for her family, but she is unable to convince her father of the moral danger. Mr Bennet allows Lydia to become a camp follower, even though she is a minor, because he has never been able to effectively manage her or any other member of his family.

Elizabeth cannot influence what is happening at Longbourn and must allow events to take their course. All she can do is maintain her dignity, behave with humility, and seek as much understanding as she can through Locke's formula. She realizes she has made many errors of judgment, some of which have contributed to the precariousness of her situation. Her future depends on interpreting correctly, acting wisely, and not expecting good fortune. Suddenly life has become a serious business for a young woman, not yet twenty-one, so certain of herself in the first half of the novel.

Volume III demonstrates Darcy's capacity for change and Elizabeth's gradual recognition of that change. The key word here is gradual, for the novel would lose much of its Lockean significance, and become less relevant as a moral story about the consequences of free will, if the hermeneutical dilemmas Elizabeth encounters on her journey into maturity were easily solved. Austen does not allow Elizabeth facile recognitions based on her feelings because, like Marianne's in *Sense and Sensibility*, her feelings are unreliable and she must learn to give primacy to reason. If her feelings now tell her she wants Darcy to love her, she needs to keep them in check.

Austen confounds Gregory's thesis that love and successful marriage depend on the female being grateful to the male. Darcy does not expect Elizabeth's gratitude for saving Lydia, or for reuniting Bingley with Jane, but what Elizabeth doesn't realize during most of volume III is how Darcy is trying to be everything she accused him of not being during their confrontation at the center of the novel. He is doing everything he can to become acceptable to her, but she is now reacting with an inappropriate passiveness, giving him signals more like those Jane gave Bingley in volume I. Complicating this, Darcy and Elizabeth are never allowed a moment alone. Their every attempt to connect is interrupted.

Ultimately it is Lady Catherine's visit to Longbourn that gives Darcy hope. The visit is intended to intimidate Elizabeth but she refuses to be intimidated. This demonstrates her suitability to be first lady of the Estate, and shows the forces of change outstaring the forces of reaction. Their confrontation must have a high level of probability about it or Austen would have been criticized for Elizabeth's lack of deference to her superiors. Elizabeth's refusal to invest Lady Catherine with an authority she does not merit is the source of her moral authority.

The preservation and salvation bestowed on Elizabeth and Darcy at Pemberley is not shared with everyone, and it is not shared indiscriminately. In the final chapter we see who is allowed to visit Pemberley, as an earthly paradise, and who will benefit from its now perfected economy. Pemberley mediates different degrees of preservation and salvation to many frail and fallen characters, some of whom have merited it more than others, some of whom have not merited it at all. That makes Pemberley a potent symbol of biblical soteriology: for example, in Jesus' description of heaven as a house with many rooms (John 14:1–4). Not every character is given a room at Pemberley. But because Austen is both biblical and contemporary in equal measure she fills those rooms with several characters that represent a society in transition: a society continually falling and continually being preserved and saved.

Mansfield Park

The seriousness of *Mansfield Park* (1814) as a social and religious commentary sets it apart from the rest of Austen's novels. The first chapter establishes a series of ineffective marriages within an extended family in Mansfield and Portsmouth, which cause disorder in Estate and Church. Three men, Sir Thomas Bertram, Reverend Norris, and Lieutenant Price, marry three sisters. The second sister, who should not marry first, captivates Sir Thomas and becomes Lady Bertram. Six years later, the first sister, unless she wishes to remain a spinster, is obliged to marry the Reverend Norris, a clergyman with education but no fortune. Finally, the third sister, to disoblige her family, marries a lieutenant of marines with neither education nor fortune. Sir Thomas, paterfamilias of the extended family, gives Mr Norris a living, and is happy to assist Mr Price. Before he can, an estrangement occurs, aided and abetted by the mischievous Mrs Norris. The Bertram and Price marriages are fertile but the Norris marriage is infertile.

Reordering Estate and Church depends on reversing the effects of these ineffective marriages, which depends on an effective marriage between two children of the estranged sisters, Fanny Price and Edmund Bertram. Their marriage reunites an extended family and banishes the forces of evil that caused and perpetuated the disorder. This marriage does not simply happen and neither is it predestined. It only occurs after the biblical stories of fall and preservation and salvation are reworked through a contemporary prism.

Three characters are crucial to understanding *Mansfield Park* as Austen's most religious novel: Sir Thomas as "first cause" and "absentee landlord," who is head of the Estate; Fanny as "suffering servant" and "anointed one," who makes a journey of self-denial and self-discovery before becoming a contemporary messiah; and Edmund as a candidate for ordination, whose moral authority and pastoral focus are at risk from worldly seduction. These three characters do not represent the Trinity but there is a Trinitarian logic about the way their relationship develops throughout the novel. Such a reading is contested, by secular critics who disagree with religious interpretations of ostensibly secular novels, and by religious critics who disagree with those who describe the more didactic and allegorical dimensions of Austen's work, but there is sufficient textual evidence to demonstrate its validity.

Every event in *Mansfield Park* has, as its "first cause," to use an Aristotelian and Scholastic term, an action or inaction of Sir Thomas. He is an "absentee landlord," a deist description of God's relationship with creation. Deism was a prominent religious philosophy in Austen's period, which believes in a supreme creator who is the ultimate source of reality and ground of value but does not intervene in natural or historical processes through providences or revelations or incarnations. Austen may not be consciously critiquing deism but she is a theist, who believes God is personal and present as well as transcendent, and a critique of deism is an extension of her contemporary presentation of the story of the fall and the drama of preservation and salvation, and her interrogation of reason and feeling. Throughout *Mansfield Park*, Austen criticizes Sir Thomas as an emotionally absent parent. The social and economic and moral disorder of the Estate and Church, which includes Sir Thomas's extended family in Mansfield and Portsmouth and his affairs in Antigua, can only improve after he recognizes how bad things are and becomes personally involved. His ability to act, however, is circumscribed by the nature of human free will.

Apart from recent losses, we do not know why Sir Thomas had to go to Antigua for most of volume I. We do know its plantations were not as viable as they once were, its soil was exhausted, there was a boycott of sugar for political and moral reasons, and recent legislation had abolished the slave trade in the colonies although slavery itself had long been abolished in the United Kingdom. Sir Thomas's income was precarious, and the reordering of his affairs in Antigua, which may have involved slavery in some way, took longer than expected. He was greatly altered on his return to England, and while he was away the moral order of his home fell apart because of his absence.

From the beginning of volume II, Sir Thomas focuses his gaze on Fanny, the only character who resisted the staging of *Lovers' Vows*, as he silently goes about doing what he can to prevent further disorder and promote renewal from within his Estate and Church. At the center of the volume, also the center of the novel, during a game of Speculation, he issues a veiled threat to Henry Crawford, telling him he is not welcome to purchase, secularize, and "improve" Thornton Lacey, a living destined for Edmund and necessary for his plan for renewal.

At the beginning of volume III, Sir Thomas enters Fanny's domain, an area of Mansfield that became hers by default because no one else wanted to use it. This domain is the east room and the white attic, which combine to represent Mansfield's mind; particularly in a neoclassical building, within a neoclassical novel, where the term attic has a double meaning. He has come to bring her news of Henry's proposal of marriage. When she refuses the proposal, he suggests she does not know her own mind, an ambiguous comment that suggests she does not know his mind either.

Is it really Sir Thomas's will that Fanny marries Henry? While it is generally assumed that it is, we cannot be sure because his will, like God's, is complex and hidden. We do know that he has already placed clear boundaries around Henry, and his visit to Fanny's domain does symbolize his shift from deism to theism. When he discovers Fanny's domain is cold, because his sister-in-law Mrs Norris never allowed her to have a fire there, he has one lit. In a novel where symbolism matters, the cold mind signifies pure reason and the hot fire signifies pure feeling. Once these rooms are warm, Fanny's mind, and Mansfield's, become more balanced.

When Fanny first came to Mansfield she had no formal education but brought with her something more important that it lacks: a religious disposition; a spirit of brotherly love. Even so, she needs to make the same journey into maturity as every Austen heroine, which means achieving the right balance of reason and feeling. But Fanny's journey is unique. She is constantly being humbled and reminded that everything she is given is a gift she is not entitled to. Her position as a servant is constantly being reinforced because, like Jesus, she has come to serve not to be served, and to give her life as a ransom for many (Matthew 20:25–8; Mark 10:42–5). Her emotional trials are necessary if she is to develop the mature religious disposition necessary for the preservation and salvation of Estate and Church.

Austen is clear about Fanny's stark choice. She can serve Edmund, who is good, and never be more to him than a sister, or she can serve Henry, who is evil, and become his wife in a loveless marriage. The choice is highlighted when her beloved brother William, who is visiting Mansfield, gives her a cross without a chain to put it on. Henry and Edmund each give Fanny a chain, so she can wear the cross to her first ball. Naturally, Henry's chain cannot bear the cross, which allows her to wear Edmund's chain with a clear conscience. So Fanny makes her debut with William's cross, which links her to Jesus, and Edmund's chain, which links her to the Church.

During their confrontation in Fanny's domain, Sir Thomas subjects his niece to the kind of emotional pressure he would never subject his daughters to. She responds with a moral conviction they do not have. She stands up to him on principle and she is the only character that does, including his son Edmund. This causes her immense pain, because she honors him above all earthly things and she is mortified that her conscience prevents her from accepting what is apparently his will. When he asks whether she agrees Edmund "has seen the woman he could love," another ambiguous observation, she is thrown into emotional chaos. Fanny is certain Mary Crawford is the wrong wife for Edmund but uncertain whether Edmund feels anything more than brotherly love for her. As she has been programmed to serve, not to be served, she cannot admit her feelings for Edmund, even to herself.

Sir Thomas hands Fanny to Crawford to be tested, just as God hands Job to Satan to be tested (Job 1:6–12), and the Holy Spirit drives Jesus into the wilderness to be tested (Matthew 4:1–11; Mark 1:12–13; Luke 4:1–13). Part of her test is banishment to Portsmouth for an extended wilderness experience that coincides with Lent and, ultimately, with the Easter season. By the end of volume III, which coincides with

Ascension and Pentecost, Fanny has survived her passion and suffering and returns to Mansfield where, as its messiah, she becomes a glorified clergy wife.

Sir Thomas's gaze has also been on Edmund. On his return from Antigua, he blames Edmund for staging *Lovers' Vows*, rather than Tom, his first son and heir, even though staging the play was Tom's idea. This does not make sense until the reader realizes Edmund, a second son destined for the Church, is meant to be his brother's keeper. Edmund represents the authority of a Church that is unable to preserve the integrity of the Estate. In this way the testing of Edmund's vocation becomes bound up with the testing of Fanny's vocation. The drama facing Edmund is the drama facing a Church that will lose its moral and spiritual authority if it allows itself to be seduced by the world, represented by Mary Crawford, and forgets its focus must be on Jesus, represented by Fanny. The Church must decide between the world and Jesus. Edmund must decide between Mary and Fanny.

Apart from that, Edmund needs to become a resident priest and not participate in the widespread culture of non-residence, which encourages some priests to become more worldly than pastoral. Early in the novel, Sir Thomas is forced to pay for Tom's dissipation and extravagance, which means giving the Mansfield living to Dr Grant. For as long as Dr Grant is incumbent, Edmund is deprived of the primary living intended for him. Thornton Lacey, another parish within the estate, is the only living left for Edmund, and establishing his residency there, as soon as he is ordained, is fundamental to Sir Thomas's plan for renewal. However, Mary Crawford supports her brother's wish to purchase and secularize and "improve" Thornton Lacey, as her asides during a game of Speculation reveal, because his wish promotes her desire "to shut out the church, sink the clergyman, and see only the respectable, elegant, modernized, and occasional residence of a man of independent fortune." She has no intention of marrying a resident priest. She will only marry Edmund if he becomes a wealthy pluralist with as many absentee livings as he can obtain.

The last chapter is delineated in broad strokes. As Mansfield Park moves forward, beyond Lent and Easter and Ascension and Pentecost, the forces of evil are banished. But those forces are not conquered. The forces of good reign, for the time being at least, since preservation and salvation are frail and contingent things and both Estate and Church will no doubt fall again. In a dramatic reversal of fortune, Lady Bertram's daughter, Maria, who is her mother's namesake, is banished from the estate with Mrs Norris, the character whose mischief promoted the original estrangement. Mrs Price's daughter, Fanny, who is her mother's namesake, returns to Mansfield Park as its messiah. Once the Estate and Church are reordered, and Sir Thomas becomes more comfortable with his theistic persona, the relationship between himself and Fanny and Edmund has every chance of developing its Trinitarian character beyond the end of the novel.

The Prototypical Destiny of the Heroine

There is a relationship between the prototype a heroine represents and whether Austen intends her to become first lady of the Estate or clergy wife in the Church. The ideal marriages established in the mansions of Delaford in *Sense and Sensibility* and Pemberley in *Pride and Prejudice* represent feeling tempered by reason, which is appropriate in a gentry couple more worldly than religious. The ideal marriages established in the parsonages of Delaford and Mansfield represent reason tempered by feeling, which is appropriate in a clergy couple more religious than worldly. Marianne Dashwood and Elizabeth Bennet suffer from an excess of feeling that needs to be tempered by reason before they assume their role as effective first lady. Elinor Dashwood and Fanny Price suffer from an excess of reason that needs to be tempered by feeling before they assume their role as effective clergy wife; neither is destined to become first lady; this is their complementary but necessary role in Austen's narrative scheme.

Emma Woodhouse, the heroine of *Emma*, and Catherine Morland, the heroine of *Northanger Abbey*, share these lay and clerical destinies, but the destiny of Anne Elliot, the heroine of *Persuasion*, is unique. Austen's last heroine is being groomed to follow in Sophia Croft's footsteps and become the effective mistress of a home without traditional boundaries. Within this global province Anne will never be able to command a ship at sea, but then she will never need to as long as she has a husband who can do it for her. Austen is clear, however, that Anne has more command on land than her future husband does, hence the way in which everyone, including her future husband, looks to her for guidance after Louisa's fall from the Cobb. This is one of the more striking and radical propositions *Persuasion* makes. Anne could have become first lady of an estate had she accepted Charles Musgrove as a husband but that was not what Austen had in mind. As Mrs Frederick Wentworth, Anne becomes a naval wife whose home is a wider and more dangerous world.

When read in this context, Austen's literary vision becomes prophetic. She represents her heroines not only as Eve, the first woman of biblical myth to have fallen, but as agents of preservation and salvation from a fall that is as contemporary as it is biblical. Her vision, then, is not unlike the vision of other prophetic women who feature strongly in the scriptures, four thousand years of Jewish and Christian history, and the nineteenth- and twentieth-century novel.

Acknowledgments

Sincere thanks are due to Dr Moira O'Sullivan RSC, Lecturer in Biblical Studies, and Right Reverend Robert Forsyth, Bishop of South Sydney, for commenting on penultimate drafts.

Bibliography

Benedict, B. M. and Le Faye D., eds (2006) *Northanger Abbey*. The Cambridge Edition of the Works of Jane Austen. Cambridge University Press, Cambridge.

Butler, M. (1975) *Jane Austen and the War of Ideas*. Oxford University Press, Oxford.

Copeland, E., ed. (2006) *Sense and Sensibility*. The Cambridge Edition of the Works of Jane Austen. Cambridge University Press, Cambridge.

Cronin, R. and McMillan D., eds (2005) *Emma*. The Cambridge Edition of the Works of Jane Austen. Cambridge University Press, Cambridge.

Duckworth, A. M. (1971) *The Improvement of the Estate: A Study of Jane Austen's Novels*. Johns Hopkins University Press, Baltimore.

Gregory, J. (1774) *A Father's Legacy to His Daughters*, intro. Gina Luria. Garland Publishing, New York (1974 edition).

Rogers, P., ed. (2006) *Pride and Prejudice*. The Cambridge Edition of the Works of Jane Austen. Cambridge University Press, Cambridge.

Todd, J. and Blank A., eds (2006) *Persuasion*. The Cambridge Edition of the Works of Jane Austen. Cambridge University Press, Cambridge.

Wiltshire, J., ed. (2005) *Mansfield Park*. The Cambridge Edition of the Works of Jane Austen. Cambridge University Press, Cambridge.

CHAPTER 31

George Gordon Byron

Wolf Z. Hirst

Byron took the Bible seriously. The thoroughness of his acquaintance with Scripture has long been known (Stevens, 1964, pp. 460–3), most of his numerous biblical references have been detailed (Looper, 1978), and his obsession with the theme of the fall is now generally recognized (Ridenour, 1960; McGann, 1976; Hirst, 1991). Yet the pervasiveness and import of the biblical atmosphere in his work – even where there are no explicit biblical allusions – is not always appreciated. We are so often struck by Byron's iconoclastic, comic, and generally pioneering usage of scriptural material that we sometimes fail to notice the traditional aspects and the underlying seriousness of his treatment. In particular critics tend to overlook the fact that in the rare instances when he copies or dramatizes a biblical narrative (as he does in his two "Mysteries," *Cain* and *Heaven and Earth*, and also in "The Vision of Belshazzar" in the *Hebrew Melodies*), despite his ingenious innovations he remains basically faithful to the plot and the spirit of his model. In these instances he also largely subordinates his own concerns to those of his source. This is not the case, however, with regard to the poet's many scriptural references when he merely quotes or paraphrases an expression, takes up an image or an idea, or alludes to an episode (without retelling it) or to a character (without recounting the story associated with him or her). Such references, whether radically revised or introduced in a more conventional manner, nearly always become secondary to Byronic themes. This chapter considers the range of biblical allusions in Byron's poetry and the complexity and variety of his treatment of biblical sources. It begins with some general examples from *Childe Harold*, *Beppo*, and *Don Juan*, then considers the collection of short poems, *Hebrew Melodies*, with special attention to "The Destruction of Semnacherib" and "She Walks in Beauty." It concludes with an extended discussion of Byron's reworking of scriptural materials in *Cain: A Mystery*. Apart from these, the works for which most biblical quotations and allusions have been listed are *Marino Faliero*, and *The Prophecy of Dante*, most from the Old Testament (especially Genesis), but also many from Matthew, John, Luke, Revelation, Corinthians and Acts (Looper, 1978).

Childe Harold

In Byron's earliest poems scriptural allusions may serve as mere ornaments (as do Adam, Eden, and the "wings of the dove" in the last two stanzas of "The First Kiss of Love"),[1] but in the mature work they are carefully integrated. When, for example, in *Childe Harold* Byron adapts the dust and clay metaphors (each of which appears well over a hundred times in his poetry), he develops the biblical sense of human transience: for example, he writes that the great Italian poets, though "distinguish'd from our common clay," are yet "resolv'd to dust" (4:56). The description of the fetters of our physical existence as "clay-cold bonds which round our being cling" (3:73) shows Byron successfully applying Holy Writ to his own use, and so does the dust image introduced at the point where these fetters are rent: "And when, at length, the mind shall be all free ... / And dust is as it should be" (3:74). Again, reading about those who "perish with the reed on which they leant" (4:22), we may remember a verse from the Second Book of Kings: "Now, behold, thou trustest upon the staff of this bruised reed, even upon Egypt, on which if a man lean, it will go into his hand, and pierce it" (18:21). This expression of human deceit (political unreliability in this instance) is unobtrusively assimilated to Byron's argument for bearing the suffering of existence – it fits in as neatly as does the figure of the wolf dying in silence in the previous stanza, or the scorpion's sting in the following stanza – but the metaphor of the treacherous reed retains its biblical connotation and purpose. In the second canto, however, Byron appropriates this image of the reed in a more original manner. Beholding the magnificent remnants of the Acropolis, the poet declares:

> ... religions take their turn:
> 'Twas Jove's – 'tis Mahomet's – and other creeds
> Will rise with other years, till man shall learn
> Vainly his incense soars, his victim bleeds;
> Poor child of Doubt and Death, whose hope is built on reeds. (2:3)

The scriptural figure of the reed is here forced to bear an antiscriptural message, because instead of evoking the idea of perfidious humanity it is made to stand for all "creeds," not excepting the Bible's. *Childe Harold* contains other instances of the same strategy: in an allusion to Psalm 90:10, Byron writes: "The Psalmist numbered out the years of man" (3:35), but in contrast to the latter's lament over the brevity of life, Byron goes on to assert: "They are enough." While undermining the source, the sentiment voiced here reflects "the fulness of satiety" experienced by Childe Harold from the outset (1:4) and, furthermore, is in keeping with – and may indeed have been influenced by – passages from the Book of Job (10:1) and Ecclesiastes (1:2, 1:9, 4:3, 5:6).

Beppo

The poet's revision of scriptural material is most obvious when he transposes it to highly extraneous contexts to achieve comic incongruity. In a digression in *Beppo* he explicitly draws on the Bible (1 Timothy 4:8) to describe his projected memoirs as "my life (to come) in prose" and concludes that "laughter / Leaves us so doubly serious shortly after" (stanza 79). This is especially true when the laughter is at the expense of the Bible. In the next stanza the biblical background and the seriousness of its implication are not immediately apparent:

> Oh, Mirth and Innocence! Oh, Milk and Water!
> Ye happy mixture of more happy days
> In these sad centuries of sin and slaughter,
> Abominable Man no more allays
> His thirst with such pure beverage. No matter,
> I love you both, and both shall have my praise:
> Oh, for old Saturn's reign of sugar-candy! –
> Meantime I drink to your return in brandy.

Whereas few readers will identify the two expressions in the opening apostrophe as a repetition from Byron's letter to Thomas Moore of December 24, 1816[2] or the rhyming of "brandy" with "sugar-candy" as taken from a nursery rhyme beginning "As I was going down Cranbourne Lane," most will recognize the allusion to the golden age in classical mythology. But the mention of Saturn, a pagan deity, hides a deeper concern. The double irony of characterizing "happy mixtures" as "pure beverage" because the concoction symbolizes the purity of the bygone era of "old Saturn's reign" may divert our attention from the biblical undertone contrasting primordial "Innocence" with post-lapserian "sin." Those for whom "Milk and Water" calls to mind the biblical "milk and honey" will in the present context think not so much of the promised "land flowing with milk and honey" (Exodus 3:8) as of the "more happy days" before the expulsion from Eden. The narrator, however, confesses that he "love[s] ... both" the "Innocence" prior to original "sin" and the corrupt world of "these sad centuries" in which we live.

Don Juan

Eden has often been represented as pure love and the fall as a loss of such love, but in *Don Juan* Byron goes beyond this. Juan's first love, his relationship with Julia, is "Like Adam's recollection of his fall; / The tree of knowledge has been pluck'd – all's known –" (1:127). Expulsion from Paradise and a satiated life (and thus a satiated love) seem inappropriate to the occasion, because Juan is still in the throes of his first passion, but we should not miss Byron's radical innovation: Eden is lost even while love is yet alive. Love still is Eden, but, paradoxically, it also constitutes a forfeiture of Eden. Byron's new conception of Eden displaces the fall's traditional temporal sequence by encompassing the notion that consciousness foredooms love to disillusion at its very inception. Since "The Tree of Knowledge is not that of Life" (*Manfred* 1.1:12), we must know that everything dies, even the purest of loves. As often in Byron, the weary satiety and sense of futility, so well known to readers of *Childe Harold*, *Manfred*, and *Cain*, and sometimes associated with Ecclesiastes, here derive directly from Adam and Eve's forbidden fruit.

Some of the references to Adam, Eve, Eden, and the fall in *Don Juan* may be pure burlesque, as in the observation "That happiness for Man – the hungry sinner! – / Since Eve ate apples, much depends on dinner" (13:99), yet there is a serious thematic intent behind most of the apparently flippant biblical allusions in Byron's great epic satire. For example, Juan is caught by Alfonso in Julia's bedroom, and his "only garment quite gave way; / He fled, like Joseph, leaving it;" to which the poet adds the editorial comment: "but there, / I doubt, all likeness ends between the pair" (1:186). This seemingly super-fluous clarification heightens the farcical effect by drawing attention to the obvious difference between a hero who resists temptation and one who succumbs. It will, however, also remind us that the similarity between Juan and Joseph does *not* end with the abandonment of a garment, because in both cases an inexperienced young man is tempted, manipulated, and ensnared by an older married woman. The reference to Joseph in Byron's masterpiece thus hints at the author's unconventional treatment of the Don Juan legend, in which the ruthless seducer is transformed into a victim of seduction.

Hebrew Melodies

Feeling no need to follow convention when dealing with biblical and Christian subjects, Byron often provoked the establishment by expressing unorthodox views, as in his attacks on the doctrine of eternal damnation in *The Vision of Judgment* (stanzas 13–14) and in *Heaven and Earth* (1.3:193–203). As Richard Cronin (2006, p. 152) points out in connection with *Don Juan*, "Byron does not repudiate any of the faiths that he encounters … but neither does he espouse any." Generally his work reflects what Robert Ryan (1990, p. 42) calls an "oscillation" and an "equipoise" between "two impulses, to doubt and to believe." Only in *Hebrew Melodies* does he unswervingly conform to biblical or traditionally religious sentiments (perhaps – as most were written not long before and shortly after their wedding – because he wished to please Annabella Milbanke, or perhaps out of loyalty to childhood memories). Either way, these senti-ments are shored up by an unusually pronounced biblical style and atmosphere, though the design and execution of the individual poems remain distinctively Byron's own. A few of them are about the exile following the destruction of the temple in Jerusalem, but this theme, together with the pervasive theme of the loss of Eden, forms the back-ground of all the pieces published as *Hebrew Melodies*.

Byron must have considered the poems that he gave to the composer Isaac Nathan to be suitable for inclusion in their anthology, even those he had already written before his association with Nathan. Although most of the Hebrew melodies are based on some Old Testament figure or incident, perhaps it can only be said of one – "The Vision of Belshazzar" – that the poet is reworking an entire biblical story (or at least one that consists of more than a single verse). In this poem he imaginatively yet faithfully retells the fifth chapter of the Book of Daniel, with four of his six stanzas focusing on the writing on the wall, to which he twice alludes satirically in *Don Juan* (3:65 and 8:134). The idea of being "weighed in the balances, and … found wanting" (Daniel 5:27), as is Belshazzar in line forty-three of the poem, is echoed repeatedly in Byron's verse (*Childe*

Harold 4:93; *Manfred* 2.3:70; *Marino Faliero* 1.2:122, 4.2:223; *Cain* 2.2:438; *The Two Foscari* 2.1:133; *Werner* 3.1:36, 4.1:250).

The poet modifies biblical material more freely and puts more of himself into the poems about the final days of Saul – Israel's first sovereign – in "Saul" and "Song of Saul Before His Last Battle" (cf. 1 Samuel 28–31), whereas "My Soul is Dark" does not at all *retell* the story of David's relieving Saul of his despondency (cf. 1 Samuel 16:14–23) but merely *alludes* to a "minstrel" (11) and his "harp" (2), so that conceivably the poet may above all be writing about his own "heavy heart" (12) (see Blackstone, 1975, p. 131). "Jephtha's Daughter" originates from the two verses in Judges comprising the victim's speech (11:36–7) out of a story of forty verses. "On Jordan's Banks" does not retell a specific biblical incident in any sense, but the scriptural theme of yearning for an end to exile is reproduced by means of a series of scriptural references: to the Jordan, Sion (Zion), Baal, Sinai, the tablets with the Ten Commandments, the warning that one cannot see God and survive, the destruction of the temple and more generally to an "oppressor's spear" (10). The poem has been seen as "a painfull registering of the terrible silence of God in the face of injustice" (Mole, 2002, p. 24), but to most readers it will probably convey a balance between lament and prayer for redemption in keeping with the prophetic tradition. Biblical parallelism in the first two lines of the poem ("On Jordan's banks ... On Sion's hill") is more pronounced in the repetition in stanza 2 ("There – where ... There – where"), and prepares for a climactic ending with the reiteration of "How long" in the last stanza (echoing, for example, Psalms 6:3 and 13:1), which culminates in a direct appeal to the Almighty.

"The Destruction of Semnacherib [Sennacherib]," frequently anthologized (it is often found suitable for school-children and it illustrates anapaestic meter, which may be seen as capturing the rhythm of biblical parallelism: Roston, 1965, p. 190), gives us the traditional scriptural theme of human frailty and insignificance in the face of divine omnipotence:

The Destruction of Semnacherib

1
The Assyrian came down like the wolf on the fold,
And his cohorts were gleaming in purple and gold;
And the sheen of their spears was like stars on the sea,
When the blue wave rolls nightly on deep Galilee.

2
Like the leaves of the forest when Summer is green,
That host with their banners at sunset were seen:
Like the leaves of the forest when Autumn hath blown,
That host on the morrow lay withered and strown.

3
For the Angel of Death spread his wings on the blast,
And breathed in the face of the foe as he pass'd;
And the eyes of the sleepers wax'd deadly and chill,
And their hearts but once heaved, and for ever grew still!

4
And there lay the steed with his nostril all wide,
But through it there roll'd not the breath of his pride:
And the foam of his gasping lay white on the turf,
And cold as the spray of the rock-beating surf.

5
And there lay the rider distorted and pale,
With the dew on his brow, and the rust on his mail;
And the tents were all silent, the banners alone,
The lances unlifted, the trumpet unblown.

6
And the widows of Ashur are loud in their wail,
And the idols are broke in the temple of Baal;
And the might of the Gentile, unsmote by the sword,
Hath melted like snow in the glance of the Lord!

Basing his poem on a single verse from the Old Testament (2 Kings 19:35, repeated almost *verbatim* in Isaiah 37:36), Byron summarizes this verse in the poem's title and expands it into twenty-four lines, with the first stanza describing the might of the Assyrian army, the second establishing the contrast between these martial forces "at sunset" (6) and "on the morrow" (8), and the last four elaborating upon the desolation and explaining its cause. Few poems are so profoundly steeped in the atmosphere of the Bible and, while creatively revising its imagery, so successfully replicate its style: anaphora (the word "And," beginning thirteen lines); the memorable redundancies; the parallelism and incremental repetition revolving around one catastrophe; the unforgettable simile of the poem's first line reminding us of the faithful shepherd. The importation of a nocturnal sea of Galilee (far from the present scene outside Jerusalem) creates a dark radiance that is reflected in the music produced, among other things, by the assonance of the "e" and alliteration of the "l" sounds in the admirable simile of lines 3–4. The eventually withering leaf, one of the central biblical symbols of human ephemerality, links the two similes of the second stanza, each comprising a full couplet, a connection reinforced by the repetition of "Like the leaves of the forest" and "That host."

The word "For" in line 9 introduces the explanation for Sennacherib's overthrow: the intervention of "the Angel of Death." Even without the repetitions in the next three verses, the mere mention of the angel tells us that the Assyrians' fate is sealed. Such explicit repetitiveness of the death scene recurs in the fourth stanza, which is focused on the "steed" introduced in line 13. The significance of "his nostril all wide" is explained in the following verse with the "But" announcing a negation and at the same time displacing the repeated "And," thus indicating that we are taking a quick look back at the opening stanza now summed up in the word "pride." Line 15 expands upon the steed and its nostrils. How superfluous to call attention to the last "gasping" of the steed, but how evocative of death-throes and the frustrations of defeated might! Biblical parallelism is imitated in the fifth stanza's first line with the two cogent adjectives "distorted and pale" (in contrast with the splendor of "purple and gold" in the poem's second line). The following three verses are each divided by caesuras into two parallel phrases, the last parallelism emphasized by the repetition of a peculiar use of a common prefix: "unlifted ... unblown."

The final stanza gives a wider perspective on the Assyrian home front. Byron first wrote "Babel" instead of "Ashur" (21), an error that shows how engrossed he was with the theme of exile and with Babylon, the place of Judah's banishment. ("Babel" or "Babylon" occurs thirty times in Byron's poetry.) The final couplet conveys the biblical message: human powerlessness before the Lord (and not the Angel of Death, who is merely the Lord's agent). Whereas "unlifted" and "unblown" reflect helplessness, the coinage "unsmote" refers to the manner of defeat of the Assyrian invader, who, in the Hebraic spirit, is now referred to as "the Gentile." "Melt" in the sense of the destruction of power is frequent in the Bible, but although "melted like snow" does not appear (snow is uncommon in the Holy Land), the expression is a stroke of genius, because it takes up the seasonal imagery of the second stanza with its withered leaves. The word "glance" also appears nowhere in the Authorized Version, but accomplishing the defeat of an army by a sheer glance suggests the omnipotence and spirituality associated with monotheism.

The essential unity of *Hebrew Melodies* is seldom appreciated. Some of the poems neither recreate a biblical episode nor make any overt biblical allusion, but their relevance becomes apparent in relation to the biblical background of the whole collection. This is true also of "She Walks in Beauty," though it has often been said that this lyric does not belong to *Hebrew Melodies* (Marchand, 1965, p. 134). At one level the poem demonstrates how the balance of light and shade in a human face conjures up a nocturnal landscape, and the subdued contrast between winning "smiles" and glowing "tints" suggests the kindness of "days in goodness spent" (15–16), a peaceful mind, a pure heart, and innocent love (17–18). Within the framework of the *Hebrew Melodies*, however, the "days in goodness spent," with their leap into the past to evoke a by-gone era, remind us of the Israelites' yearning for their happy former days, the pre-exilic period. Although "She Walks in Beauty" already existed before the question of writing the *Hebrew Melodies* arose, Murray Roston (1965, p. 187) feels that the poem "consciously aims at capturing from the *Song of Songs* [the *Song of Solomon*] the oriental luxuriance, the languorous yet rich passion for the dark beauty of the Shulamite." Among other things, Roston probably has the "raven tress" (9) in mind, reminiscent of the "raven" locks of Songs 5:11. In any event the "cloudless climes" (2) might suggest the Mediterranean, but in the context of the *Hebrew Melodies* these climes are certainly made to refer to the lands of the Bible, and "dwelling place" (12) may remind us of Balaam's prophecy (Numbers 24:21).

Before we interpret "A mind at peace with all below" (17) ironically as "a mind that is without sensitivity to the promptings of the nether parts, a mind dead to passion," and "innocent" (18) as "immune to carnal desire" (Miller, 1985, p. 66), we have to consider the pervasive contrast in Scripture and in the Christian tradition between human frailty and divine omnipotence, earthly clay and celestial essence, body and soul. In this context "below" stands in opposition to "heaven" (6). The position of "innocent" at the end of the poem and the unusual secondary stress on its last syllable resulting from the rhyme with "spent" (16) give the word double emphasis. For Byron "innocent" love is Edenic love, which fallen humanity has forfeited, so that the person described in this lyric, who retains such primordial innocence, is placed, as it were, into some transcendental realm from which she can look down on "all below" and be "at peace" with it (17). But no matter how "biblical" we may sense this lyric to be, Byron leaves his signature plainly visible, not only in the exceptional emphasis on an "innocent" love, but also in such original turns as the idiosyncratic opposition between a conventional "heaven" and the striking expression "gaudy day" (6). Like all of the *Hebrew Melodies*, even those not based on a biblical subject and more personal – such as "Oh! Snatch'd Away in Beauty's Bloom" (Ashton, 1972, p. 149) with its lament over human transience, its weeping by a river bank, even if not Jordan's or one of Babylon's, and the parallelism of its last line – "She Walks in Beauty" partakes of the biblical atmosphere of the collection while remaining unmistakably Byronic.

Cain: A Mystery

Not less distinctively Byronic is the poet's one substantial and completed rewriting of a whole biblical episode, which he calls *Cain: A Mystery* (*Heaven and Earth* is a fragment). The play has frequently been seen as an attack on the Bible and religion, yet despite Byron's development of a story about fratricide into an intriguing tragedy of human revolt against the divine order and his self-projection into the rebellious protagonist, *Cain* most impressively illustrates his essential fidelity to his particular source and to the scriptural spirit in general. As in the original story, Cain, a tiller of the soil, and Abel, his younger brother, a shepherd, make offerings to God. When Abel's sheep is accepted and Cain's fruit rejected, Cain slays his brother and is cursed from the earth, condemned to wander east of Eden as a fugitive and vagabond with a mark set on him. Readers have too often disregarded various themes Byron imports into the play from other portions of the Scriptures, his skillful development of the biblical lesson of human brotherhood, and in particular his close adherence to the account given in chapter 4 of Genesis. Perhaps this disregard is because the events of acts I and II, the dialogue preceding Abel's entry in act III, and the play's last eighty lines are largely fabrications.

Unlike the variety of circumstances in Byron's play that reveal the several attributes of his hero, in Genesis the act of fratricide is the only event that clearly establishes the character of Cain. We may assume that the murder is connected with the rejection of Cain's offering and surmise that the murderer may have acted out of spite, frustration, rebellion, hatred, or revenge, but most frequently, in Byron's age as in ours, readers have thought of "the jealous murder of Abel" (Schock, 1995, p. 204). Presumably we may take Cain's reply to the Lord's question "Where is Abel thy brother?" as a callous rejection of responsibility and as evasive and deceitful, or insolent and defiant, yet we cannot be *quite* sure: "I know not" just *might* indicate not indifference, evasion, or deceit but a sincere expression of confusion or despair, and "Am I my brother's keeper?" *might* express shocked acknowledgment of responsibility. As we cannot be absolutely certain about anything in the character of the biblical figure apart from his guilt of fratricide, when Byron creates an idealist thirsting for justice and enlightenment, a metaphysical rebel who is also a loving father, husband, and brother, it must be the Cain of the popular tradition that Byron ennobles rather than the Cain of Genesis. He does not so much change the biblical story as focus on its ambiguities, fill its gaps, and develop what is merely implied.

Chapter 4 of Genesis several times refers to Abel as Cain's "brother" (even after this fact has been established), and Byron builds on the idea of mutual responsibility suggested in being the "keeper" of one's "brother" by means of judicious usage of the latter term, which appears forty-two times in the play (with "brethren" occurring three and "sister" eight times). When Adah, Cain's sister and wife, announces Abel's arrival with the words "Our brother comes," Cain prepares us for his murderous repudiation of blood ties with the odd remark "Thy brother Abel" (III.1.161–2). As Abel falls dying and is about to forgive his murderer, he registers the bond between them: "What hast thou done, my brother?" (III.1.317); and at this point Cain, who, after a cosmic flight with Lucifer, has not even once addressed Abel as "brother," gives evidence of a sudden inner change by responding with the one-word exclamation "Brother!" (III.1.318). Henceforth he *does* repeatedly call the slain Abel "My brother" (III.1.323, 353, 375). It is the poignant reminder that Zillah (who has lost her brother and husband) "has but one brother / Now" that jolts Cain into the recognition that he himself is henceforth left "brotherless" (III.1.335–6).

A significant contribution to the moral superiority of Byron's protagonist over the long-established Cain figure is made by the poet's omission of the speech containing the Lord's admonition to Cain (Genesis 4:6–7):

> And the LORD said unto Cain, Why art thou wroth? and why is thy countenance fallen?
> If thou doest well, shalt thou not be accepted? and if thou doest not well, sin lieth at the
> door. And unto thee shall be his desire, and thou shalt rule over him.

In the Bible, it seems that an envious Cain rejects God's warning and goes on to commit premeditated homicide, but since the Bible does not explicitly mention either the envy or the premeditation (and gives no details about what happens between the warning in verse 7 and the murder in verse 8), Byron's source leaves him free to provide his own version of what "leads to the Catastrophe ... *not* premeditation or envy ... but ... rage and fury against the inadequacy of his state to his Conceptions" (*BLJ* 9:53–4). Clearly Byron's protagonist acts impetuously in a moment of mental imbalance and is shocked when "awake at last" (III.1:378), but the poet's contention that Cain's murderous blow is caused by something other than envy has been challenged. Lucifer's suggestion that Cain harbors thoughts of envy (the traditional view) puts into words what Cain feels but does not admit to himself (II.2:339, 353–6). Such sentiments may never entirely leave Cain, but in the murder scene Byron indisputably stages an act motivated not by envy but by rebellion. Cain's frustration after his journey with Lucifer produces in the usually affectionate father and brother such "rage and fury" that he envisages the possibility of killing his baby son (III.1.124–6) and in the scene of fratricide is led from protesting innocent suffering to causing it.

Deviating from Genesis, Byron combines the scene of murder with that of the sacrifice in which Abel's offering precedes Cain's, and a "whirlwind ... throw[s] down the altar of CAIN." This brings to mind God's answer "out of the whirlwind" at the end of the Book of Job (38:1) whereby the Lord breaks His long silence by asserting divine providence without answering the question of Job's innocent suffering. The ending of *Cain* also leaves unanswered the question of unmerited pain, which, like Job, the hero has repeatedly confronted with militant passion. Also like Job, Cain rejects life while grieving over death's inevitability. Job, however, lamenting the ephemerality of life (10:20 or 14:1–2), thinks of human fate in general and in his wish that he "had never been born" (3:3) refers to himself alone, whereas Cain speaks of himself in both instances: "Must I not die?" (I.1.29) and "Would I ne'er had been / Aught else but dust!" (I.1.291–2). Cain longs for death because of the senselessness of a life that ends in death (I.1.109–10), so that in Hades he declares: "Since / I must one day return here from the earth / I rather would remain; I am sick of all / That dust has shown me –" (II.2.106–9). Though, not unlike the Book of Job in tone, this expression of *taedium vitae* is more reminiscent of Ecclesiastes, with whom Cain also shares the consciousness of his limitations and of life's vanity.

The drama's most important biblical topic not based on the Cain episode itself is, as so often in Byron, the Eden story of the previous two chapters of Genesis. More than the plot of Cain's seduction by Lucifer is derived from Eve's temptation by the snake; the fall motif, rather than the Cain figure of popular tradition, also provides the essential feature of the hero's character: his mental unrest. The older curse, the burden resulting from the primal fall, something that is impersonal and remote for other haunted romantic heroes, becomes dramatically immediate when a son complains of suffering for the sins of his parents. In rebellion against God, Cain attacks the fatal tree's "bitter" fruits (I.1.78), the expulsion from Eden and man's toil (he takes no notice of woman's pain in childbirth) and focuses on the death sentence, the penalty prescribed for his transgression (Genesis 3:16–19, 23–4; 2:17). Among his first words are "Must I not die?" (I.1.29). He then taunts his parents asking "wherefore pluck'd ye not the tree of life?" (I.1.33), and upon his encounter with Lucifer he immediately laments that "the tree of life / Was withheld ... and all the fruit is death!" (I.1.105–8). In the biblical account of the death of Abel we hear nothing of Cain's preoccupation with death or any curse before the scenes of sacrifice and murder. Thus the dirge of Byron's hero over the transience of his existence, "being dust, and groveling in the dust, / Till I return to dust" (III.1.114–15), echoes words from the previous chapter of Genesis: "for dust thou art, and unto dust shalt thou return" (3:19). Cain has inherited this consciousness from his father, whom Byron makes bear a mark "upon his forehead" (II.1.75) before Cain is stained with his.

Although Byron once more rehearses the fall theme and draws on many other biblical passages in *Cain*, it is unmistakably chapter 4 of Genesis that he is rewriting. Fifteen lines of Byron's dialogue (III.1.468–82) copy almost verbatim six (verses 9–14) of the sixteen verses comprising the biblical story of the first murder. Yet a careful comparison of these two seemingly identical passages reveals the remarkable revisionary effort on the poet's part. Substituting an angel for the Lord (thus avoiding biblical anthropomorphism), Byron's version begins "Where is thy brother Abel?" which preserves the Bible's emphasis on brotherhood. But in the light of Zillah's charge that Cain, "the stronger" of the two brothers, failed to defend the weaker Abel (III.1.365–9), the rejoinder "Am I then / My brother's keeper?" (III.1.468–9) attains a new dimension. Perhaps Byron's Cain is merely repeating what we may see as his proto-type's attempt to exculpate himself (possibly even to arraign the Creator), but we have not ruled out the possibility that the biblical Cain *might* be speaking in confusion or with a shocked recognition of responsibility. The Cain of Genesis, however, apparently also conveys lack of concern, whereas such an attitude could only be pretence in the case of Byron's sensitive hero, who earlier expressed acute remorse. The poet makes two changes at this point: his honest Cain does not reiterate the outright lie "I know not" when asked where his brother is, and he adds the word "then" to "Am I my brother's keeper?" (Genesis 4:9). Following Zillah's accusation and Cain's repeated expressions of regret and sorrow, these two revisions may prompt us to consider the possibility that an intuition about being answerable for his fellows is here in the process of ripening in the hero's consciousness. Rather than trying to evade respon-sibility, he may, having internalized his sister's indictment, now be asking the Angel (or really asking himself) whether he should not have acted literally as his brother's "keeper," that is, his guard and protector. The possibility that Cain's question does not constitute rebelliousness or rejection of guilt is less remote in Byron than in Genesis.

With the repetition of the rebuke "what hast thou done?" (III.1.469) Byron retains the Bible's implicit ascription of responsibility for human acts, which he will later rein-force with an expression of irrevocability: "what is done is done" (III.1.516). In the play the voice of "[Abel's] blood cries out, / Even from the ground" (III.1.470–1), with Byron's addition of "Even" emphasizing that the earth cannot hide bloodshed. This poignant image acquires further resonance from the tradition of spilt innocent blood culminating in the crucifixion, which has just been brought to mind by Abel's Christ-like words "Forgive [Cain], for he knew not what / He did" (III.1.319–20; cf. Luke 23:34), and which the drama's repeated references to blood sacrifice richly exploit (see Steffan, 1968, pp. 88–9). In his rephrasing of verse 11, however, the poet inserts a word that jars: Abel's blood was shed by Cain's "rash" hand (III.1.473). Not only does the adjective not appear in the original, there is no hint whatsoever that the biblical Cain (who has been given a warning) might have acted as impetuously as Byron's hero. In modifying verse 12 Byron has the Angel separate the two components of "a fugitive and a vagabond," perhaps in order to let the force of each word sink in before Adah uses the compact biblical form four lines later in her plea on Cain's behalf, which replaces the biblical Cain's own words in verses 13–14.

At this point the poet breaks off his seeming transcription of verses from the Old Testament. He begins with a reversal of the source pattern: his hero courts death (III.1.482), whereas the biblical Cain has just pleaded for his life. Next he invents speeches about the yet unpeopled earth (III.1.483–4), sibling ties (III.1.490–1), and potential parricide (III.1.485–8, 492). Byron probably remembered the story of Lamech's accidental killing of his ancestor Cain from Bayle's Dictionary. At line 494 the poet resumes the scriptural account as given in verse 15: "And the Lord set a mark upon Cain," which he spins into a miniature drama. When the Angel calls "Come hither!" Cain asks "What / Would'st thou with me?" (III.1.497–8), a question that may reflect confusion, affect incomprehension, or perhaps once more breathe defiance (She-Rue, 2004, p. 132). After the Angel's reply again brings home to Cain the gravity of "such deeds as [he has] done" (III.1.499), making further evasion impossible, the murderer exclaims "No, let me die!" (III.1.500), where the death wish also serves as a last futile attempt to escape accountability. The mark, which he receives despite refusing its protection, produces the immediate effect of externalizing his remorse by "burn[ing]" his "brow" (III.1.500–1). After this point there is no further reference to the mark. The play's new, relatively more tranquil tone following the scenes of murder, Eve's curse, and Cain's confrontation with the Angel leaves little room for the frenzy usually associated with the traditional mark as the symbol of pariahdom and the curse of homelessness. The feeling of being perpetually hounded is but briefly conjured up in Cain's words "Now for the wilderness" (III.1.544) and in his description of the road "Eastward from Eden" as "the most desolate" (III.1.552–3), which replaces the biblical Cain's actual departure and settling "east of Eden" (4:16). Thus the effect becomes all the more powerful when in the play's last line, which gives Adah's farewell to the dead Abel and Cain's response, the eternal wanderer's inner turbulence suddenly finds its outlet:

ADAH. Peace be with him!
CAIN. But with *me*!

It is as if the mark were now being set on Cain's brow a second time. Even if such a reverberating ending truncates the tragedy's catharsis, it undoubtedly epitomizes the traditional Cain curse and is especially ironic because, as the result of his parents' fall, Byron's hero gives expression to such feverish restlessness *before* the murder as if already bearing the mark of the outcast: "Nothing can calm me more. *Calm!* say I? Never / Knew I what calm was in the soul" (III.1.204–5).

Despite such revisions, we should accept Byron's repeated claim that in *Cain* he is faithful to the Bible. Granted, few readers think of the Cain of Genesis as Byron does: an iconoclast questioning divine justice who possibly holds God responsible for the murder because He created Cain and failed as Keeper of Abel. In all probability none before Byron ever exercised their imagination so energetically in filling the gaps in the character of the Old Testament figure by suggesting his complex sensitivity: his love, his innate sense of isolation, his obsession with human transience (paradoxically coupled with a death wish), and his relentless pursuit of righteousness. In Byron's Cain these traits become so poignantly ironic in the light of the act of fratricide as to make it into a perfect tragic peripeteia. The fact that Cain kills his brother in Byron's drama as well as in Genesis is so obvious that it is hardly ever mentioned, but we should remember that with Cain's murder of Abel the play retains the essence of the Cain story. One might assume that the poet could easily have changed the fratricidal ending (as easily as showing us a hero named "Don Juan" being seduced) if he wished to maintain to the end the noble innocence of his romanticized seeker of justice. It is not that Byron feared he would fail to reach an audience that might be hostile to such drastic rewriting of the Bible, since he does not shrink from putting the most offensive blasphemies into the mouth of his hero, nor, in general (as we have seen), does he hesitate to break with standard practice in his treatment of Holy Writ. But to spare Cain the murder of his brother may have seemed impossible to the poet. In 1821 Lord Byron wrote to his publisher, "I am a great reader and admirer of those books [of the Bible] – and had read them through & through before I was eight years old – that is to say the *old* Testament

– for the New struck me as a task – but the other as a pleasure" (*BLJ* 8:238). The poet's loyalty to his source in *Cain*, which reproduces a full story from one of those pleasurable books he had so voraciously read in his childhood, testifies to the spell the Bible cast over him.

Notes

1   Lord Byron, *The Complete Poetical Works*, ed. Jerome J. McGann, 7 volumes (Clarendon Press, Oxford, 1980–93), 1:157. All quotations from Byron's poetry are from this edition, subsequently cited as *Works*.
2   See Leslie A. Marchand, ed., *Byron's Letters and Journals*, 12 volumes (Harvard University Press, Cambridge, 1973–82), 5:149. Further references to this edition are abbreviated as *BLJ*.

References

Ashton, Thomas L. (1972) *Byron's Hebrew Melodies*. Routledge & Kegan Paul, London.

Blackstone, Bernard (1975) *Byron: A Survey*. Longman, London.

Cronin, Richard (2006) "Words and the Word: The Diction of *Don Juan*" in *Romanticism and Religion from William Cowper to Wallace Stevens*, ed. Gavin Hopps and Jane Stabler. Ashgate, Aldershot and Burlington, VT, pp. 137–53.

Hirst, Wolf Z., ed. (1991) *Byron, the Bible, and Religion: Essays from the Twelfth International Byron Seminar*. University of Delaware Press, Newark, NJ.

Looper, Travis (1978) *Byron and the Bible: A Compendium of Biblical Usage in the Poetry of Lord Byron*. Scarecrow Press, Metuchen, NJ.

McGann, Jerome J. (1976) *"Don Juan" in Context*. University of Chicago Press, Chicago.

Marchand, Leslie A. (1965) *Byron's Poetry: A Critical Introduction*. John Murray, London.

Miller, Edmund (1985) "Byron's Moonshine: Alternative Readings in the Ironic Mode," *The Byron Journal* 13, 61–7.

Mole, Tom (2002) "The Handling of *Hebrew Melodies*," *Romanticism* 8:1, 18–33.

Ridenour, George M. (1960) *The Style of Don Juan*. Yale University Press, New Haven, CT.

Roston, Murray (1965) *Prophet and Poet: The Bible and the Growth of Romanticism*. Faber and Faber, London.

Ryan, Robert (1990) "Byron's *Cain*: The Ironies of Belief," *The Wordsworth Circle* 21, 41–5.

Schock, Peter A. (1995) "The 'Satanism' of *Cain* in Context: Byron's Lucifer and the War against Blasphemy," *Keats–Shelley Journal* 44, 182–215.

She-Rue, Kao (2004) "Byron's Cain: A Disqualified Champion of Justice," *The Byron Journal* 32:2, 131–5.

Steffan, Truman Guy (1968) *Lord Byron's CAIN: Twelve Essays and a Text with Variants and Annotations*. University of Texas Press, Austin.

Stevens, Harold Ray (1964) "Byron and the Bible: A Study of Poetic and Philosophic Development," dissertation, University of Pennsylvania.

CHAPTER 32
P. B. Shelley

Bernard Beatty

Shelley was a self-consciously determined foe of Christianity and of the Bible insofar as that presented itself as the declared Word of God. In a note to his *Queen Mab*, mainly written in 1812, he wrote: "the genius of human happiness must tear every leaf from the accursed book of God ere man can read the inscription on his heart."[1] That this attitude persisted is shown in his positioning of Nature's voice in Mont Blanc (1817) as superior to God's legislative voice on Sinai: "thou hast a voice, great Mountain, to repeal / Large codes of fraud and woe" (Norton Shelley, pp. 80–1) and also in his horror that Byron was unable to see the dependence of *Cain*, which he much admired, on the Bible (Trelawney, 1973, p. 99). He thus took for granted that Bacon was right in making knowledge of Nature independent of Revelation, as well as the Enlightenment dismissal of miracles. He concluded that the Bible's customary authority was wholly compromised by its dependence on fictions masquerading as facts. He approved whole-heartedly of the French Revolutionaries' assault on the alliance of feudal nobility and the Church, and moved readily from intense dislike of his father, to hatred of tyrants, to contemptuous enmity to any Father God.

Shelley never abandoned these confident prejudices, but unlike Godwin or Paine nevertheless undertook a "constant perusal of portions of the Old Testament – the Book of Psalms, the Book of Job, the prophet Isaiah, and others, the sublime poetry of which filled him with delight" (Oxford Shelley, p. 153). While Mary Shelley suggests her husband only read "portions of the Old Testament," Shelley seems to have read most or all of the Bible at various times (Bryan Shelley, 1994, pp. 174–86). His biblical reading habits are unsurprising. Robert Lowth's *Lectures on the Sacred Poetry of the Hebrews* (1753, English translation 1787) refers widely to the Hebrew Scriptures, but emphasizes poetic style, imagery, allegory, and their sublime aspect. He gives particular attention to the prophets, especially Isaiah and Ezekiel, and to the Psalms. When he talks about history, he is primarily concerned with the images through which it is presented, a preference Shelley echoes in *A Defence of Poetry*:

It is probable that the astonishing poetry of Moses, Job, David, Solomon and Isaiah had produced a great effect upon the mind of Jesus and his disciples. The scattered fragments preserved to us by the biographers of this extraordinary person, are all instinct with the most vivid poetry. (Norton Shelley, p. 495)

Hence Shelley can talk approvingly of the "poetry in the doctrines of Jesus Christ" (p. 495) and of "the abstract purity of Christianity" insofar as it divulges "sacred and eternal truths to mankind" (p. 496). Lowth would assume that sacred poetry conveys sacred truths founded in an actual saving history, but Shelley assumes that it is the poetry in the doctrines that is salvific and that it communicates to the exalted mind in a dehistoricized "abstract purity" of "inextinguishable thought" (p. 486), rather than speaking to the historical person. Hence "prophecy is an attribute of poetry" (p. 483), a statement that enables Shelley to resolve the tension between his contempt toward and simultaneous admiration for the Bible. This chapter suggests that Shelley uses the Bible not simply as a source of images but more significantly as a book that offers a vision of redemption, a narrative of how we moved from a tainted to an untainted world. This narrative is discussed through his references to prophecy and history, his fascination with the redemptive drama of *The Book of Job*, and his fixation on the imagination as a way of effecting salvation through hope.

Prophecy and History

Gerhard von Rad argues that our modern sense of history originates in the gradual Jewish understanding that God would act in the future in a different way than the past. This founds a specifically Jewish sense of prophecy and also authorizes history as the instructive record of a distinctly sequenced past generating, as God's responsive act, a new future. The peculiar character of Hebrew Prophecy originated with the written preservation of Amos's declaration that Israel was hopelessly doomed. Jerusalem is destroyed. Jerusalem is restored. This, roughly, was the position of Shelley in relation to the French Revolution, its failure and apparent defeat. He lived within the shadow of a cursed terrain and found in the later prophets exactly the images of a permanently renewed paradisal harmony that he longed for and in his own way believed in.

Thus *Laon and Cythna* tells the story of a Golden City ruled by a tyrant, of the peaceful revolution brought about by its ideal eponymous couple, of its destruction by the action of hostile foreign powers, the restoration of the tyrant, and the persecution and "martyrdom" by fire of Laon and Cythna who then find themselves miraculously transferred to a paradisal heaven and earth through which a celestial boat takes them in the last stanza to "The Temple of the Spirit." The Golden city is Jerusalem, Paris – before and after the Revolution, and then the Restoration – and Augustine's City of God and City of Man, but it is also a Romance invention formed by nightmares and rhetoric that heralds the wholly fictional ending. Here we lose connection with history and the city in any sense, except perhaps if we read the boat's journey as representing some real future brought about by persistent imagining induced in part by poetry. The poem's sequence – failure, consolation, failure, transformation to a different order of reality where finally appears a transformed temple which is one with the indwelling human Spirit – could not exist without the Hebrew prophets, but the modality is that of

Romance. Shelley was at pains to avoid the supernatural as such but the poem is scarcely "realistic." It displaces the activity of God by the colorings of a Romance imagination, which is a permanent possibility in human consciousness. Hence the Temple of the Spirit represents not the biblical displacement of the Temple by Christ's Body and Spirit that indwell the believer, but a purely human possibility. Nevertheless this ending's main purpose is to disguise failure. The Hebrew prophets always mirror exactly their contemporary situation that determines the doom or hope that they announce. But Shelley does not end his poem with the failure of the attempt to construct a true Golden City and the unchecked triumph of injustice because his contemporary Europe was stifling revolutionary endeavor. Instead, the form of his imagination is always at least as much in love with failure as with success.

The biggest exception to this pattern is act IV of *Prometheus Unbound*. Here, too, we have a transformed heaven and earth whose marriage is a cosmic image of the union of Prometheus and Asia in act II. This is a revisionist version of the renewed marriage of Yahweh and Israel promised in Isaiah 54 and of Christ and the New Jerusalem presaged in Revelation 21, although these marriages are between persons, not parts of the cosmos or of the psyche. Unlike Baal or Uranus, Yahweh does not marry Gaia (the earth), he marries a people. It is curious that the nuptials of Yahweh and Christ with Israel and New Jerusalem/Church are promised rather than shown, even though the reader receives the prophecies as somehow already accomplished. By contrast, Shelley portrays the mutual interpenetration of the moon and the earth in a dazzling set of ecstatic lyrics, underplaying the marriage image to highlight the experience that each has of this penetration. He also works to illustrate the effects of this experience on "Man" (400) who has been changed from "a leprous child" (388) into a "harmonious Soul" (400) ruling a transfigured world of love. Thus Shelley reworks Psalm 68 and Ephesians 4:8 – "when he ascended upon high, he led captivity captive" – into "Conquest is dragged Captive through the deep" (556). The change from "upon high" to "through the deep" is characteristic and instructive.

The Scriptures present the New Jerusalem as descending from on high "as a bride adorned for her husband" (Revelation 21). These adornments are then transferred to the precious stones that garnish the foundations of the city. The adornment of the bride and procession to the bridegroom's house is traditional, as in Psalm 45. Shelley keeps the idea of procession, but turns it into the moving together of the chariot of the moon borne on the wheels of "azure and gold" clouds (IV.214) and the sphere of earth, which, recalling the wheels within wheels of the chariot vision of God in Ezekiel I, is "as many thousand spheres" (IV.238). Each has a child as a guiding spirit. In the same way the nuptial consummation is a mutual interpenetration, which reverses the customary gendering of the earth as female and in effect neutralizes the effects of sexual difference: it is the masculine earth's colored fecundity that impregnates the white moon. In that act, we do find the motif of the adornment of the bride wonderfully transmuted in the "Life of Life" lyric so that Asia's now transfigured limbs "are burning / Through the vest which seems to hide them" (II.5.54–5). In act IV, the adornment is transferred to the glowing spheres themselves.

Shelley here most wants to avoid any idea of the bride's subordination or a union of above and below. In Revelation, there is no need of sun and moon for "the Lord God giveth them light" (22:5); in Shelley's vision, the earth is bathed "In the light which is undying / Of thine own joy" (IV.438–9). In Revelation, the promised union of Christ (as Lamb) and Jerusalem (as Bride) is the sign of hope's fulfillment but also of warning, judgment and final exclusion for "whosoever loveth and maketh a lie" (22:15). In *Prometheus Unbound*, however, Shelley flips between realized vision and the imperfect world that it is correcting (for instance, in the Earth's exultant lyrics in IV.332–55, 370–423) as though we cannot wholly settle in and trust the image without rhetorical underpinning. The vision, after all, cannot be presented as one that God "gave unto him" as in the opening words of Revelation. It depends upon a potentiality maintained by the poet.

The Bible ends with an image of marriage. The image of marriage feast is the most important of all images of the coming kingdom of heaven. But neither marriage nor feast, both of which suggest realization, can be final images for Shelley. That lies with the child and with potentiality as the final fact. This image, too, is derived from Isaiah 9:6 where the government of a transfigured world will be on the shoulders of a child that Christian exegesis has always understood to be Christ. The scriptural heaven is assured and, indeed, already realized, but it cannot be adequately imaged and, as love, retains infinity of extension. Thus the potentiality of the Divine Child and the consummation of marriage, along with the visionary potentiality of the transfigured moon and earth, always exceed any realization. Two unmarrying siblings illustrate this better than the marriage of the spheres that they inhabit. In act III, Shelley plays with the idea that the two children will have an erotic relationship themselves (III.4.86–96) but act IV turns this into the idea that the penetration of Moon and Earth is by each other's spirit (IV.327) in a more diffused sense. We could not combine this sense easily with the Earth-spirit's cheeky voice in act III or the solemn realization of the guiding Moon-Spirit in act IV as an infantine transmutation of the Ancient of Days figure from Daniel 7 with his "white robe" and white hair (IV.232–3). It is the gleeful disengagement of word and transformation from any authority outside the child-like potentiality of poet and poem that is the final fact. Here, then, we can see how Shelley's "theology" and his shifting imagery go hand in hand, as do the biblical imagery and Christian theology that he uses but counterdirects. Potentiality is his version of Christian hope, which, even in this Aeschylean context, bears the traces of the Gothicism of *Zastrossi* and *St Irvyne*, for it is always in expectation of a hitherto unapprehended intensity greater than anything yet encountered. Indeed the young Shelley argued that belief's "intensity is precisely proportionate to the degrees of excitement" (Oxford Shelley, p. 812).

The Book of Job

There are other texts by Shelley that have some anchorage in dated history (*The Mask of Anarchy*, *Hellas*) and make a bid for prophetic authority ("Ode to the West Wind"). These, however, fit Shelley's vaguer poetic model of prophecy more readily than the biblical one, which shows the interventions of the transcendent into history rather than the displacement of history by Apocalypse. The latter is more the form of Shelley's imagination than prophecy as such, but whereas that is primarily a written form ("What thou seest, write in a book": Revelation 1:11), Shelley asserts, as prophecy does, the power of voice while identifying this with poetry and the power of thought. Thus Prometheus's main action is to tell the Spirit of the Hour to "breathe into the many-folded Shell" (III.3.80) so that its "mighty music" shall be "As thunder" over all the earth. Similarly, the words of "Ode to the West Wind" are to be "the trumpet of a prophecy" and the "Shape arrayed in mail," which arises in "The Mask of Anarchy," destroys Anarchy by its footsteps, which make thoughts spring up where they tread (125). All this is a cerebralized version of the prophets' conviction that the word they utter enacts events simply by its promulgation.

The least history-related books of the Bible belong to the tradition of Wisdom writing. Despite Shelley's emphasis on the lyrical transformation of contingent reality rather than its prudential management, and his preference for the wisdom of the child rather than the sage, sapiential writings influenced him. For instance, in one of the infrequent quotations used in *The Defence of Poetry*, Shelley asserts that "The pleasure that is in sorrow is sweeter than the pleasure of pleasure itself" and quotes Ecclesiastes 7:2 in support: "It is better to go to the house of mourning, than to the house of mirth" (Norton Shelley, p. 501). We think instantly of lines such as "Our sweetest songs are those that tell of saddest thought" ("To a Skylark," 90) and even of Maddalo's claim:

> Most wretched men
> Are cradled into poetry by wrong,
> They learn in suffering what they teach in song. ("Julian and Maddalo," 544–6)

Clearly their genesis lies in prudential adage and grim paradox. The Book of Job particularly appealed to Shelley as a sublime poetry made out of suffering and wrong. Mary Shelley tells us that he planned to write his own lyrical drama on the subject (Oxford Shelley, p. 267), the equivalent, perhaps, of Byron's *Cain*. While he never attempted this drama, Shelley did leave two poems that make use of Job directly: *The Triumph of Life*, relentlessly concerned with its central dilemma and to which we return below; and a comic version of Wordsworth's "Peter Bell."

In "Peter Bell the Third" Shelley depicts his protagonist as a figure suddenly exposed to torments "that almost drove him mad," his friends acting in a burlesque parody of Job's comforters, and giving him the sanctimonious explanation that "He was predestined to damnation" (14, 20). Such humor is anchored safely in Shelley's intense dislike of the ideas of divine punishment and salvific suffering and of poetry's (here Wordsworth's) association with such ideas. Bryan Shelley (1994) similarly discusses the many allusions to Job in "Julian and Maddalo," suggesting that the maniac, like Job, begs that "the dust / Were covered in upon my body now" (315–16). He has, too, a recognizable something of Job's self-assurance:

> What Power delight to torture us? I know
> That to myself I do not wholly owe
> What now I suffer. (320–2)

Thereafter the patterns largely diverge. There can be no transforming dialogue with God, for nothing from outside the text can strike inside its calculated structure. Neither can there be any restoration of what has been lost, and the causes of suffering (instability of personality, betrayal in love) belong more to the novel or Confession genre than to parable. But Bryan Shelley does not direct us to the Maniac's friends as versions of Job's Comforters. To be sure, these are comforters who actually try to comfort rather than hypocrites ready to condemn. But the balancing of the poem is strikingly the same as that of Job. We have a suffering man who, like Job, is cradled into poetry by wrong and his outbursts are juxtaposed with dialogues of explanation from other voices about the ultimate sources, rightness, and inevitability of such suffering. Just as such a dialogic structure enables Job to critique some of the most foundational idioms and explanations of other parts of the Bible while claiming its own place alongside them within the recognized canon, so Shelley's poem upholds but also savages the heuristic commonplaces of Shelley's preferred ideology.

Redemption and Hope

Since Gregory the Great's immensely influential *Moralia in Job*, it has been common to see Job as a Christ figure. Shelley is always prepared to praise Christ as a teacher (provided that Shelley can determine which are His true doctrines), and almost all suffering figures in his poetry are shadowed by the Man of Sorrows (Bryan Shelley, 1994, p. 106). But Shelley hated the idea that Christ's sorrows, or indeed any sorrows, are redemptive in themselves, however exemplary they may be. In the "Ode to the West Wind," for example, the poet in his "chained and bowed" weakness (55) virtually prays to the West Wind to become him and give him and his words prophetic strength, but the weakness is not the cause of the wind's possible activity and, in any case, the wildly energetic opening of the poem has already shown that the poet has, despite his disclaimer, all the energies that the wind has. The wind is not a heavenly Spirit descending like the Pentecostal "sound from heaven as of a rushing mighty wind" (Acts 2:2). Instead, Shelley's wind drives the clouds and leaves horizontally across the landscape: it does not come from a world above. If any more permanently transforming help is to be had in Shelley's world, it will come from below as, for instance, Demogorgon's volcanic cave. But Demogorgon, whatever he is, has real power already. It just needs directing away from Jupiter to Prometheus and Asia. Shelley is similarly careful in his use of resurrection imagery in the poem. The seeds are "like" corpses in the grave but are not actually so. The spring wind will awake them *as* from sleep. Their death is not the agency of their rebirth. Prometheus's vision of the crucified Christ similarly exists in order to situate and bypass it by denying efficacious functionality to it, though it also makes explicit the parallels between the two. Both suffer unjustly and endure with "long suffering love" (*Prometheus Unbound* III.3.2), both wish to help humankind. The sequence from suffering body to invulnerable body and the promise of a world wholly transfigured by love is the same. But in Christ's case, unlike Prometheus, it is the obedience in suffering that is efficacious. On the other hand, Shelley is far more interested in the sheer pain that Prometheus suffers than the Passion accounts are and he is far less concerned to privilege the moment of Prometheus's unbinding by Hercules, the emblem of strength. How we get from one world to another is the main preoccupation of Shelley's thought.

His usual answer is given in the "Preface" to *The Cenci* in a formula that shows how consciously he is patterning his thought upon St Paul's even as he is rejecting it: "Imagination is as the immortal God which should assume flesh for the redemption of mortal passion" (Norton Shelley, p. 241). The shell breathed upon by the Spirit of the Hour to spread its revolutionary music as Atheism's Good News over the earth in *Prometheus Unbound* is a mythical enactment of this belief. But, of course, it cannot be exactly a belief for there is no "immortal God" to be believed in. Shelley prefers Hope to Faith. His words are enacting words not because the Word has God's enacting authority built into it but because they could change consciousness. Hence it is Hope not Faith that lies down "before the horses' feet, / Expecting with a patient eye, / Murder, Fraud, and Anarchy" (*The Mask of Anarchy* 100–1). The difficulty is that we are bound to see this exemplary patience on Hope's part in a hopeless situation as being a form of faith. We are equally bound to see its inexplicably sudden translation into an image of strength ("a Shape arrayed in mail," 110) – so that Hope now walks "ankle-deep in blood" but "with a quiet mien" – as founded on the antecedent grace in weakness. If we transfer sign to referent, that is, to the blood of the "massacred" at Peterloo leading to a change of heart and mind in public opinion, we are no better off. No figure within the poem can effect this – it can only be the poem itself. This is why most of the poem (about two-thirds of the whole) is the Earth's rhetoric inviting just such a change but claiming that it is the massacre itself that, as principal agent,

> Shall steam up like inspiration,
> Eloquent, oracular;
> A volcano heard afar. (360–4)

St Paul's and the Letter to the Hebrews' understanding of the Passion as Redemptive sacrifice could be seen as a bizarre interpretation of the execution of a "criminal" but it triumphantly fits, not least because of the way the Passion (especially in St John's account) is presented in parallel with the Passover. In Shelley's case, image and meaning do not fit exactly. The patient blood-stained maiden who suddenly rises as though from brutal death (but only "as though," just as the "winged seeds" in "West Wind" are only "like corpses"), and now walks serenely as the figure of Death flees from the scene, seems powerful indeed. Yet the power of the emblem is only trustworthy as poetic hope, which depends upon the rhetorical support of the rest of the poem rather than the other way round. In this way, it resembles the transformation of Beatrice Cenci from frightened woman into freedom fighter who will snatch a dagger from the murderers in order to incite them to action. We see a before and after but not the change itself: it is the sequence, rather than the play, that suggests this change is provoked by her rape. Outrage, as at Peterloo, transforms helpless victim into unconquerable militant. But in that case there is an uneasy complicity between institutionalized violence and the revolution that seeks to end all violence. In Revelation, Christ is both Lion of Judah and Lamb (Revelation 5:5–6). He comes first in the form of weakness and then with authority as Judge. Shelley's Hope lies down like a lamb for slaughter but the people are told in the last stanza to "Rise like lions after slumber." Shelley wishes to get energy out of his biblical images while at the same time subverting them.

The Bible reinterprets its own images constantly. The Exodus becomes a type of the return from Babylon for the prophets and a type of Baptismal immersion in Christ's death and resurrection in the Christian Bible (1 Corinthians 10:1–5). But the earlier images are not discarded. We could not understand the later ones without the earlier, and these still retain authority in their own right. Shelley inclines instead to erasure (as, for example, in the self-erasing progression in *Prometheus Unbound*) both in his sheer multiplication of images and in his subversion of precursor texts. On the one hand, this is the cause of the inimitable buoyancy of his texts. Only Shelley could successfully present the tread of his mailed figure in *The Mask of Anarchy* as "soft as wind" (118). The way in which the image shifts as the meaning shifts so that the image signifies but cannot be pictured as a whole is like that of Hebrew imagery in general. Yet the bias to erasure means that there is a gap between realized image and the life of the poem in which it inheres that is wholly unlike the Bible or indeed most poetry. He uses and subverts the Bible but sometimes seems to be mainly intent on fending it off.

Erasure is the form of the constantly expected new in Shelley's poems but, by the same token, undermines whatever is presented. In *The Triumph of Life*, however, erasure is a wholly negative experience but can be formally presented as such in an image that cannot itself be erased. It is, however paradoxical the claim, his most suc-cessfully realized poem. It works in the usual fashion by apparently subverting its precursor texts – principally, Ezekiel I, Revelation, *I Trionfi*, and *Divina Commedia*. Yet something has changed. In *The Mask of Anarchy*, Anarchy astride his horse, modeled on both Death's horse in the Apocalypse and Christ's ride into Jerusalem, is acclaimed as "King and God and Lord" (69) with hymns, prayers, and prostrations in a vicious parody of the worshipping of God by the elders in chapter 4 of Revelation. Shelley has put Death in the throne position of heaven but transferred the vision to a London street. In *The Triumph of Life*, however, erasure is the enemy rather than the enabler of the wholly new. The sun's initial freshness is deceptive for it awakens the world to repeated toil. The "shape all light" seems like the Dawn (353) but hands down a cup that brings erasure (406) and the return of a nightmare landscape. Erasure is the remorseless and inexplicable agent of repetition in this untransformable world. The Book of Revelation itself depends upon repetition but does so in the manner of reca-pitulation so as to lead finally to the wholly new with untainted expectation ("and the Spirit and the Bride say, Come": 22:17). Shelley is again not subverting but using biblical resonance in order to intensify his poem's insistence that neither the new nor hope is possible.

Imagination not Faith

If act IV of *Prometheus Unbound* is the most convincing representation of the Hebrew prophets' vision of a new heaven and earth wholly transfigured by Love since *Paradiso*, *The Triumph of Life* is equally the most convincing representation of Gehenna since *Inferno*. Shelley also turns to the question of the transition and transfiguration in *The Witch of Atlas*. This poem is the only complete illustration of Shelley's claim that

"Imagination is as the immortal God which should assume flesh for the redemption of mortal passion." The important word here is "as." What would "redemption of mortal passion" mean if carried out? We would have to have an external power capable of effecting it, assuming flesh within the world, and saving those whom it chose to save. It would have to do this freely like God in the Bible rather than like Necessity in *Queen Mab*. We would have to license the operations of supernatural power so carefully avoided in *Laon and Cythna*. In his notes to *Queen Mab*, Shelley asserts that "Christianity, like all other religions, rests upon miracles, prophecies and martrydoms" (Oxford Shelley, p. 81). Laon and Cythna are martyred, but Shelley's witch is a miracle-worker.

She herself has a miraculous conception and birth narrative (56–88), which indeed "brings to mind the nativity of Christ" (Bryan Shelley, 1994, p. 138). She is then greeted by wild animals (89–104) based both on Eve before the Fall and on the Christian application of Isaiah 60:6 to the Crib. We then jump from infancy narrative to miracles narrative, as Luke and Matthew do, which for them is a sign of the redemption of sin that is to come, but here is redemptive. Freedom from death seems to be given only to those whom she elects but not on the grounds of faith or works; instead this version of "grace" is given "To those she saw most beautiful" (593). This aesthetic Jansenism is wholly external. There is no sense, as in *Prometheus Unbound*, that human consciousness would have to been changed from within. In general, Shelley is always ready to blame but reluctant to find fault, since faults imply fault-lines and hence what Byron and Maddalo would call "this uneradicable taint of sin" (*Childe Harold's Pilgrimage* IV.1228). Only *The Triumph of Life* suggests some bewilderingly primal and universal inheritance of fault. The author of *Queen Mab* wished that "the accursed book of God" should be displaced so that "man can read the inscription on his heart." But in *The Triumph of Life* the heart's inscription is as horribly readable as the visible hearts of the damned in the Hall of Eblis in Beckford's *Vathek*.

In *The Witch of Atlas*, however, external miracles are sufficient to bring about the revision of "Life" prophesied by Isaiah ("Beating their swords to ploughshares": 645). It is not so much hearts that are altered as brains that the witch reprograms through dreams (617–19). Cause and power here derive, within the poem, from the witch's ability to make all orders of reality "do her will" (668). Outside the "visionary rhyme" (8) of the poem, it depends on all orders of reality momentarily obeying the imperatives of the poet's and reader's imagination. Shelley calls this contract "belief" but deplores the fact that nowadays it rarely exceeds our capacity to see (672). This regret for the absence of faith ends the poem. Whereas in other poems, rhetoric is necessary to accomplish the "how" of transition between worlds, in *The Witch of Atlas* it is simply the act of reading the narrative that generates belief as long as the poem lasts. Of course, this belief would not satisfy the logical requirements for correct belief that Shelley set out in his elaborate note to *Queen Mab* VII.13 (Oxford Shelley, pp. 803–5). But as he points out there, creeds exclude "us from all enquiry" (ibid., p. 797).

It is the wholly acknowledged "as if" that enables the exact correspondence between the redemption offered by Christ and that performed by Imagination. It enables, too, the poem's startlingly poised subversion of the former now that it knows that it can, authorized by "as if," do exactly what it wants to do without any fear of collapse into

"I pant, I sink, I tremble, I expire!" (*Epipsychidion*, 591). Thus we have a redemptive virgin rather than One born of a virgin, who deliberately settles for a sterile Hermaphrodite as agent rather than any transformed vocabulary of natural generation. Nevertheless, she redeems "mortal passion" by providing "timid lovers" with sexual confidence and expertise in this life (649), whereas death's sting is removed from the elect through blissfully solipsistic sleep rather than eternal life and love (610–16). Redemption is thus indeed a prank (665) in mode and content. This is because the witch-redeemer does not share the stricken condition of those whom she redeems. Salvation does not come from failure. Inevitably, therefore, the poem separates belief in the imagination from the figure who embodies it and thus can only involve faith in a wholly transferred sense. The poem defuses such problems by its openly acknowledged whimsy. In a note to *Queen Mab*, Shelley eagerly looks forward to a time when "men will laugh ... heartily at grace, faith, redemption, and original sin" (Oxford Shelley, p. 821). This poem may be seen as a much more sophisticated version of the same wish but it reveals, as the earlier prose note does not, just how much Shelley wishes for his own version of a redeemed world and can found his best hope only within a poem that has the good manners to invite no more than "a modest creed" ("The Sensitive-Plant," conclusion, 13). The most adroit example of the effrontery of this "modest creed" is its treatment of the "religion" that it seeks to replace. In the transfigured world brought about by the witch, the priests now openly admit "How the god Apis, really was a bull / And nothing more" (622–6). Thus the reality revealed by religion is exposed as a fiction within a poem whose fiction has to be taken "as" reality.

We might conclude from this and from this chapter as a whole that Shelley uses the Bible as indiscriminate quarry much as he uses Greek and other narratives like some intrepid John the Baptist of intertextual light. But this would, I think, be quite wrong. He uses the Bible because it attracts him with the most powerful version possible of something that he wants more than anything – a narrative of how we get from a tainted to an untainted world. He also thinks that the Bible – perhaps in itself, perhaps in the use made of it – represents the greatest possible threat to the accomplishment of this transition. Shelley depends upon the Bible, then, at the same time as he has to fend it off. *The Triumph of Life* and "The Witch of Atlas" in particular – in comparison, for instance, to the purely rhetorical neoplatonism that all too magnificently concludes *Adonais* – suggest that he is at his best when he is doing both.

Note

1   Percy Bysshe Shelley, *The Complete Poetical Works*, ed. Thomas Hutchinson (Oxford University Press, London, 1935), p. 799 (henceforth Oxford Shelley). All quotations from Shelley's and Mary Shelley's notes to the poems are from this edition. Quotations from *Laon and Cythna* are from *The Poems of Shelley, volume II*, ed. Kelvin Everest and Geoffrey Matthews (Longman, London, 2000) (henceforth Longman Shelley). All other quotations from Shelley's poetry and prose are from *Shelley's Poetry and Prose*, ed. Donald H. Reiman and Sharon B. Powers (W. W. Norton, New York, 1977) (henceforth Norton Shelley).

Bibliography

Barnard, Ellsworth (1937) *Shelley's Religion*. University of Nebraska Press, Minneapolis.

Bradley, Arthur (2006) "'Until Death trample it to fragments': Percy Bysshe Shelley after Postmodern Theology," in Gavin Hopps and Jane Stabler, eds, *Romanticism and Religion from William Cowper to Wallace Stevens*. Ashgate, Aldershot, pp. 191–206.

Brew, Claude (1977) "New Shelley Text: Essay on Miracles and Christian Doctrine," *Keats–Shelley Memorial Bulletin* 28, 10–28.

Brisman, Leslie (1981) "Mysterious Tongue: Shelley and the Language of Christianity," *Texan Studies in Literature and Language* 23:3, 389–417.

Burdon, Christopher (1997) *The Apocalypse in England: Revelation Unravelling 1700–1834*. Macmillan, Basingstoke, especially pp. 174–9.

Clark, David Lee (1951) "Shelley's Biblical Extracts," *Modern Language Notes* 66, 435–41.

Clubbe, John and Lovell, Ernest J. Jr (1983) *English Romanticism: The Grounds of Belief*. Northern Illinois University Press, Dekalb, pp. 115–30.

Shelley, Bryan (1994) *Shelley and Scripture: The Interpreting Angel*. Clarendon Press, Oxford.

Trelawney, Edward John (1973) *Records of Shelley, Byron, and the Author*, ed. David Wright. Penguin, Harmondsworth.

von Rad, Gerhard (1975) *Old Testament Theology. Vol II, The Theology of Israel's Prophetic Traditions*, trans. D. M. G. Stalker. SCM, London.

Wilson Knight, G. (1941) *The Starlit Dome*. Oxford University Press, Oxford.

Woodman, Ross Grieg (1964) *The Apocalyptic Vision in the Poetry of Shelley*. University of Toronto Press, Toronto.

PART V

Victorian

CHAPTER 33
Introduction

Elisabeth Jay

The Bible as Intertext

The Bible may well have been Victorian literature's chief intertext. It was a treasure trove for book titles: for novels of sensation such as Rhoda Broughton's *Cometh Up as a Flower* (1867);[1] for domestic sagas such as Margaret Oliphant's *A House Divided against Itself* (1886);[2] as well as, more understandably, Ruskin's social intervention, *Unto this Last* (1862).[3] It could be mined for small jokes: as in Trollope's naming of the philoprogenitive Mr Quiverful.[4] The choice of a biblically derived name could also provide useful plot clues: the hero of George Eliot's *Daniel Deronda* (1876) is, so to speak, set up from the start to be recognized as a Jewish leader in exile.

It was invoked as a short cut for establishing certain kinds of moral framework. Thackeray relies upon quoting the words of the preacher – "Vanitas Vanitatum" – for a suitably pious ending to *Vanity Fair* (1848), reminding readers that their business is not with the sentimental Amelia and the scheming Becky but with a world beyond. Browning uses the same phrase for his opening salvo in "The Bishop orders his tomb at St Praxed's Church" to provide the reader with the moral bearings from which to judge this particular purveyor of the Word. It is quoted at moments of high drama: Dickens particularly favored it as a short cut to moral solemnity at the moment of death. Miss Barbary, of *Bleak House* (1852), responds to a reading of the tale of the woman taken in adultery (John 8:6–7) with an apocalyptic text from Mark 13:35–7: "Watch ye therefore! lest coming suddenly, he find you sleeping," before suffering a paralytic stroke. Transformed perforce into such a "sleeper," her death is counterpointed with that of Jo, the little crossing-sweeper, who finds his death eased by his new-found access to the Word, though he has formerly eaten his crust on "the door-step of the Society for the Propagation of the Gospel in Foreign Parts," and looking up at "the great Cross on the summit of St Paul's Cathedral," without ever encountering the words of the Lord's Prayer.[5]

The precise signification of the biblical references with which some nineteenth-century novels teem can sometimes be frankly baffling, giving some weight to Bakhtin's claims that the authoritative nature of biblical text resists creative appropriation by the novel, which is, by its very nature, "uncanonical." Scripture remains "inert" so that its fixed meaning is carried into the novel, preventing us from varying our distance as readers so as to accept one text, partially accept another, and utterly reject a third.[6] Should the catena of quotations from Revelation with which *Jane Eyre* ends be read as endorsing St John Rivers's mission and faith, or is it an extension of Jane and her author's critique of her cousin?[7] A similarly indecipherable ending occurs in Rhoda Broughton's novel, *Cometh up as Flower*, whose title hints at an untimely demise for the heroine. The aptly surnamed Nelly Le Strange pauses from time to time in her rambling narrative to ruminate about Eve and her apple (p. 69), Jonah and his gourd (p. 243), or disputed points of biblical translation:

> Sometimes we feel tempted to curse God and die; it would be such a relief to us; curse God, as Job's wife is supposed to have urged her much enduring lord to do, as a cure for his boils; that is, if she did not urge him to *bless* God and die, as the word has either signification, in which case the poor woman's character for piety has been shamefully taken away for the last three or thousand years.[8]

When we arrive at the heroine's deathbed on the last page of the novel it is difficult to know what to make of her preoccupation with the New Jerusalem given that, despite being married to a loving husband, she is dying of anorexia induced by love for a former suitor now dead. Anticipating a lowly mansion in her Father's house, the last words she manages to scribble with her pencil sound more like an assignation with the dead suitor than a picture designed to remind the reader of the "passionless bliss" to come: "Oh Lord Jesus Christ! Let me be in that city by this time tomorrow night! Grant me entrance there! Open to me when in fear and trembling I knock!"[9]

The troubling thing about her final compilation of biblical quotations is that they have the touch of authenticity: the *journals intimes* of believers as different as Lord Shaftesbury and Margaret Oliphant both display that same tendency to mull over their thorniest problems by way of wrestling with biblical texts. Broughton hit an authentic note again in identifying the books of Job and Revelation as chief among her heroine's biblical interests. As William James remarked, for those who were "perplexed and baffled" by the claims of dogmatic theology but retained a sense of the religious, "the book of Job went over this whole matter once for all and definitively."[10] The Book of Revelation appealed to those who clung to the notion of the afterlife all the more tenaciously in that it remained a rich field for speculation, little touched by matters of scientific proof or orthodox teaching: along with the prophetic books of the Old Testament, it enjoyed particular popularity during unsettled periods when millennial preaching was in the ascendant.

The ten-year-old Jane Eyre's list of biblical favorites, chiefly surprising today on account of its length, would have had a familiar resonance for the novel's first readers in 1847: "I like Revelations and the book of Daniel, and Genesis and Samuel, and a little bit of Exodus, and some parts of Kings and Chronicles, and Job and Jonah."[11] Furthermore, they would probably have recognized the continuum between this child's treasured secular books and her biblical preferences: both reinforce the intensely subjective nature of this alienated orphan's outlook on life. The injustice of Jonah and Job's sufferings provides opportunities for self-identification, while the history of a people chosen for special intervention, together with apocalyptic prophecy, promises good times coming, even if current circumstances seem dire. Her skewed course of biblical reading attracts reproof from a fellow pupil at Lowood school who recommends Jane to "Read the New Testament"[12] as an antidote to her retaliatory philosophy. Furthermore, Jane's list offers a point of entry into the novel's larger concerns. Her determination to make her own biblical choices signals the fierce Protestantism of a heroine who repeatedly stands up to clerical attempts to mediate God's authority. Brontë backs her heroine's proclivity for Revelation, whose apocalyptic visions surface in Jane's dreams and paintings, in the image of the bestial Whore of Babylon cast down from the ramparts of Thornfield Hall, and in St John Rivers's keen desire to be written into the Book of Life and "fill a place in the first rank of those who are redeemed from the earth – who stand without fault before the throne of God; who share the last mighty victories of the Lamb; who are called, and chosen, and faithful."[13]

It could be argued that their Evangelical upbringing made Charlotte Brontë and her sisters into special cases – "Elle était nourrie de la Bible," recalled her Roman Catholic teacher, M. Héger[14] – but they were less atypical than might at first appear. Charlotte's admiration for Thackeray seems to have been predicated upon a sense that they shared biblically based values. How else can one explain the elaborate trope, based on 2 Chronicles 18, in the preface to the second edition of *Jane Eyre*, in which her tribute to Thackeray figures him as a modern-day Micaiah, speaking truth to power?[15] Modern criticism has emphasized the vein of combative cynicism that increasingly dominated Thackeray's later work, while dismissing as Victorian sentimentality the vignettes of Christian compassion that recur in his fiction and letters. As an adolescent Thackeray had been "accustomed to hear and read a great deal of the Evangelical (so called) doctrine," which he claimed had taught him an "extreme distaste" for the work of Evangelical divines,[16] yet he retained to the last a biblical frame of reference: his final novel was entitled *Adventures of Philip on His Way through the World; shewing who robbed Him, Who Helped Him, and Who Passed Him By.*[17] His daughter, Annie, attested that by the time she and her sister were nine and six respectively, after breakfast, and again after dinner, "smoking his cigar, Papa used to talk to us a great deal, and tell us about the Bible and Religion."[18] By their teenage years the girls were so imbued with their father's views that Thackeray's mother, who had intermittent charge of her grandaughters, reported herself unable to continue reading the Bible with them: she felt obliged to tell them that "all Scripture is given by inspiration from God" and they clung tenaciously to the view their father had felt equally duty-bound to impart that "Scripture only means a writing and Bible means a Book. It contains Divine Truths: and the history of a Divine Character: but imperfect but not containing a thousandth part of Him."[19]

The developing controversy between Evangelicalism and the Oxford Movement tended to color subsequent accounts so that they were represented as polarized opponents, relying exclusively on either biblical revelation or the authority of the Church's teaching as their route to Christianity. That prolific disseminator of Tractarian teaching, Charlotte Yonge, was emphatic in her recollection of "the great quantity of Scripture which the children were encouraged to learn by heart in connection with any subject on which they were being instructed," in John Keble's parish.[20] Faithful to this tradition she produced *Aunt Charlotte's Stories of Bible History* (1875) and a volume of *Verses on the Gospels for Sundays and Holydays* (1880), specifically designed to anchor the footnoted biblical texts in juvenile memories. Yonge's usage, however, in keeping with the Tractarian doctrine of reserve in communicating religious knowledge, remained less obtrusive than evangelically edifying literature for children, which was inclined to pepper its pages with copious biblical grapeshot. Dickens's Arthur Clennam remained haunted, even in adulthood, by memories of being "scared out of his senses by a horrible tract which commenced business with the poor child by asking him in its title, why he was going to Perdition? ... and which, for the further attraction of his infant mind, had a parenthesis in every other line with some such hiccupping reference as 2Ep.Thess. c. iii. v. 6&7."[21] Dickens is commonly reputed to have had a slim grasp on theology. The advice he passed on to his children in his will was certainly blandly permissive by the dogmatic standards of the day: they were told that they should "humbly try to guide themselves by the teaching of the New Testament in its broad spirit, and to put no faith in any man's narrow construction of its letter here or there."[22] Liberal individualism, however, should not be confused with biblical illiteracy. The referenced verses from Paul's second epistle to the Thessalonians which recommend "that ye withdraw yourselves from every brother that walketh disorderly" have informed Mrs Clennam's judgmental separatism, and, just as pertinently, omit the further instruction in verse 11 not to count such a backslider as an enemy but to "admonish him as a brother."

How far down the class system a familiarity with the Bible reached, that exceeded phrases already wholly assimilated into the language, is difficult to determine. In Hannah More's schools for the poor in late eighteenth-century Somerset, reading was taught, using the Bible as the primer, but writing was not considered essential to the work of salvation, and might in any case afford the means for seditious communication. In 1816 Coleridge confidently proclaimed the ubiquity of the Gospel: it could be found "open in the market-place, and on every window-seat, so that (*virtually*, at least) the deaf may hear the words of the Book! It is preached at every turning, so that the blind may see them."[23] Coleridge's imagery here refers to Isaiah 29:18 ("And in that day shall the deaf hear the words of the book, and the eyes of the blind shall see out of obscurity, and out of darkness") and to Mark's recollection of this when he has an admiring crowd say of Christ's miracles, "he maketh both the deaf to hear, and the dumb to speak" (Mark 7:37), but, as we shall see, when this trope of healing is transferred to the spreading of the Word, those who are on the receiving end have a tendency to be represented as impaired.

In the early and mid-Victorian period, the increasingly widespread practice of family prayers meant that domestic servants would been regularly exposed to readings from the Scriptures. Richard Altick's famous assertion that he could name the Bible and Bunyan's *Pilgrim's Progress* in outlining "pretty precisely the cultural and literary tradition the self-made reader inherited" was reliant on literary texts with their own persuasive agenda.[24] Thomas Hardy claimed that in the mid-1850s, when he was about fifteen, he was a Sunday School teacher in a parish where as a pupil in his class he had a dairy-maid four years older than himself, who subsequently appeared as Marian in *Tess of the d'Urbervilles*. "This pink and plump damsel had a marvellous power of memorizing whole chapters in the Bible, and would repeat to him by heart in class, to his boredom, the long gospels before Easter without missing a word, and with evident delight in her facility; though she was by no means a model of virtue in her love-affairs."[25] Her inconsequential party-trick is turned to parodic effect when the drunken Jude Fawley is encouraged to recite the Nicene creed in Latin to a host of ignorant Oxford undergraduates (Book II, chapter 7).[26] Yet Hardy's fictional portraits of agricultural laborers using a "semi-biblical dialect" to conscious blasphemous effect were, suggested R. Hutton, a contemporary reviewer, little more than a mouthpiece for the novelist's own skepticism.[27]

Hardy's strategy here was no more manipulative of the laboring classes than was that of the writers of evangelical tracts who loved to show the deserving poor aroused to the joint virtues of Godliness and cleanliness by the influence of the Word. Anne Brontë's *Agnes Grey* (1847) stems very much from this tradition. The eponymous heroine visits Nancy, an elderly cottager and "a woman of a serious, thoughtful turn of mind" who finds herself troubled by Calvinist fears, of the sort that had troubled Anne Brontë herself, concerning predestined election to eternal damnation. Brontë quickly finds herself in the double bind that afflicted most middle-class Evangelical proselytizers. On the one hand she is anxious to denounce anyone, in this case the local High Church Rector, who preaches against "the reprehensible presumption of individuals who attempted to think for themselves in matters connected with religion, or be guided by their own interpretation of Scripture."[28] On the other hand she requires a biddable pupil whose own interpretative attempts require remedial help: Nancy's partial readings, it might in fairness be said, go some way to justify the High Church Rector's position. In order to allow Agnes to act as the interpreter who presents the countervailing texts, Nancy has to be infantilized by developing eyesight problems that prevent her from finding these texts for herself. Her affliction is hardly accidental: the dimming of her outer eye is closely related to her spiritual myopia. Although Elizabeth Gaskell's *North and South* (1855) broadens out into wider considerations of the harm done by limited or partial readings of the Bible, it also features the same pattern of a middle-class girl, again a clergyman's daughter, trying to counter the texts loved by a working-class lass whose unhealthy fondness for the eschatological portions of the Bible is mirrored by her increasingly delirious and moribund state. By contrast, the robustly healthy insights of the heroine, Margaret Hale, are signaled by her surname.

Tennyson's poem "Rizpah" (1880), which grimly satirizes this tradition of disabling or infantilizing the poor, depends upon its readers close knowledge of biblical text. Although he cannot divest himself of his own class status, nor of the act of working-class ventriloquism this dramatic monologue requires, his poor cottager, rather than being under catechetical instruction, holds the floor and is permitted to put words into the mouth of the condescending visitor who has come to "read me a Bible verse of the Lord's good will toward men" (line 61).[29] The dying woman who has defied the law to gather up the bones of her highwayman son, hung on a gibbet for his offense, sees her Bible-visitor as an intrusive spy to be feared, flattered, and resented. Christopher Ricks's edition of Tennyson's poetry cites as his source 2 Samuel 21:8–10, in which the daughter of one of Saul's concubines protects the bones of her two sons who have been sacrificed by King David as an act of redress to the Gibeonites, but Tennyson's revision takes account of the larger tale in which Rizpah is a pawn in a grander "aristocratic" game. Her bastard sons are substituted for Saul's legitimate descendants, "because of the Lord's oath that was between them, between David and Jonathan the son of Saul." Rizpah lives in a state where the King's spies are everywhere: "And it was told David what Rizpah the daughter of Aiah, the concubine of Saul had done" (verse 11). The full irony of Tennyson's ballad stems from this after-tale to Rizpah's action. The rhythms of the biblical narrative lead us to expect that David will punish Rizpah. Instead, he is inspired by her maternal love finally to attend to collecting the bones of Saul and Jonathan from Jabesh-Gilead where they had ended up after being stolen from the place where the Philistines had first hung them (2 Samuel 21:12). In Christian Britain, however, the mother in Tennyson's poem fears that her Bible-toting visitor is part of the state's repressive network. The mother's paranoia stems from the way in which the authorities of her time had treated her attempted interventions on her son's behalf as symptoms of insubordination and lunacy:

> They seized me and shut me up: they fastened me down on my bed.
> "Mother, O mother!" – he called in the dark to me year after year.
> They beat me for that, they beat me – you know that I couldn't but hear;
> And then at the last they found I had grown so stupid and still
> They let me abroad again ... (46–50)

At the poem's ending there is more than a hint of apocalyptic reprisal for the years of injustice suffered on earth. His mother has no doubt that "My Willy 'ill rise up whole when the trumpet of judgment 'ill sound," and her dying words suggest the overthrow of the structures of this world: "And he calls to me now from the church and not from the gibbet – for hark! / Nay – you can hear it yourself – it is coming – shaking the walls" (84–5).

This sense of the Bible as an instrument of oppression also containing the seeds of its own redress is portrayed particularly forcibly in pictures of children's encounters with the Bible. Children traditionally cut their reading teeth on the Scriptures. The intimacy and sense of mutual care that could at best be inspired by time set aside for this purpose is suggested in Charlotte Brontë's *Villette* (1853) where the teacher–pupil relationship it establishes between the infant Polly and the gawky teenager Graham Bretton subsequently flowers into marriage.[30] However, Charlotte and Emily were also to give currency to versions of this experience that formed fictional templates for representing the Bible as a central adult weapon for abusing children. Neglected though their education is by Hindley and his new wife Frances, Heathcliff and Catherine Earnshaw have plenty of experience of being "set to learn a column of Scripture names, if they don't answer properly," or of being set chapters from the Bible to learn as a penance for misbehavior by the curate.[31] At Lowood school, "The Sunday evening was spent in repeating, by heart, the church catechism, and the fifth, sixth, and seventh chapters of St Matthew." Mr Brocklehurst's subsequent manipulation of the Sermon on the Mount to justify the privations of this charity school is followed by the episode in which Jane Eyre is pilloried as "the native of a Christian land, worse than many a little heathen who says its prayers to Brahma and kneels before Juggernaut," and then branded "a liar."[32]

How conscious Kipling was of this primal literary scene of biblical abuse when he came to write "Baa Baa Black Sheep" is unclear, but his fictional reshaping of his childhood misery in an "establishment run with the full vigour of the Evangelical as revealed to the Woman" reveals remarkable echoes.[33] The facility the young Kipling developed in lying, which he later saw as the "the foundation of literary effort," earned him the regular punishment of learning collects "and a great deal of the Bible."[34] In "Baa Baa Black Sheep" the fictional child "was always ready to oblige everybody. He therefore welded the story of Creation on to what he could recollect of his Indian fairy tales." Demonized by the Evangelical Woman and her son, he is sent out for a walk bearing a placard proclaiming him a "Liar," a punishment that seems to conflate Jane Eyre's "sin" with Helen Burns's punishment of having a piece of pasteboard with the word "Slattern" bound to her forehead.

The Materiality of Biblical Text

It went without saying that these children would have been learning their biblical portions from the Authorized Version, for by the Victorian period this had become established as the British gold standard. Not only did it bear the royal imprimatur and the reputation for learning of the universities of Oxford and Cambridge, but so few changes had been effected since Benjamin Blayney's edition of 1769 that it had come to be viewed as the definitively authoritative text, rather than one among a number of possible translations.[35]

Anglophone Jews had no complete translation into English of the Hebrew Bible available until Isaac Leeser (1806–68), a Prussian émigré, published his version in Philadelphia in 1845: there is no evidence of a British edition. The small number of orthodox Jews in England, would, if male, have studied the Hebrew Bible and the commentaries (the Talmud and Mishnah) in Hebrew and Aramaic. In 1845 Grace Aguilar claimed that their lack of Hebrew excluded most Jewish women raised in an Anglophone culture from their true spiritual heritage,[36] and so when she advocated studying the Bible without the commentaries she presumably assumed that Jewish readers would resort to the King James Bible. It seems probable that Jewish women continued to read the Bible in English until the 1880s when immigrants arriving from Eastern Europe brought with them so-called "women's bibles" – translations of some biblical narratives into Yiddish.

The export of the Bible, particularly under the aegis of The British and Foreign Bible Society (founded 1804), became associated with an imperial mission to spread British values. Introducing himself to a Portuguese host, George Borrow, one of the Society's agents, explained:

I did not come to Portugal with the view of propagating the dogmas of any particular sect, but with the hope of introducing the Bible, which is the well-head of all that is useful and conducive to the happiness of society, that I cared not what people called themselves, provided they followed the Bible as a guide; for that where the Scriptures were read, neither priestcraft nor tyranny could long exist, and instanced the case of my own country, the cause of whose freedom and prosperity was the Bible.[37]

However, the Society's interdenominational and international remit involved tampering with the traditional format of the Authorized Version, separating it from the 1662 Anglican Book of Common Prayer and denuding it of exegetical marginal cross-references for the home market, and including the Apocrypha for the European market. Multiple translations further unsettled assumptions as to the absolute authority of the language of the Authorized Version, by raising the visibility of "the human authorship" involved in the production of the Scriptures.[38] The nature of the outcry that greeted the Revised New Testament in 1881 (the Revised Old Testament followed in 1885), which attempted to respond to textual problems unknown to the compilers of the King James version, suggests that the aestheticization of the Bible as literary artifact rather than sacred didactic text was well under way.[39]

The vocabulary and style of the King James Version, archaic even when first published, were perceived as offering a common wellspring from which all Britain's greatest authors had drawn, even though the Geneva Bible had in fact been the version used by Shakespeare, Milton, and Bunyan, and had also, incidentally, been the version transported to the New World by the Pilgrim Fathers in 1620. Thomas Hardy purposely plays with his British readership's sense of the blasphemous as attaching more nearly to the Authorized Version than to the Godhead when Sue Bridehead taunts her more devout cousin Jude about the chapter headings of the Song of Solomon: "You needn't be alarmed: nobody claims inspiration for the chapter headings ... it seems the drollest thing to think of the four-and-twenty elders, or bishops, or whatever number they were, sitting with long faces and writing down such stuff."[40] Authors who came to doubt the Bible's absolute authority continued to reverence the Authorized Version as an aesthetic yardstick. Tennyson, who had once learned Hebrew with an eye to a poetic translation of the Book of Job, abandoned the project but continued to proclaim that "the Bible ought to be read, were it only for the sake of the grand English in which it is written, an education in itself."[41] Ruskin owned himself indebted for "the best part of my taste in literature" to learning the Bible by heart as a child. "[O]nce knowing the 32nd of Deuteronomy, the 119th Psalm, the 15th of 1 Corinthians, the Sermon on the Mount, and most of the Apocalypse, every syllable by heart, ... it was not possible for me, even in the foolishest of times of youth, to write entirely superficial or formal English."[42] In 1888, Kipling fearing that his advice might sound "queer," nevertheless advised a tyro poet and novelist to "read the Bible thoroughly and see how much can be said in how few words. I regard the Book as a great help to literary composition."[43] By 1934, believing himself to be now writing for a biblically challenged generation,[44] Kipling produced in his tale "Proofs of Holy Writ" a brief guide to the provenance of the King James version.

Whether regarded as the one thing needful for salvation, or totem of cultural literacy, the Bible was undoubtedly a hot commercial property in the early Victorian period. The output from the three publishers authorized by the Crown was still rising by mid-century.[45] Meanwhile other publishers were finding ways of enjoying the exemption from the knowledge tax on paper that only the Bible enjoyed. Part-publication of Bibles, often aimed at the lower classes, preceded Dickens's adoption of this mode for *Pickwick Papers* (1836–7) by two decades or more. The rich, and the aspiring, were able to purchase their Bibles in simple boards and then order a binding to taste. Dickens's Arthur Clennam had thus grown up with "no more real knowledge of the beneficent history of the New Testament, than if he had been bred among idolaters," because he had experienced the Word solely through the punitive regime of his mother, who on Sundays, "stern of face and unrelenting of heart, would sit all day behind a bible – bound like her own construction of it, in the hardest, barest, and straitest boards, with one dinted ornament on the cover like the drag of a chain, and a wrathful sprinkling of red upon the edges of the leaves – as if it of all books, were a fortification against sweetness of temper, natural affection, and gentle intercourse."[46]

The growth of daily household prayers encouraged further tailoring of the Bible for family reading. Editions were produced marking out passages that might usefully be omitted. Such exclusions tended to focus upon the genealogies and detailed descriptions of permitted and forbidden sexual practice to be found in the Old Testament. This fictional account by the clergyman's daughter, Rhoda Broughton, suggests why such editions became popular.

> Opposite me ... sit the servants, in clean caps and aprons, and behind them open windows, and the sun, and the green trees, and the June airs at play. It is a very long chapter; all about the Israelitish wars, how Joshua and his host took Ai and the king thereof, and the people thereof, and killed them all; and then went off to Libnah, and did the same there, and then on again ditto. *How* tired they must have got of cutting up and hacking those poor Aborigines![47]

The pathologizing of Christianity's oriental inheritance[48] was frequently furthered in illustrated editions. Those featured in Charles Knight's "Pictorial Bible," edited by the industrious Rev. John Kitto, were picked out by Margaret Oliphant as having given "additional reality to many passages which refer to the unchanging customs of Oriental life and the antique world": the inference to be drawn is of the Orient as a fossilized, primitive culture.[49]

Further commodification of the Family Bible occurred as specially designed leaves were included for recording family events. The use of the Bible as family register had probably developed in days when a Bible might have been the sole well bound book in the family's possession. Such a Bible charts the Tulliver family's fortunes in George Eliot's *The Mill on the Floss* (1860). When his household is sold up the only book left to Tulliver père is the old quarto (9 inch by 7 inch) Bible in which his and his sister Gritty's births and marriages are recorded on the flyleaf. Accustomed to paying attention to the bindings rather than contents of books (book 1, chapter 3), Tulliver has his son inscribe his promise to pursue a family vendetta on this same flyleaf.[50]

It is difficult to overestimate the visibility of biblical text in Victorian Britain: on samplers, in Gothic picture frames, on china and pottery, applied in frieze form to public buildings, painted on rural gates and barns, or chalked on college walls.[51] Lord

Shaftesbury, an enthusiastic millenarian, went so far as to have "Even so, come, Lord Jesus" stamped in Greek on the flaps of his envelopes.[52]

Hardy's Bible-saturated novel *Jude the Obscure*, provides a kind of prospectus for the products of the Bible-industry. Sue Bridehead is first discovered at work in an Anglican shop, illuminating a metal chancel scroll, while Jude's skills as a mason are frequently applied to engraving tombstones and monuments. A later drinking binge is spent in the company of Tinker Taylor, a "bankrupt ecclesiastical ironmonger." When Sue and Jude turn their talents to account in the restoration of the tablets bearing the Ten Commandments in a country church, they take a professional pleasure in this "relettering" exercise. However, their conscientious reworking of conventional morality is thrown into visible relief as the unmarried Sue's pregnant body is silhouetted against the old letters they are reinscribing and the two are dismissed from this employment.[53]

Sue was by no means the only Victorian woman to attempt to live "off" as much as "by" relettering the Bible. Sarah Trimmer's six volume *Sacred History, selected from the Scriptures, with Annotations and reflections adapted to the comprehension of Young Persons* (1782–4) started an educational trend that was to burgeon in mid-Victorian England. Since the earliest religious instruction was assumed to take place at one's mother's knee, a market soon developed for nugget-sized portions of biblical narrative laced with moral commentary. Favell Lee Mortimer was a specialist in the genre, producing best-sellers clearly designed to be read by an adult to a child, such as *The Peep of Day, or a Series of the Earliest Religious Instruction the Infant Mind is Capable of Receiving with Verses Illustrative of the Subjects* (1836), still being republished in 1909. This success was followed by *Line upon Line; or a Second Series of the Earliest Religious Instruction the Infant Mind is Capable of Receiving* (1841), *Precept upon Precept*, (1867), and *The Kings of Israel and Judah* (1872). Elizabeth Rundle Charles managed to turn a recuperative trip to the Mediterranean for her husband to good account in *Wanderings over the Bible Lands and Seas* (1861). What had begun as a genre of pious travel writing was also capable of being turned into an arena for theological knockabout. In the preface to *Jerusalem the Holy City: Its History and Hope* (1891), one of her occasional series of historical city guides, Margaret Oliphant openly declared warfare on Renan, and "the labours of half-a-dozen learned Germans working by no light except that of their own genius." Pinning her colors to the mast, she announced "the history of the Bible is above all things biographical" and stated "that to transfer my faith and confidence from the writers of the Old Testament to the Herrn Wellhausen, Kuenen, etc., would seem to me the wildest insanity. Moses I know, Samuel I know, but who are these?"[54]

Advancing through the process of producing translations, grammars, and dictionaries, women writers eventually came to engage more directly with biblical scholarship.[55]

Biblical Criticism and Literature

Developments in biblical scholarship were as centrally important to many high Victorian writers as politics had been to the Romantics. New scholarship brought the Bible into the realm of literature, linguistics, and literary criticism. The Scriptures had been dethroned from their unique position as a series of texts, written under direct inspiration from God and by virtue of this containing a historically true account of God's interactions with his Creation: instead they became a collection of antique writings whose textual history and culturally defined meaning could and should be subjected to the same forms of analysis as any other classical text. ("Lower Criticism" denoted the scholarship involved in establishing a reliable text, while "Higher Criticism" indicated the literary and historical critique employed in studying the forms and sources of texts.) Historical criticism endeavored to separate out the verifiable from the mythical, while literary approaches opened up questions as to how to read books whose forms and original purposes were as different as the Song of Songs and a Pauline epistle. To the attacks upon the inerrancy of scriptural texts mounted by those whose business, broadly speaking, was theological scholarship were added the questions raised by scientific evidence and theories that seemed to challenge biblical accounts of creation and belief in God's continuous providential intervention in human affairs.

There were some who, recognizing that the game was up, simply drew stumps and refused to continue the game. In his account of his intellectual evolution, *Phases of Faith* (1850), Francis Newman, recalled how, fresh from Oxford, he had encountered John Nelson Darby, who had not as yet joined the separatist Plymouth Brethren, but had already abandoned the cultural baggage acquired at Westminster School and Trinity College Dublin:

> He had practically given up all reading except that of the Bible; and no small part of his movement towards me soon took the form of dissuasion from all other voluntary study.
>
> In fact, I had myself more and more concentrated my religious reading on this one book: still, I could not help feeling the value of a cultivated mind. ... "But do you really think that *no* part of the New Testament may have been temporary in its object? For instance what should we have lost, if St Paul had never written the verse, "The cloak which I have left at Troas, bring with thee, and the books, but especially the parchments." He answered with the greatest promptitude: "I should certainly have lost something; for that is exactly the verse which alone saved me from selling my little library. No! every word, depend upon it, is from the Spirit, and is for eternal service."

To those who believed in plenary inspiration, and those who had been educated in the fourfold exegetical methodology, originating with the Early Fathers of the Church and still enjoying currency in early Victorian England, the advice given by Benjamin Jowett in "On the Interpretation of Scripture" would have been anathema. In this contribution to the notorious *Essays and Reviews* (1860) Jowett advocated reading Scripture "like any other book," attempting only to recover the meaning of the words "as they first struck on the ears or flashed before the eyes of those who heard and read them."[56] The advice to read the Scriptures "like any other book" achieved results almost certainly never envisaged by Jowett, who had in mind liberating biblical scholarship from the old fourfold methodology (literal, allegorical, moral, and anagogical), rather than licensing idiosyncratically individualistic uses of it. Christina Rossetti's commentary upon Revelation demonstrates the startlingly personal readings that could result when traditional modes were employed by a woman who felt herself to have "graduated" from being one of the "hearers who seek instruction of God through men" to being "a reader studying at first hand ... in direct contact with God's Word."[57] Take, for example, her poem "She Shall Be Brought unto the King," which attempts to weave together Psalm 45's account of the glorious rewards bestowed upon the Lord's anointed – "The king's daughter is all glorious within: her clothing is of wrought gold. She shall be brought unto the king in raiment of needlework: the virgins her companions that follow her shall be brought unto thee" (verses 13–14) – with Revelation's vision of "the Lamb, the Bride's wife" (21:9–11). The method involved in showing the New Testament as a fulfillment of Old Testament typology is entirely traditional. However, Rossetti, appropriated as her own the psalmist's declaration in verse 1 – "my tongue is the pen of a ready writer" – and took his invocation to the king's daughter that she should "forget thy father's house" (verse 10) as permission to transform one of several kings' daughters rendered to the Israelite king as tribute into "a high princess, / Going home to her Husband's Throne, / Virgin queen in perfected loveliness." This woman who sits in a state of suspended sexuality, enjoying the title of bride without sacrificing her virginity, next becomes a feminist symbol: "Who sits with the King in his throne? Not a slave but a Bride / With this King of all greatness and Grace Who reigns not alone / His Glory her glory, where glorious she sits at His side."[58]

Something of Jowett's principle, though again not in the spirit he advocated, had already been deliberately employed by Edward Fitzgerald in his refashioning of the unorthodox philosophy of the twelfth-century Persian astronomer-poet. Fitzgerald believed that the way in which his poem "Rubáiyát of Omar Khayyám" (1859) invoked parallels to the translation of biblical texts had *prepared all Englishmen at least for the reception of other Oriental works under the same forms*: both of *words* and *grammar*."[59] Certainly Jowett's pupil, Swinburne, was quick to seize upon the possibilities Fitzgerald's allusive technique raised and exploit them in the parodic broadsides of his own far more openly iconoclastic *Poems and Ballad* (1866).

The developments of the poetic dramatic monologue and of fiction structured around multiple narratives have both been used to argue that German Higher Criticism made mid-century Victorians simultaneously suspicious of claims to authoritative interpretation and sympathetic to more subjective readings.[60] For some authors and texts such as Emily Brontë's *Wuthering Heights* (1847) the case must be speculative, but we have ample evidence for the way in which other authors kept abreast of and became imaginatively engaged in developments in biblical scholarship. George Eliot's tear-laden translation of Strauss's *Das Leben Jesu* (1846) might be said to have set her off on the lifelong search for ethically valid interpretations of the religious impulse and the drive to incarnate these in fictional form. When Renan's *La Vie de Jesus* (1863) came out, Robert Browning was already working on "A Death in the Desert" (1864), grappling as he had done before in "An Epistle to Karshish" and "Cleon" (1855) with the ways in which one might evaluate documentary evidence so as to come at the nature of the divinity of Christ in an era when origins and ur-texts seemed so disputed. He was taken aback, therefore, not by the content, so much as the sloppy scholarship of Renan's work.[61]

Stefan Collini, in his New DNB entry for Matthew Arnold, remarks that Arnold displayed a "surprising mastery of the technicalities of Biblical history and textual criticism" in *Literature and Dogma: an Essay towards a better apprehension of the Bible* (1873) and *God and the Bible: A Review of Objections to "Literature and Dogma"* (1875). Yet his grasp of the issues is neither unique among his literary contemporaries nor surprising, given what he believed to be at stake. Arnold believed, quite simply, that for the first time since the Reformation *"the masses* [were] losing the Bible and its religion" (*Literature and Dogma: an Essay towards a better apprehension of the Bible*: 1873, p. 311): and it was to this estrangement from the ultimate guide to human conduct that Arnold attributed England's unsettled moral condition. In order to re-establish the Bible as "the great inspirer" of the conduct that he believed to make up "more than three-fourths of human life," it was imperative for Arnold to work out a viable basis upon which the Bible could still be presented to both the educated and "the masses" as a text to live by.

> Let us announce, not: "There rules a Great Personal First Cause, who thinks and loves, the moral and intelligent Governor of the universe, and *therefore* study your Bible and learn to obey this!" No; but let us announce: "There rules an enduring Power, not ourselves, which makes for righteousness, and *therefore* study your Bible and learn to obey this." For if we announce the other instead, and they reply: "First let us verify that there rules a Great Personal First Cause, who thinks and loves, the moral and intelligent Governor of the universe," – what are we to answer? We *cannot* answer.[62]

For Arnold and his brothers the intellectual heartlands of Victorian Britain were a birthright, but his niece's extraordinarily popular novel *Robert Elsmere* (1888) drew upon the experience of her parents' marriage in depicting the problems raised when an inquiring spirit found itself yoked to staunch religious conservatism. Mrs Humphry Ward's novel depicts a clergyman's daughter, as a theological "virgin intacta" moving to the tune of her dead father's Low Church Evangelicalism: her father had survived Oxford at the height of the Oxford Movement, without challenge to his convictions. His daughter, however, marries a clergyman, whose Oxford education inclines him to respond to each successive wind of nineteenth-century biblical criticism, before eventually embracing "the image of a purely human Christ – a purely, human, explicable, yet always wonderful Christianity." The last chapter has the dying husband drifting feverishly between Virgil, his favorite Romantic poets, and the pronouncements of Herbert Spencer, while Catherine still sits "with her Bible on her knee."[63]

By killing off Robert the novel evades the final showdown and leaves the Bible and literature as polarized entities. In practice leaving the Bible in the possession of conservative traditionalists seemed an impossibility to other Victorian doubters who had abandoned an earlier ministerial vocation, such as William Hale White, Arthur Hugh Clough, or Thomas Hardy. Hale White, who had been ejected in 1852 from his dissenting training college for expressing doubts as to the inerrancy of Scriptures, found it the "King Charles's head" of his future literary endeavors. To the second volume of his semi-fictional autobiography *Mark Rutherford's Deliverance* (1885) he felt impelled to add, by way of an appendix, his "Notes on the Book of Job." *The Revolution in Tanner's Lane* (1887) interrupts his excoriating picture of small town dissenting life to list a series of biblical episodes, from "the garden of Eden" and "the murder of Cain" to "the

Incarnation, the Atonement, and the Resurrection from the Dead": likening their status to nineteenth-century gossip, with the disadvantage that no authentic evidence remained to check them by.[64]

Hardy's 1861 Bible bore the legend of his phase as a Bible Christian in copious notes and markings: and the Bible was to become the literary medium through which he conducted his lifelong debate with Christianity and its supporters. In the mid-1860s he began "turning the Book of Ecclesiastes into Spenserian stanzas, but finding the original unmatchable abandoned the task."[65] His friend Edmund Gosse's claim that Hardy was an iconoclast in the Swinburnian mode receives support from *Jude the Obscure* (1895), and not just from the scene where Sue Bridehead reads from Swinburne's "Hymn to Proserpine" to celebrate the triumphant erection of her pagan altar amidst the saints, texts, and "Calvary print" in the symbolically named Miss Fontover's lodgings.[66] The rather crude literalism of this scene is less effective than the contrapuntal "readings" that punctuate the novel, in which Hardy juxtaposes biblical texts with events that bring the Providential Creator of orthodox interpretation into question. Listening to the chanting of the verse "Wherewith shall a young man cleanse his way?" from Psalm 119, in the cathedral at Christminster, Jude "could hardly believe that the psalm was not specially set by some regardful Providence for this moment of his first entry into the solemn building. And yet," the narrator reminds us, "it was the ordinary psalm for the twenty-fourth evening of the month." Later coincidences provoke harsher reflections: an organist is heard practicing the anthem from the seventy-third Psalm, "Truly God is loving unto Israel," in a nearby college chapel as Jude and Sue await the coroner's and jury's verdict on the death of their children. As Jude lies dying the antiphonal response to his recitation of Job's desolate verses, pleading for utter extinction, is formed by the repeated "Hurrahs!" wafting from the ironically named "Remembrance Games" attended by his deliberately forgetful wife, Arabella.[67]

Hardy does not confine his quarrel with the Bible in this novel to the backdrop: it is openly aired by the leading protagonists. Biblical criticism becomes the medium for depicting the emotional frissons of the developing relationship between Sue and Jude. To deflect an awkward moment of emotional intimacy with her cousin, the newly married Sue starts a conversation on "the uncanonical books of the New Testament," taking the opportunity to recommend a useful edition to him. Earlier she had taunted Jude by recollecting the way she had cut up "all the Epistles and Gospels into separate *brochures*, and re-arranging them in chronological order as written, beginning with the book of Thessalonians." The "sense of sacrilege" this provokes in Jude is aroused as much by his distaste for her mention of the previous undergraduate boyfriend who had admired this act as for her "Voltairean" audacity.[68]

Yet how, over a century later, are we to gauge the precise distances between Jane Eyre's highly selective childhood canon, the issue of the Bible in part form, Bibles with passages marked for exclusion, and Sue Bridehead's material reorderings? At what point does the reverent attempt to incorporate the master text turn into attempting to subvert it? Repositioning fragmented sacred text within the world of the literary imagination, or subjecting it to new marketing strategies, inevitably revealed the Bible too as "a literary construct." With the relegation of the Bible to literary masterpiece the nineteenth-century had in effect licensed increasingly personalized interpretations, and shifted responsibility for protecting the Word from the religious authorities to the guardians of high culture.[69]

Notes

1   Cf. Job 14:2.
2   Cf. Matthew 12:25.
3   Cf. Matthew 20:13–14.
4   Cf. Psalm 127:5.
5   C. Dickens, *Bleak House*, Ed. Stephen Gill (Oxford University Press, Oxford, 1998), pp. 28, 677, 237, 290.
6   M. M. Bakhtin, *The Dialogic Imagination*, ed. M. Holquist, trans. Caryl Emerson and Michael Holquist (University of Texas Press, Austin, 2004), pp.70, 342–4.
7   Charlotte Brontë, *Jane Eyre*, ed. Jane Jack and Margaret Smith (Clarendon Press, Oxford, 1969), pp. 578–9.
8   R. Broughton *Cometh up as a Flower* (Alan Sutton, Gloucester, 1997), pp. 69, 243, 218.
9   Ibid., pp. 284–5.
10 W. James, *The Varieties of Religious Experience: A Study in Human Nature, Gifford Lectures delivered at Edinburgh University* (1902) (Longmans, Green: London, 1929), p. 448.
11 *Jane Eyre*, p. 35.
12 Ibid., p. 66.
13 Ibid., p. 578.
14 Elizabeth Gaskell, *The Life of Charlotte Brontë* (1857), ed. Elisabeth Jay (Penguin, London, 1997), p. 173.
15 *Jane Eyre*, p. xxxi.
16 *The Letters and Private Papers of William Makepeace Thackeray*, ed. Gordon N. Ray, 4 volumes (Oxford University Press, London, 1945–6), vol. iii, pp. 93–4.
17 Cf. Luke 10:25–37.
18 *Letters of Anne Thackeray Ritchie*, ed. Hester Ritchie (John Murray, London, 1924), p. 22.
19 *Letters of Thackeray*, vol. iii, pp. 85–6, 95.
20 Charlotte Yonge, "Gleanings from Thirty Years' Intercourse with the Rev. John Keble," in *Musings over the "Christian Year" and "Lyra Innocentium"* (James Parker, Oxford and London, 1871), p. xvi.
21 C. Dickens, *Little Dorrit*, ed. H. P. Sucksmith (Clarendon Press, Oxford, 1979), p. 30.
22 *Oxford Reader's Companion to Dickens*, ed. Paul Schlicke (Oxford University Press, Oxford, 1999), p. 37.
23 S. T. Coleridge, *Lay Sermons*, ed. R. J. White. *The Collected Works. Vol. 6* (Princeton University Press, Princeton, NJ, 1972), p. 6.
24 *The English Common Reader: A Social History of the Mass Reading Public 1800–1900* (1963) (University of Chicago Press, Chicago, 1967), p. 255.
25 *The Life and Work of Thomas Hardy by Thomas Hardy*, ed. Michael Millgate (Macmillan, London and Basingstoke, 1984), p. 30.
26 T. Hardy, *Jude the Obscure*, ed. P. Ingham (Oxford University Press, Oxford, 2002), pp. 114–15.
27 R. H. Hutton, *Spectator* 19 December 1874, reprinted in R. G. Cox, ed., *Thomas Hardy, the Critical Heritage* (Routledge and Kegan Paul, London, 1970), pp. 21–7.

28   Anne Brontë, *Agnes Grey*, ed. H. Marsden and R. Inglesfield (Clarendon Press, Oxford, 1988), p. 85.

29   *The Poems of Tennyson*, ed. Chistopher Ricks, 3 volumes (Longman, Harlow, 1987), vol. iii, pp. 30–4.

30   Mary Wilson Carpenter's reading of Polly as "subjected to the pedagogical construction of the authoritative male – and his imperial bible" ignores the narrator's resentment and subsequent desire for a similarly constructed adult relationship. *Imperial Bibles, Domestic Bodies: Women, Sexuality, and Religion in the Victorian Market* (Ohio University Press, Athens, 2003), p. 82.

31   Emily Brontë, *Wuthering Heights*, ed. H. Marsden and Ian Jack (Clarendon Press, Oxford, 1976), pp. 57–8.

32   *Jane Eyre*, pp. 69, 76–77.

33   R. Kipling, *Wee Willie Winkie, Under the Deodars, The Phantom Rickshaw, and Other Stories* (1890) (Macmillan, London, 1910), pp. 271–310.

34   *Something of Myself* (1937) (Macmillan, London, 1951), pp. 6, 11.

35   See, David Norton, *A Textual History of the King James Bible* (Cambridge University Press, Cambridge, 2005).

36   G. Aguilar, *The Women of Israel; or Characters and Sketches from the Holy Scriptures and Jewish History* (Groombridge and Sons, London, 1870), p. 534. Her theological position, influenced by Evangelicalism's critique of Judaism as contaminated by rabbinic commentary, seems not to have commanded much sympathy among her peers.

37   G. Borrow, *The Bible in Spain: or The Journeys, Adventures, and Imprisonments of an Englishman in an attempt to circulate the Scriptures in the Peninsula* (1843) (Ward, Lock, London, 1890), p. 20.

38   See Leslie Howsam, *Cheap Bibles: Nineteenth-Century Publishing and the British and Foregin Bible Society* (Cambridge University Press, Cambridge, 1991).

39   See Stephen Prickett, "From Novel to Bible: The Aestheticizing of Scripture," in Mark Knight and Thomas Woodman, eds, *Biblical Religion and the Novel, 1700–2000.* (Aldershot, Ashgate, 2006), pp. 13–24.

40   *Jude the Obscure*, p. 146.

41   H. Tennyson, *Alfred Lord Tennyson: A Memoir*, 2 volumes (Macmillan, London, 1897), vol. i, 308.

42   *The Works of John Ruskin*, eds. E. T. Cook and A. Wedderburn, 39 volumes (George Allen, London, 1903–12), vol. xxvii, p. 168.

43   *The Letters of Rudyard Kipling*, ed. Thomas Pinney, 6 volumes (Palgrave Macmillan, Basingstoke, 1990–2004), vol. I, p. 248.

44   Ibid., VI, p. 88.

45   Simon Eliot, *Some Patterns and Trends in British Publishing 1800–1919* (The Bibliographical Society, London, 1994), pp. 56–7, 132–3.

46   *Little Dorritt*, p. 30.

47   *Cometh up as a Flower*, p. 195.

48   See, Carpenter, *Imperial Bibles*, pp. 34–7.

49   M. O. W. Oliphant and F. R. Oliphant, *The Victorian Age of English Literature*, 2 volumes (Percival, London, 1892), vol. ii, p. 37.

50   G. Eliot, *The Mill on the Floss*, ed. Gordon S. Haight (Clarendon Press, Oxford, 1980), pp. 16, 227, 232–3.

51   See *Jude the Obscure*, p. 112.

52   E. Hodder, *The Life and Work of the Seventh Earl of Shaftesbury*, 3 volumes (Cassell, London, 1886), vol. ii, p. 10.

53   *Jude the Obscure*, pp. 82, 171, 289–93.

54   M. O. W. Oliphant, *Jerusalem the Holy City: Its History and Hope* (Macmillan, London, 1891), pp. xii–xiv.

55   See Marion Ann Taylor and Heather E. Weir, eds, *Let Her Speak For Herself: Nineteenth-Century Women Writing on Women in Genesis* (Baylor University Press, Waco, TX, 2006).

56   Victor Shea and William Whitla, eds, *Essays and Reviews: The 1860 Text and Its Reading* (University Press of Virginia, Charlottesville, 2000), pp. 482, 538.

57   C. Rossetti, *The Face of the Deep: A Devotional Commentary on the Apocalypse* (Society for Promoting Christian Knowledge, London, 1892), p. 12.

58   *The Complete Poems of Christina Rossetti*, ed. R. W. Crump, 3 volumes (Louisiana State University Press, Baton Rouge, 1979–90), vol. ii, pp. 281–2.

59   *The Letters of Edward Fitzgerald*, ed. A. M. Terhune and A. B. Terhune, 4 volumes (Princeton University Press, Princeton, NJ, 1980), vol. ii, p. 164.

60   See Simon Marsden, "'Vain are the thousand creeds': *Wuthering Heights*, the Bible and Liberal Protestantism," *Literature and Theology* 20:3 (2006), 236–50; David Klemm, "The Influence of German Criticism on English Literature"; and T. R. Wright, "The Victorians," in A. Hass, D. Jasper and E. Jay, eds, *The Oxford Handbook to English Literature and Theology* (Oxford University Press, Oxford, 2007), pp. 131–47, 148–63.

61   *Dearest Isa: Robert Browning's Letters to Isabella Blagden*, ed. E. C. McAleer (University of Texas Press, Austin, 1951), p. 180.

62   *The Complete Works of Matthew Arnold*, ed. R. H. Super, 11 volumes (Ann Arbor, University of Michigan Press), vol. vi, p. 370.

63   Clyde de L.Ryals, *Robert Elsmere*, ed. Clyde de L. Ryals (University of Nebraska Press, Lincoln, 1967), pp. 602–3.

64   William Hale White, *The Revolution in Tanner's Lane* (Oxford University Press, London, 1936), p. 164.

65   *Life and Work of Hardy*, p. 49.

66   E. Gosse, "Mr Hardy's Lyrical Poems," *Edinburgh Review* 207 (April 1918), 272; Reprinted in *Thomas Hardy, the Critical Heritage*, pp. 444–63. In 1905 Swinburne told Hardy that he had read "in a Scotch paper": "Swinburne planteth, Hardy watereth, and Satan giveth the increase": *Life and Work of Hardy*, p. 349.

67   See *Jude the Obscure*, pp. 84–5, 326, 392–3.

68   Ibid., pp. 195, 145–6.

69   See Joss Marsh, *Blasphemy, Culture and Literature in Nineteenth-Century England* (University of Chicago Press, Chicago, 1998).

CHAPTER 34
The Brownings

Kevin Mills

Elizabeth Barrett Browning

> *We read of a prophecy concerning "angels ascending and descending upon the son of man." What if this spiritual influx and afflux is beginning? (Huxley, 1929, p. 190)*

Raising a question about the fulfillment of prophecy, and envisioning human encounters with angels, the above quotation serves to suggest not only Elizabeth Barrett Browning's comfortable familiarity with the Bible, but also the kind of motifs that were attractive to her as a writer. For example, it would be easier to list her poems that *do not* mention angels than those that do, so common are they in her work. Her early poem "The Seraphim" (published in 1838) is an account of the crucifixion of Christ from the point of view of two angels who watch it from above the earth; from then on, angels make appearances in numerous poems such as "Lady Geraldine's Courtship," "The Runaway Slave at Pilgrim's Point," and "Sonnets from the Portuguese," to name but a few of the better-known works. Their presence is suggestive of the extent to which the natural world and human existence are interwoven in Barrett Browning's poetry with a higher reality – a world of spiritual essences derived from the Christian interpretation of the Bible.

Prophecy, taken in its broadest sense, is also recurrent in her work. We might think, for example, of the revelation made in the poem "A Vision of Poets," to a would-be poet by a mysterious woman (possibly an embodiment of the Church, given the repeated references to Church architecture – niched saints, altars, aisles, and an organ). Again, a certain prophetic tone derived from biblical models can be heard in the denunciations of corrupt authority in "The Cry of the Children" and "A Curse for a Nation," and in the declamatory style of the poems about Italy's fight for independence (from Austria) and unification, "Casa Guidi Windows," "Napolean III in Italy," and "Italy and the World":

> Each Christian nation shall take upon her
> The law of the Christian man in vast:

> The crown of the getter shall fall to the donor,
> And last shall be first while first shall be last,
> And to love best shall still be, to reign unsurpassed. ("Italy and the World," 28)

When, in 1853, Barrett Browning wrote in a letter to her sister the words quoted in the epigraph to this chapter, she was expressing an opinion about the mid-century growth in spiritualism – a trend that interested and excited her – and attempting to relate it to biblical prophecy. The precise connection that she was suggesting between the quoted text and spiritualism is not very clear, but her tendency to read the world around her in terms of biblical stories, images, themes, and texts is evident, a tendency that is marked in her poetry. It appears in many forms as the outcropping of a stratum of her consciousness that underlay her poetic imagination and that ran very deep. At times she offers interesting new lights on familiar Bible stories – the crucifixion in "The Seraphim," the Fall in "A Drama of Exile," the nativity in "The Virgin Mary to the Child Jesus," the raising from the dead of Lazarus in "The Weeping Saviour." At other times biblical references appear as rhetorical reinforcements for some observation or argument: Jesus' agony in Gethsemane provides an empathetic note in "A Thought for a Lonely Death-Bed," and again in "Two Sketches"; the biblical musicians Jubal, Asaph, Miriam, and King David provide a pattern of cultural development – an encouragement to build upon past achievements in "Casa Guidi Windows"; Peter's denial of Christ serves as a model of the treachery of the French to Italy in "A View Across the Roman Compagna."

The apparent ease with which the biblical text springs to mind in her letters and in her poetry might be taken to indicate that the writer was profoundly secure not only in her knowledge of the Bible but also in the Bible's unimpeachable authority. Such confidence in the Divine origin and content of the Scriptures was quickly coming to the end of its life when Barrett Browning was writing, and something of the intellectual and spiritual conflict caused by its demise appears, albeit obliquely, in her late verse novel *Aurora Leigh* (1856). In book V a student who has studied at Göttingen in Germany displays a rationalist turn of mind; he is dismissive of Christianity, and his conversation at one point is too irreligious for the ease of his interlocutor: " 'Soft!' Sir Blaise drew breath / As if it hurt him – 'Soft! no blasphemy, / I pray you' " (V.769–71). In the same book of *Aurora Leigh*, she alludes to the work of F. A. Wolf, a German classical scholar who denied the existence of Homer, arguing that the *Iliad* was a composite work collated in the sixth century BCE. Barrett Browning's fictional poet (Aurora Leigh) characterizes him (tellingly) as Judas, and the connection felt at the time to hold between Homeric criticism and biblical criticism is evident in the way she frames her worries about Wolf:

> Wolff's [*sic*] an atheist;
> And if the Iliad fell out, as he says,
> By mere fortuitous concourse of old songs,
> Conclude as much too for the universe. (V.1254–7)

If atheistic academic practices question the integrity of the classical tradition, subjecting to historical and textual criticism works as foundational to Western culture and as revered as those of Homer, then what is to keep such approaches from being used to question the Bible's account of creation? A line seems to have been crossed in Barrett Browning's estimation, and the critical spirit has trespassed on sacred territory.

Robert Browning, too, was troubled by such questions and explicitly engaged with Wolf's treatment of Homer in his poem "Development." Some six years before *Aurora Leigh* was written he had also attempted, in his "Christmas Eve" (1850), to dismiss the rejection of biblical truth, associating the new critical discourses with the University at Göttingen – the *alma mater* of Barrett Browning's fictional student. I will return to both of these poems. Such approaches as those belittled by both Elizabeth Barrett Browning and Robert Browning would eventually shake to its foundations the kind of confidence in the Bible's authority that the former often displays in her poetry, but in the Britain of the 1840s and 1850s Bible scholarship was conservative and largely ignorant of the work being done on the continent. The literary culture continued to deploy the Scriptures as a source of privileged ideas, images, stories, and moral and spiritual teachings.

So there was nothing unusual in Elizabeth Barrett Browning's lacing her work with quotations and citations of, or allusions to, Scripture. What distinguish Barrett Browning's use of the Bible (to some degree) from the conventional biblicism of the age are the intellectual prowess and the vibrant, imaginative relish with which she engaged with its content and used it as both a source and an interpretative framework in her writing. Her intellect and her commitment to the Bible are both made clear by Margaret Forster's biography: she indicates that Barrett Browning made a serious effort to learn enough Hebrew to be able to read the "Old Testament" in its original language (Forster, 1988, p. 67). There is a trace of such study in Barrett Browning's preface to the 1844 edition of her poems when she discusses (briefly) the meaning of the Hebrew word translated as "evening" in the English versions of Genesis, as a way of justifying the lengthy Eden twilight that occurs in "A Drama of Exile" (Barrett Browning, 1844, p. x).

The latter is a long dramatic poem, written in 1844, that attempts to deal with "the new and strange experience of the fallen humanity, as it went forth from Paradise into the wilderness; with a peculiar reference to Eve's allotted grief ... more expressible by a woman than a man" (Barrett Browning, 1844, p. viii). The whole episode is understood from within an expressly Christian worldview, not only in that Christ himself puts in an appearance toward the end of the poem, promising redemption to a fallen world, but also in that it is focused through St Paul's words: "For we know that the whole creation groaneth and travaileth in pain together until now" (Romans 8:22). Thus parts of the poem are taken up with a dialogue between the banished pair and the spirits of Earth who threaten severe recriminations for the curse that has descended upon them as a result of the Fall:

> the elements shall boldly
> All your dust to dust constrain.
> Unresistedly and coldly
> I will smite you with my rain.
> From the slowest of my frosts is no receding.

The angry and scornful spirits are confronted by an outraged Adam who insists that, being made in God's image, he and Eve retain a superiority over the rest of creation: "We are yet too high, O Spirits, for your disdain."

Eve's perspective is rather different, and it is this more than anything else that allows the poem to escape the shadow of Milton – a shadow that Barrett Browning addressed directly in the preface already quoted: "I had promised my prudence to shut close the gates of Eden between Milton and myself, so that none might say I dared to walk in his footsteps. He should be within, I thought, with his Adam and Eve unfallen or falling, – and I, without, with my EXILES, – I also am an exile" (Barrett Browning, 1844, p. viii). Such self-identification as an exile might remind us of Barrett Browning's sense of being outside of a poetic tradition dominated by male writers of whom Milton is the representative figure (Gilbert and Gubar, 1979, p. xvi), but it is also a poetic strategy that enables her to inhabit the character of the fallen Eve outside the Garden of Eden and to offer an account of her that is quite unlike anything attempted by Milton.

Eve expresses deep remorse and more than a little guilt for her role in the transgressive fruit eating. Above all, she seems to feel bad about what she has done to Adam: "I now confess myself," she tells him, "thy death / And thine undoer, as the snake was mine." When Adam's response is to acknowledge his own guilt and to praise God that his punishment did not involve taking away the one thing that really mattered to him – Eve herself – she feels that she has come into some kind of redemption: "Is it thy voice? / Or some saluting angel's – calling home / My feet into the garden?" Love turns out to matter more to Eve than did Paradise, or even *to be* Paradise. Love, in its various forms, would become Barrett Browning's abiding theme, and Eden an enduring image in her work.

In "Memory and Hope," the poet explores the relationship between these two human proclivities in terms of the Edenic origins of both:

> Back-looking Memory
> And prophet Hope both sprang from out the ground;
> One, where the flashing of Cherubic sword
> Fell sad, in Eden's ward, –
> And one, from Eden earth, within the sound
> Of the four rivers lapsing pleasantly,
> What time the promise after curse was said –
> "Thy seed shall bruise his head."

Memory appears to be a product of the Fall – a kind of curse that causes the speaker to focus longingly on a lost paradise. Hope seems to be defeated by it until the appearance of Christ in Eden, as in "A Drama of Exile." Hope then takes the form of renewed communion with God, the hearing again of "the Voice which talked / To Adam as He walked."

"The Lost Bower" offers a similar consolation. In this poem, Barrett Browning tells the story of a childhood memory of discovering a spot in the middle of a woodland where a linden tree, a hawthorn, and wood-ivy formed a kind of magical enclosure that seemed more like a cultivated garden than a product of wild nature. Here, on a carpet of moss, where may-leaves fluttered "like an angel" and the music of birdsong played, the speaker felt transported: "Mystic Presences of power / Had up-snatched me to the Timeless, then returned me to the Hour." If there are echoes here of a Wordsworthian sublime in the childhood encounter with nature, there are also biblical resonances in the loss of this idyllic garden: "The next morning, all had vanished, or my wandering missed the place." The poem ends with the Eden parallel made explicit:

> Till another open for me
> In God's Eden-land unknown,
> With an angel at the doorway,
> White with gazing at His Throne;
> And a saint's voice in the palm trees, singing – "All is lost ... and won!"

The poem, then, uses the childhood memory as an image of lost youth and innocence that is both personal and a matter of wider religious significance:

> For this loss it did prefigure
> Other loss of better good,
> When my soul, in spirit-vigour,
> And in ripened womanhood,
> Fell from visions of more beauty than an arbour in a wood.

The word "Fell" – capitalized at the head of the last line of the stanza – makes its own connection, and serves to align "The Lost Bower" with those other treatments of Eden in Barrett Browning's poems. Again Eden is connected with both memory and hope, with both loss and its ultimate remediation.

That sense of loss balanced by hope of restoration is the product of seeing Eden as both history and typology – a mode of biblical interpretation that dominated Christian hermeneutics in Britain until later in the Victorian period when George Eliot began to translate works of German Higher Criticism into English. In Barrett Browning's Eden poems the literal understanding of the Creation and Fall narratives in Genesis is complemented by an interpretation that views Eden as a foreshadowing of the New Jerusalem described in the book of Revelation – the apocalyptic regaining of paradise. Thus, in "The Lost Bower" the Eden reference with which the poem closes turns the angel who in Genesis is said to guard the entrance to Eden after Adam and Eve's expulsion into a figure of welcome at the door to the New Jerusalem – characterized as "God's Eden-land unknown."

The vision of Heaven described in Revelation turns up in a number of Barrett Browning poems such as "Isobel's Child," "Earth and Her Praisers," "Sounds," and "Heaven and Earth." In "Isobel's Child" we are given a sentimental account of a mother praying for her sick child's recovery. Childhood innocence and the inevitability of losing it are once again linked with Eden:

> A solemn thing it is to me
> To look upon a babe that sleeps;
> Wearing in its spirit-deeps
> The undeveloped mystery

> Of our Adam's taint and woe,
> Which, when they developed be,
> Will not let it slumber so!

Eventually the child wakes up and gazes into its mother's eyes. In doing so, the child manages to communicate its desire to die, to be released from the mother's prayers that hold its body and soul together. Its lengthy plea for release is based upon a vision of Heaven drawn directly from the Apocalypse, received while asleep – a vision that makes it want to leave behind its earthly life:

> Oh, the sweet life-tree that drops
> Shade like light across the river
> Glorified in its for-ever
> Flowing from the Throne!
>
> ...
>
> Mother, mother, let me go
> Toward the Face that looketh so.
> Through the mystic, winged Four
> Whose are inward, outward eyes
> Dark with light of mysteries,
> And the restless evermore
> "Holy, holy, holy," – through
> The sevenfold Lamps that burn in view
> of cherubim and seraphim, –
> Through the four-and-twenty crowned
> Stately elders, white around,
> Suffer me to go to Him!

Having understood the plea, Isobel changes her prayer and lets her child die. It is a poem that feels far removed from contemporary consciousness, not least because the biblical text does not inspire us with the kind of confidence that is evident in Isobel's willingness to "loose [her] prayer and let [the child] go." To a modern reader, the act may seem callous, or at least less than motherly, but the opposite effect is intended: the mother's act of release is self-sacrificing, and based upon what she sincerely believes to be her child's best interests. Such an implicit trust – one in which life itself is at stake – not only in the veracity or trustworthiness of an ancient text, but also in the apparently unproblematical literal interpretation of so difficult, stange, and symbolistic a text as the Book of Revelation, is profoundly at odds with modern sensibilities.

Yet the Book of Revelation is almost as important to Barrett Browning's poetry as the story of Adam and Eve. Present in some form in many poems, it is frequently quoted and alluded to in Barrett Browning's most important work – *Aurora Leigh*. John Schad (1999, p. 149) writes: "The poem not only concludes with St John's vision, but also includes at least sixteen further references or allusions to Revelation." It is interesting to note, then, that interwoven with these references are almost as many allusions to Adam, Eve, and the Garden of Eden: I have counted at least fourteen. This interweaving of biblical ends and beginnings in her poetry seems to be part of a design intended to resist what she perceived to be the materialism of the age. Romney Leigh, Aurora's cousin, concludes:

> Ay, materialist
> The age's name is. God Himself, with some,
> Is apprehended as the bare result
> Of what His hand materially has made,
> Expressed in such an algebraic sign
> Called God. (VIII.635–40)

Not only is God reduced to a theorem by the age of expanding science and technology, but he is in danger of disappearing from nature altogether, a victim of "our modern thinker who turns back / The strata ... granite, limestone, coal, and clay, / Concluding coldly with, 'Here's law! where's God?"' (V.1117–19). The discoveries of geology that threatened the reliability of the biblical account of creation early in the nineteenth century are in view here. But the potential loss of sacred ground is also linked, both metaphorically and (in Barrett Browning's view) metaphysically, with the loss of innocence encoded and foreshadowed in the exile from Eden. Dorothy Mermin makes a similar point:

> In her poems, to accept God's will is to renounce earthly happiness, just as the hope of heaven replaces nostalgia for Eden; but since she does not doubt that happiness is irrevocably lost and earth's beauty just a pale reflection of heaven's, there's no need to struggle. ... Paradise (in whatever earthly form, real or mythic, remembered or imaginary) is easily relinquished in God's name. (Mermin, 1989, p. 70)

The ease with which Paradise is relinquished in Mermin's interpretation is, perhaps, overstated: if Paradise had no residual power to give rise to longing in Barrett Browning, then why did she continually return to it in her poems? A slightly more complex assessment is called for, one that does not involve writing off earth's beauty as a "pale reflection of heaven's," so much as celebrating it as imbued with the promise of its own renewal. Interweaving the image of fall with visions of apocalyptic renewal, such as that with which *Aurora Leigh* ends, keeps the way open for continued engagement with the natural world as an index of the divine: we can see that "Earth's crammed with heaven, / And every common bush afire with God" (VII.821–2), because despite our exile – whether understood as being from Eden or from youthful innocence – "the old world waits the time to be renewed ... HE shall make all new" (IX.942–9).

Robert Browning

In 1860 – the year before Elizabeth Barrett Browning died – a volume entitled *Essays and Reviews* was published. The contributions from a number of scholars brought to a wider reading public than had previously been cognizant of developments in biblical criticism a range of issues, hypotheses, and discoveries that were transforming understanding of the Bible – the history of its production, the mythological sources of its stories and imagery, the thinking underlying its interpretation, and the evidences for Christian belief. The preface to the book expressed a desire to "illustrate the advantage derivable to the cause of religious and moral truth" from a reverent and "becoming" deployment of the latest ideas of academics and theologians. In 1864, in a poem called "Gold Hair," Robert Browning noted the public impact of the book: "The candid incline to surmise of late / That the Christian faith proves false, I find; / For our Essays-and-Reviews debate / Begins to tell on the public mind."

Biblical criticism had been issuing a variety of challenges to received opinion on the validity of Christian readings of the Bible at least since Richard Simon's seventeenth-century questioning of the long-held assumption that Moses was the sole author of the Pentateuch (the first five books of the Bible) (Prickett, 1991, pp. 136–8). In the early years of the nineteenth century, scientific investigations and discoveries, especially in geology and paleontology, had given rise to new sources of doubt about the Bible's reliability as a guide to the origins and age of the earth and of life – doubts that were made more immediate by the publication of Charles Darwin's *The Origin of Species* (1859). Alongside the science, biblical criticism took on a demythologizing character, questioning the possibility of the miraculous, the supernatural, the divine interventions in history that were recorded in the Bible. Among the most significant of the works in this field was David Strauss's *Life of Jesus*, translated into English (from the German) by Marian Evans (George Eliot) in 1846. This work depicted Christianity as essentially mythological – based in neither historical fact nor deliberate fiction, but in imaginative symbols that embodied experience, feeling, and religious perceptions.

Browning's attitude to the Bible was informed, though not entirely shaped, by the wide-ranging and deeply felt debates of his day about the validity of biblical history, the sources of the biblical text, and the implications of biblical criticism for Christian beliefs. His engagement with the Bible, less extensive than Elizabeth's, tended to focus on these new approaches to the study of the Bible, and was filtered through a personal interest based on a thoughtful Christian faith that was not immune to doubt, as John Woolford observes:

> The Higher Criticism touched Browning on the raw precisely because it confirmed an existing dubiety: he had assembled a massive collection of different Bibles, learned Hebrew, gathered thirteen works of biblical criticism; all, one suspects, to try to filter out the pure white truth from these prismatic textual variants. (Armstrong, 1974, p. 32)

While other Victorian poets, such as Elizabeth Barrett Browning, Alfred Tennyson, Matthew Arnold, Arthur Hugh Clough, and Mathilde Blind, alluded to the Bible, allowed its language to echo through their lines, and even turned the contemporaneous crisis of faith into poetry, what marks out Browning's approach is that he often confronted biblical criticism directly in his verse. To some degree he shared with Tennyson a chastened faith – a continuing commitment to Christianity despite the counter-discourses that threatened its credibility. His attitude can be contrasted sharply with the religious fervor evident in the poetry of Gerard Manley Hopkins and Christina Rossetti, with the melancholy resignation of Arnold, and with the febrile rejection of faith in the work of Clough. The contrast with Clough is particularly pointed in their divergent references to the biblical criticism of Strauss.

Clough's "Epi-Strauss-ium" takes David Strauss's *Life of Jesus* to have rendered the Gospels' portrait of Christ obsolete, so that "Matthew and Mark and Luke and holy John" are said to be "Evanished all and gone!" In their place Strauss offers a clearer, if more lowly, picture – it is as if the stained glass windows of the church had been replaced with "windows plainly glassed." If the Gospels are defunct, it says, well at least "The place of worship ... with light / Is, if less richly, more sincerely bright." And now, of course, one can see out of the window too – one is no longer constrained to view the world through the lens of religious belief.

Browning was far less willing to let Strauss have things all his own way. He argued the case with him (and with the so-called Higher Criticism that he represented) in "Christmas Eve." The poem, shot through with biblical allusions and quotations, dramatizes a contrast between two extremes in Christian observance – the evangelical and the intellectual – each characterized according to its treatment of the Bible. As the poem opens, the speaker enters a little chapel to escape from the rain, and finds himself in the middle of a service attended by an array of lower class, almost Dickensian, characters and presided over by an enthusiastic interpreter of Scripture in an evangelical vein. The sermon is criticized by the narrative voice for its inept interpretative procedures:

> No sooner our friend had got an inkling
> Of treasure hid in the Holy Bible,
>
> ...
>
> Than he handled it so, in fine irreverence,
> As to hug the book of books to pieces:
> And, a patchwork of chapters and texts in severance,
> Not improved by the private dog's-ears and creases,
> Having clothed his own soul with, he'd fain see equipt yours, –
> So tossed you again your Holy Scriptures.

Underlying the comic tone that turns an untutored familiarity with the biblical text – its piecemeal deployment showing scant regard for either methodology or context – into "hug[ging] the book of books to pieces," and that rhymes "equipt yours" with "Scriptures," is a serious worry about the use and misuse of Scripture. In fact, that tricksy rhyme not only raises a smile, but also serves to suggest something of the contortion of language inflicted on the book of books by the preacher's sermonizing. The twisted syntax of the lines serves the same purpose. Before long the speaker finds such mishandling of the Bible quite unbearable:

> 'Twas too provoking!
> My gorge rose at the nonsense and stuff of it;
> So, saying like Eve when she plucked the apple,
> "I wanted a taste, and now there's enough of it."
> I flung out of the little chapel.

Comically mirroring the evangelical preacher's fondness for taking biblical texts out of context, Browning misappropriates the story of Eve's temptation – inventing a quotation in the process – as a wildly implausible pretext for leaving the meeting. While the poem's speaker appreciates both "the zeal" and "the aspiration" of the preacher, he laments not only his arbitrary patchwork of decontextualized quotations (prooftexting), but also the fact that such preaching serves only to confirm in their beliefs those already convinced, and to repel those who may be in need of convincing.

The chapel scene is contrasted with a lecture delivered on another Christmas Eve, by a "hawk-nosed high-cheek-boned Professor." While the physical description and the location (the University of Göttingen) are unrelated to him, the views expressed by the professor are pretty much those of Strauss:

> ... the penman's prejudice, expanding
> Fact into fable fit for the clime,
> Had, by slow and sure degrees, translated it
> Into this myth, this Individuum, –
> Which, when reason had strained and abated it
> Of foreign matter, left, for residuum,
> A Man!

Demythologizing the Gospels – showing how their content was shaped by the cosmogony and belief systems of their time – leaves us with a portrait of Jesus not as God incarnate, but as a mere man – albeit a good one. The speaker sees this as emptying the Christian message; to reduce Christ to a moral teacher is to deprive Christianity of its very air supply – to leave the believer in a vacuum. Thus Browning attempts to refute the case – or at least to raise objections to it – in a number of ways. First, he argues (somewhat naively) that while millions believe the Christian message, only one man – the unprepossessing Professor – has the necessary ability and inclination to demythologize it. Second, he argues, if Christ were no more than a good man, then from where did he derive his goodness and in what way does it make him superior to us? Then again, the case continues: if Christ were merely the discoverer rather than the vehicle of God's goodness, why is he worshipped? Finally, Browning asserts, Christ did not ask us to believe in his message, but to believe in *him*.

He makes a similar case in "Fears and Scruples," arguing that although the letters he has received from a friend have been called "forgery from A to Z," and the friend's absence and refusal to prove his existence are puzzling, the speaker's love of his friend is undiminished and that is ultimately what matters. The poem ends by identifying the absent friend with God, and, by extension, the letters denounced as forgeries can be seen to refer to the Bible, traduced by practitioners of the Higher Criticism.

It is tempting to suggest that Browning here, and in "Christmas Eve," stands convicted of the very charge he lays against the evangelicals: such arguments as those adduced in defense of Christian belief would convince no one not already predisposed to accept them; they are, after all, arguments that presume rather than establish the truth of Christianity. Each one could, in fact, be turned into an argument *against* belief. On the other hand, it has to be remembered that Browning was not writing a scholarly treatise; he was responding imaginatively and artistically to the emotional, psychological, and religious content of an academic, theological discourse. William O. Raymond suggests that, in doing so, he was actually adopting a kind of populist stance: "The arguments used to refute the conclusions of the Göttingen professor, in *Christmas Eve*, are those of the ordinary "Christian" man, rather than those of the theological expert" (Raymond, 1965, p. 29).

"Christmas Eve" ends with the speaker returning to the opening scene and confessing his preference for the passionate stupidity of the evangelicals over the dried up and loveless intellectual approach to the Bible. In this it has something in common with "Development" – a poem about the way in which scholarship can destroy the naive reader's engagement with, and enjoyment of, literature. It tells of Browning's gradual, developmental encounter with Homer's *Iliad*, from being told the story by his father at the age of five, through reading it in Pope's translation a few years later, and then learning to read it in the original Greek: "The very thing itself, the actual words." The excitement and passion of the process are then undermined by the appearance of the critical work of the German scholar F. A. Wolf, who argued that "there never was any Troy at all, / Neither Besiegers nor Beseieged, – nay, worse, – / No actual Homer, no authentic text." Such concerns plagued the reading of both Homer and the Bible: both kinds of critical material came "unsettling one's belief."

Ultimately Browning's overriding religious concern is with love as the heart of the Christian message; this is the burden not only of "Christmas Eve," but also of poems such as "Saul," "Karshish," "Cleon," and "A Death in the Desert." These poems take the form of dramatic monologues in which the poet imaginatively inhabits the personae of biblical figures (in much the same way Elizabeth had in "The Virgin Mary to the Child Jesus") or of fictional characters who come into contact with early believers such as Lazarus and St Paul. Like "Christmas Eve" they are often concerned with issues of the interpretation of ancient texts – a theme that is most brilliantly considered in Browning's greatest poetic work, *The Ring and the Book*. The latter deals not with the Bible but with a little two-hundred-year-old yellow book he found in a Florence market stall, containing documents from the trial of Count Guido Franceschini for the murder of his wife and her adoptive parents. The poem consists of a series of dramatic monologues, each discussing the case from a different point of view. Not only is it rich in biblical references, with each viewpoint citing carefully chosen Scriptures to show their case in its best light, it also suggests something of the conflict of interpretations that raged in Victorian culture and found expression in the publication of *Essays and Reviews*.

The Ring and the Book makes clear that Browning was all too aware that the Bible was a contested site, not only because the history and conditions of its production were coming under ever closer critical scrutiny, but also because its original meanings and contexts could not be recovered. This meant that it was subject to many different interpretations and could be used to justify widely divergent, even opposed opinions. Thus, to his defenders, Guido appears as Adam deceived by Eve (Guido's wife Pompilia), as Job tested by God, or even as St Paul fleeing Damascus under threat of persecution, while to his accusers he is a devil who invites in other devils (Matthew 12:43–5), or Judas betraying his wife with a kiss. Such strong contrasts can be sensed in other Browning poems too: his critique of predestinarian and antinomian excesses in

"Johannes Agricola in Meditation" shows one extreme, the urbane sophistication and rhetorical nicety of "Bishop Blougram's Apology" another. What is at stake in *The Ring and the Book* is the extent to which such interpretative frames put the truth beyond reach, as David Shaw points out:

> *The Ring and the Book* dramatizes Schiller's aphorism that the "truth still lives in fiction." The truth about the past is precisely what is lost. Every frame around this loss is a fiction, a story we construct over a missing history. Since it is impossible to penetrate the innermost core of this history, Browning must keep the story going, allowing the multiple frames to repeat themselves endlessly in their acknowledged incompleteness. (Shaw, 1987, p. 66)

That Browning sees the necessity for such incessant reframings of history as a problem for Christian readers of the Bible is evident in the way the interpretation of Scripture feeds into the competing accounts of the circumstances that led to the trial, and in the fact that it is used in a variety of inconsistent and partisan ways. As Dominus Hyacinthus (Guido's defence counsel) cynically puts it:

> It's hard: you have to plead before these priests
> And poke at them with Scripture, or you pass
> For heathen and, what's worse, for ignorant
> O' the quality o' the Court and what it likes
> By way of illustration of the law.

Here the Bible is a mere instrument – a catalogue of seemingly authoritative quotations, rhetorical figures, and reusable pretexts, a repertoire of cases, characters, and situations that can be drawn upon in the service of just about any conceivable purpose, and its overuse renders it little more than a kind of legal jargon adopted as badge of social acceptance and cohesion. In other words, it has been detached from its historical and religious moorings to such an extent that its power as sacred Scripture is lost, or at least devalued.

The loss of biblical truth with the passage of time is dealt with powerfully in "A Death in the Desert," a poem in which Browning takes the reader to the scene of St John's last hours of life. The immediate context for the poem was the *Essays and Reviews* debate mentioned in "Gold Hair," and it revisits some of the issues discussed in "Christmas Eve." John's imminent death is viewed by himself and those around him as of great significance for Christianity, as he is the last person alive to have been an eyewitness to the earthly ministry of Jesus: with his death, the episode begins to slip into history and to become subject to the problems of reinterpretation and doubt. "How will it be," John wonders, "when none more saith 'I saw'?" He imagines that with the passage of time doubts will strengthen, even as to his own existence:

> ... unborn people in strange lands,
> Who say – I hear said or conceive they say –
> "Was John at all, and did he say he saw?
> Assure us, ere we ask what we might see!"
>
> And how shall I assure them?

John's question is born of his sense of his own decrepitude, and an awareness that once he is gone his word will be reduced to a vulnerable text to be picked over and demythologized by skeptical minds. He foresees that as the miracles of Jesus slip further into history, belief will become more of a problem, making it increasingly difficult for readers of his Gospel to believe his account of what he has witnessed.

Browning cleverly brings John's worry home by using framing devices that keep the dying disciple's words at a distance from the reader. Adam Roberts neatly sums up the complex textuality of the poem:

> The effect of the framing device is to introduce a sense of distance. In fact, John's speech is embedded within several frames – it is reported by Xanthus, who in turn is reported by Pamphylax, who in his turn is edited and presented to us by the unnamed narrator. This technique is wholly appropriate to the subject of Browning's poem. (Woolford 1998, p. 47)

So the poem serves as kind of enactment of the very processes of history that John foresees – it is already a document that has been reframed and recontextualized. This is made all the more obvious by the addition of two further parenthetical notes – one a theological gloss on John's doctrine of the soul, based on the comments of "Theotypas," the other a note added by "Cerinthus" – a gnostic comment that also serves as a "foreshadowing" of Higher Critical attitudes.

John's answer to the critics whose work he foresees is, once again, the power of love to transcend argumentation and the gathering of textual and historical evidence, as Donald Thomas notes:

> Browning makes St John answer directly, as if specifically countering the contributors to *Essays and Reviews* as well as Strauss and Renan. With the passing of the contemporary witnesses, the "absolute blaze" of historical truth is dead. The texts which remain will yield it only if read with the love which is the essence of Christian faith. (Thomas, 1982, p. 212)

In such a commitment, as in so many other things, Robert Browning and Elizabeth Barrett Browning were at one.

References

Armstrong, Isobel, ed. (1974) *Robert Browning*. Bell, London.
Barrett Browning, Elizabeth (1844) *The Poems*. Frederick Warne and Co., London.
Forster, Margaret (1988) *Elizabeth Barrett Browning*. Chatto and Windus, London.
Gilbert, Sandra M. and Gubar, Susan, eds (1979) *Shakespeare's Sisters: Feminist Essays on Women Poets*. Indiana University Press, Bloomington.
Huxley, Leonard, ed. (1929) *Elizabeth Barrett Browning: Letters to Her Sister, 1846–1859*. John Murray, London.
Mermin, Dorothy (1989) *Elizabeth Barrett Browning: The Origins of a New Poetry*. University of Chicago Press, Chicago.

Prickett, Stephen, ed. (1991) *Reading the Text: Biblical Criticism and Literary Theory*. Blackwell, Oxford.

Raymond, William O. (1965) *The Infinite Moment and Other Essays in Robert Browning*. University of Toronto Press, Toronto.

Schad, John (1999) *Victorians in Theory: From Derrida to Browning*. New York: Manchester University Press, Manchester.

Shaw, W. David (1987) *The Lucid Veil: Poetic Truth and the Victorian Age*. Athlone Press, London.

Thomas, Donald (1982) *Robert Browning: A Life Within Life*. Weidenfeld and Nicolson, London.

Woolford, John, ed. (1998) *Robert Browning in Contexts*. Wedgestone Press, Winfield.

Further Reading

Armstrong, Isobel (1993) *Victorian Poetry: Poetry. Poetics and Politics*. Routledge, London.

Bloom, Harold and Munich, Adrienne, eds (1979) *Robert Browning: A Collection of Critical Essays*. Prentice Hall, Englewood Cliffs, NJ.

Bristow, Joseph, ed. (1987) *The Victorian Poet: Poetics and Persona*. Croom Helm, London.

Bristow, Joseph (1992) *Robert Browning*. Harvester Wheatsheaf, Hemel Hempstead.

Cosslett, Tess (1996) *Victorian Women Poets*. Longman, London.

Harrison, Antony H. (1998) *Victorian Poets and the Politics of Culture: Discourse and Ideology*. University Press of Virginia, Charlottesville.

Hawlin, Stefan (2002) *The Complete Critical Guide to Robert Browning*. Routledge, London.

Leighton, Angela (1986) *Elizabeth Barrett Browning*. Harvester, Brighton.

Leighton, Angela (1992) *Victorian Women Poets: Writing Against the Heart*. Harvester Wheatsheaf, New York.

Ward, Maisie (1969) *Robert Browning and His World*. Cassell, London.

CHAPTER 35
Alfred Tennyson

Kirstie Blair

When Hallam Tennyson came to discuss *In Memoriam* in his *Memoir*, he paused to assess Tennyson's relation to the Bible in general:

> That my father was a student of the Bible, those who have read "In Memoriam" know. He also eagerly read all notable works within his reach relating to the Bible, and traced with deep interest such fundamental truths as underlie the great religions of the world. He hoped that the Bible would be more and more studied by all ranks of people, and expounded simply by their teachers; for he maintained that the religion of a people could never be founded on mere moral philosophy: and that it could only come home to them in the simple, noble thoughts and facts of a Scripture like ours. (H. Tennyson, 1897, I, p. 308)

Passages such as this imply that Tennyson knew of and was engaged with the major nineteenth-century debates about the Bible, even if he himself did not necessarily sympathize with the complexities of these debates. The repetition of "simply ... simple" suggests that Hallam wishes to emphasize his father's (and his own) straightforward and implicitly democratic relation to Scripture. As opposed to the still-current view that only unquestioning belief in the Bible as God's revealed truth was acceptable, Tennyson was a liberal thinker who supported biblical study. Stating that such study should be available to "all ranks of people," however, implies a rejection of the more abstruse kinds of biblical analysis practiced by historical and linguistic critics of the period. To describe the Scriptures as full of "simple, noble thoughts and facts" seems a less innocuous statement if the emphasis falls on the final word, given how trenchantly the "facts" of the Bible had been questioned in the preceding decades. Hallam Tennyson clearly has a stake in securing his father's reputation as, if not a wholly orthodox nineteenth-century Christian (note the expressed interest in *all* the great religions of the world), at least an unimpeachable lover of the Bible. But as this extract demonstrates, any comment on a writer's relation to the Bible from this period is inevitably fraught with the tensions stemming from almost a century of heated debate, and even the simplest responses to Scripture take on complex connotations from their historical context.

Tennyson is not at first glance a poet who had a special or peculiar relation to the Bible. Browning, in poetry, and Arnold, in prose, directly involved themselves in what Bishop Colenso (1865, p. 5) described as "one of the great questions of the time, of which *this* generation must give account to future ages," the question of inspiration and of the literal truth or otherwise of biblical accounts. Christina Rossetti and other contemporaries wrote poetry and prose that showed an intensely personal commitment to scriptural interpretation and was steeped in biblical allusion in every line. Tennyson, in contrast, left behind few comments on his reading of "notable works ... relating to the Bible," does not appear to have been particularly excited by the debates that surrounded him, and, although he frequently alluded to the Bible in his poems, arguably did not generally accord these allusions more status than his equally frequent allusions to the classics or to earlier English poetry. He considered various projects relating to the Bible, such as writing a metrical or prose version of the Book of Job, but never began them (H. Tennyson, 1897, II, p. 52). None of his poems are included in David Jasper and Stephen Prickett's standard guide to the Bible and literature, and, in comparison to a writer like Rossetti, very little critical discussion exists on his specific engagement with the Bible. The frustration felt by critics who have tried to assess Tennyson's religious opinions, only to be thwarted by the limited and often contradictory evidence available, applies here too. As Alan Hill observes ruefully in his excellent study of Wordsworth and Tennyson's thinking on form and faith, "It is impossible to detect a consistent pattern in [Tennyson's] scattered remarks, and under stress his unstructured intuitions tended to fall apart altogether" (Hill, 1997, p. 38).

Yet Tennyson's relation to the Bible is vital perhaps precisely because such "unstructured intuitions" were more likely to mirror the thoughts of Victorian Christians of all classes and denominations than the subtler and more learned effects created by, say, Browning's "An Epistle Containing the Strange Medical Experiences of Karshish." Tennyson's status as an immensely popular poet and sage was in part founded on his ability to use biblical language and cadences for maximum appeal in *In Memoriam* (1850) and elsewhere. As I discuss below, it is often in his sentimental verse, in poems that can seem embarrassing to the modern reader, that biblical quotations take on the greatest affective power. The fact that such allusions tend to be consciously placed in the mouths of "simple" people highlights their popularity and availability. By adhering to a loose if strongly felt notion of the Bible as simultaneously a resplendent literary text, worth reading in the Authorized Version if only "for the sake of the grand English in which it is written" (H. Tennyson, 1897, I, p. 308n), and an inspirational account of human suffering and redemption that offered hope of an afterlife, Tennyson ensured that his poetry would be in sympathy with writers holding wildly differing views. Indeed, Tennyson's poetry is often important with regard to nineteenth-century biblical criticism not because the poetry engages with the criticism, but because the criticism engages with the poetry. *In Memoriam*, in particular, was appropriated equally readily by opposing camps. F. D. Maurice's controversial *Theological Essays* (1853), dedicated to Tennyson, cites the prologue to *In Memoriam* as part of an argument that men should not "let the faith in an actual Son of God be absorbed into any religious or philosophical theories or abstractions" (Maurice, 1853, p. 89). Tennyson's "We have but faith: we cannot know" (Prologue line 21 in Tennyson, 1987) is used to justify Maurice's claim

that contemporary debates about biblical inspiration were pointless and even dangerous. The same passage, however, was also cited by John William Colenso at the start
of part V of his notorious *The Pentateuch and Book of Joshua Critically Examined*. Colenso
quotes four stanzas from the prologue as an epigraph, starting from:

> Our little systems have their day;
>   They have their day and cease to be:
>   They are but broken lights of thee,
> And thou, O Lord, art more than they. (Colenso, 1865, p. 361, lines 17–20)

Here, *In Memoriam* backs up Colenso's argument that proving the logical and historical inconsistencies of parts of the Old Testament is God's will, by demonstrating that
the Bible is a "broken light," a humanly inspired system that can be rejected without
losing God's presence and love. In addition, Tennyson's "Let knowledge grow from
more to more" (Prologue, line 25) is implicitly read as supporting Colenso's quest
by giving intellectual enquiry a spiritual purpose. This is more or less the opposite of
Maurice's take on *In Memoriam*. Maurice and Colenso, once close friends, were irrevocably alienated by the publication of Colenso's research. Tennyson, as we shall see, was
substantially in sympathy with Maurice's viewpoint. But that did not prevent writers
like Colenso from admiring and appropriating his work. Indeed, in 1865 Mrs Woolner
reported to Emily Tennyson that Colenso was very disappointed to miss meeting Tennyson at her home:

> He said that your husband was the only man he had wished to see before leaving England,
> as he thought him the man who was doing more than any other to frame the Church of
> the future. (H. Tennyson, 1897, II, p. 23)

Whether he wished to be regarded as a religious teacher or not, the choice had already
been made for Tennyson. Simply by being the author of *In Memoriam*, his status as a
poet whose work had special relevance to contemporary religious controversies, including those surrounding the Bible, was assured.

As the child of a well educated and intellectual clergyman, Tennyson would have
had a certain familiarity with these controversies from an early age. George Tennyson
owned sixteen editions of the Bible or separate books of the Bible dating from 1622
onwards, in Hebrew, Latin, Greek, French, and English, several of which are annotated
in his or Tennyson's hand: Tennyson himself later possessed nine copies of the Bible in
English alone (Campbell, 1971, pp. 3, 31). Although George Tennyson's library contained relatively little higher criticism, he did own Robert Lowth's annotated translation of Isaiah from 1762, one of the most successful and well known early examples in
the field. In Somersby, the education of Tennyson and his brothers included translations from Hebrew, Latin, and Greek and study of the Scriptures as well as the classics.
As a young man, then, he would already have been aware of the difficulties of biblical
translation – and later in life, he continued to read various translations and make his
own, commenting with interest (and disappointment) on the New Authorized Version
(H. Tennyson, 1897, I, p. 322). When Tennyson went to Trinity College, Cambridge,

moreover, he came into contact with tutors who were very familiar with the latest advances in German Higher Criticism. Connop Thirlwall, a Fellow of Trinity who was in residence for the first year of Tennyson's study, 1827–8, had recently translated and introduced Schleiermacher's important essay on St Luke's Gospel. Julius Hare, classics tutor at Trinity and an ardent reader of Wordsworth and Coleridge, besides owning an impressive library of German texts, collaborated with Thirlwall on translating Niebuhr's history of Rome. These two men, in conjunction with William Whewell, "carried German biblical criticism to the Trinity common room" (Flynn, 1979, p. 705) at a time when few in England were familiar with its methods and arguments.

Unlike later writers, however, Hare and Thirlwall were relatively cautious and defensive about the impact of Higher Criticism on the Bible. Julius Hare and his brother Frederick wrote in their popular compilation *Guesses at Truth*: "In reading the apostolical epistles, we should bear in mind that they are not scientific treatises armed at all points against carpers and misconceivers" (Hare and Hare, 1827, p. 184). They argue that "Were the purportings of the Bible to be a revelation false, it would still be the truest book that ever was written" (p. 132). Thirlwall's introduction to Schleiermacher, which at over 150 pages long is an impassioned and densely argued engagement with recent German theology, is similarly hesitant about the implications of Schleiermacher's deconstruction of Luke. He circumvents the problem of revelation – the issue that if the notion that the biblical writers were directly inspired by and channeling God's words is false, then the whole truth of the Bible and Christianity must thereby be called into question – by subtly reinterpreting "inspiration" as a more general idea that the Gospel writers were "filled with that spirit, which was to lead into all truth" (Schleiermacher, 1825, p. xviii). The essential "pure and bright" whole of the Gospel, Thirlwall argues, is only occasionally "broken and obscured" by human fallibility (p. xviii).

Such appeals to the essential "truth" of the Bible, in the light of doubts about its historical accuracy and internal consistency, bear a notable resemblance to Arthur Hallam's writings of the period. His accounts show the extent to which the young men of the Apostles were engaged with these ideas. In fact, Hallam already knew of Hare when he arrived in Cambridge in 1828, writing to Gladstone, "His brother is an Oxford man: I knew him well in Italy; and no-one can know him without liking and being struck by him," and recommending *Guesses at Truth* (Hallam, 1981, p. 244). Hallam's father disapproved of Hare's influence, and was apparently even more disapproving of Hallam's rapidly growing interest in Coleridge's prose writings. By 1829, Hallam was reading Thirlwall and Hare on Niebuhr and had taken up German. He looked set to become a model young scholar of the Higher Criticism. Yet in "Theodicaea Novissima," the essay that Tennyson admired enough to argue for its inclusion in Hallam's *Remains*, Hallam defends biblical truth against all comers. He states that he is "determined" to believe that the Bible is "essentially true" and "divinely authorized" (Hallam, 1943, p. 201), if perhaps not divinely authored, and includes a passionate and defiant paragraph on the vital centrality of the Bible to faith:

Between the opposing weight of reasonings, equally inalienable from the structure of our intellect, the scale hung with doubtful inclination, until the Bible turned it. I hesitate not

> to say that I derive from Revelation a conviction of Theism, which without that assistance
> would have been but a dark and ambiguous hope. I see that the Bible fits into every fold of
> the human heart. I am a man, and I believe it to be God's book because it is man's book.
> (Hallam, 1943, p. 201)

Hallam makes the Bible's human provenance a selling point, and rests its importance
on the sense that it conveys truths felt in the heart rather than logical reasoning.
Comments such as these may also owe something to Hallam's reading of the Scottish evangelical writer Thomas Erskine, whose book *The Unconditional Freeness of the
Gospel* he presented to Emily Tennyson (Hallam, 1981, p. 447n). Erskine's emphasis
on the importance of love as central to Christianity has been noted as a source for
Hallam's similar emphasis in "Theodicaea" (see Flynn, 1979, p. 719), but perhaps
equally important is Erskine's insistence on a reverent reading of the Bible:

> We are so accustomed to the sight of a Bible, that it ceases to be a miracle to us. ... But there
> is nothing in the world like it, or comparable to it. The sun in the firmament is nothing
> to it, if it be really – what it assumes to be – an actual direct communication from God to
> man. Take up your Bible with this idea, and look at it, and wonder at it. (Erskine, 1828,
> pp. 226–7)

Although there is some ambiguity here in "what it assumes to be," hinting at the
question of whether the Bible was directly communicated or not, Erskine is definite
throughout this work on the Bible as full of "the idea and feeling of God" (p. 78). Such
language suggests that even if the Bible were proven full of historical and scientific
inaccuracies, it should still be respected and reverenced. Hallam was clearly more with
Erskine than with Schleiermacher.

As we know from Hallam's letters, Tennyson was reading Erskine in 1831 on his
strong recommendation (Hallam, 1981, p. 446). A later recollection by Benjamin
Jowett suggests that Tennyson also had knowledge of the German critical works circulating in Cambridge at the time:

> Once he said to me "I hate learning," by which I understood him to mean that he hated
> the minutiae of criticism compiled by the Dryasdusts. They seemed to him to have no life
> in them, and to arrive at no result. More than thirty years ago I remember his making
> what appeared at the time a very striking remark, namely, that "the true origin of Biblical
> criticism was to be ascribed not to Strauss, but to Niebuhr, who lived a generation earlier."
> (H. Tennyson, 1897, II, p. 463)

Tennyson owned Niebuhr in Hare and Thirlwall's translation, and this also implies
that he was familiar with Strauss's work. Tennyson's remark "I hate learning" could
be read as simply a teasing comment on Jowett's own "learning," as a scholar of the
Bible among other things. But it does seem that in later life Tennyson had little respect
for the kind of criticism that rested on a line-by-line analysis of problems with biblical
narratives, preferring a broader approach. While he obviously knew about the historical questions raised by critics and the problems created by geological and scientific

research, in relation to the Bible at least he did not share the agonized or fascinated response of many of his contemporaries. A rare comment from an 1846 letter to Mary Howitt states:

> I got your letter yesterday, and I have had so much to do in the interim that I have merely glanced over the Extracts. They seem to me to be very clever and full of a noble 19th century-ism ... but whether not too fantastic, if considered as an explanation of the Mosaic text may I think admit of doubt. Meanwhile I hail all such attempts as heralding a grander and more liberal state of opinion and consequently sweeter and more nobler modes of living. There was no more *sea* says St John in Revelation. I wonder your friend did not quote that, perhaps he does in some other part of his book. I remember reading that when a child and not being able to reconcile myself to a future when there should be no more sea. (Tennyson, 1982, I, p. 270)

The Howitts had lived in Heidelberg from 1840 to 1843 and were familiar with German theology if disapproving of its effects, and although the friend who supplied these "extracts" has not been identified, they could have been drawn from any of the several books of criticism on the Pentateuch available at this time. Tennyson writes in the apologetic tone of one who is not as interested in the reading material supplied by Howitt as she might wish him to be. While he is skeptical about the interpretation these extracts offer, he welcomes such attempts in principle and, presumably responding to the author's questioning of literal interpretations of the Bible, provides his own instance of a moment when literal interpretation proves problematic. His generally negative opinion of "dryasdust" learning was evidently not due to the conservative position that the Bible must be held as divinely inspired, but was instead a kind of impatience with critics who sought to pull apart and overinterpret a text that already "worked" in the sense of providing aesthetic pleasure in language and imagery, affective sympathy with narratives and characters, and insight into Christ's life and God's relations with man. Like Hallam, Tennyson was more interested in how the Bible fitted into "every fold of the human heart" than in disproving its authority.

This attitude becomes gradually evident in Tennyson's poems as he moves from early speakers who have little faith in their own ability to use and correctly interpret biblical tropes – or have too much faith, in the case of St Simeon Stylites – through the questionings of *In Memoriam*, to speakers who are generally more confident and trusting in their biblical readings. In several early poems, written in the decades when Tennyson was experiencing doubt and insecurity, his speakers use scriptural allusion as a critique of or ironic contrast to their doubting states. In "Supposed Confessions of a Second-Rate Sensitive Mind Not in Unity with Itself," for instance, the speaker compares himself bitterly to the scribes and Pharisees who ask Jesus for a sign in Matthew:

> That even now,
> In this extremest misery
> Of ignorance, I should require
> A sign! (Lines 7–10)

> Then certain of the scribes and the Pharisees answered, saying, Master, we would see a sign from thee. But he answered and said unto them, An evil and adulterous generation seeketh after a sign, and there shall no sign be given to it. (Matthew 12:38–9)

Tennyson's speaker, in contrasting his "damned vacillating state" (line 190) to the placid unquestioning faith of his mother, sees himself as representative of a new generation who believe that "it is man's privilege to doubt" and to "compare / All creeds till we have found the one, / If one there be?" (lines 175–7). As George Landow (1980, p. 87) notes in a consideration of the poem's use of typology, biblical allusion dramatizes this "peculiarly modern Arnoldian state of disbelief mixed with a desire for faith." Comparing himself to the "evil and adulterous generation" suggests that the speaker cannot maintain confidence in his own forward-looking attitudes. Matthew 12 haunts him as he, like his later counterpart in *In Memoriam*, wonders whether his words have any purpose or are simply condemning him: "how can ye, being evil, speak good things? For out of the abundance of the heart the mouth speaketh ... every idle word that men shall speak, they shall give account thereof in the day of judgment" (Matthew 12:34–6). The larger irony in the poem is that the speaker alludes to biblical passages and archetypes without being quite sure how or whether meaning adheres in them. He pictures his mother praying "Bring this lamb back into thy fold" (line 105), but then uses the lamb as an image of man as unquestioning beast doomed to slaughter:

> Shall man live thus, in joy and hope
> As a young lamb, who cannot dream,
> Living, but that he shall live on? (Lines 169–71)

The speaker ignores the redemptive possibilities in the parable of the lost sheep in favor of a gloomy meditation on the pointlessness of living a placid, animal-like existence when death is inevitable, thus missing the broader point that the lamb is also a type of Christ and hence a symbol of resurrection and eternal life. He finds it hard to believe that such biblical types have meaning for him. Shortly before this, he recalls his mother's reassurance that God would forgive him:

> That grace
> Would drop from his oe'r-brimming love,
> As manna on my wilderness,
> If I would pray – that God would move
> And strike the hard, hard rock. (Lines 112–16)

Landow discusses this passage along with other uses of Moses striking the rock (Numbers 20:10–11) as a good example of typological readings of the Old Testament, as the narrative of the Israelites in the wilderness becomes a metaphor for the state of the sinner's soul. Again, however, these allusions hold little meaning for the speaker. The repetition of "hard" has a nice note of self-pity and self-aggrandizement: he takes a certain pride in his doubt. It is only in the final passage of the poem that a biblical image is used without layers of irony and distance, when the speaker asks: "Let Thy dove / Shadow me over" (lines 180–1).

Somewhat similar uses of the Bible appear in "The Two Voices" and "St Simeon Stylites," two poems that like "Supposed Confessions" enact a blend of practiced cynicism and agonized doubt. As critics have noted, "The Two Voices" begins with the perversion of a biblical allusion, as the "still small voice" of God from 1 Kings 19:12 becomes the voice tempting the speaker into despair and suicide (Adler, 1974, p. 366). Yet as in "Supposed Confessions," the speaker ends by accessing feeling and admitting the potential for consolation through the Bible:

> And wherefore rather I made choice
> To commune with that barren voice,
> Than him that said "Rejoice! Rejoice!" (Lines 460–2)

The various sources for this alternate voice (Ricks cites Philippians 4:4 and Ecclesiastes 11:9, to which several of the Psalms could be added: Tennyson, 1987, I, p. 593n) suggest that the speaker finally learns to read the Bible trustingly and without dismissing its positive message. "St Simeon Stylites" sets up a different situation in that the reader is expected to recognize that the speaker's self-important references to Scripture, often designed to link him to Christ, are another aspect of his hypocrisy. He asks:

> O Jesus, if thou wilt not save my soul,
> Who may be saved? who is it may be saved?
> Who may be made a saint, if I fail here? (Lines 45–7)

Simeon echoes the astonishment of the apostles in Matthew 19 on hearing that the wealthy young man who has obeyed all the commandments may not be saved. He is being ironic because, unlike the young man in this episode, he *is* one of those who "hath forsaken houses, or brethren, or sisters, or father, or mother, or children, or lands, for my name's sake" (Matthew 19:29) and so might reasonably, in his view, expect the stated reward of everlasting life. But the irony works on two levels: the original questioners were confounded by Christ's reinterpretation of what needed to be done for salvation, and by repeating the question St Simeon Stylites asks the reader in turn to question whether his apparent confidence is justified.

Such uses of the Bible by various troubled speakers suggest its slippery potential for reinterpretation and call into question any notion that its words might have clear and fixed meanings. If the speakers find hope in their knowledge of Scripture, they also find that this knowledge cannot necessarily be trusted. Similar ideas run throughout *In Memoriam*, which has of course been read as a sustained meditation on the instability and impermanence of all language. *In Memoriam* is infused with biblical language and imagery, so that even when a direct allusion is not apparent Tennyson's words hold religious overtones. To take only one key example, the word "change" inevitably recalls the familiar phrasing of 1 Corinthians 15:51–2:

> Behold, I shew you a mystery; We shall not all sleep, but we shall all be changed, In a moment, in the twinkling of an eye, at the last trump: for the trumpet shall sound, and the dead shall be raised incorruptible, and we shall be changed.

A preoccupation with change and stasis is characteristic of Tennyson's poetry, but *In Memoriam* seems to play specifically with the many possible interpretations of "change" here. As the poem obsessively returns to the idea of change, the intertextual relation to 1 Corinthians is deepened as Tennyson interrogates what such change might consist of and what it might mean for his friendship with Hallam. In XIV, he imagines Hallam returning unchanged:

> And I perceived no touch of change,
>   No hint of death in all his frame,
>   But found him all in all the same,
> I should not feel it to be strange. (Lines 17–20)

In later sections where "change" is again rhymed with "strange" the strangeness is associated with the potential estrangement between Tennyson and Hallam once death has worked its changes on the latter, as in XLI:

> But thou art turned to something strange,
>   And I have lost the links that bound
>   Thy changes; here upon the ground,
> No more partaker of thy change. (Lines 5–8)

Removed into a different sphere, the ways in which Hallam might change, in a "tenfold-complicated" (XCIII:12) process, are unimaginable. Earlier verses of 1 Corinthians 15 also echo in such passages, especially the striking rhetoric of verses 42–4:

> So also is the resurrection of the dead. It is sown in corruption; it is raised in incorruption:
> It is sown in dishonour; it is raised in glory: it is sown in weakness, it is raised in power:
> It is sown a natural body; it is raised a spiritual body. There is a natural body, and there
> is a spiritual body.

Again, this ambiguous statement about the difference between the "natural" and the "spiritual" body seems to lie behind many of Tennyson's comments about Hallam's physical body and whether it will also remain unchanged, as well as contributing to the recurring imagery of sowing and reaping grain in the poem. Since these passages would be entirely familiar to the vast majority of Victorian readers, Tennyson does not need to cite them directly: his readers would simply be conscious that St Paul's rhetoric was subliminally present.

In Memoriam's most important use of the Bible comes in sections XXXI–XXXVI, which include a reworking of the story of Lazarus in XXXI–XXXII that can productively be read in relation to Browning's very different take on the same narrative. For Tennyson, the focus in this story is not on what we know of Lazarus's miraculous resurrection but on what we do not know:

> When Lazarus left his charnel-cave,
>   And home to Mary's house returned,
>   Was this demanded – if he yearned
> To hear her weeping by his grave?

> "Where wert thou, brother, those four days?"
>   There lives no record of reply,
>   Which telling what it is to die
>   Had surely added praise to praise.
>
> ***
>
> Behold a man raised up by Christ!
>   The rest remaineth unrevealed;
>   He told it not; or something sealed
>   The lips of that Evangelist. (XXXI:1–8, 13–16)

This is a gloss on what might have happened between Lazarus rising from the dead, in John 11:44, "And he that was dead came forth, bound hand and foot with grave-clothes," and the statement in John 12:2 that Lazarus and his sisters were present at a dinner with Jesus. The actual moment of resurrection and Christ's role in it are obscured – "When Lazarus left" makes no mention of the agency that permitted him to leave – in favor of a focus on how those left behind would respond to Lazarus's return. The implicit perspective here is that of Mary, who asks the question in line 5. "There lives no record of reply" and "The rest remaineth unrevealed" leave open the tantalizing possibility that Lazarus did respond to Mary's question, but that the writer of the St John's Gospel has either failed to record it or deliberately chosen not to reveal it to later readers. Lazarus lived, but the full "record" of his resurrection remained buried. This section raises the question of whether the eschewing of detail in this biblical narrative is due to Lazarus's own silence, a loss of historical records, or the deliberate choice of the writer of St John's Gospel. The implication is that the Evangelist may have been silenced by some higher power, that ambiguous "something."

Section XXXII again thinks about how Mary, effectively an innocent bystander to the main event, would have responded to her brother's return. It moves to John 12 and the dinner at which she anoints Jesus with precious ointment:

> Her eyes are homes of silent prayer,
>   Nor other thought her mind admits
>   But, he was dead, and there he sits,
>   And he that brought him back is there.
>
> Then one deep love doth supersede
>   All other, when her ardent gaze
>   Roves from the living brother's face,
>   And rests upon the Life indeed.
>
> All subtle thought, all curious fears,
>   Borne down by gladness so complete,
>   She bows, she bathes the Saviour's feet
>   With costly spikenard and with tears. (XXXII:1–12)

"He that brought him back" and "the Life indeed" are euphemistic or evasive ways of referring to Jesus, who appears in these sections not as the speaking and acting character of the biblical verses but as a more mysterious power. As elsewhere in *In Memoriam* and in Tennyson's other writings, female characters are perceived as enviable in their ability to maintain a trusting faith in the face of inexplicable events: the succeeding XXXIII expands upon how the simple faith of a sister should not be troubled with a "shadowed hint" from her more logically inclined brother. The comma after "But" in line 3, above, beautifully encapsulates Mary's refusal to "admit" thoughts that might trouble her joy: rather than objecting "But he was dead," she and the reader are left to accept nothing but the simple facts. The simplicity of the monosyllabic words in lines 3–4, with the repetition of "there" and the lack of detail about *where* Lazarus has been "brought back" from, emphasize the reduction of this amazing event to a family reunion while at the same time drawing attention to the difficulty of believing these stark facts. It is precisely because the resurrection is so hard to grasp that it can only be treated as a matter-of-fact occurrence, echoing the casual reference to "Lazarus ... whom he raised from the dead" in John 12:1.

Four sections later, Tennyson produced his only explicit poetic commentary on the importance of the Bible:

> For Wisdom dealt with mortal powers,
>   Where truth in closest words shall fail,
>   When truth embodied in a tale
> Shall enter in at lowly doors.
>
> And so the Word had breath, and wrought
>   With human hands the creed of creeds
>   In loveliness of perfect deeds
> More strong than all poetic thought;
>
> Which he may read that binds the sheaf,
>   Or builds the house, or digs the grave,
>   And those wild eyes that watch the wave
> In roarings round the coral reef. (XXXVI:5–16)

Human interest in narrative and character, this suggests, meant that God chose to present his truths through Christ and his actions rather than through densely argued reasoning. Christ is the embodied Word of God, and his "perfect deeds," such as the raising of Lazarus, are meaningful across classes and cultures, from "lowly" laborers to savage natives. Since actions speak louder than words, according to these stanzas, the silence surrounding Lazarus's resurrection in XXXI–XXXII now makes sense. But the obvious problem here, as we come upon "read" in line 13, is that the Bible is still a text, and thus inevitably contains linguistic ambiguities and possible misinterpretations. This section is evasive about the question that most exercised the biblical critics of Tennyson's day, that of inspiration. "Wrought /With human hands" could apply to the authors of the Gospels and suggest that God's truth was channeled through their humanity, but the "human hands" also apply to Christ, if he is the subject of "perfect deeds." The stanza implies that the "creed of creeds" consists of Christ's deeds – but someone still had to record these deeds or there would be no possibility that they could be "read." "Wrought" evasively turns away from "wrote," but these stanzas evoke what they attempt to cancel out, the question of whether the Bible itself consists of "closest words" that may fail to convey the appropriate truths. And although in the last stanza Tennyson sounds for a moment like a representative of the Society for the Propagation of the Gospel, he still ends on a note of ambiguity, as the savage and peculiarly disembodied "wild eyes" he envisions are turned not toward the Scriptures but outward on the inexplicable motions of nature.

Tennyson seems to value the Bible here primarily if not solely as a repository of "tales," recalling Emily Tennyson's account of his response to the Song of Solomon:

> He is full of the Song of Solomon, reading it in Hebrew: and he said that most people knew nothing about it, that in the coarsely-painted, misrepresented, unundertandable story, given in the Bible translation, there is hardly a trace of what he calls "The most perfect Idyll of the faithful love of a country girl for her shepherd, and of her resistance to the advances of a great king, that ever was written." (H. Tennyson, 1897, II, p. 51)

This implies that Tennyson wants to rewrite the "poetic thought" (*In Memoriam* XXXVI:8) of the King James version of the Song of Solomon into one of his own domestic idylls. The disputed sexuality of this book, which surely lies behind the anxiety here that it is "coarsely painted" and "misrepresented," would be reworked into a nice tale of a rustic maiden's fidelity to her humble lover. This might seem like Tennyson indulging in middle-of-the-road and middle-class Victorian prudishness, especially given how important the translation of Song of Solomon was for other Victorian poets, such as Christina Rossetti or Swinburne. Yet given the emphases in *In Memoriam* XXXVI, this anecdote fits with his general belief that the Bible was most accessible through easily understandable narratives, and that this accessibility was crucial.

Many of Tennyson's popular sentimental poems, from "The May Queen" to *Enoch Arden*, represent this by placing biblical allusions in the mouths of relatively humble and uneducated speakers who draw simple comfort from literal readings of God's word. The speaker of "The May Queen," for instance, addressing her mother from her death-bed, recounts how she has been comforted by their clergyman: "He taught me all the mercy, for he showed me all the sin. / Now, though my lamp was lighted late, there's One will let me in" (lines 18–19). This situates the speaker with the foolish virgins of Matthew 25, recalling her frivolity and flirtatiousness in the first part of the poem, but suggests that her story will have a happier ending than the biblical narrative: "Afterward came also the other virgins, saying, Lord, Lord, open to us. But he answered and said, Verily I say unto you, I know you not" (Matthew 25:11–12). In a similar alteration of a less than comforting passage into a reassuring promise, "The May Queen" ends with a very Victorian fantasy of Heaven as a family reunion:

> For ever and for ever, all in a blessed home –
> And there to wait a little while till you and Effie come –
> To lie within the light of God, as I lie upon your breast –
> And the wicked cease from troubling, and the weary are at rest. (Lines 57–60)

The final line is drawn from Job's first bitter and despairing lament, "Let the day perish wherein I was born, and the night in which it was said, there is a man child conceived"

(Job 3:3). As Ricks notes, there is a sharp contrast between this biblical context and the speaker's reassuring vision of God as parent (Tennyson, 1987, I, p. 460n). Tennyson's allusion effectively removes the troubling elements of the line and rewrites it as a soothing platitude, just as the story of the wise and foolish virgins is turned from a tale of exclusion to one of inclusion and forgiveness.

The important point here is that, in contrast to "Supposed Confessions" or "St Simeon Stylites," there is no sense that an ironic reading of these allusions would be appropriate. This tendency is also evident in two poems of the late 1870s, "Rizpah" (Tennyson's only poem named after a biblical character) and "In the Children's Hospital." The modern Rizpah – named for the biblical character who guards the bones of her hanged son in 2 Samuel 21 – tells the narrative of her son's execution and her rescue of his bones from the gibbet to a pious and implicitly Calvinistic lady visitor. But she rejects this visitor's doctrines:

> Sin? O yes – we are sinners, I know – let all that be,
> And read me a Bible verse of the Lord's good will towards men –
> "Full of compassion and mercy, the Lord" – let me hear it again. (Lines 60–2)

The fact that the speaker asks her visitor to read the verse to her suggests that she may be illiterate, yet she not only has the ability to recall and cite the Bible, but also incorporates its language in her own words, consciously or unconsciously, when she describes her son's bones as "flesh of my flesh" (Genesis 2:23). Her faith rests on consolatory biblical passages, and there is no suggestion in the poem that the reassurance she gains from these is misplaced. "In the Children's Hospital," a poem very seldom discussed, has a similar slant. This deeply sentimental tale of an orphaned child's death, narrated by a nurse, rests upon the text of Mark 10:14 ("Suffer the little children to come unto me") and enacts a contrast between the simple, charitable Christianity of the speaker and the brusqueness of the modern doctor called in for a consultation. When the nurse recommends prayer for a hopeless case, this skeptical materialist doctor mutters to himself: "All very well – but the good Lord Jesus has had his day" (line 22). She responds: "How could I bear with the sights and the loathsome smells of disease / But that He said 'Ye do it to me, when ye do it to these'?" (lines 25–6). As the narrative continues, the young girl Emmie overhears the doctor telling the nurse that she is unlikely to live through her imminent operation, and the nurse reports the conversation between Emmie and the child in the next bed, Annie:

> "If I," said the wise little Annie, "was you"
> I should cry to the dear Lord Jesus to help me, for, Emmie, you see,
> It's all in the picture there: "'Little children should come to me'." (Lines 48–50)

Predictably, after making her plea Emmie is found dead the next morning. "In the Children's Hospital" again has no layers of irony and the implicit and positive comparison is between the immediacy and literalness of the children's response to the painting and text, including this simplified version of the language of the King James Bible, and the nurse's equally faithful interpretation of Christ's words. The reader might have more sympathy with the advanced opinions of the French-educated vivi-sectionist doctor, but nonetheless authorial sympathy is firmly on the narrator's side. Jesus will not have had his day, the poem implies, as long as his words and image still hold meaning.

What "The May Queen," "Rizpah," and "In the Children's Hospital" show is not so much that Tennyson used the Bible for purely affective ends, but that he was prepared to write sympathetically from the perspective of speakers who did so and to value their ability to find consolation. In each poem the narrator is a relatively lower-class woman who knows the Bible intimately but interprets it in an entirely uncritical way, reminis-cent of *In Memoriam* XXXV and XXXVI. This might seem like Tennyson falling prey to the haze of Victorian sentimentality surrounding particular biblical texts or moments (of which the "Suffer the little children" passage is perhaps the best example). These poems do, however, also adhere to a particular ideology about ways of reading and using the Bible evident in works that we know Tennyson admired. In his *Theological Essays* and elsewhere, Maurice (a close friend of Tennyson's from Cambridge days onward) is strongly against reductive biblical criticism precisely because it threatens the kind of uncritical reading practiced by these Tennysonian speakers:

> In solitary chambers, among bedridden sufferers, the words of these good men have still a living force. The Bible is read there truly as an inspired book; as a book which does not stand aloof from human life, but meets it. ... It is of quite infinite importance that the con-fidence in which these humble students read, should not be set at naught and contradicted by decisions and conclusions of ours. (Maurice, 1853, p. 334)

He recommends Job because "the story is more simply human ... than any in the Old Testament" and states that "You will see bedridden women ... feeding on it and finding themselves in it," just as Tennyson's May Queen seems to do (p. 61). Maurice counsels an intensely personal reading of the Bible in which meaning is discovered through emotional affinity:

> Books of the Bible which were lying in shadow for me, in which I could see little meaning, have come forth into clearness, because I met with hard passages in myself or in society which I could not construe without their help. (p. 339)

The language used here transfers the terms of scholarship to human life and society: rather than construing passages from the Bible, Maurice suggests, it helps us to read and interpret ourselves. This follows Coleridge in his posthumously published *Confessions of an Inquiring Spirit* (1840), where he argues that "in the Bible there is more that *finds* me than I have experienced in all other books put together" (p. 43). It also resonates with the arguments of F. W. Farrar, the schoolmaster, philolo-gist, novelist, and biblical scholar; and with the widely read sermons and lectures of F. W. Robertson, whose Sunday afternoon expositions of books of the Bible to a largely working-class audience in Brighton proved highly popular. Tennyson owned several works of Farrar's, including *The Witness of History to Christ*, in which (with an epigraph from *In Memoriam* XXXVI) Farrar argues passionately that demonstrable problems or flaws in the gospels are irrelevant given how much the Bible still "calms, and comforts, and soothes us" in moments of trouble (Farrar, 1871, pp. 48, 75). He also owned Robertson's lectures on Corinthians, throughout which Robertson insists that the point of biblical exposition is not to increase critical knowledge or wrongly apply scientific ideas to a work intended as "a revelation of the Character of God" (Robertson, 1859, p. 287), but to apply "spiritual principles to those questions, and modes of action, which concern present existence, in the Market, the Shop, the Study, and the Street" (p. 2).

In one of Tennyson's late dramatic monologues, the Wycliffite martyr Sir John Old-castle, in hiding in Wales, argues that the "Heaven-sweet Evangel, ever-living word" ("Sir John Oldcastle, Lord Cobham," line 28) will humanize those who can read it in their own language: "Had he God's word in Welsh / He might be kindlier: happily come the day!" (lines 22–3). Tennyson's poem wholly supports Oldcastle's efforts to widen access to God's word. Biblical stories and characters model ways to be "kindlier" for his heroes, and he appeared most strongly interested in the Bible as a repository of stories, characters, and sayings whose value lay, as Robertson argued, in their continued relevance to modern life. The important point about this is that Tennyson's own poetry works in a similar way to the Bible, if to a lesser degree. Just as "Rizpah" is intended to make the reader pity the mother's plight and feel horror at the harsh law that executed her son for a prank, so might a biblical story invoke similar sympathetic affects. Carlyle noted of Tennyson's breakthrough 1842 collection:

> there seems to be a note of "The Eternal Melodies" in this man; for which let all other men be thankful and joyful! Your "Dora" reminds me of the *Book of Ruth*; in the "Two Voices" ... I think of passages in *Job*. For truth is quite *true* in Job's time and Ruth's as it is now. (Cited by H. Tennyson, 1897, I, p. 213)

He echoes Hallam's understanding of biblical "truth" in relation to a general notion of shared humanity. Tennyson himself, this implies, is both one of the teachers who can expound the Bible "simply" to readers of all classes and a poet who in the best Romantic tradition is inspired by God to eternal melody; like the authors of Scripture, he may be both an interpreter of God's word and a vessel for it.

References

Adler, J. (1974) "Tennyson's 'Mother of Sorrows': 'Rizpah'," *Victorian Poetry* 12, 363–9.

Campbell, N., ed. (1971) *Tennyson in Lincoln*, 2 volumes. Tennyson Society, Lincoln.

Colenso, J. W. (1865) *The Pentateuch and Book of Joshua Critically Examined*. Longman, London.

Coleridge, S. T. (1956) *Confessions of an Inquiring Spirit*, ed. H. Hart. Adam & Charles Black, London.

Erskine, T. (1828) *The Unconditional Freeness of the Gospel*, 2nd edn. Waugh & Innes, Edinburgh.

Farrar, F. W. (1871) *The Witness of History to Christ*. Macmillan, London.

Flynn, P. (1979) "Hallam and Tennyson: The 'Theodicaea Novissima' and *In Memoriam*," *Studies in English Literature* 19, 705–20.

Hallam, A. H. (1943) *The Writings of Arthur Hallam*, ed. T. H. Vail Motter. Oxford University Press, London.

Hallam, A. H. (1981) *The Letters of Arthur Henry Hallam*, ed. J. Kolb. Ohio State University Press, Columbus.

Hare, J. and Hare, F. (1827) *Guesses at Truth*, 2 volumes. John Taylor, London.

Hill, A. G. (1997) *Tennyson, Wordsworth and the "Forms" of Religion*. Tennyson Society, Lincoln.

Jasper, D. and Prickett, S., eds (1999) *The Bible and Literature: A Reader*. Blackwell, Oxford.

Landow, G. (1980) *Victorian Types, Victorian Shadows: Biblical Typology in Victorian Literature, Art and Thought*. Routledge, London.

Maurice, F. D. (1853) *Theological Essays*. Macmillan, Cambridge.

Robertson, F. W. (1859) *Expository Lectures on St Paul's Epistles to the Corinthians*. Smith, Elder, London.

Schleiermacher, F. (1825) *A Critical Essay on the Gospel of St Luke*, ed. C. Thirlwall. John Taylor, London.

Tennyson, A. (1982) *The Letters of Alfred Lord Tennyson*, 3 volumes, ed. C. Y. Lang and E. F. Shannon. Clarendon Press, Oxford.

Tennyson, A. (1987) *The Poems of Tennyson*, 2nd edn, 3 volumes, ed. C. Ricks. Longman, Harlow.

Tennyson, H. (1897) *Alfred Lord Tennyson: A Memoir*, 2 volumes. Macmillan, London.

CHAPTER 36
The Brontës

Marianne Thormählen

In the mid-nineteenth century there was much heated discussion regarding the individual's right to think for himself or herself on religious matters, including the status of the Bible as Holy Writ. Christian combatants expressed all sorts of views, ranging from a conviction of the Bible's absolute authority to the idea that every Bible reader is entitled to exercise his or her "private judgment" – a term that filled the orthodox with horror.[1] The expression "private judgment" appears memorably in Charlotte Brontë's *Shirley* (1849),[2] in a scene where the two heroines, Shirley Keeldar and Caroline Helstone, are intent on persuading the factory foreman Joe Scott that women's intellectual capabilities are equal to men's. Asked whether he allows the right of private judgment, Joe answers that he claims it "for every line of the holy Book." This freedom to pursue the meaning of Scripture according to one's own understanding should be restricted to the male sex, however: women should "take their husbands' opinion, both in politics and religion," as that is "wholesomest" for them (II.7.329).

The continued conversation in *Shirley* testifies to Charlotte Brontë's awareness that any discussion of a biblical passage involves interpretation, and that individual readers of the Bible will engage with it on their own terms. Having quoted 1 Timothy 2:11–14 to the effect that women should learn in silence and not exert authority over men, Joe challenges Miss Helstone, the rector's niece, to state her "reading" of Paul's words. Somewhat hesitantly at first, the young woman produces a remarkable reply:

> [Paul] wrote that chapter for a particular congregation of Christians, under peculiar circumstances; and besides, I dare say, if I could read the original Greek, I should find that many of the words have been wrongly translated, perhaps misapprehended altogether. It would be possible, I doubt not, with a little ingenuity, to give the passage quite a contrary turn; to make it say, "Let the woman speak out whenever she sees fit to make an objection;" – "it is permitted to a woman to teach and to exercise authority as much as may be. Man, meanwhile, cannot do better than hold his peace," and so on. (*Shirley* II.7.329–30)

The last part of Caroline Helstone's answer ("It would be possible") comes close to a parody of the right to "private judgment." The first, however, offers a sketch of the state of biblical criticism as perceived by a well informed, independent-minded Anglican in mid-1800s England: historical conditions at the very different points in time when the respective texts came into being should be taken into account when interpreting the Scriptures; and scholarly interpretation requires mastery of the original language. A reading that diverges from the prima facie meaning in the Authorized Version's English need not be a sign of impiety. Personal spiritual conviction – Caroline Helstone goes on to claim that her "notions are dyed in faster colours" than Joe's – matters more than the letter of a law made for another people at another time in another language.

The *Shirley* passage invites being read in conjunction with Samuel Taylor Coleridge's dislike of "Bibliolatry," the worship of Scripture as literally true.[3] Coleridge's posthumous *Confessions of an Inquiring Spirit* (1825, published in 1840) formulated a more flexible view of the truth of the Bible. According to Coleridge, the essence of Scripture is found in its effect on the human heart: "it finds me," as he put it in the second Letter of the *Confessions*. The sixth Letter articulates his stance in the form of a question:

> Is it safer for the Individual, and more conducive to the interests of the Church of Christ, in its twofold character of pastoral and militant, to conclude thus: The Bible is the Word of God, and therefore true, holy, and in all parts unquestionable; or thus, The Bible, considered in reference to its declared ends and purposes, is true and holy, and for all who seek truth with humble spirits an unquestionable guide, and therefore it is the Word of God?[4]

The second statement is obviously closer to the attitude expressed by Caroline Helstone than the first, which fits "thoroughly dogmatical" Joe (as she calls him) better.

Another scene from a Brontë novel in which an individual – again a young unmarried woman – asserts her right to interpret the Bible in accordance with her inmost belief occurs in Anne Brontë's *The Tenant of Wildfell Hall* (1848). Confronted with her aunt's anxiety about her future were she to marry a man whom even the infatuated girl cannot call virtuous, Helen Lawrence avers that any separation in death would only be temporary: the lake of fire would not hold her prospective husband forever, only for a long time, "till he has paid the uttermost farthing." In other words, he would spend some considerable time in purifying fires – a highly unorthodox idea; the Protestant Anglican Church rejected Purgatory as a "Papist" doctrine – before being able to join the celestial throng. Helen's aunt does not pursue the girl's tacit admission that the man she has set her heart on is unlikely to escape hellfire, be it ever- or merely long-lasting. Instead, shocked by the way her niece uses her Bible, she asks Helen whether her perusal of Holy Writ has not produced any indication that her belief may in fact be mistaken. Helen's answer resembles Caroline Helstone's in its emphasis on the possibility of alternative interpretations and the scope for uncertainty created by translation:

> No: I found indeed some passages that taken by themselves, might seem to contradict [my] opinion; but they will all bear a different construction to that which is commonly given, and in most the only difficulty is in the word which we translate "everlasting" or "eternal." I don't know the Greek, but I believe it strictly means for ages, and might signify either endless or long-enduring.[5]

Anne Brontë herself believed in "universal salvation," a radical and challenging notion rooted in the conviction that Christ died for all and not just for those who lead virtuous lives. It took courage to express that notion openly; some men who did so lost their jobs as a result.[6] Anne held this belief throughout her short adult life and herself studied the Bible systematically in pursuit of scriptural corroboration. A brief outline of her Bible project introduces the ensuing discussion of Anne Brontë and the Scriptures, a natural point of departure because of the boldness of her thinking and the availability of first-hand biographical evidence. Sections on the Bible in the novels of Charlotte and Emily Brontë follow, and the chapter concludes with a review of the Brontë sisters' position in the contemporary debate on the status and uses of the Bible.

Shortly before her twenty-second birthday, lonely and unhappy in an uncongenial governess position, Anne Brontë began to subject the Bible her godmother had given her to systematic study.[7] For a period of about one and a half years, she scrutinized the Old Testament book by book, writing down chapters and sometimes verses of special interest and underlining some of these items once, twice, or even three times.[8] Some of the passages she selected were also marked by pencil strokes alongside the actual text, and she put in crosses by some of the Psalms.[9] The passages Anne singled out deal with the prospects of the good and the wicked respectively, with prescriptions on how to lead a righteous life of the kind that will help the individual find favor in God's sight, with God's reluctance to punish his creatures and with the believer's trust in God to forgive and save. Still little more than a girl, Anne thus made use of the Protestant Christian's license to study Scripture independently and for a particular purpose, the same license she would give her fictional heroine Helen several years later. However, she faced the fact that freedom to explore the Bible does not mean that one is necessarily reassured by what one finds. Though most of the verses she selected encourage reliance on a merciful God, she also marked such lines as "There is no peace, saith my God, to the wicked" (Isaiah 50:21). A long pencil stroke by Lamentations 3 runs alongside expressions of despair as well as of hope that God will ultimately end the suffering outcast's misery. Anne Brontë worked some of these verses into the concluding paragraph of chapter 55 in *The Tenant of Wildfell Hall*, where an older, sorely tried Helen expresses her anguish in the prophet's and psalmist's laments (Helen quotes Psalm 119, listed as noteworthy by Anne). Helen remains hopeful, however, clinging to a belief in salvation for all as she sits by her dying husband's bedside, even as she sidelines a key drawback of the individual's liberty to study the Bible on his or her own: the possibility of error.[10]

In transferring authority from church, saints, and clergy to the Scriptures, the Reformation invested the individual with a new dimension of responsibility for his or her spiritual welfare. The Brontë novels represent the Protestant's freedom of religious inquiry as a priceless privilege, but they do not attempt to conceal its unsettling corollary. Answerable to nobody but God, the struggling Christian who realizes that the Bible – his or her sole tangible guide – does not supply unambiguous and practicable directions for every situation in life might easily become "somewhat afflicted with religious melancholy."[11] That is the situation in which chapter 11 of *Agnes Grey* (1847) depicts the cottager Nancy Brown, whose poverty and lack of education do not prevent her from being "of a serious, thoughtful turn of mind." Literate but unable to read because her eyes are inflamed, Nancy fails to derive any comfort even from biblical verses that used to fortify her. The chief reason for her tribulations is her sense that she does not love God or man as she should and is therefore herself cut off from God's love. The rector's obvious contempt for her ("a canting old fool," 11.92) and his suggestion that she is "one of those that seek to enter in at the strait gate and shall not be able" (10.90; Luke 13:24) add to her misery.

The turnaround point for Nancy comes when the new curate Mr Weston explicates 1 John 4 to her. In simple, concrete terms adaptable to daily life, he shows her how she can foster love both for God and for her fellow human beings (11.92–5). Once he has set her on the right path, she is able to benefit from having the Bible read to her by the narrator Agnes Grey. The contrast between the two clergymen is carefully worked out: the rector – says Agnes disapprovingly – dislikes "individuals who [attempt] to think for themselves in matters connected with religion ... guided by their own interpretations of Scripture" (10.81), and he is seen to be worse than useless when it comes to assuaging his parishioner's troubled spirit. His junior succeeds because he is able to bring out the essence of the biblical message in ways the listener can understand. In Nancy's words, Mr Weston "read bits here and there, an' explained 'em as clear as the day: and it seemed like as a new light broke in on my soul" (11.94). Nancy goes on to tell Agnes of a sermon by Mr Weston based on Matthew 11:28, "Come unto me, all ye that labour and are heavy laden, and I will give you rest" (11.95). Here, for a change, church attendance profits the religious seeker. The decisive factor – apart from the verse itself, which has given comfort to Christians from the earliest times of the Church – is neither the actual place nor the clerical rank held by the mediator of Scripture. What matters is his personality; he is "a man of strong sense, firm faith, and ardent piety" who also turns out to be benevolent and considerate (11.98–9).[12]

Anne Brontë's novels are more concerned with dogmatic–doctrinal issues than her sisters' books. She explored these issues in strikingly audacious ways, integrating biblical passages in her idiosyncratic representations of the Christian's endeavor to "stay upon his God" (Isaiah 50:10, also the last words of chapter 36 in *The Tenant of Wildfell Hall*).[13] From first to last, she sought assurance that God's love is boundless and his mercy infinite. A note in her Bible, "See A. Clark[e]," indicates her readiness to enlist the support of religious thinkers outside mainstream Anglicanism: Dr Adam Clarke was a Wesleyan preacher and Bible commentator, whose unorthodox notions comprised a conviction that even repenting Judas was not beyond God's grace.[14] At the same time, Anne's fiction, *Agnes Grey* especially, is germane to Coleridge's "insistence on the essential *practicality* of Bible study."[15] As Agnes Grey says to her former pupil Lady Ashby, "The end of Religion is ... to teach us ... how to live" (23.186). Both Anne's novels combine study of the Bible with everyday ethics at a deeper level than that of mere maxims for good conduct.

While Anne's writings contain a large number of biblical references, her sister Charlotte's prose is steeped in the language of the Authorized Version to an extent that even her youngest sister did not match; indeed, it would be difficult to find a counterpart among all the other writers of fiction at the time.[16] "Elle était nourrie de la Bible," as Constantin Heger claimed.[17] At school Charlotte impressed the other girls with her ability to quote Holy Writ from memory; her friend Ellen Nussey remembered her familiarity "with all the sublimest passages [in the Bible], especially those in Isaiah in which she took great delight."[18] Ellen's choice of words ("sublimest," "delight") is significant, suggesting a powerful aesthetic-emotional dimension to Charlotte's engagement with the Scriptures. As Christine Alexander and Margaret Smith put it in their informative entry on the Bible in *The Oxford Companion to the Brontës*, Charlotte Brontë "responded emotionally and imaginatively to its poetry and profundity."[19] Like Anne's novels, Charlotte's books allude freely to both Testaments. It is natural for New Testament references to predominate in the St John chapters in *Jane Eyre* (1847), while ten-year-old Jane quizzed by Mr Brocklehurst would just as naturally list the Old Testament books with the largest proportion of exciting narrative as her biblical favorites.[20] Attempts to use their fiction to establish any peculiar affinity on the part of the adult authors for any particular section of the Bible would be inconclusive at best; the functions of biblical material in the actual texts form a more rewarding object of study.[21]

In this respect Charlotte Brontë's novels present a more varied picture than her sisters'. The child Jane Eyre regards the Bible as a story-book; Lucy Snowe in *Villette* (1853) withstands attempts to weaken her Protestant soul partly thanks to the guidance and comfort provided by her Bible;[22] Caroline Helstone, looking ahead to the last things, acknowledges the classic paradox of expressing the inexpressible in words (*Shirley* 1.10.175), including the words of the Bible; "Biblical promises" cheer the sick and bereaved (*Shirley* I.10.180 and *The Professor* 19.148);[23] the narrator of *Shirley* halts the story to exhort readers not to forget that "Whom [God] loveth, He chasteneth" (II.9.351); St John Rivers clothes his otherworldly ambitions in the words of Revelation, whose last-but-one verse closes *Jane Eyre* (III.12.452), and implicitly (by way of Revelation 21:8) threatens Jane with hellfire if she does not comply with his wishes (III.9.417). As these examples show, the uses to which biblical references are put in Charlotte Brontë's novels are as remarkable for their range as the snippets of Scripture in her prose are for their numerousness.

The scriptural components in Charlotte Brontë's language also evince great variety, ranging from stock phrases to searching metaphor. Expressions like "this promising olive-branch" and "pearl of great price" (*Villette* 10.94 and 13.124) are little more than turns of speech, though their biblical origins give an extra edge to the narrator's irony for anyone who is aware of them.[24] On the other hand, Lucy Snowe's comparison of the sudden growth of her soul to that of Jonah's gourd (*Villette* 6.48; Jonah 4:6–11) signals trouble ahead;[25] and as Lisa Wang has shown, figurative language indebted to both Testaments informs the theological vision of *Villette*.[26] Biblical idiom in Charlotte Brontë's fiction thus incorporates both the playful and the desperately serious. Jane Eyre's references to the Psalms form a particularly poignant instance of the latter, invoking the movements between lament, supplication, and praise that are so characteristic of this the longest book in the Bible.[27] While modern Bible criticism distinguishes between different types of Psalms, "laments" being one category,[28] it is worth observing that individual psalms often comprise both personal anguish and fervent trust in God. Similar juxtapositions of hope and despair occur in Charlotte Brontë's fiction, notably in *Villette* where Lucy Snowe couches her resolution to endure the suffering she recognizes as her lot in biblical terms. The first paragraph of chapter 38 weaves passages from the Psalms and other Old Testament books and Paul's letters into a dense fabric of hope-against-hope, ending with a capitalized assertion quoted from Habakkuk, "WE SHALL NOT DIE!"

The variety seen in Charlotte Brontë's use of the Bible bespeaks an eclectic turn of mind. The coexistence of tolerance and passionate conviction is one of the most intriguing aspects of her personality, and a degree of eclecticism in religious contexts is part of this pattern. Young Charlotte's familiarity with -isms far removed from the Anglican middle ground surprised her friends, though as a devoted daughter of the Church of England she might speak of them in less than respectful terms.[29] A letter to her publisher's reader W. C. Williams illustrates the grown woman's unblinkered willingness to receive spiritual enlightenment as and when it comes, acknowledging that it is a rare thing on earth at the best of times and the monopoly of no church or sect:

> I smile at you ... for supposing that I could be annoyed by what you say respecting your religious and philosophical views, that I could blame you for not being able when you look amongst sects and creeds, to discover any one which you can exclusively and implicitly adopt as yours. I perceive myself that some light falls on Earth from Heaven – that some rays from the Shrine of Truth pierce the darkness of this Life and World – but they are few, faint, and scattered – and who without presumption can assert that he has found the *only* true path upwards?[30]

The genial tone suggests a fundamental absence of anxiety where religious inquiry is concerned. Charlotte Brontë's fearlessness in the pursuit of spiritual insight, a robust confidence that the truth can do no harm, is a feature in those contemporary religious thinkers with whom she had most in common, the Coleridge "heir" F. D. Maurice and Thomas Arnold.[31] It is also very much a Brontë family characteristic, as the case of Emily Brontë demonstrates.

The relative lack of biblical references in Emily Brontë's *Wuthering Heights* (1847) is so apparent that one may well wonder whether it betrays an anti-Christian disposition, a suspicion all the more understandable in view of the fact that such a large proportion of the references that do occur are put in the mouth of the grotesque religious hypocrite Joseph.[32] Many scholars and critics over the years have regarded Emily as a "pagan" or "heretic" figure;[33] and this glaring contrast to her sisters, in whose fiction the Bible is an almost constant intertext, could be taken to support such a view. It has, however, been ably refuted by Lisa Wang, who has pointed out that Emily Brontë was simply a far less allusive writer than Charlotte and Anne.[34] There is no reason to believe that she knew her Bible less well than her sisters because she did not bring it into her writing the way they did; there is a corresponding dearth of references to Shakespeare, for instance. Granted that Emily Brontë referred to the Bible far less frequently than Anne and Charlotte, what do those few references achieve in the text? The obvious place to go for an answer to that question is Lockwood's Branderham dream, in which half the biblical allusions in *Wuthering Heights* are clustered.

While looking at the title of a "Pious Discourse" starting out from Matthew 18:21–2 by one Jabes Branderham,[35] the narrator Lockwood falls asleep, pondering the implications of "Seventy Times Seven, and The First of the Seventy First."[36] Jesus had said that a transgressor should be forgiven "*until* seventy times seven" (emphasis added). It is certainly a very large number – practically a metaphor for infiniteness – in the context of ordinary human existence; but this is a dream, and that removes any strangeness from the idea of 491 offenses committed by one and the same person against one victim. Emily Brontë's skill in creating a realistic nightmare shows on several planes: it takes a dream for the "denominating" of cudgels as "pilgrim's staffs" to pass unchallenged (Joseph, Lockwood's companion, reproaches him for not having brought a pilgrim's staff and proudly shows off his own, "a heavy-handed cudgel"); the destination of the dreamer shifts en route, from Thrushcross Grange to the chapel of Gimmerton; the normally half-deserted chapel holds "a full and attentive congregation"; and the dreamer is not sure who is to do what to whom once he gets there. At one level, it is a hilarious piece of grotesquerie; but there are serious undercurrents beneath its absurdities, and they are channeled through the biblical references.

To begin with, the verses from Matthew are an extreme formulation of the theme of forgiveness as opposed to revenge that is so central to *Wuthering Heights*.[37] It is the first articulation of that theme in the book, apart from Cathy's teasing of Joseph (labeled "a species of dreary fun" by Lockwood). The chief combatants, the dreamer and his nemesis Jabes, call for the other chapelgoers' violent assistance in terms borrowed from representations of the wrathful God of the Old Testament. Lockwood the dreamer is the first to summon the congregation to destroy his adversary, in a plea that lends a dimension of bloodthirst even to this humdrum character: "Drag him down, and crush him to atoms, that the place which knows him may know him no more!" (I.3.19). "[T]hat the place which knows him may know him no more" comes from Job's outcry against his manifold sufferings (7:9–21, especially 10). Job is aware of his sinfulness but cannot understand why God keeps up a regime of persecution so terrible that death would be a release: "why dost thou not pardon my transgressions?" (verse 21). Verse 14 is directly relevant to Lockwood's night of horror at the Heights: "thou scarest me with dreams, and terrifiest me through visions." All that is left for Job is to protest against the unfair treatment he is subjected to. Lockwood the dreamer does the same when, in a fit of "inspiration," he suddenly rises and denounces the preacher of 490 execrable part-sermons in the speech that includes the quotation from Job.

Jabes, however, goes on the counterattack, representing the dreamer as the real culprit because he failed to appreciate the preacher's discourse as he ought to have done ("Seventy times seven didst thou gapingly contort thy visage," I.3.19). Jabes's speech begins with Nathan's accusation against David, who had robbed Uriah the Hittite of life and wife (2 Samuel 12:7): "Thou art the man" (who took the poor man's one ewe lamb rather than an animal from his own abundant flocks). If David had not freely confessed his sinfulness, he would have been destroyed; as it is, God causes his first child by Bathsheba to die as a measure of retribution. The twelfth chapter in 2 Samuel describes the averted evil as disgrace caused by internal strife ("out of thine own house"), manifest in David's "neighbor" taking possession of his wives before the public ("he shall lie with thy wives in the sight of this sun"). It has a peculiar resonance in a tale of two houses and transgressive passions, further reinforced by the evocation of civil strife in Lockwood's description of the indiscriminate brawl where "Every man's hand was against his neighbour."

The last expression recalls at least three Old Testament passages where the talk is of war between brothers and/or neighbors. One of them, Genesis 16:12, is particularly suggestive in connection with *Wuthering Heights*. Speaking to Hagar, the angel of the Lord tells her that her unborn son Ishmael will "be a wild man; his hand will be against every man, and every man's hand against him." The relevance of this verse to Heathcliff is obvious on more levels than one: this "fierce, pitiless, wolfish man" (thus described by Catherine, I.10.90) is "wild" enough; he belongs, like Ishmael, outside the sphere of legitimate inheritance; and his enmity with Hindley and Edgar may well be characterized in the quoted terms.

As pointed out above, most of the biblical references in *Wuthering Heights* are associated with Joseph. During the storm just after Heathcliff's departure, Joseph "[beseeches] the Lord to remember the Patriarchs Noah and Lot" (I.9.75), and Nelly Dean ascribes the role of Jonah to Hindley, who has already come a fair way along the "Broad road" to destruction (invoked by Joseph, I.10.92). The latter expression is one of a fairly small number of references to the New Testament in *Wuthering Heights* (Matthew 7:13). Another is found in the first biblical allusion in the novel, Lockwood's comparison of Heathcliff's dogs to the Gadarene swine of Luke 8:26–33. Like the cluster of allusions in the Branderham dream, this scriptural image has a bearing on what turns out to be a major theme in the book, in this case demoniac possession.[38] Emily's use of Scripture is hence primarily structural and symbolic, an approach to religion comparable to those of Schleiermacher and Blake, who, as Simon Marsden argues, "sought to reinterpret, not reject, Christianity."[39] Indifferent to any deity other than the "God within [her] breast,"[40] Emily Brontë would not shy away from any kind of spiritual inquiry suggested by that God, unhampered by self-doubt or fear of the world's disapproval.

That the Brontë novels met with some strongly formulated censure owing to their alleged religious unorthodoxy is well known.[41] The authors' handling of Scripture is part of that perceived unorthodoxy. While they wrote in a period where advances in biblical criticism had made literalist readings of the Bible increasingly untenable, the contemporary reading public had also experienced a certain swing back toward biblical orthodoxy.[42] Consequently, some of the Brontës' readers would find their treatment of biblical material offensive, whereas others, devout Christians included, would not. The resurgence of orthodoxy in the early nineteenth century may seem surprising to those who think of modern biblical criticism as a kind of linear chronological progress from narrow literalism to liberal allowances for "private judgment." However, the eighteenth century had seen much radical questioning of the Bible as a repository of both historical and spiritual truth. Allegorically and mythically orientated views of the Scriptures were frequently aired in England long before the Germany-based "neology" spread in the British Isles. Some of the best-known eighteenth-century works on religion from within the Anglican mainstream came into being as responses to this questioning of the Bible's status as the literal Word of God.

Occasional expressions in the Brontë fiction suggest that the authors knew about and were unworried by conflicting views of the Bible, having been used to exercising their "private judgment" as Bible readers from their early years. An example from the last volume of *Jane Eyre* may serve as an illustration: When St John Rivers rejects Jane

Eyre's statement that he speaks "as a mere pagan philosopher," he calmly corrects her, saying that there is "this difference between [him] and deistic philosophers": he believes, and he believes the Gospel (III.6.375). Most of the overt challenges to the Bible as inerrant in eighteenth-century Britain came from exponents of deism, as Charlotte Brontë was obviously aware; and she placed the difference between them and St John exactly where apologists for Protestant Christianity located the crux of the matter: in the realm of personal belief.[43]

Listening to St John reading his namesake's Revelation, Jane muses on how much she likes to hear him "[deliver] the oracles of God" (III.9.417). The phrase "oracles of God" occurs three times in the New Testament.[44] The biblical passage that seems most immediately relevant to the *Jane Eyre* context is Romans 3:2, where Paul says that the Jews have the special advantage of having been the recipients of the Old Testament – "unto them were committed the oracles of God." While the expression has been used of the whole Christian Bible,[45] it is commonly understood as referring particularly to the Old Testament (as in Romans 3), and that was the case in the eighteenth and nineteenth centuries as well.[46] It is noteworthy as a metaphor for the entire Bible in a fictional work written by the daughter of a Church of England clergyman in the mid-1800s. The meaning of the word "oracle" in connection with Holy Writ is a matter for another essay by another hand, and there is no need to go beyond its customary connotations here.[47] In a religious context, oracles are normally associated with a higher power, involving divine communications that are to be subjected to interpretation. Unless this-worldly recipients of what they deliver are able to interpret them with wisdom and skill, the guidance they offer cannot be put to any useful purpose. In their writings, fiction, poetry, and letters, the Brontë sisters showed that to them the acquisition and exercise of this interpretative ability was a matter for the free individual, acting under responsibility invested in him or her by God.

Notes

1   On this expression see Marianne Thormählen, *The Brontës and Religion* (Cambridge University Press, Cambridge, 1999), p. 51. There is a subsection on the Brontës and the Bible on pp. 156–62 in the same book.

2   References are to the World's Classics edition of *Shirley*, first published by Oxford University Press in 1981, with an introduction by Margaret Smith and notes by Herbert Rosengarten and Margaret Smith. This quotation is from vol. II, ch. 7, p. 329.

3   Coleridge did not invent the expression; see John Beer's edition of *Aids to Reflection* (Routledge and Princeton University Press, Princeton, NJ, 1993, vol. 9 in the Bollingen Collected Works of Samuel Taylor Coleridge), p. 162n5. An excellent introduction to biblical criticism in eighteenth- and nineteenth-century Britain, with extracts from various commentators on the Bible including Coleridge, is John Drury, ed., *Critics of the Bible 1724–1873* (Cambridge University Press, Cambridge, 1989); the section on Coleridge is on pp. 105–21.

4   From Letter VI in the *Confessions*; here quoted from Drury, *Critics of the Bible*, p. 110. The Brontës are likely to have read Coleridge's religious writings as well as his poetry.

5   References are to the World's Classics edition of *The Tenant of Wildfell Hall*, first published by Oxford University Press in 1993, edited by Herbert Rosengarten and with an introduction by Margaret Smith. This quotation is from ch. 20, p. 167.

6   See Thormählen, *The Brontës and Religion*, p. 88. On Anne's belief in universal salvation, see also Juliet Barker, *The Brontës* (Weidenfeld and Nicolson, London, 1994), pp. 580–1, and the poem "A Word to the Calvinists," in Edward Chitham's edition of *The Poems of Anne Brontë* (Macmillan, Basingstoke, 1979; reprinted 1987), pp. 89–90.

7   The exact point in time when Anne began her project is uncertain. According to a note of hers it was "begun about December 1841"; the wording implies that this is a piece of hindsight information.

8   It should be pointed out that in Anne Brontë's Bible, only the Old Testament bears the marks of systematic study. She may have used a separate New Testament – whose present whereabouts are unknown – for this purpose.

9   Maria Frawley's "Contextualising Anne Brontë's Bible," in Julie Nash and Barbara A. Suess, eds, *New Approaches to the Literary Art of Anne Brontë* (Ashgate, Aldershot, 2001), pp. 1–13, first drew attention to Anne's Bible, which is in the Pierpont Morgan Library in New York. While Frawley did not observe the markings in the text, overlooked the reference to Adam Clarke, and stopped short of drawing conclusions from Anne's selections, her essay was a pioneering contribution to Anne Brontë scholarship, directing researchers to a neglected source of information.

10 On Helen's motives for withholding the comfort of that hope from her husband and on the significance of Luke 16 in this context, see Thormählen, *The Brontës and Religion*, pp. 91–3.

11 *Agnes Grey*, ch. 11, p. 87 in the World's Classics edition edited by Robert Inglesfield and Hilda Marsden, with an introduction and notes by Inglesfield, first published by Oxford University Press in 1991. All references are to this edition. On daily reading of the Scriptures as a religious duty, especially for young girls, see Kate Flint, *The Woman Reader 1837–1914* (Clarendon Press, Oxford, 1993), p. 80. (Both Patrick Brontë's short works of prose fiction, *The Cottage in the Wood* (1815) and *The Maid of Killarney* (1818), stress this obligation.)

12 On Mr Weston's use of Scripture, see Jennifer M. Stolpa, "Preaching to the Clergy: Anne Brontë's *Agnes Grey* as a Treatise on Sermon Style and Delivery," *Victorian Literature and Culture* 31:1 (2003), 225–40 (232–5).

13 Anne Brontë marked the verse with a pencil stroke in her Bible. In the *Tenant* context, the narrator Helen refers to Isaiah as "the inspired writer," signaling the author's awareness of the debate on the nature and extent of divine inspiration in the Bible, which has been going on for centuries. For a helpful introductory survey, see William H. Barnes's entry on "Inspiration and Inerrancy" in Bruce M. Metzger and Michael D. Coogan, eds, *The Oxford Companion to the Bible* (Oxford University Press, New York and Oxford, 1993), pp. 302–4.

14 Clarke's multivolume commentary and critical notes on the entire Bible were completed in 1826. For most present-day students the quickest way of familiarizing themselves with Clarke and his writings, including the complete Commentary, is via the website www.godrules.net.

15 Daniel M. McVeigh, "Coleridge's Bible: *Praxis* and the 'I' in Scripture and Poetry," *Renascence* 49:3 (Spring 1997), 191–207 (191).

16 See Keith Allan Jenkins, "The Influence of Anxiety: *Bricolage* Brontë Style," dissertation, Rice University, 1993; David Norton, *A History of the Bible as Literature. Vol. II, From 1700 to the Present Day* (Cambridge University Press, Cambridge, 1993), pp. 172–5; and Lisa Wang, "The Use of Theological Discourse in the Novels of the Brontë Sisters," dissertation, Birkbeck College, 1998.

17   Chapter 11, p. 157 in the 1960 reprint of Everyman's edition of Elizabeth Gaskell's *The Life of Charlotte Brontë*, first published in 1857.

18   Quoted by Winifred Gérin in another Brontë biography that has remained a classic, *Charlotte Brontë: The Evolution of Genius* (Oxford University Press, Oxford, 1967), p. 75.

19   Published by Oxford University Press in 2003, pp. 33–4 (33).

20   Vol. I, ch. 4 in *Jane Eyre*, p. 33 in the World's Classics edition of 2000, edited by Margaret Smith with an introduction and revised notes by Sally Shuttleworth (Oxford University Press). (Revelation is the only New Testament book that the child Jane says she "likes.")

21   Other works that address Charlotte Brontë's use of the Bible in her fiction include Michael Wheeler, "Literary and Biblical Allusion in 'The Professor'," *Brontë Society Transactions* 17:1, part 86 (1976), 46–57; George P. Landow, *Victorian Types Victorian Shadows: Biblical Typology in Victorian Literature, Art, and Thought* (Routledge and Kegan Paul, London, 1980), pp. 97–100; Barry V. Qualls, *The Secular Pilgrims of Victorian Fiction: The Novel as Book of Life* (Cambridge University Press, Cambridge, 1982), pp. 43–84; Thomas Vargish, *The Providential Aesthetic in Victorian Fiction* (University Press of Virginia, Charlottesville, 1985), pp. 57–88; and M. Joan Chard, "'Apple of Discord': Centrality of the Eden Myth in Charlotte Brontë's Novels," *Brontë Society Transactions* 19, part 5 (1988), 197–205.

22   The Church of Rome was often attacked for its reluctance to allow its adherents access to the Bible; see, for instance, Thormählen, *The Brontës and Religion*, p. 31.

23   The reference is to the World's Classics edition, from Oxford University Press in 1991, of Charlotte Brontë's posthumously (1857) published first novel *The Professor*, ed. Margaret Smith and Herbert Rosengarten with an introduction by Margaret Smith.

24   On irreverent biblical allusions in *The Professor*, see Wheeler, "Literary and Biblical Allusion," 50–1. In "Charlotte on the Plain of Shinar: Biblical Connections in *Shirley*," *Brontë Society Transactions* 22 (1997), 54–8, Linda B. Figart draws attention to humorous aspects of Charlotte's use of the Bible.

25   As Tim Dolin points out in his notes to the 2000 World's Classics edition of *Villette*, this is an "ominous allusion" (p. 500). All references to *Villette* are to this edition, by Margaret Smith and Herbert Rosengarten with an introduction and notes by Tim Dolin.

26   "Unveiling the Hidden God of Charlotte Brontë's *Villette*," *Literature and Theology* 15:4 (2001), 342–57.

27   See Thormählen, *The Brontës and Religion*, pp. 158–60. On the Psalms generally, see Robert Alter's chapter on the Psalms in Robert Alter and Frank Kermode, eds, *The Literary Guide to the Bible* (Collins, London, 1987, also issued by Fontana Press in 1989).

28   See Roland E. Murphy's entry on the Psalms in Metzger and Coogan, eds, *The Oxford Companion to the Bible*, pp. 626–9, for a succinct overview.

29   For an example, see Margaret Smith, ed., *The Letters of Charlotte Brontë with a Selection of Letters by Family and Friends. Vol. I, 1829–1847* (Clarendon Press, Oxford, 1995), pp. 289–90 (a letter of Charlotte's from 1842).

30   Margaret Smith, ed., *The Letters of Charlotte Brontë with a Selection of Letters by Family and Friends. Vol. II, 1848–1851* (Clarendon Press, Oxford, 2000), p. 95.

31   For brief and illuminating introductions to Maurice and Arnold respectively, see Alec R. Vidler, *The Church in an Age of Revolution*, vol. 5 in the Penguin History of the Church (the revised edition of 1974), pp. 83–7, and Basil Willey, *Nineteenth-Century Studies: Coleridge to Matthew Arnold* (originally published by Chatto and Windus in 1949 and reissued by Penguin in 1964), pp. 72–7.

32   See Thormählen, *The Brontës and Religion*, pp. 81–2 and 158.

33 For instance, Stevie Davies's *Emily Brontë: Heretic* (The Women's Press, London, 1994) speaks of *Wuthering Heights* as mounting "two-pronged attacks on the foundations of Christian religion" (p. 147). Emma Mason adopts a more nuanced view in "'Some God of Wild Enthusiast's Dreams': Emily Brontë's Religious Enthusiasm," *Victorian Literature and Culture* 31:1 (2003), 263–77, which examines the relevance of Methodist enthusiasm to Emily Brontë's writings with special attention to her poetry. Even so, Mason also regards Emily Brontë as a critic of Christianity, who struggled to "envisage a different kind of religion" (274).

34 "The Holy Spirit in Emily Brontë's *Wuthering Heights* and Poetry," *Literature and Theology* 14:2 (2000), 160–73.

35 The name "Jabes Branderham" was probably suggested by the indefatigable Baptist compiler of "skeletal sermons" Jabez Burns (Thormählen, *The Brontës and Religion*, p. 18).

36 Vol. I, ch. 3, p. 18. All references to *Wuthering Heights* are to the World's Classics edition of 1995, ed. Ian Jack with an introduction and notes by Patsy Stoneman (Oxford University Press). The biblical references in the Branderham pages are identified on p. 304 in the notes.

37 On this theme in Emily Brontë's novel, see Thormählen, *The Brontës and Religion*, pp. 134–42. For discussions of revenge/forgiveness in relation to the Branderham dream, see Vereen M. Bell, "*Wuthering Heights* and the Unforgivable Sin," *Nineteenth-Century Fiction* 17 (1962/3), 188–91, and William A. Madden, "*Wuthering Heights*: The Binding of Passion," *Nineteenth-Century Fiction* 27 (1972/3), 127–54 (129–31, 151–4).

38 On the image of the Gadarene swine in *Wuthering Heights*, see Simon Marsden, "'Vain Are the Thousand Creeds': *Wuthering Heights*, the Bible and Liberal Protestantism," *Literature and Theology* 20:3 (2006), 236–50 (243–5). On madness in the novel, see Marianne Thormählen, "The Lunatic and the Devil's Disciple: The 'Lovers' in *Wuthering Heights*," *Review of English Studies* 48 (May 1997), 183–97.

39 "'Vain Are the Thousand Creeds'," 248.

40 "O God within my breast" is the first line of the second stanza of Emily Brontë's best-known poem, "No coward soul is mine."

41 The classic example is the review by Elizabeth Rigby (Lady Westlake) of *Jane Eyre* in the *Quarterly Review* 84 (December 1848), 153–85, easily accessible in Miriam Allott's *The Brontës: The Critical Heritage* (Routledge and Kegan Paul, London, 1974), pp. 105–12 (see especially p. 109).

42 See S. L. Greenslade, ed., *The Cambridge History of the Bible: The West from the Reformation to the Present Day* (Cambridge University Press, Cambridge, 1963), p. 256.

43 There are a number of helpful introductions to the subject of biblical criticism in eighteenth- and nineteenth-century Britain: for instance, Stephen Prickett's essay "Romantics and Victorians: from Typology to Symbolism" in Prickett, ed., *Reading the Text: Biblical Criticism and Literary Theory* (Blackwell, Oxford, 1991), pp. 182–224, and the same author's introductory history of biblical and literary criticism in David Jasper and Stephen Prickett with Andrew Hass, eds, *The Bible and Literature: A Reader* (Blackwell, Oxford, 1999), pp. 12–43. Other works by Jasper and Prickett offer additional insights, notably Prickett's *Origins of Narrative: The Romantic Appropriation of the Bible* (Cambridge University Press, Cambridge, 1996) and Jasper's *The Sacred and Secular Canon in Romanticism* (Macmillan, Basingstoke, 1999). Ch. VII in Greenslade, ed., *The Cambridge History of the Bible* is extremely useful. For more extensive scholarly discussions that go beyond Britain, see Hans W. Frei, *The Eclipse of Biblical Narrative: A Study in Eighteenth and Nineteenth Century Hermeneutics* (Yale University Press, New Haven, CT, 1974) and Hermann Graf Reventlow, *The*

Authority of the Bible and the Rise of the Modern World, trans. John Bowden (SCM, London, 1984). On the British Deists, see William Baird, *History of New Testament Research. Vol. I: From Deism to Tübingen* (Fortress Press, Minneapolis, 1992). *Biblical Interpretation* by Robert Morgan with John Barton is readable and informative (Oxford University Press, Oxford, 1988).

44   Romans 3:2, Hebrews 5:12, and 1 Peter 4:11; cf. Acts 7:38. (Unlike most biblical allusions and echoes in the Brontë fiction, this reference has not been picked up by the Oxford annotators.)

45   Notably in the words spoken as the Bible is presented during the coronation of the British Sovereign ("This is the royal Law; These are the lively Oracles of God"). See Greenslade, *The Cambridge History of the Bible*, p. 519.

46   Robert Lowth's *Lectures on the Sacred Poetry of the Hebrews*, originally delivered in Latin in 1753 and later translated into English (after first having been translated into German), are one example; a piece from Lowth where the expression occurs is found in Jasper and Prickett, eds, *The Bible and Literature*, p. 26.

47   The literal sense of the original Greek is "word," and translations into different languages have adopted a variety of expressions, including "revelation" and "word of promise."

CHAPTER 37

John Ruskin

Dinah Birch

The Christian faith that formed Ruskin's work as a young man broke down as he grew older, but he never stopped reading the Bible. There are few publications among the hundreds he produced in a lifetime of writing in which some form of reference to a biblical text cannot be demonstrated. This much is evident to anyone who turns to his work. What is less apparent is the creative and constantly developing nature of his relations with the Bible. His persistent engagement amounts to more than a legacy of habit from an evangelical childhood, lingering as a husk of piety to be stripped away in order to reveal the genuine thought beneath. It is a sustained source of intellectual energy, not a fixed authority, nor a reassuring envelope of nostalgic allusion. He was a biblical critic in a contentious and often troubled sense, and the place of the Bible in his late writing is fundamentally different from its function in his earlier work. In this he was representative of his generation. Born in 1819, he lived through a period in which the cultural role of the Bible was transformed. He was not the only Victorian writer to find himself compelled to reassess the scriptural authority that had once seemed so secure. But few did so with the rigor that characterized Ruskin's textual scrutiny. The construction of a moral framework whose roots in biblical wisdom could survive the loss of evangelical conviction was for Ruskin both a personal preoccupation and an expression of his public responsibility as a cultural critic. His pursuit of an expanded understanding of the Bible within a new and more complex intellectual context was exceptional in its intensity, but not in its direction. Many were attempting the same journey.

"That Property of Chapters": Biblical Reading and Preaching

The origins of Ruskin's thinking about the Bible, like much else in his work, lay in his family history, and more particularly in the story of the education he received at the hands of his mother. Margaret Ruskin's evangelical religion was serious, and strenuous, and the Bible stood at its heart. As soon as her son could read, she began a daily course of biblical training with him that continued throughout his childhood – in fact, until he went up to Christ Church College, Oxford as a gentleman commoner in 1837. Fifty years later, his autobiography, *Praeterita* (1885–9), looked back on the experiences that had formed his mind:

> She read alternate verses with me, watching, at first, every intonation of my voice, and correcting the false ones, till she made me understand the verse, if within my reach, rightly, and energetically. It might be beyond me altogether; that she did not care about; but she made sure that as soon as I got hold of it at all, I should get hold of it by the right end.
>
> In this way she began with the first verse of Genesis, and went straight through, to the last verse of the Apocalypse; hard names, numbers, Levitical law, and all; and began again at Genesis the next day. If a name was hard, the better the exercise in pronunciation, – if a chapter was tiresome, the better lesson in patience, – if loathsome, the better exercise in faith that there was some use in its being so outspoken. After our chapters ... I had to learn a few verses by heart, or repeat, to make sure I had not lost, something of what was already known. ...
>
> And truly, though I have picked up the elements of a little further knowledge – in mathematics, meteorology, and the like, in after life, – and owe not a little to the teaching of many people, this maternal installation of my mind in that property of chapters I count very confidently the most precious, and, on the whole, the one *essential* part of all my education. (Cook and Wedderburn, 1903–12, 35, pp. 40–3)

The process of reading and learning described here was a daily experience of the exercise of authority – the maternal rule that Margaret Ruskin represented, and also the authority of text, as Ruskin steadily proceeded through chapter and verse of the family Bible. It was an education constructed from an active process of interpretation and understanding. The Bible was a constant point of reference, but its full meaning must be worked for, with unremitting effort. Misunderstanding was a possibility, as well as understanding. If there was a right end for getting hold of a verse, it follows that there must also have been a wrong end. The account is marked by an emphasis on repetition – the cycle of return to the beginning after the end is reached, and the recital of text, as language and meaning are located in the memory. It was there that they stayed. When Ruskin quotes the Bible, it is sometimes unclear which version he is using. One reason for this is that he customarily quotes from memory. He knows the texts too well to want to transcribe the reference, but not quite well enough not to change a word or two here and there as he recalls it. The core of meaning always mattered more than the precise formulation of its translation.

As Ruskin grew, this domestic rhythm of repetition and interpretation was reinforced by the experience of hearing hundreds of sermons, each one taking the exegesis of a biblical text as its starting point. The prosperous and rapidly expanding suburbs of south London in the 1820s and 1830s were a perfect place to hear vigorous preaching, for numerous churches and chapels were springing up in the area. The Ruskin family became connoisseurs of sermons. They heard a number of preachers, for they did not give a steady allegiance to any one place of worship. There was the eccentric Anglican Reverend William Howels, the much more fashionable Congregationalist Edward Andrews, and later the eminent evangelical Henry Melvill, who preached at the Camden Chapel, and was throughout the 1830s acknowledged to be the "most popular preacher in London" (Wheeler, 1999, p. 15). It is worth remembering that such preachers were widely admired, on a scale that perhaps surprises us today. They were glamorous and charismatic figures, celebrities of their time, and they could draw huge audiences. In later life Ruskin was sardonic about preacher-worship, recalling that congregations were often more interested in the man than his message – "And not a soul in all Camden Chapel caring two straws about the young man clothed with linen, nor about Christ, but only about the tone in which their adored Mr. Melvill said 'Aha!' and his fine action over the velvet cushion!" (Evans and Whitehouse, 1956–9, 3, p. 1001). But at the time Ruskin too was impressed by Melvill's charismatic style, and spoke of his sermons as "noble," "interesting," and "admirable" (Burd, 1969, p. 62). Melvill's sermons gave much weight to the close scrutiny of the Bible, emphasizing the need to consider it as a text "to be pondered, not hurried over; a book, so to speak, that may be better read by lines than by chapters" (Melvill, 1845, p. 209; see Landow, 1971, p. 250). As an eagerly idealistic young man, Ruskin found Melvill's biblical evangelicalism an attractive model of Christian identity as it might find expression in the world.

Throughout his childhood and beyond, Ruskin's experiences among the congregations of south London allowed him to experience the moral authority of biblical interpretation within the variously masculine models he encountered in listening to those regular sermons – flamboyant, polished, or mundane. A process that had been maternal and domestic grew to include the possibility of a public role that a talented boy, eager for success, might fulfill. *Praeterita* includes a humorously self-deprecating memory of his first performances:

> I arrived at some abstract in my own mind of the Rev. Mr. Howell's sermons; and occasionally, in imitation of him, preached a sermon at home over the red sofa cushions; – this performance being always called for by my mother's dearest friends, as the great accomplishment of my childhood. The sermon was, I believe, some eleven words long; very exemplary, it seems to me, in that respect – and I still think it must have been the purest gospel, for I know it began with, "People, be good." (Cook and Wedderburn 1903–12, 35, pp. 25–6)

There is no doubt that Ruskin's affinity with the role of the preacher was rooted in his early experiences in the family home in Herne Hill, but it is also clear that this was more than a matter of the prestige that the work might offer. Years of thinking about preaching played a crucial part in Ruskin's move toward the life of a writer, rather than a clergyman – a calling in which the doctrines he would expound could move beyond the orthodoxies of any specific religious affiliation.

It is easy to underestimate the influence of the sermon on nineteenth-century literary form. When it is acknowledged, it is often with a measure of condescension or hostility – the "preachiness" of Ruskin, as Andrew Saint has described it (Saint, 2002, p. 30), is hardly considered a positive attribute. Yet the pedagogic structures of the sermon were fundamental to Ruskin's thinking and writing. Much of his mature work rests on the strategies of the preacher. He saw himself as the spiritual guide of his readers, whose method was to take a sacred text and expand and clarify its meaning to those who heard him. His first literary exercises, regularly undertaken as a child, consisted of summarizing and commenting on the Sunday sermons he heard with his family. Later, from around the age of twelve or thirteen, he began to write sermons himself. He composed, with meticulous care, a series of eighteen sermons on the first five books of the Old Testament – the Pentateuch – and recorded them in a series of handmade manuscript booklets. These dense and thoughtful expositions are based on the solid confidence in the Bible, "the very ground of our faith," that characterized evangelical religious conviction, and Ruskin insists that its truth must be "unqualifiedly" accepted (S1:5.14^v, quoted in Burd, 1981, p. 4). The more we examine and meditate upon the Bible, "the more we shall believe in the sanctity of its origin and the wisdom of its author" (S2:7.6^v, quoted in Burd, 1981, p. 4). Though the nature of his belief in the origin of the Bible was to change fundamentally as a result of the new biblical and scientific researches that transformed the religious world of his boyhood in the 1850s and 1860s, his commitment to the examination of the Bible as a source of moral and practical guidance, rooted in a wisdom beyond the vagaries of the individual will, remained constant. What changed was the definition of what might be identified as a sanctified text, and what the consequences of that recognition ought to be.

"A Subject of Thought": Sacred Texts in Nature and Art

The first and in some ways the most radical expression of Ruskin's biblical practice as a critic is to be found in *Modern Painters,* his first major work, published in five volumes between 1843 and 1860. The giant achievement of *Modern Painters* lies in its fusion of the intellectual and moral intensity of Ruskin's thinking as an evangelical Christian with the second defining imaginative drive of his early years – his engagement with the Romanticism he had encountered in the poetry of Wordsworth, Coleridge, Shelley, and Byron, and in the landscape art of J. M. W. Turner and his contemporaries. Ruskin looks at nature, and at Turner's paintings, which he sees as an expression of the truths of nature, with the same relentless searching eye for detail and for meaning that he had habitually turned on the texts of the Bible. He had heard thousands of sermons on the Bible, he had written sermons on the Bible. Now he develops the model, in order to write sermons on nature and art. His texts are mountains, clouds, leaves, rivers, the sea, or the sky. Like the texts of the Bible, these too must be precisely and actively examined, with genuine care and reverence, before their meaning can be discerned. The sky will provide a telling example. Looking at the sky is something anyone can do – just as anyone might read the Bible. But who, Ruskin asks, really looks at the sky? As he remarks, we "never attend to it, we never make it a subject of thought" (Cook and Wedderburn, 1903–12, 3, p. 344). Making the sky a subject of real thought is among the central objectives of *Modern Painters.*

> One says it has been wet; and another, it has been windy; and another, it has been warm. Who, among the whole chattering crowd, can tell me of the forms and precipices of the chain of tall white mountains that girded the horizon at noon yesterday? Who saw the narrow sunbeam that came out of the south and smote upon their summits until they melted and mouldered away in a dust of blue rain? Who saw the dance of the dead clouds,

when the sunlight left them last night, and the west wind blew them before it like withered leaves? All has passed, unregretted as unseen; or if the apathy be ever shaken off, even for an instant, it is only by what is gross, or what is extraordinary; and yet it is not in the broad and fierce manifestations of the elemental energies, not in the clash of the hail, nor the drift of the whirlwind, that the highest characters of the sublime are developed. God is not in the earthquake, nor in the fire, but in the still, small voice. (Cook and Wedderburn 1903–12, 3, pp. 344–5)

The biblical reference with which Ruskin ends this passage is a familiar one. It is from the account of the Old Testament prophet Elijah's encounter with the Lord after his flight from Ahab and Jezebel:

And behold, the Lord passed by, and a great and strong wind rent the mountains, and broke in pieces the rocks before the Lord, but the Lord was not in the wind: and after the wind an earthquake; but the Lord was not in the earthquake. And after the earthquake a fire; but the Lord was not in the fire: and after the fire, a still small voice. (1 Kings 19:11–12)

This is a biblical moment that Ruskin often refers to. The still small voice of divinity in the natural world is not to be found in what is spectacular, exceptional, or terrifying, but in the quiet detail of the natural world, to which Ruskin repeatedly directs our gaze throughout his critical writings in the 1840s and 1850s. Chapters in the first volume of Modern Painters have titles like "The Truth of Vegetation," as Ruskin demonstrates the mystery, complexity, and grace with which nature demonstrates the moral truths of harmony, truths that it should be the artist's job to explicate. The branch of a tree becomes a text for serious meditation, as Ruskin asks us to understand it:

Break off an elm bough three feet long, in full leaf, and lay it on the table before you, and try to draw it, leaf for leaf. It is ten to one if in the whole bough (provided you do not twist it about as you work) you find one form of a leaf exactly like another; perhaps you will not even have *one* complete. Every leaf will be oblique, or foreshortened, or curled, or crossed by another, or shaded by another, or have something or other the matter with it; and though the whole bough will look graceful and symmetrical, you will scarcely be able to tell how or why it does so, since there is not one line of it like another. (Cook and Wedderburn, 1903–12, 3, p. 589)

Here, as in his observation of the sky, what Ruskin wants to emphasize is the unending variety, the difficulty and changeful evanescence of detail that seems to him to distinguish and define the natural phenomena he takes as his texts in this study. Nature is not static; it performs imperfection, loss, and incompletion. Clouds dissolve and melt away, they decompose, unregretted and unseen. Leaves are crossed and shaded, each has "something or other the matter with it," though together they express an infinity of truth and form. We cannot see the whole of the shadowed meaning of nature, whose dappled changeful intricacies express both vitality and mortality. This is what leaves have to teach us – the precision and humility of perception that recognizes its own incapacities. Leaves express the imperfection of the fallen world that the human mind must inhabit. Ruskin moves from his single bough of elm to a whole tree, and then to an entire forest of beauty and incomprehensible mystery:

> The leaves then at the extremities become as fine as dust, a mere confusion of points and lines between you and the sky, a confusion which, you might as well hope to draw sea-sand particle by particle, as to imitate leaf for leaf. This, as it comes down into the body of the tree, gets closer, but never opaque; it is always transparent with crumbling lights in it letting you through to the sky: then out of this, come, heavier and heavier, the masses of illumined foliage, all dazzling and inextricable, save here and there a single leaf on the extremities: then, under these, you get deep passages of broken irregular gloom, passing into transparent, green-lighted, misty hollows; the twisted stems glancing through them in their pale and entangled infinity, and the shafted sunbeams, rained from above, running along the lustrous leaves for an instant; then lost, then caught again on some emerald bank or knotted root, to be sent up again with a faint reflex on the white under-sides of dim groups of drooping foliage, the shadows of the upper boughs running in grey network down the glossy stems, and resting in quiet chequers upon the glittering earth; but all penetrable and transparent, and, in proportion, inextricable and incomprehensible, except where across the labyrinth and the mystery of the dazzling light and dream-like shadow, falls, close to us, some solitary spray, some wreath of two or three motionless large leaves, the type and embodying of all that in the rest we feel and imagine, but can never see. (Cook and Wedderburn, 1903–12, 3, pp. 589–90)

This is a passage that takes us to the heart of Ruskin's critical thought in its earliest expression, and also toward what matters most in his approach to the Bible. The intricate texture of his language insists on confusion, inextricability, irregularity, gloom, entanglement, faint and falling light, shade and solitariness, labyrinth and mystery. The purpose of Ruskin's exegesis of the texts of vegetation is not to make things clear and simple – quite the reverse. His purpose is to make us understand that understanding is only possible when we accept that things aren't clear, and can never be simple. It is the Romantic in Ruskin who underscores the role of feeling and imagination, rather than comprehensive vision. But it is the devotion of the evangelical biblical scholar who draws our attention to the spiritual humility necessary to discern the significance of that solitary wreath of leaves, the type of what cannot be wholly seen. Their function can be compared with that of a biblical verse, "transparent with crumbling lights in it letting you through to the sky."

Critical Controversies and Social Polemics

As Ruskin's reading grew broader, and he mixed with people from a wider variety of religious and intellectual backgrounds, he encountered developments in scientific and biblical research that steadily undermined his evangelicalism. In 1851, he wrote to Henry Acland, a university friend who had become a doctor, of a faith that was fluttering "in weak rags from the letter of its old forms; but the only letters it can hold by at all are the old evangelical formulae. If only the Geologists would let me alone, I could do very well, but those dreadful Hammers! I hear the clink of them at the end of every cadence of the Bible verses" (Cook and Wedderburn, 1903–12, 36, p. 115). Though

Ruskin was later to claim that the turning point came in 1858, when "his evangelical beliefs were put away, to be debated of no more" (Cook and Wedderburn, 1903–12, 35, p. 495), this "un-conversion" took the form of a cumulative process, rather than a dramatic crisis. He wrote to the American scholar Charles Eliot Norton in 1860: "I don't believe in Evangelicalism – and my Evangelical (once) friends now look upon me with as much horror as on one of the possessed Gennesaret pigs" (Bradley and Ousby, 1987, p. 53; Matthew 8:28–32). This was the year that saw the publication of the notorious *Essays and Reviews*, the collection of essays whose sceptical biblical scholarship threw the ecclesiastical world into disarray. Ruskin's sympathies were very much with the contributors. Throughout the 1860s, he supported J. W. Colenso, the first Bishop of Natal, whose historical examination of the Pentateuch had led to his prosecution in the ecclesiastical courts (Colenso, 1862–3). He wrote as a humanist in the 1860s, gradually returning to an individual and sometimes idiosyncratic mode of Christianity in the 1870s. These shifts had the effect of revitalizing his relations with the Bible. Just as we cannot hope to understand what a forest has to teach until we acknowledge the limits of human perception, so, Ruskin argues, we cannot understand the Bible unless we accept its variety, its changefulness, its darkness and mystery.

Ruskin's views of the spiritual and moral authority of the Bible in those turbulent days are crisply summarised in *Time and Tide*, a series of letters to a working man of Sunderland dating from 1867. Ruskin here demonstrates how far his reading as a man has shifted his thinking from the position of his boyhood, when the Bible was simply the word of God. He now suggests that:

> the mass of religious Scripture contains merely the best efforts which we hitherto know to have been made by any of the races of men towards the discovery of some relations with the spiritual world; that they are only trustworthy as expressions of the enthusiastic views or beliefs of earnest men oppressed by the world's darkness, and have no more authoritative claim on our faith than the religious speculations and histories of the Egyptians, Greeks, Persians and Indians; but are, in common with all these, to be reverently studied, as containing a portion, divinely appointed, of the best wisdom which human intellect, earnestly seeking for help from God, has hitherto been able to gather between birth and death. (Cook and Wedderburn, 1903–12, 17, p. 349)

These are views that place him very much at the liberal end of the spectrum of religious belief within the period. But when Ruskin insisted that the Bible should be reverently studied, he meant it. The habit of regular biblical study that he had formed as a child did not fade as his understanding of the spiritual status of the Bible changed. Though the parallel speculations of the Egyptians, Greeks, Persians, and Indians carried equal weight and called for equal respect, it was in the cultural identity of Europe that Ruskin was chiefly interested, and the history of the Bible lay at its heart. The terms in which Ruskin approached his work as a critic changed radically in the 1860s, as he abandoned the highly wrought poetic cadences that had characterized the first volume of *Modern Painters*, and moved toward a more cool and measured style. But his central preoccupations did not change. He still directs us to look for meaning in what is uncertain and incomprehensible. In 1868, he explained the shift in his approach, and its consistency too, in a lecture called "The Mystery of Life and Its Arts":

For my thoughts have changed also, as my words have; and whereas in earlier life, what little influence I obtained was due perhaps chiefly to the enthusiasm with which I was able to dwell on the beauty of the physical clouds, and of their colours in the sky; so all the influence I now desire to retain must be due to the earnestness with which I am endeavouring to trace the form and beauty of another kind of cloud than those; the bright cloud of which it is written – "What is your life? It is even as a vapour that appeareth for a little time, and then vanisheth away." (Cook and Wedderburn 1903–12, 18, p. 146)

This is written, of course, in the Bible – in the Epistle of James (James 4:14). "The Mystery of Life and Its Arts" was published at a time when Ruskin's distance from the formal practices and beliefs of the evangelical Christianity of his youth were at their height, yet over and over again this pivotal statement of critical intent is punctuated with reference to biblical texts. The entire lecture has the structure of a secular sermon. It is a sermon that rests on what cannot be known, rather than what is certain. This was James's point – "Whereas ye know not what shall be on the morrow" (James 4:14) – and it is Ruskin's point too.

Are you sure there is a heaven? Sure there is a hell? Sure that men are dropping before your faces through the pavement of these streets into eternal fire, or sure that they are not? Sure that at our own death you are going to be delivered from all sorrow, to be endowed with all virtue, to be gifted with all felicity, and raised into perpetual companionship with a King, compared to whom the kings of the earth are as grasshoppers, and the nations as the dust of His feet? (Cook and Wedderburn, 1903–12, 18, p. 155; Isaiah 40:15, 22; Nahum 3:17; 1:3).

Of course these could not, in 1868, be matters for certainty for the audience that Ruskin was addressing. Just as he had previously insisted on the shadowed mystery in which the spiritual meaning of a forest consists, so he now insists on the mystery that clouds the central issues of human faith. Much that had seemed fixed in the Bible that he had studied throughout his life now seemed uncertain. But the deeper moral imperatives of the Bible remain, and though this lecture is among the most sceptical of his accounts of Christian faith, it is also one of the most biblical – the labyrinthine range and extent of biblical reference throughout the text is extraordinary. Biblical authority is confirmed, not erased, by its location within uncertainty. The lecture ends with one of Ruskin's most fervent and highly wrought perorations, as he returns to the deepest foundations of his biblically grounded moral discourse, and exhorts his readers to recall the unchanging tenets what he here terms "an infallible religion": Faith, Hope, and "the greatest of these, Charity" (Cook and Wedderburn, 1903–12, 18, p. 167).

A New Evangelicalism

As Ruskin moves into his most productive, innovative, and turbulent decade, the 1870s, he moves closer to an openly proclaimed Christian position, and further from the humanism of the 1860s. Recurrent reference to and interpretation of biblical text and authority becomes still more prominent in many of his varied publications through-out this decade. He does not, however, return to the evangelical doctrines of his early years, and is in fact often openly hostile to evangelical beliefs. *Fors Clavigera* (1871–84) persistently debates the question of what the proper role of biblical authority in the lives of his readers should be. In this fierce series of letters, addressed to "the workmen and labourers of Great Britain," Ruskin often uses preacherly strategies to challenge the evangelical assumptions of his readers. The thirty-sixth letter, "Traveller's Rest," pub-lished in October 1873, is in essence a celebration of the value of good public houses – not a traditionally evangelical topos, nor one that would naturally be associated with a biblical critic. Unusually forthright even for this provocative phase in his career, Ruskin begins the letter with a challenge, proclaiming that he will explain to his readers why "it is so grave a heresy (or wilful source of division) to call any book, or collection of books, the 'Word of God'" (Cook and Wedderburn, 1903–12, 27, p. 669). The Word of God, Ruskin affirms, is not confined to the Bible:

> By that Word, or Voice, or Breath, or Spirit, the heavens and earth, and all the host of them, were made; and in it they exist. It is your life; and speaks to you always, so long as you live nobly; – dies out of you as you refuse to obey it; leaves you to hear, and be slain by, the word of an evil spirit, instead of it.
>
> It may come to you in books, – come to you in clouds, – come to you in the voices of men, – come to you in the stillness of deserts. You must be strong in evil, if you have quenched it wholly; – very desolate in this Christian land, if you have never heard it at all. (Cook and Wedderburn, 1903–12, 27, pp. 669–70)

Ruskin has a very specific purpose in his mind in this passage. He wants to dis-suade his readers from their unquestioning belief that biblical teaching would frown on drinking, and he does this first by a characteristically close examination of a passage from the first epistle of Timothy, where it is affirmed, in the King James Bible, that "every creature of God is good, and nothing to be refused, if it be received with thanks-giving. For it is sanctified by the word of God and prayer" (1 Timothy 4:4–5). Ruskin goes on to question the emphasis of the Authorized Version, suggesting that a better translation would read "For it is sanctified by the word of God, and the chance that brings it." Which means, Ruskin says, "that when meat comes in your way when you are hungry, or drink when you are thirsty, and you know in your own conscience that it is good for you to have it, the meat and drink are holy to you" (Cook and Wedderburn, 1903–12, p. 670). Here we get closer to the pub, as Ruskin develops his argument:

> there cannot indeed be at present imagined a more sacred function for young Christian men than that of hosts or hospitallers, supplying, to due needs, and with proper mainte-nance of their own lives, wholesome food and drink to all men: so that as, at least, always at one end of a village there may be a holy church and vicar, so at the other end of the village there may be a holy tavern and tapster, ministering the good creatures of God, so that they may be sanctified by the Word of God and His Providence. (Cook and Wedderburn, 1903–12, 27, pp. 671–2)

Ruskin was the son of a wine merchant, and like so much of his social teaching this passage can in part be explained by his family history. In his most fervently evangelical days, he was never sympathetic to the austerities of the temperance movement. But he means something more than the advocation of moderate and healthful drinking. He turns to the Psalms, as he very often does, to develop his point, and thinks particularly about the short and resonant verses of the fifteenth Psalm: "It begins by asking God who shall abide in His tabernacle, or movable tavern, and who shall dwell in his holy hill" (Cook and Wedderburn, 1903–12, 27, p. 674). Ruskin reminds his readers of the shared etymological root of the words "tavern" and "tabernacle" in the Latin *taberna*, meaning simply a hut, or booth. This kind of word play is characteristic of Ruskin's method in his late writing. What had seemed simple – the holy tabernacle as the home of the Ark of the Covenant on the one hand, and the unholy tavern as the home of drunken indulgence on the other, turns out not to be so clear cut. This too might be a matter for uncertainty and mingled shade. But the central question of the Psalm, as Ruskin expands it to its readers in this secular letter that turns into a resolute sermon, is not ambiguous: "Who among travelling men will have God to set up his tavern for him when he wants rest?" (Cook and Wedderburn, 1903–12, 27, pp. 674–5). Ruskin's answer paraphrases the affirmations of the fifteenth Psalm, using the strategies he had heard developed in the pulpit so many times as a boy. His point is that the biblical Psalms are the Word of God to his readers, just as the works of nature are the Word of God, if they are read with active devotion. "But if your heart is dishonest and rebellious, you may read them for ever with lip-service, and all the while be 'men-pleasers,' whose bones are to broken at the pit's mouth, and so left incapable of breath, brought by any winds of Heaven" (Cook and Wedderburn 1903–12, 27, pp. 675–6).

Ruskin's polemical register in *Fors Clavigera* and other comparably challenging texts of the 1870s and 1880s returns to the evangelical methods that had formed his voice in the years in which his mother had trained him as a reader of the Bible. But he now uses these tactics in order to challenge what had come to seem to him the narrow complacencies of evangelical conviction. The Bible as he reads it does not confirm a settled claim to righteousness in those who claim its authority; instead, it demands self-questioning, uncertainty, spiritual inwardness, and persistent effort. Like nature, and like the art that serves nature, the Bible must be read with energetic and often painful attention. It also demands arduously practical and political forms of expression, for a proper comprehension of the Bible cannot be contained within the study or the pulpit, nor within unquestioning conformity to any established church. The foundation of the reforming Guild of St George alongside the publication of *Fors Clavigera*, and the exemplary schemes for practical action (road-building, street-sweeping, the purchase of a small shop to sell pure tea to the poor) that accompanied work for the Guild were as much the product of Ruskin's biblical reading as his prolific later publications. The exhortatory *Fors Clavigera*, alongside *Modern Painters* and *The Stones of Venice*, became lastingly influential, especially among those self-educated working men and women who used Ruskin's authority as a means to further their own personal and intellectual growth. It was, to take one example of its power, a formative text among those who were active in the early years of British socialist movements. Questioned in 1906 on the reading that had most influenced them, the first generation of Labour MPs cited Ruskin more often than any other author, with the Bible as a close second (Goldman, 1999). Ruskin also became a vivid source of inspiration for a generation of independently minded women reformers, like Octavia Hill, who were reluctant to accept a secondary role in the pursuit of social justice (Harris, 1999).

Traditions of biblical study have a long history of influence among those looking to question the cultural establishment, and here the association between early nineteenth-century evangelicalism and older varieties of nonconformism is worth remembering. Ruskin's assertion that formal training in school or university could not take the place of an exacting individual engagement with the meaning of the Bible, and that the practical consequences of that work would be expressed in shared action rather than private scholarship, made his thinking attractive to those who looked for the moral energies of Christianity without the constraints of its institutional or theological orthodoxies. What remains remarkable is the extent to which the largely secular range of the polemics of Ruskin's later years continues to draw on a meditation on the biblical texts that he had memorized as a child. No nineteenth-century thinker had a more diverse impact on his contemporaries and their successors than Ruskin, and none was more radically shaped by a lifelong engagement with the Bible.

References

Bradley, J. and Ousby, I., eds (1987) *The Correspondence of John Ruskin and Charles Eliot Norton.* Cambridge University Press, Cambridge.

Burd, V. A., ed. (1969) *The Winnington Letters: John Ruskin's Correspondence with Margaret Alexis Bell and the Children of Winnington Hall.* George Allen, London.

Burd, V. A. (1981) "Ruskin's Testament of his Boyhood Faith: Sermons on the Pentateuch," in R. Hewison, ed., *New Approaches to Ruskin: Thirteen Essays.* Routledge and Kegan Paul, London, pp. 1–16.

Colenso, J. W. (1862–3) *The Pentateuch and Book of Joshua Critically Examined.* Longman, London.

Cook, E. T. and Wedderburn, A., eds (1903–12) *The Works of John Ruskin*, 39 volumes. George Allen, London.

Evans, J. and Whitehouse, J. H., eds (1956–9) *The Diaries of John Ruskin*, 3 volumes. Clarendon Press, Oxford.

Goldman, Lawrence (1999) "Ruskin, Oxford, and the British Labour Movement 1880–1914," in D. Birch, ed., *Ruskin and the Dawn of the Modern.* Clarendon Press, Oxford, pp. 57–86.

Harris, Jose (1999) "Ruskin and Social Reform," in D. Birch, ed., *Ruskin and the Dawn of the Modern.* Clarendon Press, Oxford, pp. 7–33.

Landow, G. P. (1971) *The Aesthetic and Critical Theories of John Ruskin.* Princeton University Press, Princeton, NJ.

Melvill, H. (1845) *Sermons.* Rivington, London.

Saint, A. (2002) "The Danger of Giving In," *London Review of Books* 24:20, 30–1.

Wheeler, M. (1999) *Ruskin's God.* Cambridge University Press, Cambridge.

CHAPTER 38

George Eliot

Charles LaPorte

Among the many "quaintnesses" attributed to Caleb Garth, the genial land agent of George Eliot's novel *Middlemarch* (1872), is that "whenever he had a feeling of awe, he was haunted by a sense of Biblical phraseology, though he could hardly have given a strict quotation."[1] Now, what makes Garth's condition seem "quaint" may be his ineptness with quotation or his general inarticulateness or his social situation, but it can hardly be the sole fact of his being "haunted by ... Biblical phraseology." For most Victorian literary figures that we can now name were similarly haunted, with Eliot conspicuous among them. As John Holloway pointed out long ago, Eliot's writings betray her own habit of "Biblical phraseology" as surely as she betrays Garth's.[2] Like Thomas Carlyle and John Ruskin, Eliot absorbed the language of the King James translation so thoroughly as to make it a part of her idiom and manner of thinking.

Eliot's investment in the Bible, moreover, stands out in two important ways from that of other Victorian sages such as Carlyle or Ruskin. First, she was better versed in contemporary biblical criticism, especially the avant-garde tradition called "the Higher Criticism" that emerged from Germany in the first half of the nineteenth century and that she helped to translate into English. (It subsequently became the basis for mainstream anglophone biblical scholarship.[3]) Second, and partly in consequence, Eliot grappled still more extensively with the Bible's vitality in modern culture. This second point is made far less frequently than the first because literary scholars like to conceive of Eliot as an agent in a widespread process of Victorian secularization that diminishes the Bible's overall cultural importance. Yet Eliot's most characteristic literary uses of the Bible do not lend themselves to this simple view of secularization. For this reason, the following chapter will focus not just upon her use of the Bible's language, but also upon its enduring cultural function. Below, I examine both Eliot's shrewd exploration of the historical conditions of biblical hermeneutics (or theories of interpretation), and, equally importantly, some of her abundant expressions about the cultural importance of having a sacred text at all. Eliot strove to express the Bible's influence upon a great variety of religious attitudes: the zealous, the lukewarm, the antipathetic, and the utterly indifferent. And her works invariably seek to transform the terms of the Bible's influence upon their readers.

Caleb Garth's awe and haunting, for instance, are clearly prefigured in the darkly comic scene from *The Mill on the Floss* (1860) in which the hapless miller Tulliver asks his son, Tom, to record in the family Bible a curse against his enemy. His daughter, Maggie, protests against this action, and he rebukes her sharply:

> "Now write – write it i' the Bible."
>
> "O father, what?" said Maggie, sinking down by his knee, pale and trembling. "It's wicked to curse and bear malice."
>
> "It isn't wicked, I tell you," said her father fiercely. "It's wicked as the raskills should prosper – it's the devil's doing. Do as I tell you, Tom. Write."[4]

This moral episode is more complex than at first appears. By the terms of middle-class Victorian morality, Maggie's side of this argument clearly seems best: "it's wicked," after all, "to curse and bear malice." But by the terms of the Authorized Version (AV) of the King James translation, Tulliver also seems justified. His telling juxtaposition of "wicked" and "prosper" invokes the famous plaint of Jeremiah, "Wherefore doth the way of the wicked prosper? *wherefore* are all they happy that deal very treacherously?" (Jeremiah 12:1).[5] And Jeremiah presents something of a user's guide to cursing, where in chapter upon chapter, the prophet curses the impious "raskills" of Israel and Judah for their transgressions against the Lord. Maggie's refined moral ideas also may derive from the Bible, but her less articulate father seems on firmer footing here.

Eliot's novels regularly aim to upset her readers' habits of biblical reading in this manner, vexing their assumptions not so much about the Bible's significance as about the way that it ought to be appreciated. She was a masterful exegete and, as I have mentioned, a scholar of hermeneutic method from antiquity to the present. Early reaction against her youthful evangelical Christianity led to her English translation of D. F. Strauss's *Das Leben Jesu* (*The Life of Jesus*, 1835, trans. 1846), a monument of the Higher Criticism and among the most influential studies ever written on the Christian Scriptures, as well as Ludwig Feuerbach's *Das Wesen des Christenthums* (*The Essence of Christianity*, 1841, trans. 1854). Yet her intellectual achievement in this area culminates in literary writings such as *The Mill on the Floss* and *Middlemarch*. In part, this is because these works articulate not only the heart of the new sophisticated continental models of biblical hermeneutics, but also that of older, native, and even crude types of exegesis that nonetheless exercise important claims upon us.[6] Eliot winks at her readers' presumable differences with Tulliver or with the rustic Methodists Dinah Morris and Seth Bede, characters in *Adam Bede* who "drew lots, and sought for Divine guidance by opening the Bible at hazard; having a literal way of interpreting the Scriptures," but she never smirks at them or contests the private usefulness of their haphazard exegesis. Like Garth and Tulliver, Dinah and Seth find important personal truths in the Bible even when it is opened "at hazard." That the angelic Dinah Morris's truths seem entirely incommensurable with the vengeful Tulliver's is only part of the point.

Here and throughout her literary work, Eliot presents good hermeneutics as capacious, expansive, and even paradoxical. Yet, for her good hermeneutics are never entirely arbitrary: not just any manner of reading the Bible is equal to any other. Edward Casaubon, for instance, the withered scholar of *Middlemarch*, provides the most salient example in Eliot of a bad hermeneut. His quasi-erudite *Key to All Mythologies* parodies eighteenth-century critical traditions that sought in comparative mythology a confirmation of the Genesis creation account.[7] Casaubon's own methods were made obsolete by the type of German scholarship that would be translated by his author, and she traces his intellectual situation lightly but with great exactness. As his nephew Will Ladislaw summarizes the tragic obsolescence of his work: "it should be thrown away, as so much English scholarship is, for want of knowing what is being done by the rest of the world. If Mr Casaubon read German he would save himself a great deal of trouble" (p. 208). True, Casaubon's scholarly paradigm gives offense, with its self-gratifying idea that other world mythologies are mere corruptions of the Bible; whereas a modest reader like Seth Bede restricts his exegesis to his own life, Casaubon tries to make claims about other people's mythology without well enough understanding his own. But Casaubon's real sin in *Middlemarch* is his prejudiced dismissal of the German writers who, as Ladislaw notes, would disabuse him of his grandiose principle of mythic originality by turning it altogether inside out.

The German critics, instead, conveyed how quickly a comparative mythology could bring home the foreign nature of their own Christian texts, and Eliot returns to their scholarly paradigms again and again in her writings.[8] Among other things, they showed her exactly how historical and geographical distance from the social conditions of the Bible's composition risks making any modern reading a misreading.[9] Even the safest seeming interpretation may be mistaken for reasons now lost to history. Like many Victorian poets and novelists, for instance, Eliot regularly invoked scriptural condemnations of the wealthy. But when Seth Bede gives voice to his positive conviction that the Gospels discourage interest in worldly security, his mother Lisbeth responds scornfully,

> I donna see how thee 't to know as "take no thought for the morrow" means all that. An' when the Bible's such a big book, an' thee canst read all thro 't, an' ha' the pick o' the texes, I canna think why thee dostna pick better words as donna mean so much more nor what they say.[10]

Seth's reading seems unobjectionably sound, and yet his mother's *explication de texte* (or *de "texe"*) may be unanswerable. Lisbeth scrupulously points out that Christ's injunction to "take no thought for the morrow" cannot be exclusively restricted to material security. And by resisting any implication that it can, she joins the majority tradition of Victorian exegetes, who ignored the radical social implications of the Gospels in favor of less evident, yet still viable, interpretations that permitted a degree of social comfort.[11] It should already be apparent that Lisbeth's hermeneutic philosophy ("I canna think why thee dostna pick better words as donna mean so much more nor what they say") is really the flip side of Feuerbach's observation that "the Bible, as every one knows, has the valuable quality that everything may be found in it which it is desired to find."[12] So Lisbeth Bede is not especially remiss among exegetes or literary critics, who must inevitably privilege some features of a text at the expense of others. However, her method presents a genuine conundrum for a hermeneutics that seeks to be representative of the text.

Eliot makes similar comedy of the inevitable selectiveness of the biblical exegete in *Silas Marner* (1861), where the good Dolly Winthrop has either never heard of or never grasped the biblical practice of drawing lots in order to determine the will of God (found with God's seeming approbation in Joshua, 1 Samuel, and Jonah). Silas, the title character, relates to Dolly that he had been banished from his dissenting chapel community because the community relied heavily upon the practice of lots to investigate mysteries. When Silas was wrongly accused of stealing, the lots misrepresented his character to heartrending effect:

> Silas at last arrived at the climax of the sad story – the drawing of lots, and its false testimony concerning him; and this had to be repeated in several interviews, under new questions on her part as to the nature of this plan for detecting the guilty and clearing the innocent.
>
> "And yourn's the same Bible, you're sure o' that, Master Marner – the Bible as you brought wi' you from that country – it's the same as what they've got at church, and what Eppie's a-learning to read in?"
>
> "Yes," said Silas, "every bit the same; and there's drawing o' lots in the Bible, mind you," he added in a lower tone.
>
> "O dear, dear," said Dolly in a grieved voice, as if she were hearing an unfavorable report of a sick man's case.[13]

Dolly does not quickly recognize the practice of lots as biblical, but her gradual disappointment speaks volumes. Her grief is not at Silas's personal condition (which by this point is better than ever), but at the circumstance of her own Bible containing such unseemly elements and seeming to sanction them. Hence her repeated inquiry: "And yourn's the same Bible, you're sure o' that, Master Marner ...?" It is this "same Bible," and not poor Silas, that provokes the hushed tones with which they converse as at "a sick man's case."

Here is Maggie Tulliver's moral conundrum in another form. To Victorian readers, as to us, various key elements of the Bible seemed perplexing, unsavory, or simply immoral, despite the paradoxical circumstance that the Bible had done so much to form Victorian ideas about morals. This is why ethically dubious passages from the Scriptures are so relentlessly probed in what we now call the Victorian literature of "faith and doubt." Consider J. A. Froude's *The Nemesis of Faith* (1849), the quintessential novel of "faith and doubt," and a *succès de scandale* that owed at least part of its notoriety to Eliot's effusive praise in *The Westminster Review*. Froude's protagonist, Markham Sutherland, spends page upon page rehearsing the inconsistency between modern moral instincts and scriptural episodes like Saul's slaughter of the Amelkites, or Christ's apparent sanction of the idea of Hell, which Sutherland calls "a doctrine so horrible that it could only have taken root in mankind when they were struggling in the perplexities of Manicheeism."[14] *The Nemesis* no longer commands a significant readership, partly because it reads like a misshapen theological treatise. Yet in her review, Eliot lauds it as a "true product of genius," and specifies that its glory lies in uncovering "the dubious aspect which many chartered respectabilities are beginning to wear under the light of this nineteenth century," and in "its suggestive hints as to the necessity of recasting the currency of our religion and virtue."[15] In short, our chartered historical notions of "religion and virtue" may no longer be entirely compatible with the moral sense that they have done so much to form. Froude's Sutherland scandalized Victorian readers by flatly stating as much, but the more appealing narratives of Silas Marner and Maggie Tulliver slyly advance the same premise.

The German philosopher F. D. E. Schleiermacher, the most important of that contemporary school of biblical scholars whom Casaubon ignores, emphasized the role of private investment in textual interpretation as a way to make sense of this problem of the Bible's historically and culturally foreign nature. It was Schleiermacher's genius to show how such personal investment was an essential condition not only to comprehending a deeply foreign sacred book, but to hermeneutics more generally. When Samuel Taylor Coleridge wrote in the *Confessions of an Inquiring Spirit* that "in the Bible there is more that *finds* me than I have experienced in all other books put together," this personal element is unmistakable, and signals all the difference between a Dinah Morris and a Casaubon.[16] Naturally, pitfalls also attend the proposal to rely upon moral instincts and personal circumstances in order to judge the meaning of any scriptural text. Mary Holt, mother of the eponymous hero of *Felix Holt* (1866), takes this to ridiculous extremes, as when she boasts that the Bible expressly sanctions her quack medicines, and that one scriptural text in particular "might have been made for a receipt of my husband's – it's just as if it was a riddle, and Holt's Elixir was the answer."[17] This fantastic claim prompts her kindly pastor Rufus Lyon to the ever-timely reflection that "it is quite true that we may err in giving a too private interpretation to the Scripture" (p. 57). As Schleiermacher recognized, bad exegesis *à la* Mrs Holt poses a genuine problem for his system, in response to which he must appeal to the good sense of the exegete. In *Felix Holt*, the good Lyon's interpretations often fail as well. But to acknowledge as much is not to disavow good interpretation in the world of Eliot's fiction.[18] No perfect interpretation is possible, but some forms are worse than others.

Further, Shleiermacher's personal conception of interpretation remains paramount in Eliot as a key to genuine understanding even though, as she shows, the personality of the exegete always exists at odds with the unruly nature of the Scriptures, the foreign quality that Casaubon and Mrs Holt in their different ways refuse to recognize. Even in the best of cases, this personal element may seem to entail something of a guilty self-absorption, although that does not render it irrelevant. Dorothea Brooke, the heroine of *Middlemarch*, whom the narrator depicts as a modern Saint Theresa, illustrates this much in a chaste early love scene with Ladislaw, to whom she explains her religious philosophy:

> "by desiring what is perfectly good, even when we don't quite know what it is and cannot do what we would, we are part of the divine power against evil – widening the skirts of light and making the struggle with darkness narrower."
> "That is a beautiful mysticism – it is a –"

"Please not to call it by any name," said Dorothea, putting out her hands entreatingly. "You will say it is Persian, or something else geographical. It is my life. I have found it out, and cannot part with it." (p. 392)

What seems most striking about this exchange is Dorothea's apprehension that to accept her own philosophy to be originally "Persian, or something else geographical" somehow risks estranging her from it. She feels it to be personal, if not unique, and she entreats Will to recognize that personal quality: "It is my life. I ... cannot part with it." In a certain sense, this self-absorption is mirrored in Casaubon's whole school of mythological exegesis, a school unwilling to surrender any part of their own biblical mythology to the broader Mesopotamian culture from which many of its elements evidently derive. The beauty of Dorothea's confession to Will lies in the fact that he, who grasps the principles of the higher criticism, who thus sees the shortcomings of Casaubon's scholarship, and who can surely imagine "geographical" antecedents to Dorothea's mysticism, nonetheless falls in love with her particular expression of it. In a later chapter, when Will believes himself to have lost Dorothea's confidence and esteem, he cries aloud that "I never had a *preference* for her, any more than I have a preference for breathing. No other woman exists by the side of her. I would rather touch her hand if it were dead, than I would touch any other woman's living" (p. 778). It is not Dorothea's philosophy, hardly distinctive in itself, but her personal instantiation of that philosophy that moves Will. It is only her version of Saint Theresa who can save him.

Eliot revisits this theme of hermeneutic particularity in her final novel, *Daniel Deronda* (1876). When Daniel saves Mirah Lapidoth from drowning herself in the river, he understates the uniqueness of his own heroism, and Mirah contradicts him:

"It was my good chance to find you," said Deronda. "Any other man would have been glad to do what I did."

"That is not the right way of thinking about it," said Mirah, shaking her head with decisive gravity. "I think of what really was. It was you, and not another, who found me, and were good to me."

"I agree with Mirah," said Mrs Meyrick. "Saint Anybody is a bad saint to pray to."[19]

Mrs Meyrick, who here volunteers herself as a third-party arbiter of this dispute, properly points out that Mirah owes nothing to Saint Anybody – a patron whose title seems foreign to Mirah's Jewish heritage anyway – and that Mirah is right to recognize the depth and distinctiveness of her debt to Daniel. This is important, for depth and distinctiveness of religious obligation are imperative leitmotivs of *Daniel Deronda*. Mirah also invokes the terms cited above when speaking of her family, without any awareness on either her part or Daniel's that they share a common ancestry: "It was he who was given to me for my father, *and not another*. And so it is with my people. I will always be a Jewess" (p. 317, italics added). Critics from the Victorian era to the present day have balked at the artificiality of Daniel's secret Jewish ancestry, but for Eliot, the necessity of this heritage seems to grow naturally from her repeated insistence upon particularity. It may in some measure be a response to the unsettling impersonality of prominent nineteenth-century conceptions of religion from vague Romantic pantheism to Comtean positivism to Feuerbach's proposal that the divine is a mere projection of human experience. Deronda's eventual religious zeal may be no more than a psychological projection of his own finest qualities, as Feuerbach held, but it gets life from the community in which he finds himself joined through relations with Mirah and her brother Mordecai. For all three of these, "Saint Anybody is a bad saint to pray to."

Eliot's deep investment in contemporary hermeneutic theory from the primitive Methodists to the higher critics to nineteenth-century Zionism has rightly received a great deal of attention since U. C. Knopflemacher's recommendation that Eliot be studied as a "philosophic novelist" in the tradition of Feuerbach.[20] Perhaps the fullest instance of such scholarship comes from Mary Wilson Carpenter, whose *George Eliot and the Landscape of Time* (1986) traces Eliot's extensive use of the apocalyptic "Continuous History" school of contemporary biblical exegesis. Evangelical advocates of this eighteenth- and nineteenth-century hermeneutic method applied the apocalyptic Scriptures, especially Revelation, to the evolution of modern European history, so as to achieve what Mrs Meyrick describes as "making an almanac for the Millennium" (p. 318). Eliot's antipathy to contemporary evangelical exegesis is well known from her correspondence, and may be seen in her *Westminster Review* attacks on the popular minister John Cumming, whom she excoriates for, among other things, "*unscrupulosity of statement*," "*abscence of genuine charity*," and "*perverted moral judgment*" (*Critical Writings*, pp. 144–64, original italics). But Eliot found literary form in the interpretative school to which Cumming belonged:

> Although George Eliot rejected Cumming's fundamentalist interpretation and millenarian politics, the scheme of history constructed by "continuous historical" expositors seems to have provided the web on which she could position beginnings and ends and work out "meaningful form" in her narratives. (Carpenter, 1986, p. 23)

In other words, Eliot's fiction and poetry appropriate the literary power of biblical apocalyptic writing, and even of "unscrupulous" modern exegesis, and use them to great effect. Carpenter offers a detailed account of the precision with which Eliot structures her biblical allusion in *Adam Bede*, *Romola* (1862–3), *Middlemarch*, *Daniel Deronda*, and her poetic collection *The Legend of Jubal* (1874), not in lieu of nineteenth-century exegetical commentary, but in seamless conjunction with it and the texts that inspire it. "However deeply George Eliot's personal experience of isolation may inform the emotional tone of *Daniel Deronda*," she writes in a characteristic passage, "the novel takes its epic 'machinery' from the biblical literature of exile." Hence it is a Daniel, and not, say, a Solomon Deronda who converts to a philosophy of Zionism.

Studies such as Carpenter's, with her extensive and exact plotting of one form of biblical exegesis in Eliot's writing, could leave the misimpression that Eliot's every use of the Bible is charged with precisely calculable meaning. However, Victorian culture reflects the Bible in innumerable, often jarring, ways, and Eliot represents these too. For instance, Carpenter's intricate reading of *Adam Bede* links the events of the narrative to the scriptural readings of the ecclesiastical calendar of the Church of England, and, in sequence, to the evolution of Adam's spiritual understanding. But not every biblical allusion in *Adam Bede* serves this network of meaning or corresponds to the ecclesiastical calendar. To pick an obvious example, Adam's and Seth's names are not instructive in the manner of Daniel Deronda's. In Genesis, God explicitly appoints Adam's third son, Seth, as a means of continuing Adam's line and a replacement for Abel, killed by Cain. It is hard to reconcile Eliot's Seth to this biblical genealogy, since the novel presents him as Adam's earliest rival for Dinah's affections, and subsequently a bachelor uncle of their children. Such unruly examples would strike any Bible student reading a text like *Adam Bede*, though they would be tedious to enumerate for the very reason that they do not clearly lend themselves to broader patterns in the text.

More broadly speaking, the habit of biblical phraseology generates its own unruliness, as Eliot was well aware. In her evangelical girlhood, she had once sent a devotional poem to a friend, Maria Lewis, with the caveat that "You must be acquainted with the idiosyncrasy of my authorship, which is that my effusions, once committed to paper, are like the laws of the Medes and Persians that alter not." By excusing in advance any faulty verses, this letter invokes a common trope of late-Romantic women's poetry, which in 1839 was often presumed to be spontaneous, emotive, and unfinished. In brief, the future Eliot casts herself here as a sort of devotional *improvisatrice* in the manner of Letitia E. Landon. But her Danielic allusion to the "laws of the Medes and Persians" might seem to defeat this posture. In Daniel, the inflexible Median law compels King Darius to condemn to death his friend Daniel (6:16), but then God saves Daniel, and Darius alters the supposedly unalterable law (6:26). To read this letter casually is to understand that a reader's suggestions for revisions would be unwelcome, yet to follow rigorously the logic of the allusion is to understand the opposite to be true. Certainly Eliot's published poetry from the 1860s and 1870s, with its many painstaking revisions, bears a much closer resemblance to Daniel's "laws of the Medes and Persians" than to any *improvisatrice* model of Romantic poetry.

Even in cases where biblical quotations would seem to elude clear application, Eliot habitually reaches for their broad resonance of biblical quotation. Holloway suggests that this is why Dorothea is introduced in the opening chapter of *Middlemarch* as having "the impressiveness of a fine quotation from the Bible" without any specification about which quotation might be intended (p. 294). The Bible is a varied text, but its diverse parts attain a common power by keeping company with the other parts. And the nature of Eliot's metaphor for Dorothea ultimately matters less than its provenance: Bible citations claim power because they belong to the Bible. This logic is circular, but not less compelling for being so. I have already mentioned how the bookish and thoughtful Maggie Tulliver objects to her father's curses in the family Bible and remains disturbed by their place there. In a subsequent chapter of *The Mill on the Floss*, Maggie's brother Tom forces her to swear upon that same Bible that she will spurn her first lover – who, naturally, is the son of Tulliver's accursed enemy. As in the earlier passage, Maggie protests against this ritual use of the Bible, but her brother Tom insists upon its providing the context for her promise:

> "If I give you my word, that will be as strong a bond to me, as if I had laid my hand on the Bible. I don't require that to bind me."
> "Do what I require," said Tom. "I can't trust you, Maggie." (p. 445)

This brief passage invites a Feuerbachian analysis, but then refuses to corroborate it. Feuerbach, once more, felt that the Scriptures are a refracted image of humankind's best impulses and noblest conceptions, but nothing more than a refracted image. Maggie's rejection of Tom's talismanic use of the Bible seems in keeping with this idea, as does her (presumably sincere) claim that her good word "will be as strong a bond" without such ritual. By her lights, Feuerbach ought to have the final word here: the Bible at its best presents but a reflection of Maggie's own indubitable integrity, her personal goodness. But of course Feuerbach does not have the final word. Tom does, and Tom's dim sense of the importance of biblical ritual is only confirmed by Maggie's profound revulsion from it: she cannot be indifferent to the Bible of her father's curses. So we see that this unintellectual and religiously indifferent brother, an image of his father, nonetheless appreciates the power of the family Bible better than Maggie does, with her comparatively enlightened views and complex religious allegiances. A Feuerbachian analysis of her own pure motives lends the scene additional irony, but it cannot alone satisfy our sense of her complex reaction to her vow. This seems much better supplied by Tom's own rude instincts about the power of a sacred book that he personally never reads.

All this is to show how the Bible performs a role in Victorian literature, and especially in the works of Eliot, that can only be done by itself or by texts that convincingly wear its guise. Happily, such texts are innumerable, not least because the actual Bible texts are such a mystery. The illiterate Dolly Winthrop adorns her lard cakes with characters from the four Gospels:

> "There's letters pricked on 'em," said Dolly. "I can't read 'em myself, and there's nobody, not Mr Macey himself, rightly knows what they mean; but they've a good meaning for they're the same as is on the pulpit-cloth at church. What are they, Aaron, my dear?" (*Silas Marner*, p. 79)

In a similar spirit of reverent ignorance, Maggie's literate Uncle Pullet purchases "a print of Ulysses and Nausicaa" because it is a "pretty Scripture thing" (p. 154). Lisbeth Bede quotes one of Benjamin Franklin aphorisms one of the scriptural 'texes'" and becomes annoyed when Seth corrects her. And *Middlemarch* briefly describes an art auction held in a country house "furnished indeed with such large framefuls of expensive flesh-painting in the dining-room, that Mrs Larcher was nervous until reassured by finding the subjects to be Scriptural" (p. 602). For Eliot, such misidentifications only serve to embody the cultural value of that unspecified scriptural passage to which Dorothea is to be compared: Dorothea, too, is a "pretty scripture thing." The title poem from *The Legend of Jubal* presents an inversion of such generous misidentifications, in which the genuine article is rejected as a ridiculous forgery. The story extrapolates from Genesis 4:21 to recount the journey of Jubal, the inventor of the lyre, who travels from the land of his birth to beyond the mountains and back. When he returns, his descendants cannot recognize him; they misinterpret his claim to have invented their traditional songs, and kill him for the blasphemy of suggesting it. These things are a parable, as Eliot was fond of saying. *Jubal* is a metaphor both for the ritualization of sacred literature and for its independent life. Eliot scorns Dr Cumming for presenting to his congregation "the romance of Scripture," and not the real texts, "filling up the outline of the record with an elaborate colouring quite undreamed of by more literal minds" (*Critical Writings*, pp. 143–4). But of course Eliot does just this in *The Legend of Jubal* in a more thoroughgoing fashion, pushing at the boundaries of what the Bible is and ought to be.

To point to the limitations of a Feuerbachian or Straussian analysis of Eliot in this way is neither to find fault with nor to depart from the scholarly tradition of tracing their influence upon her work. But it is to reject the habit of presenting Eliot as the leading light of a generation of Victorian intellectuals who used a breezy version of German theory to get beyond the Bible or to reject its cultural importance. Consider by way of this the following dismissal of Eliot's importance in a discussion by Terry Eagleton:

> George Eliot was a devout believer in what was then known as the Religion of Humanity. God had been dethroned by an equally exotic, infinitely capacious creature known as Man. Since Christianity has rather a lot to say about God becoming Man, this smacked more of a replay than a refutation. It was not until the advent of Nietzsche, who realized that we had murdered God but cravenly refused to acknowledge it, that this bungled substitution would be laid bare.[21]

Eagleton's levity about Eliot's "craven" humanism fails to do justice to the complexity of her hermeneutics, particularly her handling of Feuerbach's "bungled substitution." In religious terms, Eliot can indeed seem like the ultimate case of what Oscar Wilde called the Victorian proposition "to carry on the business of the old firm under the new name."[22] But a critical part of Eliot's perspective is that the business of the old firm, sacred interpretation, was itself neither continuous nor even really old in the sense that it is most often taken to be. The text is profoundly diverse and profoundly foreign, and continually being remade and reimagined. And so are prior hermeneutic traditions.

Eliot's investment in the diversity and complexity of prior biblical traditions, finally, explains why her works return so often to related hermeneutic traditions that were foreign to the strict Protestantism of her adolescence. When Eliot depicts Romola as a latter-day incarnation of the Madonna ("Many legends were afterwards told in that valley about the blessed Lady who came over the sea"), she does so for a largely Protestant audience during the heyday of Virgin apparitions on the Continent.[23] In this way, medieval Catholicism in *Romola* and *The Spanish Gypsy* (1868) resembles Judaism in *Daniel Deronda*, or the role of the apocryphal Scriptures in her poetry and local English fictions. Adam Bede, the narrator more than once relates, would "read in the Apocrypha, of which he was very fond," not least of all because he "enjoyed the freedom of occasionally differing from an Apocryphal writer" (*Adam Bede*, p. 499). This emphasis upon apocryphal Scriptures and midrashic texts brings home the constructed – not to say factitious – nature of the sacred canon. Eliot's earliest publication, a lyric published during her Evangelical youth, celebrates the Bible as a "Blest volume! whose clear truth-writ page, once known / Fades not before heaven's sunshine or hell's moan," but she subsequently found this "truth-writ page" to be susceptible to fading after all, and in historically complicated ways. So it is no surprise that her later apostasy coincided with a vigorous Victorian debate around biblical translation issues in the AV. This is parodied in Eliot's very first work of fiction, *The Sad Fortunes of the Reverend Amos Barton* (1857), when a group of country clergymen gossip about one of their brethren:

> "Talking of scandal," returned Mr Fellowes, "have you heard the last story about Barton? Nisbett was telling me the other day that he dines alone with the Countess at six, while Mrs Barton is in the kitchen acting as cook."
>
> "Rather an apocryphal authority, Nisbett," said Mr Ely.
>
> "Ah," said Mr Cleves, with a good-natured humour twinkling in his eyes, "depend upon it, that is a corrupt version. The original text is, that they all dined together *with* six – meaning six children – and that Mrs Barton is an excellent cook."
>
> "I wish dining alone together may be the worst of that sad business," said the Rev. Archibald Duke, in a tone implying that his wish was a strong figure of speech.[24]

The scene is comic, and not coincidentally so. Eliot can afford to be earnest when dealing with "foreign" concepts like Catholicism and Judaism, but here, as in *The Mill on the Floss* and *Silas Marner*, she must resort to humor to evoke the scandalous question of textual authority: in this instance, whether the AV accurately represents the best manuscript authorities. Like questions posed in the misshapen *Nemesis*, this probes at the root of British Protestantism. Ely's and Cleves's concern with mistranslation represents in precise language exactly the sort of thing that inspired the translation of the New Revised Version – just as Fellowes and Duke represent conservative loyalty to the received account, however preposterous aspects of it might seem.[25] Cleves's quip about Nisbett's "corrupt version" of an "original text," in particular, also suggests the context of the Greek and Roman classics, but scholars of Cleves's (and Eliot's) fastidiousness were perfectly aware that pagan classics held a disturbingly analogous relationship with their own biblical literature: similarly fraught manuscript problems prevailed in both cases. This textual condition haunted the Victorians, and affords a dramatic instance of Stephen Prickett's argument that the Bible's palpable influence upon literary studies is usually reciprocated in the less-often-appreciated influence of literary studies upon the Bible.[26]

The apocryphal text, the secular text with pretensions to the sacred, here provides an implicit counterpoint to T. S. Eliot's famous dictum that the inclusion of any work in the literary canon changes the character of the other works. Potential substitution between apocryphal and sacred texts implies that a text might win a place in the canon, and to recognize this is to possess a great key to the way that George Eliot's understanding of the Bible helped to shape her own literary expressions throughout her career. Her letters confirm her enthusiasm for Carlyle's idea that a great writer could be "a prophet for his generation."[27] And her work increasingly aspired to this status during most of her career. She seems to have had a reverent audience in mind, for instance, when appealing to posterity in the lyric "O May I Join the Choir Invisible":

O may I join the choir invisible
Of those immortal dead who live again
In minds made better by their presence: live
In pulses stirred to generosity.
In deeds of daring rectitude, in scorn
For miserable aims that end with self,
In thoughts sublime that pierce the night like stars,
And with their mild persistence urge men's search
To vaster issues ... (p. 49)

To appreciate the tenor of this positivist hymn, one must recall that whereas today the idea of the canon has largely been secularized, Eliot clung to the promise of the nineteenth-century cult of literature, trusting that poetry would always retain something of its sacred nature. She had once written in *The Westminster Review* of Alfred Tennyson that "Whatever was the immediate prompting of 'In Memoriam' ... the deepest significance of the poem is the sanctification of human love as a religion" (*Writings*, p. 172). Only a post-Christian Victorian like Eliot would write such lines, but this apostate remained faithful to the religion of Tennyson. When her partner G. H. Lewes died in 1878, Eliot refused to attend his funeral, preferring to stay at home, "reading In Memoriam over and over and copying long sections of it into her Diary" (as Gordon Haight, 1968, describes it).[28] In light of such circumstances, it seems telling that "O May I Join" discernably echoes *In Memoriam*'s famous appeal to "mind and soul" to "make one music as before // But vaster."[29] She was sometimes a lonely practitioner of "human love as a religion," it seems, but one committed to the music described by Tennyson. And although Eliot associated this music with poetry, her novels illustrate equally well the appeal of the Victorian cult of literature. Nothing suggests her own influence more clearly than this. For Eliot's Bibles, like Tennyson's, still have their readers.

Notes

I am grateful to Kathleen Blake for helpful comments upon an earlier draft of this chapter.

1   George Eliot, *Middlemarch*, ed. Rosemary Ashton (Penguin, New York, 1994), p. 411.
2   John Holloway, *The Victorian Sage* (Norton, New York, 1965), p. 294.
3   For a general introduction, see W[illiam] Neil, "The Criticism and Theological Use of the Bible, 1700–1950," in Peter R. Ackroyd, et al., eds, *The Cambridge History of the Bible* (Cambridge University Press, Cambridge, 1963–70).
4   George Eliot, *The Mill on the Floss*, ed. A. S. Byatt (Penguin, New York, 1979), p. 356.
5   Anon., *The Holy Bible, King James Version* (Penguin, New York, 1974).
6   Harold Fisch, "Biblical Realism in *Silas Marner*," in Mark H. Gelber, ed., *Identity and Ethos* (Peter Lang, New York, 1986); Dwight H. Purdy, "The Wit of Biblical Allusion in the Mill on the Floss," *Studies in Philology* 102:2 (2005).
7   Lisa Baltazar offers the fullest and best explanation of Casaubon's hermeneutics: Lisa Baltazar, "The Critique of Anglican Biblical Scholarship in George Eliot's *Middlemarch*," *Literature and Theology* 15:1 (2001).

8   Elinor S. Shaffer, *"Kubla Khan" and the Fall of Jerusalem: The Mythological School in Biblical Criticism and Secular Literature, 1770–1880* (Cambridge University Press, Cambridge, 1975); Elisabeth Jay, *The Religion of the Heart: Anglican Evangelicalism and the Nineteenth-Century Novel* (Clarendon Press, Oxford, 1979); Mary Wilson Carpenter, *George Eliot and the Landscape of Time* (University of North Carolina Press, Chapel Hill, 1986). Suzanne Bailey, "Reading the 'Key': George Eliot and the Higher Criticism," *Women's Writing* 3:2 (1996); Charles LaPorte, "George Eliot, the Poetess as Prophet," *Victorian Literature and Culture* 31:1 (2003).

9   It is often remarked that Eliot learned from her friend Charles Christian Hennell's free-thinking circle most of what could be taught by the German critics whom she subsequently studied and translated. This seems like an overstatement. British "Higher Criticism" such as Hennell's *Inquiry Concerning the Origin of Christianity* (1838) or John William Colenso's *Pentateuch and Book of Joshua Critically Examined* (1862) is of dramatically inferior quality to the works of Strauss and Schleiermacher. Ladislaw would not have recommended Casaubon to read Hennell had *Middlemarch* been set in 1838.

10 George Eliot, *Adam Bede*, ed. Stephen Gill (Penguin, New York, 1980), p. 48.

11 Hugh McLeod discusses how Victorian social progressives frequently drew upon "the Old Testament prophets, the gospels and the epistle of James" for their "messages of equality, social justice and condemnation of the rich, while most of the clergy, drawing from the epistles of Paul and Peter, appealed for submission to God-given authority." Hugh McLeod, *Secularization in Western Europe, 1848–1914* (St Martin's Press, New York, 2000), p. 25.

12 Suzy Anger skillfully reads this passage of Eliot's Feuerbach translation in *Victorian Interpretation* (Cornell University Press, Ithaca, NY, 2005), p. 102.

13 George Eliot, *Silas Marner*, ed. Terence Cave (Oxford University Press, Oxford, 1996), pp. 138–9.

14 James Anthony Froude, *The Nemesis of Faith*, 2nd edn (J. Chapman, London, 1849), pp. 14–15.

15 George Eliot, *Selected Critical Writings*, ed. Rosemary Ashton (Oxford University Press, Oxford, 1992), p. 15.

16 Samuel Taylor Coleridge, *Confessions of an Inquiring Spirit* (Scolar Press, Menston, 1971 [1840]), p. 13.

17 George Eliot, *Felix Holt, the Radical*, ed. Lynda Muggleston (Penguin, New York, 1995), p. 57.

18 Robin Sheets, "Felix Holt: Language, the Bible, and the Problematic of Meaning," *Nineteenth-Century Fiction* 37:2 (1982).

19 George Eliot, *Daniel Deronda*, ed. Graham Handley (Oxford University Press, Oxford, 1984), p. 312.

20 In addition to works noted above by Shaffer, Jay, Carpenter, Bailey, Anger, and myself are recent works by Bronwyn Law-Viljoen and William R. McKelvy. U. C. Knoepflmacher, "George Eliot, Feuerbach, and the Question of Criticism," *Victorian Studies* 7:3 (1964); Bronwyn Law-Viljoen, "Midrash, Myth, and Prophecy: George Eliot's Reinterpretation of Biblical Stories," *Literature and Theology* 11:1 (1997). William R. McKelvy, *The English Cult of Literature: Devoted Readers, 1774–1880* (University of Virginia Press, Charlottesville, 2007).

21 Terry Eagleton, "Eat It," *London Review of Books* (June 8, 2006), 29.

22 Oscar Wilde, "The Decay of Lying," in Dorothy Mermin and Herbert F. Tucker, eds, *Victorian Literature: 1830–1900* (Harcourt, Fort Worth, TX, 2002), p. 1022.

23 George Eliot, *Romola*, ed. Andrew Sanders (Penguin, New York, 1980), p. 649.

24 George Eliot, *Scenes of Clerical Life*, ed. Thomas A. Noble (Oxford University Press, Oxford, 1985), p. 48.
25 The New Revised Version only appeared in the 1880s, but discussion about its translation dates from the beginnings of the period.
26 Stephen Prickett, "Biblical and Literary Criticism: A History of Interaction," in David Jasper and Stephen Prickett, eds, *The Bible and Literature: A Reader* (Blackwell, Oxford, 1999).
27 George Eliot, *The George Eliot Letters*, ed. Gordon Sherman Haight, 9 volumes (Yale University Press, New Haven, CT 1954), vol. 4, p. 300.
28 Gordon S. Haight, *George Eliot: A Biography* (Oxford University Press, Oxford, 1968), p. 516.
29 Alfred Tennyson, *In Memoriam*, ed. Erik Gray (Norton, New York, 2004), p. 6.

References

Anger, Suzy (2005) *Victorian Interpretation*. Cornell University Press, Ithaca, NY.

Anon (1974) *The Holy Bible, King James Version*. Penguin, New York.

Bailey, Suzanne (1996) "Reading the 'Key': George Eliot and the Higher Criticism," *Women's Writing* 3:2, 129–43.

Baltazar, Lisa (2001) "The Critique of Anglican Biblical Scholarship in George Eliot's Middlemarch," *Literature and Theology* 15:1, 40–60.

Carpenter, Mary Wilson (1986) *George Eliot and the Landscape of Time*. University of North Carolina Press, Chapel Hill.

Coleridge, Samuel Taylor (1971) *Confessions of an Inquiring Spirit*. Scolar Press, Menston (1840).

Eagleton, Terry (2006) "Eat It," *London Review of Books* June 8, 29–30.

Eliot, George (1954) *The George Eliot Letters*, ed. Gordon Sherman Haight, 9 volumes. Yale University Press, New Haven, CT.

Eliot, George (1979) *The Mill on the Floss*, ed. A. S. Byatt. Penguin, New York.

Eliot, George (1980) *Adam Bede*, ed. Stephen Gill. Penguin, New York.

Eliot, George (1980) *Romola*, ed. Andrew Sanders. Penguin, New York.

Eliot, George (1984) *Daniel Deronda*, ed. Graham Handley. Oxford University Press, Oxford.

Eliot, George (1985) *Scenes of Clerical Life*, ed. Thomas A. Noble. Oxford University Press, Oxford.

Eliot, George (1992) *Selected Critical Writings*, ed. Rosemary Ashton. Oxford University Press, Oxford.

Eliot, George (1994) *Middlemarch*, ed. Rosemary Ashton. Penguin, New York.

Eliot, George (1995) *Felix Holt, the Radical*, ed. Lynda Muggleston. Penguin, New York.

Eliot, George (1996) *Silas Marner*, ed. Terence Cave. Oxford University Press, Oxford.

Fisch, Harold (1986) "Biblical Realism in Silas Marner," in Mark H. Gelber, ed., *Identity and Ethos*. Peter Lang, New York, pp. 343–60.

Froude, James Anthony (1849) *The Nemesis of Faith*, 2nd edn. J. Chapman, London.

Haight, Gordon S. (1968) *George Eliot: A Biography*. Oxford University Press, Oxford.

Holloway, John (1965) *The Victorian Sage*. Norton, New York.

Jay, Elisabeth (1979) *The Religion of the Heart: Anglican Evangelicalism and the Nineteenth-Century Novel*. Clarendon Press, Oxford.

Knoepflmacher, U. C. (1964) "George Eliot, Feuerbach, and the Question of Criticism," *Victorian Studies* 7:3, 306–9.

LaPorte, Charles (2003) "George Eliot, the Poetess as Prophet," *Victorian Literature and Culture* 31:1, 159–79.

Law-Viljoen, Bronwyn (1997) "Midrash, Myth, and Prophecy: George Eliot's Reinterpretation of Biblical Stories," *Literature and Theology* 11:1, 80–92.

McKelvy, William R. (2007) *The English Cult of Literature: Devoted Readers, 1774–1880.* University of Virginia Press, Charlottesville.

McLeod, Hugh (2000) *Secularization in Western Europe, 1848–1914.* St Martin's Press, New York.

Neil, W[illiam] (1963–70) "The Criticism and Theological Use of the Bible, 1700–1950," in Peter R. Ackroyd, Christopher Francis Evans, G. W. H. Lampe and S. L. Greenslade, eds, *The Cambridge History of the Bible.* Cambridge University Press, Cambridge.

Prickett, Stephen (1999) "Biblical and Literary Criticism: A History of Interaction," in David Jasper and Stephen Prickett, eds, *The Bible and Literature: A Reader.* Blackwell, Oxford, pp. 12–43.

Purdy, Dwight H. (2005) "The Wit of Biblical Allusion in *The Mill on the Floss,*" *Studies in Philology* 102:2, 233–46.

Shaffer, Elinor S. (1975) *"Kubla Khan" and the Fall of Jerusalem: The Mythological School in Biblical Criticism and Secular Literature, 1770–1880.* Cambridge University Press, Cambridge.

Sheets, Robin (1982) "Felix Holt: Language, the Bible, and the Problematic of Meaning," *Nineteenth-Century Fiction* 37:2, 146–69.

Tennyson, Alfred (2004) *In Memoriam,* ed. Erik Gray. Norton, New York.

Wilde, Oscar (2002) "The Decay of Lying," in Dorothy Mermin and Herbert F. Tucker, eds, *Victorian Literature: 1830–1900.* Harcourt, Fort Worth, TX.

CHAPTER 39

Christina Rossetti

Elizabeth Ludlow

Rossetti's statement, "Neither knowledge nor ignorance is of first importance to Bible students: grace is our paramount need" (FD, p. 114),[1] is suggestive of her sense that any true understanding of the Bible is a gift from the Holy Spirit, a matter more concerned with spiritual growth than with intellectual pursuit. Not only did she claim a "devout meditative ignorance" (FD, p. 286) of the Bible, but she also suggested in her study of Revelation, *The Face of the Deep*, that she could do no more than "but quote" from its translations (FD, p. 113). Yet it is clear that Rossetti has a deft and profound grasp of these translations, often playing one version off against another in an attempt to find new theological meanings and interpretations. While she is generally dependent on the 1611 King James Version of the Bible in her poetry and prose, for example, she was also devoted to the Prayer Book Version of the Psalms, used at her own church, Christ Church, Albany Street in London, and recognized as more poetical and musical than other translations. Rossetti also compares the 1611 Bible to the 1885 Revised Version, claiming in *The Face of the Deep* that "the two translations combined kindle hope, gratitude, confidence, excite emulation" (p. 111).

Although this form of comparative study was unavailable to Rossetti for much of life, her earlier devotional poetry and prose exhibit the same passion for meditating on the specifics of the language of the Bible to inspire fellow Christians to emulate the self-sacrifice of Christ, his Old Testament predecessors, and the Christian saints of the New. This chapter discusses Rossetti's relationship with the Bible by examining her hermeneutics, as filtered through the writings of Isaac Williams, John Keble, and Augustine; assessing her commitment to biblical tradition as that which she felt urgently compelled to uphold and defend; and by exploring her presentation of biblical characters as role models for her Victorian readership. While Rossetti's work is drawn on widely here, I focus on her analysis of the book of Revelation, *The Face of the Deep*, and her introductory poem to *Annus Domini*, "Alas my Lord," as indicative of her at once systematic but always devotional approach to the Bible as a source of spiritual comfort and intellectual strength.

Williams, Keble, Augustine

Rossetti tends to introduce her interpretations of biblical passages rather hesitantly, using words like "seems" and "appears" to exhibit caution and demonstrate her fear of appearing "overbold" (FD, p. 551) in her hermeneutics. Writing in a climate that forcibly discouraged, in John Ruskin's words, women dabbling in the "dangerous science" of theology (Ruskin, 1900, pp. 79–80), Rossetti's position as a female critic of the Bible was undoubtedly precarious. The constant reminders that what her devotional works offer is more meditative than interpretative underpins a careful negotiation with this position and grounds her words firmly within the structures set out by Scripture. By lifting words from the prayers uttered by the faithful believers of the Bible and by focusing on her own emptiness in light of the corresponding "immensity of God" (FD, p. 214), Rossetti repeatedly acknowledges her willingness to be remolded by God into a vessel that is able to effectively serve His kingdom. Conflating the words of Psalm 119:105, as translated in the Prayer Book Version of the Psalms, "Thy word is a lantern unto my feet, and a light unto my path," and Proverbs 18:10, "The name of the LORD is a strongtower: the righteous runneth into it, and is safe,"[2] she writes:

> O Lord, Whose Word is a lantern unto our feet, and a light unto our paths, I pray Thee make the law of Thy mouth dearer unto us than thousands of gold and silver. O Lord, Whose name is a strong tower to the righteous, I pray Thee give us wisdom to run into it and be safe. (FD, p. 113)

By highlighting the nature of the Bible as a guidebook of life, she acknowledges it to be the means by which men and women are to be trained in righteousness so that they become "perfect, thoroughly furnished unto all good works" (2 Timothy 3:17).

Rossetti begins *Seek and Find: A Double Series of Short Studies of the Benedicite* (1879) by emphasizing the devotion that fuels her interpretations. She claims that apart from using the biblical Harmony of Isaac Williams, the only source she relies on is the text of her Bible and the "valuable alternative readings" that are found in its margins (SF, p. 3). In the introduction to his Harmony, *Thoughts on the Study of the Holy Gospels*, Williams argues that "our way of interpretation should come from Christ" (Williams, 1842, p. 146) and subsequently examines Christ's method of using Old Testament narratives to frame his parables and explain the nature of his being (ibid., p. 192). His Harmony itself contains barely any words not taken from the Bible. Indeed, it is structured throughout in the same way as the first few pages of *Seek and Find*, with parallel columns leading the reader toward a systematic, comparative reading of the gospels. Gisela Honnighausen points out that the attempts to "prove harmony in the Gospels" and articulate the "prefigurative interpretation of the Old Testament" was particularly influenced by medieval thought:

> This retreat into the thought of a previous century, suggested by the tradition of Romantic medievalism, is understandable in the light of the philosophical crises of the nineteenth century which made the certainty provided by earlier absolute faith seem desirable. (Honnighausen, 1972, p. 2)

Stephen Prickett addresses these "philosophical crises" when he writes that if, for millions, the Bible was still the "Inspired Word of God," able to speak directly to their hearts and minds, "more and more of those millions were becoming increasingly aware of the lengthy processes of mediation by which it had reached them" (Prickett, 2000, p. 64).

The theories of the German "Higher Critics," which were becoming popular in Britain by the mid-nineteenth century, focused on the problem of the mediation of the Scriptures through the ages and discounted the belief in the unshakable holiness of Scripture. A huge controversy met *Essays and Reviews*, which was published in Britain in 1860. Included in this, Benjamin Jowett's essay "On the Interpretation of Scripture" argued that the Bible should be read like any other work of literature. As the intellectual debates that culminated in *Essays and Reviews* were developing, John Keble proposed a return to the "tradition of Romantic Medievalism" of the early Church Fathers. In Tract 89, "On the Mysticism Attributed to the Fathers of the Church" (Keble, 1841, Part 1, p. 1), he writes of the Father's articulation of the remarkable discovery that could be made of "future heavenly things" in the Old Testament, and, most especially, in The Song of Solomon. John Mason Neale reaffirms Keble's claim when he speaks of the time when the early Fathers, including Clement, Jerome, and Augustine, who, being "holy men," recognized the book's typological importance and learnt more from it than from any other part of the Old Testament (Neale, 1872, p. 1). The influence of the interpretations of those "holy men" can be seen in the King James Version of the Bible, which positions The Song of Solomon in a Christian framework. The running titles it gives the book include: "The church's love unto Christ," "The calling of the Church," "The graces of the church," and "Christ's love to the Church." Despite a widespread reverence for the King James Version of the Bible, John Keble and Isaac Williams recognized that many nineteenth-century Christians held a deep-seated suspicion of the allegorical hermeneutics of the patristic Fathers. As a result, their Tracts seek to remedy the hardheartedness of the "cold, sceptical, and self-indulgent age" (Williams, 1838, p. 25) that dismisses any allegorical interpretation as remote from "common sense and practical utility" (Keble, 1841, Part 1, p. 5). Acknowledging the typological exegesis of Christ and that of the apostles, both encourage a reverential attitude in approaching the works of the Early Fathers and an acknowledgment of the marvel of the numerous instances of typological symbolism they discover.

Considering the cyclical patterns and the double visions that emerge from Rossetti's fluid typological methods, it is unsurprising that, among the works of the patristic Fathers, the one that most influenced her was St Augustine's *Confessions*. She first demonstrates her familiarity with the book in *Seek and Find* when, after reflecting upon Paul's assertion that we are all in desperate need of God's mercy, she writes that "St Augustine has illustrated a kindred lesson: One prayed, Lord take away the ungodly man: and God answered him, Which?" (SF, p. 79). In *Time Flies* (1885), she gives a short biography of the life of Augustine as she celebrates his feast day and speaks of the effect of the prayers of Augustine's mother, Monica, his recognition of divine grace, and his baptism by Ambrose (TF, p. 166–7). By imitating St Augustine's technique of illuminating the words of one passage or phrase of Scripture by quoting extensively from another, and by seamlessly conflating her own words with those of the Psalmists and the Prophets, Rossetti integrates herself and her community into the biblical schema. Thus, she is able to establish a structure of hermeneutics easily accessible to her readers.

In "A Christmas Carol for My Godchildren," Rossetti compares herself to the wise men who followed God's guiding star to their savior and demonstrates an adherence to Peter's instruction to "take heed" of the "sure word" of prophecy until "the day star arise in your hearts" (2 Peter 1:19). "My life is like their journey," she writes, "Their star is like God's Book" (lines 37–8). Utilizing this same image, she concludes *Annus Domini* with the prayer:

> O LORD Jesus Christ, the Bright and Morning Star, as once by a star Thou didst lead the Wise Men unto the sure mercies of David, so now by Thine Illuminating Spirit guide us, I pray Thee, to Thyself: that we with them, and by the Grace of the same Most Holy Spirit, may offer unto Thee gold of love, frankincense of adoration, and myrrh of self-sacrifice. Amen. (AD, p. 366)

The act of taking God's "illuminating" book as the guiding "star" of her life and encouraging others to do the same serves as the central force behind Rossetti's devotional prose and poetry. To a certain extent, as an interpreter, she considers all her readers "Godchildren" for whom she is responsible for guiding lovingly on their spiritual journey, helping them to identify the illuminating star that God has provided. In *The Face of the Deep*, she claims that saying "Give me children, or else I die" is foolish, since "the childless who make themselves nursing mothers of Christ's little ones are the true mothers in Israel" (FD, p. 312). As Robert Kachur (1997, p. 202) argues:

> By writing that "the childless who make themselves nursing mothers of Christ's little ones are the true mothers of Israel," Rossetti recalls Scripture's many references to the fathers of Israel – men ... who heard God speak directly and communicated his words to others. Rossetti's metaphorical use of the term "mother," then, allows her to posit an Apocalyptic reversal, re-envisioning women's cultural roles as house-hold mediators and nurtures; here they are powerful mediators in the household of God itself, using God's word to nurture God's people.

Certainly, Rossetti's depiction of nursing mothers as valid interpreters of Scripture challenges the construction of the ideal woman as domestic and reproductive. It also enables Rossetti to assert a greater, God-given, authority in her hermeneutics.

Upholding Tradition

In *Christina Rossetti's Feminist Theology*, Lynda Palazzo links Christina Rossetti's hermeneutical methods to those of modern feminist theologians. She claims that Rossetti was not unquestioning in her acceptance of Tractarian thought and Anglo-Catholic doctrine but instead sought to challenge them, only nominally disclaiming "a reputation for prevalent originality" (Palazzo, 2002, p. xvii). Palazzo also asserts that Rossetti's desire to transform doctrinal concepts within theology went beyond the aims of her female contemporaries who sought to use theology for social reform. While I am keen to emphasize the distinctive elements of Rossetti's feminist, albeit "domestic" hermeneutics, unlike Palazzo I do not consider her theology to be exceptionally original. Instead, I consider it to be consistent with her biblical antitypes; the Old Testament Psalmists who considered themselves vessels or, in the case of Hannah, Mary, and Elizabeth, "nursing mothers" and "household mediators" through whom God could nurture and speak to others. Meditating on John's assertion of the sanctity of the Bible, Rossetti prays:

> Fill us with reverence, I pray Thee, for Thy most holy written Word: give us grace to study and meditate in it, with prayer and firm adoring faith: not questioning its authority, but obeying its precepts and becoming imbued by its spirit. Teach us to prostrate our understandings before its mysteries; to live by its law, and abide by its promises. (AD, p. 314)

For Rosetti, that we should align ourselves with biblical characters as we apply scriptural precepts to our own lives is unquestionable: becoming "imbued" by the "spirit" of the text is a prerequisite for the believer. She writes of the sin of devaluing the holiness of the biblical text in *Letter and Spirit: Notes on the Commandments* (1883), claiming that:

> It is, I suppose, a genuine through not a glaring breach of the Second Commandment, when instead of learning the lesson plainly set down for us in Holy Writ we protrude mental feelers in all directions above, beneath, around it, grasping, clinging to every imaginable particular except the main point. (LS, p. 85)

That the Bible is the book of life and the only place wherein humans can search for their true identity as children of God is apparent throughout Rossetti's prose and poetry. Instead of "clinging to every imaginable particular" and concerning ourselves with such things as the "precise architecture of Noah's Ark" or the "astronomy of Joshua's miracle" (LS, p. 86), she advocates the Scriptures as the molding principle behind each individual believer, since it serves as the springboard for communication with the divine. However, in *The Face of the Deep*, Rossetti warns that "Interpretation may err and darken knowledge": in spite of her acknowledgment that each individual may bring aspects of themselves to their hermeneutical analysis, she highlights the dangerous temptation of pride (FD, p. 549). A letter she wrote to Frederick Shields in 1881 (Rossetti, 1997–2004, vol. 2, pp. 308–9) indicates her eagerness to avoid this sin first by prayer, and, second, by actively participating in a communal, rather than individual, hermeneutical process. By appealing to figures such as Shields, Williams, and her confessor Dr Richard Frederick Littledale, Rossetti successfully warded off the charge of unfounded creativity.

Considering her engagement with these key figures of the Oxford Movement, G. B. Tennyson (1981, p. 198) asserts that Rossetti was "the true inheritor of the Tractarian devotional mode in poetry" and that her poetry brings to fruition much of what the Oxford Movement advocated in theory and sought to put into practice.

In spite of his introductory claim that the poetry of the Oxford Movement "is as much cause and symptom as it is result" (ibid., p. 8), Rossetti's protestation against the charge of biblical scholarship has, for the most part, been taken at face value and her contribution to the doctrinal basis of the Movement's hermeneutics and, indeed, to subsequent biblical interpretation has been overlooked. However, in light of the direct impact of her poetry on the works of Littledale and John Mason Neale, Rossetti deserves to be seen more as an upholder of the Movement than as its "inheritor." Indeed, her poem "Alas My Lord" encapsulates Rossetti's sense of fighting a spiritual battle, highlighting her hermeneutical practices, and attesting to her engagement with her scriptural predecessors who sought to know and obey God. It opens Rossetti's first book of devotional prose, *Annus Domini: A Prayer for Each Day of the Year*:

> Alas my Lord,
> How should I wrestle all the livelong night
> With Thee my God, my Strength and my Delight?
>
> How can it need
> So agonized an effort and a strain
> To make Thy Face of Mercy shine again?
>
> How can it need
> Such wringing out of breathless prayer to move
> Thee to Thy wonted Love, when Thou art Love?
>
> Yet Abraham
> So hung about Thine Arm outstretched and bared,
> That for ten righteous Sodom had been spared.
>
> Yet Jacob did
> So hold Thee by the clenched hand of prayer
> That he prevailed, and Thou didst bless him there.
>
> Elias prayed,
> And sealed the founts of Heaven; he prayed again
> And lo, Thy Blessing fell in showers of rain.
>
> Gulped by the fish,
> As by the pit, lost Jonah made his moan;
> And Thou forgavest, waiting to atone.
>
> All Nineveh
> Fasting and girt in sackcloth raised a cry,
> Which moved Thee ere the day of grace went by.
>
> Thy Church prayed on
> And on for blessed Peter in his strait,
> Till opened of its own accord the gate.
>
> Yea, Thou my God
> Hast prayed all night, and in the garden prayed
> Even while, like melting wax, Thy strength was made.

Alas for him
Who faints, despite Thy Pattern, King of Saints:
Alas, alas, for me, the one that faints.

Lord, give us strength
To hold Thee fast, until we hear Thy Voice
Which Thine own know, who hearing It rejoice.

Lord, give us strength
To hold Thee fast until we see Thy Face,
Full Fountain of all Rapture and all Grace.

But when our strength
Shall be made weakness, and our bodies clay,
Hold Thou us fast, and give us sleep till day.

The publication of *Annus Domini* in 1874 was extremely well received: in its preface, H. W. Burrows writes that the prayers contained within are valuable for "their fervour, reverence, and overflowing charity, and also because they are suggestive of the use which should be made of Holy Scripture in our devotions." Each little prayer, he writes, "may be considered as the result of a meditation, and as an example of the way in which that exercise should issue in worship." The diminutive "little," Joel Westerholm (1993, p. 13) suggests, "reveals how Rossetti's praying has been safely contained within a domestic setting in Burrow's mind."

"Alas My Lord" can be seen as a microcosm of *Annus Domini* in that its simple meditative surface masks a profound typological schema and a profession of an overwhelming desire to actively "hold fast" (line 38) to God. Like the poem, the book begins by quoting various extracts from Genesis before moving systematically through the Bible, offering short prayers based upon meditations of particular passages. As in the poem, where the speaker aligns herself with various biblical characters and subsequently experiences God's protection and receives His strength, the prayers in *Annus Domini* serve to reinforce the message that contemporary readers are not so far removed from their biblical prototypes as might first appear. Rather than merely taking specific words and phrases from the biblical text and applying them to a particular personal situation, Rossetti engages with the situation of the characters she associates herself with as though she herself is working through the dilemmas they faced. The wording of the opening plea conflates at least two biblical episodes. The first, in Genesis 32, is that of Jacob wrestling with God until daybreak. This allusion can be confirmed when the poem speaks of Jacob prevailing as he held God "by the clenched hand of prayer." Indeed, in her later explication of Genesis 32:28, Rossetti acknowledges the importance of coming to an understanding of our biblical precedents in order to reach an ontological conception of our own subjectivities. She prays, "O Lord Jesus Christ, with Whom Jacob prevailed, help us with that holy patriarch by prayer to *hold Thee fast*, and by love to cleave steadfastly unto Thee, our ever-present Aid" (AD, p. 6). In *The Face of the Deep*, she again suggests that we should all imitate Jacob, writing that:

Hands emptied by showing mercy to the poor, are set free to hold fast what God will require of us; hearts emptied of self are prepared to receive and retrain all He will demand. ... Thus,

> Jacob said: "I will not let Thee go, except Thou bless me ... And He blessed him there." Yet because God Himself is to us more than all His blessings, let us rather protest with the Bride: "I found Him Whom my soul loveth: I held him, and would not let Him go." (FD, p. 96)

The conflation of Jacob's protestation with the words of the Song of Solomon's Bride (Song of Solomon 3:4) is typical of Rossetti's typological method, whereby passages that may at first seem incongruous are conflated. She had suggested the conflation between Jacob, the Bride, and the church in her earlier poem, "Advent" (PC, pp. 62–4) when she wrote "We will not let Him go / Till daybreak smite our wearied sight ... Then He shall say, 'Arise, My love, / My fair one, come away'" (lines 50–1, 55–6).

In light of the conflation between Jacob and Bride, then, the words of the penultimate verse of "Alas my Lord" can be linked to those of the Song of Solomon. Thus, the "Full Fountain of all Rapture and all Grace" (line 39) can be seen in terms of the "fountain" that the Lover in the Song describes when he speaks of his beloved as "a spring shut up, fountain sealed" (Song of Solomon 4:12). In "Three Nuns," too, Rossetti's utilization of the image of the hidden fount precedes a voiced desire for both the "Living Well" (line 142) of Paradise and the "living waters" (lines 145–6) that Christ claims he can provide (John 4:10). This selective and imaginative use of the biblical imagery that follows the patterning of the Old Testament book can be seen in terms of a struggle to construct an understanding of selfhood typologically in the context of the resurrection. Since Kachur (1997, p. 203) has suggested that Rossetti's repeated links between real women and the Bride of Christ serves to "feminize" male believers, it could be argued that in conflating Jacob and the Song of Solomon's bride, Rossetti appropriates his story for the sake of her female readers.

Reading the Bible

In certain instances Rossetti worked to erase gender boundaries, adhering to the argument in Galatians that "there is neither male nor female ... in Christ Jesus" (Galatians 3:28). Even when alluding to conventionally masculinized approaches to the Bible, such as Paul's insistence that we develop a physical relation to God, Rossetti attempts to neutralize them and break down any barriers gender might pose to the reader. The importance of holding God fast, for example, is promoted by Paul in Ephesians 6:12 when he writes "For we wrestle not against flesh and blood, but against principalities, against powers, against the rulers of the darkness of this world, against spiritual wickedness in high places." Although Jacob was wrestling with the ultimate power for good, not against "the darkness of this world," by implicitly linking the episode to the "wrestling" that Paul speaks of in her allusion to the battles concurrent with our "breathless prayer" (line 8), Rossetti brings to the fore the message that we are to use our strength on the spiritual plain rather than the physical. Indeed, choosing to begin the poem with the reference to Jacob's battle with God is significant in highlighting this truth because Jacob had to endure previous struggles with Esau and then Laban before coming to the realization that it was God with whom his ultimate battle lay.

The fact that Jacob's wrestling match is spoken of as lasting "all the livelong night" (line 2) can also be read as symbolically significant when read in the context of Rossetti's works as a whole. Throughout her writings, she alludes to the life that we are now experiencing as occurring in the nighttime of the eschatological schema and the emergence of the New Heavens and New Earth that will occur at the Second Coming as a day break. Indeed, this meaning is established in the last line of the poem when she prays "give us sleep till day" (life 42). Alongside Ephesians, another typological counterpart to Jacob's night of wrestling can be identified in Peter's response to Jesus' instruction to "launch out into the deep, and let down your nets for a draft." Peter's response was to complain "Master, we have toiled *all the night*, and have taken nothing: nevertheless at thy word I will let down the net" (italics added). Needless to say, they managed to catch a "multitude of fishes" (Luke 5:4–6).

After asking why "such wringing out of breathless prayer" is imperative in moving "Thee to Thy wonted Love" (lines 8–9), the poem moves on to remember biblical characters – Abraham and Elijah, for example – who passionately strove to receive God's blessing and whose faithfulness and prevalence proved successful. Elijah, for example, is used to highlight the power of prayer, James referring to the narrative of 1 Kings 17–18 to underline the affect of his faith: "Elias [Elijah] was a man subject to like passions as we are, and he prayed earnestly that it might not rain: and it rained not on the earth by the space of three years and six months. And he prayed again and the heaven gave rain, and the earth brought forth her fruit" (James 5:16–17). Although, as James writes, Elias was constituted of human passions, Rossetti acknowledges that his appointed task was unique: "Elijah stood alone: his ... were deeds of vengeance in a day of vengeance ... A few are charged to do judgment: every one without exception is charged to show mercy" (FD, pp. 292–3). She makes it clear, however, that his power and his strength were derived from God alone and were in no way intrinsic to his being. As his channel of communication with the Divine, prayer was his ultimate weapon. Hence, the words "Elias prayed" (line 16) convey more than is immediately apparent.

Rossetti also uses "Alas My Lord" to present her conviction that studying the Bible should naturally lead to prayer. In the seventh and eighth verses, she turns to the book of Jonah to showcase the importance of using Old Testament characters as templates for Victorian readers. From the start of the poem, Rossetti makes it clear that, in the lives of the Old Testament characters, there is a lesson for contemporary believers, beginning the poem with a "How should I"? (line 2) that culminates in a communal "our" in the last verse. The switch from individual to shared concern is particularly apparent in those verses concerning Jonah. As God forgave Jonah for his disobedience, so too he forgave "all Ninevah" (line 22) after they repented of their evil ways. The model of prayer that Rossetti alludes to by her mention of Jonah's "moan" (line 20) reads as follows:

> Then Jonah prayed unto the LORD his God out of the fish's belly, And said, I cried by reason of mine afflication unto the LORD, and he heard me ... I am cast out of thy sight; yet I will look again toward thy holy temple ... I went down to the bottoms of the mountains; the earth with her bars *was* about me for ever yet hast thou brought up my life from corruption, O LORD my God ... I will sacrifice unto thee with the voice of thanksgiving; I will pay

that that I have vowed. Salvation is of the Lord. And the Lord spake unto the fish, and it vomited out Jonah upon the dry land. (Jonah 2:1–2, 4, 6, 9–10)

The importance of praise and thanksgiving, as well as lament, is reiterated throughout the Bible and repeatedly reaffirmed by Rossetti. Indeed, her approach to studying the Bible can be aligned with the Psalmist who writes "I have rejoiced in the way of thy testimonies, *as much as* in all riches ... How sweet are thy words unto my taste! *yea, sweeter* than honey to my mouth" (Psalm 119:14, 103, italics in the original).

Exemplifying the continuity and harmony between the two testaments and contemporary Christian living, verse 9 further emphasizes the importance of thanksgiving. The book of Acts recalls how "Peter was kept in prison: but prayer was made without ceasing of the church unto God for him" (Acts 12:5). As a direct result of this prayer, an angel is sent to free Peter from his chains and lead him to freedom: "they came unto the iron gate that leadeth unto the city; which opened to them of his own accord: and they went out, and passed on through one street; and forthwith the angel departed from him" (Acts 12:10). Earlier on in Acts, a similar incident is recalled where the apostles, locked in a public jail, are released by an "angel of the Lord." After opening the prison doors for them the angel instructs them, "Go, stand and speak in the temple to the people all the words of this life" (Acts 5:20). In an analogous fashion, when Peter is freed, he is not brought to a place of worldly safety but placed in the midst of Roman persecution where he was to ensure "the word of God grew and multiplied" (Acts 12:24). Understood in the context of the "freedom" bestowed on the apostles and Peter, Rossetti's allusion to the Christian journey as "So agonised an effort and a strain" (line 5) should be read as indicative of her allegiance to the realities of the New Testament Church rather than of her own personal struggles.

A Living Scripture

Consistently through her devotional prose, Rossetti is careful not to attribute any divine power to the figures involved in Jesus' ministry but is eager to reserve all praise and thanksgiving for Christ himself. Thus, following the recollection of Peter's escape from prison, she refocuses on the sacrificial love of God. The agony that Christ went through on the cross is emphasized throughout her poetry. Indeed, several of her early poems are voiced through the mouth of Christ as he articulates his suffering and his passion. For instance, in "The Love of Christ which Passeth Knowledge," she has Jesus speak of the "six hours" on the cross, "alone, athirst, in misery" (line 22) while he waited for God to "smote" his "heart and cleft / A hiding-place" (lines 23–4) for each believer. In "A Bruised Reed Shall He not Break," she similarly has Christ tell a struggling believer "For thee I hung upon the cross in pain" (line 19). By associating the crucified Christ with the God of Isaiah 42:3, who would neither break a "bruised reed" nor quench "the smouldering flax," Rossetti both highlights his Messianic place as the fulfiller of the Scriptures and offers a method of biblical typological interpretation her readers can utilize and a pattern they can imitate. Instead of merely focusing on the crucifixion of self-centeredness and bodily desires that Jesus claims is necessary in the process of being born again in Him, in "Alas my Lord," Rossetti highlights the preparation involved in the emptying of finite selfhood. As Christ made himself "like melting wax" (line 30) in the Garden of Gethsemane, believers should, she suggests, "hold Thee fast" (line 35) as they do likewise. Her cry "Alas, alas, for me, the one that faints" (line 33) highlights the desperation and urgency of her prayer and her need for an understanding that supersedes her circumstances. It is perhaps this consistent striving for a deep understanding that most aptly characterizes Rossetti's meditations on the Bible. Considering Scripture as "living and powerful, and sharper than any two-edged sword" (Hebrews 4:12), Rossetti's conviction of the urgent need to pray for protection from the Holy Spirit in her hermeneutics is unwavering.

Notes

1   Abbreviated references to Rossetti's works are: FD, *The Face of the Deep*; SF, *Seek and Find*; TF, *Time Flies*; AD, *Annus Domini*; LS, *Letter and Spirit*; PC, *Poems, Chosen and Edited by W. M. Rossetti*. See the reference list for details.
2   Both the King James Version and the Authorized Version read "Thy word is a *lamp*."

References

Daniel, E. (1901) *The Prayer-book: Its History, Language and Contents.* Wells, Gardner, Darton & Co, London.

Honnighausen, G. (1972) "Emblematic tendencies in the works of Christina Rosetti," *Victorian Poetry,* 10, 1–15

Jowett, B. (1861) "On the Interpretation of Scripture," in *Essays and Reviews*, 5th edn. Longman, Green, Longman, and Roberts, London.

Kachur, R. M. (1997) "Repositioning the Female Christian Reader: Christina Rossetti as Tractarian Hermeneut in The Face of the Deep," *Victorian Poetry* 35:2, 193.

Keble, J. (1841) "Tract 89, On the Mysticism Attributed to the Fathers of the Church," in *Tracts for the Times by Members of the University of Oxford, 6 volumes.* J. G. F. & J. Rivington, London, p. vi.

Neale, J. M. (1872) "Sermon XXII: How Christ Is a Bundle of Myrrh," in *Sermons on the Black Letter Days Or Minor Festivals of the Church of England.* Joseph Masters, London (in http:// anglicanhistory.org, accessed April 9, 2006).

Palazzo, L. (2002) *Christina Rossetti's Feminist Theology.* Palgrave, Basingstoke.

Prickett, S. (2000) "Purging Christianity of Its Semitic Origins: Kingsley, Arnold and the Bible," in J. John, A. Jenkins and J. Sutherland, eds, *Rethinking Victorian Culture.* Macmillan, Basingstoke, p. 244.

Rossetti, C. (1874) *Annus Domini: A Prayer for Each Day of the Year.* James Parker and Co, London.

Rossetti, C. (1879) *Seek and Find: A Double Series of Short Studies of the Benedicite.* SPCK, London.

Rossetti, C. (1881) *Called to Be Saints, The Minor Festivals Devotionally Studied.* SPCK, London.

Rossetti, C. (1883) *Letter and Spirit: Notes on the Commandments.* SPCK, London and Brighton.

Rossetti, C. (1885) *Time Flies: A Reading Diary.* SPCK, London.

Rossetti, C. (1895) *The Face of the Deep: A Devotional Commentary on the Apocalypse*. SPCK, London.

Rossetti, C. G. (1904) *Poems, Chosen and Edited by W. M. Rossetti*. Macmillan & Co, London.

Rossetti, C. G. (1997–2004) *The Letters of Christina Rossetti*, ed. A. Harrison. University of Virginia Press, Charlottesville.

Rossetti, C. G. (2001) *Christina Rossetti: The Complete Poems*, ed. R. W. Crump. Penguin, London.

Ruskin, J. (1900) *Sesame and Lilies*. Houghton Miffin, Boston.

Scheinberg, C. A. (2002) *Women's Poetry and Religion in Victorian England: Jewish Identity and Christian Culture*. Cambridge University Press, Cambridge.

Tennyson, G. B. (1981) *Victorian Devotional Poetry: The Tractarian Mode*. Harvard University Press, Cambridge, MA.

Westerholm, J. (1993) "'I magnify mine office': Christina Rossetti's authoritative voice in her devotional prose," *Victorian Newsletter* 11–17.

Williams, I. (1838) Tract number 80: "On Reserve in Communicating Religious Knowledge" (Parts I–III), in *Tracts for the Times by Members of the University of Oxford, 6 volumes*. J. G. and F. Rivington, London and J. H. Parker, Oxford (in http://anglicanhistory.org, accessed March 28, 2006).

Williams, I. (1842) *Thoughts on the Study of the Holy Gospels, Intended as an Introduction to a Harmony and Commentary*. Rivingtons, London.

Williams, I. (1870) *Devotional Commentary on the Gospel Narrative, new edn. Volume 2: A Harmony of the Four Evangelists*. Rivingtons, London.

CHAPTER 40
G. M. Hopkins

Paul S. Fiddes

> He hath abolished the old drouth,
> And rivers run where all was dry,
> The field is sopp'd with merciful dew.
> He hath put a new song in my mouth,
> The words are old, the purport new,
> And taught my lips to quote this word
> That I shall live, I shall not die,
> But I shall when the shocks are stored
> See the salvation of the Lord. (Hopkins, 1967, pp. 18–19)

These lines from an early poem by Hopkins (July 1864) foreshadow the way he later draws upon Scripture in poetry soaked in scriptural images and phrases, a style that might well be expected from someone who was first a devout Anglican and then a Jesuit priest. His earlier verse is more explicit about his use of the Bible than the later, however, and so provides us with clues as to the way to read all his work. In this poem, for example, Hopkins deliberately draws attention to his use of Scripture to illuminate his own experience – "the words are old, the purport new" – and he immediately quotes "this word" from Psalm 118:17: "I shall not die, but live."[1] This is the "new song" that God has put in his mouth, a phrase taken from Psalm 40:3. But he also implicitly alludes to another Psalm, 65, in beginning with the picture of the running rivers and the fields sopping with water (Psalm 65:10–13), a reference confirmed when he paraphrases the last verse of that Psalm (14) in the final two lines of the poem:

> We shall be sheavèd with one band
> In harvest and in garnering,
> When heavenly vales so thick shall stand
> With corn that they shall laugh and sing.

The reference to Psalm 65, to which he draws no explicit attention at first, is in fact crucial for his composition, since it is from here that he draws the image of grain in both parts of the poem. Unlike the corn in the Psalm, however, this grain is eschatological; it is the faithful people whom God "stores" in his barns (alluding to Matthew 13:30), and so the poet truly shall live after death, to "see the salvation of the Lord" (here adding the Song of Simeon, Luke 2:30, to the Psalms). The word "shocks" refers to a bundling together of sheaves of wheat, and there is probably a reference to Job 5:26, where death in old age is pictured "like as a shock of corn cometh in in his season." The poet rejoices in the second verse that he and the one whom he loves – perhaps Christ himself – will be "sheaved with one band," an idea that has no precedent in Scripture but that also occurs in another early poem, "Barnfloor and Winepress": "When He has sheaved us in His sheaf" (Hopkins, 1967, p. 17).

In the first ten lines of the poem Hopkins thus weaves together references to three Psalms, two Gospels and the Book of Job. An image, here the water running in the "river of God" (Psalm 65:10), is taken as a theme, and this evokes the immediate context of the Scripture that is being drawn upon (here, the harvesting of grain), which is then further elaborated. Hopkins is not just quoting from Scripture to decorate a theme he has produced from elsewhere, but neither is he employing a close typology. Instead, a theme is taken from the scriptural passage and is then developed creatively so that it truly becomes a "new song." The earthly grain in a Psalm celebrating harvest becomes grain stored in the heavenly barns, an idea that Hopkins alludes to later in his much more well known poem "The Starlight Night":

> These are indeed the barn; withindoors house
> The shocks. This piece-bright paling shuts the spouse
> Christ home, Christ and his mother and all his hallows.

Here it is made clear that the saints are sheaved in the same harvest as Christ, the eucharistic grain. By the time of "Starlight Night," the idea of the heavenly storehouses has, moreover, undergone further theological development; they have merged in one vision with the literal, physical heavens, since Hopkins has formed a theology of Christ as incarnate in the natural world. Similarly, in "Hurrahing in Harvest," Christ can be "gleaned" from the "meal-drift" of the clouds: "I walk, I lift up, I lift up heart, eyes, / Down all that glory in the heavens to glean our Saviour ..." We might read this early poem, then, as an intimation of Hopkins's method. Employing a term suggested by George P. Landow (Landow, 1980, p. 179; cf. Korshin, 1977, pp. 147–203), we may say that he "abstracts" the essence from scriptural images rather than following a strictly typological approach, and so creates an organizing theme. As this is elaborated, first some images from the immediate context and then other scriptural texts are woven in. The development is so free, the song so new, that the scriptural allusion is often almost invisible. We might think that the image comes only from his own observation of nature, or from his reflections on philosophical theology, especially in the mature poems. We do not have to know the scriptural context for the poem to be effective, yet the more that we know of the original passage the more meaning we can find in what Hopkins is doing.

In the early poems the biblical source is more explicitly identified than in the later poems, but even here it has a freedom over against a rigid typology. In this particular poem the theme that first appears is that of life-giving water, provided by God. The poet's glad announcement that "He hath abolished the old drought" seems to have personal reflection attached to it. Hopkins's experience was of periods of spiritual and poetic dryness, and here he rejoices that this is behind him and that he has "a new song" in his mouth. In a poem of the very next year he is complaining that "My sap is sealed / My root is dry" (Hopkins, 1967, p. 169), appealing to the Gospel text "Trees by their yield / Are known" (Matthew 12:33). In the latest, despairing poems he laments "Mine, O thou lord of life, send my roots rain" (Hopkins, 1967, p. 107). The type of "the water of life" is visible, whose antitype is Christ (John 7:37–8), but through the allusion to Psalm 65 this is also associated with the harvesting of grain, and a stream of scriptural allusions connected with this image.

The image of harvesting grain that is central to "He hath abolished the old drouth" is accompanied in another early poem by the more violent image of threshing the grain, referring first to Christ and then to his followers. "Barnfloor and Winepress" explores this image:

> Sheaved in cruel bands, bruised sore,
> Scourged upon the threshing-floor;
> Where the upper mill-stone roof'd His head,
> At morn we found the heavenly Bread ...

Actually, there is no scriptural precedent for picturing the suffering and death of Christ as the threshing and grinding of grain. There is certainly a traditional Old Testament type of Christ as grapes crushed in the winepress, popularized by the use of Isaiah 63:3 in the liturgy for Holy Week, and expressed in George Herbert's poem "The Bunch of Grapes": "Ev'n God himself being pressed for my sake." At this period Hopkins was strongly influenced by Herbert, and we are not surprised to find him writing in this poem: "For us by Calvary's distress / The wine was rackèd from the press ..." Hopkins, mindful of the pairing of eucharistic bread with wine, has drawn on the Old Testament type of the manna in the wilderness (Exodus 16:15 – "at morn we found the heavenly Bread") and has then transferred the traditional images of crushing and bruising from the grapes to the grain. The theme that life can only come through bruising, crushing, pressing, and threshing is pervasive throughout Hopkins's poetry, and in this early poem we can see laid bare its scriptural sources.

The later poem "God's Grandeur" physically expresses the glory of God in the world, as that which "gathers to a greatness, like the ooze of oil / Crushed," invoking the crushing of olive seeds as another image to stand alongside those of pressing grapes and threshing grain. Nature is full of forms that are under pressure, being bruised and squeezing out life-giving fluids, as in the poem "That Nature Is a Heraclitean Fire": "in pool and rutpeel parches / Squandering ooze to squeezed / dough, crust, dust." There are frequent instances in Scripture of the pouring of oil, as a sign of the gifts of God in nature and the land (for example, "the oil of joy," Isaiah 61:3), but Hopkins prefers now to add a different scriptural image for the presence of God in the world – the hovering of the Holy Spirit over the darkness of chaos (Genesis 1:2). Perhaps there is an implicit link in the idea of anointing with oil as a symbol for the pouring out of the Spirit:

> Oh, morning, at the brown brink eastward, springs –
> Because the Holy Ghost over the bent
> World broods with warm breast and with ah! bright wings.

"The Windhover" presents another set of images of the beauty that comes from bruising and breaking. As Hopkins greets Christ in the form of the windhover, swinging and soaring on the currents of air, he finds the most intense beauty in the sudden collapse (buckling) or plummeting of the bird to earth – "oh, air, pride, plume, here / Buckle!" So Christ has stooped low in humility, his life has buckled and crumpled, but from this passion there flashes the fire of sacrifice that is the energy in the world. The "fire" or light of the sun glinting from the plumage ("AND the fire that breaks from thee then") reminds Hopkins of the beauty that emerges from other kinds of bruising: there is the way that the furrow shines as the ploughblade breaks the dark soil, and the way that dull, half-burnt embers are broken open as they fall apart to show the fire within:

> No wonder of it: sheer plod makes plough down sillion
> Shine, and blue-bleak embers, ah my dear,
> Fall, gall themselves, and gash gold-vermilion.

Images of crushing reappear in the "terrible" last sonnets of 1885–9, in which Hopkins records a sense of spiritual and aesthetic desolation. In "Patience, Hard Thing" we are to ask God to bend our wills to his, though "We hear our hearts grate on themselves" and "it kills / To bruise them dearer." While the biblical reference in "The Windhover" and "Patience" is implicit (in the latter, Paul's words about patience in Romans 2:1–11 lie in the background), the scriptural allusions cluster more explicitly in "Carrion Comfort." In this latter poem the poet feels as if he has been threshed and winnowed: "That my chaff might fly; my grain lie, sheer and clear." The chaff here is flying before the storm-wind of God's approach ("fan, / O in turns of tempest, me heaped there"), recalling the several depictions of divine judgment in Scripture as the driving away of chaff by the wind (e.g. Job 21:18; Psalms 1:4, 35:5; Hosea 13:3). That the threshing has a scriptural context is made clear by the parallel image of the poet's bones being "bruised" by a heavenly opponent, in a reference to the story of the wrestling of Jacob with God all night (Genesis 32:24–5):

> That night, that year
> Of now done darkness I wretch lay wrestling with (my God!)
> my God.

In "The Wreck of the Deutschland" Hopkins recalls two extreme moments where the elevating grace of God was released through a human experience of being afflicted and bruised. The spiritual crisis of his own life when he was called by God to the priesthood merges with God's calling of a group of nuns to martyrdom in a shipwreck. In a moment of choice that, according to the Ignatian Exercises, corresponds to God's election (Hopkins, 1959a, p. 146–59) Hopkins had said "yes / O at lightning and lashed rod" (stanza 2):

> Thou knowest the walls, altar and hour and night:
> The swoon of a heart that the sweep and the hurl of thee trod
>   Hard down with a horror of height:
>   And the midriff astrain with leaning of, laced with fire of stress.

This was one kind of storm, which is brought into a single focus with the literal storm in which the nuns make their choice for God, who is calling them to martydom. As "they fought with God's cold," the tall nun cries "O Christ, Christ, come quickly," echoing Revelation 22:20, and so "The cross to her she calls Christ to her, christens her wild-worst Best" (stanza 24). Though these are two intense moments of crisis, Hopkins places them in the more general context of the natural world, which all the time is offering the "stress" of God's grace to the human consciousness – "stroke and a stress that stars and storms deliver" – because Christ is present in all creation, "under the world's splendour and wonder" (stanza 5). Once again drawing on the image of the release of fluids, as if from pressed grapes, this grace "flushes" human hearts and so "hushes" human guilt (stanza 6). Above all, life is released through the bruising and breaking of Christ in his incarnation and passion, and here Hopkins appeals explicitly to the scriptural story (stanza 7):

> Manger, maiden's knee;
> The dense and the driven Passion, and frightful sweat:
> Thence the discharge of it, there its swelling to be,
>   Though felt before, though in high flood yet –

Taking his clue from the account of the agony of Christ in Gethsemane, where "his sweat was as it were great drops of blood falling down to the ground" (Luke 22:44), the sacrifice of Christ is told in terms of the "discharge" of grace. Elaborating this liquid image, the human heart in extremity ("midriff astrain with leaning of, laced with fire of stress") is called to respond to this sacrifice, which it may find bitter or sweet, like a fruit pressed in the mouth and bursting (stanza 8):

> How a lush-kept plushed-capped sloe
>   Will, mouthed to flesh-burst,
> Gush! – flush the man, the being with it, sour or sweet,
>   Brim, in a flash, full!

In the background there is thus the scriptural image of pressed grapes, and the accompanying image of threshed grain is certainly not absent from this story of a spiritual and literal storm. Where Scripture speaks only of *chaff* "carried before the wind," as we saw in the later poem "Carrion Comfort," Hopkins here appeals to a paradox: through the witness of the nun to Christ, this tempest might actually be carrying *grain*, the harvest of human lives (Luke 10:2): "is the shipwreck then a harvest, / does tempest carry the grain for thee?" (stanza 31). It is a broad theme of the New Testament that life only comes through death, that resurrection is reached only through the darkness of the cross. This is the way of Christ, and it is the path that his disciples follow in baptism, dying and rising again in Christ (Romans 6:3–5). Put in eucharistic language, wine is made by crushing grapes, and bread by the threshing of grain. But the idea of beauty coming through sacrifice also has a particular theological location in Hopkins's thinking, associated with the medieval scholar Duns Scotus. The thought of Scotus regarding "the Great Sacrifice" on which the whole of creation is founded had a profound effect on Hopkins's vision of the world, and lies behind all the images of breaking, crushing, and pressing that fill his poetry. Yet it is Hopkins's reflections on Plato, Pythagoras, and Parmenides (Hopkins, 1959b, pp. 86–121, 127–30), affirmed by his reading of Scotus, that give rise to his ideas of "stress" and "inscape" that so inform these biblical references to physicality.

For Hopkins, everything has a unique "self" or its own characteristic form, which he compared with Scotus's term *haecceitas* or "thisness" (Hopkins, 1959a, pp. 151, 341–3). In contrast to other scholastic thought, which aims to extract *universal* ideas from individual forms, for Scotus it is in the particular that objects and persons touch reality and from which the universal can be constructed. So Hopkins rejoices in the particularity of things, none exactly like another. While everything has its distinct identity, Hopkins gains particular pleasure from dappled and freckled things that combine shapes and colors in odd combinations. In "Pied Beauty" he celebrates:

> All things counter, original, spare, strange;
> Whatever is fickle, freckled (who knows how?)
> With swift, slow; sweet, sour; adazzle, dim ...

The universe is full of individual forms like notes in a musical scale or separate fractions in scales of light. Hopkins calls the form of these myriad selves their "inscape," denoting that they have an outer shape (scape) that expresses an inner nature:

> Each mortal thing does one thing and the same:
> Deals out that being indoors each one dwells;
> Selves – goes itself; *myself* it speaks and spells,
> Crying *What I do is me: for that I came.* (Hopkins, 1967, p. 90)

So, for instance, creatures reflect sunlight in different ways: "As kingfishers catch fire, dragonflies draw flame." Each stone makes its own kind of splash when thrown into a well, each bell makes its own ring, "finds tongue to fling out broad its name." Hopkins finds inscapes to be sustained by a charge of energy that he calls "stress," and this also makes a bridge of communication between them (see Downes, 1985, p. 21; Fiddes, 1991, pp. 117–22). One inscape delivers a surge of stress out of itself to another, and linked to the inscape this energy becomes "instress." In an early essay, Hopkins writes that "I have often felt ... the depth of an instress or how fast the inscape holds a thing" (Hopkins, 1959b, p. 127).

For Hopkins the "stress" that holds everything together is nothing less than the grace of God, and this grace depends on an eternal act of sacrifice. This is the theological basis for all the images of crushing, pressing, breaking, and bruising in Hopkins's poetry. Reading Scotus, Hopkins developed the insight that the sacrifice of the Son is God's first thought of the world, so that both the eternal generation of the Son from the Father, and the mission of Christ into the world that follows, take the form of sacrifices (Balthasar, 1986, pp. 381–3).[2] In the fellowship of the Trinity, writes Hopkins, "the first outstress of God's power was Christ" (Hopkins, 1959a, p. 197). The triune God "selves" himself, moving beyond his being into his creation with the stress of love: "He fathers-forth whose beauty is past change" (Hopkins, 1967, p. 70). The sacrificial out-stress of God is the foundation of creation: Hopkins writes in a sermon that "It is as if the blissful agony of stress or selving in God has forced out drops of sweat and blood, which drops were the world" (Hopkins, 1959a, p. 197).

If God has made all things with their own self, then, it is in order that they may exist in communion with him. When an inscape "stresses itself" or speaks itself out, it is responding to God by riding on the surge of energy that comes from God's own sacrificial presence in the world. The stress of grace, which is the work of the Holy Spirit, unites the created inscape with the divine lovescape. Hopkins's idea of "stress" therefore allows him to understand two movements going on at once as objects in creation "selve" themselves, crying "what I do is me": there is the response of the creatures to God, and the "selving" or doing-be of the triune God through them:

> For Christ plays in ten thousand places,
>   Lovely in limbs and lovely in eyes not his
>   To the Father through the features of men's faces. (Hopkins, 1967, p. 90)

Perhaps a unique contribution of Hopkins is in identifying the Great Sacrifice, in all its forms, with the Eucharist, so that from eternity the sacrifice has body and materiality in view. Creation is sacramental from the beginning (Downes 1960, pp. 36–8; Harris, 1982, p. 46). Objects in the natural world give praise to God by simply being themselves, but human beings respond at the highest level of the will. We receive a stress from an object of beauty in the natural world, accept this into ourselves ("instress" it), and then respond in adoration and surrender to God, stressing or speaking out the grace that has come from him: "his mystery must be instressed, stressed." Hopkins makes the definitive statement of this sequence in his poem "The Wreck of the Deutschland" (stanza 5):

> I kiss my hand
>   To the stars, lovely-asunder
>   Starlight, wafting him out of it; and
>   Glow, glory in thunder;
> Kiss my hand to the dappled-with-damson west;
> Since, tho' he is under the world's splendour and wonder,
>   His mystery must be instressed, stressed;
> For I greet him the days I meet him, and bless when I understand.

We meet the grace of God indwelling the beauty of nature ("wafting him out of it," "under the world's splendour"), and respond ("kiss my hand to the stars"), stressing the mystery.

All this may seem a metaphysical scheme that has merely been imposed on Scripture, but we can see that it is a creative development of the scriptural theme of the birth of the Word, and the response of Mary to bearing the Word of God: "behold the handmaid of the Lord; be it unto me according to thy word" (Luke 1:38). In Hopkins's thought, the eternal sacrifice and the eucharistic presence of Christ in the world require the participation of Mary in saying "yes" to God, so that the whole of creation itself depends upon her response. This is why she is "the mighty mother": the growth of nature in Spring, the "magnifying" of nature, which in turn magnifies (praises) God, depends upon the magnifying of the Lord by Mary (Luke 1:46): "All things rising, all things sizing / Mary sees, sympathising" (Hopkins, 1967, p. 77). Of her flesh the Word became flesh (John 1:14), and when we respond as Mary did, the Word can be born again in us and through us, making "New Nazareths in us" (Hopkins, 1967, p. 95). Thus, as we receive into our selves the stress of God's grace, Hopkins envisages that we respond with appropriate words, which echo the true Word who is Christ. As we speak the word of Christ we give birth to the Logos ("birth of a brain, / Word"; Hopkins, 1967, p. 61), just as God uttered the Word in creation and as Mary gave him birth: "so conceivèd, so to conceive thee is done" (Hopkins, 1967, p. 61). The tall nun in the shipwreck "words" the shock night "by him that present and past / Heaven and earth are word of, worded by" (John 1:1–3) and so like Mary in her "heart-throe" she "heard and kept thee and uttered thee outright" (Luke 2:19, 51).

Hopkins portrays the God who delivers stress into the world through his creative and redemptive acts in an image deriving from Scripture, and chiefly from the Psalms – that is, the Lord who reigns over the waters. Again we see Hopkins abstracting a theme, and using it as a center upon which to organize thought and other Scripture references. In "The Wreck of the Deutschland" the God who comes in a spiritual storm to Hopkins, and who comes in a physical storm to the nuns in the shipwreck, is addressed as "master of the tides," as the Lord who checks and represses the hostile waters of the sea (stanza 32):

> I admire thee, master of the tides,
>   Of the Yore-flood, of the year's fall;
>   The recurb and the recovery of the gulf's sides,
>   The girth of it and the wharf of it and the wall;
>   Stanching, quenching ocean of a motionable mind;
>   Ground of being, and granite of it; past all
>   Grasp God ...

There are many biblical echoes here. God is the one "who shuts up the sea with doors" (Job 38:8–11), and who wins a victory over the raging of the sea, symbolized as the sea-monster (Psalm 89:9–10; Isaiah 51:9–11; Job 26:12–13). As manifest in Christ, this God stilled the storm on the Lake of Gennesereth (Matthew 8:25; stanza 25). Such a God is also Lord over the unstable ocean of human minds ("a motionable mind"), for we read in James 1:6–8 that "he who wavereth is like a wave of the sea driven with wind and tossed ... a double-minded man is unstable in all his ways"; by contrast with this "motionable mind," Hopkins in a previous verse approves the nun as having "a single eye" (Luke 11:34). God is master of the "Yore-flood," whether this is the primeval waters of chaos referred to in Genesis 1:2 and the Psalms, or whether it is Noah's flood when the waters of chaos burst forth again over the earth (Genesis 7:11). The very next stanza (33) invokes the descent of Christ into Hades, to redeem the spirits in prison, who "sometime were disobedient ... in *the days of Noah*, while the ark was preparing, wherein few ... were saved by water" (1 Peter 3:20). So Hopkins celebrates the mercy of God which is like "an ark for the listener" and which "outrides / The all of water." Christ, "our passion-plunged giant risen" has descended into the very deepest waters of death to lead out the imprisoned spirits, "fetched in the storm of his strides."

This last phrase recalls Psalm 18:16, "He shall send down from on high to fetch me: and shall take me out of many waters," a verse in a Psalm which is central to an image of the Lord as master of the waters. It begins with an invocation of God as a rock, just as in the verse above God is invoked as "granite," and then proceeds to describe the God who comes down from heaven to rescue the Psalmist from the waters of death where he is about to be drowned. This is the God who controls the sea, and who has himself the characteristics of a storm, including thunder and lightning (verses 13–14). The Psalm's depiction of a God who descends from the heights of heaven and who "cast forth lightnings" (verses 13–14) has evidently had a strong impact on the poem. The poet says "yes / O at lightning and lashed rod" (stanza 2) and finds that God treads down on him from "a horror of height." God is "lightning and love," and significantly "hast thy dark descending and most art merciful then" (stanza 9). At first this description of God's descent as "dark" seems puzzling, but the Psalm explains it: "[The Lord] bowed the heavens also, and came down: and it was dark under his feet" (verse 9). As a storm God, the Lord shows aspects both of brightness and darkness: "he made darkness his secret place ... at the brightness of his presence his clouds removed" (verses 11–12). By contrast, Hopkins's poem ends with the hope of a new creation when judgment will be past, and there will be no more need for "a dooms-day dazzle in his coming nor *dark* as he came" nor for "a lightning of fire hard-hurled." This last phrase appears to combine the imagery of Psalm 18 with Jesus' rebuke to his disciples, who wanted him to command "fire to come down from heaven" (Luke 9:54–5).

It may seem that this picture of a God of storm, the "martyr-master" in whose sight "storm flakes were scroll-leaved flowers" (stanza 21), does not sit easily with the God of sacrifice who has made the world at the cost of "sweat and blood" (Hopkins, 1957a, p. 197; cf. Robinson, 1978, pp. 120–2). However, there is some coherence as well as ambiguity here. Imagery of the storm God is located within the biblical theme that God shows creative power in overcoming hostile powers, symbolized as the unruly sea. There is a hint here then of the divine sacrifice that Hopkins associates with creation. From a modern theological perspective we may say that in creation, God empties God's self out by coming into conflict with the forces of chaos that emerge from a universe to which God has given a radical freedom. Hopkins reflects the New Testament in telling us that, in Christ, God is immersed in the waters of death and is voluntarily overcome by them for a moment, in order to rise again in victory over chaos and death.

Alongside Psalm 18, Hopkins seems to have Psalm 139 in mind, especially in the first three stanzas of "The Wreck of the Deutschland." In Psalm 139 the Psalmist celebrates the God who searches all human hearts, and from whose presence no one can escape, even in the depths of the sea and Hades. For Hopkins, as we have seen, God indwells all the inscapes of the world. When the Psalmist asks, "Whither shall I go then from thy spirit? or whither shall I go then from thy presence?," the poet asks "where, where was a, where was a place?" The Psalmist reflects "If I take the wings of the morning and remain in the uttermost parts of the sea; even there also shall thy hand lead me, and thy right hand shall hold me." The poet also takes wing, and aims like a homing pigeon for the presence of Christ in the eucharistic bread: "I whirled out wings that spell / And fled with a fling of the heart to the heart of the Host." Perhaps there is here also an echo of Psalm 55:6, "O that I had wings like a dove! For then I would flee away, and be at rest." The writer of Psalm 139 confesses to God that "thou has fashioned me behind and before and laid thine hand upon me," and the poet asks "dost thou touch me afresh? / Over again I feel thy finger and find thee," though in this last phrase he also perhaps has the reference to "the finger of God" in Luke 11:20 in mind. Finally, the poet exclaims that "Thou has bound bones and veins in me, fastened me flesh." While there is a clear reference here to Job 10:11, "Thou hast clothed me with skin and flesh and hast fenced me with bones and sinews," the writer of Psalm 139 also reflects that God saw him while his bones were being fashioned in secret (verses 14–16). Thus, in the opening to his poem, Hopkins weaves together reminiscences from Psalms 18 and 139, connected by the common picture of a God who has command over the sea ("World's strand, sway of the sea") and who lays his hand upon the human personality. The imagery from the Psalms combines to show a God who is touching Hopkins and the five nuns with the stresses of affective and elective grace.

There is also a link between Psalms 18 and 139 in the motif of wings. In Psalm 18 the storm God flies "upon the wings of the wind" (verse 10), and in Psalm 139 the Psalmist too wishes that he could "take the wings of the morning and remain in the uttermost parts of the sea" (verse 9). The image of the bird ascending to heaven seems to have been a signature of Hopkins's poetry from the very beginning (Hopkins, 1967, pp. 15, 28–9, 128, 171). Above the scenes of devastation of the world, whose wild and primeval beauty is "unselved" by human selfishness and exploitation, the bird flies in the free, untamable air, truly being itself and "selving" itself in ever new and surprising ways. The sound of the lark ascending, for instance, pouring out his "rash-fresh rewinded new-skeinèd score," shames the human "shallow and frail town" whose inhabitants are breaking "down / To man's last dust" (Hopkins, 1967, p. 68). It seems unlikely that Hopkins drew this image from Scripture in the first place, but scriptural instances such as in Psalms 18, 55, and 139 (cf. Job 39:26: "is it by your wisdom that the hawk soars and spreads its wings?") reinforce an existing symbol, and give it more depth and resonance.

On the one hand, the bird stands as a symbol and an occasion for the presence of God, who rides "on the wings of the wind." The beauty and the passion of Christ can be discerned in the gliding flight of the windhover, which is "morning's minion," recalling the "wings of the morning" in Psalm 139, and in "God's Grandeur" the Holy Spirit hovers over the world like a bird with "bright wings" in the early morning. They are bright, presumably, because they reflect the early morning sun, but there may also be a recollection of the scriptural text "the sun of righteousness will arise, with healing in his wings" (Malachi 4:2). By contrast, it seems that the victims in the *Deutschland* were "O Father, *not* under thy feathers" (stanza 12; cf. Matthew 23:37). On the other hand, the ascending bird stands as a symbol for what the human spirit can be, "like a lark to glide aloof" (Hopkins, 1967, p. 113). At the moment, however, dwelling in its "bonehouse," it is often like a skylark trapped "in a dull cage" (Hopkins 1967, p. 70–1). This does not mean that Hopkins, committed as he is to a sacramental universe, is dualistic about the body and soul; in agreement with Paul, he looks for the resurrection when there will be a new kind of body (1 Corinthians 15:44), which will no more encumber the spirit than a meadow is "distressed / For a rainbow footing it." Even now, however, the particularity of a human self – say, Henry Purcell – can stand out like the distinctive marks – the "quaint moonmarks" – under the plumage of "some great storm-fowl," spreading its wings for flight (Hopkins, 1967, p. 80). The fact that, as in Psalms 18 and 139, the flight of a bird can be attributed to God *and* the human person shows that it is in the moment when an inscape receives and gives stress that the Creator and the created are open to each other in their mutual "selving":

> which two when they once meet,
> *The heart rears wings* bold and bolder
> And hurls for him, O half hurls earth for him off under his feet. (Hopkins, 1967, p. 70)

In contrast to a joyous meeting with God in the world, the group of despairing sonnets that were written toward the end of Hopkins's life sound a note of protest against the God who seems to have left Hopkins desolate (Miller, 1963, p. 335). The taste of self in the mouth is now no longer glorious "selving" ("Crying *What I do is me: for that I came*") but only bitterness:

> I am gall, I am heartburn. God's most deep decree
> Bitter would have me taste: my taste was me;
> Bones built in me, flesh filled, blood brimmed the curse. (Hopkins, 1967, p. 101)

Here the "gall" drunk by Christ on the cross in his forsakenness (Luke 23:36) is merged with the cup of God's will that is "drunk" by Christ in Gethsemane ("God's most deep decree": Luke 22:42), but the twist lies in the fact that for Hopkins "my taste was me." While in "The Wreck of the Deutschland" Hopkins rejoiced that God has "bound bones and veins in me, fastened me flesh" (echoing Psalm 139 and Job 10:8–12), here blood fills not the "course" of veins but the "curse," or "the blight man was born for" (Hopkins, 1967, p. 88–9; cf. Psalm 51:5). The story of Christ in Gethsemane fits into the scriptural tradition of pleading, contending, or arguing with God of which Hopkins gives a stark example in "Thou art indeed just, Lord," quoting from Jeremiah 12:1. Hopkins heads the poem with the verse from the Vulgate version, and then proceeds to give his own translation. Needless to say, the last phrase is Hopkins and not Jeremiah:

> Thou art indeed just, Lord, if I contend
> With thee; but, sir, so what I plead is just.
> Why do sinners' ways prosper? and why must
> Disappointment all I endeavour end?

Drawing on the tradition of complaint in the Old Testament, Hopkins is in fact ranging wider than Jeremiah 12. The quotation has, it seems, sparked off a memory of Job's complaint against God in Job 9–14, beginning with the key word "contend": "But how should man be just with God? If he will contend with him, he cannot answer him one of a thousand" (Job 9:2–3). Hopkins seems to have meditated long on these chapters in Job, where the author confronts God with what seems the injustice of his suffering. Hopkins's complaint that God could not treat him worse if he were his enemy echoes Job's cry: "Wherefore hidest thou thy face, and holdest me for thine enemy?" (Job 13:24). His final cry to God – "Mine, O thou Lord of life, send my roots rain" – recalls the complaint of Jeremiah 12 that the wicked have "taken root and grow," but also draws on Job 14:7–10: "there is hope for a tree, if it be cut down ... through the scent of water it will bud and bring forth boughs like a plant. But man dieth and wasteth away."

In this group of sonnets Hopkins constantly returns to the scene of Christ in Gethsemane, to the "frightful sweat" to which he had referred in "The Wreck of the Deutschland." We seem also to return to the image of pressed olives oozing oil since Gethsemane means "an oil press" and is situated on the slopes of the Mount of Olives. In "Patience" he confesses that "the rebellious wills / Of us we do bid God bend to him," so copying Christ's submission, "Thy will not mine be done," as Christ had bid his disciples to pray (Luke 22:42, 46). But Hopkins brings this prayer of Christ in Gethsemane into one focus with the complaints of Job. The poet is like Christ in the garden, yet his mood is not one of acceptance, but protest. Most poignantly, the sonnet "No Worst, There Is None" reads like an Ignatian meditation on Christ praying in Gethsemane, just as "Carrion Comfort" is an imaginative participation in the wrestling of Jacob with God at night.[3] The poet, like Christ, cries out in agony ("My cries heave"; cf. Hebrews 5:7). In this desolation, Mary is absent for the poet as for Christ ("Mary, mother of us, where is your relief?") But unlike Christ, it seems, the poet is not visited by an angel who comforts him (Luke 22:43):[4] "Comforter, where is your comforting?"

Hopkins, indeed, is not so much like Christ as like the disciples who accompany him, whom Christ at the end of his agony "found sleeping for sorrow" (Luke 22:45). In his meditation Hopkins puts himself imaginatively in their place:

> Here! creep,
> Wretch, under a comfort serves in a whirlwind: all
> Life death does end and each day dies with sleep.

Here is also an unmistakable reference to Job, who in his complaints is confronted by the Lord who "answered Job out of the whirlwind" (Job 38:1). Also perhaps there is an echo of Job 14 again, where Job asks "that thou wouldest hide me in the grave, that thou wouldest keep me in secret, until thy wrath be past" (verse 13). In bringing together the Christ of Gethsemane and the Job of contention, we see how Hopkins uses Scripture – abstracting a theme, yet also weaving into it the echoes of specific texts. We also see an irony: the poet who laments a loss of creativity in his final sonnets is, in that very lament, using Scripture in a profoundly creative way.

Notes

1   The Psalms in English are cited from Coverdale's version in the Book of Common Prayer, and all other scriptural quotations are taken from the King James Version of the Bible, as being two of the translations of Scripture with which Gerard Manley Hopkins would have been familiar.
2   See Scotus, *Oxoniense*, iv, dist. 10, qu. 4, cit. C. Devlin in Hopkins (1959a, pp. 113–14).
3   Generally, for the influence of the Ignatian Exercises on the last sonnets, see Paul L. Mariani (1970, pp. 209–12) and Downes (1985, pp. 99–101).
4   Vulgate: "confortans eum." However, see Hopkins's sermon on the Holy Spirit as Comforter (John 16:7; Hopkins, 1959a, pp. 70–1).

References

Balthasar, Hans Urs von (1986) *The Glory of the Lord. A Theological Aesthetics. Volume III, Studies in Theological Style: Lay Styles, trans.* Andrew Louth, John Saward, Martin Simon and Rowan Williams, ed. John Riches. T. & T. Clark, Edinburgh.

Downes, David A. (1960) *Gerard Manley Hopkins: A Study of His Ignatian Spirit.* Vision, London.

Downes, David A. (1985) *Hopkins' Sanctifying Imagination.* University Press of America, Lanham, MD.

Fiddes, Paul S. (1991) *Freedom and Limit. A Dialogue betweeen Literature and Christian Doctrine.* Macmillan, Basingstoke.

Harris, Daniel A. (1982) *Inspirations Unbidden. The "Terrible Sonnets" of Gerard Manley Hopkins.* University of California Press, Berkeley.

Hopkins, Gerard Manley (1959a) *The Sermons and Devotional Writings of Gerard Manley Hopkins,* ed. Christopher Devlin, SJ. Oxford University Press, London.

Hopkins, Gerard Manley (1959b) *The Journals and Papers of Gerard Manley Hopkins,* 2nd edn, ed. Humphry House, completed Graham Storey. Oxford University Press, London.

Hopkins, Gerard Manley (1967) *The Poems of Gerard Manley Hopkins,* 4th edn, ed. W. H. Gardner and N. H. Mackenzie. Oxford University Press, London.

Korshin, Paul (1977) "The Development of Abstracted Typology in England, 1650–1820," in Earl Miner, ed., *Literary Uses of Typology from the Middle Ages to the Present.* Princeton University Press, Princeton, NJ, pp. 147–203.

Landow, George P. (1980) *Victorian Types, Victorian Shadows: Biblical Typology in Victorian Literature, Art and Thought.* Routledge and Kegan Paul, London.

Mariani, Paul L (1970): *A Commentary on the Complete Poems of Gerard Manley Hopkins*. Cornell University Press, Ithaca, NY.

Miller, J. Hillis (1963) *The Disappearance of God: Five Nineteenth Century Writers*. Belknap Press of Harvard University, Cambridge, MA.

Robinson, John (1978) *In Extremity. A Study of Gerard Manley Hopkins*. Cambridge University Press, Cambridge.

Further Reading

Gardner, W. H. (1958) *Gerard Manley Hopkins (1844–1889): A Study of Poetic Idiosyncrasy in Relation to Poetic Tradition*, 2nd edn, 2 volumes. Oxford University Press, Oxford.

Jenkins, Alice, ed. (2006) *The Poems of Gerard Manley Hopkins: A Sourcebook*. Routledge, London.

Muller, Jill (2003) *Gerard Manley Hopkins and Victorian Catholicism: A Heart in Hiding*. Routledge, London.

CHAPTER 41
Sensation Fiction

Mark Knight

Although "sensation fiction" is often understood to refer to a group of novels written during the 1860s, the term predated the decade and continued to be applied to works written well after 1870. Moreover, the term "sensation" meant more than a particular type of fiction, as Jenny Bourne Taylor (1988, p. 2) explains:

> "Sensation" was one of the keywords of the 1860s. It encapsulated the particular way in which the middle-class sense of cultural crisis was experienced during that decade. ... In one sense this wasn't so much a coherent literary tendency or genre, more a critical term held together by the word "sensation" itself.

Scholarly attention to sensation fiction has tended to focus on the work of more familiar novelists such as Wilkie Collins, Mary Braddon and Mrs Henry Wood. However, as Andrew Maunder's *Varieties of Women's Sensation Fiction* has shown, there were a great many authors of sensation narratives who have since been forgotten. Their work was discussed at the time by a range of authors and cultural commentators, including Sigismund Smith, the fictional "sensation author" (Braddon, 1998, p. 11) who appears in the curiously self-reflexive opening to Mary Braddon's *The Doctor's Wife* (1864). Smith's work as "the author of about half a dozen highly-spiced fictions, which enjoyed an immense popularity amongst the classes who like their literature as they like their tobacco – very strong" (p. 11) – reminds us that the genre was not confined to the middle-class novels found in periodicals such as Charles Dickens's *All the Year Round*. The fictional Smith further complicates the nature of sensation fiction when he describes the sort of novels he writes as "a combination story" that "steal other people's ideas" to present "the brightest flowers of fiction neatly arranged into every variety of garland" (p. 45). His detailed account of the different titles and incidents his work draws upon initially bores his friend George Gilbert, but the boredom gives way to consternation as Smith goes on to contemplate a sensational rewrite of Oliver Goldsmith's *Vicar of Wakefield* (1766). Like many of the actual critics from the 1860s, Gilbert is alarmed at the potential reach of the sensational phenomenon and its refusal to be contained within clear boundaries.

Given the generic promiscuity of the sensation novel and the way in which it sought to compete with more sedate, established literary classics for the attention of the reading public, it is not surprising that many critics saw the genre as battling for the soul of the reader. The religious discourse permeating much of the criticism of the genre – Henry Mansel famously claimed that sensation writers were "usurping ... the preacher's office" (reprinted in Maunder, 2004, p. 32) – was perhaps inevitable in a society where Christian faith played such an integral role. For example, the author of "Decay of Spiritual Strength," published in *The Revival: An Advocate of Evangelical Truth* (8 March 1866), made it clear that reading was to be seen as a threat:

> This is a reading age. What multitudes of books are constantly pouring forth! But the majority are from the world, and for the world. Men of strong but unscrupulous minds are writing with a determinate design to poison the minds of their fellow men ... (p. 128)

In *The Reading Lesson: The Threat of Mass Literacy in the Nineteenth Century* (1998), Patrick Brantlinger explores the trope of the dangerous, poisonous text in the nineteenth century and considers its reappearance during the sensation debates of the 1860s. His argument helps to account for the religious hostility to the sensation novel, and builds upon a claim he made in 1982 that the sensation novel is a secular form of mystery, without "even a quasi-religious content" (Brantlinger, 1982, p. 4). Brantlinger's reading of the debates over sensation fiction is helpful on many levels; yet, at the same time, it is a reading that sometimes imports, uncritically, the rhetoric and assumptions of nineteenth-century critics who insisted on a strict dichotomy between religion and the "secular" sensation novel. The relationship between sensation fiction and religion is, however, less clear-cut than this, particularly when it comes to thinking about the way in which mid-nineteenth-century writers engaged with the Bible.

Publishing strategies such as serialization certainly helped to increase the public's interest in sensation fiction, although reading patterns were affected by many factors including the limited levels of literacy in the nineteenth century and the growth of other demands on people's leisure time. Nonetheless, for many mid-century religious commentators, the "secular" threat of sensation fiction was directed toward the Bible. An article titled "Character: How It Is Formed and What It Is Worth," published in the *Evangelical Magazine* (June 1866), articulated its concerns in this way:

> Are those books which he [the reader] devours so eagerly sensation novels, or good, substantial works, full of solid information and of right sentiments? ... if a man would build up for himself a strong and useful character, he must read very sparingly fiction of any kind. ... Let there be chosen, rather, books which will instruct ... let there be daily studied that one Book which speaks to us the thoughts of God. (p. 376)

It was, of course, disconcerting for religious communities to think that the public's burgeoning interest in sensation fiction might deplete the amount of time that individuals had available for reading the Bible. More surprising is the fact that some sensation novels of the period register this concern over the religious implications of changing reading habits. For example, in *The Woman in White* (1859–60), a novel that helped bring sensation fiction to the attention of the middle classes, the Bible is not read, but instead lies closed on "the largest table, in the middle of the room, ... placed exactly in the centre, on a red and yellow woollen mat" (p. 494). When its owner, Mrs Catherick, feels her respectability threatened by Walter Hartright's questions, she offers a defense based on what the Bible symbolizes rather than what it says: "I have matched the respectable people fairly and openly, on their own ground. ... Is your mother alive? Has she got a better Bible on her table than I have got on mine?" (p. 498). The changing status of the Bible is an issue that Collins implicitly returns to in *The Moonstone* (1868), where Gabriel Betteredge's comic reliance on "the one infallible remedy" (p. 518) involves opening a copy of *Robinson Crusoe* for inspiration rather than the Word of God.

The Bible is not forgotten in the world of sensation fiction, nor is it simply a parodied cultural artifact; instead, sensation fiction repeatedly draws on and engages with biblical tropes. The difficulty of exemplifying this engagement is that the more deeply a biblical text is internalized, the more diffuse its trace becomes. Dickens – one of the most influential figures in the development of sensation fiction – exemplifies the point, and the extensive scriptural trace in his work and the complex ways in which different biblical texts are juxtaposed and read against one another has been examined by Janet L. Larsen (1985). This chapter takes one example of such a trace in sensation fiction, and considers the ways in which the sensation novel might be read as a meditation on a selection of biblical texts relating to marital (in)fidelity and the fallen woman. These particular issues are central to the sensation genre, as even the most cursory glance at the critical literature on sensation fiction makes clear; they are also integral to the Bible, recurring, to give just a few examples, in descriptions of Israel, in the book of Hosea, in the figure of Mary Magdalene in the Gospel accounts, and in the comparison between Babylon and the New Jerusalem in the book of Revelation.

Sensation fiction is, then, willing to engage with biblical voices that have often been marginalized by religious communities. This is particularly evident in the case of the prostitute in the book of Hosea. As Yvonne Sherwood explains in *The Prophet and the Prostitute: Hosea's Marriage in Literary-Theological Perspective* (1996), religious communities have frequently failed to come to terms with the central conceit in Hosea. This reluctance to talk openly about prostitution in conjunction with the Bible was especially acute in the middle of the nineteenth century, and can be seen in the selective way that Mary Smith, the first-person narrator of *Out of the Depths* (Jebb, 1859), reads the Bible. Her narrative claims to be a true confession of her fall into prostitution and her subsequent conversion to a life of faith. While the text is too polemical and one-dimensional to merit unqualified description as a sensation novel, its proximity to the sensation debates of the 1860s and its shared narrative content make it a useful point of comparison. One of the dominant markers in Mary's conversion is the Bible that she carries everywhere with her. It is a text that she constantly reads and seeks inspiration from; yet while Mary occasionally mentions stories from the Gospels concerning the hope that Jesus offers to adulterous and promiscuous women (stories that can be seen as correlatives of the book of Hosea) she struggles to comprehend how religion makes space for a woman who is sexually impure. One of the signs of her inability to conceive of the possibility (described in Hosea) of unity between a prophet and a prostitute is that her confession struggles to speak clearly or openly about prostitution. For all her insistence that she is providing a frank and detailed confession, the word "prostitution" is only mentioned once, and in the latter stages of the book. Describing her conversation with Mrs Carbury, Mary writes: " 'I was once an unfortunate woman in London, ma'am – a – a prostitute! lady,' I cry, extorted by some sudden thrilling pain" (p. 290).

In contrast to Mary's pained reference, writers of sensation novels were more willing to name prostitution and other "immoral" activities. Through their reliance on what Thomas Hardy termed "moral obliquity" in his 1889 preface to *Desperate Remedies* (1871), sensation novels gave considerable space to the exploration of prostitution and they frequently extended readers' understanding of what prostitution involved. Famously, Mary Braddon's *Lady Audley's Secret* (1862) details the financial inequality faced by Victorian women in a manner that blurs the distinction between being paid for sex and earning one's financial security through marriage. In one of the novel's most disturbing scenes, Lady Audley's removal to an asylum as punishment for her deceit is preceded by a desperate attempt to fit whatever possessions she can into her case, aware that the effective dissolution of her marriage renders her financially helpless. Cultural critiques of this kind are in keeping with the critiques found in prophetic books such as Hosea, although they are far from straightforward. Not only were sensation writers constrained by the conservative aesthetics demanded by their readers; they found themselves reading a Bible that was sometimes deeply ambiguous about its attitude to unfaithful women. Hosea may conceive of the union of prophet and prostitute, but Gomer (his adulterous wife) is not given her own voice in the biblical text. The refusal to allow Gomer to speak in defence of her infidelity results in a strikingly violent punishment from God in chapter 2, raising questions about the possibility of real justice at the hands of a patriarchal writer. Hosea is constrained by his culture at the very moment in which he tries to think outside it and imagine the union of a prostitute and a prophet. A similar dilemma faces sensation writers in their response to the social plight women find themselves in, as much of the scholarship on sensation fiction has shown. Lyn Pykett explains:

> Sensation novels reproduce and negotiate broader cultural anxieties about the nature and status of respectable femininity and the domestic ideal at a time when women and other reformers were clamouring for a widening of women's legal rights and educational and employment opportunities. (Pykett, 1994, p. 10)

References to fallen women in sensation fiction are marked by a willingness to entertain the idea of union with the sacred. In this respect, the writers of these stories may be seen as more faithful readers of Scripture than many respectable nineteenth-century religious commentators, who found such ideas unimaginable. It is significant, for instance, that a number of novelists use the name "Magdalen" for their fallen female characters, recalling the figure of Mary Magdalene in the Gospels. According to tradition (the Gospels are unclear on this point), Mary Magdalene was a prostitute before she became a follower of Jesus. The possibility of redemption for fallen women is seized upon in many sensation novels and made an integral part of the narrative. It is a conceit that can also be found in some of the forerunners to the sensation novel, as the character of Nancy in Dickens's *Oliver Twist* (1837–8) illustrates. In a similar vein are the "numerous" (Zemka, 1977, p. 136) references to prostitutes in Dickens's *Dombey and Son* (1847–8), which, as Sue Zemka goes on to observe, culminate in Harriet Carker's interest in Alice Marwood leading back to the Bible rather than away from it. Like the sensation novels that followed, these accounts of prostitution in Dickens are able to conceive of falleness in conjunction with the sacred; however, the union is far from unproblematic. In many respects, the limitations to the sacred vision of sensation fiction are in keeping with the conservative undertone of any mainstream genre. Like the biblical stories they inherit, sensation novels exist in a multifaceted relation to their surrounding culture that is not easily disentangled or shaken off. My purpose here is not to insist that sensation novels be read as subversive continuations of a prophetic biblical tradition but to draw attention to the sacred dimension of the sensation novel and use it to highlight the complexity of determining what a faithful reading of the Bible, with its multiplicity of voices and counter voices, might look like.

Drawing on the work of Tina Pippin, Mary Carpenter argues in her book on women and the Bible in the nineteenth century that the apocalyptic vision found in the book of Revelation and repeated in Victorian novels such as *Jane Eyre* is permeated with a gender violence that is frequently sublimated and reinscribed. Reflecting on Jane's self-positioning as an apocalyptic seer at the end of the novel, Carpenter (2003, p. 138) suggests that her "last words may also be read as enthusiastic agreement with the 'continuous historical' interpretation of Apocalypse, and her narrative as yet another commodification of the consumption of the Whore of Babylon." The novel's difficulty in reimagining the violence of the biblical text helps to explain why it is that the sympathetic treatment of fallen women in sensation fiction is frequently accompanied by violent and excessive punishment. As the majority of scholars writing on sensation fiction have noted, the heroines of the sensation novel endure immense and disproportionate suffering. Isabel's betrayal of her husband in *East Lynne* (1860–1), for example, results in facial disfigurement and death, despite her repentance, while Miss Gwilt's sorrowful discovery that she has almost killed the wrong man at the end of *Armadale* (1864–6) culminates in her own poisoning and death rather than a new beginning. Similarly, in Dickens's *Bleak House* (1852–3), the softening of Lady Dedlock's hardness at the moment in which her past is revealed is not enough to save her from a lonely and ignoble death. In each case, the texts use death to avoid having to reimagine a resurrected state for women after their fall. What is especially noticeable is the tendency of these texts to insist that, contrary to the Protestant idea of justification by faith alone, female repentance is insufficient without additional physical confirmation that justice has been served. The use of a disfigured or lifeless body to register this physical confirmation points to a lack of agency for women in sensation fiction, one that is rooted in biblical texts such as Hosea, where the female body is merely a means to a different narrative end. Pamela Gilbert (1997, p. 4) reads the bodily emphasis in sensation fiction as symptomatic of a broader concern "with violation of the domestic body, with class and gender transgression, and most importantly, with the violation of the privileged space of the reader/voyeur, with the text's reaching out to touch the reader's body, acting directly 'on the nerves'." Gilbert's astute reading helpfully draws out the signification of the female body and connects it to the genre's preoccupation with popular fiction, consumption, and disease; however, it is a reading that should be read alongside (rather than against) the theological significance of gendered approaches to punishment in sensation fiction.

The gendered dimension to the physical suffering of several characters in the sensation novel becomes clearer when comparison is made to the experiences of Pip in Dickens's *Great Expectations* (1860–1). Pip's faithlessness is evident from the start of the novel – his guilt at forsaking his roots in the interests of great expectations haunts almost all of his childhood recollections – yet it is not punished in the same way as the mistakes of his female equivalents. In thinking further about the gendered dimension of punishment, it is worth considering the way in which Dickens's novel turns to another biblical narrative to structure its meditation on human faithlessness. As John Reed argues in *Victorian Conventions*, Pip's reckless waste of his inheritance is evidence of the novel's deliberate allusion to the parable of the Prodigal Son in Luke 15. The parable was frequently linked to Hosea by nineteenth-century preachers and commentators: while some commentators simply linked the two biblical stories to make a broader point about the faithfulness of God in the face of our faithlessness, others drew attention to differences between these stories. Having discussed the parallels between Luke and Hosea, Alfred Clayton Thiselton wrote in 1874:

> In the *latter* [Luke 15] we see the prodigal son leaving his father; but in the former [Hosea] we are shown the faithless wife leaving an all-loving, always loving husband. Both show us the exceeding sinfulness of sin and the exceeding riches of God's grace.... Both tell of full restoration to favour, of perfect reconciliation and peace between the base sinner and the holy and just God.... They both tell of all this; but as Hosea's picture has reference to those who have been brought up to the enjoyment of great Church privileges and advantages, it describes the greatest possible turpitude on the part of those who forsake the living, loving God, and show us apostasy under a figure even more marked, more striking, than that of the prodigal son. Israel, in her departure from God, is no common sinner; she is therefore presented as an ungrateful and base adulteress. (pp. 28–9)

Thiselton's distinction is a problematic one given the doctrine of grace and the emphasis in Jesus' parable on the idea that all sinners are to be welcomed home, regardless of their actions. Beyond this, however, it is difficult to ignore the troubling implication that female faithlessness, particularly in the context of marriage, is viewed as a greater sin, deserving more severe punishment. For all its openness to a marginal, female, biblical voice, the sensation novel follows the dominant testimony of the Bible in seeing marital infidelity by a woman as particularly reprehensible and emblematic of disobedience to God.

Pip's actions are not the only level on which *Great Expectations* reimagines the story of the Prodigal Son. The account in chapter 22 of Miss Havisham's past and her suffering at the hands of a profligate half brother also contains unmistakable allusions to Luke 15. Having explained how the younger half brother "turned out riotous, extravagant, undutiful," Herbert Pocket describes Miss Havisham as the proud, disapproving elder sibling. The allusion to Luke 15 casts Miss Havisham in an accusatory light, for while the father's love for the older son in Luke 15 is clear, the emphasis of the parable is on the need for the older brother to stop focusing on his own rights and start welcoming the disinherited brother. With this in mind, it is hard to avoid the conclusion that at the very moment that Miss Havisham's suffering is accounted for, she is also presented as bearing some of the responsibility. Her inability to adapt to a new situation in which an adopted son is to be valued results in a cycle of punishment. Instead of being the bride of Christ, Miss Havisham becomes a bride perpetually in waiting, having missed the opportunity of marriage to the bridegroom. Rather than directing our attention to a sympathetic reading of Miss Havisham's plight, the novel finds no space for her redemption and uses the figure of Estella to detail her legacy as a "revenge on all the male sex" (p. 167).

A similar idea of the forsaken woman who attempts to wreak revenge on the male sex dominates the narrative of Collins's *No Name* (1862–3). Unlike *Great Expectations*, however, the focus of *No Name* is on the identity of its forsaken woman rather than her punishment. Magdalen Vanstone's identity shifts throughout Collins's novel as a result of legal structures, natural circumstance, and her own use of artifice. In an attempt to enact revenge on the uncle and son who disinherit her and her sister, Magdalen assumes different identities throughout the story, to the extent that it is difficult to have any firm sense of who the "real" Magdalen is. Yet for all her multiple disguises and characteristics, Magdalen cannot escape the fact that she possesses a name, a history, and an inheritance, however fractured and arbitrary these prove to be. Her strained relation to the past provides much of the novel's interest; it also offers a helpful analogy of the relation between sensation writers and the biblical texts they inherit in the mid-nineteenth century. Like Magdalen, sensation writers begin with a biblical identity that no amount of invention can throw off completely. One solution to the complex relations that ensue is to argue that the freedom of sensation writers depends on embodying the spirit of the Bible rather than following it to the letter. This is a solution that Dickens and Collins frequently articulate in their fiction, and one that the lawyer, Pendril, vocalizes in *No Name*. In his explanation of how the law freezes Magdalen and Norah out of their rightful inheritance, Pendril acknowledges the rigidity and injustice inherent in the legal system. Recognizing that it is a system that condemns not only the two sisters but also their parents, who lived together without being married for many years, Pendril offers the following defence of the mother's youth:

> Let strict morality claim its right, and condemn her early fault. I have read my New Testament to little purpose indeed, if Christian mercy may not soften the hard sentence against her – if Christian charity may not find a plea for her memory in the love and fidelity, the suffering and the sacrifice of her whole life. (p. 103)

Pendril's juxtaposition of the New Testament spirit and the Old Testament letter ("sentence") follows a popular Protestant response to the problem of how one is to read the Old Testament law in the light of the New Testament. Yet the letter of the law is not dismissed so easily, as the rest of the novel acknowledges, and justice cannot exist outside a linguistic and material framework.

For all Magdalen's artifice and pretence, she inherits a name with a clear biblical echo, or, rather, at least two distinct biblical echoes. The Magdalene of the Gospels is a faithful follower of Jesus, but the sexually impure past ascribed to her by the Christian tradition links her to the figure of an unfaithful prostitute found in other biblical texts. Both identities inform Collins's novel and prove difficult to separate. In the end, the narrative's redemptive hope for its central figure is satisfied, but the narrative focus on Magdalen's falleness is clearly removed from the Gospels' description of Mary Magdalene as a faithful disciple of Christ. The impure taint of Mary Magdalene's fallen history is highlighted in the latter stages of *No Name* when the character of Old Mazey describes Magdalen Vanstone as a "young Jezebel" (p. 552); however, Mazey augments the slippage between the two biblical histories evoked by Magdalen's name when he goes on to offer a more sympathetic reading of Jezebel. Whereas the Bible views Jezebel negatively, treating her as a symbol of whoredom and infidelity, Old Mazey is sympathetic to the "Jezebel" (p. 552) he prevents from stealing a letter:

> But, try as hard as I may, I can't find it in my heart, you young jade, to be witness against you. I liked the make of you (specially about the waist) when you first came into the house, and I can't help liking the make of you still – though you *have* committed burglary, and though you *are* as crooked as Sin. (p. 556)

Mazey's mixed response to Magdalen acknowledges the different ways in which she is named by the Bible. The ambiguity of naming is a theme that recurs throughout *No Name*. It is most apparent when Captain Wragge and Magdalen write to one another about the identities they will assume to trick Noel Vanstone and Mrs Lecount. Magdalen's initially dismissive attitude to the name that she takes on is accompanied by a recognition that names matter. She writes: "use any assumed name you please, as long as it is a name that can be trusted to defeat the most suspicious inquiries" (p. 261). Names matter, but they also have a capacity for new identities and fresh readings, as Captain Wragge illustrates in the language he uses to explain the name that he has chosen: "The Skin which will exactly fit us, originally clothed the bodies of a family named Bygrave" (p. 263).

In the same way that Magdalen Vanstone is shaped but not fixed by the names she inherits, the Bible constrains and frees the sensation novel to tell new stories that depart from and reinterpret the sacred text. The uncomfortable nature of the resulting relationship is evident in the conflict between religious critics and sensation writers in the 1860s. Yet it would be quite wrong to conclude from these arguments that the Bible and the sensation novel were diametrically opposed. Sensation fiction is full of allusions to the biblical texts, and the emphasis on theological considerations of infidelity gives rise to complex theoretical questions as to what it means to read the Bible faithfully. Given the multivocality and open-ended nature of the biblical story, faithfulness and infidelity collide and mingle at every turn, and it is hardly a surprise that sensation fiction challenged religious sensibilities in its reading and rewriting of the Bible. In conclusion, it is helpful to recall the way in which one of the arguments arising from the sensation furore of the 1860s epitomized the difficulty of determining what faithfulness to Scripture meant. In 1860 a new periodical, *Good Words*, was launched with a view to reaching the religious and secular market. The journal included a range of material from different sources, including overt discussions of the Bible, travel writing, and sensational stories from writers such as Anthony Trollope and Margaret Oliphant.

Disquiet in some quarters regarding the new boundaries being drawn by the periodical led one religious publication, *The Record*, to offer the following complaint in 1863:

> there is a "mingle-mange" ... of persons, as well as of things, in *Good Words*, against which we indignantly protest. There is a spurious liberalism prevalent at the present day, which rejoices in seeing persons of the most opposite and antagonistic opinions brought to work, speak, or write together. (p. 5)

In light of some of the ideas explored in this chapter, it may be that the truth of this charge is precisely why Macleod's periodical and, more generally, sensation fiction were able to depart from the Bible while remaining faithful to it.

References

Anon (1873) "Apologists for Sin and Crime," *The Family Herald* 31 (September), 349–50.

Anon (1866) "Character: How It Is Formed and What It Is Worth," *Evangelical Magazine* 8, 374–9.

Anon (1866) "Decay of Spiritual Strength," *The Revival: An Advocate of Evangelical Truth* 14, 127–9.

Braddon, Mary (1998) *The Doctors Wife*, ed. Lyn Pykett. Oxford World's Classics, Oxford.

Braddon, Mary (1998) *Lady Audley's Secret*, ed. David Skilton. Oxford World's Classics, Oxford.

Brantlinger, Patrick (1998) *The Reading Lesson: The Threat of Mass Literacy in the Nineteenth Century*. Indiana University Press, Bloomington.

Brantlinger, Patrick (1982) "What Is 'Sensational' about the Sensation Novel?" *Nineteenth-Century Fiction* 37:1, 1–28.

Carpenter, Mary (2003) *Imperial Bibles, Domestic Bodies: Women, Sexuality, and Religion in the Victorian Market*. Ohio University Press, Athens.

Collins, Wilkie (1986) *The Moonstone*, ed. J. I. M. Steward. Penguin Classics, Harmondsworth.

Collins, Wilkie (1994) *No Name*, ed. Mark Ford. Middlesex Penguin Classics, Harmondsworth.

Collins, Wilkie (1995) *Armadale*, ed. John Sutherland. Penguin Classics, Harmondsworth.

Collins, Wilkie (1998) *The Woman in White*, ed. John Sutherland. Oxford World's Classics, Oxford.

Dickens, Charles (1994) *Great Expectations*. The Oxford Illustrated Dickens, Oxford.

Gilbert, Pamela (1997) *Disease, Desire, and the Body in Victorian Women's Popular Novels*. Cambridge University Press, Cambridge.

Griffin, Susan M. (2004) "The Yellow Mask, The Black Robe, and the Woman in White: Wilkie Collins, Anti-Catholic Discourse, and the Sensation Novel," *Narrative* 12:1, 55–73.

Jebb, Henry (1859) *Out of the Depths: The Story of a Women's Life*. Macmillan, Cambridge.

Larsen, Janet L. (1985) *Dickens and the Broken Scripture*. University of Georgia Press, Athens.

Mansel, Henry (1863) "Sensation Novels," *Quarterly Review* 113, 481–514.

Maunder, Andrew, gen. ed. (2004) *Varieties of Women's Sensation Fiction*, 6 volumes. Pickering and Chatto, London.

Mitchell, Sally (1981) *The Fallen Angel: Chastity, Class and Women's Reading, 1835–1880*. Bowling Green University Popular Press.

Pykett, Lyn (1994) *The Sensation Novel*. Northcote House, Plymouth.

Record Offices (1863) *Good Words: The Theology of Its Editor and of Some of Its Contributors*, 2nd edn. London.

Reed, John R. (1975) *Victorian Conventions*. Ohio University Press, Athens.

Sherwood, Yvonne (1996) *The Prophet and the Prostitute: Hosea's Marriage in Literary-Theological Perspective*. Sheffield Academic Press, Sheffield.

Taylor, Jenny Bourne (1988) *In the Secret Theatre of Home: Wilkie Collins, Sensation Narrative, and Nineteenth-Century Psychology*. Routledge, London.

Thiselton, Alfrey Clayton (1874) *Church and Home Lessons from the Book of the Prophet Hosea*. James Nisbet and Co., London.

Wood, Mrs Henry (2000) *East Lynne*, ed. Andrew Maunder. Broadview, Ontario.

Wynne, Deborah (2001) *The Sensation Novel and the Victorian Family Magazine*. Palgrave, Basingstoke.

Zemka, Sue (1997) *Victorian Testaments: The Bible, Christology, and Literary Authority in Nineteenth-Century British Culture*. Stanford University Press, Stanford, CA.

CHAPTER 42
Decadence

Andrew Tate

"Of late I have been studying the four prose-poems about Christ with some diligence," wrote Oscar Wilde in his famous prison epistle, posthumously published in 1905 as *De Profundis* (1999, p. 119). That this eccentric (and sometimes vicious) open letter to his former lover, Lord Alfred Douglas, abounds with the kind of biblical allusion that typifies so much nineteenth-century writing, both sacred and profane, is not surprising. However, Wilde's attitude of reverence toward the Gospels, read in a "Greek Testament" that he happily acquired at Christmas during his incarceration, might have astonished contemporary readers who associated the author with lurid stories of vice, dissolute self-indulgence, and corruption. Yet the sole scandal that Wilde offers is the revelation that reading Scripture has become his daily practice and chief source of pleasure. "[E]very morning, after I have cleaned my cell and polished my tins, I read a little of the Gospels, a dozen verses taken by chance anywhere. It is a delightful way of opening the day" (Wilde, 1999, p. 119). This vignette of a quotidian ritual is both playfully pious and highly aesthetic: the fact that New Testament narratives are referred to as "prose-poems about Christ" emphasizes their status as literary texts rather than divinely dictated and inerrant pieces of moral teaching. Are we to assume, then, that Wilde's interest in Scripture is primarily artistic, his allusions to the four evangelists mere decoration? In fact, the emphasis on the Gospels in *De Profundis* is the culmination of a fascination with biblical writing that spans Wilde's creative life. From his earliest published poems, short fiction and essays, via the sole, scandalous novel *The Picture of Dorian Gray* (1890–1), to his later drama including *Salome* (1893), Wilde's work is continually drawn into a mischievous, erudite, and provocative dialogue with the Jewish and Christian holy books. Wilde, in common with the vast body of interpreters before and since, is caught up in what Valentine Cunningham names "the central Western myth of the free individual self and the Open Book: the long Christian tradition of saving-encounters with the biblical text ... the Judaeo-Christian sacred text, the Big Book of God, the Bible" (Cunningham, 2002, p. 6).

This chapter explores the significance of Wilde's developing relationship with the Bible in the context of so called Decadent writing and the dawn of the modernist moment in literature. It also makes reference to the work, and in particular to the biblical predilections, of a number of Wilde's peers, forerunners, and intellectual mentors, including Walter Pater, John Ruskin, Algernon Charles Swinburne, Dante Gabriel Rossetti, and H. G. Wells. All contemporary readings of Oscar Wilde's dalliance with biblical motifs owe a debt to Ellis Hanson's groundbreaking study, *Decadence and Catholicism* (1997). A number of critics have offered valuable explorations of Wilde's complex religious sensibility (see, for example, Sloan, 2003; Schad, 2004). My chapter, however, focuses on the shape, style, and impact of scriptural allusions in Wilde's work rather than on his path to Rome or his particular religious beliefs. It addresses a variety of questions about the relationship between 1890s culture and the Bible. Does "the decadence," a phenomenon with which Wilde was intimately associated, preclude reading the Scriptures for spiritual edification rather than simply as a colorful and rich entertainment? What place can the fierce call for authenticity of the Jewish and Christian texts have among the luxuriant artifice of the *fin de siècle*? Is Wilde's recurrent interest in the teaching of Christ inconsistent with his aestheticism?

Decadent Scriptures: (Ir)religious Faith at the *Fin de Siècle*

During an era that witnessed increasing skepticism toward the truth-claims and historicity of the Bible, many nineteenth-century artists grew bolder in their readiness to exploit the once sacred narratives primarily as a source of aesthetic inspiration. For example, in his memoir of the Pre-Raphaelite Brotherhood, William Holman Hunt rebukes his fellow painter, Dante Gabriel Rossetti, for approaching "the Gospel history simply as a storehouse of interesting situations and beautiful personages for the artist's pencil, just as the Arthurian legends afterwards were to him, and in due course to his younger proselytes at Oxford" (Holman Hunt, 1905, p. 172). Rossetti's aestheticism certainly foreshadows the celebration of form, sensuality, and delight in beauty for its own sake that gained cultural weight in the 1880s and 1890s. Decadence is associated with a cultural mood of excess, indulgence, and artifice; as its etymology suggests, it also embodies the notion of society in a state of decay or slow ruin. David Weir argues, however, that "decadence," like so many other cultural designations, is fundamentally unstable and best "functions as a general or all-purpose antonym." For example, Decadent aesthetics are often seen as a repudiation of the bourgeois values dominant in the late nineteenth century (Weir, 1995, p. 10).

Decadent writing might appear to be hostile to biblically inflected thought, particularly since those who were associated with the aesthetic movement typically disliked the colorless Puritanism of Victorian bourgeois society. Yet Hanson observes that these writers, for all their attraction to Classical civilization, did not abandon the Bible as a rich literary source. "[T]he very style of the Bible can, in some of its books, be described as decadent," he argues, "especially the Canticles and Apocalypse, with their erotic spectacles, their strange profusion of symbols, their demonization of nature, and their mesmerizing repetitions" (Hanson, 1997, p. 7). Wilde's *Salome*, originally written in French and later translated by Douglas, exemplifies the exotic approach to the Scriptures in its heightened rewriting of the beheading of John the Baptist (Matthew 14:12; Mark 6:14–29). Aubrey Beardsley's distinctive and strange illustrations for *Salome* recuperate the erotic elements of the biblical narrative in a way that might have shocked Protestant England.

Writers who emerged in the 1890s had grown up in the wake of debates about the origin, purpose, and reliability of the Scriptures. The impact of *Essays and Reviews* (1860), whose contributors synthesized the radical hermeneutics of the German Higher Criticism and challenged traditional ways of understanding the inspiration of the Bible, was particularly evident. In "The Interpretation of Scripture," the collection's most influential essay, Benjamin Jowett argued that the Bible should be read in the same spirit as any other work of literature. This simple idea is ventriloquized in Wilde's essay "The Soul of Man Under Socialism" (1891), indicating just how far these ideas had been absorbed into popular culture:

> In Art, the public accept what has been, because they cannot alter it, not because they appreciate it. They swallow their classics whole, and never taste them. They endure them as inevitable. ... The uncritical admiration of the Bible and Shakespeare in England is an example of what I mean. (Wilde, 1999, p. 19)

Wilde subtly relocates the interpretation of Scripture from the ecclesiastical realm to the domain of public taste. However, one of the dominant influences on 1890s aestheticism – and on Wilde in particular – was the intensely biblicist, prophetic voice of John Ruskin (1819–1900), the polymathic critic of art, politics, and society. Ruskin's vast *oeuvre* simultaneously displays a sensuous appreciation of beauty and an energetically moral appreciation of art and nature. The Christian aesthetic that he developed from the first volume of *Modern Painters* (1843) was rooted in his lifelong engagement with the Bible: his work is replete with allusions not just to the Gospels but to the Jewish books of history, prophecy, law, and poetry that constitute, in Christian terms, the "Old Testament." Ruskin was Slade Professor of Fine Art at Oxford during Wilde's undergraduate years. Indeed, Wilde not only attended Ruskin's biblically inflected lectures but also joined his student crew in the famously quixotic road-building project (Ellmann, 1988, pp. 45–50). Another Oxford academic, Walter Pater (1839–94), once a follower of Ruskinian ideas, provided a rich counterpoint to the Slade Professor. Pater's branch of aestheticism favored an openly Hellenic approach to the world. His elegant essays, including *Studies in the History of the Renaissance* (1873), advocated an ecstatic, near Pagan celebration of the visible.

These competing influences – Hebrew and Hellene, to use the now overfamiliar and arguably too simplistic categories – are vital in the development of late nineteenth-century aesthetic debate (DeLaura, 1969). However, the body of writers, painters, and full-time aesthetes connected with the 1890s cult of decadent art – including such figures as Aubrey Beardsley, Arthur Symons, Lionel Johnson, and Ernest Dowson – were also Anglophone inheritors of a tradition given shape by a preceding generation of French writers. These beauty seekers, especially Theophile Gautier (1811–72), who originated the term "*l'art pour l'art*," and the poet Charles Baudelaire (1821–67), embodied an elegantly defiant rejection of conventional morality and usefulness as integral to aesthetics. Gautier embraced, in William Gaunt's terms, a "world of sensation":

> Forms, colours, feelings were meant to provide the refined pleasure and enjoyment of the man for whom it existed and he must turn them into art without restraint, scruple or concern as to whether this satisfied the policeman, pleased the minister of religion or elevated the shopkeeper. (Gaunt, 1975, p. 15)

This emphasis on sensuality is not necessarily inimical either to a religious disposition or to a spiritual engagement with the Bible but it certainly provided a vibrant contrast with the strict public moralizing of the evangelical worldview. The virtues of self-denial and unworldly conduct ostensibly preached throughout the canonical Jewish and Christian Scriptures might seem alien to the brashly transgressive qualities of much Decadent literature. Indeed, J. K. Huysmans's (1848–1907) infamous novel *À Rebours* (1884) – translated as *Against the Grain* or, more forcefully, *Against Nature* – seemed to provide a template for an inversion of Judeo-Christian moral absolutes. Paul Valéry even elevated the book to the status of his personal "Bible" (Pearce, 2000, p. 5). The novel's focus on dissipation and the pursuit of pleasure beyond normative concepts of sin directly foreshadow the behavior of Wilde's own chief-of-sinners, Dorian Gray. Huysmans's dedicated hedonist, as Gaunt argues, shuns "all natural and external experience ... because what was not nature was art and art was the only worthy condition of existence" (Gaunt, 1975, p. 113).

In *Dorian Gray*, the fallen hero encounters and is morally corrupted by a nameless book, frequently assumed to be *À Rebours*. Huysmans's fictional experiments with narratives of gratuitous sin and rebellion against God were not just a prelude to Wilde's preoccupation with immorality in *Dorian Gray*: in the mid-1890s Huysmans, whose work was marked by every kind of moral outrage, returned to a committed Christian practice as a member of the Roman Catholic communion. This journey foreshadowed Wilde's late – indeed, death-bed – conversion and anticipates the *rapprochement* with Catholicism of many of Wilde's peers, including Johnson, Dowson, Beardsley, Robert Ross, and Douglas (Wheeler, 2006, p. 273). Wilde's relationship with orthodox religious practice was as complex as any late Victorian or early modernist pilgrimage and, in spite of a lifelong fascination with Catholic ritual and piety, his final admission into the Church was by no means inevitable.

"When I think about Religion at all," notes Wilde in *De Profundis*, "I feel as if I would like to found an order for those who cannot believe: the Confraternity of the Fatherless one might call it ... agnosticism should have its ritual no less than faith" (Wilde, 1999, p. 98). What kind of liturgy would Wilde's imaginary sect for the dispossessed and faithless use in their hesitant, skeptical devotions? Would the preacher declaim portions of Scripture, only to mock its language and faith? Perhaps parables would be recast, rewritten, and aestheticized? Wilde's writing, so dependent on generative paradox, is predictably unpredictable in terms of its relationship with the Scriptures. *De Profundis* bears a distinctively (if also discreetly) biblical title, though one chosen by Robert Ross rather than by Wilde himself. Although the letter's most explicit scriptural debt is to the Gospels, the title signifies the text's relationship with the Jewish Scriptures. As Ian Small (2005, p. 288, cited in Wilde 2005) notes, the title is appropriated from Psalm 129 in the Vulgate, translated in Psalm 130 of the Authorized Version as "Out of the depths."

Out of the depths have I cried unto thee, O Lord.

Lord, hear my voice: let thine ears be attentive to the voice of my supplications.

If thou, Lord, shouldest mark iniquities, O Lord, who shall stand? (Psalm 130:1–3)

Ross's title is an act of interpretation that suggests continuity between Wilde's present suffering and the spiritual desolation of the Psalmist. The theologian Walter Brueggemann reads the prayer with which the Psalm begins as one of "inordinate boldness" as in a single "sweeping rhetorical move it proposes to make a link between the ruler of reality enthroned and the most extreme, remote circumstance of human need." Far from addressing God from a position of respectability, the psalm constitutes "the miserable cry of a nobody from nowhere" (Brueggemann, 1994, p. 104). Wilde's epistle similarly identifies with the dispossessed and spiritually destitute and echoes the Psalmist's hope that redemption and forgiveness are possible. *De Profundis* is caught between a rather prosaic self-aggrandizing, self-righteous spite and a psalm-like tone that describes a spiritual awakening and gradual personal transformation. In this sense, it reads like a conversion narrative that both repudiates the former self and records the pains of new birth. If the figure of Christ is a source of inspiration and devotion for Wilde, the apostle Paul is another paradigm for his experience. Indeed, the language that he uses to describe his frustrated hope that Douglas might have changed is explicitly derived from the story of the aftermath of Saul's conversion on the road to Damascus when the scales fell from his eyes in Acts 9:18: "I forced myself to believe that at last the scales had fallen from your long-blinded eyes" (Wilde, 1999, p. 77). Paul might also have appealed to Wilde as a fellow prisoner and as an apostle who was persecuted for his faith.

David Lyle Jeffrey suggests that the "vital continuance of biblical influence" on English literature at the end of the nineteenth century emerges "less vividly in the popularity of evidently Christian works ... than in the rich mastery of biblical idiom, motif, and allusion by writers notably antagonistic to orthodox religion" (Metzger and Coogan, 1993, p. 444). This might be particularly true of *The Picture of Dorian Gray*. "Be always searching for new sensations," Lord Henry Wotton, aristocratic arch tempter, instructs the novel's neophyte, eponymous anti-hero (Wilde, 2000a, p. 25). If Dorian is an 1890s iteration of Faustus or an androgynous composite of Adam and Eve, Lord Henry rejuvenates the scheming serpent in Eden (Genesis 3:1–20). He incarnates the spirit of Decadence in his espousal of a "new Hedonism" (Wilde, 2000, p. 25). As David Weir rightly notes, the "myth of the Garden of Eden, of innocence giving way to an evil tempter" is vividly signified in the first pages of *Dorian Gray*, and so too "is the Faust legend, when Dorian expresses the desire to exchange his soul for eternal youth" (Weir, 1995, pp. 110–1). In the novel's opening chapter, Basil Hallward's studio – a place "filled with the rich odour of roses" and the "heavy scent of the lilac, or the more delicate perfume of the pink-flowering thorn" – recreates the world before the fall, an echo of the earthly paradise described in Genesis 1–3. For John Sutherland (1998, pp. 196–201), the temporal impossibility of these blooms and scents coexisting in the modern space of the metropolis is an early clue to the novel's uncanny nature. In this prelapsarian space, Dorian is encountered first as Hallward's creation in a painted image. *Dorian Gray* may have scandalized many readers, but the debauched progress of its titular protagonist from innocence to experience echoes a variety of biblical narratives: for example, it has the scrupulous intensity of one of Christ's parables and, in the final revelation of Dorian's deteriorated body, it conforms to the Pauline concept that the "secrets of the heart" will be revealed within an economy of divine judgment (Ecclesiastes 12:14; 1 Corinthians 14:25).

The literature of Decadence, particularly in the case of Huysmans, tends to rejoice in the spectacle of a damned world, replete with gorgeous food, clothes, and people, but cursed by its awareness that all of this splendor is finite. The taint of mortality is everywhere in 1890s texts: the dark pleasures pursued by Dorian Gray, for example, are associated with both his murderous instincts and his paradoxical terror of death. Martin Halliwell (2001, p. 30) notes that a "cultural confusion" between "degeneration" and "decadence" was commonplace in the 1890s. Despite the still persistent tendency to conflate the terms, their emphases are split along corporeal and cultural lines: as Halliwell (2001, p. 30) states, at the *fin de siècle* degeneration generally signified "mental and bodily decline," while Decadence became synonymous with "the cultural rot of over-civilization." *Dorian Gray* is an obliquely apocalyptic text but it echoes Ruskin's belief that all wealthy cultures precipitate their own decline. In a sermonic 1858 lecture, ostensibly on art, Ruskin connected "national decline" with "luxury ... love of pleasure, fineness in Art, ingenuity in enjoyment" (Ruskin, 1905, p. 189). The association of self-indulgence with the judgment of God is derived, in Ruskin's case, from biblical warnings regarding the transience of material things and the association between opulence and luxury: "Your wealth has rotted and moths have eaten your clothes. ... The cries of the harvesters have reached the ears of the Lord Almighty" (James 5:2–4).

H. G. Wells's "scientific romance," *The Time Machine* (1895), offers a secular rewriting of these apocalyptic ideas. It also explores the idea of punishment for sin as the poor enact a gruesome revenge upon the decadent rich. When the anonymous time traveler describes the torpid, ludic, and inarticulate (apparent) future of the human race, he might be describing Decadent culture of his own historical moment: "This has ever been the fate of energy in security; it takes to art and to eroticism, and then to languor and decay" (Wells, 1953, pp. 39–40). As Weir (1995, p. 17) notes, late nineteenth-century culture is marked by a sense of mortality and transience, it sees itself "as a time when all was over, or almost over: not the end, but the ending." For explicitly religious writers, this imagined ending might have figured apocalypse as the time of promised revelation, when secrets would be uncovered and mysteries unveiled. For more skeptical, scientifically minded thinkers, the promises of Christian eschatology had evaporated. Yet Wells's fable, in tension with its outward interest in questions of technology and progress, draws on a biblical rhetoric of beginning and endings, as the earth is viewed as a finite creation facing a coming day of reckoning. Despite his secular, progressive worldview, Wells relies on the ancient language of Jewish and Christian Scriptures to describe his visionary future. In the year AD 802,701, the suburbs of London have become, in the traveler's words, "a long-neglected and yet weedless garden": the future, in other words, resembles nothing so much as a return to Eden (Wells, 1953, p. 31). The Eloi, the name of the childlike dwellers of this apparently Edenic future, is derived from Christ's words on the cross: "*Eloi, Eloi, lama sabachthani?*" ("My God, my

God, why have you forsaken me?" Mark 15:33–4). Their vicious predators, the Morlocks, are named for an Old Testament cult of worship that involved the sacrifice of children (see, for example, Leviticus 20:2–5). Wells's visionary future is apparently forsaken by God but haunted by the language of the Bible.

In *Dorian Gray* and *The Time Machine*, Wilde and Wells offer secularized re-visions of a world subject to judgment – the ravages of time, the necessary brevity of life itself – without the hope of divine saving grace. Yet the taint of death that marks Wilde's only novel is transformed in other texts by his fascination with the figure of Christ. "The supposed facts on which Christianity rests, utterly incapable as they have become of any ordinary test," wrote Walter Pater in a letter to Mary Ward, "seem to me matters of very much the same sort of assent we give to any assumption, in the strict and ultimate sense, moral. The question whether those facts were real will, I think, always continue to be what I should call one of the *natural* questions of the human mind" (Pater, 1970, pp. 64–5). Pater, the most eloquent advocate of aestheticism, was privately persuaded that the mystery of Christianity, its combination of history and faith, transcendence and materialism, ensured its continuing significance within cultural life despite the pressures of scientific enquiry. Wilde, one of Pater's intellectual inheritors, conscious or otherwise of his teacher's conviction, explored the mysteries of Christ throughout his work.

Out of Darkness: Wilde's Gospels

What G. Wilson Knight has described as the "strong Christ-like affinities" of Wilde's project disturb straightforward readings of his aestheticism as fundamentally irreligious or Pagan (1962, p. 293). Wilde's early writing displays an ambivalent concern with Scripture, religious experience, and the nature of faith. Three sonnets, in particular, written in 1877, when Wilde was an undergraduate at Oxford, are dominated by images of Christ. Indeed, the son of God is the addressee of his "Sonnet on the Massacre of the Christians in Bulgaria," a poem open in its debt to Milton's famous sonnet "On the Late Massacre in Piedmont" (1655). The opening lines are audacious in their reference to the bodily resurrection and the empty tomb. "Christ, does thou live indeed? or are thy bones / Still straitened in their rock-hewn sepulchre?" (lines 1–2). This is neither an unequivocal declaration of faith nor a rationalist rejection of Christ's miraculous resurrection. "Easter Day" (published in 1879) contrasts the majesty of the modern Pope ("Three crowns of gold rose high upon his head: / In splendour and in light the Pope passed home," lines 7–8) with the destitute, nomadic Christ of the gospels:

> My heart stole back across wide wastes of years
> To One who wandered by a lonely sea,
> And sought in vain for any place of rest:
> Foxes have holes, and every bird its nest,
> I, only I, must wander wearily,
> And bruise my feet, and drink wine salt with tears. (Lines 9–14)

This allusion to Luke 9:58 undercuts the devotional language of the octet; the turn to the Gospel's emphasis on the material poverty of Christ makes the sonnet's veneration something richer and darker. "E Tenebris" (1881) utters a cry for redemption from an overwhelming sea of spiritual despair. Both the Latin title – translated as "out of darkness" – and the sonnet's idiom pastiche the desolation of many of the psalms combined with elements of Christian liturgy: "Come down, O Christ, and help me! reach thy hand" (line 1). The poem is intensely devotional but it also encodes the experience of unbelief in specifically biblical terms: the doubt of the speaker is that of Simon Peter: "For I am drowning in a stormier sea / Than Simon on thy lake of Galilee" (lines 2–3). In addition to this reference to Christ's saving the doubting Peter as he walked on the water (Matthew 14:29–32), Fong and Beckson (2000, p. 241) identify allusions to 1 Kings 18:27 (the mocking reference to the prophets of Baal) and, finally, to Revelation 1:15. The visionary language of the final lines recuperates the eschatological hope of ultimate salvation and emphasizes both the divine glory and the human frailty of Christ:

> Nay, peace, I shall behold before the night,
> The feet of brass, the robe more white than flame,
> The wounded hands, the weary human face. (Lines 12–14)

Wilde's short stories of the 1880s combine the fantastical and grotesque elements of European fairy-tales with the demanding ethics of Christ's parables. "The Happy Prince," for example, is structured around an allegory of Christ-like self-sacrifice and compassion. Indeed, its conclusion, in which God welcomes the broken heart of the titular Prince and the dead swallow to his kingdom, is explicitly eschatological, if also rather sentimental: "for in my garden of Paradise this little bird shall sing for evermore, and in my city of gold the Happy Prince shall praise me" (Wilde, 2003, p. 11). "The Selfish Giant," included in the same collection of tales, similarly fuses elements of popular fable, myth, and parable. It is structured around a distinctively New Testament pattern of sin (destructive self-interest), penitence (a gratuitous act of generosity), and redemption (final resurrection in an eternal paradise). The sentimentality of the story is both intensified and transformed by its explicitly Christological dimension. The child whom the giant lifts into the tree is given unambiguously Christ-like features in the tale's final encounter: his hands and feet bear "the prints of two nails" described by the child as "the wounds of Love" (ibid., p. 23). He welcomes the dead giant into his own garden "which is Paradise" as a reward for his act of kindness (ibid., 23). As John Sloan (2003, p. 166) argues, suffering in Wilde's fairy-tales becomes "a means of self-realization" that is "the dark other side of aesthetic pleasure and freedom."

A number of Wilde's subtle and ambiguous "Poems in Prose" written in the mid-1890s are explicitly scriptural in both register and subject matter. These inventive parables lack the redemptive aspect of the fairy-tales. The later, frequently God-haunted (and Bible-saturated), poetic tales are not straightforwardly devotional but neither are they belligerently skeptical. Their dominant mood, however, is unnerving and uncanny. The language (as Hanson, 1997, p. 236, has observed) is self-consciously patterned on the resonant cadences of the Authorized Version. The cultural authority of this familiar, mellifluous, and rhythmic style generates a creative tension with the ambivalence of the narrative. Although Wilde's pastiche of the King James Bible is vivid and linguistically opulent, a reading that simply emphasizes an addiction to the aesthetic qualities of its idiom is wholly inadequate. The strength of these compressed parabolic poems in prose is their faculty for rendering complex theological questions without offering simple, homiletic solutions. Is humanity to be blamed for its habitual penchant for transgression? Is God culpable for creating a glorious world that men and women are then prohibited from enjoying? In "The Doer of Good" (1894), for example, an unnamed, solitary Christ visits "the city" by night and encounters a number of individuals he has healed or forgiven, only to discover that such miracles and grace are easily squandered by men and women in their ordinary fallen state. In their meticulous edition of the poems, Fong and Beckson identify allusions to all four Gospels in the prose-poem, as the mysterious figure is cast off, for example, by the leper he cured (Matthew 8:1–4; Mark 1:40–5; Luke 17:12–19), now enjoying a luxurious and pleasure-seeking existence (Wilde, 2000b, p. 304). "And when He came near he heard within the city the tread of the feet of joy, and the laughter of the mouth of gladness" (ibid., p. 174).

"The Soul of Man Under Socialism" (1891) privileges Christ as the definitive individualist: "And so he who would lead a Christ-like life is he who is perfectly and absolutely himself. He may be a great poet, or a great man of science. ... It does not matter what he is, so long as he realizes the perfection of the soul that is within him. All imitation in morals and in life is wrong" (Wilde, 1999, p. 12). Isobel Murray demonstrates Wilde's (rarely discussed) debt to Ralph Waldo Emerson (1803–82), the American Transcendentalist, former Unitarian Minister and, like Wilde, conscious heretic (Wilde, 1999, p. xi). Indeed, we might locate Wilde in the great tradition of literary heretics, a heterodox body of artists in which Valentine Cunningham (2006, pp. 1–18) includes such diverse writers as James Joyce, Emily Dickinson, John Milton, and Daniel Defoe.

Wilde's Jesus in "The Soul of Man" is the perfect individual, uninhibited by moral law or social custom, and the incarnation of human freedom. Yet the shape of his fiction is inconsistent with this belief in absolute ethical freedom: Dorian Gray's freedom, for example, mutates into destructive license for which he is eventually punished. Whatever its practical limitations, this reinterpretation of Christ as the ideal individualist competes with Swinburne's infamous vision in his "Hymn to Proserpine" (1866) of Jesus as an insipid usurper of a previous spiritual era. The poem is both an elegy for the lost gods of the Greco-Roman world and an angry rejection of Christianity. It articulates an unambiguous antipathy toward the ascension of Christ in the modern world: "Thou hast conquered, O pale Galilean; the world has grown gray from thy breath; / We have drunken of things Lethean, and fed on the fullness of death" (lines 35–6). Swinburne's flamboyant show of sympathy for pagan attitudes coupled with a marked sensuality make him a significant precursor of Decadent culture. "Hymn to Proserpine" has a typically decadent theme that emphasizes the transient nature of culture, including apparently transcendent, eternal religion: the speaker accepts that Christ has displaced the old gods but daringly claims too that "thy kingdom shall pass, Galilean, thy dead shall go down to thee dead" (line 74). In a later poem, "Before a Crucifix" (1871), Swinburne addresses an image of the crucified Christ with ferocity and ironic bile. Wilde's "The Soul of Man" offers a more generous mode of interpretation than that of his openly impious precursor; it rereads elements of the Gospels and focuses, in particular, on a narrative of sin and forgiveness:

> There was a woman who was taken in adultery. We are not told the history of her love, but that love must have been very great; for Jesus said that her sins were forgiven her, not because she repented, but because her love was so intense and wonderful. Later on, a short time before his death, as he sat at a feast, the woman came in and poured costly perfumes on his hair. His friends tried to interfere with her, and said that it was an extravagance. ... Jesus did not accept that view. ... The world worships the woman, even now, as a saint. (Wilde, 1999, pp. 11–12)

As Murray keenly observes, Wilde is guilty of conflating different female figures of the New Testament (Mary Magdalene in Luke 8:2 and the woman accused of adultery in John 8:3–11) (Wilde, 1999, p. 201). This rhetorical recreation of the Gospel is an imaginative act of rewriting designed to emphasize the liberating nature of Christ's forgiveness. Does Wilde's avowed antinomianism ("I am one of those who are made for exceptions, not for laws") render his writing more open to the radical possibility of grace (ibid., p. 98)? Or does such a transgressive approach to law suggest that the very concept of divine mercy is unnecessary? Hanson (1997, p. 237) rightly notes that in his late essays, Wilde "offers an interpretation of the Gospels in which Christ is valorized as an aesthete, a mouthpiece for Wilde's own theories about art, individualism, imagination, love, sorrow, and faith." De Profundis develops Wilde's vision of Christ as the supreme creative individual, whose "place is indeed with the poets. His whole conception of humanity sprang right out of the imagination and can only be realised by it" (Wilde, 1999, p. 110). "In Wilde's rereading of the New Testament," argues John Sloan (2003, p. 166), "Christ overcomes limited human perception by means of a supreme artistic personality that refuses the divisions and differences – self and the other, beauty and ugliness, the human and the divine – that narrow and imprison the minds of men." The prison epistle, for all Wilde's "antinomian" rhetoric, emphasizes the necessity of forgiveness: "Only one whose life is without stain of any kind can forgive sins. But now when I sit in humiliation and disgrace it is different. My forgiveness should mean a great deal to you now" (Wilde, 1999, p. 94).

The sober, melancholic, and spiritual tone of De Profundis, unpublished in his lifetime, evolves in The Ballad of Reading Gaol (1898). Wilde's autobiographical lament inspired by his experience of prison is not simply an indictment of the British legal system and the inhumanity of the death penalty; it also reads like a cry at the foot of the cross. The poem's narrative recounts the execution of a soldier, Charles Thomas Wooldridge, convicted of murdering his wife. Its theme of the spiritual wretchedness of incarceration is matched by a similarly intense hope that such misery is a necessary prelude to rebirth: "How else but through a broken heart / May Lord Christ enter in?" (lines 617–18).

And he of the swollen purple throat,
And the stark and staring eyes,
Waits for the holy hands that took
The Thief to Paradise;
And a broken and a contrite heart
The Lord will not despise. (Lines 619–25)

As Fong and Beckson note, Wilde alludes to Christ's words to the penitent thief (Luke 23:39–43) and to the emphasis on forgiveness in Psalm 51:17 (Wilde, 2000b, p. 315). The ballad is stirred by the Gospels' radical implication that Christ dwells with sinners and is most present among the dispossessed. In the penultimate stanza, Wilde antici-pates bodily resurrection ("till Christ call forth the dead," line 643) using language similar to that deployed in a number of biblical passages (see, for example, John 11:24 and Acts 24:15). The disparate convicts of Reading Gaol are linked to the figure of the suffering Christ in one striking image: on the eve of the execution, Wilde imagines the prayers of inmates for whom "bitter wine upon a sponge / Was the savour of Remorse" (lines 281–2). The taunting of Christ, dying on the cross, with wine vinegar, as described in Mark 15:36, becomes a motif for agonized and, by inference, contrite, criminals. The speaker looks in vain for a sign in the enclosed space of the prison "To tell the men who tramp the yard / That God's Son died for all" (lines 497–8).

Wilde's last great poetic statement celebrates the hope of resurrection and the pos-sibility of redemption. His fascination with Scripture and eventual conversion to Roman Catholicism foreshadows the theological turn of the modernist moment and its after-math: T. S. Eliot's bleak worldview found sanctuary in the most Catholic wing of the Anglican church, while many others including G. K. Chesterton, Evelyn Waugh, Sieg-fried Sassoon, Muriel Spark, and Graham Greene joined the Catholic communion (see Pearce, 2000). Mark Knight and Emma Mason (2006, p. 195) have observed that many critics refuse to take the *fin de siècle* turn to religion seriously, and in particular its affinities with Roman Catholicism, reading it instead as "a pose that exemplifies the Decadent fascination for the exotic and bizarre, and one that should not be mistaken for a sincerely held belief." Wilde, they note, is exceptionally ambiguous, but they rightly insist that the theological and biblical elements of his work, and of *De Profundis* in particular, ought not to be dismissed as purely "performative": "Just because the religious turn of the letter is to not be equated with a narrow, unambiguous statement of faith, it does not follow that the religion espoused has to be declared false and thus ignored" (Knight and Mason, 2006, p. 196). Decadence in Wilde's mode thrives on apparently absurd contradiction: its narratives combine a love of elegance and an enthusiasm for disintegration and ugliness; a delight in surfaces vies with a desire for profundity; the irreligious is frequently a prelude for saintly devotion. In this last sense, in particular, Wilde echoes the subversive quality of the Gospels of Christ that continu-ally invert expectations regarding true holiness and the Kingdom of Heaven.

Wilde's liberated approach to the gospels is distinctive from the Evangelical bibli-cism that characterizes the writing of Ruskin. It would, however, be too simple to argue that this fallen aesthete was only concerned with the sensuous, imaginative escape that a New Testament offered him from the reality of prison life. His turn to the Bible might be disturbing for early twenty-first century readers who fear that it will be used by conservative thinkers as evidence that liberated artists must eventually recant their freedom in favor of orthodoxy. Similarly, traditionalists should not be too quick to appropriate a writer who could celebrate Christ but maintained, in *De Profundis*, that "Religion does not help me. The faith that others give to what is unseen, I give to what one can touch, and look at" (Wilde, 1999, p. 98). Yet in the prison epistle and in much of his later work, Wilde the aesthete becomes Wilde the exegete as this most self-conscious of writers uses the horizon of scriptural language to reconfigure a world that appears to have lost its vivid pleasures.

References

Brueggemann, W. (1994) *The Message of the Psalms*. Augsburg, Minneapolis.

Cunningham, Valentine (2002) *Reading After Theory*. Blackwell, Oxford.

Cunningham, Valentine (2006) "Introduction: The Necessity of Heresy," in Andrew Dix and Jonathan Taylor, eds, *Figures of Heresy: Radical Theology in English and American Writing, 1800–2000*. Academic Press, Brighton, pp. 1–18.

DeLaura, David J. (1969) *Hebrew and Hellene in Victorian England: Newman, Arnold, and Pater*. University of Texas Press, Austin.

Ellmann, R., ed. (1969) *Oscar Wilde: A Collection of Critical Essays*. Prentice Hall, Englewood Cliffs, NJ.

Ellmann, R. (1988) *Oscar Wilde*. Penguin, London.

Gaunt, William (1975) *The Aesthetic Adventure*. Cardinal, London.

Halliwell, Martin (2001) *Modernism and Morality: Ethical Devices in European and American Fiction*. Palgrave, Basingstoke.

Hanson, Ellis (1997) *Decadence and Catholicism*. Harvard University Press, Cambridge, MA.

Holman Hunt, William (1905) *Pre-Raphaelitism and the Pre-Raphaelite Brotherhood*, 2 volumes. Macmillan, London.

Knight, M. and Mason, E. (2006) *Nineteenth-Century Religion and Literature*. Oxford University Press, Oxford.

Metzger, B. M. and Coogan, M. D., eds (1993) *The Oxford Companion to the Bible*. Oxford University Press, Oxford.

Pater, Walter (1970) *Letters of Walter Pater*, ed. Lawrence Evans. Clarendon Press, Oxford.

Pearce, Joseph (2000) *Literary Converts: Spiritual Inspiration in an Age of Unbelief*. Harper Collins, London.

Ruskin, John (1903–12) *The Works of John Ruskin*, library edn, ed. E. T. Cook and Alexander Wedderburn, 39 volumes. George Allen, London.

Schad, J. (2004) *Queer Fish: Christian Unreason from Darwin to Derrida*. Academic Press, Brighton.

Sloan, John (2003) *Authors in Context*. Oxford University Press, Oxford.

Sutherland, John (1998) *Is Heathcliff a Murderer? Puzzles in 19th-Century Fiction*. Oxford University Press, Oxford.

Weir, D. (1995) *Decadence and the Making of Modernism*. University of Massachusetts Press, Amherst.

Wells, H. G. (1953) *The Time Machine*. Pan, London.

Wheeler, M. (2006) *The Old Enemies: Catholic and Protestant in Nineteenth-Century English Culture.* Cambridge University Press, Cambridge.

Wilde, Oscar (1998) *Complete Shorter Fiction,* ed. I. Murray. Oxford University Press, Oxford.

Wilde, Oscar (1999) *The Soul of Man. De Profundis. The Ballad of Reading Gaol,* ed. Isobel Murray. Oxford University Press, Oxford.

Wilde, Oscar (2000a) *The Picture of Dorian Gray,* ed. Robert Mighall. Penguin, London.

Wilde, Oscar (2000b) *The Complete Works of Oscar Wilde: Volume 1, Poems and Poems in Prose,* ed. Karl Beckson and Bobby Fong. Oxford University Press, Oxford.

Wilde, Oscar (2003) *Complete Short Fiction,* ed. Ian Small. Penguin, London.

Wilde, Oscar (2005) *The Complete Works of Oscar Wilde: Volume II, De Profundis,* "Epistola: In Carcere et Vinculis," ed. I. Small. Oxford University Press, Oxford.

Wilson Knight, G. (1962) *The Christian Renaissance.* Methuen, London.

Modernist

CHAPTER 43
Introduction

Ward Blanton

As a religious icon and object of academic investigation, the Bible changed dramatically and in surprisingly complex ways during the modern period, all of which changes shaped indelibly the role the Bible played within modern literature. These transformations of the Bible were intimately related to the way "modernity," as both theoretical project and sociological phenomenon, began to define itself in relation to religion. For some moderns, latter day bearers of the slogans of radical Enlightenment, the appropriate way for modernity to relate to religion was by way of disenchanting or secularizing critique. For others, modernity was to be the moment of a profound repetition or appropriation of biblical myth, with the role of the artist that of making clear the modern, contemporary value of biblical texts.

Such initial schemata provide a useful way to approach the topic of the Bible in modern literature. In order to make clear how this is so, we first consider the theory and practice of modern autonomy (or self-rule) as it relates to the modern academic study of the Bible. Such considerations set the stage for analysis of how these phenomena affected rather intimately the function of the Bible in several major monuments of modern literature.

Modernity as Theoretical, Axiomatic Autonomy

In the Preface to *The Critique of Pure Reason*, the book that became perhaps the most influential piece of philosophy for the entire modern period, Kant declared famously:

> Our age is the genuine age of criticism, to which everything must submit. Religion through its holiness and legislation through its majesty commonly seek to exempt themselves from it. But in this way they excite a just suspicion against themselves, and cannot lay claim to that unfeigned respect that reason grants only to that which has been able to withstand its free and public examination. (Kant, 1999, p. 100–1/Ax)

The remark signaled an important intellectual, philosophical, and religious shift in which political forms, habits of thought, and received doctrinal formulations all became subject to doubt and subversive challenge. Indeed, Kant would go on to say that the "Copernican revolution" ushered in by his own reflections on this "age of criticism" caused him to realize that human reason operated, *even in relation to nature itself*, not by way of passive submission to an exterior authority but by way of an inversion even of this received hierarchy. Reason is "instructed by nature not like a pupil, who has recited to him whatever the teacher wants to say, but like an appointed judge who compels witnesses to answer the questions he puts to them" (Kant, 1999, p. 109/Bxiii).

All of this implied a theoretical and practical principle of life that was, again, simultaneously political, philosophical, and religious (see Taylor, 2007, pp. 84–129). Kant described the principle in terms of autonomy: "*Sapere aude*! 'Have courage to use your own reason!' That is the motto of enlightenment" (Kant, 1963, p. 3). It is as if bold exploits were needed to throw off the traditional authority of another (heteronomy), thus freeing oneself to the rule of oneself (autonomy). Such is the never-ending, and thus even paradoxical, demand of these modern formulations of *autonomia* (see Gourgouris, 2003, pp. 49–89). As we would expect, modern engagement with the Bible was marked profoundly by this first sense of the word autonomy. Biblical studies as an enterprise, for example, often tried to manifest its distinctly *modern* credentials, its operational autonomy, by way of a *disenchanting or secularizing critique* of inherited interpretations of these texts. Autonomy, in this sense, simply could not exist without an intimately related ability to make clear, and to reject as an obstruction to self-rule, an "other" that is *not* oneself. As renowned modern biblical scholar David Friedrich Strauss described it after he lost his academic post due to the scandal caused by his (significantly entitled) *Life of Jesus Critically Examined*: "If antiquity found it valuable to treat nothing as alien to humanity, the watchword of modern times is to regard everything as alien which is not human and natural" (Strauss, 1877, p. 6). That is, in order to be self-legislating, modernity necessarily had to be able to produce an "other" which it itself *was not*.

In this respect, biblical studies became a crucial placeholder within a cultural struggle whereby this distinction between modern "self" and non- or premodern "other" was produced, mirrored, and stabilized. As Strauss liked to put it, one discovers the "purely human" in the Bible by recognizing, designating, and excluding from one's analysis the "alien" other one also finds there. Strauss designated this alien otherness or alterity the "mythical" or the "dogmatic" elements of biblical texts. Excluding the *heteros* or other (identified with myth, religious interpretation) in order to discover a firm grounding in the self (*auto*), Strauss mapped biblical studies firmly onto the modern quest to achieve the "purely human," a quest often described rightly as the effort to translate theology into anthropology. Strauss's philosophical hero, G. W. F. Hegel, followed Kant in recognizing that such a judgment or distinction between self and other necessitated that modern biblical studies align itself rather closely to an aesthetic of distaste and disenchantment. Indeed, Hegel described this distinction as a modern readerly *experience*, namely that experience in which a modern finds herself struck in her reading of the ancient biblical texts with "a sense of repulsion" (see Blanton, 2007, pp. 22–66). In other words, given this first definition of autonomy, there were structural reasons for which experiences of disenchantment and distaste became an integral part of what it meant to attain to a genuinely *modern* reading of biblical texts (see Gadamer, 1998, pp. 19–42). In this first sense of autonomy, there is no reading as a modern that is not simultaneously a reading able to designate that which is *not* modern and therefore inappropriate or distasteful. To repeat all this in Kantian terms, the "tribunal" before which august traditional authorities must be paraded was therefore the aesthetic taste of the modern print market.

This realization has several very important implications for the study of the Bible and modern literature. First, it is clear that an engagement with *modern* literature and the Bible is certainly not simply about pious personal interests of authors or their literary burying away of explicit or implicit references to, or commentaries on, favorite Bible passages. Indeed, one reason the Bible was of such perennial interest to modern literature was for the "sense of repulsion" various moderns, at various points and for diverse reasons, experienced or wanted to cause others to experience through their own literary engagements with these texts. In the case of the intriguing theatrical reworkings of Gospel stories by W. B. Yeats, for example, the literary exploration of biblical texts frequently illumines the author's intuition, inherited from Friedrich Nietzsche, that biblical Christianity represented a reactionary negation of otherwise self-justifying "life." On this reading, Christianity attempts to eradicate life's properly tragic dimensions and to smooth over its senseless losses. Rather than a bold acceptance of this experience of loss, early Christianity (and particularly Pauline religiosity) divinized "pity" and lulled itself to sleep with the false assurances of an imagined universal Calculator of "good" and "bad" actions, punishments, and rewards. Such is one of the rhetorical punches of plays like Yeats's *Calvary* (1920) and *The Resurrection* (1931), and one finds similarly Nietzschean readings of Christianity in the remarkable *Apocalypse* of D. H. Lawrence (1930) or in *Man and Superman* (1903) and *Preface to Androcles and the Lion* (1912) by George Bernard Shaw.

Again, this type of intertwining of the Bible and an aesthetic of distaste was endemic to modernity as we have inherited it inasmuch as the modern project gambled on the idea that autonomy was united (by way of a privileged link) to the critique *of religion.* As Karl Marx claimed, rather remarkably in retrospect, in "criticism of religion is the premise of all criticism," the very foundation of that age Kant called "critical" (Marx and Engels, 1957, p. 41). Inasmuch as modernity gambled on the fact that "religion" could be taken as an exemplary obstruction on the way to autonomy, to that same degree the Bible became a key historical, theological, and ethical battleground in terms of which important cultural decisions about self-definition – not to mention the definition of the excluded other – were to be established and solidified.

Modernity as Practical, Institutional Autonomy

It is also important to notice that, as a phenomenon affecting the modern Bible, the principal of autonomy was not simply a theoretical axiom or an attempted reduction of theology to anthropology. Modern autonomy was also a practical and institutional reality that created a situation in which knowledge about the Bible was increasingly self-contained or self-referential and thus disconnected from many earlier and perhaps more wholistic contexts of life and faith that "the Book" had been thought to address or encapsulate. As is the case with any academic discipline, in fact, with the increasing disconnection or self-referentiality of this enterprise, modern biblical studies was free to enter into a period of rapid development and the production of increasingly sophisticated and technical interpretative strategies (Luhmann, 2002, pp. 113ff). In short, within the modern university the historical investigation of the Bible quickly became increasingly distinguishable as a technical enterprise from earlier forms of biblical interpretation in which scholars were pressed to integrate their work more directly to spiritual concerns of parishioners, the organization of ecclesiastical structures, or even the interests of a general readership.

This practical and institutional phenomenon of autonomy may be observed in the way that, at the end of the eighteenth century, Kant could still describe the biblical scholar as a "biblical theologian," assuming there to be a relatively seamless union between academic biblical interpretation and a static or "dogmatic" system of interpretation keyed to modern ecclesiastical concerns and the shoring up of shaky links between ancient and modern religious identities (Kant, 1979, p. 98; Bahti, 1992, pp. 20–2). A century later, it would have become a commonplace on all sides that "historical" or "theological" enquiries into biblical texts constitute almost incompatible modes of textual engagement, with little or nothing to assure their mutual communicability. In keeping with practical and institutional (rather than axiomatic or theoretical) autonomy, each of these enterprises had developed over this century increasingly self-referential, highly technical forms of sophistication that rendered problematic the earlier assumption that they were, essentially, the same project. As a field, in other words, the study of the Bible had undergone a similar process of *technical* modernization as the rest of the academy. As the sociologist Max Weber warned aspiring academics in a speech of 1918, the modern academy had become a fragmented whole, with individual academics becoming discrete technicians of a field of research rather than intellectuals fully aware of their significance and place within the whole. For Weber, this fragmentation of modern knowledge rendered impossible an academic life driven by earlier senses of "vocation" and its assurance that one's labor operated within a harmonious whole that transcends individual, technical sophistication. The hard modern truth for aspiring academics to realize, he suggested, was that "the individual can acquire the sure consciousness of achieving something truly perfect in the field of science only in case he [sic] is a strict specialist" (Weber, 1998, p. 134).

It is worth considering, in this light, the scholarly Casaubon in George Eliot's *Middlemarch*, hard at work on his *Key to All Mythologies*. Introduced in the novel with a quote from Cervantes's *Don Quixote*, Casaubon has shouldered the modern academic project to understand the Bible as but one part of a much more general, even global, history of religion. In shouldering this promising task, however, the scholar finds that the labor is endless, its possibilities labyrinthine, and his book is never finished. Casaubon's Sisyphean struggle merely destroys his eyesight, generating shelf upon shelf of copious fragments and notes that he is unable to synthesize into a coherent system of religious history that might return to the Christian Bible its former, premodern capacity to orient traditional piety. Autonomy (in this second sense) constituted a complexification of "the book" that seemed for many moderns to render its earlier usefulness as an orienting cultural text virtually inoperable.

One can find similar anxieties within academic biblical studies, which Eliot knew remarkably well and which informed her literary productions. Desperate to hold on to earlier and ostensibly more integrated or wholistic models of the Bible, for example, Martin Kähler penned a famous essay at the end of the nineteenth century, *The So-called Historical Jesus and the Historic Biblical Christ*. The book urges "historical research" not to forget its "modesty," those limits that would preclude too much interest, say, in the historical Jesus *behind* the New Testament writings rather than in these biblical representations of him (Kähler, 1964, p. 47). Kähler was concerned that increasingly sophisticated forms of historical analysis – particularly of the historical Jesus – had become "an obstacle to genuine attentiveness" to the biblical texts, by which he meant a more wholistic mode of attention he imagined to be more pious, believing, or religious (ibid., p. 71). For Kähler, and many others observing the technical results of nineteenth-century biblical scholarship, the excess of detail and new layers of sophistication produced by "historical research" had become a genuine obstruction to what they imagined to be a more holistic and simple engagement with the Bible through the eyes of faith. As Weber put it, the modern academy was producing a technical sophistication that occluded a reassuring and orienting sense of "vocation."

Indeed, Kähler's anxieties about technical interests in the history *leading up to* the depictions of Jesus we have in the New Testament Gospels could be repeated at many levels within modern biblical scholarship. Over the course of the century, for example, this developing field of research had replaced quaint eighteenth-century assumptions about the nondescript "poetry of the Hebrews" and popular notions about the "five books of Moses" (the first five books of the Bible) with increasingly complex reconstructions of multiple "editorial" moments, spread over centuries, in which anonymous figures like "JE" or "P" (the Yahwist, Elohist, or Priestly writers) reworked and transformed received texts for the interests of their own respective times and places in history. Not only were modern academics feeling fragmented, it seems, but their academic objects were becoming increasingly so as well. Introducing the groundbreaking work of historical scholarship by Julius Wellhausen, *Prolegomena to a History of Ancient Israel* (an initial version of which appeared in 1878), William Robertson Smith explicated this book's title by claiming, strikingly, that "the Old Testament does not furnish a history of Israel" (Wellhausen, 1885, p. vii). Indeed, academic autonomy in the sense of technical sophistication and disconnection from earlier wholes had allowed historical research to develop to the point that it had become necessary to contemplate itself reflexively, as if now at one step removed from what it earlier understood to be its object of analysis. Here the most sophisticated historical rendering of the Hebrew Bible had become a mere "prolegomena" to a deferred historical reconstruction. Biblical scholars had produced more and more complex theories about the cultural and even technological history of textual transmission to the point that Wellhausen believed the biblical texts afforded only fitful and highly censored or worked over glimpses of what many earlier nineteenth-century historians tended to assume they were finding more immediately and transparently in these texts (whether the writings of Moses, acts of God, or the actual history of Israel, all of which Smith mentions). In the modern, technical, or autonomous development of biblical studies, the immediate presence of "history" was becoming ever more deferred and mediated.

As Smith summarized, these texts "are themselves very composite structures, in which old narratives occur imbedded in later compilations, and groups of old laws are overlaid by ordinances of comparatively recent date" (Wellhausen, 1885, p. vii). Significantly, Smith explains that the complexity and scrambled narrative chronology of this evolutionary mode of interpretation challenged earlier experiences of readers who thought themselves to be reading in the Bible "the providential course of Israel's history." Layered complexity and an increasing awareness of historical contingency, Wellhausen's "twisted skein of tradition," were throwing off the rails earlier modes of reading, belief, and even modern "historical" interpretation itself (see Van Seters, 2006, pp. 223–31). Indeed, Sigmund Freud, a careful reader of W. R. Smith and other "biblical researchers," would later model the human psyche explicitly on Smith's and other modern readings of the Bible (e.g. in *Moses and Monotheism*), with the former becoming likewise fragmented, obscurely layered, and complexly historical rather than transparent or as it appears on the (conscious) surface. Allowing the complexly "edited" and fragmented Bible of modern scholarship to serve as a model for complexly edited and fragmented selves, Freud claimed that it was in the writings of that "man of genius" W. R. Smith that the psychoanalyst found "valuable points of contact with the psychological material of analysis" (Freud, 1964, p. 132).

Similarly, the New Testament Gospels came to be depicted during the same period as the result of a complex prehistory of shifting community values across geographically and historically distinct early Christian communities (Riches, 1993, pp. 50–69). The "Synoptic problem," or the question of literary interdependence among the New Testament Gospels Matthew, Mark, and Luke, replaced dominant earlier assumptions about the originality of these writings (Baird, 2003, pp. 261–87). In the process, received notions of the eyewitness character or first-hand recollection of these texts gave way, again, to a more complex history of transmission in which their putative objects were increasingly refracted. By the end of the nineteenth century, for example, there began to appear explicit and sustained reconstructions and considerations of a possible lost Gospel (now called "Q" after the German *Quelle* or source) that may have been incorporated into the Gospels of Matthew and Luke (Kloppenborg, 2000, pp. 267–352).

Already at the mid-point of the nineteenth century, D. F. Strauss could summarize the "critical" investigation of the Gospels by saying of the once coherent and relatively straightforward narratives that they now seemed to his readers disconcertingly fragmented and ungrounded:

> We see in the first three Gospels what happens to discourses that are preserved in the
> memory of another and [thus] shaped by their [later and ongoing] inscription. Severed

> from their original connection [to real events or authorial intentions] and split into smaller and smaller fragments ... when collected they give the appearance of a mosaic in which the connection of the parts is purely external and every transition a leap. (Strauss, 1846, p. 700/386)

The fragmentation engendered by technical sophistication had replaced earlier interpretations that afforded a more accessible, holistic form of identification, whether original events or authorial intentions.

It was precisely this collapse of biblical texts into fragmentation or new modes of complexity that frequently evoked the "sense of repulsion" from many modern readers of the Bible. Such was certainly the case with the English translator of Strauss's work, Mary Ann Evans (George Eliot). The bold Evans translated the radical, critical work not only of Strauss but also of his near contemporary, Ludwig Feuerbach, whose *Essence of Christianity* also attempted to translate theology into anthropology, with Christianity being read as a confused form of sociological analysis. A friend of the scandal-making Evans confides in a private letter: "We have seen more of M.A. than usual this week. She said she was Strauss-sick – it made her ill dissecting the beautiful story of the crucifixion" (Laski, 1973, p. 30). Intriguingly for our purposes, the friend suggests that Evans salved her sense of biblical fragmentation – the technical dissection of its once organic narrative body into a "mosaic" of disconnected pieces – by staring at a figurine and picture of Jesus that she kept in her room while translating Strauss's book: "Only the sight of her Christ-image and picture made her endure it." Looking to preserve that sense of orientation Weber called a "vocation," only the imagined wholeness of the visual image served to counteract the technical dissection of the New Testament narratives.

Even Friedrich Nietzsche expressed horror at the fragmented holism of life and biblical text that he discovered in Strauss's work, the philosopher declaring that one finds there only a "tattered memory and incoherent personal experience of the sort one finds in the newspapers" (Nietzsche, 1983, p. 29). Such was the result of autonomy in the second, practical and sociological, sense: life based on the Book seemed to be changing into a schizoid mosaic of the sort one finds in the newspaper's juxtaposition of otherwise disconnected stories. In fact, it is worth considering Nietzsche's reference to Strauss's newspaper psyche in terms of both our definitions of modern autonomy. It was not simply that modern axiomatic autonomy demanded that the Bible be read secularly, as one would read any "everyday" text – like a newspaper – though such was certainly the case. (As Siegfried Kracauer would write in relation to the modern Bible translation of Martin Buber and Franz Rosenzweig, "today access to truth is by way of the profane" or everyday: Kracauer, 1995, p. 201). At the same time (and in our second sense of autonomy), profane or everyday experience was one in which life had for many come to seem increasingly disjointed, technically fragmented and lacking holistic sense of orientation. Here, too, modern subject and ancient biblical object mirror each other perfectly. The Bible was not simply becoming secularized. For these writers, it was also fragmenting alongside the everyday life of modernity itself: the Bible had become a newspaper.

What *would* religion and literature do with the modern Bible in fragments? Does this "mosaic" effect destroy traditional piety or cause it to spring to life in unexpected new ways? The question is really, therefore, the one that asks what modernity does with the fragmentation of modern life more generally during this period, that experience of which the increasing specialization of biblical interpretation was but a part. Echoing the anxieties of Weber about the inability of a modern scholar to hear a holistic call of "vocation" in an otherwise fragmented form of life, T. S. Eliot's early work plays with various literary personae in order to question *how* or even *whether* moderns are able to take up earlier religious roles in a period of the increasing "dissociation of sensibility" (Prickett, 1996, p. 153). As we are pressed from all sides to ask in *The Wasteland*, is it really possible for the modern, autonomous and fragmented, to be the addressee of a divine word, to have a "vocation" in Weber's influential way of phrasing the problem? Playing with the divinely addressed "Son of Man" (as in the biblical story of the prophet Ezekiel) Eliot asks famously: "What are the roots that clutch, what branches grow / Out of this stony rubbish? Son of man, / you cannot say, or guess, for you know only/ A heap of broken images ..." (1.19–22). What will one do, and what becomes of the biblical text, once its imagery appears to constitute nothing but a heap of broken mythologies, empty and exiled from their lost origins?

Literature as the Cultural Salvation of the Bible in Fragments?

Indeed, what *was* one to do with this Bible in fragments, that great result of both axiomatic and sociological processes of modern autonomy? As Jonathan Sheehan describes in *The Enlightenment Bible*, the modern period may be read as an interpretative process in which familiar biblical texts came to seem *"strange, awkward, and new"* (Sheehan, 2005, p. 27). As we have pointed out, some interpreters, like Strauss, appropriated this awkward newness of the biblical texts at the hands of modern biblical scholars as an indication of things that were alien, threatening, and in need of expulsion from the sphere of the modern in order to attain the safe haven of the "merely human." Others, strikingly, attempted to situate themselves in relation to this uncanny newness as those who had discovered new media or modes of religious truthfulness. Thinkers of the Bible and literature as diverse as the German Romantics and James Joyce, for example, found in the very "non-modern" strangeness of the Bible an indication of its inexhaustible resources and even a model of art's own creative capacities (Prickett, 1996, pp. 180–221; Jasper, 2004, pp. 26–40).

In fact, part of the fascination with the Bible *and* or *as* "literature" and "culture" was undoubtedly a response to the powerful *historical* critiques of biblical texts that emerged from the "critical" tradition of biblical studies and the growing sense of unease with supernaturalist readings of biblical texts in which this discipline often trafficked. Matthew Arnold's influential *Literature and Dogma*, for example, informs readers that the aim of the book "is to re-assure those who feel attachment to Christianity, to the Bible, but who recognise the growing discredit befalling miracles and the supernatural" (Arnold, 1883, p. vii). Repeating Strauss's interest in reducing theology to the anthro-

pological realm of the "merely human," Arnold often described his project as the elucidation of the "natural truth" of Christianity, apart from its mythological (read:
miraculous) packaging. The enduring "substratum" of all those detachable miracle
stories or portions of biblical texts that no longer seem tasteful for modern readers was
still available, he suggested. As we might guess, this tastefully natural, verifiable, and
enduring substratum consisted, for Arnold, in the twin concepts of "literature" and
"culture."

Essentially Arnold urged his readers in works like this one not to fall into the wrong
kind of religion, in this case a religiosity that would use the Bible like a magical "talisman," a word he repeats often. Such "materialistic" (or, indeed, middle-class "Philistine") interpretations of miracles as real historical events, of hopes in a future kingdom
of God as a literal form of sovereignty, and so on, must be replaced by a religious education that teaches moderns not to treat "the Bible as Mahometans [*sic*] treat the Koran,
as if it were a talisman all of one piece, and with all its sentences equipollent" (Arnold,
1883, p. xxii). On the contrary, using fear of the European outsider to save biblical
interpretation from a mode of reading Arnold imagines to be too "materialist" or concrete, he urges his audience to understand that the "language of the Bible ... is literary,
not scientific language; language *thrown out* at an object of consciousness not fully
grasped, which inspired emotion" (ibid., pp. 30–1). While he does not mention them
as often as the religionists he opposes, such arguments could be deployed against
would-be secularist historians as well, inasmuch as they also tended to reduce the significance of biblical texts to a monolingualism of the "merely human." As a pluriform
mosaic of language "thrown out" at a utopia he calls perfection, divinity, or salvation,
Arnold presented the Bible as of inestimable value for – even inextricable from – the
striving of cultural progress (cf. Arnold, 1965, pp. 90ff, 163ff). Arnold had saved the
modern, historicized Bible, as it were, by making of the Bible a "classic," a perennial
source of inspiration and cultural education.

This biblical salvage job may appear to us a rather convenient baptism and appropriation of what was understood by many others to be a profound shock and challenge
to religion's future. It may also strike us as a conveniently classist reaction against mass
movements of the 1860s, with the fragmented and critiqued traditional authority represented by the "supernaturalist" Bible being restored in the form of an allegedly
forward-looking "literary" reading of the "educated" or "cultured" citizenry (e.g. Williams, 1980, pp. 1–8; Eagleton, 2000, pp. 1–35). Nevertheless, Arnold's rendering of
the fragmented Bible as a perennial classic also points up the way fragmentation and
even the *failure* of biblical texts effectively to represent their ostensible objects did not,
during this period, *only* afford material for a critique of religion. On the contrary, these
failures, and even deaths, of particular modes of biblical reading also served as religion's
salvation or even resurrection – and this by way of the value-inverting function of
"literature."

Several years after *Literature and Dogma* first appeared, Arnold's niece, Mary Augusta
Ward, wrote an extremely popular three-volume novel about a minister's loss of orthodox Christian faith, exploring many of these dynamics in the process. There, in *Robert
Elsmere*, a devout young evangelical goes to Oxford to sit under the teaching of a Hegelian, that great philosophical systematician of modernity. Subsequent to his formal

education, as a cleric the young Elsmere spends his mornings reading historical scholarship about the Bible and religion, eventually deciding that orthodox, apologetic biblical scholarship (like that of B. F. Westcott) operates by way of a refusal of honest
comparison of biblical ideas, texts, and tendencies with those of other ancient religions.
Westcott, Elsmere confides to his former teacher,

> who means so much nowadays to the English religious world, first isolates Christianity
> from all other religious phenomena of the world, and then argues upon its details. You
> might as well isolate English jurisprudence, and discuss its details without any reference
> to Teutonic custom or Roman law! You may be as logical or as learned as you like within
> the limits chosen, but the whole result is false! You treat Christian witness and Biblical lit-
> erature as you would treat no other witness, and no other literature in the world. And you
> cannot show cause enough. For your reasons depend on the very witness under dispute.
> And so you go on arguing in a circle, *ad infinitum*. (Ward, 1976, p. 2.315)

Despite himself, however, Elsmere finds that to try to read differently, outside the self-
reinforcing circuit within which the Christian Bible is privileged and abstracted from a
"world" of other religious and literary phenomena, leaves him feeling that he has lost
his own orientation – even his own place within the world. Disenchanted, he discovers
that his effort to read the Bible comparatively and as any other religious text is to stare
directly into the gaze of "a medusa," his own sense of piety and possibility becoming
paralyzed by this comparative enterprise (Ward, 1976, p. 2.136). Like the educated
reader in *Literature and Dogma*, Elsmere eventually loses his faith in the privileged (or
supernaturalist) reading of the Bible, declaring to himself that "*miracles do not happen!*,"
meaning in this case that no culture should be thus treated as exceptional (ibid., p.
2.291). Under the tutelage of his Hegelian advisor, however, Elsmere finds that the
collapse of the orthodox, supernaturalist position opens up the possibility for a kind of
worldly spirituality, with the apostate cleric starting a "New Brotherhood" in which
old energies of faith exist as social activism.

Disenchanting Fragmentation or Magical Collage?

Writing after two world wars, T. S. Eliot has perspectives that differ from those of predecessors like Arnold, though he also claims that "We may ... ask whether what we
call culture, and what we call religion, of a people are not different aspects of the same
thing: the culture being, essentially, the incarnation (so to speak) of the religion of a
people" (Eliot, 1948, p. 28). Eliot also sometimes relates to the Bible as to a "classic"
generative of all of Europe's "future literature" and therefore of its more general production of "culture" (ibid., p. 114). At times he also shares with thinkers like Arnold a sense
that artists must save the "spiritual organism of Europe" from a collapse into a post-
religious and quasi-mechanistic "materialism" (ibid., p. 119). As Eliot confides rather
anxiously, if "we" (Europeans) lose the Christian "unity in the common elements of
culture," which is the "true bond between us," "then all the organisation and planning

of the most ingenious minds will not help us, or bring us closer" (ibid., p. 123). Technical engineers of the merely material realm are not able to replicate that "patrimony of
culture" he imagines to be named in the word Christianity. Again, the anxiety is the
same as that expressed by Weber. Would modernity experience a holistic sense of place,
a divine "vocation," or would such intangible assurances collapse into a life of fragmentation and merely technical operations?

Interestingly enough, however, there are often times in Eliot's literary work when
it is *precisely* the fall of the Bible into the realm of the fragmentary – and even the ruined
– that allows Eliot to generate such interesting interventions in the ongoing life of biblical interpretation. Moving from disparate image to disparate image in *The Waste Land*,
for example, and this without reassuring explanatory gloss or transitional link, Eliot's
juxtaposition of prophetic, Roman, Shakespearean, urban, occult, and Medieval mythological references produces a phantasmagoria of rogue meanings in which hermeneutical frameworks are necessarily blasted open. This, however, is precisely the openness
within which one must wonder whether there may be new significations that are yet
to come to light from these ruinously displaced images, textual topics that may otherwise appear to us as well framed but exhausted.

Like Arnold's reflections on the Bible and modern literature, Eliot's work may be
read not just as a questioning of the Bible's value, but as an *embrace* of this crisis of
legitimation as a significant religious and artistic event in its own right. To affirm the
"broken images" of the modern Bible, to shuffle through them, to reorder them in
new "worlds" of relations, or to cast them into new conversations (with other religions, with banalities of everyday modern life) is, in a peculiar way, to engage in a
kind of literary alchemy, finding in violated and burned out meanings new powers
of life that may yet spring to existence. To put this slightly differently, in an ironic
twist such appropriations of the modern, blasted or fragmented, Bible may be read
as a strange *return* of biblical interpretation to a premodern mentality in which the
biblical text was imagined as pluriform, not only literal (or historical) but excessively
mystical, allegorical, tropological, analogical, and so on as well (see Prickett, 1996,
pp. 108–79). Indeed, inasmuch as it may be read as a particularly disoriented version
of this premodern plurality of meanings and contexts, one could say that Eliot's early
alchemical approach to biblical texts may be read as a kind of biblical cubism, in
which the before-and-after of our usual ways of seeing are mashed together into a
pure, magical presence. As the "English Cubist" Wyndham Lewis described the *Blast*
series in which some of Eliot's early work was published: "WE NEED THE UNCON-
SCIOUSNESS OF HUMANITY – their stupidity, animalism and dreams" (Lewis, 1969,
p. 25). Artistic imagery does not *correspond* (more or less accurately) to a world so
much as *conjure* worldhood out of the enchanted thicket of a fragmented everyday
life: "The artist of the modern movement is a savage ... [and] this enormous, jangling,
journalistic, fairy desert of modern life serves him as Nature did more technically
primitive man" (ibid., p. 28).

Indeed, in light of the power of imagistic collage and its disorienting overlay of
displaced texts in T. S. Eliot's earlier works, it is worth wondering whether this early
work is not ultimately a more provocative *religious* vision than some of those much

more predictable jeremiads about Europe's loss of Christianity that Eliot wrote *after* his joining the Church of England in 1927. Similarly, in the case of James Joyce, for example, it is precisely the break with the Church and with structures of orthodox thought that enabled his creative reworking of biblical imagery, epic biblical motifs being transformed into "profane" contexts with the occasional result rendering the everyday as an oddly mystical potency (as Lewis hoped the cityscape would be for a new kind of "savage" artist). Exploring this paradoxical link between the secularization of Christianity and the spiritualization of the everyday, Thomas Altizer imagines Joyce to stand in a long line of heterodox thinkers (and even post-Christian "apostates") like William Blake and Friedrich Nietzsche, in order to proclaim Joyce a great figure in the biblical tradition of apocalypticism. For the apocalyptic thinker, Altizer suggests, the new appears only in the proclamation that the old, indeed the world itself, is passing away. In this case, out of the very death of the old metaphysical God and the church's otherworldly beliefs in afterlife, arises a *secularized* religiosity, curiously *present* in a way it had not seemed before. The dramatic stagings of Altizer's narrations are not completely disconnected from what we observed in the modernist gesture of Marx and Strauss when they gambled that a critique of religion as external agency (heteronomy) might yet liberate new forms of selfhood, finally present and unobstructed. In such readings of modern figures like Joyce, the end of supernaturalist orthodoxy may simultaneously be read as the self-emptying, and even eucharistic self-giving, in which the death of the traditional God clears a space within which a now-mystical worldliness snaps to attention. Modernity thus produced a remarkable literature in which loss, and even the loss of religion, was itself recuperated into the life of "culture," "literature," and even religion itself. After the modern critique of the Bible, the ruin, emptiness, fragmentation, and failure of these texts ended, ironically, as striking indications of the ongoing life of religion. Such are some of the basic, if inescapable, dramas and paradoxes constituting the Bible in modern literature.

Bibliography

Anidjar, Gil (2007) *Semites: Race, Religion, Literature.* Stanford University Press, Stanford, CA.

Arnold, Matthew (1883) *Literature and Dogma.* Smith & Elder, London.

Arnold, Matthew (1965) *Culture and Anarchy.* University of Michigan Press, Ann Arbor.

Arnold, Matthew (1970) *God and the Bible: Introduction,* ed. R. H. Super. University of Michigan Press, Ann Arbor.

Bahti, Timothy (1992) *Allegories of History: Literary Historiography after Hegel.* Johns Hopkins University Press, Baltimore.

Baird, William (2003) *History of New Testament Research. Volume 2, From Jonathan Edwards to Rudolf Bultmann.* Fortress, Minneapolis.

Blanton, Ward (2007) *Displacing Christian Origins: Philosophy, Secularity, and the New Testament.* University of Chicago Press, Chicago.

Derrida, Jacques (1996) "Faith and Knowledge: The Two Sources of 'Religion' at the Limits of Reason Alone," in Jacques Derrida and Gianni Vattimo, eds, *Religion.* Stanford University Press, Stanford, CA, pp. 1–76.

Eagleton, Terry (2000) *The Idea of Culture*. Blackwell Publishers, Oxford.

Eliot, T. S. (1948) *Notes towards the Definition of Culture*. Faber & Faber, London.

Feuerbach, Ludwig (1989) *The Essence of Christianity*, trans. George Eliot. Prometheus Books, Buffalo, NY.

Freud, Sigmund (1964) *Moses and Monotheism*. trans. James Strachey. Hogarth Press, London.

Gadamer, Hans-Georg (1998) Truth and Method, trans. Joel Weinsheimer and Donald G. Marshall. Continuum, New York.

Gourgouris, Stathis (2003) *Does Literature Think? Literature as Theory for an Antimythical Era*. Stanford University Press, Stanford, CA.

Jasper, David (2004) *The Sacred Desert: Religion, Literature, Art, and Culture*. Blackwell, Oxford.

Kähler, Martin (1964) *The So-called Historical Jesus and the Historic, Biblical Christ*. Fortress Press, Philadelphia.

Kant, Immanuel (1963) *On History*, ed. Lewis White Beck. Merrill Educational Publishing, Indianapolis.

Kant, Immanuel (1979) *The Conflict of the Faculties/Der Streit der Fakultäten*, trans. Mary J. Gregor. University of Nebraska Press, Lincoln.

Kant, Immanuel (1999) *The Critique of Pure Reason*, trans. Paul Guyer and Allen Wood. Cambridge University Press, Cambridge.

Kloppenborg, John (2000) *Excavating Q: the History and Setting of the Sayings Gospel*. T & T Clark, Edinburgh.

Kracauer, Siegfried (1995) *The Mass Ornament: Weimar Essays*. Harvard University Press, Cambridge, MA.

Laski, Marghanita (1973) *George Eliot and Her World*. Scribners, New York.

Lewis, Wyndham (1969) Wyndham Lewis on Art: Collected Writings 1913–1956, ed. Walter Michel and C. J. Fox. Thames and Hudson, London.

Luhmann, Niklas (1996) *Social Systems*. Writing Science. Stanford University Press, Stanford, CA.

Luhmann, Niklas (1999) *Observations on Modernity*. Writing Science. Stanford University Press, Stanford, CA.

Luhmann, Niklas (2002) *Theories of Distinction: Redescribing the Descriptions of Modernity*. Stanford University Press, Stanford, CA.

Martin, Dale (2001) "Paul and the Judaism/Hellenism Dichotomy: Toward a Social History of the Question," in Troels Engberg-Pedersen, eds., *Paul Beyond the Judaism/Hellenism Divide*. Westminster John Knox, Louisville, KY, pp. 39–62.

Marx, Karl and Engels, Friedrich (1957) *On Religion*. Progress, Moscow.

Nietzsche, Friedrich (1983) *Untimely Meditations*, trans. R. J. Hollingdale. Cambridge University Press, Cambridge.

Prickett, Stephen (1996) *The Origins of Narrative: The Romantic Appropriation of the Bible*. Cambridge University Press, Cambridge.

Riches, John (1993) *A Century of New Testament Study*. Lutterworth Press, Cambridge.

Shaw, George Bernard (1913/2006) "The Monstrous Imposition on Jesus," in *Writings of St Paul*, ed. Wayne Meeks. Norton, New York.

Sheehan, Jonathan (2005) *The Enlightenment Bible: Translation, Scholarship, Culture*. Princeton University Press, Princeton, NJ.

Strauss, David Friedrich (1846) *The Life of Jesus Critically Examined*, trans. George Eliot. Sigler Press, Ramsey, NJ.

Strauss, David Friedrich (1877) *Das Leben Jesu*. Gessamelte Schriften 3. Verlag von Emil Strauss, Bonn.

Taylor, Mark C. (2007) *After God*. University of Chicago Press, Chicago.

Van Seters, John (2006) *The Edited Bible: the Curious History of the "Editor" in Biblical Criticism*. Eisenbrauns, Winona Lake, IN.

Ward, Mary Augusta (1976) *Robert Elsmere*. Garland Publishing, New York.

Weber, Max (1998) *From Max Weber: Essays in Sociology*. Routledge, London.

Wellhausen, Julius (1885) *Prolegemonena to the History of Israel*. A. & C. Black, Edinburgh.

Williams, Raymond (1980) *Problems in Materialism and Culture*. Verso, London.

Williams, Raymond (1984) *Culture and Society 1780–1950*. Penguin Books, Harmondsworth.

CHAPTER 44
W. B. Yeats

Edward Larrissy

If people were asked to reflect on Yeats and the sacred, the Bible would probably not be the first association to occur to many: Irish or Greek mythology, or the wisdom of the Upanishads, might understandably seem like more fruitful connections to explore. And indeed, if one were to seek either the exposition of biblical themes or the ambitious development of biblical imagery or narrative, one would have much unrewarding ground to cover before encountering examples that fit these descriptions in any straightforward sense. In some ways, this is quite surprising. Yeats's grandfather and great-grandfather were both Church of Ireland clergymen, and even allowing for the fact that the descendants do not always imitate the sires, one might at least have expected some reflection of the immersion in the Bible, both Old and New Testaments, that was typical of an Irish Protestant upbringing. But "unlike Blake and Milton, Yeats can be understood without knowing the Bible."[1] Probably a substantial part of the reason is that Yeats's was "not a conventional Irish Protestant childhood."[2] Nor was the intellectual universe his father inhabited a conventional Protestant one. His intellectual formation when a young man at Trinity College, Dublin, had been in a milieu where the discussion was of Comte, of Darwinism, of J. S. Mill.[3] And when he set out on a financially precarious career as a painter, it was the Pre-Raphaelites he first chose as models. Although W. B. Yeats was to react against the Victorian materialism encouraged by the first names on this list, the ostensible sign of this reaction is to be found in an interest in theosophy, in occult speculations, and in the esoteric connections of Blake's system.

Yet it would be superficial to claim that there was no biblical influence on Yeats simply because of the scarcity of the expected names, tales, and messages. At a profound level, Yeats's thinking bears the imprint of Christian thought, especially the doctrine of incarnation. Indeed, no knowledgeable person would dissociate his occult and esoteric influences from the Christian tradition. A salient reminder of the reasons why this must be the case is provided by the works of the esoteric thinker Anna Kingsford, a compilation of whose writings, *The Credo of Christendom* (1916), was to be found in Yeats's library. She was an acquaintance of MacGregor Mathers, one of Yeats's colleagues in the Hermetic Order of the Golden Dawn. Yeats was clearly familiar with her ideas as early as the 1880s. There is a lengthy reference to a story about her in a letter of 1888 to his friend Katharine Tynan.[4] The writings in *The Credo of Christendom* date from the

1880s and 1890s, and during his magical apprenticeship, Yeats would have come across these ideas about Christianity. They are consonant with other, less obviously Christian-looking, notions current among Golden Dawn members. Thus, Kingsford asserts in an article of 1885 in the occultist journal *Light* that "not the historic but the spiritual Christ is the real essential of Christianity, and subject."[5] This is because "The things that are truly done, are not done on the historical plane."[6] But such a view would be entirely congruent with that of Blake, who discarded the dross of literal historical interpretation of the Bible. As he says in his annotations to Bishop Watson's *Apology for the Bible* (1797), "I cannot concieve [sic] the Divinity of the ... Bible to consist either in who they were written by or at what time or in the historical evidence which may be all false in the eyes of one man & true in the eyes of another but in the Sentiments & Examples."[7] And in this sense of what it is to be a Christian, Blake, one of Yeats's most important mentors, is a Christian whose "Prophetic Books" make constant reference to the Bible. But with his avowed indebtedness, recorded in *The Marriage of Heaven and Hell*, to Paracelsus and "Jacob Behmen," as well as the importance he accords to spiritual progression and rebirth, Blake's Christianity is influenced by philosophical alchemy, and so was that of Anna Kingsford. In their remarks on resurrection, Kingsford and her collaborator Edward Maitland aver that "The Alchemic gold issues purged and resplendent from the fiery furnace, in which its constituent elements have been dissolved, segregated, sublimed, and regularised."[8] This is alchemy understood as an allegory of spiritual rebirth, and this very understanding implied that alchemical imagery was only one of the vestures worn by a perennial truth. In this spirit, Kingsford and Maitland were able to feel confident that the story of Jesus derived from Greek Mysteries, which they appear to have regarded as a purer expression of the truth than the Gospel narrative.[9] In this perspective, Yeats's comparison of Christ and Dionysus, to which we shall have occasion to refer, looks very much in accord with his own spiritual education.

Yet Christ and the Bible are not the same thing. It remains illuminating about Yeats to recall that he "uses the Old Testament lightly."[10] Psalms, Ecclesiastes, and Ezekiel are just some of the expected texts to which Yeats makes scant allusion.[11] The doctrine of the incarnation, which is the subject of Yeats's continuing reflections, is definitive of the difference between Christianity and Judaism, even if, as he was aware, the idea of incarnation appears in other religions, such as Hinduism. If one adds to this a particular interpretation of the crucifixion, one has found a way of understanding the specifically Christian connections of Yeats's early "Romantic" phase, when he had so much to say about Rose and Cross.

Rose, Cross, and Celtic Christianity

The Rose and Cross are supposed to be symbolic components of the name of Rosicrucianism, an eclectic synthesis of various esoteric traditions, including Kabbalah and philosophical alchemy, the origins of which are appropriately mysterious.[12] Its supposed doctrines were the staple of the Golden Dawn, and of those inner, "higher," or speculative orders of Freemasonry to which the Golden Dawn was indebted, and which, incidentally, would have been familiar to Yeats's Freemason uncle, George Pollexfen. It is worth recalling the pervasiveness of Freemasonry among Anglo-Irish Protestants, and pondering the question of how the exotic ritual magic practiced by the Golden Dawn might seem to Yeats to offer a ritual intensity fit to vie with that of Roman Catholicism, whose adherents were officially forbidden to be Freemasons.[13]

For all its esoteric connections, Rosicrucianism was true to its sources in Renaissance syncretism in being professedly Christian. In other words, in the same way that there might be Christian Kabbalists, neoplatonists, or philosophical alchemists, so the Rosicrucian who sought to combine all these traditions was also Christian. The Cross to which Yeats and the Rosicrucians refer is saliently, though not exclusively, the Cross of Christ. Yeats's acceptance of this association, if it needed corroboration, is suggested by his early notebook containing "The Rosy Cross Lyrics."[14] The Cross was, at the same time, other things: partly as a result of the ancient association of cross and tree, it could be the Tree of Life. This status was inseparable from the Kabbalistic symbol of the same name, according to which the aspects of God vouchsafed to human awareness could be figured as lights or spheres at different positions on the Tree of Life. There were ten such lights, the lower seven representing the world of time, a number symbolism deriving from the seven days of Creation. The Tree also had two opposed aspects, one of "justice" and one of "mercy." Christian Kabbalists could easily relate this opposition to the apparent tension between these two qualities within their own faith. Yeats was also able to relate it to other pairs of opposed principles – or "antinomies," as he called them – having been educated by his reading of Blake to think in terms of "contrary states." The particular relevance of this to the Cross resides in the ambivalent symbolism of incarnation and atonement: salvation procured through torture and death. Thus it is that what may seem harsh and painful about the Cross is ultimately redeemed. In this connection, it is important to remember also the Rose, the meaning of which had been defined by Yeats's Golden Dawn colleague A. E. Waite in *The Real History of the Rosicrucians* (1887). Waite notes that "According to the Kabbala Denudata of the Baron Knorr de Rosenroth, the Rose signifies the Shecinah," the Schechinah being the indwelling or immanence of God in the world.[15] Yeats was able to see the Rose as the blooming in the world of the eternal divine principle. He referred to it in relation to "eternal beauty." In fact, Rose and Cross symbolize another pair of mutually dependent contrary principles.

These ideas are well illustrated in a reading of Yeats's poem "To the Rose upon the Rood of Time," first published in *The Countess Kathleen and Various Legends and Lyrics* (1892), but included in subsequent collections in a section called *The Rose*.[16] The connection with Christianity is advertised by the use of the word "rood" for cross, with its ancient liturgical connotations. But the poem is dominated by the unorthodox reflections Yeats imparts to the symbol. The Rose is the leading image, in fact, and the rood (or tree) is directly referred to once as made up of "the boughs of love and hate," a description that comprises all the contrariety of our world. As for the Rose, its association with beauty permits Yeats to fulfill the role of poet and dreamer, in this case singing of the "ancient ways" of Cuchulain and Fergus, and all the sagas and romances of Ireland. As far as Yeats is concerned, the symbol of united Rose and Cross permits him to give clarity and definition to the role of the poet, which is something of a balancing act: one must find the eternal (the principle of the Rose), but it must be in this life (the Rose blooms on the Tree of Life with all its connotations of contrariety and pain). Indeed, the second stanza warns against being overpowered by the symbol of the Rose: "leave me still / A little space for the rose-breath to fill, / Lest I no more hear common things that crave." The lesson of a reading of this poem is not encouraging to the search for orthodox Christian doctrine or even the creative reworking of biblical material. The idea of incarnation is present in a broad sense, lacking in doctrinal specificity, and there is a dim allusion to the doctrine of atonement in the notion that suffering is a necessary part of a full existence, but no evidence of the doctrine itself. This remote and high-minded attitude to Christian doctrine and biblical symbolism was to remain characteristic of Yeats even where biblical references were more direct.

Even so, it is unlikely that Yeats thought of himself in the 1890s as entirely divorced from the Christian tradition. It seems more probable that he would have thought that the kind of philosophy he espoused was in accord with the Celtic Church. Of course, as *The Wanderings of Oisin* makes clear, Yeats felt that much had been lost with the coming of official Christianity to Ireland. As Oisin remarks to St Patrick,

> If I were as I once was, the strong hoofs crushing the sand and the shells,
> Coming out of the sea as the dawn comes, a chaunt of love on my lips,
> Not coughing, my head on my knees, and praying, and wroth with the bells,
> I would leave no saint's head on his body from Rachlin to Bera of ships. (P, p. 383)

Even so, Yeats probably shared the not uncommon belief that the so-called Celtic Church had inherited some of the features of the pagan, druidical beliefs in which he was so interested. Indeed, there may be a clue to this in the character of the "rood" itself, for he may have been thinking of a Celtic Cross, such as the one at the edge of Drumcliff churchyard in County Sligo, close to his childhood haunts. The way that such crosses are bounded by a circle might suggest the shape of a rose.

But what was the druid lore supposedly retained by Christianity? The point of convergence would for Yeats be summarized in the existence of beauty in living things. In common with other commentators on Celtic religion, Yeats took it for granted that the druids believed in the transmigration of souls. The ancient poem sometimes called "The Rune of St Patrick," and at other times "St Patrick's Hymn Before Tara," was seen as evidence that druid notions had survived into Celtic Christianity.[17] Yeats would certainly have known James Clarence Mangan's translation. The poem addresses "The God of the elements" and implies the identity of God and His creation:

> I place all Heaven with its power,
> And the sun with its brightness,
> And the snow with its whiteness,
> And fire with all the strength it hath,
> And lightning with its rapid wrath,
> And the winds with their swiftness along their path,
> And the sea with its deepness,
> And the rocks with their steepness,

> And the earth with its starkness; –
> All these I place,
> By God's almighty help and grace,
> Between myself and the power of darkness.[18]

This poem was compared with what was understood to be the oldest fragment of Irish poetry, "The Mystery of Amergin." A translation of this pantheist and supposedly pre-Christian utterance was designedly placed at the beginning of the influential anthology *Lyra Celtica*:

> I am the wind which breathes upon the sea,
> I am the wave of the ocean
> I am the murmur of billows
> I am the ox of the seven combats[19]

And so on, through a fairly long list, which ends by identifying the speaker as "the God who creates in the head ... the fire."[20] John Rhys, in his *Lectures on ... Celtic Heathendom* sums up the state of affairs when Ireland became Christian in a way that emphasizes mutual influence:

> Irish druidism absorbed a certain amount of Christianity; and it would be a problem of considerable difficulty to fix on the point where it ceased to be druidism and from which onwards it could be said to be Christianity in any restricted sense of that term.[21]

When Fergus, in Yeats's "Fergus and the Druid," looks into the druid's "bag of dreams," he discovers

> I have been many things –
> A green drop in the surge, a gleam of light
> Upon a sword, a fir-tree in a hill,
> An old slave grinding at a heavy quern,
> A king sitting upon a chair of gold. (P, p. 33)

This druid lore of pantheism and the transmigration of souls was not clearly separate in Yeats's mind from the mystical interpretation of Christianity that he saw as characteristically Celtic. Nor was he the only member of the Golden Dawn who discerned a link between his beliefs and those of "Celtic Christianity." In the 1890s, Aleister Crowley joined a group that called itself "The Celtic Church."[22] It is relevant to note that there were those who thought that one of the masonic rituals had originated in "I-Colm-Kill" – that is, Iona, the island of St Columba (Colm Cille).[23] Even so, it remains the case that there is no hint in Yeats of an interest in anything Christian or biblical that could not be associated with a religion of the imagination involving the transmigration of souls, reincarnation, and a spirit world, and he is happy to seek authority in non-Christian sources. As W. J. McCormack says, "Yeats's relationship to Church or doctrine was never close, despite his grandfather's holy orders. The incarnation took its place in his philosophy of history, as if he were a comparativist, not a believer."[24]

Christ and the Christian Era

Nevertheless, the figure of Christ and the nature of the Christian era become topics of renewed importance in their own right from the time in 1917 when Yeats began work on the great occult system first revealed in *A Vision* (first edition 1925). This system explains human society and personality in relation to the metaphor of the phases of the moon. A fundamental polarity (another version of "antinomies") structures this metaphor, that of the alternation between the light and the dark of the moon. The light of the moon represents subjectivity (or what Yeats called the "antithetical"), the dark of the moon objectivity (or the "primary"). The different quantities of light and dark to be found in each of the phases correspond to the different quantities of subjectivity and objectivity to be found, for instance, in real historical individuals. There is, however, the proviso that no living human being can correspond to the moon when either full or completely dark, since these phases, being perfect, can have no representatives in the imperfect world of time. Also, since the same relative quantities of light and dark occur twice each month, it is worth noting that the character of the phase is influenced by whether or not it comes before or after the full: that is, by its direction of travel. This fact underlines a fundamental aspect of the system: it describes motion, a cycle of time, for it is also at root a metaphor of the month. This explains Yeats's ambitious application of the metaphor to history, for just as an individual can possess the character of a certain lunar phase, so can a historical period. And historical periods go through the phases of the moon in the correct order. This is the reason for Yeats's renewed interest in the Christian era and the figure of Christ, since clearly, if his system were to lay claim to any powers of historical interpretation, it could hardly shirk the task of explaining a historical event of such moment, along with its unfolding consequences. *A Vision* contains a description of the character of Christ, and a detailed account of the Christian era that is essential to the understanding of the whole of Yeats's thought from 1917 onwards.

Yeats's conception is influenced by Plato's notion of "The Great Year," a cyclical period or 36,000 years after which the sun returns to the same place among the constellations that it had occupied at the beginning of the universe. Yeats did entertain a belief in some such major cycle, but he thought that it was subdivided into lesser cycles, and it is these that concern him most. Particularly significant for him was the subdivision of 2,000 years, roughly the length of time from the destruction of Troy to the birth of Christ, and also the length of time from the birth of Christ to our own era. These two periods are seen by Yeats as two opposing gyres or vortices, the first being subjective ("antithetical"), the second objective ("primary"). Despite this alternation, though, each period of 2,000 years goes through the twenty-eight phases of the moon, and is itself compounded of an alternation of relatively subjective and objective qualities. Yeats thought that the pre-Christian cycle was antithetical in character, the Christian primary. At the end of 2,000 years, the Christian era would itself give way to another dispensation, this time antithetical again. This means that there will be no apocalyptic end to history, as foreseen in orthodox Christian accounts, but only a continuing alternation of solar and lunar qualities. This is the subject of Yeats's poem "The Second

Coming" (P, p. 187). The title is ironic, for in reality it is not Christ who comes again, but the equivalent instigator of the next era, which will not be like the Christian one.

The poem begins by evoking the end of an age in terms of Yeats's system: "Turning and turning in the widening gyre / The falcon cannot hear the falconer." The gyre is the vortex of the Christian era, now far from its inception, weakened, losing touch with its fundamental inspiration. Anarchy is developing. (One must not forget the context of the period after the Great War, the Russian Revolution, and the Irish rebellion.) Yeats is clear that distinctively Christian qualities are being overwhelmed: "The ceremony of innocence is drowned." This phrase evokes the centrality of the qualities of the Christ-child to the Christian story and the religious rituals it inspires. The new dispensation will have its own birth, but it will not be an innocent little child who is born: "And what rough beast, / Its hour come round at last, / Slouches towards Bethlehem to be born?" The rough beast, Yeats's shockingly ironic interpretation of the Beast of Revelation, is the harbinger of a new post-Christian age. As he explains in *A Vision*, "as Christ was the *primary* revelation to an *antithetical* age, He that is to come will be the *antithetical* revelation to a *primary* age."[25] As such, He will represent hierarchy and domination, as opposed to any abstract idea of justice. The new dispensation will "seek no general agreement," and "may grow a fanaticism and a terror, and at its first outsetting oppress the ignorant – even the innocent – as Christianity oppressed the wise" (AVA, p. 215). Despite Yeats's general preference for the antithetical over the primary, he entertained mixed feelings about the inception of a new era, as the language of "The Second Coming" suggests. Nietzsche had taught Yeats that the perfection of the aristocracy was to be found when violent groups who had gained control of society by force were tempered by the cultivation of arts and manners. But while Yeats might admire the Renaissance court, he was understandably perturbed at the idea of his own society being under threat from some new kind of barbaric warlord, as is confirmed in a poem printed immediately after "The Second Coming" in *Michael Robartes and the Dancer*, namely "A Prayer for My Daughter," with its valuing both of settled custom and of innocence, and its air of anxious foreboding. (P, 188–90)

As for the figure of Christ himself, Yeats's account in *A Vision* is complex, an analysis in terms of the different primary and antithetical qualities that made up his personality: "we say of Him that He was love itself, and yet that part of Him which made Christendom was not love but pity, and not pity for intellectual despair, though the man in Him, being *antithetical* like His age, knew it in the Garden, but *primary* pity, that for the common lot, man's death seeing that He raised Lazarus, sickness seeing that He healed many, sin seeing that He died" (AVA, pp. 186–7[26]). More simply put, Christ's was a predominantly *antithetical* or subjective nature, but his legacy was formed from the primary elements in his character, which expressed themselves in terms of pity.

Yeats's Christian Mystery Plays

Christ himself is the central subject of two of Yeats's plays, *Calvary* (1920) and *The Resurrection* (1931): so central, in fact, that they have been referred to, by Peter

Ure, as "Yeats's Christian Mystery Plays."[27] Both of these can be categorized as "Plays for Dancers," a description Yeats applied to plays partly influenced by his acquaintance with Japanese Nōh theatre, a form involving masks, music, and stylized movement and scenes. *Calvary* was first published as one of the *Four Plays for Dancers* (1921), and *The Resurrection* in *Wheels and Butterflies (More Plays for Dancers)* (1934). The stylized character of these plays is appropriate to the themes that preoccupy Yeats in his interpretation of Christ. In *Calvary* the tension between Christ's predestined role and the free will of those with whom he associated mirrors the tension between destiny and freedom that is implied in his own historical system. *The Resurrection* is concerned with an analogous tension between the world of human mortality and the larger pattern of the Great Year, with its recurrent spiritual and divine forms.

In *Calvary*, Christ, arriving at the place of his execution, converses in turn with Lazarus, Judas, and three Roman soldiers. Christ, Lazarus, and Judas all wear masks, while the Roman soldiers have their faces "masked, or made up to resemble masks."[28] Lazarus complains to Christ: "You took my death, give me your death instead" (*Plays*, p. 331). It appears that Lazarus had no will to live: "I had been dead and I was lying still / In an old, comfortable mountain cavern." The quality of "pity," identified by Yeats as essential to Christ and his historical legacy, is here interpreted as an imposition, potentially irksome to some, on the particularities of life. Judas, by contrast, explains that he could find his freedom by betraying God: "Whatever man betray Him will be free." (*Plays*, p. 333) Christ makes the point that Judas was only acting in accord with "the commandment of God," but Judas argues that, although it was decreed "that somebody betray you," there was no decree stating that it should be himself, namely "I the man Judas, born on such a day, / In such a village, such and such his parents." (*Plays*, p. 334) The treatment of Judas explores a similar tension between freedom and the great preordained patterns to that found in the Lazarus story, but offers a slightly different way of conceiving the element in human behavior that wants to escape the pattern of destiny. Where Lazarus represents a passivity that fears life under any conception, whether as pre-destined or not, Judas would make his escape from the great pattern the opportunity for a heroic act on behalf of human freedom. In the end, though, the relationship between fate and free will remains paradoxical, but it is significant that Christ himself appears to be governed by fate. As for the soldiers, they are merely interested in which of them is to have Christ's cloak, a question they will settle by throwing dice. Yeats explains in his note to the play that the soldiers "suggest a form of objectivity that lay beyond His help" (*Plays*, p. 697). This means that their meretricious materialism cannot be redeemed by Christ's "objective" morality. It is appropriate that they use dice: they represent also a world of chance beyond the reach of any system of thought. But this is the realm in which the intelligent or the cunning may, unlike the soldiers, find some little area to exploit or shape in the name of freedom.

The central dialogue – it scarcely amounts to action – is bracketed at each end by two mysterious songs performed by Three Musicians. The first song, with which the play opens, begins thus:

> Motionless under the moon-beam,
> Up to his feathers in the stream;
> Although fish leap, the white heron
> Shivers in a dumbfounded dream. (*Plays*, p. 329)

The refrain, sung by the Second Musician, is "God has not died for the white heron."

In his own note, Yeats explains that "I use birds as symbols of subjective life. ... Certain birds, especially as I see things, such lonely birds as the heron, hawk, eagle, and swan, are the natural symbols of subjectivity. ... I have used my bird-symbolism in these songs to increase the objective loneliness of Christ by contrasting it with a loneliness, opposite in kind, that unlike His can be, whether joyous or sorrowful, sufficient to itself" (*Plays*, p. 696). At the same time, as we have seen, Christ's sympathy cannot extend to Judas or Lazarus, nor his assistance to the soldiers. This leaves him seeming both isolated and very particular in His isolation, in a way that makes it problematic to see Him as God, even though He is touched by divinity.

The Resurrection briefly brings onto the stage the figure of Christ, but He is given no speech. This is dramatically appropriate in a play that revolves around the question of how to conceive of the risen Christ. Three characters – the Hebrew, the Greek, and the Syrian – are given opinions on this question, opinions characteristic of their respective cultures. The Greek thinks that Christ, since he was a "god," must have been a spirit: "No god has ever been buried; no god has ever suffered. Christ only seemed to be born, only seemed to eat, seemed to sleep, seemed to walk, seemed to die." (*Plays*, p. 484) The Hebrew, from a religious culture not rich in notions of an afterlife, but hopeful of a Messiah, concludes that "He was nothing more than a man" (*Plays*, p. 484). The Syrian, however, not only arrives having heard the testimony of the two Marys (*Plays*, p. 488), but also has a clearer grasp of the truth as Yeats understands it: it is, perhaps, appropriate that Syria is geographically situated between Greece and Palestine, since his position can be seen as a synthesis of the other two. He believes that Christ is physically risen. In this, of course, he is orthodox, as is Yeats. "What matter if it contradicts all human knowledge?" (*Plays*, p. 489). Yeats's orthodoxy, though, is heavily qualified. For he does not think that such an intervention of spirit in the material world, and in material form, is unique: on the contrary, it is the characteristic form of the beginning of each new era. Yeats explains this in the section of *A Vision* called "Dove or Swan."[29] The Swan of Zeus instigates the classical epoch by impregnating Leda, as recalled in Yeats's "Leda and the Swan" (P, pp. 214–15). Leda gives birth to Castor and Pollux and to Helen. Castor and Pollux, by being twins, symbolize division; and Helen, by being beautiful, brings about the conflict of the Trojan War. Thus it is that an antithetical era of violence and heroism comes into being. By contrast, the Dove of the Holy Spirit, who impregnates Mary, ushers in an epoch that pursues the ideal of peace. These creatures will be succeeded by other bestial incarnations, the first of which may perhaps be one fit to give birth to a "rough beast." Each miraculous birth is only one of a series. Indeed, miraculous deaths may also, Yeats suggests, constitute a series. *The Resurrection* has a song at each end, and the opening song begins thus:

> I saw a staring virgin stand
> Where holy Dionysus died,
> And tear the heart out of his side,
> And lay the heart upon her hand
> And bear that beating heart away;
> And then did all the Muses sing
> Of Magnus Annus at the spring,
> As though God's death were but a play. (*Plays*, pp. 481–2)

In context, the intention is clear: to indicate a similarity between the myths of Dionysus and Christ. The point is emphasized by the appearance of the worshippers of Dionysus on the streets below the room where the action of the play takes place (*Plays*, p. 486) Both are dying gods. They differ in being characteristic of two contrasting eras, the pagan classical and the Christian. Dionysus's death and resurrection affirm the eternal recurrence of sexuality and the cycle of birth, death, and regeneration, and imply that the world of the gods mirrors this. Christ's death represents a moral self-abnegation occasioned by what Yeats would call his "pity," and the spiritual regeneration that may be consequent upon that. But whatever symbolic death may seem appropriate to the coming antithetical era, it will be more like that of Dionysus than that of Christ: such is the logic of the "Magnus Annus" (Great Year). For, as the song goes on to explain, "Another Troy must rise and set, / Another lineage feed the crow, / Another Argo's painted prow / Drive to a flashier bauble yet." On the other hand, the death of Christ shares something with the death of Dionysus: it exemplifies the union of what Yeats elsewhere calls "Demon and Beast" (P, pp. 185–7), the union of blood and the supernatural that is the true form of revelation, and that embodies a power far stronger than abstract thought. As the final song informs us, "Odour of blood when Christ was slain / Made all Platonic tolerance vain / And vain all Doric discipline." (*Plays*, p. 492) For, as the song goes on to explain, "Whatever flames upon the night / Man's own resinous heart has fed." With such a belief, Yeats can indeed accept the miraculous, including the resurrection of Christ, as an example of the passionately close relationship of spirit and matter. He makes this point most clearly in the poem "Vacillation" (P, 249–53), from *The Winding Stair and Other Poems* (1933): "The body of Saint Teresa lies undecayed in tomb, / Bathed in miraculous oil, sweet odours from it come, / Healing from its lettered slab." Nevertheless, having already explained that Homer's theme was original sin, he proceeds to affirm that "Homer is my example and his unchristened heart." Yeats's work makes it clear that there are occurrences of miracles outside Christianity, and in any case, his loyalty is to the affirmation of life and the singing, like Homer, of original sin. Indeed, in section VIII of "Vacillation," in a dialogue of "The Soul" and "The Heart," he contrasts Homer with Isaiah: "*The Soul*: Isaiah's coal, what more can man desire? / *The Heart*: Struck dumb in the simplicity of fire!" Isaiah himself may not have been dumb, but Yeats cannot see the point of a song that denies the variety and complexity of a life not limited by an ideal of holiness and rectitude. Yeats's esoteric Christianity does no more than concede that Christianity is true in the way that any religion must be true, according to him. At the same time, it is not even the right kind of religion, since, in what he sees as the great choice between life-denying and life-affirming faith, he thinks that Christianity belongs to the former, while one must choose the latter.

Notes

1   Dwight H. Purdy, *Biblical Echo and Allusion in the Poetry of W. B. Yeats: Poetics and the Art of God* (Bucknell University Press, Lewisburg, 1994), p. 24.
2   Ibid., p. 26.
3   Terence Brown, *The Life of W. B. Yeats* (Blackwell, Oxford, 1999), p. 10.
4   John Kelly, ed, assoc. ed Eric Domville, *The Collected Letters of W. B. Yeats*, I (Clarendon Press, Oxford, 1986), pp. 117–18.
5   Anna Kingsford, *The Credo of Chrisitanity and Other Addresses and Essays on Esoteric Chrisitanity and Some Letters by Edward Maitland*, ed. Samuel Hopgood Hart (John M. Watkins, London, 1916), p. 206.
6   Ibid.
7   David V. Erdman, ed., *The Complete Poetry and Prose of William Blake*, rev. edn (Doubleday, New York, 1988), p. 618.
8   Kingsford, *Credo*, p. 119.
9   Ibid., p. 89.
10 Purdy, *Biblical Echo*, p. 26.
11 Ibid.
12 For Yeats and Rosicrucianism, see Edward Larrissy, *Yeats the Poet: The Measures of Difference* (Harvester Wheatsheaf, Hemel Hempstead, 1994), pp. 61, 143–4.
13 For thoughts on Yeats and Freemasonry, see Larrissy, *Yeats the Poet*, pp. 17–22, 167–9.
14 See R. F. Foster, *W. B. Yeats: A Life*, I, *The Apprentice Mage 1865–1914* (Oxford University Press, Oxford, 1997), p. 117.
15 Arthur Edward Waite, *The Real History of the Rosicrucians* (George Redway, London, 1887), p. 434.
16 Richard J. Finneran, ed., *The Collected Works of W. B. Yeats*, I, *The Poems*, 2nd edn (Macmillan, New York, 1989), p. 31. Subsequent references to *The Collected Works* are given in the main text as P, followed by page numbers.
17 Kathleen Raine, "Yeats and the Creed of St Patrick," in *Yeats the Initiate: Essays on Certain Themes in the Work of W. B. Yeats* (Dolmen, Portlaoise, 1986), pp. 379–99.
18 Louise Imogen Guiney, ed., *James Clarence Mangan, His Selected Poems* (Lamson, Wolffe & Co., Boston, 1897), pp. 123, 125.
19 *Lyra Celtica: An Anthology of Representative Celtic Poetry*, ed. E. A. Sharp and J. Matthay, intro. and notes W. Sharp, reprint of 2nd edn of 1924 (John Grant, Edinburgh, 1932), p. 3 (1st edn 1896).
20 Ibid.
21 John Rhys, *Lectures on the Origin and Growth of Religion as Illustrated by Celtic Heathendom* (Williams and Norgate, London 1888), p. 224.
22 Colin Wilson, *Aleister Crowley: The Nature of the Beast* (Aquarian Press, Wellingborough, 1987), p. 41.
23 Robert Macoy, *A General History, Cyclopedia and Dictionary of Freemasonry* (Masonic Publishing Company, New York, 1869), p.1 70.
24 W. J. McCormack, *Blood Kindred. W. B. Yeats: The Life, the Death, The Politics* (Pimlico, London, 2005), p. 112.

25   W. B. Yeats, *A Vision* (privately printed by T. Werner Laurie, London, 1925), p. 169. Future references to this, the first edition of *A Vision*, are given in the main text as AVA followed by the page numbers.
26   And see also the second edition: W. B. Yeats, *A Vision* (Macmillan, London, 1937), p. 275.
27   Peter Ure, "Yeats's Christian Mystery Plays," *RES*, n.s. 11 (1960), 171–82.
28   W. B. Yeats, *The Plays*, ed. David R. Clark and Rosalind E. Clark, *The Collected Works of W. B. Yeats*, II (Palgrave, Basingstoke, 2001), p. 329. Future references are given in the main text as *Plays*, followed by page numbers.
29   Yeats, *A Vision*, 2nd edn, pp. 265–300.

Select Bibliography

Brown, Terence (1999) *The Life of W. B. Yeats*. Blackwell, Oxford.

Foster, R. F. (1997) *W. B. Yeats: A Life, I, The Apprentice Mage 1865–1914*. Oxford University Press, Oxford.

Kingsford, Anna (1916) *The Credo of Chrisitanity and Other Addresses and Essays on Esoteric Chrisitanity and Some Letters by Edward Maitland*, ed Samuel Hopgood Hart. John M. Watkins, London.

Larrissy, Edward (1994) *Yeats the Poet: The Measures of Difference*. Harvester Wheatsheaf, Hemel Hempstead.

Purdy, Dwight H. (1994) *Biblical Echo and Allusion in the Poetry of W. B. Yeats: Poetics and the Art of God*. Bucknell University Press, Lewisburg.

Raine, Kathleen (1986) "Yeats and the Creed of St Patrick," in *Yeats the Initiate: Essays on Certain Themes in the Work of W. B. Yeats*. Dolmen, Portlaoise, pp. 379–99.

Ure, Peter (1960) "Yeats's Christian Mystery Plays," *RES*, n.s. 11, 171–82.

CHAPTER 45
Virginia Woolf

Douglas L. Howard

At first glance, Virginia Woolf's interest in the Bible seems passing, at best, and with good reason. Her father, Leslie Stephen, a man whom she proudly described as "the muscular agnostic" (Woolf, 1985b, p. 115), had, after all, partly built his reputation on his attacks upon the sacred text. Woolf herself, moreover, was frequently outspoken in her contempt for religious belief – "we *do* believe," she wrote to Vita Sackville-West in 1936, "not in God though: not one anyhow" (Woolf, 1975–80, p. 377) – and, through characters such as Eleanor Pargiter in *The Years*, she (sounding very much like her father in his essay "The Scepticism of Believers": Stephen, 1893, p. 53) questioned the validity of the Bible as the basis of faith: "It was what one man said under a fig tree, on a hill. ... And then another man wrote it down. But suppose that what that man says is just as false as what this [journalist] says?" (Woolf, 1965, p. 154). In preparation for her next book, *Reading at Random* or *Turning the Page*, in the last few months before her death, Woolf even critiqued the Bible's use of language and condemned its impact on other writers: "The biblical style [is] limited & emphatic" (Silver, 1979, p. 378), she concluded and, in her essay "Anon," she warned that, "when familiar letters are written in Biblical prose, there is a limit to what can be put into words" (Woolf, 1979, p. 389). But for all of these criticisms and rejections, the Bible appears in Woolf with curious frequency. She can never completely dismiss it. Biblical references crop up in her correspondences and diary entries, and biblical patterns appear in her fiction that suggest a strange ambivalence toward it and an odd preoccupation with it, a preoccupation that, perhaps, belies some larger, more personal spiritual struggle within the author herself.

Bible Study

The Bible was clearly a controversial text for both of Woolf's parents. Not only did her father consistently criticize its authority as a sacred text, but Woolf's mother, Julia, was able to come to grips with her own loss of faith in religion and the Bible by reading Stephen's essays "in the years of her bereavement" (Lee, 1998, p. 93). Raised in this strongly agnostic household, Woolf was admittedly skeptical of religion from a young age, but, in thinking about her childhood years later, she had vague recollections of her mother breaking rank: "Once when she had set us to write exercises I looked up from mine and watched her reading – the Bible perhaps; struck by the gravity of her face, [I] told myself that her first husband had been a clergyman and that she was thinking, as she read, what he had read, of him" (Woolf, 1985b, p. 82). Woolf maintained that this memory "was a fable on [her] part" (ibid.), but Mitchell Leaska (1998, p. 43) suggests that, during her marriage to Leslie Stephen, Julia "was still *in love* with Herbert Duckworth" and so may well have found some comfort in reading through the Bible and remembering her first husband. And even a teenage Virginia, like her mother, considered the possibility of faith and planned on developing "a long picturesque essay upon the Christian religion ... proving that man has need of a God" (Woolf, 1977–84, 3, p. 271; hereafter cited as *Diary*), a demonstration, according to Louise DeSalvo (1989, p. 244), of her "independent thinking" and her ability to "challenge her father's system of belief."

Ultimately, though, Woolf went on to question the existence of God like her father and, at times, seemed to go even further, as she atheistically affirmed, in *Moments of Being*, that "certainly and emphatically there is no God" (p. 72). But the Bible still remained and, rather than abandon it, she continued to read and discuss it. In preparation for the family vacation to Salisbury in 1903, Woolf wrote in her journal that she began "putting aside books in [her] mind, to read in the summer, about October, Shakespeare for instance & the Bible" (Woolf, 1990, p. 178). After misquoting the Book of Ruth, Woolf expressed a desire, in a letter later that year, to her friend and confidante Violet Dickinson to know her "Holy Bible better" (Woolf, 1975–80, 1, p. 96; hereafter cited as *Letters*). In 1919, Woolf reported that she and Leonard listened to author Logan Pearsall Smith "read ... his stories from the bible" (*Diary*, 4, p. 282), which the Woolfs subsequently published through their Hogarth Press as *Stories from the Old Testament* in 1920. During "one of [her] last teas" with her friend and tutor Janet Case and her sister Emphie at their home in Hampstead that same year, Woolf noted that the suggested topics of conversation included "Cellini and the Bible" (*Diary*, 2, p. 50). According to Nigel Nicolson, Woolf "found time for the Old Testament" while she was starting to write *Mrs Dalloway*, but was critical of the Book of Job inasmuch as "God [did not come] well out of it" (*Diary*, 2, p. 80). Shortly after the completion of "the Dr chapter," she even quoted Psalm 100 in her diary, considering that "It is He that has made us, not we ourselves. I like that text" (*Diary*, 2, pp. 300–1). Woolf told Ethel Smyth that a walk in the country in 1932 put her "in a biblical frame of mind" (*Letters*, 4, p. 105). Leaska (1998, p. 349) notes that, from the various personal and professional issues in her life, "She had every reason to read 'rather vainly' the Book of Job" again in 1933. She was also reading the Bible for enjoyment as well as for inspiration during the writing of *The Pargiters*, although Nicolson (2000, p. 142) is quick to point out that she was interested mainly in "its language, not its doctrine." In a January 1935 diary entry, Woolf reminded herself, in fact, that she had to "buy the Old Testament" and reported that she was "reading the Acts of the Apostles [to illuminate] that dark spot in [her] reading" (*Diary*, 4, p. 271). This reading may also have been prompted by her friendship with Ethel Smyth, who was a Christian and who appeared to have encouraged Woolf's reading in this regard. (Two of Woolf's most important friendships, in fact, were with religious women, Smyth and Violet Dickinson.) In a 1935 letter, Woolf reassured

Ethel that she was reading the Bible and "the New Testament; so don't call me a heathen in the future" (*Letters*, 362); in another letter a few weeks later, she marvelled at "what a magnificent book it [was]" (*Letters*, 366). The Bible also became a topic of conversation during a 1938 dinner with Clive Bell and the novelist Janice Loeb, and Woolf noted that, from their discussion of "the word broken in the Bible [Leonard Woolf] read passages" (*Letters*, 187).

Woolf mentioned the Bible in a number of her non-fiction works as well. The highest praise that she could give Hardy's characters in her 1928 essay on "The Novels of Thomas Hardy" was that "Their speech ha[d] a Biblical dignity and poetry" (Woolf, 1966–7, 1, p. 263). Arguing passionately, Woolf used the Bible most directly in her 1938 *Three Guineas* to make her case against those patriarchal institutions that turned "the daughters of educated men" into a "Society of Outsiders." If their contributions to society were acknowledged and if women could be paid a living wage by the State for their professions, including "marriage and motherhood" (Woolf, 1966, p. 111), they would, she maintained, go on to review and reform other social institutions like religion, to read "the New Testament in the first place and ... make it their business to have some knowledge of the Christian religion and its history" (p. 112). If religion was found wanting, Woolf foresaw women, in these circumstances, helping "to create a new religion based, it might well be, upon the New Testament, but, it might well be, very different from the religion erected upon that basis" (p. 113). In either case, in her more pointed critique of the Church of England and the Report of the Archbishops' Commission on the Ministry of Women, she was quick to defend the Bible itself and to point out that the interpretation, as opposed to the text itself, was ultimately what was in question:

> What the Christian religion is has been laid down once and for all by the founder of the religion in words that can be read by all in a translation of singular beauty; and whether or not we accept the interpretation that has been put on them, we cannot deny them to be words of the most profound meaning. (p. 121)

Although she could have condemned the Bible as the basis for the oppression that had alienated women from society, Woolf instead placed the blame on those religious authorities who imposed their own dogmas on the sacred text. In the notes to her book, she went even further, specifically arguing that the Bible was "unreadable" not so much because of the way in which it had been written, but because of the way in which its readings had been prescribed and directed by the Church: "those who have not been forced from childhood to hear it thus dismembered weekly assert that the Bible is a work of the greatest interest, much beauty, and deep meaning" (p. 180n).

The Search for Paradise

Whatever personal or aesthetic value she found in the Bible, Woolf clearly had a sense of the milestones of biblical history in her fiction, and biblical references or allusions to this end functioned as a kind of spiritual vernacular through which she typically expressed and charted the development of her characters on a metaphysical level. We clearly see this development in the portrait of Rachel Vinrace in her first novel, *The Voyage Out*. Amidst all the conversations about religion and faith – Helen Ambrose tells Willoughby Vinrace that she "would rather [her] children told lies" (Woolf, 1948, p. 27) than believe in any religion, and Mrs Dalloway compares religion to "collecting beetles" (p. 56) – St John Hirst conceives that Rachel Vinrace most likely has only read "Shakespeare and the Bible" (p. 154) (Woolf's Summer reading for 1903) and is horrified to learn that Rachel may believe in God. As Rachel observes the congregation during the church service, she is struck by how people blindly "accepted the ideas that the words gave as representing goodness ... in the same way ... as one of those industrious needlewomen had accepted the bright ugly pattern on her mat as representing beauty" (p. 227). From this experience, she rejects Christianity, yet the novel ironically still toys with the possibility of biblical imagery and biblical metaphors. (Christine Froula (1988, p. 212), in fact, calls it Woolf's "*first* rewriting of Genesis"; italics added.)

Whatever experiences she may have had of life, Rachel is still an "innocent" to the extent that she has never been in love, yet she clearly pays a price in order to enjoy this experience. Walking out into the valley to read before lunch, Rachel curiously stops in front of a "strange" tree, "so strange that it might have been the only tree in the world" (Woolf, 1948, p. 174), a curious emphasis on both Woolf's and Rachel's part that recalls the tree of knowledge in Genesis. From her reading of Gibbon, Rachel becomes excited at the possibility that "all knowledge would be hers" (p. 175) and wonders about the nature of love. Prior to their expedition on the river and out into the jungle, Helen Ambrose is prophetically "shaken" by the way relationships are changing among the group, "as if beneath dead leaves she had seen the movement of a snake" (p. 263); later, when Rachel and Terence Hewet leave the rest of the party to go for a walk and admit their love, Hirst, along the same lines, warns them to "Beware of snakes" (p. 270), although the real temptation, in this case, may be something more internal and emotional and perhaps even more difficult to deny. In the jungle, Terence throws some fruit into the air, with the condition that he will begin his conversation with Rachel (and talk about their love) once the fruit has "dropped" (p. 271), and "Eden's legacy," as Froula (1988, p. 212) points out, "is felt in the heavy silence that weighs them down." Shortly thereafter, as they start to talk of marriage, Rachel feels Helen's hand upon her shoulder like "a bolt from heaven" (Woolf, 1948, p. 283), and, from her initial headache, Rachel falls prey to the fever that kills her. If love does, as Hirst believes, indeed "explain everything" (p. 312), then Rachel has acquired that knowledge, but tasting that forbidden fruit brings death into the world for her, just as it does for Adam and Eve and their progeny in the Bible.

If Woolf is thinking of a biblical cycle in the novel, then there may also be some subtle suggestions of the New Testament and of Christ here, as there most certainly are in texts like *Mrs Dalloway*. While Saint John, in his Gospel, proclaims that "the Word was God" (1:1), "St John" Hirst sarcastically bothers Helen with his poem that "practically proved that God did exist" (p. 278) and, from his contemplation of Rachel and Terence, goes on to preach his doctrine of "love" as the explanation for everything. During her fever, Rachel has visions of "an old woman slicing a man's head off with a knife" (p. 339), a beheading that could be connected to John the Baptist, who was killed by Herod through the indirect prompting of his brother's wife Herodias. Following her death, Ridley Ambrose thinks about Christ and Milton's poem "On the Morning of Christ's Nativity," and, in a strange way, Rachel is resurrected, as Evelyn Murgatroyd is "positive [that she is] not dead" (p. 362) and that she feels "Rachel in the room with her" (p. 364). If Rachel is "sacrificed" for a specific purpose, it may well be so that, in the same way that Mrs Dalloway reconsiders the meaning of life following the news of Septimus's death, the remaining tourists and travelers realize the importance of love and appreciate the value of their own lives as a result, a value that is naturally reiterated through "the flashing light" and "the broad illumination" (p. 374) that ends the novel.

Perhaps Woolf's most pronounced and effective use of biblical metaphors and biblical history, as I have argued in "Virginia Woolf's Redemptive Cycle," occurs in her 1925 novel *Mrs Dalloway*. While Clarissa and her party guests prepare for the evening's activities, they all nostalgically contemplate an Edenic past, when they were younger and felt that they were perfectly understood, in some way, by someone else. Throughout the day, Clarissa remembers that summer at Bourton, with its "walled-in" garden (Woolf, 1953, p. 114), among the hollyhocks and the dahlias "and the rooks rising, falling" (p. 3). She was a young woman, "lovely in girlhood" (p. 46), innocent, and knowing "nothing about sex [or] social problems" (p. 49). And she remembers her "religious" love for Sally Seton, a feeling that could only exist between women, women just grown up" (p. 50), that culminated in a kiss. Peter Walsh similarly remembers Bourton, "when he was so passionately in love with Clarissa" (p. 88) and how they used to go "in and out of each other's minds without any effort" (p. 94). Lady Bruton daydreams about her childhood in Devonshire with her brothers among "the beds of dahlias, the hollyhocks, the pampas grass" (p. 169), while Septimus considers how he "flowered" from "the usual seeds" (p. 128) into adulthood.

Sadly, though, these Edenic moments of youthful potential do not last, but only anticipate a fall into adulthood and the burden of mortality. As with Rachel Vinrace, for some of the characters, love leads, in part, to their fall. Clarissa suggests that "Love destroy[s]" (p. 192), and Septimus's wife Rezia thinks "To love makes one solitary" (p. 33). Both Clarissa and Peter think about their break-up "in the little garden by the fountain" (p. 10) at Bourton, a break that, she believes, was for their own good, but that nevertheless marked the beginning of their adult lives. For Clarissa, this leads to her marriage to Dalloway and to her failure to fulfill her sexual role as his wife. Peter likewise believes that he has become "a failure" (p. 64) after Bourton. Not only has he been sent down from Oxford, but his first marriage, to a woman that he "met on the boat going to India" (p. 10), is about to end in divorce, and he is involved in an illicit relationship with Daisy, "the wife of a Major in the Indian army" (p. 67). Septimus's feelings for Evans during the war may also be the cause for his fall. Although he is initially proud of himself for "feeling very little and very reasonably" (p. 130) about Evans's death, shortly thereafter, in Milan, he panics from the belief that "he [is] falling" (p. 131). Clarissa saw her "own sister killed by a falling tree" (p. 117), and in this conjunction of loss of innocence, mortality, and a fatal tree, Woolf could well be thinking of Genesis here, too.

Most of the characters in the novel have also fallen, in some way, as a result of the Great War, and they consistently refer to the negative impact that the war has had on their lives. Septimus is no longer the same after Evans is killed "just before the Armistice" (p. 130) and believes that "in the War itself he had failed" (p. 145). His wife Rezia maintains that "Every one has friends who died in the War" (p. 99). Mrs Foxcroft eats "her heart out because that nice boy was killed"; Lady Bexborough "open[s] a bazaar ... with the telegram in her hand, "John, her favorite, killed" (p. 5). Miss Kilman loses her teaching job at Miss Dolby's school, even though "her brother had been killed," because of her family's German origins as well as, "because she would not pretend that all Germans were villains" (p. 187). Mr Brewer thinks that the war is responsible for smashing "a plaster cast of Ceres, [ploughing] a hole in the geranium beds, and utterly [ruining] the cook's nerves" (p. 130). Even Clarissa laments that, "before the War, you could buy almost perfect gloves" (p. 15).

And with the fall, time marches on, and they all feel their mortality. Big Ben rings in "the hours, irrevocable." Clarissa feels "unspeakably aged" (p. 11). Evelyn Whitbread has "some internal ailment" (p. 7). Peter Walsh is desperate to believe that "he [is] not old" (p. 64). Dozing off on her sofa – dozing off like so many of the characters in the novel that day who feel the passage of time – Lady Bruton considers passing on Clarissa's party because "she [is] getting old" (p. 168). Clarissa's husband Richard encourages her to take "An hour's complete rest after luncheon ... because a doctor had ordered it once" (p. 181). Peter "[sinks] into the plumes and feathers of sleep" (p. 85) in Regent's Park, just like Septimus, who rests there before his visit to Sir William Bradshaw. Even Richard "must" yawn while Hugh Whitbread shops for his wife.

But, while human nature comes for the fallen and brings "death" (p. 138), to the wretched, Septimus comes, like Christ, to repair the damage of the fall and to die, in effect, for the sins of the fallen. Septimus, "suffering for ever, the scapegoat, the eternal sufferer" (p. 37), in fact, tells Bradshaw that "he is Christ" (p. 150) and that he has a message for the prime minister: "first, that trees are alive; next there is no crime; next love, universal love" (p. 102). Where Jesus' sermons represent, in many ways, a departure from pre-existing religious practices and where he "makes a deep impression on people because he [teaches] them with authority, and not like their own scribes" (Matthew 7:28–9), Septimus, with his message, heralds "the birth of a new religion" (p. 33). As Jesus states that he is "the good shepherd ... who lays down his life for his sheep" (John 10:11), Septimus sees "a few sheep" (p. 37) and hears "a shepherd boy's" elegy "played among the traffic" (p. 103) in Regent's Park. We are told that "he had won crosses" (p. 133) during the war. In the same way that John sees "Death and Hades ... emptied of the dead that were in them" (Revelation 20:12) for final judgment, Septimus sees Evans and the rest of the dead rising and wants to tell the world about his "astonishing revelation" (p. 106), a word that is repeated on a number of different occasions and applied to a number of different characters in the novel. And Susan Dick suggests that Septimus's last words prior to his "crucifixion" "on Mrs Filmer's area railings" – "I'll give it to you!" (p. 226) – recall Christ's dying words, "It is finished" (p. 42), just as he kills himself at the same three o'clock hour.

Although Septimus and Clarissa never physically meet, he does have a "second coming" of sorts, as his prophecies are realized through the gathering of guests at her party and as Clarissa "resurrects" Septimus by considering the meaning of his suicide at length. The dead suddenly do rise and come back to life. While Peter Walsh was "quite certain she was dead" (p. 287), Aunt Helena Parry shows up and "is placed in a chair" (p. 271). Thinking about Sally Seton and her behavior, Clarissa admits that she thought that it would "end in some awful tragedy; her death; her martyrdom" (p. 277), but she too is reborn as Lady Rosseter, the mother of "five enormous boys" (p. 261). A new Paradise is created. In praising her hostess's accommodations, Mrs Hilbery tells Clarissa that they are "surrounded by an enchanted garden" (p. 291), and "the yellow curtains with all the birds of Paradise" (p. 256) on them blow back and forth from the window, simulating their flight. And, as she stares at the old lady in the room opposite putting "out her light" (p. 283), Clarissa fully appreciates the enormity of Septimus's sacrifice that afternoon and feels "the beauty" and "the fun" of life" (p. 284). Through his death, Septimus helps her recommit to life.

Moreover, if, as Clarissa believes, "the unseen part of us ... might survive, be recovered somehow attached to this person or that" (p. 232), then Septimus does survive through Clarissa. Though the "obscurely evil" (p. 281) Sir William Bradshaw is intent on stamping out "the prophetic Christs and Christesses" (p. 150) of the world, Clarissa becomes that feminized "Christess" who completes his mission. Her party is her sacrifice, her "offering for the sake of offering" (p. 185) that makes the dead rise. She meets the prime minister when he arrives. She brings all the various characters in the novel together for the evening, and, perhaps, in doing so, she conveys his message of universal love. Thus, while the apocalypse does take place at her party and while death appears and judgments are made, John's visions in Revelation are reinvented and rescaled; this biblical story also ends in rebirth, as it applies to Clarissa and her guests, who come to some new understandings about their pasts, presents, and futures.

The biblical echoes of *To the Lighthouse* also begin with the potential of youth. Through his childhood vision of the world, James Ramsay has the ability to "[endow] the picture of a refrigerator ... with heavenly bliss" (Woolf, 1955, p. 9), and his imagination sees possibility and "wonder" (p. 9) in their trip to the lighthouse, which he later remembers as an Edenic "garden where there was none of this gloom" (pp. 275–6). But it is a possibility that the adult perceptions of his father must destroy, "making ['that happy world'] shrivel and fall" (p. 276). "The child's paradise" DiBattista explains, must "fall before the oppressive figure of the father" (p. 88), and, as the novel initially develops, within the adult fallen world, so many of its characters are alone and unsatisfied. The lonely atheist Tansley can only take a momentary pleasure in walking with Mrs Ramsay, who thinks that he is an "odious little man" (p. 26). Mr Ramsay is alienated from his children and particularly despised by James, whose dream he consistently crushes. Lily Briscoe, like the other characters in the novel (and in *Mrs Dalloway*) longs for "unity" (p. 79) with Mrs Ramsay, but is unable to legitimately achieve it. And as Louise Poresky (1981, p. 138) argues, Mr Ramsay "boom[ing] tragically" at Lily and Mr Bankes in the garden also recalls the Genesis story and "Adam and Eve, after their fall, when they hear God's voice as he walks through the garden." Though Ramsay is thinking more of himself here, the scenario works as yet another reminder to the reader that Woolf's characters are operating within a fallen world.

From the bickering rooks that she calls "Joseph" and "Mary" to her central role in the novel and her continual attempts to create unity, Mrs Ramsay becomes that "Christess" who would repair the damage of the fall and sacrifice herself so that the child's vision can be realized apocalyptically. Throughout "The Window," Mrs Ramsay is presented as a character dedicated to sacrificing herself for the happiness of others. As the morose Mr Ramsay continues to predict rain for their trip, Mrs Ramsay considers that "her husband required sacrifices" (p. 28). She also thinks about "this desire of hers to give" (p. 65), and, during her "last supper," she feels compelled to take responsibility for "the effort of merging and flowing and creating" (p. 126) and getting her boarders and dinner guests to interact.

While Mrs Ramsay dies in "Time Passes," her death, her sacrifice, is what ultimately makes the Ramsay family's trip and Lily's painting possible and successful at the end of the novel. As she waits for that "great revelation" (p. 240) of the meaning of life, Lily does her best to conjure up or resurrect Mrs Ramsay, who seems to sit next to Lily while she paints and returns "raising to her forehead a wreath of white flowers with which she went" (p. 269; see Overcarsh, 1950, p. 117). Through her contemplation of the power and influence of Mrs Ramsay, Lily, whose name prophetically foreshadows Mrs Ramsay's death as well as her return, has a sense of the landscape that is as much original as it is apocalyptic: "Here sitting on the world, ... she could not shake herself free from the sense that everything was happening for the first time, perhaps for the last time, as a traveller ... knows, looking out of the train window, that he must look now, for he will never see that town ... again" (p. 288). And, as Mrs Ramsay's "prophet" or "apostle," Lily, like Mrs Dalloway, completes her own original aesthetic vision and the aesthetic vision of the Christess Mrs Ramsay by giving of herself to Mr Ramsay and by finishing the painting that she began in the first section of the novel. As both these goals are realized, she, twice, refers to Christ's final words, "It is finished" (p. 310), words that Mrs Ramsay herself essentially parallels when she euphorically stares at the lighthouse earlier and repeatedly affirms, "It is enough" (p. 100).

In the process of completing their voyage, Mr Ramsay now praises James for steering the boat, and Cam half consciously conceives of the religious image of "a pale blue censer swinging rhythmically this way and that across her mind" and sees "a hanging garden; ... a valley, full of birds, and flowers, and antelopes" (p. 303), perhaps an apocalyptic vision akin to a "paradise regained" or the "new Jerusalem" that John envisions in Revelation 21:2. While James and his siblings were unable to make the journey and go to the lighthouse earlier, Mrs Ramsay's death and their family tragedies now demand their "unity" and inspire the trip, as the potential and possibility of youth is accomplished or "finished" through their arrival at this destination.

Woolf more dramatically and directly juxtaposes this biblical cycle with the contemporary course of human events in *The Waves*. The landscape description of the coming day – "The sun had not yet risen. The sea was indistinguishable from the sky, except that the sea was slightly creased as if a cloth had wrinkles in it" (Woolf, 1959, p. 7) – is clearly reminiscent of the opening of Genesis, of the light that God creates amidst the "formless void" and the "darkness over the deep" (1:2). As he considers their childhood later on in the novel, Bernard similarly recalls Genesis with his suggestion that, "In the beginning, there was the nursery, with windows opening on to a garden, and beyond that the sea" (p. 239), and Poresky (1981, p. 209) also believes that unity characterizes the prelapsarian state of Woolf's protagonists in the novel, inasmuch as, "In the nursery no self-consciousness separates the children." From the garden in the opening scene, the children all fall into adulthood, individuality, and jealousy, as Louis and Jinny's kiss infuriates Susan, and Bernard thinks about how their teachers take them "for fallen trees" (Woolf, 1959, p. 23). Where Louis has "a belt fastened by a brass snake" (p. 12), Jinny compares her hand to "a snake's skin" and Bernard's face to "an apple tree" (p. 23), and Neville, traumatized by the story about the dead man found in the gutter, thinks about how they are all doomed "by the apple trees, by the immitigable tree which [they] cannot pass" (p. 25).

Where Woolf turns Christ into a mentally ill war veteran in *Mrs Dalloway*, he appears in *The Waves* in the figure of the popular Percival, who is known only through the descriptions of the other characters. Neville notices him in the chapel just after thinking about seeing representations of Christ and Mary in Rome during Easter, and, watching the other students following him out of the chapel, Louis remarks that "his faithful servants [will] be shot like sheep, for he will certainly attempt some forlorn enterprise and die in battle" (p. 37). Years later, as the group dines together "to say good-bye to Percival, who goes to India" (p. 116), Neville's description of his arrival, as Lucio Ruotolo (1986, p. 156) notes, "recalls the Last Supper": "This is the place to which he is coming. This is the table at which he will sit. Here, incredible as it seems, will be his actual body" (Woolf, 1959, p. 118). Although he dismisses the idea, Bernard even wonders if they have been "drawn into this *communion* by [their] 'love of Percival'" (p. 126, italics added). And, in imagining his success in India, Bernard goes on to see him in both comically inflated and inspiring terms. Advancing on his "flea-bitten mare," the imperialistic Percival succeeds "by applying the standards of the West, by using the violent language that is natural to him" (p. 136) and, absurdly, single-handedly solves "the Oriental problem." By the same token, "the multitudes cluster round him, regarding him as if he were – what indeed he is – a God" (p. 136).

In contrast to Septimus's violent, bloody escape from Bradshaw, Percival dies when he is thrown from his horse, a freak accident, as Neville points out, that could have been prevented if someone had just "pulled the strap three holes tighter" (p. 152). Nevertheless, his death is a tragedy that impacts the other characters dramatically for the rest of the novel. Bernard mourns in the gallery near "the blue madonna streaked with tears" (p. 157). Rhoda casts her violets into the ocean as her "offer to Percival" (p. 164). Neville remembers their "last supper," "when their lives were all potential and they "could have been anything" (p. 214). Although Percival is not physically resurrected, he, like Septimus, does return through memory, as the characters continue to think about him. At the end of the novel, from his thoughts of Percival, Bernard is struck by the way in which "the dead leap out ... at street corners, or in dreams" (p. 274), and, as death approaches, he prepares for it by thinking of Percival's example, "when he galloped in India" (p. 297). Identifying the strong apocalyptic overtones at the end of the novel, Jane de Gay (2006, p. 181) sees biblical references in "the picture of Bernard riding against death on horseback, for Revelation depicts a battle in which kings and warriors and the 'Beast' are destroyed by a shadowy, god-like figure on horseback." Moreover, from this apocalyptic movement, Bernard perceives "Another general awakening" and acknowledges "the eternal renewal" (Woolf, 1959, pp. 296–7). As Maria DiBattista (1980, p. 187) explains, the landscape descriptions that frame the novel are thus "identified with both Genesis and Apocalypse, a creation and an uncovering ... of the real cycles in natural and human history," and, in coming to the end of this day, Bernard, like his friends and like Clarissa Dalloway, essentially comes to a biblical ending that is at once a new beginning, a new rise, and a new Genesis.

Christina Froula (2005, p. 198) maintains that Woolf was rewriting Eden "over the twenty-five-year span of her novels," and, even in later novels such as *Orlando* and *Flush*, Woolf finds a way to incorporate the search for Paradise into her character's lives and to contrast it with their specific circumstances. For the female Orlando, "The letter S ... is the serpent in [her] Poet's Eden" (Woolf, 1956, p. 173), and, rather than contending with the spiritual consequences of disobedience, Orlando more mundanely struggles to avoid the present participle, "the Devil himself" (p. 173). As Froula (2005, p. 186) explains, "The biblical scapegoating of women for sexuality and sin vanishes from Orlando's Eden, as does sexual hierarchy and even sexual difference." Paradise, instead, boils down to artistic inspiration and good grammar. The narrator of *Flush*, on the other hand, is quick to remind the reader that Browning's energetic cocker spaniel does not live in that Paradise "where essences exist in their utmost purity, and the naked soul of things presses on the naked nerve" (Woolf, 1961, p. 132), but must instead deal with the fallen torment of fleas that forces his owner to cut off his fur.

Like Froula, Natania Rosenfeld (2000, p. 157) also sees Genesis in Woolf's last novel *Between the Acts*, with Isa and Giles Oliver as "the new Adam and Eve." As the troubled couple is finally left alone after Miss La Trobe's pageant ends and the audience goes home, the narrator tells us how this drama will unfold. They will fight. They will embrace. And "From that embrace another life might be born. But first they must fight" (Woolf, 1969, p. 219). For Froula (1988, p. 216) this retelling amounts to a return to that "prehistoric landscape" that Lucy Swithin envisions in her Outline of History, before the creation of culture. Time and history are compressed and deflated (as they have been through the course of the novel and Miss La Trobe's play), as this night becomes "the night before roads were made, or houses" and "the night that dwellers in caves had watched from some high place among rocks" (Woolf, 1969, p. 219). Inasmuch as Woolf acknowledged the cyclical nature of biblical movements, this final Genesis also amounts to an apocalyptic denial or eradication of all that has come before it in the novel, of current events, of history, of culture, of religion (both pagan and Christian), and perhaps even of language, since the novel ends on the rather vague note that "They spoke" (p. 219). The vast allusive scope of the text is virtually eliminated and reduced to this specific moment of marital drama. And it may be fitting, in this regard, that this is Woolf's last retelling because, in *Between the Acts*, she concludes with a Bible story that is, in effect, all her own and free from any potential historical, dogmatic, or denominational trappings that might obscure her message. As opposed to Reverend Streatfield, who, according to Mr Oliver, "excruciate[s]" (p. 203) Miss La Trobe with his interpretation of her play, and those priests that Woolf condemns for "dismembering" the Bible for their listeners on a weekly basis in *Three Guineas*, for Isa and Giles, where the drama goes and how it plays out is up to them solely, and, from an aesthetic as well as spiritual standpoint, this "sacred text" may well represent the realization of Woolf's Edenic vision.

Literature and Dogma

Washington State University currently houses the library of Leonard and Virginia Woolf, which, according to Laila Miletic-Vejzovic, contains all those texts that were "still in the possession of Leonard Woolf before his death in 1969" (King and Miletic-Vejzovic, 2003). The Woolfs not only combined their own personal collections here, but Virginia also inherited a number of books from her father as well as from her mother's first husband Herbert Duckworth. Among the more intriguing aspects of the collection is not so much that the Woolfs had a Bible on their shelves, but rather that they had so many. (At least seventeen are listed in the collection, in fact, along with a copy of Smith's *Stories from the Old Testament* (ibid., p. 3) and Isaac Watts's *A Short View of the Whole Scripture History* signed by her cousin Herbert.) While most of these were probably Leonard's, Diane Gillespie points out that some of them belonged to Virginia, including "a Holy Bible inscribed to [her] by Violet Dickinson, one inscribed to her by Leonard, and two Greek New Testaments, one owned by Leonard and annotated by Virginia" ("Introduction"). The Woolfs also had two copies of Matthew Arnold's *Literature and Dogma* on their shelves, one of which was presented to Leslie Stephen by Arnold himself, and, while the extent of Woolf's interest in Arnold is certainly debatable in a diary entry for May 1929, she reminded herself that she wanted to "read the whole of Matthew Arnold" (*Diary* 3.22), Arnold's argument sets up a binary between religious and cultural readings of the Bible that is perhaps useful in accounting for Woolf's interest in it and for its consistent presence in her work. In the same way that Woolf dismissed religious readings of the Bible in *Three Guineas*, Arnold (2002, p. 302) believed that the Bible had been corrupted through the imposition of religious dogma not in the text and that "the construction [that] theologians [had] put upon [it] to be false." But he also believed that the Bible still had spiritual value that could be gleaned if the reader could process it through the lens of culture and study it with that "tact which letters, surely, alone [could] give" (p. 46). Along these lines, Woolf may have used the Bible as that cultural/metaphorical center through which she could examine spiritual patterns of history, chart her characters' spiritual development, and, ultimately, assess the nature of her own beliefs, beyond her father's or her mother's or her husband's. Within its pages, she may have found the promise of Paradise appealing and elusive and perhaps only briefly tasted in those "moments of being" where Rachel Vinrace finds love and Clarissa Dalloway reaffirms her commitment to life; she may have also found the foundations for those vicious patriarchal dogmas that made women "outsiders" and that inspired sections of her *Three Guineas*. In discussing R. L. Chambers's reading of her, Jean Love (1970, p. 71) refers to Woolf as "a religious person without a religion," and that may likely be the best description of her spiritual background. In her ambivalent and often confrontational relationship with the Bible, we find not so much her attempt to reconcile herself to a specific organizational faith or denomination, but her attempt to define the individual spirituality of a woman in a world of paradises consistently lost and regained.

References

Arnold, Matthew (2002) *Literature and Dogma: An Essay Towards a Better Apprehension of the Bible*. Fredonia Books, Amsterdam.

Chambers, R. L. (1947) *The Novels of Virginia Woolf*. Russell and Russell, New York.

de Gay, Jane (2006) *Virginia Woolf's Novels and the Literary Past*. Edinburgh University Press, Edinburgh.

DeSalvo, Louise (1989) *Virginia Woolf: The Impact of Childhood Sexual Abuse on her Life and Work*. Beacon Press, Boston.

DiBattista, Maria (1980) *Virginia Woolf's Major Novels: The Fables of Anon*. Yale University Press, New Haven, CT.

Dick, Susan (1989) *Virginia Woolf*. Edward Arnold, London.

Fernald, Anne E. (1999) "The Memory Palace of Virginia Woolf," in Sally Greene, ed., *Virginia Woolf: Reading the Renaissance*. Ohio University Press, Athens, pp. 89–114.

Froula, Christina (1988) "Rewriting Genesis: Gender and Culture in Twentieth-Century Texts," *Tulsa Studies in Women's Literature* 7:2, 197–220.

Froula, Christina (2005) *Virginia Woolf and the Bloomsbury Avant-Garde*. Columbia University Press, New York.

Gillespie, Diane F. (2003) "Introduction: Virginia Woolf and Libraries," in Julia King and Laila Miletic-Vejzovic, eds, *The Library of Leonard and Virginia Woolf*. Washington State University Press, Pullman.

Howard, Douglas L. (1998) "*Mrs. Dalloway*: Virginia Woolf's Redemptive Cycle," *Literature and Theology* 12:2, 149–58. My analysis of *Mrs. Dalloway* here is based upon this article.

The Jerusalem Bible (1968) Gen ed. Alexander Jones. Doubleday, Garden City, NY.

King, Julia (2006) "Woolf's Greek Bibles," e-mail, June 27.

King, Julia and Miletic-Vejzovic, Laila, eds (2003) *The Library of Leonard and Virginia Woolf: A Short-Title Catalog*. Washington State University Press, Pullman (http://www.wsulibs.wsu.edu/holland/masc/OnlineBooks/woolflibrary/woolflibraryonline.htm, accessed June 15, 2006).

Leaska, Mitchell A. (1998) *Granite and Rainbow: The Hidden Life of Virginia Woolf*. Farrar, Strauss, and Giroux, New York.

Lee, Hermione (1998) *Virginia Woolf*. Knopf, New York.

Love, Jean O. (1970) *Mythopoetic Thought in the Novels of Virginia Woolf*. California University Press, Berkeley.

Nicolson, Nigel (2000) *Virginia Woolf*. Viking, New York.

Overcarsh, F. L. (1950) "The Lighthouse, Fact to Face," *Accent* 10, 107–23.

Poresky, Louise A. (1981) *The Elusive Self: Psyche and Spirit in Virginia Woolf's Novels*. Delaware University Press, Newark, NJ.

Rosenfeld, Natania (2000) *Outsiders Together: Virginia and Leonard Woolf*. Princeton University Press, Princeton, NJ.

Ruotolo, Lucio P. (1986) *The Interrupted Moment: A View of Virginia Woolf's Novels*. Stanford University Press, Stanford, CA.

Silver, Brenda R., ed. (1979) "'Anon' and 'The Reader': Virginia Woolf's Last Essays," *Twentieth Century Literature* 25:3/4, 356–441.

Stephen, Leslie (1893) "The Scepticism of Believers," in *The Agnostic's Apology and Other Essays*. Putnam, New York, pp. 42–85.

Woolf, Virginia (1929) *A Room of One's Own*. Harcourt, New York.

Woolf, Virginia (1948) *The Voyage Out*. Harcourt, New York.

Woolf, Virginia (1953) *Mrs Dalloway*. Harcourt, New York.

Woolf, Virginia (1955) *To The Lighthouse*. Harcourt, New York.

Woolf, Virginia (1956) *Orlando*. Harcourt, New York.

Woolf, Virginia (1959) *The Waves*. Harcourt, New York.

Woolf, Virginia (1961) *Flush*. Harcourt, New York.

Woolf, Virginia (1965) *The Years*. Harcourt, New York.

Woolf, Virginia (1966) *Three Guineas*. Harcourt, New York.

Woolf, Virginia (1966–7) *Collected Essays*, 4 volumes, ed. Leonard Woolf. Harcourt, New York.

Woolf, Virginia (1969) *Between the Acts*. Harcourt, New York.

Woolf, Virginia (1975–80) *The Letters of Virginia Woolf*, 6 volumes, ed. Nigel Nicolson and Joanne Trautmann. Harcourt, New York.

Woolf, Virginia (1977–84) *The Diary of Virginia Woolf*, 5 volumes, ed. Anne Oliver Bell. Harcourt, New York.

Woolf, Virginia (1979) "'Anon' and 'The Reader': Virginia Woolf's Last Essays," ed. Brenda R. Silver. *Twentieth Century Literature* 25:3/4, 356–441.

Woolf, Virginia (1985a) *The Complete Shorter Fiction of Virginia Woolf*, 2nd edn, ed. Susan Dick. Harcourt, New York.

Woolf, Virginia (1985b) *Moments of Being*, 2nd edn, ed. Jeanne Schulkind. Harcourt, New York.

Woolf, Virginia (1990) *A Passionate Apprentice: The Early Journals, 1897–1909*, ed. Mitchell A. Leaska. Harcourt, San Diego.

CHAPTER 46
James Joyce

William Franke

James Joyce's employment of the Bible in his literary productions is vast and multifaceted: nevertheless, the Bible filters into Joyce's texts most intensively and persistently through the forms of the Latin liturgy of the Mass.[1] This helps us to restrict and focus the field of vision to the point where we discern that the core of the Bible as it is refracted in Joyce consists in the eucharistic celebration of the death of Christ, his offer of his flesh as nourishment for all: this rite in the Bible and in Joyce alike culminates in the symbolic resurrection of the body of Christ and in the salvation and even the sanctification of the world. Numerous figures and narratives from throughout the Old and New Testaments are alluded to by Joyce, but in the motif of the Eucharist as a re-enactment of the death and resurrection of Christ we grasp the essential dynamic of the Bible at the heart of Joyce's whole project of apocalyptic imagination – his envisioning of a final disclosure of the truth of the universe through poetic images.

My main guide for this interpretation of the biblical vision in Joyce is Thomas J. J. Altizer.[2] Altizer views the biblical revelation in Christ, and particularly in the Christ event, the death and resurrection of God, in a perspective that is derived from the Christian prophetic poets in the tradition of Dante, Milton, and Blake. For Altizer, this tradition has carried forward the authentic apocalyptic revelation of the Bible, which, according to him, has been almost universally betrayed by the whole range of Christian theologies. Interpreting James Joyce and in particular *Finnegans Wake* and *Ulysses* in the context of what he calls the Christian epic tradition, Altizer discovers Joyce as an incomparably revelatory moment in this tradition of revelation, which he understands as specifically apocalyptic in character. Dante and his successors, Milton, Blake, and finally Joyce, are seen as carrying out the mission of realizing theological revelation as apocalypse in the modern world. Their poems show the full and final meaning of human life and death in the light of Christian revelation. Beyond the plethora of thematic connections and citations of Christian and Jewish tradition, Joyce is aligned with a continuous prophetic-apocalyptic movement comprising the efforts of secular writers to extend apocalyptic revelation from the Bible into the sphere of literary artistic endeavor.[3]

In the view of other eminent interpreters as well, the connection with prophetic inspiration on the biblical model is obviously present but also vexed in Joyce. Northrop

Frye read Joyce's contribution to literature and culture in the perspective of a continuity with the Catholic tradition that remained his intellectual root: "In Joyce's personal life his break with the Catholic Church meant not that he wanted to believe in something else but that he wanted to transfer the mythical structure of the Church from faith and doctrine to creative imagination, thereby exchanging dogmatic Catholicism for imaginative catholicity."[4] Robert Alter emphasizes rather more trenchantly the Bible's purely literary canonicity, parallel to that of the *Odyssey*, in Joyce's work. Nevertheless, Alter too shows how, despite his unsparing parody and subversion of the Bible, Joyce still writes with a strong sense of continuity with the biblical tradition. Joyce counts among the modernist writers who challenge but also "reaffirm the continuing authority of the canon as a resource of collective memory and as a guide for contemplating the dense tangle of human fate."[5] Alter senses the potential of Joyce's playful and subversive deformations of biblical tradition to reinsert themselves back into that tradition and so to continue its revelatory claim: "In the extraordinarily supple and varied uses to which the Bible is put in *Ulysses*, it is converted into a secular literary text, but perhaps not entirely secular, after all, because it is reasserted as a source of value and vision" (pp. 182–3). At the very same time as it declares the secularizing force particularly of Joyce's readings of the Bible, this sentence evinces a suspicion of the still, at least covertly, theological character of disclosure – or perhaps revelation – in Joyce's writing.

Thomas Altizer's interpretation, in contrast, accentuates unequivocally the radical rupture with the Catholic tradition, insisting on Joyce's deliberate apostasy and obstinate heterodoxy – yet precisely in order to highlight the specifically biblical-apocalyptic thrust of Joyce's vision. And this apocalyptic vision he esteems to be, after all, an authentic realization of theological truth, the theological truth of apocalypse that orthodox Christian tradition all along had been betraying. Altizer sees Joyce's work, particularly *Finnegans Wake*, together with Christian epic in general, as realizing the death of God that for him is the core of true, eschatological Christian experience and, consequently, theology. He reads theologians from John and Paul through Augustine and Luther to Hegel and Nietzsche as all deeply realizing the death of God. But just as fundamental are the revelations of the poets, particularly Dante, Milton, Blake, and finally Joyce. Their epic works become eucharists in which the death of God the Word is shared out in tormented and martyred words with the readers. Readers realize in their own experience and interpretations of broken, mortified meaning the apocalypse that is proclaimed by the Christian gospel and that is actually accomplished by Christ's Crucifixion/Resurrection.

It is by ending the era of belief in a static, self-identical God, immutable in his transcendence, that the death of God, in Altizer's view, opens up a genuinely new conception of divinity. For Altizer, authentic apocalyptic Christianity stands in opposition to previous religions and their myths of eternal return. Altizer derives this idea, which remains fundamental all through the development of his thought, especially from Mircea Eliade's work in comparative religions.[6] In this perspective, Christianity inaugurates the vision of divinity revealed in a unique, irreversible historical event, an incarnation in flesh that is a final and irrevocable submission to death (as recounted particularly in Philippians 2:5–11). The self-emptying of divinity in death without return to an eternity outside of and over and above time marks for the first time in the history of religions the real and actual beginning of finite historical existence that never returns but passes toward a future that is genuinely new and apocalyptic. The past is now totally past and finally vanishes in real and irrevocable death, and a future that is not just a return of the past is now really born in all its astonishing newness. Unique, finite, historical existence is finally free to be just itself in its definitive perishing, once the past has been nailed to the cross and is thus crossed out forever. This is resurrected life, and it is no longer beholden to any past. Only now is full and absolute presence of the embodied individual and the incarnate historical act possible. And just this "total presence" is what would have been realized by Joyce in the apocalypse of *Finnegans Wake*.[7]

Altizer emphasizes the heretical character of Christian epic and at the same time the absolute necessity of Christianity as ground not only of the epic but of the whole modern world. Joyce, like other modern epic poets, in his view, performs a dialectical reversal of Christian tradition, and so of every kind of dogmatic Christianity, in favor of an apocalyptic, visionary Christianity – the original apocalyptic vision of the Bible – concerned not with conserving tradition but with ending, that is, with consummating the world. This reversal is necessary in order that Christianity be rediscovered as the religion of the *novum*, of the absolutely new, as against the return of the same. Its eternity is won precisely by ending the cycle of eternal return that dominates pre-Christian religion and also Christianity itself as grounded in an eternal and transcendent God, a God who is *only* transcendent and eternal and does not, at least not in his own person, die. The actuality of the event of Christianity is at the same time a definitive ending of the *in*actuality of the eternity outside time of all such purely transcendent religious presences. Altizer insists on the absolutely new and different eternity that is inaugurated by death, specifically the death on the Cross. This is the eternity of an event that remains forever irreversible precisely because it is the event of becoming definitively past, of perishing, never to come back again. Thus the full actuality of events is made possible by the death of God and takes place decisively in the central, literally crucial event of Christianity and of all history, the Crucifixion.

This new world and fully apocalyptic history has been apprehended and represented, according to Altizer, most completely and perspicuously, and in a contemporary language, by Joyce in *Finnegans Wake*. This can be seen most readily perhaps from the way that Crucifixion and Resurrection are deployed as key themes of the work. At the center of the *Wake*, in pages that happen also to comprise the first to be written, is an event that Altizer describes as "a divine acceptance of death." It is concentrated into the utterance: "*I've a terrible errible lot todue todie todue tootorribleday.*"[8] This phrase articulates a terrible, perhaps errant, resignation to death as due ("todue") today, as to-be-done presently – in the torrid heat and torrent of the present tense: "today" (Latin: *hodie*) becomes synonymous, by dint of quasi-homophony, with "to die" (*todie*). Altizer reads this statement as extending Joyce's total demythologization of the divine death at the end of the Proteus episode in *Ulysses*: "God becomes man becomes fish," which for Altizer describes "a victim wholly dissociated from any mythical form of Christ, a victim who is pure victim as such and no more, and hence by necessity a nameless or anonymous Christ."[9] Of course, it should not be overlooked that Joyce is also alluding to how this naked victim is inscribed into Christian symbolism, since the word for fish in Greek, ἰχθύρ, transliterated Ixthus, was used by ancient Christians as an acronym for "Jesus Christ, Son of God, Savior" (*Iesous Xristos THeou 'Uios Salvator*). Joyce's "God becomes man becomes fish" exploits a latent comic potential inhering in what was initially a reverent symbol of the holy before it came to be transformed in the course of tradition. He explodes thereby the aura of holiness that would elevate the divine victim above the material world of ordinary comestibles.

Altizer also quotes the "prayer": "Grant sleep in hour's time, O Loud!" (FW, p. 259.4), in which the name of the Lord has become just loud noise. Prayer here confesses itself to be distracted by distraction to the point where, prayer being impossible, only sleep can be wished, a wish for extinction in time, in an "hour," which is also what is most essentially "ours." Joyce is echoing, of course, the Book of Common Prayer: "Grant peace in our time, O Lord." But as this refrain reverberates in his text, it suggests that our being has been fully disclosed as temporal to its very core, and thus as most essentially a perishing. This indeed is how Altizer takes it. However, there is also another crucial implication that imposes itself as the same parodic play is pursued in further deformations of liturgical formulae such as "Loud, hear us! / Loud, graciously hear us!" (FW, p. 258.24–5). Insistent vocalization of "Lord," pronounced with a thick Gaelic accent as "Loud," mischievously exposes the resonant emptiness of language as *flatus vocis*. We hear the holy mystery of the Name of God, from which all language derives and on which it all depends in monotheistic theologies of the Divine Name, reduced to a linguistic fact or flub. We are reminded, moreover, that language conjures up what it *is not* out of thin air, out of the insubstantiality, the near immateriality, of voice, and this holds even in the case of the divine Name. The name of the Lord, which substitutes for the unspeakable Name of God, sounds aloud (literally as "Loud") this uncannily pregnant and productive nothingness into which the purported presence of God evoked in prayer is evacuated.

This voiding of the Holy Name accords with Altizer's stress on the self-emptying of God in order that he become incarnate in a profane, contemporary language. In the passage leading up to the prayer just quoted, a further phrase – "The timid hearts of words all exeomnosunt" (FW, p. 258.2–3) – by echoing the Latin *exeunt omnes*, as in the stage direction "all leave," meaning alternately "all die," likewise evokes the divine absence enshrined in every word. It bespeaks an emptiness of language that works as its omnipotence, its unlimited power of creation from nothing.

This cardinal biblical motif of creation *ex nihilo* suggests something of the full extent to which *Finnegans Wake* enfolds an interpretation of the history of civilization and cosmos in the perspective rendered uniquely possible by the Bible. The work begins with a fall that, in the context of Christian epic tradition, reads as the fall of Satan. As a literary act, moreover, it aims to embody, and perhaps succeeds in embodying, to a superlative degree, the total presence of immanent historical consciousness that coincides with a new vision of eternity. The total immanence of God in the Word, that is, the word that is broken and dispersed and profaned in the unrelenting, audacious linguistic outrages and sacrileges that make up this extraordinarily blasphemous work, is brought into clear and convincing focus by Altizer's interpretation. But it is especially the possibility of celebrating a new humanity on the basis of the total collapse of any established social and cosmic order that makes Joyce's vision apocalyptic in the originally biblical sense Altizer advocates.

The profound theological drama of the resurrectional, life-giving, sacrificial death of God in Joyce's works has been illuminated brilliantly by Altizer's ideas, and in the light they shed I would like to propose a detailed reading (independent of Altizer's own exegeses) of a couple of passages from *Finnegans Wake*. They will show how the Christ event emerges clearly as a sacrificial, liberating death, celebrated in the Christian Eucharist and re-enacted even in the most vulgar and profane banalities of ordinary people's lives as represented by Joyce. All life, however degraded in the common and contemporary world, can be seen as transfigured in the perspective of this event of sacrifice and crucifixion that itself becomes the resurrection to fully incarnate life. For in Joyce the original event narrated in the gospels as the Christ event is broken open, divided up, and scattered abroad. It is dispersed eucharistically so as to become all events – however mean and trivial – rather than remaining fixed as determined by a single narrative about one identical subject.

Language is the arena in which Joyce's poetic apocalypse is achieved. Joyce sees grammar as at least one factor accomplishing the sacrificial death of God, which runs the Crucifixion and the Resurrection (and the Incarnation) together inextricably. The sacrifice of God on the altar of grammar features as a recurrent motif, especially in the funeral elegy for H.C.E. pronounced at the end of the first chapter of *Finnegans Wake*. Joyce bases this elegy on the idea that "the grammarians of Christpatrick" (FW, p. 26.21) have violently killed and buried God, in a scene that Andrew Mitchell revealingly connects with Nietzsche's staging of the death of God in the *Gay Science*, sec. 125.[10] The novel's protagonist, as a surrogate for God (as will become clear in the sequel), is in effect put on trial posthumously as part of his sacrificial ordeal:

> our old offender was humile, commune and ensectuous from his nature, which you may
> gauge after the bynames was put under him, in lashons of languages, (honnein suit and
> praisers be!) and, totalisating him, even hammissim of himashim that he, sober serious,
> he is ee and no counter he who will be ultimendly respunchable for the hubbub caused in
> Edinborough. (FW, p. 29.30–6)

God, or his alter-ego H.C.E., and indistinguishably also Adam ("our old offender"), is made responsible ("respunchable") ultimately, in the "end" ("ultim*end*ly"), but also ill-timedly or anachronistically, for the chaos pursuant to the fall that occurred in Eden ("the hubbub caused in Edinborough"). The story of the Fall – and its modern repetitions – is thus linked to the sacrifice of the divine victim or scapegoat. In addition to being made responsible, the victim is made repeatedly punishable or more exactly *punchable*, like a thing, in Latin a *res* ("respunchable"). The sacrificial victim is lashed particularly by language ("lashons of languages"), with the intimation of his being lashed down and so bound by language, verisimilarly by grammatical rules and restrictions; but at the same time we hear that the latchings-on of language are multiple and indeed wrought in a plurality of "languages." The burgeoning multiplicity of his names, as well as of words in general, which bind him as he goes on trial and is sacrificed, is at the same time a source of untold fertility. He becomes the common humus that humbly nourishes ("humile, commune") his community. Yet this nourishment of names also plagues nature infectiously ("ensectuous"), recalling the plagues of *insects* like flies and locusts that infested Egypt (Exodus 7–11).

This ill effect is due at least in part to his being divided up by names ("bynames") into sects ("ensectuous") that totalize him ("totalisating him"). In particular, Muslim and Jew, with their languages, seem to make mincemeat of the One supposed to be God above all, making of him a hash: "even hamissim of himashim." These word-conglomerates sound like Arabic and Hebrew respectively: moreover, in English "himashim" is a third-person version of the phrase "I am that I am," by which the Lord designates himself to Moses in Exodus 3:14. Joyce's concocted locutions suggest that God is missed and mashed, and perhaps even worshipped as ham. Of course, Greek and Christian, too, totalize their conceptions of divinity and represent God as One and Being: "honnein," where the Greek *on* for Being is aspirated (as in *όv*, the One) to become *hon* and combines with German *ein* for One, but equally with *nein* for Nothing.

In this last language-family or culture, Christianity from its Greek to its German expressions, God is also simple repetition of simplicity ("he is ee and no counter"). In *Paradiso* XXVI.133–5, Dante has Adam say that *I* was the original human Name of God: "Pria ch'i' scendessi all'infernale ambascia, / *I* s'appelava in terra il sommo bene / onde vien la letizia che mi fascia" ("Before I descended to the infernal dismay, the highest good whence comes the delight that wraps me round was called *I* on the earth"). "I," which is pronounced in Italian like "e" in English, is the simplest sound the language affords; it is without the difference of a consonant, with no sound "counter" to it. It comes from Adam, in his first moment of consciousness, as an ecstatic acknowledgment of the source of all his delight, in a spontaneous act of naming and of praise for his Creator.[11] But this human utterance is offered to and, at the same time, offers up a God who will be cheered and jeered countless numbers of times ("he is ee and no counter"). Heard another way, this phrase suggests that the divine name is repeated countless times as a sort of stutter in language. Paradoxically and tragicomically, or fortunately-calamitously, the divine essence, "his nature," which is in principle absolute simplicity and the source of all goodness and healing, becomes malefic through its appropriation into human languages. The divine nature is made divisive and sectarian essentially by names ("which you may gauge after the bynames was put under him") used as instruments of appropriation that subvert divinity's sovereign impartiality. Truly, these are *bi*-names, since they inevitably split the divine nature's unity: they appropriate God by one name in one language and oppose him to another name in another language, and thus oppose one people to another.

The elegy is for the death of "the G.O.G! He's duddandgunne now" (FW, p. 25.23). At least initially, ecclesiastical authorities dispose of the legacy of the sacrificial event: "the company of the precentors and of the grammarians of Christpatrick's ordered concerning thee in the matter of the work of thy tombing" (FW, p. 26.21–3). But, of course, these preceptors, unmasked as lustful and duplicitous centaurs ("pre*centors*"), cannot control divinity and its self-sacrifice exclusively, and God is resurrected in other, popular guises. He is eulogized in this text as open at the "fore" for the laps (and lapses) of goddesses or working girls ("when you were undone in every point fore the laps of goddesses you showed our labourlasses how to free was easy," FW, p. 25.20–1). These lasses are made free of labor, laborless, by what is offered as free love, though it could of course make them laboring lasses again in another sense too. There is something divine in the freedom of this sexual activity, although it is also an undoing, presumably of pants, but also of self ("you were undone in every point"). There is thus a hint here of sacrificial self-surrender, the ultimate model for which is Christ's sacrifice, his kenosis, his being undone completely, even to the point of death on the Cross (Philippians 2:8). But coupled together with this, the arched, stiff or stolid, as well as soiled and spending, phallus looms fecund and loaded with seed as it lowers itself in the lines: "If you were bowed and soild and letdown itself from the oner of the load it was that paddyplanters might pack up plenty."

This reminiscing over his prowess and potency climaxes in the goggling exclamation elegiacally evoking the deceased with a thinly veiled "By God": "Begog but he was, the G.O.G!" The eulogized is an awkward figure whose title in this distillation of initials has a clumsy consonance with "God" (much like "Godot" in Samuel Beckett's *Waiting for Godot*). From beyond the bounds of orthography and orthodoxy, the text begins to suggest what the deceased has meant and means, or could mean, to his community at large. In the spirit of Joyce's prolific displays of the endless fecundity of linguistic corruption, this dissemination of significances would potentially embrace everything, even the most perverse things, as accepted, graced, transfigured.

"Gog" appears in Ezekiel 38–9 as the arch foe of Israel in a doomsday battle: "On that day I will give to Gog a place for burial in Israel" (39:11). Gog is defeated and becomes carrion for birds and wild animals, as well as a sacrificial meal for Israel: "Assemble and come, gather from all around to the sacrificial feast that I am preparing for you, a great sacrificial feast on the mountains of Israel, and you shall eat flesh and drink blood" (Ezekiel 39:17). Viewed typologically, this invites mixing together the vengeance on Judgment Day against the "Gog and Magog" (Revelation 20:8) with the eucharistic sacrifice of God in Christ, especially given the eating of His flesh and drinking of His blood. And, of course, Christ's sacrificial dismemberment is linked with the punishment of Man after the Fall. Joyce evidently revels in conflating together and confounding all these in fact theologically interdependent and mutually inextricable moments of biblical epic history from Creation to Apocalypse.

Even so, the crucial event, the death of God, has not yet changed things, not apparently anyway: "Everything's going on the same or so it appears to all of us, in the old holmsted here" (FW, p. 26.23–6). The work of the Church, in providing a secure home, which is instead something of a hole (as suggested by "holmsted"), goes on as God's entombing. This includes, presumably, the writing of the gospels among the linguistic means of mastering the sacrificial catastrophe and its uncontainable grace. Nevertheless, God or "Gunne," as this character is also called, making him out, not without irony, to be a big-shot, has proved to be a dud, like a shot that fails to fire ("He's dud-dandgunne now"). True to his name when dead, he is "gunne now," which evidently says that he is "gone now" but at the same time also hints that he is "going to *now*," that is, becoming actual, becoming finally present – Gunne now! This, I suggest, might be taken to be "total presence" in exactly the sense Altizer intends, the total presence made possible uniquely by the death of God as a transcendent reality beyond and inaccessible to the present.

These elucidations are meant, in the first instance, to provide an example of the potential productiveness of Altizer's frame for reading *Finnegans Wake* – and universal history as well, for that matter – in terms of the sacrificial, apocalyptic death of God. The *Wake* seems to open such a comprehensive view of everything "immarginable" (p. 4.19). Yet it does so without comprehending it. The whole story is made rather incomprehensible, at least to all familiar, available faculties and instruments of comprehension. There is definitely a sense of the sacrificial scenario as inescapable and totalizing, yet it is the unlimited equivocity of it all that comes out in Joyce's texts every time, and indeed as prior to the apocalyptically clear, final, theological sense that Altizer's reading inevitably elicits from it.

The languages that totalize God are bound and undergirded with latencies that are not actually or exhaustively revealed. The praise of him goes on as a "suit," a musical suite or hymn, but also a "following" or sequel, if we hear the French nuances of this word. The phrase "honnein suit," of course, also says "honey an' sweet," even in praising the lashes – to mention one more of the contradictory significances compressed into this phrase. Totalizing itself is changed by the gerund continuative into an ongoing process of "totalis*ating.*" This sort of wild equivocity of meanings in the unrestricted linguistic play that the text invites and even obliges us to participate in is bounded only by a principle of repetition, whereby we must be able to recognize elements that have occurred elsewhere, and so are already familiar, as being actualized here and now, albeit with other meanings pointing in different directions. These endless intricacies of repetition are incalculable at innumerable levels, as can be seen straight from the staging of the overarching theme of the "fall" on the first page of the *Wake*:

> The   fall   (babadalgharaghtakamminarronnkonnbronntonnerronntuonnthunn-
> trovarrhounawnskawntoohoohoordenenthurnuk!) of a once wallstrait oldparr is retaled
> early in bed and later on life down through all christian minstrelsy. The great fall of the
> offwall entailed at such short notice the pftjschute of Finnegan, erse solid man, that the
> humptyhillhead of humself prumptly sends an unquiring one well to the west in quest of
> his tumptytumtoes. (FW, p. 3.15–21)

This passage projects the fall of Adam and Eve, oldest human couple or pair (the "oldparr"), named at the outset of the book a few lines before, backward to the fall of Satan, "unquiring one," from among the angels, "well to the west" perhaps suggesting the setting of the morning star from Isaiah 14:12: "How art thou fallen from heaven, O Lucifer, son of the morning." The passage projects from here forward to the fall of language at the Tower of Babel (the syllables "babadal" beginning a long imitation of babalese). The trajectory of repetition reaches further into a very different register with the reference to the nursery rhyme about Humpty Dumpty's fall from a wall, as well as to an event nearly contemporary to composition, namely, the crash of the stock market, "wallstraight," in 1929. This word also hints that the confines of Eden may have been claustrophobic, such that the Fall was fortunate, as also in Milton's *Paradise Lost*, according to which, once expelled from the straits of the Garden and its wall, the human pair face an exhilarating prospect opening before them: "The world was all before them" (XII.646). These piggy-backed falls are all replayed also in the ballad "Finnegan's Wake" – which gives Joyce's work its title – about Tim Finnegan falling off a ladder and rising again on the strength of the whisky spilled at his wake.

All these fallings announce what Harry Levin indicated as the work's "central theme" of the problem of evil and original sin.[12] Typically the repetitions of falling are riotously sacrilegious reversals: this is emphatically so when they are "retaled" in Joyce's "meandertale" (FW, p. 18.22), which unearths by circuitous routes unsuspected origins and primitive ancestors. Joyce finds an emblem for this recirculation of history in language in the phoenix, cyclically reborn anew from its own ashes. He links this figure with the idea of the happy fall, the *felix culpa*, which is hailed: "O foenix culprit" (p. 23.16). The babelic fall into a multiplicity of languages is the precondition for any such exercise as the *Wake*'s own macaronic mélange of languages.

Joyce's genius is to discover the trace of patterns of recurrence compressed into words and to release it by tweaking them in such a way that everything seemingly excluded by their proper sense reappears in the deformations that devolve from the resultant, impishly perverse and corrupted form. Minimal slips and shifts of orthography can totally reverse sense and make it ridiculous, diverting it in unexpectedly devious directions. The recurrences that result entail the wildest meetings of opposites and coincidences of contraries. They also result in what it has been customary to term the "layering" of Joyce's text, ever since Richard Ellmann's observation concerning Joyce's "working in layers."[13] There are many different levels or layers at which the repetitions alluded to by the text are simultaneously operative.

In the paradoxical anti-*summa* of *Finnegans Wake*, the archives of civilization are ransacked in order to show how every past is contained in every present and will be presented again in every future. This is to continue without any end that is not destined to be repeated: "fin again." As in dream, where distinctions of tense collapse, time here consists in cyclical repetitions that at the same time evoke an eternal "wake." Already in *Ulysses*, Leopold Bloom, an undistinguished modern man on an ordinary day, was able to repeat, at whatever distance, making for pathetic parody, the fabled adventures of the Greek epic hero Odysseus known as "Ulysses" through the relay of Latin tradition. The whole story is "history repeating itself with a difference": in the opening episode Stephen thinks lucidly, "I am another now and yet the same," as he assists Buck Mulligan in performing his mock eucharistic rite and morning ablutions.[14]

In *Finnegans Wake* the possibilities of repetition are multiplied by the myriad different linguistic levels or layerings. One does not even know what language to use to decipher any given word. The text hints that every word in it might be read in seventy different ways, according to its different "types": "every word will be bound over to carry three score and ten toptypsical readings throughout the book of Doublends Jined" (FW, p. 20.14–16). Although this may well mean that "three score and ten" is the number of languages used in the book, following rabbinical and patristic tradition in envisaging a total of seventy nations and a corresponding number of separate tongues on the earth,[15] the possibilities are actually unlimited, to the extent that the languages in play are not discrete and separate but combine and generate, proliferating in new codes beyond and between their presumable boundaries. That the book makes its ends meet in doubleness ("Doublends Jined"), or, as it elsewhere says, in "doublecressing twofold truths and devising tingling tailwords" (FW, p. 288.3), suggests a self-replicating, endlessly open circulation that spills out always more from its top, or trails off still a remainder from its tail, rather than completing itself in a closed circuit.

The repetition in question, of course, displaces and in effect reoriginates whatever it repeats in an endless process that the *Wake*'s own wacky language describes as "contonuation through regeneration of the urutteration of the word in pregross" (FW, p. 284.19–21). Any "ur" utterance is but a continuation of the then not-so-original thunder (Italian: *tuono*) with which language begins as the language of the gods, according to Vico. More than a beginning or origin, it is an ongoing rumbling tone or "contonuation." The word, as a pre-existing quantity or "pregross," is actually heard, in the event, as a word *in progress*. The repetition is thus at the same time an erasure of the original, a negation through oblivion of the *arché*, in "the obluvial waters of our noarchic memory" (FW, p. 80.24). And just as any staking out of a first beginning is destined to be washed away by what comes after, so also no ending can be final in this tumultuous "chaosmos" (FW, p. 118.21).

In the passage on the "pftjschute of Finnegan" (from the French *chute* for "fall," with onomatopoeic elaboration of the initial consonant), there is a suggestion that Finnegan falls by virtue of a perversion or negation of inquiring. This sin repeats the unauthorized inquiring after knowledge of good and evil in Eden that turned it into an *un*quiring, a false note of disobedience marring cosmic harmony. His fall "well to the west," furthermore, is the repetition and, in effect, repeal of a line from the Easter Vigil liturgy: "Lucifer, dico, qui nescit occasum," about the bearer of light, who knows no setting. It alludes to Christ's rising like the morning star (Revelation 22:16 and Luke 1:78) never to set and is quoted in *Ulysses* at the very moment that "Allbright he falls, proud lightning of the intellect" (p. 50). There, too, the fall is "to evening lands," that is, to the West, just as in the *Wake* passage, with a hint that this is at the same time a Crucifixion scene ("I thirst"). There may even be a reminiscence of the Dantesque "altezza d'ingegno," height of genius or pride of intellect, which lies behind the fall of Guido Cavalcanti adumbrated in Canto X of the *Inferno* (line 59). But the *Wake*'s destitute, modern-day Satan, collapsed together with Christ crucified, falls to evening lands in quest not of high intellect but of clumsy and trivial "tumptytumtoes" at the low end of his body, as he tries to put on his drawers perhaps, having risen or rather fallen out of bed in the morning. This is a good example of how Joyce translates the liturgical past into utterly contemporary language, as Altizer compellingly maintains.

The tremendous creative power of Joyce's language flows indeed, in large measure, from its assuming the most crass, banal, meaningless language of common, contemporary life – including its advertising slogans and consumer product brand-names, its popular songs, its technical and professional jargon, the trite banter of people in pubs – and transfiguring it all within the frame of a mock-heroic epic that re-enacts revelation of everything in everything else. It thus becomes possible to see the contemporary world and its characteristic speech in an apocalyptic light as re-echoing the most holy verbal heritage of Joyce's civilization, as it is garnered and transmitted signally in the Latin liturgy of the Roman Catholic Church. Other civilizations, too, are represented by incorporations especially of otherworldly and apocalyptic motifs from texts including the Egyptian and the Tibetan Books of the Dead, the Koran, the Indian Vedas, and the Chinese Book of Changes.

Such is the powerfully syncretistic apocalyptic vision that Joyce actualizes in his epic. Still, this vision is for Joyce essentially that of the Bible. The whole history of the world is revealed in its essential dynamic by the Bible in its core narrative of the death and resurrection of Christ as celebrated in the Eucharist. Joyce's literary work continues this eucharistic breaking and dispersal of the Word in its profanation by human words. This profanation of the Word coincides with what can become the sanctification of human words: through their fragmenting and violent dismemberment they become transfigured as sacraments of Christ's self-sacrificial, saving act. Joyce's literary work thus becomes not only a verbal echo of themes from the Bible but the actual, material re-enactment in incarnation and dissemination of its central event.

Notes

1 Essential bibliography on the broad topic of Joyce and the Bible includes Robert Boyle, SJ, *James Joyce's Pauline Vision: A Catholic Exposition* (Southern Illinois University Press, Carbondale, 1978); Giuseppe Martella, *Ulisse: Parallelo biblico e modernità* (Cooperativa Libraria Universitaria, Bologna, 1997); Gian Balsamo, *Scriptural Poetics in Joyce's Finnegans Wake* (Edwin Mellon Press, Lewiston, NY, 2002); and Virginia Moseley, *Joyce and the Bible* (Northern Illinois University Press, DeKalb, 1967).

2 Altizer's theses on Christian epic are developed in detailed literary-critical studies of his selection of Christian epic poets in *History as Apocalypse* (State University of New York Press, Albany, 1985). These views are integrated, furthermore, into his general theology, especially in *Genesis and Apocalypse: A Theological Voyage Toward Authentic Christianity* (Westminster John Knox Press, Louisville, KY, 1990) and again in *The Genesis of God: A Theological Genealogy* (Westminster John Knox Press, Louisville, KY, 1993).

3 The body of this chapter is adapted from material in chapter 4 of my book *Poetry and Apocalypse: Theological Disclosures of Poetic Language*, Palo Alto, CA: Stanford University Press, 2008.

4 Northrop Frye, "Quest and Cycle in *Finnegans Wake*," in *Fables of Identity: Studies in Poetic Mythology* (Harcourt, Brace and World, New York, 1963), pp. 256–7.

5 Robert Alter, *Canon and Creativity* (Yale University Press, New Haven, CT, 2000), p. 20.

6 See Altizer's *Mircea Eliade and the Dialectic of the Sacred* (The Westminster Press, Philadelphia, 1963).

7 Altizer's *Total Presence: The Language of Jesus and the Language of Today* (Seabury Press, New York, 1980) gives an outline of this and several other guiding insights that remain crucial for him throughout his career.

8 *Finnegans Wake*, 3rd edn (Faber and Faber, London 1964 [1939]), p. 381.23–4 (hereafter cited as FW). The passage is quoted in *Genesis and Apocalypse*, p. 171.

9 Altizer, *History as Apocalypse*, p. 218.

10 Andrew John Mitchell, "'So it appeals to all of us': The Death of God, *Finnegans Wake*, and the Eternal Recurrence," *James Joyce Quarterly* 39:3 (Spring 2002), 419–34.

11 In *De vulgari eloquentia* I, iv, Dante describes Adam's first word or *primiloquium* in just these terms. In this earlier treatise, he still held Hebrew to be Adam's language in Eden, and thus

"El," the Name of God in Hebrew, to be the first word humanly spoken. The later substitution in *Paradiso* XXVI of *I* as the original human Name of God evidences a greater depth of speculative reflection.

12   Harry Levin, *James Joyce: A Critical Introduction* (Faber, London, 1960 [1941]), p. 134.

13   Richard Ellmann, *James Joyce*, rev. edn (Oxford University Press, Oxford, 1982), p. 546.

14   James Joyce, *Ulysses* (Vintage, New York, 1990 [1934]). Citations from p. 638 and p. 12.

15   See Laurent Milesi, "L'idiome babélien de *Finnegans Wake*: Recherches thématiques dans une perspective génétique," in Claude Jacquet, ed., *Genèse de Babel: Joyce et la création* (CNRS, Paris, 1985), pp. 155–215.

CHAPTER 47

D. H. Lawrence

T. R. Wright

Reading the Bible Differently

The Bible is obviously a key element in Lawrence's work. Born in 1885 to a pious, well educated, nonconformist mother, who had switched allegiance from the Wesleyan Methodism of her family to the more liberal Congregationalism she encountered on settling in Eastwood two years earlier, he grew up with a profound, almost encyclopedic, knowledge of the sacred texts. He would entertain friends at all stages of his life with impromptu performances of his favorite biblical episodes: the Chambers family, for example, who provided his second home as a young man, were treated to a dramatic rendition of Pharaoh hardening his heart against Moses (Nehls, 1957–9, I, pp. 47–8), David Garnett remembered Frieda and Lawrence enacting Judith and Holofernes in Mayrhofen in 1912 (ibid.), and H.D. would record in her novel *Bid Me to Live* how Rico (the Lawrence character) played God (his favorite role) to Frieda's growling serpent and Richard Aldington's Adam in an elaborate charade enacted at their London house in 1917 (H.D., 1984, pp. 111–12). Not just because of his beard but because of his strong personal presence and sheer religious intensity, comparisons with Christ followed him throughout his life (Ellis, 1998, p. 528). His spiritual journey would take him a long distance from the passionate Christian faith of his youth, which he abandoned at the age of twenty-one while at college in Nottingham (Worthen, 1991, pp. 174–5), but it would never remove from his mind the powerful imprint of the Bible.

The Bible, in Harold Bloom's terms, was Lawrence's most important precursor-text, the book that first inspired his imagination and against the influence of which he constantly struggled (Bloom 1973). It was through biblical images that he developed his own independent religious thinking. "Bible religion," as Paul Morel tells Miriam somewhat irreverently in one of his many letters to her in *Paul Morel*, the first draft of what was to become *Sons and Lovers*, is "a heap of rag-bag snippings ... which you cut your coat from to fit you just as you please" (PM, p. 93). And this, it could be argued, Lawrence himself proceeded to do, weaving his literary work from what remained of the Bible after his critical "snipping." Because of this, I suggest, he risks alienating both those who love the Bible as it is and therefore resent the imaginative freedom with which he treats it, and those who hate it, shying away from anything so directly religious. For Lawrence, in his own words, remained "passionately religious" long after he had abandoned orthodox Christianity (L, II, p. 165).

Looking back at the end of his life at the fixed and literal way in which he had first been taught to read the Bible, Lawrence claimed to have come himself to "resent" the Bible:

> From earliest years, right into manhood, like any other nonconformist child, I had the Bible poured every day into my helpless consciousness, till there came almost a saturation point. Long before one could think or even vaguely understand, this Bible language, these "portions" of the Bible were *douched* over the mind and consciousness till they became soaked in, they became an influence which affected all the processes of emotion and thought. (A, p. 59)

One of "the real joys of middle age," however, was "coming back to the Bible" and reading it alongside "modern research and modern criticism," putting it "back into its living connexions" with other ancient civilizations and learning to read it differently as "a book of the human race, instead of a corked up bottle of 'inspiration'" with a fixed meaning (A, pp. 59–60).

How Lawrence made this long and sometimes painful journey is a complicated story, of whose intertextual elements it is only possible to provide a brief sketch here before proceeding in the following two sections to explore two of the most significant biblical motifs in his work: a fascination with the story of Adam and Eve and their supposed Fall, and an identification with the figure of Christ, first with his crucifixion and suffering and then (in his later work) with his resurrection. The first motif demonstrates his increasingly critical treatment of the traditional Christian interpretation of the early chapters of Genesis, which tends to deplore Eve's curiosity (linked in particular with the wickedness of all flesh, the reason for God proceeding to destroy most of his creation), while the second displays an ongoing grappling with what Lawrence saw as an overemphasis in theology on the divinity of Jesus as Word at the expense of his humanity as incarnate flesh.

A propensity among Lawrence's early admirers to portray him out of context as a unique if flawed genius, encouraged perhaps by his own penchant for covering over all traces of influence, has tended to obscure how widely read and well informed he was. Virginia Hyde, however, has demonstrated his familiarity with medieval and renaissance iconographical traditions surrounding both Adam and Christ (Hyde, 1992), while Robert Mongomerie and Daniel Schneider have traced his philosophical development (Schneider, 1986; Montgomery, 1994). Less well established is his early familiarity with Higher Criticism of the Bible through his reading of secularists such as Robert Blatchford and modernist theologians such R. J. Campbell, both of whom he discussed with the Reverend Robert Reid, the minister of Eastwood Congregational Church, who not only taught him Latin but took a personal interest in his spiritual progress (L, I, pp. 36–7). Reid himself, like many leading Congregationalists, was quick to accept the findings of higher criticism (Chadwick, 1970, II, p. 105), preaching a series of sermons on the early chapters of Genesis while Lawrence was still a member of his congregation, arguing that the later patristic doctrine of the Fall should not be allowed to override the biblical account of Adam and Eve's growth in knowledge and moral awareness (Masson, 1988, pp. 171–2). The liberal Congregationalist Campbell, in his exposition of *The New Theology*, was similarly critical of doctrines such as the Fall, which he believed to be based upon a misreading of the book of Genesis, "a composite, primitive story ... in existence as oral tradition long before it became literature" whose "narrative says nothing about the ruined creation or the curse upon posterity" (Campbell, 1907, pp. 54–5). In Blatchford too Lawrence would have found an explanation of the documentary hypothesis about the different strands of Genesis (Blatchford, 1904, pp. 37–8). Renan's *Life of Jesus*, a celebration of an altogether human Christ misled into claiming divinity for himself, also occupied a prominent place in the development of the young Lawrence as of the young Morel, who is portrayed passing through "the Renan ... stage" in *Sons and Lovers* (SL, p. 267).

Another significant element in Lawrence's rejection of the traditional Christian interpretation of Genesis was probably provided by Edward Carpenter, the late Victorian guru of sexual liberation, a section of whose book *Civilization, Its Cause and Cure* (1889) is entitled "The Fall and the Return to Paradise," a theme that recurs in Lawrence's own painting, poetry and fiction (Delavenay, 1971, p. 63). The most powerful model, however, for Lawrence's strong revisionary reworking of the Bible would have been Nietzsche, whom he appears to have discovered in the winter of 1908–9, working his way through many volumes of the Levy translation of the complete works as they were published from 1909 to 1913 (Burwell, 1982, p. 69). *Human, All Too Human*, along lines to be followed by Lawrence in *Apocalypse*, distinguishes between what Nietzsche calls "an *affirmative* Semitic religion, the product of a *ruling* class," to be found in "the older parts of the Old Testament," and "a *negative* Semitic religion, the product of an *oppressed* class," exemplified in the New Testament (Nietzsche, 1994, p. 93). *The Anti-Christ* even includes a comic retelling of the opening chapters of Genesis in which God creates man out of sheer boredom and feels threatened by Eve's desire for knowledge before finally giving up on the vast majority of the race and deciding to drown them (Nietzsche, 1968, pp. 176–7). Nietzsche, like Lawrence, distinguishes between Christianity, the dogmatic religion founded by St Paul, and the charismatic figure of Jesus himself. It is the followers of Christ who are blamed for the "anti-natural castratation of a God into a God of the merely good" (ibid., p. 138). Jesus himself, according to Nietzsche's prophet Zarathustra, had he lived longer (as Lawrence would permit him in *The Escaped Cock*), "would have learned to love the earth" (Nietzsche, 1961, p. 98).

Other contributors to the way in which Lawrence learnt to read the Bible differently were theosophists such as Madame Blavatsky, J. M. Pryse, and Frederick Carter. Reading the Bible for Blavatsky is a matter of reading between the lines in order to detect traces of an older strand of sacred wisdom now lost. The early chapters of Genesis may on the surface, or "exoterically," appear to describe "a temptation of flesh in a garden of Eden," which God curses. "Esoterically," however, according to Blavatsky, God "regarded the supposed *sin* and FALL as an act so sacred, as to choose the organ, the perpetrator of the *original sin*, as the fittest and most sacred symbol to represent that God" (Blavatsky, 1970, I, pp. 375–6). Blavatsky herself doesn't celebrate the phallus as much as Lawrence, regarding not only the Fall but Creation itself as a descent from spiritual existence. Lawrence clearly distanced himself from her teaching, finding much of *The Secret Doctrine* "not quite real," but he did "glean a marvellous lot from it" when he read it in 1917 (L, III, p. 150). He would also make creative use of the theories of her followers Pryse and Carter on the book of Revelation while working on such esoteric works (in every sense) as *The Symbolic Meaning, The Plumed Serpent*, and *Apocalypse* (Wright, 2000). None of these thinkers, of course, were accepted precisely in their own terms, but they served both to stimulate and to shape some of elements of Lawrence's own creative reworking of the Bible, in particular his understanding of Adam and of Christ.

Adam and Eve Re-Enter Paradise

Variations on the story of Adam and Eve recur in Lawrence's writing from his earliest poetry to his last fiction. The early poem "Renaissance," for example, of 1909, presents Jessie Chambers as Eve and Haggs Farm as paradise, with the young Lawrence as Adam learning to embrace his animal nature, to acknowledge the whole valley "fleshed like me" (CP, p. 38). In the sequence of poems published in 1917 as *Look! We Have Come Through!* Lawrence again celebrates his recapturing of paradise, this time with Frieda. Now, however, he makes bolder changes to the biblical narrative. In a reversal of roles from Genesis 3, for example, in "Why Does She Weep," it is the two lovers

> who walk in the trees
> and call to God "Where art thou?"
> And it is he who hides. (CP, p. 231)

Another poem of this sequence, "Paradise Re-entered," like the painting of "Eve Regaining Paradise" that Lawrence produced a decade later, has the exiled lovers pass through the "flames of fierce love" back into the "sinless being" from which they were unfairly discarded, successfully storming "the angel-guarded / Gates of the long-discarded / Garden." They defy conventional morality with Nietzschean confidence, returning to a prelapsarian state "beyond good and evil" (CP, pp. 242–3). A number of poems in *Birds, Beasts and Flowers* of 1923 continue this theme: "Figs," for example, deplores Eve's original embarrassment about her nakedness, developing the one-sided biblical exchange between Eve and God, in which He curses her while she merely makes excuses, into a much more complex dialogue in which a number of sexually mature and liberated women mock their creator's narrow morality (CP, p. 284).

Adam and Eve also recur in Lawrence's prose, several passages in *Psychoanalysis and the Unconscious* (1921), *Fantasia of the Unconscious* (1922), and *Studies in Classic American Literature* lamenting a fall, as Lawrence sees it, from intuitive spontaneity into mental self-consciousness about sex. Perhaps the most powerful of these occurs during a discussion of *The Scarlet Letter* when Lawrence insists that the significant change after the theft of the apple was in the attitude of the two lovers:

They wanted to KNOW. And that was the birth of sin. Not *doing* it, but KNOWING about it. Before the apple, they had shut their eyes and their minds had gone dark. Now, they peeped and pried and imagined. They watched themselves. And they felt uncomfortable after. They felt self-conscious. So they said, "The *act* is sin. Let's hide. We've sinned."

No wonder the Lord kicked them out of the Garden. Dirty hypocrites. (SCAL, pp. 90–1)

Here even God seems to have come round to Lawrence's view that it is not sexuality as such that is sinful but a prurient self-consciousness about it. The biblical references in these polemical works are clearly designed to subvert repressive attitudes to the body that Lawrence attributes to Christian misreading of the book of Genesis.

Similarly subversive references to Eden in Lawrence's fiction are perhaps more engaging than his openly polemical prose, because they function as a mode of discovery, probing the original story to reveal something genuinely new. Even in the early novels the biblical story of the Fall is developed not merely to make a point but to uncover something more complicated, less easily reducible to paraphrase. A chapter title in *The White Peacock* (1911), for example, advertises "The Fascination of the Forbidden Apple" but the whole point of this novel is that its characters lack the courage to follow Eve's rebellion against God's prohibition on this fruit. The first person narrator Cyril Beardsall complains to his friend Emily, "You think the flesh of the apple is nothing, nothing. You only care for the eternal pips." He encourages her therefore to "snatch your apple and eat it" while she can (WP, p. 69). As one of the characters confides to Cyril, it is the Bible that is identified as the source of their nonconformist inhibitions; her husband metaphorically "wallows in bibles," she laments, even "when he goes to bed. I can feel all his family bibles sticking in my ribs as I lie by his side" (WP, p. 316).

The adulterous lovers of Lawrence's second novel, *The Trespasser* (1912), based upon the tragic experiences of his friend Helen Corke, make a brief but ultimately unsuccessful attempt to "trespass" against the most famous of the commandments. A short sojourn on the Isle of Wight momentarily lights up the world for the guilt-ridden hero Siegmund, "as if I were the first man to discover things: like Adam when he opened the first eyes of the world" (T, p. 90). The identification of the two lovers in this novel with Adam and Eve is both reinforced and complicated by references to the long poem *Adam Cast Forth* by Charles Doughty, which Lawrence had sent to Jessie Chambers on its publication in 1908 with instructions to note especially the passage "where Eve, after long separation, finds Adam," who "tells her to bind himself with vine strands, lest they be separated again by the Wind of God" (L, I, p. 95). In Doughty's poem the wind is part of God's anger and punishment for their sin, but for Lawrence it represents a repressive and destructive morality that prevents the lovers from reaching fulfillment. For a while the mere thought of escape makes Siegmund feel reborn, as if "the womb which had nourished him in one fashion for so many years, was casting him forth" (T, p. 49). The significance of Doughty's poem is here reversed, suggesting the possibility at least of the novel's Adam being cast forth not *from* paradise but *to* it. The tragedy in this novel is that the lovers fail to sustain their rebellious courage. There are times when they walk hand in hand through their paradisal island celebrating the beauty of creation. "It is good," says Helena, echoing the Creator in Genesis 1, "it is very good" (T, p. 108). But Siegmund cannot escape the ingrained feelings of guilt that force him first to return home and finally to hang himself. Lawrence succeeds in rewriting Helen Corke's Wagnerian tragedy in terms derived from Genesis only to the extent that he characterizes the lovers as Adam and Eve in at least wanting to recapture paradise.

Sons and Lovers (1912) can be seen to chart Lawrence's continuing rebellion against conventional Judeo-Christian morality through further use of imagery from Eden. In turning from Miriam, who offers him sex as a dutiful sacrifice, to Clara, who rejects the notion that it makes them "sinners," Paul Morel sees himself as recovering his "old Adam." He continues to tease Clara, imputing to her whole sex a taste for guilt: "I believe Eve enjoyed it, when she went cowering out of Paradise" (SL, p. 358). Edward Garnett characteristically cut from the manuscript Paul's development of this biblical episode, so important in all Lawrence's early writing: "And I guess Adam was in a rage, and wondered what the deuce all the row was about – a bit of an apple that the birds could peck if they wanted to" (SL, p. 358). To preach so didactically such a rebellious message was to court the rejection of his readers, already scandalized enough by the relative sexual explicitness of the novel. The "Foreword to Sons and Lovers" was equally unpublishable at the time, urging its readers to embrace the female flesh in rebellion against the patriarchal Word. The Word, Lawrence argues, tries to make "the pip that comes out of the apple, like Adam's rib, ... the mere secondary product, that is spat out." But it is the maternal pip, which is "responsible for the whole miraculous cycle" (SL, p. 470). Here, as in Study of Thomas Hardy, Lawrence protests strongly against male employment of the Bible to suppress women.

In The Rainbow (1915) it is significantly the women who lead the rebellion against patriarchal religion. When Will Brangwen attempts to represent the Genesis account of the creation of woman from Adam's rib, Anna objects to his making her "like a little marionette, ... like a doll" in comparison to his Adam, who is "as big as God." "It is impudence to say that Woman was made out of Man's body," she continues, "when every man is born of woman" (R, p. 162). Later, during their visit to Lincoln Cathedral, Anna undermines Will's "gothic ecstasies," playing the role of "the voice of the serpent in his Eden" by drawing attention to the human qualities of the individual figures of Adam and Eve (189). For a while their daughter Ursula and her lover Skrebensky promise to effect a return to paradise denied to her parents. Their kisses, for example, are described as "their final entry into the source of creation," passing for a moment "into the pristine darkness of paradise" (R, pp. 450–1). They also dance naked and unashamed, like the prelapsarian Adam and Eve, on the South Downs. Ursula, however, has to wait until Women in Love (1920) to find a more worthy Adam in the shape of Birkin, also given to wandering naked among the flowers and to pontificating about the book of Genesis. There is a terrible fall from innocence, he explains, in Hermione's false kind of knowledge, which he traces back to Eve, who chose the wrong fruit from the wrong tree (WL, pp. 41–4).

It is not until Lady Chatterley's Lover (1928), in fact, that Lawrence portrays a fully successful fictional return to paradise. In The First Lady Chatterley Constance makes this very clear, telling Parkin as she weaves flowers into his body-hair, "We are Adam and

Eve naked in the garden" (FLC, p. 174). That the lovers are to be seen as regenerate versions of Adam and Eve is also evident in the final version of the novel, the manuscript of which has the two lovers very self-consciously acting the parts of Adam and Eve as they weave flowers around each other's bodies. Mellors even addresses Constance as Eve in this passage of the manuscript, labeling his land "Paradise" (LCL, p. 360). The fact that Lawrence removed these explicit references to Genesis in the final version of the novel may indicate that he wanted his characters to appear more human than mythical to his readers, opting for greater realism over symbolic meaning. But it is clear that they remain, at one level at least, descendents of Adam and Eve rediscovering paradise.

Divorced from their artistic context in this critical condensation of Lawrence's reworking of these biblical figures, Lawrence's continual redeployments of Adam and Eve may appear programmatic, offending against his own insistence that the novel, unlike "didactic Scripture," should not "nail anything down" to a fixed meaning (STH, pp. 150–4). The gospels, he thought, were "wonderful novels" but written "with a purpose," while he counted Genesis as one of the "greater novels" in the Bible because less obviously didactic (STH, p. 157). As Jack Stewart argues, however, in relation to Paul Morel's expressionist transformation of the burning bush from the book of Exodus in his painting of trees in sunset, avant-garde, modernist art of the kind Lawrence and his character produce involves projecting their "changing sexual, religious and aesthetic passion" onto commonplace objects and familiar biblical material in order to create new and constantly evolving artistic meaning (Stewart, 2005, p. 172). There is clearly a consistent rebellion against Christian orthodoxy running through all Lawrence's versions of the loss and recovery of paradise but they are by no means identical. The symbolic figures of Adam and Eve assume different significance, operating on different literary levels, in each particular context.

Christ Crucified and Risen

If Adam, the first man, is a figure with whom Lawrence often identified, it is Jesus, the Risen Adam, who can be seen to have occupied the most prominent place in Lawrence's religious imagination. Sometimes, as with Nietzsche, it seems as if he resents the fact of Christ's priority as the precursor-poet with whom it is impossible to compete. In Lawrence's earlier writing it is mainly the crucified victim on whom he focuses. Increasingly, however, in the latter part of his career, it is the Risen Lord who plays a more important role. Having discovered a medieval bestiary depiction of a "Phoenix Rising from the Flames" along with an explanation of its traditional association with the resurrection in Katharine Jenner's book *Christian Symbolism* (Jenner, 1910, p. 150), Lawrence famously reproduced the image on the cover of *Lady Chatterley's Lover*, much to the dismay of his publisher Orioli, who complained that it looked like "a pigeon having a bath in a slop basin" (Nehls, 1957–9, III, p. 186). It has since, of course, been permanently associated with Lawrence for a whole generation of readers through its reproduction on the cover of the Penguin edition of his novels.

Lawrence's fiction initially highlights the human aspect of Jesus. "It would be cruel to give up the resurrection," Paul Morel explains to Miriam in the first version of *Sons and Lovers*, "yet the Christ-*man* is so much more real" (PM, p. 111). The rejection of this novel by Heinemann in July 1912 ironically produced a savage example of Lawrence's tendency to see himself in the role of the crucified Jesus. "Why," he asks,

> was I born an Englishman ... *why* was I sent to *them*. Christ on the cross must have hated his countrymen. "Crucify me, you swine," he must have said through his teeth. It's not so hard to love thieves also on the cross. But the high priests down there – "crucify me, you swine." (L, I, p. 422)

Lawrence, as he recounted in his essay "Christs in the Tirol," had encountered many depictions of the crucified Christ on his travels with Frieda across the Alps into Italy that summer. He expresses a clear preference for the more realistic examples, miserable though they often seem and "in need of a bit more kick," over the more baroque examples with "great gashes" and "streams of blood" found on the other side of the Brenner pass (TI, p. 46). In a fictional version of this tour in *Mr Noon*, Gilbert finds a one-sided "dark mysticism, a worship of cruelty and pain and torture and death" in these figures (MN, p. 138), shocking Johanna (the Frieda-figure) by inviting one of them down from the cross and offering him a drop of Dunkels (MN, p. 202).

Such emphasis on suffering had appeared totally appropriate to Lawrence during the Great War, when his letters and poems were full of references to the crucifixion. "The War finished me," he wrote to Cynthia Asquith in January 1915, "it was the spear through the side of all sorrows and hopes" (L, II, p. 268). One of his most powerful poems of protest at the war, published a few months later, "Eloi, Eloi, Lama Sabach-thani?," presents Jesus as a reluctant soldier, who has dreamt of love but is forced to kill (CP, pp. 741–3). Other writing around this time, however, displays a more critical dialogue with the figure of Jesus. In *Study of Thomas Hardy*, for example, he continually takes issue with Christ's teaching, complaining rather pedantically that lilies, far from taking no care for the morrow, lay down stores of food for the continuation of the natural cycle (STH, p. 7). Even the commandment to love one's neighbor, he objects, can simply encourage self-pity. He relents, however, when it comes to Christ's injunction to be born again, which he sees as fundamental to all human development (STH, p. 40).

This dialogue with Jesus overflows into the text of *The Rainbow*, most famously in Ursula's interior monologue in chapter 10, where she negotiates her relationship with Jesus. The focus of her meditation is not "the actual man, talking with teeth and lips, telling one to put one's finger into His wounds" but a more "shadowy," other-worldly and mystical figure. Like Lawrence, she engages with particular sayings of Jesus, such as his reply to the rich man in St Mark's Gospel (10:25): "It is easier for a camel to go through the eye of a needle, than for a rich man to enter into heaven." Such hyperbole, she concludes, cannot be taken literally, so she commits herself to "the non-literal application of the Scriptures" (R, p. 258). She becomes increasingly critical of conventional Christian attitudes to the body encapsulated in Christ's refusal to allow Mary Magdalen to touch her, to which she offers a direct challenge:

> Why shall I not rise with my body whole and perfect, shining with strong life? Why, when Mary says: Rabboni, shall I not take her in my arms and kiss her and hold her to my breast? Why is the risen body deadly, and abhorrent with wounds? (R, p. 262)

The manuscript of the novel contains an even bolder challenge to orthodox Christianity when Ursula subjects the Sermon on the Mount to similarly severe interrogation, objecting in turn to being "the light of the world," to possessing eternal treasure, to taking no thought of her raiment and to not casting her pearls before swine. "Is not my body holy," she asks, "and my flesh more precious than pearls" (R, p. 629). She then engages with the parable of the house built upon sand, launching into a diatribe against the Church as a prime example of such a precarious building before envisaging a time when Jesus,

> whole and glad after the resurrection ... shall give himself to the breasts of desire and shall twine his limbs with the nymphs and the oreads, putting off his raiment of wounds and sorrows, appearing naked and shining with life, the risen Christ, gladder, a more satisfying lover than Bacchus, a God more serene and ample than Apollo. (R, pp. 629–30)

The fact that these passages were omitted from the published version of the novel shows that even Lawrence recognized that Britain was not yet ready for Jesus the lover. It was not yet ready, of course, even for the self-censored version of the novel, as the suppression of the novel by court order in November 1915 would prove.

The motif of the risen Christ refusing to be bound by conventional limits on his sexuality recurs in much of Lawrence's writing from this point on. The Jesus of "Resurrection of the Flesh," for example, a poem written in 1915, removes all "heavy books of stone" that prohibit his enjoyment of Mary Magdalen's body (CP, pp. 737–8). Johanna for her part refuses in *Mr Noon* to play the role of "a weeping Magdalen" (MN, p. 129), resolving instead to take "sex as a religion" and administer the "cup of consolation" to any man in need (MN, p. 139). In "The Ladybird," the first version of which was written in 1915 and envisaged as a story about resurrection (L, II, pp. 418–20), Daphne's husband returns from the war shrinking like Christ from all forms of touch, kneeling before his wife and kissing her feet. In apparent dramatization of the celebrated Nietzschean contrast between Dionysus and the Crucified, however, she prefers to play Magdalen to her new lover Dionys (FCL, pp. 192–3). Another short story, "The Overtone," possibly stemming from this time although not published until a decade later (Kinkead-Weekes, 1996, pp. 75–80), has its heroine make a similar rebellion against conventional Judeo-Christian morality, coming to the similarly Nietzschean conclusion that "if the faun of the young Jesus had run free, seen one white nymph's brief breast, he would not have been content to die on a cross" (StM, p. 15).

Lawrence's opposition to Christianity became significantly more outspoken as the likelihood of publication (after the banning of *The Rainbow*) receded. Old Mr Crich, for example, in *Women in Love*, originally part of the same project as *The Rainbow* but continually revised and not eventually published until 1920, functions as a grotesque example of the kind of sentimental concern for the poor and subservient that Lawrence, like Nietzsche, now associated with Christianity. Rawdon Lilly in *Aaron's Rod*, begun in 1917 but not published until 1922, pronounces himself similarly "sick of Christianity" (AR, p. 78), preaching his new gospel of heroism and power to Aaron in the final two chapters of the novel. The Christian ideals of love and service, "the beastly Lazarus of our idealism," he explains, are a corpse beyond hope of resurrection: "By this time he stinketh – and I'm sorry for any Christus who brings him to life again" (AR, p. 281).

Lawrence's writing of the early 1920s maintains this hostility to traditional Christian ideals, most notably perhaps in "The Evangelistic Beasts," four poems that play subversively with the animal symbols attached to the authors of the gospels. "St Matthew" in particular prides himself on his down-to-earth masculinity, regretting Jesus's desire to be "not quite a man" and asking himself to be put "down again on the earth, Jesus, on the brown soil / Where flowers sprout" (CP, p. 331). "St John" is presented altogether unsympathetically as the formulator of the metaphysics associated with the Logos (CP, pp. 328–9). *Fantasia of the Unconscious*, to the scandal of its first readers in the *Adelphi* (Ellis, 1998, p. 135), mocks Jesus' claim not to desire domesticity, advising him to be "man enough ... to come home at tea-time and put his slippers on," thus avoiding inclusion among the world's "failures" (Fant, pp. 98–101). *Quetzalcoatl* and *The Plumed Serpent* both involve complex ceremonies in which the worship of Jesus is replaced by a new religion built upon ancient Aztec rituals. A passage in Lawrence's Mexican Notebook still recognizes Jesus as "one of the Sons of God" but by no means the only one (Ref, p. 185). Similarly, Ramon, the prophet of this new Mexican religion, insists that "the Most High has other divine Sons than Jesus" and even "divine Daughters" (Q, p. 175).

The Risen Christ plays an increasingly important role in Lawrence's writing after his remarkable recovery from illness in Mexico in 1925. He also appears in "The Resurrection," a painting of 1927, sporting an identifiably Lawrentian beard, and is described in a letter as "stepping up, rather grey in the face, from the tomb, with his old ma helping him from behind, and Mary Magdalen easing him up towards her bosom" (L, VI, p. 72). Lawrence's most sustained fictional treatment of the Risen Christ, of course, is *The Escaped Cock*, whose title was inspired by a children's toy model of a white rooster escaping from an egg, which he and his Buddhist friend Earl Brewster saw in a shop window on their Etruscan pilgrimage in 1927. It was Brewster, apparently, who suggested it would make a good title: "The Escaped Cock – A Story of the Resurrection" (Ellis, 1998, p. 356). The original short story, when it first appeared in *The Forum*, was actually entitled "Resurrection" on the front cover, while the revised novella appeared posthumously as *The Man Who Died*. It is, in Lawrence's own words,

> a story of the Resurrection, where Jesus gets up and feels very sick about everything, and can't stand the old crowd any more – so cuts out – and as he heals up, he begins to find what an astonishing place the world is, far more marvellous than any salvation or heaven – and thanks his stars he needn't have a "mission" any more. (L, VI, p. 50)

In the novella itself "the man who had died" (who is never actually named) initially repeats the *Noli me tangere* of St John's Gospel but comes quickly to recognize "that the body, too, has its ... life" (EC, pp. 53–4), a lesson reinforced in part II of the novella, in which the priestess of Isis gradually heals his scars and brings his wounded body back to life. This involves restoring, to him as to the healed Osiris, a fully functioning phallus, thus enabling a distinctly new and shocking sense to his claim, "I am risen!" (EC, p. 144).

The resurrection of the flesh in this physical sense, of course, is the central theme of *Lady Chatterley's Lover*, most conspicuously in the second version of the novel, *John Thomas and Lady Jane*, in which Tommy Dukes connects the neglect of the flesh in years of Christian asceticism with the gospel accounts of the risen Jesus refusing to be touched. This sparks off a long meditation by Lady Constance on the meaning of Jesus' words, with the suffering of men like her husband, maimed by the war, who "had all been crucified" and were now living in "the strange, dim, grey era of the resurrection ... before the ascension into new life. ... They lived and walked and spoke, but theirs was still the old, tortured body that could not be touched" (JTLJ, p. 69). Lawrence would express similar views in the essay "The Risen Lord" in 1929, criticizing the churches of his day for preaching "Christ crucified" at the expense of "Christ risen in the flesh! ... and if with hands and feet, then with lips and stomach and genitals of a man" (Phoenix, pp. 571–5). In this second version of *Lady Chatterley* Dukes's similar view that men should "rise up again, with new flesh on their spirits ... and a new fire to erect their phallus" prompts Lady Constance to ponder what "a man with a risen body" might be like (JTLJ, p. 72). Mellors, in this context, becomes a figure not only of Adam but of a risen Christ fully endowed with all that becomes a man.

Lawrence famously described the Bible as "a great confused novel" (STH, p. 169), prompting later critics to apply that epithet to his own work (Kennedy, 1982, p. 220). Kennedy contrasts Lawrence's unsystematic borrowing from the Bible with the more controlled use of mythical structure to be found in Joyce. It is a comparison that Lawrence himself, who complained bitterly about the "old fags and cabbage-stumps of quotations from the Bible ... stewed in the juice of deliberate, journalistic dirty-mindedness" in his modernist rival, would have challenged (L, VI, pp. 507–8). Readers, of course, will have their own views on which of these writers is the more systematic in his use of the Bible and which the more "dirty-minded." But what should be apparent even from this brief sketch of Lawrence's work is how important the Bible, in particular the figures of Adam and Christ, remained for him long after he took to reading it very differently from the way in which he had been first taught.

References

Lawrence

All references to Lawrence's work, unless otherwise stated, are to the Cambridge Edition of the Letters and Works of D. H. Lawrence, published by Cambridge University Press, using the following abbreviations:

A: *Apocalypse and the Writings on Revelation*, ed. Mara Kalnins, 1980.
AR: *Aaron's Rod*, ed. Mara Kalnins, 1988.

CP: *The Complete Poems of D. H. Lawrence*, ed. Vivian de Sola Pinto and Warren Roberts, 2 volumes. Heinemann, London, 1962.

EC: *The Escaped Cock*, ed. Gerald M. Lacy. Black Sparrow Press, Santa Barbara, 1978.

Fant: *Fantasia of the Unconscious and Psychoanalysis and the Unconscious*. Penguin, Harmondsworth, 1971.

FCL: *The Fox/The Captain's Doll/The Ladybird*, ed. Dieter Mehl, 1992.

FLC: *The First Lady Chatterley*. Penguin, Harmondsworth, 1973.

JTLJ: *John Thomas and Lady Jane*. Penguin, Harmondsworth, 1973.

L: *The Letters of D. H. Lawrence*, ed. James Boulton and others, 8 volumes, 1979–2000.

LCL: *Lady Chatterley's Lover*, ed. Michael Squires, 1993.

MN: *Mr Noon*, ed. Lindeth Vasey, 1984.

Phoenix: *Phoenix, The Posthumous Papers of D. H. Lawrence*, ed. Edward McDonald. Heinemann, London, 1936.

PM: *Paul Morel*, ed. Helen Baron, 2000.

PS: *The Plumed Serpent*, ed. L. D. Clark, 1987.

Q: *Quetzalcoatl: The Early Version of "The Plumed Serpent,"* ed. Louis L. Martz. Black Swan Books, Redding Ridge, CT, 1995.

R: *The Rainbow*, ed. Mark Kinkead-Weekes, 1989.

Ref: *Reflections on the Death of a Porcupine and Other Essays*, ed. Michael Herbert, 1988.

SCAL: *Studies in Classic American Literature*. Penguin, Harmondsworth, 1971.

SL: *Sons and Lovers*, ed. Helen Baron and Carl Baron, 1992.

StM: *St Mawr and Other Stories*, ed. Brian Finney, 1983.

STH: *Study of Thomas Hardy and Other Essays*, ed. Bruce Steele, 1985.

T: *The Trespasser*, ed. Elizabeth Mansfield, 1981.

TI: *Twilight in Italy and Other Essays*, ed. Paul Eggert, 1994.

WL: *Women in Love*, ed. David Farmer, Lindeth Vasey and John Worthen, 1987.

WP: *The White Peacock*, ed. Andrew Robertson, 1983.

Other References

Blatchford, Robert (1904) *God and My Neighbour*. Clarion Press, London.

Blavatsky, Helena P. (1970) *The Secret Doctrine: The Synthesis of Science, Religion and Philosophy*, 2 volumes. Theosophical University Press, Pasadena, CA.

Bloom, Harold (1973) *The Anxiety of Influence*. Oxford University Press, Oxford.

Burwell, Rose Marie (1982) "A Checklist of Lawrence's Reading," in Keith Sagar, ed., *A D. H. Lawrence Handbook*. Manchester University Press, Manchester, pp. 59–110.

Campbell, R. J. (1907) *The New Theology*. Chapman and Hall, London.

Chadwick, Owen (1970) *The Victorian Church*, 2 volumes. Adam and Charles, London.

Delavenay, Emile (1971) *D. H. Lawrence and Edward Carpenter*. Heinemann, London.

Doughty, Charles (1908) *Adam Cast Forth*. Duckworth, London.

Ellis, David (1998) *D. H. Lawrence: Dying Game 1922–1930*. Cambridge University Press, Cambridge.

H.D. (1984) *Bid Me to Live*. Virago, London.

Hyde, Virginia (1992) *The Risen Adam: D. H. Lawrence's Revisionist Typology*. Pennsylvania State University Press, Philadelphia.

Jenner, Katharine Lee (1910) *Christian Symbolism*. Methuen, London.

Kennedy, Andrew (1982) "After Not So Strange Gods in *The Rainbow*," *English Studies* 63, 220–30.

Kinkead-Weekes, Mark (1996) *D. H. Lawrence: Triumph to Exile, 1912–1922*. Cambridge University Press, Cambridge.

Masson, Margaret (1988) "The Influence of Congregationalism on the First Four Novels of D. H. Lawrence," PhD dissertation, Durham University.

Montgomery, Robert E. (1994) *The Visionary Lawrence: Beyond Philosophy and Art*. Cambridge University Press, Cambridge.

Nehls, Edward, ed. (1957–9) *D. H. Lawrence: A Composite Biography*, 3 volumes. University of Wisconsin Press, Madison.

Nietzsche, Friedrich (1961) *Thus Spoke Zarathustra*, trans. R. J. Hollingdale. Penguin, Harmondsworth.

Nietzsche, Friedrich (1968) *Twilight of the Gods/The Anti-Christ*, trans. R. J. Hollingdale. Penguin, Harmondsworth.

Nietzsche, Friedrich (1994) *Human, All Too Human*, trans. Marion Faber and Stephen Lehmann. Penguin, Harmondsworth.

Pryse, James M. (1910) *The Apocalypse Unsealed*. John M. Watkins, London.

Schneider, Daniel J. (1986) *The Consciousness of D. H. Lawrence: An Intellectual Biography*. University Press of Kansas, Lawrence.

Stewart, Jack (2005) "Forms of Expression in *Sons and Lovers*," in John Worthen and Andrew Harrison, eds, *D. H. Lawrence's Sons and Lovers: A Casebook*. Oxford University Press, Oxford.

Worthen, John (1991) *D. H. Lawrence: The Early Years, 1885–1912*. Cambridge University Press, Cambridge.

Wright, T. R. (2000) *D. H. Lawrence and the Bible*. Cambridge University Press, Cambridge.

CHAPTER 48
T. S. Eliot

David Fuller

> *The chief use of the "meaning" of a poem, in the ordinary sense, may be ... to satisfy one*
> *habit of the reader, to keep his mind diverted and quiet, while the poem does its work*
> *upon him: much as the imaginary burglar is always provided with a bit of nice meat for*
> *the house-dog. (Eliot, 1933, p. 151)*

> *I gave the references [to Dante] in my notes [to* The Waste Land*], in order to make the*
> *reader who recognised the allusion know that I meant him to recognise it, and know that*
> *he would have missed the point if he did not recognise it. (Eliot, 1965, p. 128)*

Perhaps there is no conflict between these statements, but they at least represent Eliot
permissive – poetry as verbal music or imagistic free play addressed to the unconscious
– and Eliot prescriptive – poetry addressed to a reader whose ability to respond fully
draws on traditions of knowledge, especially the literature of Greece, Rome, and Israel,
on which (as Eliot put it) Western civilization depends. Polemical about the importance
of educated elites as Eliot could be, he also expressed a desire for an audience that (like
Shakespeare's) "could neither read nor write" (Eliot, 1933, p. 152) – though of course
Shakespeare's audience knew the literature of Israel – the Bible – from hearing it read
aloud in church.

Recognizing allusion provides information about a poem, not knowledge of it as a
poem – though it can all too readily be presented as or mistaken for that. Information
can be one basis of knowledge, but attention is misdirected if readers too readily look
for information to obviate expressive lacunae. Though Eliot's views on the importance
of tradition, a canon of common reading, and cultural continuity and cohesion mean
that difficulties can be less difficult for readers educated in what he argues are the
requirements of sophisticated literacy, the range of reference in his poetry is in fact not
especially wide. Allusion is often to central texts of Western culture (the Bible, Virgil,
Dante). Where it goes beyond this it assumes that modern consciousness is international – so should grapple with Eastern religions, especially Buddhism. And inclusions
are also admittedly accidental: everybody engaged by the arts encounters work that
especially appeals to their sensibility. Eliot happened to love Wagner – who has some
claim to be the most important European artist of the age before Eliot's. Ultimately, with

certain classic texts, of which the Bible is the most notable, when readers do not recognize a story, a character, a famous phrase, they should (in Eliot's view) blame not the poet writing for a coterie, but an educational culture that fails poets and readers alike.

The kind of biblical knowledge that Eliot requires or presupposes is often straightforward. "The Hippopotamus," a satire of the Church for its worldiness, has an epigraph from St Paul (Colossians 4:16), the point of which lies not in the epistle but in the simple reference to Laodiceans, those whose religion is lukewarm (Revelation 3:14–16): religious institutions are always (the poem implies) "Wrapt in the old miasmal mist." Some of the poem's phraseology is biblical but, like "Laodicean," in a way that has passed into the language, not that requires recognition of a particular text: the Church as a rock (Matthew 16:18; *OED*, rock, *sb.*[1] 2.b); Christ as the Lamb of God (John 1:29; Revelation 7:14; *OED*, lamb, *sb.* 3.a). Likewise, "Mr Eliot's Sunday Morning Service" may be a very puzzling poem, but its biblical allusion is of the clearest – to the famous opening of St John's Gospel, "In the beginning was the Word." The problems of interpretation lie not in recognizing one of the most famous sentences in Western culture but in understanding what Eliot does with it.

"Difficulties of a Statesman" (*Coriolan* II) works similarly: beyond the initial recognition of Isaiah (40:6) – perhaps as no more than a prophetic voice – everything is in the poem. The question of the prophet is direct and bold: "What shall I cry?" And it can be answered simply: "All flesh is grass." The poet attempts to join his voice with the prophet's, which he endorses, but he is more perplexed. Recognizing the need to cry out, he asks the prophet's question, but his answers are hesitant. There is a mystery at the heart of the bustling public world, but the world does not notice, and the poet senses it only obliquely. What the reader needs to recognize is the tone of the prophet's voice, the poet's difficulty in adopting it, and the contrast with the modern situation – the languages of politics, administration, and prosaic material fact, and the hedging about of affairs these bring with them. The modern would-be prophet is enmeshed in myriad circumstances that obscure the only things of real importance: "the still point of the turning world" (*Coriolan* I); the heroic subject's aspiration after what is "Hidden in the stillness of noon"; or the depths made by the context of spiritual search to resonate from the commonplace: "Please, will you / Give us a light? / Light / Light."

J. Alfred Prufrock may know that he is not Prince Hamlet, and that (despite weeping, fasting, and praying) he is "no prophet," but he nevertheless entertains two spectacular fantasy selves which are biblical. Here Eliot assumes the reader will recognize their originals. Prufrock has seen himself as the precursor of Christ, John the Baptist, whose extravagantly weird manner of life, the most complete obverse of Prufrock's own (Matthew 3; Mark 1), is quite as relevant as the grisly manner of his death (to which the poem refers). In the biblical accounts (Matthew 14:3–12; Mark 6:17–29) John's execution and the presentation of his head is a simple act of revenge, but it is relevant with this "love song" to remember the development of the story in Oscar Wilde's *Salome*, where the execution arises from illicit and obsessive sexual desire. The Baptist focuses for Prufrock a double fantasy, as subject and as agent. His alternative biblical persona might be either of two Lazaruses. The brother of Martha and Mary (John 11:1–44) is brought back from the dead, but reports nothing about the hereafter; while in the parable of Dives and Lazarus (Luke 16:19–31), Dives hopes that Lazarus's report of Hell might transform the conduct of the living, but his return to this world is not permitted. One Lazarus returns, but tells nothing; the other could tell all, but does not return. Either would serve Prufrock equally well – able to answer "some overwhelming question," but failing to do so.

The allusion to St Matthew (12:38) in "Gerontion" is different, and more complex. The quotation marks around "We would see a sign!" prompt the reader to recognize a fragment with a context – scribes and Pharisees asking Christ for evidence of his powers, which he refuses to give. The speaker, apparently contemptuous of reading supposed "signs," recalls the demand denounced by Jesus, and the reader may feel there is a link between his implied relish of the denunciation of Jewish teachers and his anti-Semitism. But though only the Gospel quotation is marked, the whole passage ("Signs ... darkness"), incorporating phrases based on the first verse of St John's Gospel, is in fact adapted from the 1618 Nativity Sermon of Lancelot Andrewes, in which (drawing on Luke 2:12–14) "signs" are considered quite differently, as legitimate. The presence of St Luke's Gospel is perceptible in the poem without knowledge of Andrewes: "Swaddled," a term familiar principally in relation to the Christ child's cradle-clothes, draws on the Authorized Version rendering of Luke 2:7–12. Whether or not Andrewes is recognized, it is difficult to make sense of the one significant change to his text ("within" for "without"). The poem's old man, though at times wise, is also – as he knows – confused ("a dull head," "a dry brain"); and more confused than he recognizes. "I have no ghosts," he claims, in a paragraph full of them. How far his biblical scraps characterize his confusions it is not easy to decide.

Of the poems written before Eliot's conversion to Christianity in 1927, only *The Waste Land* has the Bible as a significant extended presence, and then within a frame of reference to other great sacred texts of world religions, the Buddha's Fire Sermon and the Hindu Upanishads, as well as other writings from Christian and non-Christian religious traditions (the legends of the Holy Grail, the *Divina Commedia* of Dante, the *Confessions* of St Augustine, the *Metamorphoses* of Ovid). The Bible is just one element in the "heap of broken images" that epitomizes the waste land's ignorance of its own wisdom. The poem is at one level a presentation of London after the First World War, but the framework of culturally diverse allusion implies that, while spiritual sickness may present itself in ever new forms, its substance is permanent. Or at times the comparison (contrast) implies a permanent gap between the actual and the imagined: life has consistently conceived of better than it has achieved.

The great biblical symbol of the desert is primary. In "The Burial of the Dead" the desert of Old Testament prophecy, symbol of spiritual aridity, place of trial and purgation, is the location of an authoritative and threatening voice, addressing the reader ("Son of man") as the prophet Ezekiel is addressed when he is enjoined to reclaim the apostate community. The voice uses its desert location to establish a fundamental perspective: "fear in a handful of dust" – a *momento mori*. The desert returns in "What the Thunder said," where it is the ground of intense imagination of its own opposite – a vision of an irrigated world "Where the hermit-thrush sings in the pine trees." At first the non-desert exists only in imagination and desire; "a damp gust / Bringing rain" is preface to wisdom from a different tradition, the Upanishads. But the final Sanskrit blessing, "shantih," if Eliot's notes are taken as part of the poem, is said to have a biblical "equivalent": St Paul's "Peace which passeth understanding" (Philippians 4:7). Or so texts say from the 1936 *Collected Poems* onwards. It is one of the few significant variants in Eliot's poetry: originally St Paul's phrase was "a feeble translation of the content of this word."

The Bible is a presence too behind at least the better-known versions of the Grail legends that are the poem's underlying myth of a potentially healing quest: the search for the cup used by Christ at the Last Supper in which, it is supposed, his blood was collected as he was pierced on the cross. This legendary accretion to the biblical story, though it has an aura of the sacred, has a different status from that of a sacred text. Unlike the Fire Sermon, the Upanishads, or the Bible, it is not foundational to the wisdom of a culture. And in any case Eliot's use of the Grail legends largely emphasizes the negatives – not the healing potential, but the sickness in need of healing.

The Bible is a clearer presence in occasional phrases. "Murmur of maternal lamentation" (line 367): in the context of the falling towers of Jerusalem, Rachel mourning for her children (Jeremiah 31:15; Matthew 2:18), a resonant epitome in 1922 of the sorrowing mothers of the world. "By the waters of Leman I sat down and wept" (line 182): the protagonist repeats the exile experience of the Old Testament community, but in modern isolation (Psalm 137:1; "I" for "we," a Swiss lake for an ancient river). But even such verbal reminiscence can be puzzling. The phrase from Ezekiel ("Son of man," line 20) might, without Eliot's note, more probably suggest reference to Christ (a Messianic title he uses in all four gospels). Yet more problematic is Eliot's note to "the dead tree gives no shelter, the cricket no relief" (line 23), which refers the seeker after sources to Ecclesiastes 12:5:

> And when they shall be afraid of that which is high, and fears shall be in the way, and the almond tree shall flourish, and the grasshopper shall be a burden, and desire shall fail: because man goeth to his long home, and the mourners go about the streets.

The semi-inscrutable imagery of the almond tree is clearer in context, where grinders that are few (teeth) and windows that are darkened (eyes) more obviously represent physical decrepitude. The almond tree (blossom) then represents white hair; but the grasshopper (cricket, locust) remains a challenge to interpreters. The verse is about death, and shares with Eliot's line a tree (dead in one, flourishing in the other) and an insect (absent in one, burdensome in the other). If an annotator other than the author referred Eliot's line to this source, the reader might be skeptical. There is a connection, death; but there is also a contrast (physical death as natural fact; spiritual death consequent on transformable conditions). "The Man with Three Staves ... I associate, quite arbitrarily, with the Fisher King," says Eliot's note on the Tarot pack. As with the Tarot, so with the Bible: the associations offered in Eliot's notes need not always be the reader's.

The most difficult to read biblical allusions occur in "What the Thunder said" (lines 322–30). "Torchlight ... garden ... agony ... shouting ... crying ... Prison and palace" – Eliot's notes make no reference to the Gospels, but all of this suggests the trial of Jesus: "the agony in the garden" (the usual phrase for Christ's praying in Gethsemane the night before the crucifixion), the torchlight accompanying his arrest, his interrogation in the palace of the Jewish high priest, his scourging in the prison of the Roman governor, the shouts of the crowd for his death, and the lamentation of the women who follow his cross. "He who was living is now dead": after the trial the crucifixion; or, once a living presence in the culture, Christ is now present only in moribund forms. But "reverberation / Of thunder of spring over distant mountains" intrudes an element that has no immediate connection with these scenes – an element that looks forward to the message the poem derives from the Upanishads. The death of the hanged god of Western culture is vividly recalled, but recall is not tied entirely to that unique example. So it is too with the other element of the myth, the god's return to life, in Christian terms first revealed on the road to Emmaus (Luke 24:13–35). Eliot recalls this through a manifestation of incomprehensible presence drawn from contemporary life – the experience under conditions of extreme physical and psychological pressure of Antarctic explorers. And here there is no reference to the language of the Gospels: the parallel is drawn in the notes, but is present in the poem only by implication.

If there is a source of religious wisdom among the "broken images" of *The Waste Land* it is found as much in the Upanishads and the Buddha's Fire Sermon as in writings from Christian tradition. In *The Hollow Men* intimations of a mode of consciousness beyond that of "headpieces filled with straw" can only grope toward fragments of the Lord's Prayer (Matthew 6:9–13). After his conversion to Christianity in 1927 the presence of the Bible in Eliot's poetry changed. The change is most obviously signaled in Eliot's published work in "Religion and Literature" (1935, see Eliot, 1951, pp. 388–401). There he endorses treating the Authorized Version as a literary work, but only with major reservations: the literary importance of the Bible is not separable (he argues) from its having been considered the report of the Word of God. An unpublished address of 1932 delivered in King's Chapel Boston describes at greater length a similar fundamental view. Eliot begins by affirming that he cannot treat the Bible as literature because of its special religious status, which places on the reader special responsibilities about seriousness of ethical response – as the epigraph from Revelation (5:4) makes clear: "And I wept much, because no man was found worthy to open and to read the book, neither to look thereon."[1] Eliot goes on to consider the use and effect of the Bible for contemporary poets, arguing that borrowing must not be purely for the beauty of phrase or image – that a writer who borrows from the Bible must enter into its spirit, which means having purposes that are either akin to or consciously and pointedly diverse from those of the source text. The issue is (as Eliot puts it) about "the relation of word to flesh." This view is fundamental to understanding Eliot's practices of biblical allusions in poetry written after his conversion.

This began with commissioned work for the Faber series, "Ariel Poems," the first two of which, *Journey of the Magi* and *A Song for Simeon*, constitute a pair: poems for Epiphany and Candlemas, both markers of the end of Christmas – the end of the period of festival, and the end of the ecclesiastical season. Both poems are as much concerned with death as with their obvious subjects of birth and visionary promise: desire for literal death, because spiritual knowledge entails a heightened awareness of pain; metaphorical death, because new spiritual awareness entails a radically different state of being. With both poems the biblical subject is mediated through the Church. This mediation – through liturgy's set forms and the ministry of the Word – demonstrated for Eliot the close relationship between Church and Scripture often denied by the "inner light" Protestantism that he especially deplored, which sets the Bible and the Church in opposition. For Eliot they are continuous. The Church is established in the Gospels by Christ's commandment to the disciples to preach, and by the accounts of the early Church in Acts and the New Testament Epistles.[2] The Church is therefore the authorized and authoritative interpreter of the Bible, while the inner light is "the most untrustworthy and deceitful guide that ever offered itself to wandering humanity" (Eliot, 1934, p. 59). Ministry of the Word, in this view, is not personal exegesis. How uneasy Eliot was about exposition of biblical texts by anybody uninstructed in Catholic traditions of exegesis he made clear in the prologue to the one sermon he preached (in the chapel of Magdalene College Cambridge in 1948), which is a homily of moral reflection, not biblical exposition.[3] Preaching in a tradition of disciplined meditation, reimagining the words and substance of a biblical text in terms of lights cast on it throughout the history of the Church, was best exemplified for Eliot in Anglican tradition by Lancelot Andrewes. To Andrewes Eliot applied Dante's words of St Bernard, that in this world he tasted the peace of heaven. He is one in whom (Eliot's highest praise) "intellect and sensibility were in harmony" (Eliot, 1951, p. 345). Working within the broadly Catholic exegetical tradition, "Andrewes takes a word and derives the world from it; squeezing and squeezing the word until it yields a full juice of meaning which we should never have supposed any word to possess" (ibid., p. 347). For Eliot he was the most important preacher in the history of Anglicanism.

Journey of the Magi has a New Testament source (Matthew 2:1–12), but more important than the source itself is the implied contrast with the way it is sometimes developed in Christian tradition, particularly in painting: Eliot contradicts the saccharine Christmas card tableau. As he indicates by quotation marks, the poem also draws on Andrewes's 1622 Christmas Day sermon (on Matthew 2:1–2), from which Eliot took not only (in free paraphrase) the opening lines of the poem, but also the fundamental idea of imagining the background to the biblical account with prosaic realism. As sometimes in paintings of the Christ child, the poem also contains premonitions of the gospel accounts of Christ's sufferings and death, as well as a hint of his ultimate triumph: "three trees" (the crucifixion), "pieces of silver" (for which he was betrayed), "dicing" (for his robe by the soldiers who crucified him), a "white horse" (Christ as King of kings: Revelation 6:2, 19:11–14). These details give new life to the meaning of the biblical gift of myrrh, which looks forward both to the crucifixion (where it is offered as an anaesthetic: Mark 15:23) and to death more generally (because of its use in anointing for burial). Eliot conveys this Gospel premonition of suffering and death through other biblically derived details suited to the poem's harsh travelogue, which is described without picturesque aspects that might prompt feelings of historical distance or conventional piety. A preacher's manner of firm instruction ("set down this," which Eliot also derived from Andrewes), introduces the central question: "were we led all that way for / Birth or Death?" Apparent conviction turns out to be profound uncertainty – a birth so like death as to unsettle everything; an experience so alienating as to prompt a desire for oblivion. It is a reimagining of the biblical account quite different from that sanctioned by tradition.

A *Song for Simeon* also has a New Testament source (Luke 2:25–35), but again there is an intermediary – the liturgical use of the Lucan text in the Book of Common Prayer service of evensong, important because of its daily use in the offices of the Church. The evensong canticle "Nunc dimittis" is drawn directly from the Gospel – the words of Simeon when Jesus is brought to the Temple for the first time, as required by Jewish Law. Parts of the "Nunc dimittis" are worked into the poem, from the first word (the first word of the canticle), "Lord." The canticle's personal plea, "now lettest thou thy servant depart in peace," is translated into the more general "Grant us thy peace" (from "dona nobis pacem" in the "Agnus Dei" of the Mass). And much else in the poem is drawn from the canticle and its Gospel context, with one intervention from Andrewes – the Christ child as "the still unspeaking and unspoken word" (from a sermon on St John's Gospel that Eliot also used in *Gerontion* and *Ash-Wednesday*). "And a sword shall pierce thy heart, / Thine also" (from Luke 2:35) looks forward to Mary's sufferings, while the final lines of the poem are taken directly from the canticle. "According to thy word" refers to Simeon's revelation "that he should not see death, before he had seen the Lord's Christ" (Luke 2:26), but Eliot deploys the endorsement more generally: the Bible will provide inspiration for saints and martyrs in every generation. Simeon also allusively foresees the crucifixion (the flagellation; the lamentation of the women who follow the cross; the stations of the cross – its stages as formalized from the Gospel narratives in Catholic tradition; the seven sorrows of the Virgin, again formalized in Catholic tradition from the Gospel accounts). And he looks beyond the crucifixion to the sack of Jerusalem in AD 70, which Christ prophesies in Luke (19:41–4, 21:23–4, 23:28–31). A tissue of quotations and allusions, largely from the evensong canticle, but absorbed into the balanced, musical voice created for its speaker, *A Song for Simeon* is Eliot's most biblical poem.

Alongside these commissioned poems Eliot began writing more personal poetic meditations on his own spiritual state, which in 1930 cohered into the sequence *Ash-Wednesday*. As a poem named from the first day of Lent, three biblical texts underlie this: the central text of the Ash Wednesday liturgy, "dust thou art, and unto dust shalt thou return" (Genesis 3:19); and the two fundamental texts of the ecclesiastical season, the gospel accounts of the temptation in the desert (Matthew 4:1–11; Luke 4:1–13). Eliot does not refer to these, but he would assume knowledge of them, and all are relevant: the Genesis sentence as a reminder of mortality and because of its context (God's judgment on the sin of Adam and Eve); the gospel narratives as epitomes of one significance of Lent, a season in which to exercise the disciplines of abstinence that evince resolutions of repentance. The poem begins in this register: temptation, sin, judgment, penitence. What leads this Lent toward the light of Easter is also derived from the Bible, but less directly: the figure of the Virgin Mary as developed in Catholic tradition, and particularly as embodied in the *Divina Commedia* in relation to that poem's central female figure, Beatrice. Like Andrewes, Dante wrote in a tradition of exegesis sanctioned by the Church. While Eliot's symbolic writing invites much more free play of the reader's imagination, the separate sections of *Ash-Wednesday* in earlier forms (partly as published, partly in typescript) were given titles from Dante, and some of the poem's weirdness is analogous to the visions of Hell, Purgatory, and Paradise that Dante drew in large measure from biblical sources.

Part II epitomizes this mixture of the Dantean and the biblical: a Beatrice-like Lady "honours the Virgin in mediation"; a lyric addressed to the Virgin-Mother on her all-encompassing paradoxes; and extravagantly strange biblical images, such as leopards satiated on human viscera (God's agents of destruction in Jeremiah 5:6 and Hosea 13:7, emblems of ferocity in Isaiah 11:6); fragments from Ezekiel's vision of the valley of dry bones (Ezekiel 37:1–10). As the main Old Testament foreshadowing of the resurrection of Christ, in Christian tradition Ezekiel's vision brings to mind the focus of Lent in Easter Day. In Ezekiel the bones are restored to life: here they are a death-and-dissolution prelude to resurrection. "This is the land which ye / Shall divide by lot" is also from Ezekiel (48:29). There, after exile in Babylon Israel is re-established: here, remaking the individual is followed by a more fragmentary reordering of the community. In the final chapters of Ezekiel division of the land matters very much: it is the basis of the ordered unity of the nation, symbolic of the ideal relationship between God and his people. Here, that "Neither division nor unity / Matters" is a stage of development – abnegation of the ego, willingness to be "dissembled" (disassembled), a beginning to being remade. Like other endings, it looks forward to further stages of the Lenten journey.

Progress in a Dantean mounting of Purgatorial stairs (III) is sealed by allusion to the first of several biblical texts that are used liturgically in the poem: a fragment from the story of the centurion at Capernaum who asks Christ to heal his servant, though without entering the house of one unworthy to receive him (Matthew 8:5–13). The incident is notable for Christ's endorsement of the faith shown by a Gentile. Words adapted from the centurion's demonstration of faith are used in Roman Catholic liturgy by the priest immediately before taking the sacrament, though here with the significant omission, "and I shall be healed." This Lenten journey is not so near conclusion, but there is further positive movement under the influence of the Beatrice-like Lady, who comes to seem almost an avatar of the Virgin. Eliot echoes St Paul (Ephesians 5:15–16; Colossians 4:5): "Redeem / The time. Redeem / The unread vision in the higher dream" (IV). The contexts in St Paul have no special bearing on this unusual use of "redeem": "save (time) from being lost" (*OED*, redeem, *v*. 8). The focus is on the unusual use, urgently repeated – St Paul wrestling with words and meanings – and the inscrutability of dream-vision, which, for all its restorative effects, though it can be conveyed by signs is not otherwise articulate. Apparently inscrutable symbolic dreams, which the prophet (Daniel, in Daniel 4) or the God-favored leader (Joseph, in Genesis 41) is able to interpret, are a repeated biblical motif. Eliot describes the triumphal car of Beatrice (*Purgatorio*, 29), which is based on a collocation of biblical images, as belonging to that world of "the *high dream*" (Eliot, 1951, p. 262). In *Ash-Wednesday* "the higher dream" is symbolic thinking that can be genuinely reanimated, "restoring / With a new verse the ancient rhyme." This attempt to recover St Paul's meaning ("redeem") and reimagine biblical–ecclesiastical–Dantean symbols (the Virgin, the Lady) is followed by help from Andrewes in giving new life to another crucial biblical term: "word" ("Word").

"The token of the word unheard, unspoken" is taken up (V) with a meditation on the presence of Christ in the world developed from the opening of St John's Gospel on Christ as the Eternal Word. Again the biblical text is partly filtered through Andrewes: "The Word without a word" is from his Christmas sermon of 1618. And as elsewhere (III, VI) Eliot incorporates a biblical sentence (Micah 6:3) that has an important liturgical use, this time in the Good Friday offices of the Roman Catholic Church, in the reproaches uttered by the priest (in the voice of Jesus) against the ingratitude of those by whom Christ is crucified. This invocation of the Good Friday offices recalls the focus of Lent in the celebration of Easter. There is "a garden in the desert": the great biblical locations of fecundity and drought are present in the poem's pasture and fountains, dry air and dry bones. Quite who spits out "the withered apple-seed" of Original Sin (Genesis 3) Eliot's fluid syntax leaves uncertain. If it is the terrified who, like St Peter (Matthew 26:69–75), *in extremis* deny, even this can be overcome through the process begun on Ash Wednesday.

Contrary to the willed effort in the first poem to construct a ground of rejoicing in approved holy terms that turn their back on the secular – an effort that signally fails – the last poem (though it judges this "lost," "weak," "blind," and "empty") records a spontaneous experience of rejoicing in the natural world. The speaker may retain pious delusions about what constitutes spiritual health: he discovers ways out of desolation despite these. The poem also recapitulates: the speaker has shored fragments against his ruin. Dante, the liturgy, and the Bible are drawn together in the closing prayer. "And let my cry come unto Thee" (Psalm 102:1) is a final biblical text better known through its liturgical use, as a congregational response to the priest's "Hear my prayer, O Lord." The Psalm allows Eliot to introduce singular personal pronouns, a transition that is also effected by the incorporation of words from the Catholic prayer "anima Christi" ("suffer me not to be separated"). Though Eliot does not present the experiences of the poem in personal terms, he aimed to be true to his own experience of beginning in desolation and moving toward regeneration, analogous to the movement of the ecclesiastical season of Lent toward Easter. The biblical-liturgical quotations allow him to speak in a personal register – "I am not worthy"; "let my cry ..." – but to do so while uniting an individual voice with the religious experience of historic communities, Christian and Jewish.

In *Ash-Wednesday* Eliot is at his most elusive. In the *Choruses from "The Rock"* – the most biblical work in the *Collected Poems* – he is at his most perspicuous. From a pageant written to raise funds for the restoration of London churches, these choruses are principally based on the obvious Old Testament analogy for their fund-raising cause, the prophecy of Nehemiah, an account of the rebuilding of the temple in Jerusalem after the exile in Babylon, and the social processes of communal repentance and return to God that accompany that rebuilding. In Eliot's view Europe in the 1930s had similarly lost a living sense of its religious foundations: the Enlightenment had given rise to perspectives in which political and economic creeds had replaced Christianity, with ruinous results. Writing for a Christian audience on a Christian subject Eliot clearly felt that a range of biblical analogies and allusions would be resonant and could be frequent and various. The Rock is God (2 Samuel 22:2–3), Christ (1 Corinthians 10:4), and the Church (Matthew 16:18) – an image biblical in origin, but familiar enough to have passed into common use. From Isaiah (63:3) he took Messianic prophecies of apocalyptic change (the winepress; Chorus I), and of Christ as the chief cornerstone (28:16; Chorus II). By reference to Jeremiah (17:9) he articulates the view that a secular society with no practice of penitential self-examination is likely to be always self-deceiving (Chorus V). The Chorus as a body – and, when the texts are incorporated into the *Collected Poems*, in effect Eliot himself – adopts the posture of all Old Testament prophecy ("the word of the Lord came to me," Chorus III), and reference ranges widely, beyond the prophets, from Genesis (Chorus VII) to the Psalms (Chorus III) and the Gospels.

Eliot's theme – the moral bankruptcy of a society that has turned away from the Church – is also biblical: failure to obey the injunction of the law and the prophets to care for the poor and disadvantaged, the injunction of Leviticus (19:18) incorporated into Christ's summary of the law and the prophets: "love your neighbour as yourself" (Matthew 22:39; Chorus II). The spiritual condition of Britain in the 1930s is epitomized by the state of the unemployed, whose keynote is struck using Christ's parable of the labourers in the vineyard: "No man has hired us" (Matthew 20:7). This became a central social theme with Eliot in the 1930s. It is one of the lines of thought that makes *The Idea of a Christian Society* – which in some ways appears (and appeared in its time) backward-looking – also so modern: insistence on the non-exploitation of labor and of nature. The politics of *The Idea of a Christian Society* are in contemporary terms "green," environmentally conscious in advance of their time, an emphasis that is allied to biblical precepts about care of God's creation and care by a community of all its members.

The Rock is the most didactic of Eliot's poems. Despite Eliot's stress on "incantation" and beauty of language, and the arts of verbal music that he so skillfully exercises, the basis in biblical narrative, the adoption of a prophetic voice, and the copious biblical allusions all signal these choruses as Christian polemic written for an audience of believers. The non-Christian reader may acknowledge aspects of the argument as valid independent of their basis in Eliot's beliefs, but the work's polemical stance is too distinctly Christian to be subsumed into a less doctrinal, more general acceptance of the importance of spiritual perspectives.

Not so *Four Quartets*: though explicitly religious, they are less biblical than much of Eliot's later work and more doctrinally open. The sequence is about states of spiritual awareness, moments not characterized by the deflections from full consciousness that (in Eliot's account) time characteristically engenders. Eliot exemplifies by re-creating experiences, describing and defining, often by paradox, and calling upon other forms of testimony, not all of which are Christian, or even religious, but which include the Bible. Congruent with the relatively pellucid nature of the verse – Eliot's only major poetry written after he began addressing a wider audience through the theater – knowledge of other texts is rarely assumed, and the processes of allusion are straightforward. *Burnt Norton* (V) sets a pattern with its single biblical reference, to the Gospels (Matthew 4:1–11; Luke 4:1–13):

> Words strain,
> Crack and sometimes break, under the burden,
> Under the tension, slip, slide, perish,
> Decay with imprecision, will not stay in place,
> Will not stay still. Shrieking voices
> Scolding, mocking, or merely chattering,
> Always assail them. The Word in the desert
> Is most attacked by voices of temptation.

The spiritual states that Eliot describes and embodies can be created or sustained by poetry. The temptation in the desert of Christ, the Word (John 1:1), by the Devil – the attempt to make Jesus fail by compromising with the worldly – is analogous to the verbal precision essential to poetry assailed by the forces that cause language to decay. While Eliot's late writings about culture and education offer views on how the modern desert might be irrigated, the poem presents this form of the struggle between Word and world as perpetual.

In *East Coker* Eliot adopts the rhetoric of Old Testament Wisdom, and revises the Theological Virtues of St Paul. The balance and antithesis of a time for x and a time for y – "a time for building / ... / And a time for the wind to break the loosened pane" (I) – are taken directly from Ecclesiastes (3:1–8). Ecclesiastes offers a more purely human wisdom than the prophets: the writer presents himself as King Solomon, a man of such wealth and power that, insofar as one individual can, he claims to say what life adds up to on the basis of having experienced all it has to offer. His often gloomy, even atheistic, wisdom fits so uneasily with Old Testament expectations that some readers take his more consolatory statements as the interpolations of an editor. Eliot discusses Ecclesiastes in his King's Chapel address. On the basis of his initial distinction between reading the Bible as revelation or as poetry, he further distinguishes Ecclesiastes from "inspired" work – the writings of the prophets, or of the psalmist. But he insists nevertheless that, when Ecclesiastes is understood within the Old Testament as a whole, what makes it cohere from the point of view of readers who treat the Bible as revelation is precisely what seems extraneous to readers who treat it as poetry, its moral statements – often fierce, but nevertheless consolatory because they see purpose in life. In accordance with this emphasis, while deploying in *East Coker* the book's balanced acceptance of opposites, Eliot gives this a context that contradicts the Preacher's best-known verdict on existence: "vanity of vanities: all is vanity." Though the poem finds so much of life "filled with fancy and empty of meaning," it does not present this as life's necessary condition.

While the Preacher is recruited for his rhetoric, St Paul is invoked for a substantial revision of the virtues faith, hope, and love (1 Corinthians 13; *East Coker*, III). All are, or can be, ways of looking to the future, and so they potentially distract the mind from its own fundamental emptiness, which *East Coker* would have us face as the first step toward wisdom. Eliot changes St Paul's valuation. He also changes his hierarchy. This is not a critique of St Paul but a view from a different perspective – temporal, not eternal. For the Apostle hope will eventually be fulfilled, and faith finally subsumed in knowledge, so the greatest of his virtues, the only one that is eternal, is love. But for Eliot, concerned with spiritual perspectives in this life, hope and love are both likely to deceive, and even faith can be endorsed no more than partially. "The faith and the love and the hope are all in the waiting": learning to wait properly requires mastering the disciplines that resolve the paradoxes central to *Four Quartets* by which "the darkness shall be the light, and the stillness the dancing."

It is important to the status and tone of Eliot's biblical allusions in *Four Quartets* that they are not presented as decisive points of reference but as permanent possessions of the culture that can, within limits, be reread and reshaped in new contexts. Eliot is not like Pound, drawing together, with slashing "guide to kulchur" confidence, a light from

Eleusis and philosophies of ancient China. On the contrary, Eliot was aware from his Sanskrit studies how difficult it is to enter into the ethos of a culture based on fundamentally different traditions. Nevertheless, even though writing as a Christian, Eliot does not treat Catholic Christianity as a unique repository of wisdom. Expression is culturally dependent; wisdom can be translated. In *Four Quartets* Christian texts other than the Bible are also presented as authoritative – the *Revelations of Divine Love* of Julian of Norwich, and the *Divina Commedia*, which Eliot admired partly because of the breadth of the biblical, Classical and Christian culture, philosophy, and theology that it drew into a genuine synthesis. But in *The Dry Salvages* Eliot also goes beyond Christian tradition with new ways of addressing what was implied by the drawing together of St Augustine and the Buddha, or the Sanskrit blessing annotated from St Paul, in *The Waste Land*. Like the Bible, the *Mahabharata* distils from a broad cultural base a wisdom that is permanent. Being in accordance with things as they really are, this wisdom is not only derived from a text but can be heard "in the rigging and the aerial / ... a voice descanting ... / ... and not in any language." Eliot offers a "translation" that is in part a free rendition of gists and piths, but he also quotes specifically from the *Bhagavadgita* (8:6). *The Dry Salvages* could not be more a Christian poem: its fundamental points of reference are the Annunciation (II) and the Incarnation (V). But the Bible is scarcely a presence. "The bitter apple and the bite in the apple" (II) recalls the primal act of disobedience in Eden (Genesis 3). The "ragged rock in the restless waters" may be taken simply as a symbol of permanence in the midst of change, though it may also assume biblical resonances of Christ and the Church. Christianity is present in myth and doctrine, but the sacred text of *The Dry Salvages* is the *Bhagavadgita*.

The choice of symbolic location for *Little Gidding* – a High Church Anglican community founded in the embattled situation of the reign of Charles I – appears to promise the opposite – sectarian polemic. But the poem is explicitly non-sectarian: opponents are "folded in a single party" (III). Eliot is not specific, but the context suggests opponents of the English Civil War including Charles I ("a king at nightfall") and Milton ("who died blind and quiet"). The poem's biblical allusions are congruent with this inclusiveness.

> The dove descending breaks the air
> With flame of incandescent terror
> Of which the tongues declare
> The one discharge from sin and error.
> The only hope, or else despair
>   Lies in the choice of pyre or pyre –
>   To be redeemed from fire by fire.
>
> Who then devised the torment? Love. (IV)

This Dove is the Holy Spirit that descended on the disciples at Pentecost as "cloven tongues like as of fire" (Acts 2:1–4). The force behind the terrifying descent is named by reference to the First Letter of John: "God is Love; and he that dwelleth in love dwelleth in God, and God in him" (4:16). The tongues of flame reverse the curse of Babel:

in place of fragmentation and incomprehension, the ability to speak so that every ear may hear. But though the image and its articulation are biblical, and the terms offered emphatically unitary ("one discharge … only hope … we only live"), the pains associated with adequate and inadequate response are imagined in other terms. Love's "intolerable shirt of flame / Which human power cannot remove" recalls Hercules and the poisoned shirt of Nessus; the imagery of entrapment in the secular world ("Consumed by … fire") recalls, not how Christian tradition has imagined the forces ranged here against the Spirit, but the Sermon of the Buddha that Eliot made central to *The Waste Land*.

The close of *Little Gidding* looks forward to a condition in which apparently opposite pathways of the sequence as a whole will be found to lead to the same end: the ways of vacancy and plenitude (*Burnt Norton*, III); the way up and the way down (*Burnt Norton*, epigraph; *The Dry Salvages*, III); severe spiritual disciplines and openness to the unexpected moment; the tongues of flame of the Holy Spirit and the vision of the rose garden at Burnt Norton. That allusions to Ecclesiastes, the Gospels, the Acts of the Apostles, and St Paul are set in a broad context of other sacred writings, Christian and non-Christian, plays a part in making Eliot's last poems inviting to readers for whom the Bible is what Eliot stressed it could not be to him: a literary work with the same status as any other.

Notes

1   Houghton Library, Harvard, bMS Am 1691 (26). This seventeen-page carbon typescript is headed (in the hand of John Carroll Perkins, minister of King's Chapel Boston), "Read by T. S. Eliot / before the Women's Alliance King's Chapel / Dec. 1, 1932." Perkins also recorded that this is an uncorrected copy – implying that the copy from which Eliot read (now in the collection of Mrs Valerie Eliot) contained changes. A copy identical to the Harvard typescript (another carbon from the same original) exists in the archives of King's Chapel. I am grateful to Mrs Eliot and the Eliot Estate for permission to transcribe this typescript, and to the British Academy for funding this research.

2   See E. S. Abbott et al., *Catholicity: A Study in the Conflict of Christian Traditions in the West*, especially section II. Eliot was one of fourteen co-authors of this report, which was presented to the Archbishop of Canterbury "with complete unanimity" (preface).

3   Something of Eliot's private reading of the Bible can be gleaned from a copy he owned (a plain text of the Authorized Version including the Apocrypha), now in the Hayward Collection of King's College, Cambridge (London, Oxford UP, n.d.). Lyndall Gordon notes two markings in Isaiah, on personal redemption, and the forgiveness of sin (Isaiah 43.1, 43.25; *Eliot's New Life*, pp. 244, 494). There are also markings in New Testament epistles, as follows: Romans, 5.10 and 6.3 ("we shall be saved by his life," and "were baptized into his death" underlined), 6.16, 7.24 ("O wretched man that I am! who shall deliver me from the body of this death?" marked by marginal lines), 8.24–25, 8.28, 8.35 (that no trials need separate the believer from the love of Christ), 11.6; 1 Corinthians, 1.23, 2.13, 4.7 (on not taking pride in one's abilities since they are the gift of God), 6.16–17; and Ephesians, 6.12.

References and Further Reading

Writings by T. S. Eliot

Collected Poems: 1909–1962. Faber, London, 1963.

Selected Essays, 3rd edn. Faber, London, 1951.

The Use of Poetry and the Use of Criticism. Faber, London, 1933.

After Strange Gods: A Primer of Modern Heresy. Faber, London, 1934.

The Idea of a Christian Society and Other Writings, ed. David L. Edwards. Faber, London, 1939 and 1982.

Notes towards the Definition of Culture. Faber, London, 1948.

To Criticize the Critic and Other Writings. Faber, London, 1965.

Untitled address delivered in King's Chapel Boston, 1932 ("The Bible as Scripture and as Literature"). Houghton Library, Harvard, bMS Am 1691 (26).

Catholicity: A Study in the Conflict of Christian Traditions in the West, E. S. Abbott et al. (including T. S. Eliot). Dacre Press (A. & C. Black Ltd), Westminster, 1947.

"The Language of the New English Bible" (1962), in Dennis E. Nineham, ed., *The New English Bible Reviewed*. Epworth Press, London, 1965, pp. 96–101.

Scholarship and Criticism

This list is confined to books and essays that discuss or bear upon Eliot's use of or relation to the Bible.

Cook, Cornelia (1996) "The Hidden Apocalypse: T. S. Eliot's Early Work," *Literature and Theology* 10, 68–80.

Cook, Cornelia (2001) "Fire and Spirit: Scripture's Shaping Presence in T. S. Eliot's Four Quartets," *Literature and Theology* 15, 85–101.

Gordon, Lyndall (1999) *T. S. Eliot: An Imperfect Life*. Norton, New York.

Jones, Florence (1966) "T. S. Eliot among the Prophets," *American Literature* 38, 285–302.

Schmidt, A. V. C. (1983) "Eliot's Intolerable Wrestle: Speech, Silence, Words and Voices," *UNISA English Studies*, 17–22.

Wright, Terence R. (2001) "The Writings in the Church: T. S. Eliot, Ecclesiastes and the *Four Quartets*," in John Schad, ed., *Writing the Bodies of Christ: the Church from Carlyle to Derrida*. Ashgate, Aldershot, pp. 25–39.

CHAPTER 49

The Great War Poets

Jane Potter

For those who experienced the Great War, whether as combatants or non-combatants, on the battlefields or on the home front, the Bible was a central and resonant force. It consoled and inspired, and its language was an intrinsic part of everyday as well as literary speech. This chapter considers the ways in which the poets of the Great War drew on and reinterpreted biblical themes, imagery, and language to make sense of and bear witness to the trauma of 1914–18.

The "poets of the Great War" were not a homogeneous group, made up solely of those now in the "canon" of war literature, such as Wilfred Owen, Siegfried Sassoon, and Isaac Rosenberg. It is important to bear in mind that hundreds of other lesser known – and admittedly less accomplished – poets were writing and publishing verse that appeared in newspapers, magazines, individual volumes, and edited collections often "sold for the benefit of charities." The contents of the 1915 collection *The Fiery Cross*, for instance, are indicative of the outpouring of verse – and the public's appetite for it. Pride of place is given to Rupert Brooke's "The Soldier" (discussed below), but the work of poets who were enormously popular in their day, yet almost unknown to us now, such as Alfred Noyes, Owen Seaman, and Alice Meynell, is also included. And for them the Bible was a key source of inspiration and expression. Noyes's "Veterans," for example, draws on the book of Revelation:

> When the great réveillé sounds
> For the terrible last Sabaoth,
> All the legions of the dead shall hear the trumpet ring!

Seaman's "For the Red Cross" echoes the story of the Crucifixion:

> That lonely Cross on Calvary's hill
> Red with the wounds of Christ;
> By that free gift to none denied,
> Let Pity pierce you like a sword.

And Meynell's "Summer in England, 1914" develops the Gospel of John: "Who said 'No man hath greater love than this, / To die to serve his friend'?" *The Fiery Cross*, like other collections, reflects the ways in which the Bible is both an overt source for, and a subtle influence on, literary expression.

The Victorians and Edwardians were steeped in the stories and language of the Authorized Version and it is easy to forget just how widespread was this familiarity: "Everyone in the English-speaking world, literate and illiterate, pious and worldly, was once, to some degree, familiar with it" (Spurr, 2006, p. 199). Sunday Schools, in particular, "would have exerted lasting influences particularly on older members of the war generation cohort" (Schweitzer, 2003, p. 6). Yet is it important to make the distinction between *familiarity* with biblical narrative and the *practice* of Christianity. Attendance at church services had fallen dramatically in the latter years of the nineteenth century and engendered much debate about the rising tide of secularism.

Religious practice at the front is documented – and often derided – in countless letters and literary recollections. In 1917, Ivor Gurney noted: "Here I am at the billet instead of being at Church Parade. C of E is on my Identification Disk, but only for burial purposes" (Hurd, 1978, p. 87). And David Jones's *In Parenthesis*, "the nearest equivalent to an epic that the Great War produced in English," according to Bergonzi (1996, p. 195), describes how

> The official service was held in the field; there they had spread a Union Jack on piled biscuit tins, behind the 8 in. siege, whose regular discharges made quite inaudible the careful artistry of the prayers he read.
>
> He preached from the Matthew text, of how He cares for us above the sparrows. The medical officer undid, and did up again, the fastener of his left glove, behind his back, throughout the whole discourse. They sang *Onward Christian Soldiers* for the closing hymn. (Jones, 1978, p. 107)

Such sacred hymns were often debunked by soldiers who applied very different words to the solemn tunes. "When This Lousy War is Over" was sung to the melody of "What a Friend We Have in Jesus":

> When this lousy war is over no more soldiering for me,
> When I get my civvy clothes on, oh how happy I shall be.
> No more church parades on Sunday, no more begging for a pass.
> You can tell the sergeant-major to stick his passes up his arse.

It was not organized religion or its ordained ministers but simple, ordinary actions that the soldiers valued. The medical officer in the above quotation "was popular" because he "glossed his technical discourses with every lewdness" and his "heroism and common humanity reached toward sanctity" (Jones, 1978, p. 13). Jones contrasts the "official service" with a very different Last Supper where it is the *soldiers'* administration of the sacrament that is most moving as "No. 1 section gathered, bunched, in the confined traverse":

> They bring for them,
> for each and for several;
> he makes division, he ordains:
> three ration biscuits,
> one-third part of a loaf
>
> ...
>
> Come off it Moses – dole out the issue,
> Dispense salvation,
> Strictly apportion it,
> Let us taste and see,
> Let us be renewed,
> For Christ's sake let us be warm. (Jones, 1978, 72–3)

Yet leaders of the Church of England, like their political counterparts in government, continued to use the language of the Bible as patriotic rhetoric. It was equally depicted as a "crusade against the German infidels," a Holy War, in which Britain was symbolically "linked to God's chosen people," the Israelites (Robb, 2002, p. 14). Germany was often portrayed as the Beast from Revelation.

Between 1914 and 1916 "a staggering 40 million religious tracts, prayer books, bibles, and hymn books [were distributed] to British servicemen" by numerous organizations (Schweitzer, 2003, p. 31). While there are countless stories of Bibles kept in pockets stopping bullets – the physical text could literally save a man's life – just how many of these were actually read is open to debate. Edmund Blunden recalled that of all the books he carried, including Francis Thomson's *Night Thoughts* and the poems of Shelley, the New Testament (given to him by a commanding officer, "a timid, fragile man") went "mainly unconsulted" (Blunden, 1928, p. 22). Charles Hamilton Sorley, while waiting near the front lines to advance on Loos, wrote to his friend Arthur Watts and declared, "Give me *The Odyssey*, and I return the New Testament to store" (Wilson, 1985, p. 215).

Nevertheless, the Bible had a profound impact on their poetic interpretations of the conflict. For Wilfred Owen in particular it was his "earliest and probably ... most important literary influence" (Owen, 1994, p. xxi). Church discourse was one of Owen's "speech communities" and although he rejected organized religion, "there was no unremembering the scriptures which had been [his] daily reading for the best part of two decades" (Kerr, 1995, p. 72).

Pastoral Idyll: The Lost Eden

By and large, the poets of 1914–18 were Georgians, steeped in the pastoral, with a concern for the elements of everyday life, and with an ear for direct speech. The landscape, especially the English landscape, was precious to them. Rupert Brooke did not live long enough to see the ravaged earth wrought by the war, but his sonnet "The Soldier" proclaims his confidence that if he "should die" and be buried in "some corner of a foreign field," "There shall be / In that rich earth a richer dust concealed." This oblique reference to Genesis 3:19: "till thou return unto the ground; for out of it wast thou taken: for dust thou art, and unto dust shalt thou return," also invokes the Church of England burial service: "ashes to ashes, dust to dust." Dean Inge in his 1915 Easter sermon at Westminster Abbey praised the sonnet, saying it owed much to Isaiah 26:19: "The dead shall live, my dead bodies shall arise. Awake and sing, ye that dwell in the dust." Yet while Inge praised Brooke's "pure and elevated patriotism," he felt "The Soldier" "fell somewhat short of Isaiah's vision" (cited in Hassell, 1964, p. 502). "The Soldier" was later damned (unfairly) by critics as the voice of naive optimism, partly for having been exploited by propagandists. On reading it, Ivor Gurney for one commented: "I do not like it ... his manner has become a mannerism, both in rhythm and diction. I do not like it" (Hurd, 1978, p. 56).

Edmund Blunden, who survived four years of fighting without injury, saw the world through "a countryman's eye" and was overwhelmed by the destruction of the French landscape. In his memoir *Undertones of War*, he claims to be untouched by the treacherous serpent – "No destined anguish lifted its snaky head to poison a harmless young shepherd in a soldier's coat" (Blunden, 1928, p. 226). Yet he *is* poisoned: "the knowledge that the remaining countryside of Picardy has been ravaged" (Fussell, 1975, p. 267) emerges in his poems – thirty-one are appended to the prose text – and later writing. Blunden could never escape the horrors of the violated landscape, the lost Eden, and its generation of young men.

The Tree of Life that stood in the biblical Garden of Eden is evoked in poems that describe the "hellscape" of the Western Front, which was characterized not just by trenches, mud, rotting corpses, and rats but by shattered, broken trees, "suggestive of crosses" (Stallworthy, 2008, p. 110). Paul Nash represented this landscape from a painterly perspective, but the language of the war poets is equally visual. David Jones describes "a splintered tree [that] scattered its winter limbs, [and] spilled its life low on the ground," "the spilled bowels of trees, splinter-like, leper-ashen, sprawling the receding, unknowable, wall of night," and "low sharp-stubbed tree-skeletons, [that] stretched slow moving shadows" (Jones, 1978, pp. 21, 31, 44). Wilfred Owen portrayed the Western Front as "hideous ... everything unnatural, broken, blasted" and it is no surprise that he hoped "to take a cottage and orchard in Kent Surrey or Sussex" (Owen, 1967, pp. 431, 446).

A lost Eden is quietly evoked in Edward Thomas's "As the Team's Head Brass." The "couple" who "disappeared into the wood" recall Adam and Eve; the "felled" elm the damaged Tree of Life; and the country idyll marred by the loss of the village's young men in the trenches recalls the Paradise lost. The poem's central message, "Everything / Would have been different. For it would have been another world" is a poignant reminder of the peace and the lives that have been shattered.

"The mire of the trenches" and the guns that "bark all night-long" destroy "our Paradise" in Ivor Gurney's "De Profundis," while the Eden in which "Earth is bursting into song" in Charles Hamilton Sorley's "All the Hills and Vales Along" is quickly disrupted by satire: "And the singers are the chaps / Who are going to die perhaps." The mocking rhyme-scheme of these lines parodies the cant phrases of propagandists as Paradise is sullied by the deaths of so many men: "Strew your gladness on earth's bed, / So be merry, so be dead."

Old Testament Narratives

Many poets, such as those represented in *The Fiery Cross*, relied on traditional motifs and certainties to make sense of the slaughter, but others subverted and reworked them to demonstrate how the old ways and especially the "Old Men" – generals, politicians, and clerics – betrayed a generation. For these, the Great War represented a break with the past, with the certainties of the Victorian age. The "conviction that the war had empowered the elderly to send the young to their deaths" (Hynes, 1990, p. 246) was prevalent. A potent Old Testament story was the *akedah*, the Binding of Isaac in Genesis 22:1–19. The first fourteen lines of Owen's "The Parable of the Old Man and the Young" are a close wording of the biblical narrative, but Owen departs from the story with his final couplet, itself set apart from the main section: "But the old man would not so, but slew his son, / And half the seed of Europe, one by one." Here the old man ignores the Angel's final injunction not to slaughter his son – and extends the sacrifice to "half the seed of Europe." The phrase "one by one," set off as it is by a comma, reinforces the ritualistic nature of the killing and challenges the perception that in mechanized warfare individual identity is obscured. Owen's rage is directed "not so much against a cruel god, as against a generation of European 'fathers' who have sent their sons to slaughter in the trenches" (Jasper and Prickett, 1999, p. 113). Richard Aldington's "The Blood of the Young Men" is a similar reworking of the Genesis story, but its imagery is more graphic as cannibalistic old men feast on the "Blood of the young, dear flesh of the young men" (Winter, 1995, p. 200).

In Robert Graves's "Goliath & David," not only is the usual order of the names reversed in the poem's title, but the victor of the Old Testament tale is now the vanquished: David is killed and "Steel-helmeted and grey and grim / Goliath straddles over him," an image recalling propaganda cartoons of the "Hun." As in Owen's parable, the reader's assumptions are challenged by the "reversing of the traditional outcome" (Fussell, 1975, p. 241) of biblical narrative.

Although heavily resonant of Tennyson and Donne, Owen's "Futility" has clear biblical antecedents. The reference to "clay" and the questioning by the speaker, "Was it for this the clay grew tall?" echoes Isaiah 45:9: "Shall the clay say to him that fashioneth it, What makest thou?" But in Isaiah, God's anger is directed at man, who questions His power and His plan: "Woe unto him that striveth with his Maker." In Owen's poem the speaker deliberately dares to ask, and then to reject such a plan in the frustrated final lines: "Oh what made fatuous sunbeams toil / To break the earth's sleep at all?"

The Language of the Old Testament

Verbal parallelism and verbal repetition are key rhetorical features of the Bible. Genesis, for instance, is particularly notable for its echoing "And." May Wedderburn Cannan in her poem "Rouen" (the most anthologized Great War poem by a woman) employs these verbal techniques in a catalogue of a day in the life of the busy port city during the war:

> Early morning over Rouen, hopeful, high, courageous morning,
> And the laughter of adventure and the steepness of the stair,
> And the dawn across the river, and the wind across the bridges,
> And the empty littered station and the tired people there. (Lines 1–4)

The recording of the incidentals of experience ground the poem in the immediacy of the Great War: "the coming of provisions"; "the little piles of Woodbines"; "the Drafts just out from England," but the rhythm of speech, the repetitive questioning "Can you," blend these within a lyrical memory. As in the story of Genesis where the use of "And" reinforces the ever-developing creation, so too does Cannan's use of the word in "Rouen." It also suggests a "suppressed intensity of feeling – an imprisoned feeling, as it were, for which there is no outlet but a repeated hammering at the confining walls of language" (Leech, 1969, p. 79). There is so much she wishes to communicate, but she does so within the ordered form of verse and the containment of the day-to-night structure. The repetition, moreover, of the insistent questions "can you recall," "can you forget," "can I forget" accelerates the tempo of accumulating memories.

Verbal repetition contributes to the pathos of Ivor Gurney's "Pain," a poem that echoes the suffering catalogued in such Old Testament books as Job and the Psalms. The lines "Pain, pain continual; pain unending" (line 1) and "Grey monotony lending / Weight to the grey skies, grey mud where goes / An army of grey bedrenched scarecrows in rows" (lines 5–7) makes vivid the dementia and torment of those "men broken, shrieking even to hear a gun" (line 12). Gurney ends his poem with the Job-like "The amazed heart cries angrily out on God."

Isaac Rosenberg "looked to biblical and Jewish history for the language with which to describe the horrors of the Western Front" (Matalon, 2002, p. 36), and some critics have argued for Rosenberg's standing as a specifically Jewish poet. Others assert that Rosenberg himself was more concerned with being an *English* poet. His "vision was cosmic rather than sectarian, personal and unique rather than specifically Jewish" (Rosenberg, 1979, p. xxi). Fascinated by myth and legend, Rosenberg was nevertheless steeped in both the Old and New Testaments of the Authorized Version. "Scriptural and sculptural are the epithets I would apply to him" (Rosenberg, 1977, p. vii), said Siegfried Sassoon. Like an Old Testament prophet "anticipating the destruction of civilizations" (Cohen, 1975, p. 108), Rosenberg in "On Receiving News of the War" talks of "Some spirit old" that "Hath turned with malign kiss / Our lives to mould." The description in the fourth stanza is reminiscent of the sufferings of Job, yet the capitalization of "His" and "He" suggests that it is God Himself who suffers the violence of war:

> Red fangs have torn His face.
> God's blood is shed.
> He mourns from His lone place
> His children dead.

The cry of the final stanza

> O! ancient crimson curse!
> Corrode, consume.
> Give back this universe
> Its pristine bloom.

echoes the many supplications contained in the Psalms: for instance, "O Lord, open thou my lips; and my mouth shall shew forth thy praise" (Psalm 51:15) and "Make haste, O God, to deliver me; make haste to help me, O Lord" (Psalm 70:1).

In "Break of Day in the Trenches," the dust that is so extolled in Brooke's "The Soldier" (being, as it is, the remains of a "body of England") is invoked in an altogether more ironic way in the final lines:

> Poppies whose roots are in men's veins
> Drop and are ever dropping;
> But mine in my ear is safe –
> Only a little white with the dust.

The speaker of the poem has not, as he claims, made the flower "safe," for having plucked it, it will die. Nor has he made himself any safer, for the red poppy marks him out as a target. The dust that mars the vibrant color is derived from the remains of the dead, among which the speaker will also mingle. The prophecy of Isaiah 26:19, "The dead shall live, my dead bodies shall arise. Awake and sing, ye that dwell in the dust," cannot be fulfilled in the trenches.

Whereas other war poets such as Edmund Blunden and Edward Thomas use nature to "represent peace, beauty, normality," Rosenberg's earth has a "jealous devouring power" (Liddiard, 1975, p. 219). Nowhere is this better exemplified than in the epic "Dead Man's Dump." It contains few specific biblical references, but the imagery, language, and syntax of the Scriptures are unmistakable. Christ's passion is clearly referred to in the line "stuck out like many crowns of thorns" (line 3) and the crucifixion more obliquely but no less effectively suggested in "They left this dead with the older dead, / Stretched out at the cross roads" (lines 62–3). But it is the Old Testament of which "Dead Man's Dump" is so movingly resonant. "Man born of man, and born of woman" (line 11) is a clear echo of Job (14:1). The questions and exclamations that punctuate the poem – "What fierce imaginings their dark souls lit?"; "Who hurled them out?"; "Will they come?"; "Earth! have they gone into you!"; "Dark Earth! dark Heavens!" – are typical of the historical and prophetic books. While Rosenberg's vision is grounded in the landscape of the Western Front, the "shattered track," shells, shrapnel, and stretcher-bearers, it is informed and inspired by Old Testament narratives of warfare, destruction, and death. The hellish scenes Rosenberg describes recall the "valley of slaughter" described in Jeremiah 7:32 and the "grievous deaths" in which those slain "shall not be lamented; neither shall they be buried; but they shall be as dung upon the face of the earth" in Jeremiah (16:4). We also hear echoes of the prophecies of desolation contained in Isaiah, in which the dead will be cast out of their graves "like an abominable branch" (Isaiah 14:19) and their stink shall come up out of their carcases (Isaiah 34:2–3). The "sinister faces" that are "burnt black by strange decay" are reminiscent of the suffering of Lamentations: "Their visage is blacker than a coal; they are not known in the streets: their skin cleaveth to their bones; it is withered, it is become like a stick" (4:8). The bones that are such a disturbing feature of the poem are equally resonant images in Old Testament narrative from Psalm 22 ("I am poured out like water, and all my bones are out of joint"; "I may tell all my bones") to Ezekiel 37 ("The hand of the Lord was upon me, and carried me out in the spirit of the Lord, and set me down in the midst of the valley which was full of bones"). Unlike in Ezekiel where the bones are given new life by the Lord God, the remains of these soldiers are not resurrected. Yet for all its horror "Dead Man's Dump" expresses "an overwhelmingly compassionate tenderness," an "infinite sadness" that "reinvests the dead with human dignity" (Cohen, 1975, p. 62).

Christ's Teachings, Suffering, and Sacrifice

In Matthew 18:21–2 Jesus instructs Peter that he should forgive his brother not "Until seven times: but, Until seventy times seven." David Jones invokes this passage when he describes the tense anticipation of the men as they wait to "go over the top":

> But they already looked at their watches and it is zero minus seven minutes.
> Seven minutes to go ... and seventy times seven times to the minute
> this drumming of the diaphragm (Jones, 1978, p. 155–6)

The inherent contrast suggests that the reader should question the validity of the fighting in light of the teachings of Christ in which forgiveness is a central tenet. The biblical commandment "Thou Shalt Not Kill" and Jesus' sustained advocacy of pacifism was difficult for many to square with the imperatives of war. Wilfred Owen is particularly candid:

> Already I have comprehended a light which never will filter into the dogma of any national church: namely, that one of Christ's essential commands was: Passivity at any price! Suffer dishonour and disgrace but never resort to arms. Be bullied, be outraged, be killed; but do not kill. (Owen, 1967, p. 461)

Calling himself "a conscientious objector with a very seared conscience," and quoting John 15:13, "Greater Love hath no man than this, that a man lay down his life for his friends," he argues that pure Christianity will not fit in with pure patriotism (Owen, 1967, p. 462). His poem "Greater Love," which begins "Red lips are not so red / As the stained stones kissed by the English dead," returns to this theme. The sensuousness Owen learned from Swinburne combines with the biblical proclamation to provide a contrast between romantic love and Christ-like sacrificial love such as that shown by the soldiers (Spear, 1975, p. 37).

This pivotal New Testament narrative of the suffering and death of Christ is one that was used by countless poets, journalists, preachers, and politicians who saw parallels between the sacrifice proclaimed in the Gospels and that of the soldiers in the trenches: "the conjunction, the conflation, of Christ and soldier is as old as St Paul's Epistle to the

Ephesians (6:11–17)" (Stallworthy, 2008, p. 110). But Owen goes further to suggest that "the love that the soldiers show in sacrificing themselves is greater than that shown by a lover and as great as that shown by Christ himself" (Hibberd in Owen, 1973, p. 115). The monosyllables are striking and "give to the poem the quality of the Law and the Commandments" (Spear, 1975, p. 37), as in the final line, "Weep, you may weep, for you may touch them not," itself a reminder of Jesus' words to Mary Magdalene in John 20:15–17.

The crucifixion and resurrection of Christ that is alluded to in "Greater Love" is also evoked in Owen's "Spring Offensive." The "last hill" and the "end of the world" at which the soldiers arrive in the poem's opening line suggest both Calvary and Armageddon, while the biblical language, especially that contained in the narratives of the Last Supper, "slept – watched – hour – blessed – sorrowing – sun – culminate in the renewal of Christ's sacrificial act as the soldiers die in the offensive" (Spear, 1975, p. 38).

Siegfried Sassoon's "The Redeemer," set in a trench on a dark mid-winter night, describes how the flare of a rocket illuminates the face of a figure he declares is Christ, wearing not a crown of thorns but the "woollen cap" (line 19) of "an English soldier" (line 20). Like the mortal soldiers, "like any simple chap" (line 21), he has learned the lessons of trench warfare and will "endure / Horror and pain" (lines 25–6), re-enacting the suffering on the road to Calvary: "reeling in his weariness, / Shouldering his load of planks, so hard to bear" (lines 28–9). The direct speech, especially "the explosive colloquialism of the last line" – "Mumbling: 'Oh Christ Almighty, now I'm stuck!' " – is a language Sassoon learned from Hardy (Stallworthy, 2002, p. 65).

Like most of Sassoon's war poems, "The Redeemer" is "launched at the reader like a hand-grenade" (Stallworthy, 2002, p. 68). So too is "Christ and the Soldier." The exhausted "gasping" soldier who falls before the image of Christ, declaring "O blessed crucifix, I'm beat!" receives no relief from the aloof proclamation "My son, behold these hands and feet." Christ's pat answer mimics those used by the Established Church: organized religion offered no consolation to those suffering at the front. Similarly, "Stand-to: Good Friday Morning" demonstrates how "traditional belief in Christ's res-urrection has very little significance in the hell of the trenches" (Quinn, 1994, p. 174). The speaker who has "been on duty from two till four" in a waterlogged trench "prays" for a "blighty," an injury that will send him back home. But the prayer is not sincere, it is a bargain:

> "O Jesus, send me a wound to-day,
> And I'll believe in Your bread and wine,
> And get my bloody old sins washed white!"

As discussed earlier, Charles Sorley's "All the Hills and Vales Along" prefigured such uncomfortable representations. It is layered with New as well as Old Testament resonances:

> Jesus Christ and Barabbas
> Were found the same day.
> This died, that went his way. (Lines 12–14)

The sing-song rhythm mocks the too-easy association of the Gospels and the Happy Warrior ideal:

> Earth that blossomed and was glad
> 'Neath the cross that Christ had,
> Shall rejoice and blossom too
> When the bullet reaches you. (Lines 23–6)

The patriotic and propagandistic celebrations of the fighting "chaps" are also debunked by David Jones as he recalls the soldiers' agony of waiting to go over the top, embedding it with a reference to Christ's Agony in the Garden (Matthew 26:39): "O my Father, if it be possible, let this cup pass from me":

> Perhaps they'll cancel it.
>
> ...
>
> Or you read it again many times to see if it will come different:
> you can't believe the Cup wont pass from
> or they wont make a better show
> in the Garden.

Bernard Bergonzi has argued that Jones did not express pity like Owen but "was, however, very aware of the sacrificial elements in the soldiers' experience, which he understood in Christian terms" (Bergonzi, 1996, p. 200).

Owen's interpretation of Christ's Agony took different forms. "Strange Meeting" offers an oblique parallel between His suffering and that of soldiers on the Western Front in the line "Foreheads of men have bled where no wounds were." As Hilda Spear (1975) has pointed out, this is reminiscent of Luke 22:44: "And being in an agony he prayed more earnestly: and his sweat was as it were great drops of blood falling down to the ground." In a letter, Owen described how

> For 14 hours yesterday I was at work – teaching Christ to lift his cross by numbers, and how to adjust his crown. ... With a piece of silver I buy him every day, and with maps I make him familiar with the topography of Golgotha. (Owen, 1967, p. 561)

It is not difficult to see why the seared landscape of the Western Front could have been compared with "the place of skull" – in Latin "Calvary," in Hebrew "Golgotha." Blunden, for instance, recalls in *Undertones of War*:

> Looking back towards safety from the Auchonvillers trenches, one daily saw a high crucifix at the end of the town, silvered and silhouetted in the sunset. Before we came away, this sad sculpture had fallen, and it was penitential weather. (Blunden, 1928, p. 112)

In his poem "On Reading that the Rebuilding of Ypres Approached Completion," he describes

the hillock's signifying tree, that choked and gouged and miry
Was like a cross, but such a cross that there no bleeding Figure
Might hang without tautology.

The town, addressed as a lost lover, remembers him like the mad man healed of his unclean spirit by Christ in Mark 5:9: "My name is Legion."

The lifelike models of the crucifixion that stand at many crossroads in France, which Sassoon evokes in "Christ and the Soldier" and called "merely a reminder [to the soldiers] of the inability of religion to cooperate with the carnage and catastrophe they experienced" (Sassoon, 1983, p. 47), is also exploited by Wilfred Owen in "At a Calvary Near the Ancre." Drawing on his experience of fighting near the French river, Owen relates how "One ever hangs where shelled roads part" (line 1). There are direct correlations to the Gospel story: "But His disciples hide apart" (line 3) echoes Matthew 26:56, "Then all his disciples forsook him, and fled"; "And now the Soldiers bear with Him" (line 4) relates to Matthew 27:36, "And sitting down they watched him there," though it must be noted that the soldiers did so while gambling for Christ's belongings. "Near Golgotha strolls many a priest" (line 5) reflects Matthew 27:41, "Likewise also the chief priests, mocking him, with the scribes and the elders." In Owen's version, the priest refers to those sent to the front to minister to the troops. "[T]hey were flesh-marked by the Beast" (line 7) not only suggests their wounding at the hands of the Germans for which they take "pride," but is a clear echo of Revelation 14:9–10: "If any man worship the beast and his image, and receive his mark in his forehead, or in his hand." Dominic Hibberd has shown that there is a further meaning here: the organized Church whose "hatred of Germany puts it in the Devil's following; and the priests' wounds are signs not so much of opposition to the Devil Germany as of allegiance to the Devil War" (Owen, 1973, p. 116).

The Book of Revelation

This final book of the Bible, containing St John's prophetic and apocalyptic visions, also armed many Great War poets with potent symbols with which "ironically to demonstrate the gap between ... civilisation's ideals and its practices" (Sinfield, 1982, p. 339). Owen's "Soldiers' Dream" recalls Revelation 12:7 ("And there was war in heaven: Michael and his angels fought against the dragon; and the dragon fought") in its final lines, "But God was vexed, and gave all power to Michael; / And when I woke he'd seen to our repairs." The bishop in Sassoon's "They" similarly twists the biblical message when he compares the sacrifice of "the boys" to the battle in Revelation: "they lead the last attack / On Anti-Christ" (lines 3–4). But the reply of "the boys" themselves refutes the idea that "their comrades' blood has bought / New right to breed an honourable race" (lines 4–5) with examples of wounds that are not glorious badges: from losing both one's legs, to blindness, to syphilis. Yet the bishop will not accept the futility of war, saying " 'The ways of God are strange!' " Owen's "The End" recalls Ezekiel 37:1–6 and Revelation 21:4, but refutes "the assured statements of St

John the Divine" in the lines "Mine ancient scars shall not be glorified, / Nor my titanic tears, the seas, be dried" (Spear, 1975, p. 36).

Revelation is also a point of reference for David Jones, whether it be the satiric portrait of the unlikable orderly sergeant – "Here comes bloody Anti-Christ with a packet for each us'n's" (Jones, 1978, p. 114) – or the ominous description of the "malign chronometer" of the "heavy battery ... ticking off with each discharge an exactly measured progress toward a certain and prearranged hour of apocalypse" (Jones, 1978, p. 135). The image of "Riders on pale horses loosed / and vials irreparably broken" evokes Revelation 6:8 ("And I looked, and behold a pale horse") and equates the Great War with the epic battle of salvation. But the lines immediately following undercut the grand associations, albeit it in a poignant way:

> an' Wat price bleedin' Glory
> Glory
> Glory Hallelujah
> and the Royal Welsh sing:
> Jesu
>   lover of me soul ...

The Battle of the Somme is the constant presence in Jones's epic and "the martial apocalypse more than lives up to its scriptural counterpart" (Dilworth, 1979, p. 17).

Owen's "Mental Cases" owes much to Dante, presenting as it does a vision of hell on earth for those "purgatorial shadows" (line 2), the "men whose minds the Dead have ravaged" (line 10), but also refers "back beyond Dante to a Biblical vision of Heaven" (Sinfield, 1982, p. 339) contained within Revelation 7:13–17, which begins:

> What are these which are arrayed in white robes? and whence came they?
> ... These are they which came out of great tribulation, and have washed
> their robes, and made them white in the blood of the Lamb. Therefore are
> they before the throne of God, and serve him day and night in his temple.

Owen's use of the colloquial phrase "slob their relish" (line 3) grounds the poem in the same ways as the references to mechanized warfare such as "Batter of guns and shatter of flying muscles" (line 16), but the biblical resonances are pervasive. The stigmata of Christ are alluded to in the description of the dawn that "breaks open like a wound that bleeds afresh" (line 22) and his flogging in the "rope-knouts of their scourging" (line 26). Forced to kill, "to violate their humanity" (Sinfield, 1982, p. 341), these emaciated figures are tormented in their dreams and their waking hours: "Memory fingers in their hair of murders" (line 11). They have escaped death, but cannot verbally articulate the "Multitudinous murders they once witnessed" (line 12) – their *bodies* are the mirror of that suffering: "They are, in a sense, both the saved and the damned" (Sinfield, 1982, p. 341).

Conclusion: Bearing Witness

"*Neither will they understand,*" proclaimed Edmund Blunden in his preface or "prelimi-nary" to *Undertones of War*, quoting from Psalm 82:5: "They know not, neither will they understand; they walk on in darkness: all the foundations of the earth are out of course." The younger generation and those not directly involved in the Great War will never be able to comprehend the enormity of what survivors have witnessed. Blunden was compelled to "go over the ground again," a reference both to his previous attempt to record his war in *De Bello Germanico* (1918) and to what was a lifelong compulsion to revisit his memories of 1914–18. Many of his poems are elegiac, lyrical reminis-cences, but "II Peter ii, 22 (1921)" is more Sassoon-like in its sarcasm and anger. Blunden draws on the book of Proverbs: "But it is happened unto them, according to the true proverb, The dog is turned to his own vomit again; and the sow that was washed to her wallowing in the mire." Although the "new year succeeds the dead" and the war is "farther away," the passage of time does little to assuage his painful memories of "the heights that crowned a deadlier year." Indeed, Blunden could never escape. He once asserted, "My experiences in the First World War have haunted me all my life and for many days I have, it seemed, lived in that world rather than this" (quoted in Fussell, 1975, p. 256).

For Blunden, naming was a key force of literary witnessing. The titles of his poems record such places as "Vlamertinghe: Passing the Château," "A House at Festaubert," "Third Ypres," and "The Zonnebeke Road," and they memorialize the landscape and villages through which the young soldier passed and for which he fought. As in May Cannan's "Rouen," naming is itself an act of piety and of remembrance. So too it is with David Jones:

> But that was on the right with
> the genuine Taffies
>   but we are rash levied
> from Islington and Hackney
> and the purlieus of Walworth
> flashers from Surbiton
> men of the stock of Abraham
> from Bromley-by-Bow. (Jones, 1978, p. 160)

The catalogue of London places mirrors the catalogue of French towns that had become synonymous with fighting and suffering. Where the men have come from is as impor-tant as where they went to die.

Like Blunden and Cannan, Jones is "the voice of the survivor" (Stallworthy, 2002, p. 185). Yet those who did not physically survive – among them Owen, Rosenberg, Thomas, Sorley, Brooke – left behind records of witnessing, their poems. Together they not only echo the messenger in the Book of Job ("I alone am escaped to tell thee") but follow in the footsteps of the poet of the heroic age who "was not primarily a warrior. His function was to ensure that his friends did not die unsung. He must escape that he might tell: bear witness" (Stallworthy, 1982, p. 6). The Evangelists, Matthew, Mark, Luke, and John, were also witnesses, and the poets of the Great War who similarly employed direct speech, colloquialisms, and the specific details of life as they knew it documented the experiences of a generation. Other less accomplished, though no less sincere, poets witnessed as well, and together with those we now include in "the canon," they made poetry itself an act of remembrance. The poets of the Great War have, as Jay Winter has observed, "become both the psalmists and the prophets of our century" (Winter, 1995, p. 204).

Bibliography

Atwan, R. and Wieder, L., eds (2000) *Chapters into Verse: A Selection of Poetry in English Inspired by the Bible from Genesis through Revelation*. Oxford University Press, Oxford.

Bergonzi, B. (1996) *Heroes' Twilight: A Study of the Literature of the Great War*, 3rd edn. Carcanet, Manchester.

Blunden, E. (1928) *Undertones of War*. Cobden-Sanderson, London.

Blunden, E. (1996) *Overtones of War: Poems of the First World War*, ed. M. Taylor. Duckworth, London.

Cohen, J. (1975) *Journey to the Trenches: The Life of Isaac Rosenberg 1890–1918*. Robson Books, London.

Cox, S. (2006) *The New Testament in Literature: A Guide to Literary Terms*. Open Court, Chicago.

Dilworth, T. (1979) *The Liturgical Parenthesis of David Jones*. Golgonooza Press, Ipswich.

Edwards, M. C. and Booth, M., eds (1915) *The Fiery Cross: An Anthology*. Grant Richards, London.

Fussell, P. (1975) *The Great War and Modern Memory*. Grant Richards, London.

Hassell, C. (1964) *Rupert Brooke: A Biography*. Faber & Faber, London.

Hipp, D. (2005) *The Poetry of Shellshock: Wartime Trauma and Healing in Wilfred Owen, Ivor Gurney and Siegfried Sassoon*. McFarland & Co., Jefferson, NC.

Hurd, M. (1978) *The Ordeal of Ivor Gurney*. Oxford University Press, Oxford.

Hynes, S. (1990) *A War Imagined: The First World War and English Culture*. Collier Books/ Macmillan Publishing Company, New York.

Jasper, D. and Prickett, S., eds (1999) *The Bible and Literature: A Reader*. Blackwell, Oxford.

Jones, D. (1937/1978) *In Parenthesis: seinnyessit e gledyf ym penn mameu*. Faber & Faber, London.

Kerr, D. (1995) *Wilfred Owen's Voices*. Oxford University Press, Oxford.

Leech, G. N. (1969) *A Linguistic Guide to English Poetry*. Longman, Harlow.

Liddiard, J. (1975) *Isaac Rosenberg: The Half Used Life*. Gollancz, London.

Matalon, A. (2002) "Difference at War: Siegfried Sassoon, Isaac Rosenberg, U. Z. Grinberg, and Poetry of the First World War," *Shofar: An Interdisciplinary Journal of Jewish Studies* 21:1, 25–43.

Owen, W. (1967) *Collected Letters*, ed. H. Owen and J. Bell. Oxford University Press, London.

Owen, W. (1973) *Wilfred Owen: War Poems and Others*, ed. D. Hibberd. Chatto & Windus, London.

Owen, W. (1994) *The War Poems of Wilfred Owen*, ed. J. Stallworthy. Chatto & Windus, London.

Quinn, P. J. (1994) *The Great War and the Missing Muse: The Early Writings of Robert Graves and Siegfried Sassoon*. Susquehanna University Press, Sellingsgrove.

Reilly, C. (1981) *Scars Upon My Heart: Women's Poetry of the First World War*. Virago, London.

Robb, G. (2002) *Popular Culture in the First World War*. Palgrave, Basingstoke.

Rosenberg, I. (1977) *The Collected Poems of Isaac Rosenberg*, ed. G. Bottomley and D. Harding. Chatto & Windus, London.

Rosenberg, I. (1979) *The Collected Works of Isaac Rosenberg*, ed. I. Parsons. Chatto & Windus, London.

Sassoon, S. (1983) *War Poems of Siegfried Sassoon*, ed. R. Hart-Davis. Faber & Faber, London.

Schweitzer, R. (2003) *The Cross and the Trenches: Religious Faith and Doubt among British and American Great War Soldiers*. Praeger, Westport, CT.

Sinfield, M. (1982) "Wilfred Owen's 'Mental Cases': Source and Structure," *Notes and Queries* (August), 339–41.

Spear, H.D. (1975) " 'I Too Saw God': The Religious Allusions in Wilfred Owen's Poetry," *English* 24:119, 35–40.

Spurr, B. (2006) *Studying Poetry*, 2nd edn. Palgrave Macmillan, Basingstoke.

Stallworthy, J. (1982) "Survivors' Songs in Welsh Poetry," Annual Gwyn Jones Lecture.

Stallworthy, J. (2002) *Anthem for Doomed Youth: Twelve Soldier Poets of the First World War*. Constable and Robinson, London.

Stallworthy, J. (2008) *Survivors' Songs: From Maldon to the Somme*. Cambridge University Press, Cambridge.

Wilson, J. M. (1985) *Charles Hamilton Sorley: A Biography*. Cecil Woolf, London.

Winter, J. (1995) *Sites of Memory, Sites of Mourning: The Great War in European Cultural History*. Cambridge University Press, Cambridge.

Index

Note: The index does not include the reference works cited in the footnotes and bibliographies of each chapter. Please consult the end of individual chapters for detailed listings of editors and critics. The index lists the first or key entry of texts discussed in individual chapters.